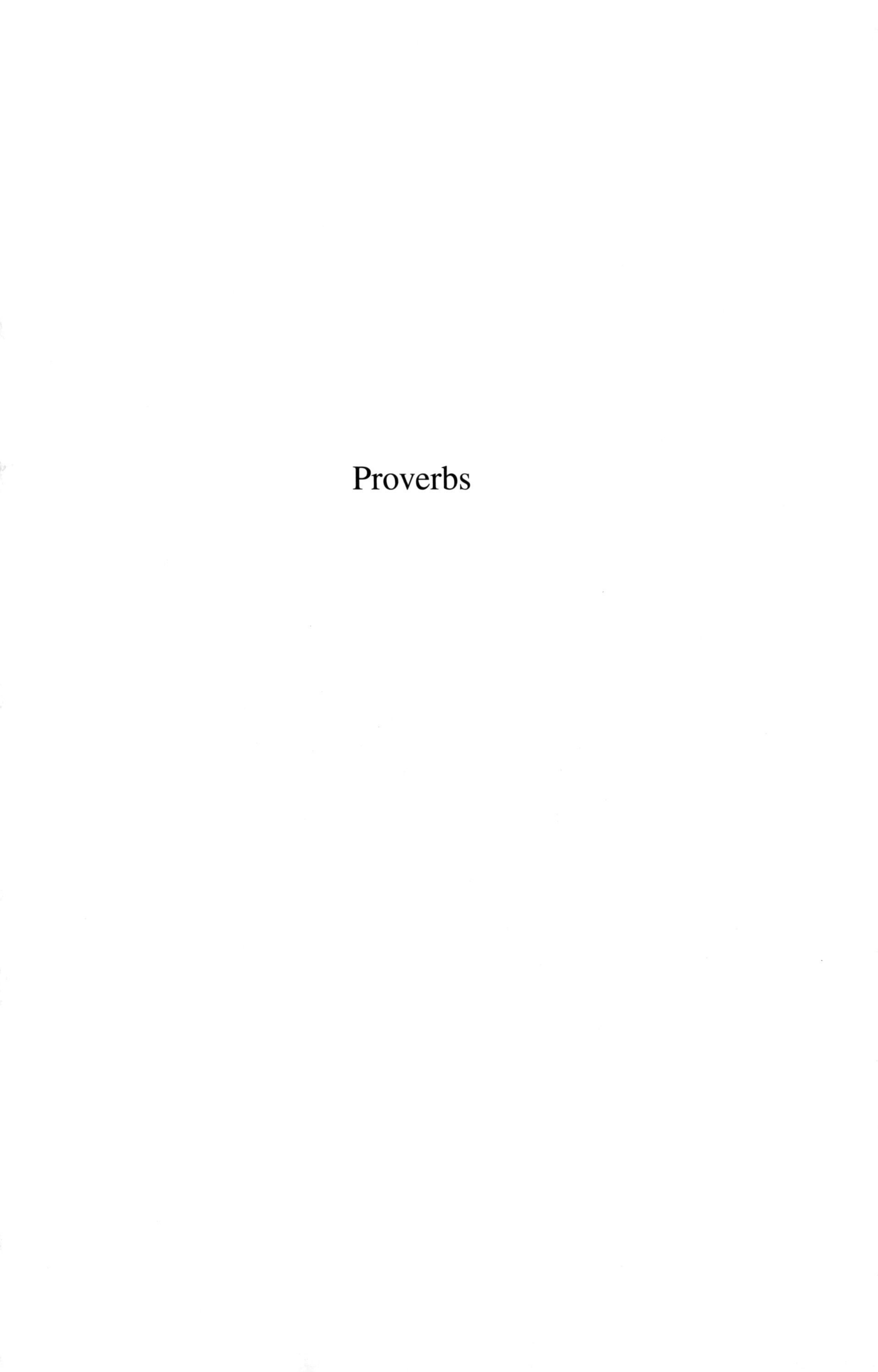

Proverbs

OLD TESTAMENT AND CPH EDITOR

Christopher W. Mitchell

NEW TESTAMENT EDITOR

Curtis P. Giese

CONCORDIA COMMENTARY VOLUMES

Leviticus, John W. Kleinig

Joshua, Adolph L. Harstad

Ruth, John R. Wilch

1 Samuel, Andrew E. Steinmann

**2 Samuel*, Andrew E. Steinmann

**1 Kings 1–11*, Walter A. Maier III

Ezra and Nehemiah, Andrew E. Steinmann

Proverbs, Andrew E. Steinmann

Ecclesiastes, James Bollhagen

The Song of Songs, Christopher W. Mitchell

Isaiah 40–55, R. Reed Lessing

Isaiah 56–66, R. Reed Lessing

Ezekiel 1–20, Horace D. Hummel

Ezekiel 21–48, Horace D. Hummel

Daniel, Andrew E. Steinmann

Amos, R. Reed Lessing

Jonah, R. Reed Lessing

Matthew 1:1–11:1, Jeffrey A. Gibbs

Matthew 11:2–20:34, Jeffrey A. Gibbs

Mark 1:1–8:26, James W. Voelz

Luke 1:1–9:50, Arthur A. Just Jr.

Luke 9:51–24:53, Arthur A. Just Jr.

John 1:1–7:1, William C. Weinrich

Romans 1–8, Michael P. Middendorf

Romans 9–16, Michael P. Middendorf

1 Corinthians, Gregory J. Lockwood

Galatians, A. Andrew Das

Ephesians, Thomas M. Winger

Colossians, Paul E. Deterding

Philemon, John G. Nordling

Hebrews, John W. Kleinig

2 Peter and Jude, Curtis P. Giese

1–3 John, Bruce G. Schuchard

Revelation, Louis A. Brighton

For subscription information and a current list of available Concordia Commentary volumes, visit our website: cph.org/commentary.

*In preparation

CONCORDIA COMMENTARY

A Theological Exposition of Sacred Scripture

PROVERBS

Andrew E. Steinmann

THE SCRIPTURES
TESTIFY TO ME

Concordia Publishing House
Saint Louis

Copyright © 2009 Concordia Publishing House
3558 S. Jefferson Avenue, St. Louis, MO 63118-3968
1-800-325-3040 • www.cph.org

Unless otherwise indicated, Scripture quotations are the author's translation.

The SymbolGreek II, NewJerusalem, JacobiteLS, and TranslitLS fonts used to print this work are available from Linguist's Software, Inc., PO Box 580, Edmonds, WA 98020-0580, USA; telephone (425) 775-1130; www.linguistsoftware.com.

Manufactured in the United States of America

Library of Congress Cataloging-in-Publication Data

Steinmann, Andrew.
Proverbs / Andrew E. Steinmann.
p. cm. — (Concordia commentary: a theological exposition of sacred scripture)
Includes bibliographical references and indexes
ISBN 978-0-7586-0320-3
ISBN 0-7586-0320-7
1. Bible. O.T. Proverbs—Commentaries. I. Title. II. Series.
BS1465.53.S74 2009
223'.7077—dc22

2009001082

3 4 5 6 7 8 9 10 11 12 26 25 24 23 22 21 20 19 18 17

In memoriam
Melvin Louis Steinmann
August 19, 1927–August 9, 1999
Confirmed into the Christian faith
March 29, 1942
יִֽשְׂמַח־אָבִ֥יךָ וְאִמֶּ֑ךָ וְ֝תָגֵ֗ל יֽוֹלַדְתֶּֽךָ׃
Proverbs 23:25

Contents

Editors' Preface

What may a reader expect from the Concordia Commentary: A Theological Exposition of Sacred Scripture?

The purpose of this series, simply put, is to assist pastors, missionaries, and teachers of the Scriptures to convey God's Word with greater clarity, understanding, and faithfulness to the divine intent of the original Hebrew, Aramaic, or Greek text.

Since every interpreter approaches the exegetical task from a certain perspective, honesty calls for an outline of the presuppositions held by those who have shaped this commentary series. This also serves, then, as a description of the characteristics of the commentaries.

First in importance is the conviction that the content of the scriptural testimony is Jesus Christ. The Lord himself enunciated this when he said, "The Scriptures … testify to me" (Jn 5:39), words that have been incorporated into the logo of this series. The message of the Scriptures is the Good News of God's work to reconcile the world to himself through the life, death, resurrection, ascension, and everlasting session of Jesus Christ at the right hand of God the Father. Under the guidance of the same Spirit who inspired the writing of the Scriptures, these commentaries seek to find in every passage of every canonical book "that which promotes Christ" (as Luther's hermeneutic is often described). They are *Trinitarian* and *Christological* commentaries.

As they unfold the scriptural testimony to Jesus Christ, these commentaries expound Law and Gospel. This approach arises from a second conviction—that Law and Gospel are the overarching doctrines of the Bible itself and that to understand them in their proper distinction and relationship to each other is a key for understanding the self-revelation of God and his plan of salvation in Jesus Christ.

Now, Law and Gospel do not always appear in Scripture labeled as such. The palette of language in Scripture is multicolored, with many and rich hues. The dialectic of a pericope may be fallen creation and new creation, darkness and light, death and life, wandering and promised land, exile and return, ignorance and wisdom, demon possession and the kingdom of God, sickness and healing, being lost and found, guilt and righteousness, flesh and Spirit, fear and joy, hunger and feast, or Babylon and the new Jerusalem. But the common element is God's gracious work of restoring fallen humanity through the Gospel of his Son. Since the predominant characteristic of these commentaries is the proclamation of that Gospel, they are, in the proper sense of the term, *evangelical.*

A third, related conviction is that the Scriptures are God's vehicle for communicating the Gospel. The editors and authors accept without reservation that the canonical books of the Old and New Testaments are, in their entirety, the inspired, infallible, and inerrant Word of God. The triune God is the ultimate author of the Bible, and every word in the original Hebrew, Aramaic, and Greek is inspired by the Holy Spirit. Yet rather than mechanical dictation, in the mysterious process by which the Scriptures were divinely inspired (e.g., 2 Tim 3:16; 2 Pet 1:21), God made use of the human faculties, knowledge, interests, and styles of the biblical writers, whose individual books surely are marked by distinctive features. At the same time, the canon of Scripture has its own inner unity, and each passage must be understood in harmony with the larger context of the whole. This commentary series pays heed to the smallest of textual details because of its acceptance of *plenary and verbal inspiration* and interprets the text in light of the whole of Scripture, in accord with the analogy of faith, following the principle that *Scripture interprets Scripture.* The entirety of the Bible is God's Word, *sacred* Scripture, calling for *theological* exposition.

A fourth conviction is that, even as the God of the Gospel came into this world in Jesus Christ (the Word Incarnate), the scriptural Gospel has been given to and through the people of God, for the benefit of all humanity. God did not intend his Scriptures to have a life separated from the church. He gave them through servants of his choosing: prophets, sages, evangelists, and apostles. He gave them to the church and through the church, to be cherished in the church for admonition and comfort and to be used by the church for proclamation and catechesis. The living context of Scripture is ever the church, where the Lord's ministry of preaching, baptizing, forgiving sins, teaching, and celebrating the Lord's Supper continues. Aware of the way in which the incarnation of the Son of God has as a consequence the close union of Scripture and church, of Word and Sacraments, this commentary series features expositions that are *ecclesiological* and *sacramental.*

This Gospel Word of God, moreover, creates a unity among all those in whom it works the obedience of faith and who confess the truth of God revealed in it. This is the unity of the one holy Christian and apostolic church, which extends through world history. The church is to be found wherever the marks of the church are present: the Gospel in the Word and the Sacraments. These have been proclaimed, confessed, and celebrated in many different cultures and are in no way limited nor especially attached to any single culture or people. As this commentary series seeks to articulate the universal truth of the Gospel, it acknowledges and affirms the confession of the scriptural truth in all the many times and places where the one true church has been found. Aiming to promote *concord* in the confession of the one scriptural Gospel, these commentaries seek to be, in the best sense of the terms, *confessional, ecumenical*, and *catholic.*

All of those convictions and characteristics describe the theological heritage of Martin Luther and of the confessors who subscribe to the Book of Concord (1580)—those who have come to be known as Lutherans. The editors and authors forthrightly confess their subscription to the doctrinal exposition of Scripture in the Book of Concord. As the publishing arm of The Lutheran Church—Missouri Synod, Concordia Publishing House is bound to doctrinal agreement with the Scriptures and the Lutheran Confessions and seeks to herald the true Christian doctrine to the ends of the earth. To that end, the series has enlisted confessional Lutheran authors from other church bodies around the world who share the evangelical mission of promoting theological concord.

The authors and editors stand in the exegetical tradition of Martin Luther and the other Lutheran reformers, who in turn (as their writings took pains to demonstrate) stood in continuity with faithful exegesis by theologians of the early and medieval church, rooted in the hermeneutics of the Scriptures themselves (evident, for example, by how the New Testament interprets the Old). This hermeneutical method, practiced also by many non-Lutherans, includes (1) interpreting Scripture with Scripture according to the analogy of faith, that is, in harmony with the whole of Christian doctrine revealed in the Word; (2) giving utmost attention to the grammar (lexicography, phonetics, morphology, syntax, pragmatics) of the original language of the Hebrew, Aramaic, or Greek text; (3) seeking to discern the intended meaning of the text, the "plain" or "literal" sense, aware that the language of Scripture ranges from narrative to discourse, from formal prose to evocative poetry, from archaic to acrostic to apocalyptic, and it uses metaphor, type, parable, and other figures; (4) drawing on philology, linguistics, archaeology, literature, philosophy, history, and other fields in the quest for a better understanding of the text; (5) considering the history of the church's interpretation; (6) applying the text as authoritative also in the present milieu of the interpreter; and (7) above all, seeing the fulfillment and present application of the text in terms of Jesus Christ and his corporate church; upholding the Word, Baptism, and the Supper as the means through which Christ imparts salvation today; and affirming the inauguration, already now, of the eternal benefits of that salvation that is yet to come in the resurrection on the Last Day.

To be sure, the authors and editors do not feel bound to agree with every detail of the exegesis of our Lutheran forefathers. Nor do we imagine that the interpretations presented here are the final word about every crux and enigmatic passage. But the work has been done in harmony with the exegetical tradition that reaches back through the Lutheran confessors all the way to the biblical writers themselves, and in harmony with the confession of the church: grace alone, faith alone, Scripture alone, Christ alone.

The editors wish to acknowledge their debt of gratitude for all who have helped make possible this series. It was conceived at CPH in 1990, and a couple of years of planning and prayer to the Lord of the church preceded its formal launch on July 2, 1992. During that time, Dr. J. A. O. Preus II volunteered his enthusiasm for the project because, in his view, it would nurture and advance the faithful proclamation of the Christian faith as understood by the Lutheran church. The financial support that has underwritten the series was provided by a gracious donor who wished to remain anonymous. Those two faithful servants of God were called to heavenly rest not long after the series was inaugurated.

During the early years, former CPH presidents Dr. John W. Gerber and Dr. Stephen J. Carter had the foresight to recognize the potential benefit of such a landmark work for the church at large. CPH allowed Dr. Christopher W. Mitchell to devote his time and energy to the conception and initial development of the project. Dr. Mitchell has remained the CPH editor and is also the Old Testament editor and the author of the commentary on the Song of Songs. Dr. Dean O. Wenthe served on the project since its official start in 1992 and was the general editor from 1999 until 2016; he is also the author of the commentaries on Jeremiah and Lamentations. Julene Gernant Dumit (M.A.R.) has been the CPH production editor for the entire series. Dr. Jeffrey A. Gibbs served on the editorial board as the New Testament editor from 1999 until 2012 and is the author of the commentaries on Matthew. Dr. Curtis P. Giese, author of the commentary on 2 Peter and Jude and the commentary on James, joined the board in 2011 and now serves as the New Testament editor.

CPH thanks all of the institutions that have enabled their faculty to serve as authors and editors. A particular debt of gratitude is owed to Concordia Theological Seminary, Fort Wayne, Indiana, for kindly allowing Dr. Dean O. Wenthe to serve on the editorial board and to dedicate a substantial portion of his time to the series for many years. CPH also thanks Concordia Seminary, St. Louis, Missouri, for the dedication of Dr. Jeffrey A. Gibbs during his tenure as the New Testament editor. Moreover, Concordia University Texas is granting Dr. Curtis P. Giese a reduced load to enable him to carry on as the New Testament editor of the series. These institutions have thereby extended their ministries in selfless service for the benefit of the greater church.

The editors pray that the beneficence of their institutions may be reflected in this series by an evangelical orientation, a steadfast Christological perspective, an eschatological view toward the ultimate good of Christ's bride, and a concern that the wedding feast of the King's Son may be filled with all manner of guests (Mt 22:1–14).

> Now to him who is able to establish you by my Gospel and the preaching of Jesus Christ, by the revelation of the mystery kept secret for ages past but now revealed also through the prophetic Scriptures, made known to all the nations by order of the eternal God unto the obedience of faith—to the only wise God, through Jesus Christ, be the glory forever. Amen! (Rom 16:25–27)

Author's Preface

Attempting to comment on the wisdom of Proverbs is a humbling task for anyone who takes the Word of God seriously. Never does one feel quite up to the task. But commentaries on the Bible are a necessity for any number of reasons. When I was first asked by the editors of the Concordia Commentary series to undertake this task, I wondered whether it was even possible to complete this volume in a reasonable amount of time and with the high quality it deserves. Due to circumstances that developed beyond my expectations, I was able to complete the manuscript much more quickly than I anticipated. I will leave the judgment on its quality to others. Though I had studied Proverbs for at least a decade before writing this commentary, I was surprised at the insights into this book's wisdom that were revealed as I wrote. One simply cannot exhaust the wonderful wisdom of God that is contained in Proverbs.

In a way, that means that this commentary, or any other biblical commentary, is never a finished work. This is true because our finite human minds and spirits cannot ever completely grasp the truths revealed to us in Scripture by the infinite God. It is also true because in every generation the church faces the challenge of communicating the Gospel of Jesus Christ in new situations.

The Gospel of course is not limited in its power in any situation. As the truth of God, it contains the power of the Almighty to reconcile to himself all people, to build up the faithful, and to comfort all who grieve. That power of the Gospel is what has made Proverbs a loved and cherished book among God's people for generations. In it the Father reveals the glory of his Son as Wisdom, who would, generations after Solomon's day, become flesh. That Wisdom is the one greater than Solomon (Mt 12:42), and he is the Wisdom that Solomon reveals to us. I am grateful that I have been given the opportunity to learn of Christ as I studied this book and wrote this commentary.

Many people are responsible for this commentary. My thanks are due to the library staff at Concordia University Chicago for aiding me in acquiring a great many bibliographic materials. I would also like to thank Dr. Christopher Mitchell and Mrs. Julene Dumit for their helpful comments and suggestions during the editorial process. The encouragement and prayers of my colleagues at Concordia University Chicago are greatly appreciated. In addition, my wife contributed to this commentary in ways that she will never fully appreciate. Her love and support, at times given at great distance in space but in closeness of spirit, were essential to my work.

I pray that by God's grace this commentary may prove useful to the church and may lead many to Christ, the Wisdom of God.

February 22, 2009
The Transfiguration of Our Lord

Principal Abbreviations

Books of the Bible

Gen	2 Ki	Is	Nah	Rom	Titus
Ex	1 Chr	Jer	Hab	1 Cor	Philemon
Lev	2 Chr	Lam	Zeph	2 Cor	Heb
Num	Ezra	Ezek	Hag	Gal	James
Deut	Neh	Dan	Zech	Eph	1 Pet
Josh	Esth	Hos	Mal	Phil	2 Pet
Judg	Job	Joel	Mt	Col	1 Jn
Ruth	Ps (pl. Pss)	Amos	Mk	1 Thess	2 Jn
1 Sam	Prov	Obad	Lk	2 Thess	3 Jn
2 Sam	Eccl	Jonah	Jn	1 Tim	Jude
1 Ki	Song	Micah	Acts	2 Tim	Rev

Books of the Apocrypha and Other Noncanonical Books of the Septuagint

1–2 Esdras	1–2 Esdras
Tobit	Tobit
Judith	Judith
Add Esth	Additions to Esther
Wisdom	Wisdom of Solomon
Sirach	Sirach/Ecclesiasticus
Baruch	Baruch
Ep Jer	Epistle of Jeremiah
Azariah	Prayer of Azariah
Song of the Three	Song of the Three Young Men
Susanna	Susanna
Bel	Bel and the Dragon
Manasseh	Prayer of Manasseh
1–2 Macc	1–2 Maccabees
3–4 Macc	3–4 Maccabees
Ps 151	Psalm 151
Odes	Odes
Ps(s) Sol	Psalm(s) of Solomon

Reference Works and Scripture Versions

AC	Augsburg Confession
AE	*Luther's Works*. St. Louis: Concordia, and Philadelphia: Fortress, 1955– [American Edition]
ANE	*The Ancient Near East: An Anthology of Texts and Pictures*. Vol. 1. Edited by J. B. Pritchard. Princeton: Princeton University Press, 1958
ANET	*Ancient Near Eastern Texts Relating to the Old Testament.* Edited by J. B. Pritchard. 3d ed. Princeton: Princeton University Press, 1969
ANF	*The Ante-Nicene Fathers.* Edited by A. Roberts and J. Donaldson. 10 vols. Repr., Peabody, Mass.: Hendrickson, 1994
Ap	Apology of the Augsburg Confession
BDAG	Bauer, W., F. W. Danker, W. F. Arndt, F. W. Gingrich. *A Greek-English Lexicon of the New Testament and Other Early Christian Literature.* 3d ed. Chicago: University of Chicago Press, 2000
BDB	Brown, F., S. R. Driver, and C. A. Briggs. *A Hebrew and English Lexicon of the Old Testament.* Oxford: Clarendon, 1979
BHS	*Biblia Hebraica Stuttgartensia*
DCH	*The Dictionary of Classical Hebrew.* Edited by D. J. A. Clines. Sheffield: Sheffield Academic Press, 1993–
Ep	Epitome of the Formula of Concord
FC	Formula of Concord
FF	*Fauna and Flora of the Bible.* 2d ed. Helps for Translators. London: United Bible Societies, 1980
ESV	English Standard Version of the Bible
ET	English translation
FC	Formula of Concord
GKC	*Gesenius' Hebrew Grammar.* Edited by E. Kautzsch. Translated by A. E. Cowley. 2d ed. Oxford: Clarendon, 1910
HALOT	Koehler, L., W. Baumgartner, and J. J. Stamm. *The Hebrew and Aramaic Lexicon of the Old Testament.* Translated and edited under the supervision of M. E. J. Richardson. 5 vols. Leiden: Brill, 1994–2000
Jastrow	Jastrow, M., comp. *A Dictionary of the Targumim, the Talmud Babli and Yerushalmi, and the Midrashic Literature.* 2 vols. Brooklyn: P. Shalom, 1967

Joüon	Joüon, P. *A Grammar of Biblical Hebrew.* Translated and revised by T. Muraoka. 2 vols. Subsidia biblica 14/1–2. Rome: Editrice Pontificio Istituto Biblico, 1991
KJV	King James Version of the Bible
LC	Large Catechism by M. Luther
LSB	*Lutheran Service Book.* St. Louis: Concordia, 2006
LSB Agenda	*Lutheran Service Book: Agenda.* St. Louis: Concordia, 2006
LSJ	Liddell, H. G., R. Scott, and H. S. Jones. *A Greek-English Lexicon.* 9th ed. with revised supplement. Oxford: Clarendon, 1996
LXX	Septuagint
MT	Masoretic Text of the Hebrew Old Testament
NAB	New American Bible
NASB	New American Standard Bible
NIV	New International Version of the Bible
NJB	New Jerusalem Bible
NKJV	New King James Version of the Bible
NPNF[1]	*The Nicene and Post-Nicene Fathers.* Series 1. Edited by P. Schaff. 14 vols. Repr., Peabody, Mass.: Hendrickson, 1994
NPNF[2]	*The Nicene and Post-Nicene Fathers.* Series 2. Edited by P. Schaff and H. Wace. 14 vols. Repr., Peabody, Mass.: Hendrickson, 1994
NRSV	New Revised Standard Version of the Bible
NT	New Testament
OT	Old Testament
Payne Smith	Payne Smith, R. *A Compendious Syriac Dictionary.* Oxford: Clarendon, 1903
PG	Patrologia graeca. Edited by J.-P. Migne. 161 vols. Paris, 1857–1866
PL	Patrologia latina. Edited by J.-P. Migne. 217 vols. Paris, 1844–1855
SA	Smalcald Articles
SC	Small Catechism by M. Luther
SD	Solid Declaration of the Formula of Concord

TDOT	*Theological Dictionary of the Old Testament.* Edited by G. J. Botterweck, H. Ringgren, and H.-J. Fabry. Translated by J. T. Willis et al. 15 vols. Grand Rapids: Eerdmans, 1974–2006
TLH	*The Lutheran Hymnal.* St. Louis: Concordia, 1941
TLOT	*Theological Lexicon of the Old Testament.* Edited by E. Jenni and C. Westermann. Translated by M. E. Biddle. 3 vols. Peabody, Mass.: Hendrickson, 1997
TWOT	*Theological Wordbook of the Old Testament.* Edited by R. L. Harris, G. L. Archer Jr., and B. K. Waltke. 2 vols. Chicago: Moody, 1980
WA	*D. Martin Luthers Werke: Kritische Gesamtausgabe.* 73 vols. in 85. Weimar: Böhlau, 1883– [Weimarer Ausgabe]
WA DB	*D. Martin Luthers Werke: Kritische Gesamtausgabe. Die Deutsche Bibel.* 12 vols. in 15. Weimar: Böhlau, 1906–1961 [Weimarer Ausgabe Deutsche Bibel]
WA TR	*D. Martin Luthers Werke: Kritische Gesamtausgabe. Tischreden.* 6 vols. Weimar: Böhlau, 1912–1921 [Weimarer Ausgabe Tischreden]
Waltke-O'Connor	Waltke, B. K., and M. O'Connor. *An Introduction to Biblical Hebrew Syntax.* Winona Lake, Ind.: Eisenbrauns, 1990

Hebrew and Aramaic Verbal Systems

Hebrew Verbal System

	G-Stem System[1] *Basic*	D-Stem System *Doubling*[2]	H-Stem System *H-Prefix*
Active	G (Qal)	D (Piel)	H (Hiphil)
Passive	Gp (Qal passive)	Dp (Pual)	Hp (Hophal)
Reflexive/Passive	N (Niphal)	HtD (Hithpael)	

Aramaic Verbal System

	G-Stem System *Basic*	D-Stem System *Doubling*	H-Stem System *H-Prefix*[3]
Active	G (Peal)	D (Pael)	H (Haphel)
Passive	Gp (Peil)	Dp (Pual)	Hp (Hophal)
Reflexive/Passive[4]	HtG (Hithpeel)	HtD (Hithpaal)	HtH (Hishtaphal)

1 "G" is from the German *Grundstamm,* "basic stem."

2 This also includes other doubling patterns such as Polel (D), Pilpel (D), Polal (Dp), Polpal (Dp), Hithpolel (HtD), and Hithpalpel (HtD).

3 This also includes Aphel (H), where the ה is written as א, and the Shaphel (H), with the prefix שׁ.

4 This also includes patterns where the ה is written as א: Ithpeel (HtG) and Ithpaal (HtD).

Icons

These icons are used in the margins of this commentary to highlight the following themes:

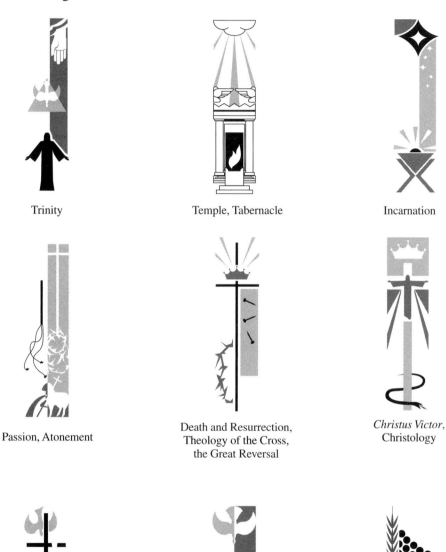

Trinity

Temple, Tabernacle

Incarnation

Passion, Atonement

Death and Resurrection,
Theology of the Cross,
the Great Reversal

Christus Victor,
Christology

Baptism

Catechesis,
Instruction, Revelation

Lord's Supper

Ministry of Word and Sacrament,
Office of the Keys

The Church,
Christian Marriage

Worship

Sin, Law Breaking,
Death

Hope of Heaven,
Eschatology

Justification

Bibliography

Ackroyd, P. R. "The Meaning of Hebrew דור Considered." *Journal of Semitic Studies* 13 (1968): 3–10.

Albright, William F. "A New Hebrew Word for 'Glaze' in Proverbs 26:23." *Bulletin of the American Schools of Oriental Research* 98 (1945): 24–25.

Aletti, J. N. "Séduction et parole en Proverbes I–IX." *Vetus Testamentum* 27 (1977): 129–44.

Andersen, Francis I., and A. Dean Forbes. *The Vocabulary of the Old Testament.* Rome: Pontificio Istituto Biblico, 1989.

Andrew, M. E. "Variety of Expression in Proverbs XXIII 29–35." *Vetus Testamentum* 28 (1978): 102–3.

Archer, Gleason L. "Proverbs 22:6 and the Training of Children." Pages 273–75 in *Learning from the Sages: Selected Studies on the Book of Proverbs.* Edited by Roy B. Zuck. Grand Rapids: Baker, 1995.

Barker, Kenneth L. "Proverbs 23:7—To Think' or 'To Serve Food'?" *Journal of the Ancient Near Eastern Society of Columbia University* 19 (1989): 3–8.

Barr, James. "בארץ ~ μόλις: Prov. xi. 31, I Pet. iv. 18." *Journal of Semitic Studies* 20 (1975): 149–64.

Berman, Joshua. "The 'Sword of Mouths' (Jud. III 16; Ps. CXLIX 6; Prov. V 4): A Metaphor and Its Ancient Near Eastern Context." *Vetus Testamentum* 52 (2002): 291–303.

Bernat, David. "Biblical *Waṣf*s beyond Song of Songs." *Journal for the Study of the Old Testament* 28 (2004): 327–49.

Blenkinsopp, Joseph. "The Social Context of the 'Outsider Woman' in Proverbs 1–9." *Biblica* 72 (1991): 457–73.

Boorer, Suzanne. "A Matter of Life and Death: A Comparison of Proverbs 1–9 and Job." Pages 187–204 in *Prophets and Paradigms: Essays in Honor of Gene M. Tucker.* Edited by Stephen B. Reid. Journal for the Study of the Old Testament: Supplement Series 229. Sheffield: Sheffield Academic Press, 1996.

Bricker, Daniel P. "The Doctrine of the 'Two Ways' in Proverbs." *Journal of the Evangelical Theological Society* 38 (1995): 501–17.

Brown, William P. *Character in Crisis: A Fresh Approach to the Wisdom Literature of the Old Testament.* Grand Rapids: Eerdmans, 1996.

———. "The Didactic Power of Metaphor in the Aphoristic Sayings of Proverbs." *Journal for the Study of the Old Testament* 29 (2004): 133–54.

Brueggemann, Walter. "A Neglected Sapiential Word Pair." *Zeitschrift für die alttestamentliche Wissenschaft* 89 (1977): 234–58.

Bryce, Glendon E. "Another Wisdom-'Book' in Proverbs." *Journal of Biblical Literature* 91 (1972): 145–57.

———. " 'Better'-Proverbs: An Historical and Structural Study." Pages 343–54 in vol. 2 of *Book of Seminar Papers.* Edited by Lane C. McGaughy. Missoula, Mont.: Society of Biblical Literature, 1972.

Budge, E. A. Wallis. "The Precepts of Life by Amen-em-apt, the Son of Ka-nekht." Pages 431–46 in *Recueil d'études égyptologiques dédiées à la mémoire de Jean-Françios Champollion.* Paris: Librairie Ancienne Honoré Champion, 1922.

———. *The Teaching of Åmen-em-åpt, Son of Kanekht: The Egyptian Hieroglyphic Text and an English Translation, with Translations of the Moral and Religious Teachings of Egyptian Kings and Officials Illustrating the Development of Religious Philosophy in Egypt during a Period of about Two Thousand Years.* London: Hopkinson, 1924.

Burns, John Barclay. "Proverbs 7,6–27: Vignettes from the Cycle of Astarte and Adonis." *Scandinavian Journal of the Old Testament* 9 (1995): 21–36.

Byargeon, Rick W. "The Structure and Significance of Prov 9:7–12." *Journal of the Evangelical Theological Society* 40 (1997): 367–75.

Camp, Claudia V. *Wisdom and the Feminine in the Book of Proverbs.* Bible and Literature Series 11. Decatur, Ga.: Almond, 1985.

Carasik, Michael. "Who Were the 'Men of Hezekiah' (Proverbs XXV 1)?" *Vetus Testamentum* 44 (1994): 289–300.

Cathcart, Kevin J. "*Beḥopnāw* in Proverbs XXX 4." *Vetus Testamentum* 48 (1998): 264–65.

———. "Proverbs 30,4 and Ugaritic ḪPN, 'Garment.' " *Catholic Biblical Quarterly* 32 (1970): 418–20.

Chemnitz, Martin. *The Two Natures in Christ.* Translated by J. A. O. Preus. St. Louis: Concordia, 1971.

Clements, Ronald E. "The Concept of Abomination in the Book of Proverbs." Pages 211–25 in *Texts, Temples, and Traditions: A Tribute to Menahem Haran.* Edited by Michael V. Fox et al. Winona Lake, Ind.: Eisenbrauns, 1996.

———. "The Good Neighbour in the Book of Proverbs." Pages 209–28 in *Of Prophets' Visions and the Wisdom of Sages: Essays in Honour of R. Norman Whybray on His Seventieth Birthday.* Edited by Heather A. McKay and David J. A. Clines. Journal for the Study of the Old Testament: Supplement Series 162. Sheffield: Sheffield Academic Press, 1993.

Clifford, Richard J. "Observations on the Text and Versions of Proverbs." Pages 47–61 in *Wisdom, You Are My Sister: Studies in Honor of Roland E. Murphy, O. Carm., on the Occasion of His Eightieth Birthday.* Catholic Biblical Quarterly Monograph Series 29. Edited by Michael L. Barré. Washington, D.C.: Catholic Biblical Association of America, 1997.

———. *Proverbs: A Commentary.* Old Testament Library. Louisville: Westminster John Knox, 1999.

———. "Your Attention Please! Heeding the Proverbs." *Journal for the Study of the Old Testament* 29 (2004): 155–63.

Cody, Aelred. "Notes on Proverbs 22,21 and 22,23b." *Biblica* 61 (1980): 418–26.

Cohen, Jeffrey M. "An Unrecognized Connotation of *NŠQ PEH* with Special Reference to Three Biblical Occurrences." *Vetus Testamentum* 32 (1982): 416–24.

Cook, Johann. "אִשָּׁה זָרָה (Proverbs 1–9 Septuagint): A Metaphor for Foreign Wisdom?" *Zeitschrift für die alttestamentliche Wissenschaft* 106 (1994): 458–76.

———. "The Dating of Septuagint Proverbs." *Ephemerides theologicae lovanienses* 69 (1993): 383–99.

———. "The Law of Moses in Septuagint Proverbs." *Vetus Testamentum* 49 (1999): 448–61.

———. "The Origin of the Tradition of the יצר הטוב and יצר הרע." *Journal for the Study of Judaism in the Persian, Hellenistic and Roman Period* 38 (2007): 80–91.

———. *The Septuagint of Proverbs: Jewish and/or Hellenistic Proverbs? Concerning the Hellenistic Colouring of LXX Proverbs.* Supplements to Vetus Testamentum 69. Leiden: Brill, 1997.

Crenshaw, James L. "The Expression *Mî Yôdēaʿ* in the Hebrew Bible." *Vetus Testamentum* 36 (1986): 274–88.

———. *Old Testament Wisdom: An Introduction.* Atlanta: John Knox, 1981.

Dahood, Mitchell. "Immortality in Proverbs 12,28." *Biblica* 41 (1960): 176–81.

———. "The Hapax *Ḥārak* in Proverbs 12,27." *Biblica* 63 (1982): 60–62.

———. "Honey That Drips: Notes on Proverbs 5,2–3." *Biblica* 54 (1973): 65–66.

———. "Proverbs 8,22–31: Translation and Commentary." *Catholic Biblical Quarterly* 30 (1968): 512–21.

Daube, D. "A Quartet of Beasties in the Book of Proverbs." *Journal of Theological Studies* 36 (1985): 380–86.

Davies, Eryl W. "The Meaning of *Qesem* in Prv 16, 10." *Biblica* 61 (1980): 554–56.

Deist, Ferdinand. "Prov. 31:1: A Case of Constant Mistranslation." *Journal of Northwest Semitic Languages* 6 (1978): 1–3.

Delitzsch, Franz. *Biblical Commentary on the Proverbs of Solomon.* Translated by M. G. Easton. 2 vols. 1874–1875. Repr., Grand Rapids: Eerdmans, 1978.

Dell, Katharine J. *The Book of Proverbs in Social and Theological Context.* Cambridge: Cambridge University Press, 2006.

Dietrich, M., O. Loretz, and J. Sanmartín. "Die angebliche ug.-he. Parallele *spsg* || *sps(j)g(jm)*." Pages 37–40 in vol. 8 (1976) of *Ugarit-Forschungen: Internationales Jahrbuch für die Altertumskunde Syrien-Palästinas*. Edited by Kurt Bergerhof, Manfried Dietrich, and Oswald Loretz. Kevelaer: Butzon & Bercker, 1977.

Donald, Trevor. "The Semantic Field of 'Folly' in Proverbs, Job, Psalms, and Ecclesiastes." *Vetus Testamentum* 13 (1963): 285–92.

Driver, G. R. "Problems in the Hebrew Text of Proverbs." *Biblica* 32 (1951): 173–97.

Emerton, J. A. "The Interpretation of Proverbs 21,28." *Zeitschrift für die alttestamentliche Wissenschaft* 100 (1988 Supplement): 161–70.

———. "Looking on One's Enemies." *Vetus Testamentum* 51 (2001): 186–96.

———. "The Meaning of Proverbs XIII. 2." *Journal of Theological Studies* 35 (1984): 91–95.

———. "A Note on Proverbs II. 18." *Journal of Theological Studies* 30 (1979): 153–58.

———. "A Note on Proverbs xii. 26." *Zeitschrift für die alttestamentliche Wissenschaft* 76 (1964): 191–93.

———. "A Note on the Hebrew Text of Proverbs i. 22–3." *Journal of Theological Studies* 19 (1968): 609–14.

———. "Notes on Some Passages in the Book of Proverbs." *Journal of Theological Studies* 20 (1969): 202–20.

———. "A Problem in Proverbs 3:35." Pages 9–24 in *Sefer Moshe: The Moshe Weinfeld Jubilee Volume: Studies in the Bible and the Ancient Near East, Qumran, and Post-Biblical Judaism*. Edited by Chaim Cohen, Avi Hurvitz, and Shalom M. Paul. Winona Lake, Ind.: Eisenbrauns, 2004.

———. "The Teaching of Amenemope and Proverbs XXII 17–XXIV 22: Further Reflections on a Long-Standing Problem." *Vetus Testamentum* 51 (2001): 431–65.

Eshel, Hanan. "6Q30, a Cursive *Šîn*, and Proverbs 11." *Journal of Biblical Literature* 122 (2003): 544–46.

Estes, Daniel J. *Hear, My Son: Teaching and Learning in Proverbs 1–9*. New Studies in Biblical Theology. Grand Rapids: Eerdmans, 1997.

Fee, Gordon D. "Wisdom Christology in Paul: A Dissenting View." Pages 251–79 in *The Way of Wisdom: Essays in Honor of Bruce K. Waltke*. Edited by J. I. Packer and Sven K. Soderlund. Grand Rapids: Zondervan, 2000.

Finegan, Jack. *Handbook of Biblical Chronology.* Rev. ed. Peabody, Mass.: Hendrickson, 1998.

Finkbeiner, Douglas. "An Analysis of the Structure of Proverbs 28 and 29." *Calvary Baptist Theological Journal* 11/2 (Fall 1995): 1–14.

Fishbane, Michael. "Torah and Tradition." Pages 275–300 in *Tradition and Theology in the Old Testament*. Edited by Douglas A. Knight. Philadelphia: Fortress, 1977.

Fontaine, Carole R. "The Proof of the Pudding: Proverbs and Gender in the Performance Arena." *Journal for the Study of the Old Testament* 29 (2004): 179–204.

———. *Traditional Sayings in the Old Testament: A Contextual Study*. Bible and Literature Series 5. Sheffield: Almond, 1982.

Forti, Tova. "Animal Images in the Didactic Rhetoric of the Book of Proverbs." *Biblica* 77 (1996): 48–63.

———."The *Isha Zara* in Proverbs 1–9: Allegory and Allegorization." *Hebrew Studies* 48 (2007): 89–100.

Fox, Michael V. "ʾ*Amon* Again." *Journal of Biblical Literature* 115 (1996): 699–702.

———. "Ethics and Wisdom in the Book of Proverbs." *Hebrew Studies* 48 (2007): 75–88.

———. "Ideas of Wisdom in Proverbs 1–9." *Journal of Biblical Literature* 116 (1997): 613–33.

———. "The Pedagogy of Proverbs 2." *Journal of Biblical Literature* 113 (1994): 233–43.

———. "Preface." *Journal for the Study of the Old Testament* 29 (2004): 131–32.

———. *Proverbs 1–9: A New Translation with Introduction and Commentary.* Anchor Bible 18A. New York: Doubleday, 2000.

———. "The Rhetoric of Disjointed Proverbs." *Journal for the Study of the Old Testament* 29 (2004): 165–77.

———. "The Social Location of the Book of Proverbs." Pages 227–39 in *Texts, Temples, and Traditions: A Tribute to Menahem Haran.* Edited by Michael V. Fox et al. Winona Lake, Ind.: Eisenbrauns, 1996.

———. "Who Can Learn? A Dispute in Ancient Pedagogy." Pages 62–77 in *Wisdom, You Are My Sister: Studies in Honor of Roland E. Murphy, O. Carm., on the Occasion of His Eightieth Birthday.* Catholic Biblical Quarterly Monograph Series 29. Edited by Michael L. Barré. Washington, D.C.: Catholic Biblical Association of America, 1997.

Franklyn, Paul. "The Sayings of Agur in Proverbs 30: Piety or Skepticism?" *Zeitschrift für die alttestamentliche Wissenschaft* 95 (1983): 238–52.

Franzmann, Majella. "The Wheel in Proverbs XX 26 and Ode of Solomon XXIII 11–16." *Vetus Testamentum* 41 (1991): 121–23.

Freedman, David Noel. "Proverbs 2 and 31: A Study in Structural Complementarity." Pages 47–55 in *Tehillah le-Moshe: Biblical and Judaic Studies in Honor of Moshe Greenberg.* Edited by Mordechai Cogan et. al. Winona Lake, Ind.: Eisenbrauns, 1997.

Garrett, Duane A. *Proverbs, Ecclesiastes, Song of Songs.* New American Commentary 14. Nashville: Broadman, 1993.

———. "Votive Prostitution Again: A Comparison of Proverbs 7:13–14 and 21:28–29." *Journal of Biblical Literature* 109 (1990): 681–82.

Gerhard, Johann. *On the Nature of God and on the Most Holy Mystery of the Trinity.* Theological Commonplaces. Translated by Richard J. Dinda. St. Louis: Concordia, 2007.

Gibbs, Jeffrey A. *Matthew 1:1–11:1.* Concordia Commentary. St. Louis: Concordia, 2006.

Giese, Ronald L., Jr. "Compassion for the Lowly in Septuagint Proverbs." *Journal for the Study of the Pseudepigrapha* 11 (1993): 109–17.

———. "Qualifying Wealth in the Septuagint of Proverbs." *Journal of Biblical Literature* 111 (1992): 409–25.

———. "Strength through Wisdom and the Bee in LXX-Prov 6,8[a-c]." *Biblica* 73 (1992): 404–11.

Gluck, J. J. "Proverbs XXX 15a." *Vetus Testamentum* 14 (1964): 367–70.

Goldingay, John. "The Arrangement of Sayings in Proverbs 10–15." *Journal for the Study of the Old Testament* 61 (1994): 75–83.

Greenfield, Jonas C. "The Seven Pillars of Wisdom (Prov 9:1)—A Mistranslation." *Jewish Quarterly Review* 76 (1985): 13–20.

Greenspahn, Frederick E. "A Mesopotamian Proverb and Its Biblical Reverberations." *Journal of the American Oriental Society* 114 (1994): 33–38.

Grossberg, Daniel. "Two Kinds of Sexual Relationships in the Hebrew Bible." *Hebrew Studies* 35 (1994): 7–25.

Habel, Norman C. "The Symbolism of Wisdom in Proverbs 1–9." *Interpretation* 26 (1972): 131–57.

Haran, Menahem. "The Graded Numerical Sequence and the Phenomenon of 'Automatism' in Biblical Poetry." Pages 238–67 in *Congress Volume: Uppsala 1971*. Supplements to Vetus Testamentum 22. Leiden: Brill, 1972.

Harland, P. J. "בצע: Bribe, Extortion or Profit?" *Vetus Testamentum* 50 (2000): 310–22.

Harris, Scott L. *Proverbs 1–9: A Study of Inner-Biblical Interpretation*. Society of Biblical Literature Dissertation Series 150. Atlanta: Scholars, 1996.

Harstad, Adolph L. *Joshua*. Concordia Commentary. St. Louis: Concordia, 2004.

Hawkins, Tom R. "The Wife of Noble Character in Proverbs 31:10–31." *Bibliotheca sacra* 153 (1996): 12–23.

Heim, Knut Martin. *Like Grapes of Gold Set in Silver: An Interpretation of Proverbial Clusters in Proverbs 10:1–22:16*. Beihefte zur Zeitschrift für die alttestamentliche Wissenschaft 273. Berlin: De Gruyter, 2001.

Hermisson, Hans-Jürgen. *Studien zur israelitischen Spruchweisheit*. Neukirchen-Vluyn: Neukirchener, 1968.

Hildebrandt, Ted. "Motivation and Antithetic Parallelism in Proverbs 10–15." *Journal of the Evangelical Theological Society* 35 (1992): 433–44.

———. "Proverbial Pairs: Compositional Units in Proverbs 10–29." *Journal of Biblical Literature* 107 (1988): 207–24.

———. "Proverbial Strings: Cohesion in Proverbs 10." *Grace Theological Journal* 11 (1990): 171–85.

———. "Proverbs 22:6a: Train Up a Child?" *Grace Theological Journal* 9 (1988): 3–19. Reprinted as pages 277–92 in *Learning from the Sages: Selected Studies on the Book of Proverbs*. Edited by Roy B. Zuck. Grand Rapids: Baker, 1995.

Hoglund, Kenneth G. "The Fool and the Wise in Dialogue: Proverbs 26:4–5." Pages 161–80 in *The Listening Heart: Essays in Wisdom and the Psalms in Honor of Roland E. Murphy, O. Carm.* Edited by Kenneth G. Hoglund et. al. Sheffield: Sheffield Academic Press, 1987. Reprinted as pages 339–52 in *Learning from the Sages: Selected Studies on the Book of Proverbs.* Edited by Roy B. Zuck. Grand Rapids: Baker, 1995.

Holladay, William L. "Indications of Segmented Sleep in the Bible." *Catholic Biblical Quarterly* 69 (2007): 215–21.

Humbert, Paul. " 'Etendre la main' (Note de lexicographie hébraïque)." *Vetus Testamentum* 12 (1962): 383–95.

Humphreys, W. Lee. "The Motif of the Wise Courtier in the Book of Proverbs." Pages 177–90 in *Israelite Wisdom: Theological and Literary Essays in Honor of Samuel Terrien.* Edited by John G. Gammie, et. al. New York: Union Theological Seminary, 1978.

Hurowitz, Victor Avigdor. "Nursling, Advisor, Architect? אמון and the Role of Wisdom in Proverbs 8,22–31." *Biblica* 80 (1999): 391–400.

———. "Paradise Regained: Proverbs 3:13–20 Reconsidered." Pages 49–62 in *Sefer Moshe: The Moshe Weinfeld Jubilee Volume: Studies in the Bible and the Ancient Near East, Qumran, and Post-Biblical Judaism.* Edited by Chaim Cohen, Avi Hurvitz, and Shalom M. Paul. Winona Lake, Ind.: Eisenbrauns, 2004.

———. "Proverbs 29.22–27: Another Unnoticed Alphabetic Acrostic." *Journal for the Study of the Old Testament* 92 (2001): 121–5.

———. "Two Terms for Wealth in Proverbs VIII in Light of Akkadian." *Vetus Testamentum* 50 (2000): 252–57.

Hurvitz, Avi. "Toward a Precise Definition of the Term אמון in Proverbs 8:30" [Hebrew]. Pages 647–50 in *The Bible in Light of Its Interpreters: Sarah Kamin Memorial Volume.* Edited by S. Japhet. Jerusalem, 1994.

Irwin, William A. "Where Shall Wisdom Be Found?" *Journal of Biblical Literature* 80 (1961): 133–42.

Irwin, William H. "The Metaphor in Prov 11,30." *Biblica* 65 (1984): 97–100.

Jobes, Karen H. "Sophia Christology: The Way of Wisdom?" Pages 226–50 in *The Way of Wisdom: Essays in Honor of Bruce K. Waltke.* Edited by J. I. Packer and Sven K. Soderlund. Grand Rapids: Zondervan, 2000.

Johnson, John E. "An Analysis of Proverbs 1:1–7." *Bibliotheca sacra* 144 (1987): 419–32.

Johnson, Timothy. "Implied Antecedents in Job XL 2B and Proverbs III 6A." *Vetus Testamentum* 52 (2002): 278–84.

Jones, John N. " 'Think of the Lilies' and Prov 6:6–11." *Harvard Theological Review* 88 (1995): 175–77.

Jones, Scott C. "Wisdom's Pedagogy: A Comparison of Proverbs VII and 4Q184." *Vetus Testamentum* 53 (2003): 65–80.

Kaiser, Walter C., Jr. "True Marital Love in Proverbs 5:15–23 and the Interpretation of Song of Songs." Pages 106–16 in *The Way of Wisdom: Essays in Honor of Bruce K. Waltke*. Edited by J. I. Packer and Sven K. Soderlund. Grand Rapids: Zondervan, 2000.

Kassis, Riad Aziz. *The Book of Proverbs and Arabic Proverbial Works*. Supplements to Vetus Testamentum 74. Leiden: Brill, 1999.

———. "A Note on שָׁלָל (Prov. XXXI 11b)." *Vetus Testamentum* 50 (2000): 258–59.

Kelly, J. N. D. *Early Christian Creeds*. 3d ed. New York: Longman, 1972.

Kidner, Derek. *Proverbs: An Introduction and Commentary*. Tyndale Old Testament Commentaries. Leicester: Intervarsity, 1964.

Kitchen, Kenneth A. "The Basic Literary Forms and Formulations of Ancient Instructional Writings in Egypt and Western Asia." Pages 235–82 in *Studien zu altägyptischen Lebenslehren*. Edited by Erik Hornung and Othmar Keel. Freiburg: Universitätsverlag, 1979.

———. "Proverbs and Wisdom Books of the Ancient Near East: The Factual History of a Literary Form." *Tyndale Bulletin* 28 (1977): 69–114.

Kleinig, John W. *Leviticus*. Concordia Commentary. St. Louis: Concordia, 2003.

Krantz, Eva Strömberg. " 'A Man Not Supported by God': On Some Crucial Words in Proverbs XXX 1." *Vetus Testamentum* 46 (1996): 548–53.

Kruger, Paul A. "Promiscuity or Marriage Fidelity? A Note on Prov 5:15–18." *Journal of Northwest Semitic Languages* 13 (1987): 61–68.

Kselman, John S. "Ambiguity and Wordplay in Proverbs XI." *Vetus Testamentum* 52 (2002): 545–48.

Kuntz, J. Kenneth. "Affirming Less as More: Scholarly Engagements with Aphoristic Rhetoric." *Journal for the Study of the Old Testament* 29 (2004): 205–42.

Lang, Bernhard. "Women's Work, Household and Property in Two Mediterranean Societies: A Comparative Essay on Proverbs XXXI 10–31." *Vetus Testamentum* 54 (2004): 188–207.

Lenzi, Alan. "Proverbs 8:22–31: Three Perspectives on Its Composition." *Journal of Biblical Literature* 125 (2006): 687–714.

Lessing, R. Reed. *Amos*. Concordia Commentary. St. Louis: Concordia, 2009.

Lichtenstein, Murray H. "Chiasm and Symmetry in Proverbs 31." *Catholic Biblical Quarterly* 44 (1982): 202–11. Reprinted as pages 381–90 in *Learning from the Sages: Selected Studies on the Book of Proverbs*. Edited by Roy B. Zuck. Grand Rapids: Baker, 1995.

Loader, J. A. "Wisdom by (the) People for (the) People." *Zeitschrift für die alttestamentliche Wissenschaft* 111 (1999): 211–33.

Lockwood, Gregory J. *1 Corinthians*. Concordia Commentary. St. Louis: Concordia, 2000.

Loewenstamm, Samuel E. "Remarks on Proverbs XVII 12 and XX 27." *Vetus Testamentum* 37 (1987): 221–24.

Longman, Tremper. *Proverbs.* Baker Commentary on the Old Testament Wisdom and Psalms. Grand Rapids: Baker, 2006.

Lyons, Ellen Louise. "A Note on Proverbs 31.10–31." Pages 237–45 in *The Listening Heart: Essays in Wisdom and the Psalms in Honor of Roland E. Murphy, O. Carm.* Edited by Kenneth G. Hoglund et. al. Sheffield: Sheffield Academic Press, 1987.

Macintosh, Andrew A. "A Consideration of Hebrew נער." *Vetus Testamentum* 19 (1969): 471–79.

———. "A Note on Proverbs XXV 27." *Vetus Testamentum* 20 (1970): 112–14.

Malchow, Bruce V. "A Manual for Future Monarchs." *Catholic Biblical Quarterly* 47 (1985): 238–45. Reprinted as 353–60 in *Learning from the Sages: Selected Studies on the Book of Proverbs.* Edited by Roy B. Zuck. Grand Rapids: Baker, 1995.

Martin, James D. *Proverbs.* Old Testament Guides. Sheffield: Sheffield Academic Press, 1995.

McCreesh, Thomas P. *Biblical Sound and Sense: Poetic Sound Patterns in Proverbs 10–29.* Journal for the Study of the Old Testament: Supplement Series 128. Sheffield: Sheffield Academic Press, 1991.

———. "Wisdom as Wife: Proverbs 31:10–31." *Revue biblique* 92 (1985): 25–46. Reprinted as pages 391–410 in *Learning from the Sages: Selected Studies on the Book of Proverbs.* Edited by Roy B. Zuck. Grand Rapids: Baker, 1995.

McKane, William. *Proverbs: A New Approach.* Philadelphia: Westminster, 1970.

Meinhold, Arndt. *Die Sprüche.* Zürcher Bibel. 2 vols. Zurich: Theologischer, 1991.

———. "Das Wortspiel רצון–רזון in Prov 14,28–35." *Zeitschrift für die alttestamentliche Wissenschaft* 110 (1998): 615–16.

Miller, Cynthia L. "A Linguistic Approach to Ellipsis in Biblical Poetry (Or, What to Do When Exegesis of What Is There Depends on What Isn't)." *Bulletin for Biblical Research* 13 (2003): 251–70.

Mitchell, Christopher W. *The Song of Songs.* Concordia Commentary. St. Louis: Concordia, 2003.

Montgomery, David J. " 'A Bribe Is a Charm': A Study of Proverbs 17:8." Pages 134–49 in *The Way of Wisdom: Essays in Honor of Bruce K. Waltke.* Edited by J. I. Packer and Sven K. Soderlund. Grand Rapids: Zondervan, 2000.

Moore, Rick D. "A Home for the Alien: Worldly Wisdom and Covenantal Confession in Proverbs 30,1–9." *Zeitschrift für die alttestamentliche Wissenschaft* 106 (1994): 96–107.

Murphy, Roland E. "A Brief Note on Translating Proverbs." *Catholic Biblical Quarterly* 60 (1998): 621–25.

———. *Proverbs.* Word Biblical Commentary 22. Nashville: Thomas Nelson, 1998.

———. "Proverbs 22:1–9." *Interpretation* 41 (1987): 398–402.

———. "Wisdom and Eros in Proverbs 1–9." *Catholic Biblical Quarterly* 50 (1988): 600–603.

———. *Wisdom Literature: Job, Proverbs, Ruth, Canticles, Ecclesiastes, and Esther.* Forms of the Old Testament Literature 13. Grand Rapids: Eerdmans, 1981.

———. "Wisdom's Song: Proverbs 1:20–33." *Catholic Biblical Quarterly* 48 (1986): 456–60.

Murphy, Roland E., and Elizabeth Huwiler. *Proverbs, Ecclesiastes, Song of Songs.* New International Biblical Commentary, Old Testament, 12. Peabody, Mass.: Hendrickson, 1999.

Niccacci, Alviero. "Analysing Biblical Hebrew Poetry." *Journal for the Study of the Old Testament* 74 (1997): 77–93.

North, Francis Sparling. "The Four Insatiables." *Vetus Testamentum* 15 (1965): 281–82.

Novick, Tzvi. " 'She Binds Her Arms': Rereading Proverbs 31:17." *Journal of Biblical Literature* 128 (2009): 107–13.

O'Connell, Robert H. "Proverbs VII 16–17: A Case of Fatal Deception in a 'Woman and the Window' Type-Scene." *Vetus Testamentum* 41 (1991): 235–41.

Ogden, Graham S. "The 'Better'-Proverb (Tôb-Spruch), Rhetorical Criticism, and Qoheleth." *Journal of Biblical Literature* 96 (1977): 489–505.

Overland, Paul. "Did the Sage Draw from the Schema? A Study of Proverbs 3:1–12." *Catholic Biblical Quarterly* 62 (2000): 424–40.

———. "Structure in *The Wisdom of Amenemope* and Proverbs." Pages 275–91 in *"Go to the Land I Will Show You": Studies in Honor of Dwight W. Young.* Edited by Joseph E. Coleson and Victor H. Matthews. Winona Lake, Ind.: Eisenbrauns, 1996.

Paul, Shalom M. "Unrecognized Biblical Legal Idioms in the Light of Comparative Akkadian Expressions." *Revue biblique* 86 (1979): 231–39.

Peels, Hendrik G. L. "Passion or Justice? The Interpretation of *B*^{e}*yôm Nāqām* in Proverbs VI 34." *Vetus Testamentum* 44 (1994): 270–74.

Perdue, Leo G. "Wisdom Theology and Social History in Proverbs 1–9." Pages 78–101 in *Wisdom, You Are My Sister: Studies in Honor of Roland E. Murphy, O. Carm., on the Occasion of His Eightieth Birthday.* Catholic Biblical Quarterly Monograph Series 29. Edited by Michael L. Barré. Washington, D.C.: Catholic Biblical Association of America, 1997.

Plass, Ewald M., comp. *What Luther Says.* St. Louis: Concordia, 1959.

Rabin, Chaim, ed. *The Zadokite Documents.* Rev. ed. Oxford: Clarendon, 1958.

Rad, Gerhard von. *Wisdom in Israel.* Nashville: Abingdon, 1972.

Reif, S. C. "A Note on נער." *Vetus Testamentum* 21 (1971): 241–44.

Rendsburg, Gary A. "Bilingual Wordplay in the Bible." *Vetus Testamentum* 38 (1988): 354–57.

———. "Double Polysemy in Proverbs 31:19." Pages 267–74 in *Humanism, Culture, and Language in the Near East: Studies in Honor of Georg Krotkoff.* Edited by Asma Afsaruddin and A. H. Mathias Zahniser. Winona Lake, Ind.: Eisenbrauns, 1997.

Renfroe, F. "The Effect of Redaction on the Structure of Prov 1,1–6." *Zeitschrift für die alttestamentliche Wissenschaft* 101 (1989): 290–93.

Rogers, Cleon L., III. "The Meaning and Significance of the Hebrew Word אמון in Proverbs 8,30." *Zeitschrift für die alttestamentliche Wissenschaft* 109 (1997): 208–21.

Ross, Allen P. "Proverbs." Pages 881–1134 in vol. 5 of *The Expositor's Bible Commentary*. Grand Rapids: Zondervan, 1991.

Roth, Wolfgang M. W. "The Numerical Sequence x/x + 1 in the Old Testament." *Vetus Testamentum* 12 (1962): 300–311.

Rothstein, David. "The Book of Proverbs and Inner-Biblical Exegesis at Qumran: The Evidence of Proverbs 24,23–29." *Zeitschrift für die alttestamentliche Wissenschaft* 119 (2007): 75–85.

Ruffle, John. "The Teaching of Amenemope and Its Connection with the Book of Proverbs." *Tyndale Bulletin* 28 (1977): 29–68. Reprinted as pages 293–331 in *Learning from the Sages: Selected Studies on the Book of Proverbs.* Edited by Roy B. Zuck. Grand Rapids: Baker, 1995.

Scherer, Andreas. "Is the Selfish Man Wise? Considerations of Contexts in Proverbs 10.1–22.16 with Special Regard to Surety, Bribery and Friendship." *Journal for the Study of the Old Testament* 76 (1997): 59–70.

Schmid, Hans Heinrich. *Wesen und Geschichte der Weisheit: Eine Untersuchung zur altorientalischen und israelitischen Weisheitsliteratur.* Beihefte zur Zeitschrift für die alttestamentliche Wissenschaft 101. Berlin: Töpelmann, 1966.

Scott, R. B. Y. *Proverbs, Ecclesiastes.* Anchor Bible 18. New York: Doubleday, 1965.

———. "Wisdom in Creation: The *ʾĀmôn* of Proverbs VIII 30." *Vetus Testamentum* 10 (1960): 213–23.

Seely, Francis M. "Note on GʿRH with Especial Reference to Proverbs 13:8." *Bible Translator* 10 (1959): 20–21.

Skehan, Patrick W. "The Seven Columns of Wisdom's House in Proverbs 1–9." *Catholic Biblical Quarterly* 9 (1947): 190–98.

———. "A Single Editor for the Whole Book of Proverbs." *Catholic Biblical Quarterly* 10 (1948): 115–30.

———. "Wisdom's House." *Catholic Biblical Quarterly* 29 (1967): 468–86.

Sneed, Mark. "The Class Culture of Proverbs: Eliminating Stereotypes." *Scandinavian Journal of the Old Testament* 10 (1996): 296–308.

Snell, Daniel C. "The Most Obscure Verse in Proverbs: Proverbs XXVI 10." *Vetus Testamentum* 41 (1991): 350–56.

———. " 'Taking Souls' in Proverbs XI 30." *Vetus Testamentum* 33 (1983): 362–65.

———. *Twice-Told Proverbs and the Composition of the Book of Proverbs.* Winona Lake, Ind.: Eisenbrauns, 1993.

———. "The Wheel in Proverbs XX 26." *Vetus Testamentum* 39 (1989): 503–7.

Stallman, Robert C. "Divine Hospitality and Wisdom's Banquet in Proverbs 9:1–6." Pages 117–33 in *The Way of Wisdom: Essays in Honor of Bruce K. Waltke* Edited by J. I. Packer and Sven K. Soderlund. Grand Rapids: Zondervan, 2000.

Steinmann, Andrew E. *Daniel.* Concordia Commentary. St. Louis: Concordia, 2008.

———. *The Oracles of God: The Old Testament Canon.* St. Louis: Concordia, 1999.

———. "Proverbs 1–9 as a Solomonic Composition." *Journal of the Evangelical Theological Society* 43 (2000): 659–74.

———. "Three Things … Four Things … Seven Things: The Coherence of Proverbs 30:11–33 and the Unity of Proverbs 30." *Hebrew Studies* 42 (2001): 59–66.

Steinmann, Andrew E., and Michael Eschelbach. "Walk This Way: A Theme from Proverbs Reflected and Extended in Paul's Letters." *Concordia Theological Quarterly* 70 (2006): 43–62.

Stek, John H. "Proverbs: An Introduction." *Calvin Theological Journal* 36 (2001): 365–71.

Storøy, Solfrid. "On Proverbs and Riddles: Polar Word Pairs and Other Poetical Devices, and Words for 'Poor and Needy' in the Book of Proverbs." *Scandinavian Journal of the Old Testament* 7 (1993): 270–84.

Tångberg, Arvid. "Notes on the Text and Interpretation of Proverbs 8:22–31." Pages 296–305 in *Built on Solid Rock: Studies in Honor of Professor Ebbe Egede Knudsen on the Occasion of His 65th Birthday, April 11th, 1997.* Oslo: Novus, 1997.

Thiele, Edwin R. *The Mysterious Numbers of the Hebrew Kings.* 3d ed. Grand Rapids: Zondervan, 1983.

Thomas, D. Winton. "אֵו in Proverbs XXXI 4." *Vetus Testamentum* 12 (1962): 499–500.

———. "The Meaning of חַטָּאת in Proverbs X. 16." *Journal of Theological Studies* 15 (1964): 295–96.

———. "A Note on דַּעַת in Proverbs XXII. 12." *Journal of Theological Studies* 14 (1963): 93–94.

———. "Notes on Some Passages in the Book of Proverbs." *Vetus Testamentum* 15 (1965): 271–79.

Torrey, Charles C. "Proverbs, Chapter 30." *Journal of Biblical Literature* 73 (1954): 93–96.

Tov, Emanuel. "Recensional Differences between the Masoretic Text and the Septuagint of Proverbs." Pages 43–56 in *Of Scribes and Scrolls: Studies on the Hebrew Bible, Intertestamental Judaism, and Christian Origins Presented to John Strugnell on the Occasion of His Sixtieth Birthday.* College Theology Society Resources in Religion 5. Lanham, Md.: University Press of America, 1990.

Toy, Crawford H. *A Critical and Exegetical Commentary on the Book of Proverbs.* International Critical Commentary. Edinburgh: T&T Clark, 1899.

Trible, Phyllis. "Wisdom Builds a Poem: The Architecture of Proverbs 1:20–33." *Journal of Biblical Literature* 94 (1975): 509–18. Reprinted as pages 179–89 in *Learning from the Sages: Selected Studies on the Book of Proverbs.* Edited by Roy B. Zuck. Grand Rapids: Baker, 1995.

Ulrich, Eugene, et al. *Qumran Cave 4.XI: Psalms to Chronicles.* Discoveries in the Judaean Desert 16. Oxford: Clarendon, 2000.

Van der Toorn, Karel. "Female Prostitution in Payment of Vows in Ancient Israel." *Journal of Biblical Literature* 108 (1989): 193–205.

Van Leeuwen, Raymond C. "The Background to Proverbs 30:4aα." Pages 102–121 in *Wisdom, You Are My Sister: Studies in Honor of Roland E. Murphy, O. Carm., on the Occasion of His Eightieth Birthday.* Catholic Biblical Quarterly Monograph Series 29. Edited by Michael L. Barré. Washington, D.C.: Catholic Biblical Association of America, 1997.

———. "The Book of Proverbs: Introduction, Commentary, and Reflections." Pages 17–264 in vol. 5 of *The New Interpreter's Bible.* Nashville: Abingdon, 1997.

———. "Building God's House: An Exploration in Wisdom." Pages 204–11 in *The Way of Wisdom: Essays in Honor of Bruce K. Waltke* Edited by J. I. Packer and Sven K. Soderlund. Grand Rapids: Zondervan, 2000.

———. *Context and Meaning in Proverbs 25–27.* Society of Biblical Literature Dissertation Series 96. Atlanta: Scholars, 1988.

———. "Cosmos, Temple, House: Building and Wisdom in Mesopotamia and Israel." Pages 67–90 in *Wisdom Literature in Mesopotamia and Israel.* Edited by Richard J. Clifford. Atlanta: Society of Biblical Literature, 2007.

———. "Proverbs XXV 27 Once Again." *Vetus Testamentum* 36 (1986): 105–14.

———. "Proverbs 30:21–23 and the Biblical World Upside Down." *Journal of Biblical Literature* 105 (1986): 599–610.

———. "A Technical Metallurgical Usage of יצא." *Zeitschrift für die alttestamentliche Wissenschaft* 98 (1986): 112–13.

———. "Wealth and Poverty: System and Contradiction in Proverbs." *Hebrew Studies* 33 (1992): 25–36.

Vawter, Bruce. "Prov 8:22: Wisdom and Creation." *Journal of Biblical Literature* 99 (1980): 205–16.

Von Soden, Wolfram. "Kränkung, nicht Schläge in Sprüche 20,30." *Zeitschrift für die alttestamentliche Wissenschaft* 102 (1990): 120–21.

Waltke, Bruce. K. "The Authority of Proverbs: An Exposition of Proverbs 1:2–6." *Presbytérion* 13 (1987): 65–78.

———. *The Book of Proverbs.* 2 vols. New International Commentary on the Old Testament. Grand Rapids: Eerdmans, 2004–2005.

———. "The Book of Proverbs and Ancient Wisdom Literature." *Bibliotheca sacra* 136 (1979): 221–38. Reprinted as pages 49–65 in *Learning from the Sages: Selected Studies on the Book of Proverbs*. Edited by Roy B. Zuck. Grand Rapids: Baker, 1995.

———. "Does Proverbs Promise Too Much?" *Andrews University Seminary Studies* 34 (1996): 319–36.

———. "Lady Wisdom as Mediatrix: An Exposition of Proverbs 1:20–33." *Presbytérion* 14 (1988): 1–15. Reprinted as pages 191–204 in *Learning from the Sages: Selected Studies on the Book of Proverbs*. Edited by Roy B. Zuck. Grand Rapids: Baker, 1995.

Washington, Harold C. *Wealth and Poverty in the Instruction of Amenemope and the Hebrew Proverbs*. Society of Biblical Literature Dissertation Series 142. Atlanta: Scholars, 1994.

Weeks, Stuart. "The Context and Meaning of Proverbs 8:30a." *Journal of Biblical Literature* 125 (2006): 433–42.

Westermann, Claus. "Die Beobachtungsgedichte im Alten Testament." Pages 234–47 in *Wisdom, You Are My Sister: Studies in Honor of Roland E. Murphy, O. Carm., on the Occasion of His Eightieth Birthday*. Catholic Biblical Quarterly Monograph Series 29. Edited by Michael L. Barré. Washington, D.C.: Catholic Biblical Association of America, 1997.

———. "Der Frieden (*Shalom*) im Alten Testament." Pages 196–229 in vol. 2 of Claus Westermann, *Forschung am Alten Testament: Gesammelte Studien*. Munich: Kaiser, 1974.

———. *Roots of Wisdom: The Oldest Proverbs of Israel and Other Peoples*. Louisville: Westminster/John Knox, 1995.

Whitley, C. F. "The Positive Force of the Hebrew Particle בל." *Zeitschrift für die alttestamentliche Wissenschaft* 84 (1972): 213–19.

Whybray, Roger Norman. *The Book of Proverbs: A Survey of Modern Study*. History of Biblical Interpretation 1. Leiden: Brill, 1995.

———. "City Life in Proverbs 1–9." Pages 243–50 in *"Jedes Ding hat seine Zeit ...": Studien zur israelitsichen und altorientalischen Weisheit: Diethelm Michel zum 65. Geburtstag*. Edited by Anja A. Diesel et al. Beihefte zur Zeitschrift für die alttestamentliche Wissenschaft 241. Berlin: De Gruyter, 1996.

———. *The Composition of the Book of Proverbs*. Journal for the Study of the Old Testament: Supplement Series 168. Sheffield: Sheffield Academic Press, 1994.

———. *Wealth and Poverty in the Book of Proverbs*. Journal for the Study of the Old Testament: Supplement Series 99. Sheffield: Sheffield Academic Press, 1990.

———. *Wisdom in Proverbs: The Concept of Wisdom in Proverbs 1–9*. Naperville, Ill.: Allenson, 1965.

Wilch, John R. *Ruth*. Concordia Commentary. St. Louis: Concordia, 2006.

Williams, Daniel H. "Proverbs 8:22–31." *Interpretation* 48 (1994): 275–79.

Williams, James G. "The Power of Form: A Study of Biblical Proverbs." *Semeia* 17 (1980): 35–58. Reprinted as pages 73–97 in *Learning from the Sages: Selected Studies on the Book of Proverbs.* Edited by Roy B. Zuck. Grand Rapids: Baker, 1995.

———. *Those Who Ponder Proverbs: Aphoristic Thinking and Biblical Literature.* Bible and Literature Series 5. Sheffield: Almond, 1981.

Wilson, Frederick M. "Sacred and Profane? The Yahwistic Redaction of Proverbs Reconsidered." Pages 313–34 in *The Listening Heart: Essays in Wisdom and the Psalms in Honor of Roland E. Murphy, O. Carm.* Edited by Kenneth G. Hoglund et. al. Sheffield: Sheffield Academic Press, 1987.

Wilson, Gerald H. " 'The Words of the Wise': The Intent and Significance of Qohelet 12:9–14." *Journal of Biblical Literature* 103 (1984): 175–92.

Wolters, Al. "Proverbs XXXI 10–31 as Heroic Hymn: A Form-Critical Analysis." *Vetus Testamentum* 38 (1988): 446–57.

———. "*Ṣôpiyyâ* (Prov 31:27) as Hymnic Participle and Play on *Sophia*." *Journal of Biblical Literature* 104 (1985): 577–87.

Yee, Gale A. "An Analysis of Prov 8:22–31 according to Style and Structure." *Zeitschrift für die alttestamentliche Wissenschaft* 94 (1982): 58–66. Reprinted as pages 229–36 in *Learning from the Sages: Selected Studies on the Book of Proverbs.* Edited by Roy B. Zuck. Grand Rapids: Baker, 1995.

———. " 'I Have Perfumed My Bed with Myrrh': The Foreign Woman (*ʾiššâ zārâ*) in Proverbs 1–9." *Journal for the Study of the Old Testament* 43 (1989): 53–68.

Yoder, Christine Roy. *Wisdom as a Woman of Substance: A Socioeconomic Reading of Proverbs 9:1–9 and 31:10–31.* Beihefte zur Zeitschrift für die alttestamentliche Wissenschaft 304. Berlin: De Gruyter, 2001.

———. "The Woman of Substance (אשת־חיל): A Socioeconomic Reading of Proverbs 31:10–31." *Journal of Biblical Literature* 122 (2003): 427–47.

Zhu-En Wee, John. "The Meaning of הוקר לבב in *Ahiqar* Saying 15[1]." *Vetus Testamentum* 54 (2004): 556–60.

Zimmerli, Walter. "Concerning the Structure of Old Testament Wisdom." Pages 175–207 in *Studies in Ancient Israelite Wisdom.* New York: KTAV, 1976.

———. "Ort und Grenze der Weisheit im Rahmen der alttestamentlichen Theologie." Pages 300–15 in *Gottes Offenbarung: Gesammelte Aufsätze zum Alten Testament.* Theologische Bücherei 19. Munich: Kaiser, 1963.

Introduction

Authorship and Date[1]

Proverbs is a much-loved book of wisdom whose guidance has practical applications to lives in every age. It is often included (with Psalms) in small editions of the Bible that contain the NT. Unfortunately, Proverbs is often seen as a collection of disconnected, almost random sayings that are studied individually without the benefit of context. Indeed, the bulk of the book, beginning in 10:1 and extending almost to the end, consists of short, pithy sayings that often invite such treatment, especially in English translation, where many of the connections to the larger context that are evident in the Hebrew cannot be sustained.

More than a random collection of sayings, Proverbs is a thoughtfully arranged and richly ornamented book of wisdom that derives not merely from human experience, but from God, who grants his people "the fear of Yahweh" (e.g., 1:7; 2:5) and guides them to understand his wise ways. However, the very organization of Proverbs leads many to view it as best understood by contemplation of individual sayings of practical advice. It is organized into several parts, and all but the first part (Proverbs 1–9) and the last (31:10–31) are mostly short sayings. It is not until one understands the essential role that Solomon played in composing the bulk of this book that its treasury of wisdom can be opened wide and seen as an interconnected series of instructions in godly wisdom.

Proverbs is one of only two OT books that are self-described as resulting from composite authorship. The other is Psalms, whose superscriptions cite the various authors, principally David. Proverbs contains notices of authorship in 1:1; 10:1; 22:17; 24:23; 25:1; 30:1; and 31:1. In addition, most scholars consider the acrostic poem that concludes the book (31:10–31) to be a separate composition whose author is not mentioned. If one takes the book's authorial notices at face value, as does this commentary, the book divides into eight sections as shown in figure 1.

Some of these attributions of authorship have been challenged by critical scholars and even by a few scholars who are otherwise generally conservative and evangelical.[2] The rejection of the book's notices of authorship is especially

---

1 Much of this section is adapted from Andrew E. Steinmann, "Proverbs 1–9 as a Solomonic Composition," *Journal of the Evangelical Theological Society* 43 (2000): 659–74.

2 E.g., Kidner, *Proverbs*, 22. One example of a section whose authorship has been questioned—even though an author is named—is the latter part of chapter 30. Agur is named in 30:1 and the simplest conclusion is that he authored all of chapter 30. However, some interpreters argue that 30:15–33 was written by a different author or authors. See the discussion in Whybray, *The Book of Proverbs*, 86–87. Those who attribute 30:15–33 to another author or authors cite two reasons: (1) unlike the material attributed to Agur in 30:1–14, the material in 30:15–33 is primarily numerical sayings, and (2) in the LXX, 30:1–14 is placed before 24:23–34, and 30:15–33 is placed after 24:23–34. See further the commentary on 30:1a and on 30:11–33.

common in expositions of the first section of the book, Proverbs 1–9. It contains lengthy discourses rather than the short sayings that characterize the other two sections by Solomon (10:1–22:16 and chapters 25–29).

Figure 1

The Authors of the Sections of Proverbs

Section	*Author*
1:1–9:18	Solomon
10:1–22:16	Solomon
22:17–24:22	Wise people
24:23–34	Wise people
25:1–29:27	Solomon (as copied by Hezekiah's men)
30:1–33	Agur, son of Jakeh
31:1–9	Lemuel (or his mother)
31:10–31	Unknown

Though admitting some conceptual connections between chapters 1–9 and the two other sections attributed to Solomon, critical scholars uniformly regard chapters 1–9 as composed later than Solomon's time,[3] usually in the early Persian period.[4] They believe that these chapters were composed later as an introduction to the book as a whole. Critical scholars often argue that these longer discourses represent a more developed Israelite wisdom with greater theological reflection than the short sayings of the other sections attributed to Solomon.[5] Behind this approach is an evolutionary assumption regarding both wisdom in ancient Israel and Israelite theology: both moved from shorter, less coherent forms to longer, more integrated forms.

Even some evangelical scholars, who tend to dispute this evolutionary model of Israelite wisdom and theology, often reject Solomon's authorship of chapters 1–9. These scholars understand 1:1, "the proverbs of Solomon son of David, king of Israel," as a general heading for the entire book and not an

---

3 Hermisson, *Studien zur israelitischen Spruchweisheit*, 15–18; McKane, *Proverbs*, 9, 17–18; Scott, *Proverbs, Ecclesiastes*, 9–10; Skehan, "A Single Editor for the Whole Book of Proverbs."

4 Van Leeuwen, "Proverbs," 20–21; Whybray, *The Book of Proverbs*, 62–71, 150–57; Williams, *Those Who Ponder Proverbs*, especially p. 16.

5 Some claim to find in Proverbs 1–9 Hebrew reactions to Greek philosophy (e.g., Fox, *Proverbs 1–9*, 6), though this is difficult to prove and often speculative. Fox admits that such a reading of Proverbs 1–9 is not certain when he opines: "These features [that allegedly suggest an early Hellenistic setting] would not be impossible prior to the Macedonian conquest [of Palestine by Alexander the Great in 332 BC] but are more likely after it. These considerations, however, are far from decisive. While the characteristics of Part I [Proverbs 1–9] allow for a Hellenistic dating, they do not prove it" (p. 49).

indication of the authorship of chapters 1–9.[6] Kidner believes that 1:1 could be read either as indicating the authorship of chapters 1–9 or as a general heading for the entire book. He opts for the latter, contending that if the heading in 1:1 were intended to indicate that Proverbs 1–9 was authored by Solomon, then the heading in 10:1 would have been worded as "these *also* are proverbs of Solomon."[7]

Nevertheless, the Solomonic authorship of Proverbs 1–9 does have its defenders among evangelical scholars. For example, Garrett views Proverbs 1–9 as a Solomonic composition.[8] He bases his analysis on the work of Kitchen, who has studied the formal structure of ancient Near Eastern wisdom literature.[9] Kitchen divides instructional wisdom texts into two types. Type A begins with a title and then moves directly to the subject matter of the text. Type B begins with a title and a prologue and then moves to the text's subject matter. The prologues in type B texts were short or medium in length in the third and second millennia BC, but around 1000 BC, about Solomon's time, they tended to become longer. Type B literature also contains what Kitchen labels "subtitles" and "titular interjections." Subtitles occur within the body of a work and name the author of subsections. Titular interjections are breaks in the narrative in which the author directly addresses the reader. They are less formal than subtitles but still delineate subsections. In addition, type B works, especially in the third and second millennium BC, often had epilogues, but these epilogues began to disappear in the first millennium.

Garrett views Proverbs 1–24 as a wisdom text typical of type B texts of the first millennium BC.[10] If Garrett, following Kitchen, is correct, the prologue (1:2–7) is followed by four main text sections, each preceded by its own title, subtitle, or titular interjection. The organization of the first part of Proverbs would be something like that shown in figure 2.

This analysis would also answer the objection of Kidner that 10:1 implies that chapters 1–9 are not from Solomon. According to Kitchen's analysis, 10:1 is a typical subtitle and not the titular interjection that Kidner would prefer, but either a subtitle or a titular interjection is acceptable in this type of literature, and Solomon uses both. This analysis also implies that main texts 3 and 4 were compiled by Solomon from other wise people and were included by him as commendable wisdom.[11] The remainder of the book—the proverbs of

---

[6] E.g., Ross, "Proverbs," 904.

[7] Kidner, *Proverbs*, 22 (emphasis added). Kidner bases his argument on 24:23 and 25:1. Prov 22:17 introduces proverbs from "wise people," and 24:23 adds "these *also* are by wise people." Prov 25:1 begins with "these also are the proverbs of Solomon."

[8] Garrett, *Proverbs, Ecclesiastes, Song of Songs*, 39–44.

[9] Kitchen, "The Basic Literary Forms and Formulations of Ancient Instructional Writings in Egypt and Western Asia" and "Proverbs and Wisdom Books of the Ancient Near East."

[10] Garrett, *Proverbs, Ecclesiastes, Song of Songs*, 43–44.

[11] As is well-known, there have been many scholarly attempts to link 22:17–24:22 with the Wisdom of Amenemope. It is possible that some of this section is related to Amenemope or

Solomon copied by Hezekiah's men (chapters 25–29), the sayings of Agur (chapter 30) and Lemuel (31:1–9), and the acrostic poem (31:10–31)—consists of later additions.

Figure 2

The Organization of Proverbs 1–24*

Section	*Text*	
Title	1:1	"The proverbs of Solomon son of David, king of Israel."
Prologue	1:2–7	
Main text 1	1:8–9:18	
Subtitle	10:1	"The proverbs of Solomon."
Main text 2	10:1–22:16	
Titular interjection	22:17	"Open your ears and listen to the words of wise people, and set your heart on my knowledge."
Main text 3	22:18–24:22	
Titular interjection	24:23	"These also are by wise people."
Main text 4	24:23–34	

* This follows Garrett, *Proverbs, Ecclesiastes, Song of Songs*, 43.

If this model drawn from the work of Kitchen and Garrett is correct, there are three types of material in Proverbs:

- Authored by Solomon: chapters 1–9; 10:1–22:16; chapters 25–29
- Included and commended by Solomon, but authored by others: 22:17–24:22; 24:23–34
- Authored by others: chapter 30; 31:1–9; 31:10–31

How are we to choose between the view that Solomon authored chapters 1–9 and the view that 1:1 is simply a title for the whole book but does not mean that Solomon is the actual author of chapters 1–9? A simple test would involve comparing chapters 1–9 to 10:1–22:16 and to chapters 25–29. If these three sections (chapters 1–9; 10:1–22:16; and chapters 25–29) are all by Solomon, they should contain indicators of his vocabulary, thought, and modes of expression despite the fact that Proverbs 1–9 differs in its style and intent from the two

---

other Egyptian wisdom. See the excursus "The Words of Wise People (Prov 22:17–24:22) and Its Relationship to the Wisdom of Amenemope" in the commentary on chapter 22. However, the relationship has been hotly disputed. See Whybray, *The Book of Proverbs*, 6–14. A reasonable suggestion that Solomon did adapt Egyptian wisdom is provided by Ruffle, "The Teaching of Amenemope."

later sections by Solomon. Different sections of material in differing styles and with differing concerns should not be expected to match each other completely even when they are by the same author. However, the vocabulary, thought, and modes of expression in sections by the same author probably would bear some similarities, especially since all those in Proverbs are within the same genre of proverbial Wisdom literature.

We would expect that the sections included by Solomon but attributed to other authors (22:17–24:22; 24:23–34) should not be as close to Solomon's style, but since he would have included material that he had himself studied, these sections by others may have influenced his writing to some degree. Therefore, we should find less correspondence between Proverbs 1–9 and 22:17–24:22; 24:23–34 than between Proverbs 1–9 and Solomon's writings in 10:1–22:16 and chapters 25–29, but we may still find some influence or correspondence. One example of such correspondence might be 6:11 (by Solomon) and 24:34 (from wise people), since the two verses are almost identical.

We would expect the sections at the end of the book that were not authored by Solomon nor included by him (chapter 30; 31:1–9; 31:10–31) would have even less correspondence with Proverbs 1–9. There should be some correspondence, since these are also proverbial Wisdom texts, but we can also expect some indications that these texts are not as close to each other as are the sections authored by Solomon and those from other authors that Solomon himself added to the book.

We will now examine similarities and differences between the sections of material in Proverbs based on an analysis of their vocabulary, thought, and modes of expression, especially comparisons and other uses of טוֹב, "good, better."

Vocabulary

One test of the common authorship of Proverbs 1–9; 10:1–22:16; and chapters 25–29 is vocabulary usage. While we might attempt to apply this test to the entire vocabulary of Proverbs, many of the common Hebrew words are used so frequently throughout biblical literature that it would be difficult to determine a particular author's usage preferences.[12] However, a particular author's preference for less frequently used words is more easily detected.

An examination of words occurring less than fifty times in the MT of the entire OT yields interesting results. A detailed analysis has shown precisely what the model based on the suggestions by Kitchen and Garrett would predict: chapters 1–9 were authored by Solomon, and 10:1–22:16 and chapters 25–29

[12] However, even some common words can suggest whether or not a single author is responsible for different texts. For instance, the word תָּוֶךְ, "middle, midst," which usually is used in construct with the preposition בְּ, בְּתוֹךְ, "in the midst/middle of," occurs 420 times in the MT and only eight times in Proverbs. All of these eight occurrences are in sections by Solomon: Proverbs 1–9 (five times); 10:1–22:16 (twice); and chapters 25–29 (once).

have the highest percentage of his preferred words.[13] Prov 22:17–24:22 and 24:23–34, which are proverbs that Solomon received and adapted from "wise people," have a lesser percentage of words that Solomon used in chapters 1–9. That is to be expected because Prov 22:17–24:22 and 24:23–34 were not originally Solomon's own work. However, since he had studied these sayings, they have a higher percentage of his preferred words than do chapters 30–31, which were not Solomon's own work nor part of works that he studied.

Of course, statistics alone could mean that chapters 1–9 come from some other author than Solomon who was mimicking the vocabulary of other sections by Solomon (10:1–22:16 and chapters 25–29). However, these vocabulary differences in low-usage lemmas are extremely subtle. No one, to my knowledge, has ever been aware of them, and it required state-of-the-art computer technology to have the means to discover them.[14] It is much more likely that they indicate a common author for chapters 1–9; 10:1–22:16; and chapters 25–29, as indicated by the authorial notices in the text of Proverbs itself.

Thought

It is not possible in this introduction to analyze all of the concepts in Proverbs and their use in the various sections of the book. A look at the distribution of one of these concepts will suffice to reinforce the conclusion drawn from the vocabulary analysis above.[15] One of the best-known expressions of Proverbs is יִרְאַת יְהוָה, "the fear of Yahweh." What has often been overlooked is the distribution of this phrase throughout the book. It occurs in Proverbs 1–9 (1:7, 29; 2:5; 8:13; 9:10); in 10:1–22:16 (10:27; 14:26–27; 15:16, 33; 16:6; 19:23; 22:4); and only twice in non-Solomonic sections (23:17; 31:30). This argues against the view that the concept of the fear of Yahweh was simply picked up from chapters 10–31 by another author besides Solomon to use in Proverbs 1–9 as that author's introduction to the rest of the book. The fear of Yahweh is not a major theme throughout the entire rest of the book (chapters 10–31), but it is only a major theme in the Solomonic proverbs in 10:1–22:16. This supports the view that chapters 1–9, like 10:1–22:16, are by Solomon.

At the same time, we should note that the concept of fearing God can also be expressed by the imperative clause יְרָא אֶת־יְהוָה, "fear Yahweh." This clause occurs much less frequently than "the fear of Yahweh": only twice, once (3:7) in the introductory chapters (1–9) and once (24:21) in the proverbs Solomon

---

[13] For details, see Steinmann, "Proverbs 1–9 as a Solomonic Composition," 662–66.

[14] Note that even the extensive computer study by Andersen and Forbes, *The Vocabulary of the Old Testament*, would not enable one to discover these differences, since that study only treats the book of Proverbs as a whole. However, the learned Lutheran scholar Franz Delitzsch, writing in the 1870s long before the invention of the computer, did recognize vocabulary affinities between 10:1–22:16 and chapters 25–29 (*Proverbs*, 1:31–32).

[15] While space does not permit the analysis of other themes, we should note that there are several that point to common authorship of the Solomonic sections, for example, עֵץ־חַיִּים, the "tree of life," in 3:18; 11:30; 13:12; 15:4.

adapted from the words of wise people (22:17–24:22 and 24:23–34). This confirms that Solomon was not writing in a vacuum. Occasionally Solomon may have borrowed concepts from other wise people, and after incorporating and perhaps adapting these concepts in his own writing, Solomon also commended them to others.

But how are we to account for the absence of "the fear of Yahweh" or "fear Yahweh" in the set of Solomon's proverbs in chapters 25–29? Perhaps Hezekiah's men (25:1), the compilers of the Solomonic collection that begins in chapter 25, had a different concern. They certainly included some proverbs that were from the Solomonic collection that begins in chapter 10 (21:9 || 25:24; 18:8 || 26:22; 22:3 || 27:12; 20:16 || 27:13) or that were nearly identical to them (22:13 || 26:13; 19:24 || 26:15; 19:1 || 28:6; 12:11 || 28:19; 22:2 || 29:13). However, their thematic interests were different than those of Solomon in chapters 1–9 and 10:1–22:16 so they did not include proverbs with the fear of Yahweh theme when they copied Solomon's proverbs.

Specifically, chapters 25–29 are concerned with what Crenshaw characterizes as "the powerful individual [ruler] with whom all subjects had to reckon."[16] These chapters seldom mention "wisdom" (only in 28:26; 29:3, 15). Moreover, they do not explicitly connect wisdom with Yahweh, who, likewise is seldom mentioned (only in 25:22, 28:5, 25; 29:13, 25–26). One of the concerns of chapters 1–9 and the Solomonic proverbs beginning in 10:1 is the gaining of wisdom and life and their connection with Yahweh. This expressed concern is nearly absent from chapters 25–29. Instead, when Yahweh is mentioned, it is often in a juridical connection, parallel to the juridical power of the king. For instance, Yahweh determines rewards (25:22) and is connected with understanding justice (28:5) and meting out justice (29:26). This accords well with the observations by Bryce and Malchow that these chapters may have been collected to train courtiers and kings.[17] These chapters are not directly concerned with the more theoretical discussion of gaining wisdom and life but with the more practical concern of governing. Thus the proverbs chosen and collected by Hezekiah's servants did not include "(the) fear (of) Yahweh" because that phraseology was not closely connected with proverbs on the themes in which they were interested.

In addition, how can one explain the use of "the fear of Yahweh" in 31:30? A number of scholars have concluded that the poem in 31:10–31, which concludes Proverbs, was placed at the end of the book intentionally to mirror the theme of Lady Wisdom in the book's first part.[18] If this is the case, then the

---

[16] Crenshaw, *Old Testament Wisdom*, 75.

[17] Bryce, "Another Wisdom-'Book' in Proverbs"; Malchow, "A Manual for Future Monarchs."

[18] Camp, *Wisdom and the Feminine in the Book of Proverbs*, 90–97; Garrett, *Proverbs, Ecclesiastes, Song of Songs*, 246–52; McCreesh, "Wisdom as Wife"; Murphy on Proverbs in Murphy and Huwiler, *Proverbs, Ecclesiastes, Song of Songs*, 154–56; Ross, "Proverbs," 1128–30; Van Leeuwen, "Proverbs," 257. See further the commentary on 31:10–31.

author of this poem was specifically drawing upon the concept of the fear of Yahweh, most probably in 8:13.

The almost complete absence of "(the) fear (of) Yahweh" in the non-Solomonic sections of Proverbs, in contrast to its frequency in both Proverbs 1–9 and also in 10:1–22:16, is a strong indication that both Proverbs 1–9 and 10:1–22:16 are by the same author, namely, Solomon.

Modes of Expression

While chapters 1–9 differ greatly in overall style from 10:1–22:16 and chapters 25–29, if these three sections all come from the hand of the same author, there should be some consistent indications of that author's modes of expression in each of them. While there are many of modes of expression that could be examined, an analysis of only one of them in detail will demonstrate the frequent and quite intricate connections between Proverbs 1–9 and the other two Solomonic sections.

One of Solomon's modes of expression may be sayings using the word טוֹב, "good," which can be used in comparative constructions to mean "better/greater." The adjective טוֹב (including the feminine form טוֹבָה) occurs sixty-one times in Proverbs. These sixty-one occurrences are fairly evenly distributed throughout the book, as one would expect with such a common word, which occurs around five hundred times in the whole OT. The proverbs that use טוֹב, "good, better," often define blessing and its opposite, detriment, through comparisons. These comparisons, whether direct or implied, are intended to lead the readers from the more general concepts in Proverbs 1–9 to the more specific applications given in later chapters, especially 10:1–22:16 and chapters 25–29.

Direct Comparisons

Many of the occurrences of טוֹב, "good," are in formulaic sayings. The most studied of these are those that use the comparative formula טוֹב ... מִן, "better/greater ... than."[19] Included in this category are eighteen proverbs that begin with טוֹב, "good, better" (8:19; 12:9; 15:16–17; 16:8, 19, 32; 17:1; 19:1; 21:9 || 25:24; 21:19; 25:24; 28:6), the feminine equivalent טוֹבָה, "good, better" (27:5), כִּי טוֹב, "because better/greater ..." (3:14; 25:7), or the feminine equivalent כִּי טוֹבָה, "because better ..." (8:11), and two in which such a comparison is drawn in a subsequent line (19:22; 27:10). In addition, it is possible to draw the same comparison without using the word טוֹב, "good, better," as part of the comparative formula with מִן, "than." טוֹב, "good, better," is gapped (omitted but implied) in the comparisons in the first line of 22:1 and in the second half of 3:14; 8:19; and 16:32. In all four of these cases, טוֹב, "good, better,"

[19] See Ogden, "The 'Better'-Proverb," for a summary of the history of research into this formula. Also see the treatments of Hermisson, *Spruchweisheit*, 155–56, and Bryce, " 'Better'-Proverbs," and the summary in Murphy, *Wisdom Literature*, 66–67.

occurs explicitly in another line of the same verse, so it clearly is the word that is implied where it is gapped.[20]

> A good reputation is to be chosen rather than great wealth.
> Favor is better than silver and gold. (22:1)

Bryce has pointed out that these proverbs come in two forms, the simple comparison (A is better than B) and a more sophisticated version that involves a binary opposition comparison (A in view of B is better than A' in view of B').[21]

There is an interesting distribution of these two types of proverbs. All but three of the binary opposition comparisons are in 10:1–22:16:

> Better to be a nobody and have a servant
> than to pretend to be important and lack food. (12:9)

> Better a little with the fear of Yahweh
> than great wealth with turmoil. (15:16)

> Better a meal of vegetables where there is love
> than a fatted calf and hatred with it. (15:17)

> Better a little with righteousness
> than a large income without justice. (16:8)

> Better to be humble in spirit with oppressed people
> than to share in stolen goods with haughty people. (16:19)

> Better a bit of stale food and quietness with it
> than a house filled with sacrificial feasts of [with] quarreling. (17:1)

> Better is a poor person walking in his integrity
> than a person with crooked lips who is a fool. (19:1)

> Better to live on the corner of a roof
> than in a home shared with a quarrelsome wife. (21:9 || 25:24)

> Better to live in desert country
> than with a quarrelsome and ill-tempered wife. (21:19)

The other binary comparisons are in chapters 25–29. One of them is 25:24, which is identical to 21:9. These are the others:

> A neighbor who is near is better
> than a relative who is far away. (27:10)

> Better is a poor person walking in his integrity
> than a person who is twisted [in his] ways and is rich. (28:6)

---

[20] Bryce, " 'Better'-Proverbs," 352, notes the omission of the element טוֹב, "good, better," in several of the comparative sayings in Sirach 30:14–17. Ogden, "The 'Better'-Proverbs," 492–93, notes that the omission also occurs in Ecclesiastes (4:2; 4:17 [ET 5:1]; 7:1b; 9:17). With Sirach 30:14–17 and with all of the Ecclesiastes verses except 4:17 (ET 5:1), there are comparative sayings in the immediate context that do have the element טוֹב, "good, better."

[21] Bryce, " 'Better'-Proverbs," 349; cf. Murphy, *Wisdom Literature*, 67.

What do the binary comparisons of these proverbs teach? They teach that blessing does not always come in the most obvious ways. What appears at first to be a blessing can be a detriment. For example, 15:16 says that a situation that seems to be an obvious blessing from God (riches) can be anything but a blessing if it brings turmoil. On the other hand, a situation that many would readily judge to be a curse from God (relative poverty) can be a blessing. Thus these proverbs serve to define what the wise know about blessing and detriment: they often depend on the attendant circumstances of a particular situation and not the situation itself.

Only three טוֹב proverbs in 10:1–22:16 are direct comparisons:[22]

Better to be a patient person than a hero,
and [better to be] a person who controls his temper than one who captures a city. (16:32)

A person's desire [should be for] his [Yahweh's] mercy,
so it is better to be poor than a liar. (19:22)

A good reputation is to be chosen rather than great wealth.
Favor is better than silver and gold. (22:1)

Prov 19:22b is probably an explanation of the circumstances under which "mercy" (חֶסֶד) is desirable. Therefore, it is probably to be grouped with the binary טוֹב, "good, better," proverbs. The two other direct comparisons do not show the circumstances under which the first element is made into a blessing while the second becomes a detriment. The implication is that these situations are inherently better. They need no attendant circumstances to make them better.

The טוֹב ... מִן, "better ... than," proverbs of chapters 1–9 are the direct comparison type:

Blessed is the person who finds Wisdom
and the person who acquires Understanding,
because her [Wisdom's] profit is greater [better] than profit from silver,
and her harvest better than fine gold. (3:13–14)

Take my [Wisdom's] discipline, and not silver,
and knowledge rather than fine gold,
because Wisdom is better than jewels,
and all desirable things cannot equal her. (8:10–11)

My [Wisdom's] fruit is better than gold and than pure gold,
and what I produce [is better] than fine silver. (8:19)

---

22 Bryce contends that 16:32 and 22:1 are actually binary comparisons with the middle elements implied (" 'Better'-Proverbs," 350). However, Murphy is probably correct in discounting this possibility (*Wisdom Literature*, 67).

When the readers of Proverbs carefully compare these טוֹב, "good, better," proverbs in chapters 1–9 with the ones from 10:1–22:16 they are led to the following conclusions:

1. Unlike most of the blessings described in 10:1–22:16, wisdom in chapters 1–9 is an inherently good thing that always brings blessing.
2. When wisdom is compared using טוֹב, "good, better," it is always compared favorably to silver and gold. So is a good reputation in 22:1. Therefore, wisdom will lead to a reputation worth having: that of being wise.
3. The more general blessing of wisdom described in Proverbs 1–9 will lead to the ability to distinguish blessing from detriment in more concrete situations, such as those of the binary comparisons in the טוֹב, "good, better," proverbs of 10:1–22:16 (and also those in chapters 25–29).

Indirect Comparisons

"Not Good!" and "How Good!"

However, the comparative formula מִן ... טוֹב, "better ... than," is not the only formula using the word טוֹב, "good, better." Another common formula is the "not good" (לֹא טוֹב) proverb.[23] There are seven "not good" proverbs, five in 10:1–22:16 (16:29; 17:26; 18:5; 19:2; 20:23) and two in chapters 25–29 (25:27; 28:21).[24] A parallel expression uses the term "disgusting thing, abomination" (תּוֹעֵבָה). All uses of this term but one occur in the sections attributed to Solomon.[25] Once תּוֹעֵבָה, "disgusting thing," is used in parallel with "not good":

> Differing weights are a disgusting thing to Yahweh,
> and dishonest scales are not good. (20:23)

While there are no לֹא טוֹב, "not good," proverbs in Proverbs 1–9, there are three passages that use תּוֹעֵבָה, "disgusting thing," and two of them (3:32 and 6:16–19), which describe things that are disgusting to Yahweh, are closely parallel to two proverbs from 10:1–22:16, namely, 11:20 and 12:22. The first tie between these sections involves the semantic overlap of the words עִקֵּשׁ, "twisted, perverted," and נָלוֹז, "crooked" (cf. 2:15, where this pair occurs in parallel), and the roots תמם, "have integrity, be blameless," and ישׁר, "be upright" (cf. 2:7, 21; 29:10, where words from these roots occur in parallel, and 11:3, 5; 28:10, where they occur together).

---

[23] A less severe form of this formula uses the expression לֹא־נָאוֶה, "[it is/they are] not fitting, proper" (17:7; 19:10; 26:1). For a general discussion of these types of proverbs, see Hermisson, *Spruchweisheit*, 154–55, and Murphy, *Wisdom Literature*, 66.

[24] On the anomalous לֹא טוֹב, "not good," proverb in the sayings of the wise (24:23), see " 'Good' in the Words of Wise People" below.

[25] In chapters 1–9, the word occurs in 3:32; 6:16; 8:7. In 10:1–22:16, it occurs in 11:1, 20; 12:22; 13:19; 15:8–9, 26; 16:5, 12; 17:15; 20:10, 23; 21:27. In chapters 25–29, it occurs in 26:25; 28:9; and 29:27 (twice). Outside of the sections attributed to Solomon, the term occurs once in the Words of Wise People (24:9).

A *crooked person* is a *disgusting thing to Yahweh*,
but Yahweh's confidential advice is with *upright people*. (3:32)

Those with a *perverted* heart are a *disgusting thing to Yahweh*,
but his favor is [upon] those people whose way has *integrity*. (11:20)

In both of these passages, the comparison is between the reprobation of God against deviousness and the delight of God with godliness.

The second tie involves the abomination of lying:

Six things Yahweh hates,
and seven are *disgusting things to his very being*:
an arrogant pair of eyes,
a *lying* tongue ... (6:16–17b)

Lying lips are a *disgusting thing to Yahweh*. (12:22a)

Both of these passages involve an implicit comparison between God's attitude toward honesty and his attitude toward lying (see also 12:22b). Thus the "not good" and related proverbs are another tie between Proverbs 1–9 and 10:1–22:16 involving a common mode of expression. The tie does not directly involve the uses of the word טוֹב, "good," but rather its antonym תּוֹעֵבָה, "disgusting thing." Here the concept of detriment as the opposite of blessing is brought to the fore. The proverbs which use לֹא טוֹב, "not good," do not explicitly state why the things described are not good. However, of the twenty proverbs that state that something is a "disgusting thing," twelve state that it is a disgusting thing to Yahweh. The implication is clear: people who do disgusting acts will not receive blessing from Yahweh.

The "not good" proverbs are complimented by two "how good" (מַה־טּוֹב) proverbs (15:23; 16:16) and one "only good" proverb (אַךְ־טוֹב, 11:23). One of these shows a direct connection with the "good, better" proverbs concerning wisdom in Proverbs 1–9:

How much better it is to acquire wisdom than gold,
and to acquire understanding is to be chosen rather than silver. (16:16)

Just as the "not good" proverbs have a corresponding form in proverbs using the concept of "disgusting thing, abomination," the "how good" proverbs have a corresponding form in proverbs that use the word רָצוֹן, God's gracious "favor."[26] All fourteen of these occur in Proverbs 1–9 or 10:1–22:16.[27] Four of these use "favor" in antithetical parallelism to "disgusting thing" (11:1, 20; 12:22; 15:8). In addition, three others use "good" with "favor" (11:27; 12:2; 18:22). Prov 11:27 equates eagerness for "good" with searching for "favor."

רָצוֹן, "favor," also provides a link between Proverbs 1–9 and 10:1–22:16:

---

[26] Cf. Zimmerli, "Ort und Grenze," 309; Hermisson, *Spruchweisheit*, 155.

[27] The fourteen occurrences are in 8:35; 10:32; 11:1, 20, 27; 12:2, 22; 14:9, 35; 15:8; 16:13, 15; 18:22; 19:12.

Whoever finds me [Wisdom] finds life,
and he obtains favor from Yahweh. (8:35)

The man who finds a wife finds a good thing,
and he obtains favor from Yahweh. (18:22)

These proverbs define blessing as Yahweh's favor. The parallel between 8:35 and 18:22 helps the readers understand the blessing of Yahweh. The more abstract concept "Wisdom" (personified as a woman) is later replaced by the more concrete godly "wife." To find either—or both—is to find blessing in the form of God's favor. In fact, seven of these proverbs (fifty percent) are concerned with Yahweh's favor (8:35; 11:1, 20; 12:2, 22; 15:8; 18:22).

Good People

Another use of טוֹב, "good," in Proverbs that ties Proverbs 1–9 to 10:1–22:16 is as a substantive to denote a "good person." טוֹב, "good," is only used this way in these two sections of Proverbs. In three proverbs it is used in the plural; in two it is used in the singular:

... so that you walk in the way of good people
and stay on the paths of righteous people. (2:20)

Evil people will bow down in front of good people,
and wicked people [will bow down] at the gates of a righteous
person. (14:19)

The eyes of Yahweh are everywhere,
watching evil people and good people. (15:3)

A good person will obtain favor from Yahweh,
but he will condemn a schemer. (12:2)

A good man leaves an inheritance to his grandchildren,
but a sinner's wealth is treasured up for a righteous person. (13:22)

The distinction between the plural "good people" and the singular "good person" is an important one. The use of the plural is for more general, theoretical concepts: broad counsel (2:20), the outcome of righteous behavior (14:19), or the omniscience of God (15:3). The singular is used for more concrete situations: the act of scheming (12:2) or of leaving an inheritance (13:22). It is significant that the only time טוֹב is used in this sense in Proverbs 1–9 it is plural ("good people" in 2:20). The general relationship of theoretical principles preceding more practical advice is apparent when comparing Proverbs 1–9 with 10:1–22:16. While the theoretical can be found in 10:1–22:16 and the practical in Proverbs 1–9, the predominant progression is from theoretical in Proverbs 1–9 to practical in 10:1–22:16.

Good Reputation, Good Sense

A final binding motif in the טוֹב, "good, better" proverbs is the phrase שֵׂכֶל־טוֹב, "good sense." This phrase occurs only four times in the OT. 2 Chr

30:22 uses it in the sense of "good skill." In Ps 111:10 it is used in a Wisdom setting that is very similar to Proverbs:

> The beginning of wisdom is the fear of Yahweh.
> [It is] good sense to all who do it.

שֶׂכֶל־טוֹב, "good sense," is used in similar ways in Proverbs 1–9 and 10:1–22:16:

> Then you will find favor and *good sense*
> in the eyes of God and humans. (3:4)

> *Good sense* yields grace,
> but the way of treacherous people is unchanging. (13:15)

Those verses are similar to each other since in both "good sense" is connected with receiving "favor" (חֵן). In 3:4 the believer receives both "favor" and "good sense," while in the second the gift of "good sense" yields "favor." This similarity involving "good sense" appears to be a deliberate device by the common author, as were also the previous types of טוֹב, "good, better," proverbs. It is unlikely that another, later author of Proverbs 1–9 would have created such a subtle connection between the two sections (Proverbs 1–9 and 10:1–22:16). Such attention to fine detail in using the word טוֹב, "good, better," to bind these two sections of Proverbs is more likely to be the careful, systematic work of a single author (Solomon) who wrote both sections.

"Good" in the Words of Wise People (Prov 22:17–24:34)

What is the explanation for the occurrences of טוֹב, "good," outside Proverbs 1–9; 10:1–22:16; and chapters 25–29? When its occurrences in the Words of Wise People (24:13–14, 23, 25) are carefully examined, one can see that these proverbs are not by Solomon, but they are Solomon-like. Several proverbs in this section are similar to proverbs in 1:1–22:16.[28] This is also true of the טוֹב, "good," proverbs in the Words of Wise People. One of these is 24:23:

> To show partiality when administering justice is not good.

This "not good" proverb differs from the ones in 10:1–22:16 in that it uses the negative בַּל for "not" instead of לֹא. The negative בַּל occurs five times in proverbs originally by Solomon (9:13; 10:30; 12:3; 14:7; 19:23) and five times in the collections of proverbs that Solomon adapted from other wise people (22:29; 23:7; 23:35 [twice]; 24:23). Since the collections from other wise people (22:17–24:22; 24:23–34) are much shorter than those sections by Solomon, בַּל is most heavily concentrated in the proverbs adapted from other wise people. Prov 24:23 is Solomon-like, but different from the other "not good" proverbs.

---

[28] Compare, for example, 23:9 with 9:7; 23:12 with 2:2; 23:20–21 with 21:17; 23:26–28 with 5:1–6 and 22:14; and 24:1–2 with 3:31–32.

Another טוֹב, "good," proverb in the Words of Wise People is 24:13–14:

My son, eat honey, because it is good,
and flowing honey is sweet upon your palate.
In the same way, know that wisdom is [like this] for your soul.
If you find [it], then there is a future,
and your hope will never be cut off.

This proverb not only uses טוֹב, "good," but also speaks of finding "wisdom" (חָכְמָה), a definite Solomon-like statement, since "wisdom" is a major theme in the proverbs by Solomon and "to find [מָצָא] wisdom" is a concept in Solomon's proverbs (3:13; 10:13). Thus the occurrences of טוֹב, "good," proverbs in the Words of Wise People are one indication as to why they were included in the book: they are similar to Solomon's wisdom and can be commended for study.[29]

"Good" as Applied to the Ideal Wife (Prov 31:10–31)

The other two occurrences of טוֹב in Proverbs are in the acrostic poem about the ideal wife (31:10–31). This poem begins with a rhetorical question that recalls the "better than" proverb in 8:11, which has the same comparison "than jewels," and the "finds a good thing" proverb in 18:22, which also speaks of finding a wife:

Who can find a wife with strong character?
Her value is beyond that of jewels. (31:10)

The two uses of טוֹב, "good," in 31:12 and 31:18, while not conforming to any of the formulaic uses of טוֹב in Proverbs, were probably designed to draw a connection with the Solomonic portions of the book. This may be especially true in the case of 31:18, which comes at the end of the first major section of this acrostic poem.[30] The placement of this acrostic poem—which has connections to the Solomonic sections via the טוֹב, "good," proverbs—at the end of the book accomplishes at least three purposes:

1. It makes the non-Solomonic appendix to Proverbs (chapters 30–31) Solomon-like, justifying its incorporation in the book.[31]
2. Its first verse (31:10) recalls the proverbs in 8:11 and 18:22, which have טוֹבָה and טוֹב (respectively), "good." This recollection extends the binding motif of the טוֹב, "good," proverbs from Proverbs 1–9 through 10:1–22:16 to the end of the book.

---

[29] טוֹב, "good," also occurs in 24:25 in a simple adjectival sense. It is impossible to determine whether this is an imitation of the material in chapters 1–9 and 10:1–22:16 or simply the use of a common adjective.

[30] Lichtenstein, "Chiasm and Symmetry," demonstrates that this poem is structured as a nine-verse unit (31:10–18), a two-verse chiasm (31:19–20), a second nine-verse unit (31:21–29), and a closing two-verse coda (31:30–31). See also McCreesh, "Wisdom as Wife," and the commentary on 31:10–31.

[31] For additional connections between this acrostic poem and Solomon's proverbs, see the commentary on 31:10–31.

3. It ends the book with an explicit contrast between blessing and detriment (cf. 31:10, 12, 28), a contrast that is evident throughout the book of Proverbs.

It should be noted that *none of the uses of* טוֹב*, "good," in this section share any of the formulaic features of the Solomonic sections*. This dissimilarity supports the view that 31:10–31 is a section written by an author other than Solomon. The section stands in sharp contrast to chapters 1–9, which show every sign of a close relationship to the other Solomonic sections (the proverbs of Solomon in 10:1–22:16 and chapters 25–29, proverbs from Solomon copied by Hezekiah's men). That relationship is most easily explained by accepting that the three Solomonic sections (chapters 1–9; 10:1–22:16; and chapters 25–29) come from the pen of a single author.

Conclusion about Authorship

On every level examined—vocabulary, thought, and mode of expression—chapters 1–9 indicate that they come from the same author as 10:1–22:16 and chapters 25–29. This is exactly what the book itself indicates: these three sections come from "Solomon" (1:1; 10:1; 25:1). While "the fear of Yahweh" motif is obvious to readers, the טוֹב, "good, better," proverbs in the Solomonic sections are similar to each other in sophisticated ways. It would require an extremely sensitive reading of 10:1–22:16 (and chapters 25–29) if, according to critical theory, a different writer had read them and then produced such a closely aligned text as chapters 1–9. Therefore, the probabilities of Proverbs 1–9 coming from someone other than Solomon are extremely low. Moreover, the vocabulary shared by Proverbs 1–9; 10:1–22:16; and chapters 25–29 argues for a common author, because it would have been unthinkably difficult for a different author to have produced such a similar pattern of word usage.

At the same time, the inclusion (but not authorship) of the Words of Wise People (22:17–24:34) most probably should also be attributed to Solomon. These are somewhat like his writings and may have influenced him to some extent. On the other hand, he may have recognized in them thoughts similar to his own and included them for that reason.

Thus the authorship of Proverbs can be assigned to five categories:

- Solomon: 1:1–22:16; chapters 25–29
- Wise people: 22:17–24:34
- Agur: chapter 30
- Lemuel (or his mother): 31:1–9
- Unknown author: 31:10–31

That Solomon himself wrote under divine inspiration as he was led by the Holy Spirit (cf. 2 Pet 1:21) accounts for the theological content of his proverbs. The portrait of him in the historical books during his faithful years shows him acting under divine influence. He is the first heir of the promise given to his father, David (2 Samuel 7 || 1 Chronicles 17). He is endowed with unsurpassed wisdom (1 Kings 3–4 || 2 Chronicles 1) and is inspired to build the Jerusalem temple and accomplish other feats of greatness (1 Kings 5–10 || 2 Chronicles 2–9). We may assume that under inspiration Solomon judiciously copied and perhaps edited the proverbs from the wise people. As for the concluding portions by other authors, the contents of chapters 30–31 must have been recognized in Israel as authentic divine revelation when those sections were appended to the Solomonic portions to form the canonical book.

From the above discussion, it is clear that the majority of Proverbs originated from Solomon's pen. However, since not all of the book is from Solomon, the book in the form we have it must have been compiled after the time of Solomon. The dating of the book's several parts is difficult, but probably can be outlined in the following steps.

Solomon wrote 1:1–22:16 and compiled the Words of Wise People (22:17–24:34). Since the book addresses Solomon's son or sons, especially in Proverbs 1–9, he probably did not write 1:1–22:16 until after he had at least one son and had also received wisdom from God. His reception of wisdom happened shortly after his coronation in Jerusalem in about 971 BC (1 Ki 3:4–15 || 2 Chr 1:3–13).[32] Solomon's eldest son, Rehoboam, was born before Solomon became king, since Solomon reigned for forty years (1 Ki 11:42 || 2 Chr 9:30), and Rehoboam was forty-one years old when he succeeded his father (1 Ki 14:21 || 2 Chr 12:13). Therefore, the earliest date for the initial writing of 1:1–22:16 is 971 BC, but Proverbs 1–24 probably was finished later in Solomon's reign, as this would have given him time to collect the wisdom of other sages to include at the end of his own collection. Since it appears that Solomon added the second set of Words of Wise People sometime after the first, we can probably assume that he may not have completed Proverbs 1–24 until sometime late in his reign, which ended in 931 BC.

Hezekiah's men copied, edited, and arranged some more sayings from Solomon, probably from the official court archives, to produce chapters 25–29. This was most likely the work of Hezekiah's secretary Shebnah and his recorder Joah son of Asaph (2 Ki 18:18, 37). Since these sayings contain some sayings from Proverbs 1–24, but many more that are not from those chapters, it is clear that they were not simply relying on the document that became Proverbs 1–24. Instead, they were probably copying and arranging some of the three thousand proverbs that Solomon spoke (1 Ki 5:12 [ET 4:32]) and that were most likely preserved by Solomon's court secretaries Elihoreph and Ahijah, the sons of Shisha, or his recorder Jehoshaphat son of Ahilud, who had also served as David's recorder (1 Ki 4:3; 1 Chr 18:15). This activity would have taken place sometime in Hezekiah's reign (715–686 BC).

It is impossible to determine the dates of the composition by Agur (Proverbs 30), since we cannot determine with certainty who he was. (See the textual notes on 30:1a.) However, a clue may be found in the word מַשָּׂא, "oracle," which is

---

[32] All dates for the reigns of Israelite/Judean kings are taken from Finegan, *Handbook of Biblical Chronology*, 245–61.

used in 30:1 to describe his composition.[33] This word is first attested in this sense in Hebrew during the late ninth century in the reigns of Jehu (2 Ki 9:25; 841–813 BC) and Joash (2 Chr 24:27; 835–796 BC). However its most common use is among the Judean prophets of the eighth, seventh, and sixth centuries: Isaiah, Jeremiah, Ezekiel, Nahum, and Habakkuk.[a] It is used only sparingly after this by later prophets (Zech 9:1; 12:1; Mal 1:1). Since other portions of Proverbs that are appended to the original work of Solomon also indicate a seventh century date, the most likely date for Agur's composition is the seventh century, perhaps during the reign of Hezekiah.

(a) Is 13:1; 14:28; 15:1; 17:1; 19:1; 21:1, 11, 13; 22:1; 23:1; 30:6; Jer 23:33–34, 36, 38; Lam 2:14; Ezek 12:10; Nah 1:1; Hab 1:1

Since Lemuel's short work (Prov 31:1–9) contains several Aramaisms (see the first textual note on 31:2; the textual note on 31:3; and the second textual note on 31:4), it is likely that he composed his work after Aramaic became widespread as an international language. It had established itself as such in Hezekiah's day (2 Ki 18:26). Because Lemuel is called a king (Prov 31:1), the most likely candidate for his identity is Hezekiah (715–686 BC) or Josiah (640–609 BC), with Hezekiah being more likely (see the first textual note on 31:1). Unless Lemuel was a non-Judean king (which is unlikely, given his name), the latest possible date for the composition of 31:1–9 is the fall of Judah in 587 BC.

The final editor of the book probably wrote the final acrostic poem (31:10–31) as he drew on concepts and vocabulary in Solomon's proverbs. He may have also been responsible for adding the notice of editorial activity in 25:1 and the notices of authorship in 30:1 and 31:1. Since he probably worked sometime after the reign of Hezekiah, the earliest possible date for his activity is 686 BC. Because it is unlikely that any book written after the early Persian period was received into the canon,[34] the latest date is probably the time of Ezra (458–457 BC).

The growth of the book of Proverbs can then be reconstructed as shown in figure 3.

Wisdom in Proverbs

When Solomon first began to record his wisdom, he was heir to a centuries-old tradition of wisdom writings. Though scholars have pointed out that a precise definition of what constituted the genre of wisdom writings in the ancient Near East cannot be formulated, a number of works that can be classified as wisdom literature survive from Egypt, Syria, and Mesopotamia. In these works we find a number of motifs that are shared by Proverbs:

- Wisdom is divine. It is revealed by the gods (or to Israel, by the one true God) through authorities such as the head of the family or the king.
- Wisdom does not address society as a whole in order to transform it (as Israel's prophets often did), but it addresses individuals, who will then have an effect on society.

---

[33] Some take this word as a proper noun, "Massa," a kingdom in Arabia. See the third textual note on 30:1a.

[34] See Steinmann, *The Oracles of God*, especially pp. 190–93.

Figure 3

The Growth of Proverbs

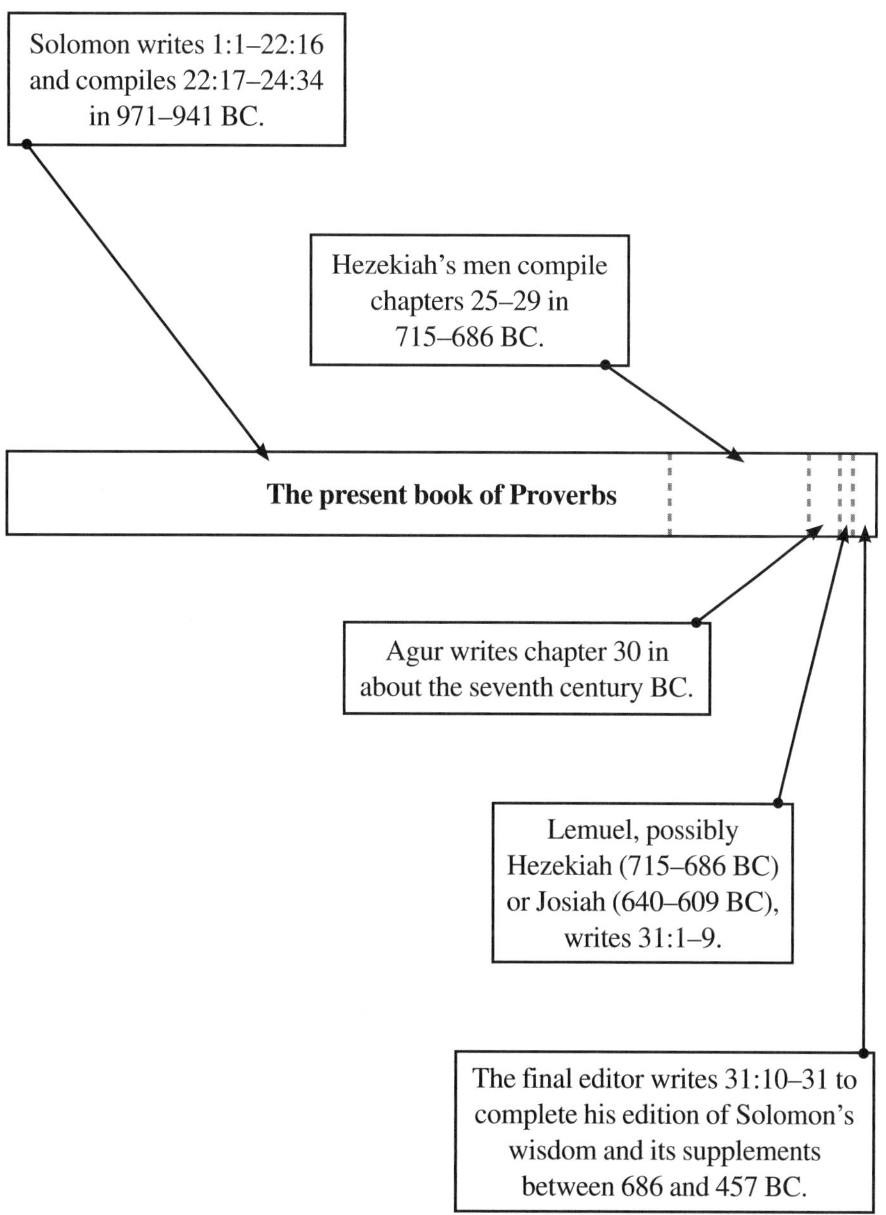

Solomon writes 1:1–22:16 and compiles 22:17–24:34 in 971–941 BC.
Hezekiah's men compile chapters 25–29 in 715–686 BC.
The present book of Proverbs
Agur writes chapter 30 in about the seventh century BC.
Lemuel, possibly Hezekiah (715–686 BC) or Josiah (640–609 BC), writes 31:1–9.
The final editor writes 31:10–31 to complete his edition of Solomon's wisdom and its supplements between 686 and 457 BC.

- Wisdom most often addresses practical knowledge instead of theoretical knowledge. It emphasizes what to do and how to do it and what the consequences will be. This focus on the practical presupposes the unexpressed greater principles reflected in living wisely. In Proverbs this is generally the case, though it extols divine wisdom itself and does contain passages that set the forth the theological principles of wisdom.

The oldest wisdom literature in Egypt stems from the Old Kingdom (twenty-seventh through twenty-second centuries BC). Already at this early period, Egyptians produced instructional literature, words of wisdom from a father to a son. This type of literature proved to have a long life, and instructional literature also survives from the First Intermediate Period (twenty-second and twenty-first centuries), the Middle Kingdom (between the twenty-first and seventeenth centuries), the New Kingdom (between the sixteenth and eleventh centuries), and even into Hellenistic rule as late as the fourth century BC. The parallel to the book of Proverbs is obvious, as Proverbs 1–9 is exactly this type of literature in the form of wisdom from a father to a son, as are the Words of Wise People that begin in 22:17. Solomon probably used this type of literature as a model for Proverbs 1–9, and it is likely that he borrowed and adapted some sayings from Egyptian wisdom to include in the Words of Wise People.[35] However, it would be going too far to say that Solomon's proverbs reflect Egyptian thought. Instead, while Solomon's wisdom and Egyptian wisdom have certain points of contact, especially when speaking of practical matters, the theology of Solomon's proverbs is thoroughly Israelite and demonstrates a continuity with the earlier revelation of God in the OT Scriptures.[36] In turn, later prophets reveal a familiarity with Solomon's wisdom.[37] In addition, Clifford notes:

> Taken as a whole, the instructions in Proverbs 1–9 are distinctive. … They are less specific than their Egyptian and Mesopotamian prototypes. They urge readers to seek wisdom rather than to do or not do particular actions. To put it another way, Proverbs emphasizes character rather than acts.[38]

Mesopotamian and Syrian wisdom instruction often takes the form of shorter sayings, similar to the ones found in 10:1–22:16 and chapters 25–29. These also have a long history, from early Sumerian wisdom through the sixth century BC Aramaic work the Words of Ahiqar.[39] Scholars have noted some parallels between the short sayings of Ahiqar and certain proverbs of Solomon.

---

35 See the excursus "The Words of Wise People (Prov 22:17–24:22) and Its Relationship to the Wisdom of Amenemope" in the commentary on chapter 22.

36 See the excursus "The Use of Deuteronomy 6:4–9 in Proverbs 3:1–12 and 6:20–22" in the commentary on chapter 3.

37 See the excursuses "The Relationship between Proverbs 1:16 and Isaiah 59:7" and "The Relationship of Proverbs 1:20–33 to Jeremiah 7 and Zechariah 7" in the commentary on chapter 1.

38 Clifford, *Proverbs*, 18.

39 *ANET*, 427–30; *ANE*, 245–49.

However, these ancient Near Eastern texts with shorter sayings have only slight parallels to Proverbs, and their influence on Solomon is doubtful. Instead, the older texts demonstrate that Solomon also adapted this type of wisdom expression for the purpose of relaying the truths revealed to him by Israel's God, Yahweh. Again, Clifford has noted the differences:

> The concise saying ... has been distinctively reshaped. Akkadian and Syro-Palestinian sayings were extremely diverse and included witty sayings, observations on life, jokes, wordplays, humorous or ironic maxims, and proverbs. Proverbs 10–31 is less inclusive and, more important, has made all the sayings bicolon in form. Though some earlier sayings were already in parallel lines, many of them were not. Israelite authors created a subgenre, the bicolon proverb, which attained definitive shape well before the late eighth century, when King Hezekiah's clerks added their collection to an already existing one.[40]

In Proverbs, wisdom is first and foremost an attribute of God. All true wisdom is godly wisdom, and any wisdom that people possess is a result of his gift of wisdom. This, however, often can only be perceived by understanding that it is the assumption lying behind Proverbs' teaching on wisdom. Rarely does the book make explicit statements about God's wisdom. Instead it assumes that God is all-wise and that the person who wants wisdom needs to receive it from him.

Perhaps the clearest statement on wisdom as God's possession is found in 3:19:

> Yahweh founded the earth by Wisdom;
> he established the heavens by Understanding.

Wisdom here is not a human attribute, because it predates humans. The eternal God utilized his wisdom when he formed the creation itself (see also Prov 8:22–31 as well as Job 28:12–28; 38:4–13). Wisdom is Yahweh's to use and to grant. This is stated in Prov 2:6:

> Yahweh gives wisdom;
> from his mouth [come] knowledge and understanding.

Only when the reader can understand that wisdom is God's alone and that real human wisdom is a gift of God, do the instructions of this book begin to make sense. This explains why "the fear of Yahweh" is the source and wellspring of wisdom:

> The fear of Yahweh is the beginning of knowledge. (1:7)

> The fear of Yahweh is the beginning of wisdom.
> The knowledge of the Holy One is understanding. (9:10)

> The fear of Yahweh is discipline that leads to wisdom. (15:33)

---

[40] Clifford, *Proverbs*, 18–19.

That a relationship with Yahweh through the "the fear of Yahweh," or faith,[41] leads to wisdom emphasizes that wisdom is God's. Proverbs also emphasizes that what humans consider wisdom is not true wisdom, for it cannot stand against God and his wisdom:

> Do not consider yourself wise.
> Fear Yahweh, and turn away from evil. (3:7)
>
> There is no wisdom, no cleverness,
> and no advice [that can stand up] against Yahweh. (21:30)

Thus essential for understanding the wisdom of Proverbs is discerning that wisdom is God's. This is also the key to comprehending the Gospel in Proverbs. Wisdom is God's great gift to his people throughout the book. Wisdom is what God bestows. It is God's gracious blessing that enlightens humans, and ultimately it is God as he comes to humanity in the person of his incarnate Son.

Wisdom is more than an attribute that describes God. In Proverbs, wisdom first is personified as a woman who invites those who hear her to partake of God's gift of wisdom. This choice of a woman to portray wisdom is partly based on the grammatical gender of the Hebrew word חָכְמָה, "wisdom." Because it is feminine, Wisdom is a woman. Yet the choice of a woman is more than simply adopting grammar as a guide. Since Proverbs 1–9 is addressed to Solomon's son, Lady Wisdom is intended to present an image of wisdom that is attractive to the son and that counters the attraction of the foolish world and its sinful ways. This is accomplished by contrasting the offer that Wisdom makes to the doom of those who reject her (1:20–33). It is also portrayed again in 9:1–18, where Wisdom is contrasted to another woman, Foolishness. This contrast is in the final section of the opening chapters (1–9) of Proverbs and is designed to leave a lasting impression on the son of the value of divine wisdom that God freely offers to all.

Another implicit contrast to personified Wisdom in Proverbs 1–9 is the adulteress.[42] Solomon pursues a strategy of commending Wisdom by a positive link between Wisdom and a wife, in contrast to the negative link between the adulteress and Foolishness. He uses Law to condemn the foolish son who strays from God's ways into adultery and foolishness. At the same time, he uses the Gospel in the form of Wisdom to proclaim God's benefits, confer God's favor, and bestow life.

As the reader of Proverbs encounters the figure of Wisdom in Proverbs, two passages in particular stand out. These passages in chapters 3 and 8 go beyond a mere personification of God's divine attribute. In 3:13 Wisdom is introduced and her value is extolled. In 3:19 Wisdom is explicitly connected to God's creative acts, making Wisdom an active participant in creation. In this passage,

---

[41] See "יִרְאַת יְהוָה, 'the Fear of Yahweh,' and יְרֵא יְהוָה, 'One Who Fears Yahweh' " below.

[42] See further the excursus "Wisdom and the Adulteress in Proverbs 1–9" in the commentary on chapter 2.

Solomon portrays the eternal second person of the Trinity, through whom all things were made (John 1:3; Col 1:16; Heb 1:2). That Christ is called "the Word (of God)" (e.g., Jn 1:1, 14; 1 Jn 1:1; Rev 19:13) recalls the words God spoke to cause the creation in Genesis 1. The identification of Wisdom as the agent of creation serves to draw the son who listens to his father's instructions closer to Yahweh. Wisdom is valuable because Wisdom is God, who offers his gracious blessings to the son listening to the father's word. Therefore, Wisdom in this passage is not merely personified, but it is a hypostasis.[43] That is, we are shown the unique person of God the Son, who shares the same divine essence as the Father and the Spirit. The one triune God created all things and is the bestower of all good gifts through the Gospel.

The reader meets hypostasized Wisdom again in Proverbs 8. Wisdom is the one by whom rulers rule, who grants riches and honor, and who grants inheritances (8:12–21). Here, once again, Wisdom is connected with God's creation of all things (8:22–31). This depiction emphasizes the eternal generation of Wisdom from the Father (8:22–26). The Christian will recognize this as Solomon's description of the second person of the Trinity.[44] Indeed, this is the NT's understanding. For example, Christ is clearly identified as the Wisdom of God in 1 Cor 1:24, 30. Furthermore, in stating that "Christ [is] the power of God and the Wisdom of God" (1 Cor 1:24), Paul plainly shows that he has Proverbs 8 in mind (see Prov 8:14; see also Job 12:13).

Garrett's argument that Paul did not have Proverbs 8 in mind because he was addressing the scandal of the cross[45] misses the point. The scandal of the cross is precisely that the eternal God, the Wisdom who existed before time, through whom the world was created and by whose power it is governed, humbled himself to die on the cross for sinful humanity before rising from the dead.

---

[43] The Greek term ὑπόστασις, *hypostasis*, is used in Heb 1:3 to say that the Son is "the express image of his [the Father's] *person*" (KJV) or "the exact representation of His *nature*" (NASB). The original Creed of Nicaea confirmed this biblical doctrine by anathematizing those who maintained that the Son was of a different ὑπόστασις *(hypostasis*, "divine nature, essence") than the Father (Kelly, *Early Christian Creeds*, 216). The Athanasian Creed emphasizes the one divine nature and the divine attributes shared by the three coequal persons of the one God. In doctrinal theology from the early church through the Reformation, "hypostasis" and "hypostatic" were used for the personal union of the divine and human natures in the one person of Jesus Christ. See Chemnitz, *The Two Natures in Christ*, especially pp. 67–169. The *unio hypostatica* (literally, "hypostatic union," often translated as "personal union") is affirmed in FC SD VIII, "The Person of Christ," for example, §§ 14, 23, and 76. See also the discussion of ὑπόστασις (*hypostasis*, "divine nature, essence") in Gerhard, *On the Nature of God and on the Most Holy Mystery of the Trinity*, 309–17.

[44] The Athanasian Creed affirms that the Father, Son, and Spirit are uncreated, coeternal, and one. The Son is generated or begotten of the Father from eternity, and the Holy Spirit proceeds from the Father and the Son. "The Son is neither made nor created, but begotten of the Father alone. The Holy Spirit is of the Father and of the Son, neither made nor created nor begotten, but proceeding" (vv 21–22 of the Athanasian Creed [*LSB*, p. 320]). See also the Nicene-Constantinopolitan Creed, which speaks of the Son as "begotten, not made" and of the Spirit "who proceeds from the Father and the Son."

[45] Garrett, *Proverbs, Ecclesiastes, Song of Songs*, 112–13.

This scandal is what makes God's foolishness wiser than human wisdom and God's weakness stronger than human strength (1 Cor 1:25). Also unconvincing is the argument of Fee that Paul was "demythologizing" the Corinthians' concept of wisdom and not actually connecting Wisdom with Christ.[46] Fee maintains that Paul was merely anchoring Christ in history by calling him "God's Wisdom." However, Christ is the Wisdom that was preexistent before history and was active at the beginning of history in the creation. He is anchored in history from its very beginning. He is the goal of history ("all things were created through him and *for him*," Col 1:16), and he physically entered earthly history in his incarnation.

St. Paul's references to Christ as God's Wisdom do not consist only of those in 1 Cor 1:24, 30. In Col 2:2–3 he states, "... so that they may know the mystery of God, [that is] Christ, in whom are hidden all of the treasures of the wisdom and knowledge of God" (see also 1 Cor 2:7–8). Paul evidently has in mind Prov 8:9–11, 21. In addition, Paul is not the only one in the NT to point to Christ as Wisdom. In Mt 12:42 (|| Lk 11:31), Jesus says that the Queen of Sheba will judge his hearers' generation because she came to hear Solomon's wisdom, but they do not understand that one greater than Solomon is here among them. The reference to "one greater than Solomon" is intended to point to Wisdom that is greater than Solomon's wisdom. Wisdom in Proverbs 1–9, and especially in Proverbs 8, is, by Solomon's own admission, greater than he. It is by Wisdom that Solomon reigned. In addition, in Lk 11:49 Jesus says, "The Wisdom of God said, 'I will send them prophets and apostles, and they will kill some of them and persecute others.' " This "Wisdom of God" who speaks is the Word, Jesus himself, who also says, "Therefore, I am sending you prophets, wise men, and scribes. Some of them you will kill and crucify, and others you will flog in your synagogues and persecute from city to city" (Mt 23:34). Finally, when Jesus is accused of being a drunk and glutton, he once again identifies himself as Wisdom (Mt 11:19 || Lk 7:34–35).

Therefore, in Proverbs, the concept of wisdom is completely theocentric and Christocentric. Without this understanding of wisdom, one cannot fathom the role of the Gospel throughout Proverbs. Wisdom is to be comprehended as God's gracious gift to his people in Christ. By it they are able to follow his Law and obey his commands (cf. Rom 13:8–10). The Gospel grants the power to implement the agenda for one's life that is set forth in this book. That agenda depends solely on God's love in Christ, which empowers and motivates his people to obtain wisdom and live wisely.

While wisdom is foremost an attribute and hypostasis of God in Proverbs, by his gift it also becomes an attribute of his people. Unlike God, God's people do not fully possess wisdom. Rather, through faith they acquire righteousness, knowledge, and wisdom from Christ, who strengthens them. As God's people ponder his Word, they will grow in wisdom.

---

[46] Fee, "Wisdom Christology in Paul," 255–57.

Proverbs employs a wide range of terms to describe what wisdom is and how it is displayed by those to whom God has given it. These terms show the broad scope of the concept of wisdom and its application to all areas of life.

חָכְמָה, "Wisdom," and Related Words

The abstract feminine noun חָכְמָה, "wisdom," occurs thirty-nine times in Proverbs. The cognate adjective חָכָם, used as a noun, "wise person," appears forty-seven times, and the verb חָכַם "to be wise," fourteen times.

The most prominent words relating to God's people as wise are these words from the root חכם. It must be borne in mind that חָכְמָה is not completely equivalent to the English word "wisdom." חָכְמָה is knowledge *and* ability to apply what one knows. In some passages in the OT, it denotes craftsmanship and proficiency in a occupation (e.g., Ex 35:31). In Proverbs wisdom has a wider sense denoting the ability to live in accordance with God's plan and will (10:8). It can manifest itself in practical matters and in interpersonal relationships (16:14, 23). Wisdom depends on reasoning and the aptitude and willingness to learn (1:5–6; 9:9; 13:10). It also is characterized by insight into the ways that God has ordered the world and into the ways that sin corrupts the world (14:8; 16:14). Coupled with this is foresight, the ability to anticipate the consequences of one's actions, so that one can avoid sinful and harmful situations (14:16). Wisdom also imparts the ability to teach others the way of wisdom (13:14; 15:2).

דַּעַת, "Knowledge," and יָדַע, "to Know"

The noun דַּעַת, "knowledge," occurs thirty-nine times in Proverbs, and the cognate verb יָדַע, "to know," thirty-five times. דַּעַת, "knowledge," signifies more than knowledge in the sense of facts that one has learned. It also denotes awareness of one's situation and the ability to integrate the facts one has learned into one's life in everyday situations. In addition, knowledge of God implies a relationship with him through faith that guides one's life (2:5). In many passages, דַּעַת, "knowledge," is used as a synonym for wisdom (e.g., 2:6).

שֵׂכֶל, "Good Sense," and הִשְׂכִּיל, "to Act Sensibly"

The noun שֵׂכֶל, "good sense," occurs six times (3:4; 12:8; 13:15; 16:22; 19:11; 23:9), and the cognate Hiphil (H) verb הִשְׂכִּיל, "to act sensibly," thirteen times. In Proverbs "good sense" is not the ability to exercise common sense, but rather the ability to follow God's ways even when circumstances seem to indicate some other course of action may be desirable or prudent (19:11). Such a person is spiritually and morally prudent.

בִּינָה, "Understanding," and Related Words

From the root בין come these words: the noun בִּינָה, "understanding," which occurs fourteen times; the noun תְּבוּנָה, "understanding," nineteen times; the substantized Niphal (N) participle נָבוֹן, "person with understanding, discerning person," nine times; the substantized Hiphil (H) participle מֵבִין, "person with understanding/discernment," six times; the Qal (G) verb בִּין, "to understand," fourteen times (including the Qere in 21:29); and הֵבִין (Hiphil [H]), "to understand," five times.

Of the two nouns for "understanding," the first one, בִּינָה, conveys the more theoretical or conceptual idea. It is used most often to describe the overall conceptual framework of one's reasoning and knowledge (23:4; 30:2). Therefore, it is used in the passages that speak of understanding in general terms (4:5, 7; 8:14). While the second and more common noun, תְּבוּנָה, can be used in this more general sense, it often takes on a more specific meaning: applied understanding. The person with this quality knows when to be patient and to hold his temper (14:29; 17:27). A ruler who lacks this quality oppresses his people (28:16).

עָרוּם, "Prudent," and עָרְמָה, "Prudence"

The adjective עָרוּם, "prudent," occurs eight times, and the cognate noun עָרְמָה, "prudence," three times (1:4; 8:5, 12). While these words often take on a sinister tone in the OT and denote the cunning wiles a person may use to obtain his goals (e.g., עָרְמָה in Ex 21:14; Josh 9:4; cf. Gen 3:1), in Proverbs they signify the use of intelligence and wisdom to accomplish things that are aligned with God's will and that exhibit godly knowledge (8:12; 13:16; 22:3).

מוּסָר, "Discipline," and יָסַר, "to Discipline"

The noun מוּסָר, "discipline," occurs thirty times, and the cognate verb יָסַר, "to discipline," five times.

Wisdom is not acquired all at once, but requires a lifelong process of learning and contemplation. To accomplish this, one needs discipline. Most often this word signifies correction, the intervention of some authority to turn one from harmful, self-destructive ways and sins. This may be a verbal warning (12:1; 13:1, 18), corporal punishment (13:24; 22:15), or some intervention of God into one's life (3:11). Discipline may also come from within oneself, a form of self-correcting thought (24:32). Since discipline is never meant simply as the venting of an authority's anger, but as a way of teaching and guiding in the way of life (6:23), מוּסָר can simply take on the meaning of instruction (4:1, 13).

מְזִמָּה, "Insight, Foresight"

The noun מְזִמָּה, which occurs eight times, is often used to portray inner thought and planning. In Proverbs 1–9 it refers to the aptitude of "insight" or "foresight" that God gives to his believing people together with divine wisdom (1:4). It can denote "insight" into the present situation that enables one to live according to God's Word. It can also refer to eschatological "foresight" about the eventual outcome of one's way of life: either the way of wisdom, which eventuates in eternal life, or the way of foolish infidelity, which ends in death and Sheol. This divine gift guards and preserves the believer's way of life (2:11), and the believer in turn is to "guard" it (3:21; 5:2). In chapter 8, which highlights preexistent Wisdom as the second person of the Trinity and the agent of creation

(8:22–31), "insight, foresight" is a divine attribute of Wisdom itself (8:12). In contrast, later in Proverbs it signifies evil scheming (12:2; 14:17; 24:8).

תּוּשִׁיָּה, "Sound Judgment"

Wisdom helps one evaluate and make judgments concerning one's world and the best course of action in it. The noun תּוּשִׁיָּה, "sound judgment," which occurs four times (2:7; 3:21; 8:14; 18:1), not only is applied to the faculty that produces such decisions (8:14), but also, as with תְּבוּנָה, "understanding," to the practical execution of those decisions (18:1).

תַּחְבֻּלוֹת, "Guidance"

Without a plan of action, wisdom remains only an intellectual exercise. The abstract plural noun תַּחְבֻּלוֹת, which occurs five times (1:5; 11:14; 12:5; 20:18; 24:6), refers to the guidance or even plan of action that one devises or is given. The wise in Proverbs have guidance that leads them to success (20:18; 24:6). However, the foolish and evil can also have plans and guidance that leads to destruction (12:5).

(b) Prov 1:7, 29; 2:5; 8:13; 9:10; 10:27; 14:26–27; 15:16, 33; 16:6; 19:23; 22:4; 23:17

עֵצָה, "Advice," and יוֹעֵץ, "Advisor"

The noun עֵצָה, "advice," occurs ten times, and the cognate substantized Qal (G) participle יוֹעֵץ, "advisor," four times (11:14; 12:20; 15:22; 24:6).

The wise person knows that he has received his wisdom from God. Divine "advice" (עֵצָה) forms a deep reservoir from which the wise person can draw (20:5). This wisdom comes not only in God's Word but also in the advice one receives from others (19:20), including pastors. The Lutheran Confessions affirm that the Gospel comes to us through God's Word and Sacraments and also "through the mutual conversation and consolation of brethren"[47] as we receive biblically informed advice from other Christians. A wise person accepts advice from those who are wise in the ways of God (12:15).

One ignores good advice to one's peril (1:25, 30). Advice that runs counter to the will of God will prove worthless (21:30).

יִרְאַת יְהוָה, "the Fear of Yahweh," and יְרֵא יְהוָה, "One Who Fears Yahweh"

The important phrase יִרְאַת יְהוָה, "the fear of Yahweh," occurs fourteen times in Proverbs[b] and only seven times elsewhere in the OT.[c] In Proverbs the noun יִרְאָה, "fear" (perhaps a feminine form of the infinitive construct, "to fear"), is never used by itself, but always in this phrase. The imperative of יָרֵא, "to fear," occurs twice with אֶת־יְהוָה, "Yahweh," as its direct object (3:7; 24:21). As either a participle or as a verbal adjective, יָרֵא, "fearing, one who fears," occurs in construct with "Yahweh" in 14:2 and (feminine) in 31:30. It pertains to fearing God's "commandment" in 13:13 and turning away from evil in 14:16.

(c) Is 11:2–3; 33:6; Pss 19:10 (ET 19:9); 34:12 (ET 34:11); 111:10; 2 Chr 19:9

[47] SA III IV, "The Gospel," citing Mt 18:20.

Finite forms of יָרֵא occur in 3:25 and 31:21 exhorting believers not to fear dangers other than God.

The fear of Yahweh can denote fear of God's wrath (24:21–22). More often, however, it denotes a positive, filial relationship to God through faith that causes a person to want to please the heavenly Father (8:13). God, who bestows blessings for temporal and eternal life and leads people to wisdom, initiates this positive relationship. The objective saving relationship with God is established by Christ, the Wisdom of God (Prov 8:1–36; 1 Cor 1:24, 30).

Thus "the fear of Yahweh" is first and foremost a filial relationship initiated by God when he reckons sinners as righteous through faith (Gen 15:6; Is 53:11; Hab 2:4). Justified believers can then have a positive relationship with God, who has forgiven them and made them his children. Proverbs speaks of this filial relationship with God by using the phrase "the fear of Yahweh." It was God alone who established this relationship with his people when he called their ancestor Abraham (Gen 17:7; Deut 29:13–14 [ET 29:14–15]) and when he delivered them from Egypt and graciously promised to be their God.[d] *Therefore, the theme and guiding principle of Proverbs is the Gospel, initiated by God and sustained by him.* This Gospel relationship to Yahweh is encapsulated in the phrase "the fear of Yahweh." In Proverbs all wisdom obtained by humans comes through this relationship established by God's own redemptive work—by grace alone—and received by believers through faith.

(d) E.g., Ex 6:7; Lev 11:45; 22:32–33; 25:38; Num 15:41; Jer 11:4

The Relationship between Wisdom and Righteousness in Proverbs

Wisdom and righteousness are seldom directly equated in Proverbs, but some sayings portray or at least presuppose the relationship between them. In 10:31 it is the "righteous person" (צַדִּיק) who is able to speak "wisdom" (חָכְמָה), implying that the divine gift of righteousness through faith (Gen 15:6; Hab 2:4) is a necessary prerequisite for a person before he is able to impart wisdom to others. Similar is the message of other proverbs in the context that refer to the "righteous" and the benefits they can convey to others by speaking to them (10:11a, 20a, 21a, 32a). Chapter 10 also refers to other blessings besides wisdom that are given by God to the "righteous" (see, e.g., 10:3, 6, 16, 24, 25, 30), and the immediate context presupposes that the righteous have "the fear of Yahweh" (10:27).

Wisdom and righteousness are intimately linked through the phrase "the fear of Yahweh" also in chapter 9:

> Do not warn a mocker, otherwise he will hate you.
>   Warn a *wise person*, and he will love you.
> Give [advice] to a *wise person* [חָכָם], and he will become even *wiser*.
>   Teach a *righteous person* [צַדִּיק], and he will add [to his] learning.
> *The fear of Yahweh* is the beginning of *wisdom*.
>   The knowledge of the Holy One is understanding. (9:8–10)

In this passage, a person who is wise is equated with a person who is righteous. Wisdom is inseparable from righteousness. When given divine advice and teaching, the wise and righteous person grows in learning, and this learning is predicated on the fear of Yahweh. This salvific fear includes not only dread of God's wrath at sin according to his Law, but also faith in God as Savior and love for God.

Like 9:9, a second passage where the "righteous person" (צַדִּיק) is parallel to, and equated with, the "wise person" (חָכָם) is 11:30. It is similar to 10:31 in that it has an evangelistic message about how God can save and bless others through the righteous and wise person:

> The fruit of a *righteous person* is a tree of life,
> and one who harvests souls is *wise*. (11:30)

In chapter 11 the "righteous" are delivered and saved (11:8, 9, 21; cf. 11:28) and so receive life. Moreover, the righteous person is able to offer "life" to others just as a tree yields fruit for the benefit of others (11:30a), and in this way the believer can "harvest souls" (11:30b). He is declared to be "wise" (11:30b). Again, God's gift of righteousness through faith is the prerequisite for a person who is wise. The distinct emphasis here is that through this righteous and wise person God proffers life and salvation to others too.

That emphasis is also conveyed in a third passage where a "righteous person" (צַדִּיק) is parallel to, and equated with, a "wise person" (חָכָם):

> The father of a *righteous person* will cheerfully rejoice.
> The man who begets a *wise person* will find joy in him. (23:24)

Here the father's son is both "righteous" and "wise." The context emphasizes that the son has acquired these qualities because he has listened to the divine wisdom taught to him by his father (23:19, 22), and the son is exhorted to "have the fear of Yahweh all the time" (23:17).

Throughout Proverbs this fundamental connection between wisdom, righteousness, and justification through faith is assumed even though it is seldom discussed. *Only the righteous—those who, through faith, have received God's imputed righteousness for the sake of Christ—have access to divine wisdom* (cf. Col 1:9, 28; 2:3). The righteous alone have the fear of Yahweh, a relationship with him based on the Gospel. "Righteousness" gives everlasting "life" with "no death" (Prov 12:28; cf. 21:21), and Yahweh "loves" a person who pursues "righteousness" (15:9; cf. Mt 5:6). The eternal Wisdom of God became incarnate in Jesus, and faith in God the Son is the way to receive righteousness and all wisdom.[48] While reading Proverbs it is vital to keep this in mind.

If these proverbs are read as only practical advice for tinkering with everyday situations, they will fall far short of the expectations readers place upon

---

48 See also the commentary on 1:1–7; 3:13–20; 8:22–31; 30:1b–10; and the excursus "Proverbs 8, Wisdom, Christology, and the Arian Controversy" in the commentary on chapter 8.

them. The advice they present does not always lead to an easy life and in fact can lead to decisions that make life more difficult (29:10). The proverbs in this book are not intended to make life easier and more comfortable, to be practical from a worldly point of view. Instead they are intended to make life more godly, to reinforce the relationship the righteous have with Yahweh through his grace, which they receive in his Word as it comes to them in Scripture and in the wisdom of others who fear him. At times this may make their life better, but when this happens it is a secondary benefit.

According to the sages, the search for an easy life through human plans and schemes comes at the expense of a positive relationship with Yahweh.[e] The wise person understands this and has his relationship with Yahweh as his first priority. For him it is the beginning and end of wisdom (9:10; cf. 4:7). The person who has his own worldly welfare as his first priority and is too shortsighted to see that his long-term welfare actually lies in the hands of Yahweh is portrayed in Proverbs as a fool.

(e) Prov 10:3; 12:2; 14:2; 15:16, 25; 20:22; 23:17

Fools in Proverbs

Proverbs teaches by both positive and negative examples. The most common positive example is the wise person, the person to whom God has given wisdom and who in turn seeks God and his ways. This positive example is held up as the ideal to which readers of the book should strive. The most common negative example is the fool, the person who has cut himself off from God and his guidance. Fools come with a range of attitudes and behaviors, from those who do not realize that they are cut off from God and blindly do things of which God disapproves to hardened fools who purposely cut themselves off from God and delight in doing things God detests. One needs to keep in mind that foolishness is not the same as lack of intelligence. In Proverbs fools are said to be able to think and reason, often with much sophistication. It is not lack of intelligence but *lack of faith and trust in God* that ultimately classifies one as a fool.

פֶּתִי, "Gullible Person"

The person who is foolish but least culpable for his foolishness is the פֶּתִי, "gullible person," which occurs fourteen times. This kind of person is inexperienced and immature (14:15; 22:3; 27:12). He is open to the influences of other fools and can easily be deceived and misled (9:16). Given enough exposure to the ways of foolishness, this person can become a fool who delights in his foolishness and waywardness from God, eventually suffering the punishment that awaits all fools (1:22, 32; 7:7). However, this type of fool is also the easiest to reach with the Gospel and can be led toward wisdom (1:4; 8:5; 9:4, 6; 19:25; 21:11). Yet, as long as he continues to be naïve, he remains a fool.

כְּסִיל, "Fool," and כְּסִילוּת, "Foolishness"

The generic noun for a "fool" in Proverbs, כְּסִיל, occurs forty-nine times, and the cognate abstract noun כְּסִילוּת, "foolishness," occurs once (9:13). The essence of a fool is his smug confidence in himself and his own powers rather than trust in God (28:26). In fact, he often is characterized as hating God and godly virtues (1:22), but loving and rejoicing in immorality (10:23; 13:19). He blunders into all kinds of harmful situations because of his lack of insight and foresight and his inability to learn wisdom (14:16; 17:16). His speech betrays his foolishness, because he is self-centered and selfish instead of humble and reliant on God and his mercy (10:18; 12:23; 15:2; 18:2; 26:7). This also leads him to bring grief and trouble to others (10:1; 13:20; 17:12, 21). In Proverbs the sages hold out little hope for changing the fool (26:11). Only the threat of punishment can keep him from doing foolish things (19:29; 26:3).

אֱוִיל, "Stubborn Fool," and אִוֶּלֶת, "Stupidity"

"Stubborn fool," אֱוִיל, occurs nineteen times, and the cognate abstract noun אִוֶּלֶת, "stupidity," twenty-three times. A fool who willfully rejects good and chooses evil is an אֱוִיל. This "stubborn fool" despises wisdom (1:7), rejoices in sin and rejects repentance (14:9), cannot control his emotions (12:16; 20:3), and considers himself clever because of his folly (12:15). He is so caught up in his foolishness that his way of life is called אִוֶּלֶת, "stupidity," by the sages (13:16; 14:8, 17; 26:11). This fool is so stubborn that he is nearly irredeemable (24:7; 27:22). Yet by God's grace and with the discipline of wisdom, stupidity can be driven out of a person (22:15).

נָבָל, "Complete Fool," and נָבַל, "to Be a Complete Fool"

The noun נָבָל, "complete fool," occurs three times (17:7, 21; 30:22), and the cognate verb נָבַל, "to be a complete fool," once (30:32). The most hopelessly foolish person in Proverbs is the נָבָל. This person has not only rejected God, but as the psalmist says, he rejects the very existence of God and mocks him as if he has no power (Pss 14:1; 53:2 [ET 53:1]; 74:22). This type of fool is the most dangerous since he is completely caught up in foolishness. When he is given prosperity in this life, he is insuperable (Prov 30:22).

Proverbs not only employs general words for fools, it also contains several words or phrases that characterize specific types of foolish persons and their behavior.

חֲסַר־לֵב, "Lacking Sense"

The construct phrase חֲסַר־לֵב, "lacking sense" (literally, "lacking a heart"), occurs eleven times. Fools often lack sense to comprehend the consequences of their actions (6:32; 12:11). Such fools are often the "gullible" (פֶּתִי, 7:7; 9:4, 16). This lack of sense leads them into danger and destruction (10:21).

בַּעַר, "Stupid"

Brutish stupidity that appears as ignorant as the actions of a dumb animal (בַּעַר) is mentioned twice in Proverbs. The person who resents being corrected is said to possess this quality (12:1). However, Agur uses the term for himself as he confesses his ignorance of God and his ways (30:2), and the context shows that Agur is humbly admitting his deficiencies but still is a believer in Yahweh.

גֹּבַהּ, "Arrogance," and Related Words

The noun גֹּבַהּ, "arrogance," occurs once (16:18), the adjective גְּבַהּ, "arrogant," once (16:5), and the verb גָּבַהּ, "to be arrogant," twice (17:19; 18:12). High-handed arrogance is the hallmark of a truly foolish person. The chief characteristic of the arrogant person is that he places himself above God, which merits God's contempt (16:5). This arrogance blinds a person to the self-destructive nature of his actions (16:18; 17:19; 18:12).

רְמִיָּה, "Laziness"

The feminine noun רְמִיָּה, "laziness," occurs four times. The person who thinks that there is a short cut around work or who thinks that he can survive without labor is characterized as shortsighted and inviting hunger and poverty by his laziness (10:4; 12:27; 19:15). Such people bring even harsher labor conditions on themselves because others will be forced to compel them to work (12:24).

לֵץ, "Mocker," and לָצוֹן, "Mocking, Scoffing"

The participle לֵץ, "mocker," occurs fourteen times, and the cognate noun לָצוֹן, "mocking, scoffing," occurs twice (1:22; 29:8). The most disgusting foolish behavior in Proverbs is that of the mocker. The לֵץ is arrogant and insolent, disdaining all that is godly and delighting in foolishness (1:22; 21:24). Mockers despise and deride those who offer them correction and wisdom (9:7–8). They produce quarrels and strife by their derision (22:10; 29:8) and thereby become detested by decent people (24:9).

Types of Sayings in Proverbs

Proverbs is known for its short wisdom sayings. While some parts of the book, notably Proverbs 1–9, contain longer, extended discourses of a father to his son, much of the book consists of short maxims that are commonly known as proverbs. These proverbs occur even within the extended wisdom instruction in Proverbs 1–9. Proverbs are constructed in several ways. Understanding a few of the basic methods used by Solomon and Israel's other wise people to construct their maxims allows one to appreciate their artistry as well as gain a better understanding of their message.

Complete Sentence

Some proverbs are composed of complete sentences:

Whoever places his trust in his wealth will fall,
  but righteous people will sprout like foliage. (11:28)

These sayings leave the least to the imagination of the reader, and their style is the least obscured in translation.

Juxtaposition

Often the sage will place two things or persons next to one another without a verb:

> A gold ring in a pig's snout—
> a beautiful woman without discretion. (11:22)

While there is some connection between the two things juxtaposed, this style requires more from the reader, who is required to make the connection:

> The fruit of a righteous person a tree of life,
> and one who harvests souls wise. (11:30)

In this case the connection is simple. One simply adds the copula "is":

> The fruit of a righteous person [is] a tree of life,
> and one who harvests souls [is] wise.

In other cases the connection is not so obvious, so the proverb itself supplies the connection by stating the characteristic common to all the elements:

> Heaven for height and earth for depth,
> kings' heart—there is no search. (25:3)

All three elements in this proverb (heaven, earth, heart) are unsearchable. In translating these sayings one must often obscure the stylistic features of the saying to make them flow legibly in English:

> [Like] heaven for height and earth for depth,
> so there is no searching the heart of kings.

Juxtaposition is sometimes used to emphasize a result that is seen as highly likely or certain:

> The plans of a hardworking person: only to abundance,
> but every person in a hurry: only toward poverty. (21:5)

Once again, the style of the Hebrew proverb must be obscured to produce a more natural translation:

> The plans of a hardworking person [lead] only to abundance,
> but every person in a hurry [progresses] only toward poverty.

Unfortunately, much of the stylistic flair of the proverbs is lost in translation. This is especially true for proverbs that use juxtaposition. While this commentary attempts to produce understandable English translations for the proverbs, readers who have knowledge of Hebrew are urged to consult the original.

Comparison

Some proverbs compare two things or persons:

> Like snow during the summer and rain during the harvest,
> so honor is not fitting for a fool. (26:1)

At other times the comparison is implicit:

A city broken into [and] without a wall [is]
a person who lacks self-control. (25:28)

The comparison enables the sage to teach either by moving from the well known to the lesser known or from a concrete situation to a general truth. In addition, comparisons were also used to add a measure of humor:

A person who grabs a dog by the ears [is]
a passerby who meddles in a quarrel that is not his. (26:17)

A door turns on its hinges,
and a lazy person [turns] on his bed. (26:14)

Good and Better Sayings[49]

A more subtle way of comparing two things is the use of "good, better" sayings. The simple statement declaring something "good" or "not good" is an implied comparison.

Differing weights are a disgusting thing to Yahweh,
and dishonest scales are not good. (20:23)

In the case of this proverb, the comparison is to honest weights and measures. A way that proverbs make a finer distinction among classes of things is the use of "better" sayings. In these sayings two things are compared. The simplest is the direct comparison, which takes the form A is better than B:

A good reputation is to be chosen rather than great wealth.
Favor is better than silver and gold. (22:1)

A more complicated form that allows for more subtlety in the comparison is the binary opposition comparison (A in view of B is better than A' in view of B'):

Better a little with righteousness
than a large income without justice. (16:8)

Better to be humble in spirit with oppressed people
than to share in stolen goods with haughty people. (16:19)

The binary opposition comparison allows the sage to state under which circumstances something is better than something else.

Numerical Sayings

Some sayings are organized numerically. The simplest of these is the saying involving a number followed by a list:

Four things are small on the earth,
yet they are wiser than the wisest people:
Ants are a species without strength,
but they store their food in summer.

---

[49] For a more complete treatment of these "good, better" sayings, see "Modes of Expression," "Direct Comparisons," and "Indirect Comparisons" in "Authorship and Date" above.

Rock badgers are a species without power,
  but they make their home in a cliff.
Locusts have no king,
  but they all go forth in ranks.
A lizard you can hold in [your] hands,
  but it is in palaces of a king. (30:24–28)

A more advanced form is the graded numerical saying. These sayings advance from one number to a greater one. In Proverbs the advance is always the addition of one to the first number. A list then follows that contains the same number of elements as the second, higher number.

Three things stride with majesty,
  four walk with majesty:
a lion, the mightiest among the animals—
  it does not turn away from anything;
a rooster or a male goat;
  and a king presiding over his army. (30:29–31)

These numerical proverbs allow the sage to draw an extended comparison over several elements.

The Spectrum of Advice in the Short Sayings

The book of Proverbs is often read for advice and guidance in life. It is important to realize that the several types of sayings that offer advice give different amounts of it. Some sayings offer no guidance. Others imply what one is to do without stating it directly. Still others flatly tell the reader what to do or avoid.

Observation of Life

Some sayings simply observe the way life is. They are not meant to offer advice as much as to inform the reader of the realities of life in the fallen, sinful world of humans.

A rich person's wealth is his strong city.
  Poverty is the ruin of poor people. (10:15)

One person pretends to be rich, but has nothing.
  [Another] person pretends to be poor, but has great wealth. (13:7)

Neither of these proverbs gives any explicit guidance. They tell what life is like without recommending a course of action. They reveal misplaced trust (10:15a) and despair (10:15b) as well as hypocrisy and façades (13:7). When encountering such proverbs, it is important not to assume that they are recommending that readers imitate the people they describe. Instead these proverbs enlighten readers about the vicissitudes and pitfalls of earthly life and the deceptiveness of human pretenses.

Observation and Conclusion

Some proverbs not only observe life, but they also offer a conclusion about what has been observed. These sayings *imply* that a wise person will take a certain a course of action without directly commending that course of action. In some sayings, the implication is gentle:

> A desire being fulfilled is sweet to the soul,
> but it is a disgusting thing to fools to turn from evil. (13:19)

Some have a stronger implication as to the correct mode of behavior that a godly person will have:

> Insolence only produces strife,
> but wisdom [is] with those who take advice. (13:10)

Still others come close to commending a course of action without actually recommending it:

> Whoever walks with wise people becomes wise,
> but a companion of fools will be harmed. (13:20)

The majority of the sayings in Proverbs fall into this category of observation and conclusion.

Command or Prohibition

A number of sayings in proverbs commend certain actions. Other sayings forbid some actions. In many cases these two are found in the same proverb:

> Discipline your son while there is hope,
> and do not make yourself responsible for his death. (19:18)

> Do not love sleep, or you will become poor.
> Keep your eyes open, and you will have enough to eat. (20:13)

However, some sayings contain only one:

> Commit your efforts to Yahweh,
> and your plans will be established. (16:3)

Occasionally a command or prohibition will also include the reason for the advice that is given:

> Do not rob a poor person because he is poor,
> and do not crush an oppressed person in the [city] gate,
> because Yahweh will defend their cause
> and deprive those who deprive them of life. (22:22–23)

> Do not befriend a hot-tempered person,
> and do not associate with a hothead,
> otherwise you will learn his path
> and set a trap for yourself. (22:24–25)

The Spectrum of Advice

All of these differing levels of advice in Proverbs are meant to help the reader ponder God's wisdom as it is revealed in the book. Each saying must be understood in its own right as falling somewhere on a spectrum of advice that offers some amount of guidance and leaves some amount of choice to the reader as to how and when to implement the advice. The spectrum could be diagrammed as in figure 4.

Figure 4

The Spectrum of Advice in Proverbs

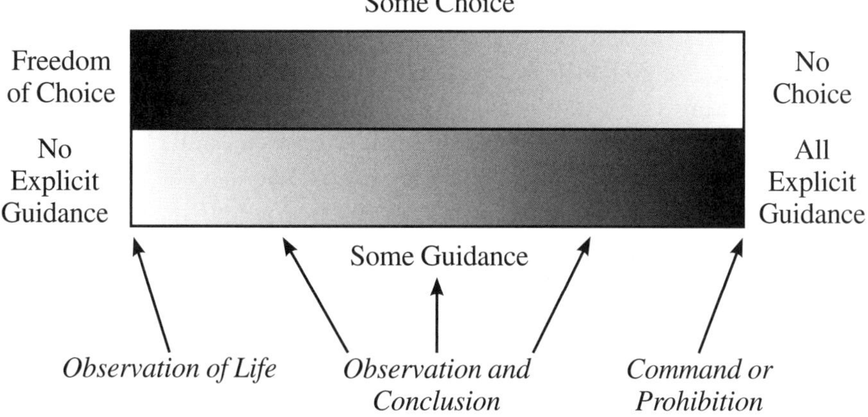

Understanding and Applying Proverbs

Those who read Proverbs today, like all modern readers of Scripture, are separated by a great distance in time and place from the original writers and audience. The challenge of applying the proverbs to contemporary life can be daunting when they refer to long past customs and situations that no longer exist (e.g., arbitration in the city gate). However, the timeless advice of Proverbs has spoken to every generation since the proverbs it contains were first written. In order to take advantage of the wisdom offered by this book, we need to explore a number of principles that apply to the unique challenges of interpreting this Wisdom book.

As with all proverbs, the surface meaning is not necessarily an indication of the scope of its proper application. For instance, consider the adage "don't count your chickens before they're hatched." On the surface this maxim is about animal husbandry, but its meaning goes well beyond chickens and eggs. The advice it offers about the dangers of overconfidence applies to all areas of life. In the same way, the sayings in the book of Proverbs are not necessarily to be restricted to their surface meaning. Take, for instance, this very similar pair of proverbs:

> Do not move an ancient boundary marker
> that your ancestors made. (22:28)

Do not move an ancient boundary marker,
    and do not enter the fields of orphans,
because their redeemer is strong.
    He will defend their cause against you. (23:10–11)

All that is needed to understand the surface meaning of the first proverb is the information that in ancient times boundary markers guarded property rights for subsequent generations; modern surveying techniques had not yet been invented. This proverb prohibits land fraud and is set in the midst of several proverbs dealing with economic fraud.

On the surface the second proverb seems to be the same. However, its setting is quite different. The proverbs in its immediate vicinity are not economic proverbs, and this proverb specifically mentions orphans, a generally poor and disenfranchised class of people in the ancient Near East. This proverb may go beyond the surface meaning to a metaphorical sense. Moving a boundary marker may represent changing laws and customs to the disadvantage of the defenseless, and entering a field of orphans may be a metaphor for using one's might to intimidate them. Thus context and subtle differences in similar proverbs can be clues as to their application, not only in ancient times but also today.

The larger context can be difficult to use for interpreting many of the sayings in Proverbs because they seem to be a nearly random collection of isolated maxims, especially when read in translation. Yet context is not completely lacking in Proverbs, even in the collections of short sayings that begin in 10:1. Some proverbs are collected together by theme. Others are connected by a *catchword*—a word, verbal root, or phrase they share in common with the context, though often used in differing senses. Still others may be connected because of similar sounding words. Knowing the reason why two proverbs are next to one another can be a great aid in interpreting them. While one cannot in every case determine the reason behind the organization of the sayings in Proverbs, in many instances it can be determined with a high degree of certainty. Throughout this commentary these organizational features will be pointed out as an aid to understanding their meaning.

Many Christians have turned to Proverbs for answers to questions that their lives have posed to them. They want to know the correct way to live and the correct moral and ethical decisions to make. However, the sayings in this book seldom give direct answers to life's questions. Instead, they require contemplation and growth in wisdom so that one can learn to apply them properly. God grants the power to acquire wisdom and to learn to apply these sayings properly. Therefore, one needs not only the proverbs themselves but also the insight that allows one to know the situation to which each proverb applies. For instance, 23:4–5 advises:

Do not wear yourself out getting rich.
    Have the insight [to know when] to stop.
Will your eyes glimpse it before it is gone?
    For it will quickly make a pair of wings for itself;
    like an eagle it will fly into the sky.

The principle of this proverb is easy to understand: do not seek riches in excess of what you need and can use charitably, since worldly wealth is transitory. However, the application of this proverb is difficult. When does one reach the point where one should no longer pursue money? For the desperately poor, this point may never come in earthly life. For the fabulously wealthy, this point has long since passed. It is easy to determine how the rich and the poor should appropriate this proverb. Those persons somewhere between need the wisdom to assess their situation and know when to pursue other interests.

Another example of needing insight to evaluate one's situation so that one can properly apply a proverb is the case of the twin proverbs in 26:4–5:

> Do not answer a fool according to his stupidity.
>   Otherwise you too will be like him.
> Answer a fool according to his stupidity.
>   Otherwise he will consider himself wise.

In any given situation, should you answer a fool or not? Will answering him benefit him or make you into a fool too? Only the God-given wisdom and insight that Proverbs commends can guide a person who seeks to implement this advice. The same is true of most of the proverbs. One cannot expect them to be a simple, follow-the-instructions textbook to life. Instead, they are designed to help the reader grow in wisdom and learn how to use them through a life that increases in the knowledge of the Gospel that alone brings fallen sinners to God and empowers them to live according to his will.

Law and Gospel in Proverbs

Throughout the Scriptures it is essential to distinguish between God's Law and his Gospel. The Law expresses God's holy will and demands that people conform to it by obeying his commands. The Gospel is his free gift of righteousness, salvation, and everlasting life on account of the perfect life, suffering, death, and resurrection of Christ. While we sinners are unable to satisfy the demands of God's Law, through his Gospel he bestows his gifts of grace and justifies all believers through faith alone.

The Law is the subject of much of Proverbs. The book also pays close attention to the principles of life in this fallen world. For these reasons, Proverbs is often seen as a book with little or no Gospel. It is true that Proverbs has few passages that are nothing but Gospel, but it is not true that Proverbs is without the Gospel. In fact, all of Proverbs presupposes the Gospel. This can be seen by its use of the Law.

Of the three uses of the Law,[50] the first and third uses predominate. These two uses of the Law match Proverbs' view of humans as foolish or wise, wicked

[50] The Law's three uses are these: "(1) to maintain external discipline against unruly and disobedient men, (2) to lead men to a knowledge of their sin, (3) after they are reborn, and although the flesh still inheres in them, to give them on that account a definite rule according to which they should pattern and regulate their entire life" (FC Ep VI 1).

or righteous. Fools can be restrained from their sinful ways only through the first use of the Law. Yet the Law guides righteous people, who are endowed with divine wisdom (Deut 4:5–6; Prov 2:6–7; Eph 1:7–8, 17); this application is its third use. The second use of the Law is seldom explicitly employed in Proverbs, though it is always present implicitly, since *lex semper accusat*, "the Law always accuses." Believers are simultaneously sinners and saints (as St. Paul confesses about himself in Romans 7; 1 Tim 1:15), and to the extent that we still act like fools, the sayings in Proverbs condemn our foolishness.

The relative lack of the overt second use of the Law points us to the primary intended audience of Proverbs: it is written to speak to God's people, those who are forgiven and justified, who have a living relationship with him through faith in his Gospel promise. In OT terms, Proverbs was intended for the instruction of young men who had been incorporated into God's people through the promise connected with their circumcision (Gen 17:10–14; Ex 12:48; Deut 10:16; 30:6; cf. Rom 4:11). It is not intended for the unregenerate and therefore does not presuppose that readers are unbelievers who need to be driven to repentance by the condemnation of their sins. In NT terms, it speaks to the baptized people of God, who have been brought into God's kingdom and regenerated through this Sacrament, who have been brought to repentance and faith and are heirs of the OT promises (Gal 3:26–29; Col 2:11–13; Titus 3:4–6). Thus few passages in Proverbs speak the Law directly in order to apply it in its second use, which is its proper theological use.[51] However, since human nature is fallen and even in the regenerate people of God sin persists in this life, the Law in Proverbs will always remind us of our sin and drive us to daily repentance. Daily we need to die to sin and rise to new life in Christ (Rom 6:1–11).

The civil use of the Law to restrain sin is especially employed to combat the foolish behavior toward which sinful human nature inclines. This is often found in threats of punishment and suffering:

They would not accept my advice,
    and they despised all my warning.
They will eat the fruit of their way,
    and they will be gorged with their own advice.
Therefore, the apostasy of gullible people kills them,
    and the complacency of fools destroys them. (1:30–32)

A little sleep, a little slumber,
    a little folding of the hands to lie down,
and your poverty will come like a drifter,
    and your need like an armed robber. (6:10–11)

At the death of a man who is wicked, hope will perish,
    and confidence in strength perishes. (11:7)

---

[51] "The chief function or power of the law is to make original sin manifest and show man to what utter depths his nature has fallen and how corrupt it has become" (SA III II 4).

The person who repays evil for good—
evil will never leave his house. (17:13)

Some proverbs promise benefits for those who follow the Law:[52]

Like the coldness of snow on a harvest day
is a trustworthy messenger to those who send him.
He revives his masters' soul. (25:13)

When there is no more wood, a fire goes out,
and without a gossiper, a quarrel dies down. (26:20)

Some proverbs use both a threat of punishment and a promise of benefits:

A faithful man benefits himself,
but a cruel man brings trouble on himself. (11:17)

A person who is greedy for ill-gotten gain troubles his own household,
but a person who hates bribes will live. (15:27)

This use of the Law to discourage sin and encourage civil righteousness is needed even by the regenerate people of God, since they remain in their sinful flesh as long as they are in this life. For this reason Proverbs contains some of the Scripture's sharpest images of the punishment that God can meet out to those who fail to keep his Law (e.g., 7:22–27; 9:18).

The use of the Law as a guide for the person who by faith knows God and wants to please him is found throughout Proverbs. For instance, those who have been made Yahweh's children are encouraged to keep the Third Commandment by praying to him:

Yahweh is far away from wicked people,
but he hears the prayer of righteous people. (15:29)

Often Proverbs assumes that readers are among God's believing people when it presents the Law's precepts:

Honor Yahweh with your wealth
and the first part of your entire harvest. (3:9)

Do not reject Yahweh's discipline, my son,
and do not despise his warning,
because Yahweh warns the one whom he loves
like a father [warns] a son with whom he is pleased. (3:11–12)

In many cases God's promises are used to encourage his people to do good:

The person who spreads blessing will prosper,
and the person who refreshes others will be refreshed. (11:25)

---

52 The Lutheran Confessions "maintain that the law was given by God first of all to restrain sins by threats and fear of punishment and by the promise and offer of grace and favor" (SA III II 1).

Proverbs therefore often assumes that its readers are children of God through faith, presupposing that the Gospel has brought them into his kingdom and that they understand their adoption by grace into the family of Yahweh. Its sayings are intended to encourage them to good works even though the sinful world may weigh heavily upon them. It seeks to provide guidance in the way of God's holy Law as they live their lives. The same dynamic is found in the NT, which exhorts believers to obey God's Law and be diligent in good works—not in order to be saved by obedience and works, but precisely because God in Christ has already granted salvation by grace alone (e.g., Romans 13; Eph 2:8–10).

While Proverbs does not have a large number of well-known Gospel passages, nevertheless, it is animated by the Gospel. The forgiveness of God by his grace alone (e.g., Psalm 32) and the righteousness he credits to his people through faith alone (e.g., Gen 15:6; Hab 2:4) form the basis for many of the proverbs, which assume that readers have a positive relationship with him. Most notable of the passages with much Gospel content are the three discourses of Solomon about Wisdom (1:20–33; 8:1–36; 9:1–18) as well as Solomon's second address to his son (2:1–22), which are fulfilled in the Gospel of God's Son, Wisdom incarnate.[53] In addition, scattered throughout Proverbs are a number of Gospel proverbs that point to God's work in the lives of his people:

> Whoever places his trust in his wealth will fall,
> *but righteous people will sprout like foliage.* (11:28)
>
> In the path of righteousness [there is] life,
> *and the way of its pathway is no death.* (12:28)

In Proverbs sayings that apply the Law are far more frequent than sayings that bring the comfort of the Gospel. Yet the Gospel predominates in this book, for the sole source of its comfort for those who have fallen short of God's expectations is the Good News of God's forgiveness and free salvation. The Gospel is what empowers them to live as God's forgiven and reconciled people and therefore to grow in wisdom and righteous living.[54]

Reading and Understanding Proverbs

Given all that has been said about Proverbs to this point, how are we to read this book profitably and understand it correctly? Several conclusions suggest themselves from the stages of composition, organization, and content of the book.

If the theory on the growth of the book presented above is correct, it also implies that one needs to read the book in light of the historical process used by the Holy Spirit to produce the final form of the book that we have today. In its earliest stage Proverbs consisted of the portions produced by Solomon under

[53] See "Wisdom in Proverbs" above.

[54] Note the parallels between, for example, Prov 9:1–6 and Is 25:6–9; 55:1–7; Jn 4:10–14; 6:28–29, 35; 7:37–39; Rom 3:21–25; Rev 22:17.

the guidance of divine inspiration: Proverbs 1–24. This contains Solomon's long opening section (Proverbs 1–9), his collected sayings (10:1–22:16), and his two collections of sayings edited from the words of other wise people (22:17–24:34). This implies that Proverbs 1–9 is the introduction to his work and is intended to set forth his wisdom in a more systematic way than could be accomplished in collections of shorter sayings. Therefore, one needs to understand well the wisdom of this introductory section and then read the shorter sayings that follow in light of this introduction. Since the introduction treats Christ as wisdom, and since the climax of this section is Proverbs 8, we must read all of Proverbs in light of God's revelation in Christ, especially the portrait of Christ in this chapter.[55] In addition, Proverbs 9 is clearly a transitional chapter intended to prepare the reader for the contrast of wisdom and foolishness that underlies the sayings in Proverbs 10–24. The message of chapter 9 cannot be neglected or ignored if one wishes to understand the later sayings properly because it defines and explains what wisdom and foolishness are.

When one then moves into the sayings of Proverbs 10–24, it becomes obvious that they should be understood in light of the exposition of godly wisdom and wise, godly living as Solomon has explained in Proverbs 1–9. From this perspective, it should be understood that Solomon, under the inspiration of the Holy Spirit, was led to include (and perhaps modify) the wisdom of others, including non-Israelites, in the sayings of 22:17–24:34.[56] At the same time, one should not view Proverbs 10–24 as a random collection of sayings. Instead one should read those chapters as having an organization of their own.[57]

Likewise, the addition of the proverbs of Solomon copied by Hezekiah's men (chapters 25–29) should be understood as having been attached to the earlier work of Solomon because they are part of a common view of wisdom and share a common theology centering on Christ as God's Wisdom. By inspiration, a later editor was led to attach these sayings to the earlier work because they also bring the Gospel to bear on the lives of God's people. Like the earlier sayings of Solomon, these are not randomly collected proverbs, but they are organized in their own way in order to lead the reader in learning wisdom.

The sayings of Agur (chapter 30) and Lemuel (31:1–9) were also attached to the book because an inspired editor understood that they reinforced the message communicated through Solomon's God-given wisdom. Agur's words are a consciously constructed work based on Solomon's earlier proverbs and other passages from the OT.[58] They need to be read as a further exposition of the wisdom that leads to Christ.[59]

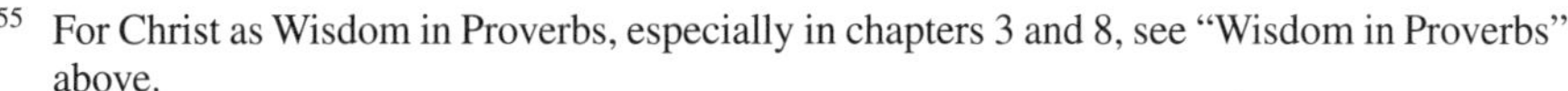

[55] For Christ as Wisdom in Proverbs, especially in chapters 3 and 8, see "Wisdom in Proverbs" above.

[56] See the excursus "The Words of Wise People (Prov 22:17–24:22) and Its Relationship to the Wisdom of Amenemope" in the commentary on chapter 22.

[57] See the excursus "The Organization of the Sayings in Solomon's Proverbs in Proverbs 10:1–22:16" in the commentary on chapter 10.

[58] See the commentary on 30:1b–10.

[59] See the commentary on 30:4.

Finally, the poem that concludes Proverbs (31:10–31) was undoubtedly written by an author who had in mind the figure of Lady Wisdom (e.g., 1:20–33; 7:4; 9:1–6) and the sayings about a wife of strong character (e.g., 12:4).[60] It was appended, and perhaps written, by the inspired final editor of Proverbs to close out the book's final form. Once again, it needs to be read in relation to the rest of the book, especially Proverbs 1–9.

Within each section of Proverbs, the individual units exhibit an organization. Sometimes this organization is rather tight and explicit, as in the discourses in Proverbs 1–9, while in other places the organization is loose and implicit, as in Proverbs 10:1–22:16. In addition, each section of Proverbs, except the closing poem (31:10–31), contains a number of discrete units and can be read individually. For example, 2:1–22 is an address to a son and can be read as a unit by itself. Most of the sayings in Proverbs 10–29, and many in Proverbs 30–31, can be read as individual units, often one verse at a time. While there is nothing inherently wrong with studying them as discrete units, they should never be read and interpreted apart from their context—both the narrower context of the sayings or units around them and the wider context of the entire book, which is part of the OT and which needs to be interpreted in light of the NT fulfillment in Jesus Christ.

Reading any proverb apart from its context runs the risk of detaching it from the book's emphasis on the Gospel of Christ, the incarnate Wisdom of God.[61] Such a procedure will lead to a misunderstanding of the theological nature of any and every unit in the book. Such isolated readings have led some scholars to view Proverbs as essentially a book of humanly devised wisdom. Instead of that approach, the wider context of Proverbs—with its emphasis on Christ, the Wisdom of God—must play an essential role and serve as the interpretive guide even in the places where the immediate context is not always a readily apparent guide to the meaning of a proverb (as in much of chapters 10–29). Moreover, since there are a large number of verses in Proverbs that are repeated in whole or in part elsewhere in the book, the book itself invites a cross-contextual reading that points to the Gospel as a feature that permeates Proverbs and gives it unity.

Finally, one must read and interpret Proverbs with an eye to its overall content. Important themes such as wisdom, foolishness, the metaphor of the path,[62] righteousness, and wickedness run throughout the book as threads that create a warp and woof for the fabric of its message. The first and third uses of the Law, the uses that predominate in Proverbs, need to be used as important guides when interpreting individual sayings. Most importantly, as noted already, the theme that unites the book is Christ as God's Wisdom, and no passages can be prop-

---

[60] See further the commentary on 31:10–31.

[61] See "Wisdom in Proverbs" above.

[62] See the excursus "The Metaphor of the Path in Solomon's Wisdom" in the commentary on chapter 10.

erly interpreted if one's understanding of any part of Proverbs is not informed by this aspect of the Gospel.[63]

The Text of Proverbs

In general, the text that forms the basis for this commentary is the Hebrew MT as preserved in the great medieval manuscripts, especially Codex Leningradensis. However, at several places this text is extremely difficult and perhaps corrupt.[64] In most of these cases, this commentary adopts as a solution a repointed text using different vowels but the same consonants as the MT (since the original Hebrew text had no vowel pointing). In a few cases, guidance from the ancient versions, especially the LXX, provides a readable and understandable reconstruction of the Hebrew text. All of these departures from the MT are explained in the textual notes.

The discovery of the ancient scrolls hidden in caves beside the Dead Sea has shed little light on the textual problems in Proverbs. Only several scraps of leather containing text from Proverbs were preserved, all of them from cave 4. Variants from the MT are few and not very significant. The texts preserved consist of parts of 1:27–2:1; 13:6–9; 14:5–10, 12–13, 31–35; 15:1–8, 19–31; and possibly 7:9–11.[65] Manuscript 6Q30 may contain parts of 11:5, 6, 7, 10.[66] In addition, there is a quotation of 15:8 in the *Damascus Document*. All of the variants in these scrolls are discussed in the textual notes on the particular verses.

The ancient Greek translation of Proverbs probably was produced in the second century BC.[67] The translator's main objective seems to have been to make an understandable version of Proverbs for his Greek readers. At times he follows a text very similar to the MT fairly closely, though in most of the proverbs he deviates from the Hebrew text in some way. At other times he seems to paraphrase, interpret, or even rewrite the Hebrew text, probably in the attempt to make it more relevant to his audience. In addition, the LXX omits a number of verses in the MT and adds quite a few more (see figure 5). Some of these expansions show signs of being Hellenistic,[68] making it likely that the LXX's different text is most likely secondary.[69] It also rearranges the end of the book, placing 30:1–14 between 24:22 and 24:23; 30:15–31:9 between 24:34 and 25:1; and 31:10–31 after 29:27. At the same time, it removes all mention of authors or editors other than Solomon, making it likely that these rearrangements are

---

63 See "Wisdom in Proverbs" above.

64 See, for example, the first and third textual notes on 30:1b.

65 Ulrich et. al., *Qumran Cave 4.XI*, 181, 183.

66 Eshel, "6Q30, a Cursive *Šîn*, and Proverbs 11."

67 Cook, "The Dating of Septuagint Proverbs," 399; Fox, *Proverbs 1–9*, 362.

68 For example, see the second textual note on 6:8.

69 Tov ("Recensional Differences") argues that the LXX sometimes represents a different Hebrew recension of Proverbs. I find his argument doubtful.

secondary and designed to attribute the entire book to Solomon.[70] Due to these features of the LXX, it is only occasionally useful for text critical investigations in Proverbs, though in the past it has been invoked regularly to solve textual problems, whether real or perceived.[71]

Like the LXX, other ancient versions are of limited use in text critical work in Proverbs. The Syriac Peshitta is at times fairly faithful to the MT. In other cases it is heavily influenced by the LXX. The Targum to Proverbs is directly dependent on the Peshitta, so that the Targum rarely has any independent text critical value. The Vulgate is very dependent on a form of the text that is very close to the MT. It preserves few variants compared to the MT and only occasionally supports one of the other versions.

When reading the church fathers, it is important to keep in mind that their text of Proverbs was the LXX or versions dependent upon it, such as the Old Latin. Therefore, they often understand passages in Proverbs to be saying something quite different than the Hebrew text. For instance, one of Augustine's favorite passages in Proverbs is LXX 8:35b: καὶ ἑτοιμάζεται θέλησις παρὰ κυρίου, "and the will is prepared by the Lord."[72] This is quite different from the Hebrew וַיָּ֥פֶק רָ֝צ֗וֹן מֵיְהוָֽה, "and he obtains favor from Yahweh."

In general, the translation of Proverbs in this commentary strives for natural and understandable English, avoiding a slavish dependence on the form of the Hebrew text that would make the English read awkwardly. However, the translation may seem somewhat unnatural since some forms present in the Hebrew are important to the meaning of the text. Thus the translation attempts to balance Hebrew form and English function for a reader who is assumed to be advanced enough to go beyond a completely natural English translation that would obscure most, if not all, of the distinctive features of the Hebrew text.

Brackets are used to enclose words that are supplied—that do not render any Hebrew word but are implied by the Hebrew. The only major exception to this rule is the frequent use of some form of the English copula without brackets, even where no Hebrew copula exists in the text. The proper name of God, יהוה, is translated as "Yahweh," the way the surviving evidence indicates that it was pronounced in ancient times.[73]

---

[70] Washington, *Wealth and Poverty*, 126–27.

[71] The opinion of Cook, *The Septuagint of Proverbs*, 334, is helpful:

> The Septuagint version of Proverbs should be treated with the utmost caution when utilised for text-critical purposes. By far the greatest number of differences compared to the MT are the result of the translator's creative approach. To me at least it would seem that the Hebrew parent text from which this Greek version was constructed did not differ extensively from the Massoretic text.

[72] Augustine, *On the Merits and Forgiveness of Sins, and on the Baptism of Infants*, 2.30 (*NPNF*[1] 5:56); *Against Two Letters of the Pelagians*, 1.36; 2.20; 4.12–13, 26 (*NPNF*[1] 5:388, 400, 422, 429); *On Grace and Free Will*, 32 (*NPNF*[1] 5:457); *On Rebuke and Grace*, 17 (*NPNF*[1] 5:478); *On the Predestination of the Saints*, 1.42 (*NPNF*[1] 5:518).

[73] See D. N. Freedman, M. P. O'Connor, and H. Ringgren, "יהוה," *TDOT* 5:501–12.

Figure 5

Differences between the MT and the LXX in Proverbs

MT	LXX	MT	LXX	MT	LXX
1:16	**Missing in some MSS**	12:13	*Expansion*	20:14–19	**Missing**
1:18	*Expansion*	13:9	*Expansion*	20:20–22	After 20:9
3:16	*Expansion*	13:13	*Expansion*	21:5	**Missing**
3:22	*Expansion*	15:18	*Expansion*	22:6	**Missing**
4:7	**Missing**	15:27	*Expansion (16:6)*	22:8	*Expansion*
4:27	*Expansion*	15:28	*Expansion*	22:9	*Expansion*
6:8	*Expansion*	15:29	*Expansion (16:8–9)*	22:14	*Expansion*
6:11	*Expansion*	15:31	**Missing**	23:23	**Missing**
7:1	*Expansion*	16:1	**Missing**	24:22	*Expansion*
8:21	*Expansion*	16:3–4	**Missing**	25:10	*Expansion*
8:32b–33	**Missing**	16:6	After 15:27	25:20	*Expansion*
9:10	*Expansion*	16:8–9	After 15:29	26:11	*Expansion*
9:12	*Expansion*	17:6	*Expansion*	27:20	*Expansion*
9:18	*Expansion*	17:16	*Expansion (17:19b; repetition of 17:20bβ)*	27:21	*Expansion*
10:4	*Expansion*	17:19b	After 17:16	28:17	*Expansion*
11:4	**Missing**	18:22	*Expansion*	30:1–14	Before 24:23
11:16	*Expansion*	18:23–19:2	**Missing**	30:15–31:9	After 24:34
12:11	*Expansion*	20:9	*Expansion (20:20–22)*	31:25–26	Reversed

Proverbs 1:1–7

The Superscription and Solomon's Preface

Proverbs 1:1–7

The Superscription and Solomon's Preface

Translation

1 [1]The proverbs of Solomon son of David, king of Israel:
[2]to know wisdom and discipline,
to understand words of understanding,
[3]to acquire discipline for acting sensibly:
righteousness, justice, and fairness,
[4]to give to gullible people prudence,
to a young man knowledge and foresight—
[5]may a wise person listen and increase [his] learning,
and may a person with understanding acquire guidance—
[6]to understand a proverb and an enigma,
the words of wise people and their riddles.
[7]The fear of Yahweh is the beginning of knowledge.
Stubborn fools despise wisdom and discipline.

Textual Notes

1:1 מִשְׁלֵי שְׁלֹמֹה בֶן־דָּוִ֑ד מֶלֶךְ יִשְׂרָאֵל׃—The Hebrew title of the book of Proverbs is the first word, which is the plural construct of מָשָׁל. The noun מָשָׁל usually means "proverb" (*HALOT*, 2) or "wisdom saying … didactic speech … parable" (*HALOT*, 3). Often a מָשָׁל involves a comparison. The verbal root מָשַׁל means "to compare." The noun often refers to an observation about life based on some comparison, a saying or maxim (26:7, 9), an allegory (Ezek 17:2), or a familiar saying (1 Sam 10:12; Ezek 18:2). The noun is used in Proverbs to denote the wise sayings that constitute this book (1:1, 10:1; 25:1) as well as more generally to refer to any proverb that encapsulates divine wisdom (1:6; 26:7, 9).

The *athnach* on דָּוִ֑ד suggests that the last phrase in apposition, מֶלֶךְ יִשְׂרָאֵל, "king of Israel," is intended to describe the earlier person, Solomon, rather than David.

1:2 לָדַעַת חָכְמָה וּמוּסָר—The Qal (G) infinitive לָדַעַת is from יָדַע with לְ. The infinitives construct that begin each verse in 1:2–4, as well as לְהָבִין beginning 1:6 and the second half of 1:2, express purpose: the purpose of the book of Proverbs is to bestow divine wisdom. This could be clarified by rendering 1:1–2 as "the proverbs of Solomon son of David, king of Israel, [given to you, the reader, so that you may] know wisdom and discipline …"

For the nouns חָכְמָה and מוּסָר, see "חָכְמָה, 'Wisdom,' and Related Words" and "מוּסָר, 'Discipline,' and יָסַר, 'to Discipline' " in "Wisdom in Proverbs" in the introduction. Wisdom in Proverbs is not mere worldly insight, but it is the insight and foresight given by the Holy Spirit to those who know God through faith and seek to do his will in accord with his Word. מוּסָר, "discipline," occurs thirty times in Proverbs, including twice more in this preface (1:3, 7). While it can refer to the correction or instruction that a parent or other authority uses to train a child (5:12; 19:27), it also means the *self-discipline* of a person who is consciously striving to live in a way that pleases Yahweh (23:23).

לְהָבִין אִמְרֵי בִינָה׃—In Proverbs the Hiphil (H) of בִּין often has the meaning "to understand" (*HALOT*, 1). The identical Hiphil infinitive construct לְהָבִין begins 1:6, and the Niphal (N) participle נָבוֹן is in 1:5. Here the accusative direct object is the construct phrase אִמְרֵי בִינָה, "words of understanding," which has the cognate noun בִּינָה. See "בִּינָה, 'Understanding,' and Related Words" in "Wisdom in Proverbs" in the introduction.

1:3 לָקַחַת מוּסַר הַשְׂכֵּל—The object of the Qal (G) infinitive construct (קַחַת, from לָקַח, with the preposition לְ) is the noun מוּסָר in construct with the Hiphil (H) infinitive absolute הַשְׂכֵּל. The construction means "to acquire discipline for acting sensibly" (cf. Waltke-O'Connor, § 35.3.3, example 9). The verb לָקַח meaning "to acquire, receive" wisdom is common in Proverbs (e.g., also 2:1; 4:10; 8:10). For מוּסָר, "discipline," see the first textual note on 1:2.

צֶדֶק וּמִשְׁפָּט וּמֵישָׁרִים׃—This phrase also occurs in 2:9. "Righteousness" (צֶדֶק) for humans is thought and behavior that conforms to God's standard. See "The Relationship between Wisdom and Righteousness in Proverbs" in "Wisdom in Proverbs" in the introduction. "Justice" (מִשְׁפָּט) denotes decisions that are correct and in keeping with God's standard. "Fairness" (the abstract plural מֵישָׁרִים) is what is correct and lacks guile or deviousness. The noun comes from the Hebrew root ישׁר, which denotes straightness, in contrast to Hebrew nouns for deviousness and craftiness, many of which come from roots that denote something that is "twisted" or "crooked" (e.g., עִקְּשׁוּת in 4:24; 6:12; נִפְתָּל in 8:8; נָלוֹז in 2:15; 3:32; 14:2; and הֲפַכְפַּךְ in 21:8).

1:4 לָתֵת לִפְתָאיִם עָרְמָה—The noun פֶּתִי denotes a "gullible, naïve person" (see *HALOT*). See "פֶּתִי, 'Gullible Person' " in "Fools in Proverbs" in the introduction. The feminine noun עָרְמָה is often translated as "prudence," which in English implies a cautious, conservative approach to life. However, the concept behind this word is insight into a situation so that one can determine the proper course of action (8:5, 12). The related adjective עָרוּם, "prudent," is used, for example, in 13:16; 22:3; and 27:12 to encourage insightful use of knowledge, not merely a conservative, cautious attitude. See "עָרוּם, 'Prudent,' and עָרְמָה, 'Prudence' " in "Wisdom in Proverbs" in the introduction.

לְנַעַר דַּעַת וּמְזִמָּה׃—For the feminine nouns דַּעַת and מְזִמָּה, see "דַּעַת, 'Knowledge,' and יָדַע, 'to Know,' " as well as "מְזִמָּה, 'Insight, Foresight' " in "Wisdom in Proverbs" in the introduction.

1:5 יִשְׁמַע חָכָם וְיוֹסֶף לֶקַח—The purpose clauses in 1:2–4 and 1:6 are interrupted by the exhortations in the two clauses of 1:5. The Hiphil (H) verb יוֹסֶף is jussive in form, and probably the Qal (G) יִשְׁמַע is jussive too, hence "*may* a wise person listen and increase …" Divine Wisdom is pleading with the reader or hearer of Proverbs to receive this saving knowledge in faith. "The Holy Scriptures … are able to make you *wise unto salvation* through faith in Christ Jesus" (2 Tim 3:15).

The noun לֶקַח, "learning," literally means "what is received," and is cognate to the verb לָקַח, translated as "to acquire," that began 1:3. The noun recurs in 4:2; 7:21; 9:9; 16:21, 23. The apostle declares about the Supper, "I received from the Lord what I also passed on to you" (1 Cor 11:23), and he uses similar phraseology about the Gospel (1 Cor 15:3).

וְנָבוֹן תַּחְבֻּלוֹת יִקְנֶה׃—The Niphal (N) participle נָבוֹן, used as a substantive, "a person with understanding," is from the verb בִּין, whose Hiphil (H) infinitive begins 1:6 and the second half of 1:2 (see the second textual note on 1:2). For the feminine abstract plural noun תַּחְבֻּלוֹת, see "תַּחְבּוּלוֹת, 'Guidance' " in "Wisdom in Proverbs" in the introduction. The Qal (G) verb יִקְנֶה probably is jussive, "*may* a person acquire," like the two jussives in the preceding clause. In this context קָנָה, "acquire," is a synonym of לָקַח, "receive, acquire," at the start of 1:3. קָנָה recurs in Proverbs referring to the acquisition of wisdom.[a] See also the first textual note on 8:22. קָנָה has the commercial nuance "to buy, purchase" in 20:14; 23:23.

(a) Prov 4:5, 7; 15:32; 16:16; 17:16; 18:15; 19:8

1:6 לְהָבִין מָשָׁל וּמְלִיצָה דִּבְרֵי חֲכָמִים וְחִידֹתָם׃—The verb לְהָבִין, "to understand," is repeated from the second half of 1:2. Here it does double duty since this single verb takes direct objects in both halves of 1:6. The first noun in the first half, מָשָׁל, "proverb," is repeated from 1:1. The second noun, מְלִיצָה, "enigma," only occurs here and in Hab 2:6, where it refers to a bitter satirical condemnation of sinful behavior. It is from the root ליץ, which usually denotes showing contempt or mocking. Both times in the OT מְלִיצָה is used with מָשָׁל, "proverb," and חִידוֹת, "riddles." Here it either denotes a saying characterized by its biting cleverness, or a saying that is enigmatic and allusive to those who do not know wisdom (*HALOT*).

The final noun חִידָה, "riddle," occurs seventeen times in the OT, most often in Judges 14, where Samson tells his riddle. In 1 Ki 10:1 the queen of Sheba poses riddles to test Solomon's wisdom. Here it denotes a saying that is not easily understood by those without divine knowledge or understanding (see *HALOT* and BDB, 1).

1:7 יִרְאַת יְהוָה—This important phrase, "the fear of Yahweh," occurs fourteen times in Proverbs[b] and only seven times elsewhere in the OT.[c] The fear of Yahweh can denote fear of God's wrath (Prov 24:21–22). More often, however, it denotes a positive, filial relationship to God that causes a person to want to please the heavenly Father. God, who bestows blessings for temporal and eternal life and leads people to wisdom, is the one who initiates this positive relationship. The believer responds by fleeing evil and seeking to do the will of the heavenly Father (8:13). See further "יִרְאַת יְהוָה, 'the Fear of Yahweh,' and יְרֵא יְהוָה, 'One Who Fears Yahweh' " in "Wisdom in Proverbs" in the introduction.

(b) Prov 1:7, 29; 2:5; 8:13; 9:10; 10:27; 14:26–27; 15:16, 33; 16:6; 19:23; 22:4; 23:17

(c) Is 11:2–3; 33:6; Pss 19:10 (ET 19:9); 34:12 (ET 34:11); 111:10; 2 Chr 19:9

רֵאשִׁית דָּעַת—Phrases similar to "the beginning of knowledge" are in 4:7 and 9:10. God-given faith, which fears and loves God, is the beginning in the sense that it is prerequisite and absolutely essential for receiving divine knowledge. Without faith it is impossible to please God or to know him. Without faith, a person, no matter how clever, is a fool.

חָכְמָה וּמוּסָר אֱוִילִים בָּזוּ׃—The first two nouns, חָכְמָה וּמוּסָר, are the direct objects of the verb בָּזוּ, "despise," whose subject is the plural of אֱוִיל. This type of fool is stubborn and thick-headed,[1] a "stubborn fool." He clings to his foolish behavior because he has rejected God's gracious offer of wisdom, righteousness, and life in Christ. See "אֱוִיל, 'Stubborn Fool,' and אִוֶּלֶת, 'Stupidity' " in "Fools in Proverbs" in the introduction.

Commentary

The Superscription (1:1)

Prov 1:1 is the book's superscription. This introductory verse can be understood in two ways: (1) as applying to the entire book, with Solomon as the principal (but not the sole) author, or (2) as applying to 1:8–9:18 as having been composed by Solomon. Since the reader is left with the impression that what follows is from Solomon's pen and most of the rest of the book is of the same character, it is best to understand this verse as applying especially to the first nine chapters of Proverbs, although it is also a general characterization of most of the rest of the book. See further "Authorship and Date" in the introduction.

By naming "Solomon" as the "son of David," the superscription gives the entire book of Proverbs a Christological orientation.[2] The book, its inspired author, and its divine wisdom anticipate the greater "Son of David" (Mt 1:1), Jesus Christ, who embodies the sum total of all divine wisdom (1 Cor 1:18–31; Col 2:3). Although he has always been true God, as true man from the time of his conception, Christ had a fully human development, and as a child he grew in wisdom (Lk 2:40, 52). Those who heard him were astonished at his wisdom (Mk 6:2).

The title of Solomon as "king of Israel" (Prov 1:1) also points toward Christ as "the King of Israel" (Jn 1:49; 12:13). Christ is greater and wiser than Solomon:

> The queen of the South … came from the ends of the earth to hear the *wisdom* of Solomon, and behold, someone greater than Solomon is here! (Mt 12:42; cf. 1 Ki 10:1–13)

Christ's threefold office is that of Prophet, Priest, and King. "He has taken us as his own, under his protection, in order that he may *rule us* by his righteousness, *wisdom*, power, life, and blessedness" (LC II 30; emphasis added). He dispenses divine wisdom through the preached and written Word of his Gospel, and this wisdom is apprehended through faith in him.[d]

(d) 1 Cor 2:6–7; Eph 1:8, 17; 3:10; Col 1:9, 28; 3:16; James 1:5; 3:17

Solomon's Preface (1:2–7)

Solomon has placed at the beginning of the book a preface designed to set the stage for the reader who wishes to learn about God-given wisdom and to receive this divine wisdom through the book of Proverbs. These verses are

---

1 Cf. L. Goldberg, "אֱוִיל," *TWOT* 1:19.

2 See "Solomon, Wisdom, and Christology" in Mitchell, *The Song of Songs*, 34–38.

stair-like parallelism, with each line forming an additional step until the climax is reached in 1:7. Three key concepts for understanding and applying the wisdom in Proverbs are introduced as we climb the stairs: knowledge, discipline, and spiritual growth.

The first concept is knowledge, which is the essential foundation. "To know wisdom" (1:1) means to know the Lord himself. "This is eternal life, that they should know you, the only true God, and the one whom you sent, Jesus Christ" (Jn 17:3). Unbelievers have no true knowledge of God; such knowledge only comes through faith. Hence St. Paul says to Christian converts, "When you did not know God, you were enslaved to those that by nature are not gods. But now that you know God, or rather, are known by God ..." (Gal 4:8–9). *Thus Proverbs is not simply about the natural knowledge of God that even unbelievers can glean from viewing creation and to which their conscience testifies* (Rom 1:18–22, 32; 2:14–16). *Proverbs is about the saving knowledge of God that comes through his Son, Jesus Christ.*

The second concept is discipline, which follows knowledge. Discipline allows the believer to act wisely. The book of Proverbs has the purpose of enabling the reader "to acquire discipline for acting sensibly: righteousness and justice and fairness" (1:3). Solomon tells us exactly what actions flow from knowledge exercised with discipline. They are not necessarily the behaviors that the world considers shrewd, but instead they are the types of behaviors that characterize God himself: righteous, just, and true acts. These he enables his justified believers to do (Eph 2:8–10; Phil 2:12–13).

The third concept is growth in wisdom. Those who know God still face the risk that they could be led away from wisdom and life toward foolish behavior and death. Especially the gullible and the young have much to learn from Solomon's wisdom: "to give to gullible people prudence, to a young man knowledge and foresight" (1:4). Even those who are already wise through faith will benefit from reading and rereading Proverbs: "may a wise person listen and increase [his] learning, and may a person with understanding acquire guidance" (1:5). Prov 1:5 interrupts the stair-like ascent and allows the reader to contemplate the value of maturing in wisdom throughout life. No matter how wise and knowledgeable we may consider ourselves to be, we have much more to learn. Now we only "know in part"; only in the eschaton shall we "know fully" (1 Cor 13:12).

Solomon continues the ascent in Prov 1:6 by assuring the reader that his proverbs are able to teach us to understand wisdom in its most enigmatic forms, just as Solomon could solve the perplexing riddles that the queen of Sheba posed to him. This leads to 1:7, the proverb of Solomon that is placed at the climax to the preface to guide our reading of this entire book. (Note the similarity of the first line of 1:7 to the better-known first line of 9:10.) Here Solomon first explicitly introduces the wisdom of Proverbs as godly wisdom flowing from a positive relationship with Yahweh.

This relationship with God is established by Christ, the incarnate Wisdom of God (Prov 8:1–36; 1 Cor 1:18–31). Thus wisdom is received through Christ and the content of wisdom is Christ himself. This wisdom brings the recipient into a favored relationship with God the Father. "The fear of Yahweh" (Prov 1:7) is first and foremost a filial relationship initiated by God when he reckons sinners as righteous through faith on account of his Son (Gen 15:6). God declares Christ to be "my Son" (Ps 2:7; Mt 2:15; Lk 9:35; cf. 2 Sam 7:14 || 1 Chr 17:13), and all baptized believers in Christ are sons of God (Gal 3:26–29). They share Christ's filial relationship with God the Father, who has forgiven them and made them his children.

Prov 1:7 emphasizes this filial relationship with God under the rubric "the fear of Yahweh." It was God who established the filial relationship of the people of Israel with himself when he called their ancestor Abraham (Gen 17:7; Deut 29:13–14 [ET 29:14–15]) and when he redeemed Israel, whom he called "my son" (Hos 11:1; cf. Mt 2:15) and "my firstborn son" (Ex 4:22), from Egypt and graciously promised to be Israel's God.[e] "The fear of Yahweh" as well as "the Spirit of wisdom and understanding" are embodied in the Davidic Messiah, the "shoot from the stump of Jesse" (Is 11:1–3). Jesse was the father of David and the grandfather of Solomon, and all three are ancestors of Jesus Christ (Ruth 4:17–22; Mt 1:1–7; Lk 3:31–32). Yet divine wisdom offers to all believers a filial relationship to God through faith that is even stronger than genetic ancestry (cf. Mt 3:9).

(e) E.g., Ex 6:7; Lev 11:45; 22:32–33; 25:38; Num 15:41; Jer 11:4

Therefore, *the theme and guiding principle of Proverbs is the Gospel of Jesus Christ.* By the same Gospel fully revealed in the NT, God called his OT people into existence, redeemed them, and sustained them by his grace. This Gospel relationship to Yahweh, encapsulated in the phrase "the fear of Yahweh" (Prov 1:7) is the beginning, source, and sustaining power of all wisdom. From the outset Solomon is laying down the theology essential for understanding the entire book of Proverbs:

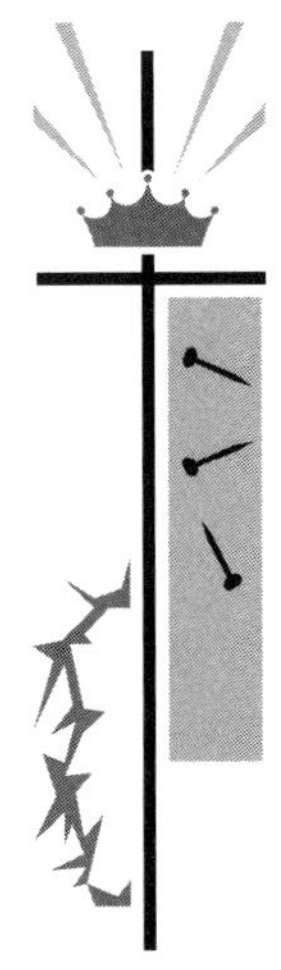

- Wisdom comes from God through Christ.
- Wisdom is a free gift from God, received through faith.
- Wisdom cannot be possessed apart from God's gracious work in Christ.
- Wisdom conveys Christ himself and hence confers sonship, righteousness, and everlasting life.

God had declared Solomon himself to be "my son" when he designated Solomon as the one who would inherit God's kingdom, reign on David's throne, and build the temple (1 Chr 22:10; 28:6)—all in anticipation of the incarnate Christ, whom God declares to be his "Son" at Christ's Baptism (Mt 3:17; Lk 3:22; cf. Mt 2:15) and transfiguration (Mt 17:5; Lk 9:35) and resurrection (Rom 1:4; cf. Acts 13:30–34). Christ reigns on the throne of David as the eternal King of Israel (Is 9:5–6 [ET 9:6–7]), and his advent has brought the kingdom of God in grace.

In the following proverbs (1:8–9:18), Solomon, uttering divine wisdom, will issue a call, repeated fifteen times, for "my son" to pay attention to his father's instruction.[f] These admonitions to "my son" are in ten sections.[3] A "son" who is endowed with divine wisdom is a son of God by his grace in his Son (Mt 5:9; Jn 1:12; Rom 8:14–15; Gal 3:26; 1 Jn 3:1).

(f) Prov 1:8, 10, 15; 2:1; 3:1, 11, 21; 4:10, 20; 5:1, 20; 6:1, 3, 20; 7:1

The same triune God who bestows wisdom and blessings for temporal and eternal life in Christ is the one who initiates and sustains the believer's filial relationship until he calls the believer through death to resurrection and eternal glory (Dan 12:2–3; Rom 8:11, 16–21). The Lord works through his Word and appointed means of grace (in the church age, Christian Baptism and the Lord's Supper) to regenerate the heart of man and fill him with his Spirit (Jn 3:3–5; Acts 2:38–39; Titus 3:4–6) and thus to lead him to "fear, love, and trust in God above all things" (SC I 1). Yet believers remain *simul iustus et peccator*, "simultaneously saint and sinner," throughout this earthly life. Their sinful nature shuns God and fears his wrath. Therefore the Christian life is one of continual repentance, or penitence. The Lutheran Confessions explain penitence as having into two parts, contrition and faith, and this explains what is included in "the fear of Yahweh" (Prov 1:7):

> Contrition is the genuine terror of a conscience that feels God's wrath against sin and is sorry that it has sinned. This contrition takes place when the Word of God denounces sin. For the sum of the proclamation of the Gospel is to denounce sin, to offer the forgiveness of sins and righteousness for Christ's sake, to grant the Holy Spirit and eternal life, and to lead us as regenerated men to do good. …
>
> As the second part of our consideration of penitence, we therefore add faith in Christ, that amid these terrors the Gospel of Christ ought to be set forth to consciences—the Gospel which freely promises the forgiveness of sins through Christ. … This faith strengthens, sustains, and quickens the contrite. … This faith gradually grows and throughout life it struggles with sin to conquer sin and death. But love follows faith. … *Filial fear can be clearly defined as an anxiety joined with faith, where faith consoles and sustains the anxious heart.*[4]

The final line of Prov 1:7 turns from believers with "the fear of Yahweh" to the opposite scenario: unbelievers, who lack fear of and faith in Yahweh. They are "stubborn fools" who "despise wisdom and discipline." This sheds light on what makes a stubborn fool so stubborn. Believers have their new, regenerate nature as children of God as well as their old, sinful nature (see the apostle Paul's description of his own Christian life in Romans 7). Fools, however, have only their corrupt, stubborn nature as children of the devil (Jn 8:44; 1 Jn 3:8–10). Fools have chosen to despise God, leading them to despise the wisdom and discipline that God bestows on those who fear him. The divine wisdom of the Gospel proffers the knowledge of God, but judgment awaits "those who do not

[3] The ten sections are (1) 1:8–19; (2) 2:1–22; (3) 3:1–20; (4) 3:21–35; (5) 4:10–19; (6) 4:20–27; (7) 5:1–23; (8) 6:1–19; (9) 6:20–35; and (10) 7:1–27.

[4] Ap XII 29, 35–38 (emphasis added).

know God," who are "those who do not submit to the Gospel of our Lord Jesus" (2 Thess 1:8; cf. 1 Thess 4:5).

The line of condemning Law that concludes Solomon's preface (1:7b) mirrors to the reader the sinful foolishness of the unregenerate human heart, driving the reader to repent and embrace the wisdom that God freely offers to all.

Proverbs 1:8–9:18

Solomon's Extended Discourses on Wisdom

Excursus

Proverbs 1–9, Christ, and the Ten Commandments

One of the most striking features of the extended discourses on wisdom in the first nine chapters of Proverbs is the call, issued fifteen times, for "my son" to pay attention to his father's instruction.[a] These admonitions to "my son" are in ten sections.[1] There is also one section that is an address to plural "sons" (4:1–9) and three poems about wisdom (1:20–33; 8:1–36; 9:1–18). This organization was part of the author's scheme to instruct his son in the wisdom of living by the guidance of God's Word, so that the son might receive the manifold blessings of wisdom and hence live—both in this life and for eternity.

(a) Prov 1:8, 10, 15; 2:1; 3:1, 11, 21; 4:10, 20; 5:1, 20; 6:1, 3, 20; 7:1

This Wisdom is Christ himself.[2] Jesus Christ is the only one who, during his earthly life, actually lived in full conformity to the many wise commands and exhortations in Proverbs. The ten addresses from father to son in Proverbs can be viewed in light of the NT affirmation about Christ that "although he was a Son, he learned obedience from what he suffered" (Heb 5:8). God the Father spoke to his Son, who was wholly obedient to his Father's will. The Son's perfect life is credited to the believer simply through faith in him, so that the believer is justified forensically and enjoys a filial relationship with God (see the commentary on 1:7). Christ alone enables the believer to begin to live with what the Lutheran Confessions call "the new obedience"[3] according to God's Word, including the portrait of wisdom and the wise man in Proverbs.

The ten addresses of father to son in Proverbs 1–9 are intended to call the reader to consider those addresses in light of what are usually called the Ten Commandments (Ex 20:1–17), which are at the heart of God's address to his people from Sinai. God's covenant with Israel through Moses is summarized in the Ten Commandments. However, these commandments are not numbered in the text of Exodus 20 or in Deuteronomy 5, nor are they called "commandments" in the Torah except in Ex 20:6. Instead, elsewhere in the Torah we are told that God inscribed "the ten words/sayings" (עֲשֶׂרֶת הַדְּבָרִים) that he gave

---

1 The ten sections are (1) 1:8–19; (2) 2:1–22; (3) 3:1–20; (4) 3:21–35; (5) 4:10–19; (6) 4:20–27; (7) 5:1–23; (8) 6:1–19; (9) 6:20–35; and (10) 7:1–27.

2 See "Wisdom in Proverbs" in the introduction. See also the commentary on 1:1–7; 3:13–20; 8:22–31; 30:1b–10; and the excursus "Proverbs 8, Wisdom, Christology, and the Arian Controversy" in the commentary on chapter 8.

3 In AC VI, "The New Obedience," the Lutheran confessors declare: "It is also taught among us that such faith should produce good fruits and good works and that we must do all such good works as God has commanded, but we should do them for God's sake and not place our trust in them as if thereby to merit favor before God." The new obedience is also described in FC Ep and SD III, "The Righteousness of Faith before God"; FC Ep and SD IV, "Good Works"; and FC Ep and SD VI, "The Third Use of the Law."

on the mountain on two tablets of stone (Ex 34:28; Deut 4:13; 10:4). Therefore, "Decalogue" (from the Greek for "ten words/sayings") may be the most accurate title for them.

The Decalogue expresses how God's covenant people are to live, now that he has redeemed them from slavery in Egypt, claimed them as his own, and declared himself to be their saving God (Ex 20:2; Deut 5:6). The Lord commanded the Israelites to teach these ten sayings to their children and to live by them (Deut 4:13; 5:1; 11:18–19). As a father teaching his son, Solomon, on God's behalf, calls the reader "my son" and implores him to listen and live by his ten addresses to his son.

The First Commandment, "you shall have no other gods before me" (Ex 20:3; Deut 5:7), can be expressed positively, "you shall love the Lord your God with all your heart and with all your soul and with all your might" (Deut 6:5; see also Mt 22:37). It is "the great and first commandment" (Mt 22:38). Transgressions against any of the other commandments ultimately are transgressions against the First Commandment and the God who gave all the commands. Likewise, all ten of the addresses from father to son in Proverbs ultimately center on "the fear of Yahweh" (1:7), that is, on obedience to, faith in, and love for the Lord above all else.

The four addresses in Proverbs 1–9 that refer to adultery (the second, seventh, ninth, and tenth) should be understood in light of Scripture's correlation between sexual fidelity and spiritual fidelity to God, and between sexual immorality and spiritual harlotry and idolatry.[4] Hence these addresses pertain to the First Commandment in that way.

Since each of the ten addresses calls on the son to heed his father's instruction, they all encourage observance of the Fourth Commandment (Ex 20:12; Deut 5:16). In addition, each calls on the son to contemplate specific applications of the Decalogue:

The first address (Prov 1:8–19) advises the son to avoid the company of sinners because they might lead him to shed blood and steal (Fifth and Seventh Commandments, Ex 20:13, 15; Deut 5:17, 19).

The second address (Prov 2:1–22) advises the son especially to avoid adultery (Sixth Commandment, Ex 20:14; Deut 5:18).

The third address (Prov 3:1–20) advises the son to trust Yahweh with all his heart, a summary of the First Table of the Law (First through Third Commandments, Ex 20:3–11; Deut 5:7–15), similar to the summaries of the First Table by Moses in Deut 6:5 and by Jesus in Mt 22:37 and Mk 12:30 (cf. Lk 10:27).

The fourth address (Prov 3:21–35) advises the son to treat his neighbor properly, a summary of the Second Table of the Law (Fourth through Tenth

---

[4] For other biblical passages that reveal the correlation between spiritual and sexual fidelity or unfaithfulness, see, for example, Hosea; Ezekiel 16 and 23; the Song of Songs; 1 Cor 6:9–20; Gal 5:19–25; and Eph 5:21–33.

Commandments, Ex 20:12–17; Deut 5:16–21), similar to the summaries of the Second Table by Moses in Lev 19:18; by Jesus in Mt 22:39 and Mk 12:31 (Lk 10:27); by Paul in Rom 13:9 and Gal 5:14; and by James (2:8).

The fifth address (Prov 4:10–19) commands the son to stay away from the path of wicked people, encompassing all Ten Commandments. Compare Ps 1:1–2, where avoidance of wicked people is linked to observance of the (entire) Torah.

The sixth address (Prov 4:20–27) not only advises the son to avoid evil in general, but 4:24 also pointedly commands him to avoid dishonesty and deceptive speech (Eighth Commandment, Ex 20:16; Deut 5:20).

The seventh address (Prov 5:1–23), like the second, ninth, and tenth addresses, warns about the dangers of adultery (Sixth Commandment, Ex 20:14; Deut 5:18).

The eighth address (Prov 6:1–19) has four subsections. First, 6:1–5 advises against financial entanglements that can tempt one to break the Seventh Commandment (Ex 20:15; Deut 5:19). Second, Prov 6:6–11 warns against laziness, which can lead to poverty and the temptation to break the Seventh Commandment (Ex 20:15; Deut 5:19). Third, Prov 6:12–15 cautions against dishonesty (Eighth Commandment, Ex 20:16; Deut 5:20). Fourth, the seven abominations in Prov 6:16–19 include offenses against the Fifth and Eighth Commandments (Ex 20:13, 16; Deut 5:17, 20) and also sins of the heart (Ninth and Tenth Commandments, Ex 20:17; Deut 5:21).

The ninth address (Prov 6:20–35) once again warns against breaking the Sixth Commandment, and it is the only one of the ten addresses that uses the same verb for "commit adultery" as the command through Moses (נָאַף in Prov 6:32 as in Ex 20:14; Deut 5:18).

The tenth address (Prov 7:1–27) is the fourth warning about adultery and violating the Sixth Commandment (Ex 20:14; Deut 5:18).

These ten addresses, then, cover the entire Ten Commandments and are designed to lead the reader to conclude that Solomon's counsel is not simply human advice, but divine wisdom for life—that the reader "may have life and have it abundantly" (Jn 10:10). These ten addresses contain instructions for life in human society. While most of them focus on commandments from the Second Table of the Law (Fourth through Tenth Commandments), they presuppose the First Table of the Law (First through Third Commandments). The First and Second Tables of the Law are summarized by Jesus in what he calls"the great and first commandment" and the "second," respectively (Mt 22:37–40). All ten of the addresses emphasize wisdom for believers living not just in the world, but among and within the whole people of God, in a community redeemed by his grace.

Dispersed throughout these ten addresses are three poems about wisdom (1:20–33; 8:1–36; 9:1–18) and an eleventh address, this one to plural "sons" (4:1–9). These extol the value of divine wisdom. In this way Solomon emphasizes that wisdom is more than mechanically following a list of ten do's and don't. Nor is it a formula for becoming righteous through one's own effort or a guide for imposing legalistic requirements on the people of God. Instead, this Wisdom is Christ and flows to the wise person through Christ, as especially 3:19–20 and 8:1–36 demonstrate. The faith, motivation, and power to follow the Law, therefore, is found in the Gospel freely offered by Wisdom through the Word. Wisdom invites the reader to receive life (3:16, 18, 22; 8:35). The reader responds to this gift of God by clinging to the Gospel (4:8) with its gift of forgiveness and new life through the death and resurrection of Christ (e.g., Rom 6:1–11). For this reason believers willingly and gladly follow God's wise advice in his Word.

Proverbs provides insight and foresight as it reveals God's Gospel, which creates and increases love for the Lord and delight in all his commands and wise ways (Psalms 19 and 119). By its antithesis of wisdom and folly, Proverbs edifies and warns. It enables pupils of wisdom to avoid situations that could lead them away from the Lord and toward eternal death in hell (Prov 5:5; 7:27; 9:18). Through this biblical book is fulfilled the psalm of the author's father, David:

> He leads me in paths of righteousness for the sake of his name. (Ps 23:3)

Proverbs 1:8–19

First Address to a Son: Avoid the Company of Sinners

Translation

1 [8]Listen, my son, [to] your father's discipline,
and do not forsake your mother's teaching
[9]because they are a garland of grace for your head
and a chain for your neck.
[10]My son, if sinners entice you,
do not be willing [to go along].
[11]If they say, "Come with us; let's set an ambush to [shed] blood;
let's hide to [ambush] an innocent person without cause;
[12]we will swallow them alive like Sheol [does]
and whole like those who go down to the pit;
[13]we will find all wealth and treasure;
we will fill our homes with plunder;
[14]cast your lot among us;
there will be one coffer for all of us"—
[15]my son, do not walk along a road with them.
Keep your foot from their pathway,
[16]because their feet run to [do] evil,
and they rush to shed blood.
[17]For it is useless for a net to be spread in the sight of any bird.
[18]Yet they set an ambush for their own blood.
They hide for [ambushing] their own lives.
[19]Thus are the paths of every person who is greedy for ill-gotten gain.
It takes away the life of those who possess it.

Textual Notes

1:8 שְׁמַע בְּנִי מוּסַר אָבִיךָ—The Qal (G) of שָׁמַע meaning "hear with attention, listen to" often takes an accusative object (BDB, 1 f), but English translation requires the preposition "to." The direct object in the construct phrase, מוּסָר, "discipline," may take on the connotation of "warning" (*HALOT*, 3), while still expressing the self-discipline that the father hopes to inculcate in this son. See "מוּסָר, 'Discipline,' and יָסַר, 'to Discipline' " in "Wisdom in Proverbs" in the introduction.

וְאַל־תִּטֹּשׁ תּוֹרַת אִמֶּךָ׃—This identical clause recurs in 6:20b. The Qal (G) of נָטַשׁ, "to forsake, abandon," recurs again but as an imperative in 17:14.

The noun תּוֹרָה, *torah*, occurs thirteen times in Proverbs.[a] Frequently it is translated as "Law." However, in many OT passages it also encompasses doctrinal Gospel,

(a) Prov 1:8; 3:1; 4:2; 6:20, 23; 7:2; 13:14; 28:4 (twice), 7, 9; 29:18; 31:26

such as in the many instances where it refers to the Torah of Moses.[1] Here and often elsewhere in Proverbs (e.g., 28:4), it has the broad meaning "teaching," especially the teaching of God's Word, including both Law and Gospel. Supporting this general meaning is the fact that in Proverbs תּוֹרָה never occurs with a definite article.[2] In at least three instances, it refers to a mother's teaching, which she imparts to her children (1:8; 6:20; 31:26). Elsewhere in Proverbs it can refer to a father's teaching (3:1; 4:2) or God's teaching (28:4, 7, 9; 29:18).

1:9 כִּ֤י ׀ לִוְיַ֤ת חֵ֓ן הֵ֭ם לְרֹאשֶׁ֑ךָ—The noun לִוְיָה, "garland, wreath," occurs in the OT only in the construct phrase לִוְיַת חֵן in Prov 1:9 and 4:9. The noun חֵן, usually meaning "grace," occurs thirteen times in Proverbs.[b] Usually it refers to God's grace, that is, his undeserved mercy and favor which he shows to his believing people. It is derived from the verb חָנַן, which refers to God as "being gracious," in, for example, Ex 33:19 and Num 6:25. The construct phrase לִוְיַת חֵן recurs in 4:9a. It could be a genitive of material, "a garland [made out] of grace," or an epexegetical genitive, "a [metaphorical] garland that is [God's] grace."

(b) Prov 1:9; 3:4, 22, 34; 4:9; 5:19; 11:16; 13:15; 17:8; 22:1, 11; 28:23; 31:30

וַ֝עֲנָקִ֗ים לְגַרְגְּרֹתֶֽךָ׃—The noun עֲנָק occurs elsewhere only in Judg 8:26 and Song 4:9. Its plural is translated as "chain," meaning a piece of jewelry, not an instrument of bondage.[3] Here in Prov 1:9 the LXX translates it as κλοιὸν χρύσεον, "a golden chain." Note that the parents' instruction (1:8) gives true (spiritual) wealth in contrast to the stolen earthly wealth that sinners (1:10) promise in 1:13–14.

The plural reduplicated noun גַּרְגְּרוֹת, which has the singular meaning "neck," occurs in the OT only in Proverbs. It always has the second masculine singular suffix and always refers to the part of the body around which divine wisdom is to be affixed metaphorically (1:9; 3:3, 22; 6:21).

1:10 בְּנִ֡י אִם־יְפַתּ֥וּךָ חַ֝טָּאִ֗ים—The Piel (D) of פָּתָה, "to entice," can also mean "to seduce" in sexual contexts (Ex 22:15 [ET 22:16]; Judg 14:15; 16:5), and so the enticement by sinners here may allude to the theme of seduction by the adulteress[4] and by Lady Foolishness in 9:13–18. The verb is cognate to the noun פֶּתִי. See "פֶּתִי, 'Gullible Person' " in "Fools in Proverbs" in the introduction.

אַל־תֹּבֵֽא׃—The Qal (G) of אָבָה means "to be **willing**" or "to consent to" (*HALOT*, 3), to do what the sinners propose. The א (instead of ה) in the second masculine singular jussive תֹּבֵא may reflect Aramaic influence (GKC, § 75 hh) or a northern Hebrew dialect.

1:11 נֶאֶרְבָ֥ה לְדָ֑ם—The sinners use the Qal (G) cohortative of אָרַב to propose, literally, "let's set an ambush for blood" (cf. לְדָמָ֣ם יֶאֱרֹ֑בוּ in 1:18 and אֱרָב־דָּ֑ם in 12:6). The phrase לִשְׁפָּךְ־דָּם in 1:16 (cf. 6:17) clarifies that "for blood" means "in order to

---

1 See the textual note on תּוֹרָה in Josh 1:7 and the commentary on 1:7–8 in Harstad, *Joshua*, 75–77, 81–87.

2 G. Liedke and C. Petersen, "תּוֹרָה," *TLOT* 3:1416.

3 See the textual note on the singular in Song 4:9 in Mitchell, *The Song of Songs*, 832. The denominative cognate verb עָנַק, "serve as a necklace," occurs in Ps 73:6.

4 See the excursus "Wisdom and the Adulteress in Proverbs 1–9" in the commentary on chapter 2.

shed blood." Here and in the next clause (also twice in 1:18) the preposition לְ indicates disadvantage, "for" a hostile purpose of attack (BDB, 5 g (*b*) (γ)).

נִצְפְּנָה לְנָקִי חִנָּם—The cohortative נִצְפְּנָה is from the Qal (G) of צָפַן, "to hide," which recurs in 1:18; 2:1, 7; 7:1; 10:14; 13:22; 27:16 and often means "store up, treasure." נָקִי refers to an "innocent person" (BDB, 1), who has done nothing to provoke the attack and would not expect it. The adverb חִנָּם, which recurs in 1:17; 3:30; 23:29; 24:28; 26:2, here means "gratuitously, without any cause or reason." The person whom the sinners propose to ambush has done no wrong to the attackers. The plan may be to assault someone for no better reason than the amusement of the gang members.

1:12 נִבְלָעֵם כִּשְׁאוֹל חַיִּים—The same vocabulary is in Num 16:30–33, where the Lord caused the earth to open up and "swallow" (בָּלַע) Korah and his people so that they "descended" (יָרַד, the verb in Prov 1:12b) "alive" (חַיִּים) to "Sheol" (שְׁאוֹל). In Proverbs שְׁאוֹל, "Sheol," is synonymous with death and the grave (also 5:5; 7:27; 9:18; 15:11, 24; 23:14; 27:20; 30:16). Some passages emphasize its nuance of being the place of spiritual and eternal death for the damned, that is, hell (e.g., 7:27; 9:18). Some interpreters have asserted that Sheol is a place for all the dead, and therefore they claim the OT has no teaching of an afterlife. However, that is not the case, since Proverbs speaks of the hope for the righteous beyond the grave (23:18; 24:14, 20).[5] Christians recognize this hope as the resurrection on the Last Day (e.g., Dan 12:2–3; Mt 25:31–46; Rev 20:11–15).

וּתְמִימִים כְּיוֹרְדֵי בוֹר׃—The plural adjective תְּמִימִים "whole," like the parallel adjective חַיִּים, "alive," refers back to the object suffix on נִבְלָעֵם, "we will swallow *them*." "Those who go down to the pit," יוֹרְדֵי בוֹר, with the plural participle of יָרַד in construct, refers to the damned who descend into hell, both here and (without כְּ) in other passages such as Ezek 26:20; 32:24–25, 29–30 (cf. Is 14:15, 19). בּוֹר can refer to a literal "pit" into which a person can be thrown, either dead (Gen 37:20) or alive and whole (Gen 37:22, 24). As a metaphor, the "pit" (בּוֹר) often designates death and hell, and is a synonym for Sheol, as here and in Prov 28:17. The Lord saves his redeemed people from the pit (Pss 30:4 [ET 30:3]; 40:3 [ET 40:2]).

1:14 גּוֹרָלְךָ תַּפִּיל בְּתוֹכֵנוּ—Here the imperfect תַּפִּיל (Hiphil [H] of נָפַל) has imperatival force, "you should cast" or "cast!" (cf. Joüon, § 113 m). The idiom "cast your lot [גּוֹרָלְךָ] among us" means "join us," "share our fate." This appeal of the gang to the young man shows that its members consider their lives to be a game of random chance and fate; they do not entrust their lives to the God who is Lord over all that happens.

כִּיס אֶחָד יִהְיֶה לְכֻלָּנוּ׃—The noun כִּיס can refer to a "coffer/purse" (Prov 1:14) with gold (Is 46:6) or to a "bag" for weights (Prov 16:11). The "one coffer/purse" means that they will divide and share the wealth equally.

1:15 בְּנִי אַל־תֵּלֵךְ בְּדֶרֶךְ אִתָּם—The noun דֶּרֶךְ is often translated as "way," meaning a road or street. It is used frequently in Proverbs (seventy-six times), usually as a metaphor for a pattern of behavior, either evil (as here) or righteous (e.g., 2:8). The idiom here, "to walk" (the Qal [G] of הָלַךְ) "in/along a way" (בְּדֶרֶךְ) occurs also in 2:13, 20;

5 Cf. R. L. Harris, "שְׁאוֹל," *TWOT* 2:893.

7:19 (cf. 3:23; 16:29). דֶּרֶךְ is parallel to its synonym נְתִיבָה, "pathway," in 1:15; 3:17; 7:25; 12:28 (cf. 8:2).[6]

1:16 כִּי רַגְלֵיהֶם לָרַע יָרוּצוּ—Both clauses of 1:16 are repeated almost verbatim in Is 59:7.[7] The noun רֶגֶל, "foot, leg," is feminine, as are most Hebrew words for body parts that occur in pairs, but its suffixed dual (רַגְלֵיהֶם, "their feet") is the subject of the masculine verb יָרוּצוּ, "they run," probably because of the preference for the third masculine plural imperfect instead of the rare third feminine plural imperfect (GKC, § 145 u). Or perhaps the whole persons are envisioned as the subject of the verb, as seems to be the case with the verb in the following clause, the Piel (D) imperfect וִימַהֲרוּ, "they rush."

The preposition לְ with the noun רַע, "evil, injury, wrong" (BDB, s.v. רַע II, 2) is, literally, "for [the purpose of doing] evil." This is confirmed by the parallel phrase in the next clause, the Qal (G) infinitive expressing purpose: לִשְׁפָּךְ־דָּם, "to shed blood." לָרַע (pausal: לָרָע) or לְרַע occurs in the same sense in Is 59:7; Ps 56:6 (ET 56:5); Eccl 8:9. In form לָרַע could have the generic article (contracted from לְהָרַע, "for *the/that which is* evil"), but לְ without the article often is pointed לָ when prefixed to a monosyllabic noun (here רַע) and when a following word contains the principal pause (the main disjunctive accent in the verse), as does יָרוּצוּ here (GKC, § 102 h).

1:17 כִּי־חִנָּם מְזֹרָה הָרָשֶׁת—The adverb חִנָּם is repeated from 1:11 but here has the nuance "it is useless, futile." The feminine noun רֶשֶׁת, "net" (here in pause with the article: הָרָשֶׁת) recurs in Proverbs only in 29:5. It is the subject of the feminine Pual (Dp) participle מְזֹרָה. Elsewhere זָרָה in active stems usually means "to scatter, spread" and passive stems have corresponding passive meanings. A bundled-up net could be "spread" by throwing it so that it expanded and captured birds on the wing or upon the ground. Or a net could also be spread on the ground, and after birds landed on it, it could be pulled together with a drawstring. However, neither method would work if the birds saw the net in time to escape from it.

Garrett claims that זָרָה cannot be used to describe the spreading of a net.[8] He understands the verse as saying that a bird cannot distinguish between the net and the seed scattered (spread) on it, luring the bird to be caught in the net. In the same way, the gang members cannot perceive the connection between the lure of ill-gotten gain and the trap they are setting for themselves. However, it is difficult to understand how a net (unless it is of a very fine mesh) could be baited with seed merely by scattering seed in it. It is more likely that the verse refers to the action of throwing the net, and the net is spread or unfurled by throwing it outward toward the birds.

בַּעַל כָּנָף׃—Translated as "bird" above, the phrase is, literally, "master/owner of a wing." The noun כָּנָף, "wing," recurs in Proverbs only in 23:5. (For צִפּוֹר, "bird," see 6:5; 7:23; 26:2; 27:8.) This phrase is a poetic way of referring to a bird's unsurpassed skill in flight, since "בַּעַל indicates the owner of an object which embodies his manner,

---

6 See the excursus "The Metaphor of the Path in Solomon's Wisdom" in the commentary on chapter 10.

7 See the excursus "The Relationship between Proverbs 1:16 and Isaiah 59:7."

8 Garrett, *Proverbs, Ecclesiastes, Song of Songs*, 70, including n. 15.

his character or his occupation" (*HALOT*, A 6). בַּעַל is often used in construct with a word designating a skill, inclination, or occupation, for example, בַּעַל הַחֲלֹמוֹת, "master of dreams," that is, "expert dreamer" (Gen 37:19); בַּעַל אַף, "master of anger," that is, "hot-tempered person" (Prov 22:24); בַּעַל נֶפֶשׁ, "master of an appetite," that is, "person with a big appetite" (Prov 23:2); בַּעַל פְּקִדֻת, "master of the mustered army," that is, "[army] officer" (Jer 37:13); בַּעֲלֵי חִצִּים, "masters of arrows," that is, "archers" (Gen 49:23). Thus the meaning here is "a bird, a skillful master of swift and evasive flight." It does no good to set a trap in plain sight of the birds it is designed to trap since the birds that see it can easily avoid being captured.

1:18 וְהֵם לְדָמָם יֶאֱרֹבוּ יִצְפְּנוּ לְנַפְשֹׁתָם׃—The verbs אָרַב and צָפַן are repeated from 1:11. The two prepositional phrases (לְדָמָם ... לְנַפְשֹׁתָם) use לְ with the nuance of disadvantage (see the first textual note on 1:11). The suffixes in the prepositional phrases refer to the subjects of the verbs and have a reflexive meaning: "for *their own* blood … for *their own* lives." The noun נֶפֶשׁ, "life, soul," occurs fifty-six times in Proverbs and does not simply denote physical life. Rather, it refers to life in communion with God, including spiritual life. Unbelievers may be physically healthy and rich, but still lack "life," as in 1:19b.

1:19 כֵּן אָרְחוֹת כָּל־בֹּצֵעַ בָּצַע—The noun אֹרַח, "path," is a synonym of דֶּרֶךְ and נְתִיבָה (see the first textual note on 1:15). The Qal (G) participle בֹּצֵעַ of בָּצַע, "be greedy, gain dishonestly," takes the cognate noun בֶּצַע (in pause: בָּצַע), "ill-gotten gain," as its object. The accent on the participle recedes from the second syllable (צֵ֫עַ-) to the first, penultimate syllable (-בֹּ) in order to avoid two adjacent stressed syllables (בֹּ-צֵ֫עַ בָּ-צַע). See Joüon, § 31 c.

אֶת־נֶפֶשׁ בְּעָלָיו יִקָּח׃—The noun בֶּצַע, "ill-gotten gain," in the preceding clause is the implied subject of the verb יִקָּח, "take away," and the referent of the objective pronominal suffix on בְּעָלָיו, "those who possess *it*."

Commentary

The first of the ten addresses in chapters 1–9 from father to son[9] begins with an appeal to a son to learn from the instruction given by both parents ("father … mother," 1:8). This instruction is not only characterized as "teaching" but also as "discipline." While discipline may involve punishment, God and good parents mete out discipline in love (Eph 6:4; Heb 12:5–11; Rev 3:19). The positive aspect of discipline is mentioned here: discipline will lead to attractive personal qualities, just as a garland or jewelry are intended to make a person's outward appearance attractive. This theme will be expanded by Solomon in 3:1–20, where he connects jewelry and other valuables to wisdom, which comes to the believer through Christ (see the commentary on 3:1–20 and 4:9).

It is noteworthy that both parents are mentioned here and elsewhere in Proverbs as involved in the training of a child. Some understand the address

9 For the ten addresses from father to son in Proverbs 1–9, see the excursus "Proverbs 1–9, Christ, and the Ten Commandments."

as coming from a sage to his pupil, who is not his biological child.[10] While a sage could address his student as "son" (Sirach 7:3), the continued reference throughout Proverbs to both mother and father as instructors and trainers of children—and their pride in children who do well, and their shame when their children go astray (e.g., 10:1)—indicates that this is instruction from actual parents. Also note that Solomon mentions learning the same lessons from his own parents (4:3). The responsibilities of parents to train children are, therefore, taken seriously in Proverbs, especially in the opening chapters (1–9; see Eph 6:4).

Of course, only Christ fulfilled the role of obedient Son perfectly as he obeyed his heavenly Father's will (e.g., Mt 26:42; Lk 22:42; Heb 10:7–9; cf. Mt 6:10) as well as his earthly parents (Lk 2:51). Although we cannot obey our earthly parents or our heavenly Father perfectly, through faith in Christ his perfect obedience and his righteousness are imputed to us (Rom 5:19; 2 Cor 5:21), and we receive wisdom to grow in grace as he did (Lk 2:40) and to be obedient (Rom 6:16; 16:19; 1 Tim 3:4; 1 Pet 1:2). Solomon will expand this theme later (see the commentary on Prov 3:1–20).

The parents' instruction to their son recognizes that he is old enough to succumb to the pressure to leave the family and conform to his peers. The temptation to join the gang is portrayed as attractive in several ways. First, the gang offers the thrill of wanton violence (1:11–12). Second, it entices the young man with seemingly easily gained wealth (1:13). Finally, it offers companionship (1:14). These are powerful inducements that still lure youth into gangs and lives of crime and violence. However, the lure that Solomon describes is not to be seen simply as gang life. It is but one example of the pressure that peers can assert in youth and adulthood. It serves as a reminder that God's people need to be constantly on guard against any societal pressures that would tempt them to various sins against God and their neighbor.

Solomon appeals to his son not to adopt the ways of this gang by extending the metaphor of the path (1:15–16).[11] He begins by describing the behavior of the gang as a road or path. After warning his son not even to set foot on that path, he describes the feet of the gang members as running along the path in their hurry to do evil and commit murder. The metaphor is made powerful by the rush of the wicked to carry out their schemes. The path leads to sin, but they are more than anxious to accomplish their treacherous conspiracy. In this way Solomon uses this metaphor to demonstrate the foolishness of their ways.

A second metaphor is introduced in 1:17. The figure is of a hunter who is attempting to catch birds in a net. It is useless to put a net out where the birds can easily see it and avoid being captured. Instead, fowlers generally

---

[10] Murphy on Proverbs in Murphy and Huwiler, *Proverbs, Ecclesiastes, Song of Songs*, 18.

[11] See the excursus "The Metaphor of the Path in Solomon's Wisdom" in the commentary on chapter 10.

sneaked up on birds from behind and threw their net over the birds.[12] However, the gang members cannot see the very obvious trap they are setting for themselves. Solomon employs irony by depicting them as ambushing themselves. Prov 1:18–19 then concludes the first address by pointing out that this trap is the deadly outcome for all who are greedy. It is not only the gang members who plan violence who fall into such a trap, but also every greedy person who seeks to take advantage of his neighbor. Solomon is warning against greed leading to every kind theft including fraud, embezzlement, and unethical business practices. By demonstrating the inglorious end of the gang members, he is attempting to curb the desire to join others in their sin.

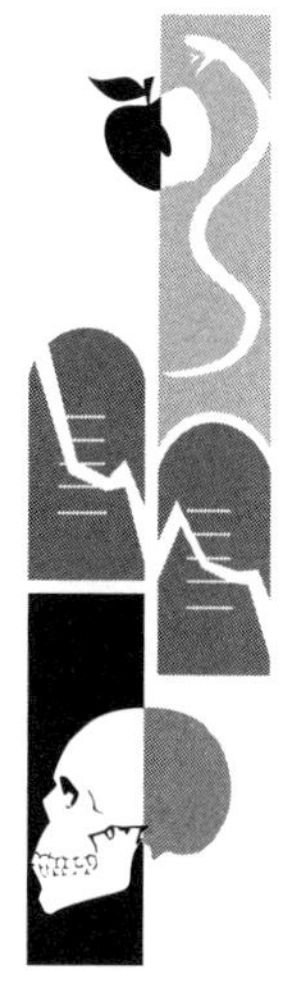

Moreover, the behavior of the gang members is eternally damaging. They are setting an ambush for their own lives (1:18). They risk dying eternally because of their actions that alienate them from God. Those who are alienated from God, rather than being reconciled to him through the blood of Jesus, shed their own blood and ruin their own spiritual lives.[13] They seek to devour others like Sheol (1:12), but if they perish in sin and unbelief, they will be condemned to Sheol (5:5; 7:27; 9:18) in eternal disgrace (Is 66:24; Dan 12:2). The father and mother are warning their son that though he may have faith now, the lure of the world, the flesh, and the devil are powerful. Paul offered the same advice to the young pastor Timothy and even gave him an example of those who did not listen to Wisdom's words:

> This charge I entrust to you, my child Timothy, in accordance with the previous prophecies about you, that by them you may wage the good fight, having faith and a good conscience, which some have rejected and made shipwreck of their faith. Among them are Hymenaeus and Alexander, whom I have handed over to Satan so that they may learn not to blaspheme. (1 Tim 1:18–20)

Luther urges us to pray the Lord's Prayer, especially the Sixth Petition, "and lead us not into temptation" (καὶ μὴ εἰσενέγκῃς ἡμᾶς εἰς πειρασμόν, Mt 6:13),[14] so that we constantly plead with our heavenly Father that he

> would guard and keep us so that the devil, the world, and our sinful nature may not deceive us or mislead us into false belief, despair, and other great shame and vice. Although we are attacked by these things, we pray that we may finally overcome them and win the victory.[15]

---

[12] Waltke, *Proverbs* 1:195.

[13] The Apology of the Augsburg Confession notes that faith in Christ, which justifies people before God, cannot exist with mortal sin (e.g., Ap IV 48, 64, 115).

[14] For a discussion of this Sixth Petition and of the closely related Seventh Petition, "but deliver us from the evil one" (ἀλλὰ ῥῦσαι ἡμᾶς ἀπὸ τοῦ πονηροῦ, Mt 6:13), a translation that Luther advocated (LC III 113), see Gibbs, *Matthew 1:1–11:1*, 317–18, 337–45.

[15] SC III 18 (*Luther's Small Catechism with Explanation* [St. Louis: Concordia, 1986, 1991], 19).

Excursus

The Relationship between Proverbs 1:16 and Isaiah 59:7

That there is some connection between Prov 1:16 and the first half of Is 59:7 is beyond dispute, considering their similarity. They share six Hebrew words that, except for two minor spelling variations (יָר֑וּצוּ versus יָרֻ֔צוּ and לִשְׁפָּךְ־ versus לִשְׁפֹּ֖ךְ), are identical even as to their inflections, prepositions, suffixes, and word order. The only significant differences are that the first Hebrew word of Prov 1:16 is not in Is 59:7 and the last Hebrew word of the first half of Is 59:7 is not in Prov 1:16. These differences are translated in italic:

כִּ֣י רַ֭גְלֵיהֶם לָרַ֣ע יָר֑וּצוּ וִֽ֝ימַהֲר֗וּ לִשְׁפָּךְ־דָּֽם׃

… *because* their feet run to [do] evil, and they rush to shed blood. (Prov 1:16)

רַגְלֵיהֶם֙ לָרַ֣ע יָרֻ֔צוּ וִֽימַהֲר֕וּ לִשְׁפֹּ֖ךְ דָּ֣ם נָקִ֑י

Their feet run to [do] evil, and they rush to shed *innocent* blood. (Is 59:7)

Prov 1:16 is missing in three important LXX manuscripts: Codex Vaticanus, Codex Sinaiticus, and Codex Ephraemi Rescriptus. However, it is present in many other LXX manuscripts, including Codex Alexandrinus, and it was added to Codex Sinaiticus by the first corrector. Several commentators have asserted that 1:16 is a secondary addition to Proverbs based on three reasons: (1) the mixed textual evidence in the LXX; (2) the belief that 1:16 breaks the connection between 1:15 and 1:17; and (3) the general assumption by many critical scholars that Proverbs 1–9 is the latest portion of the book and was compiled from a variety of sources.[1] To add to the problem, some LXX manuscripts that include 1:16 insert it after 1:17, which could indicate that 1:16 is a later addition to those LXX manuscripts.

However, there is good reason to assume that 1:16 is part of the original text of Proverbs. First, missing verses are far from rare in the LXX of Proverbs. The LXX omits a number of verses that are present in the MT (see figure 5 in the introduction). For example, 16:1 and 18:23–19:2 are missing from most LXX manuscripts. Also, the LXX contains numerous additions. For example, see the second textual note on 6:8 for what is most probably a long Hellenistic addition to LXX Proverbs. Therefore the absence or presence of verses in the LXX carries very little weight in determining what is genuine in the MT. In fact, the absence of the verse in the LXX could well reflect a case of parablepsis on

---

1 For the general critical assumption, see "Authorship and Date" in the introduction. Clifford, *Proverbs*, 39; Delitzsch, *Proverbs*, 1:65; Murphy, *Proverbs*, 10; Toy, *Proverbs*, 17; and Fox, *Proverbs 1–9*, 87, offer the possibility that both Proverbs and Isaiah are quoting a common proverb.

the part of the Greek translator: his eyes skipped from the כִּי ("because") at the beginning of 1:16 to the כִּי ("for") at the beginning of 1:17, thereby omitting 1:16, which was later added again to most LXX manuscripts.[2]

Nor is the belief that 1:16 breaks the connection between 1:15 and 1:17 a convincing argument. In fact, 1:16 forms an appropriate conclusion for the sentence begun in 1:15b: in 1:15b the father counsels the son to keep his "foot" (the singular of רֶגֶל) from the path of sinners, and then 1:16 explains the evil purposes for which the sinners' "feet" (the dual of רֶגֶל) run along their path. The relationship between 1:15 and 1:17 is more distant than that between 1:15 and 1:16. Moreover, the connection between 1:15 and 1:17 is far from certain, especially considering the debate over what exactly the action described in 1:17 means. It is debated whether מְזֹרָה in 1:17 means that a net is "spread" by throwing it or that the net is laid on the ground and baited. In any case, 1:17 seems rather abrupt whether it follows 1:15 or 1:16, since 1:17 is the only passage in chapters 1–9 that refers to either a "net" or to a bird "wing" (see the textual notes and commentary on 1:17).

There are several reasons why 1:16 should be viewed as an original part of Proverbs. First, 1:16 is present between 1:15 and 1:17 in all extant Hebrew manuscripts, and the Hebrew manuscript tradition of Proverbs is an older and more reliable textual tradition than the Greek tradition(s) represented by the LXX manuscripts. Second, 1:16 matches the thought and style of Proverbs 1–9, especially the last lines of 6:17 and 6:18:

וְ֝יָדַ֗יִם שֹׁפְכ֥וֹת דָּם־נָקִֽי

... a pair of hands that sheds innocent blood. (6:17)

רַ֝גְלַ֗יִם מְמַהֲר֥וֹת לָר֥וּץ לָרָעָֽה

... a pair of feet quickly running to [do] evil. (6:18)

Note the number of words that those lines in 6:17–18 have in common with 1:16: the Qal (G) of שָׁפַךְ, "to shed"; דָּם, "blood"; רֶגֶל, "foot, leg"; the Piel (D) of מָהַר, "to rush, do quickly"; and the Qal (G) of רוּץ, "to run." Note also the close pair of nouns, רָעָה, "evil," in 6:18 and רַע, "evil," in 1:16, both with the preposition לְ. Thus every word in 1:16 except the conjunction כִּי is repeated in these two lines of 6:17–18. Also, these two lines contain only two words that do not appear in 1:16: (1) יָד, "hand," in 6:17, which clearly serves as a parallel to רֶגֶל, "foot," in 6:18; and (2) נָקִי, "innocent," in 6:17, which appears in the immediate context of 1:16 in 1:11. This close correspondence between 1:16 and 6:17–18 casts doubt on the critical assumption that a later editor who supposedly was shaping Proverbs 1 would have gone to Isaiah to find a line for Prov 1:16 when similar lines were already available in Proverbs itself.

Moreover, if some editor of Proverbs was borrowing from Is 59:7, why did he omit the word נָקִי, "innocent," which is in Is 59:7 (and also in Prov 6:17) but

[2] This idea was proposed by David Noel Freedman according to Fox, *Proverbs 1–9*, 369.

is not in 1:16? Are we to assume that because the words דָּם, "blood," and נָקִי, "innocent," appear in 1:11 (though in separate clauses), the editor purposely omitted נָקִי, "innocent," but included דָּם, "blood," in 1:16? That seems unlikely. If an editor was copying Is 59:7, there is no apparent reason why he would have omitted "innocent."

In addition, there are a number of indicators that the author of Is 59:7 could have borrowed from Proverbs. This is historically possible according to the traditional view that Proverbs 1–9 was written by Solomon in the tenth century BC and the whole book of Isaiah was written by Isaiah ben Amoz during his long ministry (ca. 739–686 BC). The OT contains plenty of other examples of biblical authors, writing under inspiration, who apparently were led to draw on earlier written portions of God's sacred Word, as when, for example, the prophets and psalmists drew on the Torah.[3]

In addition to the six identical Hebrew words shared by Is 59:7 and Prov 1:16 as noted above, there are twelve other Hebrew words in Is 59:6–9 that appear in Proverbs as shown in figure 6.

Given the large proportion of vocabulary in Is 59:6–9 that occurs in Proverbs and the close association of this section of Isaiah with Prov 1:15–16; 3:17; and several verses in Proverbs 6, it would appear that Isaiah 59 is drawing on Proverbs, not the other way around. The addition of the word נָקִי, "innocent," in Is 59:7 is probably due to its use in Prov 6:17 and perhaps 1:11. It appears that Isaiah was consciously adopting a Wisdom theme to indict God's people.[4] The description of "sinners" in Prov 1:10–19 had become, in his day, an apt description of the Israelites. They hadn't lived by wisdom, but instead they did the things that are labeled foolish in Proverbs. Isaiah is clearly using passages in Proverbs that, therefore, must predate Isaiah 59.

The direction of borrowing is important since it confirms the interest in wisdom in Hezekiah's day ("these also are the proverbs of Solomon, which the men of King Hezekiah of Judah transcribed," 25:1) and the chronology of the composition of Proverbs proposed in the introduction of this commentary.[5] Isaiah, the prophet most closely associated with Hezekiah's court (see Is 1:1 and chapters 36–39), borrowed from Proverbs, especially Proverbs 1. This small bit of information confirms the traditional attribution of all of Isaiah to the Judean prophet. It also refutes the critical notion that later chapters of Isaiah are from the postexilic period.[6] At the same time, Is 59:6–9 confirms that Proverbs 1–9

---

[3] See, for example, the excursus "Amos' Use of Earlier Biblical Texts" in Lessing, *Amos*, 289–92.

[4] Fox, *Proverbs 1–9*, 87, notes: "Isaiah 59:1–8 draws heavily upon Wisdom usages."

[5] See "Authorship and Date" in the introduction and the excursus "The Organization of Solomon's Proverbs Copied by Hezekiah's Men (Prov 25:1–29:27)" in the commentary on chapter 25.

[6] Contemporary critical scholars commonly propose that Isaiah 40–55 is from the exilic era (sixth century BC) and Isaiah 56–66 is from the postexilic era.

was already a part of the book of Proverbs when Hezekiah's men starting adding proverbs from Solomon (Proverbs 25–29) to the book. This corroborates the view advocated in the introduction that Prov 1:1 is not just a general ascription of some later parts of the book to Solomon; instead, 1:1 attributes to Solomon the authorship of the early chapters (1–9) of Proverbs as well as later chapters.[7]

[7] See "Authorship and Date" in the introduction.

Figure 6

Additional Words Shared by Isaiah 59:6–9 and Proverbs

Word	*Is 56:6–9*	*Proverbs*
אָוֶן, "wickedness"	59:6–7 (also 59:4)	nine times, including 6:12, 18
חָמָס, "violence"	59:6	seven times, including 3:31
מַחֲשָׁבוֹת , "plans"	59:7 (twice, including מַחְשְׁבוֹת אָוֶן, "wicked plans")	eight times, including 6:18 (מַחְשְׁבוֹת אָוֶן, "wicked plans")
שָׁבַר, "to break, destroy," or the noun שֶׁבֶר, "destruction"	59:7 (noun)	verb (three times, including 6:15); noun (four times)
דֶּרֶךְ, "way"	59:8	seventy-six times, including 1:15; 3:17; 6:6, 23
שָׁלוֹם, "peace"	59:8 (דֶּרֶךְ שָׁלוֹם, "way of peace")	three times, including 3:17 ("all her pathways [נְתִיבוֹת] are peace")
מִשְׁפָּט, "justice"	59:8–9 (also 59:11, 14–15)	twenty times
מַעְגָּל, "pathway"	59:8	seven times (out of sixteen times in the OT; forty-four percent)
נְתִיבָה, "pathway"	59:8	six times including 1:15; 3:17
עָקַשׁ, "to be crooked," or the cognate adjective עִקֵּשׁ, "crooked"	59:8 (verb)	verb (twice); adjective (seven times for a total of nine times out of sixteen times in the OT; fifty-six percent)
צְדָקָה, "righ-teousness"	59:9 (also 59:14, 16–17)	eighteen times
אֲפֵלָה, "darkness"	59:9	twice (out of ten times in the OT; twenty percent)

Proverbs 1:20–33

First Poem about Wisdom: Wisdom's Call and the Fate of Those Who Refuse to Listen

Translation

1 [20]Wisdom calls aloud publicly.
In the open squares she raises her voice.
[21]At the head of the noisy streets she calls out.
At the entrances to the city gates she speaks her words.
[22]"How long will you gullible people love being gullible,
and [how long] will mockers delight in their mocking,
and [how long] will fools hate knowledge?
[23]If you turn to my warning,
I will pour out my Spirit for you;
I will make my words known to you.
[24][However,] because I called and you refused [to listen];
I stretched out my hand, and no one paid attention;
[25]you ignored all my advice;
you did not accept my warning—
[26]so I will laugh at your calamity.
I will make fun [of you] when your fear strikes,
[27]when your fear strikes like a violent storm,
when your calamity strikes like a windstorm,
when trouble and distress come upon you.
[28]Then they will call to me, but I will not answer;
they will look for me, but they will not find me
[29]because they hated knowledge
and they did not choose the fear of Yahweh.
[30]They would not accept my advice,
and they despised all my warning.
[31]They will eat the fruit of their way,
and they will be gorged with their own advice.
[32]Therefore, the apostasy of gullible people kills them,
and the complacency of fools destroys them.
[33]But whoever listens to me will live in safety
and will be secure, without fear of evil."

Textual Notes

1:20 חָֽכְמוֹת בַּחוּץ תָּרֹנָּה—The abstract plural of חָכְמָה in the form חָכְמוֹת refers to personified or hypostatized "Wisdom" in 1:20; 9:1; 24:7 (cf. 14:1) and also Ps 49:4 (ET

49:3). The form is somewhat unusual because the expected pointing of the plural would be חֲכָמוֹת (Joüon, § 88M k). It is the subject of the Qal (G) third feminine plural imperfect תָּרֹנָּה from רָנַן, "*cry aloud*, in summons, exhortation" (BDB, 3). The same plural verb form recurs in 8:3 (תָּרֹנָּה), where its subject is the feminine singular חָכְמָה (8:1).

The noun חוּץ can simply mean "outside" (*HALOT*, 1 a and 2), as in 22:13. Wisdom is pictured here as taking her message outside, that is, making it public. Here בַּחוּץ is often translated as "in the streets," to match the urban plural parallel בָּרְחֹבוֹת, "in the open squares," in the next clause. However, the more general adverbial rendering "outside" or "publicly" is better.

בָּרְחֹבוֹת תִּתֵּן קוֹלָהּ׃—The noun רְחֹב refers to an open area or plaza in a city (*HALOT*). The idiom נָתַן קוֹל, literally, "to give one's voice," means "to raise one's voice, speak up." The implied subject of the feminine singular verb תִּתֵּן and the referent of the feminine singular pronominal suffix on קוֹלָהּ is the feminine plural "Wisdom" (חָכְמוֹת) in the preceding clause.

1:21 בְּרֹאשׁ הֹמִיּוֹת תִּקְרָא—The participle הֹמִיּוֹת is from the verb הָמָה, "to make a noise" (*HALOT*, 1), which can describe a noisy crowd or as here, noisy, bustling streets. For this form of the Qal (G) feminine plural participle, see GKC, § 75 v. For the first two Hebrew words, the LXX has ἐπ' ἄκρων δὲ τειχέων, "and on top of the walls," apparently reading חֹמוֹת instead of הֹמִיּוֹת.

בְּפִתְחֵי שְׁעָרִים בָּעִיר—The noun פֶּתַח is the "opening" in which a door fits, and thus it denotes an "entrance" (*HALOT*, 1).

1:22 עַד־מָתַי ׀ פְּתָיִם תְּאֵהֲבוּ פֶתִי—This is, literally, "until when will you gullible people love gullibility?" For the adjective and substantive פֶּתִי, see "פֶּתִי, 'Gullible Person' " in "Fools in Proverbs" in the introduction. For the pointing of the Qal (G) imperfect תְּאֵהֲבוּ, "you will love," see GKC, § 63 m. The second person verb shows that Wisdom is addressing the gullible directly in the vocative, "*you* gullible people." For the lack of an article on the vocative פְּתָיִם, see Joüon, § 137 g. The noun פְּתִי (so BDB) in pause (פֶּתִי), "gullibility, naïveté," is the direct object of the verb. It occurs only here in the OT and obviously is cognate to the adjective.

וְלֵצִים לָצוֹן חָמְדוּ לָהֶם—See "לֵץ, 'Mocker,' and לָצוֹן, 'Mocking, Scoffing' " in "Fools in Proverbs" in the introduction. The participle לֵצִים and the cognate noun לָצוֹן are adjacent in Hebrew, but English translation requires separating them: literally, "and mockers desire for themselves [חָמְדוּ לָהֶם] mocking."

וּכְסִילִים יִשְׂנְאוּ־דָעַת׃—See "כְּסִיל, 'Fool,' and כְּסִילוּת, 'Foolishness' " in "Fools in Proverbs" in the introduction for the noun כְּסִיל, which recurs in 1:32. For the noun דַּעַת, which recurs in 1:29, see "דַּעַת, 'Knowledge,' and יָדַע, 'to Know' " in "Wisdom in Proverbs" in the introduction. The verb שָׂנֵא, "to hate," is the antonym of אָהַב, "to love," in 1:22a, but in context both denote foolish behavior.

1:23 תָּשׁוּבוּ לְתוֹכַחְתִּי הִנֵּה …—The Qal (G) of שׁוּב often means "to turn" to God in repentance, that is, in contrition and faith (cf. BDB, 6 c, d, e). It is followed by the particle הִנֵּה, "behold," here used here to introduce a concluding sentence (*HALOT*, 7). This implies that the imperfect תָּשׁוּבוּ introduces a conditional clause: "*if* you turn, *then* [הִנֵּה] I will pour out …" (cf. GKC, § 159 d).

The noun תּוֹכַחַת occurs sixteen times in Proverbs, including 1:25, 30. It is derived from the verb יָכַח (see the first textual note on 3:12). The noun denotes a "reproof" (*HALOT*, 1 b), that is, a "criticism." However, in Proverbs it is often used in the sense of constructive criticism intended for the good of the hearer or reader. The English word "warning" or "correction" fits well here and elsewhere in Proverbs. A good indication of this is 15:31, which uses the phrase תּוֹכַחַת חַיִּים, which denotes a warning that preserves the life of those who heed it, a "life-giving warning."

אַבִּיעָה לָכֶם רוּחִי—The Hiphil (H) stem of the verb נָבַע has the transitive meaning "to pour out" here. It recurs in negative contexts in 15:2, 28, where a mouth of a fool or wicked person "spouts" stupidity or evil. In the Qal (G) in 18:4, it refers to a stream "flowing" with water.

The direct object, "my Spirit," is the only time in Proverbs where רוּחַ refers to the Holy Spirit, the third person of the Trinity. The collocation of a verb associated with water and the "Spirit" may recall Gen 1:2. Later, prophets speak Yahweh's promise to pour out his Spirit as life-giving water (Is 44:3) and to sprinkle his people with cleansing water as he confers his Spirit (Ezek 36:25–27; cf. Eph 5:26). The NT affirms that God bestows his Spirit and regenerates through Baptism into Christ.[a]

(a) E.g., Acts 2:38–39; Titus 3:5–6; 1 Pet 3:21; cf. Mt 3:16; 28:19; Jn 3:5; Eph 4:4–5

1:24 וְאֵין מַקְשִׁיב׃—This is, literally, "and there was not [anyone] paying attention." The Hiphil (H) of קָשַׁב means "heed, give one's attention to." It refers positively to listening to divine wisdom in 2:2; 4:1, 20; 5:1; 7:24. It negatively refers to believing lies in 17:4 and 29:12.

1:25 וַתִּפְרְעוּ כָל־עֲצָתִי—The Qal (G) of פָּרַע often means "let go, let loose," but in Proverbs it means "ignore, neglect" (1:25; 8:33; 13:18; 15:32) or "avoid" (4:15). For the noun עֵצָה, which recurs in 1:30, see "עֵצָה, 'Advice,' and יוֹעֵץ, 'Advisor' " in "Wisdom in Proverbs" in the introduction.

וְתוֹכַחְתִּי לֹא אֲבִיתֶם׃—"You did not accept my warning" renders this clause with אָבָה, "to be willing" or "to consent to" something (*HALOT*, 3). See also the textual note on 1:30, where it recurs.

1:26 גַּם־אֲנִי בְּאֵידְכֶם אֶשְׂחָק—The noun אֵיד, "calamity, disaster, ruin," recurs in 1:27; 6:15; 17:5; 24:22; 27:10. God "laughs" (שָׂחַק) at the wicked also in Pss 2:4; 37:13; 59:9 (ET 59:8), showing his supreme power over them and their evil schemes. See also the next textual note.

אֶלְעַג בְּבֹא פַחְדְּכֶם—The verbs שָׂחַק and לָעַג, "make fun of, mock," are parallel with God as subject also in Pss 2:4; 59:9 (ET 59:8). Compare לָעַג alone with God as subject in Job 9:23. In Proverbs לָעַג recurs in 17:5 and 30:17 referring to sinful human ridicule.

The use of בְּ with an infinitive construct (בֹּא) forms a temporal clause: "*when* your fear comes." בְּבֹא recurs twice in 1:27. However, in English idiom, fear does not "come" but "strikes." Using "come" here would be understandable, but may be taken by an English reader to indicate something unusual or awkward in the underlying Hebrew, since this is not the normal English construction. However, the Hebrew expression is *not* indicating anything usual and is not awkward Hebrew. Therefore, the correct corresponding English phrasing has been used in this and the following verse.

Note that the noun for "fear" in 1:26–27 is not יִרְאָה, which is used to denote "the fear of Yahweh" (e.g., 1:7, 29), the positive relationship of the child of God to the heavenly Father. Instead, the noun פַּחַד in 1:26–27 is "fear" that leads to panic when a recalcitrant unbeliever must face the consequences of his sins without Christ as his mediator before a wrathful God. However, this kind of "fear" is removed for the believer; see פַּחַד in 1:33 and 3:25 and the verb פָּחַד in 3:24 (cf. Mt 28:5, 10; Mk 5:36; 1 Jn 4:18).

1:27 כְשֹׁאָוה—The Qere is כְּשׁוֹאָה, while the Kethib is כְּשַׁאֲוָה, which appears to be a metathesis with ו and א interchanged. The noun שׁוֹאָה refers to a storm with violent consequences (*HALOT*, 1 c). שׁוֹאָה recurs in 3:25. Modern Hebrew uses it to refer to the holocaust. The Kethib, שַׁאֲוָה, also would mean "devastating storm" (BDB). The parallel noun in the next clause, סוּפָה, "windstorm" (used also in 10:25), is a synonym that has the same preposition, כְּ, forming another simile ("like").

צָרָה וְצוּקָה׃—These are more general terms that refer literally (not in a simile) to the consequences of rejecting divine Wisdom. The feminine noun צָרָה, "trouble, distress, straits," recurs in 11:8; 12:13; 17:17; 21:23; 24:10; 25:19 and derives from the verb צָרַר, "bind, be cramped, be in distress." The rare feminine noun צוּקָה, "distress," is a synonym that occurs elsewhere in the OT only in Is 8:22; 30:6.

1:28 יִקְרָאֻנְנִי ... יְשַׁחֲרֻנְנִי ... יִמְצָאֻנְנִי׃—These three third masculine plural imperfects each have a paragogic *nun* (-נְ-) before the first common singular suffix (-נִי). See GKC, §§ 47 m and 60 e.

1:29 תַּחַת כִּי—This combination of preposition and conjunction occurs only here and in Deut 4:37 (cf. Is 51:6). It means "for the reason that" (*HALOT*, תַּחַת, 4 c), as the Greek γάρ often does (e.g., Mt 1:20; Rom 1:19).

1:30 לֹא־אָבוּ לַעֲצָתִי—The verb אָבָה is repeated from 1:25b but here with the indirect object "to my advice" (לְ with עֲצָתִי, which was in 1:25a). The proper English idiom to express consent to advice received is "take advice" or "accept advice."

1:31 וְיֹאכְלוּ מִפְּרִי דַרְכָּם—The Qal (G) of אָכַל, "eat," can have the figurative meaning "of receiving [the] consequences of [one's] action, good or [as here] bad" (BDB, 1), as also in 18:21. The consequences are מִפְּרִי דַרְכָּם, literally, "from the fruit of their way." The preposition מִן is used idiomatically here and in the next clause with verbs of eating or being filled "from" a source of food. See BDB, s.v. מִן, 2 b (*b*).

וּמִמֹּעֲצֹתֵיהֶם יִשְׂבָּעוּ׃—The Qal (G) of שָׂבַע, "be filled, satiated," can be used with the preposition מִן attached to the food eaten (BDB, 1 c; *HALOT*, 6). Here the eating is metaphorical; the food in this case is the result of the "advice" (the plural of מֹעֵצָה) of those who reject divine Wisdom. The verb שָׂבַע is used with מִן with a similar metaphorical meaning in 12:14; 14:14; 18:20.

1:32 כִּי מְשׁוּבַת פְּתָיִם תַּהַרְגֵם—The noun מְשׁוּבָה means "turning away" from God or "apostasy" (*HALOT*). It is the subject of the feminine Qal (G) imperfect תַּהַרְגֵם, "will kill/kills them." Those who abandon the advice and guidance of divine Wisdom do so to their own peril. 4QProv[a] contains the variant reading מושכת,[1] to be vocalized מוֹשְׁכֹת, the plural of מוֹשֶׁכֶת in construct: "cords of." It may be that a scribe was bothered by the

[1] Ulrich et. al., *Qumran Cave 4.XI*, 181–82.

"turning" that kills, since the root of the noun מְשׁוּבָה is the verb שׁוּב, which was used positively meaning "to turn (to God), repent" in 1:23. So the scribe borrowed the plural noun מוֹשְׁכוֹת from Job 38:31 (the only OT occurrence of מוֹשְׁכָה) in order to change the text to mean "the cords of gullible people kill them." Alternately, מושכה may be a simple case of graphic confusion of כ for ב and the later addition of a ו as a *mater lectionis* in the wrong place.[2]

וְשַׁלְוַת כְּסִילִים תְּאַבְּדֵם׃—The feminine noun שַׁלְוָה can refer positively to "quietness" (17:1), but here it denotes the lack of concern that a sinner ought to have, but does not have. Thus "complacency" is an appropriate translation. It is the subject of the feminine imperfect תְּאַבְּדֵם. The Piel (D) of אָבַד has a causative meaning: "to cause to perish, destroy."

1:33 וְשֹׁמֵעַ לִי יִשְׁכָּן־בֶּטַח—The noun בֶּטַח, "safety, security," occurs four times in Proverbs and always has an adverbial meaning, "safely, securely," whether it has the preposition לְ (3:23, 29) or does not (1:33; 10:9). Twice it modifies a verb for "live, dwell": שָׁכַן here and יָשַׁב in 3:29. Twice it modifies הָלַךְ, "to walk, go": in 3:23 and 10:9.

וְשַׁאֲנַן מִפַּחַד רָעָה׃—The verb שָׁאַן occurs only in the Palel (D) stem (see GKC, § 55 d) and means "to be secure, at rest." The preposition מִן has a privative sense, "without," and the construct phrase פַּחַד רָעָה contains a genitive of source, "fear at/caused by evil."

Commentary

This first of three poetic descriptions of Wisdom reveals Wisdom's message.[3] The section is a tightly constructed chiasm:[4]

- A Wisdom addresses the crowds (1:20–21)
  - B Wisdom calls out to fools (1:22)
    - C Wisdom's invitation and offer (1:23)
      - D Wisdom's offer was rejected (1:24–25)
        - E Wisdom's condemnation (1:26–27)
      - D' Wisdom's reaction to those who rejected her offer (1:28–30)
    - C' The consequence of not accepting Wisdom's invitation (1:31)
  - B' Wisdom speaks about the self-destruction of fools (1:32)
- A' Wisdom addresses the crowds (1:33)

The description of Wisdom begins by clearly indicating that Wisdom is available to all (A; 1:20–21). Wisdom declares her song publicly. The four lines of 1:20–21 cover the entire city: outside or publicly; in the open squares; at the head of the crowded, noisy streets; and at the gates, the entrances to the city. Solomon emphasizes that no one has an excuse for being without Wisdom, which God offers to all freely.

---

[2] Clifford, "Observations on the Text and Versions of Proverbs," 49.

[3] Solomon's two later poems about Wisdom are in 8:1–36 and 9:1–18. For this commentary's Christological view of wisdom, see "Wisdom in Proverbs" in the introduction. See also the commentary on 1:1–7; 3:13–20; 8:22–31; 30:1b–10; and the excursus "Proverbs 8, Wisdom, Christology, and the Arian Controversy" in the commentary on chapter 8.

[4] Trible, "Wisdom Builds a Poem."

After describing Wisdom's availability by grace, the poem presents her song in her own words. The "how long" (עַד־מָתַי, 1:22) that opens her call to the foolish (B) sounds a note of exasperation as she raises the question about the continued ignorant behavior of gullible people, mockers, and fools. This is followed by her invitation (C; 1:23).[5] Wisdom's appeal here begins with the Law and moves quickly to the Gospel. She speaks of a warning that is intended to drive her hearers to see their need for God's Spirit, whom God promises to "pour out"[6] and who works though his Word. This is divine Wisdom speaking: God himself offers enlightenment that cures foolishness.[7]

(b) See Is 50:2; 66:4, 65:12; Jer 7:13, 24–27; Ezek 3:7; Hos 11:2

(c) Mt 23:29–37; 26:56; Lk 24:25–27; cf. Mt 5:12

The rejection of Wisdom's offer (D; 1:24–25) mirrors the experience of the prophets when they brought God's message.[b] This culminates in the rejection suffered by Israel's greatest Prophet, Jesus.[c] He is the Wisdom of God incarnate, but the world deems the Gospel of Christ crucified to be foolishness (1 Cor 1:18–31). The stretching out of the hand as a gesture of invitation (Prov 1:24) serves to heighten the contrast between Wisdom's gracious offer and the callous rejection it received.

The center of Wisdom's song (E; 1:26–27) brings her condemnation in two carefully constructed verses involving interlocked chiasms.[8] This highlights the vulnerability of those who reject Wisdom's offer. Note the major chiasm:

26So I will laugh at *your calamity* [אֵידְכֶם].
    I will make fun [of you] when *your fear* [פַּחְדְּכֶם] strikes,
    27when *your fear* [פַּחְדְּכֶם] strikes like a violent storm,
when *your calamity* [אֵידְכֶם] strikes like a windstorm.

The two verbs in 1:26 are parallel to each other ("I will laugh at … I will make fun") as are the two nouns in 1:27 ("a violent storm … a windstorm"). In addition, 1:26 is itself chiastic in its word order. The first line of 1:26 concludes with a prepositional phrase with בְּ ("at, when") and a first person verb, then the second line begins with a first person verb and prepositional phrase with בְּ ("at, when"). These are reflected in this literal translation:

---

5 Murphy, "Wisdom's Song," would read 1:23 as an accusation, which would begin "you turned aside from my reproof." However, he is forced then to argue that the sense of the next line, "I will pour out my Spirit for you," is "I will pour out my wrath on you." However, there is no biblical precedent for understanding the Spirit as an agent of "wrath" and judgment in this way. Emerton, "A Note on the Hebrew Text of Proverbs i. 22–3," would read 1:23a as a question, "when will you turn to my reproof?" To accomplish this he proposes that the last two lines of 1:22 ("[how long] will mockers delight in their mocking, and [how long] will fools hate knowledge?") are a secondary insertion of an independent proverb into the text. Neither of these proposals is convincing.

6 See the second textual note on 1:23.

7 Note how the parallel to Prov 1:24b in Is 65:2a confirms this understanding of Wisdom's invitation as God's invitation. Just as Wisdom stretched out her hand in invitation in Proverbs (tenth century BC), so in Isaiah (eighth–seven centuries BC), God stretches out his hands.

8 Trible, "Wisdom Builds a Poem," 513–14.

At your calamity I will laugh. בְּאֵידְכֶם אֶשְׂחָק
I will make fun of when comes your fear. אֶלְעַג בְּבֹא פַחְדְּכֶם

The two verbs are adjacent in the center of 1:26, surrounded on either side by prepositional phrases. This word order forms a sharp contrast with 1:25, where the verbs were at the start and end of the verse and their direct objects were adjacent in the center, as reflected by this literal translation:

You ignored all my advice. וַתִּפְרְעוּ כָל־עֲצָתִי
My warning you did not accept. וְתוֹכַחְתִּי לֹא אֲבִיתֶם

Finally, 1:27 forms its own chiasm. Its first and third lines have the same grammatical structure: a verbal temporal clause (בְּבֹא) with the subject noun(s) last. The second line has the inverse structure: the subject noun is first, and the verb is last. This is reflected in this literal rendition:

When comes like a storm your fear, בְּבֹא כְשַׁאֲוָה ׀ פַּחְדְּכֶם
your calamity like a windstorm arrives, וְאֵידְכֶם כְּסוּפָה יֶאֱתֶה
when comes upon you trouble and distress. בְּבֹא עֲלֵיכֶם צָרָה וְצוּקָה

The rejection of Wisdom's offer (D; 1:24–25) is carefully matched to Wisdom's reaction against those who rejected her offer (D'; 1:28–30) by the repetition of several verbs and nouns.

- I called (קָרָאתִי, 1:24).
- They will call to me (יִקְרָאֻנְנִי, 1:28).

- You did not accept (לֹא אֲבִיתֶם, 1:25).
- They would not accept (לֹא־אָבוּ, 1:30).

- All my advice (כָל־עֲצָתִי, 1:25).
- My advice (לַעֲצָתִי, 1:30).

- And my warning (וְתוֹכַחְתִּי, 1:25).
- All my warning (כָּל־תּוֹכַחְתִּי, 1:30).

Note that 1:29 is not included in this echo of 1:24–25. Instead, 1:29 echoes 1:7, and it also stands out as the chief theological accusation, the reason why the rejecters will suffer the consequences. It explains why Wisdom will now reject them (as stated in 1:28). They have elected not to have "knowledge" and "the fear of Yahweh" (1:29), key terminology from the declaration that is foundational and programmatic for the entire book: "the fear of Yahweh is the beginning of knowledge" (1:7). This serves as a stark warning to those who read Wisdom's song. They are not to neglect the benefits Proverbs offers from its very beginning (1:7).

The self-destruction of those who are determined to be fools (B'; 1:32) stands in contrast to Wisdom's call to fools (B; 1:22). Now we see the result of gullible people's love for their gullibility (1:22): they kill themselves (1:32a). In a similar vein we are told the result of fools' hatred of knowledge and complacency in the face of Wisdom's offer: they destroy themselves (1:32b).

A close parallel exists between the warning that those who reject Wisdom will seek her but not find her (Prov 1:28) and the warning by Jesus that those who reject him will seek him but not find him (Jn 7:32–36).[9] This applies especially to Judgment Day, when all unbelievers will be overcome by everlasting "fear" and "distress" (Prov 1:26–27), yet it will be too late for them to repent and be saved (cf. Dan 12:2–3; Mt 25:31–46).

Yet despite the fools' rejection of Wisdom and her consequent rejection of them, she ends her song with another call to everyone who will listen (1:33). The promise contrasts the panic of fools who reject her offer (1:26–27) to the security of all who respond to her call. This, of course, is the everlasting security that God offers to all in the Gospel of Christ with the free invitation for anyone and everyone to believe and be saved (e.g., Jn 3:14–16; 6:47; 7:37–38; 11:25–26). Jesus reassures his flock that they have this security under his loving care when he promises:

> My sheep hear my voice, and I know them, and they follow me. I give them eternal life and they will never perish. Neither will anyone pluck them out of my hand. (Jn 10:27–28)

The father's third section of instruction to his son about Wisdom (3:1–20) and the second poem on divine Wisdom (8:1–36) both directly point to the second person of the Trinity: God the Son, Jesus Christ.[10] This first poem on Wisdom in 1:20–33 points to him only indirectly, via the verbal and theological parallels to the words of Jesus in the Gospels (cf. also 1 Cor 1:18–31). Nevertheless, Wisdom surely is divine here, because she offers security of life that the world cannot offer (1:33). This everlasting life comes through the work of all three persons of the Godhead.

Therefore, we see in this first poem on divine Wisdom that Solomon, the wise teacher, begins by introducing Wisdom without burdening his students with many details. Later he refines his words and further defines Wisdom as his son or his readers learn more and can understand more details. He introduces Wisdom in this poem, gives more Christological information about Wisdom in his third address (3:1–20), and climaxes with a full-blown treatment of Christ, the preexistent Wisdom of God, in the second Wisdom poem in 8:1–36.

---

[9] See also Hos 5:6; Amos 8:12; Jn 8:21; 13:33. For other OT parallels, see the excursus "The Relationship of Proverbs 1:20–33 to Jeremiah 7 and Zechariah 7."

[10] See "Wisdom in Proverbs" in the introduction. See also the commentary on 1:1–7; 3:13–20; 8:22–31; 30:1b–10; and the excursus "Proverbs 8, Wisdom, Christology, and the Arian Controversy" in the commentary on chapter 8.

Excursus

The Relationship of Proverbs 1:20–33 to Jeremiah 7 and Zechariah 7

The call of divine Wisdom in 1:20–33 is ignored by the foolish with the result that Wisdom will ignore them when they call. When calamity comes, these unbelievers will seek God and the Wisdom they rejected but will find no relief. This passage by Solomon in the tenth century BC will be echoed a millennium later in the words of Jesus.[1] Before then it is also echoed in the prophets, especially Jeremiah (sixth century BC) and Zechariah (fifth century BC). Compare the following verses:

יַ֣עַן קָ֭רָאתִי וַתְּמָאֵ֑נוּ
נָטִ֥יתִי יָ֝דִ֗י וְאֵ֣ין מַקְשִֽׁיב׃

[However,] because I called and you refused [to listen];
I stretched out my hand, and no one paid attention … (Prov 1:24)

אָ֣ז יִ֭קְרָאֻנְנִי וְלֹ֣א אֶֽעֱנֶ֑ה
יְ֝שַׁחֲרֻ֗נְנִי וְלֹ֣א יִמְצָאֻֽנְנִי׃

Then they will call to me, but I will not answer.
They will look for me, but they will not find me. (Prov 1:28)

וְעַתָּ֗ה יַ֛עַן עֲשׂוֹתְכֶ֥ם אֶת־כָּל־הַֽמַּעֲשִׂ֥ים הָאֵ֖לֶּה נְאֻם־יְהוָ֑ה
וָאֲדַבֵּ֨ר אֲלֵיכֶ֜ם הַשְׁכֵּ֤ם וְדַבֵּר֙ וְלֹ֣א שְׁמַעְתֶּ֔ם
וָאֶקְרָ֥א אֶתְכֶ֖ם וְלֹ֥א עֲנִיתֶֽם׃

"And now, because you have done all these things," declares Yahweh,
"I spoke to you repeatedly, but you did not hear,
I called you and you did not answer …" (Jer 7:13)

וְדִבַּרְתָּ֤ אֲלֵיהֶם֙ אֶת־כָּל־הַדְּבָרִ֣ים הָאֵ֔לֶּה וְלֹ֥א יִשְׁמְע֖וּ אֵלֶ֑יךָ
וְקָרָ֥אתָ אֲלֵיהֶ֖ם וְלֹ֥א יַעֲנֽוּכָה׃

"You will say all these things to them, but they will not listen to you.
You will call to them, but they will not answer you." (Jer 7:27)

וַיְהִ֥י כַאֲשֶׁר־קָרָ֖א וְלֹ֣א שָׁמֵ֑עוּ
כֵּ֤ן יִקְרְאוּ֙ וְלֹ֣א אֶשְׁמָ֔ע אָמַ֖ר יְהוָ֥ה צְבָאֽוֹת׃

When he called, they did not listen.
"So when they call, I will not listen," says Yahweh of armies.
(Zech 7:13)

---

[1] Compare Prov 1:28 especially to Jn 7:32–36. See the latter part of the commentary on Prov 1:20–33.

Several scholars have noted the particularly close relationship between Jeremiah 7 and Prov 1:20–33.[2] There are numerous similarities of vocabulary and phrasing.[3] Jeremiah delivers his message in the gate (Jer 7:2) as Wisdom does (Prov 1:21). Those who hear Wisdom are promised that they will be secure, without fear (Prov 1:33), and Yahweh through Jeremiah offers security in the land for those who heed his message (Jer 7:3). Several ties with other parts of Jeremiah can be noted, especially Jeremiah 20, where everyone mocks and laughs at the prophet (Jer 20:7), which is what divine Wisdom will do to those who refuse to listen to her (Prov 1:26–27).

That there is a connection between Jeremiah and Proverbs and between Zechariah and Proverbs is probable. However, what is the direction of the influence? Critical scholars often assume that Jeremiah 7 is the text that influenced Proverbs[4] since they date Proverbs 1–9 late, perhaps as late as the Achaemenid period.[5] These scholars tend to base their theory on perceived social conditions that are reflected in these chapters, a method that is highly subjective and "largely theory-driven," as conceded by Fox.[6]

No convincing argument can be made on the basis of the text of Jeremiah 7 or the text of Prov 1:20–33 that Jeremiah influenced Proverbs. In fact, the dependence can just as easily be seen as flowing in the opposite direction. The traditional view, which this commentary affirms, is that Proverbs 1–9 is by Solomon in the tenth century BC.[7] There may be good reason for reading the sixth century BC prophet Jeremiah in this light. The prophet is depicting the lack of divine wisdom among the Israelites during his era, shortly before the Babylonian conquest of Judah and the destruction of Jerusalem and the temple. Similar to Wisdom in Prov 1:21, who calls at the city gates (שְׁעָרִים), Yahweh's prophet calls to the people from the "gate" (שַׁעַר) of the Lord's house (Jer 7:2), but they do not have the wisdom to listen. Just as do those who reject Wisdom cause their own death and destruction (Prov 1:31–32), so the impenitent Israelites harm themselves by arousing God's wrath and judgment (Jer 7:19–20). Just as the fools in Prov 1:7 and 5:12, 23 do not accept "discipline" (מוּסָר),[8] neither does Jeremiah's audience (מוּסָר, Jer 7:28). The father urges his son to "incline" his "ear" (הַטֵּה אָזֶן, Prov 4:20; 5:1; cf. 2:2; 5:13), but the people of Jerusalem did not "incline" their "ear" (הַטָּה אָזֶן, Jer 7:24, 26). Those who do not accept Wisdom's "advice" (עֵצָה, Prov 1:30) "will be gorged with their own

---

[2] Fox, *Proverbs 1–9*, 104–5; Harris, *Proverbs 1–9*, 67–109.

[3] See especially the list in Harris, *Proverbs 1–9*, 93–94.

[4] See, for example, Harris, *Proverbs 1–9*, 1–3.

[5] See Fox, *Proverbs 1–9*, 48–49; 104–5. Fox notes that the scholarly tendency is to date Proverbs 1–9 to the middle of the fifth century BC, but he seems to favor a Hellenistic date.

[6] Fox, *Proverbs 1–9*, 48.

[7] See "Authorship and Date" in the introduction.

[8] See further "מוּסָר, 'Discipline,' and יָסַר, 'to Discipline' " in "Wisdom in Proverbs" in the introduction.

advice" (plural of מֹעֵצָה, Prov 1:31), and the foolish inhabitants of Jerusalem follow their own "advice" (plural of מֹעֵצָה, Jer 7:24).

Thus it would appear that Jeremiah is drawing on Wisdom motifs from Proverbs, primarily 1:20–33, but also from other places in Proverbs 1–9, in order to rebuke the obdurate Israelites facing imminent judgment during his ministry. The likely direction of dependence is that Jeremiah, under divine inspiration, borrowed from the Proverbs authored by Solomon. (It is a much less defensible position to argue that in addition to Prov 1:20–33, several scattered texts in Proverbs 1–9 were influenced by Jeremiah 7.)

This makes Jeremiah's condemnation of God's people even more poignant. Through his prophet, Yahweh is trying to show his people that for some four centuries, they had already received the wisdom they now needed for their desperate situation. However, they consciously rejected not just Jeremiah's message but also the longstanding message of Solomon. Thus Jeremiah's message was not a new one. It was the same message of Law and Gospel—of the need for repentance and of salvation through faith—that the people of Israel had previously received from God's spokesmen, including Israel's wisest king.[9]

In this light, it becomes even easier to read Zech 7:13. It immediately follows the accusation that the Israelites had refused to pay attention to the words of Yahweh through earlier prophets (Zech 7:7–12). Then God states that "when he called, they did not listen. 'So when they call, I will not listen,' says Yahweh" (Zech 7:13). This reference to God's call includes his words through two earlier spokesmen: Solomon and Jeremiah.

Thus the intertextual connections with Prov 1:20–33 not only give evidence that this section of Proverbs predates Jeremiah and Zechariah, they also testify to how these later prophets understood this chapter and applied it to their contemporary generations. The impenitent Israelites in the sixth and fifth centuries BC serve as case studies of people who rejected Wisdom's call and suffered the consequences—the same consequences contained in Wisdom's warning against all who ignore her call (Prov 1:31–32). They killed and destroyed themselves (Jer 7:32–8:3; Zech 7:14), as do all who reject the only Savior sent by Israel's God (Jn 7:32–36; cf. Jn 1:11–13; 1 Jn 5:11–13).

---

9 See further "Law and Gospel in Proverbs" in the introduction.

Proverbs 2:1–15

Wisdom Comes from God to Protect You

Translation

2 1 My son, if you accept my words
and treasure my commands inside you,
2 in order to pay attention to wisdom with your ear
and reach out with your heart for understanding—
3 if indeed you call for intelligence,
[if] you raise your voice for understanding,
4 if you search for it like money
and hunt for it as [if it were] hidden treasure—
5 then you will understand the fear of Yahweh
and find the knowledge of God,
6 because Yahweh gives wisdom;
from his mouth [come] knowledge and understanding.
7 He stores up sound judgment for upright people;
[he is] a shield for those who walk in integrity,
8 to protect [those who walk on] paths of justice.
He guards the way of his godly ones.
9 Then you will understand righteousness, justice, and uprightness—
every good pathway,
10 because wisdom will come into your heart,
and knowledge will be pleasant to your soul.
11 Foresight will stand guard over you;
understanding will protect you,
12 to save you from the evil way,
from the man who speaks perverse things—
13 [from] those who abandon upright paths
to walk in the ways of darkness,
14 those who enjoy doing evil
and rejoice in the perversity of evil,
15 whose paths are crooked,
and devious things are in their pathways.

Textual Notes

2:1 וּמִצְוֺתַ֗י תִּצְפֹּ֥ן אִתָּֽךְ׃—This clause is repeated verbatim in 7:1b. This is the first of ten occurrences of מִצְוָה, "command," in Proverbs. The same suffixed plural as here, "my commands," recurs in 3:1; 4:4; 7:1–2.[1]

---

1 See the excursus "Proverbs 1–9, Christ, and the Ten Commandments" in the commentary on Proverbs 1.

The Qal (G) verb צָפַן means "hide" for the evil purpose of setting an ambush in 1:11, 18 (see the second textual note on 1:11). But here and in 2:7; 7:1; and 10:14 it has the positive meaning of "store up, treasure" divine wisdom and its blessings. The suffix on the prepositional phrase אִתָּךְ (pausal for אִתְּךָ), literally, "with you," is masculine singular, referring back to בְּנִי, "my son," earlier in the verse. Here it is best rendered as "inside you" because it refers to the internal appropriation of God's words through faith.

2:2 לְהַקְשִׁיב לַחָכְמָה אָזְנֶךָ— In this address the noun חָכְמָה recurs in 2:6, 10. See "חָכְמָה, 'Wisdom,' and Related Words" in "Wisdom in Proverbs" in the introduction. It is parallel to תְּבוּנָה, "understanding," in the second clause of 2:2. חָכְמָה and תְּבוּנָה are parallel also in 2:6; 3:13, 19; 5:1; 8:1; 21:30; 24:3 (cf. 10:23), always with חָכְמָה in the first clause and תְּבוּנָה in the second clause.

This construction is unusual for the Hiphil (H) of קָשַׁב, which normally means "pay attention, listen attentively" (see the textual note on 1:24). Here and in Ps 10:17, it is accompanied by אָזְנֶךָ, "your ear." A first possibility is that in Prov 2:2 (and Ps 10:17) the Hiphil has a causative meaning and אָזְנֶךָ is its direct object: "*cause your ear* to pay attention to the wisdom" (cf. Joüon, § 125 x). The parallel construction in the second clause of the verse is a transitive Hiphil verb with a direct object (see the next textual note). A second possibility, reflected in the translation above, is that the Hiphil has its usual meaning, "pay attention," with no direct object and אָזְנֶךָ means "*with* your ear," either as an "accusative of the organ or means by which the action is performed" (GKC, § 117 s; cf. Waltke-O'Connor, § 10.2.1h) or perhaps as an adverbial accusative (GKC, § 118 q). A third possibility is that אָזְנֶךָ is to be regarded as the subject: "so that your ear pays attention to the wisdom" (cf. GKC, §§ 144 l and 144 m (*b*)).

תַּטֶּה לִבְּךָ לַתְּבוּנָה׃—This is, literally, "you may turn your heart to understanding." The Hiphil (H) of נָטָה with the transitive meaning, "to turn (something), incline, direct," takes the object לֵב or לֵבָב, "heart," also in 21:1 (in a longer construction) and, for example, Josh 24:23 and Ps 119:36. For לֵב, see the first textual note on Prov 2:10.

In this address the noun תְּבוּנָה recurs in 2:2–3, 6, 11. The cognate noun and synonym בִּינָה occurs in the first clause of 2:3. The cognate verb בִּין occurs in the clause אָז תָּבִין, "then you will understand," in 2:5a, 9a. For this vocabulary, see "בִּינָה, 'Understanding,' and Related Words" in "Wisdom in Proverbs" in the introduction. Although the noun בִּינָה is usually translated in this commentary as "understanding," in 2:3 it is translated as "intelligence" to contrast it with תְּבוּנָה.

2:4 אִם־תְּבַקְשֶׁנָּה כַכָּסֶף—This is the first of fourteen occurrences in Proverbs of the Piel (D) of בָּקַשׁ, "to seek." Its third feminine singular suffix (ֶ‍נָּה) could refer back to any of the three feminine nouns for "wisdom" (חָכְמָה) or "understanding" (תְּבוּנָה or בִּינָה) in 2:2–3.

This is the first of thirteen occurrences in Proverbs of כֶּסֶף, which usually refers to "money" in general, as here and also, for example, in 7:20, but it is translated as "silver" when it is paired with "gold" (3:14; 8:10, 19; 16:16). The LXX translates כֶּסֶף here literally with ἀργύριον, which can mean either "silver" or "money" (e.g., Mt 25:18, 27; Mk 14:11; Acts 8:20).

2:5 אָז תָּבִין יִרְאַת יְהוָה—See "יִרְאַת יְהוָה, 'the Fear of Yahweh,' and יְרֵא יְהוָה, 'One Who Fears Yahweh' " in "Wisdom in Proverbs" in the introduction. See also the first textual note and the commentary on 1:7.

וְדַעַת אֱלֹהִים תִּמְצָא׃—In this address the noun דַּעַת recurs in 2:6, 10. See "דַּעַת, 'Knowledge,' and יָדַע, 'to Know' " in "Wisdom in Proverbs" in the introduction.

2:6 כִּי־יְהוָה יִתֵּן חָכְמָה מִפִּיו דַּעַת וּתְבוּנָה׃—The parallelism between יְהוָה יִתֵּן, "Yahweh gives," and מִפִּיו, "from his mouth," shows that חָכְמָה ... דַּעַת וּתְבוּנָה, divine "wisdom ... knowledge and understanding," come through faith in the Word of God, spoken by him and recorded in the Scriptures.

2:7 וִצְפֹּן לַיְשָׁרִים תּוּשִׁיָּה—In light of the Gospel assurance expressed with the imperfect in 2:6, יִתֵּן, "Yahweh *gives* wisdom," preferable here is the Qere, the imperfect יִצְפֹּן, "he stores up," instead of the Kethib, the perfect וְצָפַן. For the verb צָפַן, see the textual note on 2:1. For the direct object of the verb, see "תּוּשִׁיָּה, 'Sound Judgment' " in "Wisdom in Proverbs" in the introduction.

The adjective יָשָׁר, "straight, right," occurs twenty-five times in Proverbs. Here and often it is used as a substantive, "upright person, just/righteous person." It refers to a person whose life displays the result of receiving the gifts of divine wisdom and righteousness through faith. See "The Relationship between Wisdom and Righteousness in Proverbs" in "Wisdom in Proverbs" in the introduction.

מָגֵן לְהֹלְכֵי תֹם׃—The noun מָגֵן describes God as a "shield" again in 30:5 (see also, e.g., Pss 3:4 [ET 3:3]; 28:7; 115:9–11).

"Those who walk in integrity" is a construct chain formed by לְ on the plural participle of הָלַךְ, "walk," in construct with the absolute state noun תֹּם, "integrity." The construct relationship here includes an adverbial genitive. The phrase is a synonym of יְשָׁרִים, "upright people" (see the previous textual note). תֹּם, "integrity," is a synonym of "righteousness" and is a highly valued attribute in Proverbs, denoting honesty and blamelessness. It recurs with a participle of הָלַךְ in 10:9; 19:1; 20:7; 28:6; with דֶּרֶךְ, "way," in 13:6; and as a substantive, "person with integrity," in 10:29 (cf. 29:10). In 10:29–30 it is parallel with "righteous person" and is contrasted with its antonyms "evildoers" and "wicked people." A person who walks/lives with "integrity" is pronounced "righteous" in 20:7 and is guarded by "righteousness" in 13:6. The masculine noun תֹּם is synonymous with the feminine noun תֻּמָּה in 11:3. It is cognate to the adjectives תָּם (29:10) and תָּמִים, "person of integrity, blameless person" (see the second textual note on 2:21).

2:8 לִנְצֹר אָרְחוֹת מִשְׁפָּט—The verb נָצַר, "to protect," is a synonym of שָׁמַר, "keep, guard," in 2:8b. The two verbs recur together in 2:11 and also in 4:6; 5:2; 13:3; 16:17; 27:18. For נָצַר, see further the second textual note on 3:1.

Here the noun מִשְׁפָּט, "justice," probably involves an ellipsis that refers to people: "to guard [those who walk on] paths of justice." This fits with 2:7, since its two clauses refer to people ("upright people ... those who walk in integrity"). It also fits with the next clause about "godly ones" and with 2:9, which uses the same noun to describe people: those who "will understand ... justice."

וְדֶרֶךְ חֲסִידָו יִשְׁמֹר׃—The adjective חָסִיד is used substantivally here. It means "faithful, godly" (*HALOT*) and occurs only here in Proverbs. The plural Qere חֲסִידָיו is the preferred reading here instead of the singular Kethib, חֲסִידוֹ.

2:9 אָז תָּבִין צֶדֶק וּמִשְׁפָּט וּמֵישָׁרִים כָּל־מַעְגַּל־טוֹב׃—The Masoretic cantillation of the verse implies the following syntax:

> Then you will understand righteousness and justice,
> and uprightness—every good pathway.

However, it is best to read the three nouns צֶדֶק וּמִשְׁפָּט וּמֵישָׁרִים as a group, with all three as direct objects of the verb תָּבִין, as in the translation above, and in many modern translations.[2] An inferior alternative is to emend וּמֵישָׁרִים to תִּשְׁמֹר, as does Toy (following the LXX's κατορθώσεις), or to וּמְשַׁמֵּר, as does Driver.[3]

2:10 כִּי־תָבוֹא חָכְמָה בְלִבֶּךָ—The "heart" (לֵב or לֵבָב) denotes more than the seat of emotions as in English. In Hebrew the heart is the source of emotions such as joy (Is 24:7), fear (Josh 2:11), and despair (Eccl 2:20), and it is also the seat of intellectual capacities such as insight (Prov 2:2) and critical evaluation (Josh 14:7) as well as the locus of the human will (2 Sam 7:3; 1 Ki 8:17). Here divine wisdom enters the heart of Solomon's son when he believes and lives according to God's words. The father's instruction to his son in Proverbs 1–9 often speaks of the son taking wisdom to heart. "Heart" occurs twenty-one times in these chapters and ninety-nine times in Proverbs as a whole. Wisdom is a desirable attribute of the heart for it can guide a person's entire existence.[4] Such a wise person is above all else justified, that is, reckoned righteous by God through faith (Gen 15:6). God grants wisdom to those who believe his Word (Prov 2:6). Wisdom transforms the heart, leading to the sanctified life that characterizes a person as wise in his attitude and behavior.

וְדַעַת לְנַפְשְׁךָ יִנְעָם׃—The feminine noun דַּעַת is the subject of the masculine imperfect יִנְעָם probably because of the preference for the more common masculine forms of verbs (Joüon, § 150 k; cf. GKC, § 145 u).

The verb נָעֵם, "to be pleasant, delightful," recurs in a positive sense in regard to divine wisdom in 24:25. Foolishness uses it deceptively to advertise the pleasure of sin in 9:17. The cognate noun נֹעַם, "pleasantness, pleasure," refers to wisdom's ways in 3:17 and to gracious words in 15:26 and 16:24. Solomon's father, David, desired to dwell in Yahweh's house and temple all his days to gaze upon Yahweh's "pleasantness" there (Ps 27:4). Since the Jerusalem temple was not constructed during his lifetime, David probably refers to the beatific vision of God in everlasting life in the heavenly temple (cf. Ps 23:6; Rev 3:12; 7:15). The cognate adjective נָעִים, "pleasurable, pleasant" (Prov 22:18; 23:8; 24:4) refers to "pleasures" in God's presence after resurrection in Ps 16:11 (see also Ps 16:6). Compare עֵדֶן, *Eden*, "pleasure, delight," the name of the first paradise (Gen 2:8, 10, 15).

---

2 NIV; NRSV; see Garrett, *Proverbs, Ecclesiastes, Song of Songs*, 75, including n. 34; Waltke, *Proverbs*, 1:214, including n. 13.

3 Toy, *Proverbs*, 39; Driver, "Problems in the Hebrew Text of Proverbs," 174. Driver translates 2:9b as "and (thou art) regarding every good path."

4 See F. Stolz, "לֵב," *TLOT* 2:638–42.

2:11 מְזִמָּה תִּשְׁמֹר עָלֶיךָ—See "מְזִמָּה, 'Insight, Foresight' " in "Wisdom in Proverbs" in the introduction. In this context the word signifies not only insight that allows one to understand the present situation but most importantly "foresight" that allows one to avoid future difficulties (2:12–19). The context here ascribes this quality to God himself since it/he is able to "stand guard over" (שָׁמַר עַל-) the believer and preserve him in salvation.

תְּבוּנָה תִנְצְרֶכָּה׃—The *dagheshforte* in the suffix (-כָּה) reflects an energic *nun* that has been assimilated (for -ֶנְכָה with *daghesh lene*). See GKC, § 58 i.

2:12 לְהַצִּילְךָ מִדֶּרֶךְ רָע—The identical Hiphil (H) infinitive construct with לְ and the pronominal suffix -ךָ and followed by the preposition מִן begins 2:16. The Hiphil of נָצַל, "to save, deliver," occurs ten times in Proverbs. The Niphal (N) in 6:3, 5 has the reflexive sense, "save oneself" from entanglements with one's neighbor. The meaning of the verb is not always just physical, but usually it is also spiritual and eschatological. It refers to salvation that God bestows already now and that is evident in the life of the redeemed believer. Yet this salvation given by God through the wisdom imparted by his Word (2:6) will continue even after death in the resurrection to everlasting life (e.g., Dan 12:2–3).

מֵאִישׁ מְדַבֵּר תַּהְפֻּכוֹת׃—Divine wisdom intends to save the believer "from the man who speaks perverse things." Here the feminine plural noun תַּהְפֻּכוֹת is a true plural, "perverse things." In 2:14 it is an abstract plural, "perversity," and it recurs in 6:14; 8:13; 10:31–32; 16:28, 30; 23:33. Compare Waltke-O'Connor, § 7.4.2a, example 1, which suggests that it could have the meaning of an abstract plural here.

2:13–15 These verses are phrased in the plural, referring to evil men and their practices. They give an expanded description of the various kinds of people who are associated with the singular phrase in 2:12b (see the previous textual note). Divine wisdom intends to save the believer also from the kinds of wicked people portrayed in 2:13–15. The translation adds "from" to the start of 2:13 to clarify that the plural participles in 2:13–15, הָעֹזְבִים, "those who abandon," and הַשְּׂמֵחִים, "those who enjoy," are loosely in apposition to the phrase with a singular participle אִישׁ מְדַבֵּר, "the man who speaks," in 2:12b.

2:13 הַעֹזְבִים אָרְחוֹת יֹשֶׁר—Normally the article before ע has *qamets* (-הָע) but הַעֹזְבִים is an exception (Joüon, § 35 d). Another exception occurs in 2:17. Both verses have Qal (G) participles of עָזַב, "to abandon, leave, forsake." This verb occurs eleven times in Proverbs and generally signifies unbelief, apostasy from God, and departure from his ways.[a]

(a) Prov 2:13, 17; 3:3; 4:2, 6; 9:6; 10:17; 15:10; 27:10; 28:4, 13

The noun יֹשֶׁר, "straightness, uprightness," serves as an adjectival genitive in the construct phrase, hence "upright paths." It is cognate to יְשָׁרִים, "upright people," in 2:7 and to מֵישָׁרִים, "uprightness," in 2:9.

2:15 אֲשֶׁר אָרְחֹתֵיהֶם עִקְּשִׁים—The adjective "crooked" (עִקֵּשׁ) is an antonym to the words for "straight(ness), upright(ness)" in the preceding textual note. It recurs in 8:8; 11:20; 17:20; 19:1; 22:5; 28:6. The cognate verb עָקַשׁ, "to twist," occurs in 10:9 and 28:18. Elsewhere in the OT the adjective עִקֵּשׁ can describe the corrupt sinful heart (Ps 101:4) or a whole twisted generation of unfaithful people (Deut 32:5; cf. Acts 2:40; Phil

2:15). The advent of God in Christ requires—and causes—"the crooked places" to be made straight (τὰ σκολιά, Lk 3:5).

וּנְלוֹזִים בְּמַעְגְּלוֹתָם:—This Niphal (N) plural participle of the verb לוז, "depart, deviate," is used substantivally to denote "devious, perverted things." Forms of the verb recur in 3:21, 32; 4:21; 14:2 and the cognate noun לְזוּת occurs in 4:24. Solomon uses לוז to drive home the sinister harmfulness of sin against one's neighbor. He is teaching his son that sinners make conscious decisions to deceive and injure others. Sin has so corrupted all human thought and deliberation (Rom 3:10–18) that the sinners may actually rationalize and justify their actions as somehow beneficent (cf. Jn 16:2; Rom 6:1).

Commentary

Chapter 2 is the second address in Proverbs 1–9 from a father to a son.[5] It consists of twenty-two verses, the number of letters in the Hebrew alphabet. Although this is not a formal acrostic as is the poem in 31:10–31, it is built on the alphabet by employing the first and twelfth letters, א and ל, respectively.[6] The first letter, א, *aleph,* represents the first half of the alphabet (the first eleven letters) and the twelfth letter, ל, *lamed,* represents the second half of the alphabet (the second eleven letters). Just as an acrostic poem indicates completeness because it covers all the letters, so this poem signifies that divine wisdom confers every blessing and gift of grace from God (cf. Dan 1:4; Eph 1:8; Col 1:28).

The first letter of the alphabet, א, *aleph,* is featured in 2:1–11. The protasis (2:1–4) features a word beginning with א, namely, אִם, "if." Each apodosis (2:5–8 and 2:9–11) starts with a word beginning with א, namely, אָז, "then."

The twelfth letter of the alphabet, ל, *lamed,* dominates 2:12–22. Each of the three sections begins with a purpose clause with ל as the first letter, namely, לְהַצִּילְךָ, "to save you," in 2:12 and 2:16, and לְמַעַן, "so that," in 2:20.

- 2:1–4: אִם, "if." These verses form the protasis of the father's conditional sentence. He coaxes his son into seeking divine wisdom by repeating אִם, "if," three times (2:1, 3–4).
- 2:5–8: אָז, "then." These verses form the first apodosis, which begins with אָז, "then" (2:5). It contains the promise of obtaining wisdom given by Yahweh.
- 2:9–11: אָז, "then." The second apodosis also begins with אָז, "then" (2:9). It contains the promise of being protected by divine wisdom.
- 2:12–15: לְהַצִּילְךָ, "to save you." This purpose clause (2:12) introduces the intent of divine wisdom to save the son from evil, especially the actions of evil men (2:12b–15).
- 2:16–19: לְהַצִּילְךָ, "to save you." This purpose clause (2:16) introduces the goal of divine wisdom to save the son from the trap of illicit sex with a woman.
- 2:20–22: לְמַעַן, "so that." This third purpose clause (2:20) introduces the sanctifying benefit of divine wisdom. It enables righteous behavior (2:20) and reaps the blessing of enduring life (2:21).

---

[5] For the ten addresses from father to son in Proverbs 1–9, see the excursus "Proverbs 1–9, Christ, and the Ten Commandments" in the commentary on chapter 1.

[6] Murphy, *Wisdom Literature*, 56; Clifford, *Proverbs*, 45–46; Waltke, *Proverbs*, 1:216–17.

This chapter is a tightly organized poem. The conditional promise of wisdom ("if … then") occupies the first half and is divided into three sections, which consist of four verses (2:1–4), four verses (2:5–8), and three verses (2:9–11). After the customary address בְּנִי, "my son," in 2:1, each of the first three sections begins with the first letter of the first half of the alphabet, א, *aleph.*

The salvific purpose of wisdom occupies the second half of the poem, likewise divided into three sections, which consist of four verses (2:12–15), four verses (2:16–19), and three verses (2:20–22). Each section begins with the first letter of the second half of the alphabet, ל, *lamed.* The effect of this arrangement is to focus the son on wisdom as God's comprehensive gift and to help him desire it above all the sinful enticements of the world.

2:1–4 In the protasis the father begins his instruction by appealing to the son's inner desire to have wisdom. All people yearn to know their Creator, and the words from God spoken by the father to his son kindle faith and strengthen the resolve to understand God more intimately. The father speaks of his son accepting and treasuring his inspired words (2:1). He then guides his son to a more active role in his education as the son searches for wisdom by paying attention and reaching out (2:2). The son's desire both to learn of God and to live according to wisdom are the result of God himself working in him through his Word and Spirit (cf. Acts 10:44; Eph 1:13; Phil 2:13; 1 Thess 1:5–6). Finally, the father pictures his son as moving beyond simply being his student; the son matures into adulthood and is motivated to call for wisdom and search for it because of its supreme value (Prov 2:3–4). The father is setting forth a program of growth in divine knowledge and sanctification that is to occupy the son throughout his life.

2:5–8 In the first apodosis the father reminds his son of God's promise to confer knowledge. Here the father implies that the advice he is giving his son is not simply human insight. Instead the father is passing on God's wisdom, for God alone gives true knowledge and understanding through his Word (2:6). To those who listen to his Word, God promises to give the fear of Yahweh (faith), divine knowledge, and saving wisdom (2:5–6). God blesses his people with the ability to make sound judgments based on divine wisdom (2:7) instead of being seduced by sinful desires and the world (see 2:16–19). This ability is one way God protects his people as they live (2:7–8). These verses also introduce the metaphor of life's conduct as to "walk" along "paths" or a "way" (2:7–8). This metaphor is developed through 2:15 as the contrasting paths of wisdom and sin are explored.[7]

2:9–11 The second apodosis continues the metaphor of the path, linking it with three attributes that flow from wisdom: "righteousness," "justice," and "uprightness" (2:9). The promise of wisdom is expanded in two ways: it will be pleasant (2:10), and it will offer protection for everlasting life so that the son

[7] See further the excursus "The Metaphor of the Path in Solomon's Wisdom" in the commentary on chapter 10.

will not end up on the evil path (2:11–12), which leads to everlasting death and perdition (2:18; see also 5:5; 7:27; 8:36; 9:18).

2:12–15 Prov 2:12 begins the first of three sections in the chapter describing the redemptive purpose of wisdom: preservation from this evil path. The evil path is populated by those who have rejected wisdom and adopted the dark ways of sin (2:13–15), in contrast to 2:3–5, where the son is urged to seek wisdom and its enlightenment with understanding and knowledge. The father notes that such wicked people not only enjoy evil, they find joy in its very perversity (2:14; cf. Rom 1:22–32). Their fiendish delight contrasts with the pleasure that the son will find in knowing God's wisdom, which is "pleasant to your soul" (Prov 2:10). These contrasts are intended to function together to move the son to love wisdom. The promises draw the son toward God and his wisdom, while the description of the evil path is designed to lead the son to reject as harmful the perverse ways of those who engage in the twisted behaviors of sin. This interplay of Law and Gospel is designed to skillfully accomplish the purpose of bringing the son to find comfort and joy in God's wisdom:

> When law and Gospel are opposed to each other, … the Gospel is … a comforting and joyful message which does not reprove or terrify but comforts consciences that are frightened by the law, directs them solely to the merit of Christ, and raises them up again by the delightful proclamation of God's grace and favor acquired through the merits of Christ. (FC Ep V 7)

Proverbs 2:16–19

An Example of Wisdom's Protection: Protection from the Adulterous Woman

Translation

2 [16]To save you from the woman who is a stranger,
from the foreign woman who makes her words smooth,
[17]who abandons the companion of her youth
and forgets the covenant of her God.
[18]Therefore, she sinks down to death, her house,
and her pathways [sink] to the souls of the dead.
[19]All who go into her never return,
nor do they [ever] reach the paths of life.

Textual Notes

2:16 לְהַצִּילְךָ מֵאִשָּׁה זָרָה—This verse begins with the same infinitive construct as 2:12a, expressing the purpose of divine wisdom. See the first textual note on 2:12 and the commentary on 2:12–15. The father implored his son in 2:10–12 to allow Yahweh to fill his heart with wisdom "*to save you* from the evil way, *from the man* …" (לְהַצִּילְךָ מִדֶּרֶךְ רָע מֵאִישׁ …, 2:12). Now 2:16 adds the corresponding promise that divine wisdom intends "*to save you from the woman* …" (לְהַצִּילְךָ מֵאִשָּׁה …).

This woman is described as זָרָה, the feminine of the adjective זָר, which may be the participle of the verb זור (so BDB), "be a stranger; be foreign." Describing a person, the adjective signifies someone who is alien or incompatible in some way, either a foreigner or a person who is unauthorized, prohibited, or illicit (*HALOT*). Often translated as "strange," the point here is that she is a stranger to the son who is being instructed in divine wisdom. It does not mean that she is a "strange woman" in the sense that something is wrong about her appearance or mannerisms.

There has been much discussion about the identity of this woman. Is she the same as the other seductive women in Proverbs 1–9? The אִשָּׁה זָרָה is mentioned again in the similar purpose clause in 7:5a. In 5:3, 20 the woman is simply זָרָה, while in 6:24 we find אֵשֶׁת רָע, "a woman of evil," that is, "an evil woman," and in 6:26 אִשָּׁה זוֹנָה, "a woman (who is) a prostitute," and אֵשֶׁת אִישׁ, "a wife of a[nother] man," that is, "a married woman." Prov 7:10 describes "a woman [אִשָּׁה] … dressed as a prostitute [זוֹנָה]." אִשָּׁה זָרָה in 2:16 and 7:5; זָרָה in 5:20; and אֵשֶׁת רָע in 6:24 are all parallel to נָכְרִיָּה, "a foreign woman."

These are best understood as varying descriptions of the same type of woman, just as the varying descriptions of knowledge, insight, and understanding in 2:10–11 are all aspects of the same concept, wisdom.[1] In describing this woman as a "stranger" and

---

1 Yee, "I Have Perfumed My Bed with Myrrh," 54.

a "foreign woman," Solomon is not necessarily describing a non-Israelite woman. In fact, this woman is depicted as participating in Israel's sacrificial system (7:14). Rather, he is indicating that the woman is not his son's wife and so is "foreign" to his son, and 2:17 implies that she is another man's wife. She tempts young men with illicit sex, but this would violate the biblical mandate that the marriage of a man and his wife is the only legitimate and holy relationship in which sexual intimacy is permitted by God.

מִנָּכְרִיָּה אֲמָרֶיהָ הֶחֱלִיקָה׃—The identical clause, literally, "from the foreign woman—her words she makes smooth," recurs in 7:5b. The Hiphil (H) of חָלַק, "make smooth, slippery, deceptive," occurs in 2:16; 7:5; 28:23; 29:5, all referring to words or speech. It could be rendered to "flatter" (so KJV) or to attempt verbally to "deceive, seduce." The related noun חֵלֶק, "smoothness, seductiveness" of speech, occurs in 7:21, and the synonymous noun חֶלְקָה is in 6:24. The adjective חָלָק, "smooth, deceptive," refers to speaking in 5:3 and 26:28.

2:17 הַעֹזֶבֶת אַלּוּף נְעוּרֶיהָ—The feminine participle of עָזַב may apply to present time, "who abandons, who is now forsaking, leaving," in contrast to a verbal construction that would clearly refer to past time. This may suggest that the woman is still married to another man, so she is an adulteress, not a divorcee or widow. "The companion of her youth" refers to the woman's husband. In the biblical era, marriage normally was after physical maturity but still at a relatively young age. The abstract plural נְעוּרִים, "youth," is used with suffixes elsewhere to describe the wife of a man's youth (Prov 5:18; Mal 2:14–15) and a bridegroom betrothed to a virgin in her youth (Joel 1:8). The word is also used figuratively for Israel as Yahweh's spiritual bride (Is 54:6; Jer 2:2).

Normally the article before ע has *qamets* (-הָע) but הַעֹזֶבֶת is an exception (Joüon, § 35 d). For another exception with a participle of the same verb, see the textual note on 2:13.

וְאֶת־בְּרִית אֱלֹהֶיהָ שָׁכֵחָה׃—This is the only occurrence of בְּרִית in Proverbs. "The covenant of her God" is her marriage. The marriage covenant is not just between a man and woman, but also between both of them and God. Mal 2:14 refers to marriage as a "covenant" (בְּרִית), and Yahweh testifies against any unfaithful husband because God is the one who has joined the spouses (Mal 2:15). שָׁכֵחָה is the pausal form of the Qal (G) perfect. The perfect aspect of verbs of cognition is often used with a present meaning, so it is translated as "forgets."

2:18 כִּי שָׁחָה אֶל־מָוֶת בֵּיתָהּ—This means "therefore, she sinks down to death, [which is] her house." The rare verb שׁוּחַ, "sink down, descend," probably is related to nouns for a "pit" (שׁוּחָה, שִׁיחָה, and שַׁחַת). Since שָׁחָה is a feminine perfect, the masculine noun בַּיִת cannot be its subject.[2] The woman must be the subject, even though the result is that it becomes difficult to interpret the syntax of אֶל־מָוֶת בֵּיתָהּ. However, the syntactical awkwardness is intentional in order to call the son's attention to the woman's deadly abode.[3] The LXX translates this difficult clause as ἔθετο γὰρ παρὰ τῷ θανάτῳ τὸν οἶκον

---

2 Longman, *Proverbs*, 123–25, ignores the grammatical inconsistency and translates בַּיִת as the subject of שָׁחָה. He then denies that there is any awkwardness in the syntax of this line.

3 Waltke notes the awkwardness of this verse and gives a history of attempts to deal with it (*Proverbs*, 1:215–16, n. 24).

αὐτῆς, "for she sets her house next to death." However, בֵּיתָהּ, "her house," should be understood as an appositive to מָוֶת, defining "death." That is, the woman's "house" *is* "death."[4] This is where she lives once she chooses to commit adultery. This image is intended to frighten the son so that he is not attracted to her.

Emerton proposes that שָׁחָה be repointed to the noun שַׁחָה, "pit," so that the clause would be nominal and mean "for her house [is] a pit (leading) to death."[5] The implication of the passage would be the same, but it is better to follow the awkward syntax of the clause rather than emend in order to eliminate it.

וְאֶל־רְפָאִים מַעְגְּלֹתֶיהָ:—The noun רְפָאִים, which recurs in 9:18 and 21:16, is always plural in the OT and denotes the dead (*HALOT*, b) whose souls have departed their bodies for שְׁאוֹל (9:18).

2:19 כָּל־בָּאֶיהָ—The verb בּוֹא with the preposition אֶל, "to go into, enter," is a common euphemism for sexual intercourse.[a] The pronominal suffix on the plural participle here serves as an indirect object in lieu of a preposition; כָּל־בָּאֶיהָ means "all who go into her" (see Joüon, § 121 n; GKC, §§ 116 h and i).

(a) E.g., Gen 16:2; 29:21; 30:3, 16; 38:8, 16; Judg 15:1; 2 Sam 16:21–22; 20:3; Ps 51:2 (ET: superscription)

As usual in Hebrew, the participle is continued by finite verb forms (Joüon, § 121 j), the two negated imperfects later in the verse: לֹא יְשׁוּבוּן, literally, "they will not return," and וְלֹא־יַשִּׂיגוּ (from נָשַׂג), literally, "they will not attain, reach."

Commentary

These verses (2:16–19) continue the father's second address to his son (2:1–22).[6] Just as the father's first example of divine wisdom's purpose was to keep his son safe from the evil man (2:12b, and evil men in 2:13–15), so this second example mentions safety from the evil woman, the adulteress. Her temptation imitates and mirrors the appeal of divine wisdom, which comes from Yahweh's mouth through his Word (2:6). Similarly, in the NT when the devil tempts Christ, he cites (but misconstrues) the Word of God (Mt 4:1–11; cf. 2 Cor 11:14).

It is the words of this seductive woman, not her appearance or her actions, that the father depicts as her appeal ("who makes her words smooth," 2:16).[7] This woman is portrayed as abandoning her husband and her marriage covenant, made before her God (2:17), just as evil men abandon God's upright paths (2:13). The father depicts the temptation to adultery as a sinkhole, leading inescapably to death (2:18). This description is intended to horrify the son so that he will flee this trap from which there is no chance of escape to obtain life (2:19).

While the father's exhortation is first of all a direct warning against breaking the Sixth Commandment, it also serves as a warning against spiritual adultery, straying from God to worship foreign gods or allowing anything to take God's

---

4 Kidner, *Proverbs*, 62.

5 Emerton, "A Note on Proverbs II. 18."

6 For the structure of the chapter as a whole, see the commentary on 2:1–15.

7 Aletti, "Séduction et parole en Proverbes I–IX"; Yee, "I Have Perfumed My Bed with Myrrh"; Murphy, "Wisdom and Eros in Proverbs 1–9."

place, including (but not limited to) one's sexual desires.[8] This is signaled by the description of the woman as someone who "forgets the covenant of her God," which first refers to her violation of her marriage covenant (see the second textual note on 2:17). Yet the phraseology reminds the son that straying from one's spouse has a spiritual counterpart: straying from one's God, whose covenant at Sinai made the people of Israel his own (Jer 31:32). God's people were to remain faithful to him just as a spouse is to remain faithful. Adultery and other sexual sins are incompatible with faith, and unless one repents of them, they will prevent a person from entering the eternal kingdom of God (e.g., Rom 1:18–32; 1 Cor 6:9–20; Gal 5:19–21).

This is why the woman "sinks down to death" and her pathways lead those who sin with her down to the abode of dead souls (Prov 2:18). Surely both Solomon and his son know that adultery does not necessarily result in physical death immediately (although bodily death may be one of its consequences). Yet 2:18 is not simply hyperbole about the consequences of adultery. Instead Solomon is inviting his son and his readers to contemplate the analogy of marriage to the relationship between God and his people, an analogy that is found throughout Scripture.[9] Abandoning God by losing one's faith (or never receiving faith) is so serious that perishing in unbelief results in an irreversible state of eternal death (Heb 6:4–6). The father urgently calls on his son to consider what he would lose if he were to succumb to the lure of the temptations presented by the world, the devil, and the sinful flesh.[10] They lead away from Christ and his blessings, and toward death and eternal condemnation.

---

[8] See further the excursus "Wisdom and the Adulteress in Proverbs 1–9" after the commentary on 2:16–19, as well as the excursus "Proverbs 1–9, Christ, and the Ten Commandments" in the commentary on chapter 1.

[9] For this theme in Scripture, see, for example, Song of Songs; Is 61:10; Ezekiel 16 and 23; Hosea 1–3; Jn 3:29; 2 Cor 11:2; Eph 5:21–33.

[10] While writing this warning, Solomon may have borne in mind the troubles, some of them deadly, caused by the adultery of his father, David, with his mother, Bathsheba (2 Samuel 11–20).

Excursus

Wisdom and the Adulteress in Proverbs 1–9

Even the most casual reader of Proverbs 1–9 cannot help but notice that one particular sin is condemned repeatedly in these chapters: adultery. It is a major topic in the father's second address (2:1–22) and is the topic under discussion in the seventh, ninth, and tenth addresses (5:1–23; 6:20–35; 7:1–27).[1] Why this concentration on one particular sin? Was it more widespread in Solomon's day? The Scriptures give no indication that this was the case. Instead the contrast between divine Wisdom and the adulterous woman is an important way for Solomon to commend Wisdom and turn his son from foolishness.[2]

There are a number of similarities between Wisdom and the adulteress that serve in the end to contrast the two (see also the figure 7, "Contrasts between the Two Women," in the commentary on 6:20–35). Both attempt to attract the young man by their words. However, only the adulteress is depicted as making her words deceptively smooth (2:16; 7:5; cf. 26:23). The metaphor of the path is applied to both.[3] Wisdom's path is pleasant (3:17), whereas the adulteress' path leads to spiritual and everlasting death (2:18; 5:5; 7:27; 9:18; see also the rejection of Wisdom in 8:36). This leads to the impression that Wisdom is the opposite of the adulteress, just as Lady Wisdom is the opposite of the woman Foolishness in Proverbs 9.[4]

This impression is reinforced by the similarities between Wisdom and a good wife. Proverbs encourages one to "find" Wisdom (מָצָא, 3:13; 8:17, 35) just as one "finds" a good wife (מָצָא, 18:22; 31:10). Especially important in this regard are 8:35 and 18:22. In 8:35 the one who finds Wisdom finds "life," and "he obtains favor from Yahweh" (וַיָּפֶק רָ֝צ֗וֹן מֵיְהוָֽה). In 18:22 the one who finds a wife "finds a good thing" (טוֹב), and "he obtains favor from Yahweh" (וַיָּפֶק רָ֝צ֗וֹן מֵיְהוָֽה). Moreover, Proverbs encourages one to "love" Wisdom (אָהֵב, 4:6; 8:17, 21) and "embrace" her (the Piel [D] of חָבַק, 4:8). A man is to love his wife (cf. אֲהָבִים, "loving," in 5:19) and not "embrace" the adulteress (the Piel of חָבַק, 5:20). Wisdom will help the young man avoid the adulteress (7:4–5) as will a wife (5:15–20). In fact, the son is to address Wisdom as his wife; he

---

1 For the ten addresses from a father to his son in Proverbs 1–9, see the excursus "Proverbs 1–9, Christ, and the Ten Commandments" in the commentary on chapter 1.

2 See also the commentary on 2:16–19.

3 See the excursus "The Metaphor of the Path in Solomon's Wisdom" in the commentary on chapter 10.

4 The commentary on 9:13–18 discusses the similar language used for the woman Foolishness and the adulteress. It also discusses the sexual imagery in the depiction of the woman Foolishness.

should call her "my sister" (אֲחֹתִי, 7:4) the same term of endearment Solomon applies to his wife (Song 4:9–10, 12; 5:1–2).[5]

Solomon's strategy, then, is to commend Wisdom by a positive and a negative analogy to concrete human relationships, marriage and adultery, since each physical relationship also has its spiritual implications. Negatively, sexual immorality shows a lack of faith and therefore excludes the immoral from the everlasting kingdom of God (1 Cor 6:9–20; Gal 5:19–21; cf. Rev 2:20–23). Positively, the faithful marriage of believers is a picture of the great mystery of Christ's salvific union with his bride, the church (Eph 5:21–33). Yet it is not a human wedding that saves, but union with Christ by faith and membership in his bride, the church, which includes all baptized believers, whether single or married, divorced or widowed (Eph 5:26; Revelation 21–22).

The faithful son will find benefits in Wisdom just as he does in his wife. The son will find sin and death in Foolishness (Prov 9:13–18; and in rejecting Wisdom, 8:36) just as he does in the adulteress (2:18; 5:5; 7:27). Solomon wants his readers to take seriously his condemnation of adultery, the sin that was punished by death in the OT (Lev 20:10; Deut 22:22–24) and that kills marriage (Mt 5:32; 19:9). At the same time, the negative example of adultery is intended to reinforce the greater positive message about divine Wisdom and its power to deliver believers from all kinds of sin and preserve them in a life of faithfulness. God's Wisdom, incarnate in Christ, saves all believers and preserves them to life everlasting in union with the triune God.

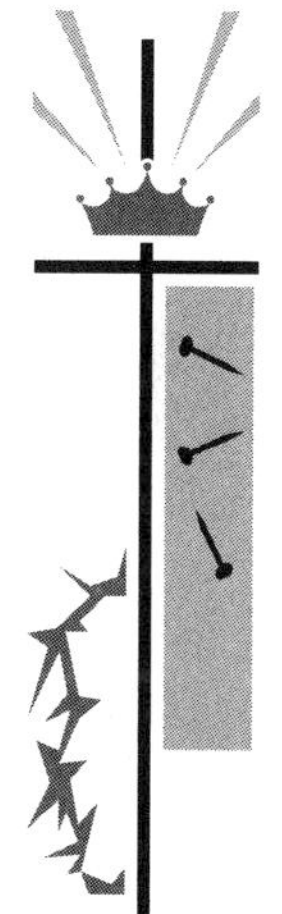

This interplay between Wisdom and the wife, the adulteress and Foolishness, underscores Solomon's use of Law and Gospel throughout Proverbs 1–9.[6] The Law condemns the foolish son who strays from God's Law into adultery and foolishness. The Gospel, in the form of Wisdom, proclaims God's benefits, brings God's forgiveness and gracious favor, and bestows everlasting life (8:35).

Since Wisdom is ultimately Christ, the incarnate Wisdom of God,[7] Solomon is employing these positive and negative analogies to draw his son and his readers toward the Savior, to allow them to see him as more attractive than sinful enticements in the world, although to the world the Suffering Servant is most "despised and rejected among men" and "like one from whom men hid their faces" (Is 53:3); Christ crucified is "foolishness" (1 Cor 1:18–24). The world finds sexual licentiousness attractive and views marriage as nothing more than

---

[5] For the Song verses with "my sister," one may see Mitchell, *The Song of Songs*, 825–26, including n. 23, who compares "my sister" in the Song to Prov 7:4 and to 1 Cor 9:5, where the apostle refers to ἀδελφὴν γυναῖκα, "a sister-wife," that is, a Christian wife, who is a sister in Christ.

[6] See further "Law and Gospel in Proverbs" in the introduction.

[7] For Wisdom as incarnate in Christ and as God's saving gift to all believers, see "Wisdom in Proverbs" in the introduction. See also the commentary on 1:1–7; 3:13–20; 8:22–31; 30:1b–10; and the excursus "Proverbs 8, Wisdom, Christology, and the Arian Controversy" in the commentary on chapter 8.

a human convenience.[8] Its contempt for Christ is parallel to its disregard for the holiness of marriage as an institution created by God. Solomon wants his son to see beyond the world's distorted view so that he understands that in Christ one finds what is not only attractive but also the only true and enduring blessing that satisfies the desires of the soul. The contrast between Wisdom and the adulteress allows Solomon to vividly portray this truth to his son.

---

[8] In modern times some have even attempted to redefine marriage as possibly applying to other relationships besides the lifelong union of one man and one woman. Such redefinitions are contrary to God's Word and are condemned by it.

Proverbs 2:20–22

Admonition to Live Righteously

Translation

2 [20]**So that you walk in the way of good people**
and stay on the paths of righteous people,
[21]**because upright people will live in the land,**
and people of integrity will remain in it,
[22]**but wicked people will be cut off from the land,**
and treacherous people will be torn out from it.

Textual Notes

2:20–22 לְמַעַן—These verses begin with a purpose clause, "so that …" This compound preposition (לְ with מַעַן) is parallel to the preposition לְ on the infinitive לְהַצִּילְךָ, "to save you," in 2:12, 16. See the commentary on 2:1–15 for an explanation of the acrostic significance of לְ and for how 2:20–22 fits into the structure of chapter 2 as a whole.

טוֹבִים ... צַדִּיקִים ... יְשָׁרִים ... וּתְמִימִים ... וּרְשָׁעִים ... וּבוֹגְדִים—Masculine plural forms are used here to denote people in general, not males in particular. The previous two sections used אִישׁ (2:12) and אִשָּׁה (2:16) specifically for a pernicious "man" and adulterous "woman," respectively. This section speaks of people of both sexes: God's faithful believers in 2:20–21 and apostate unbelievers in 2:22. Hebrew commonly uses the masculine plural to denote groups consisting of people of both genders, whereas feminine plurals normally refer to groups of women only. Here the father wants the son to see that the path he is to take is one for both men and women who fear Yahweh (2:20–21), whereas the both wicked men and women will perish eternally (2:22).

2:20 טוֹבִים—See "Good People" in "Authorship and Date" in the introduction.

צַדִּיקִים—Regarding "righteous people," see "The Relationship between Wisdom and Righteousness in Proverbs" in "Wisdom in Proverbs" in the introduction.

2:21 יְשָׁרִים—For "straight, upright people," see the first textual note and the commentary on 2:7.

וּתְמִימִים—In 1:12 this means "whole." Here is the first time in Proverbs that the adjective תָּמִים is used substantively in the theological sense of "person of/with integrity, blameless person," as also in 11:5; 28:10, 18 (cf. 11:20). It connotes forensic justification and so is a synonym of צַדִּיק, "righteous (person)," in 2:20. It implies that all sins are forgiven by grace alone, and it also involves a sanctified life with righteous behavior. תָּמִים is synonymous with the adjective תָּם in 29:10. Both are cognate to the noun תֹּם and תֻּמָּה, "integrity, blamelessness," for which, see the second textual note on 2:7. The NT uses several terms to call believers "blameless." See, for example, ἄμωμος in Eph 1:4; Col 1:22; Jude 24; Rev 14:5 and ἄμεμπτος in Lk 1:6; Phil 2:15 (cf. 1 Thess 3:13). These passages reveal that this involves both justification and sanctification. It

is the work of God in Christ (not human striving) that renders a person blameless and with integrity. See also ἄμωμος, "blameless, without blemish," applied to the whole church in Eph 5:27.

2:22 וּרְשָׁעִים מֵאֶרֶץ יִכָּרֵתוּ—This is the first of seventy-eight occurrences of the adjective רָשָׁע in Proverbs. It means "*wicked ... guilty of hostility* to God or his people ... *guilty of sin*, against either God or man" (BDB). Usually the adjective is used as a substantive, as here: "wicked people."

In Proverbs כָּרַת is always used in the Niphal (N), which has the passive meaning "be cut off" (2:22; 10:31; 23:18; 24:14). The eschatological implication of the verb is clear in 23:18 and 24:14, which refer to future, end-time hope. For the wicked to be "cut off" refers not only to temporal death but also to everlasting separation from God and his life (cf. Gen 17:14; Ex 31:14; Num 15:30–31).

וּבוֹגְדִים יִסְּחוּ מִמֶּנָּה׃—The verb בָּגַד means "deal treacherously with" (*HALOT*, 1) or "act deceitfully, faithlessly." In Proverbs it always occurs as a participle used substantivally, "treacherous people" (also 11:3, 6; 13:2, 15; 23:28; and the singular in 21:18; 22:12; 25:19). The verb can refer to violating the covenant with God (Hos 6:7; cf. Is 48:8); to acting treacherously toward other members of God's people so as to violate his covenant (Mal 2:10); or to being unfaithful to the marriage covenant, which is an offense against God (Mal 2:14–15; cf. Jer 3:8, 11, 20; Prov 2:17).

The verb נָסַח, "tear away/out," occurs elsewhere only in the covenant curse in Deut 28:63 that unfaithful Israel will be torn from the promised land; in Ps 52:7 (ET 52:5); and again in Proverbs in 15:25. The Qal (G) imperfect here יִסְּחוּ, with an active meaning, is preceded by its direct object, וּבוֹגְדִים, literally, "they shall tear out the treacherous (people) from it [the land]." The impersonal verb is best translated as a passive (GKC, § 144 g; cf. Waltke-O'Connor, § 23.6.1d) with its object as the subject: "treacherous people will be torn out from it."

Commentary

The father's third and concluding purpose clause (2:20–22) in the chapter once again uses contrast to draw the son to God's promise.[1] Life, as opposed to the seductress' trap of death (2:16–19), is the destination of the path that the son is urged to take (2:20–21). At the same time, the son is once again led to reject the sinful behavior of wicked people by the portrayal of their rejection by God in violent terms: "cut off" and "torn out" (2:22). Unlike God's active role in conferring the blessing of wisdom in 2:6, the passive verb in 2:22a and the impersonal construction in 2:22b only hint at God as the one who will mete out everlasting punishment to sinners. In this way Solomon emphasizes that God's desire is to lead the son and all people to wisdom. The God of grace takes no delight in punishing the wicked (Ezek 18:23, 32). God is "our Savior, who desires all people to be saved and to come to the knowledge of the truth" (1 Tim

[1] For the structure of chapter 2, see the commentary on 2:1–15.

2:3–4; cf. 2 Pet 3:9). Yet when the wicked refuse to repent, God will judge them according to his justice.[2]

Remaining in the land or being torn out of it implies more than physical life or death; it points to eternal consequences. Prov 2:21–22 are the first two verses in the book to refer to אֶרֶץ, which can refer more narrowly to the "land" or more broadly to the whole "earth." Solomon's immediate focus likely is on the land of Israel—the promised land, which Yahweh had graciously given his covenant people as their home. It was in this land that Yahweh dwelt incarnationally in the midst of his people through his temple, where he furnished the forgiveness of sins and everlasting life (see 1 Kings 8). During the era of Solomon, life in this land meant life with the God of Israel, and to be cut off from this land meant separation from God and loss of spiritual life.

Yet this passage also has universal and eschatological implications. Israel would forfeit the promised land during the exile, and the covenant nation would end forever in AD 70, when the Romans destroyed the Jerusalem temple, never again to be rebuilt. In the NT era, Jesus the Messiah redefined the kingdom of God as his worldwide kingdom of grace: the universal church, the body of Christ. In this light, אֶרֶץ points to the whole "earth," as the Hebrew term is usually understood in Ps 37:11: "the meek/humble will inherit the earth." Jesus employs the Greek equivalent γῆ in the beatitude:

> Blessed are the meek,
> for they shall inherit the earth. (Mt 5:5)

The real goal of God's people is not any land or city on this earth, nor any position or possessions in this life. Rather, believers look forward to the new heavens and new earth (Isaiah 11; 65:17–25). They "desire a better land, that is, a heavenly one. Therefore God is not ashamed to be called their God; indeed, he has prepared a city for them" (Heb 11:16; cf. Heb 12:22, 13:14; Revelation 21).

---

2 See the discussion of God's will in justification and damnation in FC SD XI ("Eternal Foreknowledge and Divine Election") 81–84.

Proverbs 3:1–20

Third Address to a Son: Wisdom Leads to a Proper Relationship with Yahweh

Translation

3 [1]My son, do not forget my teaching,
and let your heart keep my commands,
[2]because they will add length of days, years of life,
and wholeness to you.
[3]Do not allow mercy and truth to leave you.
Fasten them around your neck;
write them on the tablet of your heart.
[4]Then you will find favor and good sense
in the eyes of God and humans.
[5]Trust in Yahweh with all your heart,
and do not rely on your own understanding.
[6]In all your ways acknowledge him,
and he will make your paths straight.
[7]Do not consider yourself wise.
Fear Yahweh, and turn away from evil.
[8]Then your body will be healed,
and your bones will be refreshed.
[9]Honor Yahweh with your wealth
and with the first part of your entire harvest.
[10]Then your barns will be filled to capacity
and your winepresses will burst with fresh wine.
[11]Do not reject Yahweh's discipline, my son,
and do not despise his warning,
[12]because Yahweh warns the one whom he loves
like a father [warns] a son with whom he is pleased.

[13]Blessed is the person who finds Wisdom
and the person who acquires Understanding,
[14]because her profit is greater than profit from silver,
and her harvest [is better] than gold.
[15]She is more valuable than jewels,
and all the things you desire cannot equal her.
[16]In her right hand is length of days;
in her left hand are riches and honor.
[17]Her ways are pleasant ways,
and all her pathways are peace.
[18]She is a tree of life for those who hold on to her;
those who cling to her are blessed.

19Yahweh founded the earth by Wisdom;
he established the heavens by Understanding.
20By his knowledge the deep waters were divided,
and the clouds drip dew.

Textual Notes

3:1 בְּנִי תּוֹרָתִי אַל־תִּשְׁכָּח—For תּוֹרָה, see the second textual note on 1:8.

וּמִצְוֹתַי יִצֹּר לִבֶּךָ׃—Since יִצֹּר is parallel to the negative command, אַל־תִּשְׁכָּח, in the preceding clause, this form of נָצַר probably is jussive: "*let* your heart keep," serving as an exhortation. נָצַר generally means "keep watch, watch over" or "protect, preserve" (*HALOT*, 1, 2). The father is not simply exhorting his son to keep the father's teaching in his heart, but also to be vigilant about preserving that teaching since it is designed to give the son Wisdom and is a revelation of God's holy Word (cf. 2:6). This verb occurs nineteen times in Proverbs (including the Qere in 23:26), and Solomon exploits its semantic range, bringing out its various nuances. It can be a synonym of the more common verb שָׁמַר, "keep, guard," and occur together with it, as in 2:8, 11. But it can have other meanings, as in, for example, 27:18, where it means "tend" a fig tree. Thus it is translated with several different words, depending on context. However, it always implies diligence and vigilance.

3:2 כִּי אֹרֶךְ יָמִים וּשְׁנוֹת חַיִּים וְשָׁלוֹם יוֹסִיפוּ לָךְ׃—The three divine gifts—the direct objects—are emphasized by placing them before the verb, literally, "because length of days and years of life and peace they will add to you." The implied subject ("they") of the verb probably is both of the feminine nouns in 3:1, the singular תּוֹרָתִי, "my teaching," and the plural מִצְוֹתַי, "my commandments," even though the verb here, יוֹסִיפוּ, is masculine.

The construct phrase אֹרֶךְ יָמִים, "length of days," occurs twice in this chapter (3:2, 16) and seven times elsewhere in the OT (Deut 30:20 [with a suffix]; Pss 21:5 [ET 21:4]; 23:6; 91:16; 93:5; Job 12:12; Lam 5:20). It denotes long life under God's grace and blessing and has the eschatological nuance of eternal life in God's presence (Pss 21:5 [ET 21:4]; 23:6). Similar in meaning are expressions with the Hiphil (H) of the verb אָרַךְ and the object יָמִים, "to prolong (one's) days," that is, to enjoy long (and everlasting) life, in divine promises in Prov 28:16 and also, for example, Ex 20:12; Deut 4:40; 5:16, 33; 6:2; 32:47.

The construct phrase שְׁנוֹת חַיִּים, "years of life," occurs in the OT only in Prov 3:2; 4:10; 9:11 (cf., e.g., Gen 23:1; 25:7). It too is an indefinite time period that extends into the eschatological future, anticipating the resurrection to eternal life.

Frequently translated as "peace," שָׁלוֹם denotes wholeness or completeness of a condition.[1] Its nuance depends on the context. It can denote health and well-being (Gen 29:6) or political peace (Judg 4:17), as well as many other ideal conditions. Here it denotes a fullness of life that comes as God's blessing on the one who takes the father's

1 "The primary meaning of the word can be characterised as the healthiness, or the completeness, or the intactness of a community" (*HALOT*, 1507, citing Westermann, "Der Frieden (*Shalom*) im Alten Testament," 200).

instruction to heart. Without the blessing of God, life cannot be full or complete (cf. Jn 10:10b).

3:3 חֶסֶד וֶאֱמֶת אַל־יַעַזְבֻךָ—The noun חֶסֶד, "mercy, kindness," is difficult to translate. It denotes a special attitude or act toward someone that exceeds the normal, expected attitude or action.[2] Scripture repeatedly affirms that Yahweh's חֶסֶד endures forever.[a] Thus חֶסֶד often points to God's grace, his attitude and actions toward his people, who cannot by their own merits expect his mercy or kindness.

(a) Jer 33:11; Pss 100:5; 106:1; 107:1; 118:1–4, 29; 136:1–26; 138:8; Ezra 3:11; 1 Chr 16:34, 41; 2 Chr 5:13; 7:3, 6; 20:21

The phrase חֶסֶד וֶאֱמֶת is the subject of the negated third person jussive אַל־יַעַזְבֻךָ, literally, "may mercy and truth not leave you." However, it is the son or reader who would cause "mercy and truth" to leave by disbelieving and rejecting them. Therefore the verb is translated as second person: "do not allow mercy and truth to leave you."

קָשְׁרֵם עַל־גַּרְגְּרוֹתֶיךָ—The identical Qal (G) imperative of קָשַׁר, "to fasten, bind, tie," with third masculine plural suffix recurs in similar contexts in 6:21 and 7:3. This language recalls Deut 6:8.[3] Contrast Prov 22:15, where stupidity is "fastened, bound tightly" (קְשׁוּרָה) to the heart of a youth. For גַּרְגְּרוֹתֶיךָ, "your neck," see the second textual note on 1:9.

כָּתְבֵם עַל־לוּחַ לִבֶּךָ׃—The identical clause recurs in 7:3b. For the form of the Qal (G) imperative with suffix, כָּתְבֵם, see Joüon, § 64 a. The noun לוּחַ, "tablet," is the same word used in Ex 24:12 to denote the stone tablets upon which the Ten Commandments were written. The Qal of כָּתַב, "to write," whose imperative is here (כָּתְבֵם), is the same verb as in Ex 24:12, where Yahweh states that he "wrote" the Decalogue on the tablets. Moreover, in Ex 24:12 Yahweh said that he wrote "the teaching and the commandment" (וְהַתּוֹרָה וְהַמִּצְוָה), and the plural of the second noun refers to the father's "commands" in Prov 3:1.

Therefore Solomon, the father, is consciously comparing his commands (3:1) to God's commands to Israel at Sinai, because Solomon is writing under divine inspiration and his teaching is the revealed Word of God. Just like the Torah of Moses, the Proverbs of Solomon with their divine Wisdom are spoken by Yahweh himself (cf. 2:6). The book of Proverbs is authoritative and normative just like the other books of sacred Scripture.

To appropriate God's Word rightly involves more than reading it. Its teaching also needs to be internalized, which can only be accomplished by the Spirit of God working through the Word itself. The Spirit, working through Solomon's inspired words, grants the believer the power to do what the father invites the son to do. The commands of the father echo the commands of God himself, through which the Spirit works. The Lutheran Confessions emphasize that Christians should not attempt to find or be led by the Spirit apart from God's Word and Sacraments, since it is through these external means of grace that the Spirit works and God speaks to us clearly:

---

[2] For a discussion of חֶסֶד as shown by God and by his faithful people, see Wilch, *Ruth*, 30–37, 64–78.

[3] See the excursus "The Use of Deuteronomy 6:4–9 in Proverbs 3:1–12 and 6:20–22" after the commentary on 3:1–20.

> God will not deal with us except through his external Word and sacrament. Whatever is attributed to the Spirit apart from such Word and sacrament is of the devil. For even to Moses God wished to appear first through the burning bush and the spoken word, and no prophet, whether Elijah or Elisha, received the Spirit without the Ten Commandments. John the Baptist was not conceived without the preceding word of Gabriel, nor did he leap in his mother's womb until Mary spoke. St. Peter says that when the prophets spoke, they did not prophesy by the impulse of man but were moved by the Holy Spirit [2 Pet 1:21]. (SA III VIII 10–13)

3:4 וּמְצָא־חֵן וְשֵׂכֶל־טוֹב—After the imperatives in 3:3, the imperative וּמְצָא, "and find," here serves to introduce a result clause and promise: "then you will find" (see GKC, § 110 f; Joüon, § 116 f). For חֵן, "grace," see the first textual note on 1:9. The emphasis here is on God's gracious disposition toward the wise believer, but the next clause states that "grace" here also includes the favor and goodwill of other people.

In this context "good sense" (שֵׂכֶל־טוֹב) seems to imply that God and other humans will recognize the good sense possessed by a person who follows the instructions set forth here. See "שֵׂכֶל, 'Good Sense,' and הִשְׂכִּיל, 'to Act Sensibly' " in "Wisdom in Proverbs" in the introduction.

בְּעֵינֵי אֱלֹהִים וְאָדָם׃—"In/with the eyes of" is used sixteen times in Proverbs and over three hundred times in the OT. Sometimes it has a literal meaning (1:17; 6:13). However, it usually refers to the attitude or opinion of the person(s) in the following genitive, here "God and humans." Since here אָדָם is contrasted with אֱלֹהִים, "God," its sense is "humans" in general, not specifically "men" versus women (cf. *HALOT*, 1).

Perhaps a less figurative English idiom would be "in the opinion of" or "in the consideration of." See also the first textual note on 3:7. Of course, when something is esteemed by God, is it unquestionably good and right since his authoritative viewpoint takes precedence over all others.

3:5 בְּטַח אֶל־יְהוָה בְּכָל־לִבֶּךָ—This is the first of ten occurrences in Proverbs of the verb בָּטַח, "to trust."[b] Usually it takes the preposition בְּ, "to trust *in*," but sometimes it takes עַל or, as here, אֶל (BDB, s.v. בָּטַח, I 5). Frequently it refers to faith in God and reliance on him (3:5; 16:20; 28:25; 29:25), but often it is used negatively in warnings not to put one's trust in wealth (11:28), oneself (28:26), or other people or things. For both meanings in direct contrast, see Jer 17:5–7. The verb is cognate to the noun בֶּטַח used adverbially, "safely, securely" (see the first textual note on 1:33).

(b) Also Prov 11:15, 28; 14:16; 16:20; 28:1, 25–26; 29:25; 31:11

Saving faith in God can be defined simply as trust in him and his mercy in Jesus Christ. The Lutheran Confessions affirm this often, for example:

> Righteousness and godliness in God's sight come from faith and trust when we believe that God receives us into his favor for the sake of Christ, his only Son. (AC XXVII 37)

> If we must hold to the proposition, "Christ is the mediator," then we must defend the proposition, "Faith justifies." For how will Christ be the mediator if we do not use him as mediator in our justification and believe that for his sake we are accounted righteous? But to believe means to trust in Christ's merits, that because of him God wants to be reconciled to us. (Ap IV 69; see also Ap IV 43–45)

Like Proverbs, the Lutheran Confessions also warn against trusting in anything besides God:

> We must do all such good works as God has commanded, but we should do them for God's sake and not place our trust in them as if thereby to merit favor before God. For we receive forgiveness of sin and righteousness through faith in Christ. (AC VI 1–2)
>
> For without faith human nature cannot possibly do the works of the First or Second Commandments. Without faith it does not call upon God, expect anything of God, or bear the cross, but it seeks and trusts in man's help. (AC XX 36–37)

3:6 בְּכָל־דְּרָכֶיךָ דָעֵהוּ—The imperative דָעֵהוּ from יָדַע, "to know," with third masculine singular suffix ("him") referring back to יְהוָה in 3:5, in this context clearly means more than can be denoted by the English word "know." יָדַע can mean "know personally" (see *HALOT*, 5 a) or "recognise, admit, acknowledge, confess" (BDB, 1 f). Nearly all English versions understand it to mean "acknowledge" here.

3:7 אַל־תְּהִי חָכָם בְּעֵינֶיךָ—Literally, "do not be wise in your own eyes," this is translated idiomatically: "do not consider yourself wise." For בְּעֵינֵי, see the second textual note on 3:4.

יְרָא אֶת־יְהוָה—This imperatival clause, "fear Yahweh," relates to the common nominal phrase. See the first textual note and the commentary on 1:7.

וְסוּר מֵרָע׃—The combination of the Qal (G) verb סוּר with the preposition מִן, "to turn away from, avoid, depart from," and the noun רַע (pausal: רָע), "evil," recurs in 13:19; 14:16; 16:6, 17. See also the Hiphil (H) of סוּר with מֵרָע in 4:27.

3:8 רִפְאוּת תְּהִי לְשָׁרֶּךָ וְשִׁקּוּי לְעַצְמוֹתֶיךָ׃—The subject of the feminine jussive תְּהִי (without *waw*; Joüon, § 116 i) is the feminine abstract noun רִפְאוּת, "healing." This verse literally means "let healing be to your navel and a drink to your bones," which is awkward and extremely wooden in English. Such slavishly form-equivalent translations distract the reader and obscure the meaning and force of sentences like this. A better translation that conveys the actual meaning is reflected above. לְשָׁרֶּךָ is, literally, "to your navel" or "to your umbilical cord." It is one of the rare instances in the OT where the consonant ר has a *daghesh* (GKC, § 22 s). The noun שֹׁר is used as synecdoche for the entire body, as suggested in *HALOT*, s.v. שֹׁר, b, and reflected in most English versions. The suggestion that לְשָׁרֶּךָ should be emended to לִבְשָׂרֶךָ ("to your flesh") or לִשְׁאֵרֶךָ ("to your body"), following τῷ σώματί σου in the LXX,[4] is unwarranted. It is highly unlikely that a scribe would have substituted a rare word like שֹׁר for a more common one.[5]

3:9 וּמֵרֵאשִׁית כָּל־תְּבוּאָתֶךָ׃—The noun תְּבוּאָה is derived from the verb בּוֹא, "to come," and in the Hiphil (H), "to bring." It refers to "what is brought in" from the field, the produce or yield harvested from the land (*HALOT*, 1).

---

4 Longman, *Proverbs*, 128.

5 Ross, "Proverbs," 918.

3:10 וְיִמָּלְאוּ אֲסָמֶיךָ שָׂבָע—The noun אָסָם means "storehouse" (see *HALOT*). In the context of a harvest, the plural refers to "barns" or "silos." The noun שָׂבָע, "plenty, satiety," is a synonym of שֹׂבַע. Here it is an adverbial accusative, translated as "filled *to capacity*."

וְתִירוֹשׁ יְקָבֶיךָ יִפְרֹצוּ׃—The noun תִּירוֹשׁ is an adverbial accusative: "*with* fresh wine your winepresses will burst." See Joüon, § 125 d.

3:11 וְאַל־תָּקֹץ בְּתוֹכַחְתּוֹ׃—The verb קוּץ, "loathe, abhor," denotes a strong negative emotional response.[6] Here "despise" fits well.

For the noun תּוֹכַחַת, "warning," see the first textual note on 1:23. For the verb יָכַח, from which it is derived, see the next textual note.

3:12 כִּי אֶת אֲשֶׁר יֶאֱהַב יְהוָה יוֹכִיחַ—The relative phrase אֶת אֲשֶׁר means "whomever, the one whom" Yahweh loves, and it introduces the object of the final verb יוֹכִיחַ. This is one of the few times in the OT אֵת does not have *maqqeph* but instead another conjunctive accent (GKC, § 16 b).

Perfect forms of the verb אָהַב, "to love," usually refer to the past and present ("he has loved, now loves"). The Qal (G) imperfect יֶאֱהַב has the nuance that Yahweh "loves, continues to love," signifying "repeated, constant action" (Joüon, § 113 a). יֶאֱהַב recurs in 15:9, 12; 16:13 (cf. 9:8).

The verb יָכַח always occurs in Proverbs in the Hiphil (H).[c] Its range of meanings, depending on context, can include "decide, judge, argue, convince, convict, rebuke, warn," and "correct." It is cognate to the noun תּוֹכַחַת, "warning," in 3:11. The context of the verb here shows that God performs this action out of love for each of his people. This can involve condemnation of sin and warning of eternal death and judgment, as in 2:18; 5:5, 23; 7:23; 8:36; 9:18. However, God's purpose in warning through divine Wisdom is to turn the believer away from evil (3:7), to protect him (2:8, 11), and preserve him to everlasting life (3:2, 18, 22). See further the commentary.

(c) Prov 3:12; 9:7–8; 15:12; 19:25; 24:25; 25:12; 28:23; 30:6

וּכְאָב אֶת־בֵּן יִרְצֶה׃—This is somewhat difficult syntactically. If אָב were the subject of יִרְצֶה, this would simply mean "like a father is pleased with a son." But it is more likely that אָב is the subject of an implied verb. The verb יוֹכִיחַ, "warns," at the end of the preceding clause does double duty and is implied as the main verb in this clause too. The object clause is אֶת־בֵּן יִרְצֶה, which involves a relative clause, "[like a father warns] a son *whom* he favors" or "a son *with whom* he is pleased," as in most English translations. This understanding considers the object clause to be parallel to the object clause in the first half of the verse, which includes a relative clause: אֶת אֲשֶׁר יֶאֱהַב, "the one whom he loves." (Both verbal clauses of 3:13 also involve a relative clause.)

The verb רָצָה, "show favor to, be pleased with," occurs in Proverbs only in 3:12; 16:7; and as the Kethib in 23:26, but the cognate noun רָצוֹן, "favor, grace," occurs more often; see the second textual note on 8:35.

This is the only place in Proverbs where God is likened to a father. Some other OT passages make this explicit comparison.[d] More often God's people are likened to his son or sons. The NT, of course, uses filial language for the relationship between God the

(d) E.g., 2 Sam 7:14 || 1 Chr 17:13; Jer 31:9; Mal 1:6; 2:10; Ps 103:13; cf. also Deut 1:31; 8:5

[6] Cf. L. J. Coppes, "קוּץ," *TWOT* 2:794.

Father and God the Son, including the verbal parallels at Christ's Baptism and transfiguration, where the Father declares that he is "pleased" with his Son (Mt 3:17 and 17:5 and parallels; 2 Pet 1:17). God the Father is also pleased with—favorable and gracious toward—all in Christ (cf. Lk 2:14; 1 Cor 1:21).

Perhaps the rarity of OT depictions of Yahweh as a father is what led the LXX to read וּכְאָב as וְיַכְאִב, "and he causes pain." It translated the clause as μαστιγοῖ δὲ πάντα υἱὸν ὃν παραδέχεται, "but he whips every son whom he receives."

3:13 אַשְׁרֵי אָדָם מָצָא חָכְמָה—The plural noun in construct אַשְׁרֵי is, literally, "oh the blessedness of …" However, in the OT it always serves as an exclamatory declaration about a person or persons: "blessed is/are …" In Proverbs it recurs in 8:32, 34; 14:21; 16:20; 20:7; 28:14. It is cognate to the verb אָשַׁר, for which, see the second textual note on 3:18. It is an eschatological term that depicts the blessed state of grace that each believer now has under God and that will eventuate in everlasting life in the world to come. See, for example, אַשְׁרֵי at the start of Psalm 1 (Ps 1:1) and the eschatological perspective with which the psalm concludes (Ps 1:5–6).

The Qal passive (Gp) participle בָּרוּךְ, "blessed" (Prov 5:18), is a broader synonym of אַשְׁרֵי. The participle בָּרוּךְ can apply to God, people, or even things as "blessed" or "praised," either in a declarative statement or a prayer ("let your fountain be blessed," 5:18). בָּרוּךְ is generally equivalent to εὐλογητός, which in the NT applies to God as "blessed" (e.g., Lk 1:68; Eph 1:3), or to εὐλογημένος (e.g., Mt 21:9; Mk 11:10; Lk 1:42). However, אַשְׁרֵי is applied only to people, who are blessed by grace through faith and Wisdom. Moreover, אַשְׁרֵי is generally confined to declarative statements in OT Wisdom literature. It is usually translated in the LXX by μακάριος, which is the Greek equivalent in the NT, as in the Beatitudes (Mt 5:3–11; see also, e.g., Mt 16:17; Jn 20:29).

Both verbs in Prov 3:13 serve as relative clauses: מָצָא, "the person *who* finds," and יָפִיק, "the person *who* acquires."

In this chapter, the nouns חָכְמָה and תְּבוּנָה are parallel again in 3:19.

וְאָדָם יָפִיק תְּבוּנָה׃—The verb פּוּק II occurs only in the Hiphil (H) and means "acquire, obtain, gain." It recurs in 8:35; 12:2; 18:22. It is parallel to מָצָא, "find," in 3:13; 8:35; 18:22.

3:14 כִּי טוֹב סַחְרָהּ מִסְּחַר־כָּסֶף—For the comparative construction טוֹב … מִן, "better … than," see "Direct Comparisons" in the introduction. The second half of the verse has the same comparison but טוֹב is implied there. The segholate noun סַחַר, "profit, gain from commerce," recurs in 31:18. The cognate participle סוֹחֵר in 31:14 refers to a "merchant, commercial trader."

The feminine pronoun on סַחְרָהּ, "her profit," that is, "profit gained from having her," and the referent of the feminine forms ("she" and "her") in 3:14b–18, probably is חָכְמָה, "Wisdom," in 3:13a but could be תְּבוּנָה, "Understanding," in 3:13b.

3:15 יְקָרָה הִיא מִפְּנִיִּים—The adjective יְקָרָה, "valuable, costly," recurs in 6:26 and is the feminine form of יָקָר (1:13; 12:27; 24:4). The Qere, מִפְּנִינִים, "than jewels," is preferable to the Kethib, מִפְּנִיִּים, whose meaning is uncertain. Proposed translations for פְּנִינִים, which always occurs in the plural, are "corals" (BDB; cf. *HALOT*) and "rubies," since

Lam 4:7 says that פְּנִינִים are red. Whatever its exact meaning, in all its occurrences in Scripture, it denotes a valuable commodity.[e]

(e) Job 28:18; Prov 3:15; 8:11; 20:15; 31:10; Lam 4:7

וְכָל־חֲפָצֶיךָ לֹא יִשְׁווּ־בָהּ׃—The identical clause recurs in 8:11b except that there the noun חֲפָצִים lacks a suffix. The noun חֵפֶץ denotes a desire (31:13) or, as here and in 8:11, something that is desired. The verb שָׁוָה, "to be like, equal, comparable," recurs in the Qal (G) in 8:11 and 26:4, and in the Niphal (N) in 27:15.

3:17 דְּרָכֶיהָ דַרְכֵי־נֹעַם—The construct phrase "ways of pleasantness" has an adjectival genitive: "pleasant ways." The noun נֹעַם, "pleasantness, pleasure," is cognate to the verb נָעֵם, "to be pleasant, delightful." See the second textual note on 2:10.

וְכָל־נְתִיבוֹתֶיהָ שָׁלוֹם׃—This construction with a predicate noun (שָׁלוֹם) expressing a quality is rare in Hebrew, literally, "and all her pathways [are] peace." See Joüon, § 154 e (5); see also § 131 c, including note 2.

3:18 עֵץ־חַיִּים הִיא לַמַּחֲזִיקִים בָּהּ—The construct phrase עֵץ־חַיִּים, "a tree of life," here refers to divine Wisdom itself. It recurs in 11:30 and 15:4, where it refers to the righteous person's life and words, which benefit others. In 13:12 it refers to a fulfilled desire of a godly person. The identical construct phrase with the article refers to "the tree of life" in Eden (Gen 2:9; 3:22, 24). Eschatologically, see the fruit-bearing "tree" in Ezek 47:7, 12 and "the tree of life" in the future paradise promised to all believers in Christ ([τὸ] ξύλον [τῆς] ζωῆς, Rev 2:7; 22:2, 14, 19).

The Hiphil (H) of חָזַק, "be strong," often takes the preposition בְּ and means "to grasp, hold on to," as also in 4:13; 7:13; 26:17. It is a synonym of תָּמַךְ in the next clause.

וְתֹמְכֶיהָ מְאֻשָּׁר׃—The Qal (G) of תָּמַךְ, "grasp, attain, take hold of, retain," occurs eight times in Proverbs (3:18; 4:4; 5:5; 11:16 (twice); 28:17; 29:23; 31:19) and the passive Niphal (N) once (5:22). The unusual construction here has as its subject the plural Qal participle of תָּמַךְ with a feminine singular object suffix (ֶיהָ-) referring back to חָכְמָה, "wisdom," in 3:13. The predicate is the singular Pual (Dp) participle of אָשַׁר, "be blessed." The plural participle has a distributive meaning: "all who hold on to her are blessed" (cf. Waltke-O'Connor, § 15.6c, including example 10). The verb אָשַׁר is used mainly in the Writings and especially in Wisdom literature, and it always refers to a person who is blessed, never to God as blessed. The Pual here is best understood as having an objective and factual meaning, with God as the implied agent: "are [actually, in fact] blessed [by God]." In other contexts the verb can refer to verbal human pronouncements about blessing. The Piel (D) in 31:28 has the active meaning "to declare/consider a person to be blessed" and refers to sons speaking about their mother. אָשַׁר in 3:18; 31:28 is a synonym of the more common verb בֵּרַךְ, "to bless," for which see the textual note on 3:33.

3:19 יְהוָה בְּחָכְמָה יָסַד־אָרֶץ—The verb יָסַד, "to found, establish," occurs in Proverbs only here. Other texts use it to refer to Yahweh creating the universe (e.g., Pss 24:2; 89:12 [ET 89:11]; Job 38:4) or to founding (laying the foundation of) the temple (Qal [G] in Ezra 3:12; Piel [D] in 1 Ki 5:31 [ET 5:17]; Ezra 3:10; cf. Ezra 3:6, 11).

כּוֹנֵן שָׁמַיִם בִּתְבוּנָה׃—The verb כּוּן occurs twenty times in Proverbs. The Polel (D), "to establish," is used only here in Proverbs, but in other texts it refers to God establishing the world (e.g., Pss 24:2; 119:90), the heavenly bodies (Ps 8:4 [ET 8:3]), or his sanctuary (Ex 15:17). The synonymous Hiphil (H) occurs six times in Proverbs. In the book the passive Niphal (N), "be established, prepared, preserved, enduring," is used eleven times, and the synonymous Hophal (Hp; 21:31) and Hithpolal (HtD; 24:3) each occur once.

Commentary

This third address in Proverbs 1–9 from a father to a son[7] is divided into two parts. Prov 3:1–12 is the father's teaching to his son in six sayings with promises attached to each command. Prov 3:13–20 is a meditation on the surpassing benefits of Wisdom. These two parts function together to impress upon the son his father's teaching. It is the second part that brings balance to the entire address. If the first part is read by itself, the reader might conclude that obtaining blessings from God is simply a matter of following instructions. However, the second part reminds the reader that Wisdom comes before obedience to the commands. Wisdom was with God from the beginning (3:19–20), as Solomon will reveal more fully in 8:22–31. Moreover, Wisdom grants life and makes it pleasant (3:17–18). This description transcends a personification; here Wisdom is a hypostasis, the second person of the triune God. The preexistent Son and eternal Word was the agent of creation and is incarnate in Jesus Christ.[8]

Solomon wants his readers to see that Christ, God's Wisdom, grants the blessings of understanding and life—now and forevermore. The promises attached to the commands in the first part of this address are not to be regarded as things that people can achieve by their own efforts or earn by their merit. Rather, they are gifts from God, received by grace alone as the Holy Spirit works faith and grants increasing knowledge of Christ. The promises portray the blessings of wisdom as it is lived out in the lives of those who respond to the Gospel. This divine wisdom is lived out in the lives of those who respond to the Gospel. These commands, therefore, ultimately are not demands of the Law, but invitations of the Gospel. Wisdom gives the reader the power to respond to the invitations in the first section of this address. This third address involves the Gospel and the power it bestows to follow God's Law (FC Ep VI 6–7; FC SD VI 17–21).

Six Commands and Promises (3:1–12)

The first part of this address consists of six main commands, each with a promise that follows:[9]

---

[7] For the ten addresses from father to son in Proverbs 1–9, see the excursus "Proverbs 1–9, Christ, and the Ten Commandments" in the commentary on chapter 1.

[8] See further "Wisdom in Proverbs" in the introduction. See also the commentary on 1:1–7; 8:22–31; and the excursus "Proverbs 8, Wisdom, Christology, and the Arian Controversy" in the commentary on chapter 8.

[9] Cf. Waltke, "Does Proverbs Promise Too Much?" 320–21.

Verse	*Command*	*Verse*	*Promise*
3:1	Do not forget my teaching	3:2	Lasting, whole life
3:3	Do not allow mercy and truth to leave you	3:4	Favor before God and people
3:5	Trust in Yahweh	3:6	Straight paths
3:7	Do not consider yourself wise, but fear Yahweh	3:8	Health
3:9	Honor Yahweh	3:10	Prosperity
3:11	Do not reject Yahweh's discipline	3:12	Yahweh loves you as your Father

This first section's coherence is emphasized by the mentioning of the "son" at its beginning in 3:1 and twice at its end in 3:11–12, and by the use of כִּי, "because," to introduce only the first and last promises (3:2, 12). This inclusio or bracketing technique helps the reader to see that these commands are all versions of the same thought: place Yahweh at the center of your life. Prov 3:1 opens with the father urging his son to obey his commands and internalize them through faith. The promise connected with this is long life (3:2), which by God's grace endures beyond the grave into eternity.

The second invitation urges the son to retain "mercy and truth" (חֶסֶד וֶאֱמֶת, 3:3) and internalize them by writing these attributes on his heart. However, this does not exclude their external manifestations in what the son will do and say. This is evident from the frequent use of the verbal idiom עָשָׂה חֶסֶד, "to do/show mercy."[f] Both חֶסֶד, "mercy," and אֱמֶת, "truth," can be used together as objects of the verb עָשָׂה, "to do, show," with a believer as the subject (Gen 24:49; 47:29; Josh 2:14; cf. Zech 7:9). Moreover, the promise attached to this command—that both God and other people will recognize these attributes in the faithful believer (Prov 3:4)—assumes that these are not merely internal, but also are put to use.

(f) E.g., Gen 21:23; 40:14; 47:29; Josh 2:12, 14; Judg 1:24; cf. Gen 19:19; Ex 20:6; Deut 5:10

While the first two invitations might be considered the sage father's wise advice, the third invitation (3:5) emphasizes that this is not mere human counsel, but divine guidance. The invitation to trust in Yahweh contrasts with relying on one's own human reason or emotions. This trust in Yahweh is equated with acknowledging him, that is, openly admitting that God's favor and love, conferred by his guidance in his Word, are better than human judgment. The promise of straight paths (3:6) is especially poignant because paths in ancient Israel were often winding, tortuous roads that took much effort on the part of travelers. A straight path, which would be relatively easy to traverse, was rare. "He will make your paths straight" does not necessarily mean that one's course in life will be comfortable and trouble free. It does mean that through his Word God will reveal the right direction and destination, even if bearing the cross is required in order to get there (cf. Mt 10:38; 16:24).

The fourth invitation (Prov 3:7) builds on the third. Here the fear of Yahweh is linked with not considering oneself wise. This points out another component of the cluster of concepts that make up the fear of Yahweh.[10] The believer possesses this attitude through faith and understands God's kindness in revealing his wisdom to humans. This person, therefore, does not rely on human wisdom, which often leads to evil, but instead turns from evil. The promise connected with this invitation is health (3:8). While some believers may have good physical health and experience healing now, the fulfillment of this eschatological promise will come in "the resurrection of the body, and the life everlasting" (Apostles' Creed). See, for example, Job 19:25–27; Dan 12:2–3; 1 Corinthians 15.

The fifth invitation (Prov 3:9) is one of the few verses in Proverbs that mentions worship. Honoring God with the first part of the harvest is part of the Torah stipulations for worship (Lev 2:14; Deut 26:2–4). However, the focus here is not so much on formal worship in the annual calendar as it is on continual trust and ongoing worshipful faith in God (see Sirach 7:29–31). To give God the part of the crop that ripens first is to trust that God will not allow the rest of the crop to be ruined by disease, pests, or bad weather that leaves the believer with no sustenance; God will provide (cf. Deut 8:3). Such trust is rewarded with the promise of an overabundant harvest (Prov 3:10). This promise too is eschatological: the new creation and new earth will provide superabundance (e.g., Is 65:9–10, 17–25; Amos 9:13–14).

The final invitation (Prov 3:11) is once again focused upon the fear of Yahweh, this time by mentioning its opposite, despising Yahweh's actions. Here the father reminds his son that God often uses what humans perceive as misfortune in life as discipline to warn and correct those whom he loves (Heb 12:4–11). The promise that God is like a father who is favorably pleased with his son (Prov 3:12) is placed purposely at the end of these invitations. Solomon, the father who began this instruction by taking advantage of his good relationship with his son (3:1), now uses that relationship as an analogy for God's relationship with his people. This points toward Christ, the Son of God, who kept these commands perfectly. Through baptismal incorporation and faith in the Son, we have received adoption as sons of God with whom he is favorably pleased (e.g., Rom 6:1–4; 8:15; Gal 3:26–29; 4:4–5).

The promises attached to these six invitations paint a picture of God's faithful people who are constantly experiencing life's best: long life, heath, success, and wealth. However, other passages in Proverbs as well as many other biblical books plus our personal observations tell us that even the most faithful believers do not always encounter such things. Some of the most pious of God's people have hardships that seem to fly in the face of these promises. Christ himself possessed no material wealth and was crucified in the prime of his earthly life. His ministry appeared to be a failure on Good Friday, and to some even on Easter

[10] See "יִרְאַת יְהוָה, 'the Fear of Yahweh,' and יְרֵא יְהוָה, 'One Who Fears Yahweh' " in "Wisdom in Proverbs" in the introduction.

Sunday (cf. Lk 24:10–11, 19–24). Most of his apostles were martyred, and few could be considered a success by worldly standards.

Waltke has addressed this problem and offered some solutions to this dilemma:[11]

- These promises are only partially realized in this life.
- The epigrammatic nature of proverbs only allows them to express truth in a terse way. Their compact nature prevents them from expressing the whole truth at length. These proverbs are generally true, but they must be read in light of other proverbs that state that piety does not invariably lead to benefits in this life (15:16–17; 16:8, 19; 17:1; 19:22; 22:1; 28:6).[12]
- These promises are realized eschatologically in God's eternal kingdom (11:4; 12:7, 28; see Wisdom 2:23).

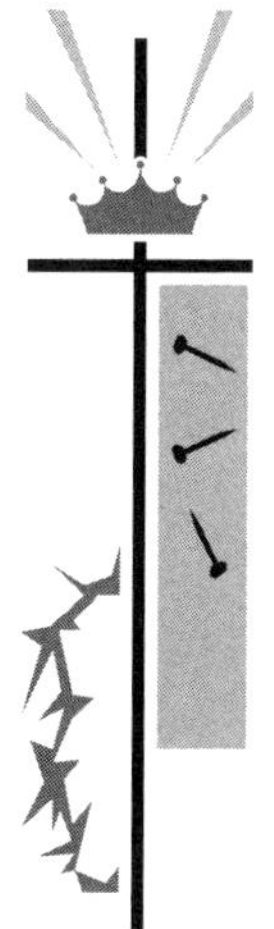

Waltke's observations are correct. The NT revelation of God's Wisdom in Christ shows more fully the cruciform life of believers; the eschatological nature of God's promises in light of the first and second advents of Christ; and that the world's perceptions about wisdom and blessing are the opposite of God's (e.g., Mt 5:3–12; 11:19; 1 Cor 1:18–31).

We must add another important observation: None of us follows the advice of these six invitations perfectly. We as sinners often fall short of having the trust in God that we ought to have. Thus we cannot claim these promises by our merits, but only by the grace of God given to us in the merits of Christ, who kept God's Law perfectly and grew in wisdom (Lk 2:40; Heb 5:8). As people who remain sinners as long as we remain in this life, we cannot expect or demand that we receive the benefits of these promises fully in this life. We also fail to recognize the extent of the blessings we already have, especially when we compare ourselves with those who have more. Yet we also know that all God's promises are yes in Christ (2 Cor 1:20), and we who are heirs of those promises shall receive their benefits in full on the Last Day.

The Benefits of Wisdom, Who Is Hypostasized in Jesus Christ (3:13–20)

Solomon moves on to the second part of his address, the blessings of Wisdom. This address is divided into two parts. Prov 3:13–18 tells of the blessings of Wisdom and is set off by an inclusio that begins with אַשְׁרֵי, "blessed" (3:13), and ends with the Hebrew cognate מְאֻשָּׁר, "blessed" (3:18). Then 3:19–20 speaks of Wisdom's role in creation.

In 3:13–18 Solomon connects Wisdom with promises attached to his invitations in 3:1–12. Wisdom brings a better profit than the harvest of the crops (compare 3:14 with 3:9–10). Wisdom offers long life (compare 3:16a with 3:2) and honor (compare 3:16b with 3:4). Wisdom bestows pleasant and peaceful paths (compare 3:17 with 3:6).

---

[11] Waltke, "Does Proverbs Promise Too Much?" 325–33.

[12] Cf. Van Leeuwen, "Wealth and Poverty: System and Contradiction in Proverbs."

These benefits of Wisdom are gifts freely bestowed by God. They are compared to riches (3:14) and jewels (3:15). These treasures far outweigh earthly valuables. That is why in the NT Jesus uses the parables of the treasure in a field and the valuable pearl to teach the same lesson (Mt 13:44–46). He urges us to store up treasure in heaven rather than on earth (Mt 6:19–21). These treasures, of course, are not accumulated by our own efforts, but are stored up for us in Christ, in whom we have the riches of his grace along with wisdom and insight (Eph 1:7–8).

To emphasize that Wisdom and blessing come through God the Son, Solomon reminds his son that Wisdom is divine. He connects Wisdom with creation both in 3:18 and in 3:19–20. The first connection is "the tree of life" (3:18).[13] Part of God's creation in Eden, "the tree of life" was able to bestow eternal life on those who ate its fruit (Gen 2:9). Therefore, after Adam and Eve fell into sin, God banned them (and all fallen humans) from the garden so they could not partake of this tree's fruit and thereby forever remain in their sin in a state of condemnation. He placed cherubim as guards to prevent sinful people from gaining access to it (Gen 3:22, 24).

The promise here is that Wisdom is even more beneficial than that tree was after the expulsion of the first people from the garden of Eden. As "the tree of life," Wisdom first conveys salvation from sin through forgiveness by grace, and then she bestows everlasting life in the state of redemption. Those who enter God's eternal kingdom will eat the fruit of this tree eternally (Rev 2:7; 22:2, 14, 19). For this reason a number church fathers identified "the tree of life" with Christ.[14] The cross of Christ is called "the tree" (τὸ ξύλον) in 1 Pet 2:24; see ξύλον also in, for example, Acts 5:30; 13:29; Gal 3:13. However, it is probably best to understand the tree of life here as a metaphor for Christ and not as a literal identification of Jesus as "the tree of life" in Eden or in John's vision in Revelation since Solomon also compares "the fruit of a righteous person," "desire fulfilled," and "a tongue that brings healing" to "a tree of life" (Prov 11:30; 13:12; 15:4).

The connection between Wisdom and creation is clearly extended in 3:19–20, which portrays Yahweh creating the world through the agency of Wisdom.[15] Creation as an act of building is a common motif connected with

---

[13] Murphy does not connect the tree of life here with the tree of life in Genesis (Murphy and Huwiler, *Proverbs, Ecclesiastes, Song of Songs*, 24). However, given the creation theme in 3:19–20, the connection between 3:18 and Genesis is certain.

[14] Clement of Alexandria, *Stromata*, 5.11 (*ANF* 2:461); Methodius, *The Banquet of the Ten Virgins*, 9.3 (*ANF* 6:346); Gregory of Nyssa, *On Virginity*, 23 (*NPNF*² 5:368); *On the Making of Man*, 19 (*NPNF*² 5:409); Hilary of Poitiers, *Homilies on the Psalms*, on Psalm 1 (*NPNF*² 9:239–40); Ephraim Syrus, *Nineteen Hymns on the Nativity of Christ in the Flesh*, 1 (*NPNF*² 13:223). This identification is mentioned as a possibility by Augustine, *The City of God*, 20.26 (*NPNF*¹ 2:446–47).

[15] The discussion in this paragraph and the next is based on Van Leeuwen, "Cosmos, Temple, House." Van Leeuwen notes that creation and building are common cosmological themes in Mesopotamian wisdom as well as in the Bible.

Wisdom in Proverbs (the verb בָּנָה in 9:1; 14:1; 24:3) and the verbs "found" and "establish" in 3:19 are synonyms of "build." This passage also resembles 24:3–4, since both passages refer to "wisdom," "understanding," and "knowledge" in that order. Moreover, both use the verb "establish" (forms of כּוּן in 3:19; 24:3) in connection with "understanding" (תְּבוּנָה, 3:19; 24:3).

What God creates he also fills and provides—a theme connected again with Wisdom in Proverbs (9:1–6). This filling and provisioning is evident already in Genesis 1, where on the first three days God creates the heavens, the sea, and the dry ground and then on the fifth and sixth days he fills them with birds, fish, and animals. Moreover, God blesses humans so that they can be fruitful and fill the earth (Gen 1:22, 28). The same pattern is found in building both the tabernacle and the temple: God provides wisdom for the building of both structures,[16] and then at their consecrations, he fills them with his glory (Ex 40:34–35; 1 Ki 8:10–11; 2 Chr 5:13–14; 7:2). Thus the tabernacle—and later the temple—is a microcosm of creation, which itself is built by God and filled with his glory (Is 6:3). Finally, we should note that the wise woman of Proverbs 31 also fills her house with products of her work and investments (31:10–31) in performing her godly and God-imitating vocation as wife and mother.

Wisdom in 3:19–20 is clearly divine: through Wisdom Yahweh himself forms the creation ("founded," "established") and fills it with what is needed to provide for and sustain all life ("the clouds drip dew").[17] Prov 3:19–20 goes beyond comparing Wisdom to the created "tree of life" (3:18) to presenting Wisdom as the means through which God created earth and heaven. The parallelism "earth … heavens" (3:19) recalls Gen 1:1 and makes Wisdom an active participant in creation. This identifies Wisdom as Christ, by whom all things were made (Jn 1:3; Col 1:16). Prov 3:20 reminds us that Christ was not a mere observer of the Father's creative acts but was himself the agent of creation, through whom the Father divided the waters. "The deep waters [תְּהוֹמוֹת] were divided" (Prov 3:20) alludes to the "deep" (תְּהוֹם) in Gen 1:2 and the separation of the sea from the dry land (Gen 1:9–10), providing habitations for the fish (Gen 1:20–23) as well as the terrestrial plants (Gen 1:11–13), the animals (Gen 1:24–25), and man (Gen 1:26–28). Likewise, the "deep (waters)" (the singular and plural of תְּהוֹם) in Prov 8:24, 27–28 alludes to the original creation as it affirms the preexistence of divine Wisdom.

This identification of Wisdom as preexistent and as at one with the Creator serves to draw the son who listens to his father's instructions closer to Yahweh. Wisdom is valuable because Wisdom is God, who offers his gracious blessings

[16] Note that God filled Bezalel with "wisdom, understanding, and knowledge" (Ex 31:2–3; 35:30–31; see also Ex 35:35–36:1) to build the tabernacle and its furnishings, and later God filled Hiram with the same three abilities to build the temple (1 Ki 7:13–14). In both cases the order of these three abilities is identical to their order in Prov 3:19–20 and 24:3–4.

[17] For "dew" as a blessing that sustains creation, see, for example, Gen 27:28; Deut 33:28; Ps 133:3. For "dew" associated with resurrection, see Is 26:19 and Ps 110:3.

to the son listening to the father's word. Therefore, Wisdom in this passage is not merely personified, but is a hypostasis. That is, we are shown the unique essence of God the Son, who, together with the Father and Spirit, was Creator of all things and is the bestower of all good gifts through his Gospel.

Although most modern commentators have not understood Wisdom in Prov 3:13–20 to be Christ, the church fathers often made this identification. Moreover, this passage, especially 3:19, figured prominently in the Arian controversy. The Arians denied the preexistence and divinity of Christ and instead supposed that Christ was a created being. The orthodox church fathers disproved that heresy. Among the fathers who cite verses in Proverbs 3 as speaking of Christ—the preexistent second person of the Godhead, through whom all things were made—are Athanasius[18] and Ambrose.[19] Irenaeus cites 3:19–20 but identifies Wisdom as God the Holy Spirit. Yet in the larger context he argues that the Word (the Son) and Wisdom (the Holy Spirit) have always been with the Father and were present and active when the one triune God created the world.[20] Irenaeus and Athanasius rightly argue that Wisdom in 3:19–20 is a divine hypostasis and cannot be a created being since the passage states that God founded the earth and heavens by Wisdom and Understanding.[21] Since Wisdom is an eternal person of the Trinity who existed before the creation, Wisdom is uncreated, these fathers demonstrate.

However, this passage did not prove decisive in the debate. The Arians countered that Wisdom/Christ was created first and was not part of either heaven or earth, but then became the agent through whom heaven and earth were created. While 3:13–20 does teach that God the Father created all things through preexistent Wisdom, which supports the orthodox doctrine of the Trinity, the Arian controversy was not decided on the basis of the statements about Wisdom in Proverbs 3 since it does not specifically or directly discuss the eternal generation of the Son from the Father nor the eternal procession of the Spirit from the Father and the Son. Of course, other biblical passages do clearly teach these truths and the doctrine of the Trinity. Based on these biblical passages, the Nicene and Athanasian Creeds affirm the full divinity of Christ, his preexistence, his eternal generation from the Father, and his unity with the Father.[22]

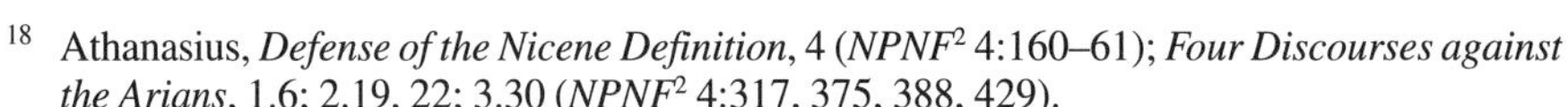

[18] Athanasius, *Defense of the Nicene Definition*, 4 (*NPNF*^{2} 4:160–61); *Four Discourses against the Arians*, 1.6; 2.19, 22; 3.30 (*NPNF*^{2} 4:317, 375, 388, 429).

[19] Ambrose, *Exposition of the Christian Faith*, 5.2 (*NPNF*^{2} 10:288).

[20] Irenaeus, *Against Heresies*, 4.20 (*ANF* 1:487–88).

[21] This is clear not only in the MT but also in the literal translation of Prov 3:19 in the LXX: ὁ θεὸς τῇ σοφίᾳ ἐθεμελίωσεν τὴν γῆν ἡτοίμασεν δὲ οὐρανοὺς ἐν φρονήσει, "God by Wisdom founded the earth and prepared the heavens through understanding."

[22] See further the excursus "Proverbs 8, Wisdom, Christology, and the Arian Controversy" in the commentary on chapter 8. For the view that Christ is the Wisdom of God, see also "Wisdom in Proverbs" in the introduction and the commentary on 1:1–7 and 8:22–31.

Excursus

The Use of Deuteronomy 6:4–9 in Proverbs 3:1–12 and 6:20–22

Several scholars have noted that two passages in Proverbs have connections to Deut 6:4–9.[1] The most obvious connection is that Prov 6:20–22 mirrors language from Deut 6:4–9. In the Torah Moses issues these commands:

4 שְׁמַ֖ע יִשְׂרָאֵ֑ל יְהוָ֥ה אֱלֹהֵ֖ינוּ יְהוָ֥ה ׀ אֶחָֽד׃
5 וְאָ֣הַבְתָּ֔ אֵ֖ת יְהוָ֣ה אֱלֹהֶ֑יךָ בְּכָל־לְבָבְךָ֥ וּבְכָל־נַפְשְׁךָ֖ וּבְכָל־מְאֹדֶֽךָ׃
6 וְהָי֞וּ הַדְּבָרִ֣ים הָאֵ֗לֶּה אֲשֶׁ֨ר אָנֹכִ֧י מְצַוְּךָ֛ הַיּ֖וֹם עַל־לְבָבֶֽךָ׃
7 וְשִׁנַּנְתָּ֣ם לְבָנֶ֔יךָ וְדִבַּרְתָּ֖ בָּ֑ם בְּשִׁבְתְּךָ֤ בְּבֵיתֶ֙ךָ֙ וּבְלֶכְתְּךָ֣ בַדֶּ֔רֶךְ וּֽבְשָׁכְבְּךָ֖ וּבְקוּמֶֽךָ׃
8 וּקְשַׁרְתָּ֥ם לְא֖וֹת עַל־יָדֶ֑ךָ וְהָי֥וּ לְטֹטָפֹ֖ת בֵּ֥ין עֵינֶֽיךָ׃
9 וּכְתַבְתָּ֛ם עַל־מְזֻז֥וֹת בֵּיתֶ֖ךָ וּבִשְׁעָרֶֽיךָ׃

4*Hear*, Israel, Yahweh our God, Yahweh is one. 5You shall love Yahweh your God with all your heart and with all your soul and with all your strength. 6These words that I am **commanding** you this day shall be on your heart. 7You shall impress them on your children and speak them when you sit in your house, when you **walk** on the road, when you **lie down**, and when you *get up*. 8You shall **fasten** them as a sign on your hand, and they shall be markings between your eyes. 9And you shall write them on the doorposts of your house and on your gates. (Deut 6:4–9)

Solomon reflects the words of Moses in this exhortation to his son:

20 נְצֹ֣ר בְּ֭נִי מִצְוַ֣ת אָבִ֑יךָ וְאַל־תִּ֝טֹּ֗שׁ תּוֹרַ֥ת אִמֶּֽךָ׃
21 קָשְׁרֵ֣ם עַל־לִבְּךָ֣ תָמִ֑יד עָ֝נְדֵ֗ם עַל־גַּרְגְּרֹתֶֽךָ׃
22 בְּהִתְהַלֶּכְךָ֙ ׀ תַּנְחֶ֬ה אֹתָ֗ךְ
בְּֽ֭שָׁכְבְּךָ תִּשְׁמֹ֣ר עָלֶ֑יךָ וַ֝הֲקִיצ֗וֹתָ הִ֣יא תְשִׂיחֶֽךָ׃

20*Keep*, my son, your father's **command**,
    and do not forsake your mother's teaching.
21**Fasten** them on your heart permanently,
    and tie them around your neck.
22When you **walk** around, she will lead you.
    When you **lie down**, she will stand guard over you.
    When you *wake up*, she will talk with you. (Prov 6:20–22)

The employment of a number of words and similar concepts from Deuteronomy is an important link that Solomon forges between the wisdom

---

[1] Fishbane, "Torah and Tradition," 284, notes the connection between Deut 6:4–9 and Prov 6:20–22. Overland, "Did the Sage Draw from the Shema? A Study of Proverbs 3:1–12," discusses the connection between Deut 6:4–9 and Prov 3:1–12 (cf. McKane, *Proverbs*, 291).

he imparts and the divine instruction in Deuteronomy.[2] In effect, he makes the entire passage (6:20–35) a commentary on Deuteronomy's call to love God (see the commentary on 6:20–35). In fact, in 6:20–35 the avoidance of the adulteress is a commentary on loving God and his Wisdom.[3] Note that Solomon not only repeats key words from Deuteronomy 6 (words in bold in the passage above), but he also employs near synonyms to mimic Deuteronomy (words in italics above). In addition he uses the imagery of fastening ancestral wisdom to parts of the body. While Deuteronomy 6 commands fastening God's words to the hand and between the eyes, Solomon urges fastening his wisdom teachings to the heart and neck. He purposely inverts the order implied by the body parts in Deuteronomy:

Deuteronomy	hand (outward actions)	forehead (inward thought)
Proverbs	heart (inward thought)	neck (outward actions)

In this way Solomon emphasizes the importance of internalizing Wisdom so that it will guide outward actions.

Solomon's commentary on Deut 6:4–9 is even more pronounced in Prov 3:1–12. As noted in the commentary on 3:1–20, this section is divided into six commands, each with a promise. The connections of these six commands and promises with Deut 6:4–9 are as follows:

The Second Command and Promise (Prov 3:3–4)

קָשְׁרֵם עַל־גַּרְגְּרוֹתֶיךָ כָּתְבֵם עַל־לוּחַ לִבֶּךָ

Fasten them around your neck;
write them on the tablet of your heart. (Prov 3:3b–c)

וּקְשַׁרְתָּם לְאוֹת עַל־יָדֶךָ ... וּכְתַבְתָּם עַל־מְזוּזֹת בֵּיתֶךָ וּבִשְׁעָרֶיךָ

You shall **fasten** them as a sign on your hand. ... And you shall **write** them on the doorposts of your house and on your gates. (Deut 6:8–9)

Note that the (outward) "neck" and then the (inward) "heart" in Prov 3:3 present the same sequence of inward thought then outward action as in Deut 6:8. This makes Prov 3:1–12 an even closer parallel to Deut 6:4–9 than is Prov 6:20–22.

The Third Command and Promise (Prov 3:5–6)

בְּטַח אֶל־יְהוָה בְּכָל־לִבֶּךָ

Trust in **Yahweh with all your heart**. (Prov 3:5)

---

[2] An example of another obvious link between Deuteronomy and Proverbs is the construct phrase "an abomination/disgusting thing to Yahweh," which occurs in the OT only in these two biblical books, and it occurs often in each. See the first textual note on 3:32.

[3] See the excursus "Wisdom and the Adulteress in Proverbs 1–9" in the commentary on chapter 2.

וְאָהַבְתָּ אֵת יְהוָה אֱלֹהֶיךָ בְּכָל־לְבָבְךָ

You shall love **Yahweh** your God **with all your heart**. (Deut 6:5)

The Fourth Command and Promise (Prov 3:7–8)

7 אַל־תְּהִי חָכָם בְּעֵינֶיךָ יְרָא אֶת־יְהוָה וְסוּר מֵרָע׃
8 רִפְאוּת תְּהִי לְשָׁרֶּךָ וְשִׁקּוּי לְעַצְמוֹתֶיךָ׃

7Do not **consider yourself wise**.
Fear Yahweh, and turn away from evil.
8Then **your body will be healed**,
and **your bones will be refreshed**. (Prov 3:7–8)

וְאָהַבְתָּ אֵת יְהוָה אֱלֹהֶיךָ בְּכָל־לְבָבְךָ וּבְכָל־נַפְשְׁךָ

You shall love Yahweh your God with all your heart and **with all your soul**. (Deut 6:5)

Since Solomon has already established the connection with Deuteronomy 6, he now feels free to depart from its actual words to expound on its meaning. He here contemplates the meaning of בְּכָל־נַפְשְׁךָ, "with all your soul." He connects it with the inner being, first by a humble assessment of one's wisdom so as not to regard oneself as wise. Then the attached promise depicts health as an inward quality of healing in the body and refreshment in the bones, rather than a matter of outward appearance. This may also involve a play on words involving parts of the body. נֶפֶשׁ, "soul," in Deut 6:5 can sometimes mean "throat." The idiomatic phrases in Prov 3:7–8 involve body parts: אַל־תְּהִי חָכָם בְּעֵינֶיךָ is, literally, "do not be wise in your own eyes"; שֹׁר, translated as "body," is literally "navel"; and עֲצָמוֹת is "bones."[4]

The Fifth Command and Promise (3:9–10)

כַּבֵּד אֶת־יְהוָה מֵהוֹנֶךָ וּמֵרֵאשִׁית כָּל־תְּבוּאָתֶךָ׃

Honor Yahweh with your wealth
and with the first part of **your entire harvest**. (Prov 3:9)

וְאָהַבְתָּ אֵת יְהוָה אֱלֹהֶיךָ בְּכָל־לְבָבְךָ וּבְכָל־נַפְשְׁךָ וּבְכָל־מְאֹדֶךָ׃

You shall love Yahweh your God with all your heart and with all your soul and **with all your strength**. (Deut 6:5)

The common word מְאֹד usually serves as an adverb, "very, exceedingly." It is used as a substantive in only two passages in the OT: in Deut 6:5, where it is customarily translated as "strength," and 2 Ki 23:25, which echoes the Deuteronomy passage. The LXX translates it as δύναμις, "power," in Deut 6:5 and ἰσχύς, "strength," in 2 Ki 23:25. The NT quotes or paraphrases Deut 6:5

4 Overland, "Did the Sage Draw from the Shema?" 429–31.

four times, translating מְאֹד as διάνοια, "mind" (Mt 22:37); διάνοια … καὶ … ἰσχύς, "mind … and … strength" (Mk 12:30); ἰσχύς, "strength" (Mk 12:33); and ἰσχύς … καὶ … διάνοια, "strength … and … mind" (Lk 10:27). Clearly, מְאֹד is the broadest of the three terms ("heart … soul … strength") in Deut 6:5 that are involved in one's devotion to God. From the example of Josiah in 2 Kings 23 and the various NT translations, it seems to refer to love for God with all of one's person, including whatever intellect and other resources one may have. In Prov 3:9 Solomon focuses on expressing love for God through the use of one's material resources: "your wealth … your entire harvest." This is demonstrated elsewhere in the way Josiah used his office and wealth (2 Kings 23) and the Good Samaritan's use of his resources (Lk 10:25–37).

Thus Prov 3:1–12 is a meditation on what it means to love God. The first command and promise call on the son to listen to these words (3:1–2); the second through fifth focus on what it means to love God (3:3–10); and the sixth emphasizes God's love for humans (3:11–12). In this way Solomon points to the fear of Yahweh (3:7) not only as the result of God's Law and fear of his punishment, but also as an attitude of faith that flows from the Gospel, which is God's gracious love for his people (3:11–12).[5]

[5] See further the first textual note and the commentary on 1:7 and "יִרְאַת יְהוָה, 'the Fear of Yahweh,' and יְרֵא יְהוָה, 'One Who Fears Yahweh' " in "Wisdom in Proverbs" in the introduction.

Proverbs 3:21–35

Fourth Address to a Son: Wisdom Leads to a Proper Relationship with Your Neighbor

Translation

3 21 My son, do not take your eyes off them—
guard sound judgment and insight.
22 They will be life for your soul
and grace for [adorning] your neck.
23 Then you will go safely on your way,
and you will not stub your toe.
24 When you lie down, you will not be afraid.
When you lie down, your sleep will be pleasant.
25 You do not need to be afraid of sudden terror
or of the destruction of wicked people when it comes,
26 because Yahweh will be your confidence.
He will keep your foot from being caught.
27 Do not withhold [anything] good from those who deserve it
when it is within your power to do.
28 Do not say to your neighbor, "Go away! Come back [some other time].
Tomorrow I will give [it to you]," although it is with you.
29 Do not plan harm against your neighbor
when he is living with you peacefully.
30 Do not quarrel with a person for no good reason
when he has done you no harm.
31 Do not envy a violent person,
and do not choose any of his ways,
32 because a crooked person is a disgusting thing to Yahweh,
but Yahweh's confidential advice is with upright people.
33 Yahweh's curse is on the wicked person's house,
but he blesses the home of righteous people.
34 Although he mocks the mockers,
he gives grace to the humble.
35 Wise people inherit honor,
but fools, because of pride, [inherit] disgrace.

Textual Notes

3:21 אַל־יָלֻזוּ מֵעֵינֶיךָ נְצֹר תֻּשִׁיָּה וּמְזִמָּה׃—The Qal (G) of לוּז, "turn aside, depart," occurs only here in the OT; for the Niphal (N), see the second textual note on 2:15. The form of יָלֻזוּ is jussive, so with the negative, the literal meaning of the first clause is "*do not let* [them] *depart* from your eyes." The subject of the masculine plural verb יָלֻזוּ appears to be the two feminine nouns that are delayed to the second clause of this verse: תֻּשִׁיָּה וּמְזִמָּה. See "תּוּשִׁיָּה, 'Sound Judgment' " and "מְזִמָּה, 'Insight, Foresight' " in "Wisdom in Proverbs" in the introduction. The dash in the translation above ("them—") indicates that the compound subject is delayed until the second clause. Some translations (e.g., NIV) simplify the syntax by placing 3:21b before 3:21a.

3:22 וְחֵ֥ן לְגַרְגְּרֹתֶֽיךָ׃—For חֵן, "grace," see the first textual note on 1:9. For לְגַרְגְּרֹתֶיךָ, see the second textual note on 1:9.

3:23 אָ֭ז תֵּלֵ֣ךְ לָבֶ֣טַח דַּרְכֶּ֑ךָ—For the noun בֶּטַח used adverbially, "safely," see the first textual note on 1:33. לָבֶטַח recurs with the same adverbial meaning in 3:29.

וְ֝רַגְלְךָ֗ לֹ֣א תִגּֽוֹף׃—This is, literally, "and you will not strike your foot." To an English reader this form-equivalent translation reads as if the son would be striking his own foot, which is clearly not what the Hebrew means. The English equivalent is "and you will not stub your toe."

3:24 אִם־תִּשְׁכַּ֥ב לֹא־תִפְחָ֑ד—The particle אִם can be used to set up a conditional sentence. It can signal a condition that will be realized or one that cannot be realized (*HALOT*, 1, 2). In this case it sets up a condition that will be realized. The son will lie down to sleep. However, an English sentence that began "*if* you lie down" would raise some doubt about whether the son would lie down to sleep. Therefore, it is better in this case to signal to an English reader that the father expects the son to lie down to sleep. In this sentence "when" is more appropriate than "if" would be and is used in most English versions. Note that the second sentence in 3:24 is also a conditional sentence that mirrors the first sentence, but both the protasis and apodosis are coordinated with *waw* instead of אִם.

The verb פָּחַד, "to be afraid," occurs in Proverbs only here and in 28:14. It is cognate to the noun פַּחַד, "fear, terror," in 1:26–27, 33; 3:25. This noun and verb usually have a negative connotation of dread and aversion, whereas the synonyms יָרֵא, "to fear" (as in 3:25), and the noun יִרְאָה, "fear," more often refer to fear engendered by faith in God.

3:25 אַל־תִּ֭ירָא מִפַּ֣חַד פִּתְאֹ֑ם—The negative אַל with an imperfect (here תִּירָא) can express that something should not happen (GKC, § 109 e; Joüon, § 114 k), hence, "you *do not need* to be afraid," as the same clause means in Job 5:22.

וּמִשֹּׁאַ֥ת רְ֝שָׁעִ֗ים כִּ֣י תָבֹֽא׃—For the noun שׁוֹאָה, see the first textual note on 1:27.

3:26 כִּֽי־יְ֭הוָה יִהְיֶ֣ה בְכִסְלֶ֑ךָ—The noun כֶּסֶל occurs in Proverbs only here. It can mean "confidence," as here and also in Ps 78:7; Job 8:14; 31:24. Yet it can also mean "foolishness," and it is cognate to כְּסִיל, "fool," and כְּסִילוּת, "foolishness," which occur elsewhere in Proverbs. The preposition בְּ here is the *beth essentiae* (GKC, § 119 i), meaning "Yahweh will *be* your confidence."

וְשָׁמַ֖ר רַגְלְךָ֣ מִלָּֽכֶד׃—This is, literally, "he will keep your foot from capture." The noun לֶכֶד (pausal: לָכֶד), which occurs only here in the OT, is translated verbally as "being caught." Using the cognate verb, Ps 9:16 (ET 9:15) states this about the wicked: "their foot is captured" (נִלְכְּדָה רַגְלָם).

3:27 אַל־תִּמְנַע־טוֹב מִבְּעָלָיו—This is, literally, "do not withhold good from its owners." Here the noun בַּעַל signifies "one to whom good is due" (BDB, s.v. בַּעַל, 1), those who have the right to possess the good item in question. In this context, "those who deserve it" is the intended sense, as recognized by English versions such as NIV and ESV.

בִּהְיוֹת לְאֵל יָדֶיךָ לַעֲשׂוֹת׃—The infinitive of הָיָה with בְּ forms a temporal clause: literally, "when it is/belongs to the power of your hand to do." However, translating most Hebrew idioms into English with a form-equivalent translation yields awkward or misleading English. The translation above, "when it is within your power to do," reflects an idiom-for-idiom translation rather than a word-by-word translation.

There are several words spelled אֵל in Hebrew. The one here means "power" (BDB, s.v. אֵל II, 7; *HALOT*, s.v. אֵל IV) and is always used idiomatically with לְ and יָד to refer to possessing the power or ability to do something. In these idioms elsewhere, יָד is always singular (Gen 31:29; Deut 28:32; Micah 2:1; Neh 5:5), so the singular Qere, יָדְךָ, "your hand," is preferable to the plural Kethib, יָדֶיךָ.

The infinitive לַעֲשׂוֹת, "to do," is ambiguous. It could refer to the action of withholding what is good, in which case the verse means "do not withhold good … even when you have the power to (withhold good)." Or it could mean "do not withhold good … when you have the ability to do (good)—to give what is good to those who deserve it." In either case, the verse warns against committing a sin of omission: not doing something that a believer should do.

3:28 לְרֵעֶיךָ—The singular Qere, לְרֵעֲךָ, "to your neighbor" (as in 3:29), is preferable to the plural Kethib לְרֵעֶיךָ because of the two following singular Qal (G) imperatives, לֵךְ וָשׁוּב, which are addressed to the neighbor.

לֵךְ וָשׁוּב וּמָחָר אֶתֵּן וְיֵשׁ אִתָּךְ׃—The quoted words, are literally, "go and return, and tomorrow I will give." The implied subject of וְיֵשׁ אִתָּךְ, "and *it* is with you," is the "good thing" (טוֹב) that you have and should not withhold (3:27a) and that you have the ability to give (3:27b).

3:29 אַל־תַּחֲרֹשׁ עַל־רֵעֲךָ רָעָה—The Qal (G) of חָרַשׁ can mean "to engrave" or "to plow," as in 20:4. But elsewhere in Proverbs it means "to devise, plan." Only once is its object טוֹב, a "good" plan or goal (14:22b). Usually, as here, its object is an "evil" (רָעָה or רַע, 6:14; 12:20; 14:22a) plot or scheme, or "wicked" (אָוֶן, 6:18) plans.

וְהוּא־יוֹשֵׁב לָבֶטַח אִתָּךְ׃—For a similar idiom, see the first textual note on 1:33. Here the neighbor is "dwelling securely with you," meaning that he is living peacefully with good will and in trust.

3:30 אַל־תָּרִוב עִם־אָדָם חִנָּם—The Qal (G) of רִיב, "to quarrel" (*HALOT*, 2), recurs in 22:23; 23:11; 25:8–9. The Qere, תָּרִיב, is preferable to the Kethib, תָּרוֹב, which would be a synonymous by-form verb רוֹב, attested only here in the OT.

The adverb חִנָּם can mean "without cause." However, "do not quarrel with a person without cause" sounds to the English reader that it is acceptable to quarrel if one thinks there is a reason to do so, no matter how flimsy the reason might be. The Hebrew, however, is implying that one must have a good, upright reason to engage in strife. Thus it is better to translate "for no good reason." While the Christian should avoid strife and quarrels (Rom 14:1; 2 Tim 2:14; James 4:2), there are times when one cannot avoid conflict, and it is the Christian's duty to engage in spiritual warfare, especially when the faithful proclamation of the Gospel offends unbelievers (Mt 10:34–36; Lk 12:51–53).

אִם־לֹ֖א גְמָלְךָ֣ רָעָֽה׃—This circumstantial clause means "if/when he has not done to you any evil." The Qal (G) of גָּמַל, "to do to, deal out to," has a suffix that serves as the indirect object ("to you"). The verb recurs in 11:17 and 31:12, where it refers to doing good.

3:31 אַל־֭תְּקַנֵּא בְּאִ֣ישׁ חָמָ֑ס—In Proverbs the verb קָנָא, "envy, be jealous of," always occurs in the Piel (D) imperfect negated by אַל with the preposition בְּ prefixed to an expression for the wicked, expressing the command not to envy sinners (3:31; 23:17; 24:1, 19). The construct phrase אִישׁ חָמָס ("a man of violence") recurs in 16:29 and has an adjectival genitive: "a violent man." The noun חָמָס, "violence," occurs five other times in Proverbs (4:17; 10:6, 11; 13:2; 26:6).

3:32 כִּ֤י תוֹעֲבַ֣ת יְהוָ֣ה נָל֑וֹז—For נָלוֹז, "crooked person/thing," see the second textual note on 2:15. This Niphal (N) participle of לוּז is the subject in the nominal clause.

(a) Prov 11:1, 20; 12:22; 15:8–9, 26; 16:5; 17:15; 20:10, 23

The predicate is the construct phrase תוֹעֲבַת יְהוָה, literally, "an abomination of/to Yahweh." This phrase represents God's ultimate revulsion for a sinful attitude or behavior. It is used frequently in Proverbs.[a] Elsewhere in the OT it occurs only in Deuteronomy.[b] This suggests that Solomon is deliberately borrowing the language of Moses in order to expound upon the Torah.[1]

(b) Deut 7:25; 12:31; 17:1; 18:12; 22:5; 23:19 (ET 23:18); 25:16; 27:15

וְֽאֶת־יְשָׁרִ֥ים סוֹדֽוֹ׃—Here אֵת must be the preposition "with." The noun סוֹד can denote a confidential discussion or "counsel"; a secret; or a circle of confidants, a "council" (see BDB and *HALOT*). Yahweh's faithful prophets were privy to the divine counsel revealed in the divine council (e.g., Jer 23:18; Amos 3:7; cf. 1 Ki 22:14–23).[2] In this context סוֹד appears to be the confidential advice in the divine wisdom that God gives to his believing people (as in Ps 25:14), but God withholds it from unbelievers (Mt 13:11–17). סוֹד recurs in Prov 11:13; 15:22; 20:19; 25:9.

3:33 מְאֵ֣רַת יְ֭הוָה בְּבֵ֣ית רָשָׁ֑ע וּנְוֵ֖ה צַדִּיקִ֣ים יְבָרֵֽךְ׃—The nouns בַּיִת, "house," and נָוֶה, "home," are synonyms. However, the verse has two pairs of antonyms. The first is רָשָׁע, "a wicked person" (see the first textual note on 2:22), versus צַדִּיקִים, "righteous people." See "The Relationship between Wisdom and Righteousness in Proverbs" in "Wisdom in Proverbs" in the introduction.

The noun מְאֵרָה, "a curse" (also in 28:27), is derived from the verb אָרַר, "to curse" (absent from Proverbs, but see, e.g., Gen 3:14, 17; 4:11). They are the strongest antonyms to the noun בְּרָכָה, "blessing" (see the first textual note on Prov 10:6), and the verb בָּרַךְ, "to bless." Here מְאֵרָה is in construct with its agent: מְאֵ֣רַת יְ֭הוָה, "Yahweh's curse," means that the wicked man's house, and by metonymy the wicked man himself, is cursed by Yahweh. Yahweh pronounced curses upon the serpent and the creation after the fall into sin (אָרַר in Gen 3:14, 17) and upon Cain, the first murderer (אָרַר in Gen 4:11). Unless the wicked repent, Yahweh will carry out his curse on the Last Day

[1] See the excursus "The Use of Deuteronomy 6:4–9 in Proverbs 3:1–12 and 6:20–22" after the commentary on 3:1–20.

[2] See Lessing, *Amos*, 208, 221.

by publicly pronouncing all unbelievers as cursed and by damning them for eternity (Mt 25:41, 46).

Yahweh (Prov 3:33a) is the implied subject of יְבָרֵךְ, the Piel (D) of בֵּרַךְ, "to bless." Here it has the eschatological meaning that God already now pronounces his blessing upon the habitation of the righteous (cf. נָוֶה also in 21:20; 24:15), and on the Last Day he shall publicly declare their blessedness when he grants them their inheritance of everlasting life in the new creation (Mt 25:34, 46). The Piel (D) of בָּרַךְ can also refer to human benedictions, as in Prov 27:14 and 30:11. The Pual (Dp) of בָּרַךְ in 20:21 and 22:9 means "to be blessed" by God in an eschatological sense. The only other occurrence of בָּרַךְ in Proverbs is the Qal passive (Gp) participle בָּרוּךְ, "blessed," in 5:18, where it refers to one's wife.

3:34 אִם־לַלֵּצִים הֽוּא־יָלִיץ וְלַעֲנָיִּים יִתֶּן־חֵֽן׃—The construction אִם ... וְ marks the first clause as concessive: "although ..."[3] This verse is translated by the LXX as κύριος ὑπερηφάνοις ἀντιτάσσεται ταπεινοῖς δὲ δίδωσιν χάριν, "the Lord opposes the proud, but he gives grace to the humble." The LXX rendition is quoted in James 4:6 and 1 Pet 5:5, but with ὁ θεός substituted for κύριος.

For the participle לֵצִים and the verb לִיץ, "to mock," see the second textual note on 1:22 and "לֵץ, 'Mocker,' and לָצוֹן, 'Mocking, Scoffing' " in "Fools in Proverbs" in the introduction.

The Qere, וְלַעֲנָוִים, is the plural of the adjective and substantive עָנָו, "humble, meek, afflicted." It occurs in Proverbs only as the Qere in 3:34; 14:21; 16:19. The Kethib, וְלַעֲנִיִּים, is the plural of the synonym עָנִי, "humble, afflicted," which is the Kethib in 3:34; 14:21; 16:19 and occurs five other times in Proverbs (15:15; 22:22; 30:14; 31:9, 20; cf. עֳנִי, "affliction," in 31:5).

For חֵן, "grace," see the first textual note on 1:9.

3:35 וּכְסִילִים מֵרִים קָלֽוֹן׃—The Hebrew text may mean "but disgrace lifts up fools," as in KJV: "but shame shall be the promotion of fools." Since מֵרִים, "lift up," is a masculine singular Hiphil (H) participle, the masculine singular noun קָלוֹן, "disgrace," probably is its subject, and then כְּסִילִים ("fools") would be its object.

Some translations construe the plural וּכְסִילִים, "and fools," as the subject and קָלוֹן as the object: "but fools get disgrace" (RSV, ESV; cf. NASB). However, this is grammatically inconsistent with the singular participle.

Another construal is to consider Yahweh to be the implied subject of the participle: "but he lifts up fools [to] disgrace," as in NIV: "but fools he holds up to shame." However, that would require supplying an implied preposition before קָלוֹן or taking it as an adverbial accusative.

The solution proposed by Emerton[4] and adopted here understands וּכְסִילִים as the subject and קָלוֹן as the object. It assumes that the implied verb in 3:35b is יִנְחָֽלוּ, "inherit," which ends 3:35a and does double duty as the verb for both clauses of the verse. Finally, it emends מֵרִים to מֵרוּם, assuming that a scribe confused the ו for י. The

---

[3] Driver, "Problems in the Hebrew Text of Proverbs," 176.

[4] Emerton, "A Problem in Proverbs 3:35," 23–24.

noun רוּם means "arrogance, pride" in Is 2:11, 17, and it occurs in an idiom for pride in Prov 21:4. (In Prov 25:3 רוּם has the physical meaning "height.") The preposition מִן attached to it would have a causal meaning: "but fools [וּכְסִילִים], because of pride [מֵרוּם], [inherit, יִנְחֲלוּ] disgrace [קָלוֹן]."

Commentary

This is the fourth address in Proverbs 1–9 from a father to a son.[5] It has three sections:

- 3:21–24: The benefits of wisdom
- 3:25–32: Five warnings
- 3:33–35: Three sayings contrasting evil and righteous people

The benefits of wisdom (3:21–24) are described in ways already used in previous addresses: "life" (חַיִּים, 3:22, as in 3:2, 18; cf. 2:19) and "grace" (חֵן, 3:22, as in 1:9; 3:4; see also 3:34). Moreover, to the promise of safety on a path—a metaphor used heretofore[6]—is added security when sleeping (3:24), a time of great vulnerability (cf. Pss 3:6 [ET 3:5]; 4:9 [ET 4:8]; 121:4).

Once the son is assured of the benefits of wisdom, the father offers five pieces of advice in the form of warnings (3:25–32). First is the advice to not be concerned about sudden terrors or the destruction of wicked people (3:25). Instead the son is counseled to place his confidence in Yahweh, who is absolutely trustworthy and will prevent the son from being caught as he walks in wisdom's ways (3:26). This first warning with its promissory counsel is foundational for the other warnings that follow. Faith in Yahweh grants to the son the confidence of salvation, which enables him to live sacrificially in gratitude and deal with others honestly and without malice (3:27–32).

Without that confidence, however, he would be afraid of what may happen to him, knowing that God would punish him along with the rest of the wicked, and he could not follow God's Law. What fulfills the Law is love—love from God, which instills love for God and one's neighbor (Mt 22:36–40; Rom 13:10). Jesus promises his people that they will not be punished with the wicked; rather, they will be separated from them in the final judgment as his sheep, who inherit "eternal life" in paradise (Mt 25:32–46). This is represented by the "tree of life" in Prov 3:18 and "life" in 3:2, 22. Believers are freed by Christ to follow God's commands in this life and to inherit the life of the world to come.

The other warnings remind the son to have integrity in his dealings with his neighbor: not to misuse power and fail to do what is right, and not to withhold possessions borrowed from a neighbor or refrain from giving generously to him (3:27–28), not to take advantage of a neighbor who trusts him (3:29), not to engage in useless quarrels (3:30), and not to envy those who use violence

---

5 For the ten addresses from father to son in Proverbs 1–9, see the excursus "Proverbs 1–9, Christ, and the Ten Commandments" in the commentary on chapter 1.

6 See, for example, 1:15, 19, 31; 2:8, 12–15; 3:6, 17. See also the excursus "The Metaphor of the Path in Solomon's Wisdom" in the commentary on chapter 10.

(3:31), perhaps as an easy way to riches or a forceful way to gain power. Prov 3:32, which speaks of God's attitude toward crooked and upright people, reinforces all the warnings in 3:27–31. It highlights Yahweh's utter disgust with perverse people and promises that God provides his counsel to the son and to all who are upright.

The three sayings that contrast evil and righteous people (3:33–35) are examples of God's own actions flowing out of his two attitudes depicted in 3:32. The "crooked person" who is the object of Yahweh's disgust in 3:32 is further characterized as a "wicked person" (3:33) and one of the "mockers" (3:34) and "fools" (3:35). In contrast, the "upright people" in 3:32 are further characterized as "righteous people" (3:33), "the humble" (3:34), and "wise people" (3:35). Therefore, the people who are upright have been made so by God, who has justified them. This means that God has declared them righteous through faith on account of Jesus' merit. Moreover, they are humble. That is, they do not stand before God relying on their own righteousness; instead, they humbly repent of their sins and rely on God's grace and mercy to provide forgiveness and new life. Finally, they are wise because God has given them wisdom. This means that Yahweh's "confidential advice," or counsel (3:32), is what is summarized elsewhere as "the fear of Yahweh," that is, the fear and love for God that result from saving faith and that grow with divine wisdom.[7]

This theme of "grace to the humble" and "honor" for the "wise" (3:34–35) is explored in the NT by both James and Peter, who quote Prov 3:34 from the LXX. James uses this passage to exhort his Christian readers to "humble yourselves before the Lord," adding the promise that "he will exalt you" (James 4:6–10). Similarly, Peter urges us to display humility toward all people (1 Pet 5:5). He echoes the words of both Solomon and James when he writes: "Humble yourselves, therefore, under the mighty hand of God so that he may exalt you at the proper time" (1 Pet 5:6). Of course, neither Solomon nor the apostles are teaching that through humility we can earn glory from God. Rather, they are reminding us that in humility we depend on Christ and his redemptive work, since only he fulfilled the demand for perfect humility and obedience. He is the one who has obtained everlasting glory for us (Rom 8:30).

"Grace" (חֵן, Prov 3:22, 34) is something that is not earned. Augustine notes that God freely gives his grace to the humble through the work of Christ: "Therefore is it grace because [it is] given gratuitously. And therefore is it given gratuitously, because it is not rendered as a reward."[8]

The apostle Paul urges us to adopt the humility shown by Christ himself:

> Therefore if there is any encouragement in Christ, any comfort from love, any communion from the Spirit, any compassion and mercy, complete my

---

[7] See the first textual note and the commentary on 1:7 and "יִרְאַת יְהוָה, 'the Fear of Yahweh,' and יְרֵא יְהוָה, 'One Who Fears Yahweh' " in "Wisdom in Proverbs" in the introduction.

[8] Augustine, *Sermons on Selected Lessons of the New Testament*, 94, on Jn 16:8 (*NPNF*[1] 6:538).

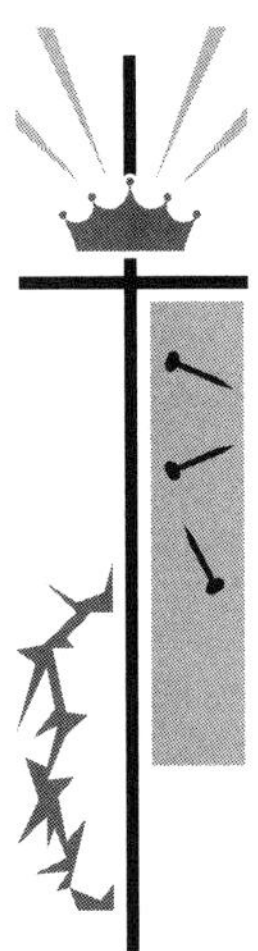

joy by being of the same mind, having the same love, being spiritually united and thinking the same thing. Do nothing from rivalry or conceit, but in humility consider others as better than yourselves. Let each of you watch out not only for his own interests, but also for the interests of others. Have this mind among yourselves, which was also in Christ Jesus, who, though he was in the form of God, did not count being equal with God a thing to be grasped, but emptied himself, taking the form of a servant, being born in the likeness of men. And being found in form as a man, he humbled himself, being obedient until death, even death on a cross. Therefore God highly exalted him and bestowed on him the name that is above every name, so that at the name of Jesus every knee should bow, of those in heaven and on earth and under the earth, and every tongue confess that Jesus Christ is Lord, to the glory of God the Father. (Phil 2:1–11)

Proverbs 4:1–9

An Address to Sons: Solomon's Parents Taught Him to Value Wisdom

Translation

4 **[1]Listen, sons, [to] a father's discipline,**
and pay attention to learn understanding,
[2]because I have given you good instruction.
Do not abandon my teaching.
[3]When I was son to my father,
a tender and only child in front of my mother,
[4]he used to teach me and say to me,
"Cling to my words wholeheartedly.
Obey my commands so that you may live.
[5]Acquire Wisdom;
acquire Understanding.
Do not forget, and do not turn away
from the words of my mouth.
[6]Do not abandon her, and she will watch over you.
Love her, and she will guard you."
[7]The beginning of Wisdom [is to] acquire Wisdom.
With all you possess, acquire Understanding.
[8]Cherish her, and she will exalt you.
She will honor you when you embrace her.
[9]She will bestow a garland of grace for your head.
She will present you with a beautiful crown.

Textual Notes

4:1 שִׁמְעוּ בָנִים מוּסַר אָב—Similar calls for plural "sons" (בָּנִים, with no pronominal suffix) to "listen" (שִׁמְעוּ) are in 5:7; 7:24 (where the parallel verb is וְהַקְשִׁיבוּ, as here); and 8:32. A few translations add the pronoun "my": "my sons" (NIV) or "my children" (NKJV). However, in the Hebrew Solomon does not identify the "sons" that he addresses as his own. Neither does he call himself their father, only "*a* father" (אָב). However, in the next verse Solomon states, "I have given you good instruction" (4:2), referring to previous instruction, probably Proverbs 1–3. Therefore, it is most likely that the sons referred to here are Solomon's own sons and that the instruction he is giving them is a father's, that is, the type of instruction any godly father ought to give to his sons.

וְהַקְשִׁיבוּ לָדַעַת בִּינָה׃—The sons are exhorted to "pay attention" (הַקְשִׁיבוּ; see the textual note on 1:24) in order "to learn understanding." Here דַּעַת is not the noun but the infinitive construct of יָדַע with לְ (pointed -לָ since the following syllable has the tone) to express purpose. The verb יָדַע is used widely in the OT and has a large semantic range. One cannot simply always translate it as "know." In this case it means "to learn" (*HALOT*, 2). For its direct object noun, see "בִּינָה, 'Understanding,' and Related Words" in "Wisdom in Proverbs" in the introduction. Since the action expressed by the verb לָדַעַת, "to learn," is a synonym of the abstract noun בִּינָה, "Understanding," the construction לָדַעַת בִּינָה can be called an accusative of the internal object (Joüon, § 125 q).

4:2 כִּי לֶקַח טוֹב נָתַתִּי לָכֶם—For the noun לֶקַח, "instruction," see the first textual note on 1:5.

תּוֹרָתִי אַל־תַּעֲזֹבוּ׃—For תּוֹרָה, "teaching," see the second textual note on 1:8. For the verb from which it is derived, see the first textual note on 4:4.

The negative command "do not abandon" (אַל with the imperfect of עָזַב) recurs in 4:6.

4:3 כִּי־בֵן הָיִיתִי לְאָבִי—Here the conjunction כִּי has the temporal meaning "when" (BDB, 2 a). It refers to the past time described in 4:3–6.

4:4 וַיֹּרֵנִי וַיֹּאמֶר לִי—In this context the two imperfects with *waw* consecutive have an iterative force: "he used to teach me [frequently, repeatedly] and say to me." וַיֹּרֵנִי is the Hiphil (H) of יָרָה, "to teach," which occurs in Proverbs only in 4:4, 11; 6:13, and the substantivized participle occurs in 5:13. It is the verbal root of the noun תּוֹרָה, "teaching, Torah," in, for example, 4:2.

יִתְמָךְ־דְּבָרַי לִבֶּךָ—With the Qal (G) jussive of תָּמַךְ (see the second textual note on 3:18), this clause is, literally, "may your heart retain/cling to my words." However, "your heart" refers to young Solomon—the whole person, not just a part of him (*pars pro toto*). Therefore the jussive verb can be translated as an imperative and the subject noun can be rendered adverbially: "cling to my words wholeheartedly." Compare the second textual note on 22:21, where the noun אֱמֶת functions adverbially.

שְׁמֹר מִצְוֺתַי וֶחְיֵה׃—This clause is repeated verbatim in 7:2a. The Qal (G) of שָׁמַר can mean "to keep, observe, obey" a command or "fulfill" an obligation (see BDB, 3 c, and *HALOT*, 8), as here. It can also mean "to watch over, preserve, protect" (see BDB, 4 a, and *HALOT*, 1), as it does in 4:6 (וְתִשְׁמְרֶךָּ). Note that Solomon plays on the different meanings of the word in 4:4 and 4:6. In Proverbs the sages frequently use such plays on words, making it difficult to translate a repeated Hebrew word or root by the same English word.

The imperative of חָיָה, "to live," with *waw*, וֶחְיֵה (cf. GKC, § 75 n), forms a purpose clause: "*so that* you may live," as also in 7:2a and 9:6a (see Joüon, § 116 f). The only other instance of חָיָה in Proverbs is in the eschatological promise of 15:27. In all these verses "to live" conveys the divine promise of everlasting life, as does the noun חַיִּים, "life," in, for example, 3:2, 18, 22; 4:10.

4:5 קְנֵה חָכְמָה קְנֵה בִינָה—The Qal (G) imperative of קָנָה, "to acquire," occurs twice in the alliterative clause here and twice again in 4:7.

וְאַל־תֵּט מֵאִמְרֵי־פִי׃—The Qal (G) of נָטָה means "stretch out, extend" in 1:24. Here its jussive with the preposition מִן in the construction תֵּט מִ־ means "deviate/turn away from."

4:6 אַל־תַּעַזְבֶהָ וְתִשְׁמְרֶךָּ אֱהָבֶהָ וְתִצְּרֶךָּ׃—The feminine singular suffixes ("her … her") on the Qal (G) imperfect תַּעַזְבֶהָ (of עָזַב), "to leave, abandon," and Qal imperative אֱהָבֶהָ (of אָהַב; see Joüon, § 64 a), "to love," could refer to either of the feminine singular nouns חָכְמָה, "Wisdom," or בִּינָה, "Understanding," since both nouns occur in both 4:5 and in 4:7. אָהַב, "to love," refers to loving divine "wisdom" (חָכְמָה) in 29:3. In 8:17, 21 אָהַב could refer to loving either "Wisdom" (8:12) or "Understanding" (8:14). (It refers to loving "discipline" and "knowledge" in 12:1.)

Whether חָכְמָה or בִּינָה, the same noun would be the subject ("she … she") of both of the third feminine singular imperfects, וְתִשְׁמְרֶךָּ … וְתִצְּרֶךָּ, "will watch over … will guard." The Qal (G) forms of שָׁמַר and נָצַר are parallel synonyms, as they are in, for example, 2:8, but in reverse order. See the first textual note on 2:8.

4:7 The LXX omits this entire verse. Based on this, some commentators have suggested that it is a later insertion and ought to be deleted.[1] However, the verse's abruptness, which may have puzzled the LXX translators, is part of the literary artistry of the verse.

רֵאשִׁית חָכְמָה קְנֵה חָכְמָה—The initial construct phrase recalls רֵאשִׁית דָּעַת (see the second textual note on 1:7). This clause with the imperative קְנֵה (repeated in the next clause) is, literally, "the beginning of Wisdom—acquire Wisdom." The abrupt syntactical break signals that Solomon has shifted from quoting his father's words (with the simple commands in 4:4–6) to imparting his own instruction based on what his father had taught him. In 4:7–9 the imperatives and other second person forms are all singular. Instead of reverting to plural second person forms like those Solomon used to address "sons" in 4:1–2, he uses singular forms to address each son individually. These singular forms in 4:7–9 correspond to the singular forms David used to address Solomon himself, which are quoted in 4:4–6.

וּבְכָל־קִנְיָנְךָ קְנֵה בִינָה׃—Note another play on words, which could be rendered as, literally, "and with all you have acquired, acquire Understanding." The noun קִנְיָן, "possession, what one has acquired," is from the verb קָנָה, "to acquire," whose imperative קְנֵה follows the noun.

4:8–9 As in 4:6, the feminine singular suffixes and feminine singular verbs could refer either to חָכְמָה, "Wisdom," or בִּינָה, "Understanding," since both occur in 4:5 and in 4:7.

4:8 סַלְסְלֶהָ וּתְרוֹמְמֶךָּ תְּכַבֵּדְךָ כִּי תְחַבְּקֶנָּה׃—Note the chiasm: the first and last words (סַלְסְלֶהָ … תְּחַבְּקֶנָּה) refer to the actions the hearer/reader should perform, while the middle two adjacent verbs (וּתְרוֹמְמֶךָּ תְּכַבֵּדְךָ) refer to divine Wisdom's actions in exalting the believing recipient.

Each of the first two verbs is a duplicated, emphatic form similar to the Piel (D) form of the second two verbs. סָלַל means "lift up," and the Pilpel (GKC, §§ 55 f; 67 l; 72 m) imperative סַלְסְלֶהָ has the metaphorical meaning "exalt her … esteem highly, prize" (BDB) or "cherish her." וּתְרוֹמְמֶךָּ is the Polel (GKC, § 72 m) imperfect of רוּם, meaning "and she will exalt you."

[1] Toy, *Proverbs*, 88; Clifford, *Proverbs*, 60; Scott, *Proverbs, Ecclesiastes*, 49, 51.

4:9 תִּתֵּן לְרֹאשְׁךָ לִוְיַת־חֵן—For the construct phrase לִוְיַת־חֵן, see the first textual note on 1:9.

עֲטֶרֶת תִּפְאֶרֶת תְּמַגְּנֶךָּ׃—The noun עֲטָרָה, "crown," recurs in 12:4; 14:24; 16:31; 17:6. David spoke of how Yahweh sets the עֲטָרָה, "crown," upon the king's head and grants blessings, everlasting life, salvation, and majesty (Ps 21:4–7 [ET 21:3–6]). The same noun also refers to the "crown" worn by King Solomon on his wedding day in Song 3:11. Metaphorically, Yahweh himself is the "crown" for his faithful people (Is 28:5), and he makes his people into "a crown of beauty" by his gifts of righteousness and salvation (Is 62:1–3; cf. the wedding imagery in Is 62:5).

The construct chain עֲטֶרֶת תִּפְאֶרֶת, "a crown of beauty" (as also in Is 62:3; Jer 13:18; Ezek 16:12; 23:42; Prov 16:31), has an adjectival genitive: "a beautiful crown." The second, abstract noun describes a quality of the noun in construct. This type of construct phrase is frequently used in Proverbs. For another example, see מַעְגְּלֵי־יֹשֶׁר, "upright pathways," in 4:11.

The verb מִגֵּן occurs only thrice in the OT, always in the Piel (D), meaning either "deliver up" (Gen 14:20; Hos 11:8) or, here, "to give as a gift" (*HALOT*, 2) or "to present." Its direct object is the preceding construct phrase, and its suffix (ךָּ-) is the indirect object, "(to) you."[2]

Commentary

Solomon[3] in this address (4:1–9) breaks from the four previous and the six following addresses to an individual son,[4] whom he calls "my son" (e.g., 3:21; 4:10). This section is addressed to several "sons" (4:1). Here Solomon reminds the sons of the good instruction he has given them in the past and exhorts them not to abandon what he has taught them. To reinforce the wisdom of his teachings, he reminds them that his instruction to them is the same as his father's instruction was to him. In 4:4–6 he quotes teaching from his father. He declares that "my father" (4:3), David, taught him in the presence of "my mother" (4:3), Bathsheba (see 2 Sam 12:24–25). The mention of a "mother" is intended to recall the first address to a son (Prov 1:8–19), where Solomon called "my son" to listen to the instruction of "your father" (Solomon himself) and "your mother" (1:8).

Solomon summarizes David's teaching as a series of short commands (4:4–6). David's instruction to Solomon was simple: learn what I am teaching, for it is divine Wisdom! Hold on to it and love it. In three cases a command is expanded with a promise (4:4c, 6a–b). The three promises attached to David's instruction echo those of the previous addresses. First, "so that you may live" (וֶחְיֵה, 4:4) recalls the promises of "life" (חַיִּים) in the third address (3:2, 18) and

---

2 BDB, s.v. מִגֵּן, under the root נגן, recognizes that the suffix is the indirect object. *HALOT*, s.v. מגן I, 2, somewhat misleadingly states that the verb here takes two accusatives.

3 See "Authorship and Date" and especially "Conclusion about Authorship" in the introduction.

4 For the ten addresses from father to son in Proverbs 1–9, see the excursus "Proverbs 1–9, Christ, and the Ten Commandments" in the commentary on chapter 1.

the fourth address (3:22). Second, "and she will watch over you" (וְתִשְׁמְרֶךָּ, 4:6) evokes the use of same verb, שָׁמַר, "watch, keep," in the second address (2:8, 11, 20) and the fourth address (3:26). The third promise, "and she will guard you" (וְתִצְּרֶךָּ, 4:6), pairs the verb נָצַר, "to guard," with שָׁמַר, "watch, keep" (4:6a), just as the two verbs were paired in the previous promises of protection in the second address (2:8, 11). These connections between the quoted words of David and Solomon's previous addresses serve to emphasize to the sons that Solomon's instructions are not his alone, but were passed down to him from his father, Israel's most faithful king.

Israel's wisest king (1 Ki 5:11 [ET 4:31]) then proceeds to elaborate on his father's words with his own commentary on his father's instruction (Prov 4:7). The father reminds his sons that the beginning of Wisdom is to seek Wisdom above all else. He tells his sons to put the highest priority on getting Wisdom by placing it above possessions (4:7), by cherishing it (4:8a), and by embracing it (4:8b). He motivates his sons to value Wisdom in these ways by reminding them of the benefits of Wisdom: exaltation and honor (4:8), which are reinforced by the metaphor of a beautiful headdress (4:9). The metaphor "a garland of grace" (4:9, as in 1:9) recalls his first address, where he noted that Wisdom would grace the head of those who have her (1:9). The "garland" that is made "of"—or that is—"grace" and the "beautiful crown" indicate that Wisdom confers royal majesty upon the believer (see the textual notes on 4:9) so that he will reign with Christ (Rom 5:17; 2 Tim 2:12; Rev 22:5). The "garland" and the "crown" anticipate the NT references to God's gifts of grace in Christ, "the crown of righteousness" (2 Tim 4:8), "the crown of glory" (1 Pet 5:4), and "the crown of life" (James 1:12; Rev 2:10; cf. Rev 3:11; 4:4, 10) to be received by each believer on the Last Day.

In this address to sons, therefore, Solomon is not only recalling the instruction that his father, David, gave him, but he is also calling on the sons to recall their previous instruction from him in Proverbs. He references all four of his previous addresses in order to connect his teaching with that of his father. Just as David handed down to Solomon divine guidance, both personally (cf. 1 Ki 2:1–12) and through the many psalms that he authored, so now Solomon is handing down to his sons the same Wisdom that will make them wise unto salvation (cf. 2 Tim 3:15).

Therefore, this address should be read in light of the previous ones, and the father's commendation of Wisdom should be understood as pointing the sons once again to God and his gifts to believers in Christ. Of course, neither the sons nor we today can keep the commands of David and Solomon perfectly. However, the Son of David, Jesus Christ, the Wisdom of God incarnate, did obey his Father perfectly and fulfilled all the Scriptures. All who believe in him receive the saving gifts of righteousness, wisdom, and knowledge through his grace.[5]

---

[5] For Christ as the Wisdom of God incarnate, see "Wisdom in Proverbs" in the introduction. See also the commentary on 1:1–7; 3:13–20; 8:22–31; 30:1b–10; and the excursus "Proverbs 8, Wisdom, Christology, and the Arian Controversy" in the commentary on chapter 8.

Proverbs 4:10–19

Fifth Address to a Son: Wisdom Teaches the Difference between Wicked and Righteous People

Translation

4 [10]Listen, my son, and accept my words,
so that the years of your life will be many.
[11]I have taught you the way of wisdom.
I have led you along upright pathways.
[12]When you walk, your stride will not be restricted.
Even if you run, you will not stumble.
[13]Hold on to discipline; do not let go.
Guard it, because it is your life.
[14]Do not go on the path of wicked people,
and do not walk on the way of evil people.
[15]Avoid it; do not travel on it!
Turn away from it and pass on,
[16]because they cannot sleep unless they are doing wrong,
and their sleep is stolen unless they are making someone stumble,
[17]because they eat food obtained from wickedness,
and wine obtained by violence they drink.
[18]But the path of righteous people is like the light of dawn,
shining brighter until the day is established.
[19]The way of wicked people is like the darkness:
they never know over what they stumble.

Textual Notes

4:10 וְיִרְבּוּ לְךָ שְׁנוֹת חַיִּים׃—This is, literally, "years of life will be many for you." This promise that believers will have everlasting life is similar to the promises with חַיִּים, "life," in, for example, 3:2, 18, 22; 4:13, and with חָיָה, "to live," in 4:4; 7:2; 9:6; 15:27. For "years of life," see the first textual note on 3:2.

4:11 בְּדֶרֶךְ חָכְמָה הֹרֵתִיךָ—See "חָכְמָה, 'Wisdom,' and Related Words" in "Wisdom in Proverbs" in the introduction. For דֶּרֶךְ, "way," see the excursus "The Metaphor of the Path in Solomon's Wisdom" in the commentary on chapter 10. הֹרֵתִיךָ is the Hiphil (H) perfect of יָרָה, "to teach," for which, see the first textual note on 4:4.

הִדְרַכְתִּיךָ בְּמַעְגְּלֵי־יֹשֶׁר׃—The Hiphil (H) of the verb דָּרַךְ, which occurs only here in Proverbs, is cognate to the noun דֶּרֶךְ, "way," in the preceding clause. It has the causative meaning "to lead, cause (someone) to walk along a way." See the second textual note on 4:9 for another phrase with an adjectival genitive similar to בְּמַעְגְּלֵי־יֹשֶׁר, literally, "in pathways of uprightness." That construct phrase occurs only here in the OT, but see בְמַעְגְּלֵי־צֶדֶק, "in pathways of righteousness," in Ps 23:3.

4:12 לֹא תִכָּשֵׁל׃—The verb כָּשַׁל means "to stumble, trip" over something in both the Qal (the Kethib in 4:16) and the Niphal (4:12, 19; 24:16–17). For the Hiphil (the Qere in 4:16), see the third textual note on that verse.

4:13 הַחֲזֵק בַּמּוּסָר אַל־תֶּרֶף—See "מוּסָר, 'Discipline,' and יָסַר, 'to Discipline' " in "Wisdom in Proverbs" in the introduction. The same point is conveyed by a positive and then by a negative command. First, the Hiphil (H) imperative of חָזַק with בְּ means "to take hold of, hold on to." The second command is the negated (אַל־) Hiphil imperfect of the antonym רָפָה, "do not let drop, let go of" it.

נִצְּרֶהָ כִּי־הִיא חַיֶּיךָ׃—Since מוּסָר in 4:13a is a masculine noun, the feminine suffix on the Qal (G) imperative נִצְּרֶהָ, "guard it," and feminine pronoun הִיא, "it," probably refer back to חָכְמָה, "wisdom," in 4:11. For נָצַר, "to guard," see the first textual note on 2:8 and the second textual note on 3:1. The *daghesh forte dirimens* in the צּ in נִצְּרֶהָ makes the *shewa* more audible (GKC, § 20 h).

4:14 וְאַל־תְּאַשֵּׁר בְּדֶרֶךְ רָעִים׃—Probably the verb אָשַׁר, whose Qal (9:6) and Piel (4:14) forms mean "to walk, go straight ahead" (and whose Piel has a causative meaning in 23:19), is a homograph of אָשַׁר, "to bless" in 3:18 and 31:28, rather than a different meaning of the same verb (so *HALOT* contra BDB).

4:15 פְּרָעֵהוּ אַל־תַּעֲבָר־בּוֹ שְׂטֵה מֵעָלָיו וַעֲבוֹר׃—Note the play on two different meanings of עָבַר. First, the negated imperfect תַּעֲבָר with בְּ means "do not go/pass along a way, travel on it" (see BDB, 5 h, and *HALOT*, 1). Second, the imperative וַעֲבוֹר means "pass by, pass on" (see *HALOT*, 3 a) and so is a synonym of פָּרַע, "to avoid" (for which, see the first textual note on 1:25). שָׂטָה, "turn aside," here with מֵעַל־, "away from," recurs in 7:25. The three masculine singular pronominal suffixes (פְּרָעֵהוּ ... בּוֹ ... מֵעָלָיו) all must refer to the "path" (אֹרַח) or "way" (דֶּרֶךְ) in 4:14, both of which usually are masculine.

4:16–17 כִּי ... כִּי—These two verses that give reasons why the son should turn away from the evil path (4:15) are each introduced with the causal conjunction כִּי, "for, because."

4:16 כִּי לֹא יִשְׁנוּ אִם־לֹא יָרֵעוּ—The *metheg* with the *hireq* (ִֽ) in יִֽשְׁנוּ shows that it is defectively written for יִישְׁנוּ and is the Qal (G) imperfect of יָשֵׁן, "to sleep," rather than a form of שָׁנָה. See Joüon, § 14 c (1). Confirming this, the cognate feminine noun שֵׁנָה with suffix, שְׁנָתָם, "their sleep," occurs in the next clause.

וְנִגְזְלָה שְׁנָתָם—The verb גָּזַל means "to rob" (*HALOT*, 3), and the Niphal (N) feminine perfect has the corresponding passive meaning: "their sleep is stolen." This is the apodosis of a conditional sentence, whose protasis follows.

אִם־לֹא יַכְשִׁולוּ׃—The Kethib is the pausal plene Qal (G) יִכְשׁוֹלוּ, "unless they stumble." However, in this context the Qere is preferable: the Hiphil (H) יַכְשִׁילוּ, "unless they cause (others) to stumble."

4:17 לָחֲמוּ לֶחֶם רֶשַׁע וְיֵין חֲמָסִים יִשְׁתּוּ׃—Note the chiasm of this verse:

A verb
B pair of object nouns
B' pair of object nouns
A' verb

The initial verb לָחֲמוּ, "they eat," is followed by its two object nouns, לֶחֶם רֶשַׁע, "bread of wickedness," a concrete noun in construct with an abstract genitive. Then two more object nouns, וְיֵין חֲמָסִים, "and wine of violence," another concrete noun in construct with an abstract genitive, precede the final verb that governs them, יִשְׁתּוּ, "they drink." This chiasm emphasizes that the entire life of the wicked depends on their doing evil. The genitive constructions לֶחֶם רֶשַׁע and יֵין חֲמָסִים are adverbial and denote the evil means by which the food and drink were obtained.

4:18 וְאֹרַח צַדִּיקִים כְּאוֹר נֹגַהּ—Citing the *waw* that begins this verse, some want to place 4:19 before 4:18, claiming that 4:19 follows more logically after 4:17.[1] However, the *waw* should be understood as adversative, drawing a contrast between the wicked in 4:16–17 and the righteous people in 4:18.

This nominal clause is, literally, "and the way of righteous people [is] like light of brightness." The noun נֹגַהּ often refers to the "brightness" of theophany (e.g., Is 4:5; 60:3; Ezek 1:4, 27–28), and so it is appropriate for describing God's gracious gift of his own righteousness, as here and in Is 62:1. In the context of Prov 4:18b, נֹגַהּ, "brightness," represents the dawn; see the Aramaic cognate נְגַהּ in Dan 6:20 (ET 6:19). It grows in intensity until the night is gone and the full light of the sun establishes the day.

הוֹלֵךְ וָאוֹר—This idiomatic construction juxtaposes the Qal (G) participle of הָלַךְ with another verb, here the Qal participle of אוֹר, to "*become light, shine* of sun (esp[ecially] in early morn[ing])" (BDB). The verbal coordination expresses continuing and increasing action: "shining brighter (and brighter)." See GKC, § 113 u, and Joüon, § 123 s.

4:19 דֶּרֶךְ רְשָׁעִים כָּאֲפֵלָה—The noun אֲפֵלָה, "gloom, deep darkness" recurs in 7:9. With the article and the preposition כְּ, it is antonymous to כְּאוֹר נֹגַהּ, "like light of brightness/dawn," in 4:18a. אֲפֵלָה is used in a simile describing wickedness also in Jer 23:12. It refers to the plague of supernatural darkness in Ex 10:22 and is in the covenant curse of Deut 28:29.

Commentary

This is Solomon's fifth address in Proverbs 1–9 expressed as a father speaking to his son.[2] It builds on the previous address to plural "sons" (4:1–9). Here the father repeats the promise of life (compare 4:10 with 4:4). He then emphasizes that he has taught his son the way of wisdom (4:11), recalling how he had received the instruction from his father, David, before passing it on (4:3–6).

Prov 4:10–19 reintroduces the metaphor of life as a path (featured previously in, e.g., 3:6, 17, 23, 31). It depicts the father as leading his young son

---

1 Delitzsch, *Proverbs*, 1:111; Toy, *Proverbs*, 93.

2 For the ten addresses from father to son in Proverbs 1–9, see the excursus "Proverbs 1–9, Christ, and the Ten Commandments" in the commentary on chapter 1.

along the proper path of wisdom.[3] This path enables true freedom in life and leads to the resurrection to eternal life (the "tree of life" in 3:18; see also, e.g., 1:33; 2:21; 3:2, 22; 4:4, 10, 13; and, e.g., Dan 12:2–3) because it is the path of the Gospel. Solomon is, therefore, teaching his son to value the Gospel in which he is declared righteous before God, solely by grace, apart from any human effort (see, e.g., "righteousness" in 1:3; 2:9 and "righteous" in 2:20; 3:33; 4:18). The Gospel sets people free from the bondage of sin and death to live a new and everlasting life by the power of Christ (Jn 8:31–32, 36; Rom 6:17–22; 8:2; Gal 5:13; 1 Pet 2:16).

A stride that is not restricted and a path that will not cause runners to stumble (Prov 4:12) symbolize this freedom. The father urges his son to hold on to this Gospel liberty that he has found because it is his very life (Prov 4:13). Similarly, Paul urged the Galatians to stand firm in their freedom in Christ: "For freedom Christ has set us free; stand fast, therefore, and do not submit again to a yoke of slavery" (Gal 5:1). The Lutheran Confessions quote that passage to denounce human ordinances and regulations that some churches impose on their people as necessary for salvation:

> It is necessary to preserve the teaching of Christian liberty in Christendom, namely, that bondage to the law is not necessary for justification, as St. Paul writes in Gal. 5:1. … For the chief article of the Gospel must be maintained, namely, that we obtain the grace of God through faith in Christ without our merits; we do not merit it by services of God instituted by men" (AC XXVIII 51–52).

Solomon then reminds his son that another path is available to him—one that he should avoid (Prov 4:14). It is the path that wicked people take. To underscore the danger of this path, he forbids his son from considering such a course in life with a series of terse, sharp imperatives (4:15). To suppress every desire for what can seem to be an attractive way in life, the father describes the pathetic state of those who take the evil path. They cannot sleep, eat, or drink unless they are engaged in some sinful activity (4:16–17). They are enslaved to the sinful life that they have chosen. As Jesus explained:

> Everyone who practices sin is a slave to sin. The slave does not remain in the house forever; the Son remains forever. Therefore if the Son sets you free, then you shall be free indeed. (Jn 8:34–36)

Solomon closes out this address by introducing another metaphor, that of light and darkness, and combining it with the metaphor of the path. He compares the path that righteous people walk to light that increases in brightness (Prov 4:18). Solomon depicts for his son the growth in grace and knowledge of God that is given in the Gospel. Note that the righteous themselves are not the light, but the way in which they are to walk is the light. This way is Christ, who is both "the way" or path (Jn 14:6) and the light of the world (Jn 8:12; see also

---

[3] See the excursus "The Metaphor of the Path in Solomon's Wisdom" in the commentary on chapter 10.

Is 9:1–6 [ET 9:2–7]; 60:1–6; Mt 2:9–10; 1 Thess 5:5). As we walk in Christ, guided by the light of the knowledge of God, the dawn of the new day grows brighter and nearer.[a] When the Last Day finally dawns, all darkness shall be banished and we shall enter the new creation of everlasting day and light (Rev 21:23; 22:5).

(a) Rom 13:12; 2 Cor 4:4–6; Eph 5:8–14; 2 Pet 1:19; 1 Jn 2:8; Rev 2:26–28; 22:16

The path of wicked people is depicted as the opposite (Prov 4:19). It is dark, and consequently, they stumble (Jn 12:35; 1 Jn 2:11). The contrast between the safety God gives the righteous on the path of wisdom versus the danger faced by the wicked on their evil path is heightened by the threefold use of the verb "stumble" (כָּשַׁל, Prov 4:12, 16, 19). Solomon promises his son that even if he should run on the righteous path, he "will not stumble" (4:12). Those on the evil path try to trip others; they are always "making someone stumble" (4:16). Yet their wickedness causes their own downfall; they themselves stumble, and because they are in the dark, "they never know over what they stumble" (4:19). They shall be consigned to everlasting gloom and night.[b]

(b) Is 8:20–22; Joel 2:2; Amos 5:18–20; 2 Pet 2:17; Jude 13

Jesus used this same contrast between walking with faith in him, the light of the world, versus stumbling in darkness without him, before he raised Lazarus from the dead:

> If anyone walks in the day, he does not stumble because he sees the light of this world. But if anyone walks in the night, he stumbles because the light is not in him. (Jn 11:9–10)

So also, Solomon calls on his son—and on each reader of Proverbs—to walk in God's light so that he can walk through this life, and to everlasting life, with Wisdom as his guide.

Proverbs 4:20–27

Sixth Address to a Son: Advice for Living a Righteous Life

Translation

4 [20]**My son, pay attention to my words;**
open your ears to what I say.
[21]**Do not let them escape from your sight.**
Keep them within your heart,
[22]**because they are life to those who find them,**
and healing for the entire body.
[23]**With all diligence guard your heart,**
because the source of life [comes] from it.
[24]**Turn yourself away from perverse speech,**
and keep corrupt lips far away from you.
[25]**Let your eyes look straight ahead,**
and let your gaze be directly in front of you.
[26]**Make a level pathway for your feet,**
and all your ways will be secure.
[27]**Do not bend to the right or the left.**
Turn your feet away from evil.

Textual Notes

4:20 הַט־אָזְנֶךָ׃—The Hiphil (H) imperative הַט is from the verb נָטָה, "to turn, incline." Its Hiphil with the object אֹזֶן, "ear," is a common idiom in Proverbs (4:20; 5:1, 13; 22:17) as well as in Jeremiah[a] and Psalms.[b] It is a synonym of the Hiphil verb הַקְשִׁיבָה, "pay attention," in the preceding clause. While the literal English "incline thine ear" (KJV) is archaic, a little of the form of the Hebrew can be retained by the more familiar "open your ears." Note the play on words with 4:27, the last verse in this section, where תֵּט, the Qal (G) imperfect of נָטָה, "to incline" to one side or the other, means "bend."

(a) Jer 7:24, 26; 11:8; 17:23; 25:4; 34:14; 35:15; 44:5

(b) Pss 17:6; 31:3 (ET 31:2); 45:11 (ET 45:10); 49:5 (ET 49:4); 71:2; 78:1; 86:1; 88:3 (ET 88:2); 102:3 (ET 102:2); 116:2

4:21 אַל־יַלִּזוּ מֵעֵינֶיךָ—Literally, "let them not depart from your eyes," this clause with the Hiphil (H) of לוּז, "to depart," is synonymous with the clause with the Qal (G) of לוּז in 3:21. See the textual note on 3:21. Instead of the expected form יָלִיזוּ the preformative has a short vowel (-ַי) and the following consonant takes a *daghesh forte* (-לּ-). See GKC, § 72 ee. The implied subject of the plural verb יַלִּזוּ is "my words" (דְּבָרַי and/or אֲמָרָי) in 4:20. That is also the referent of the plural pronoun הֵם, "they," in 4:22a.

4:22 כִּי־חַיִּים הֵם לְמֹצְאֵיהֶם—"They are life" recalls other promises about divine wisdom bestowing "life" (חַיִּים, e.g., 3:2, 18, 22; 4:10, 13), and it anticipates the promise in the next verse (4:23b). This clause refers to people in the plural: לְמֹצְאֵיהֶם, "to those (people) who find them [the words of wisdom]."

וּֽלְכָל־בְּשָׂרוֹ מַרְפֵּֽא׃—This is, literally, "and to all his flesh [they/the words are] healing." The referent of the pronoun ("his") on בְּשָׂרוֹ must be one individual out of the (plural) people in the previous clause who find the words. מַרְפֵּא, "healing," a noun from the verb רָפָא with the nominal prefix מ, recurs seven more times in Proverbs.[c]

(c) Prov 6:15; 12:18; 13:17; 14:30; 15:4; 16:24; 29:1

4:23 מִכָּל־מִשְׁמָר נְצֹר לִבֶּךָ—This difficult clause is, literally, "from all guarding guard your heart." The noun מִשְׁמָר here must refer to the quality of the act of guarding, so many English versions have "with diligence" or "with vigilance," which probably are accurate expressions of the meaning. The LXX translates the clause with an instrumental dative: πάσῃ φυλακῇ τήρει σὴν καρδίαν, "*with* all guarding guard your heart," and the Vulgate and Syriac translate similarly. Based on this, the editors of *BHS* assume that the ancient translations were from a Hebrew text that had the preposition בְּ in בְּכָל־, "with all … ," instead of the preposition מִן (on מִכָּל־), even though they favor following the reading of the MT. However, this assumption is not necessarily true. Occasionally מִן can be understood as meaning "with, using," in the same sense as בְּ, as with the parallel words בַחֲלֹמוֹת וּמֵחֶזְיֹנוֹת in Job 7:14. Compare also וּמִשִּׁירִי אֲהוֹדֶנּוּ in Ps 28:7 to אֲהַלְלָה ... בְשִׁיר in Ps 69:31 (ET 69:30). Another possibility is that מִן has a comparative force here: "more than all other guarding, guard your heart." Either understanding could have led to the LXX's perfectly defensible translation.

כִּֽי־מִמֶּנּוּ תּוֹצְאוֹת חַיִּֽים׃—The noun תּוֹצָאוֹת, from יָצָא, "to go out," always occurs as a plural, usually "extremities, edges of a border." Only here in the OT is it apparently an abstract plural meaning "source, origin," hence "source of life."

4:24 הָסֵר מִמְּךָ עִקְּשׁוּת פֶּה—This is, literally, "cause to turn away from yourself crookedness of mouth." The Hiphil (H) imperative of סוּר, "turn aside," has a causative meaning and recurs in 4:27b. The only other instance of the Hiphil in Proverbs is the participle in 28:9, but the Qal (G) is common. See, for example, the third textual note on 3:7.

The construct phrase עִקְּשׁוּת פֶּה is an idiom here and in 6:12 that signifies corrupt speech. The abstract feminine noun עִקְּשׁוּת occurs in the OT only in this phrase in 4:24 and 6:12, but it is cognate to the adjective עִקֵּשׁ, "crooked," and verb עָקַשׁ, "be crooked, twisted," for which see the first textual note on 2:15. The son is to avoid a "crooked mouth" of another person by ignoring corrupt speech. He is also to avoid having his own "crooked mouth" by speaking crooked words.

וּלְזוּת שְׂפָתַיִם—The construct phrase "deviation of lips" also signifies corrupt, perverse speech. The feminine noun לְזוּת, "crookedness, deviation," with the abstract ending וּת-, occurs only here in the OT. It is cognate to the verb לוּז, "deviate, depart," in 2:15; 3:21, 32; 4:21; 14:2 (see the second textual note on 2:15).

4:25 וְעַפְעַפֶּיךָ יַיְשִׁרוּ נֶגְדֶּֽךָ׃—Literally, "let your eyelids look straight before you," this refers to the son keeping his gaze straight ahead of him, as does the parallel first clause of the verse. He is not to look to the side, become distracted, and walk off the path. The reduplicated noun עַפְעַף, "eyelid," is from the verb עוּף, "to fly," and perhaps suggests the fluttering motion of blinking eyes. The noun recurs in 6:4, 25; 30:13.

The two verbs in this verse, יַבִּיטוּ (Hiphil [H] of נָבַט) and יַיְשִׁרוּ are each imperfect in form, but they each have the modal meaning of a jussive: "let your … ," that is, a form of command (see Joüon, § 113 m). The Hiphil of יָשַׁר, "be straight," occurs in the OT only here, in Ps 5:9, and possibly as the Kethib in Is 45:2. יַיְשִׁרוּ is an example of an uncontracted Hiphil imperfect (GKC, § 70b); the expected form would be יֵישִׁרוּ. Here the Hiphil apparently has the intransitive meaning "look straight" ahead (BDB). The cognate adjective יָשָׁר, "straight, upright," and cognate nouns are common in Proverbs, and so this verbal clause is part of the book's language for the Gospel and righteousness, versus the sin and condemnation involved in being crooked or deviating from the way.

4:26 פַּלֵּס מַעְגַּל רַגְלֶךָ—The Piel (D) verb פִּלֵּס is denominative, that is, it is formed from the noun פֶּלֶס "scale, balance." The verb is used here and in 5:6, 21 as well as in Is 26:7 and Ps 78:50 to mean "make (something) level" or "weigh (something)" (see BDB) with the extended meaning of "examine" (*HALOT*). The object of the Piel imperative is the construct phrase מַעְגַּל רַגְלֶךָ, literally, "the pathway of your foot." For מַעְגָּל, see the excursus "The Metaphor of the Path in Solomon's Wisdom" in the commentary on Proverbs 10.

וְכָל־דְּרָכֶיךָ יִכֹּנוּ׃—This clause with יִכֹּנוּ, the Niphal (N) imperfect of כּוּן, "be established, secure," probably serves as a promise attached to the preceding imperatival clause: "make level … and then [God promises that] all your ways will be secure." Many English versions understand the clause in that way, although KJV and NKJV take the verb as a modal imperfect, resulting in another command: "and let all your ways be established" (NKJV; cf. NIV).

4:27 אַל־תֵּט־יָמִין וּשְׂמֹאול—The identical negated verb אַל־תֵּט was in 4:5. It is the Qal (G) jussive of נָטָה, "turn aside, bend." Here the two nouns יָמִין וּשְׂמֹאול are adverbial accusatives indicating direction: "do not bend *(to the) right or (to the) left*." The only other proverb with both nouns is 3:16.

The LXX accurately translates this clause and the second clause of the verse in the MT. Then at the end of the verse the LXX adds this:

ὁδοὺς γὰρ τὰς ἐκ δεξιῶν οἶδεν ὁ θεός
    διεστραμμέναι δέ εἰσιν αἱ ἐξ ἀριστερῶν
αὐτὸς δὲ ὀρθὰς ποιήσει τὰς τροχιάς σου
    τὰς δὲ πορείας σου ἐν εἰρήνῃ προάξει.

For God knows the ways on the right,
    but those on the left are perverted.
He himself will make your paths straight
    and guide your travels in peace.

This addition changes the significance of the right and left directions in the first clause of this verse. That clause proscribes any deviation either to the right or to the left. The LXX addition makes the way on the right a positive direction, and only the left is negative.

The Western church fathers, who used the LXX version of Proverbs, generally emphasize that the Christian must go straight ahead and not turn in either direction.[1]

---

1 Origen, *Commentary on the Gospel of John*, 6.103 (Fathers of the Church 80:197–98); John Chrysostom, *Homilies on the First Epistle of Paul to the Thessalonians*, 9 (*NPNF*[1] 13:364);

Augustine notes that "the paths on the right hand are praised," but he still understands this passage as discouraging turning off the path in either direction (in harmony with 4:27a but contrary to the LXX's addition that commends turning to the right).[2]

In the Torah Yahweh commands his people to follow his Word and not deviate from it either to the right or the left (Deut 5:32; 17:11, 20; 28:14), and later passages echo that language (Josh 1:7; 23:6; 2 Ki 22:2 || 2 Chr 34:2). Yet there are some passages that support the divine favor shown to those on the right in the addition to LXX Prov 4:27. Jacob confers greater blessing with his right hand than with his left on the grandsons in Gen 48:13–14. In Eccl 10:2 Solomon associates going to the right with wisdom and going to the left with foolishness. In the final judgment, Jesus declares that believers will be gathered to his right before they are welcomed into the eternal kingdom and that unbelievers will be on his left before they are condemned (Mt 25:33–34, 41; cf. Is 63:12; Ps 109:31). After his resurrection and ascension, Jesus himself was enthroned at the right hand of the Father, fulfilling Ps 110:1 (see, e.g., Mt 26:64; Acts 2:33; 7:55–56; Rom 8:34; Col 3:1).

Commentary

In this sixth address in Proverbs 1–9 from a father to a son,[3] Solomon instructs his son to avoid evil by focusing on the body. He mentions ten parts of the body: ears (אָזְנֶךָ, 4:20); eyes (twice: עֵינֶיךָ, 4:21, and עֵינֶיךָ, 4:25); heart (twice: לְבָבֶךָ, 4:21, and לִבֶּךָ, 4:23); the whole body (בְּשָׂרוֹ, 4:22); mouth (the literal meaning of פֶּה in 4:24); lips (שְׂפָתַיִם, 4:24); eyelids (the literal meaning of עַפְעַפֶּיךָ in 4:25); foot (twice: רַגְלֶךָ in 4:26 and רַגְלְךָ in 4:27); the right side/hand (יָמִין, 4:27); and the left side/hand (שְׂמֹאול, 4:27). He also organizes his thoughts into ten mandates:[4]

1. 4:20a: "Pay attention to my words."
2. 4:20b: "Open your ears to what I say."
3. 4:21a: "Do not let them escape from your sight."
4. 4:21b: "Keep them within your heart."
5. 4:23: "Guard your heart."
6. 4:24: "Turn yourself away from perverse speech."
7. 4:25: "Let your eyes look straight ahead."
8. 4:26: "Make a level pathway for your feet."
9. 4:27a: "Do not bend."
10. 4:27b: "Turn your feet away from evil."

Gregory of Nazianzus, *Orations*, 2.34 (*NPNF*[2] 7:212); John Cassian, *On the Institutes of the Coenobia*, book 11 ("Of the Spirit of Vainglory"), chapter 4 (*NPNF*[2] 11:276).

2 Augustine, Letter 215 (*NPNF*[1] 5:440). See also *On the Merits and Forgiveness of Sins, and on the Baptism of Infants*, 2.57 (*NPNF*[1] 5:67).

3 For the ten addresses from father to son in Proverbs 1–9, see the excursus "Proverbs 1–9, Christ, and the Ten Commandments" in the commentary on chapter 1.

4 The imperative in 4:24b and the command in 4:25b simply restate and emphasize the mandates in 4:24a and 4:25a. As such, they are not additional mandates, but extensions of the two mandates they serve to reinforce.

The weaving of the ten body parts through the ten mandates in this address serves to unite them into one instruction. Especially the early mandates in this section can serve as Gospel invitations to receive and believe God's Word and so be saved and be preserved in that salvation throughout this life, until the hearing son or believer enters the fullness of everlasting "life" (4:22–23). While these imperatives could easily be seen as only commands, so that this section would be primarily Law (God's demands for what people must do), it should be understood within the larger context as one of the ten speeches from the father to his son, which have a predominantly Gospel emphasis.[5] They are invitations to walk in the light of the Gospel. For those who are already believers, they also can serve as the third use of the Law, which presupposes the Gospel.[6]

The address opens with the familiar admonition to heed and accept the father's instruction (4:20–21). However, Solomon makes this admonition unique by his introduction of parts of the body. He tells his son the reason why he should accept his instruction: his words are "life" and "healing" (4:22). This twofold promise emphasizes both the temporal blessings of life and health now and also the eternal promise of God for the resurrection to eternal life hereafter. The assurance that the divine words of wisdom passed down from the father[7] will be "healing for the entire body" (4:22) will be fulfilled by the resurrection of the body on the Last Day (Dan 12:2–3), when our bodies shall be glorified to be like that of the risen Christ (1 Corinthians 15). Yet already now the believer has eternal life and may receive healing; Christians are touched physically by God through his Sacraments of Baptism and Communion (see also the commentary on Prov 12:18).

By concluding each of the opening verses of his address with a reference to a part of the body (4:20b, 21b, and 22b, plus, literally, "eyes" in 4:21a), Solomon emphasizes his use of parts of the body throughout this address.

Prov 4:23–25 speaks of ways that the son should guard his heart. The unusual phrasing of 4:23 (see the first textual note on 4:23) accents the diligence with which the son should do these things. That the son needs to guard his heart refers to his spiritual, emotional, and intellectual life as well as his ability to critically evaluate situations and use his will.[8] The reason for this mandate is that the source of life comes from it. While the NIV and a number of commentators[9] understand 4:23 as saying that the heart itself *is* the source of life, the Hebrew text clearly says that "the source of life" comes "*from*" the heart.

---

5 For the ten addresses from father to son in Proverbs 1–9, see the excursus "Proverbs 1–9, Christ, and the Ten Commandments" in the commentary on chapter 1.

6 See further "Law and Gospel in Proverbs" in the introduction.

7 In 4:3–6 Solomon noted that he had received words of divine wisdom through his father, David, before passing them down to the "sons" (4:1).

8 For לֵב, "heart," see the first textual note on 2:10.

9 Clifford, *Proverbs*, 64–65; Garrett, *Proverbs, Ecclesiastes, Song of Songs*, 88–89.

This is an allusion to the indwelling of the Holy Spirit, who through the Word of God and Baptism dwells in the heart of each believer and flows forth with life-giving power.[10] The power of the Spirit is what will enable the son to follow his father's advice. He needs to guard his heart so that he does not grieve and abandon the Spirit, the source of life. The NT affirms that the Spirit gives life (e.g., Jn 6:63; 2 Cor 3:6; cf. Rom 8:11; 1 Cor 15:45), and drawing on this biblical language, the Nicene Creed confesses that the Holy Spirit "is the Lord and giver of life."

The way to guard one's heart is explained in Prov 4:24–25. First, 4:24 invites the son to turn away from sinful speech. While many versions (e.g., NIV, NRSV) understand this as only instructing the son not to say inappropriate things, the Hebrew text is more ambiguous. It says that the son must avoid a perverse mouth and keep corrupt lips far away. This certainly means that the son himself is not to speak such things, yet it can also mean that the son is not to be where others speak such language, and he is to avoid those who teach false doctrine and espouse perverse ideas (Rom 16:17–18). The ambiguity is probably intended: the son is counseled not to speak lies and falsehoods, which originate from the devil (Jn 8:44; cf. Eph 4:25; 1 Jn 2:4, 22; 4:20), and he is also not to place himself where pernicious speech can be heard so that he does not learn and believe it. Then Prov 4:25 reminds the son to stay focused on his course in life, looking in front of him and not allowing his eyes to wander in other directions. It functions as a transition to the closing of this address (4:26–27), which reintroduces the metaphor of the path.[11]

The last verses of this address urge the son once again to live according to the father's instruction. When the son puts his father's instruction to work by acting on it, he makes his path level and easy to travel (4:26). God promises to offer him (and every believer) security. The son is also advised to remain upright, not to lean or bend to the right or the left, since this could lead him off the path (4:27). He is also urged purposely to turn away from evil.

The caution of the involvement of one's body in sin is highlighted even more forcefully in Jesus' use of hyperbole when he instructs his disciples:

> If your right eye causes you to sin, gouge it out and throw it away from you. For it is better for you that one of your members should perish so that your whole body will not be thrown into hell. And if your right hand causes you to sin, cut it off and throw it away from you. For it is better for you that one of your members should perish so that your whole body will not go away into hell. (Mt 5:29–30; see also 1 Cor 6:9–20)

---

[10] See, for example, Is 44:3; Ezek 11:19–20; 36:25–27; Joel 3:1–2 (ET 2:28–29); Jn 3:5; 4:14; 7:38–39; Acts 2:38–39; Rom 8:9–11 (cf. Rom 6:1–4); 1 Cor 3:16; Titus 3:4–7. Note how many of these passages describe the gift of the Spirit with water imagery or specifically promise that God will pour out his Spirit on those who receive the Sacrament of Baptism into Christ.

[11] See the excursus "The Metaphor of the Path in Solomon's Wisdom" in the commentary on Proverbs 10.

Just as Solomon warns his son about misusing the mouth for evil, James writes to his readers about the dangers of the misuse of the tongue:

> So also the tongue is a small member, yet it boasts great things. Look how such a small fire sets ablaze such a great forest! And the tongue is a fire. The tongue is a world of unrighteousness set among our members, staining the whole body, setting on fire the whole course of life, and set on fire by hell. For every kind of wild animal and bird, of reptile and sea creature, can be tamed and has been tamed by mankind, but no person can tame the tongue, a restless evil full of deadly poison. With it we bless our Lord and Father, and with it we curse people who are made in the likeness of God. From the same mouth come blessing and cursing. My brothers, these things ought not to be so. (James 3:5–10)

Proverbs 5:1–23

Seventh Address to a Son: Wisdom Teaches You to Avoid Adultery

Translation

5 **[1]My son, pay attention to my wisdom.**
Open your ears to my understanding
[2]so that you may keep insight
and your lips may guard knowledge,
[3]because the lips of a woman who is a stranger drip with honey
and her palate is smooth with olive oil,
[4]but in the end she is bitter like wormwood
and sharp like a double-edged sword.
[5]Her feet go down to death;
her steps proceed to Sheol.
[6]She does not make the path of life level.
Her pathways wander, and she doesn't realize it.

[7]Now sons, listen to me.
Do not turn away from the words from my mouth.
[8]Keep your way far from her,
and do not go near the doorway of her house.
[9]Otherwise you will give your strength to others
and your years to a cruel person.
[10]Otherwise your work will make strangers content,
and your labors [will be] in a foreigner's house.
[11]But you will groan when your end [comes],
when your body and flesh are consumed.
[12]Then you will say, "Oh how I hated discipline,
and my heart despised warning!
[13]I didn't listen to my teachers' voice,
and I didn't open my ears to [hear] my instructors.
[14]I soon reached total ruin
in the midst of the assembly and congregation."

[15]Drink water from your own cistern
and running water from your own well.
[16]Why should [water from] your springs be dispersed in public,
[your] streams [be dispersed] in the open squares?
[17]They should be yours, yours alone,
and none are for strangers [who are] with you.
[18]Let your fountain be blessed,
and rejoice because of the wife you married in your youth,

[19]a loving doe and a graceful ibex—
let her breasts satisfy you at all times;
always be intoxicated with her love.
[20]Why should you be intoxicated, my son, with a woman who is a stranger
and embrace the bosom a foreign woman?

[21]For the ways of a man are in front of the eyes of Yahweh,
and he examines all of his pathways.
[22]The evil deeds of the wicked man will capture him,
and he will be bound by the cords of his sin.
[23]He will die for lack of discipline,
and he will go astray because of his great stupidity.

Textual Notes

5:1 בְּנִי לְחָכְמָתִי הַקְשִׁיבָה—See "חָכְמָה, 'Wisdom,' and Related Words" in "Wisdom in Proverbs" in the introduction. בְּנִי and the emphatic Hiphil (H) imperative הַקְשִׁיבָה were also in 4:20a.

לִתְבוּנָתִי הַט־אָזְנֶךָ׃—For the noun תְּבוּנָה, which is cognate to בִּינָה, see "בִּינָה, 'Understanding,' and Related Words" in "Wisdom in Proverbs" in the introduction. For the idiom with the Hiphil (H) of נָטָה and אֹזֶן, "to open the ear," which in this chapter recurs in 5:13, see the textual note on 4:20.

5:2 לִשְׁמֹר מְזִמּוֹת—See "מְזִמָּה, 'Insight, Foresight' " in "Wisdom in Proverbs" in the introduction. Previously in Proverbs only the singular מְזִמָּה was used (1:4; 2:11; 3:21). However, here and in the rest of the book (8:12; 12:2; 14:17; 24:8) only the plural is used, perhaps as an intensive plural, "keen insight."

וְדַעַת שְׂפָתֶיךָ יִנְצֹרוּ׃—For the object noun דַּעַת, see "דַּעַת, 'Knowledge,' and יָדַע, 'to Know' "in "Wisdom in Proverbs" in the introduction. Even though שָׂפָה, "lip," is a feminine noun, its suffixed dual, שְׂפָתֶיךָ, is the subject of the masculine verb יִנְצֹרוּ due to the Hebrew preference for the more common masculine verb forms (GKC, § 145 u). The imperfect verb יִנְצֹרוּ continues the idea of purpose expressed by the infinitive construct לִשְׁמֹר at the start of the verse: "so that you may keep insight and your lips *may* guard knowledge" (see Joüon, § 124 q).

5:3 כִּי נֹפֶת תִּטֹּפְנָה שִׂפְתֵי זָרָה—In form זָרָה is the feminine participle of זוּר. It is rendered as "a woman who is a stranger" here and in 5:20. See the first textual note on 2:16, which has the fuller phrase אִשָּׁה זָרָה. The masculine plural participle זָרִים is rendered as "strangers" in 5:10, 17.

The dual construct (שִׂפְתֵי) of the feminine noun שָׂפָה, "lip," is the subject of the Qal (G) feminine plural imperfect (תִּטֹּפְנָה) of נָטַף, "to drip," and the noun נֹפֶת is an adverbial accusative, "*with* honey." Solomon uses the same vocabulary in Song 4:11 (נֹפֶת תִּטֹּפְנָה שִׂפְתוֹתַיִךְ, "your lips drip with honey"), but there he is praising the sweet lips of his "bride" (כַּלָּה), not another woman.[1] See also the textual note on Prov 5:15–20.

---

1 For a philological analysis and theological commentary, see Mitchell, *The Song of Songs*, 835–36, 860–61.

וְחָלָק מִשֶּׁמֶן חִכָּהּ׃—The adjective חָלָק, "smooth, deceptive, seductive," is cognate to the verb חָלַק, which can refer to seductive speech; see the second textual note on 2:16. The adjective refers to a "smooth/seductive mouth" in 26:28. Here the preposition מִן on שֶׁמֶן probably denotes cause, hence "smooth from/with olive oil." The noun חֵךְ, "palate," recurs in 8:7 and in 24:13, which refers to a palate sweet with honey. See also חֵךְ in Song 2:3; 5:16; 7:10 (ET 7:9).

5:4 וְאַחֲרִיתָהּ מָרָה כַלַּעֲנָה—The noun אַחֲרִית, "end," recurs in 5:11 and often later in Proverbs. It can have an eschatological meaning, referring to the last days and pointing toward eternity in heaven or hell. See, for example, Is 2:2 || Micah 4:1; Hos 3:5; Dan 8:19; 10:14; see also the Aramaic cognate in Dan 2:28.

"Wormwood" (לַעֲנָה) is one of several species of the genus *artemisia*. The *artemisia judaica* is native to Palestine. Its juice has a bitter taste and, if drunk without being diluted, can be mildly poisonous. If diluted properly, it can be used medicinally.[2]

חַדָּה כְּחֶרֶב פִּיּוֹת׃—The noun חֶרֶב is feminine, hence the feminine (חַדָּה) of the adjective חַד, which describes the sword as "sharp" (see also Is 49:2; Ezek 5:1; Ps 57:5 [ET 57:4]). The construct phrase חֶרֶב פִּיּוֹת, literally, "a sword of mouths," means "a double-edged sword." The NT refers to swords as δίστομος, "two-mouthed," in Heb 4:12; Rev 1:16; 2:12. The plural form of פֶּה, "mouth," פִּיּוֹת, has bothered some commentators since it occurs only here in the OT and the reduplicated plural form פִּיפִיּוֹת is used to describe a double-edged sword in Is 41:15 and Ps 149:6.[3] However, the similar form פֵּיוֹת is used in Judg 3:16 to describe a double-edged sword. See GKC, § 96, s.v. פֶּה, and Joüon, § 98 e (10).

5:5 מָוֶת שְׁאוֹל צְעָדֶיהָ יִתְמֹכוּ׃—In the Hebrew "death" and "Sheol" are adjacent, emphasizing that Sheol is the place of eternal death. See the first textual note and the commentary on 1:12. The two are parallel to each other also in 7:27. Instead of the usual meaning of תָּמַךְ, "to hold, grasp," here יִתְמֹכוּ means that the steps of her feet "proceed" to Sheol (*HALOT*, 4 a).

5:6 אֹרַח חַיִּים פֶּן־תְּפַלֵּס—"The paths of life, lest she make level" is difficult. *BHS* proposes reading בַּל or perhaps לֹא instead of פֶּן, though this is not necessary, since פֶּן can negate a verb and mean "not."[4] (It is translated as "otherwise" in 5:9–10.) For the Piel (D) verb פִּלֵּס, "make level," see the first textual note on 4:26. Note the play on two meanings of the verb here and in 5:21, where it means "examine, evaluate."

5:9 פֶּן־תִּתֵּן לַאֲחֵרִים הוֹדֶךָ—Usually the noun הוֹד means "splendor, majesty," but here it refers to "manly *vigour*" (BDB, 3 c) and is translated as "strength." It is a synonym of כֹּחַ, for which, see the next textual note.

5:10 פֶּן־יִשְׂבְּעוּ זָרִים כֹּחֶךָ—Literally, this is "lest/otherwise strangers will be full/satisfied [with] your strength." Here כֹּחַ, normally "strength," refers by metonymy to the "work" a person accomplishes using his strength—the fruit of his labor, the goods a

---

2 *FF*, 198.

3 E.g., Delitzsch, *Proverbs*, 1:120.

4 Cf. V. P. Hamilton, "פֶּן," *TWOT* 2:726–27.

person works for and earns. "Strangers" (זָרִים) will gain possession of them and so "be satisfied, content" (שָׂבַע) because of them.

וַעֲצָבֶיךָ בְּבֵית נָכְרִי׃—The noun עֶצֶב can mean "pain, hurt" (e.g., Gen 3:16; Prov 10:22; 15:1), but here and in 14:23, it means "toil, work, labor."

5:11 וְנָהַמְתָּ—This rare form meaning "then you will groan" was apparently read by the LXX as the more familiar וְנִחַמְתָּ and translated with καὶ μεταμεληθήσῃ, "and you will repent."

בִּכְלוֹת—This infinitive construct of כָּלָה is used temporally here. כָּלָה means "to be finished, be complete" and can have the sense "be consumed."[5]

5:12 וְאָמַרְתָּ אֵיךְ שָׂנֵאתִי מוּסָר—For the noun מוּסָר, which in this chapter recurs in 5:23, see "מוּסָר, 'Discipline,' and יָסַר, 'to Discipline' " in "Wisdom in Proverbs" in the introduction.

וְתוֹכַחַת נָאַץ לִבִּי׃—For the noun תּוֹכַחַת, "warning," see the first textual note on 1:23.

5:13 מוֹרָי וְלִמְלַמְּדַי—Note the chiastic placement of these two plural participles for "my teachers/instructors" in the center of the verse. In form מוֹרָי is the Hiphil (H) participle of יָרָה, "to teach" (see the first textual note on 4:4).

The Qal (G) of לָמַד means "to learn" (30:3), and the Piel (D) has the causative meaning, "to teach, instruct."

5:14 כִּמְעַט הָיִיתִי בְכָל־רָע—Literally, "like a little I was in all evil." The combination of כְּ and מְעַט can mean "almost, nearly" when describing an unrealized action (see BDB, s.v. מְעַט, 2 a; *HALOT*, s.v. מְעַט, 6 a). It can also mean "soon, quickly, in a short time" (see BDB, 2 b and c; *HALOT*, 6 a), and this meaning is supported by the depiction of the disaster that has already happened to the son in 5:11.

The noun רַע has a wide semantic range and denotes all kinds of things that are harmful and injurious as well as things that are intrinsically evil (see the large number of nuances for this word in *HALOT*). In this case the phrase, literally, "in all evil/harm" signifies the everlasting ruin of the sinner. Thus "total ruin" or similar phraseology is the translation favored by most English versions.

5:15–20 Much of the vocabulary and imagery in 5:15–20 pertaining to the relationship between husband and wife is also found in the Song of Songs. These similarities are easily explained if the interpreter accepts that Solomon is the author of both the Song of Songs (as stated in Song 1:1)[6] and the author of Proverbs 1–9.[7] See also the textual notes on Prov 5:3, which point out vocabulary shared with the Song.

5:15 שְׁתֵה־מַיִם מִבּוֹרֶךָ—The noun מַיִם is a term for water that also occurs in the portrayal of the wife in Song 4:15. The noun בּוֹר, "cistern, pit," is sometimes spelled באר and can be a synonym of בְּאֵר, "well," in the second clause of the verse.

---

5 Cf. J. N. Oswalt, "כָּלָה," *TWOT* 1:439–40.

6 For the Song verses cited in the following notes, see Mitchell, *The Song of Songs*, who interprets the Song as authored by Solomon.

7 See "Authorship and Date" in the introduction.

וְנֹזְלִים מִתּוֹךְ בְּאֵרֶךָ׃—The plural participle of נָזַל, "to flow," can be used as a substantive for "running water" or "streams" of water, as also in, for example, Is 44:3; Ps 78:16; and Song 4:15, where, as here, the word is a metaphor for a wife. So also בְּאֵר, "well," is a metaphor in the Edenic description of the wife in Song 4:15.

5:16 יָפוּצוּ מַעְיְנֹתֶיךָ חוּצָה—Hebrew questions need not be marked by any interrogative word, and in the larger context here, this verse must be a question (GKC, § 150 a). The imperfect יָפוּצוּ must have a modal meaning: "*why should* [water from] your springs *be dispersed* … ?" This verb does double duty as the implied verb in the next clause. The noun מַעְיָן, "a spring (of water)," is a metaphor for the wife also in the paradisiacal Song 4:12, 15. חוּצָה, with locative *he*, can mean "publicly," as did בַּחוּץ in 1:20; see the first textual note on 1:20. It is a synonym of בָּרְחֹבוֹת, "in the (open) squares," in the next clause.

בָּרְחֹבוֹת פַּלְגֵי־מָיִם׃—The construct phrase פַּלְגֵי־מָיִם is, literally, "streams of water," but the English equivalent is simply "streams."

While Hebrew often marks bodies of water to indicate that they are not dry, for example, עֵין הַמַּיִם, "a spring of water" (Gen 16:7; compare NIV to NRSV), English marks them only when they are dry, for example, "a dry well" or "a dry riverbed." The reason for the preferences is due to the geography and climate in which the languages were first used. In Palestine water is scarce, and one could not always expect to find water in a river or a well, so the body of water was often marked by the addition of "of water" to indicate that water was present. English was formed in a climate where water was relatively abundant, and bodies of water could be expected to contain water most of the time. The marking "of water" is superfluous and unnatural in English. Therefore, when translating into English, it is often unnecessary to include "of water" even when it is explicitly in the Hebrew text. On the other hand, it is sometimes necessary to include "dry" where the Hebrew text does not explicitly have such a word.

5:17 יִהְיוּ־לְךָ לְבַדֶּךָ וְאֵין לְזָרִים אִתָּךְ׃—The imperfect יִהְיוּ has the modal force of an injunction: "they *should/must* be yours, yours alone." In the second clause, the particle וְאֵין has a similar but negative verbal force (see GKC, § 152 o).

5:18 יְהִי־מְקוֹרְךָ בָרוּךְ—"Let your fountain be blessed" exhorts the husband to have the attitude of thanks and praise to God for his wife. This faith-filled disposition includes his exclusive marital devotion to her alone. He should also consider his believing wife to be a source ("fountain") of blessing. The noun מָקוֹר, "fountain," recurs in the phrase "fountain of life," which describes the benefits of a righteous person who speaks up (10:11; contrast 25:26), divine wisdom (13:14; 16:22), and the fear of Yahweh (14:27). It also occurs in "fountain of wisdom" in 18:4.

The Qal passive (Gp) participle בָּרוּךְ, which occurs in Proverbs only here, is a synonym of אַשְׁרֵי, "blessed," for which, see the first textual note on 3:13. The formula with the jussive יְהִי … בָּרוּךְ is used to bless or praise God in 1 Ki 10:9 ‖ 2 Chr 9:8 (cf. Ps 113:2; Job 1:21). Besides Prov 5:18, that formula's only other use in the OT to refer to a person is in Ruth 2:19, where Naomi prays for God to bless the person (Boaz) who graciously allowed Ruth to glean in his field, providing sustenance for the life of Ruth and Naomi.

The LXX has ἡ πηγή σου τοῦ ὕδατος ἔστω σοι ἰδία, "let your fountain of water be yours alone." This is probably a misreading of בָּרוּךְ as לְבַדְּךָ under the influence of 5:17, where לְבַדֶּךָ ended the first clause.

מֵאֵשֶׁת נְעוּרֶךָ׃—This construct chain has an adjectival genitive specifying time. Thus the phrase means "because of the wife *you married in your youth*."

5:19 אַיֶּלֶת אֲהָבִים—Deer and similar animals are symbols of grace, agility, and beauty also in the Song. The masculine noun אַיָּל, "hart, stag, deer," is used in similes for Solomon the bridegroom in Song 2:9, 17; 8:14. The feminine form אַיָּלָה, "doe, hind," occurs in Song 2:7 and 3:5. Here it is in construct with the plural of אַהַב, "love," which occurs only here and in Hos 8:9, although it is cognate to the common noun אַהֲבָה in 5:19c. The construct phrase is rendered with an adjectival genitive: "a doe of loves" means "a loving doe," as in some translations ("loving" in KJV, NIV, NASB). The next construct phrase is similar in meaning. However, others take the construct phrase to mean that the doe is the "(object) of [the husband's] love" (Joüon, § 129 g), a "beloved hind" (Waltke-O'Connor, § 9.5.3b, example 4).

וְיַעֲלַת־חֵן—Literally, "an ibex of grace," this phrase with an adjectival genitive is rendered "a graceful ibex." For חֵן, "grace," see the first textual note on 1:9. The male ibex (יָעֵל) is mentioned in 1 Sam 24:3 (ET 24:2); Ps 104:18; Job 39:1. The feminine יַעֲלָה, "female mountain goat" or "ibex" (the LXX has πῶλος, "colt") is often translated as "deer" in English versions, perhaps because "goat" has a negative connotation in English and because the female ibex is only mentioned here in the entire OT.[8]

דַּדֶּיהָ יְרַוֻּךָ בְכָל־עֵת—The rare noun דַּד (only here and in Ezek 23:3, 8, 21) is a synonym of שַׁד, "breast," as in, for example, Song 1:13; 4:5; 7:4, 8–9 (ET 7:3, 7–8); 8:1, 8, 10. דַּד always occur in the dual, as does שַׁד except in Lam 4:3, where it refers to the breast of a jackal. Oddly, both words are grammatically masculine; here דַּדֶּיהָ is the subject of the masculine verb יְרַוֻּךָ. The Qal (G) of רָוָה in Prov 7:18 means "to drink one's fill." יְרַוֻּךָ is Piel (D), which can have the intransitive meaning "to be intoxicated, drunk" (BDB, 1; cf. שָׁגָה, "to be intoxicated," in 5:19c, 20a). However, the suffix (ךָ-, "you") shows that it must have the transitive meaning, literally, "to drench, water abundantly," or figuratively, "to satisfy." The imperfect יְרַוֻּךָ has a jussive meaning: literally, "may/let her breasts satisfy you in every time."

בְּאַהֲבָתָהּ—The noun אַהֲבָה can refer to God's "love" or to "love" in human relationships, as in its other occurrences in Proverbs (10:12; 15:17; 17:9; 27:5). It refers to "love" in marriage here and also in, for example, Song 2:4–5; 5:8; 8:6–7.

5:19–20, 23 תִּשְׁגֶּה ... תִשְׁגֶּה ... יִשְׁגֶּה׃—The Qal (G) of שָׁגָה can mean "to be intoxicated, drunk (with/on)," when accompanied by a prepositional phrase with בְּ, "with," as in 5:19 (בְּאַהֲבָתָהּ), again in 5:20 (בְזָרָה), and also in 20:1. This probably is the meaning intended in 5:19–20. Even though שָׁגָה can also mean "to go astray, sin," often inadvertently,[9] the father speaking Proverbs 5 is not implying that his son goes astray or sins by enjoying his wife's love. However, in 5:23 (also 19:27) the Qal of שָׁגָה does

---

8 Cf. *FF*, 46–47.

9 V. P. Hamilton, "שָׁגָה," *TWOT* 2:904.

denote foolish straying into sin (see also the Hiphil participle in 28:10, which has the corresponding causative meaning). A play on the various connotations of this word is formed when 5:23 is contrasted with 5:19–20.

5:20 וּתְחַבֵּק חֵק נָכְרִיָּה׃—The Piel (D) of חָבַק, "to embrace," was also in 4:8. חֵק is the defectively written construct form of the noun חֵיק, which here refers to the female "bosom" as rarely elsewhere (1 Ki 3:20). More often it refers to a man's embrace of a woman (e.g., Gen 16:5; 2 Sam 12:8) or a man's chest (Prov 6:27) or lap (Prov 16:33). נָכְרִיָּה, "a foreign woman," is a synonym of זָרָה, "a woman who is a stranger" (5:3, 20a). See the first textual note on 2:16.

5:21 וְכָל־מַעְגְּלֹתָיו מְפַלֵּס׃—Here the Piel (D) of פָּלַס means "examine, evaluate." See the first textual notes on 4:26 and 5:6.

5:22 עֲוֹונֹתָיו יִלְכְּדֻנוֹ אֶת־הָרָשָׁע—The subject of 5:21b is Yahweh, but in 5:22–23 the focus changes abruptly to הָרָשָׁע, "the wicked man." This clause is, literally, "his iniquities will capture him—the wicked man." The noun עָוֹן, "iniquity," is common in the Torah and the Prophets but recurs in Proverbs only in 16:6. The third masculine singular suffix on the verb יִלְכְּדֻנוֹ with paragogic *nun* (cf. GKC, § 60 e) is proleptic or anticipatory (Joüon, § 146 e (2)) and is the first direct object. Then אֶת־הָרָשָׁע is a second direct object or an object complement that clarifies the referent of the suffix.

5:23 וּבְרֹב אִוַּלְתּוֹ—The preposition בְּ here has a causal force (BDB, III 5): literally, "because of the magnitude of his foolishness." See "אֱוִיל, 'Stubborn Fool,' and אִוֶּלֶת, 'Stupidity' " in "Fools in Proverbs" in the introduction.

Commentary

This is the seventh address in Proverbs 1–9 from a father to a son.[10] The subject of this address is chastity.[11] It is organized into four distinct sections:

- 5:1–6: First warning against adultery
- 5:7–14: Second warning against adultery
- 5:15–20: Encouragement to marital faithfulness
- 5:21–23: Yahweh's examination and punishment of the sinner

First Warning against Adultery (5:1–6)

Solomon begins this address as he does others, calling on the son to listen and acquire wisdom. His address links this instruction to the previous one in two ways. First, 5:1 employs the clause הַט־אָזְנֶךָ, "open your ears," first used in 4:20. Second, Prov 5:2 states that the son will learn to use his lips wisely, in

[10] For the ten addresses from father to son in Proverbs 1–9, see the excursus "Proverbs 1–9, Christ, and the Ten Commandments" in the commentary on chapter 1.

[11] "Chastity" is used in this commentary with its basic meaning: "refraining from sexual intercourse that is contrary to God's Law." Thus it refers to refraining from sexual intercourse except within the holy covenant marriage: the lifelong, exclusive union of one man and one woman. Throughout Proverbs 1–9 Solomon warns his son against engaging in any kind of fornication or adultery with a strange or foreign woman, that is, any woman other than the son's wife. Of course, homosexual relations are intrinsically sinful and are contrary to God's Word. See the excursus "Homosexuality" in Lockwood, *1 Corinthians*, 204–9.

contrast to the corrupt lips of 4:24. The use of the wisdom the son is gaining is then applied to a specific situation: the temptation to seduction by a woman who is a stranger. The contrast between the lips serves immediately to cause the son to be wary of this woman: the son's lips are to guard knowledge (5:2b), while the seductress's lips are inviting, dripping with honey (5:3a). Her honeyed lips and oiled palate (5:3) appear desirable, but the son, whose lips are to safeguard divine knowledge, is given pause to consider whether she is as attractive as she first appears.

What is the purpose of the woman's lips? Are they seductive because of the words she speaks, or are they desirable to kiss, as the use of "palate" in the parallel line (5:3b) might suggest? In 2:16 the woman's words are "smooth"; here her palate is "smooth." The Hebrew text is purposely ambiguous, suggesting that she seduces with kisses as well as words, as she does later in 7:13–20.

The suspicions aroused by the contrasting use of lips in 5:2–3 are confirmed in 5:4, where her words become a double-edged sword, literally, "a sword of mouths." The son is told that she is not as attractive as she seems because later on she and her words lead to bitterness, violence, and even death (5:4–5; see also, e.g., 2:18; 5:23). "Sword" is often used as a metaphor for violence and death under God's curse for violating his covenant (Lev 26:25, 33, 36–37; Deut 32:25; Lam 5:9; contrast the covenant blessing in Lev 26:6).

Prov 5:5–6 once again introduces the metaphor of the path,[12] this time speaking of the adulterous woman's path. The son is discouraged from adultery as the father offers the son the benefit of his foresight into the end of the woman's path, upon which the son also might be tempted to walk. It leads to "death" and "Sheol" (5:5), that is, everlasting condemnation in hell. Moreover, the adulterous woman does not make her path in life level nor realize where it is leading (5:6). These are direct contrasts to the father's previous instructions, where he informed his son that the way of divine wisdom leads to everlasting life and bodily healing, that is, resurrection (4:22), and where he urged his son to make a level path for his feet (4:26).[13] By depicting the adulteress in this contrasting way, the father is discouraging the son from being like her. If he would join her in her adultery, he also would abandon the wisdom his father gave him and fail to use the foresight available to him through God's words. By lampooning the adulteress' inability to see the consequences of her acts, the father is powerfully preaching the Law to his son in order to keep him from foolish behavior.[14]

---

[12] See the excursus "The Metaphor of the Path in Solomon's Wisdom" in the commentary on Proverbs 10.

[13] Some have noted that the third feminine singular verbs in 5:6 could be read as second masculine singular so that the son is said not to consider the path of life and not realize where he is being led. (See Garrett, *Proverbs, Ecclesiastes, Song of Songs*, 91–92; Murphy, *Proverbs*, 29–30.) Such a reading, while grammatically possible, is not probable considering that the antecedent of the first verb in 5:6 is the feminine singular suffix in 5:5 and the antecedent of the second verb is the feminine singular suffix in 5:6.

[14] See further "Law and Gospel in Proverbs" in the introduction.

Second Warning against Adultery (5:7–14)

Prov 5:7 repeats the opening appeal of 5:1 in different words. The signal that this is a reprise of the opening appeal in the middle of an address (and not the beginning of a new address) is the phrase וְעַתָּה בָנִים, "and now sons," which always occurs in the middle of an address to resume the father's instruction (7:24; 8:32). In addition, this phrase hints that the addresses are not intended only for one particular son. Instead, like the address to plural "sons" in 4:1–9, they apply to all the father's sons, and indeed to all who hear the father's words recorded in the Scriptures. "He who has ears to hear, let him hear" (Lk 8:8; 14:35).

Prov 5:8 makes explicit the warning implied in 5:5–6. Here the father simply tells the son to keep his distance from the adulteress. Prov 5:9–14 makes explicit the consequences of adultery for the son. The consequences of lack of chastity were explicit for the adulteress in 5:5–6, but only implied for the son. Prov 5:9–10 states that the punishment for adultery will somehow cause the son to work for others. His years and strength will belong to them. They will benefit from his God-given abilities, but he will not. The identity of those who will benefit from his efforts is hidden from the reader. The son is left to guess about whom the father is speaking. Is it the adulterous woman, her cuckolded husband, or someone else who will exploit the son's sinful choice? The ambiguity implies that it could be any number of people who take advantage of the son. This is intended to point out the vulnerability of a person who places himself in such a foolish position.

Prov 5:11–12 depicts the son later in life expressing his regrets over his sin and its consequences. Prov 5:11 may be a reference to a sexually transmitted disease, which has ravaged the body of the son ("when your body and flesh are consumed"). It may, on the other hand, be speaking of the physical and psychological manifestations of the feelings of guilt and remorse over sin. Certainly 5:12–13 depicts the son as speaking of his remorse for not having heeded the warnings of his teachers, who would include especially his father and mother (1:8; 4:3–4; 6:20). In 5:14 the son notes that he had suffered "total ruin" among "the assembly and the congregation" (קָהָל וְעֵדָה). The קָהָל, "assembly," usually signifies the community of Israel as a legal body, whereas עֵדָה, "congregation," signifies Israel as a religious assembly.[15] The son is regretting the ruinous consequences of his sin as it has destroyed his standing both as a citizen and as a child of God.

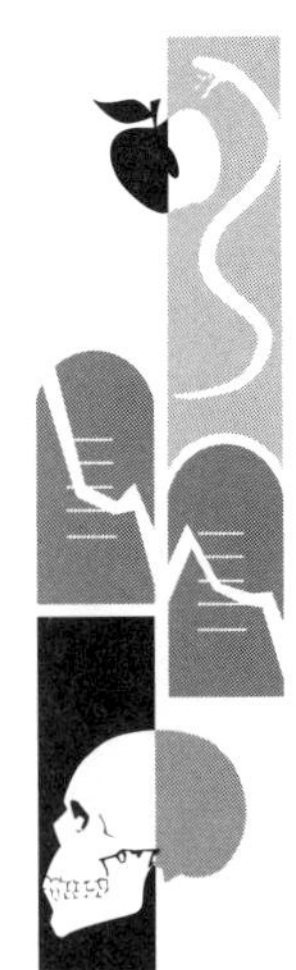

Sin destroys relationships in the family and society as well as in the church and with God. Without repentance and forgiveness, the adulterer will suffer everlasting ruin ("death … Sheol," the destination of the adulteress herself in 5:5). This is in harmony with the Torah penalty for adultery in Lev 20:10 and the NT warnings in, for example, 1 Cor 6:9–10; Gal 5:19–21; Heb 13:4; Rev 22:15.

---

[15] Cf. G. Sauer, "יעד," *TLOT* 2:553, and H.-P. Müller, "קָהָל," 3:1121.

Encouragement to Marital Faithfulness (5:15–20)

Now that the father has discouraged his son from adultery, he goes on to encourage his son to enjoy sexual relations within marriage (5:15–20). The metaphors introduced in 5:15–18 all involve water: a "cistern," "running water," "well," "springs," "streams," and "fountain." The wife is described as a cistern and well providing water for the son alone (5:15). Solomon uses similar metaphors for his bride in Song 4:12, 15.[16]

The rhetorical question in Prov 5:16 draws a contrast between the son's wife and the adulteress, who seeks many illicit relationships.[17] The son should attach his affections to his wife instead of seeking to make the adulteress his spring. The adulteress will always stray; she is found in the streets (7:12) and is never the partner of only one man. By going to an adulteress, the son is drawing water from another cistern or spring, and he makes that woman his (illicit) "streams" (5:16). However, those "streams" flow in public, so others can drink from them; the adulteress will not remain faithful to the adulterous husband, but instead will stray and have liaisons with others. To avoid the public dispersal of his precious water, the son must remain faithful to his wife and not drink from public "streams" from which strangers too imbibe (5:17).[18] In Palestine, where water is a scarce and valuable commodity, to have one's own source of water was a great blessing. The metaphor of the wife as a private "cistern" and source of "running water" (5:15) depicts her as a great blessing to her husband (see also Gen 49:25; Ps 128:3; Song 4:12, 15).

The consequence of fidelity is God's blessing, part of which is the delight in the sexual relationship that God has given (Prov 5:18). This blessing is intended to emphasize that God favors humans with the gift of marriage. It is not merely a human invention, but a divinely created and hallowed estate that God has given to promote the well-being of the church and every human society.[19] Luther understands marriage in this way:

---

[16] There Solomon calls his bride "a locked spring, a sealed fountain" (Song 4:12) and "a fountain of [watering] gardens, a well of living waters, and flowing streams" (Song 4:15). Only the husband has the privilege to enter the locked garden and eat and drink, as Solomon declares he has done with his wife in Song 5:1. For an interpretation of Song 4:12, 15 as describing premarital chastity and fidelity within marriage and as also pointing to the great mystery of Christ and his baptismal union with his bride, the church, see Mitchell, *The Song of Songs*, 837–40, 844–47, 868–73.

[17] Kruger, "Promiscuity or Marriage Fidelity?"

[18] The interpretation above takes the water imagery in 5:15 as referring to the son's wife, and the water imagery in 5:16 as referring to the adulteress after the son has joined himself to her and thereby made her his "streams." If, however, all of the water imagery in 5:15–17 refers to the son's wife, then 5:16–17 could imply that if the husband commits adultery, his "streams," that is, his wife (5:16) will be available to others ("strangers," 5:17). The adulterous husband violates and terminates the exclusive bond of marriage, and so he may cause his (former) wife to become the wife of another man. This may be why Jesus states in Mt 5:32a that a man who divorces his wife causes *her* to commit adultery. See Gibbs, *Matthew 1:1–11:1*, 291, 294.

[19] Based on the Scriptures, clergy should not be prohibited from entering this holy estate. See AC XXIII, "The Marriage of Priests," and Ap XXIII, "The Marriage of Priests."

> Significantly he [God] established it as the first of all institutions, and he created man and woman differently (as is evident) not for lewdness but to be true to each other, be fruitful, beget children, and support and bring them up to the glory of God. God has therefore most richly blessed this estate above all others. … For it is of the highest importance to him that persons be brought up to serve the world, promote knowledge of God, godly living, and all virtues, and fight against wickedness and the devil. …
>
> It is not an exceptional estate, but the most universal and the noblest, pervading all Christendom and even extending throughout all the world. …
>
> Parents and magistrates have the duty of so supervising youth that they will be brought up to decency and respect for authority and, when they are grown, will be married honorably in the fear of God. Then God will add his blessing and grace so that men may have joy and happiness in their married life. (LC I 207–8, 210, 218)

The description of the wife as a doe and an ibex (Prov 5:19) is probably a reference to the gracefulness of these wild animals. Solomon is explicit, but not crude, in his exhortation for the son to enjoy his wife when he mentions "her breasts" and "her love." In this context "love," as at times in English, includes sexual intimacy. A double wordplay is used in 5:19.[20] First, אֲהָבִים in the phrase "a *loving* doe" (the plural of אַהַב) is cognate to the noun אַהֲבָה in "always be intoxicated with her *love*."[21] Second, the word here for "breast," דַּד, is similar to a different Hebrew word for "love," the plural of דּוֹד, used negatively in 7:18 but positively by Solomon in the Song.[22]

The verb "to satisfy," רָוָה, carries the connotation of being satisfied with drink,[23] and so it is a reminder of the water imagery in Prov 5:15–18. The rhetorical question of 5:20 confirms that the rhetorical question in 5:16 is a reference to the son seeking sex outside of marriage. This question in 5:20 stands in the same relationship to the exhortation in 5:19 as the question in 5:16 does to the exhortation in 5:15. Each question highlights the foolishness of not heeding the prior exhortation.

Note the chiastic arrangement of the themes in 5:19–20:

A Let your wife's breasts satisfy you (5:19b)
  B Be intoxicated with your wife's love (5:19c)
  B' Why be intoxicated with an adulteress? (5:20a)
A' Why embrace an adulteress' bosom? (5:20b)

This chiasm serves to bind 5:19 and 5:20 together to highlight the difference between God's gift of sex within marriage and the sinful sexual relationship

---

20 Cf. Kaiser, "True Marital Love," 108–9.

21 In contrast, the plural of אַהַב, "love," occurs in a context of infidelity in Hos 8:9, and another cognate, the plural of אֹהַב, "love," is in the context of infidelity in Prov 7:18.

22 The plural of דּוֹד refers to holy married "love" in Song 1:2, 4; 4:10; 5:1; 7:13 (ET 7:12). In many of these passages, the context suggests the wedded couple's sexual intimacy. The singular of דּוֹד is frequent in the Song and refers to Solomon as the "lover," the one who loves his bride. See "The Song's Vocabulary for Love" in Mitchell, *The Song of Songs*, 562–65.

23 The same verb is used by the seductress in Prov 7:18.

offered by the adulteress. The wife's breasts satisfy; the adulteress' do not. The wife offers intoxication with God-pleasing love, the adulteress mere intoxication. The effect is to pull the son toward God's intended blessing within marriage while at the same time repelling him from illicit relationships.

Yahweh's Examination and Punishment of the Sinner (5:21–23)

Prov 5:21 reminds the son that not only humans notice his behavior (5:14) but also God. Solomon reintroduces the metaphor of the path so that the son will recall the end of the path that the adulteress walks (5:5–6). He then notes that people's sins capture, enslave, and bind them, so that there is no way for them to effect their own escape (5:22). Sin captures the sinner because of lack of "discipline" (5:23), one of the synonyms for wisdom in Proverbs. This lack of discipline is equated with extreme "stupidity" (a synonym of "foolishness"), which leads the sinner astray without his even realizing it. Prov 5:22–23 is not simply stating some inevitable law of cause and effect. Instead it is illustrating how God allows the sins to catch up with those who stray from the path of divine wisdom. This retribution is an expression of his anger against sin as he examines human lives (Rom 1:18–32).

Sexual imagery in Proverbs is never far away from the image of Christ and his betrothed bride. The same is true in the NT writings of Paul, whether the bride is portrayed as faithful (Eph 5:21–33) or as straying from her Bridegroom (2 Cor 11:2–4). However, in Proverbs 5 the spiritual union of God with his people is moved into the background, and sexual relations between men and women in this life become foregrounded. This happens at times in the NT also. For instance, Paul, like Solomon, urges his readers to live faithfully within marriage, to delight in each other, and to satisfy the spouse's natural sexual desires:

> But because of sexual immoralities, each man should have his own wife and each woman should have her own husband. The husband should give to his wife her conjugal due, and likewise the wife to her husband. For the wife does not have authority over her own body, but the husband does. Likewise the husband does not have authority over his own body, but the wife does. Do not deprive one another, except perhaps by agreement for a limited time, that you may devote yourselves to prayer; but then come together again, so that Satan may not tempt you because of your lack of self-control. (1 Cor 7:2–5)

Luther takes this up in the Large Catechism under the heading of the Sixth Commandment (Ex 20:14; Deut 5:18):

> Let it be said in conclusion that this commandment requires everyone not only to live chastely in thought, word, and deed in his particular situation (that is, especially in the estate of marriage), but also to love and cherish the wife or husband whom God has given. For marital chastity it is above all things essential that husband and wife live together in love and harmony, cherishing each other wholeheartedly and with perfect fidelity. This is one of the chief ways to make chastity attractive and desirable. Under such conditions chastity always follows spontaneously without any command. This is why St. Paul so urgently admonishes husbands and wives to love and honor each other. (LC I 219–20)

Proverbs 6:1–5

Wisdom Allows You to Avoid Entanglements with Your Neighbor

Translation

6 **[1]My son, if you guaranteed your neighbor's debts,**
struck hands for a stranger,
[2]you are trapped by the words of your mouth,
captured by the words of your mouth.
[3]Do this then, my son, and save yourself
because you have fallen into your neighbor's hands:
go, humble yourself, and pester your neighbor.
[4]Do not allow your eyes to sleep
or your eyelids to slumber.
[5]Save yourself like a gazelle from the hand [of a hunter]
and like a bird from the hand of a fowler.

Textual Notes

6:1 בְּנִי אִם־עָרַבְתָּ לְרֵעֶךָ—The Qal (G) of עָרַב means to become legally liable for paying off a debt, archaically called "*go surety* … for the debts of" someone (BDB, s.v. עָרַב II, 1; cf. *HALOT*, s.v. ערב I, 1). It is best translated into idiomatic English as "guarantee a debt." The person who does this guarantees that he will repay someone else's loan if the person defaults. Proverbs warns repeatedly about the dangers of this practice.[a]

(a) Prov 6:1; 11:15; 17:18; 20:16; 22:26; 27:13

Often the verb takes the accusative of the person whose debts are being guaranteed. However, here (לְרֵעֶךָ) and in the next clause (לַזָּר), the preposition לְ introduces the person "for" whom the son guarantees the debt or makes a deal.

תָּקַעְתָּ לַזָּר כַּפֶּיךָ׃—Striking hands was a public way of sealing a deal in front of witness (see also 11:15; 17:18; 22:26). In a society where few, if any, business deals were by written contract, this act before witnesses functioned like a signature on a contract.

6:2 נוֹקַשְׁתָּ בְאִמְרֵי־פִיךָ—The verb יָקַשׁ occurs only here in Proverbs. Its Niphal (N) means "be trapped." For its cognate noun יָקוּשׁ, "fowler," see the second textual note on 6:5. For its cognate noun מוֹקֵשׁ, "a snare, trap," see the first textual note on 12:13.

נִלְכַּדְתָּ בְּאִמְרֵי־פִיךָ׃—The verb לָכַד, "capture," is used again in the Niphal (N) in 11:6 for being "captured" by the consequences of foolish behavior, as is the Qal (G) in 5:22.

6:3 וְהִנָּצֵל—The Niphal (N) imperative of נָצַל recurs in 6:5. In both verses it has a middle or reflexive sense, "save yourself," meaning to extricate yourself from the legal predicament caused by your unwise actions. Elsewhere in Proverbs the verb is used in the Hiphil (H), most often with the theological meaning that God saves his people through the gift of divine wisdom (e.g., 2:12, 16) and righteousness (10:2; 11:4, 6).

בָאתָ בְכַף־רֵעֶךָ—This is, literally, "you have come into your neighbor's hand." The verb בּוֹא is usually translated as "come." However, the corresponding expression in English for the meaning of the Hebrew is "you have *fallen* into your neighbor's hands."

לֵךְ הִתְרַפֵּס וּרְהַב רֵעֶיךָ׃—The first in this series of three imperatives is from הָלַךְ, "to go." The second verb, רָפַס, means "to stomp, trample, tread on." The Hithpael (HtD) here is usually understood as having the middle or reflexive meaning: "trample yourself" in the metaphorical sense of humbling yourself to "become a suppliant" (BDB).[1] The third verb, רָהַב, can mean "to storm, assault, press" (*HALOT*), but those meanings do not fit this context. In Is 3:5 it means "to be boisterous." On analogy, in this passage it is often understood to mean metaphorically "to press" one's neighbor, that is, "to pester" him.[2]

6:4 אַל־תִּתֵּן שֵׁנָה לְעֵינֶיךָ—Literally, this is "do not give sleep to your eyes." The Qal (G) of נָתַן with an indirect object marked with לְ can mean to "permit, allow" (BDB, s.v. נָתַן, 1 g; cf. *HALOT*, 8). The noun שֵׁנָה, "sleep," occurs also in, for example, 3:24; 4:16; 6:9–10.

וּתְנוּמָה לְעַפְעַפֶּיךָ׃—The noun תְּנוּמָה, "slumber," is a synonym of the preceding parallel noun שֵׁנָה, "sleep." The two words (there plural) recur in parallel in 6:10 and the verbatim repetition in 24:33. For עַפְעַף, "eyelid," see the textual note on 4:25.

6:5 כִּצְבִי—The noun צְבִי can mean "beauty." It (or a homograph) also designates an animal considered to be gracefully attractive[3] and swift (2 Sam 2:18; 1 Chr 12:9 [ET 12:8]). Most identify it as the gazelle, either *gazella dorcas* or *gazella arabica*.[4]

וּכְצִפּוֹר מִיַּד יָקוּשׁ׃—The noun יָקוּשׁ, "fowler, bird trapper," is derived from the verb יָקַשׁ, "to trap," used in 6:2a. Other references to catching birds are in 1:17 and 7:23 (cf. 26:2; 27:8).

Commentary

Prov 6:1–19 comprises the eighth address in Proverbs 1–9 from a father to a son.[5] It consists of four distinct sections. Because these four sections are quite specific about the behaviors that are proscribed in them, some critical scholars have judged them to be a secondary insertion into Proverbs 1–9.[6] However, it has been pointed out that the four types of vices treated in this address all speak of character faults that might impede a person from having or exercising wisdom, making the verses consonant with the rest of Proverbs 1–9.[7]

---

1 See also Delitzsch, *Proverbs*, 1:137.

2 See Delitzsch, *Proverbs*, 1:138.

3 צְבִי is a simile for Solomon in Song 2:9, 17; 8:14. The feminine צְבִיָּה is used in reference to Solomon's bride in Song 4:5 and 7:4 (ET 7:3).

4 *FF*, 33–34.

5 For the ten addresses from father to son in Proverbs 1–9, see the excursus "Proverbs 1–9, Christ, and the Ten Commandments" in the commentary on chapter 1.

6 E.g., Toy, *Proverbs*, 119; Murphy, *Proverbs*, 37.

7 Clifford, *Proverbs*, 73.

Moreover, these four sections are linked together by catchwords that bind them into one coherent address:[8]

- 6:1–5: “Go” (לֵךְ, 6:3) and “slumber” (תְּנוּמָה, 6:4)
- 6:6–11: “Go” (לֵךְ, 6:6) and “slumber” (תְּנוּמָה, 6:10)
- 6:6–11: “Armed robber” (אִישׁ מָגֵן, literally, “a man of a shield,” 6:11)
- 6:12–15: “Wicked person” (אִישׁ אָוֶן, literally, “a man of wickedness,” 6:12)[9]
- 6:12–15: “Spreads conflict” (the Piel [D] of שָׁלַח with מְדָנִים, 6:14)
- 6:16–19: “Spreads conflict” (the Piel [D] of שָׁלַח with מְדָנִים, 6:19)

Prov 6:1–2 advises the son not to guarantee the debts of others or take on a potentially limitless liability of a business deal with someone else. This counsel applies regardless of whether the other person is a “neighbor” (6:1, 3), that is, a fellow member of God’s people, or a “stranger” (6:1), someone whom the son does not know well, perhaps a non-Israelite or an unbeliever (cf. 1 Cor 6:4–6; 2 Cor 6:14–15).

The father is counseling his son for prudent behavior. Some business deals may seem to promise a high rate of return for the investor but may turn out instead to be a larger burden than anticipated and may incur a loss rather than a gain. The wise son avoids temptations that would entrap him by their appeal to his desire to become rich. The trap is not only that the son will be weighed down with huge debts but also that financial concerns will lead him away from God and the source of wisdom; he might lose his faith and salvation (see 1 Tim 6:9–10).

The wise son avoids such situations altogether, being content with God’s blessings, which never fail. This corresponds to the advice from the writer to the Hebrews: “Let your way of life be free from love of money, and be content with what you have, for he himself [God] has said, ‘I will never leave you nor forsake you’ ” (Heb 13:5). The son and all believers are “to do good, to be rich in good works, to be eager to share, generous—storing up treasure for themselves as a good foundation for the future, so that they may take hold of that which truly is life” (1 Tim 6:18–19).

However, if the son finds himself trapped by his own pledge or promise, he is to use all available resources to free himself, including abject humility and tenacity (Prov 6:3–5). His fight to extricate himself from his unfortunate situation should be like that of a trapped wild animal that never stops struggling to escape. The point the father is making is that the son is not to resign himself to the circumstances in which he finds himself, but he should aggressively seek to move the debtor to pay off the debts.[10] Then the son will conform to the apostolic mandate: “owe nothing to anyone, except to love each other, for he who loves another person has fulfilled the Law” (Rom 13:8).

---

[8] Cf. Garrett, *Proverbs, Ecclesiastes, Song of Songs*, 95–96.

[9] Note that אִישׁ מָגֵן in 6:11 rhymes with אִישׁ אָוֶן in 6:12.

[10] Giese, “Strength through Wisdom and the Bee in LXX-Prov 6,8[a-c],” 406.

Proverbs 6:6–11

Wisdom Is Not Compatible with Laziness

Translation

6 [6]**Go to the ant, lazybones!**
Observe its ways and become wise.
[7]**Although it has no overseer, officer, or ruler,**
[8]**it stores its food in summer;**
it gathers its sustenance at harvest time.
[9]**How long will you lie there, lazybones?**
When will you get up from your sleep?
[10]**A little sleep, a little slumber,**
a little folding of the hands to lie down,
[11]**and your poverty will come like a drifter,**
and your need like an armed robber.

Textual Notes

6:6 לֶךְ־אֶל־נְמָלָה עָצֵל—This section begins with the same imperative, the catchword לֵךְ, as 6:3c. See the commentary on 6:1–5. The harvester ant (נְמָלָה) is found throughout Palestine. It stores grain in its nests.[1] This ant is again used as an illustration of industriousness in 30:25. The damage it causes to farmers is not mentioned in Proverbs and is not a concern since both passages use it to commend self-directed productivity.

The adjective עָצֵל means "slow, idle" (*HALOT*). It is obviously used here as a vocative and a pejorative address to a lazy person. The English "lazybones" corresponds to the usage here. It recurs as a vocative in 6:9 and a total of fourteen times in Proverbs. The lack of an article on it may suggest that it does not mean that Solomon's son is lazy; rather it applies to any other person (not present with Solomon and his son) who is lazy (Joüon, § 137 g 4 (c); Waltke-O'Connor, § 13.5.2c, including example 13).

6:7 אֲשֶׁר אֵין־לָהּ קָצִין שֹׁטֵר וּמֹשֵׁל׃—This relative clause introduced with אֲשֶׁר refers back to the ant. The feminine noun נְמָלָה in 6:6 is the referent of the feminine suffix in לָהּ. The clause is concessive: "although it has no overseer, officer, or ruler."

6:8 תָּכִין בַּקַּיִץ לַחְמָהּ—The Hiphil (H) of כּוּן first occurs in Proverbs here. It means "to prepare, make ready" (*HALOT*, Hiphil, 1). לֶחֶם can specifically mean "bread" or have the more general meaning "food," a synonym of מַאֲכָל in the next clause. This sentence speaks of the ant's summer (קַיִץ) task of readying its food for winter. Translations such as "prepares its food" (see ESV, NASB, NRSV) give the English reader the image of the ant cooking since that is what "prepare food" normally indicates in English. A more accurate translation is reflected above since the ant readies its food by storing it for future consumption.

---

1 *FF*, 1.

אָגְרָה בְקָּצִיר מַאֲכָלָהּ׃—The verb אָגַר, "to gather," occurs only in Deut 28:39 as well as here and in Prov 10:5, all in reference to gathering food. קָצִיר can refer to the "summer" (as קַיִץ in the preceding clause usually does) or to the time (or action) of the "harvest."

At the end of this verse, the LXX contains its most well-known addition to the text of Proverbs:

ἢ πορεύθητι πρὸς τὴν μέλισσαν
    καὶ μάθε ὡς ἐργάτις ἐστὶν
    τήν τε ἐργασίαν ὡς σεμνὴν ποιεῖται,
ἧς τοὺς πόνους βασιλεῖς καὶ ἰδιῶται πρὸς ὑγίειαν προσφέρονται,
ποθεινὴ δέ ἐστιν πᾶσιν καὶ ἐπίδοξος·
καίπερ οὖσα τῇ ῥώμῃ ἀσθενής,
    τὴν σοφίαν τιμήσασα προήχθη.

Or go to the bee,
    and learn how industrious it is
    and how seriously it does its work,
whose products kings and commoners use for health.
It is desired by all and respected.
Although it is weak physically,
    by honoring wisdom it has obtained distinction.

It is generally agreed that this addition reflects Hellenistic thought, in which the bee was an example of wisdom. The thought in this addition is similar to Sirach 11:3, where the bee's success comes from wisdom despite its physical inferiority.[2]

6:10–11 These verses are repeated in 24:33–34. The only differences are two orthographic changes and that the Piel (D) participle here, כִּמְהַלֵּךְ, is replaced by the Hithpael (HtD) participle מִתְהַלֵּךְ in 24:34.

6:10 מְעַט שֵׁנוֹת מְעַט תְּנוּמוֹת—The adverb מְעַט, "a little," occurs thrice in this verse. For the parallel nouns שֵׁנָה, "sleep," and תְּנוּמָה, "slumber," see the textual notes on 6:4. The plural forms may be plurals of generalization (Joüon, § 136 j).

6:11 וּבָא־כִמְהַלֵּךְ רֵאשֶׁךָ—The meaning of the Piel (D) participle of הָלַךְ (with the preposition כְּ) is uncertain. It is often translated as "robber" on the theory that it means "one who frequents highways," that is, a "highwayman." However, it probably means "one who is habitually traveling," such as a vagabond or drifter (see *HALOT*, Piel, 3). The noun רֵאשׁ, "poverty," is also spelled רִישׁ or רֵישׁ. It occurs only in Proverbs.[a]

(a) Prov 6:11; 10:15; 13:18; 24:34; 28:19; 30:8; 31:7

וּמַחְסֹרְךָ כְּאִישׁ מָגֵן׃—The noun מַחְסוֹר, "lack, need, want," from the verb חָסֵר, "to lack, need," recurs in 11:24; 14:23; 21:5, 17; 22:16; 24:34; 28:27. The construct phrase כְּאִישׁ מָגֵן, literally, "like a man of [with] a shield," is usually understood to be an armed robber.[3]

---

2 Giese, "Strength through Wisdom and the Bee in LXX-Prov $6,8^{a-c}$."

3 Garrett (*Proverbs, Ecclesiastes, Song of Songs*, 97, n. 120) suggests that the Ugaritic root *mgn*, "beg," is intended here so that poverty is depicted as a beggar. That suggestion is interesting but doubtful.

Commentary

This passage (6:6–11) is the second section of the eighth address in Proverbs 1–9 from a father to a son.[4] The discussion of diligence, like the kind needed to escape an unwise business deal (6:3–5), continues in the second lesson in 6:1–19 that Solomon teaches his son. This second lesson in the eighth address is divided into two subsections (6:6–8 and 6:9–11).

The Value of Industriousness (6:6–8)

This first subsection exhorts the son to learn from the ant. The specific lesson to be learned is disciplined self-motivation to work. The point the father is making is that ants do not need someone to supervise them (6:7). They do their work and are able to store food for the future (6:8). The son is to see the practical wisdom of such self-directed activity (6:6). By attending to his work, the son too can store up what is needed for the future.

This advice is good for all readers. The Scriptures often commend honest work and foresight in the use of wealth. There is nothing wrong with saving one's money for future needs.

However, there is another danger: trusting in one's savings and wealth rather than relying on God. This is the point of Jesus' parable of the rich man who built barns to store his crops but was not "rich toward God" (Lk 12:16–21). In the same way, Jesus declares in the Sermon on the Mount:

> Therefore I tell you, do not be anxious about your life, what you will eat or what you will drink, nor about your body, what you will put on. Is not life more than nourishment, and the body more than clothing? Look at the birds of the air, for they do not sow or reap or gather into barns, and your heavenly Father feeds them. Are you not more valuable than they?" (Mt 6:25–26)

Jesus is not contradicting Solomon. Instead, Jesus is warning us about losing faith in God's providence and becoming worried and anxious about our physical needs so that they become our gods.

Solomon, in contrast, is advising his son to make proper use of what God has provided. He is not encouraging reliance upon human effort, but urging the proper use of God's gift of work, which can lead to abundance and even wealth through diligence and thrift. The Christian will receive these as part of God's bounty, but not as idols to be cherished for their own sake. Instead, they are gifts from God the Creator, the result of God's providence. Indeed the Christian will continue to trust in God's forgiving grace in Christ alone. "For you know the grace of our Lord Jesus Christ, that for your sake he became poor even though he was rich, so that you—by his poverty—might become rich" (2 Cor 8:9).

---

4 See the commentary on 6:1–5. For the ten addresses from father to son in Proverbs 1–9, see the excursus "Proverbs 1–9, Christ, and the Ten Commandments" in the commentary on chapter 1.

The Danger of Laziness (6:9–11)

The second subsection makes the same point by ridiculing the human tendency to choose present pleasures over future rewards that come with wise use of one's time. The combination of "a little" with the plural forms of "sleep" and "slumber" (6:10) serves to show the son how ridiculous the excuses of a lazy person can be. Such bit-by-bit procrastination leads to poverty that can seem to come randomly or accidentally, like a drifter who happens along or an armed robber whose choice of victims seems random and opportunistic (6:11). This skillful portrayal of the consequences of choices the son may make is using the Law to discourage unwise and self-destructive behavior.

In the same way, in the NT Paul discourages laziness, holding himself up as an example of diligence:

> Now we command you, brothers, in the name of our Lord Jesus Christ, that you keep away from any brother who is walking with idleness and not according to the tradition that they received from us. For you yourselves know how it is necessary to imitate us, because we were not idle when we were with you, nor did we eat bread from anyone for free, but with toil and labor we worked night and day, that we might not burden any of you. It was not because we do not have that right, but to give you ourselves as an example to imitate. For even when we were with you, we would give you this command: if anyone is not willing to work, neither let him eat. For we hear that some among you walk in idleness, not busy at work, but busybodies. Now such persons we command and encourage in the Lord Jesus Christ that while working quietly they should eat their own bread. (2 Thess 3:6–12)

Just as divine Wisdom, Christ himself, would lead and motivate Solomon's son to shun laziness, so Paul encourages the Thessalonians "in the Lord Jesus Christ" to work and earn a living.

Proverbs 6:12–15

Dishonesty Leads to Disaster

Translation

6 [12]A good-for-nothing individual, a wicked person—
going about with a corrupt mouth,
[13]winking with his eye,
signaling with his foot,
gesturing with his fingers,
[14]perverse things in his heart, plotting evil at all times—
he spreads conflict.
[15]Therefore, suddenly his disaster will come upon him.
Immediately he will be broken, and there will be no remedy.

Textual Notes

6:12 אָדָם בְּלִיַּעַל—Proverbs often uses either אָדָם or אִישׁ, "a man," in construct with a more specific noun or substantive that indicates a certain attribute or quality that characterizes the person (see GKC, § 128 s and t). See also the next textual note. In such construct phrases אָדָם or אִישׁ does not always need to be translated. For example, אִישׁ כָּזָב, "a man who is a liar," can just be rendered as "a liar" (19:22).

The compound noun בְּלִיַּעַל is from בְּלִי, "not, without," and a nominal form of the verb יָעַל, "to be useful, beneficial." This word often is used to characterize people who are not just "useless" but malicious and destructive.[a] "Good for nothing" is a good, generic translation (*HALOT*, 2). A Greek variant of this Hebrew word, Βελιάρ, is used by Paul as a term for Satan in 2 Cor 6:15.

(a) E.g., Deut 13:14 (ET 13:13); Judg 19:22; 1 Sam 1:16; 2:12; 25:25; 2 Sam 16:7; 1 Ki 21:13; 2 Chr 13:7

אִישׁ אָוֶן—This construct phrase with an adjectival genitive, "a man of wickedness," means "a wicked man." See also the first textual note on 6:18. The noun אָוֶן occurs nine times in Proverbs.[b]

הוֹלֵךְ עִקְּשׁוּת פֶּה׃—This is, literally, "walking [with] crookedness of mouth." See the first textual note on 4:24 for the construct phrase עִקְּשׁוּת פֶּה.

(b) Prov 6:12, 18; 10:29; 12:21; 17:4; 19:28; 21:15; 22:8; 30:20

6:13 קֹרֵץ בְּעֵינָו מֹלֵל בְּרַגְלָו—The Kethib readings of the two nouns are singular, בְּעֵינוֹ ... בְּרַגְלוֹ, "with his eye ... with his foot," whereas the Qere readings are dual, בְּעֵינָיו ... בְּרַגְלָיו, "with his eyes ... with his feet." The Kethib in both cases is the better reading. "Winking" (the verb קָרַץ) involves only one eye at a time, and most foot gestures usually use only one foot. The Qere probably arose under the influence of the plural in the last clause of the verse, בְּאֶצְבְּעֹתָיו, "with his fingers," which makes sense since many hand gestures involve more than one finger.

The verb מָלַל means "speak," but the literal "speaking with his foot" makes no sense in English. The intended concept is that some movement of the foot is an attempted communication, a signal.

:מְרֶה בְּאֶצְבְּעֹתָיו—The Hiphil (H) of יָרָה means "to teach," as in 4:4, 11. The participle here probably notes habitual or repeated action. Once again the literal "teaching with his fingers" makes little sense in this context for an English reader. The idea is that the wicked man often uses hand gestures as some kind of sign or signal to his confederates.

6:14 תַּהְפֻּכוֹת ׀ בְּלִבּוֹ—For תַּהְפֻּכוֹת, see the second textual note on 2:12.

חֹרֵשׁ רָע בְּכָל־עֵת—For the combination of the verb חָרַשׁ, "devise, plot," and the noun רַע or רָעָה, "evil," see the first textual note on 3:29. חָרַשׁ occurs with אָוֶן in 6:18.

:מְדָנִים יְשַׁלֵּחַ—The Kethib is מְדָנִים, and the Qere is מִדְיָנִים. Both are plural forms of the noun מָדוֹן, "strife, conflict, fighting" (so BDB, s.v. מָדוֹן I, under the root דין). מְדָנִים is the sole reading in 6:19 and 10:12, and other forms of מָדוֹן occur thirteen times in Proverbs (e.g., 15:18; 16:28). Here it is the object of the Piel (D) of שָׁלַח, which normally means "to send out, send away" (BDB, 1–2). The person described here constantly "sends out conflict," meaning that he is the source and instigator of conflict. The Hebrew idiom recurs in 6:19 and 16:28. The English idiom for it is "spreads conflict."

6:15 :פִּתְאֹם יָבוֹא אֵידוֹ פֶּתַע יִשָּׁבֵר וְאֵין מַרְפֵּא—In both of the verbal clauses, the adverbial occurs first for emphasis. פִּתְאֹם, "suddenly," is one of the few true Hebrew adverbs. The noun פֶּתַע, "suddenness," is used as an adverbial accusative: "immediately." The two adverbs are used together also in Num 6:9; Is 29:5; 30:13. For the noun in the nominal clause וְאֵין מַרְפֵּא, literally, "and there is no healing," see the second textual note on 4:22.

The two clauses פֶּתַע יִשָּׁבֵר וְאֵין מַרְפֵּא are repeated at the end of 29:1.

Commentary

This passage (6:12–15) is the third section of the eighth address in Proverbs 1–9 from a father to a son.[1] This third lesson is a description of a devious person who is always hatching plots and involving others in them. Prov 6:12–14 is a single sentence whose basic message is this: "a good-for-nothing individual, a wicked person … spreads conflict." The list of means by which he spreads conflict fills in the ellipsis. In the Hebrew text each of these descriptions contains a participle and part of the body. The participles signal habitual behavior: this devious person is repeatedly doing these things. The parts of the body signify his outward actions ("mouth," "eye," "foot," and "fingers" in 6:12–13) as coming from his corrupted character ("heart" in 6:14). While the corrupt character is his alone, the actions seek to involve others in his perversity. Whether by persuasion (mouth) or by innuendo (the body language of his eyes, feet, and fingers), he spreads conflict by the messages he sends, seeking to destroy others by harming their reputation and by playing on the willingness of people to listen to disparaging things about others. The other two passages

[1] See the commentary on 6:1–5. For the ten addresses from father to son in Proverbs 1–9, see the excursus "Proverbs 1–9, Christ, and the Ten Commandments" in the commentary on chapter 1.

in Proverbs that use בְּלִיַּעַל, "good-for-nothing," also speak of harming reputations (16:27; 19:28).

Solomon the father warns his son that such a person will meet sudden destruction without any means of salvaging himself. This is not only a warning to the son not to become a devious person, but it is also a warning against associating with devious people who spread rumors and gossip about others. The danger is that an unwary person could be taken in by their message, adopt their habit of slander, and be destroyed with them.

In the NT James offers a theological rationale for avoiding this type of behavior:

> Do not speak evil against each another, brothers. He who speaks against a brother or judges his brother speaks evil against the Law and judges the Law. But if you judge the Law, you are not a doer of the Law but a judge. There is only one Lawgiver and Judge: he who is able to save and to destroy. But who are you to judge your neighbor? (James 4:11–12)

The one who does these things is judging others and supplanting God as the "Lawgiver and Judge." The destruction wrought by such a judgmental person will lead to his own judgment by God. That is why Solomon warns his son that such a good-for-nothing person will experience sudden disaster: "immediately he will be broken, and there will be no remedy" (6:15). By indirectly saying that "God will judge," Solomon actually paints a more vivid and frightening picture of God's wrath than if he had been more plainspoken.

Luther affirms these points as he explains the Eighth Commandment (Ex 20:16; Deut 5:20; cf. Prov 25:18; see also the textual notes and commentary on 6:19):

> Whatever is done with the tongue against a neighbor, then, is forbidden by God. This applies to false preachers with their corrupt teaching and blasphemy, to false judges and witnesses with their corrupt behavior in court and their lying and malicious talk outside of court. It applies particularly to the detestable, shameful vice of back-biting or slander by which the devil rides us. … It is a common vice of human nature that everyone would rather hear evil than good about his neighbor. Evil though we are, we cannot tolerate having evil spoken of us; we want the golden compliments of the whole world. Yet we cannot bear to hear the best spoken of others.
>
> To avoid this vice, therefore, we should note that nobody has the right to judge and reprove his neighbor publicly, even when he has seen a sin committed, unless he has been authorized to judge and reprove. There is a great difference between judging sin and having knowledge of sin. Knowledge of sin does not entail the right to judge it. I may see and hear that my neighbor sins, but to make him the talk of the town is not my business. If I interfere and pass sentence on him, I fall into a greater sin than his. When you become aware of a sin, simply make your ears a tomb and bury it until you are appointed a judge and authorized to administer punishment by virtue of your office. (LC I 263–66; see also LC I 267–73)

Proverbs 6:16–19

Seven Things That Are an Abomination to Yahweh

Translation

6 [16]Six things Yahweh hates,
and seven are disgusting things to his very being:
[17]an arrogant pair of eyes,
a lying tongue,
a pair of hands that sheds innocent blood,
[18]a heart devising wicked plans,
a pair of feet quickly running to [do] evil,
[19]a false witness who breathes lies,
and a person who spreads conflict among brothers.

Textual Notes

6:16 וְשֶׁ֣בַע תּוֹעֲב֣וֹת נַפְשׁוֹ׃—Because of the numeral שֶׁבַע, "seven," the plural Kethib, תּוֹעֲבוֹת, "disgusting things," is preferable to the singular Qere, תּוֹעֲבַת. For the noun תּוֹעֵבָה, see the first textual note on 3:32. The noun נֶפֶשׁ can mean one's personality, one's inner being (*HALOT*, 6). Thus the actions are depicted here as disgusting to God's very essence and being.

6:17–19 עֵינַיִם … וְיָדַיִם … רַגְלַיִם—The dual forms (all feminine) for the "eyes … hands … feet" signal the actions of a single person, just as do the singular forms (all masculine) for "tongue … heart … witness" and "spreads conflict." Note that according to Masoretic pointing עֵינַיִם and יָדַיִם are always dual, even when referring to the collective "eyes" or "hands" of several people, but רַגְלִים is pointed as plural, not the dual as here, when it refers to the "feet" of more than one person (e.g., Jer 12:5).

Some of the vocabulary in 6:17c and 6:18b is shared by Prov 1:16 and Is 59:7. See the excursus "The Relationship between Proverbs 1:16 and Isaiah 59:7" in the commentary on chapter 1.

6:17 עֵינַ֣יִם רָמ֑וֹת—The feminine plural participle of רוּם is used adjectivally. Here and elsewhere it can denote a haughty arrogance (*HALOT*, 6 a iv).

לְשׁ֣וֹן שָׁ֑קֶר—This construct phrase has an objective genitive: "a tongue of [that utters] falsehood," that is, "a lying tongue." The phrase recurs in 12:19; 21:6; 26:28.

6:18 לֵ֗ב חֹ֭רֵשׁ מַחְשְׁב֣וֹת אָ֑וֶן—For לֵב, "heart," see the first textual note on 2:10. The participle חֹרֵשׁ was also in 6:14. The construct phrase מַחְשְׁב֣וֹת אָ֑וֶן has an adjectival genitive: literally, "plans of wickedness" means "wicked plans." For אָוֶן, "wickedness," see the second textual note on 6:12.

רַ֝גְלַ֗יִם מְמַהֲר֥וֹת לָר֥וּץ לָרָעָֽה׃—For this vocabulary, see the textual note on 1:16. Here מְ֝מַהֲר֗וֹת לָר֥וּץ is, literally, "hurrying to run." The dual (רַגְלַיִם, "a pair of feet") of the feminine noun רֶגֶל is the subject of the feminine plural participle מְמַהֲרוֹת, "hurrying." However, the participle functions adverbially ("*quickly* running"), and the second verb, the infinitive construct לָרוּץ, "to run," is the main verb. While 1:16 had the masculine noun with preposition לָרַע, the feminine noun is used here with the same preposition: לָרָעָה.

6:19 יָפִיחַ כְּזָבִים עֵד שָׁקֶר—When the construct phrase עֵד שָׁקֶר is the object of the verb עָנָה, "to give, bear," it has an adjectival genitive and means "testimony that is false," as in the Eighth Commandment, Ex 20:16, and in Prov 25:18. However, here the construct phrase has an objective genitive: "a witness [who gives testimony that is] false," as the construct phrase means also in Deut 19:18 and Prov 14:5. The construct phrase with the plural genitive, עֵד שְׁקָרִים, "a witness [who gives testimonies that are] falsehoods," occurs in Prov 12:17; 19:5, 9. In English idiom these construct phrases referring to people are best rendered as "a false witness." The plural "false witnesses" occurs in Ps 27:12.

Here the noun עֵד is the subject of the verb יָפִיחַ, the Hiphil (H) of פּוּחַ, meaning to "breathe out, utter" (BDB, 3). The Hiphil (H) recurs with the same meaning in 12:17; 14:5, 25; 19:5, 9 (it has a different sense in 29:8). The verb's object is כְּזָבִים, "lies," again in 14:5, 25; 19:5, 9.

וּמְשַׁלֵּחַ מְדָנִים בֵּין אַחִים׃—For the Piel (D) of שָׁלַח (here the participle) with the object מְדָנִים, see the third textual note on 6:14.

Commentary

This passage (6:16–19) is the fourth section of the eighth address in Proverbs 1–9 from a father to a son.[1] This is also the first of the five passages with graded numerical sayings in Proverbs.[2] There are four graded numerical sayings in Proverbs 30, each of which has the pattern "three … four" (30:15, 18, 21, 29; cf. 30:24), as also does Amos 1:3–2:16.[3] Some other OT passages too involve the pattern "x … x + 1," while others use different patterns, for example, "x … 10x" (e.g., 1 Sam 18:7).

While this saying has the pattern "six … seven," it gives a total of seven (not six) attitudes and actions that God finds repulsive. The rhetorical device of the numerical saying not only makes these seven memorable, but it also allows Solomon to emphasize God's attitude toward them so that his son will hopefully adopt the same attitude as God. "Seven" is chosen here, as elsewhere in Proverbs, to signify comprehensiveness (6:31; 9:1; 24:16; 26:16; "seven disgusting things" in 26:25). See further the commentary on 30:11–33 and 31:10–31.

---

1 See the commentary on 6:1–5. For the ten addresses from father to son in Proverbs 1–9, see the excursus "Proverbs 1–9, Christ, and the Ten Commandments" in the commentary on chapter 1.

2 See "Numerical Sayings" in "Types of Sayings in Proverbs" in the introduction.

3 See "The Staircase Numerical Pattern" in "Introduction to Amos 1:3–2:16: Judgments against the Nations" in Lessing, *Amos*, 100–102.

The first five "disgusting things" (6:16) are made more vivid by associating them with parts of the body from head to toe: "eyes ... tongue ... hands ... heart ... feet" (6:17–18). All seven typify things condemned elsewhere in Proverbs by Solomon: arrogance (8:13; 11:2; 15:25; 16:18–19; 21:24; 29:23), lying (the phrase "lying tongue" is used also in 12:19; 21:6; 26:28), shedding innocent blood (1:11; cf. 1:16), plotting evil (3:29; 14:22; note especially 6:14 and 12:20, where לֵב, חָרַשׁ, and רַע are used together), rushing to do evil (1:16), false witness (the same or a similar phrase as the one in 6:19 is used also in 12:17; 14:5; 19:5, 9; 25:18; see also 14:25), and spreading conflict (6:14; 10:12; 15:18; 16:28; 28:25; 29:22). The phrase "seven disgusting things" is also used in 26:25.

But why are these seven sins chosen above all others to group together? With the exception of the third—murder—all of these sins are difficult, if not impossible, for human authorities to control. They are either internal attitudes (arrogance, plotting evil, a disposition to do evil), behaviors that are hard to prove (lying, false witness), or behaviors for which blame is hard to assign (spreading conflict). Murder, which can be punished by human authorities, is included because the taking of human life is the most heinous of crimes against humanity. Since murder is the most serious of crimes, and since human authorities cannot effectively punish the rest of these sins, Solomon invokes the power of God to discourage these attitudes and behaviors. God alone can mete out punishment for all these sins.

Jesus also warns of the internal attitudes that defile humans:

> For from within, out of the heart of men, come forth evil thoughts, sexual immoralities, thefts, murders adulteries, kinds of greediness, varieties of wickedness, deceit, sensuality, a wicked eye [envy], blasphemy, arrogance, foolishness. All these evil things come out from within, and they defile a person. (Mk 7:21–23; cf. Mt 15:19–20)

Solomon's words anticipate Jesus' condemnation of the human heart, and the king's sayings reflect that his teaching is the teaching of the Wisdom of God.[4]

[4] See also the introduction.

Proverbs 6:20–35

Ninth Address to a Son: A Father Teaches His Son to Avoid Fornication

Translation

6 [20]**Keep, my son, your father's command,**
and do not forsake your mother's teaching.
[21]**Fasten them on your heart permanently,**
and tie them around your neck.
[22]**When you walk around, she will lead you.**
When you lie down, she will stand guard over you.
When you wake up, she will talk with you,
[23]**for a command is a lamp,**
and teaching is a light,
and warnings coming from discipline are a road of life,
[24]**to guard you from an evil woman,**
from the smooth tongue of a woman who is a stranger.
[25]**Do not desire her beauty in your heart,**
and do not let her captivate you by her eyes,
[26]**because a prostitute's price is a loaf of bread,**
but a married woman hunts precious life.
[27]**Can a man take fire into his lap**
and his clothes not be burned?
[28]**If a man walks on hot coals,**
will his feet not be scorched?
[29]**So it is with the man who goes into his neighbor's wife.**
No one who touches her will be found innocent.
[30]**No one despises a thief when he steals**
to satisfy his appetite when he is starving,
[31]**but when he is caught he will have to repay sevenfold.**
He will have to give up all the wealth of his house.
[32]**Whoever commits adultery with a woman lacks sense.**
He who does it destroys himself.
[33]**He will find disease and dishonor,**
and his disgrace will never be wiped out,
[34]**because jealousy [arouses] a husband's anger,**
and he will not show mercy when he gets revenge.
[35]**He will not accept any compensation.**
He will not give in even if you increase the bribe.

Textual Notes

6:20 The first half of this verse resembles 1:8a. The second half repeats 1:8b verbatim. See the textual notes on 1:8.

6:21 קָשְׁרֵם עַל־לִבְּךָ תָמִיד—The identical Qal (G) imperative of קָשַׁר, "to fasten, bind, tie," with suffix occurs in similar contexts in 3:3 and 7:3. See the second textual note on 3:3. The third masculine plural suffix on קָשְׁרֵם ("fasten *them*") refers to the two feminine singular nouns מִצְוָה, "command," and תּוֹרָה, "teaching," in 6:20. Hebrew prefers masculine suffixes even when the referents are feminine (see Joüon, § 149 b).

עָנְדֵם עַל־גַּרְגְּרֹתֶךָ׃—The verb עָנַד, "bind, tie," occurs in the OT only here and in Job 31:36. For גַּרְגְּרֹתֶךָ, "your neck," see the second textual note on 1:9.

6:22 תַּנְחֶה ... תִּשְׁמֹר ... הִיא תְשִׂיחֶךָ׃—The verbs are third feminine singular. There is no feminine singular antecedent in 6:21, but either of the two feminine singular nouns in 6:20, "command" and "teaching," could be the subject ("*she* will") of these verbs. Some interpreters have cited this as a grammatical difficulty that they "solve" by moving 6:22 to immediately following 5:19, so that the feminine antecedent would be "the wife you married in your youth" (5:18).[1] However, there is no need for such a radical reconstruction. Instead, when in 6:22 Solomon begins to personify the instruction he and his wife are giving his son, he pictures it as a woman who will be with the son to guard him from the temptation of the evil woman.

תִּשְׁמֹר עָלֶיךָ—This same clause occurs in 2:11 with "foresight, insight" as the subject.

תְשִׂיחֶךָ׃—The Qal (G) verb שִׂיחַ here means "*talk* (with)" (BDB, 3 b).

6:23 כִּי נֵר מִצְוָה וְתוֹרָה אוֹר—English translation cannot reflect the chiastic structure. In the first nominal clause, the predicate noun is first, and in the second nominal clause, the subject noun precedes the predicate noun:

A נֵר, "lamp"
  B מִצְוָה, "command"
  B' תּוֹרָה, "teaching"
A' אוֹר, "light"

וְדֶרֶךְ חַיִּים תּוֹכְחוֹת מוּסָר׃—Although "way" is used to translate דֶּרֶךְ in most instances, "way of life" is an English phrase that has become so disconnected with a physical path that "road of life" is better here to convey the concrete image of the Hebrew. Other proverbs that promise "life" (חַיִּים) through divine wisdom include 3:2, 18, 22; 4:10, 13, 22, 23. For the noun תּוֹכַחַת, "warning," see the first textual note on 1:23. For the noun מוּסָר, see "מוּסָר, 'Discipline,' and יָסַר, 'to Discipline' " in "Wisdom in Proverbs" in the introduction.

6:24 לִשְׁמָרְךָ מֵאֵשֶׁת רָע—The construct phrase אֵשֶׁת רָע has an adjectival genitive: "evil woman" (see GKC, § 128 w). This construct phrase occurs only here in the OT. The LXX has γυναικὸς ὑπάνδρου, "a woman who is under a man; married woman." Apparently, the LXX vocalized the consonants as מֵאֵשֶׁת רֵעַ, "a neighbor's wife," a phrase

[1] Scott, *Proverbs, Ecclesiastes*, 55, 58; Clifford, *Proverbs*, 71.

that would occur only here in the OT, but that phrase with a suffix (-אֵשֶׁת רֵעַ, "your/his neighbor's wife") occurs eleven times in the OT, including the Tenth Commandment (Ex 20:17; Deut 5:21). The LXX reading may also have been influenced by אֵשֶׁת רֵעֵהוּ in Prov 6:29. Some have adopted the LXX reading as a better fit with the parallel נָכְרִיָּה in the next clause.[2] However, the LXX translator may have imposed that vocalization precisely because it is a better fit and resembles the common suffixed expression.

מֵחֶלְקַת לָשׁוֹן נָכְרִיָּה׃—For the noun חֶלְקָה, "smoothness, seductiveness" of speech, see the second textual note on 2:16. חֶלְקַת לָשׁוֹן, "smoothness of tongue," has an adjectival genitive: "a smooth tongue." נָכְרִיָּה is a synonym of the phrase אִשָּׁה זָרָה, for which, see the first textual note on 2:16. For both, see also the excursus "Wisdom and the Adulteress in Proverbs 1–9" in the commentary on Proverbs 2.

6:25 אַל־תַּחְמֹד יָפְיָהּ בִּלְבָבֶךָ—The same verb, חָמַד, "to desire, covet," is used in the Tenth Commandment (Ex 20:17; Deut 5:21) to prohibit desire for the wife of another. The noun יֳפִי, "beauty," recurs in Prov 31:30.

וְאַל־תִּקָּחֲךָ בְּעַפְעַפֶּיהָ׃—Here the verb לָקַח is used idiomatically to mean that the woman would "capture" or "captivate" the man (see *HALOT*, 10). For עַפְעַף, literally, "eyelid," see the textual note on 4:25. Here עַפְעַפֶּיהָ is translated more generally as "her eyes," although it might refer to "her eyelashes."

6:26 כִּי בְעַד־אִשָּׁה זוֹנָה עַד־כִּכַּר לָחֶם—A strictly form-equivalent translation of these words would be "because in behalf of a woman prostitute as far as a loaf of bread." Note the use of two nouns in apposition in the phrase אִשָּׁה זוֹנָה, "a woman (who is) a prostitute." This kind of apposition uses the second noun to indicate a species of the first noun. Note the similar אִשָּׁה־אַלְמָנָה, "a woman (who is) a widow" (2 Sam 14:5; 1 Ki 7:14; 11:26; 17:9–10) or אִישׁ כֹּהֵן, "a man (who is) a priest" (Lev 21:9). The combination of the accents *ʿoleh* and *yored* on כִּכַּר לָחֶם mark the end of the first half of the verse since in Proverbs (as well as in the Psalms and Job), this combination is a stronger disjunctive than the *athnach* on אִישׁ later in the verse.

וְאֵשֶׁת אִישׁ נֶפֶשׁ יְקָרָה תָצוּד׃—The construct phrase אֵשֶׁת אִישׁ, "a wife of a man," denotes "a married woman" (ESV). She is the subject of the feminine verb תָּצוּד, "hunts," and the direct object is נֶפֶשׁ יְקָרָה, "a valuable soul/life." The context, which warns against adultery, and the hostile sense of צוּד, "to hunt," imply that the woman is married to someone else, not to the "son" (6:20) Solomon is addressing. She is seeking to kill or take the life of the son, who is her prey or quarry. This interpretation is consistent with Lev 20:10, which prescribes the death penalty for a man who commits adultery with אֵשֶׁת אִישׁ, "a wife of a[nother] man, a married woman." Here some translations render וְאֵשֶׁת אִישׁ as "adulteress" (e.g., KJV, NIV, NASB). צוּד can be used when people "hunt" and kill animals (e.g., Gen 27:3, 5; Lev 17:13). In Ezek 13:18, 20 false prophetesses or witches "hunt" (צוּד) the "lives" or "souls" (נְפָשׁוֹת) of other Israelites.

This difficult verse has spawned many conjectures for translation or emendation. Yet it seems clear that the verse expresses two situations, one bad and the other worse.

---

2 NRSV; Scott, *Proverbs, Ecclesiastes*, 61; Clifford, *Proverbs*, 77–78; cf. Murphy, *Proverbs*, 36.

The distinction has usually been understood in one of two different ways. A first possibility is that the cost of hiring a prostitute is a loaf of bread (6:26a), whereas the cost of having an affair with a married woman is one's own life (6:26b). This understanding is reflected in, for example, the LXX and NRSV. A second possibility is that 6:26a means that frequenting prostitutes reduces a man to poverty (see 29:3) so that all he has left is a loaf of bread, while adultery with a married woman takes away all that a man has (cf. NKJV, NASB). Either makes sense, but in the first possibility, the parallelism is stronger and the distinction is greater: the price of a prostitute is bread, but the price tag for adultery with a married woman is your precious life and very soul.

The verse may be compared to Jesus' warning in Mt 16:26 that unbelief will cost a man his very soul and life, which cannot be repurchased by any wealth. And in 1 Cor 6:9–20 the apostle Paul exhorts Christians to avoid sexual immorality "because you were bought with a price" (1 Cor 6:20).

6:28 וְ֝רַגְלָ֗יו לֹ֣א תִכָּוֶֽינָה׃—The feminine dual רַגְלָיו (with suffix) is the subject of the third feminine plural imperfect תִּכָּוֶינָה. The verb כָּוָה occurs only twice in the OT, both times in the Niphal (N) meaning "to be burned, scorched," and both times referring to a person who walks (הָלַךְ) through/on fire (Is 43:2; Prov 6:28).

6:29 כֵּ֗ן הַ֭בָּא אֶל־אֵ֣שֶׁת רֵעֵ֑הוּ—On the idiom בּוֹא אֶל, "go into," as a euphemism for sexual intercourse, see the textual note on 2:19. The construct phrase אֵשֶׁת רֵעֵהוּ, "his neighbor's wife," also occurs in the prescription of capital punishment for adultery in Lev 20:10.

לֹ֥א יִ֝נָּקֶ֗ה כָּל־הַנֹּגֵ֥עַ בָּֽהּ׃—In Proverbs the verb נָקָה, "to be innocent, guiltless," always occurs in the Niphal (N) in the negated phrase לֹא יִנָּקֶה, "he will not be found innocent, will not go unpunished."[a]

(a) Prov 6:29; 11:21; 16:5; 17:5; 19:5, 9; 28:20

Like בּוֹא אֶל in 6:29a, the Qal (G) of נָגַע, "to touch," can be another euphemism for sexual contact (see Gen 20:6; 26:11; Ruth 2:9).

6:30 לֹא־יָב֣וּזוּ לַ֭גַּנָּב כִּ֣י יִגְנ֑וֹב—The plural impersonal construction "they do not despise" is translated as singular, "no one despises," to express the general statement. The object noun גַּנָּב, "thief," is derived from the following verb גָּנַב, "to steal."

לְמַלֵּ֥א נַ֝פְשׁ֗וֹ—The idiom "to fill his life/soul" means "to satisfy his appetite" (see *HALOT*, s.v. מלא, Piel, 9).

6:31 וְ֭נִמְצָא יְשַׁלֵּ֣ם שִׁבְעָתָ֑יִם—The verb מָצָא in the Niphal (N) can mean "to be found out, be caught in the act" (see *HALOT*, 2). The imperfect יְשַׁלֵּם has the nuance of obligation (cf. Joüon, § 113 m): "he will *have to* repay." The feminine dual form (שִׁבְעָתַיִם) of the numeral שִׁבְעָה, "seven," is used to mean "seven-fold, seven times as much" (BDB, s.v. שִׁבְעָתַיִם, 1).

6:32 נֹאֵ֣ף אִשָּׁ֣ה חֲסַר־לֵ֑ב—The Qal (G) of נָאַף, "to commit adultery," has "a woman/wife" (אִשָּׁה) as its direct object also in Lev 20:10 (cf. Jer 29:23), but English idiom requires "*with* a woman." The Qal is in the Sixth Commandment (Ex 20:14; Deut 5:18). The verb recurs in Proverbs only in 30:20 in the Piel (D), where it is a woman who commits adultery. The construct phrase חֲסַר־לֵב, literally, "devoid of a mind," is used frequently in Proverbs. See "חֲסַר־לֵב, 'Lacking Sense' " in "Fools in Proverbs" in the introduction.

מַשְׁחִית נַפְשׁוֹ הוּא יַעֲשֶׂנָּה׃—Literally, "(the one) destroying himself/his soul, he does it," this means "he who does it destroys himself." The noun נֶפֶשׁ can be used reflexively to refer to oneself (*HALOT*, 6 b), and here it is the direct object of the Hiphil (H) participle of שָׁחַת. The pronoun הוּא refers back to the participial phrase מַשְׁחִית נַפְשׁוֹ, literally, "(the one) destroying himself." The third feminine singular suffix ("it") on the verb יַעֲשֶׂנָּה refers to the abstract idea of committing adultery, the verbal action described in the first clause of the verse (נֹאֵף אִשָּׁה).

6:33 נֶגַע־וְקָלוֹן יִמְצָא—The noun נֶגַע occurs only here in Proverbs. Elsewhere in the OT it often refers to "a disease, regarded as sent by a divine chastisement" (BDB, 2), and that is its likely meaning here. The noun קָלוֹן, "dishonor, shame," occurs seven other times in Proverbs.[b]

(b) Prov 3:35; 9:7; 11:2; 12:16; 13:18; 18:3; 22:10

6:34 כִּי־קִנְאָה חֲמַת־גָּבֶר—The noun קִנְאָה can refer to the "jealousy" of a husband betrayed by his wife. It can also refer to God's jealousy for his people (e.g., Is 9:6 [ET 9:7]; 37:32; 42:13), including when they as his spiritual "wife" are unfaithful (Ezek 16:38, 42; 23:25). In this case the "jealousy" is that of a husband who has caught someone committing adultery with his wife (cf. 27:4). The infidelity provokes חֲמַת־גָּבֶר, literally, "the anger of a man." Since גֶּבֶר can be a synonym for אִישׁ (as recognized by BDB and *HALOT*), and אִישׁ often means "husband," that is the likely meaning of גֶּבֶר in this context, as acknowledged in some English versions (NIV, NKJV, NRSV).

בְּיוֹם נָקָם׃—The combination of the preposition בְּ and the noun יוֹם can simply mean "when, at that time" (see *HALOT*, s.v. יוֹם, 10 a–b). Thus in this context "on the day of revenge" means "when he gets revenge."

6:35 לֹא־יִשָּׂא פְּנֵי כָל־כֹּפֶר—"To lift up a face" (נָשָׂא פָּנִים) is an idiom for looking favorably on something and thus considering it for acceptance (see *HALOT*, s.v. פָּנֶה, A 3 g i). The noun כֹּפֶר, "compensation," signifies a ransom price, a sum to be paid to deliver another from debt, bondage, or crime (see *HALOT*, s.v. כֹּפֶר IV). The enraged husband of the adulterous woman will not accept any payment as a ransom for the life of the adulterer.

וְלֹא־יֹאבֶה כִּי תַרְבֶּה־שֹׁחַד׃—The verb אָבָה, "to be willing," in this context is translated as "give in." Here כִּי is concessive: "even though/if" (see Joüon, § 171 b). The noun שֹׁחַד usually denotes a "bribe" intended to circumvent or pervert justice. The just penalty for adultery is death (Lev 20:10).

Commentary

This is the ninth address in Proverbs 1–9 from a father to a son.[3] Its opening (6:20–21) is very similar to the opening of the first address (1:8–9). In fact, 1:8 and 6:20 are nearly identical, differing by only two words in the first line. Prov 1:9 describes the parents' teaching as a graceful garland for the head and a chain to adorn the neck, hoping to persuade the son to internalize the instruction (in his "head") and to show it in his actions (his outwardly visible "neck").

[3] For the ten addresses from father to son in Proverbs 1–9, see the excursus "Proverbs 1–9, Christ, and the Ten Commandments" in the commentary on chapter 1.

The third address to the son (3:1–20) also exhorts him to affix attributes of wisdom to his "neck" (3:3; see also 3:22) and to guard them in his "heart" (3:1, 3; see also 3:5). The opening of the ninth address recalls the earlier passages as well as Deuteronomy[4] in what now is a familiar way for Solomon to refer to the blessings that God bestows: the riches of Jesus Christ.[5] Prov 6:21 goes a step farther by commanding the son to internalize the instruction "permanently" in his "heart" and to show it in his actions, represented by his "neck."

In 6:22 the divine instruction given through the parents is personified as a woman (see the first textual note on 6:22) who will be a guide, guard, and companion to the son. Then the metaphor for the instruction quickly shifts to a light source and then again to a path of life (6:23). This piling up of metaphors is intended to reinforce the value of the parents' instruction as a protection against an adulteress (6:24). Especially important here is the contrast between the woman representing the instruction (6:22) and the adulteress (6:24–26). This contrast between two women is a constant theme in Proverbs 1–9 as shown in figure 7.

Figure 7

Contrasts between the Two Women

The Woman Whose Ways Bring Life	*The Woman Whose Ways Bring Death*
Wisdom (1:20–33)	Adulteress (2:16–19)
Wife (5:15–20)	Adulteress (5:3–6, 20)
Parents' instruction (6:22)	Adulteress (6:24–26)
Wisdom (7:4)	Adulteress (7:5–27)
Wisdom (9:1–6)	Foolishness (9:13–18)

From this pattern it can be seen that the parents' instruction is not presented as merely their personal advice, but as divine Wisdom itself. This is reinforced by the metaphor of the light source, which is an OT metaphor for God's enlightenment (2 Sam 22:29; Ps 119:105), and the metaphor of the path of life (note especially Prov 12:28, where "life" and "path, way" occur again in close proximity). This path of course is Jesus the Savior, who is "the way, the truth, and the life" (Jn 14:6).

Therefore, the parents are guiding the son by the Gospel promise of God. The Gospel will protect him and empower him so that he does not give in to the

---

4 See the excursus "The Use of Deuteronomy 6:4–9 in Proverbs 3:1–12 and 6:20–22" in the commentary on Proverbs 3.

5 For Christ as the source and hypostasis of wisdom, see "Wisdom in Proverbs" in the introduction. See also the commentary on 1:1–7; 3:1–20; 8:22–31; and the excursus "Proverbs 8, Wisdom, Christology, and the Arian Controversy" in the commentary on Proverbs 8.

temptation of adultery. It is not the commands in 6:21 that impart this power to the son, but the evangelical promises of 6:22–24. God's Law commands us to do what is right and to avoid sin, but only the Gospel grants us the power by the Holy Spirit to believe and live according to God's Word.[6]

Prov 6:25–35 contains three warnings against adultery:

- 6:25–26: The price of an affair with a married woman is high.
- 6:27–31: Adultery will cost you all that you have.
- 6:32–35: Committing adultery shows a lack of sense.

The first warning cautions against allowing one's judgment to be clouded by beauty. While 6:26 is difficult (see the textual notes on this verse), most likely it warns that adultery costs one's own life.

The second warning cautions against adultery by comparing it to playing with fire (6:27–28). The consequences of adultery (6:29) are compared to the consequences of a desperate, starving man who steals some food. Even this man, who elicits sympathy from others because of his hunger, will be made to pay for his crime (6:30–31). By implication, the adulterer, who had no such desperate need, will be punished even more. The punishment mentioned for the thief, repaying seven times the value of what was stolen, is in excess of the greatest fines for robbery found in the Law of Moses, in some cases a fivefold or fourfold restitution, though in other cases only twofold (Ex 21:37–22:3 [ET 22:1–4]). The use of "sevenfold" (Prov 6:31) signals the comprehensiveness of the punishment.[7]

The third warning reminds the son that committing adultery betrays a lack of good sense. The fact that 6:32 uses the same Hebrew verb for "commit adultery" as the Sixth Commandment (נָאַף as in Ex 20:14; Deut 5:18) indicates that Solomon is building on the Decalogue.[8] The Torah of Moses prescribes capital punishment for adultery (Lev 20:10). Even if a person avoids legal conviction and punishment, Solomon warns that adultery has inescapable consequences. The adulterer senselessly destroys himself (Prov 6:32b). He should expect to suffer from sexually transmitted disease and loss of reputation (6:33), as well as the revenge that will be sought by the cuckolded husband, who will not be deterred from acting out his jealous anger (6:34–35).

The NT extends the foresight a Christian ought to possess by emphasizing the eternal consequences of sexual sins. Paul reminds the Corinthians:

> Do you not know that the unrighteous will not inherit the kingdom of God? Do not be deceived: neither the sexually immoral nor idolaters nor adulterers

---

[6] See, for example, Ap IV 122–36 and 265–70, and "Law and Gospel in Proverbs" in the introduction.

[7] For the significance of seven, see the commentary on 6:16–19.

[8] See further the excursus "Proverbs 1–9, Christ, and the Ten Commandments" in the commentary on chapter 1.

> nor effeminate homosexuals nor sodomites[9] … will inherit the kingdom of God. (1 Cor 6:9–10)

The writer to the Hebrews agrees and urges chastity:

> Let marriage be held in honor among all, and let the marriage bed be undefiled, for God will judge those who are sexually immoral or adulterous. (Heb 13:4)

It is interesting to note that Paul includes idolatry in the midst of several sexual sins. This hints at the frequent scriptural characterization of unfaithfulness to God as adultery,[10] and this same characterization may also lie behind the father's concern in Proverbs. Unfaithfulness seldom manifests itself in only one aspect of life. The son who is foolish enough to commit adultery risks losing (or perhaps has already lost) saving faith. By urging restraint in the face of sexual temptation, Solomon is also urging restraint from idolatry and unfaithfulness to Wisdom, hypostasized as God himself.[11] It is tragic that in the end Solomon did not follow his own advice (1 Ki 11:1–13).

---

[9] While English translations vary widely, the apostle uses two specific Greek terms here. μαλακοί refers to homosexual men who attempt to play the role of a female, while ἀρσενοκοῖται refers to homosexual men who play the male role.

[10] Biblical passages that connect sexual fidelity with faith in God, and harlotry or adultery with apostasy from God include Hosea; Ezekiel 16 and 23; the Song of Songs; 1 Cor 6:9–20; Gal 5:19–25; and Eph 5:21–33. See also the excursus "Wisdom and the Adulteress in Proverbs 1–9" in the commentary on Proverbs 2.

[11] See "Wisdom in Proverbs" in the introduction.

Proverbs 7:1–27

Tenth Address to a Son: Wisdom Will Keep You from Adultery and Its Final Result, Death

Translation

7 **[1]My son, guard my words,**
and treasure my commands inside you.
[2]Obey my commands so that you may live,
and [protect] my teachings like the pupil of your eye.
[3]Tie them on your fingers;
write them on the tablet of your heart.
[4]Say to wisdom, "You are my sister,"
and call understanding "[my] relative,"
[5]to keep yourself from a woman who is a stranger,
from a foreign woman who makes her words smooth.

[6]For from a window in my house
I gazed through my lattice.
[7]I was looking at gullible people.
I noted among the young men a youth without sense.
[8]He was crossing the street near her corner,
walking on the road to her house
[9]in the twilight in the evening of the day,
in the dark of the night and the gloom.
[10]A woman meets him
dressed as a prostitute and having ulterior motives!
[11]She is loud and rebellious;
her feet will not stay at home.
[12]One moment [she is] outside, the next moment in the open squares.
She is on the prowl near every corner.
[13]She grabs him and kisses him,
and she brazenly says to him,
[14]"Fellowship offerings are required of me.
Today I must fulfill my vows.
[15]That's why I came out to meet you:
to eagerly seek you, and now I have found you!
[16]I've covered my couch with a bedspread,
colored cloth of Egyptian yarn.
[17]I've sprinkled my bed
with myrrh, aloes, and cinnamon.

18Come, let's drink our fill of love until morning.
Let's enjoy making love,
19because my husband isn't home.
He's gone on a long trip.
20He took the bag of money with him.
He'll come home at the [next] full moon."
21She deceives him with much persuasion;
with smooth lips she seduces him.
22Following after her immediately,
like a steer he goes to slaughter,
like a deer prances into bondage,
23until an arrow pierces his liver,
like a bird darting into a trap.
He does not realize it is at the cost of his life.

24Now, sons, listen to me,
and pay attention to the words of my mouth.
25Do not let your heart turn to her way.
Do not wander on her pathways,
26because she has brought down many victims,
and all she has killed are countless.
27Her house is the way to Sheol,
going down to the chambers of death.

Textual Notes

7:1 וּמִצְוֺתַי תִּצְפֹּן אִתָּךְ׃—This is repeated verbatim from 2:1b. See the textual note on 2:1. Since the preceding clause has an imperative (שְׁמֹר), the imperfect תִּצְפֹּן, "treasure," has the force of an imperative (Joüon, § 113 m).

7:2 שְׁמֹר מִצְוֺתַי וֶחְיֵה—This clause is repeated verbatim from 4:4c. See the third textual note on 4:4. As noted there, repeated Hebrew words often are best translated with different nuances depending on the immediate context. The imperative שְׁמֹר is rendered as "guard" in 7:1a and as "obey" in 7:2a (as in 4:4c). It does double duty in 7:2 since it is also the implied verb, translated as "protect," in 7:2b. The infinitive of שָׁמַר is rendered as "to keep" in 7:5a.

וְתוֹרָתִי כְּאִישׁוֹן עֵינֶיךָ׃—For תּוֹרָה, "teaching," see the second textual note on 1:8. Here and in Deut 32:10 and Ps 17:8, אִישׁוֹן refers to the "pupil" ("apple" in KJV; NIV; ESV) of the eye as a metaphor signifying something that is most precious and essential. (The word has different significance in Prov 7:9b and as the Kethib in 20:20.)

7:3 קָשְׁרֵם עַל־אֶצְבְּעֹתֶיךָ—See the second textual note on 3:3 and the first textual note on 6:21, both of which have the identical suffixed imperative קָשְׁרֵם. As in 6:21, the masculine plural suffix refers to the two feminine nouns מִצְוָה and תּוֹרָה in the preceding verse (7:2, as in 6:20).

כָּתְבֵם עַל־לוּחַ לִבֶּךָ׃—See the third textual note on 3:3.

7:4 אֱמֹר לַחָכְמָה אֲחֹתִי אָתְּ—See "חָכְמָה, 'Wisdom,' and Related Words" in "Wisdom in Proverbs" in the introduction. The noun אָחוֹת can refer to a biological "sister" (e.g., Song 8:8). A man can also use "my sister" as a term of endearment for his beloved wife, as Solomon does in Song 4:9–10, 12; 5:1–2. This use does not imply that the wife is a biological sister. Rather, it alludes to the one-flesh union of husband and wife and to marriage as the closest of all relationships of love. Compare 1 Cor 9:5, where the apostle uses ἀδελφή, "sister," to refer to a Christian wife. Therefore Prov 7:4, in which Solomon invites his son to regard wisdom as "my sister," is consistent with the passages in Proverbs where Wisdom is portrayed as a woman whom the son (and every believer) is to love and embrace (e.g., 3:13–18; 4:7–9; 9:1–6; cf. 5:18–19).

וּמֹדָע לַבִּינָה תִקְרָא׃—The noun מֹדָע, "a relative, kinsman," occurs in the OT only here and as the Qere in Ruth 2:1. It is derived from the verb יָדַע, "to know (someone)," that is, a known, close relative. Like "my sister," it signifies that the son is invited to enjoy an intimate and enduring relationship with divine "understanding." See "בִּינָה, 'Understanding,' and Related Words" in "Wisdom in Proverbs" in the introduction.

7:5 לִשְׁמָרְךָ מֵאִשָּׁה זָרָה—See the first textual note and the commentary on 2:16, which has a similar verb with מֵאִשָּׁה זָרָה.

מִנָּכְרִיָּה אֲמָרֶיהָ הֶחֱלִיקָה׃—For this identical clause, see the second textual note on 2:16.

7:6 בְּעַד אֶשְׁנַבִּי נִשְׁקָפְתִּי׃—The noun אֶשְׁנָב, a "lattice" used as a screen in a window, occurs only here and in Judg 5:28. The verb שָׁקַף is used only in the Niphal (N), as here, and the Hiphil (H). In both stems it means "look down (from); look, gaze (through)."

7:7 וָאֵרֶא בַפְּתָאיִם—The combination רָאָה בְּ, literally, "to look at," can mean "to watch carefully, observe, study, ponder." For the object noun, see "פֶּתִי, 'Gullible Person' " in "Fools in Proverbs" in the introduction.

אָבִינָה בַבָּנִים נַעַר חֲסַר־לֵב׃—The first person singular verb אָבִינָה is cohortative in form (see GKC, § 108 h), but the cohortative does not always require translation with a volitive meaning (Joüon, § 114 b (A)), and no such meaning is evident here. Waltke-O'Connor, § 34.5.3a–b (see example 2), calls such forms "pseudo-cohortative." The Qal (G) of בִּין when used with a direct object can mean "to see" (*HALOT*, 1). However, it still contains an element of understanding or cognition (BDB, 3 a). Thus the father is saying that as he studied the young men, he "noted" one in particular. On occasion בָּנִים, literally, "sons," can mean "young men" (*HALOT*, s.v. בֵּן I, 3). Note the play on words with "my son" in 7:1. Solomon doesn't want his son to be like these "sons/young men." In particular, Solomon took interest in a certain "youth" (נַעַר) "without sense." See "חֲסַר־לֵב, 'Lacking Sense' " in "Fools in Proverbs" in the introduction.

7:8 פִּנָּהּ—Apparently this is a shortened form of the feminine noun פִּנָּה, "corner," with third feminine singular suffix. The expected form would be פִּנָּתָהּ (GKC, § 91 e).

7:9 בְּאִישׁוֹן לַיְלָה וַאֲפֵלָה׃—Literally, "in the pupil of the night" signifies the darkest part of the night, just as the pupil is the darkest part of the eye. אִישׁוֹן is used similarly as the Kethib in 20:20. This meaning is reinforced by אֲפֵלָה, "deep darkness, gloom."

7:10 וְהִנֵּה אִשָּׁה לִקְרָאתוֹ—This is, literally, "behold, a woman to meet him." The interjection הִנֵּה is translated by the exclamation point at the end of the sentence to convey its dramatic force. לִקְרָאתוֹ is the Qal (G) infinitive construct of קָרָא II, "to meet, encounter." Its Qal infinitive occurs only with the preposition לְ. It implies that the woman was waiting for and expecting the young man. This implication is reinforced when she uses לִקְרָאתֶךָ in 7:15.

שִׁית זוֹנָה—The noun שִׁית, "garment," occurs only here and figuratively in Ps 73:6. The construct phrase "garment of a prostitute" must refer to what she is wearing. This terse phrase is designed to give the Hebrew text a quick pace. However, English cannot be that terse, so "dressed like a prostitute" is used by most English versions.

וּנְצֻרַת לֵב׃—The Qal passive (Gp) participle of נָצַר can refer to "secret" or "hidden" things (Is 48:6; 65:4). Here the feminine singular participle is in construct, literally, "a guarded thing of (in) her heart." This phrase signifies her hidden, ulterior motives. She is "wily minded" (BDB, s.v. נָצַר I, 4).

7:11 הֹמִיָּה הִיא וְסֹרָרֶת—The Qal (G) feminine singular participle of הָמָה, "to be loud, boisterous," refers to the woman Folly in 9:13. The plural refers to bustling streets in 1:21. All three of these passages use the alternate form of the feminine participle that retains the original third radical י before the feminine ending: here and in 9:13 הֹמִיָּה instead of הֹמָה (see GKC, § 94 d). The second Qal feminine participle is from סָרַר, "to be stubborn, rebellious," which occurs only here in Proverbs.

7:12 פַּעַם ׀ בַּחוּץ פַּעַם בָּרְחֹבוֹת—The repetition of the noun פַּעַם, "a moment, time," signifies moment-to-moment restlessness (*HALOT*, 5 a). The nouns חוּץ, "outside," and רְחֹב, "open square," are used together also in 1:20; 5:16; 22:13.

תֶאֱרֹב׃—The Qal (G) of אָרַב denotes lying in wait to ambush or surprise someone (*HALOT*). It was used earlier in 1:11, 18 and recurs in 12:6; 23:28; 24:15, all referring to people with malicious intent to harm others. An equivalent idiom in English for describing prostitutes is "on the prowl."

7:13 הֵעֵזָה פָנֶיהָ וַתֹּאמַר לוֹ׃—Literally, this is "she strengthens her face and she says to him." The first clause functions adverbially, modifying the second clause: "and she *brazenly* says to him." Joüon, § 125 b, renders it as "she was impudent enough to [say to him]." She takes on a demeanor to deceive, that is, she brazenly lies.[1] This idiom with the Hiphil of עָזַז and the object פָּנִים, "face," recurs in 21:29 (which also has the preposition בְּ), where a wicked man shows this countenance. For the form of הֵעֵזָה, see GKC, § 67 dd.

Normally the imperfect of אָמַר with *waw* consecutive has *patach* only when it is in pause, with the accent on the final syllable, immediately preceding a quotation of the words spoken, for example, וַיֹּאמַר, "and he said, '…' " (Gen 14:19). Normally it takes *seghol* and is accented penultimately if other words intervene before the quote, for example, וַיֹּאמֶר לִי, "and he said to me, '…' " (Prov 4:4). Only here does it have *patach* (וַתֹּאמַר) even though it is accented penultimately and another word (לוֹ) precedes the quote. See GKC, § 68 d.

7:14 זִבְחֵי שְׁלָמִים עָלָי—This is, literally, "sacrifices of peace offerings are upon me." This is not stating that the woman has the meat from sacrifices she has already offered,

[1] Garrett, "Votive Prostitution Again."

as many translations imply (e.g., NIV, NRSV, NAB, NJB). עַל here does not denote possession. Instead, it indicates obligation and duty. See BDB, s.v. עַל, II 1 c, which cites this verse and the similar Ps 56:13 (ET 56:12). The woman is stating the pretext for her prostitution: she needs the money so that she can pay for and offer sacrifices in fulfillment of her vows.[2] Phrases with זֶבַח in construct with שְׁלָמִים denote "peace offerings" (e.g., Lev 7:18, 29, 32, 34). Peace offerings could be sacrificed to fulfill a vow, as described in Lev 7:16–18.[3] In Prov 7:14b the prostitute claims that her peace offerings will fulfill her vows.

הַיּוֹם שִׁלַּמְתִּי נְדָרָי׃—The Piel (D) of שָׁלֵם, "to fulfill," is often used with "vow" as its object. Proverbs refers to "vows" (the plural of נֶדֶר) also in 20:25 and 31:2. Vows are fulfilled with the offering of sacrifices also in, for example, Lev 7:16; Jonah 2:10 (ET 2:9); Pss 50:14; 66:13. Most translations interpret the perfect verb (שִׁלַּמְתִּי) as referring to past, completed action: "today *I have fulfilled* my vows." However, this does not fit the context. Instead, the harlot is claiming that she needs the income from prostitution in order to pay for sacrifices that will fulfill her vows (see the preceding textual note). Therefore the verb is translated with the same force as the preposition עַל had in the preceding clause: "today *I must fulfill* my vows." The LXX renders the verb in the present tense: σήμερον ἀποδίδωμι, "today I repay."

7:15 לְשַׁחֵר פָּנֶיךָ—Literally, this is "to seek your face." The Piel (D) of שָׁחַר can mean "to seek early (in the morning)" or, as here, "to seek diligently, earnestly." The object noun פָּנִים, "face," can signify a person's presence or even the person himself (BDB, I 2 a; *HALOT*, A 3 f). The woman is saying to the young man that she was specifically looking for him, not anyone else.

7:16 מַרְבַדִּים רָבַדְתִּי עַרְשִׂי—The noun מַרְבַד occurs only in the plural and only in 7:16 and 31:22. It is derived from the cognate verb רָבַד, "to cover, spread over," which occurs only here. The noun refers to a "bedspread" or "covering" for the "couch" (עֶרֶשׂ), which can be used for reclining and embracing (Song 1:16).

חֲטֻבוֹת אֵטוּן מִצְרָיִם׃—The noun חֲטֻבוֹת occurs only here. Semitic cognates suggest that it refers to multicolored cloth (see BDB and *HALOT*, s.v. חטב II). אֵטוּן also occurs only here, but Aramaic cognates indicate that it means "yarn."

7:17 נַפְתִּי מִשְׁכָּבִי—Usually נוּף appears in the Hiphil (H) and means "to swing, wave." The Qal (G) appears only here and apparently means "to sprinkle" handfuls of spices as the woman waves her hand back and forth over the "bed" (מִשְׁכָּב).

מֹר אֲהָלִים וְקִנָּמוֹן׃—The same three fragrant spices perfume the Edenic garden that represents the beloved bride in Song 4:14. Myrrh and/or aloes occur in other Song passages as perfumes that adorn married love.[4] The textual notes on Prov 5:3 and 5:15–20 point out other vocabulary and imagery shared by Solomon's Proverbs and his Song of Songs. The holy oil for anointing in the tabernacle was perfumed with myrrh and cin-

---

2 Van der Toorn, "Female Prostitution in Payment of Vows in Ancient Israel."

3 Leviticus 3 gives the general prescriptions for the peace offering. See Kleinig, *Leviticus*, 33–43 and 83–96. Lev 7:28–36 is about the priest's portion of the peace offerings (see Kleinig, *Leviticus*, 177–82).

4 See Song 1:13; 3:6; 4:6; 5:1, 5, 13. See also Mitchell, *The Song of Songs*, 842–44.

namon (Ex 30:23). Myrrh and aloes perfume the royal messianic wedding in Ps 45:9 (ET 45:8).

These parallel passages imply that the prostitute uses perfumes in order to imitate a sacred marriage context and to disguise that her adultery is an evil counterfeit. Compare 7:14, where she invokes the pretext of fulfilling vows by offering sacred sacrifices.

"Myrrh" (מֹר) is a dark red gum with a strong aroma and bitter taste that is exuded from a tree of the family *burseraceae.* It grows in Arabia, Ethiopia, and Somalia, but is not native to Palestine. Consequently, it was an expensive imported product.[5]

"Aloes" (אֲהָלִים) are an aromatic resin of the eaglewood tree native to India and Southeast Asia. The tree can reach a height of over one hundred feet. Especially when old, it secretes resin, which was an imported product in Israel.[6] The plural feminine form (אֲהָלוֹת) is used in Song 4:14 and Ps 45:9 (ET 45:8).

"Cinnamon" (קִנָּמוֹן) is made from the inner bark of an evergreen tree belonging to the laurel family. It is a native of Sri Lanka and the Malay Peninsula and was imported into ancient Israel.[7]

7:18 לְכָה נִרְוֶה דֹדִים עַד־הַבֹּקֶר—The Qal (G) of רָוָה, "to drink one's fill," takes a Hebrew direct object (Joüon, § 125 d), but English idiom requires a genitive, "*of* love." The imperfect here has a cohortative meaning, "*let us* …" (cf. Joüon, § 114 b, note 1), as does the parallel cohortative verb נִתְעַלְּסָה in the next clause. The Piel (D) of רָוָה has a sexual meaning in 5:19; see the third textual note on 5:19. For דֹּדִים, "love," see the commentary.

נִתְעַלְּסָה בָּאֳהָבִים׃—The Qal (G) of the rare verb עָלַס means "rejoice" (Job 20:18). The cohortative here is in the Hithpael (HtD), which may have a middle meaning ("delight ourselves") or a reciprocal meaning ("give delight to each other"). The noun אֹהַב is derived from the verb אָהֵב, "to love." This noun occurs only in Hos 9:10, referring to a loved idol, and here, where the plural has the "carnal sense" (BDB) of "making love."

7:19 כִּי אֵין הָאִישׁ בְּבֵיתוֹ—Literally, this is "because the man is not in his house." At times an article is used in Hebrew to denote something that is specific in the mind of the speaker. In this case the woman uses "the man" (הָאִישׁ) to refer specifically to her husband, so the sense is "my husband."

הָלַךְ בְּדֶרֶךְ מֵרָחוֹק׃—Literally, "he went on a road from afar," this clause denotes a long trip (see *HALOT*, s.v. רָחוֹק, 5 b).

7:20 לְיוֹם הַכֵּסֶא—Literally, "at the day of the full moon," this refers to the time of the next full moon, which could be up to a month away. The noun כֶּסֶא (pausal: כֵּסֶא) occurs elsewhere in the OT only in Ps 81:4 (ET 81:3), where it is spelled כֶּסֶה.

7:21 הִטַּתּוּ בְּרֹב לִקְחָהּ—The Hiphil of נָטָה (here the third feminine singular perfect with third masculine singular suffix) can mean "to cause [someone] to apostatize" from God or to entice the heart away from proper devotion (see BDB, 3 c). Here the woman

---

5 *FF*, 147–48.

6 *FF*, 90.

7 *FF*, 108.

entices the man into sin. The noun לֶקַח usually refers to godly "instruction" (see the first textual note on 1:5), but here it signifies the art of deceptive persuasion (cf. *HALOT*, 2).

בְּחֵלֶק שְׂפָתֶיהָ תַּדִּיחֶנּוּ׃—Literally, this is "by the smoothness of her lips she seduces him." For the noun חֵלֶק, "smoothness, seductiveness," in reference to speech, see the second textual note on 2:16. The Hiphil (H) of נָדַח means "entice" and in sexual situations "seduce" (*HALOT*, 3–4).

7:22 וּכְעֶכֶס אֶל־מוּסַר אֱוִיל׃—This is, literally, "and like an anklet to the discipline of a fool." The ancient versions (LXX, Vulgate, and Peshitta) vary widely. Most interpreters assume that the Hebrew text has been damaged by scribal mistakes. A large number of reconstructions have been suggested. Those who understand the noun עֶכֶס as "shackles" rely on an uncertain derivation of the meaning of this word based on Arabic cognates.[8] However, the only other occurrence of the noun is in Is 3:18, where the plural refers to "ankle bracelets" worn by women. The cognate Piel (D) of עָכַס in Is 3:16 refers to women who "prance" to shake or rattle their ankle bracelets as they walk. The safest assumption appears to be that this line, like the parallel lines of Prov 7:22b and 7:23b, mentions an animal. The translation adopted here follows the reconstruction by Scott, which involves only minor adjustments to the MT.[9] The text וּכְעַכֵּס אֶל־מוֹסֵר אַיָּל would mean "like a deer [אַיָּל] prances [the Piel infinitive עַכֵּס with כְּ] into bondage [אֶל־מוֹסֵר]." The noun מוֹסֵר, "bondage, chain, captivity," is from the verb אָסַר, "to tie, bind, imprison."

7:23 וְלֹא־יָדַע כִּי־בְנַפְשׁוֹ הוּא׃—The preposition on בְּנַפְשׁוֹ is the *bet pretii*, the בְּ of "price" or "cost" (BDB, s.v. בְּ, III 3 a), indicating that his sin is "at the cost of" his very life and eternal soul (נַפְשׁוֹ).

7:24 The same two imperatives and the vocative בָנִים were in 4:1.

7:25 אַל־יֵשְׂטְ אֶל־דְּרָכֶיהָ לִבֶּךָ—The Qal (G) of שָׂטָה, "to turn aside, away," has a similar sense in Num 5:12, 19–20, 29, where it refers to a woman who does (or does not) stray by being unfaithful to her husband.

אַל־תֵּתַע בִּנְתִיבוֹתֶיהָ׃—The Qal (G) of תָּעָה, "to wander, go astray," recurs in 14:22 and 21:16. The causative Hiphil is in 10:17 and 12:26.

7:26 כִּי־רַבִּים חֲלָלִים הִפִּילָה—It is unusual for an attributive adjective (here רַבִּים) to precede its noun (חֲלָלִים), but this sometimes happens with רַב, "many": "*many* victims she has brought down" (Waltke-O'Connor, § 14.3.1b, example 8; see also Joüon, § 141 b). The Hiphil of נָפַל has the causative meaning "to bring down, cause to fall, to fell." In light of 7:27 as well as 5:5 and 9:18, the verb refers to seducing people into sins that lead to eternal damnation in hell. חָלָל, "slain corpse, victim," refers to dead unbelievers condemned to eternal perdition also in, for example, Is 66:16; Jer 25:33; Ezek 28:8; 31:17–18; 32:21–25.

וַעֲצֻמִים כָּל־הֲרֻגֶיהָ׃—The adjective עָצוּם, which often means "strong, mighty," means "countless" here, where it stands in poetic parallelism to רַב (*HALOT*, s.v. עָצוּם).

---

8 See, for example, Delitzsch, *Proverbs*, 1:169.

9 Scott, *Proverbs*, *Ecclesiastes*, 64.

The Qal passive (Gp) participle הֲרֻגֶיהָ, literally, "her killed ones," has a suffix that denotes the agent of the action, hence "those killed *by* her" (cf. GKC, § 116 l).

7:27 דַּרְכֵי שְׁאוֹל בֵּיתָהּ—The plural construct phrase דַּרְכֵי שְׁאוֹל, "ways of/to Sheol," may be due to the plural reference to דְּרָכֶיהָ, "her ways," in 7:25. English idiom requires the singular: "[going to] her house is the *way* to [go to] Sheol."

יֹרְדוֹת אֶל־חַדְרֵי־מָוֶת׃—The feminine plural participle יֹרְדוֹת, "going down, descending," modifies the feminine plural noun דַּרְכֵי, "ways," in the preceding clause. Here חֶדֶר, "room, chamber," may be an ironic double entendre since in some contexts it refers to a bedroom for consummating marriage (Judg 15:1; Joel 2:16; Song 1:4; 3:4).

Commentary

The tenth and last address in Proverbs 1–9 from a father to his son returns to the theme of avoiding adultery.[10] This address divides into three sections: the opening admonition (7:1–5), an incident that the father observed (7:6–23), and a closing warning (7:24–27).

The opening admonition (7:1–5) is similar to the other opening words of the previous addresses. The father once again attaches the promise of life to his commands ("so that you may live," 7:2; see, e.g., 3:2, 18, 22; 4:4). As in the previous address, the son is to appropriate the teachings to shape his behavior ("fingers") and internalize them ("heart," 7:3; see 6:21). Prov 7:4–5 once again draws a contrast between Wisdom and the adulteress as potential mates. When the son is told to call Wisdom "my sister" and "relative" (7:4), the implication is that the son should marry himself to Wisdom, just as Solomon calls his bride "my sister" in his Song.[11] If the son is faithful to Wisdom, he will keep himself from the adulteress and her tempting words (7:5).

The father now begins an object lesson for his son, describing an incident he observed through his window (7:6–23). Since windows in the ancient Near East had no glass, they were covered by a lattice that kept birds out but allowed air in (Judg 5:28; see also 2 Sam 6:16; 2 Ki 9:30; Song 2:9). Through his window the father was observing people who were foolish in their behavior. He picks out one particular young man "without sense" (Prov 7:7) who will provide an example to drive home the point of his previous address ("lacks sense" in 6:32). In the only action that the young man is depicted as taking, he walks toward the adulteress' house in the evening (7:8–9). Referring to the woman by the pronominal suffix alone ("her" twice in 7:8) heightens the drama and allows the reader to draw the conclusion about her identity. The young man's path is the wrong one, and his choice places him in the wrong location at the wrong time.

---

[10] For the ten addresses from father to son in Proverbs 1–9 and for their main themes, see the excursus "Proverbs 1–9, Christ, and the Ten Commandments" in the commentary on chapter 1. For the theme of avoiding adultery, see the excursus "Wisdom and the Adulteress in Proverbs 1–9" in the commentary on Proverbs 2.

[11] See Mitchell, *The Song of Songs*, 825–26, who compares the usage of "my sister" in Song 4:9–10, 12; 5:1–2 with that in Prov 7:4.

The description now switches to the woman. She comes out to meet the young man dressed seductively as a prostitute (cf. 6:26), but with a motive that is not apparent to him (7:10). The father describes her as "loud," which explains why he can report the ensuing conversation (7:11). She is also "rebellious." Her rebellion is against God's Law, especially the Sixth Commandment. While Ex 20:14; Lev 20:10; Deut 5:18; and Prov 6:32 all use the same verb for "commit adultery," her violation of that commandment is depicted in Proverbs 7 by her straying from home (7:11–12). The young man too obviously is not meeting his wife at his home.

The places she frequents ("outside ... the open squares," 7:12) are the same areas visited by divine Wisdom (1:20). The similarities between Wisdom and this woman are important. They signal to the reader that believers must make discriminating choices. The difference between a wise course of action and a foolish, sinful, and deadly one is not always immediately obvious. Insight and foresight from God's Word are needed in order to discern the right path. Heedless choices and reckless decisions will lead to death and hell (7:26–27).

However, two important differences exist between Wisdom and this woman. First, Wisdom is never found on the "corner." פִּנָּה refers to a street "corner" in Proverbs only in 7:8, 12, where stands the adulteress. (When פִּנָּה recurs in 21:9 and 25:24, it refers to the "corner" of a roof.) Second, Wisdom never "ambushes" or "lies in wait" (the verb אָרַב, translated as "is on the prowl" in 7:12). Only the adulteress and wicked men do this (see the second textual note on 7:12).

The woman takes the initiative. She grabs the young man, kisses him, and then shamelessly lies to him (7:13). She claims that she has an obligation to offer sacrifices to fulfill her vows to God (as in Lev 7:16–18). Her excuse for her prostitution is that it is a way for her to earn the money for the sacrifices, even though the Torah of Moses specifically forbids sacrifices paid for by prostitution (Deut 23:19 [ET 23:18]). Later she will claim to be bereft of funds since her husband has taken the money with him on a long trip (Prov 7:20). The mention of sacrifices is a ploy to ease the conscience of the young man. She is religious after all, and her purported motive is to fulfill her promises to God.[12]

Such religion, however, is an abomination to God. It purports that the end justifies the means, that sinful actions that violate God's Word are okay if you can construe them as necessary to accomplish outwardly pious purposes. However, the motivation and real purpose are purely evil. It is a convenient religion designed to soothe consciences through lowering or perverting the requirements of the Law to make it easier to claim to be good person. This kind of religion rejects God's offer of justification through faith alone for the sake of Christ alone because that would require admitting one's sin, total depravity, and utter reliance on the Savior (see AC XII 3–6). Instead such religion simply

[12] Garrett, "Votive Prostitution Again," 682.

redraws the rules to allow one to ignore or explain away sin and the total need for Christ's redemption (see SA III III 10). All religions besides the one true saving faith revealed throughout the Scriptures are manmade religions. They ultimately are of the devil and lead to eternal damnation (7:26–27).

Though the woman claims that she was looking for this particular young man ("you" three times in 7:15), these assertions are part of her lies intended to seduce the young man. She would just as gladly have taken advantage of any other fool. The seduction continues with her description of the preparations she has made (7:16–17). She has prepared her "couch" (עֶרֶשׂ, 7:16) and her "bed" (מִשְׁכָּב, 7:17) for lovemaking. This same furniture is associated with married lovemaking in Solomon's Song (עֶרֶשׂ, "couch," in Song 1:16; מִשְׁכָּב, "bed," in Song 3:1). She has also perfumed her bed with myrrh, aloes, and cinnamon. Elsewhere in the OT these spices are associated with physical attraction and love within the divinely sanctioned context of marriage.[13] The reference is ironic, however, because myrrh and aloes are also associated with death since they were used to embalm bodies (Jn 19:39). Perhaps cinnamon also was used in this connection since it or its close cousin cassia[14] was an ingredient in perfumes and oils (Ex 30:23–25; Ps 45:9 [ET 45:8]; Sirach 24:15).

After baiting the trap, she makes her proposition (Prov 7:18). Once again she uses the vocabulary of what is sacred but profanes it. She speaks of drinking of "love" (see also Song 5:1). The abstract plural noun דֹּדִים, "love," occurs only here in Proverbs but is common in Solomon's Song, where it always refers to holy marital love,[15] which is "the flame of Yah[weh]" (Song 8:6). Again, the seductress is counterfeiting the holy and the divine.

She assures the young man that it is safe to accept her offer since her husband is away on an extended business trip and won't be home until the middle of the lunar month (7:19–20). When the quotation of the woman ends, the father concludes that the woman has seduced the man and led him astray with her persuasion and her lips (7:21). "Smooth" characterizes both her words (7:5) and her lips (7:21), and especially the latter alludes to her kisses (7:13). Note the chiasm created between the father's description of her actions leading up to her speech (7:13) and his conclusion (7:21):

A "She … *kisses* him" (7:13a).
  B "She brazenly *says* to him" (7:13b).
  B' She deceives him with much [verbal] *persuasion*" (7:21a).
A' "With smooth *lips* she seduces him" (7:21b).[16]

---

13 Ps 45:9 (ET 45:8); Song 1:13; 3:6; 4:6, 14; 5:1, 5, 13; Esth 2:12. For the significance of spices and perfumes in the context of holy matrimony, see Mitchell, *The Song of Songs*, 862–68.

14 *FF*, 104–5.

15 For this term and other vocabulary for love in the Song, see Mitchell, *The Song of Songs*, 562–65 and 582–88.

16 Note that many translations miss the chiasm. Concentrating of the parallelism of 7:21 alone, they assume that her "smooth lips" pertain only to her talk, not to her kissing (e.g., NIV, NRSV, NJB).

The young man is pictured as passively following her into her snare and is compared to three animals (7:22–23): a "steer" about to be slaughtered; apparently a "deer"[17] felled by a hunter's arrow; and a "bird" caught in a trap. The foolishness of the young man makes him as vulnerable as any of these dumb animals. Like them, he does not realize his actions will lead to his own death.

As pointed out above in the textual notes and commentary, the woman's speech shares much with the imagery of love found in Song of Songs. However, the sexual relationship is entirely different.[18] In Proverbs only the woman speaks.[19] In the Song the bride utters more of the poetry, but both spouses speak abundant praises to each other. In Proverbs only the woman takes action, grabbing the young man and kissing him. In the Song the bride yearns for her husband to kiss her (1:2) and to lead her (1:4), and he does. Ultimately, it is God who enables both married lovers to take action as he animates them through the power of divine love, which is stronger than death or Sheol (8:6). The mutuality of the Song signals sexual love as God intended within marriage, with the husband as the head—the protagonist "lover" (e.g., Song 1:13)—and the wife as his "beloved, friend" (e.g., Song 1:9), his "sister" and "bride" (e.g., Song 4:9–10).[20] The distorted relationship proposed by the woman in Prov 7:14–20 is selfishly intended to fulfill her own economic desire and the equally selfish sinful lust of the young man. In the Song of Songs love overcomes even death and the grave (Song 8:6–7; cf. 1 Corinthians 13) and gives the believer eschatological hope.[21] In Proverbs 7 the false imitation of sacred love leads to death and the eternal grave (7:22–23, 26–27).

In the closing warning (7:24–27), after once again calling on his "sons" to listen (7:24, as in 4:1 and 5:7), the father returns to the metaphor of the path to tell his sons not to adopt the "way(s)" of the woman (דְּרָכֶיהָ, 7:25).[22] This is in contrast to the foolish young man, who chose to walk the "road" or "way" to the woman's house (דֶּרֶךְ, 7:8). The father wants his sons to exercise foresight so that they can see the consequences of adultery and avoid this sin. He

[17] See the textual note on 7:22.

[18] Cf. Grossberg, "Two Kinds of Sexual Relationships in the Hebrew Bible."

[19] Although note that the wise son is told to speak (7:4).

[20] See the extensive study of "Roles in the Song" in Mitchell, *The Song of Songs*, 380–428. On one hand, the Song expresses the headship and leadership of the husband in a way that prefigures divine monergism in salvation, with Christ the Bridegroom fully accomplishing by himself the salvation of his bride, the church. On the other hand, the Song portrays the bride as the joyful recipient and fully active partner in the marriage of divine love, even as the church, the bride of Christ, is enabled by his grace to respond to his love with loving action. The portrayal of the relationship and roles in the Song is consistent with that of Christian husbands and wives in Eph 5:21–33 and with that of Christ and the church in that passage and throughout the Scriptures.

[21] Compare the joyful eschatological yearning of the bride in Song 2:17 and 8:14 with "maranatha" in 1 Cor 16:22 and the continual prayer of the church still on earth in Rev 22:17, 20.

[22] See further the excursus "The Metaphor of the Path in Solomon's Wisdom" in the commentary on Proverbs 10.

portrays the consequences in terms of death and Sheol (7:27) as he did in his seventh address (5:5). The portrayal extends the metaphor of the path by picturing the house of the adulteress as the entrance to the path that leads down to death. This is a clear contrast to the path that leads to life, a contrast found in other passages about the adulteress (2:19; 5:6). Because of this contrast, death should not be understood only as physical death but also as eternal death at the end of the path that leads away from God.

The self-centered nature of the desire expressed in this tenth and final address to Solomon's son stands in stark contrast to the mutual relationship intended by God in marriage (Col 3:18–19; 1 Pet 3:1–7). Paul discusses this mutuality when he urges husbands to love their wives even as Christ has loved the church (Eph 5:25–33a) and exhorts wives to submit to their husbands even as the church submits to Christ (Eph 5:22–24, 33b). This is the opposite of the illicit relationship between the woman and the foolish young man in Proverbs 7.

Of course, the proper marriage relationship mirrors the relationship between Christ and his church (Eph 5:21–33). The improper relationship in which the foolish young man finds himself in Proverbs 7 inverts the proper order and therefore is a picture of apostasy. It does not merely portray a human relationship that is a perversion of marriage, but it also is intended by Solomon to demonstrate apostasy from divine Wisdom, that is, faithlessness and separation from God. The fool allows the devil, the world, and his sinful flesh to invert the proper relationships God intends in this life, leading ultimately to his own death and eternal condemnation. The wise son, in contrast, will rejoice in God's ordering of the world and receive eternal life through God's grace according to the order of salvation in Christ. Instead of heeding the siren call of the "foreign" woman who is a "stranger" (7:5)—any woman who is not his wife and who entices him into an illicit relationship—the wise son heeds the call of God, who initiates a proper relationship of everlasting love through Wisdom, who is Christ.[23]

[23] For Christ as Wisdom incarnate, see "Wisdom in Proverbs" in the introduction. See also the commentary on 1:1–7; 3:13–20; 8:22–31; 30:1b–10; and the excursus "Proverbs 8, Wisdom, Christology, and the Arian Controversy" in the commentary on Proverbs 8.

Proverbs 8:1–11

Wisdom's Invitation to All People

Translation

8 **[1]Does not Wisdom call out,**
and Understanding raise her voice?
[2]On the hills above the roads,
she takes her stand at the crossroads.
[3]Beside the gates, at the access to the city,
[at the] entrance to doorways she cries out.
[4]"To you people I call,
and [I raise] my voice to children of mankind.
[5]You gullible people, obtain prudence.
You fools, obtain a heart.
[6]Listen, because I am speaking noble things.
The opening of my lips [speaks] upright things,
[7]for my palate declares truth,
and wickedness is a disgusting thing to my lips.
[8]All the words of my mouth [are spoken] with righteousness.
There is nothing twisted or crooked in them.
[9]All of them are plain to those who have understanding,
and [they are] upright things to those who find knowledge.
[10]Take my discipline, and not silver,
and knowledge rather than fine gold,
[11]because Wisdom is better than jewels,
and all desirable things cannot equal her."

Textual Notes

8:1 הֲלֹא־חָכְמָה תִקְרָא וּתְבוּנָה תִּתֵּן קוֹלָהּ׃—The parallel verbal clauses קָרָא, "to call out," and נָתַן קוֹל, "to give/raise the voice," were also in 2:3. The same two verbal clauses would be parallel in 8:4, but the second clause has only קוֹל, and the verb נָתַן is implied, so the translation of 8:4b adds "I raise."

For the parallel nouns חָכְמָה and תְּבוּנָה, see the first textual note on 2:2. See also "חָכְמָה, 'Wisdom,' and Related Words" and "בִּינָה, 'Understanding,' and Related Words" in "Wisdom in Proverbs" in the introduction.

8:2 בְּרֹאשׁ־מְרוֹמִים עֲלֵי־דָרֶךְ—Literally, this is "on the head of heights over a road." The plural noun מְרוֹמִים, "heights," recurs in 9:3, 14. עֲלֵי is a poetic variant of the preposition עַל.

בֵּית נְתִיבוֹת נִצָּבָה׃—The construct phrase, literally, "house of pathways" is an idiom for "crossroads" (*HALOT*, s.v. נְתִיבָה). The Niphal (N) of נָצַב, "to take one's stand," occurs only here in Proverbs, but the Hiphil (H) is used in 15:25.

8:3 לְיַד־שְׁעָרִים לְפִי־קָרֶת—"To a hand" is an idiom for "beside" (*HALOT*, s.v. לְ, 2). As a parallel to שְׁעָרִים, the city "gates," here פֶּה, "mouth," refers to the point of "access" or entrance to a "city" (קֶרֶת).

מְבוֹא פְתָחִים תָּרֹנָּה׃—The noun מָבוֹא, "entrance," occurs only here in Proverbs. The plural of the noun פֶּתַח, here translated as "doorways," refers to "openings" or "entrances" into a city also in 1:21b. "Entrance of/to doorways" describes the area near the city gate through which all people must pass before gaining access to the different streets and many houses within the city. The first part of the verse uses prepositional phrases with לְ to indicate the place where Wisdom calls, but מְבוֹא פְתָחִים is simply an accusative of location (Joüon, § 126 h).

The same third feminine plural verb form תָּרֹנָּה is used in 1:20 with the abstract plural חָכְמוֹת, "Wisdom," as its subject. See the first textual note on 1:20. Here its subject could be both of the feminine singular nouns in 8:1, חָכְמָה and תְבוּנָה, in which case "*they* cry out." However, the singular verb נִצָּבָה in 8:2 and the singular forms in 8:4 (אֶקְרָא וְקוֹלִי), in 8:6, and later in the pericope suggest that the plural verb תָּרֹנָּה can be translated as singular with חָכְמָה, "Wisdom," in 8:1 as its implied subject.

8:4 אֲלֵיכֶם אִישִׁים אֶקְרָא וְקוֹלִי אֶל־בְּנֵי אָדָם׃—Both אִישׁ (*HALOT*, 4) and בְּנֵי אָדָם (*HALOT*, s.v. אָדָם I, 1 c) may be used to denote humans in general (instead of males in particular). That appears to be the case here: Wisdom calls to everyone ("people … children of mankind") regardless of gender.

The common plural form of אִישׁ is אֲנָשִׁים. The rare form here, אִישִׁים, "people," occurs elsewhere only in Is 53:3 and Ps 141:4. Critical scholars often claim that it is a late form since they presume that Psalm 141 is late, and not from David as the superscription states, and that Isaiah 53 is postexilic.[1] However, אִישִׁים merely follows the more common pattern of Hebrew masculine plural nouns. It may be improvised for poetic purposes since it only occurs in poetry, and therefore it is not an indicator of date. In Prov 8:4 Solomon may have chosen this form to enhance the catchy line. Each of the three words in the first line, and a total of five words in the verse, begins with the glottal stop (אֲלֵיכֶם אִישִׁים אֶקְרָא … אֶל־ … אָדָם). The first line also ends with the second glottal stop in אֶקְרָא. The rare form אִישִׁים includes two long *hireq* vowels (ִי), whereas the common form אֲנָשִׁים has only one, and the suffix on וְקוֹלִי provides a third long *hireq*. The verse also includes two instances of the long *tsere* vowel (אֲלֵיכֶם … בְּנֵי).

This provides a stunning, ear-catching opening line for Wisdom to speak because of the combination of glottal stops and long vowels, supplemented by the rare plural form. (The wording with the normal plural form, אֲלֵיכֶם אֲנָשִׁים אֶקְרָא, has an extra syllable and does not have the same effect.) Similarly, אִישִׁים may have been chosen by Isaiah ben Amoz for repetitive effect since it is followed by the singular: the sound of his wording, אִישִׁים אִישׁ, emphasizes his message that the Suffering Servant truly is a human among humans; Jesus Christ is true man as well as true God. The wording אֲנָשִׁים אִישׁ would not convey the same emphasis.

---

[1] Cf., e.g., J. Kühlewein, "אִישׁ," *TLOT* 1:98.

8:5 הָבִ֣ינוּ פְתָאיִ֣ם עָרְמָ֑ה וּ֝כְסִילִ֗ים הָבִ֥ינוּ לֵֽב׃—The Hiphil (H) imperative of בִּין appears twice in this verse. It usually means "to get or obtain understanding" (see *HALOT*, Hiphil, 1 b). Both clauses specify the particular type of understanding. In the first clause the object is עָרְמָה, "prudence" (see the first textual note on 1:4 and also "עָרוּם, 'Prudent,' and עָרְמָה, 'Prudence' " in "Wisdom in Proverbs" in the introduction). In the second clause the object is לֵב, "a heart" (see the first textual note on 2:10). In both clauses the verb should be translated "obtain" with the expressed direct object in place of the word "understanding" (used in the definition above).

In light of אֲלֵיכֶם אִישִׁים ("to you people") in 8:4, both פְתָאיִם and וּכְסִילִים are translated as vocatives, "you gullible people ... you fools." For פְתָאיִם, see "פֶּתִי, 'Gullible Person' " in "Fools in Proverbs" in the introduction. For וּכְסִילִים, see "כְּסִיל, 'Fool,' and כְּסִילוּת, 'Foolishness' " in "Fools in Proverbs" in the introduction.

8:6 שִׁ֭מְעוּ כִּֽי־נְגִידִ֣ים אֲדַבֵּ֑ר—The adjective (used as a substantive) נָגִיד, "a noble thing," is used in Proverbs only here and in 28:16, where it refers to a "prince" or "ruler."

מֵ֝ישָׁרִֽים׃—This plural noun, "upright things," is a cognate and synonym of יְשָׁרִים in 8:9, which is translated identically. מֵישָׁרִים occurred previously as an abstract plural meaning "fairness" (see the second textual note on 1:3) or "uprightness" (2:9). It is used also in 23:16, 31.

8:7 כִּֽי־אֱ֭מֶת יֶהְגֶּ֣ה חִכִּ֑י—The direct object noun אֱמֶת here and in many other OT passages refers to spoken "truth" (BDB, 4 a). Its antonym in the next clause is רֶשַׁע, "wickedness." It can also refer to "faithfulness" or "certainty." It often is paired with חֶסֶד (see the first textual note on 3:3). It recurs in Proverbs in 11:18; 12:19; 14:22, 25; 16:6; 20:28; 22:21 (twice); 23:23; and 29:14.

Except for in Josh 1:8, the Qal (G) of הָגָה I, "to declare, utter," is used only in poetry. It recurs in Proverbs in 15:28 and 24:2. For the subject noun, חֵךְ, "palate," see the second textual note on 5:3.

וְתוֹעֲבַ֖ת שְׂפָתַ֣י רֶֽשַׁע׃—For תּוֹעֵבָה, see the first textual note on 3:32.

8:8 בְּצֶ֥דֶק—Regarding צֶדֶק and related vocabulary, see "The Relationship between Wisdom and Righteousness in Proverbs" in "Wisdom in Proverbs" in the introduction.

אֵ֥ין בָּ֝הֶ֗ם נִפְתָּ֥ל וְעִקֵּֽשׁ׃—The Niphal (N) participle נִפְתָּל, "twisted," appears only here in Proverbs. For the recurring adjective עִקֵּשׁ, "crooked," see the first textual note on 2:15. Both of these terms are antonyms of the vocabulary in Proverbs for "straight," "upright," "true," and "righteous." See the second textual note on 1:3.

8:9 כֻּלָּ֣ם נְ֭כֹחִים לַמֵּבִ֑ין—The adjective נָכֹחַ means "straightforward" (*HALOT*, 2). Thus the words of Wisdom are "plain," "clear," or "uncomplicated." This adjective has not appeared before in Proverbs, but it recurs referring to words in 24:26. The Hiphil (H) participle of בִּין has the intransitive meaning "to understand." See the second textual note on 1:2.

וִ֝ישָׁרִ֗ים לְמֹ֣צְאֵי דָֽעַת׃—For יָשָׁר, "straight, right," here as a substantive, "upright thing," see the first textual note and the commentary on 2:7. For דַּעַת (here in pause), which recurs in this pericope in the second clause of 8:10, see "דַּעַת, 'Knowledge,' and יָדַע, 'to Know' " in "Wisdom in Proverbs" in the introduction as well as the commentary on 1:4, 7.

8:10–11 A clause with a negated verb occurs in 8:10a (see the first textual note on 8:10) and 8:11b. The second clause of 8:10 and the first clause of 8:11 express similar comparative ideas, each with the preposition מִן. Therefore the two verses contain a chiasm:

A Negated verbal clause (8 :10a)
  B Comparative statement with מִן (8:10b)
  B' Comparative statement with מִן (8:11a)
A' Negated verbal clause (8:11b)

8:10 קְחוּ־מוּסָרִי וְאַל־כָּסֶף—For the noun מוּסָר, see the first textual note on 1:3 and "מוּסָר, 'Discipline,' and יָסַר, 'to Discipline' " in "Wisdom in Proverbs" in the introduction. The particle אַל normally negates a verb, and the implied verb it negates is the imperative in the first clause, קְחוּ, a verb that does double duty. Therefore the second clause means "and [do] not [take] silver." Taken together, the two clauses in 8:10a suggest the comparative idea that Wisdom's discipline is much more valuable than silver.

וְדַעַת מֵחָרוּץ נִבְחָר—The noun חָרוּץ, "gold," is used with the preposition מִן also in 3:14; 8:19; 16:16. The Niphal (N) participle נִבְחָר means "chosen." The Hebrew idiom "chosen gold" corresponds to the English idiom "fine gold." The same participle is used with כֶּסֶף to refer to "fine silver" in 8:19 and 10:20.

8:11 כִּי־טוֹבָה חָכְמָה מִפְּנִינִים—This is one of Solomon's "better than" (טוֹבָה ... מִ־) proverbs. See "Direct Comparisons" in "Authorship and Date" in the introduction. For מִפְּנִינִים, "than jewels," see the first textual note on 3:15.

וְכָל־חֲפָצִים לֹא יִשְׁווּ־בָהּ׃—See the second textual note on 3:15, which has the identical clause except for the suffix there on חֲפָצֶיךָ.

Commentary

The first poem about Wisdom in Proverbs (1:20–33) was after the first of the ten addresses couched as a father teaching his son.[2] The second poem about Wisdom (8:1–36) begins as the first poem did (1:20–21), with a description of Wisdom's call and the places where she proclaims her Gospel invitation. This poem opens with a rhetorical question instead of a statement, but the meaning is the same: Wisdom freely and graciously makes herself available to all (8:1–3; 1:20–21). This is reinforced by 8:4, where Wisdom specifically states that her message is for all "people" and "children of mankind" (for similar uses of בְּנֵי אָדָם, see especially Deut 32:8; Pss 11:4; 14:2 || 53:3 [ET 53:2]). The parallel lines in Prov 8:5 remind the reader that all humans are inclined to foolishness since all are conceived and born with a sinful nature (see, e.g., Psalm 51 and Romans 3). Therefore Wisdom's call to the gullible and foolish is the call to everyone and anyone to repent and believe the divine message.

Wisdom continues by describing her message as consisting of "noble things" and "upright things" (מֵישָׁרִים, 8:6), as the "truth" and not "wickedness" (8:7), as spoken "with righteousness" and not "twisted" or "crooked"

---

2 For the ten addresses from father to son in Proverbs 1–9 and for their main themes, see the excursus "Proverbs 1–9, Christ, and the Ten Commandments" in the commentary on chapter 1.

(8:8), and as "plain" and "upright things" (וִישָׁרִים) to the wise (8:9). That her palate declares "truth" and her lips abhor "wickedness" (8:7) forms a direct contrast to the adulteress, whose lips drip honey and whose palate is smooth with oil (5:3).[3] While many of these terms have been used before in Proverbs by Solomon to describe Wisdom's message, this is the first passage in the book where Wisdom herself declares that her message consists of "upright things" and "truth" and is spoken with "righteousness" (8:6–9). It is also the first passage to use the terms translated as "noble things" (8:6) and "plain" (8:9). Moreover, the opposites of Wisdom, "wickedness," "a disgusting thing," and "crooked" (8:7–8) have previously applied to sinful unbelievers or their actions, but they have not been used before this point by Wisdom herself as antonyms that contrast with her own words. By quoting Wisdom herself in this way, Solomon is in effect introducing Wisdom anew, making her fresh, although she has been mentioned throughout the previous seven chapters.

The power of Wisdom to enlighten is assumed in 8:9. Those who have Wisdom (represented by the synonymous terms "understanding" and "knowledge") are able to comprehend Wisdom's message and assent to it as "upright." The implication is that those who do not have Wisdom—ignorant fools, unbelievers (Pss 14:1 || 53:2 [ET 53:1])—are unenlightened. They do not and indeed cannot assent to Wisdom's message since "the natural person does not accept the things of the Spirit of God, for they are foolishness to him, and he is not able to know because they are discerned spiritually" (1 Cor 2:14; cf. Rom 8:7). No person can teach himself divine Wisdom, just as no person can contribute anything to his conversion and salvation. Only as God the Holy Spirit works through the Word and the Sacraments to create and sustain faith does a person receive God's saving grace in Jesus Christ and knowledge of divine things, as the Lutheran Confessions amply demonstrate from Scripture (e.g., FC Ep II 1–6; FC SD II 9–27).

Wisdom's invitation to "take my discipline" is made attractive by noting that its value surpasses silver, gold, jewels, or anything else that humans desire (Prov 8:10–11). These comparisons repeat for emphasis the supreme and eternal value of Wisdom as presented in earlier chapters (2:1–5; 3:13–15; see the commentary on 3:1–20 on the riches of Christ). Moreover, coming directly after Proverbs 7, where the adulteress offers the young man sex in exchange for money, 8:1–11 draws a sharp contrast between the seductress and Wisdom. Divine Wisdom freely offers something of greater value than anything on earth. She demands no exchange, whereas the adulteress does. Wisdom's offer is pure Gospel, God's grace alone: the most valuable gift of God, free and available to all, makes all who receive it "wise unto salvation" (2 Tim 3:15; cf. Rom 16:19).[4]

---

3 See further the excursus "Wisdom and the Adulteress in Proverbs 1–9" in the commentary on Proverbs 2.

4 For Jesus Christ as the hypostasis of divine Wisdom, see "Wisdom in Proverbs" in the introduction. See also the commentary on 1:1–7; 3:13–20; 8:22–31; 30:1b–10; and the excursus "Proverbs 8, Wisdom, Christology, and the Arian Controversy" in the commentary on chapter 8.

Proverbs 8:12–21

Wisdom's Benefit

Translation

8 12 "I, Wisdom, live with prudence,
and I find knowledge of foresight.
13 The fear of Yahweh is to hate evil.
I hate haughtiness, arrogance, an evil way, and a perverse mouth.
14 Advice and sound judgment are mine.
I, Understanding, have strength.
15 By me kings reign,
and rulers govern with justice.
16 By me princes rule,
as well as nobles [and] all just judges.
17 I myself love those who love me,
and those who eagerly look for me find me.
18 Riches and honor are with me,
everlasting wealth and righteousness.
19 My fruit is better than gold and than pure gold,
and what I produce [is better] than fine silver.
20 I walk on the path of righteousness,
in the middle of the pathways of justice,
21 to give an inheritance of property to those who love me,
and I fill their treasuries."

Textual Notes

8:12 אֲנִי־חָכְמָה שָׁכַנְתִּי עָרְמָה—Wisdom speaks in the first person. Here the verb שָׁכַן, "to live, dwell," takes an accusative noun (עָרְמָה) that denotes the place at which or the thing with which she dwells (GKC, § 117 bb): "I live *with* prudence." This identifies divine Wisdom, the second person of the Trinity, as the source of the "prudence" God makes available for believers. For עָרְמָה, see the first textual note on 1:4 and also "עָרוּם, 'Prudent,' and עָרְמָה, 'Prudence' " in "Wisdom in Proverbs" in the introduction.

וְדַעַת מְזִמּוֹת אֶמְצָא׃—This identifies divine Wisdom as the source of the "knowledge" and "insight, foresight" that Proverbs often mentions as God's gifts to discerning believers. The construct phrase וְדַעַת מְזִמּוֹת emphasizes one area of knowledge: "knowledge of foresight." For דַּעַת, see "דַּעַת, 'Knowledge,' and יָדַע, 'to Know' " in "Wisdom in Proverbs" in the introduction as well as the commentary on 1:4, 7. מְזִמּוֹת is an abstract plural as also in 5:2; 12:2; 14:17; 24:8. See "מְזִמָּה, 'Insight, Foresight,' " in "Wisdom in Proverbs" in the introduction.

8:13 יִרְאַת יְהוָה שְׂנֹאת רָע—For the construct phrase יִרְאַת יְהוָה, see the first textual note and the commentary on 1:7 as well as "יִרְאַת יְהוָה, 'the Fear of Yahweh,' and

יְרֵא יְהוָה, 'One Who Fears Yahweh' " in "Wisdom in Proverbs" in the introduction. The Qal (G) infinitive construct שְׂנֹאת (from שָׂנֵא, "to hate," which recurs in the next clause) has a quiescent א and is formed as if the verb were שָׂנָה, with ה as the third root letter. Yahweh himself "hates" evil things (6:16–19), and he calls his people to do the same.

גֵּאָה וְגָאוֹן—These two nouns are both from the verbal root גאה, "rise up, be exalted." The use of both a feminine noun (גֵּאָה) and a masculine noun (גָּאוֹן) from the same root can express entirety (GKC, § 122 v), which here could be paraphrased as "I hate *every kind of* haughtiness and arrogance." The traditional translation of גֵּאָה is "pride" (BDB). This feminine form used as a noun occurs only here in the OT, but it could be the feminine form of the adjective גֵּאֶה, "proud" (BDB). However, in the context of 8:13, "pride" is an inappropriate translation for it in contemporary English. While "pride" in some contexts can still mean a haughty attitude, today it usually means a warranted sense of self-worth or appreciation for a relative or friend—a child, parent, student, coworker—or for one's school, city, and so forth. One can rightly be proud of or boast in Christ, his cross, and his church, despite the world's scorn. Therefore it is preferable to render גֵּאָה as "haughtiness."

וּפִי תַהְפֻּכוֹת שָׂנֵאתִי׃—For תַּהְפֻּכוֹת, "perversity," see the second textual note on 2:12. The construct phrase "a mouth of perversity" has an adjectival genitive: "a perverse mouth," meaning a mouth that speaks perverse things.

8:14 לִי־עֵצָה וְתוּשִׁיָּה אֲנִי בִינָה לִי גְבוּרָה׃—For the first three nouns, see "עֵצָה, 'Advice,' and יוֹעֵץ, 'Advisor' "; "תּוּשִׁיָּה, 'Sound Judgment' "; and "בִּינָה, 'Understanding,' and Related Words" in "Wisdom in Proverbs" in the introduction. Some translations render אֲנִי בִינָה weakly as "I *have* understanding/insight" (NIV, RSV), but at the very least it means "I *am* understanding" (KJV, NASB). Elsewhere in Proverbs בִּינָה can be a synonym of חָכְמָה (e.g., 1:2; 4:5, 7; 7:4; 9:10), so the clause here can mean "I, Understanding, …" Divine Wisdom (חָכְמָה) starts speaking in 8:12, and here she calls herself by the appositive בִּינָה, "Understanding."

8:15 וְרוֹזְנִים יְחֹקְקוּ צֶדֶק׃—The Qal (G) participle רוֹזְנִים recurs in 31:4, and both times it is used as a substantive: "rulers, princes." The verb חָקַק occurs in the Qal (G) in 8:27, 29. Its Poel here means "to govern, decree, make laws." Its Pual (Dp) participle in 31:5 means "what is decreed." Here צֶדֶק is an adverbial accusative: "*with* justice/righteousness."

8:16 בִּי שָׂרִים יָשֹׂרוּ—The plural of the noun שַׂר, "a prince," is the subject of the cognate verb שָׂרַר, "to act as a prince; rule."

שֹׁפְטֵי צֶדֶק׃—The construct phrase, literally, "judges of justice/righteousness," has an adjectival genitive: "just judges."

8:17 אֲנִי אֹהֲבַיה אֵהָב—The redundant pronoun אֲנִי is emphatic: "I myself …" The suffixed plural participle of אָהַב, "to love," has an object suffix referring to Wisdom. The Kethib of the participle, אֹהֲבֶיהָ, "those who love *her*," does not fit with the first person words that precede (אֲנִי) and follow (אֵהָב, imperfect of אָהַב). The Qere of the participle, אֹהֲבַי, "those who love *me*," fits the context and is supported by the ancient versions. It is also repeated in 8:21, where too it refers to love for God kindled by God's own gifts of faith and love by the power of the Holy Spirit. אֵהָב (pausal for אֹהֵב) is an unusual contracted form of the first singular imperfect of אָהַב, whose usual form is אֹהַב (Joüon, § 73 g (1); GKC, § 68 f).

"I myself love those who love me" may be compared to Gen 12:3: וַאֲבָרְכָה֙ מְבָ֣רְכֶ֔יךָ, "I will bless those who bless you [Abram]." Compare Jn 14:21 and also Ex 20:6; Jn 15:10; 1 Jn 5:2–3.

וּ֝מְשַׁחֲרַ֗י יִמְצָאֻֽנְנִי׃—For the Piel (D) of שָׁחַר, "to seek diligently, eagerly look for," see the textual note on 7:15, which also has מָצָא, "to find." Wisdom's promise here, "those who eagerly look for me (will) find me," may be compared to Deut 4:29 and the words of Jesus in Mt 7:7.

8:18 ה֣וֹן עָ֝תֵ֗ק וּצְדָקָֽה׃—The adjective עָתֵק, "everlasting" (or perhaps "eminent, surpassing"), occurs in the OT only here, but it is cognate to other words such as עַתִּיק, the "Ancient [of Days]" (Dan 7:9, 13, 22). Regarding צְדָקָה, see "The Relationship between Wisdom and Righteousness in Proverbs" in "Wisdom in Proverbs" in the introduction.

8:19 ט֣וֹב פִּ֭רְיִי מֵחָר֣וּץ וּמִפָּ֑ז—Like 8:11, this is one of Solomon's "better than" (טוֹב ... מִן) proverbs. See "Direct Comparisons" in "Authorship and Date" in the introduction. For מֵחָרוּץ, see the second textual note on 8:10.

וּ֝תְבוּאָתִ֗י מִכֶּ֥סֶף נִבְחָֽר׃—The noun תְּבוּאָה usually refers to what the land produces, the crop or harvest (see the textual note on 3:9). Here, however, it does not refer to what Wisdom harvests from people, as if people were able to produce such fruit. Instead, it refers to what Wisdom *produces* in people by God's grace, as confirmed by the parallel word in the preceding clause, פִּ֭רְיִי, "my fruit," the fruit produced by divine Wisdom in believers. Similar are "the fruit of the Spirit" in Gal 5:22–23 and "the fruit of righteousness" in Phil 1:11. This interpretation is consistent with Prov 8:21 (see the textual notes on that verse).

For נִבְחָר, translated as "fine" silver, see the second textual note on 8:10, where the same Niphal (N) participle refers to "fine" gold.

8:20 בְּאֹֽרַח ... נְתִיבוֹת—For this vocabulary, see the excursus "The Metaphor of the Path in Solomon's Wisdom" in the commentary on Proverbs 10.

8:21 לְהַנְחִ֖יל אֹהֲבַ֥י ׀ יֵ֑שׁ—An infinitive construct with לְ can express purpose or result or both: Wisdom is on the path to grant an inheritance to all people who are on the same path, that is, to all who love her. The Hiphil (H) of נָחַל, "to cause (someone) to inherit (something)," reinforces that divine Wisdom grants believers an inheritance by grace. The reward is God's own free gift, not pay or wages earned by the believers' good works. The same Hebrew verb refers to Yahweh giving Israel the gift of the promised land (e.g., Deut 12:10; through Joshua as a type of Christ in Deut 31:7; Josh 1:6). For אֹהֲבַי, "those who love me," see the first textual note on 8:17, where it is the Qere. Their motivation of love is a response to God's prior and greater love (cf. Deut 6:5; Mt 22:37; 1 Jn 4:10).

The inheritance is designated by יֵשׁ. Although this particle usually expresses existence, in this verse it apparently is a noun meaning "property" (*HALOT*, 1; *DCH*, 2). It is used in a similar way in Sirach 42:3.

וְאֹצְרֹתֵיהֶם אֲמַלֵּא׃—As usual in Hebrew, an infinitive construct (לְהַנְחִיל in the first part of the verse) is continued by a finite verb, here אֲמַלֵּא. The causative Piel (D), "to fill, make/cause to be full," reinforces that the treasures received by believers are the result of divine Wisdom's gracious action, not the results of the believers' own decisions, actions, or aspirations.

Both lines of 8:21 teach divine monergism in salvation and preclude the errors of semi-Pelagianism, legalism, works-righteousness, human ability to earn rewards from God, and any kind of "name it and claim it" theology, as in the "Word-Faith" Movement.

Commentary

In 8:12 Wisdom identifies herself with vocabulary from the introduction to Wisdom in 1:2–7. Prov 8:12 associates Wisdom with "prudence" (עָרְמָה), "knowledge" (דַּעַת), and "foresight, insight" (the plural of מְזִמָּה). These three nouns are mentioned together elsewhere in the OT only in 1:4.[1] Prov 8:13 then echoes 1:7 with "the fear of Yahweh," defining it now as "to hate evil." This "evil" is further defined by four qualities that Wisdom says, "I hate": "haughtiness," "arrogance," "an evil way," and "a perverse mouth." Prov 8:14 equates Wisdom with Understanding (בִּינָה),[2] who possesses "advice" (עֵצָה) and "sound judgment" (תּוּשִׁיָּה) as well as "strength" (גְּבוּרָה), which prepares for the rulers in 8:15–16.

Three attributes of Wisdom in 8:14 are closely related to the description of God in Job 12:13 and identify Wisdom as divine: "advice" (עֵצָה), "understanding" (בִּינָה; Job uses another noun from the same root, תְּבוּנָה, as in Prov 8:1), and "strength" (גְּבוּרָה). Moreover, these serve to identify Wisdom as Christ, who is said to possess the Spirit sevenfold. Upon him rests "the Spirit of Yahweh" (Is 11:2; see Mt 3:16; Jn 1:32–33), further identified with six wisdom attributes of the Spirit in Is 11:2. All six of these are claimed by Wisdom as a name or an attribute in Prov 8:12–14. See figure 8.

Is 11:3–5 then repeats "the fear of Yahweh" (יִרְאַת יְהוָה, Is 11:3) and goes on to describe how Christ will reign in righteousness and execute justice. This is parallel to Prov 8:15–16. Those in authority need the Spirit and divine Wisdom as well as strength and sound judgment if they are to rule in righteousness and bring about justice. Wisdom provides these ("I will pour out my Spirit for you," Prov 1:23). However, since in this passage Wisdom/Understanding states that rulers only govern "by me" (Prov 8:15–16), it also implies that Wisdom is divine since only God establishes rulers (e.g., Dan 2:37–38; Neh 9:37; Jn 19:10–11; Rom 13:1–4).

---

1 Prov 1:4 and 8:12 are the only two verses that have both Hebrew words translated as "prudence" and "knowledge," or that have those rendered as "prudence" and "insight." "Knowledge and "foresight, insight" occur together also in 5:2.

2 See the textual note on 8:14.

Figure 8

Wisdom Attributes of the Spirit in Isaiah 11:2 and Proverbs 8

The Gift of the Spirit in Is 11:2	*Use in Proverbs 8*
Wisdom (חָכְמָה)	8:1, 11–12
Understanding (בִּינָה)	8:14
Advice (עֵצָה)	8:14
Strength (גְּבוּרָה)	8:14
Knowledge (דַּעַת)	8:9–10, 12
The fear of Yahweh (יִרְאַת יְהוָה)	8:13

Wisdom, however, does not benefit rulers who reject her nor anyone else who refuses to listen to her; instead, they perish (Prov 1:24–32). Only those who love her will be loved by her. Note the parallel to Jesus' claim that he is the only way to the Father (Jn 14:6; cf. Acts 4:12). The contrast between Wisdom and the adulteress that extends throughout Proverbs 1–9[3] is evident in Wisdom's promise in 8:17b: only those who "eagerly look for" (the Piel [D] of שָׁחַר) her will "find" (the Qal [G] of מָצָא) her. The same verbs were used for the adulteress (who disguises herself and imitates Wisdom) in 7:15, but the roles were reversed: it was she who "sought" (the Piel of שָׁחַר) the young man and "found" (the Qal of מָצָא) him. The promise that the seeker will find Wisdom may be behind James' encouragement to ask God for wisdom (James 1:5–8).

In Prov 8:18–19 Wisdom affirms what was already stated in 8:10–11 about the supreme value of Wisdom. However, Wisdom begins not by simply stating that her worth far exceeds precious metals, but also by using agricultural terms, "my fruit" (פִּרְיִי) and "what I produce" (תְּבוּאָתִי), to underscore her surpassing benefits. This emphasizes Wisdom's worth because, unlike precious metals, fruit and produce are perennial wealth that can be had year after year, that can nourish and that can in turn be planted for a future yield.

Once again Solomon's description of Wisdom's riches matches the NT description of God's grace in the person of Jesus Christ. Compare "everlasting wealth" in Prov 8:18 to the words of Jesus in, for example, Lk 12:21, 33–34. Paul names Christ as the source of eternal riches for all baptized believers (Eph 1:7, 18; 2:7; Phil 4:19; Col 1:27; 2:2; 1 Tim 6:19). However, the most important passage relating to Proverbs 8, especially 8:12–21, is Eph 3:8–10:

> To me, the very least of all the saints, was given this grace: to preach to the Gentiles the unsearchable riches of Christ, and to enlighten for everyone what is the plan of the mystery that was hidden for ages in God, who created all

[3] See the excursus "Wisdom and the Adulteress in Proverbs 1–9" in the commentary on Proverbs 2 and also figure 7, "Contrasts between the Two Women" in the commentary on 6:20–35.

things, so that through the church the manifold Wisdom of God might now be made known to the rulers and authorities in the heavenly places.

Note the following parallels shown in figure 9.

Figure 9

Parallels between Proverbs 8 and Ephesians 3:8–10

Proverbs 8	*Eph 3:8–10*
Wisdom gives riches (8:10–11, 18–19).	Christ gives riches (3:8).
Preexistent Wisdom participated in creation (8:22–31).	Wisdom is linked to the God who created all things (3:9).
God's Wisdom empowers rulers and authorities (8:15–16).	God's Wisdom in Christ is made known to rulers and authorities in the heavenly places (3:10).

Also note that Paul states that the preaching of Christ enlightens or brings light to everyone (φωτίσαι πάντας, Eph 3:9), while Prov 6:23 speaks of Wisdom's teaching as a "lamp" (נֵר) and "light" (אוֹר). (For the theme of divine light, see also 4:18; 13:9; 29:13.)

Prov 8:20 once again uses the metaphor of the path.[4] Here, however, instead of wise believers, it is divine Wisdom who walks the path; the triune God establishes and is himself the way of righteousness and salvation. It is called "the path of righteousness" (אֹרַח־צְדָקָה) to identify it with the path that righteous people take (אָרְחוֹת צַדִּיקִים, 2:20; אֹרַח צַדִּיקִים, 4:18). Wisdom is on this path in order to give those who walk it the inheritance of her riches (8:21). Christians will once again note the similarity to Christ, who is "the way, the truth, and the life" (Jn 14:6). He has already trod the way through suffering, death, and resurrection so that we can follow on his way. Everlasting life in his eternal kingdom is given to all in Christ as their inheritance solely by grace (e.g., Mt 25:34; 1 Cor 6:9–11; Eph 1:14, 18; 1 Pet 1:4).

[4] See the excursus "The Metaphor of the Path in Solomon's Wisdom" in the commentary on Proverbs 10.

Proverbs 8:22–31

Wisdom Is God the Son, the Preexistent Craftsman of Creation

Translation

8 [22]**"Yahweh possessed me at the beginning of his way,**
before his works of old.
[23]**From eternity I was appointed, from the beginning,**
from before the earth.
[24]**When there were no deep waters, I was given birth,**
when there were no springs filled with water.
[25]**Before the mountains were settled in place,**
before the hills, I was given birth,
[26]**when he had not yet made land or fields**
or the beginning of the dust of the world.
[27]**"When he established the heavens, I was there.**
When he marked out the horizon on the surface of the ocean,
[28]**when he established the clouds above,**
when he secured the fountains of the deep waters,
[29]**when he set his decree for the sea so that the waters would not overstep his command,**
when he marked out the foundations of the earth,
[30]**I was beside him as a master craftsman.**
I was [his] joy day after day,
rejoicing in his presence at all times,
[31]**rejoicing in his inhabited world,**
and my joy was with the human race."

Textual Notes

8:22 יְהוָה קָנָנִי רֵאשִׁית דַּרְכּוֹ—The verb קָנָנִי is קָנָה with the first person object suffix (GKC, § 59 f). This clause has been interpreted and translated in several divergent ways. In the majority of occurrences, the Qal (G) of קָנָה, means "to get, acquire, possess" (see BDB, 1–2, and *HALOT*, 1–2). These are meanings it has elsewhere in Proverbs.[a] Moreover, it would seem that 8:22–26 is saying that God has done from eternity past what humans are urged to do in 1:5 and 4:5, 7: to possess and retain Wisdom. The Vulgate (*Dominus possedit me initium viarum suarum*) as well as Aquila, Symmachus, and Theodotion (all three of which have ἐκτήσατο) all support the translation that Yahweh "possessed, had" Wisdom.

(a) Prov 1:5; 4:5, 7; 15:32; 16:16; 17:16; 18:15; 19:8; 20:14; 23:23

The construct phrase רֵאשִׁית דַּרְכּוֹ is an adverbial accusative of time (cf. Waltke-O'Connor, § 10.2.2c): Yahweh had already possessed Wisdom "at the beginning of his way." Note that this phrase does *not* refer to the beginning of *Wisdom*, who is speaking—and who has no beginning. Rather, it refers to the beginning of God's activities in relation to his creation, which does have a beginning (Gen 1:1). דֶּרֶךְ, "way," can refer to God's "creative activity" as in Job 26:14; 40:19 (BDB, 6 e (a)), or more generally to his administration of his creation, including his later and ongoing activities (see BDB, 6 e (b); *DCH*, 6 b). The identical construct phrase occurs nowhere else. The construct chain in Job 40:19 is different: הוּא רֵאשִׁית דַּרְכֵי־אֵל, "he is the first of the ways of God." It describes Behemoth, who is a created being since God states, "I made" him (עָשִׂיתִי, Job 40:15; see also הָעֹשׂוֹ, "the one who made him," in Job 40:19).

The NT echoes the language of Prov 8:22 and affirms its theology when it acclaims the eternal Christ as the "beginning," meaning the originator (ἀρχή, Rev 3:14; 22:13; cf. Rev 21:6). See further the commentary on Prov 8:22–26.

קָנָה Supposedly Means "Create" in Proverbs 8:22

Some interpreters have argued that קָנָה can be translated here as "create." In the attempt to support this meaning, some cite the translations of this clause by the LXX (κύριος ἔκτισέν με ἀρχὴν ὁδῶν αὐτοῦ),[1] the Syriac Peshitta (ܡܪܝܐ ܒܪܢܝ ܒܪܫܝܬ ܒܪܝܬܗ), and the Targum (ייי בראני בריש ברויתיה). Both the Peshitta and the Targum translate with Aramaic cognates to the Hebrew verb בָּרָא, "create" (e.g., Gen 1:1, 21, 27; 2:3–4), even though both languages have cognates to קָנָה, "acquire, possess" (ܩܢܳܐ and קְנֵי), which these versions could have used instead. However, the LXX, Peshitta, and Targum often are periphrastic and unreliable for determining the meaning of the MT, which has קָנָה, not בָּרָא.

Some scholars try to justify the meaning "create" in Prov 8:22 while admitting that קָנָה has only one basic meaning. For example, Fox argues that קָנָה means "acquire," but that the verb can mean "acquire by creating" and so should be translated as "created" here.[2] However, there is no other place in the OT where קָנָה denotes *creatio ex nihilo* ("creation of something from nothing") as it would need to mean in Prov 8:22 to justify that translation/interpretation. Since there is no other Hebrew evidence for that asserted meaning, it is simply without foundation, and this argument cannot be sustained.

Others have argued for the meaning "create" based on the theory that קָנָה in Hebrew stems from two originally different roots: (1) קנו* > קָנָה, "acquire," and קני* > קָנָה, "create."[3] This theory is built on two kinds of evidence. The first is from the root *qny* in other Semitic languages, including Mishnaic Hebrew. However, there is scant evidence that this root must or even can mean "create."[4] The second line of evidence is a set of up to eight passages in the OT (other than Prov 8:22) where קָנָה is alleged to have the

---

1 See further the discussion of the MT, the LXX, and church fathers in the excursus "Proverbs 8, Wisdom, Christology, and the Arian Controversy."

2 Fox, *Proverbs 1–9*, 279.

3 See Vawter, "Prov 8:22: Wisdom and Creation," 209–10.

4 Vawter, "Prov 8:22: Wisdom and Creation," 210. For Mishnaic Hebrew, see Jastrow svv קְנֵי, קָנָה and קְנֵי, קְנָא II. None of the Mishnaic Hebrew passages cited require the meaning "create," and most refer to commercial or legal transactions.

(b) Gen 4:1; 14:19, 22; Ex 15:16; Deut 32:6; Pss 74:2; 78:54; 139:13

meaning "create,"[b] although none of them require the verb to mean "create"; it could simply mean "acquire" or "possess."[5]

Other Passages Where קָנָה Supposedly Means "Create"

It is doubtful that Eve in Gen 4:1 (קָנִיתִי אִישׁ) means to say, "*I* have *created* a man [Cain]" in the sense of *creatio ex nihilo*, since she continues with אֶת־יְהוָה, either meaning "with [the help of] Yahweh" or, if the phrase is in apposition, "a man who is Yahweh," thinking that her first son was the fulfillment of the promise of the divine Messiah in Gen 3:15. Rather, she must mean that she "acquired" or "had" the male child. Likewise, the participial phrase קֹנֵה שָׁמַיִם וָאָרֶץ in Gen 14:19, 22 does not necessarily mean "*Creator* of the heavens and the earth." It could just as easily mean that God is the "Possessor," that is, Lord or Owner, of heaven and earth.

In the Song of Moses, Ex 15:16 (עַם־זוּ קָנִיתָ) does not sing to Yahweh about "this people [Israel] whom you *created*" (as in the NIV footnote), but confesses that Yahweh has "acquired" or "purchased" them as his people (as in the LXX, NIV text, NRSV, NJB), as confirmed by the close verbal parallel in Ex 15:13, עַם־זוּ גָּאָלְתָּ, "this people whom you *redeemed*."

In Deut 32:6, the suffixed participle in הֲלוֹא־הוּא אָבִיךָ קָּנֶךָ is often understood as meaning "Is he not your Father and *your Creator*?" based on the following words, הוּא עָשְׂךָ וַיְכֹנְנֶךָ, "he who *made* you and established you." However, קָּנֶךָ could just as easily refer to God as the one who "bought" (KJV, NKJV, NASB) or "acquired" his people, as in the LXX (ἐκτήσατο), Vulgate (*possedit*), and Syriac Peshitta (which translates with the cognate participle ܩܢܝܟ), especially since this poem uses several metaphors for how Israel became God's people, for example, Yahweh "*found* him [Israel]" in the desert (יִמְצָאֵהוּ, Deut 32:10).

The ancient versions did not understand קָנָה in either Ps 74:2 or Ps 78:54 as meaning "create." For those verses the LXX used κτάομαι, the Vulgate *possideo*, and the Syriac Peshitta ܩܢܐ. Likewise, most modern versions do not have "create" in Ps 74:2 or Ps 78:54 (see, e.g., KJV, RSV, NIV, NRSV, NASB, NJB). Some interpreters assert that Ps 139:13 is the most obvious passage in which קָנָה means "create" since כִּי־אַתָּה קָנִיתָ כִלְיֹתָי appears to mean "for you [God] *formed* my kidneys." This has even led some to posit that the verb סָכַךְ in the parallel line means "knit" or "weave" instead of its usual meaning, "to overshadow, protect." However, since "kidney" can mean one's innermost being, the psalmist is expressing the thought that God "acquired" his innermost being and "protected" him in his mother's womb, a theme that runs throughout Psalm 139. The ancient versions use the same verbs for "acquire" (κτάομαι, *possideo*, and ܩܢܐ) in Ps 139:13 (138:13 in the LXX, Vulgate, and Peshitta) as they did in Ps 74:2; 78:54 (73:2; 77:54 in the LXX, Vulgate, and Peshitta).

קָנָה Supposedly Means "Beget"

Still other interpreters have proposed that in Prov 8:22 and at least some of the passages cited in "Other Passages Where קָנָה Supposedly Means 'Create,' " the verb

---

[5] Vawter, "Prov 8:22: Wisdom and Creation," 208–13.

means "become the parent of, beget."[6] This is reflected by the NIV: "brought me forth." However, the evidence and arguments set forth for this position are tenuous at best since the meaning "acquire, possess, have" is possible in all of these passages, especially Gen 4:1 and Deut 32:6. Nevertheless, these scholars claim that "beget" fits the context of Prov 8:22 better since twice in 8:24–25 Wisdom declares, "I was given birth" (חוֹלָלְתִּי). However, the imagery of 8:24–25 does not preclude the meaning "acquire" for קָנָה in 8:22 since in Hebrew poetry in general, and often in Proverbs, imagery does not remain static; it can shift quickly.

Conclusion for קָנָה in Proverbs 8:22

This verse means "Yahweh had acquired me when his way began" or "Yahweh possessed me at the beginning of his way." This view is consistent with some of the ancient versions (the Vulgate, Aquila, Symmachus, and Theodotion). It is also reflected in many English translations, beginning with the KJV (first published in 1611) and continuing in more recent translations (e.g., NKJV, ESV, NASB). The rendition "the LORD created me" in the RSV, first published in 1952 (and repeated in the NRSV), was from a group of translators that included many who deny the divinity of Christ. That rendition is an unfortunate return to the Arian heresy prevalent in the fourth century AD, a heresy that contradicts the OT and NT and the historic Christian understanding of this passage.

קֶדֶם מִפְעָלָיו מֵאָז׃—This phrase describes the preexistence of Wisdom in the person of Christ, the eternal second person of the Trinity. The noun קֶדֶם can have a spatial meaning, "front; east," or a temporal meaning, "ancient time, aforetime." It occurs in Proverbs only in 8:22–23, and in both places it refers to time before the creation, that is, from eternity past. In both verses the best English translation is with the temporal preposition "before." קֶדֶם is used to describe the preexistence of the Messiah also in Micah 5:1 (ET 5:2), which predicts that the "Ruler" will come from Bethlehem in Judah, yet his true origins are מִקֶּדֶם מִימֵי עוֹלָם, "from eternity, from days everlasting." The noun מִפְעָל, "work, deed," occurs in the OT only here in Prov 8:22 and refers to God's activity in creation. The adverb אָז, "then," with preposition מִן is often used with the temporal meaning "in *time past*, of *old*," including the distant past, the time of creation (BDB, s.v. מֵאָז, (a), under אָז).

8:23 מֵעוֹלָם נִסַּכְתִּי מֵרֹאשׁ—The Hebrew accents indicate that the syntax is, literally, "from eternity, I was appointed from the beginning," but English requires placing the comma after "appointed." The noun עוֹלָם can convey a range of meanings from "eternity" to "perpetuity" to "old, ancient" or even to the "distant future" (see *HALOT*, 2–3). It does not always refer to "eternity," but in many cases it refers to the past or future beyond the experience of the writer/speaker and his audience (as in 22:28; 23:10).[7]

In some verses עוֹלָם is repeated or used with synonyms to emphasize that the speaker means "eternity" and not merely the distant past or future (e.g., מֵעוֹלָם וְעַד־עוֹלָם, 1 Chr 29:10; לְעוֹלָם וָעֶד, Ps 9:6 [ET 9:5]). Thus this word's particular meaning in any

---

6 See Irwin, "Where Shall Wisdom Be Found?" Longman, *Proverbs*, 204, also favors this view and prefers "begot."

7 Cf. A. A. Macrae, "עלם," *TWOT* 2:672; E. Jenni, "עוֹלָם," *TLOT* 2:852.

given instance is determined by context. An abundance of synonyms and temporal phrases are used in Prov 8:22–26 to clarify that Solomon is referring unambiguously to the preexistence of divine Wisdom, a hypostasis of the eternal Trinity. Thus when עוֹלָם refers to the era before the creation of the world, as it does here, or when it refers to God's continuing existence into the eternal future, its meaning is "eternity." Sometimes it is best rendered with an adjective, "everlasting, eternal."

This verb נָסַךְ, "set, install" (BDB, s.v. נָסַךְ III) or "appoint," occurs elsewhere in the OT only in Ps 2:6 in the Qal (G), where Yahweh declares about his "Anointed One/ Messiah/Christ" (Ps 2:2), "I have installed my King on Zion, my holy hill" (Ps 2:6). The Niphal (N) here has the corresponding passive meaning: "appointed, installed." Since a more common homograph (or perhaps the same verb) can mean "pour out" (BDB, s.v. נָסַךְ I), the Qal in Ps 2:6 might mean "anoint," and the Niphal (N) here could mean "anointed," which would have more specifically messianic connotations (cf. מָשִׁיחַ and Χριστός, "Anointed One, Messiah, Christ").

מִקַּדְמֵי־אָרֶץ׃—"From before the earth" is essentially synonymous with 8:22b. See the second textual note on 8:22. This is the only use in the OT of the plural form of קֶדֶם.

8:24 בְּאֵין־תְּהֹמוֹת חוֹלָלְתִּי—The preposition בְּ with אַיִן forms a temporal clause: "when there were not," that is, before creation. The combination is repeated at the start of the next line. In this context בְּאֵין־ is essentially synonymous with בְּטֶרֶם and לִפְנֵי in 8:25, both of which mean "before" creation.

The plural noun תְּהֹמוֹת, "deep waters," is also in 3:20, which alludes to the original creation (תְּהוֹם in Gen 1:2). The noun תְּהוֹם recurs in the singular in Prov 8:27–28.

The verb חוֹלָלְתִּי, repeated at the end of 8:25, is the Polal (Dp) of חוּל or חִיל. The Polal usually means "to be given birth" (see *HALOT*, Polal, 1), and it is used by David to refer to his own birth in Ps 51:7 (ET 51:5). In Job 15:7 Eliphaz uses it to question sarcastically whether Job was born before the hills (casting doubt upon Job's wisdom). The Polal has the passive of a common meaning of the Qal (G) and Polel (D) stems. In the Qal חוּל usually signifies to twist or writhe in pain. It can refer literally to a woman giving birth (Is 45:10), but more often it is used metaphorically: instead of an ordinary female mother, the one giving birth can be the nation Israel (Is 26:17–18), or Yahweh himself can give birth to his people through Zion/Jerusalem as their mother (Is 66:7–8). The Polel can literally mean to writhe in travail, as when Sarah (Is 51:2) or animals give birth (Ps 29:9; Job 39:1). Yet the Polel does not always have a female subject; it can refer to Yahweh himself producing the earth (Ps 90:2; cf. the Hophal [Hp] in Is 66:8) and birthing his people Israel (Deut 32:18).

בְּאֵין מַעְיָנוֹת נִכְבַּדֵּי־מָיִם׃—The plural of the noun מַעְיָן, "a spring (of water)," is also in 5:16, and the singular occurs in 25:26. Apparently the noun is masculine because it is modified here by the masculine plural of the Niphal (N) participle of כָּבֵד, "be heavy," in construct. "To be heavy with water" probably is an idiom for "fountains abounding in water" (BDB, s.v. כָּבֵד, Niphal, 1 a) or "filled with water." *HALOT*, s.v. כבד, Niphal, 5, would emend נִכְבַּדֵּי־ to נִבְכֵי־, the plural construct of נֵבֶךְ, "sources of" water, which occurs elsewhere only in the construct phrase נִבְכֵי־יָם in Job 38:16.

8:25 בְּטֶרֶם הָרִים הָטְבָּעוּ—When referring to past action בְּטֶרֶם, "before," usually is used with an imperfect verb (Joüon, § 113 j), but a perfect (הָטְבָּעוּ) is used here, perhaps because הָרִים intervenes (GKC, §§ 107 c and 152 r). The Hophal (Hp) of טָבַע means "be settled" (*HALOT*, Hophal) in the sense of "be founded, established" (not "settled by settlers"). It refers to God establishing the world at the creation also in Job 38:6.

8:26 וְחוּצוֹת וְרֹאשׁ עַפְרוֹת תֵּבֵל׃—The noun חוּץ, "outside," when plural (וְחוּצוֹת) can mean "fields" (*HALOT*, B 1). The plural of עָפָר, "dust" (in construct: עַפְרוֹת), may refer to the large quantities (cf. GKC, § 124 l) that comprise the "world" (תֵּבֵל; see the first textual note on 8:31).

8:27 בְּחוּקוֹ חוּג עַל־פְּנֵי תְהוֹם׃— For תְּהוֹם, see the first textual note on 8:24. The verb חָקַק can mean "inscribe" (*HALOT*, 2) or "make a mark, mark out." Its Qal (G) infinitive construct with בְּ forms a temporal clause: "*when* he marked out ..." This denotes God marking the place where the horizon should be above the waters. The identical suffixed infinitive construct (בְּחוּקוֹ) recurs with the same meaning in 8:29b. This form is patterned as if the verb were חוּק, since normally a double-*ayin* verb such as חָקַק would have a short vowel (-חֻ- instead of חוּ) and mark the assimilation of the repeated root letter (קק) by *daghesh*, that is, בְּחֻקּוֹ (GKC, § 67 r; cf. Joüon, § 82 l). Compare the cognate noun חֹק with suffix, חֻקּוֹ, "his decree," in 8:29a.

8:28 בְּאַמְּצוֹ שְׁחָקִים מִמָּעַל—The stative verb אָמֵץ, "be strong," has a causative meaning in the Piel (D): "strengthen." In this context, it probably signifies establishing the "clouds" (שְׁחָקִים) in their place in the heavens "above" (מִמָּעַל).

בַּעֲזוֹז עִינוֹת תְּהוֹם׃—The pointing of the plural of עַיִן, "spring," in construct, עִינוֹת, is unusual; the expected form is עֵינוֹת (GKC, § 93 v). The Qal (G) infinitive construct עֲזוֹז with בְּ likely has an intransitive meaning: "when the fountains of the deep *were strong*." Many commentators propose interchanging the last two consonants (-וֹז) and repointing to the suffixed Piel (D) infinitive construct, בְּעַזְּזוֹ, "when he strengthened, made firm, secured," producing the translation above.[8] Although עָזַז does not occur elsewhere in the OT in the Piel, this proposed reading would match the preceding parallel verb בְּאַמְּצוֹ. The Syriac Peshitta translates both verbs identically, with the Aphel (H) verb ܐܚܡ, "he strengthened, set firmly." Resorting to the preceding verb could suggest that the Syriac translators were unsure how to render בַּעֲזוֹז. The LXX and the Vulgate translate the two verbs differently, but only the LXX might support the proposed reading בְּעַזְּזוֹ.

8:29 בְּשׂוּמוֹ לַיָּם ׀ חֻקּוֹ—The noun חֹק, "decree, statute," is cognate to the verb חָקַק in 8:15, 27, 29b; 31:5 (see the textual note on 8:27). The suffix on the noun חֻקּוֹ could refer to יָם, "when he set for the sea *its* decree," but the parallel word in the next clause, פִּיו, makes it more likely that the suffix refers to God, emphasizing his authority over the sea: "when he set for the sea *his* decree." In either case, the clause refers to the coastline, the boundary and limit for the sea. See the similar idea in Job 38:8.

וּמַיִם לֹא יַעַבְרוּ־פִיו—This is a purpose or result clause: "*so that* the water would not transgress/cross over his command." While פֶּה usually means "mouth," it can, by metonymy, mean a spoken "command" (*HALOT*, 7).

---

8 E.g., Clifford, *Proverbs*, 92; Longman, *Proverbs*, 203; Murphy, *Proverbs*, 48.

8:30 וָאֶהְיֶה אֶצְלוֹ אָמוֹן—Literally, this is "I was beside him (as) a master craftsman." The masculine noun אָמוֹן is used even though it refers back to (the feminine) חָכְמָה (8:1, 11–12). Compare GKC, § 122 f, and the third textual note on 8:30, where the feminine מְשַׂחֶקֶת refers to Wisdom.

"Master craftsman" as the meaning of אָמוֹן is confirmed by Jer 52:15, where אָמוֹן has the collective meaning "artisans, craftsmen." It is also supported by the cognate noun אָמָּן, "craftsman," in Song 7:2 (ET 7:1). אָמוֹן is a noun of the form *qātôl*, which can have the active meaning of someone who practices a profession (GKC, § 84ª k (*c*)).[9] Further support is provided by the Vulgate, *conponens*, "builder, arranger, composer," and by the Syriac Peshitta, ܡܬܩܢܐ, the Pael (D) participle of ܬܩܢ, "construct, fashion, arrange," a verb "used esp[ecially] of the work of the Son" (Payne Smith, s.v. ܬܩܢ, Pael). The LXX has the participle ἁρμόζουσα, from ἁρμόζω, which can mean "set in order, regulate, govern" (LSJ, I 4; cf. ἁρμοστής, "governor"). "Craftsman" is also the interpretation of Wisdom in the Apocrypha (Wisdom 7:21 [ET 7:22a]; 8:6; 14:2).

Some object to "master craftsman" and assert that elsewhere Wisdom is depicted only as observing creation, not as participating in it. However, that assertion is not true, especially when Proverbs 8 is interpreted in light of its larger context in Proverbs 1–9. Many critical scholars consider Proverbs 8 to be a separate poem, with no connection to the rest of Proverbs 1–9. They view the various parts of these chapters as separate compositions that were only later collected together. However, Proverbs 8 has obvious connections to several other sections of Proverbs 1–9 (see, e.g., the commentary on 8:1–11 and 8:12–21). Therefore it should not be viewed as a completely separate composition. It ought to be noted that in 3:19–20 Wisdom has already been depicted as active in creation (see the commentary on 3:19–20). Therefore "master craftsman" is in harmony with what Solomon has already said about Wisdom.

A second proposed meaning for אָמוֹן, "little child, ward," is based on the ancient Greek translation of Aquila, τιθηνουμένη, the present passive participle of τιθηνέω, meaning "nursed, brought up." It may presuppose a different pointing, the Qal passive (Gp) participle אָמוּן, "nursed, nourished, brought up" (cf. the active participle in 2 Sam 4:4; Ruth 4:16; and the passive participle in Lam 4:5). Those who favor this meaning often claim that "little child" fits the context better because Wisdom is said to be given birth before the creation (8:24–25) and is depicted as "joy" (שַׁעֲשֻׁעִים, 8:30–31) and as "rejoicing" or "playing" (מְשַׂחֶקֶת, 8:30–31). However, of thirty-six occurrences of the verb שָׂחַק in the OT, only one, Zech 8:5, uses it to refer to children "playing"; the predominant use is to refer to activities by adults (see the third textual note on Prov 8:30). The noun שַׁעֲשֻׁעִים, "joy," is never used elsewhere to describe children (see the next textual note). So neither word necessarily refers to childlike behavior. Nothing else in the context implies that אָמוֹן means "little child." The preexistence of Wisdom from eternity past—the eternal generation or begetting of Wisdom before creation began—does not mean that Wisdom is depicted as a child at the time of creation.

---

[9] Hurvitz, "Toward a Precise Definition of the Term אמון in Proverbs 8:30."

A third proposed meaning for אָמוֹן is to understand it as an adverbial modifier and to derive its meaning from the verb אָמַן, "be faithful." The Targum has מהימנותא, "trustworthy, faithful." The clause would then be translated as "I was *faithfully* beside him." Apparently similar was the understanding of Theodotion and Symmachus, both of whom translated it with ἐστηριγμένη, the perfect passive participle of στηρίζω, meaning "firmly established, fixed, reliable." Unfortunately for this proposal, no other uses of אָמוֹן in this sense can be documented.[10] One interpreter has recently defended אָמוֹן as "faithful" because 8:30 apparently is set following the completion of creation.[11] According to this view, Wisdom cannot be a master craftsman because the work of crafting creation is over by the time the reader gets to 8:30. However, the point of 8:30 is that Wisdom was rejoicing during the process of the creation, especially in humans as the crown of creation. This, it should be noted, is in keeping with Wisdom as the "master craftsman" who finds pride of accomplishment in a job well done (see Gen 1:31a). Thus "master craftsman" is the probable meaning of this word.[12]

וָאֶהְיֶה שַׁעֲשֻׁעִים יוֹם ׀ יוֹם—This is, literally, "and I was joy day [after] day." שַׁעֲשֻׁעִים is an abstract plural noun (Waltke-O'Connor, § 7.4.2a) that recurs with a suffix in 8:31b. It may be a reduplicated form derived from the root שׁעע (BDB). Elsewhere in the OT שַׁעֲשֻׁעִים can refer to God's own joy or delight in his covenant people (Jer 31:20; metaphorically in Is 5:7) or to God's Word as the source of a believer's joy (Ps 119:24, 77, 92, 143, 174). In Prov 8:30–31 Wisdom is claiming to be divine "joy" in its purest form. Although here שַׁעֲשֻׁעִים lacks any suffix, the likely intended meaning is that Wisdom was "*his* [Yahweh's] joy," as reflected by the LXX (ἐγὼ ἤμην ᾗ προσέχαιρεν, "I was the one in whom he found delight") and most modern versions. The interpretation "*I* was filled with delight day after day" (NIV; emphasis added) is unwarranted.

מְשַׂחֶקֶת לְפָנָיו בְּכָל־עֵת׃—The Piel (D) of שָׂחַק can refer to "rejoicing" before God or because of his salvation.[c] The Qal (G) means "rejoice" in Eccl 3:4, but has the connotation of scorn in Prov 1:26; 29:9; 31:25. The feminine Piel (D) participle מְשַׂחֶקֶת refers back to the feminine noun חָכְמָה, "Wisdom," which last occurred in 8:1, 11–12. The identical participle recurs in 8:31a. The masculine Piel participle occurs in 26:19.

(c) 1 Sam 18:7; 2 Sam 6:5, 21; Jer 30:19; 31:4; 1 Chr 13:8; 15:29

8:31 מְשַׂחֶקֶת בְּתֵבֵל אַרְצוֹ—The noun תֵּבֵל can simply mean the "earth" or "world," as in 8:26. In OT poetry it is frequently a synonymous parallel of אֶרֶץ. Only here and in Job 37:12 is תֵּבֵל in construct with אֶרֶץ. Here and in some other passages, תֵּבֵל means the "*inhabited* land" (see *HALOT*, 2). The construct phrase בְּתֵבֵל אַרְצוֹ, literally, "in the inhabited land of his world," probably means "in his inhabited world." As the next clause will show clearly, Wisdom delights not simply in the planet earth, but especially in the people whom God created to inhabit the earth. After the first people fell into sin

[10] Besides Prov 8:30 and Jer 52:15, where אָמוֹן means "craftsman," its only other occurrences in the OT are as a proper name (1 Ki 22:26; 2 Ki 21:18–19, 23–25; Jer 1:2; 25:3; 46:25; Nah 3:8; Zeph 1:1; Neh 7:59; 1 Chr 3:14; 2 Chr 18:25; 33:20–23, 25).

[11] Weeks, "The Context and Meaning of Proverbs 8:30a."

[12] Several other interpretations of אָמוֹן have also been offered. See Scott, "Wisdom in Creation"; Fox, "ʾ*Amon* Again."

(Genesis 3), Wisdom was pleased to become incarnate as a person—the man Jesus Christ—for the sake of redeeming all people.

וְשַׁעֲשֻׁעַ֗י אֶת־בְּנֵ֥י אָדָֽם׃—In this nominal clause אֶת־ must be the preposition, "and my joy [was] *with* the human race," not the direct object marker. For the noun שַׁעֲשֻׁעִים, see the second textual note on 8:30. For the construct phrase בְּנֵי אָדָם, literally, "the sons of Adam/man," see the textual note on 8:4. Since in this context it denotes all mankind, "the human race" is the proper English equivalent.

Commentary

This part of Wisdom's speech covers two topics: Wisdom's divinity and existence from eternity before creation (8:22–26) and Wisdom's role in creation as the master craftsman (8:27–31). Prov 8:22 tells us that God had acquired and possessed Wisdom from eternity past. The same verb is used when humans are exhorted to "acquire" Wisdom in 1:5 and 4:5, 7. Thus Solomon urges his sons (and all believers) to imitate God, even as the NT exhorts believers to imitate God (Eph 5:1) and Christ (1 Cor 11:1; 1 Thess 1:6). Since Wisdom is Christ,[13] those who imitate God and get Wisdom thereby acquire the attitude of Christ (Phil 2:5–8). Since Wisdom preexisted from eternity past and was the active craftsman of the creation, Prov 8:22–31 supports the biblical doctrine of Christ's preexistence and his eternal generation from God the Father. The passage is part of the biblical foundation for the orthodox doctrine of the Trinity, one eternal God in three persons: God the Father, God the Son, and God the Holy Spirit.

Despite this, 8:22–31 became a battleground during the Arian controversy in the fourth century AD. Arius held that Jesus was a creature, albeit the first created being. Therefore as part of the creation, Jesus would not be the eternal Son of God. The orthodox Christians rejected the Arian perversion of Christology because Scripture clearly states that Jesus is God (e.g., Jn 1:1). God the Son is uncreated, preexistent, and eternally begotten of the Father. The orthodox view is consistent with—and indeed required by—Prov 8:22–31 and the rest of the Scriptures.[14]

Wisdom's Divinity and Eternal Generation (8:22–26)

Prov 8:22–26 speaks of Wisdom as preexistent. Prov 8:22–23 speaks of Christ's eternal divine nature and his eternal generation from the Father. God had already "possessed" him (the perfect aspect of the verb in 8:22 indicates an already completed situation) when the triune God began to create. Wisdom's words "from eternity I was appointed, from the beginning" (8:23) are echoed at the start of the Gospel of John and are applied to Jesus Christ as God (Jn 1:1–2; see also 1 Jn 1:1; 2:13–14).

---

[13] See "Wisdom in Proverbs" in the introduction. See also the commentary on 1:1–7 and 3:13–20, and the excursus "Proverbs 8, Wisdom, Christology, and the Arian Controversy."

[14] See further the excursus "Proverbs 8, Wisdom, Christology, and the Arian Controversy."

Some interpreters misconstrue the references to the "beginning" of creation in Prov 8:22–23 as meaning that Wisdom—that is, Christ—had a beginning. However, Christ is the originator and agent of this creation (Jn 1:3–5; Col 1:15–20). He is also the goal of history, the purpose for which this creation continues up to the end of this world and into the new creation (see 2 Pet 3:1–13; Revelation 21–22). "Beginning" in Prov 8:22–23 expresses the same truth as when the eternal Christ is acclaimed as "*the beginning* of the creation of God" (ἡ ἀρχὴ τῆς κτίσεως τοῦ θεοῦ, Rev 3:14).

Christ himself declares, "I am the Alpha and the Omega, the first and the last, *the beginning* and the end" (ἐγὼ τὸ ἄλφα καὶ τὸ ὦ, ὁ πρῶτος καὶ ὁ ἔσχατος, ἡ ἀρχὴ καὶ τὸ τέλος, Rev 22:13). This verse obviously does *not* mean that Christ himself had a "beginning" nor that he will have an "end" and cease to exist. Instead, he was the agent of the creation at *its* "beginning," and he is also the one who will bring this universe to its "end" when he returns in glory to institute the new heavens and the new earth (which he has already done in the context of Rev 22:13 in the prophetic vision). In Rev 1:8 it is "the Lord *God*" (κύριος ὁ θεός) who calls himself "the Alpha and the Omega," and in Rev 21:6, it is "the one sitting on the throne" (Rev 21:5), probably God the Father, who says, "I am the Alpha and the Omega, the beginning and the end." These parallel verses show that when Christ appropriates the same title, "the Alpha and the Omega," together with "the beginning and the end" in Rev 22:13, Christ is affirming that he is fully divine; God the Son possesses the same divinity as God the Father and God the Spirit.

Prov 8:24–25 emphasizes Christ's eternal generation from the Father by using the analogy of birth, but a timeless birth from eternity, before time and before creation. Wisdom's repeated assertion "I was given birth" (8:24–25) is consistent with the statement in 8:22a that God "possessed" Wisdom in the beginning. Prov 8:22–26 fits with other Scripture passages that refer to the Father and the Son, and to the Son as begotten by the Father.[d] The language in these verses carefully avoids any hint that Wisdom is a created being, a creature. Instead, divine Wisdom is coexistent with God. Like the Father, God the Son is eternal, preexistent from eternity past, and lives forevermore. Therefore Prov 8:22–26 is part of the biblical basis for the church's confession of Christ, as in the Nicene Creed:

> [I believe] in one Lord Jesus Christ, the only-begotten Son of God, begotten of His Father before all worlds, God of God, Light of Light, very God of very God, begotten, not made, being of one substance with the Father.

And the Athanasian Creed affirms that God the Son is "uncreated" and "eternal."[15] It confesses:

> The Son is neither made nor created, but begotten of the Father alone.[16]

(d) E.g., 2 Sam 7:14; Pss 2:7, 12; 89:27–28 (ET 89:26–27); 1 Chr 22:10; Mt 3:17; 11:27; 28:19; Jn 1:14, 18; 10:36; Acts 13:33; Heb 1:5; 5:5; 2 Pet 1:17; 1 Jn 1:3; cf. Is 7:14; 9:5 (ET 9:6)

---

[15] *LSB*, p. 319, verses 8, 10.

[16] *LSB*, p. 320, verse 21.

The mistranslation of 8:22 as "the LORD *created* me" (RSV and NRSV; emphasis added) or even as "the LORD brought me forth *as the first of his works*" (NIV; emphasis added) implies that Wisdom was created, even if it was the first of God's creations. For those who deny that Wisdom is Christ,[17] this does not appear at first blush to pose a problem for Christology. However, that position fails to account for the biblical parallels that apply language and theology in 8:22–31 to Christ himself. The view that 8:22–31 depicts Wisdom as the preincarnate Christ and as the agent of creation is the view that is most consistent with the rest of Scripture.[18] Other OT passages speak of God the Son as eternal; his origins are from eternity past (e.g., Micah 5:1 [ET 5:2]), and he will reign forevermore (e.g., Is 9:5–6 [ET 9:6–7]; cf. Psalms 2 and 110). The NT clearly identifies Jesus Christ as the eternal Son of God and as the Wisdom of God.[19]

Paul clearly identifies Christ in this way in 1 Cor 1:18–31. Furthermore, in stating that "Christ [is] the power of God and the Wisdom of God" (Χριστὸν θεοῦ δύναμιν καὶ θεοῦ σοφίαν, 1 Cor 1:24; see also 1:30), Paul plainly shows that he has Proverbs 8 in mind (see Prov 8:14; Job 12:13).[20] Yet 1 Corinthians is not the only epistle in which Paul refers to Christ as God's Wisdom. In his epistle to the Colossians, he states that his struggle as an apostle of Christ is to provide "knowledge of the mystery of God, [which is] Christ, in whom are hidden all of the treasures of wisdom and knowledge" (εἰς ἐπίγνωσιν τοῦ μυστηρίου τοῦ θεοῦ, Χριστοῦ, ἐν ᾧ εἰσιν πάντες οἱ θησαυροὶ τῆς σοφίας καὶ γνώσεως ἀπόκρυφοι, Col 2:2–3; see also 1 Cor 2:7–8). Paul evidently has in mind Prov 8:9–11, 21.

In addition, Paul is not the only one in the NT to point to Christ as Wisdom. In Mt 12:42 (and its parallel Lk 11:31), Jesus himself declares that the Queen of Sheba will judge the generation of his contemporaries because she came to hear Solomon's wisdom, but most of his hearers did not perceive that the one greater than Solomon was there among them. The reference to the one "greater than Solomon" is intended to point to the fullness of divine Wisdom in Christ himself, who is far greater than Solomon and the wisdom he was given (1 Kings 3). Wisdom in Proverbs 1–9, and especially Proverbs 8, is, by Solomon's own admission, greater, older, and loftier than he.

Jesus has more to say. For example, in Lk 11:49 he is able to speak for divine Wisdom: "The Wisdom of God said, '*I will send* them prophets and apostles, and they will kill some of them and persecute others' " (ἡ σοφία τοῦ θεοῦ εἶπεν· ἀποστελῶ εἰς αὐτοὺς προφήτας καὶ ἀποστόλους, καὶ ἐξ αὐτῶν ἀποκτενοῦσιν

---

[17] See, for example, Garrett, *Proverbs, Ecclesiastes, Song of Songs*, 112–13. Garrett, following von Rad (*Wisdom in Israel*, 156), views Wisdom as an attribute of creation, not as the second person of the Trinity nor as an attribute of God.

[18] A recent commentator who rightly interprets Wisdom in 8:22–31 as Christ is Longman, *Proverbs*, 64–69.

[19] See "Wisdom in Proverbs" in the introduction. See also the commentary on 1:1–7 and 3:13–20, and the excursus "Proverbs 8, Wisdom, Christology, and the Arian Controversy."

[20] See further "Wisdom in Proverbs" in the introduction.

καὶ διώξουσιν). This speaking Wisdom of God is Jesus himself, the incarnate Word of God (Rev 19:13), since Jesus also said, "Therefore, *I am sending* you prophets, wise men, and scribes. Some of them you will kill and crucify, and others you will flog in your synagogues and persecute from city to city" (διὰ τοῦτο ἰδοὺ ἐγὼ ἀποστέλλω πρὸς ὑμᾶς προφήτας καὶ σοφοὺς καὶ γραμματεῖς· ἐξ αὐτῶν ἀποκτενεῖτε καὶ σταυρώσετε καὶ ἐξ αὐτῶν μαστιγώσετε ἐν ταῖς συναγωγαῖς ὑμῶν καὶ διώξετε ἀπὸ πόλεως εἰς πόλιν, Mt 23:34). As a final example, Jesus once again identified himself as Wisdom when he was accused of being a drunkard and a glutton (Mt 11:19; Lk 7:34–35).

Wisdom as the Craftsman of Creation (8:27–31)

From the discussion in 8:22–26 of divine Wisdom existing before all things, in 8:27 the scene shifts to creation, where Wisdom is present during the establishing of the world (cf. Jn 1:1–3). The imagery of Prov 8:27–29 is a poetic picture of Gen 1:6–10, during the second and third days of creation. Prov 8:27 begins with the heavens, and 8:29 ends with the foundations of the earth, forming a unit encompassing all creation (Gen 1:1; note the contrast between "the heavens" and "the foundations of the earth" in Jer 31:37). Other occurrences of "the foundations of the earth" (מוֹסְדֵי אָרֶץ) are in Is 24:18; Micah 6:2; Ps 82:5.

In the first line of Prov 8:30, Wisdom moves from speaking about being present at creation to his role in creation as "master craftsman." Despite the grammatically feminine gender of the noun חָכְמָה, "Wisdom" (8:1, 11–12), which is the referent of the feminine participle מְשַׂחֶקֶת, "rejoicing" (8:30–31), the noun אָמוֹן, "master craftsman," is decidedly masculine, both in form and in meaning, since it describes an occupation normally performed by men (אָמוֹן, "craftsmen," in Jer 52:15). This militates against construing Wisdom as a feminine person of the Trinity or a feminine aspect of God. It also precludes the view of some critical scholars that the figure of Wisdom in the OT is a vestige of ancient goddess worship.

Instead, this "master craftsman"[21] is the second person of the Trinity, God the Son, who participated in creation (Jn 1:3, 10; 1 Cor 8:6; Col 1:16; Heb 1:2). The second and third lines of Prov 8:30 speak of the relationship between the Father and the Son and their unity in the Godhead.[e] Christ is "joy"—the Father's joy, the one in whom the Father delights.[22] Christ, in turn, rejoices in the Father's presence. In the NT the Father verbally declares his delight in Christ at his Baptism and at his transfiguration:

(e) See Mt 11:27 || Lk 10:22; Jn 5:19–21; 6:57; 10:15, 30, 38; 14:7, 10–11, 20; 1 Cor 8:6; 1 Jn 1:1–3

[21] Jesus is the builder of God's house in Heb 3:3, and the builder is God himself in Heb 3:4. Compare Hebrews 11–12, which first speaks of the original creation (Heb 11:3) and then describes God as the "craftsman and builder" of the city with foundations (τεχνίτης καὶ δημιουργός, Heb 11:10). This heavenly Jerusalem is the city that is the eternal home of all the OT and NT saints (Heb 11:16; 12:22). Jesus, through the sprinkling of his blood, is the mediator of the covenant that enables believers to inherit this city (Heb 12:23–24).

[22] See the second textual note on 8:30.

> This is my Son, my beloved, in whom I am well pleased. (Mt 3:17; 17:5; cf. Mk 1:11; 9:7; Lk 3:22; 9:35; 2 Pet 1:17)

Prov 8:31 moves from this "joy" within the triune Godhead to the preincarnate Christ's "joy" in humanity, expressing the love of the Father and the Son (Jn 15:9) that would be revealed fully in the redemption of humanity through the unblemished life, vicarious suffering, atoning death, and glorious bodily resurrection of the Son. Wisdom emphasizes God's favor toward mankind by skipping over the creation of other creatures and even plants (Gen 1:11–25) to the creation of "the sons of Adam," or "the human race" (Prov 8:31; see Gen 1:26–30). This divine favor flowing from the Father through the Son (favor that is received through faith created by God the Holy Spirit) is highlighted by the chiasm that binds the last two lines of Prov 8:30 to the two lines of 8:31:

A I was joy (וָאֶהְיֶה שַׁעֲשֻׁעִים, 8:30b)
  B rejoicing (מְשַׂחֶקֶת, 8:30c)
  B' rejoicing (מְשַׂחֶקֶת, 8:31a)
A' my joy (וְשַׁעֲשֻׁעַי, 8:31b)

Moreover, 8:30–31 is the climax of Proverbs 8. After these verses, the chapter quickly moves to a close, as signaled by the resumptive "and now, sons," beginning 8:32 (וְעַתָּה בָנִים, as in 5:7; 7:24). As much as this chapter says about Wisdom, the high point is the presentation of the Gospel as God's favor in Christ, whose delight is in humans. From this pinnacle the reader can see the entire chapter and be drawn to Wisdom as Christ, God the Son, who shaped creation and who, in the fullness of time (Gal 4:4), assumed the human flesh of those in whom he had delighted—Adam and Eve before their fall into sin. He became fully human like us—but without sin—in order to offer himself as the perfect sacrifice that atones for all our sins and renders us righteous (2 Cor 5:21; 1 Jn 3:5). Through sacramental incorporation and faith in the second Adam, we descendants of the first Adam once again become children of God in whom he delights (Rom 5:12–21).

Excursus

Proverbs 8, Wisdom, Christology, and the Arian Controversy

From the earliest Christian writings, Wisdom in Proverbs 8 has been identified as Christ. This is not only true in the NT,[1] but also in the church fathers. They refer to Wisdom in Prov 8:22–31 as Christ and also see Christ as the Wisdom spoken of throughout Proverbs 8[2] as well as in Proverbs 3.[3] All this is true even though the fathers generally did not rely on the Hebrew text of Proverbs, but on the LXX. At times the LXX is significantly different than the MT, and some of its different wording can pose a challenge for identifying Wisdom as Christ. Nevertheless, the vast majority of the fathers easily overcame that challenge by using the analogy of faith.

The comparison of the two texts of 8:22–31 in figure 10 highlights the differences. Words in italic indicate a significant difference between the meaning of the Hebrew and Greek texts, so that the overall message of the LXX is altered. Bold words indicate places where there is no corresponding wording in the parallel version (Hebrew or Greek).

Clearly, there are a number of significant differences in these two versions of Proverbs 8. Most important are the LXX translator's words used to describe the generation of Wisdom by God. Whereas in the MT, Wisdom declares that "Yahweh possessed me" (8:22), "I was appointed" (8:23), and "I was brought forth/given birth" (8:24–25),[4] in the Greek text, Wisdom says, "The Lord created me" (8:22), "He founded me" (8:23), and "He has begotten me" (8:25). The LXX translator seems to have attempted to define the relationship between God and Wisdom as one in which Wisdom is a creation of God, who is a father to his created world and its creatures (cf. Is 63:16; 64:7 [ET 64:8]; Jer 31:9; Prov 3:12). Thus the LXX translator changed the imagery of God possessing and giving birth to Wisdom, to the image of God creating and begetting Wisdom. His change of "possessed" to "created" and "appointed" to "founded" may have been based on the reasoning that Wisdom could not have been "possessed" or

---

1 See the commentary on 8:22–31 and "Wisdom in Proverbs" in the introduction.

2 Early church authors who cite earlier passages in Proverbs 8 to speak of Christ as Wisdom include an epistle attributed to Ignatius, *Epistle to Mary at Neapolis*, 3, citing Prov 8:17 (*ANF* 1:122); Victorinus of Pettau (died 303/304), *Commentary on the Apocalypse of the Blessed John*, 1.13, citing LXX Prov 8:20 (*ANF* 7:344); Eusebius, *Ecclesiastical History*, 1.2, citing LXX Prov 8:12, 15–16 (*NPNF*[2] 1:83–84); Athanasius, *Four Discourses against the Arians*, 1.6, citing Prov 8:12 (*NPNF*[2] 4:317); 3.30, citing LXX Prov 8:14 (*NPNF*[2] 4:429); Gregory of Nyssa, *Against Eunomius*, 3.2, citing LXX Prov 8:12 (*NPNF*[2] 5:140); and Hilary of Poitiers, *On the Trinity*, 12.44, citing LXX Prov 8:21 (*NPNF*[2] 9:229).

3 See the commentary on 3:13–20.

4 See the discussion in the textual notes on 8:22–25.

Figure 10

Comparison of MT and LXX Proverbs 8:22–31

Hebrew Text	*Septuagint Text*
22 Yahweh *possessed* me [קָנָנִי] at the beginning of his way, *before* his works **of old** [מֵאָז].	22 The Lord *created* me [ἔκτισέν με] as the beginning of his ways, *for* his works.
23 From eternity I was *appointed* [נִסַּכְתִּי], from the beginning,	23 Before the age he *founded* me [ἐθεμελίωσέν με] in the beginning,
from before the earth. 24 When there were no deep waters, **I was given birth** [חוֹלָלְתִּי], when there were no springs **filled** [נִכְבַּדֵּי־] with water.	24 before **he made** [τοῦ … ποιῆσαι] the earth, before **he made** [τοῦ … ποιῆσαι] the depths, before he brought forth the springs of waters,
25 Before the mountains were settled in place, before the hills, *I was given birth* [חוֹלָלְתִּי],	25 before the mountains were settled in place, before **all** [πάντων] the hills, *he begets me* [γεννᾷ με].
26 **when he had not yet** [עַד־לֹא] made land or fields *or the beginning of the dust of the* inhabited world.	26 **The Lord** [κύριος] made countries and uninhabited places *and* inhabited *heights under the heavens.*
27 When he *established* the heavens, I was *there.* When he *marked out the horizon on the surface of the ocean,*	27 When he *prepared* the heavens, I was *with him,* when he *set apart his throne upon the winds.*
28 when he established the clouds above, when he secured the fountains *of the deep waters,*	28 When he strengthened the clouds above, as he secured the springs *under the heavens,*
29 **when he set his decree for the sea so that the waters would not overstep his command,** when he *marked out* the foundations of the earth,	29 and when he *strengthened* the foundations of the earth,
30 I was beside him as a master craftsman. I was [his] joy day after day, rejoicing in his presence at all times,	30 I was beside him as a craftsman;* I was the one in whom he found delight every day; I rejoiced in his presence at all times,
31 [*I was*] rejoicing in his inhabited world, and *my* joy was with the human race.	31 when *he* rejoiced in *having completed* the inhabited world, and *he* rejoiced in the human race.

* For the meaning of this word, see the first textual note on 8:30.

"appointed" (MT 8:22–23) before being "created" (LXX 8:22) or "begotten" (LXX 8:25).[5] Thus when the translator used ἔκτισέν με, "created me," he was not seeking a direct and faithful translation of the Hebrew קָנָנִי, "possessed me" (8:22). Instead, the LXX is an ideological rendering that does not reflect the translator's actual understanding of the meaning of the Hebrew verb קָנָה any more than his use of ἐθεμελίωσεν, "founded," reflects his understanding of the verb נָסַךְ, "appoint, install" (8:23).[6]

The changes in the LXX as compared to the MT did not inhibit the church fathers who lived before the outbreak of the Arian controversy from identifying Wisdom as Christ and as begotten of the Father. In fact, γεννᾷ με ("has begotten me") in LXX 8:25 directly supports orthodox Christology. Furthermore, many fathers connected John 1 with Proverbs 8. For instance, Ignatius of Antioch (ca. AD 35–ca. 107) wrote:

> How could such a one be a mere man, receiving the beginning of His existence from Mary, and not rather God the Word, and the only-begotten Son? For "in the beginning was the Word, and the Word was with God, and the Word was God" [Jn 1:1]. And in another place, "The Lord created Me, the beginning of His ways, for His ways, for His works. Before the world did He found Me, and before all the hills did He beget Me" [LXX Prov 8:22–23, 25].[7]

Similarly, Justin Martyr (ca. AD 100–ca. 165) asserted on the basis of Proverbs 8 that Jesus was begotten before creation. He is also a distinct person of the Trinity, God the Son to be distinguished from God the Father:

> And it is written in the book of Wisdom: "If I should tell you daily events, I would be mindful to enumerate them from the beginning. The Lord created me the beginning of His ways for His works. From everlasting He established me in the beginning, before He formed the earth, and before He made the depths, and before the springs of waters came forth, before the mountains were settled; He begets me before all the hills" [LXX Prov 8:21c–25]. When I repeated these words, I added: "You perceive, my hearers, if you bestow attention, that the Scripture has declared that this Offspring was begotten by the Father before all things created; and that that which is begotten is numerically distinct from that which begets, any one will admit."[8]

Irenaeus (second century) also made similar statements, although he equated divine Wisdom with the third person of the Trinity, the Holy Spirit. Nevertheless, the fact that the Greek translator used "created" (LXX 8:22) did not keep Irenaeus from citing Proverbs to demonstrate that as Wisdom, the Spirit is uncreated and eternal God together with the Father and the Son:

---

5 In 8:24 the LXX translator simply omitted any reference to birthing.

6 This means that the LXX rendering "created me" (ἔκτισέν με, LXX 8:22) cannot be used to assert that קָנָה, "acquire" (MT 8:22), can mean "create." See the first textual note on 8:22.

7 Ignatius, *Epistle to the Tarsians*, 6 (*ANF* 1:108).

8 Justin Martyr, *Dialogue with Trypho*, 129 (*ANF* 1:264).

> I have also largely demonstrated, that the Word, namely the Son, was always with the Father; and that Wisdom also, which is the Spirit, was present with Him, anterior to all creation, He declares by Solomon: "God by Wisdom founded the earth, and by understanding hath He established the heaven. By His knowledge the depths burst forth, and the clouds dropped down the dew" [Prov 3:19–20]. And again: "The Lord created me the beginning of His ways in His work: He set me up from everlasting, in the beginning, before He made the earth, before He established the depths, and before the fountains of waters gushed forth; before the mountains were made strong, and before all the hills, He brought me forth" [LXX Prov 8:22–25]. And again: "When He prepared the heaven, I was with Him, and when He established the fountains of the deep; when He made the foundations of the earth strong, I was with Him preparing [them]. I was He in whom He rejoiced, and throughout all time I was daily glad before His face, when He rejoiced at the completion of the world, and was delighted in the sons of men" [LXX Prov 8:27–31].[9]

Origen (ca. AD 185–ca. 254) interpreted Wisdom as God the Son and pointedly mentioned both the divine and human natures in Christ as he discussed Proverbs 8:

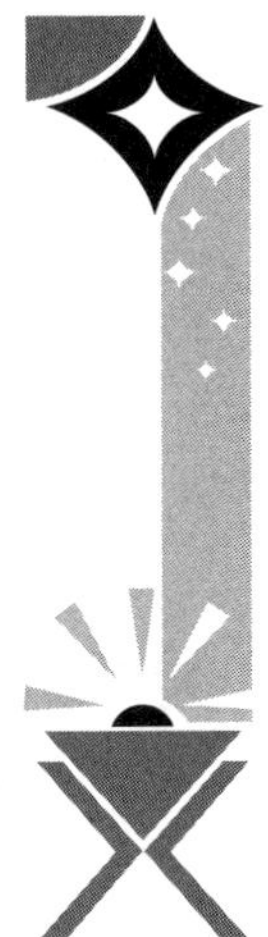

> In the first place, we must note that the nature of that deity which is in Christ in respect of His being the only-begotten Son of God is one thing, and that human nature which He assumed in these last times for the purposes of the dispensation (of grace) is another. And therefore we have first to ascertain what the only-begotten Son of God is, seeing He is called by many different names, according to the circumstances and views of individuals. For He is termed Wisdom, according to the expression of Solomon: "The Lord created me—the beginning of His ways, and among His works, before He made any other thing; He founded me before the ages. In the beginning, before He formed the earth, before He brought forth the fountains of waters, before the mountains were made strong, before all the hills, He brought me forth" [LXX Prov 8:22–25]. He is also styled First-born, as the apostle has declared: "who is the first-born of every creature" [Col 1:15]. The first-born, however, is not by nature a different person from the Wisdom, but one and the same. Finally, the Apostle Paul says that "Christ (is) the power of God and the wisdom of God" [1 Cor 1:24].[10]

That quotation from Origen helps illustrate why the fathers who wrote before the Arian controversy could overlook the plain force of the word "created" in LXX Prov 8:22. Using the analogy of faith, they read Proverbs 8 in the light of the NT passages that clearly depict Jesus as eternal God and as coexisting with the Father before creation. (In the quote above, Origen cited Col 1:15 and 1 Cor 1:24.) Similar treatments of Proverbs 8 can be found in Athenagoras

---

9 Irenaeus, *Against Heresies*, 4.20.3 (*ANF* 1:488).

10 Origen, *De Principiis*, 1.2.1 (*ANF* 4:245–46); see also Origen, *Commentary on the Gospel of John*, 1.111 (Fathers of the Church 80:56–57).

(ca. AD 133–ca. 190),[11] Tertullian (ca. AD 155–ca. 230),[12] Cyprian (ca. AD 200–258),[13] and Lactantius (ca. AD 240–ca. 320).[14] Because the fathers interpreted Scripture with Scripture and understood every text in a way that was consistent with the faith taught throughout the inspired Word of God, the Greek verb "created" in LXX Prov 8:22 did not become an impediment to orthodox Christology before Arius.

One of the few pre-Nicene fathers to have wrestled with the verb ἔκτισεν, "created," was Dionysius of Alexandria (died AD 265). He referred to false leaders who cited Proverbs 8 to support their fatal doctrinal errors. He explained that the verb can and must be understood rightly, in a way that was consistent with the divinity and eternal generation of Christ:

> But neither are they less to be blamed who think that the Son was a creation, and decided that the Lord was made just as one of those things which really were made; whereas the divine declarations testify that He was begotten, as is fitting and proper, but not that He was created or made. It is therefore not a trifling, but a very great impiety, to say that the Lord was in any wise made with hands. For if the Son was made, there was a time when He was not; but He always was, if, as He Himself declares, He is undoubtedly in the Father [see Jn 14:11]. ... The leaders of this view seem to me to have given very little heed to these things, and for that reason to have strayed absolutely, by explaining the passage otherwise than as the divine and prophetic Scripture demands. "The Lord created me the beginning of His ways" [LXX Prov 8:22]. For, as ye know, there is more than one signification of the word "created"; and in this place "created" is the same as "set over" the works made by Himself—made, I say, by the Son Himself. But this "created" is not to be understood in the same manner as "made." For to make and to create are different from one another. "Is not He Himself thy Father, that hath possessed thee and created thee?" [LXX Deut 32:6] says Moses in the great song of Deuteronomy. And thus might any one reasonably convict these men. Oh reckless and rash men! was then "the first-born of every creature" [Col 1:15] something made?—"He who was begotten from the womb before the morning star?" [LXX Ps 109:3 (MT/ET 110:3)]—He who in the person of Wisdom says, "Before all the hills He begot me?" [LXX Prov 8:25]. Finally, any one may read in many parts of the divine utterances that the Son is said to have been begotten, but never that He was made. From which considerations, they who dare to say that His divine and inexplicable generation was a creation, are openly convicted of thinking that which is false concerning the generation of the Lord.[15]

Dionysius employed two forms of argumentation in order to refute that Christ was created. One was to refer to other passages in Scripture that show

[11] Athenagoras, *A Plea for the Christians*, 10 (*ANF* 2:133).

[12] Tertullian, *Against Hermogenes*, 18, 20 (*ANF* 3:487–88); *Against Praxeas*, 6–7 (*ANF* 3:601).

[13] Cyprian, *Three Books of Testimonies against the Jews*, 2.1 (*ANF* 5:515–16).

[14] Lactantius, *Divine Institutes*, 4.6 (*ANF* 7:105).

[15] Dionysius, *Against the Sabellians*, 2 (*ANF* 7:365).

that Christ is eternal (Dionysius quoted or referred to LXX Deut 32:6; Ps 109:3 [MT/ET 110:3]; Prov 8:25; Jn 14:11; Col 1:15). The other was to posit that the verb κτίζω can mean "to set (someone) over (the creation)" and that it does not have to involve creating or making something new. However, that supposition about the Greek verb's meaning is wrong. In classical Greek the verb always has a meaning such as "create, produce, found, establish, plant" (see LSJ), and in Christian literature, it always refers to creating or making something, although it can refer to God bringing about the new creation in Christ (see BDAG). Therefore it may have been inevitable that the LXX's use of ἔκτισεν in Prov 8:22 would become a problem for the church.

About AD 320, Arius, a presbyter in Alexandria, Egypt, began to teach the following related heresies:

1. The Word (John 1) and the Father were not of the same substance (οὐσια).
2. The Son was a created being (κτίσμα, a noun cognate to the verb κτίζω in LXX Prov 8:22).
3. The Son, though he existed before earthly time and was creator of all things, came into existence at some juncture. Therefore, the Son was not eternal or preexistent, since there was a moment at which he came into being. Before that moment he did not exist.

Prov 8:22 was at the center of the Arian heresy and can even be characterized as a trigger for it. Most pointedly, LXX Prov 8:22 says that Wisdom was "created," and nearly every prominent Christian from St. Paul onward agreed that Proverbs 8 was about Christ. The orthodox fathers during and after the Council of Nicaea (AD 325) took great pains to explain that Christ, the Wisdom of God, is the eternal Son of God. At times they argued that LXX Prov 8:22 must be read in the light of "beget" (γεννάω) in LXX Prov 8:25 (MT 8:25 has חוֹלָלְתִּי, "I was given birth") and in the light of various NT passages that use "beget" (γεννάω).[16]

A form (the aorist passive participle γεννηθέντα) of this same verb, γεννάω, "beget," that is in LXX Prov 8:25 and in the NT is used twice in the Nicene Creed, which confesses:

> We believe … in one Lord Jesus Christ, the only-begotten [μονογενῆ] Son of God, begotten [γεννηθέντα] from the Father before all ages, light from light, true God from true God, begotten [γεννηθέντα] not made, of one substance [ὁμοούσιον] with the Father, through Whom all things came into existence."[17]

The later Athanasian Creed affirms the same Christology in more detail:

---

[16] Passive forms of the verb γεννάω, "begotten, conceived, born," refer to Christ in, for example, Mt 1:16, 20; 2:1, 4; Lk 1:35. Jesus uses a perfect passive form of the verb for himself in Jn 18:37. Active forms of the verb γεννάω, "beget, be the father of," refer to God the Father begetting God the Son in quotes of Ps 2:7 in Acts 13:33; Heb 1:5; 5:5.

[17] Kelly, *Early Christian Creeds*, 297.

> Whoever desires to be saved must, above all, hold the catholic faith. Whoever does not keep it whole and undefiled will without doubt perish eternally. And the catholic faith is this, that we worship one God in Trinity and Trinity in Unity, neither confusing the persons nor dividing the substance. For the Father is one person, the Son is another, and the Holy Spirit is another. But the Godhead of the Father and of the Son and of the Holy Spirit is one: the glory equal, the majesty coeternal. Such as the Father is, such is the Son, and such is the Holy Spirit: the Father uncreated, the Son uncreated, the Holy Spirit uncreated; ... the Father eternal, the Son eternal, the Holy Spirit eternal. ... The Son is neither made nor created, but begotten of the Father alone. ... And in this Trinity none is before or after another. ... Jesus Christ, the Son of God, is at the same time both God and man. He is God, begotten from the substance of the Father before all ages; and He is man, born from the substance of His mother in this age.[18]

The analogy of Scripture and the analogy of faith require that the interpretation of Proverbs 8 must be consistent with this truth about Christ.

A first line of orthodox theological reasoning was that "created" in LXX Prov 8:22 cannot be applied to the person of Christ in a literal way or does not apply to his essence or divine nature, because that would cause the verse to contradict the preponderance of other biblical texts that affirm the eternal generation of the Son from the Father. Other texts are sufficient to establish the eternal generation of the Son from the Father and to settle the matter. No single verse (such as LXX Prov 8:22) should be understood in a way that contradicts other verses. Some of these fathers argued that the verse means that Christ was made the beginning of the way of salvation (Jn 14:6).[19] Some compared the verse to metaphorical statements that Christ was made a door, a sheep, and a high priest.[20] This reasoning presupposes the unity and inerrancy of Scripture: every Scripture passage is true, and each individual passage must be understood in harmony with Scripture as a whole. For instance, Athanasius (ca. AD 293–373) wrote:

> Therefore let them tell us, from what teacher or by what tradition they derived these notions concerning the Saviour? "We have read," they will say, "in the Proverbs, 'The Lord created me a beginning of His ways unto His works' " [LXX Prov 8:22]; this Eusebius and his fellows used to insist on, and you write me word, that the present men also, though overthrown and confuted by an abundance of arguments, still were putting about in every quarter this passage, and saying that the Son was one of the creatures, and reckoning Him with things originated. But they seem to me to have a wrong understanding of this passage also; for it has a religious and very orthodox sense, which had they understood, they would not have blasphemed the Lord of glory. For on comparing what has been above stated with this passage, they will find a great difference between them. For what man of right understanding does

[18] *LSB*, pp. 319–20.

[19] E.g., Augustine, *On the Trinity*, 1.12 (*NPNF*[1] 3:31).

[20] E.g., Basil the Great, Letter 8.8 (*NPNF*[2] 8:120).

> not perceive, that what are created and made are external to the maker; but the Son, as the foregoing argument has shewn, exists not externally, but from the Father who begat Him? for man too both builds a house and begets a son, and no one would reverse things, and say that the house or the ship were begotten by the builder, but the son was created and made by him; nor again that the house was an image of the maker, but the son unlike him who begat him; but rather he will confess that the son is an image of the father, but the house a work of art, unless his mind be disordered, and he beside himself. Plainly, divine Scripture, which knows better than any the nature of everything, says through Moses, of the creatures, "In the beginning God created the heaven and the earth" [Gen 1:1]; but of the Son it introduces not another, but the Father Himself saying, "I have begotten Thee from the womb before the morning star" [LXX Ps 109:3 (MT/ET 110:3)]; and again, "Thou art My Son, this day have I begotten Thee" [Ps 2:7]. And the Lord says of Himself in the Proverbs, "Before all the hills He begets me" [LXX Prov 8:25]; and concerning things originated and created John speaks, "All things were made by Him" [Jn 1:3]; but preaching of the Lord, he says, "The Only-begotten Son, who is in the bosom of the Father, He declared Him" [Jn 1:18]. If then son, therefore not creature; if creature, not son; for great is the difference between them, and son and creature cannot be the same, unless His essence be considered to be at once from God, and external to God.[21]

Athanasius also rightly argued, in harmony with the Nicene Creed, that the Son has the same divine essence as the Father:

> It is plain from this that the Arians are not fighting with us about their heresy; but while they pretend us, their real fight is against the Godhead Itself. For if the voice were ours which says, "This is My Son" [e.g., Lk 9:35], small were our complaint of them; but if it is the Father's voice, and the disciples heard it, and the Son too says of Himself, "Before all the mountains He begat me" [LXX Prov 8:25], are they not fighting against God, as the giants in story, having their tongue, as the Psalmist says, a sharp sword for irreligion [LXX Ps 56:5 (MT 57:5; ET 57:4)]? For they neither feared the voice of the Father, nor reverenced the Saviour's words, nor trusted the Saints, one of whom writes, "Who being the Brightness of His glory and the Expression of His subsistence" [Heb 1:3], and "Christ the power of God and the Wisdom of God" [1 Cor 1:24]; and another says in the Psalm, "With Thee is the well of life, and in Thy Light shall we see light" [LXX Ps 35:10 (MT 36:10; ET 36:9)], and "Thou madest all things in Wisdom" [LXX Ps 103:24 (MT/ET 104:24)]; and the Prophets say, "And the Word of the Lord came to me" [e.g., Jer 1:4]; and John, "In the beginning was the Word" [Jn 1:1]; and Luke, "As they delivered them unto us which from the beginning were eye-witnesses and ministers of the Word" [Lk 1:2]; and as David again says, "He sent His Word and healed them" [LXX Ps 106:20 (MT/ET Ps 107:20)]. All these passages proscribe in every light the Arian heresy, and signify the eternity of the Word, and that He is not foreign but proper to the Father's Essence.[22]

---

[21] Athanasius, *Defense of the Nicene Definition*, 3.13 (*NPNF*^{2} 4:158).

[22] Athanasius, *Four Discourses against the Arians*, 2.18 (*NPNF*^{2} 4:365). Although Athanasius refers to several OT passages, the NT passages carry the primary weight of his argument.

Similar argumentation can be found in Gregory of Nazianzus (ca. AD 329–ca. 389)[23] and Hilary of Poitiers (ca. AD 300–ca. 367).[24] The whole passage (Prov 8:22–31) is similarly interpreted by the greatest Lutheran systematic theologian, Johann Gerhard (1582–1637), who relied on the Hebrew and consulted other ancient versions in addition to the LXX.[25]

In response to this first line of reasoning, certainly we must agree that it is a vital hermeneutical principle to interpret difficult and obscure passages in the light of clearer passages. However, LXX Prov 8:22 is hardly an opaque passage. Instead this ancient *version* (translation) of Scripture is most pointed: God "created" Wisdom.

A second orthodox line of theological reasoning is related to the first, but can be considered to be more nuanced. It holds that the verb "created" in LXX Prov 8:22 cannot refer to Christ's eternal divine nature, but may refer to his human nature, which the eternal Son assumed when he was conceived by the power of the Holy Spirit in the womb of the Virgin Mary. This application of the verb only to the human nature of Christ (1) recognizes the true meaning of the Greek verb ("created" rather than "set over") and, at the same time, (2) enables this passage to be understood in a way that is fully in harmony with orthodox Christology based on other passages, since Christ assumed his human nature at a certain time in earthly history.[26] Like the first orthodox line of reasoning, this one too presupposes both the inerrancy of Scripture and the unity or doctrinal harmony of all Scripture. This argument about LXX Prov 8:22 was set forth by Augustine (AD 354–430)[27] and was often used by Ambrose (ca. AD 340–397).[28] It was employed by Didymus the Blind (ca. AD 313–ca. 398),[29] Gregory of Nyssa (ca. AD 335–after 394),[30] and Athanasius (ca. AD 293–373).[31] Gregory of Nazianzus also allowed for it.[32]

[23] Gregory of Nazianzus, *Orations*, 30.2 (*NPNF*[2] 7:310).

[24] Hilary of Poitiers, *On the Trinity*, 1.35; 4.11 (*NPNF*[2] 9:50, 74). Hilary goes on to cite Prov 8:28–31 as proof of the preexistence of the Son so that 8:22 cannot mean that he was created (*On the Trinity*, 4.21 [*NPNF*[2] 9:77–78]).

[25] Gerhard, *On the Nature of God and on the Most Holy Mystery of the Trinity*, 142, 397. See Gerhard's detailed discussion of Prov 8:22–31 on pages 378–82.

[26] See, for example, FC SD VIII 6–7, 13. The orthodox Lutheran confessors also duly noted that once the personal union of the divine and human natures in Christ had taken place at his conception, the divine and human natures remain united in the one person of Christ henceforth into the future for all eternity. This understanding of the personal union is necessary for a correct understanding of the Lord's Supper. See, for example, FC Ep VIII.

[27] Augustine, *On Christian Doctrine*, 1.34 (*NPNF*[1] 2:532). See also Augustine, *On the Trinity*, 1.12 (*NPNF*[1] 3:31), and *Confessions*, 7.21 (*NPNF*[1] 1:114, including n. 13).

[28] Ambrose, *Exposition of the Christian Faith*, 1.15; 3.7 (*NPNF*[2] 10:217, 249); *Three Books on the Holy Spirit*, 2.6 (*NPNF*[2] 10:121).

[29] Didymus, *Commentary on the Proverbs of Solomon*, on 8:22. (PG 39:1629–32).

[30] Gregory of Nyssa, *Against Eunomius*, 2.10 (*NPNF*[2] 5:117).

[31] Athanasius, *Statement of Faith*, 3–4 (*NPNF*[2] 4:85).

[32] Gregory of Nazianzus, *Orations*, 30.2 (*NPNF*[2] 7:310).

However valid this argument may be, it clearly runs against the grain of the LXX version of Proverbs 8 to apply the passage *only to the human nature* in Christ and not to his whole person. The passage unambiguously states that the Lord "created" and "founded" (LXX Prov 8:22–23) Wisdom (as a whole, not just one of two natures possessed by Wisdom). Although it is clear in the LXX that this action of creating and founding took place "in the beginning," before the world's creation (LXX Prov 8:22–24), it still made Wisdom the first created being, just as the Arians held.

In conclusion, the argument from other passages of Scripture, especially the NT, eventually carried the day. *The orthodox theology of the Nicene fathers prevailed despite the clear reading of LXX Prov 8:22.* Thus in a very real sense the orthodox let Scripture as a whole prevail over the meaning of one specific text, LXX Prov 8:22, which Arius clearly understood. Nevertheless, the orthodox were arguing for the meaning of the original, inspired Hebrew text of Prov 8:22, although many of them may not have realized it since many had no faculty with the original language, although some apparently did.[33] The normative text of Proverbs is the Hebrew text, which does *not* say that Wisdom was "created." Instead, the original Hebrew of Prov 8:22 states that Yahweh had "possessed" Wisdom eternally, from eternity past, "at the beginning of his way, before his works of old." The LXX mistranslation of Prov 8:22 is unmistakably counter not only to the original Hebrew, but also to the clear Christological passages in the NT that affirm the eternal generation of Christ's divine nature. Since the eternal generation of God the Son from God the Father is essential to the Christian Gospel as declared by Jesus and his apostles in the NT—precisely fulfilling (not contradicting) all the promises in the original, inspired OT—the Arian position is a pernicious heresy incompatible with saving faith in Christ. It cannot be maintained.

This leads then to a cautionary note: the church faced a grave threat to its very existence in the Arian heresy, but that heresy was able to germinate and flourish because the church had abandoned its knowledge of the original Hebrew and Aramaic languages of the OT. Had the fathers maintained a working knowledge of Hebrew, they could have expounded the true meaning of the original Hebrew text of Proverbs 8, and the error of Arius might never have occurred—or if it still had, it would have been much more easily refuted. Thus also in our day it is important that pastors and leaders in the church maintain fluency in the original languages of Scripture. Even the best, most well-intended translation may contain ambiguous or misleading wording that can lead to false doctrine, apostasy, and loss of salvation. Study of the *ipsissima verba,* the "very words"

[33] Gregory of Nyssa, *Against Eunomius*, 2.10 (*NPNF*[2] 5:117), is one father who rightly stated that "the Hebrew text does not read 'created,' and we have ourselves read in more ancient [Greek] copies 'possessed' instead of 'created.' "

that God inspired in the original languages, is also the best way to inculcate knowledge of the Scriptures and the doctrine they teach.[34]

Luther believed that the right understanding of the Gospel would remain in the church only as long as the church's leaders retained knowledge of the original languages:

> For though the Gospel has come and is daily coming through the Holy Spirit alone, we cannot deny that the languages [Hebrew, Aramaic, and Greek] were the means through which it came. …
>
> We shall have a hard time preserving the Gospel without the languages. The languages are the sheath in which this sword of the Spirit is contained. They are the case in which we carry this jewel. They are the vessel in which we hold this wine.[35]

In particular, Luther colorfully wrote about the need for pastors to master Hebrew:

> You, too, as future teachers of religion, should apply yourselves to the task of learning this language, unless you want to be taken for dumb cattle and uninstructed rabble. … We need theological leaders, we must have fighters … who are teachers, judges, and masters in this language.[36]

Scripture—the inspired Word of God in the original languages—is the highest authority in the church, the sole source and norm (*norma normans*, the "norm" that "norms" or "judges" all other standards) for the Christian faith and life. The three ecumenical Creeds—Apostles', Nicene, and Athanasian—are true presentations of the theology of the Scriptures. As such, they serve as *norma normata*, "normed norms" that concisely proclaim what the Christian faith is and that continue to protect the church from error.[37]

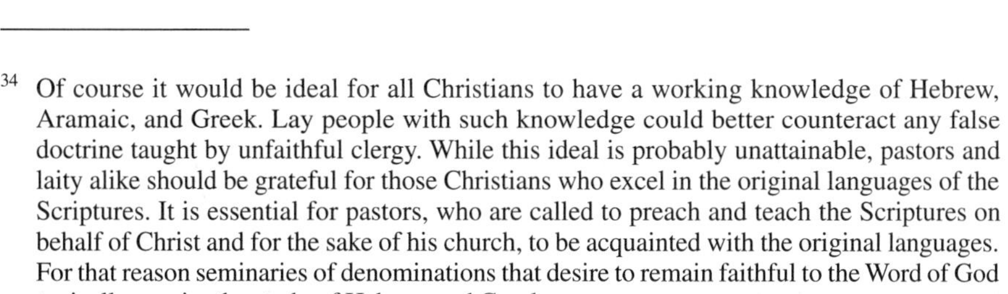

[34] Of course it would be ideal for all Christians to have a working knowledge of Hebrew, Aramaic, and Greek. Lay people with such knowledge could better counteract any false doctrine taught by unfaithful clergy. While this ideal is probably unattainable, pastors and laity alike should be grateful for those Christians who excel in the original languages of the Scriptures. It is essential for pastors, who are called to preach and teach the Scriptures on behalf of Christ and for the sake of his church, to be acquainted with the original languages. For that reason seminaries of denominations that desire to remain faithful to the Word of God typically require the study of Hebrew and Greek.

[35] Plass, *What Luther Says*, § 2273, quoting WA 15.37–38; cf. AE 45:358–60.

[36] AE 12:199. Luther also declared: "Those who produced the Septuagint did not really know the Hebrew language. Their translation has, therefore, no real value at all" (Plass, *What Luther Says*, § 2272, quoting WA TR 3, § 3271a).

[37] The *Book of Concord* therefore begins with the three ecumenical Creeds before the other documents that, together with the Creeds, comprise the Lutheran Confessions. These Confessions are a pure and unadulterated explanation of the divine Word, and as such they furnish a more detailed and comprehensive presentation of normative theology that preserves, defends, and proclaims the Gospel.

Proverbs 8:32–36

Wisdom as the Giver of Life

Translation

8 [32]"And now, sons, listen to me,
since blessed are those who keep my ways.
[33]Listen to discipline and become wise,
and do not neglect [it].
[34]Blessed is the person who listens to me
so that he watches at my doors day after day,
so that he guards the doorposts framing my doorways,
[35]because whoever finds me finds life,
and he obtains favor from Yahweh,
[36]but whoever sins against me harms himself.
All who hate me love death."

Textual Notes

8:32 וְעַתָּה בָנִים שִׁמְעוּ־לִי—This clause is repeated verbatim from 5:7 and 7:24, where it was spoken by Solomon. See the textual notes and commentary on those verses.

וְאַשְׁרֵי דְּרָכַי יִשְׁמֹרוּ׃—Although this line is simply introduced with *waw*, it serves as an explanation of the reason for the preceding imperative clause, שִׁמְעוּ־לִי, "listen to me." Therefore it is translated with a causal conjunction: "*since* blessed …" For the construct plural אַשְׁרֵי, see the first textual note and the commentary on 3:13. אַשְׁרֵי is repeated at the start of 8:34. Here the construct form governs the following verbal clause (דְּרָכַי יִשְׁמֹרוּ), which serves as a relative clause: "blessed are *those who* keep my ways." See GKC, §§ 130 d and 155 n (*c*); Joüon, § 158 d.

8:32b–33 וְאַשְׁרֵי … תִּפְרָעוּ׃—The LXX omits any translation of the second line of 8:32 and all of 8:33. One reason for the omission could be the lack of close syntactical connection between 8:32b–33 and the first clause of 8:32. On the other hand, this may be a simple case of haplography: the translator's eye skipped from וְאַשְׁרֵי in 8:32b to אַשְׁרֵי at the beginning of 8:34.

8:33 שִׁמְעוּ מוּסָר וַחֲכָמוּ—See "מוּסָר, 'Discipline,' and יָסַר, 'to Discipline' " in "Wisdom in Proverbs" in the introduction. After the first imperative, שִׁמְעוּ, "listen," the second imperative, וַחֲכָמוּ, forms a purpose or result clause: "*so that you* become wise."

וְאַל־תִּפְרָעוּ׃—For the Qal (G) of פָּרַע, "ignore, neglect," see the first textual note on 1:25.

8:34 לִשְׁקֹד עַל־דַּלְתֹתַי יוֹם ׀ יוֹם—The Qal (G) verb שָׁקַד, "keep watch, guard," occurs only here in Proverbs but is a close synonym of שָׁמַר in the following parallel clause. The repeated יוֹם ׀ יוֹם has a distributive meaning, "day after day, each day."

לִשְׁמֹר מְזוּזֹת פְּתָחָי׃—The construct phrase מְזוּזֹת פְּתָחָי, literally, "doorposts of my doorways," presupposes that the doorposts form the doorway, hence "the doorposts framing my doorways." While פֶּתַח is often translated as "door," it actually refers to the doorway. The door itself is denoted by דֶּלֶת.[1]

8:35 כִּי מֹצְאִי מָצָאי חַיִּים—The translation follows the Qere. The Qere has the singular Qal (G) participle with a singular object suffix, מֹצְאִי, "a person finding me," followed by the singular Qal perfect מָצָא, "has found life [חַיִּים]." The Kethib apparently points the participle as plural with a plural suffix, מֹצְאַי, "people finding me," and points the following verb as the same plural participle in construct, מֹצְאֵי־חַיִּים, "are finders of life." For the noun חַיִּים, "life," in the eschatological sense of everlasting life by God's grace, see, for example, 3:2, 18, 22; 4:10, 13, 22–23. See also the next textual note.

וַיָּפֶק רָצוֹן מֵיְהוָה׃—The identical clause recurs in 18:22b. An equivalent clause with an imperfect verb without *waw* consecutive occurs in 12:2. For the Hiphil (H) verb פּוּק, "acquire, obtain," see the second textual note on 3:13.

The noun רָצוֹן, "favor, grace," clearly describes "life" (8:35a) as God's free and gracious gift of everlasting salvation, not as something earned or merited. The noun occurs fourteen times in Proverbs. It unmistakably refers to "favor, grace" shown by Yahweh also in 12:2 and 18:22, whereas in 11:1, 20; 12:22; and 15:8, it refers to the fruit of faith in believers—the righteous, who do what is pleasing or delightful to God (and to the king in 16:13). The king, on behalf of God, shows "favor" to the righteous in 14:35; 16:15; 19:12. In sacrificial and liturgical contexts, the noun רָצוֹן refers to the "favor" or "grace" God shows to his people because of the vicarious sacrifices that atone for sin (e.g., Lev 1:3; 22:19–21; Is 56:7). The same is true of the cognate verb רָצָה (e.g., Lev 1:4; 7:18; 22:27). This OT theme is fulfilled in Jesus Christ, who announces the time of God's "grace, favor" (Lk 4:19, quoting Is 61:2) and who offers himself as the perfect, all-sufficient sacrifice that makes vicarious atonement for the sin of the world, so that all baptized believers in him receive divine favor by his grace alone. This is because God the Father "is favorable" toward his sinless Son (רָצָה, usually translated as "in whom my soul *delights*," in Is 42:1, part of the OT background of the Father's words at Jesus' Baptism and transfiguration; see Mt 3:17; 12:18; 17:5).

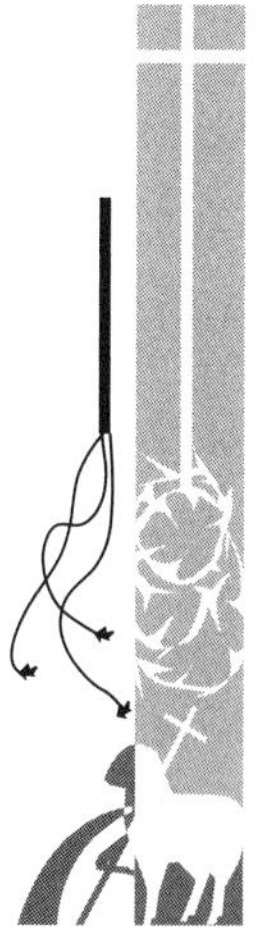

The cognate verb רָצָה, "be favorable, show favor to," occurs thrice in Proverbs. It refers to Yahweh being pleased and graciously showing his favor in 16:7 and, in a comparison to the favor shown by a father to a son, in 3:12. In 23:26 a father implores his son to let his eyes be favorable to the father's ways, that the son may follow in his righteous ways (cf. 23:24) and avoid sin and death (23:27–35).

8:36 וְחֹטְאִי חֹמֵס נַפְשׁוֹ—This is the first instance of the verb חָטָא, "to sin," in Proverbs. Here the participle חֹטְאִי has a suffix ("me") referring to divine Wisdom, the speaker, as the indirect object (a dative of disadvantage), and so it has the nuance "whoever sins *against* me." The participle חוֹטֵא is used as a substantive, a "sinner," in 11:31; 13:22; 14:21. The participle has the absolute meaning (with no object), "(he) sins," in 19:2. A phrase similar to the one here, but shorter, is used in 20:2: חוֹטֵא נַפְשׁוֹ, literally, "sins

[1] V. P. Hamilton, "דֶּלֶת," *TWOT* 1:189–90; V. P. Hamilton, "פֶּתַח," 2:743.

against his own life/soul," meaning "endangers his (own) life/soul." For the use of נֶפֶשׁ as an object referring to injuring "oneself" or one's own "soul," see the second textual note on 6:32. The phrase here, חֹמֵס נַפְשׁוֹ, is, literally, "does violence to his own life/soul." The verb חָמַס occurs only here in Proverbs, but the cognate noun חָמָס, "violence," occurs seven times (see the textual note on 3:31).

כָּל־מְשַׂנְאַי אָהֲבוּ מָוֶת׃—This clause points to the result of spurning divine Wisdom—a result that unbelievers probably do not intend, and perhaps are not even aware of, so it could be rendered as "all who hate me *must* love death," because they bring death on themselves. The verbs שָׂנֵא, "to hate," and אָהַב, "to love," are direct antonyms. They occur together also in 1:22; 9:8; 12:1; 13:24; 14:20; 27:6. The Piel (D) of שָׂנֵא occurs in Proverbs only here and may have an intensive meaning as compared to the Qal (G) in, for example, 1:22, 29. The suffix on the Piel participle מְשַׂנְאַי is objective: "those who hate *me*."

Commentary

Having presented the Gospel in 8:22–31, Wisdom now addresses her hearers as "sons," signaling her desire for a close relationship with them (8:32), just as Solomon had done when he addressed "sons" (4:1; 5:7; 7:24). She invites them into this relationship with a gracious promise of blessing: "blessed are those who keep my ways" (8:32). Therefore the following imperatives, "listen to discipline and become wise" (8:33), do not signal a negative demand of the Law, but a Gospel invitation to believe and be saved. This is the Gospel call that creates, sustains, and encourages faith. To leave no doubt that this is the case, Wisdom follows this with another promise of blessing, "blessed is the person who listens to me," where listening to Wisdom is compared to paying close attention to the door of Wisdom's house (8:34).

The hearers are encouraged to watch so that they may find and listen to Wisdom when she comes through the door (8:34). This is parallel to Jesus entering the door of the sheepfold to call his sheep; they listen to his voice and follow him (Jn 10:1–4). Jesus, the legitimate shepherd, uses the door to enter the sheepfold instead of climbing over the wall like a thief. In the same way, Wisdom enters her house through the door, whereas those who seek other entry are illegitimate purveyors of wisdom. Therefore, one needs only to wait for her at the door of her house. See also Prov 1:21 and 8:3, where divine Wisdom utters her Gospel invitation at "entrances, doorways" (the plural of פֶּתַח, as in 8:34). Where is this doorway? It is wherever divine Wisdom speaks—wherever the Word of God is faithfully read and proclaimed, and the Sacraments are rightly administered. There one will find the Word of God incarnate: Jesus, the door (Jn 10:7, 9).

Finding Wisdom is also equated with finding "life" (Prov 8:35; see Prov 3:18; Jn 8:51; 10:9–10). Note the contrast to the foolish young man at the adulteress' door (Prov 5:8); he finds death (7:27). Finding Wisdom is then further equated with obtaining God's "favor" or "grace" (8:35). These identifications of Wisdom with "life" and "favor, grace" once again reveal that Wisdom is Christ, through whom alone we obtain "life" (Jn 1:4) and "grace" (Jn 1:14–17).

However, there is another side to Wisdom's message: her preaching of condemnation according to the Law to warn those who refuse to listen to her. Those who reject her, sin against her, and by doing so they harm themselves (8:36). Note well that if they are harmed, it is not Wisdom's doing. She does not intend to hurt them in any way. This is a reminder that God does not want sinners to be lost in their sin, but to turn from their sin and receive life from him (1 Tim 2:3–4; 2 Pet 3:9; cf. Rom 2:4). Their rejection of the Gospel is called hating Wisdom. Since they reject the way to life, they are pictured as loving death (Prov 8:36; see Jn 3:20; 15:18).

Proverbs 9:1–6

Lady Wisdom Invites Everyone to Her Banquet

Translation

9 **[1]Wisdom has built her house;**
she has carved out her seven pillars.
[2]She has prepared her meat;
she has mixed her wine;
also, she has set her table.
[3]She has sent out her servant girls;
she calls from the highest of the heights in the city,
[4]"Whoever is gullible, let him turn in here."
To someone who lacks sense she says,
[5]"Come, eat my food,
and drink the wine that I have mixed.
[6]Abandon gullibility, and live.
Travel the road to understanding."

Textual Notes

9:1 חָכְמוֹת בָּנְתָה בֵיתָהּ—For the abstract plural חָכְמוֹת as the divine hypostasis "Wisdom," see the first textual note on 1:20. "Wisdom" (חָכְמָה) and "house, temple" (בַּיִת) occur together in reference to the temple of Solomon in 1 Ki 10:4 || 2 Chr 9:3. The common verb בָּנָה, "build," can refer to constructing an altar (e.g., Ex 24:4; Deut 27:5–6) or the temple (e.g., 2 Sam 7:5, 13; 1 Ki 5:19, 32 [ET 5:5, 18]; 6:1–2, 14; 8:13). God also promises to David, "I will build a house for you" (בַּיִת אֶבְנֶה־לָּךְ, 2 Sam 7:27), referring to the dynasty culminating in Christ, the new temple (Jn 2:19–22) who will reign forever (e.g., Is 9:5–6 [ET 9:6–7]).

חָצְבָה עַמּוּדֶיהָ שִׁבְעָה׃—The meaning of חָצַב is "cut out, mine, quarry." Its participle is used in 1 Chr 22:2 for "stonecutters, masons" whom David gathered to build the "house" (בַּיִת) of God.[1] The object phrase is, literally, "her pillars, seven." This implies that her "house, temple" has seven pillars. עַמּוּד, "pillar," occurs only here in Proverbs but often in the architectural descriptions of the tabernacle (e.g., Ex 27:10–17; 40:18) and of Solomon's temple (e.g., 1 Ki 7:15–22, 41–42). Compare Yahweh's theophany as "a pillar of cloud" and "a pillar of fire" (Ex 13:21–22; 14:19, 24).

---

[1] Cf. T. E. McComiskey, "חָצַב," *TWOT* 1:313. Some would emend this verb to הִצִּבָה, "she has erected," on the basis of the LXX translation ὑπήρεισεν (Clifford, *Proverbs*, 101–2; Murphy, *Proverbs*, 56; Scott, *Proverbs*, *Ecclesiastes*, 74; Longman, *Proverbs*, 214–15). However, as pointed out in the first textual note and the commentary on 8:22, the LXX is not always a reliable guide to the meaning of the Hebrew.

9:2 טָבְחָה טִבְחָהּ—The verb טָבַח refers to slaughtering an animal for its meat. The clause here with the verb and the cognate accusative noun טֶבַח, literally, "she has slaughtered her slaughter," refers to slaughtering an animal in the process of preparing meat for a meal. This job usually was done by men (*HALOT*, s.v. טבח, 1), but here it is accomplished by the woman Wisdom.

מָסְכָה יֵינָהּ—"To mix" (מָסַךְ) "wine" (יַיִן) refers to the addition of spices to improve the taste before it was drunk. The same vocabulary is repeated in 9:5. Compare Is 5:22.

עָרְכָה שֻׁלְחָנָהּ׃—The verb עָרַךְ means "arrange." The reference is to arranging items on the table for a meal, not the placing of the table in the banquet hall. Thus the corresponding English idiom is "*set* her table." The same phraseology is in Ps 23:5, where it is Yahweh who sets the table for David.

9:3 שָׁלְחָה נַעֲרֹתֶיהָ תִקְרָא—The Masoretic *athnach* places both verbs on the same, first line: "she has sent out her servant girls; she calls." Then the second line of the verse, like the first line, has three accented units: עַל־גַּפֵּי מְרֹמֵי קָרֶת, literally, "on the heights of the elevations of the city." However, most translations move the second verb (תִקְרָא, "she calls") to the start of the second line. Only here in the OT does גַּף refer to a "height" (BDB, 2, under the root גפף).

9:4 מִי־פֶתִי יָסֻר הֵנָּה—Here the interrogative pronoun מִי, "who?" is used as a general relative pronoun, "whoever" (Joüon, § 144 fa). For the noun, see "פֶּתִי, 'Gullible Person' " in "Fools in Proverbs" in the introduction. The plural of פֶּתִי in 9:6 probably has an abstract meaning. The Qal (G) verb יָסֻר is an unusual jussive form; the expected jussive form is יָסֹר (Joüon, § 80 k). The jussive can be translated as an indirect imperative: "*let* him turn in here." This clause is repeated in 9:16a.

חֲסַר־לֵב אָמְרָה לּוֹ׃—See "חֲסַר־לֵב, 'Lacking Sense' " in "Fools in Proverbs" in the introduction. The syntax is, literally, "one lacking sense—she speaks to him." The initial construct phrase חֲסַר־לֵב is a *casus pendens*, and the final prepositional phrase לוֹ indicates that it is an indirect object: "*to* someone who lacks sense she says, …" This clause is repeated (with the addition of two occurrences of *waw*) in 9:16b.

9:5 לְכוּ לַחֲמוּ בְלַחֲמִי וּשְׁתוּ בְּיַיִן—Twice here the preposition בְּ is used with something consumed: after the verb לָחַם, "eat," and after the verb שָׁתָה, "drink" (see GKC, § 119 m).

9:6 עִזְבוּ פְתָאיִם וִחְיוּ—Elsewhere in Proverbs the plural of פֶּתִי refers to gullible people, but that concrete meaning is out of place here. The NIV understands the plural to mean "simple ways." However, it is better to understand the plural as an abstract intensive meaning "gullibility" (cf. NRSV, NASB, NAB, NJB). Similar eschatological promises of eternal life are expressed with singular imperatives of חָיָה, "live," in 4:4 and 7:2. The plural imperative with *waw* here, וִחְיוּ, is also used in prophetic promises in Ezek 18:32; Amos 5:4, 6. In all these passages, the imperative could be rendered as a purpose clause: "so that you may live."

וְאִשְׁרוּ בְּדֶרֶךְ בִּינָה׃—The Qal (G) of אָשַׁר, "to walk, travel," here an imperative, has the same meaning as the Piel (D) in 4:14. For the noun, see "בִּינָה, 'Understanding,' and Related Words" in "Wisdom in Proverbs" in the introduction.

Commentary

The third and final poem about Wisdom in chapters 1–9 begins with a description of a banquet that she prepares.[2] Wisdom begins by building a house with seven pillars (9:1). Some of this vocabulary ("wisdom," "build," "house/temple," "pillars") was also applied to the tabernacle built by Moses and the temple built by Solomon (see the textual notes on 9:1), and those holy structures represented the entire universe with God at the center. However, "seven pillars" is a phrase that occurs only here in the Scriptures (cf. 1 Ki 7:17). The features of this house have been interpreted in many ways.[3]

Perhaps the best proposal is that Wisdom's house is a reference to the world inhabited by humans, since Wisdom's "joy was with the human race" (Prov 8:31). In several passages the world is spoken of as a house having foundations (e.g., Ps 104:5; Job 38:6; Prov 8:29) or pillars (e.g., 1 Sam 2:8; Ps 75:4 [ET 75:3]). The seven pillars then would signal that Wisdom inhabits the entire world.[4] In Proverbs the number seven often signals comprehensiveness (6:16, 31; 24:16; 26:25; see the commentary on 30:11–33 and 31:10–31). A typical Israelite house might have had one or two supporting columns, but a house with seven pillars would have been a large one. This large house that Wisdom inhabits is the world. While the world now may be a place of foolishness (8:1–5), it was not designed to be that way. Wisdom designed the world (8:22–31), and she seeks to rescue fools from their sinfully foolish ways.

More importantly, the choice of the number seven reminds readers that Wisdom is divine. Just as God created the world in seven days (Gen 1:1–2:3), so also Wisdom has built a house with seven pillars. Thus Wisdom in Proverbs 9 is the same divine Wisdom—a hypostasis, one person of the triune God—who is eternal and so was already present at the creation of the world (Prov 8:22–31). This Wisdom is God's Word, through whom everything was made (Jn 1:1–3; Col 1:15–20), and who became incarnate in Jesus Christ (Jn 1:14–18; Col 2:2–3, 9).

Wisdom next prepares the food and sets the table (Prov 9:2). She then sends out her servant girls as her messengers through whom she invites all people—even the gullible and senseless—to the banquet (9:3–4). The call, of course, is the invitation of the Gospel to come to a rich banquet of divinely prepared nourishment (Is 25:6–9). This banquet is free by grace: Wisdom charges no admission fee, nor do diners have to pay any bill after the meal. Those who have

---

[2] Proverbs 1–9 contains ten addresses from a father to his son as well as three poems about Wisdom: (1) 1:20–33; (2) 8:1–36; and (3) 9:1–18. See the excursus "Proverbs 1–9, Christ, and the Ten Commandments" in the commentary on chapter 1.

[3] Greenfield, "The Seven Pillars of Wisdom," lists the following: seven firmaments or heavens, seven planets, seven regions or climates, seven days of creation, seven books of the law, seven gifts of the Spirit (Is 11:2), seven church eras, seven sacraments, seven liberal arts, and the first seven chapters of Proverbs. Greenfield proposes his own: seven predeluvian sages.

[4] Ross, "Proverbs," 947–48; cf. Scott, *Proverbs, Ecclesiastes*, 76–77.

no money are invited to imbibe water and wine and milk (Is 55:1). Compare Jesus' parable of the wedding feast: the king himself makes all the preparations and sends out his messengers to bring in all kinds of guests so that his dining hall might be filled (Mt 22:1–10). Jesus freely offers living waters to all who are thirsty (Jn 4:10, 14; 7:37–39; see also Rev 22:17).

Wisdom's invitation is especially directed to everyone who is "gullible" and "lacks sense" (Prov 9:4), who is characterized by foolishness and susceptible to deception. This is a description of the natural state of all humans as they are conceived and born in sin (Ps 51:7 [ET 51:5]; Rom 3:9–20). Their inclination is not to Wisdom, but she calls to them nevertheless. When they eat her banquet, they receive spiritual nourishment and growth (Prov 9:5–6). They begin to lose their gullibility; they obtain everlasting life; they start to "travel the road to understanding" (9:6). This is a description of the walk of life in faith. It includes justification through faith in Christ alone, sanctification in the wider sense, and enlightenment by the power of the Holy Spirit, who enables the believer to grow in knowledge and in making wise choices in life, until the believer is finally brought by God's grace into the fullness of eternal life.[5]

Eating Wisdom's banquet is synonymous with eating the feast of "the bread of life" offered "for the life of the world" (Jn 6:32–59). Just as Wisdom offers food and drink, so Jesus offers his flesh and blood (Jn 6:52–56) as nourishment. Wisdom exhorts:

> Abandon gullibility, and live.
> Travel the road to understanding.

Likewise Jesus promises:

> As the living Father sent me and I live because of the Father, so whoever feeds on me will also live because of me. … Whoever feeds on this bread will live forever. (Jn 6:57–58)

Gregory of Nyssa explains:

> "Eat of my bread" [Prov 9:5], is the bidding of Wisdom to the hungry; and the Lord declares those blessed who hunger for such food as this, and says, "If any man thirst, let him come unto Me, and drink" [Jn 7:37].[6]

---

[5] See further "Wisdom in Proverbs" in the introduction.

[6] Gregory of Nyssa, *On the Making of Man*, 19.1 (*NPNF*^{2} 5:409).

Proverbs 9:7–12

Lady Wisdom’s Proverbs

Translation

9 [7]“Whoever corrects a mocker invites insults,
  and whoever warns a wicked person [invites] abuse.
[8]Do not warn a mocker, otherwise he will hate you.
  Warn a wise person, and he will love you.
[9]Give [advice] to a wise person, and he will become even wiser.
  Teach a righteous person, and he will add [to his] learning.
[10]The fear of Yahweh is the beginning of wisdom.
  The knowledge of the Holy One is understanding,
[11]because through me your days will become numerous,
  and years of life will be added to you.
[12]If you are wise, you are wise to your own advantage.
  And [if] you mock, you alone will bear [the consequences].”

Textual Notes

9:7 יֹסֵ֤ר ׀ לֵ֗ץ לֹקֵ֣חַ ל֣וֹ קָל֑וֹן—For the verb יָסַר, “to correct, discipline,” see “מוּסָר, ‘Discipline,’ and יָסַר, ‘to Discipline’ ” in “Wisdom in Proverbs” in the introduction. The direct object of the participle יֹסֵר is another participle, לֵץ. See “לֵץ, ‘Mocker,’ and לָצוֹן, ‘Mocking, Scoffing’ ” in “Fools in Proverbs” in the introduction. The one who “corrects a mocker” is described as, literally, “receiving [לֹקֵחַ] for himself [לוֹ] dishonor [קָלוֹן].” The participle of לָקַח is difficult here, and *HALOT* (s.v. קָלוֹן, 2 b) considers it part of an idiom with קָלוֹן. “Receiving for himself dishonor” probably means “invites insults” (cf. ESV, NRSV, NIV) given the parallelism to the next clause and the use of קָלוֹן to mean “insult” elsewhere in Proverbs (12:16; 22:10).

וּמוֹכִ֖יחַ לְרָשָׁ֣ע מוּמֽוֹ׃—For the Hiphil (H) of יָכַח, “to warn,” see the first textual note on 3:12. This clause uses its participle (מוֹכִיחַ) while 9:8 has the imperfect (תּוֹכַח) and imperative (הוֹכַח). The participle לֹקֵחַ in the preceding clause does double duty and is the implied predicate with the object מוּמוֹ, literally, “[receives] his blemish, fault.” The noun מוּם often refers to a physical defect or deformity, but here refers to a “moral defect” or “shame” (see BDB, 2, under the root מאם). The pronominal suffix on מוּמוֹ refers back to the “wicked man” (רָשָׁע). Hence the one giving the warning receives treatment deserved by the wicked man he is trying to help. “Abuse” seems to be contextually accurate.

9:9 הוֹדַ֥ע לְ֝צַדִּ֗יק וְי֣וֹסֶף לֶֽקַח׃—The Hiphil (H) imperative of יָדַע, “to make known,” is rendered as “*teach* a righteous person.” This is the protasis of a conditional sentence (GKC, § 109 h). The apodosis uses וְיוֹסֶף, the Hiphil (H) jussive of יָסַף, “to increase, add.” (Its plural imperfect וְיוֹסִיפוּ is in 9:11.) For the segholate noun לֶקַח, “instruction, learning,” see the first textual note on 1:5.

9:10 תְּחִלַּת חָכְמָה יִרְאַת יְהוָה—Similar wording is in 1:7 (cf. also 15:33), but the noun תְּחִלָּה, "beginning," occurs only here in Proverbs.

וְדַעַת קְדֹשִׁים בִּינָה׃—For the noun in construct, see "דַּעַת, 'Knowledge,' and יָדַע, 'to Know' " in "Wisdom in Proverbs" in the introduction as well as the commentary on 1:4, 7. קְדֹשִׁים could be a plural of majesty or an intensive plural, "the *Most* Holy One" (see GKC, § 124 h; cf. Joüon, § 136 d, and Waltke-O'Connor, § 7.4.3b, including example 6). The identical construct phrase דַּעַת קְדֹשִׁים recurs in 30:3, though aside from 30:3 קָדוֹשׁ, "holy," never occurs elsewhere in Proverbs. For the predicate noun here, see "בִּינָה, 'Understanding,' and Related Words" in "Wisdom in Proverbs" in the introduction.

9:11 וְיוֹסִיפוּ לְּךָ שְׁנוֹת חַיִּים׃—The Hiphil (H) verb is, literally, "*they will add* to you years of life." However, the impersonal plural is best rendered as a passive (cf. Joüon, § 155 c), as in the translation above and in the LXX (προστεθήσεται), Vulgate, and Peshitta. The same verb (יוֹסִיפוּ) and construct phrase for "years of life" (שְׁנוֹת חַיִּים) is in a similar eschatological promise in 3:2, and another similar eschatological promise in 4:10 also uses the construct phrase.

9:12 The LXX contains a major expansion after 9:12 and before 9:13 warning of the consequences of lying.

אִם־חָכַמְתָּ חָכַמְתָּ לָּךְ—The sequence with a perfect verb (the first of the two occurrences of חָכַמְתָּ) in this line followed by *waw* attached to another perfect verb (וְלַצְתָּ) beginning the next line juxtaposes two contrasting situations: "if you are wise … , *but* if you *are a mocker* …" (Waltke-O'Connor, § 32.3c, including example 8). The preposition לְ is often used to express advantage (BDB, 5 g (*b*)). לָּךְ ("to your own advantage") is pausal for לְּךָ with conjunctive *daghesh.*

וְלַצְתָּ לְבַדְּךָ תִשָּׂא׃—The conditional particle אִם, "if," at the start of the first clause of the preceding line does double duty for the first clause of this line too (GKC, § 159 ff; Joüon, § 167 p). The verb לִיץ, "mock, scoff," is often used elsewhere in Proverbs in the form of a participle. See "לֵץ, 'Mocker,' and לָצוֹן, 'Mocking, Scoffing' " in "Fools in Proverbs" in the introduction. The verb נָשָׂא can mean "*bear* guilt, or punishment" (BDB, Qal, 2 b).

Commentary

The Integrity of Proverbs 9:7–12

This central section of the final poem on Wisdom (9:1–18) has been challenged by a number of scholars as a secondary insertion into the text. Some would delete parts of it, and others would rearrange the verses or transfer them elsewhere in this chapter or in the book.[1] Critical scholars usually note that one Hebrew manuscript is missing 9:9–10 while another is missing 9:10–12 and the LXX adds three novel verses after 9:12. Often they assert that the passages about Wisdom (9:1–6) and Foolishness (9:13–18) are obviously connected as contrasting parallels, while the intervening verses (9:7–12) disrupt the connection.

---

1 See, for example, Clifford, *Proverbs*, 101–3; Fox, "Who Can Learn?" 63–69; McKane, *Proverbs*, 368–69; Scott, *Proverbs, Ecclesiastes*, 76–77; Toy, *Proverbs*, 192–93; Whybray, *The Composition of the Book of Proverbs*, 45–48.

However, 9:7–12 contains a number of features that (1) exhibit the coherence of these verses as a section and that (2) demonstrate that this section of verses belongs here in the chapter as an original part of Proverbs 9 because this section (9:7–12) is connected to the preceding (9:1–6) and following (9:13–18) sections.[2]

To demonstrate the first point, note that 9:7–12 is held together chiastically, showing that it is a coherent section:

A לֵץ, "mocker" (9:7–8a)
 B חָכָם, "wise person" (9:8b–9a)
  C וְיוֹסֶף, "and he will add" (9:9b)
   D "The fear of Yahweh … understanding" (9:10)
  C' וְיוֹסִיפוּ, "will be added" (9:11)
 B' חָכַמְתָּ, "you are wise" (twice in 9:12a)
A' וְלַצְתָּ, "and [if] you mock" (9:12b)

Then one can cite at least three kinds of links between this section and the surrounding sections.

First, there are three cases of paronomasia (play on sound) that link this section (9:7–12) to the preceding section (9:1–6) and to the following section (9:13–18). Each of these involves a repetition that occurs in all three sections:

1. The repetition of the three consonants in יָסֻר (from the verb סוּר), "let him turn in," in 9:4, 16, is also found in יֹסֵר (from the verb יָסַר), "whoever corrects," in 9:7. (The whole of 9:4 is repeated in 9:16.)
2. The repetition of the initial consonant and vowel of לֵב, "heart," in 9:4, 16 is also found in לֵץ, "mocker," in 9:7.
3. The repetition of לוֹ, "to him(self), to someone" in 9:4, 7, and 16 (although translated differently in 9:7).

Second, 9:12 is linked to 9:13 by the chiastic arrangement of the consonants of the last word of 9:12, תִּשָּׂא, and the first word of 9:13, אֵשֶׁת. This forms the sequence תשא אשת.

Third, a larger-scale pattern is created by three terms for fools in Proverbs 9 and the order in which these three terms occur. In 9:1–6 the fool is introduced as פֶּתִי, "gullible (person)," in 9:4. Then in 9:7–12 the fool is introduced as לֵץ, "mocker," in 9:7–8. Finally, in 9:13–18 the fool is introduced as the woman כְּסִילוּת, "Foolishness" (9:13). These three terms, one in each section of chapter 9, are given in the same order as in Wisdom's first words in Proverbs. In 1:22, the terms for fools are, in order, פְּתָיִם, "gullible people," then לֵצִים, "mockers," and finally כְּסִילִים, "fools." Thus in Proverbs 1–9, the first poem about Wisdom (1:20–33) and the last poem about Wisdom (9:1–18) form an inclusio. However, this pattern would be ruined if 9:7–12 was eliminated from Proverbs 9.

---

2 Cf. Byargeon, "The Structure and Significance of Prov 9:7–12."

The Message of Proverbs 9:7–12

What, then, is the purpose of 9:7–12 and its placement between the banquets prepared by Wisdom (9:1–6) and by Foolishness (9:13–18)? These are the words of Wisdom that allow the gullible person to learn. The Holy Spirit works through Wisdom's words—the Word of God—so that even the most ignorant and uneducated person receives divine knowledge. This gift enables a person to make an informed choice to be wise and not to be foolish, that is, to choose Wisdom and to reject Foolishness, who are the two women in Proverbs 9. Conversion from unbelief to faith is, of course, not the result of human reason or free will; God alone can accomplish this.[3] Likewise, even after conversion, the believer's decision to heed Wisdom and ignore Foolishness is not the product of human willpower; rather, God alone works within the believer to enable God-pleasing decisions and actions (see, e.g., Phil 2:12–13).

Wisdom's first piece of advice is that when attempting to correct a person who is a complete fool, one should not expect success, but instead should expect resistance (9:7–8a). Obdurate unbelievers who have rejected God and his Wisdom will heap abuse on the believer who is trying to help them. However, the wise person, the one who has been enlightened by God's Wisdom, will receive her advice, which will keep him on the path of righteousness (9:8b–9).

The center of this section and of Proverbs 9 is the saying "the fear of Yahweh is the beginning of wisdom" (9:10). This mirrors the last verse in Solomon's introduction to the book (see the commentary on 1:7). Here "the fear of Yahweh" is then equated with "the knowledge of the Holy One" (9:10). This is not simple cognitive knowledge, but the knowledge coming from God's own self-revelation, knowledge received through the Word in faith—a positive relationship with God based on his grace and favor. Moreover, "the beginning of wisdom" is further connected with "understanding." The person who is wise will understand the differences between wisdom and foolishness, even though the differences are sometimes presented in this life in ways that are quite subtle. The discernment of their nuances can only come through the enlightenment offered by Wisdom (Rom 2:12; 1 Cor 2:14–15). This understanding is not an inherent quality in people; it is not naturally possessed by sinful humans. It is solely a gift from God in Jesus Christ, the preexistent Wisdom who would become incarnate.[4]

Once again Wisdom attaches a promise to those who take her advice (9:11). The phrase "because through me" (כִּי־בִ֭י, placed up front in the Hebrew of 9:11 for emphasis) signals that 9:7–12 consists not simply of sagacious words inserted into this chapter, but these words are also the words of Wisdom herself. Through Wisdom comes the promise of "life." The noun חַיִּים in 9:11 is cognate to the verb חָיָה, "to live," whose imperative, וִֽחְי֑וּ, was in 9:6. Thus once

---

[3] See, for example, Jn 15:16 and FC SD II, "Free Will or Human Powers."

[4] See "Wisdom in Proverbs" in the introduction. See also the commentary on 1:1–7; 3:13–20; 8:22–31; 30:1b–10; and the excursus "Proverbs 8, Wisdom, Christology, and the Arian Controversy" in the commentary on chapter 8.

again Wisdom is Christ, and those who eat at Wisdom's banquet have everlasting "life" (Jn 6:35; see the commentary on Prov 9:1–6).

This section is summarized in 9:12. The wise benefit from the wisdom given them by God (see FC Ep XI 5). Mockers, on the other hand, cannot blame God when they suffer for their sins, since they alone are responsible (see FC Ep XI 12).

Therefore, 9:7–12 serves as a hinge between the descriptions of Wisdom's banquet (9:1–6) and of the imitation banquet offered by Foolishness (9:13–18). This section sets forth principles that help the reader to distinguish between wisdom and foolishness in life, and it invites the reader to value Wisdom and her promise of eternal life.[5]

---

5 For the noun חַיִּים, "life," in the eschatological sense of everlasting life by God's grace, see also, for example, 3:2, 18, 22; 4:10, 13, 22–23. For the verb חָיָה, "to live," see the third textual note and the commentary on 4:4 as well as 7:2; 9:6; 15:27, verses in which it conveys the divine promise of everlasting life.

Proverbs 9:13–18

Lady Foolishness Invites Everyone to Her Banquet

Translation

9 **[13]The woman Foolishness is loud.**

[She is] gullibility, and she does not know anything.

[14]She sits at the doorway of her house,

on a throne on the heights in the city,

[15]in order to call to those who pass by on the street,

who go straight on their paths,

[16]"Whoever is gullible, let him turn in here."

And to someone who lacks sense she says,

[17]"Stolen waters are sweet,

and food eaten in secret is tasty."

[18]But he does not know that the souls of the dead are there,

that her guests are in the depths of Sheol.

Textual Notes

9:13 אֵשֶׁת כְּסִילוּת הֹמִיָּה—The construct phrase אֵשֶׁת כְּסִילוּת has an epexegetical genitive: "the woman of/*who is* Foolishness." The feminine noun כְּסִילוּת (with the abstract ending וּת-) occurs only here in the OT but is cognate to the common noun כְּסִיל. It signifies the essence of being a fool, hence, "Foolishness" (here personified). See "כְּסִיל, 'Fool,' and כְּסִילוּת, 'Foolishness' " in "Fools in Proverbs" in the introduction. The same Qal (G) feminine participle הֹמִיָּה, "be loud," describes the adulterous woman in 7:11.

פְּתַיּוּת—This is another feminine abstract noun ending in וּת- that occurs only in this verse, but the cognate adjective and noun פֶּתִי is common. See "פֶּתִי, 'Gullible Person' " in "Fools in Proverbs" in the introduction. The feminine noun signifies the essence of being gullible: "gullibility." There is no need to emend it to a more familiar form.[1] This form was chosen to match כְּסִילוּת in the preceding clause.

וּבַל־יָדְעָה מָּה׃—The adverb בַּל, "not," is a less common poetic synonym of לֹא. It occurs eight more times in Proverbs.[a] Usually מָה is an interrogative pronoun: "what?" But here it serves as an indefinite pronoun: "and she does not know *anything*" (see BDB, s.v. מָה, 3; GKC, § 137 c; and Joüon, § 144 f). Partly because of the difficult syntax, some

(a) Prov 10:30; 12:3; 14:7; 19:23; 22:29; 23:7, 35; 24:23

---

[1] Contra Garrett, *Proverbs, Ecclesiastes, Song of Songs*, 116, n. 194; McKane, *Proverbs*, 366–67; Scott, *Proverbs, Ecclesiastes*, 75; Toy, *Proverbs*, 191–92. These commentators and the note in *BHS* are unjustifiably skeptical of the form.

would emend מָה to כְּלִמָּה, "shame," on the basis of the LXX's αἰσχύνη.[2] However, a few other passages use מָה similarly (e.g., 2 Sam 18:22–23).

9:14 וְיָשְׁבָה—The perfect with *waw* consecutive continues the timeless statement of the noun clause in 9:13a ("… is loud"). It has an imperfective sense best rendered in the English present tense: "(and) she *sits*" (Waltke-O'Connor, 32.2.4a, including example 11).

עַל־כִּסֵּא מְרֹמֵי קָרֶת׃—The noun כִּסֵּא, "throne," recurs later in Proverbs only in royal contexts as the seat of the king (16:12; 20:8, 28; 25:5; 29:14). The identical construct phrase מְרֹמֵי קָרֶת, "the heights of/in the city," concludes 9:3.

9:15 הַמְיַשְּׁרִים אֹרְחוֹתָם׃—The Piel (D) of יָשַׁר has a causative meaning in 3:6 and 11:5, "make straight," but here, literally, "those making straight their [own] paths" can be rendered as "[those] going straightforward on their paths" (BDB, Piel, 1), as similarly in 15:21.

9:16 מִי־פֶתִי יָסֻר הֵנָּה—See the first textual note on 9:4 for this identical clause.

וַחֲסַר־לֵב וְאָמְרָה לּוֹ׃—See the second textual note on 9:4 for this clause. A *waw* is added here twice.

9:17 מַיִם־גְּנוּבִים יִמְתָּקוּ—"Water" (מַיִם, 5:15) and other water imagery in 5:17–18 is a metaphor for the conjugal relationship of marital intimacy. Here "water" that is "stolen" (גְּנוּבִים, the Qal passive [Gp] participle of גָּנַב, "steal") metaphorically represents adultery, as does the water imagery in 5:16. The Qal (G) of מָתֹק, "be sweet, pleasant," refers to water also in Ex 15:25, where a divine miracle caused the water to "become sweet," that is, potable. The verb occurs only here in Proverbs, but the cognate noun מֶתֶק, "sweetness," is found in 16:21 and 27:9.

וְלֶחֶם סְתָרִים יִנְעָם׃—The noun סֵתֶר means "secrecy" (BDB, 3). In the construct phrase here, it functions adverbially: "food of secrecy" means "food eaten *in secret*." The verb נָעֵם means "be pleasant" and can take on the sense "taste good" (*HALOT*, 2). For positive usages of the verb, see the second textual note on 2:10.

9:18 וְלֹא־יָדַע כִּי־רְפָאִים שָׁם—For רְפָאִים, see the second textual note on 2:18.

בְּעִמְקֵי שְׁאוֹל קְרֻאֶיהָ׃—The noun עֵמֶק, "depth," recurs in 25:3. For שְׁאוֹל, "Sheol," which is synonymous with everlasting death, see the first textual note and the commentary on 1:12. The suffix on the Qal passive (Gp) participle קְרֻאֶיהָ specifies the agent: "those called/invited by her" (see GKC, § 116 l), that is, "her guests."

The LXX contains a major expansion after 9:18 providing further exhortation not to drink the water offered by Foolishness.

Commentary

Solomon has presented Wisdom as the preexistent Christ.[3] He closes his third and final poem about Wisdom with a contrast to another woman,

---

2 E.g., Scott, *Proverbs, Ecclesiastes*, 75.

3 See "Wisdom in Proverbs" in the introduction. See also the commentary on 1:1–7; 3:13–20; 8:22–31; 30:1b–10; and the excursus "Proverbs 8, Wisdom, Christology, and the Arian Controversy" in the commentary on chapter 8.

Foolishness.[4] Like the adulteress in Proverbs 7, she is described as "loud" (הֹמִיָּה, 7:11; 9:13), which makes her the opposite of a quiet and godly wife (1 Pet 3:4; see also 1 Tim 2:12).[5] "Foolishness" (כְּסִילוּת) is further defined as "gullibility" (פְּתַיּוּת). This explains why individual "fools" (כְּסִלִים) can also be described as "gullible people" (פְּתָיִם); both terms are used in 1:22, 32 and 8:5. (The singular of "gullible" is in 9:16.) To reinforce the complete ignorance of "Foolishness," the introductory verse concludes by stating that "she does not know anything" (9:13).

The location of Foolishness as she sits "at the doorway of her house" (לְפֶתַח בֵּיתָהּ, 9:14) reminds the reader of the father's earlier warning to his son to avoid the adulteress and not to go "to/near the doorway of her house" (אֶל־פֶּתַח בֵּיתָהּ, 5:8). Yet despite her obvious flaws and similarity to the adulteress, Foolishness is also depicted as falsely imitating Wisdom. It is Wisdom who utters a blessing upon anyone who listens to her and waits attentively for her to come through the doorway of her house (see the commentary on 8:34), since she brings everlasting life and divine favor (8:35). Just as Wisdom calls from "the heights in the city" (מְרֹמֵי קָרֶת, 9:3), so also Foolishness calls out from "the heights in the city" (מְרֹמֵי קָרֶת, 9:14) to the passers by. However, whereas Wisdom is on "the highest of [עַל־גַּפֵּי] the heights in the city" (9:3), Foolishness is arrogantly "on a throne" (עַל־כִּסֵּא, 9:14) on the heights. This self-aggrandizement makes Foolishness look even more foolish (cf. Gen 11:4–9). Who is she to challenge God, and how can she think she will possibly escape judgment for her hubris?

Her call in Prov 9:16 is the same as Wisdom's call in 9:4 (the two verses are nearly identical in Hebrew). Despite the overt similarities between Foolishness and the adulteress, and the obvious differences in character between those two women and Wisdom, the initial words of Foolishness and Wisdom are hard to distinguish. Solomon is showing his readers that when we are confronted with choices in this life, it is not always easy to distinguish between the wise and the foolish, the godly choice and the sinful choice. On the surface they may, at least at first, appear almost the same. Only through the foresight that God can provide is a person able to discern the difference.[6] Note that Paul tells his readers that even Satan disguises himself as an angel of light (2 Cor 11:14).

The lure of Foolishness is the thrilling temptation to sin (Prov 9:17). "Stolen waters" may appear and even taste sweeter than wine, not because they have been mixed with care like the beverage at Wisdom's banquet (9:2, 5), but because of the way they are obtained. Her offer of "stolen waters" has sexual

---

[4] Proverbs 1–9 contains ten addresses from a father to his son along with three poems about Wisdom: (1) 1:20–33; (2) 8:1–36; and (3) 9:1–18. See the excursus "Proverbs 1–9, Christ, and the Ten Commandments" in the commentary on chapter 1.

[5] See also the contrasts between Wisdom and the adulteress highlighted in the excursus "Wisdom and the Adulteress in Proverbs 1–9" in the commentary on chapter 2.

[6] See "מְזִמָּה, 'Insight, Foresight,' " in "Wisdom in Proverbs" in the introduction.

overtones. In the context of 5:15, 17–19 water imagery is used to describe sexual fulfillment within the holy estate of marriage, which God desires to be intoxicating for the spouses. In this case the imagery of "stolen waters" indicates the illicit nature of the sexual liaison envisioned in Foolishness' words. This is in direct contrast to the sexual relationship within marriage, which is described as drinking one's own water (5:15). "Food eaten in secret" (לֶחֶם סְתָרִים, 9:17) is another expression that carries overtones of sin. It recalls the sin of joining the unrighteous in their schemes to obtain "food" from wickedness (לֶחֶם, 4:17), and the "food" involved in committing adultery (לָחֶם, 6:26).

The implications of this veiled sexual imagery is used here not only to reinforce what has been said throughout Proverbs 1–9 about the dangers of sexual sins, but also to remind the reader once again of Scripture's frequent use of sexual unfaithfulness as a metaphor for unfaithfulness to God.[7] To follow Foolishness is to abandon Christ, the Wisdom of God. The result is eternal death (9:18; see also the commentary on 2:16–19).

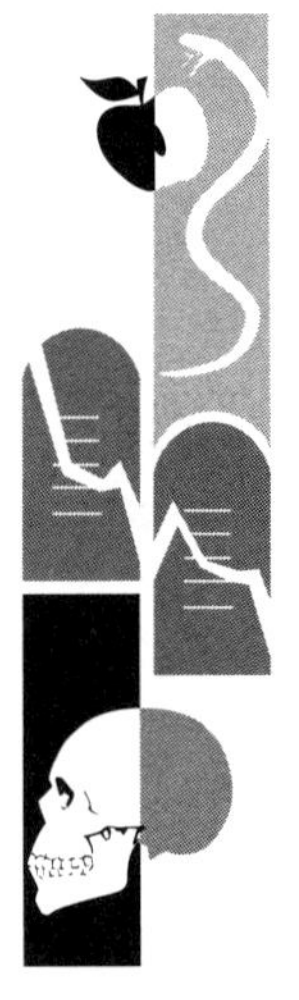

The seduced fool who joins Foolishness in her banquet is as ignorant as she is: "he does not know" (9:18), just as "she does not know" (9:13). He doesn't understand the everlasting consequences of entering her house, which are the opposite of the everlasting benefits of Wisdom's supper (to "live," 9:6). This matches Paul's description of the Gentiles who do not know Christ:

> Therefore I say this and testify in the Lord, that you must no longer walk as the Gentiles walk in the futility of their minds, being darkened in their understanding, alienated from the life of God because of the ignorance that is in them, due to the hardness of their heart. They have become callous and have given themselves up to sensuality, unto the practice of every kind of uncleanness with greed. (Eph 4:17–19)

Foolishness brings unending death, in contrast to the everlasting life that Wisdom offers (Prov 9:6, 11). The description of Foolishness' banquet as the dwelling place of "the souls of the dead" (רְפָאִים, 9:18) is eerily reminiscent of the house of the adulteress in 2:18–19 (the word translated as "the souls of the dead," רְפָאִים, is in 2:18). This echo that reverberates across Proverbs 1–9 is a powerful use of the Law as a curb on sinful behavior as it utilizes the greatest of human fears to discourage the foolishness of rejecting Wisdom's offer. The contrast between Wisdom and Foolishness here is the same stark contrast stated in plain words by Paul in Romans:

> The wages of sin is death, but the gift of God is eternal life in Christ Jesus our Lord. (Rom 6:23)

---

[7] See the excursus "Wisdom and the Adulteress in Proverbs 1–9" in the commentary on Proverbs 2.

Proverbs 10:1–22:16

More of Solomon's Proverbs

Excursus — *The Organization of the Sayings in Solomon's Proverbs in Proverbs 10:1–22:16*

Excursus — *The Metaphor of the Path in Solomon's Wisdom*

10:1–12:28 A Wise Son: Introduction to Wisdom and Righteousness

10:1–5 Introduction to Wisdom and Righteousness, Which Saves the Wise Son from Death

10:6–23 Proverbs about the Use of the Mouth

10:24–32 Contrast between the Righteous and the Wicked

Excursus *"Disgusting Thing"* (תּוֹעֵבָה) *in Solomon's Proverbs*

11:1–31 Righteous Behavior, Part 1

12:1–28 Righteous Behavior, Part 2

13:1–15:19 A Wise Son: Wise Ways to Live

13:1–25 Wise Ways to Live, Part 1

14:1–35 Wise Ways to Live, Part 2

15:1–19 Wise Ways to Live, Part 3

15:20–17:24 Advice to a Wise Son

15:20–16:7 Advice to a Wise Son, Part 1

16:8–24 Wisdom for a King and His Subjects

16:25–17:6 Advice to a Wise Son, Part 2

17:7–24 Introduction to Fools and Foolishness: The Consequences of Being a Fool

17:25–19:12 A Foolish Son: Avoiding Fools and Foolishness

17:25–18:24 Avoiding Fools and Foolishness, Part 1

19:1–12 Avoiding Fools and Foolishness, Part 2

19:13–22:16 A Foolish Son: Dealing with Fools and Foolishness

19:13–29	Dealing with Fools, Part 1
20:1–30	Dealing with Fools, Part 2
21:1–31	Wise and Foolish Behaviors, Part 1
22:1–16	Wise and Foolish Behaviors, Part 2

Excursus

The Organization of the Sayings in Solomon's Proverbs in Proverbs 10:1–22:16

The contrasts between Proverbs 1–9 and the proverbs of Solomon that begin in chapter 10 are so obvious that virtually every reader immediately notices the differences. Both collections are labeled at their beginning as "the proverbs of Solomon" (מִשְׁלֵי שְׁלֹמֹה in both 1:1 and 10:1), and that ascription of authorship is often used by scholars as a title for one or both of the collections.[1] However, Proverbs 1–9 contains longer poems that are deliberately organized according to an overarching theme.[2] In contrast, in 10:1–22:16 it is virtually impossible to find a saying that is longer than two lines of poetry. Moreover, one is hard pressed to find some overall plan of organization for these sayings. While some adjacent proverbs seem to share a common theme, the overall impression, especially when 10:1–22:16 is read in translation, is that they skip from topic to topic almost randomly. To make sense of this collection, several commentaries include a topical index of these sayings.[3] However, the lack of obvious organization has led some commentators to view this collection as a mostly haphazard compilation in which the context (adjacent sayings and larger sections) contributes almost nothing of value for the interpretation of the individual sayings.[4]

Despite this seeming disorganization, there is a growing consensus among scholars that these proverbs are not a random collection. There are at least four kinds of evidence for their organization based on small-scale features in nearby proverbs. Moreover, there are at least three kinds of evidence for large-scale organizational schemes.

Small-Scale Evidence for Organization in Proverbs 10:1–22:16

First, one may note the presence of paronomasia (a play on sounds) that binds some proverbs to their neighbors. For instance, 14:19–22 is bound

---

1 This commentary's view is that both of these collections were authored by Solomon himself. See "Authorship and Date," including figure 1, in the introduction.

2 Proverbs 1–9 contains ten addresses from a father to his son along with three poems about Wisdom: (1) 1:20–33; (2) 8:1–36; and (3) 9:1–18. The ten addresses expound the Ten Commandments. See the excursus "Proverbs 1–9, Christ, and the Ten Commandments" in the commentary on chapter 1.

3 E.g., Ross, "Proverbs," 897–903; Scott, *Proverbs, Ecclesiastes*, 130–31.

4 Kidner, *Proverbs*, 22–23; McKane, *Proverbs*, 413.

together by the similar-sounding words רַע, *raʿ*, "evil" (14:19, 22), and רֵעַ, *reaʿ*, "neighbor" (14:20–21).

Second, catchwords sometimes are used to form groups of proverbs.[5] For example, 16:27–29 forms a group because each of the three Hebrew verses begins with אִישׁ, "a person." In addition, all three of these proverbs deal with evil speech, in contrast to a preceding group of four proverbs (16:21–24) that deals with wise speech.

Third, the rhetorical device of chiasm is used to unite some proverbs to one another. For example, 10:2 is linked to 10:3 by the chiasm "wickedness, righteousness; righteous, wicked" (see the commentary on 10:3).

Fourth, occasionally several proverbs share a common motif. One example is 10:6–23, in which most proverbs contain some reference to the use of one's mouth.

Large-Scale Evidence for Organization in Proverbs 10:1–22:16

Some larger organizational schemes can be observed in this collection.[6] A first observation is about the predominant kind of parallelism, which is related to the usual message or theme. Proverbs 10–15 contains mostly antithetical parallelism,[7] and the usual message is to contrast wise behavior with foolish behavior. On the other hand, 16:1–22:16 mostly uses either synonymous parallelism or synthetic parallelism,[8] and the usual message is to emphasize the relationship between character and its consequence or between action and its consequence. After the 184 verses in Proverbs 10–15, this change in the predominant type of parallelism takes place in 16:1. Figure 11 uses a line with diamonds to show the steep rise in the number of verses using antithetical parallelism in chapters 10–15, and then that number levels off in 16:1–22:16. Conversely, the line with squares shows the low number of verses using synonymous and synthetic parallelism in chapters 10–15, but then that line rises dramatically in 16:1–22:16. By 22:16, the two lines nearly meet, showing that in all of 10:1–22:16 the total number of verses using antithetical parallelism is about equal to the total number of verses using synonymous or synthetic parallelism.

5 Many of these are cataloged in Murphy, *Wisdom Literature*, 68–74.

6 See Clifford, *Proverbs*, 108; Goldingay, "The Arrangement of Sayings in Proverbs 10–15"; Murphy on Proverbs in Murphy and Huwiler, *Proverbs, Ecclesiastes, Song of Songs*, 47, 79.

7 In antithetical parallelism the message of the first parallel line is the opposite of or directly contrasts with the message of the second line in the parallelism.

8 In synonymous parallelism each of the two parallel lines conveys essentially the same message, although usually in different words. In synthetic parallelism, the second line expands on, explains, or completes the message begun in the first line, so that the two lines must be read together in order to understand the message of the whole verse.

Figure 11

Predominant Kinds of Parallelism in Proverbs 10:1–22:16

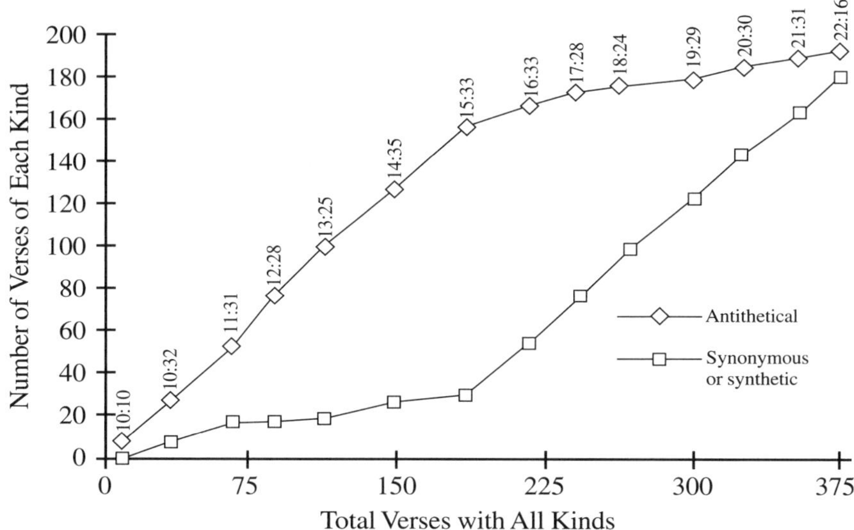

This organization is for didactic purposes: these proverbs move from easier sayings to more difficult ones. The proverbs that use antithetical parallelism are generally easier to understand because of the sharp contrasts they employ. Most of these antithetical proverbs were placed first in the collection to initiate the readers into the important thoughts and theological themes of wisdom, allowing them to learn to interpret and apply wisdom sayings. After readers have learned the basic wisdom teachings, the more difficult proverbs that employ synonymous and synthetic parallelism are presented later in the collection.

A second large-scale indication of organization in 10:1–22:16 is the distribution of certain vocabulary words. Proverbs 10–15 uses "righteous" (צַדִּיק) thirty-nine times, but it occurs in the later section (16:1–22:16) only ten times. Proverbs using "Yahweh" (יהוה) are clustered in Proverbs 15–16, on either side of the border (16:1) between these two sections. In 10:1–22:16, twenty of the fifty-five sayings that use יהוה (that is, thirty-six percent of the total) are in these two chapters (Proverbs 15–16).

A third large-scale organizational scheme present in the collection of Solomon's proverbs in 10:1–22:16 is related to the organization of Proverbs 1–9. Those nine chapters were largely organized around Solomon's ten addresses to his son.[9] Likewise, the proverbs in 10:1–22:16 can be seen as making use of

[9] Proverbs 1–9 contains ten addresses from a father to his son along with three poems about Wisdom: (1) 1:20–33; (2) 8:1–36; and (3) 9:1–18. The ten addresses expound the Ten Commandments. See the excursus "Proverbs 1–9, Christ, and the Ten Commandments" in the commentary on chapter 1.

strategically placed proverbs about "a wise son" (בֵּן חָכָם) or "a foolish son" (בֵּן כְּסִיל). One can organize 10:1–22:16 into the following sections, each headed by a proverb about a wise son or a foolish son, and the entire collection begins with a proverb that refers to both "a wise son" and "a foolish son" (10:1). See the chart that makes up the first part of figure 12.

As indicated in the column about the number of sayings in each section, the proverbs that speak of "a wise son" and/or "a foolish son" do not mark off sections of exactly the same size. Nevertheless, these proverbs are fairly evenly distributed in 10:1–22:16 as shown the diagram that comprises the second part of figure 12.

This diagram makes evident an approximately linear increase in the total number of verses as the reader progresses through each of the sections in 10:1–22:16. This linear increase suggests that the author had an organizational scheme that tied these sayings to Proverbs 1–9. Solomon addressed his "son" (and sometimes "sons") in Proverbs 1–9 with focused, coherent, and lengthy units of verses, and now he offers more general and diffuse counsel that pertains to any wise or foolish "son." While the sections in 10:1–22:16 are much looser, the references to a "son"[10] connect them to the tighter sections in Proverbs 1–9. However, since the increase shown in the diagram is not strictly linear, the organization of sections in 10:1–22:16 probably was not intended to be precise or formal, but flexible and informal. The proverbs about a wise or foolish son were placed less by a conscious decision to adhere to a mathematical formula than by the author's intuition.

Conclusion

That there are some deliberate editorial groups of sayings in 10:1–22:16 is, therefore, without question. However, one cannot find in this part of the book a tightly organized overall structure such as was in Proverbs 1–9. Instead, these sayings were compiled so that the reader could ponder them individually and in relation to one another and then draw any number of inferences with abundant connections to many other sayings. They are not intended, therefore, to be outlined in a one-dimensional, unidirectionally linear fashion, but to be studied in several dimensions, with connections reaching out in many different directions.

Therefore, the evidence suggests that Solomon wants readers to have a somewhat continuous and seamless reading of these short, self-contained sayings. The proverbs stand as individual sayings but simultaneously flow, sometimes easily, at other times with more turbulence, from one into another from the beginning in 10:1 to the end in 22:16. Links within shorter spans invite readers to contemplate these proverbs with regard for their immediate context.

---

[10] This connection is reinforced by the use of "son" twice in 10:1 and twice in 10:5, forming an inclusio around the first passage of 10:1–22:16. See the commentary on 10:1–5.

At the same time, the proverbs that repeat words and lines from earlier proverbs invite the reader to read cross-contextually. Simultaneously, the proverbs about a wise or foolish "son" invite the reader to compare the short individual units with the longer, extended discussions in Proverbs 1–9 addressed by Solomon to his "son" (or "sons").

This loose, but purposeful, organization makes context less reliable for interpreting individual proverbs than it would be for interpreting other, more tightly organized literature. Nevertheless, context is not completely lacking as a guide. Sayings were attached to one another not only because of literary features, but also because of thematic and semantic characteristics. Therefore, one must be careful to examine the surrounding sayings to see how they shed light on a particular proverb. This is especially true of repeated proverbs (e.g., 14:12 ‖ 16:25). Like all proverbs in all languages, they can take on varied applications in different situations. This is, perhaps, one reason some sayings are repeated: they exhibit different nuances in association with different sayings.

No outline can succinctly capture the arrangement of the sayings here, nor can any one scheme explain all the anomalies in organization found in these proverbs of Solomon.[11] The best one can do is offer a scheme to make some sense of the organization while realizing at the same time that these sayings are not as tightly organized as is narrative. This looser organization is characteristic of Wisdom writing. Note, for instance, the ongoing debate about the structure of each of the two other canonical Wisdom books by Solomon: Ecclesiastes and the Song of Songs.

The outline presented in this commentary is not intended to be an exhaustive or definitive outline of this section. Instead it notes that the general organizational features of 10:1–22:16 are parallel to the tighter organization of Proverbs 9 that immediately precedes it.

The first half (10:1–17:6) with its mainly antithetical parallelism is advice for wise behavior, parallel to the invitation of the woman Wisdom to her banquet in 9:1–6. The proverbs in chapters 15–16, though still about wise behavior, signal a transition with their concentration of sayings about Yahweh. They are approximately parallel to the middle section (9:7–12) in Proverbs 9, which centers on "the fear of Yahweh" (9:10). The second half (17:7–22:16) of these proverbs mainly consists of warnings against foolishness, and so it is roughly parallel to the invitation of the woman Foolishness to her banquet in 9:13–18.

Within that broad outline, smaller sections begin with proverbs that speak of "a wise son" (בֵּן חָכָם) or "a foolish son" (בֵּן כְּסִיל), in imitation of Solomon's addresses to his "son" (and "sons") in Proverbs 1–9.

---

[11] Contrary to the efforts of Hildebrandt, "Proverbial Strings" and "Proverbial Pairs," or Heim, *Like Grapes of Gold Set in Silver.*

Figure 12

Sections in Proverbs 10:1–22:16 That Start with a Saying about a Wise or a Foolish Son

Section	*A Wise or a Foolish Son*	*Number of Sayings*
10:1–12:28	A wise son and a foolish son (10:1)	91
13:1–15:19	A wise son (13:1)	79
15:20–17:24	A wise son (15:20)	71
17:25–19:12	A foolish son (17:25)	40
19:13–22:16	A foolish son (19:13)	94

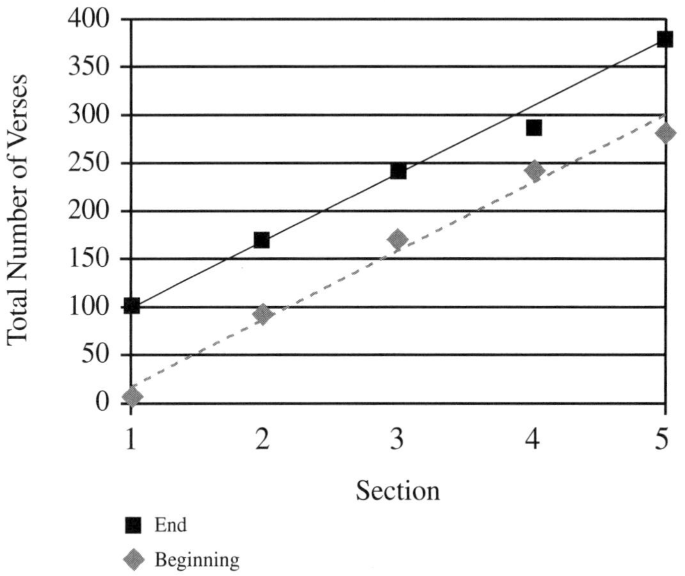

Total Number of Verses

400
350
300
250
200
150
100
50
0

1 2 3 4 5

Section

■ End
◆ Beginning

Excursus

The Metaphor of the Path in Solomon's Wisdom

Perhaps the most common metaphor employed in Proverbs is the metaphor of the path. This metaphor uses a path or road to describe the faith and resulting conduct that characterize one's way of life. Hebrew nouns for "way," "path," or "road" occur in 82 of Proverbs' 915 verses, that is, in 9% of the verses in the book. Nearly all of the occurrences of these words are in this metaphorical sense.[1] The nouns and their distribution in Proverbs are shown in figure 13.

Figure 13

Nouns for "Way, Path" and Their Distribution in Proverbs

Noun	*Translations**	*Occurrences in Proverbs*	*Occurrences in the OT*	*Percent in Proverbs*
אֹרַח	path, course	19	57	33%
דֶּרֶךְ	way, road, street, trip	75	706	11%
מְסִלָּה	highway	1	27	4%
מַעְגָּל	pathway, track	7	16	44%
נְתִיבָה	pathway	6	21	29%

* These are the translations used for these words in this commentary.

All of these nouns occur more often in Proverbs than in an average passage of the OT as a whole.[2] The most common noun used in the metaphor of the path, דֶּרֶךְ, is more frequently used in Proverbs than any other book of the

[1] Only a few occurrences could arguably be excluded since they use these words in what may be a literal sense (although a metaphorical sense is often possible too). For example, 7:8 refers to a man crossing a "street" near the corner of an adulteress and traveling on the "road" to her house, where she invites him in with the assurance that her husband has gone away on a "long trip" (7:19).

[2] Proverbs contains 6,967 Hebrew words (separately written vocables). The OT contains 308,678 Hebrew words. Thus Proverbs is 2.25% of the OT by word count. However, all of the nouns listed in the chart have a higher percentage of occurrences in Proverbs than the expected average of 2.25% for all words. (While the one occurrence of מְסִלָּה in Proverbs comprises 4% of the total occurrences in the OT, a single instance is not statistically significant.)

OT except Ezekiel.[3] Clearly the metaphor of the path is an important figure of speech in Proverbs. This is especially true of the Solomonic sections of the book. The five nouns used in the metaphor are used in seventy-six verses in the sections attributed to Solomon (1:1–22:16; 25:1–29:27), but in the non-Solomonic sections (22:17–24:34; chapters 30–31), three of the five nouns do not occur at all, and the other two occur in only six verses.[4]

Therefore, this metaphor is especially important to Solomon's wisdom. It is most prominent in 1:1–22:16, the first two Solomonic portions of Proverbs (chapters 1–9 and 10:1–22:16).[5]

By means of this metaphor, Solomon was able to balance Law and Gospel in his sayings.[6]

Law Expressed by the Metaphor of the Path

When treating the Law—God's judgment against human sin, which deserves nothing but punishment and death—Solomon shows the negative implications of a sinful path. This kind of path is characterized as evil (2:12; 8:13); crooked, devious, and wandering (2:15; 5:6; 10:9; 14:2); dark (2:13; 4:19); disgusting to Yahweh (15:9); and full of thorns and snares (15:19; 22:5). It leads to everlasting death and Sheol (2:18; 7:27; 14:12; 16:25). Those who frequent such paths are described as wicked and evil (4:14, 19; 12:26; 15:9), arrogant (8:13), crooked (2:15), greedy (1:19), lazy (15:19), stupid (19:3), treacherous (13:15), violent (3:31; 16:29), and stubborn fools (12:15). These are people who speak perverse things (2:12; 8:13), who despise God (14:2), and who abandon upright paths (2:13).

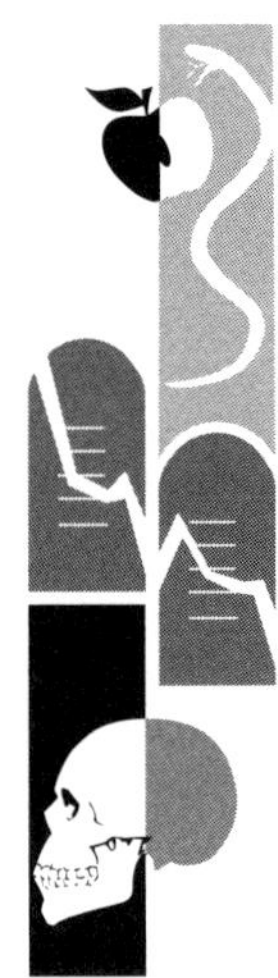

These contexts with the metaphor of the path allow Solomon to proclaim the Law with all three of its uses. First, it can act as a curb and a deterrent to prevent people from carrying out sinful behavior, as when he warns that the evil path is harmful, causing people to stumble (4:19), presenting danger (15:19; 22:5) and leading them to death (1:19; 2:18; 7:27; 16:25; 21:16). No sensible person would want to meet this end.

Second, this metaphor allows Solomon to use the Law as a mirror to help others recognize their own sin. The path subtly depicts one's own sinful urges,

---

[3] דֶּרֶךְ is used 107 times in Ezekiel, the only book where it is used more often than in Proverbs. However, since Ezekiel (18,912 words) is a much longer book than Proverbs (6,967 words), דֶּרֶךְ is used with almost twice the frequency in Proverbs. Occurrences of דֶּרֶךְ comprise 1.08% of all the words in Proverbs, whereas in Ezekiel they comprise only 0.57% of all the words.

[4] In the non-Solomonic sections, אֹרַח occurs once (22:25), and דֶּרֶךְ occurs eight times (23:19, 26; 30:19 [four times]; 30:20; 31:3). These nine occurrences are 0.76% of the 1,183 words in the non-Solomonic sections. These same two nouns are used ninety-nine times in the portions of the book attributed to Solomon; they are 1.71% of the 5,784 words in those sections.

[5] In chapters 25–29, which consist of proverbs from Solomon edited by Hezekiah's men, the word דֶּרֶךְ is used five times and the four other nouns are not used at all. Unlike Solomon himself, the Hezekian editors of this section of Solomon's proverbs did not often include proverbs that use the metaphor of the way.

[6] See further "Law and Gospel in Proverbs" in the introduction.

and a reader can see that he or she has already, at times, taken some steps down this path. Thus 3:31 reminds readers of their own envy when it admonishes:

> Do not envy a violent person,
> and do not choose any of his ways.

And 10:9 moves those who consider it to look at their own secret sins when it says:

> Whoever walks with integrity walks securely,
> but whoever makes his ways crooked will be found out.

In addition, in 5:6 the adulteress is characterized as being on the evil path, perhaps without even knowing how bad her way of life is:

> She does not make the path of life level.
> Her pathways wander, and she doesn't realize it.

Those who think about these statements are led to consider times when they have been like the adulteress. Readers recall instances when they did not consider the path of life, when they acted out their sinful impulses, when they wandered into sin. At the time they may not have even realized what they were doing and their culpability before God. In this way the warning about the adulteress is more than a warning about breaking the Sixth Commandment; it is also a warning about the insidious nature of all sin and the self-destructive foolishness that the adulteress represents.[7]

At times this accusing feature of the Law is made explicit by contrasting sinful behavior to a better way or to God's way:

> Go to the ant, lazybones!
> Observe its ways and become wise. (6:6)

> The way of a wicked person is a disgusting thing to Yahweh,
> but he loves those who pursue righteousness. (15:9)

Moreover, since all people are sinful and sin clouds one's own process of self-evaluation, no one is able to comprehend the enormity of his own iniquity:

> All of a person's ways are pure in his own eyes,
> but Yahweh weighs motives. (16:2)

> There is a way that appears to be correct to a person,
> but its end is the way of death. (16:25)

These accusatory proverbs are intended to drive the reader to repent because each has already walked down the path of evil, even if one has tried to justify past actions or is unaware of the extent of his own errors. This imparts an awareness of one's own guilt, which merits divine judgment. This is intended to move

---

7 See the excursus "Wisdom and the Adulteress in Proverbs 1–9" in the commentary on Proverbs 2. Regarding the Sixth Commandment, see also the excursus "Proverbs 1–9, Christ, and the Ten Commandments" in the commentary on Proverbs 1.

the reader to repent and acknowledge his or her need for forgiveness, salvation by grace alone, and everlasting life (see, e.g., 8:35).

Finally, the metaphor of the path can serve the third use of the Law, namely, to teach and guide the believer in godly living. This can be accomplished both by the proverbs that depict the blessings of walking on God's path and by those that portray the dangers of straying down other pathways. Some proverbs overtly depict the Law as a guide for those to whom God grants knowledge and life by the Gospel:

> Then you will understand righteousness, justice, and uprightness—
> every good pathway. (2:9)

> For a command is a lamp,
> and teaching is a light,
> and warnings coming from discipline are a road of life. (6:23)

Gospel Expressed by the Metaphor of the Path

In contrast to the evil path, the righteous path of the Gospel does not originate from human impulses, but belongs to God, since his way is from eternity past (8:22–31; cf. 3:19–20). The ability to walk on this path is a gift from God, received through faith, that is, simple trust in God (3:4–6; 10:29). This path is the path of the Wisdom of God (3:17; 8:20), who is Christ.[8] This godly path is characterized as straight and level (3:6; 4:26; 9:15; 11:5), upright (4:11), having justice (2:8), possessing and leading to life (2:19; 5:6; 6:23; 10:17; 12:28; 15:24), having righteousness (8:20; 12:28; 16:31), bringing peace (3:17), creating understanding (9:6), enabling wise judgment (21:16), and having wisdom (4:11). Since this path originates from God and is purely a gift from God to each believer, it is not a product of the human will (16:9; 20:24). Note the picturesque way in which the path of righteous people is depicted as coming to them without their aid and independent of their will, just like the rising of the sun:

> But the path of righteous people is like the light of dawn,
> shining brighter until the day is established. (4:18)

Therefore Proverbs teaches that salvation is by grace alone; no synergism, human cooperation, decision, or freedom of will is involved.[9] While verses from Proverbs are often cited by those who advocate semi-Pelagian theology, the larger context of the whole book shows that redemption is purely God's own work. However, it is possible for people to exercise their will in order to

---

8 See further "Wisdom in Proverbs" in the introduction. See also the commentary on 1:1–7; 3:13–20; 8:22–31; 30:1b–10; and the excursus "Proverbs 8, Wisdom, Christology, and the Arian Controversy" in the commentary on Proverbs 8.

9 In the course of presenting the doctrine of justification by grace alone, the Lutheran confessors cite verses from Proverbs in, for example, Ap IV 240–43, 327, and FC Ep III 7 and FC SD III 17.

reject God and his Gospel.[10] Even believers, now saved through faith, have the option to leave this path and forfeit the gift of everlasting salvation, so they are urged not to abandon it (2:11–13, 20; 10:17; 15:10).

Those who are on the godly path are accounted righteous (2:20; 4:18; 12:26), upright (14:2; 15:19; 16:17; 21:29), and good (2:20). Since they are empowered by the Gospel, God's work of sanctification is evident in their lives: they practice discipline (10:17), are given insight (15:24), have integrity (11:5, 20; 13:6), are prudent (14:8), please God (16:7), and make their paths level (4:26).

Solomon often uses the metaphor of the path as a means to make more vivid the promises of the Gospel, both temporal and eternal:

> [Yahweh is] a shield for those who walk in integrity,
> to protect [those who walk on] paths of justice.
> He guards the ways of his godly ones. (2:7–8)
>
> Then you will go safely on your way,
> and you will not stub your toe. (3:23)
>
> The way of Yahweh is a fortress for the person of integrity. (10:29a)
>
> In the path of righteousness [there is] life,
> and the way of its pathway is no death. (12:28)
>
> Righteousness guards the person whose way has integrity. (13:6a)
>
> The path of life leads upward for a person with insight,
> so that he may turn away from Sheol below. (15:24)
>
> When Yahweh is pleased with a man's ways,
> he makes even his enemies to be at peace with him. (16:7)
>
> Gray hair is a beautiful crown.
> It is found in the way of righteousness. (16:31)

Other times the metaphor of the path is used as the invitation of the Gospel to repentance, faith, and trust:

> In all your ways acknowledge him,
> and he will make your paths straight. (3:6)
>
> Make a level pathway for your feet,
> and all your ways will be secure. (4:26)
>
> Abandon gullibility, and live.
> Travel the road to understanding. (9:6)

Ultimately these are eschatological promises. The path of faith and knowledge of God leads through and beyond death (10:2; 11:4; 12:28; 13:14) to everlasting life in God's presence. These promises will be fulfilled by the power of Christ's own resurrection from the dead, which guarantees the promise of

[10] See further FC Ep and SD II, "Free Will."

resurrection to eternal life for all who believe. Jesus himself is "the way" (Jn 14:4–6), and his Gospel is the "way" of salvation (e.g., Mt 7:14; Lk 1:79; Acts 16:17; 18:25–26). Hence the Christian faith and the church of Christ can also be called "the Way" (Acts 19:9, 23; 22:4; 24:14, 22).

That eschatological perspective helps explain why the metaphor of the path is a constant and vivid figure of speech throughout Solomon's proverbs. It is Solomon's way of applying both Law and Gospel to bring others to the Wisdom of God: Christ, who leads them on the path of righteousness so that they will dwell with their Lord forever (Ps 23:3, 6).

Proverbs 10:1–5

Introduction to Wisdom and Righteousness, Which Saves the Wise Son from Death

Translation

10 **[1]The proverbs of Solomon:**
A wise son brings joy to [his] father,
but a foolish son brings grief to his mother.
[2]Treasures gained by wickedness are not profitable,
but righteousness saves from death.
[3]Yahweh will not allow a righteous person to starve,
but he frustrates the desire of wicked people.
[4]Lazy hands make poverty,
but hardworking hands bring riches.
[5]Whoever gathers in summer is a son with insight.
Whoever sleeps at harvest time is a disgraceful son.

Textual Notes

10:1 מִשְׁלֵי שְׁלֹמֹה—This title at the beginning of 10:1 is repeated from 1:1; see the first textual note on 1:1. However, in 10:1 the title is missing from the LXX, the Syriac, and some manuscripts of the Vulgate. Instead of weakening the assertion that these sayings are from Solomon, this omission may have been part of the LXX editor's scheme to strengthen it.[1] See also "Authorship and Date" in the introduction, which argues that the repeated title ascribes the authorship of both chapters 1–9 and of 10:1–22:16 to Solomon himself.

בֵּן חָכָם יְשַׂמַּח־אָב—This statement about any (indefinite) "wise son" (בֵּן חָכָם) is a more general form of teaching than Solomon's earlier addresses specifically to "my son" (בְּנִי in, e.g., 1:8, 10). The Piel (D) of שָׂמַח has the causative meaning "to cause [someone] to be joyful/rejoice" as compared to the stative meaning of the Qal (G), "to rejoice" (e.g., 5:18). The Piel recurs in 12:25; 15:20, 30; 27:9, 11; 29:3.

The imperfect יְשַׂמַּח and the following nominal clause both are best translated as English present tense ("brings") to indicate repeated, habitual, or durative action. See Waltke-O'Connor, § 31.3e, including example 13, and Joüon, § 113 c.

וּבֵן כְּסִיל תּוּגַת אִמּוֹ׃—This nominal sentence is, literally, "a foolish son [is] the grief of his mother." Most translations render it with a verb. The noun תּוּגָה, "grief (caused by suffering)" is from the verb יָגָה, "to suffer." The noun recurs in 14:13 and 17:21.

---

1 Washington, *Wealth and Poverty*, 126–27.

10:2 לֹא־יוֹעִילוּ אוֹצְרוֹת רֶשַׁע—The verb יָעַל recurs only in 11:4, where too the Hiphil (H) imperfect, "to be profitable, beneficial; to avail," is negated in an eschatological statement about the ultimate uselessness of wealth. The construct chain אוֹצְרוֹת רֶשַׁע expresses a genitive of source: "treasures of/gained by wickedness."

וּצְדָקָה תַּצִּיל מִמָּוֶת׃—The identical clause is repeated in 11:4, and a similar statement is in 11:6. For the noun צְדָקָה, "righteousness" imputed through faith for Christ's sake, and for related vocabulary, see "The Relationship between Wisdom and Righteousness in Proverbs" in the introduction. The feminine noun is the subject of the feminine Hiphil (H) imperfect (תַּצִּיל) of נָצַל, "to save, rescue, deliver," for which, see the first textual note on 2:12. In this context it certainly has an eschatological meaning, as does מָוֶת, everlasting "death" in both a physical and a spiritual sense. "To save from death" is synonymous with the gift of everlasting life (e.g., 3:18; 4:4; 7:2; 8:35; 9:6, 11).

10:3 לֹא־יַרְעִיב יְהוָה נֶפֶשׁ צַדִּיק—The Hiphil (H) of a stative verb could have a causative meaning, but both OT occurrences of the Hiphil (H) of רָעֵב, "to be hungry," have the tolerative nuance, "to let, allow (someone) to be hungry," as in Deut 8:3, where too Yahweh is the subject. The noun נֶפֶשׁ can refer to the "appetite" (see BDB, 5 a) when used with verbs of hunger or satiety, but this need not be reflected in English, and the construct phrase נֶפֶשׁ צַדִּיק can simply be translated as "a righteous person."

וְהַוַּת רְשָׁעִים יֶהְדֹּף׃—The parallelism implies that God is spoiling the plans of wicked people. The noun הַוָּה can mean "destruction, disaster" (as in 17:4; 19:13), and when it means "desire," it always has an evil connotation, as here and when it recurs in 11:6. The verb הָדַף literally means "to push away" (*HALOT*), but for its idiomatic use here, "frustrate" works well (cf. ESV, NIV, NRSV).

10:4 רָאשׁ עֹשֶׂה כַף־רְמִיָּה—The challenging syntax is, literally, "he becomes poor working [with] a hand of laziness." רָאשׁ is the Qal (G) participle of רוּשׁ or רִישׁ, "to be/become poor, in need." This verb occurs mainly in Proverbs, where its most common use is as a Qal participle,[a] usually used substantively: "poor (man, person)." The Hithpolel (HtD) participle occurs once (13:7). The participle form with א recurs but in the plural in 13:23 (see GKC, §§ 23 g and 72 p).

(a) Prov 10:4; 13:8, 23; 14:20; 17:5; 18:23; 19:1, 7, 22; 22:2, 7; 28:3, 6, 27; 29:13

The participle עֹשֶׂה, "he who works, working," is followed by the construct phrase כַף־רְמִיָּה, "a hand of laziness," which serves as an adjectival genitive phrase: "a lazy hand." The noun רְמִיָּה II, "slackness, laziness," recurs in 12:24, 27; 19:15; and elsewhere in the OT only in Jer 48:10. See "רְמִיָּה, 'Laziness' " in "Fools in Proverbs" in the introduction. The construct phrase could be an accusative object of the participle עֹשֶׂה (Joüon, § 126 l): "doing a lazy hand." But it is best translated as an instrumental accusative: "working *with* a lazy hand" (GKC, § 117 t).

וְיַד חָרוּצִים תַּעֲשִׁיר׃—This is, literally, "the hand of diligent people makes/gets rich." The feminine noun יָד in construct is the subject of the feminine verb תַּעֲשִׁיר. The Hiphil (H) of עָשַׁר, "to be rich," can have a causative meaning, "to make (someone) rich," but its internally transitive meaning, "to gain/obtain riches," fits better here (so also BDB, 2). The adjective and substantive חָרוּץ, "diligent, hardworking," recurs in the identical construct phrase in 12:24 and also in 12:27; 13:4; 21:5.

10:5 אֹגֵר בַּקַּיִץ בֵּן מַשְׂכִּיל—Literally, "one gathering during the summer is a son with good sense." The verb אָגַר, "to gather," the noun קַיִץ, "summer," and the parallel noun in the next clause, קָצִיר, "harvest time," earlier referred to the industriousness of the ant; see the first and second textual notes on 6:8. The Hiphil (H) participle מַשְׂכִּיל here is used as an adjective; see "שֵׂכֶל, 'Good Sense,' and הִשְׂכִּיל, 'to Act Sensibly' " in "Wisdom in Proverbs" in the introduction.

נִרְדָּם בַּקָּצִיר בֵּן מֵבִישׁ׃—Literally, this is "one sleeping during the harvest is a son causing disgrace."

Commentary

A Wise Son: Introduction to Wisdom and Righteousness (10:1–12:28)

The first informal section (10:1–12:28) of Solomon's further proverbs (10:1–22:16) is a collection of sayings that serve as a basic primer in righteous living and its foundation in godly wisdom.[2] It contains several subsections that show some conscious organization by Solomon:

- Prov 10:1–5 serves as a basic introduction to righteous living through honest labor.
- Prov 10:6–23 is mainly a collection of sayings about the use of one's mouth.
- Prov 10:24–32 contrasts the righteous and the wicked.
- The balance of the proverbs in this section (11:1–12:28) encourages righteous behavior.

Much of the time in this part of Proverbs, "righteousness" and "the righteous" are characterized by behavior that could simply be described as civil righteousness—righteous actions toward one's neighbor and other members of society, behavior enjoined by the Torah and more generally by God's Law throughout the Scriptures. Righteousness is not always clearly depicted as forensic justification (e.g., Gen 15:6), the righteousness through faith for Christ's sake, which comes through the Gospel and forgives the sinner, enabling one to stand before God and to be accounted as holy and blameless.

However, there are a number of proverbs that point to the Gospel and the righteousness that God imputes to the sinner by grace alone (as in, e.g., Num 6:24–27). Among these is Prov 10:6, which mentions the blessings of God on the righteous person. The similar proverbs in 10:2 and 11:4, 6 state that righteousness eternally saves a person from death, which can only be a reference to the righteousness of God imputed to sinful humans who trust in his promises—the righteousness that grants a person everlasting life. Some proverbs in this section point to this Gospel righteousness by hinting that the righteous deeds of God's people flow from their appreciation for his graciousness toward

---

2 For the loose structure of the sections in this part of Proverbs, see the excursus "The Organization of the Sayings in Solomon's Proverbs in Proverbs 10:1–22:16" at the beginning of the commentary on Proverbs 10.

them (11:5, 30; 12:10). Other proverbs that should be noted for their Gospel emphasis include 10:3, 24, 25, 28; 11:8, 30; and 12:3.

Righteousness Saves the Wise Son from Death (10:1–5)

10:1–5 This passage is marked as an introduction for all of 10:1–22:16 by an inclusio. Both its first (10:1) and its last verse (10:5) refer to a "son" twice. In each verse one "son" is wise, the other foolish. A main theme throughout this passage is the blessing of honest gain through labor, a blessing that comes to the entire family (including the son's "father," 10:1).

10:1 The placing of this proverb first in this collection is designed to link the whole collection (10:1–22:16) with Proverbs 1–9, which has ten sections addressing a son.[3] This proverb is one of a number in Proverbs that connects the character or behavior of a son to the welfare of his parents.[b] The son's faithful reception of God's Word establishes godly communion between father, mother, and son, as emphasized at the start of the entire book of Proverbs (1:8; see also, e.g., 3:12; 4:1, 3; 6:20).

(b) Prov 15:20; 17:25; 19:13, 26; 23:24–25; 28:7; 29:3

The saying in 10:1 is a string of three merisms (couplings of opposites):

1. "A wise son" versus "a foolish son"
2. "Makes … rejoice" versus "brings grief"
3. "[His] father" and "his mother"

Like this proverb, Jesus exhorts his disciples to believe the Gospel and do good works that reflect well on their heavenly Father (Mt 5:14–16).

10:2 This verse not only discourages theft and fraud (violations of the Fifth Commandment [Ex 20:15; Deut 5:19][4]), but also contrasts them with righteousness, implying that one of the fruits of righteousness is honest work. This proverb also implies that Yahweh is the one who determines the issue of profitability, especially since the verse is closely linked with the following one (see the commentary on 10:3). In this life it may appear that it is profitable to gain treasures dishonestly, but from the perspective of eternity, it is God who determines what is profitable (cf. James 4:13–15). Moreover, it is only his gift of righteousness that delivers a person from eternal death, as the NT also affirms (e.g., Rom 6:23; 1 Corinthians 15).

10:3 This proverb is linked to the preceding one because both begin with the negative particle לֹא־, "not," and an imperfect verb. This verse creates a chiasm with 10:2:

A רֶשַׁע, "wickedness" (10:2)
  B וּצְדָקָה, "but righteousness" (10:2)
  B' צַדִּיק, "a righteous person" (10:3)
A' רְשָׁעִים, "wicked people" (10:3)

---

3 For the ten addresses from father to son in Proverbs 1–9, see the excursus "Proverbs 1–9, Christ, and the Ten Commandments" in the commentary on chapter 1.

4 See further the excursus "Proverbs 1–9, Christ, and the Ten Commandments" in the commentary on chapter 1.

The righteous person who depends on Yahweh is rewarded in 10:3a, fulfilling the promise in 10:2b. In contrast, those who gain riches through devious means achieve no true profit according to 10:2a, and they are accounted as the wicked whom Yahweh will frustrate according to the warning in 10:3b. Both the promise and the warning are eschatological: the righteous may not seem prosperous in this life, while the wicked may appear to flourish, but on the Last Day the great assize will take place, and the eternal state of the righteous and the wicked will manifest the truth of 10:2–3.

This saying (10:3) stands at the center of this opening collection of proverbs (10:1–5) and emphasizes one's relationship to God. The righteousness given through faith is clearly in view here and is the defining feature of the introduction to this section of the book (10:1–12:28). This verse defines who "a wise son" (10:1) is: he is anyone who is righteous through faith. It also defines the righteousness that saves a person from death (10:2): it is God's own righteousness, imputed to the sinner by grace alone, on account of Christ, who is the Wisdom of God.[5] This proverb also tempers the sayings in 10:4–5 about diligence, reminding that it is not human effort alone that brings material blessing.

10:4 This verse is a chiasm in the order of the Hebrew words. The first and last words are verbs, while two different nouns for "hand" are near the center of the verse. These words can be translated literally as follows:

A רָאשׁ, "becomes poor"
  B כַּף־, "hand of"
  B' יַד־, "hand of"
A' תַּעֲשִׁיר, "brings riches"

Ironically, the lazy hands that appear to be doing nothing are actually accomplishing something: poverty. This imagery is quite striking.

10:5 This verse not only encourages diligent work, but also closes out this passage (10:1–5) by its links to 10:1. The "wise son" (10:1) is the "son with insight" (10:5). He is anyone who recognizes the proper time for work and the proper time for rest, something that the "foolish son" (10:1), who is also a "disgraceful son" (10:5), cannot grasp. The application is not simply to the harvest season, but to the God-given insight to recognize when a truly profitable opportunity is available. Compare the English aphorism "strike while the iron is hot," and see Is 55:6–7; Lk 4:16–30; 12:54–56; Heb 3:7–19.

---

[5] See "Wisdom in Proverbs" in the introduction. See also the commentary on 1:1–7; 3:13–20; 8:22–31; 30:1b–10; and the excursus "Proverbs 8, Wisdom, Christology, and the Arian Controversy" in the commentary on chapter 8.

Proverbs 10:6–23

Proverbs about the Use of the Mouth

Translation

10 [6]Blessings [crown] the head of a righteous person,
but the mouth of wicked people covers violence.
[7]The remembrance of a righteous person is a blessing,
but the name of wicked people will rot.
[8]The person who is wise in heart accepts commands,
but a chattering stubborn fool will be thrown down.
[9]Whoever walks with integrity walks securely,
but whoever makes his ways crooked will be found out.
[10]Whoever winks causes pain,
and a chattering stubborn fool will be thrown down.
[11]The mouth of a righteous person is a fountain of life,
but the mouth of wicked people covers violence.
[12]Hate stirs up a quarrel,
but love covers all sins.
[13]Wisdom is found on the lips of a person with understanding,
but a rod is for the back of someone who lacks sense.
[14]Wise people store up knowledge,
but the mouth of a stubborn fool is in the vicinity of ruin.
[15]A rich person's wealth is his strong city.
Poverty is the ruin of poor people.
[16]The wages of a righteous person [bring him] to life.
The harvest of a wicked person [brings him] to sin.
[17]Whoever practices discipline is [on] the path to life,
but whoever abandons a warning leads [others] astray.
[18]Whoever conceals hatred has lying lips,
and whoever spreads gossip is a fool.
[19]When there are many words, sin does not stop,
but whoever restrains his lips has insight.
[20]The tongue of a righteous person is fine silver.
The heart of a wicked person is of little [value].
[21]The lips of a righteous person feed many,
but stubborn fools die for lack of sense.
[22]The blessing of Yahweh makes one rich,
and hard work adds nothing to it.
[23]Like laughter to a fool when he carries out a scheme
is wisdom to a person with understanding.

Textual Notes

10:6 בְּרָכוֹת לְרֹאשׁ צַדִּיק—This is the first of eight occurrences of the noun בְּרָכָה, "blessing," in Proverbs.[a] It always includes God's eschatological blessings by grace upon believers, who are "righteous" (צַדִּיק here) through faith. Prov 10:22 names the source of all blessings; every blessing ultimately is "the blessing of/from Yahweh." Occasionally "blessing" also involves human praise in thanksgiving for God's gracious work through the believer (10:7; 11:26).

(a) Prov 10:6–7, 22; 11:11, 25–26; 24:25; 28:20

For the Piel (D) of בָּרַךְ, "to bless" (3:33; 27:14; 30:11), and the Pual (Dp) "blessed" (20:21; 22:9), see the textual note on 3:33. See also the second textual note on 3:18, which has מְאֻשָּׁר. The Qal passive (Gp) participle בָּרוּךְ, "blessed," only occurs in 5:18. See also the first textual note on 3:13, which has אַשְׁרֵי.

The preposition לְ with the construct phrase לְרֹאשׁ צַדִּיק implies a verb of motion with God as the agent of the action, that is, "blessings [come from Yahweh] to the head of a righteous person." The construction is poetically rendered with the verb "crown."

וּפִי רְשָׁעִים יְכַסֶּה חָמָס׃—This identical clause is repeated in 10:11b. For the noun חָמָס, "violence," see the textual note on 3:31. Some take חָמָס as the subject and פִּי רְשָׁעִים as the object: "violence covers the mouth of wicked people" (see KJV, NKJV). However, the construction more likely is the reverse: by means of lies and falsehood, "the mouth of wicked people covers/conceals violence" (see ESV, NASB). This understanding better fits the antithetical parallelism of the clause in 10:11b with 10:11a, where פִּי צַדִּיק, "the mouth of a righteous person," clearly is the subject. It also fits with 10:18a.

10:8 וֶאֱוִיל שְׂפָתַיִם יִלָּבֵט׃—This clause is repeated verbatim in 10:10b; see the second textual note on 10:10. In this pericope, אֱוִיל recurs also in 10:14, 21. The genitive relationship in the construct phrase וֶאֱוִיל שְׂפָתַיִם, literally, "a fool of lips," signifies the character of the fool: he is all lips, all talk. Equivalent English expressions would be "chattering stubborn fool" or "babbling stubborn fool." For the meaning of אֱוִיל, see "אֱוִיל, 'Stubborn Fool,' and אִוֶּלֶת, 'Stupidity' " in "Fools in Proverbs" in the introduction. The "fool of lips" contrasts with the person who is חֲכַם־לֵב, literally, "wise of heart" (10:8a). Wisdom permeates his inner thoughts and being, not just his outward speech.

The verb לָבַט occurs only thrice in the OT (Hos 4:14; Prov 10:8, 10), all in the Niphal (N), meaning "be thrust down, out, or away" (BDB) and always representing God's judgment on the apostate or unbelievers.

10:9 הוֹלֵךְ בַּתֹּם יֵלֶךְ בֶּטַח—For the verb הָלַךְ, "walk," with the noun תֹּם, "integrity," see the second textual note on 2:7. For the noun בֶּטַח, "security," used as an adverbial accusative, see the first textual note on 1:33. בֶּטַח is used with הָלַךְ also in 3:23.

וּמְעַקֵּשׁ דְּרָכָיו יִוָּדֵעַ׃—The verb עָקַשׁ occurs in Proverbs only twice. The Piel (D), used here, has the transitive, causative meaning, "to make crooked; to pervert," with the direct object דְּרָכָיו, "his ways." The Niphal (N) in 28:18 means "to be crooked, twisted." The cognate adjective עִקֵּשׁ, "crooked," is more common in Proverbs; see the first textual note on 2:15.

The passive Niphal (N) imperfect יִוָּדֵעַ, "will become known," leaves unstated whether it is God or other people—or both—who will know all about the crooked person. On the Last Day, God will publicly reveal all that unbelievers try to keep secret (e.g., Mt 10:26; Rom 2:5, 16; 1 Cor 3:13).

10:10 קֹ֣רֵץ עַ֭יִן יִתֵּ֣ן עַצָּ֑בֶת—Literally, this is "one winking an eye gives pain." For קָרַץ and עַיִן, see the first textual note on 6:13. The verb נָתַן can mean "to be the cause of" (*HALOT*, 2).

וֶאֱוִ֥יל שְׂ֝פָתַ֗יִם יִלָּבֵֽט׃—This line is repeated from 10:8b; see the first textual note on 10:8. Here, however, the line is not antithetical to the first line of the verse, whereas most other sayings in this chapter have antithetical parallelism. For that reason some interpreters argue that this line was accidentally copied from 10:8 and should be emended based on the LXX:[1] ὁ δὲ ἐλέγχων μετὰ παρρησίας εἰρηνοποιεῖ, "but the one who boldly corrects makes peace." However, there is no reason to assume that *all* the proverbs in this context must be antithetical, so there is no need for this change.[2]

10:11 מְק֣וֹר חַ֭יִּים פִּ֣י צַדִּ֑יק—"Fountain of life" occurs five times in the OT and four times in Proverbs (10:11; 13:14; 14:27; 16:22). For the noun חַיִּים, "life," in the eschatological sense of everlasting life by God's grace, see also, for example, 3:2, 18, 22; 4:10, 13, 22–23.

Here "the mouth of a righteous person" (פִּ֣י צַדִּ֑יק) is this fountain, yet "righteous" implies that the ultimate source is God, the one who justifies all believers by his grace. Ps 36:10 (ET 36:9) and Prov 14:27 establish a clear connection between "fountain of life" and Yahweh as the gracious bestower of life, which is not just physical and temporal, but spiritual and eternal, with the promise of the bodily resurrection. "Fountain of life" recalls the description of divine Wisdom as a "tree of life," which alludes to the same tree in Eden and, eschatologically, to the perpetually fruit-bearing tree in Ezekiel and Revelation; see the first textual note and the commentary on Prov 3:18. "Fountain of life" too alludes to the first paradise (Gen 2:9–14) and anticipates the eternal state in the new creation; see Ezek 47:1–14 and Rev 7:17; 21:6; 22:1–2, 17. According to Jer 2:13 and 17:13, Yahweh himself is "the fountain of living waters" (מְקוֹר־מַיִם חַיִּים). See also Zech 13:1. Similar is the claim of Jesus himself: he is the source of living waters, which he freely gives to all who believe (Jn 4:10, 14; 7:38).

10:12 שִׂ֭נְאָה תְּעֹרֵ֣ר מְדָנִ֑ים—For מְדָנִים, "strife," see the third textual note on 6:14. The verb עוּר, "arouse," occurs only here in Proverbs, in the Polel (D), meaning "stir up, provoke."

וְעַ֥ל כָּל־פְּ֝שָׁעִ֗ים תְּכַסֶּ֥ה אַהֲבָֽה׃—This is, literally, "over all transgressions love covers." The abstract noun אַהֲבָה, "love," refers to that of one's wife in 5:19. Here, and when it recurs in 15:17; 17:9; 27:5, it has the more general meaning of divine love that is shown by believers in their gracious, forgiving relationships with other people. The idiom "cover transgression" (the Piel of כָּסָה with the object noun פֶּשַׁע) recurs in 17:9 and, in a different sense, in 28:13. David uses different phrases with כָּסָה and פֶּשַׁע in Ps 32:1 to proclaim the blessedness of every person whose sin is forgiven by God. Ps

---

[1] NRSV, NAB, and Kidner, *Proverbs*, 86.

[2] Most of the sayings in 10:1–15:33 exhibit antithetical parallelism, but not all do. See the excursus "The Organization of the Sayings in Solomon's Proverbs in Proverbs 10:1–22:16," especially figure 11, at the beginning of the commentary on chapter 10.

32:1–2 is a key text cited by the apostle Paul (Rom 4:7–8) in his exposition of justification through faith alone, apart from works, as the doctrine taught in the OT as well as by Jesus and his apostles (see Romans 3–5). Prov 10:12 and 17:9 show justified believers acting out divine grace in their relationships with others by covering transgression.

10:13 בְּשִׂפְתֵי נָבוֹן תִּמָּצֵא חָכְמָה—For the Niphal (N) participle נָבוֹן, "a person with understanding," see the second textual note on 1:5. In that verse, נָבוֹן is parallel to חָכָם, "a wise person" (1:5a). Similarly here the "person with understanding" is associated with חָכְמָה, "wisdom," which in this pericope is repeated on 10:23. See "חָכְמָה, 'Wisdom,' and Related Words" in "Wisdom in Proverbs" in the introduction.

וְשֵׁבֶט לְגֵו חֲסַר־לֵב׃—The phrase שֵׁבֶט לְגֵו, literally, "a rod for the back of," recurs in 26:3. In that verse it is the "back" of "fools" (כְּסִילִים) that is or should be struck with the "rod" (שֵׁבֶט; cf. 19:29). Here it is the back of a senseless fool; see "חֲסַר־לֵב, 'Lacking Sense' " in "Fools in Proverbs" in the introduction. In this chapter, the construct phrase חֲסַר־לֵב recurs in 10:21.

10:14 חֲכָמִים יִצְפְּנוּ־דָעַת—See "דַּעַת, 'Knowledge,' and יָדַע, 'to Know' " in "Wisdom in Proverbs" in the introduction as well as the commentary on 1:4, 7.

וּפִי־אֱוִיל מְחִתָּה קְרֹבָה׃—Literally, this is "but the mouth of a stubborn fool—ruin [is] near." The feminine noun מְחִתָּה, "ruin, destruction; terror," is from the verb חָתַת, "be shattered, broken; terrified." It occurs six more times in Proverbs,[b] always in this same section of Solomon's proverbs (10:1–22:16). Its use here with the adjective קָרוֹב, "near," means that the mouth of the fool is always near to—that is, in the vicinity of—ruin. This implies that it is the fool's harmful words that cause the destruction.

(b) Prov 10:15, 29; 13:3; 14:28; 18:7; 21:15

10:16 פְּעֻלַּת צַדִּיק לְחַיִּים—The preposition לְ on חַיִּים ("[bring him] *to* life") avoids a direct statement that the wages (פְּעֻלָּה) earned by a righteous person *are* life, which could be taken as crass works-righteousness: salvation at least partly by works instead of by grace alone. Instead, this statement with the prepositional phrase is akin to 12:28 and 21:21 and also, for example, Rom 5:17–18, 21; 6:13; Phil 1:11. The person who is righteous through faith leads a life of good works and receives the gift of everlasting life.

10:17 אֹרַח לְחַיִּים שׁוֹמֵר מוּסָר—The verb שָׁמַר can mean "do something carefully" or "devote oneself to" (*HALOT*, 5, 9 a), hence to "practice" something, such as a doctor "practices" medicine. For the object practiced here, מוּסָר, see "מוּסָר, 'Discipline,' and יָסַר, 'to Discipline' " in "Wisdom in Proverbs" in the introduction.

וְעוֹזֵב תּוֹכַחַת מַתְעֶה׃—For תּוֹכַחַת, "warning," see the first textual note on 1:23. Compared to the Qal (G) of תָּעָה, which would simply mean that the unrepentant person himself "goes astray," the Hiphil (H) participle here, מַתְעֶה, has the stronger meaning that he, literally, "causes [others] to go astray." This results in greater condemnation; see Mt 18:6.

10:18 וּמוֹצִא דִבָּה—The noun דִּבָּה, "report, rumour" (*HALOT*), recurs in 25:10. In both contexts it could refer to *true* but damaging words about other people, as in Gen 37:2. Therefore "spreads gossip" is better than "spreads slander." "Gossip" also is consistent with the Hiphil (H) participle מוֹצִא, literally, "brings out," that is, "divulges, spreads."

10:20 כֶּ֣סֶף נִ֭בְחָר—"Fine silver" is similar to an earlier phrase about gold. See the second textual note on 8:10.

10:21 שִׂפְתֵ֣י צַ֭דִּיק יִרְע֣וּ רַבִּ֑ים—The Qal (G) of רָעָה can have the transitive meanings "to shepherd, care for, provide (food) for." Here with "lips" (שִׂפְתֵ֣י) as the subject, it implies that the righteous person feeds others with God's Word, through godly "teaching" (BDB, s.v. רָעָה I, Qal, 1 c).

10:22 בִּרְכַּ֣ת יְ֭הוָה הִ֣יא תַעֲשִׁ֑יר—For the feminine noun בְּרָכָה, see the first textual note on 10:6. It is the referent of the feminine pronoun הִ֣יא and the subject of the feminine verb תַעֲשִׁ֑יר, "make rich," which in this context refers more to granting spiritual wealth (as in 1 Sam 2:7) than to money. See also the identical verb in Prov 10:4 (with an intransitive sense) in the context of 10:2–3. The second line of 10:22, literally, "and hard work [עֶ֫צֶב] does not add [לֹא־יוֹסִף] with it [עִמָּֽהּ]," that is, hard work adds nothing to Yahweh's blessing, reinforces that divine blessing comes by grace alone and good works cannot contribute in any way to salvation.

Commentary

The sayings in 10:6–23 largely share a common theme. All but five of the proverbs (10:9, 15–17, 22) in this passage have some connection to the mouth, including references to the "lips" (10:13, 18–19, 21), the "tongue" (10:20), and the "mouth" itself (10:6, 11, 14); words spoken by the mouth, including a "name" (10:7) and a "warning" (10:17); and expressions that involve verbal activity done by the mouth, such as "chattering" (10:8, 10) and "laughter" (10:23). For the loose structure of the sections in this part of Proverbs, see the excursus "The Organization of the Sayings in Solomon's Proverbs in Proverbs 10:1–22:16" at the beginning of the commentary on this chapter.

10:6 This verse is connected to 10:2–3 and 10:7 through the contrast of "righteous" and "wicked" people. It is also connected to 10:7 by the catchword "blessing." Moreover, the second line of 10:6 is repeated word-for-word in 10:11, but each verse has a different first line, and in the context of this different preceding line, the second line takes on a different emphasis. Prov 10:6 contrasts the blessings God bestows upon righteous people with the violence spawned by the mouths of wicked people, who incite others and may engage in violence themselves (1:10–19).

10:7 This verse continues the contrast in 10:6 between the righteous and the wicked. God grants the blessing of remembrance for the righteous person. The proverb does not specify who will remember the righteous person, whether it is God or other people, and probably both are intended. This leads the reader to think of remembrance in terms other than mere worldly fame. God's enduring memory of his saints promises them salvation and resurrection to eternal life on the Last Day. See, for example, Pss 25:7; 106:4; Lk 23:42–43.

10:8 This verse is the first of a triplet of sayings (10:8–10) with similar Hebrew syntax.[3] Each of these three verses has four Hebrew words in the first clause and then three words in the second clause. Each verse concludes with a Niphal (N) imperfect, and those in 10:8 and 10:10 are identical:

יִלָּבֵט, "will be thrown down" (10:8)
יִוָּדֵעַ, "will be found out" (10:9)
יִלָּבֵט, "will be thrown down" (10:10)

Prov 10:8 contrasts the wise person, who obeys the Decalogue and other divine commands,[4] with the fool, who is so busy with his own chatter (literally "a fool of lips") that he does not obey God's Word. He "will be thrown down," by God as the implied agent of the passive verbs. His destruction will be for eternity, and possibly also in this life—if he is punished by temporal authorities in power or excommunicated from the church (cf. 1 Cor 5:5).

10:9 This verse does not have any imagery connected to the mouth. Nevertheless, 10:9a relates to 10:8a, and "crooked" in 10:9b is thematically linked with 10:10–12, which speaks of various people who are corrupt and perverse in their ways. Such people can never be secure in what they do because their actions and motives will be revealed and judged by God.

10:10 This verse mentions a person who causes pain by winking. This is probably a reference to winking as a signal to others involved in his sinful schemes. The LXX includes the interpretive addition μετὰ δόλου, winking "with treachery" (followed by NIV). Winking is always a negative gesture in Proverbs (קָרַץ also in 6:13; 16:30), and it is malicious in the one other OT passage with the same verb (קָרַץ in Ps 35:19). The second line of Prov 10:10, repeated from 10:8, then takes on the idea that the fool's chattering is part of his scheming and collusion with others.

10:11 This verse is bound to 10:10 by the paronomasia between their first lines (קֹרֵץ עַיִן, *qorets ʿayin*, 10:10; מְקוֹר חַיִּים, *meqor ḥayyim*, 10:11).[5] This saying first portrays the righteous person as supplying the water of life to others. This person has received life from God (Ps 36:10 [ET 36:9]) and shares it with others through his words. His speech communicates the Gospel of Jesus, who supplies the water of life (Jn 7:37–38). "The mouth of a righteous person" (פִּי צַדִּיק) is then contrasted with the following, similar Hebrew phrase, "the mouth of wicked people" (וּפִי רְשָׁעִים). Unlike the righteous person, the wicked use their words to conceal sinful "violence." The parallelism implies that the consequence of their deceptive speech is everlasting death, the opposite of eternal "life." Not only will the wicked be punished, but they also inflict death upon all who believe their false and pernicious teaching.

---

[3] Goldingay, "The Arrangement of Sayings in Proverbs 10–15," 77.

[4] See the excursus "Proverbs 1–9, Christ, and the Ten Commandments" in the commentary on Proverbs 1.

[5] Hildebrandt, "Proverbial Strings," 176.

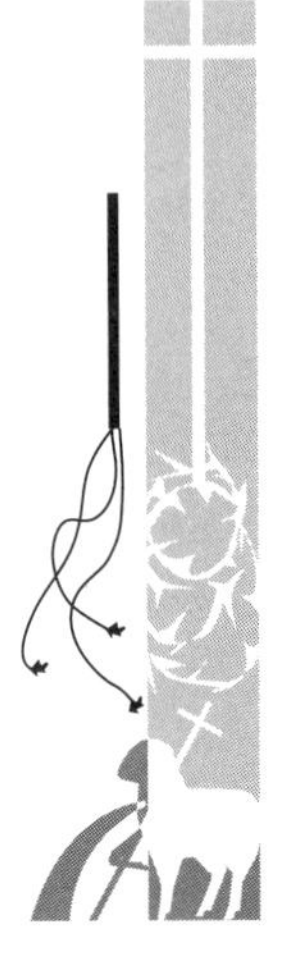

10:12 This verse is bound to 10:11 by the catchword "covers" (יְכַסֶּה in 10:11 and תְּכַסֶּה in 10:12), the second-to-last Hebrew word in each verse. Yet there is a striking contrast: in 10:11 what is covered (concealed) is "violence," whereas in 10:12 it is "love" that "covers" (forgives) "all sins." Note the close verbal parallels in the NT:

> Above all, continue to love one another earnestly, since love *covers* a multitude of sins. (1 Pet 4:8)

> Whoever brings a sinner back from his wandering will save his soul from death and will *cover* a multitude of sins. (James 5:20)

The Lutheran Confessions include a substantial exposition of how the "love" spoken of in Prov 10:12 as well as in 1 Peter is not mere human love, but is God's own redeeming love, which his people then show to each other as they are motivated by the Gospel to absolve and pardon others. Only the love of God in Jesus Christ has the power to atone for sin (Ap IV, "Justification," 238–43).

10:13 This verse is the first in a trio of sayings bound by a chain of catchwords: "wisdom" (חָכְמָה) in 10:13 connects to "wise people" (חֲכָמִים) in 10:14, and then "ruin" (מְחִתָּה) is repeated in 10:14 and 10:15. Prov 10:13 is a stark contrast between the person with understanding, who is able to offer wisdom to others, and the person without sense, who has nothing to offer, but who receives correction in the form of corporal punishment. Compare the saying of Jesus in Lk 12:47–48 about corporal and eschatological punishment.

The second line of this proverb is similar to 19:29b and 26:3b.

10:14 This verse continues the contrast, but in reverse: wise people receive and store up knowledge, while the fool speaks and loses. Taken together, these two proverbs teach the wise person to choose words carefully since words not only affect the speaker, but they also have a powerful effect on others. Similar is the counsel St. Paul gives to the young pastor Timothy about his preaching and teaching (1 Tim 4:16).

10:15 This is the first of a set of three proverbs (10:15–17) in this section that do not have any connection to the use of the mouth. The first line of this proverb is repeated as the first line of 18:11.

This verse does not endorse any particular behavior. Instead, it is an observation about life. The resources of the wealthy function as their defense like a walled, fortified city protects its inhabitants. This is true enough about earthly riches as a defense against worldly dangers. However, only the God-given treasure of the knowledge of salvation (10:14a) is a fortress that will endure forever (Psalm 46). The poor have no material resources to defend themselves. Yet the kingdom of God is open to them (Is 61:1; Lk 6:20).

10:16 This verse is placed beside 10:15 to warn that righteousness does not necessarily lead to riches in this life, nor is wealth necessarily a harbinger of everlasting life. While the wise and faithful person may accumulate wealth, the true and lasting benefit is "life" with God. Moreover, even if a wicked person becomes rich, he will still be held accountable for his sin. Wealth may seem like an unqualified blessing, but it can point to either of two opposite directions for one's eternity, depending on how it was gained: either through righteousness on the road to "life" or through sinful living on the road to everlasting death (see 10:2).

10:17 This verse connects to 10:16 through the catchword "life." It continues the theme of righteous living in contrast to sin. The second line states that sinners can lead others astray by their purposeful abandonment of God's Word, including its warnings. This suggests that the first line may also have implications for others in addition to the wise/righteous person. Those who heed discipline and demonstrate their faith in their life can have a salutary influence on others. This type of influence is seen in the book of Acts in the person of Barnabas, who influences the early part of Paul's Christian life (Acts 9:27; 11:22–26).

10:18 This verse returns the focus to the use of the mouth, as in most of the sayings in this collection. Two errors are spoken of here. First, concealing one's hatred involves hypocrisy. The second line, however, is about expressing hatred by careless, thoughtless, or even slanderous use of the mouth. Such speech is a violation of the Eighth Commandment (Ex 20:16; Deut 5:20) and also the Second Commandment, the false invocation of God's name (Ex 20:7; Deut 5:11).[6]

10:19 This verse warns against idle chatter. In the context of 10:18, the reader is led to surmise that the speech here is slander or gossip (see James 3:1–12), and possibly the misuse of God's name. The second line counsels that the insightful person will break a cycle of recriminations by maintaining silence.

10:20 This verse places 10:19 in perspective by depicting righteous speech—the positive fulfillment of the Second (Ex 20:7; Deut 5:11) and Eighth (Ex 20:16; Deut 5:20) Commandments. One is not to remain forever silent. The righteous person can speak things of great value. However, a person who has rejected God's grace has nothing of value in his heart. The wicked are unable to bring forth speech that is helpful. Jesus makes the same observation when he says:

> But what comes out of the mouth proceeds from the heart, and they are the things that defile a person. For out of the heart come evil thoughts, murders, adulteries, sexual immoralities, thefts, false testimonies, slanders. (Mt 15:18–19)

10:21 This verse continues the theme of righteous speech, this time defining the value of it as nourishment and guidance (יִרְעוּ, "feed," could be rendered as "shepherd, guide"). Righteous lips are able to offer spiritual food for others from what they have received from God. The contrast to fools also ties this

[6] See the excursus "Proverbs 1–9, Christ, and the Ten Commandments" in the commentary on Proverbs 1.

saying to the previous one since "lack of sense" is, literally, "lacking a heart," and "heart" (לֵב) is also in 10:20. The fool who has rejected God dies. Therefore, fools cannot nourish even themselves, much less others.

10:22 This verse ties the spiritual prosperity of 10:20–21 to the material prosperity spoken of in 10:15. Riches of any kind are a blessing from God. Yet Solomon here observes that hard work does not automatically lead to abundance in this world. The implication is that one should receive any food and material goods with thanksgiving to God instead of self-congratulation.

10:23 This verse compares the glee of a fool caught up in the cleverness of his scheme with the wise person who finds his enjoyment in the wisdom that God grants. The fool is preoccupied with himself and his own cleverness. The person with understanding is preoccupied with God and finds joy in divine Wisdom, that is, in Christ.[7]

---

[7] See "Wisdom in Proverbs" in the introduction. See also the commentary on 1:1–7; 3:13–20; 8:22–31; 30:1b–10; and the excursus "Proverbs 8, Wisdom, Christology, and the Arian Controversy" in the commentary on Proverbs 8.

Proverbs 10:24–32

Contrast between the Righteous and the Wicked

Translation

10 24What the wicked person dreads will come upon him,
but he [Yahweh] will grant the desire of righteous people.
25When the storm has passed, the wicked person is no more,
but the righteous person [has] an everlasting foundation.
26Like vinegar to the teeth,
and like smoke to the eyes,
so is a lazy person to those who send him [to do a job].

27The fear of Yahweh will add days,
but the years of wicked people will be short.
28The hope of righteous people [is] joy,
but the aspirations of wicked people will perish.
29The way of Yahweh is a fortress for the person of integrity,
but destruction for evildoers.
30A righteous person will never be moved,
but wicked people will not dwell on earth.
31The mouth of a righteous person bears the fruit of wisdom,
but a perverse tongue will be cut off.
32The lips of a righteous person know favor,
but the mouth of wicked people [knows] perverse things.

Textual Notes

10:24 מְגוֹרַ֣ת רָ֭שָׁע הִ֣יא תְבוֹאֶ֑נּוּ—The construct phrase מְגוֹרַת רָשָׁע, literally, "the dread of a wicked person," has a subjective genitive: "the thing that the wicked person dreads." The feminine noun מְגוֹרָה, "dread," occurs in Proverbs only here. It is the referent of the feminine pronoun הִיא and the subject of the feminine imperfect verb תְּבוֹאֶנּוּ, which has an eschatological sense: "will (eventually, finally) come upon/befall him." For its dative suffix, see Joüon, § 125 ba.

וְתַאֲוַ֖ת צַדִּיקִ֣ים יִתֵּֽן׃—The construct phrase וְתַאֲוַת צַדִּיקִים, literally, "the desire of righteous people," is another phrase with a subjective genitive: "the thing that righteous people desire." The noun תַּאֲוָה, "desire," is in the identical construct phrase in 11:23 and recurs in 13:12, 19; 18:1; 19:22; 21:25–26. It is derived from the verb אָוָה (e.g., 13:4; 21:10, 26). Yahweh is the implied masculine singular subject of the verb יִתֵּן, which has an eschatological nuance: "will (eventually, finally) give." Similar are the promises of Jesus in, for example, Mt 7:7–11 and Lk 18:1–8.

10:25 וְצַדִּ֗יק יְס֣וֹד עוֹלָֽם׃—Literally, this is "and a righteous person [is] a foundation of eternity." The noun יְסוֹד, "foundation," occurs only here in Proverbs. The cognate verb יָסַד is used in 3:19 to state that Yahweh "founded, established" the world. The implication here is that Yahweh establishes the righteous so that they will endure for eternity. Most translations render the noun as a verb (e.g., "is established" in ESV). Some reword so that Yahweh is the referent, for example, "the righteous *has* an everlasting foundation" (NASB).

10:26 כַּחֹ֤מֶץ ׀ לַשִּׁנַּ֗יִם וְכֶעָשָׁ֥ן לָעֵינָ֑יִם—The two dual nouns form an internal rhyme: שִׁנַּיִם, *shinnayim*, and עֵינַיִם, *'eynayim.* The dual שִׁנַּיִם, "teeth," refers to the two corresponding sets of teeth, in the upper and lower jaw. Compare Song 4:2 and 6:6, where each tooth has its match in the other set.

לְשֹׁלְחָֽיו׃—The implication of the participle of שָׁלַח, "send," is that the lazy person is a messenger or envoy sent to carry out a mission. This identical suffixed plural participle with preposition recurs in 25:13, and the plural participle with preposition and a different suffix occurs in 22:21. This participle may be a plural of majesty (see Joüon, § 136 e; cf. GKC, § 124 k), in which case God could be the one who has sent the person who here, nevertheless, is lazy.

10:27 יִרְאַ֣ת יְ֭הוָה תּוֹסִ֣יף יָמִ֑ים—Similar promises of everlasting life use the Hiphil (H) of יָסַף in 3:2 and 9:11. Here the feminine noun יִרְאָה, "fear," is the subject of the feminine imperfect תּוֹסִיף, "will add." See "יִרְאַת יְהוָה, 'the Fear of Yahweh,' and יְרֵא יְהוָה, 'One Who Fears Yahweh' " in "Wisdom in Proverbs" in the introduction. See also the first textual note and the commentary on 1:7.

10:28 תּוֹחֶ֣לֶת צַדִּיקִ֣ים שִׂמְחָ֑ה—The noun תּוֹחֶלֶת, "hope," recurs in 11:7 and 13:12. It is derived from the verb יָחַל, "to hope," which is absent from Proverbs but is a common expression in Psalms for saving faith (e.g., Pss 31:25 [ET 31:24]; 33:18, 22; 130:7). The noun שִׂמְחָה, "joy," recurs in 12:20; 14:10, 13; 15:21, 23; 21:15, 17. Because this noun is not the same part of speech as the verb "perish" in the following parallel line, some would emend it to a verb such as צָמְחָה, "sprouts,"[1] or שָׂמְחָה, "springs up" (proposed from Akkadian and Arabic cognates).[2] However, parallelism need not be exactly symmetrical, especially when it is antithetical, as here, so no emendation is needed.

וְתִקְוַ֖ת רְשָׁעִ֣ים תֹּאבֵֽד׃—Since the noun תִּקְוָה, normally rendered as "hope," is from a different root than תּוֹחֶלֶת, "hope," in the preceding line, it is translated collectively as "aspirations" here. Note the close verbal parallel between this line and וְדֶרֶךְ רְשָׁעִים תֹּאבֵד, "the way of the wicked will perish," in Ps 1:6.

10:29 מָע֣וֹז לַ֭תֹּם דֶּ֣רֶךְ יְהוָ֑ה—The noun מָעוֹז, "fortress," is a common metaphor in Psalms for God (e.g., Pss 27:1; 28:8; 31:3, 5 [ET 31:2, 4]). For the noun תֹּם, "integrity, blamelessness," see the second textual note on 2:7.

וּ֝מְחִתָּ֗ה לְפֹ֣עֲלֵי אָֽוֶן׃—For the noun מְחִתָּה, "ruin," see the second textual note on 10:14.

---

[1] Footnote in *BHS*.

[2] Driver, "Problems in the Hebrew Text of Proverbs," 179. See also Garrett, *Proverbs, Ecclesiastes, Song of Songs*, 122, n. 213.

10:30 צַדִּיק לְעוֹלָם בַּל־יִמּוֹט—This is, literally, "the righteous person forever shall not be moved." צַדִּיק, "righteous," is the subject of בַּל־יִמּוֹט, the negative particle (בַּל) with the Niphal (N) imperfect of מוֹט, "be shaken, moved." Most of this vocabulary is repeated in 12:3b.

10:31 פִּי־צַדִּיק יָנוּב חָכְמָה—The Qal (G) of נוּב, "bear fruit," describes righteous believers also in Ps 92:15 (ET 92:14), and its only other OT occurrence is in Ps 62:11 (ET 62:10). The noun חָכְמָה, "wisdom," syntactically may be an accusative of result (Joüon, § 125 o; cf. GKC, § 117 z).

וּלְשׁוֹן תַּהְפֻּכוֹת תִּכָּרֵת׃—For the abstract plural noun תַּהְפֻּכוֹת, "perversity," which is repeated at the end of 10:32, see the second textual note on 2:12.

For the Niphal (N) of כָּרַת, "be cut off" in an eschatological sense, see the first textual note on 2:22.

10:32 שִׂפְתֵי צַדִּיק יֵדְעוּן רָצוֹן—Here with "lips" as the subject, the verb יָדַע, "to know," could have the nuance "to be familiar with, acquainted with" (that is, the lips of the righteous person frequently speak with favor and grace) or "to be skilled in" (that is, those lips are skilled in speaking favorably, graciously). For the noun רָצוֹן, "favor, grace," see the second textual note on 8:35.

Commentary

Eight of these nine sayings contrast the wicked and the righteous (10:26 is the lone exception). A main theme in Proverbs 10 is the difference between the righteous and the wicked. The substantivized adjectives רָשָׁע, "wicked person," and צַדִּיק, "righteous person," each occur six times in 10:24–32. For the loose structure of the sections in this part of Proverbs, see the excursus "The Organization of the Sayings in Solomon's Proverbs in Proverbs 10:1–22:16" at the beginning of the commentary on this chapter.

10:24 This verse is linked to 10:23 through the alliteration of תְּבוֹאֶנּוּ, *tebo'ennu*, "will come upon him" (10:24), with תְּבוּנָה, *tebuna*, "understanding" (10:23).[3] The contrast in 10:24 of outcomes for the wicked and the righteous not only implies that Yahweh is the one who controls these outcomes, but it also implies that the righteous desire what God desires, especially the salvation of people (God's antecedent will; see 1 Tim 2:4), while the wicked dread what God desires: the punishment of sin (God's consequent will; see Ezek 18:24, 32). For the righteous the motivation is the Gospel. For the wicked, their fear comes from the Law. On the Last Day God shall execute his punishment upon all who have persisted in unbelief, and he will grant the full salvation of all who have believed in him.

10:25 This verse is linked to 10:24 by the catchwords "wicked" and "righteous." This proverb clarifies 10:24 by defining the outcomes implied there. This saying may lie behind the close of the Sermon on the Mount: Jesus depicts each believer as a wise person who has built his house on a rock, and it will withstand

3 Goldingay, "The Arrangement of Sayings in Proverbs 10–15," 77.

the storm, while the foolish person has built his house on sand, and it will collapse (Mt 7:24–27).

10:26 This verse beings with the preposition כְּ, as did 10:25 (“when”), though here it signals a comparison (“like”). This is the first of several comparison proverbs that use the formula ... כֵּן ... כְּ, “like ... so ...” (see also 26:1–2, 8; 27:8, 19). Here the compared elements are all irritants: vinegar, smoke, and a lazy person who doesn’t complete his mission. This irritation may be seen in Jesus’ parable of the man who entrusted money to his servants before going on a journey (Mt 25:13–30). The servant with one talent was “lazy” (ὀκνηρός, Mt 25:26) and thereby provoked his master’s wrath, meriting punishment that would not end (Mt 25:30).

10:27 This verse begins a series of proverbs that conclude this chapter on the central theme of the righteous versus the wicked. The “wicked” are mentioned in 10:27–28, 30, 32, and the “righteous” are in 10:28, 30–32. In 10:27 the righteous are not mentioned explicitly but are implied to be ones who have the fear of Yahweh. While one can find instances where a righteous person dies young or a wicked person lives a long life, this saying is generally true. The righteous who seek to follow God’s ways avoid behavior that endangers life, either temporal or spiritual. Conversely, the wicked often engage in behavior that shortens life. This difference between believers and unbelievers can be seen in, for example, their contrasting attitudes toward abortion and euthanasia: the righteous seek to protect life from conception to natural death, whereas the wicked allow life to be cut short unjustly.

Eschatologically, this saying (“add days ... will be short”) will come true through God’s gift of eternal life for all who are righteous through faith and through the condemnation of the wicked to death in hell (Ps 1:6; Rom 6:23; Rev 20:6; 21:8).

10:28 This verse contrasts the future expectations of the righteous and the wicked. The joy of the righteous is a present possession based on the certainty of God’s promises, which are fulfilled in the crucified and risen Christ (Rom 15:8–13; 1 Pet 1:3–9). The hopes of the wicked, however, have no such guarantee, so apart from God, they will perish.

10:29 This verse is the only saying in Proverbs to use the phrase דֶּרֶךְ יְהוָה, “the way of Yahweh.” However, it relates to other proverbs that speak of the “ways” of Wisdom (3:17–20; 8:32) and of Yahweh’s “way” (8:22). Those passages stress the preexistence of divine Wisdom as a hypostasis of the eternal Trinity. That Jesus Christ is God’s Wisdom and “the way” (Jn 14:6) is the basis for this proverb about “the way of Yahweh.”[4] Contrary to the many proverbs that speak of two different ways, the contrast here is between the two different

---

[4] For Christ as Wisdom, see “Wisdom in Proverbs” in the introduction. See also the commentary on 1:1–7; 3:13–20; 8:22–31; 30:1b–10; and the excursus “Proverbs 8, Wisdom, Christology, and the Arian Controversy” in the commentary on chapter 8.

effects that the one way of Yahweh has on the two different types of people.[5] The person of integrity—the believer, who seeks to do the will of the one who has loved him from eternity through Wisdom (8:30–31)—is made secure for eternity by God's way (2:7; 10:9; 13:6). However, those without that integrity cannot escape from God's way. They will experience it in a different manner: when the Wisdom of God condemns them to their own destruction (Mt 11:19–24; cf. those who reject "the Way" in Acts 19:9, 23).

The second line of this saying is identical to the second line of 21:15.

10:30 This verse restates the truths of 10:29, but it also serves to define the person of integrity as "righteous," that is, as forensically justified by God through faith in the promised Messiah (Gen 15:6; Is 53:11). It also defines the "destruction" for evildoers in Prov 10:29 as removal from the earth.

10:31 This verse may perhaps refer to 3:18, where Wisdom is depicted as "a tree of life." The righteous person is depicted as bearing the fruit of this tree, as also in 11:30 (cf. 15:4). For a similar use of the verb נוב, "to bear fruit," see Ps 92:13–16 (ET 92:12–15), where the fruit is able to nourish others. The perverse tongue, which produces no good fruit, is cut off, just as a tree is pruned of an unproductive branch. Jesus uses this same picture of unproductive branches to warn those who do not produce fruit that they will literally be taken away (Jn 15:1–2). See also Mt 3:10; 7:17–19.

10:32 This verse is linked to 10:31 by the catchwords "mouth" and "perverse." This saying explains how the mouth of a righteous person bears fruit. His lips "know favor," that is, they proclaim the favor and gracious will of God, who desires to save all people (see the commentary on 10:24 and 10:28). They refrain from speaking about the perverse things that occupy the speech of wicked people. This description of a "righteous person" finds its fulfillment in the Righteous One, Jesus Christ, who proclaimed that the time of God's "favor" had arrived in him (Lk 4:19).

---

[5] The excursus "The Metaphor of the Path in Solomon's Wisdom" at the beginning of the commentary on this chapter shows that the metaphor can express either Law or Gospel.

Excursus

"Disgusting Thing" (תּוֹעֵבָה) in Solomon's Proverbs

One unique feature of the proverbs by Solomon is the characterization of certain attitudes and behaviors as תּוֹעֲבַת יְהוָה, traditionally, "(an) abomination to the LORD" (KJV), rendered in this commentary as "a disgusting thing to Yahweh." This construct phrase occurs only in portions of the book authored by Solomon.[1] Elsewhere in the OT the phrase occurs only in Deuteronomy, so Solomon is drawing on the phraseology of Moses in order to explain and apply the Torah.[2] Even when it is not joined to the name "Yahweh," most of the other uses of תּוֹעֵבָה, "disgusting thing," are in proverbs by Solomon.[a] In fact, out of the total of twenty-one instances of תּוֹעֵבָה in Proverbs, only one is in a non-Solomonic section of the book, and there it has a different nuance because it does not denote the revulsion of God, but of people (24:9).

(a) Prov 6:16; 8:7; 13:19; 16:12; 21:27; 24:9; 26:25; 28:9; 29:27

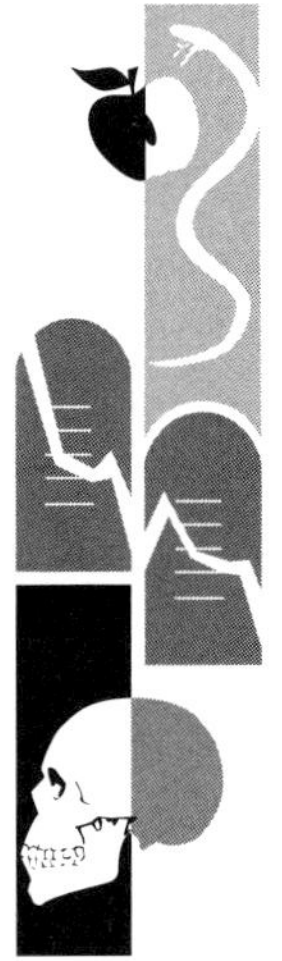

The noun תּוֹעֵבָה signifies something that is theologically and morally repulsive. It should also be innately and aesthetically reprehensible, but the natural reason and discernment of sinful people is so thoroughly corrupted because of the fall into sin that they may fail to recognize the depravity of disgusting things (see Rom 1:18–32). At times in Scripture this term is a synonym for an "idol" (Deut 7:26), like שִׁקּוּץ, "detestable thing," which denotes cultic uncleanness, especially idolatry.[3] Both of these terms are used together in 2 Ki 23:13 and Jer 16:18, and by the priest-prophet Ezekiel to condemn Israel for its idolatry, which defiled the holy temple (Ezek 5:11; 7:20; 11:18, 21). In Deuteronomy, the only other biblical book with "a disgusting thing to Yahweh," this phrase most often is connected with proscribed idolatrous or sacrilegious worship practices.[b]

(b) Deut 7:25; 12:31; 17:1; 18:12; 23:19 (ET 23:18); 27:15

Thus the phrase תּוֹעֲבַת יְהוָה denotes things that are incompatible with Yahweh's holiness and divine nature; therefore they are disgusting and abhorrent to him.[4] Prov 6:16–19 lists seven things that are disgusting to Yahweh (see below). Apart from that passage, other proverbs include six categories of human conduct that are described as "a disgusting thing to Yahweh" (תּוֹעֲבַת יְהוָה).

---

[1] Prov 3:32; 11:1, 20; 12:22; 15:8–9, 26; 16:5; 17:15; 20:10, 23. For a discussion of the authorship of the various sections of the book, see "Authorship and Date" in the introduction, especially figure 1.

[2] In Deuteronomy the phrase occurs in Deut 7:25; 12:31; 17:1; 18:12; 22:5; 23:19 (ET 23:18); 25:16; 27:15. For another clear example of Solomon citing from the Torah, see the excursus "The Use of Deuteronomy 6:4–9 in Proverbs 3:1–12 and 6:20–22" after the commentary on 3:1–20.

[3] R. F. Youngblood, "תּוֹעֵבָה," *TWOT* 2:977.

[4] E. Gerstenberger, "תעב," *TLOT* 3:1430.

1. General sinful behavior:

   ... because a crooked person is a disgusting thing to Yahweh,
   but Yahweh's confidential advice is with upright people. (3:32)

   The way of a wicked person is a disgusting thing to Yahweh,
   but he loves those who pursue righteousness. (15:9)

2. Sinful attitudes and thoughts:

   Those with a perverted heart are a disgusting thing to Yahweh,
   but his favor is [upon] those people whose way has integrity. (11:20)

   The plans of a wicked person are a disgusting thing to Yahweh,
   but pleasant words are pure [to him]. (15:26)

   Everyone with an arrogant attitude is a disgusting thing to Yahweh.
   Be sure of this: that person will not go unpunished. (16:5)

3. Sinful speech:

   ... for my [Wisdom's] palate declares truth,
   and wickedness is a disgusting thing to my lips. (8:7)[5]

   Lying lips are a disgusting thing to Yahweh,
   but those who act truthfully [receive] his favor. (12:22)

4. Worship by those who are wicked, that is, those who do not repent and are not righteous through faith:

   A sacrifice offered by wicked people is a disgusting thing to Yahweh,
   but a prayer by upright people [receives] his favor. (15:8)

   A sacrifice offered by wicked people is a disgusting thing—
   how much more when they bring it with evil intent! (21:27)[6]

5. Perverted justice:

   Acquitting the guilty person and convicting the innocent person—
   both of them are a disgusting thing to Yahweh. (17:15)

6. Fraud:

   Dishonest scales are a disgusting thing to Yahweh,
   but an accurate weight [has] his favor. (11:1)

   Differing weights and differing measures—
   both of them are a disgusting thing to Yahweh. (20:10)

---

[5] While this proverb does not speak of "Yahweh," divine Wisdom is speaking, so "my lips" refers to God.

[6] In this proverb it is implicit that the sacrifice is a disgusting thing *to Yahweh*. This is clear when the proverb is compared to 15:8. The three Hebrew words that comprise 21:27a (זֶבַח רְשָׁעִים תּוֹעֵבָה, "a sacrifice offered by wicked people is a disgusting thing") are the first three Hebrew words in 15:8a, which then ends with "... to Yahweh."

> Differing weights are a disgusting thing to Yahweh,
> and dishonest scales are not good. (20:23)

It is interesting to note that of the seven disgusting things to Yahweh listed in 6:16–19, five of them fall into one of these six categories, whereas only two do not: murder and spreading conflict.[7] With the exception of murder, all of these sins are difficult for human authorities to detect and to punish. The ease with which such sins can be hidden from other humans is emphasized by 26:25, where a wicked person's speech may appear to be gracious, but it conceals seven disgusting things in his heart.

Therefore, Proverbs may call sins "a disgusting thing to Yahweh" to emphasize that even if a person succeeds in hiding these sins from other people and/or escapes human castigation for them, he still falls under God's approbation, and unless he repents, he will not escape the threat of divine punishment.

Prov 10:1–22:16 contains most of the uses of תּוֹעֵבָה. Only two of the proverbs in that part of the book speak of something being disgusting to someone other than Yahweh. The saying in 13:19 describes turning from evil as "a disgusting thing to fools." Whereas repentance is pleasing to God, fools, whose attitude is diametrically opposite to God's attitude, find it disgusting. However, as Solomon emphasizes throughout the book, the things that God finds disgusting are delightful to fools.

The other "disgusting thing" (תּוֹעֵבָה) proverb in 10:1–22:16 that does not mention God is 16:12. In this case "to do wickedness" is said to be "a disgusting thing to kings." As God's representative over the particular nation, a king is to have the same attitude toward sins as God does. Especially relevant are the expressions of God's will in the commandments in the Second Table of the Decalogue,[8] since these commandments pertain to social relationships and are just as applicable to unbelieving peoples as they are to God's people.

Only three "disgusting thing" (תּוֹעֵבָה) proverbs are found in those proverbs of Solomon that were copied by Hezekiah's men (25:1–29:27). Besides 26:25 (see above), 28:9 and 29:27 employ this term. In this section of Solomon's proverbs, the "disgusting thing" (תּוֹעֵבָה) is never explicitly said to be disgusting to Yahweh. Prov 28:9 speaks of someone rejecting "instruction" (תּוֹרָה; see the second textual note on 1:8), and such a person's prayer is disgusting. Set in the context of worship practices, the implication is that God finds this person himself disgusting and unacceptable. This leads to the conclusion that the "instruction" is not mere human pedagogy, but the instruction from God in his Word of Law and Gospel, "instruction" imparted by faithful teachers of the Word (as in, e.g., 1:1–2, 8).

---

[7] The other five in 6:16–19 are rushing to do evil (general sinful behavior); arrogance and plotting (both are sinful attitudes and thoughts); lying and false witness (sinful speech and/or perverted justice). See further the commentary on 6:16–19.

[8] See further the excursus "Proverbs 1–9, Christ, and the Ten Commandments" in the commentary on Proverbs 1.

The last proverb in the book to use "disgusting thing" (תּוֹעֵבָה) is 29:27, which employs it twice. First, it states that "an unjust person is a disgusting thing to righteous people," since the attitude of the righteous is conformed to that of God. While baptized believers in Christ still retain their sinful nature during this life and by God's grace they must battle against it (e.g., Romans 6–7), the regeneration and renewal of the Holy Spirit (Titus 3:5–6) forms in believers the mind and attitude of Jesus Christ himself (Rom 12:2; 1 Cor 2:16; Eph 4:23; Phil 2:5; 1 Pet 4:1), which includes revulsion at sin. Second, Prov 29:27 cautions that "a person whose way is upright is a disgusting thing to a wicked person." The wicked, who are opposed to God, find a righteous person to be disgusting, just as they find God's ways disgusting. This attitude underlies the rejection of the sinless Christ himself during his earthly ministry, culminating in his crucifixion, and the persecution of the church of Christ and the rejection of his Gospel, which continues to be reviled throughout the unbelieving world to this day.

Therefore the dual teaching in 29:27 about a "disgusting thing" is the same as that by the apostle Paul:

> For the mind [φρόνημα] of the sinful flesh is death,
> but the mind [φρόνημα] of [instilled by] the Spirit is life and peace.
> (Rom 8:6)

Proverbs 11:1–31

Righteous Behavior, Part 1

Translation

11 **[1]Dishonest scales are a disgusting thing to Yahweh,**
but an accurate weight [has] his favor.
[2]When arrogance comes, then comes shame,
but with humility [comes] wisdom.
[3]The integrity of upright people guides them,
but the crookedness of treacherous people destroys them.
[4]Riches are of no help on the day of fury,
but righteousness saves from death.
[5]The righteousness of a person of integrity makes his way straight,
but because of his wickedness, a wicked person falls.
[6]The righteousness of upright people saves them,
but treacherous people are trapped by their own desire.
[7]At the death of a man who is wicked, hope will perish,
and confidence in strength perishes.
[8]A righteous person is rescued from trouble,
and a wicked person takes his place.
[9]By [his] mouth the godless person destroys his neighbor,
but by knowledge righteous people are rescued.
[10]When righteous people prosper, a city rejoices,
and when wicked people perish, [there is] a shout of joy.
[11]By the blessing of upright people, a city is raised up,
but by the mouth of wicked people, it is torn down.
[12]A person who lacks sense despises his neighbor,
but a person with understanding keeps silent.
[13]Someone who goes about gossiping betrays a confidence,
but one who is trustworthy in spirit keeps a [private] matter confidential.

[14]Without guidance a nation falls,
but many advisors [bring] victory.
[15]Trouble will come to one who guarantees a loan for a stranger,
but one who hates striking [hands] remains secure.
[16]A gracious woman takes hold of honor,
but ruthless men take hold of riches.
[17]A faithful man benefits himself,
but a cruel man brings trouble on himself.
[18]A wicked person earns deceptive wages,
but the person who sows righteousness [earns] a true reward.

[19]Just as righteousness [leads] to life,
so the person who pursues evil [leads] to his own death.

[20]Those with a perverted heart are a disgusting thing to Yahweh,
but his favor is [upon] those people whose way has integrity.
[21]Be sure of this: the evil person will not go unpunished,
but those who are righteous will escape.
[22]A gold ring in a pig's snout—
a beautiful woman without discretion.

[23]The desire of righteous people [leads] only [to] good;
the hope of wicked people [leads to] fury.
[24]One person scatters [his wealth], but it increases more,
while another holds back what he owes, but it only [leads] to poverty.
[25]The person who spreads blessing will prosper,
and the person who refreshes others will be refreshed.
[26]The people will curse a person who hoards grain,
but a blessing will be on the head of the person who sells [it].

[27]The person who eagerly looks for good seeks [God's] favor,
but whoever seeks evil, it will come to him.
[28]Whoever places his trust in his wealth will fall,
but righteous people will sprout like foliage.
[29]Whoever troubles his family will inherit wind,
and a stubborn fool will be a slave to a person who is wise in heart.

[30]The fruit of a righteous person is a tree of life,
and one who harvests souls is wise.
[31]If a person who is righteous on earth is paid back,
how much more a wicked person or a sinner!

Textual Notes

11:1 מֹאזְנֵי מִרְמָה תּוֹעֲבַת יְהוָה—The dual noun מֹאזְנַיִם refers to scales or a balance: a lever with one pan connected to each end. A weight is placed in one pan, and an equal weight of the commodity being sold is placed in the other pan so that they balance. The dual noun is in construct with the noun מִרְמָה, "deception," which can take on the denotation of dishonesty or fraud (*HALOT*, 1). The construct phrase, literally, "scales of deception" is an adjectival genitive phrase: "dishonest scales." The identical construct phrase recurs in 20:23. The opposite, מֹאזְנֵי מִשְׁפָּט, "scales of justice," that is, "accurate scales," is in 16:11.

For תּוֹעֲבַת יְהוָה, "an abomination/a disgusting thing to Yahweh," see the first textual note and the commentary on 3:32 and the excursus " 'Disgusting Thing' (תּוֹעֵבָה) in Solomon's Proverbs" at the beginning of the commentary on Proverbs 11.

וְאֶבֶן שְׁלֵמָה רְצוֹנוֹ׃—Literally, "a complete stone [is] his favor," this refers to a stone weight that is as heavy as it is supposed to be. אֶבֶן is feminine, so it is modified by the feminine form of the adjective שָׁלֵם.

The noun רָצוֹן, which in this chapter recurs in 11:20, 27, usually refers to God's gift of "favor, grace." See the second textual note on 8:35. This is the first of four proverbs that contrast תּוֹעֲבַת יְהוָה, "a disgusting thing to Yahweh," and רְצוֹנוֹ, "his favor," referring to a person or behavior that receives God's gracious approval. The other three verses are 11:20; 12:22; 15:8.

11:2 בָּא־זָדוֹן וַיָּבֹא קָלוֹן—The perfect בָּא and parallel imperfect with *waw* consecutive, וַיָּבֹא, both have a gnomic, timeless meaning (Waltke-O'Connor, § 33.3.1b, including example 14).

וְאֶת־צְנוּעִים חָכְמָה׃—In this context אֶת must be the preposition "with." צָנוּעַ occurs only here in the OT. The plural צְנוּעִים could be an adjective (BDB) used as a substantive: "with humble people is wisdom." However, since 11:2a had the two abstract nouns זָדוֹן, "arrogance," and קָלוֹן, "shame" (singular nouns that rhyme), most likely צְנוּעִים is an abstract plural, "humility" (cf. *HALOT*).

11:3 תֻּמַּת יְשָׁרִים תַּנְחֵם—The feminine noun תֻּמָּה, "integrity," occurs only here in Proverbs. For the masculine synonym תֹּם, see the second textual note on 2:7. The substantive תָּמִים, "person of integrity," is in 11:5, 20.

The feminine noun תֻּמָּה is the subject of the feminine Hiphil (H) imperfect תַּנְחֵם (from נָחָה, "to lead, guide"), and the masculine plural suffix ("them") on the verb refers back to יְשָׁרִים. For יָשָׁר as a substantive, "upright person, righteous person," see the first textual note and the commentary on 2:7.

וְסֶלֶף בּוֹגְדִים וְשָׁדֵּם׃—The noun סֶלֶף, "crookedness," occurs in the OT only here and in 15:4. For the cognate verb, see the second textual note on 13:6. For the participle of בָּגַד, "treacherous person," see the second textual note on 2:22. The Qere יְשָׁדֵּם, "it [their crookedness] destroys them," is the Qal (G) imperfect of שָׁדַד with suffix (GKC, § 67 n; Joüon, § 82 g). It is preferable to the Kethib, which probably would be vocalized as וְשַׁדָּם, the Qal perfect of שָׁדַד with *waw* conjunctive and suffix: "and it destroyed them."

11:4 לֹא־יוֹעִיל הוֹן בְּיוֹם עֶבְרָה—The initial wording is similar to that in 10:2, which also warns that riches "are not profitable" (לֹא־יוֹעִילוּ) eschatologically. "On a day of fury" points toward the Last Day: the day that Christ returns in glory is the day when God will fully execute his judgment against all sinners who have refused to repent. Similar is "the day of Yahweh" theme in the Prophets, for example, Amos 5:18–20.

וּצְדָקָה תַּצִּיל מִמָּוֶת׃—See the second textual note and the commentary on 10:2, which has the identical clause. In this pericope, צְדָקָה recurs in 11:5–6, 18–19. Similar to this clause is 11:6a.

11:5 צִדְקַת תָּמִים תְּיַשֵּׁר דַּרְכּוֹ—For תָּמִים, "person of integrity, blameless person," see the second textual note on 2:21. The Piel (D) of יָשַׁר has a causative meaning here, "to make straight," as in 3:6.

וּבְרִשְׁעָתוֹ יִפֹּל רָשָׁע׃—For רָשָׁע, "wicked person," which recurs in this chapter in 11:7–8, 10–11, 18, 23, 31, see the first textual note on 2:22. The cognate noun רִשְׁעָה has the abstract meaning "wickedness," and it occurs elsewhere in the book only in 13:6.

11:6 וּבְהַוַּת בֹּגְדִים יִלָּכֵדוּ׃—Literally, this is "and by the desire of treacherous people, they [the treacherous people] are captured, caught." For the noun הַוָּה, evil "desire," see the second textual note on 10:3.

11:7 וְתוֹחֶלֶת אוֹנִים אָבָדָה׃—The noun תּוֹחֶלֶת, "hope," is parallel to תִּקְוָה, "hope, aspiration, confidence" (11:7a), also in 10:28. The noun אוֹן, "strength," is used only twelve times in the OT, sometimes as an intensive plural, as here and in, for example, Is 40:26. It can refer to virility or reproductive power (Deut 21:17; Ps 78:51). It also can denote wealth (Hos 12:9 [ET 12:8]; Job 20:10).

Note that the imperfect of אָבַד in the preceding clause, תֹּאבַד, is parallel to the perfect of the same verb, the pausal form אָבָדָה, in this clause (see Waltke-O'Connor, § 31.1.1e, including example 6).

11:8 צַדִּיק מִצָּרָה נֶחֱלָץ—The verb חָלַץ occurs in Proverbs only in the Niphal (N), "to be rescued," in these adjacent verses: the perfect נֶחֱלָץ here and the imperfect יֵחָלֵצוּ in 11:9.

11:9 בְּפֶה חָנֵף יַשְׁחִת רֵעֵהוּ—The adjective חָנֵף, "profane, ungodly," is used as a substantive here: someone who is "alienated from God, **godless**" (*HALOT*).

וּבְדַעַת צַדִּיקִים יֵחָלֵצוּ׃—See "דַּעַת, 'Knowledge,' and יָדַע, 'to Know' " in "Wisdom in Proverbs" in the introduction, as well as the commentary on 1:4, 7.

11:10 בְּטוּב צַדִּיקִים ... וּבַאֲבֹד—Both clauses begin with the preposition בְּ used in a temporal sense: "when." The noun טוּב can refer to blessings from Yahweh (Pss 27:13; 65:5 [ET 65:4]) or have the more abstract meaning "prosperity" (BDB, 3 c). The first clause can be rendered idiomatically as "when things go well for the righteous" or "when the righteous prosper."

11:11 בְּבִרְכַּת ... וּבְפִי—The preposition בְּ is used instrumentally twice here. It signifies the means through which something is done. Note that 11:10–11 forms a nice play on the various meanings of this preposition. Both proverbs are in two lines, and in both the first line begins with the preposition בְּ and the second line begins with the conjunction and the preposition בְּ.

For the noun בְּרָכָה, "blessing," see the first textual note on 10:6. The construct phrase בִּרְכַּת יְשָׁרִים serves as an objective genitive phrase, "the blessing of [given by Yahweh to] upright people," similar to the construct phrase that began 11:10, טוּב צַדִּיקִים, literally, "the prosperity of [given by Yahweh to] the righteous."

11:12 בָּז־לְרֵעֵהוּ חֲסַר־לֵב—The verb בּוּז, "to despise," was first used in 1:7, where the subject was "fools." The identical verb with object, בָּז־לְרֵעֵהוּ, "he despises his neighbor," recurs in 14:21. For the subject here, see "חֲסַר־לֵב, 'Lacking Sense' " in "Fools in Proverbs" in the introduction.

וְאִישׁ תְּבוּנוֹת יַחֲרִישׁ׃—The abstract plural of תְּבוּנָה, "understanding," is related to cognate synonyms. See "בִּינָה, 'Understanding,' and Related Words" in "Wisdom in Proverbs" in the introduction. The only other instance of the Hiphil (H) of חָרַשׁ, "to be silent," in Proverbs is in 17:28.

11:13 הוֹלֵךְ רָכִיל מְגַלֶּה־סּוֹד—Literally, "one walking around as a slanderer reveals counsel," this vocabulary is repeated in 20:19a.

וְנֶאֱמַן־ר֝֗וּחַ מְכַסֶּ֥ה דָבָֽר׃—Literally, "one who is faithful of [in] spirit covers a matter," the context (the parallelism to the preceding clause) makes clear that "covers a matter" does not denote concealing wrongdoing (as can the English idiom "cover up") but means "keeps a [private] matter confidential." This saying is a good example of why many proverbs must be rendered in idiomatic English rather than in a strictly form-equivalent translation.

11:14 בְּאֵ֣ין תַּ֭חְבֻּלוֹת יִפָּל־עָ֑ם—See "תַּחְבּוּלוֹת, 'Guidance' " in "Wisdom in Proverbs" in the introduction.

וּ֝תְשׁוּעָ֗ה בְּרֹ֣ב יוֹעֵֽץ׃—Literally, this is "victory [is] with a multitude of counselor." The singular participle יוֹעֵץ must have a collective meaning here, hence "many advisors" (see GKC, § 123 b; Waltke-O'Connor, § 7.2.2b, example 10).

11:15 רַע־יֵ֭רוֹעַ כִּי־עָ֣רַב זָ֑ר—Literally, "(with an) injury he will be injured because he guaranteed a loan (for) a stranger." The noun רַע can denote an "injury" or "harm" (BDB, s.v. רַע II, 2). Cognate to the noun is the denominative verb רָעַע, to "suffer hurt" (BDB, Niphal) or "be injured," whose Niphal is found in the OT only as the imperfect יֵרוֹעַ here and in 13:20. For the form of the verb, see GKC, § 67 t, and Joüon, § 82 m. For the next verb, עָרַב, "to guarantee a loan," see the first textual note on 6:1.

תֹּקְעִ֣ים—For the idiom "to strike [תָּקַע] hands" in order to agree on and close a transaction, see the second textual note on 6:1. Here the object "hands" is assumed.

11:16 אֵֽשֶׁת־חֵ֭ן תִּתְמֹ֣ךְ כָּבֹ֑וד—The construct phrase אֵֽשֶׁת־חֵן, "a woman of grace," occurs only here in the OT, and it has an adjectival genitive: "a gracious woman." For חֵן, "grace," see the first textual note on 1:9. The verb תָּמַךְ in the positive context here could be rendered as "attain, receive," but it is translated neutrally as "take hold of" both here and in the following clause, where the context is negative.

וְ֝עָרִיצִ֗ים יִתְמְכוּ־עֹֽשֶׁר׃—The adjective עָרִיץ means "violent, powerful" or "acting violently" (*HALOT*, 1 a–b). In this context it describes someone who acts with violence without regard for justice or the welfare of others. Thus in context it means "ruthless," and the verb תָּמַךְ could be rendered as "seize, take" wealth (עֹשֶׁר). The LXX expands this verse as follows:

γυνὴ εὐχάριστος ἐγείρει ἀνδρὶ δόξαν,
θρόνος δὲ ἀτιμίας γυνὴ μισοῦσα δίκαια.
πλούτου ὀκνηροὶ ἐνδεεῖς γίνονται,
οἱ δὲ ἀνδρεῖοι ἐρείδονται πλούτῳ.

A gracious woman procures honor for her husband,
but a seat of dishonor is a woman who hates righteous things.
The lazy become destitute,
but the aggressive support themselves with wealth.

There is no need to follow this expansion (as does NRSV) and no reason to suspect that the additional lines added by the LXX were somehow lost in the MT.

11:17 גֹּמֵ֣ל נַ֭פְשׁוֹ אִ֣ישׁ חָ֑סֶד וְעֹכֵ֥ר שְׁ֝אֵר֗וֹ אַכְזָרִֽי׃—Both "his soul" (נַפְשׁוֹ) and "his flesh" (שְׁאֵרוֹ) are used as reflexive pronouns to refer to the person himself. The sense *is not* that a righteous person (אִ֣ישׁ חָ֑סֶד, literally, "a man of fidelity, faithfulness") is able to improve his spiritual or physical life by his own power. Rather, God's own grace and fidelity to his promises result in the blessings that the righteous person may receive, both physical and spiritual blessings.

Similarly, an evil person brings harm to both his physical and his spiritual life. The Qal of עָכַר, "to trouble" or "bring disaster" (*HALOT*), has a distinctly eschatological meaning in Josh 6:18; 7:25. Achan's violation of the divine ban brings God's wrathful judgment upon all Israel. Joshua declares to Achan that "Yahweh troubles you this day" (Josh 7:25), and Israel stones Achan, "the troubler of Israel" (1 Chr 2:7). The implication of "to trouble" in all four of its occurrences in Proverbs (11:17, 29; 15:6, 27) is that infidelity brings everlasting condemnation by God.

11:18 פְּעֻלַּת־שָׁקֶר ... שֶׂכֶר אֱמֶת׃—Both construct phrases are examples of adjectival genitive phrases. The noun שֶׁקֶר denotes a lie, a statement intended to deceive (see *HALOT*, 4). The wages (פְּעֻלָּה) earned by the wicked are deceptive since they deceive both the one paying the wages as well as the recipient, who rationalizes that he deserves them despite his dishonesty. In contrast, שֶׂכֶר אֱמֶת, "a true reward," accrues to the person who "sows righteousness" (וְזֹרֵעַ צְדָקָה). Hos 10:12 ("sow for yourselves righteousness") shows that this agricultural terminology refers to seeking God in repentance and faith.

11:20 עִקְּשֵׁי־לֵב—For the adjective עִקֵּשׁ, "crooked," see the first textual note on 2:15.

וּרְצוֹנוֹ תְּמִימֵי דָרֶךְ׃—For רְצוֹנוֹ, see the second textual note on 11:1. The construct phrase תְּמִימֵי דָרֶךְ is, literally, "people with integrity of way," but it must be rephrased in English. For תָּמִים, "person of integrity," that is, one who is righteous through faith, see the second textual note on 2:21.

11:21 יָד לְיָד—This expression, literally, "hand to hand," is used here and in 16:5. It probably means "surely, certainly, without a doubt" (see *HALOT*, s.v. יָד, 3). It may derive from the custom of striking hands with someone to close a transaction (see 11:15b and the second textual note on 6:1).

לֹא־יִנָּקֶה רָּע—Literally, this is "an evil person will not be considered innocent." See the second textual note on 6:29. רָּע is one of the few instances in the OT where the consonant ר admits a *daghesh* (GKC, § 22 s).

וְזֶרַע צַדִּיקִים נִמְלָט׃—This is, literally, "and the seed of righteous people will escape." זֶרַע, "seed," in Is 53:10 refers to those who are redeemed by the Suffering Servant and who believe and are saved.

11:22 וְסָרַת טָעַם׃—The verb סוּר means "turn aside," and can take on the connotation of "abandon, desist" or "leave off, stop" (*HALOT*, 4, 6). Its feminine Qal (G) participle is in construct with what the woman lacks. The noun טַעַם means "taste" and can be used in a way that is similar to the English word, as in "bad taste." Here its combination with the verb means "without discretion" (*HALOT*, s.v. טַעַם, 2).

11:24 יֵשׁ מְפַזֵּר וְנוֹסָף עוֹד—The combination of יֵשׁ ("there is"), the particle of existence, and a substantival participle is used here and in 12:18; 13:7, 23; 18:24 to mean "there is a type of person who" or, more simply, "one [type of] person does …" (see Waltke-O'Connor, § 37.5f, example 28, and *HALOT*, s.v. יֵשׁ, 4).

The Piel (D) of פִּזַּר, "scatter," can mean "spend money." It refers to, or at least includes, giving alms and charitable financial gifts both here and in Ps 112:9. There is no stated subject of the Niphal (N) verb וְנוֹסָף, literally, "and it is added, increased," so this is not necessarily a divine promise of gaining more money; instead God promises everlasting riches.

וְחוֹשֵׂךְ מִיֹּשֶׁר—Literally, this is "one who withholds from what is upright." The noun יֹשֶׁר often means "straightness" or "uprightness," but in this context it means "what would be right to pay," that is, one's financial obligation to support the church as well as pay one's civil debts.

11:25 וּמַרְוֶה גַּם־הוּא יוֹרֶא׃—The Piel (D) of רָוָה, "give to drink, intoxicate," was in 5:19. The Hiphil (H) participle מַרְוֶה, literally, "one who gives drinks to others," has the more general or metaphorical meaning "one who refreshes others." יוֹרֶא in the Leningrad Codex must be a Hophal (Hp) form of the same verb, "be given a drink; be refreshed," with א- instead of ה-. However, many Hebrew manuscripts have the expected spelling, יוֹרֶה. The Hophal (Hp) of רָוָה occurs only here in the OT. The expected form of the Hophal (Hp) imperfect would be יוּרֶא, but sometimes -וֹ- appears instead of -וּ- (GKC, § 69 w).

11:27 יְבַקֵּשׁ רָצוֹן—As in 11:1, 20, the noun רָצוֹן refers to God's gracious gift of his "favor." See the second textual note on 8:35.

11:29 וְעֶבֶד אֱוִיל לַחֲכַם־לֵב׃—For the subject of this nominal clause, אֱוִיל, see "אֱוִיל, 'Stubborn Fool,' and אִוֶּלֶת, 'Stupidity' " in "Fools in Proverbs" in the introduction. The predicate is וְעֶבֶד ... לַחֲכַם־לֵב, "(will be) a slave ... to a person who is wise of heart." The construct phrase חֲכַם־לֵב is antonymous to the more common construct phrase חֲסַר־לֵב, "a person who lacks sense," as in 11:12.

11:30 עֵץ חַיִּים—For "a tree of life," see the first textual note and the commentary on 3:18.

וְלֹקֵחַ נְפָשׁוֹת חָכָם׃—The pointing in the Leningrad Codex, -שׁ-, must be an error for נְפָשׁוֹת, the plural of נֶפֶשׁ. Therefore this clause is, literally, "one taking souls [is] wise." In connection with a tree or plant, לָקַח means "to pick" or "harvest" its fruit (e.g., Gen 3:6, 22; 40:11; Num 13:20; Deut 1:25). In light of the previous clause with "a tree of life," the meaning here is "to harvest souls" by helping to bring them to eternal life by God's grace. The verb does not mean "to take lives, kill," as does לָקַח when it has the singular (not plural) object נֶפֶשׁ, as in 1 Ki 19:4; Ezek 33:6; Jonah 4:3; Ps 31:14 (ET 31:13).[1]

The emendation of חָכָם, "wise," to חָמָס, "violence," based on the LXX, is suggested by some interpreters and followed by NRSV and NAB. However, that misunderstands the idiom "to harvest souls." It also destroys the catchword link of "wise" here with 11:29.

11:31 הֵן צַדִּיק בָּאָרֶץ יְשֻׁלָּם—The particle הֵן can be used to mean "if" (*HALOT*, 2), a usage that may be an Aramaism.

This clause does not promise that the righteous will be paid back while they are still on this earth (contrary to many English translations). Rather it means that those

---

[1] Cf. Irwin, "The Metaphor in Prov 11,30."

who are righteous on earth (justified through faith while still alive in this world) will indeed be rewarded by grace.[2] The LXX may have read the letters of בָּאָרֶץ in a different order: either בְּצָרָא (the equivalent of בְּצָרָה) or בַּצַּר, both of which could mean "in deficiency, with lack," and translated it as μόλις, "scarcely," adding a slight emphasis to the verse without substantially altering its meaning. LXX Prov 11:31 is reflected in 1 Pet 4:18 almost word for word:

> καὶ εἰ ὁ δίκαιος μόλις σῴζεται, ὁ ἀσεβὴς καὶ ἁμαρτωλὸς ποῦ φανεῖται;
>
> If the righteous person scarcely is saved, the ungodly and the sinner—what will appear/happen [to him]?

Commentary

Though a chapter division occurs between 10:32 and 11:1, there is no sharp break in content or style. In general, the chapter divisions in 10:1–22:16 should be thought of as a reference system, not as a guide to literary divisions. For the loose structure of the sections in this part of Proverbs, see the excursus "The Organization of the Sayings in Solomon's Proverbs in Proverbs 10:1–22:16" in the commentary on Proverbs 10. The topic of this chapter is the behavior of the righteous; their justification by grace alone yields the fruit of good works and sanctified living. This relationship between justification by grace and the fruit ("sows righteousness," 11:18) of good works is the same as in the NT, as, for example, the apostle Paul describes in Romans 6 and Eph 2:8–10. See also "The Relationship between Wisdom and Righteousness in Proverbs" in "Wisdom in Proverbs" in the introduction.

11:1 This verse is linked to 10:32 by the catchword "[God's] favor." This proverb demonstrates God's ultimate condemnation of a practice that is easily concealed: using dishonest weights and measures. Since in ancient Israel people could not easily regulate commerce based on weight (and it is still difficult to police this today), this proverb was designed to curb fraud by placing the force of God's condemnation on it. At the same time, God's gracious favor toward the faithful who are honest in their dealings is a positive motivation.

11:2 This verse begins with striking alliteration and rhyme: בָּא־זָדוֹן וַיָּבֹא קָלוֹן, literally, "comes arrogance [*zadon*] and comes shame [*qalon*]." It warns against a haughty self-importance that elevates oneself over God—breaking the First Commandment (Ex 20:3; Deut 5:7).[3] Humility, considering oneself in proper relationship with God and others, is connected here with God's gift of wisdom. Jesus makes this point at least three times in the Gospels (Mt 23:12; Lk 14:11; 18:14). The apostle Paul exhorts Christians to have the same mindset of humility as the Lord Jesus himself (Phil 2:5–11; cf. Rom 12:3; Eph 5:21).

[2] Cf. Barr, "בארץ ~ μόλις: Prov. xi. 31, I Pet. iv. 18," 162–64.

[3] See the excursus "Proverbs 1–9, Christ, and the Ten Commandments" in the commentary on Proverbs 1.

The traditional translation of זָדוֹן as "pride" is inappropriate in contemporary English. While "pride" in some contexts can still mean a haughty attitude, in contemporary usage it can also denote a God-pleasing sense of admiration or appreciation for a child, parent, student, coworker, school, and so on.

11:3–11 These verses form a group of proverbs that contrast righteous and wicked people. They are interlocked by a number of catchwords, some of which overlap:[4]

- יָשָׁר, "upright person" (11:3, 6, 11), and the Piel (D) of יָשַׁר, "make straight" (11:5)
- תֻּמָּה (11:3) and תָּמִים (11:5), "integrity"
- בּוֹגְדִים, "treacherous people" (11:3, 6)
- צְדָקָה, "righteousness" (11:4–6)
- הִצִּיל, "to save" (11:4, 6)
- מָוֶת, "death" (11:4, 7)
- צְדָקָה, "righteousness" (11:5–6), or צַדִּיק, "righteous person" (11:8), as the verse's first word
- רָשָׁע, "wicked person" (11:5, 7–8, 10–11)
- בְּ, "at, by, when," as the verse's first letter (11:7, 9–11)
- אָבַד, "to perish" (11:7, 10)
- צַדִּיק, "righteous person" (11:8–10)
- חָלַץ in the Niphal (N), "to be rescued" (11:8–9)
- פֶּה, "mouth" (11:9, 11)
- קִרְיָה (11:10) and קֶרֶת (11:11), "city"

11:3 This verse is the most general of the sayings in this group and probably was placed first for this reason. The contrast between integrity guiding and crookedness destroying is not necessarily one of polar opposites all the time. Integrity does not guarantee a lack of trouble or calamity in one's life now, but it does guide the believer away from the ultimate judgment of God that wicked people eventually will face.

11:4 This verse does not condemn wealth, but notes its eschatological limitations. Righteousness, which God imputes to the repentant sinner, has no such limitation. See further "The Relationship between Wisdom and Righteousness in Proverbs" in "Wisdom in Proverbs" in the introduction.

11:5 This verse combines the thoughts of 11:3 and 11:4.

11:6 This verse states clearly that righteousness saves. The OT insists that God alone is Savior.[a] Righteousness in 11: 6 should be understood as the righteousness God imputes to every believer through faith alone (Gen 15:6), not to a righteousness merited by obedience to the Law nor to relative righteousness compared to other people.

(a) E.g., 2 Sam 22:3; Is 43:3, 11; 49:26; 60:16; 63:8; Jer 14:8; Hos 13:4; Pss 17:7; 106:21

---

[4] As an example of overlap, in addition to a word from the root צדק, "righteousness" or "righteous person," being the first word of the verse in 11:5–6, 8, the word צַדִּיק, "righteous person," is repeated as a catchword in 11:8–10.

11:7 This verse expresses the truth that there is no hope beyond the grave for those who die in their sin; their worldly powers cannot help them. The writer to the Hebrews says the same thing: "it is appointed for people to die once, and after that [comes] judgment" (Heb 9:27).

Because of the unusual length of the first line of this saying, some have suggested eliminating the word אָדָם, "person," to shorten it.[5] However, the sound pattern of the saying would be altered, making it unlikely that this is a proper emendation.[6]

11:8 This verse speaks of God's justice as it is worked out in this world. God can use one event to both rescue the righteous from distress and punish the wicked by that same distress (cf. Genesis 19; Rom 8:28; 1 Pet 3:18–22).

11:9 This verse stresses that knowledge can aid righteous people in exposing slander for what it is. However, it also reminds readers of the powerfully destructive force of words, which is the reason behind the Eighth Commandment (Ex 20:16; Deut 5:20).[7]

11:10 This verse notes that those who are righteous by grace alone benefit the general public. The people of God practice righteousness in the civil realm, which improves the living conditions for all people. On the other hand, public corruption eventually corrodes all of society, causing public joy when the corrupting powers perish.

11:11 This verse builds on 11:10 by noting the power of public speech, which can uplift and better a society or can tear down a society by spreading strife, hatred, and acrimony. Though this proverb ends the group that began with 11:3, it also connects to 11:12 by the paronomasia of the final words of each verse: תֵּהָרֵס, "it is torn down" (11:11), and יַחֲרִישׁ, "(he) keeps silent" (11:12).

11:12 This verse is practical advice on getting along with one's neighbor. Showing open contempt is asking for trouble, but the wise person says nothing, even if he does not find his neighbor pleasant or perfect.

11:13 This verse extends the theme of keeping silent to encourage respect for a neighbor's privacy as demanded by the Eighth Commandment (Ex 20:16; Deut 5:20). Note the similarity of the first line of this proverb with the first line of Prov 20:19.

11:14 This warning is especially relevant for those with political power, such as Solomon's sons. The guidance in the first line is expanded to many advisors in the second line. This proverb reminds readers that to be effective, those who govern must rely on a broad range of advice, and most of all they need guidance from God's Word and his faithful people. The second line of this proverb is identical to the second line of 24:6.

---

5 E.g., Toy, *Proverbs*, 225.

6 McCreesh, *Biblical Sound and Sense*, 138–39.

7 See the excursus "Proverbs 1–9, Christ, and the Ten Commandments" in the commentary on Proverbs 1.

11:15 This verse is one of several proverbs that warn against taking part in risky schemes to get rich. Such schemes often involve guaranteeing someone else's loan (see the commentary on 6:1; see also 17:18; 20:16; 22:26). Despite being outlawed, so-called "pyramid schemes" and "Ponzi schemes" continue today: fraudulent managers deceive investors, who unwittingly are paying debts owed to other investors, until the entire scheme is exposed and collapses.

11:16 This verse appears to use gender to make the contrast between a woman who gains honor and ruthless men who gain riches. However, the proverb most likely is making the point that riches can be acquired by any number of means, but graciousness—the ability to be kind and forgiving—is the key to true honor.[8] Paul urges the same type of attitude because of Christ's forgiveness:

> Be kind to one another, compassionate, freely forgiving one another, just as God in Christ freely forgave you. (Eph 4:32)

11:17 This verse is a saying that is counterintuitive. The kind person seems to go out of his way to benefit others, often at his own expense, whereas the cruel person appears to be driven by selfish and self-centered ambitions. The proverb does not say how these people benefit or hurt themselves. The ambiguity allows this proverb to function in a number of situations, so that the benefit or trouble may come from others or from God. Both the promise to anyone with saving faith and the warning against the cruel will be fulfilled on Judgment Day.

11:18 This verse highlights the transitory nature of worldly prosperity that is the result of sin.[9] The second line hints of an eternal reward for those who spread the message of the righteousness that God bestows solely by his grace. Note how the play on word-sounds between שֶׁקֶר, "deceptive," and שֶׂכֶר, "reward," heightens the contrast between the sinner (who gets "deceptive wages") and the righteous person (who receives the "reward").

11:19 This verse is linked to 11:18 by the word "righteousness." It speaks of the eternal life that righteousness brings, by the merits of the crucified and risen Christ. That life contrasts with the death of the person who seeks evil. The person who sows righteousness for others looks forward to receiving an eternal reward (11:18), but the person who selfishly pursues evil merits something he was not looking for: death.

11:20 This verse speaks of God's revulsion toward those with a perverted heart—one that has rejected God's Word and ways—and contrasts such people with people who have integrity. The faith of the latter leads them to make a commitment to live according to God's ways. Since only God can search the heart and see who is righteous through faith (see Jer 12:3; 17:10; Ps 26:2; 1 Chr 29:17), God's approbation alone can deter one from abandoning integrity.

---

8 Ross, "Proverbs," 962.

9 Scott, *Proverbs, Ecclesiastes*, 88.

11:21 This verse is a reminder that, despite the way things may appear in the world, God's eventual judgment on sinners and his rescue of his righteous people are certain.

11:22 This verse uses a caricature that paints a vivid image to teach men about choosing a wife (cf. 31:18, 30). Beauty is like the gold ring; lack of godly wisdom is like the pig. No matter how attractive, the unclean animal that sports the lure is not worth having in one's house. "Discretion" is a synonym of wisdom and the gift of faith, which provides the ability to make God-pleasing moral and ethical decisions.

11:23 This verse is the first of two quite different proverbs connected by the catchword "only" (אַךְ־ in 11:23a and 11:24b). While simple enough to understand, this proverb raises questions as to its application: "good" for whom—the person or others or both? "Fury" from whom—God (as in 11:4) or other humans or both? The ambiguity is probably designed to allow those who ponder it to think of the many ways in which God will fulfill it.

11:24 This verse encourages generosity, promising an increase. Those who give sacrificially to the church and to needy fellow believers will gain more—not necessarily more money, but eternal riches (Mt 19:29; Lk 18:22). The miser who refuses to make charitable donations or even pay off his debts would seem to have more, but this leads to poverty.

Paul encourages the same type of generosity in the light of God's generous grace in Christ:

> Whoever sows sparingly will also reap sparingly, and whoever sows bountifully will also reap bountifully. Let each one do as he has purposed in his heart, not begrudgingly or by compulsion, for God loves a cheerful giver. And God is able to make all grace abound to you, so that having all contentment in all things at all times, you may abound in every good work. As it is written, "He has scattered, he has given to the poor; his righteousness endures forever." (2 Cor 9:6–9, quoting Ps 112:9, which has the same verb, the Piel of פָּזַר, "to scatter," as Prov 11:24)

11:25 This verse continues the theme of encouraging generosity and graciousness. Jesus' statement in Mk 9:41 seems to recall the second part of this proverb:

> For truly, I say to you, whoever gives you to drink a cup of water in the name, because you are of Christ, will by no means lose his reward.

11:26 This verse is tied to 11:25 by the catchword "blessing," but explores the opposite of generosity. Hoarding grain, especially during times of shortage, is a common problem. The person who is willing to sell his excess to others takes the risk that he too could eventually be without food. This proverb's promise is meant to encourage such selfless behavior.

11:27 This verse depicts the person who seeks ways to do good as seeking God's favor (רָצוֹן), which he already has by grace (see "his [God's] favor" in, e.g., 11:1, 20; 12:22). The contrast to the person seeking evil is ironic, even comic. He does not have to search very long for evil; he too already has it, and its consequences will quickly find him!

11:28 This verse is one of any number of passages in Scripture that remind us not to trust in wealth. As Jesus declared, no one can serve both God and mammon (Mt 6:24; Lk 16:13). The comparison of the righteous to a flourishing plant is also a common theme in Scripture (e.g., Ps 1:3).

11:29 This verse depicts two types of fools. The first is a person who causes trouble for his own family. This seems to refer especially to dishonoring his parents, in violation of the Fourth Commandment (Ex 20:12; Deut 5:16), so that when they die, they leave him no inheritance, only the "wind." The second is the person who is so incorrigibly foolish that he will spend his life in servitude to the wise person.

11:30 This verse recalls the image of the tree of life in the garden of Eden (see the commentary on 3:18). As in 11:19, here too "life" has its full, eschatological meaning, as also in, for example, Jn 10:10; 20:31; 1 Jn 5:12. The first line of Prov 11:30 pronounces the believer as "righteous." The second line adds that he is also "wise," and it transforms him from a tree of life—a tree from which others can pick the fruit of eternal life—to the harvester of souls, imagery that Jesus applies to Christian ministry (Jn 4:35–38).

11:31 This verse is bound to 11:30 by the catchword "righteous (person)." The proverb promises God's reward for those who possess righteousness through faith already in this life, but it also warns of the coming punishment for unrepentant sinners (cf. Mt 25:31–46; Rom 2:6–10).

Proverbs 12:1–28

Righteous Behavior, Part 2

Translation

12 [1]A person who loves discipline is a person who loves knowledge,
but a person who hates correction is stupid.
[2]A good person will obtain favor from Yahweh,
but he will condemn a schemer.
[3]A person cannot be secure in wickedness,
but the root of righteous people will never be shaken.

[4]A woman with strong character is a crown to her husband,
but a shameful woman is like rot in his bones.

[5]The plans of righteous people are just,
but the guidance of wicked people is deceitful.
[6]The words of wicked people are a deadly ambush,
but the mouth of upright people will save them.
[7]Wicked people are overthrown, and they are no more,
but the house of righteous people continues to stand.

[8]A person is praised according to the good sense that he speaks,
but the person with a twisted heart will be despised.

[9]Better to be a nobody and have a servant
than to pretend to be important and lack food.
[10]A righteous person knows the needs of his livestock,
but the compassion of wicked people is cruel.
[11]The person who works his land will have enough food,
but whoever pursues fantasies lacks sense.

[12]A wicked man desires a net belonging to evil people,
but the root of righteous people bears [fruit].
[13]The transgression of [his] lips [is] the trap for an evil person,
but a righteous person gets out of trouble.
[14]A person is filled with good from the fruit of his mouth,
and the labor of a person's hands returns to him.
[15]The way of a stubborn fool appears to him to be correct,
but whoever listens to advice is wise.
[16]A stubborn fool immediately lets his annoyance be known,
but a prudent person overlooks an insult.
[17]The one who utters the truth proclaims righteousness,
but a witness [who tells] lies is deceitful.

[18]Some speak thoughtlessly like the thrusts of a sword,
but the tongue of wise people [brings] healing.
[19]A truthful lip is established forever,
but a lying tongue [lasts only] until the blink of an eye.
[20]Deceitfulness is in the heart of those who plan evil,
but for those who advise peace [there will be] joy.
[21]Complete disaster will not happen to the righteous person,
but wicked people are filled with trouble.
[22]Lying lips are a disgusting thing to Yahweh,
but those who act truthfully [receive] his favor.
[23]A man who is prudent conceals [his] knowledge,
but the heart of fools proclaims stupidity.

[24]A hardworking hand will rule,
but laziness results in forced labor.
[25]Anxiety in a person's heart makes it depressed,
but a good word brings it joy.
[26]A righteous person guides his neighbor,
but the way of wicked people leads them astray.
[27]A lazy person does not roast his game,
but a diligent person [obtains] valuable wealth.
[28]In the path of righteousness [there is] life,
and the way of its pathway is no death.

Textual Notes

12:1 אֹהֵב מוּסָר אֹהֵב דָּעַת—The Qal (G) participles of the verbs אָהֵב, "to love" (twice in this clause), and שָׂנֵא, "to hate" (in the next clause), are antonyms forming antithetic parallelism, as also in 13:24 and 27:6. For מוּסָר, see "מוּסָר, 'Discipline,' and יָסַר, 'to Discipline' " in "Wisdom in Proverbs" in the introduction. For דַּעַת, see "דַּעַת, 'Knowledge,' and יָדַע, 'to Know' " in "Wisdom in Proverbs" in the introduction as well as the commentary on 1:4, 7.

וְשֹׂנֵא תוֹכַחַת בָּעַר׃—For תּוֹכַחַת, "warning, correction," see the first textual note on 1:23. בָּעַר is the pausal form of the noun בַּעַר; see "בַּעַר, 'Stupid' " in "Fools in Proverbs" in the introduction.

12:2 טוֹב יָפִיק רָצוֹן מֵיְהוָה—The adjective טוֹב is used as a substantive, "a good person," and as the subject in this clause. The Hiphil (H) of פּוּק, "to obtain"; the object noun רָצוֹן, God's gift of "favor, grace"; and the prepositional phrase all are also in 8:35 and 18:22; see the second textual note on 8:35. In this chapter, the noun רָצוֹן recurs in 12:22.

In context here, especially in light of 12:3, the imperfect יָפִיק has an eschatological connotation: while the believer obtains divine favor now and already has everlasting life through faith (see 12:28), God's grace toward all believers will become fully evident only on the Last Day, when they shall be raised to everlasting life. See, for example, Dan 12:2–3. See also "live" in Prov 4:4; 7:2; 9:6; 15:27.

וְאִישׁ מְזִמּוֹת יַרְשִׁיעַ׃—Earlier in Proverbs the noun מְזִמָּה has a salutary meaning; see "מְזִמָּה, 'Insight, Foresight,' " in "Wisdom in Proverbs" in the introduction. However, here and in its two later occurrences in Proverbs (14:17; 24:8), the plural has an evil meaning: "schemes, wicked plans." The construct phrase has an adjectival genitive: "a scheming person/schemer." The implied subject of the verb יַרְשִׁיעַ is "Yahweh" in the preceding clause (מֵיְהוָה). The Hiphil (H) imperfect יַרְשִׁיעַ has an eschatological connotation: the unbeliever is now condemned and will be damned on the Last Day.

12:3 לֹא־יִכּוֹן אָדָם בְּרֶשַׁע—For the Niphal (N) imperfect of כּוּן, "be established, secure," see the second textual note on 4:26. Its feminine, תִּכּוֹן, occurs in a positive context with לָעַד, "forever," in 12:19a.

וְשֹׁרֶשׁ צַדִּיקִים בַּל־יִמּוֹט׃—For similar wording, see the textual note on 10:30.

12:4 אֵשֶׁת־חַיִל—For the meaning of "a woman with strong character," see the first textual note on 31:10 and the commentary on 31:10–31.

מְבִישָׁה׃—The Hiphil (H) of בּוֹשׁ often has a causative meaning, "cause shame, put to shame," but it can have an intransitive meaning, "act shamefully," as here and in 14:35 and 17:2. See also הֹבִישָׁה in reference to Israel as an adulterous woman in Hos 2:7 (ET 2:5).

12:5 תַּחְבֻּלוֹת רְשָׁעִים מִרְמָה׃—This is the only proverb where תַּחְבּוּלוֹת refers to the "guidance" of wicked people. See "תַּחְבּוּלוֹת, 'Guidance' " in "Wisdom in Proverbs" in the introduction.

12:6 אֱרָב־דָּם—Literally, this is "to ambush blood." אֱרָב is the infinitive construct is of the verb אָרַב, "ambush," which was used with לְדָם, "for blood," in 1:11 (see also 1:18a). דָּם has an adverbial force: an ambush that leads to/results in bloodshed (see *HALOT*, דָּם, 4 a), hence "a deadly ambush."

וּפִי יְשָׁרִים יַצִּילֵם׃—Earlier proverbs state that wisdom (2:10–12, 16) and righteousness (10:2; 11:4, 6) are able "to save" (the Hiphil [H] of נָצַל). The promise that "the mouth of upright people will save them" is in harmony with the promise of Jesus in Mt 10:32 || Lk 12:8 and of the apostle Paul in Rom 10:9. By metonymy "mouth" (פֶּה) refers to words that confess faith in the one true saving God. See also Prov 12:8a. Some critics have proposed that the pronominal suffix on יַצִּילֵם should be eliminated, since they allege that it is syntactically difficult.[1] However, it should be retained. The suffix fits into the multiple sound patterns of this proverb; the verb is the fourth word that ends with *mem* (רְשָׁעִים ... דָּם ... יְשָׁרִים יַצִּילֵם ...). The antecedent of the pronoun ("them") is the preceding noun יְשָׁרִים, "upright people." The *mem* on the last word in the verse could also be retained as an enclitic *mem*.[2]

12:7 הָפוֹךְ רְשָׁעִים וְאֵינָם—The Qal (G) infinitive absolute הָפוֹךְ with רְשָׁעִים as its object, literally, "to overthrow, destroy the wicked," implies that God is the agent of the action. Most translations render it as a passive: "wicked people are overthrown." The infinitive can function as present tense (Joüon, § 123 w (4)). God is also the implied

---

[1] Toy, *Proverbs*, 244.

[2] Cf. McCreesh, *Biblical Sound and Sense*, 108–9.

agent of the action in the following clause: he is the one who enables the righteous to continue to "stand" (יַעֲמֹד).

12:8 לְפִי־שִׂכְלוֹ יְהֻלַּל־אִישׁ—Literally, "according to the mouth of his good sense a man is praised," this is an idiomatic use of the noun פֶּה, "mouth" (see *HALOT*, 10 b i). See "שֵׂכֶל, 'Good Sense,' and הִשְׂכִּיל, 'to Act Sensibly' " in "Wisdom in Proverbs" in the introduction. This is the only proverb with the Pual (Dp) of הָלַל, "to praise," but other proverbs use the Piel (D) (27:2; 28:4; 31:28, 31) or Hithpael (HtD) (20:14; 25:14; 27:1; 31:30).

וְנַעֲוֵה־לֵב יִהְיֶה לָבוּז׃—The Niphal (N) participle of עָוָה, "be twisted, perverted," is in construct with לֵב, meaning "be perverted *in* (respect to his) heart." עָוָה occurs only here in Proverbs, but for other synonyms, see the second textual note on 1:3. The noun בּוּז, "contempt, derision," recurs in 18:3. The idiom in the predicate יִהְיֶה לָבוּז is, literally, "he will *become* contempt," but usually it is translated verbally as a passive, "will be despised."

12:9 טוֹב נִקְלֶה וְעֶבֶד לוֹ—The adjective טוֹב and the preposition מִן (on מִמְּתַכַּבֵּד in the next line) form a comparison: "better ... than ..." See "Direct Comparisons" in "Authorship and Date" in the introduction. The Niphal (N) participle of קָלָה, "be insignificant, contemptible," is generally understood in this proverb to signify a person of humble means who lacks exalted status or social standing (see ESV, NASB, NIV). The suffix on לוֹ refers back to נִקְלֶה. The preposition לְ in the phrase וְעֶבֶד לוֹ denotes possession: "and *have* a servant." The phrase is read as עֹבֵד לוֹ, "serves himself," in one Hebrew manuscript, and is so translated by the LXX and Syriac Peshitta.

מִמְּתַכַּבֵּד וַחֲסַר־לָחֶם׃—The pointing of the first word is strange in Leningradensis. Most manuscripts have מִמִּתְכַּבֵּד, the preposition מִן on the Hithpael (HtD) participle of כָּבֵד, which has a reflexive or middle meaning: "glorify/honor oneself" or "be pretentious, pretend to be important."

12:10 נֶפֶשׁ בְּהֶמְתּוֹ—Yet another idiomatic use of נֶפֶשׁ appears in this proverb. Here this noun signifies the state or condition of life and its necessities. The righteous person is aware of the condition of his livestock (בְּהֵמָה) and is, therefore, cognizant of their needs.

וְרַחֲמֵי רְשָׁעִים אַכְזָרִי׃—The plural noun in construct רַחֲמֵי has a singular meaning, "mercy, compassion," and so the predicate adjective אַכְזָרִי, "cruel," is singular (GKC, § 145 h).

12:11 וּמְרַדֵּף רֵיקִים חֲסַר־לֵב׃—The adjective רֵיק means "empty, frivolous, vain" (*HALOT*, 3), and its plural is used here substantivally to mean empty or unrealistic desires, "fantasies." See "חֲסַר־לֵב, 'Lacking Sense' " in "Fools in Proverbs" in the introduction.

12:12 The Hebrew of this verse is difficult, and many emendations have been proposed. The translation above follows the MT.

וְשֹׁרֶשׁ צַדִּיקִים יִתֵּן׃—In context, a "root" (שֹׁרֶשׁ) that "gives" (יִתֵּן) probably means that it sprouts and "bears [fruit]" (cf., e.g., 11:30; 12:14; 31:31; as well as Ezek 34:27; Ps 1:3).

12:13 בְּפֶשַׁע שְׂפָתַיִם מוֹקֵשׁ רָע—Literally, "in a transgression of lips [is the] snare of an evil man," meaning that an evil person (רָע) is ensnared by the transgression (פֶּשַׁע) he utters with his lips (שְׂפָתַיִם). The noun מוֹקֵשׁ, "a snare, trap," recurs in 13:14; 14:27; 18:7; 20:25; 22:25; 29:6, 25. It is derived from the verb יָקַשׁ, whose Niphal (N) in 6:2 means "be trapped." Most translations render the noun מוֹקֵשׁ here as a passive verb, for example, "an evil man is ensnared" (ESV).

וַיֵּצֵא מִצָּרָה צַדִּיק׃—Literally, "a righteous person comes out from distress," this is an eschatological promise pointing to final deliverance on the Last Day (cf. Rev 21:4).

12:14 מִפְּרִי פִי־אִישׁ יִשְׂבַּע־טוֹב—This is, literally, "from the fruit of the mouth of a man, he will be full of good." For the metaphorical meaning of שָׂבַע, "be filled," with the preposition מִן, see the second textual note on 1:31.

וּגְמוּל יְדֵי־אָדָם יָשׁוּב לוֹ׃—The Qal (G) reading of the Kethib, יָשׁוּב, is preferable: "the recompense/labor [גְּמוּל] of the hands of a man *will return* to him." The Hiphil (H) Qere, יָשִׁיב, would make the line read as "and he *returns* the labor of the hands of a man to him," implying that God rewards good and hard work and punishes evil deeds.

12:15–16 אֱוִיל ... אֱוִיל—See "אֱוִיל, 'Stubborn Fool,' and אִוֶּלֶת, 'Stupidity' " in "Fools in Proverbs" in the introduction.

12:15 דֶּרֶךְ אֱוִיל יָשָׁר בְּעֵינָיו—Literally, "the way of a stubborn fool is straight in his (own) eyes," this means the stubborn fool thinks he is traveling on the correct path. For the idiomatic meaning of בְּעֵינֵי, see the second textual note on 3:4.

וְשֹׁמֵעַ לְעֵצָה חָכָם׃—See "עֵצָה, 'Advice,' and יוֹעֵץ, 'Advisor' " in "Wisdom in Proverbs" in the introduction.

12:16 אֱוִיל בַּיּוֹם יִוָּדַע כַּעְסוֹ—Literally, this is "a stupid fool—on the [same] day his annoyance becomes known." The prepositional phrase בַּיּוֹם can mean "at once, immediately" (see *HALOT*, s.v. יוֹם I, 10 b ii).

וְכֹסֶה קָלוֹן עָרוּם׃—The verb כָּסָה usually is used in the Piel (D) and means "cover, conceal." The synonymous Qal (G) occurs twice in Proverbs, both times in this chapter (12:16, 23), and both times as the participle with עָרוּם, "a prudent person," as its subject. The thought expressed here is not that a prudent person actively seeks to conceal wrongdoing. Rather, he is wise enough to ignore an insult and go on with his life. The noun קָלוֹן means "ignominy, disgrace" (see *HALOT*, 1). English versions are generally agreed that in this proverb it denotes some type of slight or insult (see ESV, NIV, NRSV).

12:17 יָפִיחַ אֱמוּנָה יַגִּיד צֶדֶק—Although this clause lacks any conditional particles, the imperfect verb יָפִיחַ forms the protasis of a conditional sentence, whose apodosis also has an imperfect, יַגִּיד (see GKC, § 159 c). This could be rendered as "if one utters the truth, then he proclaims righteousness." For the Hiphil (H) of פּוּחַ meaning "utter," see the first textual note on 6:19. The noun אֱמוּנָה, "truth, truthfulness, faithfulness," recurs in 12:22 and 28:20.

12:18 יֵשׁ בּוֹטֶה כְּמַדְקְרוֹת חָרֶב—For יֵשׁ with a participle (here בּוֹטֶה [GKC § 75 qq]), see the first textual note on 11:24. The Qal (G) of בָּטָה, "speak thoughtlessly, rashly," occurs only here in the OT. The synonymous Piel (D) is found in Lev 5:4 and Ps 106:33.

The phrase כְּמַדְקְר֣וֹת חָ֑רֶב is, literally, "like piercings of/with a sword." The noun מַדְקֵרָה is found only here in the OT. It is derived from the verb דָּקַר, "to pierce," which normally refers to inflicting fatal wounds, for example, in Num 25:8; 1 Sam 31:4; see also Zech 12:10, quoted in Jn 19:37, where it is applied to the crucifixion of Christ.

12:19 שְֽׂפַת־אֱ֭מֶת ... לְשׁ֣וֹן שָֽׁקֶר׃—Both construct phrases, literally, "a lip of truth ... a tongue of falsehood," are adjectival genitive phrases. Similar is שִׂפְתֵי־שָׁ֑קֶר, "lips of falsehood," in 12:22. Regarding תִּכּ֣וֹן in 12:19, see the first textual note on 12:3.

וְעַד־אַ֝רְגִּ֗יעָה—The verb is the Hiphil (H) imperfect of רָגַע. This clause could mean, literally, "as long as I ... wink with the eyelashes" (GKC, § 108 h; similar is BDB, s.v. רָגַע I, Hiphil), or perhaps "as long as I grant rest" (*HALOT*, s.v. רגע, Hiphil, 3). The verb is probably related to the noun רֶגַע, "a moment." This clause is translated nominally: "until the blink of an eye."

12:20 For the combination of the verb חָרַשׁ, "devise, plan," and the noun רַע or רָעָה, "evil," see the first textual note on 3:29.

12:21 לֹא־יְאֻנֶּ֣ה לַצַּדִּ֣יק כָּל־אָ֑וֶן—Literally, this is "entire calamity [כָּל־אָ֑וֶן] will not be allowed to happen [לֹא־יְאֻנֶּה] to the righteous person." The Piel (D) of the rare verb אָנָה means "allow to happen, allow to come" (*DCH*), and the Pual (Dp) here has the corresponding passive meaning. God is the implied agent who does not allow the righteous to be utterly destroyed. This is an eschatological promise; כָּל־אָ֑וֶן should not be taken as meaning that God will not permit "*any* disaster" to happen to his people in this life.

12:22 תּוֹעֲבַ֣ת יְ֭הוָה ... רְצוֹנֽוֹ׃—See the textual notes on 11:1, which also contrasts תּוֹעֲבַת יְהוָה, "a disgusting thing to Yahweh," and רְצוֹנוֹ, God's gift of "his favor, grace." For רָצוֹן, see also the second textual note on 8:35. And see the excursus " 'Disgusting Thing' (תּוֹעֵבָה) in Solomon's Proverbs" in the commentary on Proverbs 11.

12:23 אָדָ֣ם עָ֭רוּם—The adjective עָרוּם is often used substantivally in Proverbs, so the use of אָדָם, "a man," here is pleonastic. For a similar construction with two nouns, see the first textual note on 6:12. For עָרוּם, see "עָרוּם, 'Prudent,' and עָרְמָה, 'Prudence' " in "Wisdom in Proverbs" in the introduction.

12:24 יַד־חָרוּצִ֥ים תִּמְשׁ֑וֹל—The adjective חָרוּץ means "hardworking, diligent," as also in 10:4; 12:27; 13:4; 21:5 (see *HALOT*, s.v. חָרוּץ VI). Hence this is, literally, "the hand of hardworking people will rule." The feminine noun יָד is the subject of the feminine verb תִּמְשׁוֹל.

12:25 דְּאָגָ֣ה בְלֶב־אִ֣ישׁ יַשְׁחֶ֑נָּה—This probably means, literally, "anxiety in the heart of a man causes it [his heart] to be depressed/brought low." This proverb shows several grammatical difficulties. The forms were probably chosen regardless of grammar for the sake of sound.[3]

This is the only proverb with the feminine noun דְּאָגָה, which can denote "anxiety, dread," as in Ezek 4:16; 12:18–19. This noun must be the subject of the verb יַשְׁחֶ֑נָּה, even though the verb is masculine. The verb שָׁחָה occurs in the Qal (G) only in Is 51:23 ("bow down"). Its Hiphil (H) is found only here, where it has the causative meaning,

---

[3] McCreesh, *Biblical Sound and Sense*, 40–42.

"subdue, oppress" (*HALOT*) or "weigh down, cause to be depressed." The verb יַשְׁחֶנָּה has a feminine suffix. Normally the noun לֵב, "heart," is masculine, but apparently here it is construed as feminine, since it must be the referent of the suffix on this verb. לֵב must also be the referent of the feminine suffix on יְשַׂמְּחֶנָּה in the next line; see the next textual note.

וְדָבָר טוֹב יְשַׂמְּחֶנָּה׃—Literally, this is "and a good word causes it to rejoice." The referent of the feminine suffix ("it") on the Piel (D) verb יְשַׂמְּחֶנָּה must be לֵב, "heart," in the preceding clause.

12:26 יָתֵר מֵרֵעֵהוּ צַדִּיק—This clause is difficult. If the unique form יָתֵר is related to the verb יָתַר, whose Hiphil (H) can mean "be excellent, preeminent," this clause with מִן (on מֵרֵעֵהוּ, apparently "from/than his neighbor") could be comparative and mean "the righteous is more excellent than his neighbour" (KJV). However, יָתֵר is best understood as a Hiphil (H) imperfect of תּוּר, "lead or guide."[4] The clause then means that "a righteous person [צַדִּיק] guides [יָתֵר] his neighbor" (similar are ESV and NASB), although it is then a challenge to explain the force of the preposition on מֵרֵעֵהוּ. Other interpreters have suggested various emendations to make better sense.

וְדֶרֶךְ רְשָׁעִים תַּתְעֵם׃—The feminine noun דֶּרֶךְ, "way," is the subject of the feminine Hiphil (H) imperfect of תָּעָה, which here has a causative meaning, "cause to go astray." The suffix on תַּתְעֵם refers back to רְשָׁעִים. Compare 10:17b, where the Hiphil (H) of תָּעָה has the same causative meaning.

12:27 לֹא־יַחֲרֹךְ רְמִיָּה צֵידוֹ—This clause is challenging. Most take the feminine noun רְמִיָּה, "laziness," as concretely representing a foolish, lazy man. See "רְמִיָּה, 'Laziness' " in "Fools in Proverbs" in the introduction. If so, then the man could be the subject of the masculine verb יַחֲרֹךְ, a hapax whose meaning is unknown. It is usually understood to mean "to roast" on the basis of its Aramaic cognate and its use in postbiblical Hebrew. "A lazy person does not roast his game" would mean that the foolish hunter might eat his game raw, without cooking it. Compare the prohibition against eating the Passover lamb raw in Ex 12:9.

וְהוֹן־אָדָם יָקָר חָרוּץ׃—This difficult line is, literally, "the wealth of a man, precious, diligent." Many interpreters change the order of the words to attempt to make sense of it. For חָרוּץ, "diligent (person)," see the textual note on 12:24. Both the noun הוֹן, "wealth," and the adjective יָקָר, "precious, valuable," are common elsewhere in Proverbs. The translation here follows the MT without resorting to shuffling the Hebrew words.

12:28 חַיִּים—"Life" has its full eschatological sense, eventuating in the bodily resurrection to eternal life, as also in, for example, 3:2, 18, 22; 4:10, 13, 22–23. This is confirmed by the parallel "no death" in the next clause.

וְדֶרֶךְ נְתִיבָה אַל־מָוֶת׃—Probably נְתִיבָה is the masculine noun נָתִיב, "pathway," with the third feminine singular suffix lacking *mappiq* (Joüon, §§ 25 a and 94 h). דֶּרֶךְ נְתִיבָה is a construct phrase, "the way of her path." The suffix refers back to the feminine noun

---

[4] This is the view of BDB as well as Murphy, *Proverbs*, 88, and R. F. Youngblood, "תּוּר," *TWOT* 2:967.

צְדָקָה, "righteousness," in the preceding clause. See the excursus "The Metaphor of the Path in Solomon's Wisdom" in the commentary on Proverbs 10.

GKC, § 152 g, explains אַל־מָוֶת as a legitimate compound word, "*not-death* (immortality)," while Waltke-O'Connor gives "no death" (§ 39.3.3a, note 59). Since the particle אַל, "no, not," normally negates a verb (e.g., וְאַל־יָמֹת, "and may he [Reuben] not die," Deut 33:6), some have proposed emending it to אֶל, "to," following the LXX's εἰς θάνατον, "(in)to death," but that requires further emendations of other words in the second line of this proverb to make sense of it.[5] "The way of its pathway [that of righteousness (12:28a)] is/has no death" is a literal and intelligible rendition of the Hebrew. "Life" and "no death" are balanced semantic parallels. This understanding is consistent with other biblical promises of everlasting life, for example, Is 25:8, בִּלַּע הַמָּוֶת לָנֶצַח, "he will swallow up death forever" (quoted in 1 Cor 15:54).

Commentary

Chapter 12 concludes the first section of the proverbs of Solomon found in 10:1–22:16. The theme of this section (10:1–12:28) has been an introduction to wisdom and righteousness for the benefit of a wise son. See the commentary on 10:1–5 as well as the excursus "The Organization of the Sayings in Solomon's Proverbs in Proverbs 10:1–22:16" in the commentary on Proverbs 10.

12:1 This verse reminds the believer that when mistakes are made, there is great value in learning from the correction others can offer. Learning from one's mistakes is one of the most valuable lessons in life. When those mistakes are sins, it is even more important to accept correction, whether from other people or from God.

12:2 This verse is linked back to 11:31 and forward to 12:3 by the root רשע. It has a verb from that root, יַרְשִׁיעַ, "he will condemn," while 11:31 had the substantive רָשָׁע, "wicked person," and 12:3 has the noun רֶשַׁע, "wickedness."

This verse is the first טוֹב ("good/better") proverb in this chapter. The next such proverb is 12:9. See "Good and Better Sayings" in the introduction. In this case טוֹב is used as a substantive meaning "a good person." In this saying the good person is contrasted to the schemer, implying that the person is adjudged good because of his spiritual disposition and attitude, not his resulting outward actions. He is reckoned as righteous through faith alone and by grace alone (Gen 15:6; Is 53:11), and his good works are the fruit of this imputed righteousness. Yahweh's declaration of favor for this person, in contrast to his condemnation for the schemer, is intended to inculcate obedience to the Ninth and Tenth Commandments (Ex 20:17; Deut 5:21), since the inner disposition (either of coveting or of being satisfied with what God has given) is something that is beyond the reach of human correction.[6]

---

5 See Murphy, *Proverbs*, 88; McKane, *Proverbs*, 450–52.

6 See further the excursus "Proverbs 1–9, Christ, and the Ten Commandments" in the commentary on chapter 1.

12:3 This verse observes that "wickedness" never leads to security, peace of mind, or contentment. The sinful human nature always focuses on the world and temporal human existence and is always anxious (cf. 12:25) about the loss of worldly possessions and honor. However, righteous people have their roots in God and his eternal promises in Christ, from whom they cannot be shaken or taken (Jn 10:28–29). They have the peace of mind that the wicked cannot know (Jn 14:27; Phil 4:7).

12:4 This verse has no catchword or strong thematic link to the sayings that precede or follow it. It speaks of "a woman/wife with strong character," the same phrase that opens the concluding poem of Proverbs (31:10–31). In the context here it is probably intended more as advice to a young man in choosing a wife than as advice to women as to which course to choose in life. (A shameful woman probably would not worry about the effect of her actions on her husband, so this proverb would not be meaningful to her.) However, it can instruct both the Christian man who is looking for a wife and a Christian woman who desires to enter into a successful marriage. This proverb, along with others that speak of the value of a good wife, reminds us that the holy estate of marriage is intended for the mutual benefit of husband and wife (see 31:11, 28–31 and the commentary on 5:1–23; 6:20–35; 7:1–27; see also 1 Corinthians 7; Eph 5:21–33).

12:5 This verse is the first of three proverbs joined by the catchword רְשָׁעִים, "wicked people." These three sayings progress from the nature of the words of righteous and wicked people to the effect of their words and then to their final state, either in everlasting paradise or perdition (12:7). This proverb reminds those who heed it that advice can be either righteous or deceptive. Counsel must be weighed, and one of the most important considerations is whether it comes from sinful or righteous motives. The reliable standard by which all human words may be judged is God's own Word, including the inspired book of Proverbs.

12:6 This verse states why the advice of wicked people mentioned in 12:5 is to be avoided: because it will ambush those who follow it. The verse also reminds us that upright and righteous people not only serve others with good advice, but also serve themselves well because their own words can save them in perilous situations. Believers will be remembered for not leading others astray with their words, and they will escape the punishment meted out to those whose counsel was harmful and malicious.

Athanasius applies 12:5 and 12:6 together with 15:28 to warn against those who claim to preach the Gospel, but are actually proclaiming false doctrine:

> But when they proceed from those who are hired to advocate the cause of heresy, and since, according to the divine proverb, "The words of the wicked are to lie in wait" [12:6], and "The mouth of the wicked poureth out evil things" [15:28], and "The counsels of the wicked are deceit" [12:5], it becomes us to watch and be sober, brethren, as the Lord has said, lest any deception arise

from subtlety of speech and craftiness; lest any one come and pretend to say, "I preach Christ," and after a little while he be found to be Antichrist.[7]

12:7 This verse is chiastic in form, which serves to close off the group of three proverbs that began with 12:5. This is the Hebrew word order:

A Verb: הָפ֣וֹךְ, "are overthrown"
- B Masculine plural noun: רְשָׁעִ֣ים, "wicked people"
  - C Conjunction plus particle of negative existence: וְאֵינָ֑ם, "and they are no more"
  - C' Conjunction plus noun: וּבֵ֖ית, "but the house"
- B' Masculine plural noun: צַדִּיקִ֣ים, "of righteous people"

A' Verb: יַעֲמֹֽד, "continues to stand"

It notes once again that wicked people have no eternal security (see 12:3) but that the righteous can depend on God's everlasting blessings for themselves and for their posterity. Compare the end of the Sermon on the Mount (Mt 7:24–27) to this proverb. See also the commentary on Prov 10:25.

12:8 This verse, like 12:4, has no catchword or strong thematic link to the sayings that precede or follow it. This saying links the praise or dishonor one receives from others to one's character. However, this praise is linked to how one's character becomes evident in one's words and advice to others. Humans cannot judge what is in the heart, as only God can (see 12:2), but they can form judgments about a person's character based on what that person says.

12:9 This verse, the second טוֹב ("good, better") proverb in this chapter (see 12:2), is the first of three proverbs dealing with concerns of the working class. Prov 12:9 and 12:11 form an inclusio through the repetition of the noun לֶחֶם, "food," and the root עבד, the noun עֶבֶד, "servant," in 12:9, and the participle עֹבֵד, "the person who works," in 12:11. Prov 12:9 is one of many proverbs that speak against hypocrisy. It reminds us that ego can be self-destructive, even to the point of depriving one of the basic necessities for life.

12:10 This verse contrasts the compassion that righteous people have to that which wicked people have. Righteous people's compassion extends even to animals. In this they imitate God. As Jesus counseled, "Consider the birds of the air: they neither sow nor reap nor gather into barns, and yet your heavenly Father feeds them" (Mt 6:26; cf. Lk 12:24). Wicked people's compassion is no compassion at all, but cruelty. They have no regard for others, but are caught up in the self-centeredness of sin, classically defined as *incurvatus in se*, "directed inward toward itself."

12:11 This verse commends work that is possible using one's God-given resources, rather than pursuing unrealistic goals or sinful schemes. Note the nearly identical proverb in 28:19, which differs only in the last two Hebrew words.

---

[7] Athanasius, *To the Bishops of Egypt*, 1.9 (*NPNF*[2] 4:227); cf. *Four Discourses against the Arians*, 3.30, where he quotes 12:5 and 12:6 in a similar way (*NPNF*[2] 4:426).

12:12 This verse is paired with 12:13 by the catchword צַדִּיק, "righteous person." This saying first depicts a wicked person as desiring to use the schemes and plots employed by other evil people. This education in sinfulness is the opposite of learning wisdom. In contrast, the righteous person, whose roots are in God (see 12:3), does not set a trap to catch others, but bears fruit by the power of the Gospel (Mt 13:8, 23; Jn 15:4–5; Eph 3:17; Col 2:7; contrast Mt 13:5–6, 20–21).

12:13 This verse begins a series of proverbs concerning the mouth that extends through 12:23. Among these proverbs, only 12:21 does not mention the mouth or communication. Prov 12:13 once again calls attention to the harmful effects that sinful, devious words have on those who listen to them. However, it also points out the ability of God to deliver a righteous person through God's gift of righteousness.[a]

(a) See Pss 36:7 (ET 36:6); 71:2; Prov 10:2; 11:4, 6; see also Is 63:1; Jer 23:6; 33:16; Ezek 14:14, 20; 33:12

12:14 This verse connects two positive attributes of righteous people, who are justified by grace alone: (1) they are enabled to speak things that are beneficial, not only to others (cf. 12:8a), but especially to themselves, and (2) they work fruitfully (cf. 12:11–12). Both bring them rewards. The first line of this proverb has only one different Hebrew word than the first line of 13:2.

12:15 This verse is another reminder of the importance of heeding advice that accords with God's Word. The fool mentioned here is particularly stubborn in his foolishness, so much so that he will not listen to such advice, but insists that his own way is correct. Correction for this foolishness is offered in 3:5–6, and its eschatological end is depicted in 14:12 and 16:25.

12:16 This verse is connected to 12:15 by the catchword אֱוִיל, "stubborn fool." The obduracy of the fool in this case is shown by him failing to have a calm, measured response to insults. Instead, he is "like an injured animal and so his opponent knows that he has been wounded."[8] A prudent person knows of better ways to handle his emotions.

12:17 This verse could apply to a variety of situations, including the ministry of a faithful pastor and the testimony to the Gospel by any believer in Jesus Christ, but it is worded to apply specifically to legal testimony.

12:18 This verse warns against speaking before considering the consequences of one's words. Such reckless talk can wound even if it is not intended to do harm. Its opposite is the words of wise people, since they bring "healing." Since the wise in Proverbs are those who know God's grace, their words can heal because of the power of the Gospel, which brings "healing" (מַרְפֵּא) and "life" (חַיִּים) to troubled consciences through the forgiveness of sins (4:22; 15:4). The same Hebrew noun for "healing" (מַרְפֵּא) used in these proverbs is in the promise of the advent of the Messiah in Mal 3:20 (ET 4:2), and healing was a major part of Jesus' earthly ministry. He could heal merely by his Word (Mt 8:8–9, 13; Jn 4:50–53; 11:43–44). All believers will receive the ultimate

[8] McKane, *Proverbs*, 442.

healing on the Last Day through the resurrection of their bodies to everlasting life.

12:19 This verse is linked to 12:18 by the catchword לָשׁוֹן, "tongue." The saying emphasizes the endurance of those who speak truthfully in order to encourage the adoption of a long-term perspective—living in light of eternity—rather than the short-term gain that seems so appealing to liars.

12:20 This verse is coupled to 12:21 through the catchword רַע, "evil," translated as "trouble" in 12:21. The contrast between "deceitfulness in the heart" and "joy" (12:20) is the genius in this proverb, since the locus of "joy" is left unexpressed. Is this "joy" in the heart of those who make peace, or is the "joy" in the hearts of others as the result of the peacemaking? The proverb is ambiguous. Probably we are to understand that peacemakers anticipate the "joy" to come (Mt 25:21, 23). "Peace" signifies not only lack of conflict but also a positive social climate. The incarnation and atonement of the Savior have brought "peace" through the reconciliation of sinful humanity to God and to one another (Lk 2:14, 29; 19:38; Rom 5:1, 10).

12:21 This verse expresses a truth about righteous people. Often translated misleadingly as "*no harm befalls* the righteous person," it actually says, "*complete disaster* [כָּל־אָוֶן] *will* not happen" to a righteous person, since, as Jesus promises, "they will never perish" (Jn 10:27–28). God guards each believer from the ultimate disaster: eternal separation from God and his grace. In contrast, the wicked have no end of trouble, already now and all the more after Judgment Day.

12:22 This verse, like other sayings that speak of things that are disgusting (תּוֹעֲבָה) to Yahweh, is designed to discourage behavior that is often difficult for people to monitor. Some lies can be detected, but often they are cleverly concealed and remain so. Conversely, one cannot always determine who is telling the truth, but God's favor is promised to the truthful even when other people do not recognize their honesty.[9]

12:23 This verse is another saying about discretion and self-control (see 12:16). The fool is not only without wisdom, but he also does not know enough to keep his stupidity to himself.[10]

12:24 This verse once again commends honest work (see 12:11) and notes that it will lead to rewards, whereas laziness, which seems to offer an immediate reward, will result in even more drudgery in the long run. "Forced labor" (מַס) hints at eternal servitude (Mt 5:26; 18:34–35).

12:25 This verse expresses a well-understood truth: anxiety can lead to depression. It is a burden, but encouragement can lift that burden. This is

---

[9] Prov 12:22a has a parallel in the Wisdom of Amenemope, chapter 10 (13:15–16). See *ANET*, 423; *ANE*, 240. See also the excursus "The Words of Wise People (Prov 22:17–24:22) and Its Relationship to the Wisdom of Amenemope" in the commentary on Proverbs 22.

[10] This saying is thematically similar to the Wisdom of Amenemope, chapter 21 (22:15–16). See *ANET*, 424; *ANE*, 242.

especially true when the anxiety is spiritual in nature and the "good word" is the Gospel.

12:26 This verse is rendered various ways by English translations because of the difficulty of the verb form (see the first textual note) and the apparently weak parallelism. The proverb appears to say that a righteous person seeks to use his wisdom not only for himself but also in service to his neighbor, whereas the wicked, who refuse to be guided by the sage counsel of others (12:15), are led astray by their own foolishness.

12:27 This verse is another saying showing the outcome of laziness and the reward of work in a godly vocation. The first line is ironic comedy in which a man hunts and captures game, but is too lazy to roast it. The second line extols the value of diligence and the wealth obtained through it. This is a picturesque way of speaking of the rewards that accompany dedicated labor. Often faithful work can receive temporal rewards, but the true reward of serving God in faith is eternal wealth (cf. Eccl 9:11; Lk 16:9–11; Rom 10:12; Eph 1:7, 18).

12:28 This proverb and 12:26 both contain וְדֶרֶךְ, "and/but the way," and a word from the root צדק, either "righteous person" (צַדִּיק, 12:26) or "righteousness" (צְדָקָה, 12:28). This may explain the close proximity of these sayings.

This verse declares that "life" is given to those who are on the path of righteousness. Everlasting life is available for anyone, since Wisdom invites all people to travel along her path and receive "righteousness" (1:3; 2:9; 8:18, 20).

The second line expresses the same thought by saying that "the way of its [righteousness'] pathway" leads to no death (see Jn 11:25–26; Rev 20:6).

Proverbs 13:1–25

Wise Ways to Live, Part 1

Translation

13 [1]A wise son [heeds] a father's discipline,
but a mocker does not listen to a reprimand.

[2]From the fruit of a person's mouth he eats well,
but the appetite of treacherous people [is for] violence.
[3]Whoever guards his mouth preserves his life.
Whoever opens his lips wide—ruin is his.
[4]A lazy person desires [something] and has nothing [for] his appetite,
but the appetite of hardworking people is more than satisfied.

[5]A righteous person hates a lie,
but a wicked person brings disgrace and causes shame.
[6]Righteousness guards the person whose way has integrity,
but wickedness perverts a sinner.

[7]One person pretends to be rich, but has nothing.
[Another] person pretends to be poor, but has great wealth.
[8]A ransom for the life of a man [may be] his riches,
but a poor man does not hear a threat.
[9]The light of righteous people rejoices,
but the lamp of wicked people will be extinguished.
[10]Insolence only produces strife,
but wisdom [is] with those who take advice.
[11]Wealth from nothing dwindles,
but the person who gathers gradually makes it grow.
[12]Hope delayed makes a heart sick,
but desire fulfilled is a tree of life.
[13]The person who despises a saying will pay for it,
but the person who fears a command will be rewarded.
[14]The teaching of a wise person is a fountain of life,
to turn [someone] from snares of death.
[15]Good sense yields grace,
but the way of treacherous people is unchanging.
[16]Every prudent person acts out of knowledge,
but a fool displays stupidity.
[17]A wicked messenger falls into trouble,
but a trustworthy envoy [brings] healing.
[18]A person who ignores discipline [gets] poverty and shame,
but the one who conforms to correction will be honored.

[19]A desire being fulfilled is sweet to the soul,
but it is a disgusting thing to fools to turn from evil.
[20]Whoever walks with wise people becomes wise,
but a companion of fools will be harmed.
[21]Trouble pursues sinners,
but good repays righteous people.
[22]A good man leaves an inheritance to his grandchildren,
but a sinner's wealth is treasured up for a righteous person.
[23]Even though poor peoples' farmland [may produce] much food,
a [poor] person may be swept away without justice.
[24]The person who withholds his rod hates his son,
but the one who loves him promptly administers discipline.
[25]A righteous person eats until his appetite is satisfied,
but the stomach of wicked people is always empty.

Textual Notes

13:1 בֵּן חָכָם מוּסַר אָב—This first clause lacks a verb, but the verb in the second clause, שָׁמַע, "heed, listen to," does reverse double duty. For the noun מוּסָר, which in this chapter recurs in 13:18, 24, see "מוּסָר, 'Discipline,' and יָסַר, 'to Discipline' " in "Wisdom in Proverbs" in the introduction.

וְלֵץ לֹא־שָׁמַע גְּעָרָה׃—See "לֵץ, 'Mocker,' and לָצוֹן, 'Mocking, Scoffing' " in "Fools in Proverbs" in the introduction. The noun גְּעָרָה denotes a harsh rebuke or "reprimand," and it occurs in Proverbs only in 13:1, 8; 17:10.

13:2 יֹאכַל טוֹב—Literally, this is "he eats (what is) good." The adjective טוֹב is translated adverbially: "eats well."

וְנֶפֶשׁ בֹּגְדִים חָמָס׃—The noun נֶפֶשׁ can mean "appetite,"[1] as it does here and in 13:4. For the participle בֹּגְדִים, see the second textual note on 2:22.

13:3 פֹּשֵׂק שְׂפָתָיו מְחִתָּה־לוֹ׃—The verb פָּשַׂק, "part, open wide" (BDB), is found in the OT only here and, in the Piel (D), in Ezek 16:25, where it is usually paraphrased. The indefinite Qal (G) participle פֹּשֵׂק (like the parallel participle נֹצֵר in the preceding clause) is best rendered as present tense with an indefinite pronoun: "whoever opens ..." (see Waltke-O'Connor, § 24.3.1b, example 4). For the noun מְחִתָּה, "ruin," see the second textual note on 10:14.

13:4 מִתְאַוָּה וָאַיִן נַפְשׁוֹ עָצֵל—The feminine noun נֶפֶשׁ is the subject of the feminine Hithpael (HtD) participle מִתְאַוָּה, so this means "his appetite—[that of] a lazy person—desires [but obtains] nothing." Some have proposed eliminating נַפְשׁוֹ, "his appetite," or deleting its pronominal suffix, since נַפְשׁוֹ עָצֵל, "his appetite, the lazy person," is an Aramaizing construction. However, the repetition of נֶפֶשׁ in both lines of this verse

---

1 Cf. B. K. Waltke, "נֶפֶשׁ," *TWOT* 2:587–91.

is important in this proverb, and there are similar constructions elsewhere in the OT.[2] GKC, § 131 n, lists other examples of this construction.

וְנֶפֶשׁ חָרֻצִים תְּדֻשָּׁן׃—The Pual (Dp) of דָּשֵׁן means "become fat." In this clause too the subject of the feminine verb is נֶפֶשׁ. The concept of an appetite "becoming fat" must mean something like "is more than satisfied" (see ESV, NIV). For חָרֻצִים, "diligent, hardworking people," see the second textual note on 10:4.

13:5 דְּבַר־שֶׁקֶר יִשְׂנָא צַדִּיק—The direct object is the construct phrase דְּבַר־שֶׁקֶר, which is placed first in the clause for emphasis (GKC, § 142 f 2 (a)).

וְרָשָׁע יַבְאִישׁ וְיַחְפִּיר׃—The Hiphil (H) of בָּאַשׁ literally means "cause to stink" (as in Ex 5:21) or "make odious" (see BDB, 2). Forms of the verb are often used metaphorically to denote causing someone to appear disgraceful or shameful in someone else's eyes (see, e.g., the Hiphil [H] in Gen 34:30; the Niphal [N] in 1 Sam 13:4).

13:6 צְדָקָה תִּצֹּר תָּם־דָּרֶךְ—Literally, "righteousness keeps [a person with] integrity of way." Yahweh safeguards those whom he has gifted with integrity through faith (see Prov 2:7; 10:29). Most consider the construct phrase תָּם־דָּרֶךְ to have the abstract noun תֹּם, "integrity, blamelessness" (so BDB, s.v. תֹּם, 3, citing the parallel in Job 4:6). For תֹּם, see the second textual note on 2:7. דֶּרֶךְ refers to the justified believer's "way" of life.

וְרִשְׁעָה תְּסַלֵּף חַטָּאת׃—Literally, this is "wickedness perverts sin." The abstract noun חַטָּאת is translated concretely as "a sinner." The Piel (D) of סָלַף, "pervert, twist, make crooked," recurs in 19:3; 21:12; 22:12. It is cognate to the noun סֶלֶף, for which, see the second textual note on 11:3.

13:7 יֵשׁ מִתְעַשֵּׁר—For this construction with יֵשׁ and a participle, see the first textual note on 11:24. Both the Hithpael (HtD) participle of עָשַׁר, "be rich," and the Hithpolel (HtD) participle in the next clause, מִתְרוֹשֵׁשׁ, from רוּשׁ or רִישׁ, "be poor" (see the first textual note on 10:4), "denote esteeming or presenting oneself in a state" (Waltke-O'Connor, § 26.2f; see example 13). Here they both have the connotation of false pretense: "pretends to be rich … pretends to be poor."

13:9 אוֹר־צַדִּיקִים יִשְׂמָח—The personified figure of light (אוֹר) is the subject of the verb יִשְׂמָח, "rejoices." The supposed awkwardness of this personification has led many critical commentators needlessly to attempt to emend the verb to לָנֶצַח, "(is) forever," on the basis of the LXX's διὰ παντός.[3]

13:10 רַק־בְּזָדוֹן יִתֵּן מַצָּה— The particle רַק introduces a restrictive clause (GKC, § 153): literally, "only by insolence does one produce strife," that is, "insolence only produces strife." The term for arrogance, זָדוֹן, "insolence," recurs in 13:10 and 21:24, and is cognate to the adjective זֵד, which often describes unbelievers who oppose the efforts of godly people (e.g., Jer 43:2; Pss 86:14; 119:21, 51, 69, 78, 85, 122). The noun

---

[2] McCreesh, *Biblical Sound and Sense*, 127–28, citing 2 Sam 19:1 (ET 18:33); Jer 52:20; Ezek 10:3.

[3] Footnote in *BHS*.

מַצָּה II, "strife, contention" (BDB), derived from the verb נָצָה II, recurs in 17:19 and occurs elsewhere in the OT only in Is 58:4.

:וְאֶת־נוֹעָצִים חָכְמָה—Here אֵת must be the preposition "with." The Niphal (N) participle of יָעַץ has the meaning "take advice" (*HALOT*, 1).

13:11 הוֹן מֵהֶבֶל יִמְעָט—The noun הֶבֶל means "breath, vapor" and is commonly translated as "vanity" in Ecclesiastes. It signifies something that is insubstantial and fleeting, something that, like a vapor, has little substance and cannot be grasped. The meaning is difficult here, as seen by the wide variety of translations offered by the English versions (see, e.g., ESV, NASB, NIV). "From nothing" is literally accurate. Some emend to the Pual (Dp) participle מְבֹהָל, "in haste";[4] another form of that participle is in 20:21.

:וְקֹבֵץ עַל־יָד יַרְבֶּה—From the parallelism of this saying, "one who gathers by hand" must mean one who gathers a little bit at a time (see ESV, NIV), that is, gradually.

13:12 תּוֹחֶלֶת מְמֻשָּׁכָה מַחֲלָה־לֵב—The feminine noun תּוֹחֶלֶת, "hope," is the subject of both feminine participles, מְמֻשָּׁכָה and מַחֲלָה: "hope (that is) delayed makes a heart sick." The Pual (Dp) participle מְמֻשָּׁכָה means "be drawn out," here in a temporal sense, "be delayed" (see *HALOT*, 1). מַחֲלָה, the Hiphil (H) participle of חָלָה, "be sick," has the causative meaning "make sick; sicken," and לֵב is its direct object.

וְעֵץ חַיִּים—See the first textual note and the commentary on 3:18.

:תַּאֲוָה בָאָה—The accent on the final syllable shows that בָּאָה is the feminine participle of בּוֹא, "coming, arriving," that is, "a desire (being) fulfilled," rather than the feminine perfect of בּוֹא, which could mean that the desire "has (already) come, was fulfilled." This has implications for eschatology; see the commentary. Similar is the Niphal (N) feminine participle in תַּאֲוָה נִהְיָה, "a desire coming to pass, being fulfilled," beginning 13:19.

13:14 תּוֹרַת חָכָם מְקוֹר חַיִּים— For תּוֹרָה, "teaching," see the second textual note on 1:8. For מְקוֹר חַיִּים, "fountain of life," see the textual note on 10:11.

13:15 שֵׂכֶל־טוֹב יִתֶּן־חֵן—See "שֵׂכֶל, 'Good Sense,' and הִשְׂכִּיל, 'to Act Sensibly' " in "Wisdom in Proverbs" in the introduction. For חֵן, "grace," see the first textual note on 1:9.

:וְדֶרֶךְ בֹּגְדִים אֵיתָן—For the participle בֹּגְדִים, see the second textual note on 2:22. אֵיתָן means "permanent, enduring, unchanging." It can refer to a stream that is always flowing (Deut 21:4), which is an exception rather than the rule in Palestine, where most streams flow only after a rain. Some emend this word to אֵידָם, "(is) their disaster," on the basis of the LXX (ἐν ἀπωλείᾳ) or to תֹּאבֵד, "will perish" (as in Ps 1:6) on the basis of the Targum.[5] However, the emendation is not needed, and it destroys the contrast in this proverb between those with good sense, who change their situation by obtaining grace, and those who remain treacherous and also remain in the same futile situation.

13:16 כָּל־עָרוּם יַעֲשֶׂה בְדָעַת—For the subject noun, see "עָרוּם, 'Prudent,' and עָרְמָה, 'Prudence' " in "Wisdom in Proverbs" in the introduction, and see also the first textual

[4] Murphy, *Proverbs*, 94; Longman, *Proverbs*, 282; *BHS* footnote.

[5] Footnote in *BHS*; see also Murphy, *Proverbs*, 95; Longman, *Proverbs*, 282.

note on 1:4. Regarding בְּדָעַת, see "דַּעַת, 'Knowledge,' and יָדַע, 'to Know' " in "Wisdom in Proverbs" in the introduction as well as the commentary on 1:4, 7.

וּכְסִיל יִפְרֹשׂ אִוֶּלֶת׃—This is a rare example of a Hebrew clause with the word order subject, verb, object, literally, "a fool spreads out (his) stupidity." For the direct object, see "אֱוִיל, 'Stubborn Fool,' and אִוֶּלֶת, 'Stupidity' " in "Fools in Proverbs" in the introduction. The idiom "spreads out stupidity" is used metaphorically of the moron placing his idiocy on display for all to see (*HALOT*, s.v. פרשׂ, 1 g). McKane explains that the fool is like a peddler who puts his wares out for others to inspect.[6]

13:17 מַלְאָךְ רָשָׁע יִפֹּל בְּרָע—Some suggest repointing יִפֹּל, "falls," the Qal (G) of נָפַל, to its defective Hiphil (H) imperfect יַפִּל, "causes (others) to fall into trouble," that is, "brings trouble on others," for the sake of closer parallelism.[7] However, the kind of antithetical parallelism that predominates in this part of Proverbs does not require such strict correspondence. See "Large-Scale Evidence for Organization in Proverbs 10:1–22:16" in the excursus "The Organization of the Sayings in Solomon's Proverbs in Proverbs 10:1–22:16" in the commentary on chapter 10.

וְצִיר אֱמוּנִים מַרְפֵּא׃—Literally, this is "an envoy of faithfulness is healing." The abstract plural אֱמוּנִים serves as an adjectival genitive: "a faithful envoy." For מַרְפֵּא, see also 4:22; 12:18; 16:24; 29:1.

13:18 וְשׁוֹמֵר תּוֹכַחַת יְכֻבָּד׃—The Pual (Dp) יְכֻבָּד has a factitive meaning, "will (in fact/actuality) be honored, glorified" (see Waltke-O'Connor, § 25.2a, including n. 4). The imperfect forms an eschatological promise, pointing to the resurrection on the Last Day (see Rom 8:17, 30).

13:19 סוּר מֵרָע׃—See the third textual note on 3:7.

13:20 הָלוֹךְ אֶת־חֲכָמִים וֶחְכָּם—The two Kethib readings present the sequence of the Qal (G) infinitive absolute הָלוֹךְ followed by the Qal imperative וַחֲכָם, which forms a promise: literally, "*walk* with the wise men *and you will become wise*" (Joüon, § 116 f (3)). The Qere readings have the sequence of the participle הוֹלֵךְ followed by the imperfect יֶחְכָּם: "whoever walks … becomes/will become wise." The Qere is followed by the translation above.

וְרֹעֶה כְסִילִים יֵרוֹעַ׃—The rare verb רָעָה II means "associate with" (BDB) or "be a companion, friend." Its Qal (G) participle, used here, recurs in 28:7 and 29:3, and its Hithpael (HtD) is in 22:24. For יֵרוֹעַ, the Niphal (N) of רָעַע, "be injured," see the first textual note on 11:15.

13:21 וְאֶת־צַדִּיקִים יְשַׁלֶּם־טוֹב׃—The sign of the definite direct object, אֵת, precedes the object noun צַדִּיקִים even though it is indefinite, perhaps because the "righteous" are a distinct category of people (GKC, § 117 c). God could be the implied subject of the verb יְשַׁלֶּם, "will reward, repay," in which case the verb takes two accusatives, although English requires adding the preposition "with" before the second accusative, טוֹב: "he [God] will reward the righteous (with) good" (see GKC, § 117 ff). However, none of the surrounding verses explicitly refer to God. Many English versions render

---

6 McKane, *Proverbs*, 456.

7 Scott, *Proverbs, Ecclesiastes*, 94; Toy, *Proverbs*, 273; NRSV.

the impersonal active verb as a passive, "the righteous are rewarded with good" (ESV; similar are KJV and NASB), which leaves God as the unstated but implied agent of the action. The translation above is more literal: it takes טוֹב as the subject of the verb יְשַׁלֶּם, "good repays the righteous" (similar is RSV).

13:23 רָב־אֹכֶל נִיר רָאשִׁים—Literally, "an abundance of food (is) the fallow ground of the poor," this whole clause may be the protasis of a conditional sentence, "even though … ," with the apodosis in the following line. The rare noun נִיר II means "fallow ground" (BDB) or "farmland, arable land." In form רָאשִׁים could be the plural of רֹאשׁ, "head," but it is the plural Qal (G) participle of רוּשׁ or רִישׁ, "be poor." See the first textual note on 10:4.

וְיֵשׁ נִסְפֶּה בְּלֹא מִשְׁפָּט׃—In Proverbs the construction of יֵשׁ plus a participle (here נִסְפֶּה) usually refers to a kind of person; see the first textual note on 11:24. Hence this could mean "there is a type of [poor] person who is swept away without justice/unjustly." This kind of person represents a situation that appears to be a travesty of justice. Usually לֹא negates a verb; when used with a noun, it forms an emphatically strong negative statement: "without (any) justice (at all)." Similar is its force in Is 53:9: וְלֹא מִרְמָה בְּפִיו, "(absolutely) no deceit (was) in his mouth," referring to the sinless Suffering Servant (taken away מִמִּשְׁפָּט, "without justice," Is 53:8).

13:24 וְאֹהֲבוֹ שִׁחֲרוֹ מוּסָר׃—This can be rendered as "the one loving him promptly gives him discipline." The verb שָׁחַר II in the Piel (D) means "be on the lookout for" (*HALOT*, 1) or "seek early." The force of this verb is not that the father is looking for excuses to discipline his son, but that he is careful to discipline when needed in a timely manner. The verb takes two accusatives: its pronominal suffix (שִׁחֲרוֹ) and the noun מוּסָר, "discipline" (GKC, § 117 ff).

13:25 צַדִּיק אֹכֵל לְשֹׂבַע נַפְשׁוֹ—Literally, this is "a righteous person eats for the satisfaction of his appetite." The noun שֹׂבַע is rendered verbally: "until his appetite is satisfied."

וּבֶטֶן רְשָׁעִים תֶּחְסָר׃—Literally, "the stomach of wicked people will lack," this refers to a want of food, what in English is often termed an "empty stomach." The imperfect תֶּחְסָר can be understood to mean "will *continue* to lack," that is, "is *always* empty." Contrast Ps 23:1: לֹא אֶחְסָר, "I shall not (ever) lack (anything)."

Commentary

A Wise Son: Wise Ways to Live (13:1–15:19)

"A Wise Son: Wise Ways to Live" is a general description of this second informal section (13:1–15:19) of 10:1–22:16 that begins with another saying about a wise son.[8] The advice in these proverbs covers a wide range of topics. While much of it can be classified as Law, primarily aimed at its first and third

8 Proverbs 1–9 contains ten addresses by Solomon phrased as from a father to "my son," and several to (plural) "sons." See the excursus "Proverbs 1–9, Christ, and the Ten Commandments" in the commentary on Proverbs 1. For the loose structure of the sections in 10:1–22:16, see the excursus "The Organization of the Sayings in Solomon's Proverbs in Proverbs 10:1–22:16" as well as the commentary on 10:1–5.

uses, the role of the Gospel should not be overlooked.[9] Not only does the third use of the Law presuppose the Gospel, but many proverbs in this section also specifically apply the Gospel.

For instance, the proverbs about righteous people (e.g., 13:5, 9, 21, 22, 25) describe one who has been justified, that is, has received God's free gift of righteousness by grace alone through faith alone. Believers during the OT era, just like those in the church age, were saved on account of the perfect life, atoning death, and resurrection of Jesus Christ. Prov 14:9 applies the central promise of the Gospel—namely, the forgiveness of sins—to those who confess their guilt and receive God's mercy through faith. Two sayings—13:12 and 15:4—mention the "tree of life," a Gospel motif that occurs also in two earlier passages in Proverbs (3:18; 11:30).[10] Likewise, 13:9 speaks of the righteous as shining with brightness, a reference to eternal glory by grace alone (see the commentary on 13:9). Some of the more prominent proverbs in this section that highlight the Gospel are 13:6, 9, 12, 21, 22, 25; 14:2, 9, 11, 14, 16, 19, 26, 27; 15:4, 6, 8, 11.

Wise Ways to Live, Part 1 (13:1–25)

13:1 This verse once again returns to the parental relationship (see also, e.g., 4:1–9) and the handing down of wisdom—the theme that began the book (1:1–7). The lack of any verb in the first line makes it especially powerful: "a wise son—a father's instruction." While the translation offered above supplies the verb "heeds" on the basis of parallelism with the second line, the Hebrew allows for more densely packed meaning. A wise son not only heeds his father's instruction, but also *is* a product of his father's instruction. The focus is as much on the father's responsibility to teach as it is on the son to learn.

The second line speaks of a "mocker" not listening to a "reprimand" (גְּעָרָה). This word denotes not merely a rebuke, but also passionate anger and its physical expression, that is, shouting.[11] The mocker has no respect for any correction, no matter how forcefully expressed. Nor does he respect wisdom from any authority, human or divine.

13:2 This verse is a short study in opposites, with one person's mouth producing fruit to feed himself while another person's appetite produces violence that harms others. The irony is that treacherous, deceitful people are said to have an appetite but are not fed, while the wise person who merely speaks and produces fruit is fed well. This proverb is the first of three that are linked by the word נֶפֶשׁ. In 13:2 and 13:4 נֶפֶשׁ is used in the sense of "appetite," while

---

[9] See further "Law and Gospel in Proverbs" in the introduction.

[10] See the commentary on 3:18. See also "life" in 13:14; 14:27, 30; 15:4. All these are eschatological promises that will be consummated by the bodily resurrection of all believers to eternal life on the Last Day.

[11] Macintosh, "A Consideration of Hebrew גער," and Reif, "A Note on גער." Both of these authors also say that when God is the one who reprimands, the terminology denotes both his anger and the working out of that anger.

in 13:3 it denotes "life." The first line of this saying is nearly identical to the first line of 12:14.

13:3 This verse is linked to 13:2 by the word פֶּה, "mouth," as well as by נֶפֶשׁ, "appetite" or "life." The contrast with 13:2 is striking. In the preceding proverb the mouth is connected mostly with eating but also with speaking. In this one it is connected only with speaking. The lesson in this proverb is the wisdom of maintaining control over one's mouth. The wise person knows that one should not always speak, but the foolish person's constant need to speak reveals his foolishness and leads to his own ruin (see Mt 12:37).

13:4 This verse returns to the "appetite" (as in 13:2), but this time in the literal sense. The lazy person has a desire, but undertakes no action to fulfill his desire (see 21:17). The person who not only works, but also is diligent in his work has more than enough. This is wisdom at its most practical application for temporal existence, with implications also for a person's spiritual and eternal existence.

13:5 This verse contrasts the attitude of the righteous, which by implication keeps them from being humiliated, with that of the wicked person, who brings disgrace. The proverb's second line is purposely elliptical, not stating whether the wicked person brings disgrace upon himself or others. The lesson to be learned is not only to avoid being wicked, but also to avoid the company of wicked people. Paul offered the Corinthians the same advice: "Do not be unequally yoked with unbelievers. For what partnership has righteousness with lawlessness? Or what communion has light with darkness?" (2 Cor 6:14; see also 1 Cor 15:33).

13:6 This verse is linked to 13:5 by the roots צדק ("righteous person," צַדִּיק, and "righteousness," צְדָקָה) and רשׁע ("wicked person," רָשָׁע, and "wickedness," רִשְׁעָה). This saying reminds those who contemplate it that God's gift of "righteousness," which is imputed through faith (Gen 15:6; cf. Is 53:11), guards the person of integrity. Wickedness, the opposite of both integrity and righteousness, only serves to add to the corruption of those who reject God's gracious offer of "righteousness" (e.g., Prov 1:3; 2:9; 8:18, 20; see also Mt 6:33; Rom 3:18–2).

13:7 This verse is a simple observation of life, without offering or implying any endorsement of a certain attitude or behavior. Some people pretend to be what they are not.[12] It reminds us that appearances often deceive, even regarding something that should be so obvious as one's wealth or poverty.

13:8 This verse points out that riches can have their disadvantages because the rich person may have to use his riches to defend himself. However, being poor has its own disadvantages. The poor person cannot defend himself and so

[12] Garrett's proposal that the verbs do not necessarily mean "pretend to be" but rather "appear to be" (*Proverbs, Ecclesiastes, Song of Songs*, 136, including n. 261) ignores one common use of the Hithpael (HtD), which for some verbs means "pretend to be" or "esteem oneself as," but never simply "appear [to others] to be" (see Waltke-O'Connor, § 26.2f).

ignores even the most forceful threat (גְּעָרָה; see the comments on 13:1). Since he does not have the means to mount a defense, he simply has to endure the difficulties he may encounter. This proverb is linked to the previous one by the roots עשׁר ("be rich," מִתְעַשֵּׁר; "riches," עֹשֶׁר) and רושׁ or רישׁ ("be poor," מִתְרוֹשֵׁשׁ and רָשׁ). Like 13:7, it is an observation of life and does not endorse an attitude or behavior.

13:9 This verse refers primarily to the eternal state of the righteous and the opposite one of the wicked. It may or may not be evident for either during their temporal existence. The righteous shine brightly as they anticipate the promised eternal life God gives them. This brightness reflects the glory of Christ that is already now given to his faithful people as a gift of his bountiful grace (Ex 34:29–30; 2 Cor 4:6; Phil 2:15). Nevertheless, while still in this life, God's people continue to groan under the weight of sin that infests this world. This groaning is shared with all creation and will continue until the end, as Paul reminds us, "as we wait eagerly for adoption as sons, the redemption of our body" (Rom 8:22–23). Believers know that their lights will shine even more brightly in the world to come, after the resurrection (Dan 12:2–3; Mt 13:43).

The wicked, however, have no such hope. Their lamp will not shine beyond this life. The second line of this proverb is identical to the second line of 24:20.

13:10 This verse advises against insolence, an arrogant attitude that places one's own opinion over that of others, no matter how good their insight and advice may be. McKane notes that such a person is guilty of hubris that creates strife, inflames passions, and wounds feelings.[13] This kind of person does not possess true wisdom, which only comes with a willingness to believe God's Word and consider the advice of others who have learned from him.

13:11 This verse advises against financial speculation and "get rich quick" schemes. Instead it counsels one to look for gradual growth of wealth. Since Solomon placed this proverb immediately after 13:10, the application may be wider than economics. It could also be read as the way to a wealth of wisdom (see "riches" and "wisdom" in Eph 1:7–8, 17–18). The insolent person who is full of his own wisdom corresponds to the speculator who thinks riches can be quickly gained, whereas the wise person gradually grows in wisdom as he gathers the collected wisdom of other believers.

13:12 This verse is a saying formed by the juxtaposition of terms without a finite verb. The order of the terms in Hebrew is chiastic, as shown by this literal translation:

Hope delayed [subject]	תּוֹחֶלֶת מְמֻשָּׁכָה
sickens a heart [predicate],	מַחֲלָה־לֵב
but a tree of life [predicate]	וְעֵץ חַיִּים
desire coming [subject].	תַּאֲוָה בָאָה

---

[13] McKane, *Proverbs*, 453–54.

While this proverb could be viewed merely as an observation of life, it probably also suggests diagnostic analysis of the reason for someone's despair so that encouragement can be offered. The connection of desire that is *being* fulfilled (see the third textual note on this verse) with a tree of life not only is an observation about the invigorating nature of any hope that is at least partially realized, but also an implication that the ultimate desire of the righteous is eternal life. God has already granted this life now through faith, but the full fulfillment of the promise of eternal life will only come in the eschaton. The distinction between realized and future eschatology is evident in the adjacent promises of Jesus: "whoever believes in me, even though *he dies*, shall he live; he who lives and believes in me will *never die*" (Jn 11:25–26). See the commentary on Prov 3:18; 11:30; and 15:4. See also the promise by the exalted Christ to the believer about his future access to the tree of life after the resurrection: "to the one who overcomes I *will* grant to eat from *the tree of life*, which is in the paradise of God" (Rev 2:7; see also Lk 23:43).

13:13 This verse once again counsels readers to heed advice, noting the cost of ignoring it. Some advice comes in the form of commands. Obedience to them brings rewards. However, the advice and the command here are not simply human speech, but divine instruction, even if mediated through believers. The participle or verbal adjective יָרֵא, "one who fears," is in construct with its objective genitive, "a command." Similar are 14:2 and 31:30, where יְרֵא is in construct with the objective genitive "Yahweh." The construct phrase "one who fears Yahweh" recalls the construct phrase with the noun יִרְאָה, "fear": "the fear of Yahweh" (יִרְאַת יְהוָה; see the first textual note and the commentary on 1:7). All of these phrases imply obedience that flows from faith and a positive relationship to God, not simply fear of punishment. As Luther explains each of the Second through Tenth Commandments: "we should *fear and love God* so that we … ," which flows from the First Commandment, which Luther explains as "we should *fear, love, and trust in God* above all things."[14] This comes from a filial relationship with God through baptismal incorporation into his Son (e.g., 1 Cor 12:12–13; Gal 3:26–29).[15]

Thus the person who despises advice is the one who despised God's Word, and the person who fears the command is a believer motivated by the Gospel to obey God's Law (the third use of the Law).[16]

13:14 This verse is the only proverb in this chapter that does not employ antithetical parallelism. Instead, it has synthetic parallelism because the second line completes and further clarifies the first line. Characterizing the wise per-

---

[14] SC I (*Luther's Small Catechism with Explanation* [St. Louis: Concordia, 1986, 1991], 9–11; emphasis added).

[15] Of the five uses of the verb יָרֵא, "to fear," in Proverbs, only two denote being afraid (3:25; 31:21), and in both cases not being afraid is under discussion. In the other cases (3:7; 14:16; 24:21), the verb implies a relationship based on saving faith.

[16] See further "Law and Gospel in Proverbs" in the introduction.

son as "a fountain of life" implies that the wisdom spoken of here is not secular, human insight, but divinely granted wisdom that is alone able to rescue from eternal death and bestow life everlasting.

13:15 This verse speaks of the results of wisdom, which comes from God originally, since God the Son is the personal Wisdom of God.[17] Wisdom brings the blessing of God's "grace," and it can also elicit the graciousness or favor of other sagacious people. By contrast, an evil heart full of treachery brings no change in the status of a person before God, but causes the unbeliever to continue his unchanging descent into sin and death.

13:16 This verse notes that knowledge precedes an action by a wise person, even if that is not evident to those who observe his actions. However, a fool puts his foolishness on display for all to see.

13:17 This verse notes that messengers and envoys are given important responsibilities and that their faithfulness to their mission often determines success for them and for others. Garrett would confine the meaning of יִפֹּל בְּרָע, "falls into trouble," and מַרְפֵּא, "healing," to the effect that the messenger's actions have on himself.[18] Others would emend the first line to indicate that the messenger causes trouble for others (see the first textual note). In reality, the proverb is quite general about who is affected by the troubles or receives the benefits. The evil messenger falls into trouble that may harm both himself and others. The faithful messenger benefits himself and as well as others—those who commissioned him and those to whom he is sent to bring healing (cf. Mt 4:24–25; 10:8).

13:18 This verse speaks of the economic and social consequences of failing to learn from the discipline that one receives. However, the consequences of learning from correction do not automatically lead to economic blessing, though conforming to correction from God's Word will result in everlasting glory (1 Cor 15:43; 2 Cor 3:7–18). This proverb contains a play on words between קָלוֹן, "shame," from a verb (קָלָה II, related to קָלַל) meaning "be insignificant, lightweight," and יְכֻבָּד, "is honored, glorified," since the verb כָּבֵד can also mean "be heavy."

13:19 This verse is difficult.[19] However, contemplation of this proverb leads to the conclusion that fools will never experience the fulfillment of any God-pleasing, "sweet" or "pleasant" desire, because they refuse to turn from evil and instead remain on a course toward destruction.

13:20 This verse is a proverb about being influenced by the company one keeps. Note the play on words in the second line between רֹעֶה, "a companion,"

---

[17] See "Wisdom in Proverbs" in the introduction. See also the commentary on 1:1–7; 3:13–20; 8:22–31; 30:1b–10; and the excursus "Proverbs 8, Wisdom, Christology, and the Arian Controversy" in the commentary on chapter 8.

[18] Garrett, *Proverbs, Ecclesiastes, Song of Songs*, 138, including n. 270.

[19] Toy even proposes that it was made up of the fragments of two proverbs, each of which lost its parallel line (*Proverbs*, 274–75).

and יֵרוֹעַ, "be harmed, injured." The second line is akin to the saying "if you lie down with dogs, you'll get up with fleas." St. Paul in 1 Cor 15:33, quoting the poet Menander,[20] also reminds us that "bad company ruins good morals."

13:21 This verse is an observation about the consequences of behavior. While some have seen this proverb as teaching that absolute justice always takes place already in this life, note that it states that "trouble *pursues* sinners." It may or may not catch up to them in this life, but it surely will at God's judgment. In the same way, good repays righteous people, but *when* they are repaid is not stated. They may not receive this payment until God rewards them in eternity. This is pictured at the end of Jesus' parable of the talents: "Well done, good and faithful servant. You have been faithful over a little. I will set you over much. Enter into the joy of your lord" (Mt 25:21).

13:22 This verse is linked to 13:21 by the catchwords "good" (טוֹב is the last word of 13:21 and the first word of 13:22) and "righteous" (צַדִּיק). This proverb also appears to teach about justice in this life, especially if the inheritance in the first line is understood to be material wealth. However, good people do not always leave a substantial estate to their grandchildren. They do, however, bequeath to them the good that they have in the Gospel, an inheritance that can benefit future generations (see 2 Tim 1:5). Sinners, however, are focused only on temporal benefits in this world. Their wealth will not ultimately benefit either them or their heirs, but the righteous, who are heirs through Baptism and faith in Christ, will inherit all things (Rom 8:17; Gal 3:26–29; Titus 3:5–7; cf. Heb 1:2).

13:23 This difficult verse was paraphrased and interpreted in different ways by the ancient versions: the LXX, Peshitta, Targum, and Vulgate. It could be an explanation for the failure of some poor people to benefit even when God blesses their land. When government is corrupt, the powerful easily prey upon the poor, so that even the bounty of their land, which they worked for, is taken away. On the other hand, it could be Solomon's instruction to his sons about the need for just government to ensure that even the most economically disadvantaged person in society can have an opportunity to prosper.

13:24 This verse is about the counterintuitive nature of disciplining one's children. At times it is difficult for parents to administer punishment on the children they love. It is equally difficult for children to understand that proper discipline from parents is a sign of their love. This proverb looks beyond the immediate pain caused by discipline to the more lasting pain caused by a lack of discipline. This verse may allow corporal punishment, but it does not command believers to use it. Certainly the proverb should not be interpreted literalistically as requiring parents to beat their children with a rod. The form of discipline should be appropriate for the infraction and also for the learning ability and sensitivity of the child. The key word is "loves" (cf. 22:15; 23:13–14).

---

[20] Menander, *Thais*, 218.

13:25 This verse characterizes the righteous as content with the sufficient blessings of God, who will never leave or forsake them (1 Tim 6:8; Heb 13:5). They are grateful for the necessities of life and do not seek more than they need (cf. Ex 16:4–5, 20, 27). The wicked are never content and are always hungry for more. While the proverbs in Prov 13:23–25 may seem to have little in common, they are linked by the root אכל: "food," אֹכֶל, in 13:23 and "eats," אֹכֵל, in 13:25. Compare Is 55:1–3 and Rev 22:17.

Proverbs 14:1–35

Wise Ways to Live, Part 2

Translation

14 [1]**A wise woman builds her house,**
but a stupid one tears it down with her own hands.
[2]**The person who walks in his uprightness is one who fears Yahweh,**
but the one who is devious in his ways despises him.
[3]**In the mouth of a stubborn fool is a branch of haughtiness,**
but the lips of wise people protect them.

[4]**Without cattle the feeding trough is empty,**
but a great harvest is [gained] by an ox's strength.
[5]**A trustworthy witness does not lie,**
but a false witness breathes lies.

[6]**A mocker seeks wisdom, and there is none [to be found],**
but knowledge is easy for a discerning person.
[7]**Get away from a foolish person,**
since you cannot learn [from him how to have] lips of knowledge.
[8]**The wisdom of a prudent person is to understand his way,**
but the stupidity of fools is deception.
[9]**Stubborn fools mock confessing one's sin,**
but his [God's] favor is among the upright.
[10]**A heart knows the bitterness of its soul,**
and no stranger can share its joy.

[11]**The house of wicked people will be destroyed,**
but the tent of upright people will flourish.
[12]**There is a way that appears to be correct to a person,**
but its end is the way of death.
[13]**Even in laughter a heart can ache,**
and the end of joy may be grief.
[14]**A backslider in heart is satiated from his ways,**
but a good person [is satiated] from his [ways].

[15]**A gullible person trusts anything,**
but a prudent person considers his steps.
[16]**A wise person is one who fears [Yahweh] and who turns away from evil,**
but a fool meddles [with it] in [his] overconfidence.
[17]**A short-tempered person acts stupidly,**
and a schemer is hated.

18 Gullible people inherit stupidity,
but prudent people will surround knowledge.

19 Evil people will bow down in front of good people,
and wicked people [will bow down] at the gates of a righteous person.
20 A poor person is shunned even by his neighbor,
but those who love a rich person are many.
21 The person who despises his neighbor sins,
but the one who is kind to oppressed people—he is blessed.
22 Don't those who plan evil go astray?
But those who plan good [find] mercy and truth.

23 In all hard work is gain,
but idle talk only [leads] to poverty.
24 The crown of the wise is their wealth,
but the stupidity of fools is [always] stupidity.
25 A truthful witness saves lives,
but a liar breathes deceit.

26 In the fear of Yahweh is strong confidence,
and his children will have a refuge.
27 The fear of Yahweh is a fountain of life,
to turn [a person] away from the snares of death.

28 A large population is an honor for a king,
and without people ruin comes to a ruler.
29 A patient person has much understanding,
but an impatient person exalts stupidity.
30 A tranquil heart [gives] life to the body,
but jealousy [causes] rotting of the bones.
31 The person who oppresses the poor insults his Maker,
but the person who is gracious to a needy person honors him [God].
32 A wicked person is brought down by his own evildoing,
but a righteous person finds refuge even at his death.
33 Wisdom rests in the heart of a discerning person;
even among fools it will be recognized.
34 Righteousness lifts up a nation,
but sin [brings] shame to countries.
35 A king's favor is toward a servant who has insight,
but his fury is [for] one causing shame.

Textual Notes

14:1 חַכְמ֣וֹת נָ֭שִׁים בָּנְתָ֣ה בֵיתָ֑הּ—The phrase חַכְמ֣וֹת נָ֭שִׁים, literalistically, "wisdoms of women," has been the subject of much discussion because it is the subject of the feminine singular verb בָּנְתָ֣ה, "builds." The absolute form of the abstract plural חָכְמוֹת refers to personified or hypostatized "Wisdom" in 1:20; 9:1; 24:7. Here the abstract plural is in construct, and it refers to a state or condition of being "wise" (see Waltke-O'Connor, § 7.4.2b; cf. GKC, § 145 k, note 3). The genitive נָשִׁים indicates genus, what kind of wise person: one of the women (see Waltke-O'Connor, § 9.5.3i). Therefore the plural phrase should probably be understood as a singular "wise woman," matching the verb.

ESV takes it as a superlative: "the wisest of women." RSV renders it as abstract "wisdom."

וְאִוֶּלֶת בְּיָדֶיהָ תֶהֶרְסֶנּוּ׃—This second, antithetical clause also has an abstract feminine noun as its subject, but אִוֶּלֶת, "stupidity," is singular. See "אֱוִיל, 'Stubborn Fool,' and אִוֶּלֶת, 'Stupidity' " in "Fools in Proverbs" in the introduction. In this chapter, the concrete masculine noun אֱוִיל, "stubborn fool," is in 14:3, 9. Some translations render the noun here as an abstract, "folly" (RSV, ESV), but most render it concretely, "foolish/stupid (woman)," to match the "wise woman" in the preceding clause.

14:2 הוֹלֵךְ בְּיָשְׁרוֹ יְרֵא יְהוָה—The noun יֹשֶׁר, "uprightness," literally, "straightness," is a Wisdom synonym of God's gracious gift of righteousness, which includes justification and sanctification. For the participle or verbal adjective יָרֵא in construct with "Yahweh," see the commentary on 13:13. See also the first textual note and the commentary on 1:7, which has the nominal phrase יִרְאַת־יְהוָה, "the fear of Yahweh."

וּנְלוֹז דְּרָכָיו בּוֹזֵהוּ׃—The Niphal (N) participle נָלוֹז, "devious (one)," is one of the Wisdom words literally meaning "twisted" or "crooked" that are antonyms of words from the root ישׁר, which denotes straightness or uprightness, including יֹשֶׁר in the preceding clause. See the second textual note on 1:3. The participle is in construct with the suffixed noun (דְּרָכָיו) it affects: "perverse in his ways" (GKC, § 116 k). בּוֹזֵהוּ, "despises him [Yahweh]," is the suffixed participle of בָּזָה, "despise," which recurs in Proverbs only as the participle in 15:20 and 19:16. This verb is a biform and homonym of the more common בּוּז (eight times in Proverbs), whose participle begins 14:21.

14:3 חֹטֶר גַּאֲוָה—The noun חֹטֶר occurs only here and in Is 11:1, where it denotes a shoot from the stump of a tree. It probably refers to a "(tree) branch" that is used as a whip. It is in construct with גַּאֲוָה, "arrogance" (*HALOT*, 3) or "haughtiness."

תִּשְׁמוּרֵם׃—This suffixed imperfect form of שָׁמַר, "keep, protect," is anomalous and appears to be singular. See GKC, § 47 g, and Joüon, § 44 c. At least one Hebrew manuscript has תִּשְׁמְרוּם, apparently used as the suffixed feminine plural imperfect, which agrees with its subject, שִׂפְתֵי, the plural construct of the feminine noun שָׂפָה, "lip." The ancient versions read a plural verb.

14:4 בָּר—While this adjective normally means "pure," in this proverb it describes a trough without grain in it, hence an "empty" (*HALOT*, 2) trough.

14:5 עֵד אֱמוּנִים—The abstract plural functions as an adjectival genitive, "a trustworthy witness," analogous to צִיר אֱמוּנִים, "a trustworthy envoy," in 13:17.

וְיָפִיחַ כְּזָבִים עֵד שָׁקֶר׃—See the first textual note on 6:19, which has nearly the identical clause.

14:6 בִּקֶּשׁ־לֵץ—The participle לֵץ is the subject of the Piel (D) verb בִּקֶּשׁ. See "לֵץ, 'Mocker,' and לָצוֹן, 'Mocking, Scoffing' " in "Fools in Proverbs" in the introduction.

וְדַעַת לְנָבוֹן נָקָל׃—See "דַּעַת, 'Knowledge,' and יָדַע, 'to Know' " in "Wisdom in Proverbs" in the introduction, as well as the commentary on 1:4, 7. Here דַּעַת, which is normally feminine, is construed as masculine. It is the subject of נָקָל, a masculine Niphal perfect from קָלַל, which here can mean that knowledge is "easy" to learn (BDB, 2) or perhaps that it "comes quickly" to a person with discernment (cf. BDB, 1). The Niphal (N) participle נָבוֹן, "discerning person," recurs in this chapter in 14:33 and is from the same root (בין) as other common Wisdom vocabulary. See "בִּינָה, 'Understanding,' and Related Words" in "Wisdom in Proverbs" in the introduction.

14:7 כְּסִיל—See "כְּסִיל, 'Fool,' and כְּסִילוּת, 'Foolishness' " in "Fools in Proverbs" in the introduction. In this chapter כְּסִיל recurs in 14:8, 16, 24, 33.

וּבַל־יָדַעְתָּ שִׂפְתֵי־דָעַת׃—Literally, this is "you cannot learn lips of knowledge." For the negative בַּל, see the third textual note on 9:13. Suggestions to emend it are unconvincing. Just as unconvincing is the suggestion of Whitley that בַּל is to be understood in a positive sense and that this line should be translated as "for *surely* you are concerned with lips of knowledge."[1] Here the verb יָדַע probably is used in the sense of "learn" (*HALOT*, 2). The point of this saying appears to be that you should avoid a fool because you cannot learn from him how to speak knowledgably. See "דַּעַת, 'Knowledge,' and יָדַע, 'to Know' " in "Wisdom in Proverbs" in the introduction, as well as the commentary on 1:4, 7.

14:8 חָכְמַת עָרוּם— See "עָרוּם, 'Prudent,' and עָרְמָה, 'Prudence' " in "Wisdom in Proverbs" in the introduction. See also the first textual note on 1:4. עָרוּם recurs in this chapter in 14:15, 18.

14:9 אֱוִלִים יָלִיץ אָשָׁם—The plural "stubborn fools" is the subject of the singular imperfect of לִיץ, "mock," whose participle was in 14:6. The object noun אָשָׁם can denote objective culpability or "guilt" in God's sight caused by sin, even if the guilty are unaware that what they have done is a sin (Gen 26:10; Jer 51:5; Ps 68:22 [ET 68:21]), or, more often, the "guilt offering" (e.g., Lev 5:1–26 [ET 5:1–6:7]), a sacrifice prescribed by God to atone for the guilt of sin.[2] The cognate verb אָשַׁם, "be guilty," can describe the subjective human sense of responsibility for sin: "realize (one's) guilt" (e.g., Lev 4:13, 22, 27). The cognate verb can also mean "be punished because of guilt," as in Prov 30:10, the only other occurrence of the root in Proverbs (see BDB, s.v. אָשַׁם, 3). Here the noun אָשָׁם involves the awareness of one's own objective guilt before God, and it refers especially to the acknowledgment or confession of one's sin. This confession could be accompanied by the offering of a sacrifice, and it would include the knowledge of God's eventual punishment if one's sin is not forgiven. See further the commentary.

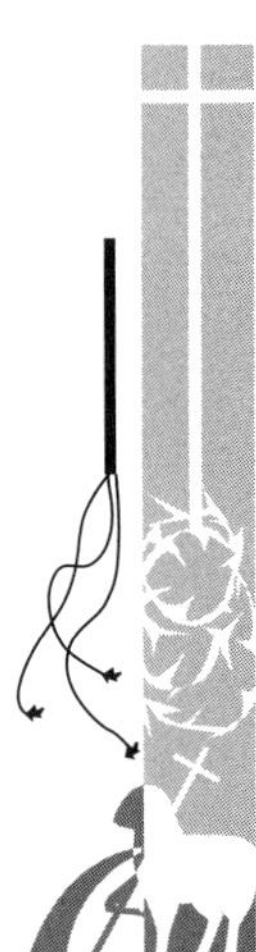

וּבֵין יְשָׁרִים רָצוֹן׃—The noun רָצוֹן usually refers to God's gracious gift of "favor." In the context here, this refers to the forgiveness of sins, received through faith alone. See the second textual note on 8:35.

14:10 לֵב יוֹדֵעַ מָרַּת נַפְשׁוֹ—The noun לֵב is the subject of the masculine participle יוֹדֵעַ and the referent of the masculine pronoun on נַפְשׁוֹ. (Contrast the construal of לֵב as feminine in 12:25.) The noun מָרָה, "bitterness," in construct here, is one of the rare instances where the consonant *resh* admits a *daghesh* (מָרַּת). See GKC, § 22 s, and Joüon, § 23 a.

---

[1] Whitley, "The Positive Force of the Hebrew Particle בל."

[2] Cf. G. H. Livingston, "אָשַׁם," *TWOT* 1:78–79.

14:11 וְאֹהֶל יְשָׁרִים יַפְרִיחַ׃—The verb פָּרַח means "to bud, sprout, send out shoots," in the Qal (G), and the Hiphil (H) can have that same meaning, as in reference to a tree in Job 14:9. Since a "tent," אֹהֶל, cannot literally "sprout," English versions are generally agreed that the Hiphil (H) is used metaphorically here to speak of success, and they translate it as "flourish" (ESV, NASB, NIV, NRSV). Similarly, the verb refers to the "righteous" in Ps 92:13–14 (92:12–13).

14:12 יֵשׁ דֶּרֶךְ יָשָׁר לִפְנֵי־אִישׁ—Literally, this is "there is a way [that appears to be] straight in front of a man." יָשָׁר is used in the same way in 12:15a and 21:2a to refer to a "way" that only seems to be "straight, correct" in human estimation (בְּעֵינָיו, literally, "in his eyes," 12:15; 21:2) but is not in God's estimation, and God's view establishes definitive and absolute truth.

וְאַחֲרִיתָהּ דַּרְכֵי־מָוֶת׃—The feminine suffix on וְאַחֲרִיתָהּ refers to the feminine noun דֶּרֶךְ, "way," in the preceding clause. For the eschatological meaning of the noun אַחֲרִית, "end," see the first textual note on 5:4. מָוֶת, "death," refers not just to physical death, but also to everlasting "death" (as in, e.g., 2:18; 5:5; 7:27; 8:36; 10:2) under God's judgment in Sheol (see the first textual note and the commentary on 1:12) or hell. The plural דַּרְכֵי, literally, "*ways* of death," could be an intensive plural for emphasis. Compare the first textual note on 7:27, which has the plural דַּרְכֵי שְׁאוֹל, literally, "ways of/into Sheol."

14:13 וְאַחֲרִיתָהּ שִׂמְחָה תוּגָה׃—The feminine suffix on וְאַחֲרִיתָהּ is proleptic and refers to the feminine noun שִׂמְחָה, literally, "but its end—[the end of] joy—[may be] grief." The noun תּוּגָה is repeated from 10:1 and recurs in 17:21.

14:14 מִדְּרָכָיו יִשְׂבַּע סוּג לֵב—The subject is סוּג, which may be an unusual form of Qal (G) active participle (BDB) or a verbal adjective (GKC, § 72 p) from סוּג, "backslide, be recalcitrant toward God." It is in construct with לֵב, meaning "a backslider in heart" (BDB, s.v. סוּג I, Qal). For the metaphorical meaning of שָׂבַע, "be filled, satiated," with the preposition מִן, see the second textual note on 1:31.

The verb יִשְׂבַּע also does double duty as the implied verb in the second clause of the verse, which includes the preposition מִן on the suffixed preposition עַל in a causative sense: וּמֵעָלָיו, "but from/because of his [ways]."

14:15 פֶּתִי יַאֲמִין לְכָל־דָּבָר—Literally, this is "a gullible person believes every word." See "פֶּתִי, 'Gullible Person' " in "Fools in Proverbs" in the introduction. Its plural occurs in 14:18.

לַאֲשֻׁרוֹ׃—The noun אָשׁוּר, "a step, stride," occurs only here in Proverbs but is part of the metaphorical vocabulary for one's way of life. See the excursus "The Metaphor of the Path in Solomon's Wisdom" in the commentary on chapter 10.

14:16 חָכָם יָרֵא וְסָר מֵרָע—יָרֵא could be the verbal adjective or a participle (see the commentary on 13:13): "a wise person is one who fears [Yahweh]." Or it could be an example of the perfect of a stative verb used gnomically: "a wise person fears [Yahweh]" (see Waltke-O'Connor, § 30.5.3c, example 9). Likewise, סָר could be a participle or a third masculine singular perfect used gnomically. For the combination of the verb סוּר and prepositional phrase מֵרָע, see 3:7; 13:19; 16:6, 17.

וּכְסִיל מִתְעַבֵּר וּבוֹטֵחַ׃—The meaning of the Hithpael (HtD) participle of עָבַר is uncertain. It could be related to עֶבְרָה, "fury, arrogance," and mean "be arrogant" (BDB, s.v. עָבַר denominative Hithpael). God is its subject in Deut 3:26; Pss 78:21, 59, 62; 89:39 (ET 89:38), where it means "become infuriated." Or this Hithpael could be related to the common verb עָבַר in the sense of "overstep, cross into." This verb occurs in the Hithpael with a human subject only in Proverbs (14:16; 20:2; 26:17). In 20:2 it denotes intruding into the king's anger, and in 26:17 it denotes meddling in someone else's quarrel. Therefore, basic force of this verb in the Hithpael appears to be "inject oneself into a situation." In this case the fool מִתְעַבֵּר וּבוֹטֵחַ, literally, "meddles and is trusting," that is, he meddles with the evil that the wise person avoided, and he (wrongly) trusts that it will not harm him. The participle וּבוֹטֵחַ is translated adverbially: "in [his] overconfidence."

14:17 קְצַר־אַפַּיִם יַעֲשֶׂה אִוֶּלֶת—In this saying, the construct phrase קְצַר־אַפַּיִם, literally, "(one who is) short of anger," denotes what is called in English "a short-tempered person." See also the textual note on 14:29. The predicate יַעֲשֶׂה אִוֶּלֶת is, literally, "does stupidity," but the object noun is translated as an adverb: "acts stupidly."

וְאִישׁ מְזִמּוֹת יִשָּׂנֵא׃—For מְזִמּוֹת meaning "schemes, wicked plans," see the second textual note on 12:2. The construct phrase is translated as "schemer." The Niphal (N) imperfect יִשָּׂנֵא means "is hated," but the LXX apparently read this word as יִשָּׂא, "bears up, endures." It translated the second line as ἀνὴρ δὲ φρόνιμος πολλὰ ὑποφέρει, "but a sensible man endures many things." This may be an attempt by the LXX translator to sharpen the contrast between the two lines.[3]

14:18 וַעֲרוּמִים יַכְתִּרוּ דָעַת׃—The verb כָּתַר occurs six times in the OT. In four of the other five cases it means "to surround," twice (Hab 1:4; Ps 142:8 [ET 142:7]) in the Hiphil (H), as here, and twice (Judg 20:43, Ps 22:13 [ET 22:12]) in the Piel (D). (In Job 36:2 the Piel means "wait.") Only here have some interpreters understood it to mean "be crowned." This is a longstanding interpretation going back to some ancient versions.[4] Almost all English translations have "will be crowned." This is based on the related noun כֶּתֶר, "a crown," and Rabbinic Hebrew usage of the Hiphil of כָּתַר, meaning "to tie a wreath, to offer a crown" (Jastrow). This view probably is influenced by עֲטָרָה, "a crown," in 14:24 as well as by the frequent use of metaphorical images in Proverbs, especially the inheritance metaphor in the first line of 14:18. The translation "be crowned" has, in turn, led some to emend נָחֲלוּ, "inherit," in the first line to נֶחְלוּ, "are adorned with."[5]

However, there is no need to assign anything other than the normal meaning, "to surround," to יַכְתִּרוּ. Nor is there any reason to emend the preceding line.

14:20 גַּם־לְרֵעֵהוּ יִשָּׂנֵא רָשׁ—The Qal (G) of שָׂנֵא normally means "to hate," and the Niphal (N) usually has the corresponding passive meaning, "to be hated," as at the

---

3 English translations generally follow the MT, but Garrett (*Proverbs, Ecclesiastes, Song of Songs*, 143, including nn. 289–90) advocates the LXX's interpretation.

4 Toy (*Proverbs*, 293) notes that Theodotion and the Targum are two such ancient versions and that the medieval Jewish interpreters Saadia Gaon and Rashi, as well as Luther (see WA DB 10/2.46–47), all take this verb to mean "crowned" here.

5 Driver, "Problems in the Hebrew Text of Proverbs," 181; McKane, *Proverbs*, 467; Garrett, *Proverbs, Ecclesiastes, Song of Songs*, 144, including n. 291.

end of 14:17. The preposition לְ (on לְרֵעֵהוּ) introduces the agent of the passive action (GKC, § 121 f): literally, "hated *by* his neighbor." The nuance of "hated" here depends on the contrast with the parallel line, where many "love" a rich person. Since the second line implies that everyone wants to be in the company and favor of a rich person, the implication of יִשָּׂנֵא in the first line is that people avoid or shun a poor person. This is confirmed by the following proverb, 14:21, which notes two attitudes toward others: despising them or treating them kindly.

14:21 For בָּז־לְרֵעֵהוּ, literally, "he despises his neighbor," see the first textual note on 11:12.

אַשְׁרָיו׃—This is the interjection אַשְׁרֵי with suffix, "blessed is he." See the first textual note on 3:13.

14:22 חֹרְשֵׁי רָע ... חֹרְשֵׁי טוֹב—For the combination of the verb חָרַשׁ, "devise, plot," and noun רַע or רָעָה, "evil," see the first textual note on 3:29. The verb חָרַשׁ usually means "plough" or "engrave." However, here as well as most of its other uses in Proverbs, it is used twice metaphorically to mean "plan, devise," first with "evil" as its object and then with "good."

וְחֶסֶד וֶאֱמֶת—For these two nouns, see the first textual note on 3:3. Their syntactical relationship to the rest of the clause here is unclear, but the meaning must be that "mercy and truth" are benefits received, and perhaps bestowed, by "those who plan good."

14:23 וּדְבַר־שְׂפָתַיִם אַךְ־לְמַחְסוֹר׃—The construct phrase "a word of lips" is used idiomatically here to denote talking that is idle chatter and does not contribute to useful purposes. Since the contrast is to "hard work" (עֶצֶב in the preceding clause), a good translation is "idle talk." The restrictive phrase אַךְ־לְמַחְסוֹר, literally, "only to poverty," was also in 11:24 and recurs in 21:5; 22:16.

14:24 אִוֶּלֶת כְּסִילִים אִוֶּלֶת׃—Literally, "the stupidity of fools (is) stupidity," this clause is difficult. Many interpreters would emend the first אִוֶּלֶת to וְלִוְיַת, "and a wreath," to match עֲטֶרֶת, "crown," in the first line. (Both of these nouns occur together in 4:9.) Some would go farther and emend the first line to, for example, "the crown of the wise is their wisdom."[6] Scott would emend the last word of the first line from עָשְׁרָם, "their riches/wealth," to יָשְׁרָם, "their virtue."[7] However, no emendation is needed for either line. The first line depicts the everlasting wealth and royal glory that accrue to those who receive divine wisdom through faith, as in 3:16; 8:18; 10:22. The second line, then, states that the consequence for those who reject divine wisdom will be that they will always remain characterized by stupidity.

14:25 מַצִּיל נְפָשׁוֹת עֵד אֱמֶת—Similar proverbs declare that righteousness (10:2; 11:4, 6) or the mouth of the upright (12:6) are able "to save" (the Hiphil [H] of נָצַל). The construct phrase עֵד אֱמֶת, "a witness of truth," has an adjectival genitive similar to עֵד אֱמוּנִים in 14:5.

וְיָפִחַ כְּזָבִים מִרְמָה׃—Probably the plural כְּזָבִים, "lies," means "a witness who tells lies," since that is the meaning of עֵד־כְּזָבִים in 21:28. It is translated as the singular "liar"

6 Toy, *Proverbs*, 296–97.

7 Scott, *Proverbs, Ecclesiastes*, 97.

and as the subject of the singular verb וְיָפִחַ, whose direct object is the abstract feminine noun מִרְמָה, "deceit."

14:26 בְּיִרְאַת יְהוָה—The same construct phrase, but without בְּ, begins 14:27. See the first textual note and the commentary on 1:7 and "יִרְאַת יְהוָה, 'the Fear of Yahweh,' and יְרֵא יְהוָה, 'One Who Fears Yahweh' " in "Wisdom in Proverbs" in the introduction.

14:27 מְקוֹר חַיִּים ... מָוֶת׃—For "fountain of life," see the textual note and the commentary on 10:11. "Life," חַיִּים, has the full eschatological sense of everlasting life by God's grace, eventuating in the resurrection to eternal life on the Last Day, as also in, for example, 3:2, 18, 22; 4:10, 13, 22–23. Conversely, מָוֶת, "death," has the same eschatological sense pointing to eternal perdition in hell as in, for example, 2:18; 5:5, 23; 7:27; 8:36; 10:2. See also Sheol in, for example, 5:5; 7:27.

14:29 אֶרֶךְ אַפַּיִם ... וּקְצַר־רוּחַ—In this saying, literally, "(one who is) long of anger" or "slow to anger" denotes what in English is called "a patient person." אֶרֶךְ אַפַּיִם, "long of anger," recurs in 15:18 and 16:32, and similar expressions are in 19:11 and 25:15. (See also the first textual note on 14:17.) The opposite of this is "(one who is) short of spirit," a short-tempered, easily angered, impatient person. See the second textual note on 17:27 for the similar phrase קַר־רוּחַ, "cool of spirit," meaning "even-tempered."

14:30 חַיֵּי בְשָׂרִים לֵב מַרְפֵּא—Literally, this is "life of flesh (is) a heart of healing." The plural of בָּשָׂר, "flesh," occurs only here in the OT and may be an abstract plural encompassing all the physical qualities of life (cf. GKC § 124 d). The plural may be due to influence of the preceding abstract plural חַיִּים (in construct), "life." "A heart of healing" may mean "a healed heart" or perhaps the heart of a person who gives healing to others. Most likely, however, here it signifies a heart that is free from envy, in contrast to קִנְאָה, "jealousy," in the next clause. Thus this heart is at peace and tranquil (see ESV, NASB, NIV, NRSV).

14:31 עֹשֵׁק־דָּל חֵרֵף עֹשֵׂהוּ—The Qal (G) participle עֹשֵׁק, "the person/one who oppresses," occurs also in 22:16 and 28:3. (The Qal passive [Gp] participle עָשׁוּק, "oppressed, burdened," is in 28:17.) In 22:16, as here, the object of the participle is the adjective דָּל, "poor," used substantively and collectively: "the poor." Prov 28:3 uses as the object the plural of the same adjective: דַּלִּים, "poor/needy people."

The person oppressing the poor חֵרֵף עֹשֵׂהוּ, "insults his Maker," a phrase that recurs in 17:5a, which is a thematic parallel to 14:31a (see the first textual note on 17:5). חֵרֵף is the Piel (D) perfect of חָרַף, which in both the Qal and the Piel means to "reproach" (BDB, s.v. חָרַף I), "taunt" (*HALOT*, s.v. חרף II), or "insult." (The Qal participle with suffix חֹרְפִי, "anyone who taunts me," is used in 27:11.) עֹשֵׂהוּ is the Qal participle of עָשָׂה, "to make, form," with a third masculine singular suffix, "his Maker," that is, God. Grammatically, the referent of the suffix ("his") could be either of the singular words עֹשֵׁק, "the person who oppresses," or דָּל, "the poor." Theologically, both are possible, since God is the one who has made both (and indeed, he has made all people). However, in context the emphasis most likely is on the poor person as the one whom God has made, so that the abuse offends God, "his [the poor person's] Maker."

וּמְכַבְּדוֹ חֹנֵן אֶבְיוֹן׃—The subject is the Qal (G) participle חֹנֵן, "the person who is gracious, kind." This word is spelled plene, חונן, in 4QProv[b] compared to the MT's defective spelling.[8] The direct object of the participle is אֶבְיוֹן, "a poor, needy person," which recurs in 30:14; 31:9, 20. English requires a preposition: "kind *to* the needy." The object suffix on the Piel (D) participle וּמְכַבְּדוֹ, "but honors *him*," must refer back to עֹשֵׂהוּ, "his Maker," that is, God, in the first clause of the verse.

14:32 וְחֹסֶה בְמוֹתוֹ צַדִּיק׃—This means "but a righteous person [צַדִּיק] finds refuge [חֹסֶה] even at his death [בְמוֹתוֹ]." The participle חֹסֶה does not just mean that the righteous person "seeks/looks for refuge," but that he truly "finds refuge" in God. It is cognate to the noun מַחְסֶה, "a refuge," in the divine promise in 14:26 for the children of a person who fears Yahweh. This clause is consistent with other proverbs that promise believers everlasting "life" (e.g., 3:2, 18, 22) that extends beyond the grave and that promise escape from eternal death (e.g., 10:2; 11:4).

In place of "in/even at his death," the LXX has τῇ ἑαυτοῦ ὁσιότητι, "in his holiness," apparently reading the Hebrew as בְּתוּמּוֹ, "in his integrity," a metathesis of מ and ת. Those who deny that Proverbs has any teaching about life beyond the grave favor this reading.[9] However, this leaves the insipid "a righteous person seeks refuge in his integrity."[10] 4QProv[b] from Qumran supports the MT.[11]

14:33 בְּלֵב נָבוֹן תָּנוּחַ חָכְמָה—The construct phrase לֵב נָבוֹן, "the heart of a discerning person," recurs in 15:14 and 18:15. "Wisdom [חָכְמָה] rests [תָּנוּחַ]" in such a heart, and it seeks (15:14) and acquires (18:15) knowledge. For נָבוֹן, see the second textual note on 14:6. The verb נוּחַ recurs in the Qal (G) in 21:16 and in Hiphil (H) in 29:17.

וּבְקֶרֶב כְּסִילִים תִּוָּדֵעַ׃—The subject of the feminine Niphal (N) imperfect תִּוָּדֵעַ is the feminine noun חָכְמָה, "wisdom," in the preceding clause. Since "fools" (כְּסִילִים) are said to be ignorant about wisdom throughout the book of Proverbs, it is unlikely that the Niphal of יָדַע means that divine wisdom "will be known, understood," that is, comprehended and believed, by fools. Instead, it probably has the meaning that wisdom "will be recognized" by them externally, even though they have not internally appropriated wisdom through faith. The LXX adds a negative adverb: ἐν δὲ καρδίᾳ ἀφρόνων οὐ διαγινώσκεται, "but in the heart of fools it is *not* known." The LXX translator was apparently bothered by the concept that wisdom could be known among fools. See further the commentary.

14:34 צְדָקָה תְרוֹמֵם־גּוֹי—For the penultimate accent on the verb תְּרוֹמֵם (the Polel of רוּם) before the monosyllable object noun גּוֹי, see GKC, § 72 bb.

וְחֶסֶד לְאֻמִּים חַטָּאת׃—Commentators agree that חֶסֶד here is not the common word for "kindness, mercy," but a homonym that means "shame, disgrace," and is attested also in Lev 20:17 (see *HALOT*, s.v. חֶסֶד I; see also the cognate verb in Prov 25:10). 4QProv[b] reads וחסר,[12] "poverty, lack," which would make the second line of this prov-

---

[8] Ulrich et. al., *Qumran Cave 4.XI*, 185.

[9] Garrett, *Proverbs, Ecclesiastes, Song of Songs*, 146–47, including n. 297; McKane, *Proverbs*, 475; Murphy, *Proverbs*, 102; Scott, *Proverbs, Ecclesiastes*, 98; Toy, *Proverbs*, 300.

[10] Clifford, *Proverbs*, 142–43.

[11] Ulrich et. al., *Qumran Cave 4.XI*, 185.

[12] Ulrich et. al., *Qumran Cave 4.XI*, 183, 185.

erb mean "but sin [brings] poverty for peoples." The difference in readings is the graphic confusion between the similarly shaped ד and ר.

14:35 רְצוֹן־מֶלֶךְ לְעֶבֶד מַשְׂכִּיל—This is the first proverb where רָצוֹן refers to a person's favor or goodwill, rather than God's gracious gift of "favor" (see the second textual note on 8:35). The "favor" of a king or kings is also in 16:13, 15; 19:12.

Commentary

These verses continue the second informal section (13:1–15:19) of the proverbs of Solomon in 10:1–22:16. See "A Wise Son: Wise Ways to Live (13:1–15:19)" in the commentary on 13:1–25 as well as the excursus "The Organization of the Sayings in Solomon's Proverbs in Proverbs 10:1–22:16" in the commentary on Proverbs 10.

14:1 This verse begins a set of three proverbs united by the word "wisdom" in the first line of 14:1 and "wise people" in the last line of 14:3. The inclusion of 14:2 ("one who fears Yahweh") serves to connect wisdom with the fear of Yahweh, as in 1:7. Prov 14:1 offers a contrast between the wise and the foolish woman. The two women who embody wisdom and foolishness, respectively, are repeated from 9:1–18. Since in Israel the household was the focus of a woman's work (see 31:10–31), the image in 14:1 of building a house or tearing it down is especially appropriate for these two women. The activity here should be understood as encompassing not only domestic chores, but also rearing children; the wise woman raises them in the one true saving faith (see 31:26, 30; see also 2 Tim 1:5; 3:15), whereas the foolish woman does not.

14:2 This verse speaks of the motivation behind one's behavior. The fear of Yahweh, that is, repentance caused by God's accusatory Law and faith created and formed by the Gospel, motivates and enables one to live according to God's Word, whereas the lack of faith and actively despising God and his Word lead to sinful behavior. See "יִרְאַת יְהוָה, 'the Fear of Yahweh,' and יְרֵא יְהוָה, 'One Who Fears Yahweh' " in "Wisdom in Proverbs" in the introduction.

14:3 The first line is understood by many to say that a fool suffers the consequences of his own prideful behavior. However, the Hebrew text is less specific. It merely says that the fool's mouth wields a branch, probably used as a whip to inflict pain. It does not say whom the whip harms. We are probably to understand that others are harmed by it, but ultimately the fool also harms himself (see, e.g., 12:26). The contrast is to wise people, whose language can protect themselves and others from the words of fools while also protecting them from harming themselves with their own words. The speech of wise people, shaped by God's Word in various forms, guards, edifies, and engenders joyful thanksgiving (Eph 5:19–20; Col 3:15–17).

14:4 This verse has two sides to its truth. Without cattle, the feeding trough does not need to be filled; one does not have the expense of feeding them. However, one also does not have the means to fill the trough. With cattle to aid in the work of farming, a large harvest is ensured, more than offsetting the expense of feeding them. This proverb seems to counsel the proper use of resources and investments, discouraging foolish, short-sighted economics (as in the English proverb "penny wise and pound foolish"). The same type of foolish economy can be practiced in spiritual matters, as noted by Jesus when he said, "Woe to you, scribes and Pharisees, hypocrites! For you tithe mint and dill and cumin, but you have neglected the weightier matters of the Law: justice and mercy and faith. These you ought to have done, without neglecting those" (Mt 23:23). Christians can become so preoccupied with adiaphora that they lose sight of the essential wisdom of the Gospel (Col 2:16–23; see also Romans 14).

14:5 This verse is not simply defining the difference between the veracity of different witnesses, but the key is in the second line, a nearly verbatim repetition of the first line of 6:19: a false witness *breathes* lies. This is a warning against being deceived by a witness to whom lying comes as naturally as exhaling (cf. Jn 8:44; 1 Jn 1:10; 5:10).

14:6 This verse depicts the mocker's vain search for wisdom. Implied is that his search is impeded by his own arrogance, which will not allow him to learn from others (cf. 13:1). For people with discernment, knowledge is easily acquired, because they are willing to learn from God and other wise people.

14:7 This verse builds on 14:6 and is linked to it by the catchword דַּעַת, "knowledge." A wise person will not waste time trying to learn from fools, but will avoid them (see Rom 16:17–20).

14:8 This verse is linked to 14:7 by the catchword כְּסִיל, "fool." This saying counsels reflection on one's life and self-examination based on God's Word. A prudent person not only acquires knowledge, but also seeks to use that knowledge. Thus a prudent person is wise enough to think about whether he has put knowledge into practice. Fools, on the other hand, are guided by stupidity that deceives them into accepting their sinful ways without adequately examining them—whether they are pleasing to God or helpful to others and themselves in the long run.

14:9 This verse builds upon 14:8 by defining a particular type of examination of one's life. Stubborn fools (אֱוִלִים)[13] mock the idea of admitting their own sin and guilt (אָשָׁם). The root אשׁם has a wide range of meanings, all connected with the concept of guilt.[14] The noun אָשָׁם is used most often in the OT to denote the guilt offering (e.g., Lev 5:1–26 [ET 5:1–6:7]). When this offering was made, an act of confession was required (Lev 5:5). In this saying, the focus is on the act of confession, though the sacrificial offering may also be in view.

In light of the first line, the second line leads us to understand what it means to be יָשָׁר, "upright." It does *not* mean to be without sin; if that were the case, no one would be upright. Rather, the proverb implies that God's favor is with

---

[13] See "אֱוִיל, 'Stubborn Fool,' and אִוֶּלֶת, 'Stupidity' " in "Fools in Proverbs" in the introduction.

[14] See the first textual note on 14:9.

those who confess their sin and rely solely on his grace and mercy for forgiveness. They are upright because God justifies them for Christ's sake, and their behavior is upright because they are strengthened by the Gospel, which enables them at least to begin to live according to God's Word.

This proverb, therefore, teaches the same theology as Ps 32:1–5; James 5:16; 1 Jn 1:8–2:6. This theology underlies the church's practice of confession and absolution on a regular basis. No believer ever progresses beyond the need for this means of grace, so it is appropriate for it to be part of the weekly Christian worship service. In fact, daily self-examination is healthy, and it always reveals the need to confess one's sins and be forgiven. Pastors are available for this reason to hear private confession and administer absolution.[15]

14:10 This verse continues the focus on one's inner being by noting that the deepest emotions, whether of bitterness or joy, cannot be completely shared with others. It is advice against shallow attempts at empathy.

14:11 This verse is the first of four proverbs linked by a concatenation of catchwords. The link with 14:12 is יָשָׁר, whose plural refers to "upright people" in 14:11, and whose singular in 14:12 refers to a way that only appears "straight, correct." This proverb illustrates the benefit of living by the Gospel. It not only brings life to the individual, but it also benefits his family. Wicked people may seem to be more prosperous by worldly standards (they have a "house," compared to the "tent" of the upright), but real flourishing is impossible without the Gospel.

14:12 This verse highlights the contrast between flawed human perception of right and wrong versus God's unchanging and perfect standard of righteousness. It also is one of the verses that continue the prominent theme of the two different "ways"—that of divine wisdom and that of sinful human rationalizing. See the excursus "The Metaphor of the Path in Solomon's Wisdom" in the commentary on chapter 10.

This verse counsels against relying on human reason, including one's own moral judgment, instead of the guidance in God's immutable and eternal Word (Is 40:8; Ps 119:160; 1 Pet 1:25). Humans can justify many actions that God judges to be sinful. The fool allows human reason to have a magisterial role as the highest authority, arbiter, and judge, but the end result of this pathway is death.

The wise person assigns a ministerial role to human reason under the supreme authority of God's Word, which determines what is right and wrong. Wisdom from the Word rules over his reason as he contemplates an action (3:5). This proverb is repeated in 16:25.

14:13 This verse is linked to 14:12 by the repetition of וְאַחֲרִיתָהּ, "but/and its end." This saying first notes that inner emotions can be masked by outward

[15] See AC XI, "Confession"; Ap XI, "Confession"; and SC V, "Confession" (*LSB*, p. 326).

behavior. The second line probably means that when the laughter that masked the pain is over, the grief remains.

14:14 This verse is linked to 14:13 by the repeated word לֵב, "heart." This proverb is difficult because it is so laconic. The translations that render יִשְׂבַּע as "will be repaid" are adopting a meaning for שָׂבַע that is otherwise unattested. Instead, its usual meaning, "be full, satiated, satisfied," is intended here. This saying indicates that the person who turns from God has an appetite for sin and that appetite is sated with sin. A good person's appetite is likewise sated on his ways as he is directed by Yahweh through faith (3:5–6), since God feeds him with the Gospel. Peter uses a similar metaphor to encourage Christians to feed on the Word of God and grow in grace:

> As newborn infants, desire the pure spiritual milk, so that by it you may grow up in salvation—if indeed you have tasted that the Lord is good. (1 Pet 2:2–3)

14:15 This verse begins a group of four proverbs contrasting wise and foolish people. Prov 14:15 and 14:18 form an inclusio by the use of the words פֶּתִי, "gullible person," and עָרוּם, "prudent person." The first line of this proverb is virtually a definition of the פֶּתִי, "gullible person": he trusts anything and does not possess the wisdom to discriminate between good and bad choices. The opposite is the prudent person, who not only has knowledge to discern good from bad, but also has the wisdom to use his knowledge to consider his choices and pick wisely.[16]

14:16 This verse builds on the last line of 14:15 by noting that it is the fear of Yahweh, a positive, Gospel-based relationship with God through faith, that leads a wise person to turn away from evil (see the commentary on 1:7). The fool, on the other hand, has no fear of God, even in the crass sense of fear of God's punishment. He thinks he can meddle in evil, and in his overconfidence, he supposes that he is immune from harm.

14:17 This verse depicts two types of foolish persons. The first is stupid because he acts rashly without thinking out what he does. The second thinks about what he does; however, his thoughts are not guided by the fear of Yahweh, but by the sinful human heart. He earns the hatred of God and other people.

14:18 This verse contrasts what gullible people eventually inherit with what prudent people obtain. In both cases they receive something. An inheritance of stupidity awaits the gullible, since they cannot and do not distinguish between wisdom and foolishness. Prudent people, however, can and do steer a course toward wisdom. The parallel verbs ("inherit … will surround") envision the eternal state, when God will recompense each according to what he has done. The foolish will be left with nothing, and the wise will gain even more as

---

[16] This proverb is said to have a parallel with the Wisdom of Amenemope, chapter 13 (16:1–2), but the connection is obscure. See *ANET*, 423; *ANE*, 241. See also the excursus "The Words of Wise People (Prov 22:17–24:22) and Its Relationship to the Wisdom of Amenemope" in the commentary on chapter 22.

they surround the throne of God, the source of all wisdom and knowledge (Mt 13:12; 25:29; 1 Cor 3:9–13; Rev 4:4, 10–11; 7:9–12).

14:19 This verse is the first of four proverbs linked by the similar words רַע, "evil," (14:19, 22) and רֵעַ, "neighbor" (14:20–21). This proverb equates evil people with wicked people and good people with righteous people. It helps define the good person in Proverbs as one who is righteous, that is, not good because he does not sin, but good because through faith he receives the righteousness of God promised in Christ (Gen 15:6). While the righteous may see this proverb fulfilled in this life, its ultimate fulfillment is seen when every knee will bow to Jesus (Psalm 110; Phil 2:10; cf. Rom 14:10–11). The exalted Christ also promises the faithful believer that in the end unbelievers will do this: "Behold, I will make them come and bow down before your feet, and they will know that I have loved you" (Rev 3:9).

14:20 This verse is another proverb that states realities of life without endorsing them or advocating these particular behaviors. It is perhaps a word of caution to those with wealth about the nature of those who may seek their friendship.

14:21 This verse contrasts hatred toward one's neighbor with love that seeks to provide for one's neighbor. It states God's disapproval of the person who ignores the temporal needs of others. It also encourages kindness by declaring God's eschatological pronouncement of "blessed" upon those who believe and do his will (see "blessed" also in Mt 5:3–12; 25:34).

14:22 This verse extends the internal attitude of hating one's neighbor in 14:21a to the scheming of sinners, noting that their actions lead them astray. It then draws a contrast with the good intentions of those who fear Yahweh. They find mercy and truth, two aspects of the blessing in 14:21. "Blessed are the merciful, for they will receive mercy" (Mt 5:7).

14:23 This verse warns wise people to be more afraid of idle talk than hard work.[17]

14:24 This verse contrasts wisdom, which furnishes its own reward, with stupidity, which never offers any reward.

14:25 "A truthful witness saves lives" either by sparing someone who is falsely accused or by protecting society from a malefactor, whom his testimony helps condemn. On the other hand, a liar whose lies flow as easily as his breath (see 14:5) deceives others and thwarts justice, endangering many, especially the vulnerable.

14:26 This verse notes that a relationship with Yahweh based on the Gospel brings confidence to faith so that it can withstand the vicissitudes of life. The benefits of this can be passed on to one's children if they too believe the Gospel that they see operative in the life of their parents (see Ex 20:5–6;

---

[17] Ross, "Proverbs," 988.

Prov 1:8; and the ten addresses from father to son in Proverbs[18]). This proverb is paired with 14:27, which also begins with "the fear of Yahweh."

14:27 This verse is nearly identical to 13:14, except for the different first two Hebrew words: here "the fear of Yahweh"; in 13:14 "the teaching of a wise person." Therefore this proverb serves to define what a wise person teaches, namely, the Gospel, the fear and love of the one true God.[19] It also serves to define the "strong confidence" and "refuge" mentioned in 14:26. They are the deliverance from eternal "death" to everlasting "life" (see the textual note on 14:27), which God offers in the Gospel.

14:28–35 Both 14:28 and 14:29 use a word from the root רבב: "large" (רֹב in 14:28) or "much" (רַב in 14:29). An inclusio is formed by 14:28 and 14:35 with the repetition of מֶלֶךְ, "king," and the wordplay between רָזוֹן, "ruler" (14:28), and רָצוֹן, "favor" (14:35).[20] This inclusio serves to place all the sayings in 14:28–35 into a royal context. Therefore these sayings are prime advice for rulers and leaders, and 14:34 focuses on how the reign—promoting either righteousness or sin—affects the entire nation. However, the proverbs in 14:29–33 do not limit themselves to matters of governance, and they have broader applications to all people, since almost everyone can exercise some form of leadership in various ways in different social relationships (e.g., at work, in the family, and in the community).

14:28 This proverb reminds rulers and leaders that they are not great on their own, but they are great only when God blesses them with people to rule or lead faithfully. It is designed to curb a powerful person's appetite to aggrandize himself while impoverishing and driving away his followers. Instead, when the people grow and flourish, so do their leaders.

14:29 This verse returns to the subject of a short temper, first treated in 14:17. Since it is linked with 14:28, it may be especially aimed at leaders whose anger is easily displayed. Patience with underlings is advised, since a hair-trigger temper will drive away subjects as they perceive their ruler's stupidity. This advice is not only good for rulers, but it is also good advice for everyone. James advises:

> Know this, my beloved brothers: let every person be quick to hear, slow to speak, slow to anger; for the anger of man does not accomplish the righteousness of God. (James 1:19–20)

14:30 This verse builds on 14:29 by urging a tranquil heart, implying that it will dampen a short temper and also invigorate one's physical being. Jealousy, however, which may manifest itself in a short temper, destroys from the inside.

---

[18] See the excursus "Proverbs 1–9, Christ, and the Ten Commandments" in the commentary on Proverbs 1.

[19] See the "יִרְאַת יְהוָה, 'the Fear of Yahweh,' and יְרֵא יְהוָה, 'One Who Fears Yahweh' " in "Wisdom in Proverbs" in the introduction, as well as the commentary on 1:7.

[20] Meinhold, "Das Wortspiel."

14:31 Anyone who oppresses a poor person insults God, the Maker of poor and rich people alike. Three proverbs express the teaching that God is the Maker of the poor and/or the rich (14:31; 17:5; 22:2) and so emphasize its importance. Of course, many other Scripture passages affirm that God created all things, including all people (e.g., Genesis 1; Jonah 1:9; Ps 33:6–9; Jn 1:1–3; Acts 4:24; 14:15). This truth is the First Article of the Apostles' Creed: "I believe in God, the Father Almighty, maker of heaven and earth." This proverb warns every person not to abuse any other, since all mankind originally was created in the image of God (Gen 1:26–27; James 3:9), and believers are being restored to the image of God through his grace in his Son, Jesus Christ.[a] The second line of the proverb restates the truth in a positive way: the person who is kind to the neediest of God's children honors God himself.[b]

This proverb has special relevance for rulers and leaders, since they wield power that they could abuse by oppressing the weak. Authorities are to be God's representatives for order in this world. "There is no authority except from God" (Rom 13:1–7). Rulers are reminded that despite their exalted position, they come from the same Maker as their lowliest subordinates. When rulers' policies are kind toward the poor, they bring honor to God, who placed them in their position of authority.

(a) See Rom 8:29; 1 Cor 15:49; 2 Cor 3:18; 4:4; Col 1:15; 3:10

(b) Cf. Mt 25:40; Lk 8:21; Jn 1:12; 11:52; 1 Jn 3:10

14:32 This verse reminds us that sinful behavior can cost us our position in life. God, who is insulted when we abuse others (14:31), can remove even the most powerful person from office in any number of ways. However, a righteous person, even when threatened with death (perhaps by martyrdom), finds refuge in God, who gives eternal life (see, e.g., Acts 7:54–60; cf. the *Martyrdom of Polycarp*). This counsel applies to rulers, who must pursue godly policies, even if they should risk deposition and death (perhaps by assassination).

14:33 This verse once again counsels the need for and the surpassing worth of wisdom from God. The second line is difficult, since Proverbs generally does not ascribe any knowledge of wisdom to fools. The force of this line may be that even foolish leaders can recognize wisdom among their subjects when they see it in them, even though the leaders themselves fail to use it, and such failure to take advantage of wisdom is itself a kind of foolishness. The imperfect verb translated as a future, wisdom "*will be* recognized," also has an eschatological connotation: on the Last Day even fools will acknowledge the Wisdom of God in Jesus Christ (Mt 11:19; 1 Cor 1:18–31), even though it will be too late for them personally to benefit from it by appropriating it through faith. Nevertheless, they shall bow before the righteous one; see the commentary on Prov 14:19.

14:34 This verse is designed to draw rulers' attention to the way they govern and the example they set for the entire nation. If the leader serves God faithfully and establishes what is righteous and good in God's sight, the whole nation may enjoy God's blessing and become preeminent. Conversely, a leader who legislates what is unrighteous and who sets an example of ungodliness leads his subjects into condemnation and prompts them to imitate his own sin.

He not only debases himself, but he also brings the entire nation under divine judgment.

14:35 This verse points out the necessity for leaders to show their appreciation to those who serve them and aid them in their labor. It encourages those who work for others to seek and employ wisdom. It also points out that there is a time for well-considered fury (instead of the short temper of 14:29) against underlings whose behavior is disgraceful. Since all people, even the most powerful, are servants under God and will be held accountable to him, this proverb encourages faithful service to God in all areas of life, mindful of the Last Day, when our King will evaluate the service rendered to him (Mt 18:23–35; 25:34–40; 1 Tim 6:13–16).

Proverbs 15:1–19

Wise Ways to Live, Part 3

Translation

15 [1]A gentle answer turns away rage,
but a harsh word stirs up anger.
[2]The tongue of wise people presents knowledge as good,
but the mouth of fools spouts stupidity.
[3]The eyes of Yahweh are everywhere,
watching evil people and good people.
[4]A tongue that brings healing is a tree of life,
but crookedness in it [produces] a shattered spirit.

[5]A stubborn fool despises discipline from his father,
but whoever heeds correction is prudent.
[6]The house of a righteous person is great wealth,
but trouble is stirred up with the income of a wicked person.
[7]The lips of wise people spread knowledge,
but the heart of fools is not that way.
[8]A sacrifice offered by wicked people is a disgusting thing to Yahweh,
but a prayer by upright people [receives] his favor.
[9]The way of a wicked person is a disgusting thing to Yahweh,
but he loves those who pursue righteousness.

[10]Stern discipline is for someone who leaves the path,
and the person who hates correction will die.
[11]Sheol and Abaddon [lie open] before Yahweh;
how much more [do] human hearts!
[12]A mocker does not love anyone who corrects him;
he will not go to wise people.

[13]A joyful heart makes a cheerful face,
but when a heart is sorrowful, a spirit is stricken.
[14]The heart of a discerning person seeks knowledge,
but the mouth of fools grazes on stupidity.
[15]All the days of an oppressed person are miserable,
but a cheerful heart has a continual feast.
[16]Better a little with the fear of Yahweh
than great wealth with turmoil.
[17]Better a meal of vegetables where there is love
than a fattened calf and hatred with it.

[18]A hothead stirs up a fight,
but a patient person calms a dispute.

[19]The way of a lazy person is like a thorny hedge,
but the path of upright people is a highway.

Textual Notes

15:1 מַעֲנֶה־רַּךְ יָשִׁיב חֵמָה—The noun מַעֲנֶה, "an answer," is modified by the adjective רַךְ, "tender, soft, gentle." Exceptionally, the consonant *resh* admits a conjunctive *daghesh* (GKC, §§ 20 c and 22 s). Compare לָשׁוֹן רַכָּה, "a soft/gentle tongue," in 25:15. מַעֲנֶה is the subject of the transitive Hiphil (H) verb: יָשִׁיב חֵמָה, "turns away rage."

וּדְבַר־עֶצֶב יַעֲלֶה־אָף׃—The construct phrase דְּבַר־עֶצֶב is, literally, "a word of pain," that is, a hurtful or harmful word. For עֶצֶב, see the second textual note on 5:10. In form, יַעֲלֶה could be Qal (G), but in context here, it must be the transitive Hiphil (H) with אָף as its object, literally, "causes anger to arise," parallel to the phrase with the transitive Hiphil (H) in the preceding clause.

15:2 לְשׁוֹן חֲכָמִים תֵּיטִיב דָּעַת—For the adjective and substantive חָכָם, "wise," which in this chapter recurs in 15:7, 12, 20, 31, see "חָכְמָה, 'Wisdom,' and Related Words" in "Wisdom in Proverbs" in the introduction. The (usually) feminine noun לָשׁוֹן, "tongue," is the subject of the feminine verb תֵּיטִיב, the Hiphil (H) of יָטַב. For the direct object noun דַּעַת, "knowledge," which recurs in this chapter in 15:7, 14, see "דַּעַת, 'Knowledge,' and יָדַע, 'to Know' " in "Wisdom in Proverbs" in the introduction, as well as the commentary on 1:4, 7. Since divine "knowledge" is already intrinsically good, the Hiphil (H) of יָטַב probably means that wise people articulate knowledge in such a way that other people may perceive that it is good; their tongue presents knowledge as something good, that is, "commends" (NIV, ESV) knowledge. Another view is that the verb means "do [something] well" and that דָּעַת is the infinitive construct of יָדַע, so that the wise "know well" (BDB, s.v. יָטַב, Hiphil, 3), that is, show that they have a good knowledge of wisdom.

וּפִי כְסִילִים יַבִּיעַ אִוֶּלֶת׃—For כְּסִילִים, see "כְּסִיל, 'Fool,' and כְּסִילוּת, 'Foolishness' " in "Fools in Proverbs" in the introduction. פֶּה (in construct) is the subject of the singular verb יַבִּיעַ, the Hiphil (H) of נָבַע, which has the transitive meaning "to spout" both here, where the mouth of a fool "spouts" stupidity, and in 15:28, where the mouth of wicked people "spouts" evil things. See the second textual note on 1:23, where the Hiphil (H) of נָבַע means "to pour out." For the object noun here, אִוֶּלֶת, "stupidity," which in this chapter recurs in 15:14, 21, see "אֱוִיל, 'Stubborn Fool,' and אִוֶּלֶת, 'Stupidity' " in "Fools in Proverbs" in the introduction. The cognate אֱוִיל occurs in 15:5.

15:3 בְּכָל־מָקוֹם עֵינֵי יְהוָה צֹפוֹת ...—This is, literally, "on every place [are] Yahweh's eyes, watching ..."

15:4 מַרְפֵּא לָשׁוֹן עֵץ חַיִּים—This is, literally, "healing of [brought by] a tongue is a tree of life." For מַרְפֵּא, "healing," see the second textual note and the commentary on 4:22, where too it is associated with חַיִּים, "life," as well as the commentary on 12:18, where the tongue of wise people brings healing. For עֵץ חַיִּים, "a tree of life," see the first textual note and the commentary on 3:18.

וְסֶלֶף בָּהּ שֶׁבֶר בְּרוּחַ׃—This is, literally, "but crookedness in it [brings] shattering in the spirit," the feminine pronominal suffix on בָּהּ ("in it") refers to the "tongue" (לָשׁוֹן)

in the previous clause. It cannot refer to either of the masculine words in עֵץ חַיִּים, "a tree of life." For סֶלֶף, "crookedness," see the second textual note on 11:3.

15:5 אֱוִיל יִנְאַץ מוּסַר אָבִיו—The central theme that a "father" (אָב) imparts "disciple" (מוּסָר) was introduced in 1:8. See "מוּסָר, 'Discipline,' and יָסַר, 'to Discipline' " in "Wisdom in Proverbs" in the introduction and the excursus "Proverbs 1–9, Christ, and the Ten Commandments" in the commentary on Proverbs 1.

וְשֹׁמֵר תּוֹכַחַת יַעְרִם׃—For תּוֹכַחַת, "warning, correction," which in this chapter recurs in 15:10, 31–32, see the first textual note on 1:23. The verb עָרַם occurs in Proverbs only here and in 19:25. Both verses have the identical Hiphil (H) imperfect with the intransitive (internally transitive) meaning "be prudent." The verb is cognate to an adjective and noun that are common in Proverbs; see "עָרוּם, 'Prudent,' and עָרְמָה, 'Prudence' " in "Wisdom in Proverbs" in the introduction as well as the first textual note on 1:4.

15:6 וּבִתְבוּאַת רָשָׁע נֶעְכָּרֶת׃—Probably this means "by the income of a wicked person [he gains only] trouble." The noun תְּבוּאָה often refers to a "harvest" (see the textual note on 3:9). Here it refers more generally to "income," whether from farming or another occupation. The feminine Niphal (N) participle נֶעְכָּרֶת does not seem to serve as a verb nor to modify any word in the context. Most likely it functions as an abstract noun, meaning "trouble." For the connotation of עָכַר, "to trouble," involving eschatological judgment, see the textual note on 11:17.

15:8 תּוֹעֲבַת יְהוָה … רְצוֹנוֹ׃—See the textual notes on 11:1, which also contrasts תּוֹעֲבַת יְהוָה, "a disgusting thing to Yahweh," and רְצוֹנוֹ, God's gift of "his favor, grace." For רָצוֹן, see also the second textual note on 8:35. Of the eleven verses in Proverbs that use תּוֹעֲבַת יְהוָה, "a disgusting thing to Yahweh," four of them contrast it with רְצוֹנוֹ, "his favor" (11:1, 20; 12:22; 15:8). See the excursus " 'Disgusting Thing' (תּוֹעֵבָה) in Solomon's Proverbs" in the commentary on Proverbs 11.

This verse first equates the masculine noun זֶבַח, "sacrifice," with the feminine noun תּוֹעֵבָה, "disgusting thing," and then the feminine noun תְּפִלָּה, "prayer," with the masculine noun רָצוֹן, "favor" (cf. Waltke-O'Connor, § 6.4.3a, note 39).

15:9 וּמְרַדֵּף צְדָקָה יֶאֱהָב׃—The imperfect יֶאֱהָב, Yahweh "loves," refers to God's continual, constant love, as when the identical form is used in 3:12 (see Joüon, § 113 a). See also 16:13, where "a king" is the implied subject, and contrast 15:12, where the verb is negated and "a mocker" is the subject.

15:10 מוּסָר רָע לְעֹזֵב אֹרַח—The adjective רַע, usually "evil," here modifies the noun מוּסָר, "discipline," which is good. רַע does not always refer to something that is intrinsically evil; it can denote something that is "harsh, severe" (see *HALOT*, 4 d). In this case it describes discipline that is unyielding or stern. A similar use is found in 15:15.

Regarding אֹרַח, see the excursus "The Metaphor of the Path in Solomon's Wisdom" in the commentary on Proverbs 10. In this chapter, אֹרַח recurs in 15:19, 24.

15:12 לֹא יֶאֱהַב־לֵץ הוֹכֵחַ לוֹ—See "לֵץ, 'Mocker,' and לָצוֹן, 'Mocking, Scoffing' " in "Fools in Proverbs" in the introduction. The Hiphil (H) infinitive absolute הוֹכֵחַ is of the verb יָכַח, which is the root of the noun תּוֹכַחַת, "correction" (see the second textual note on 15:5). The infinitive absolute (here used in lieu of an infinitive construct) with prepositional phrase הוֹכֵחַ לוֹ, literally, "to correct him," is a verbal complement that serves as the object of יֶאֱהַב (Waltke-O'Connor, § 35.5.4a–b). It could be translated as "being corrected" or, more concretely in view of 15:12b, as "*anyone* who corrects him."

15:13 לֵב שָׂמֵחַ יֵיטִב פָּנִים—Literally, "a joyful heart makes a face good," this means that the face has a cheerful expression (see *HALOT*, s.v. יָטַב, Hiphil, 3).

רוּחַ נְכֵאָה׃—This phrase recurs in 17:22 and 18:14. The adjective נְכֵאָה, "broken, crushed, stricken," is feminine to match רוּחַ. Similar are רוּחַ נִשְׁבָּרָה, "a broken spirit," in Ps 51:19 (ET 51:17) and the plural דַּכְּאֵי־רוּחַ, "crushed of/in spirit," in Ps 34:19 (ET 34:18).

15:14 לֵב נָבוֹן—For "the heart of a discerning person," see the first textual note on 14:33.

וּפְנֵי כְסִילִים יִרְעֶה אִוֶּלֶת׃—The subject of the singular Qal (G) imperfect יִרְעֶה, "feeds, grazes," must be the Qere, וּפִי, the "mouth of" fools, not their (plural) "face," which is the meaning of the Kethib, וּפְנֵי.

15:15 כָּל־יְמֵי עָנִי רָעִים—Here the plural adjective רָעִים means "miserable." See the textual note on 15:10.

וְטוֹב־לֵב—This is, literally, "one who is good of heart." Most English versions render it as "a/the cheerful heart" (e.g., NIV, NASB).

15:16 בְּיִרְאַת יְהוָה—See the first textual note and the commentary on 1:7 and "יִרְאַת יְהוָה, 'the Fear of Yahweh,' and יְרֵא יְהוָה, 'One Who Fears Yahweh' " in "Wisdom in Proverbs" in the introduction.

15:18 אִישׁ חֵמָה יְגָרֶה מָדוֹן—The construct phrase, literally, "a man of rage" denotes a person who is characterized by rage. Such a person is called "a hothead" in English. The noun מָדוֹן, "strife, a fight," recurs in twelve later proverbs, and it is the object of יְגָרֶה, "stirs up," also in 28:25 and 29:22.

וְאֶרֶךְ אַפַּיִם—Here, literally, "(one who is) long of anger" means "a patient person." See the textual note on 14:29.

15:19 כִּמְשֻׂכַת חָדֶק—This is, literally, "like a hedge of a thorn bush." The noun מְשֻׂכָה, also spelled מְסוּכָה (Micah 7:4), is a "hedge" that could be used to keep animals out of cultivated land (cf. מְשׂוּכָּה, "hedge," in Is 5:5). חֵדֶק is some type of thorny plant, though the species cannot be determined.[1] The only other occurrence of חֵדֶק in the OT is Micah 7:4, where it is used in close proximity with מְסוּכָה.

וְאֹרַח יְשָׁרִים סְלֻלָה׃—The feminine noun אֹרַח, "path," is the referent of סְלֻלָה, "thrown up, lifted up," the feminine Qal passive (Gp) participle of סָלַל, which occurs elsewhere only in Jer 18:15. This word is spelled סוללה in 4QProv[b].[2] Most English versions agree that the "path … lifted up" is made into a "highway," as the cognate noun מְסִלָּה means in Prov 16:17.

Commentary

These verses (15:1–19) conclude the second informal section of proverbs in 10:1–22:16. See "A Wise Son: Wise Ways to Live (13:1–15:19)" in

[1] See *FF*, 184–86.

[2] Ulrich et al., *Qumran Cave 4.XI*, 183, 186.

the commentary on 13:1–25, as well as the excursus "The Organization of the Sayings in Solomon's Proverbs in Proverbs 10:1–22:16" in the commentary on chapter 10 and the commentary on 10:1–5.

15:1 This verse begins a set of four sayings, three of which deal with speech. This proverb reminds believers that in addition to the content of our speech, our manner of delivery can reveal God's grace—or fail to express the Gospel. Others receive our answer favorably or unfavorably not just on the basis of *what* is said, but also on the basis of *how* it is said. See 1 Pet 3:15. The incident in 1 Sam 25:2–42 illustrates this. Nabal's reply to David was unacceptable because of its tone as well as its content. Abigail's request was received not so much because of the things she offered David but because of the gentle way in which she made her request.

15:2 This verse has been translated in a number of different ways in attempts to interpret תֵּיטִ֣יב דָּ֑עַת: "makes knowledge acceptable" (NASB), "commends knowledge" (NIV), "dispenses knowledge" (NRSV). Perhaps it is best to understand this verb in its plain sense: wise people's speech "makes knowledge good" by presenting it well (see 15:1). The mouth of fools, however, "spouts" (יַבִּ֣יעַ, "gushes, pours fourth") nothing but stupidity; no matter what factual knowledge fools may have, their words accomplish nothing good. This proverb reminds us that human knowledge in and of itself does not lead to wisdom. Rather, wisdom comes from God alone, and its source is Jesus Christ.[3] He teaches his people to use knowledge in constructive and beneficial ways (1 Cor 8:1–3).

15:3 This verse stresses that God knows all that humans are doing (see Ps 11:4). His eyes are everywhere (see Zech 4:10; Rev 2:18–19). He is present in all places, not just in heaven or in holy places like the OT temple and Christian churches. In addition, this verse uses God's omniscience and omnipresence to apply both Law and Gospel (see 1 Pet 3:12). He can punish the wicked (see the commentary on Prov 5:21–23). He can and does bless those who are righteous through faith with strength (2 Chr 16:9) and eternal benefits (e.g., Prov 3:13; 8:32, 34; 10:6, 22; 16:20; 20:7). Everyone will be called to give an account of their actions in front of the One who knows all that they have done (Rom 14:10; Heb 4:13; Rev 20:12–13).

This proverb is the only one of the four sayings in 15:1–4 that does not specifically focus on speech. Yet it is tied to the others in two ways. First, "good people" (טוֹבִ֣ים) is from a root (טוב) that is a by-form of the Hiphil (H) of יָטַב, "makes … good," in 15:2. Second, its inclusion of "eyes" forms the middle of a short chiasm of three proverbs mentioning body parts: "tongue" (15:2), "eyes" (15:3), "tongue" (15:4).

---

[3] See "Wisdom in Proverbs" in the introduction. See also the commentary on 1:1–7; 3:13–20; 8:22–31; 30:1b–10; and the excursus "Proverbs 8, Wisdom, Christology, and the Arian Controversy" in the commentary on Proverbs 8.

15:4 This verse is linked to 15:2 by לָשׁוֹן, "tongue," and is linked to 15:1 thematically as it considers the dual effects of one's words. The comparison of a tongue that brings healing to a tree of life emphasizes that the healing is not merely for social or psychological benefit, but is especially for spiritual benefit. The tongue that brings healing brings true wisdom, the Gospel of life, and applies it as medicine to heal souls (see the commentary on 3:18; 10:31; 11:30; 13:12).

The second line reminds us of the destructive power of sinful words that break a spirit instead of healing it.

15:5 This verse begins a series of proverbs (15:5–9) that contrast fools with wise people (15:5, 7) and righteous people with wicked people (15:6, 8–9). This proverb reminds us that fools resent correction itself; the sinful human nature rebels against God's Law (Rom 7:23; FC SD V 20). Believers, however, are prudent people who take advantage of the opportunity to learn from God's Word, and they delight in his Law (Psalm 119; Rom 7:22). In this life even the wisest believers need, at times, to be prodded to do what is right (FC SD VI 7–9). The writer to the Hebrews reminds us that God uses the Law to discipline his believing children, and such chastisement is an essential part of being a son or daughter of God through faith in his Son:

> If you are without discipline, in which all have participated, then you are illegitimate children and not sons. (Heb 12:8; cf. 1 Cor 10:1–13)

15:6 This verse contrasts the house of the righteous person with the income of the wicked. The parallel is not exact, and that contributes to the proverb's message. Righteous people have an enduring wealth that is already theirs in the Gospel (see the commentary on 3:1–20). Wicked people merely have monetary income, which can fluctuate and disappear altogether. On the Last Day, money will be useless, and the wicked will have everlasting "trouble" (see the textual note).

15:7 This verse involves another inexact parallel between lips and a heart, one externally observed, the other hidden to human eyes. The point of this saying is that wise people spread God's gracious gift of wisdom—their most valuable possession—to others through the words of their "lips," whereas fools are not inclined to share what they value in their "heart."

15:8 This verse compares the way God receives those whose worship is insincere because their hearts have rejected him, with those who have relied on his Gospel to make them upright so that they can follow his Word. Even if people outwardly conform to divine commands regarding worship, if their hearts lack faith, their worship is not acceptable (Micah 6:6–8; Mt 23:23). God's rejection of the worship of wicked people is a common theme in Scripture.[a]

(a) E.g., 1 Sam 15:22; Is 1:10–17; Ps 40:7–9 (ET 40:6–8); Prov 15:29; 21:3, 27; 28:9

The first line of this saying is repeated as the first line of 21:27 without יהוה, "Yahweh." A slightly different form of this proverb is quoted in the *Damascus Document*:[4]

זבח רשעים תועבה
ותפלת צדקם כמנחת רצון

A sacrifice of [offered by] wicked people is a disgusting thing,
but a prayer by righteous people is an offering of [that receives God's] favor.

15:9 This verse is tied to 15:8 by the catchwords תּוֹעֲבַת יְהוָה, "a disgusting thing to Yahweh," and רָשָׁע, "wicked (person)." This proverb serves as an explanation for God's rejection of or favor toward different people's worship. For other biblical exhortations to pursue righteousness, see Is 51:1; Mt 6:33; 1 Tim 6:11.

15:10 This verse describes the action to be taken with those who leave the path of righteousness. They need the "stern discipline" of God's Law so that they repent; only after that contrition would it be appropriate to apply the pardon of the Gospel to them. The saying then issues a warning to those who are not inclined to return. This warning also explains why the harshness of the Law needs to be applied to those who abandon the path: they will die if they do not repent and return. As confirmed by the next verse (15:11), the verb מוּת, "to die," has an eschatological sense pointing to eternal perdition in hell as also in, for example, 5:23; 10:21; 23:13. Similar is the nuance of the noun מָוֶת in, for example, 2:18; 5:5; 7:27; 8:36; 10:2.

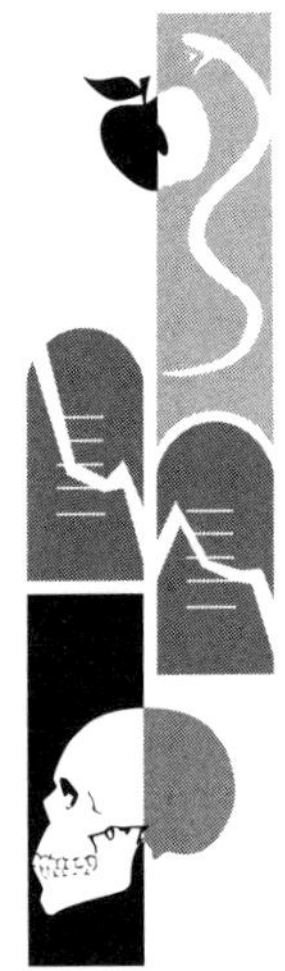

15:11 This verse has one of six occurrences in the OT of אֲבַדּוֹן, "Abaddon," a proper noun meaning "destruction" (Ps 88:12 [ET 88:11]; Job 26:6; 28:22; 31:12; Prov 15:11; 27:20).[5] The Greek equivalent is used in Rev 9:11. The most common noun paired with אֲבַדּוֹן is שְׁאוֹל, "Sheol," as here (Job 26:6; Prov 15:11; 27:20). "Sheol" is synonymous with everlasting death and the grave.[b] See the first textual note and the commentary on 1:12.

(b) Prov 1:12; 5:5; 7:27; 9:18; 15:11, 24; 23:14; 27:20; 30:16

Elsewhere "Abaddon" is paired with death (Job 28:22) or the grave (Ps 88:12 [ET 88:11]). Thus אֲבַדּוֹן is especially associated with eschatological themes involving the end of temporal life and what lies beyond it. God knows things beyond the grave that humans in this life can only know from what he reveals about them in his Word. This demonstrates God's omniscience and leads to the conclusion that he also knows the condition of the human heart. The application of God's knowledge of the heart is left to the reader. It portends Law and judgment for unbelievers, whose thoughts and motives are counter to God's will. Yet its application is the Gospel of forgiveness and eternal life for believers, whose hearts have been cleansed and renewed by the Holy Spirit,

[4] The Hebrew is cited from Rabin, *The Zadokite Documents*, 59.

[5] It is spelled וַאֲבַדֹּה in Prov 27:20, and the Qere in most manuscripts is וַאֲבַדּוֹ. Some manuscripts, however, have as the Qere the more common וַאֲבַדּוֹן, the same form as in 15:11.

who works regeneration and sanctification. See, for example, the baptismal allusions in Ezek 36:24–27; Jn 3:3–8; Eph 5:25–27; Titus 3:3–7. See also Ps 51:7–14 (ET 51:5–12); Ezek 11:19.

15:12 This verse explains why mockers will not consult wise people. Not only do they hold wisdom in contempt, but they also know that a wise person will attempt to correct their deviant ways in order to save them from their own destruction (15:10–11).

15:13–17 This set of five proverbs is bound by catchwords. Prov 15:13–15 all use לֵב, "heart," while 15:15–17 are united by their use of טוֹב, "good" (translated as "cheerful" in 15:15 and as "better" in 15:16–17). In addition, 15:14 and 15:15 are thematically linked by the concept of eating, which occurs in the second line of both proverbs.

15:13–15 These verses all state truths about how the inward state of a person affects his emotional and intellectual life. A good disposition makes one cheerful (15:13). The heart of an intelligent, God-fearing person seeks knowledge (15:14).[6] A heart that is cheerful—signifying emotional and especially spiritual joy on account of God's grace and love—has plenty on which to feast (15:15). In contrast, a depressed person is crushed by the weight of his sorrow (15:13), and people who are oppressed often are inwardly embittered (15:15a).

Fools, whose hearts are alienated from wisdom, graze like animals on their own stupidity and the stupidity of others (15:14). A literal example of this is in Daniel 4: God humbled arrogant Nebuchadnezzar by inflicting him with insanity and zoanthropy, causing him to eat grass like an ox.[7] In contrast, a cheerful heart enjoys a "continual feast" (Prov 15:15b). The OT provided annual feast days for the worshiping community of Israel, notably at Passover, the Feast of Weeks (Pentecost), and the Feast of Booths. Yet in a spiritual sense God always provides the believer with sustenance. The psalmist David acclaims:

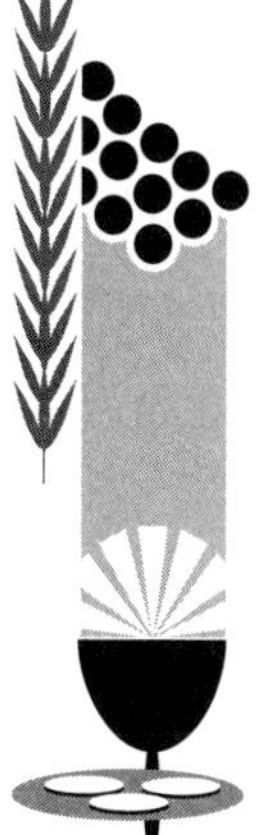

> You set before me a table
> in the presence of my enemies;
> you anoint my head with oil;
> my cup overflows. (Ps 23:5)

The Fourth Petition of the Lord's Prayer is "give us this day our daily bread" (Mt 6:11). The Christian feasts continually on Jesus Christ, the bread of life, through faith in his life-giving Word (Jn 6:27–63; cf. Is 55:1–2; Jn 4:13–14; 7:38–39; Rev 21:6; 22:17). The gathered church has the opportunity to feast on the true body and blood of Christ, given and shed for the forgiveness of sins, in the Lord's Supper (1 Cor 11:23–32), a foretaste of the everlasting feast, the wedding supper of the Lamb (Rev 19:6–9).

---

6 Note that the heart of such a person also acquires knowledge according to the first line of 18:15, which, except for the verb, is identical to the first line of 15:14.

7 See Steinmann, *Daniel*, 235–53.

15:16–17 These verses build on the last line of 15:15 by noting that prosperity is not an unmixed blessing if it is accompanied by situations that can embitter one's existence. It is better to have less material wealth and dine on a relationship with Yahweh by grace, so that one has the love of God, family, and friends.[8]

15:18 This verse returns to the theme of 15:1. אֶרֶךְ אַפַּיִם, literally, "(one who is) long of anger," does not denote a person who never gets angry, but one who can hold his anger and be longsuffering even when provoked, unlike the hothead who flies into a rage with little provocation. Note that the first line of this proverb is identical to the first line of 29:22 with the exception that 29:22 substitutes the synonym אַף, "anger," for חֵמָה, "rage." In both passages the specific noun for anger is subsumed in the translation "hothead."

15:19 This verse notes that a lazy person finds his way blocked by his own sloth. He finds the effort required to be diligent in his tasks too painful, like the thorns on a hedgerow (see the first textual note on this verse). In contrast, the path of upright people, who are conscientious in their work, is smooth and level like a well-engineered highway. The Hebrew translated as "highway" is cognate to the noun מְסִלָּה, "highway," in, for example, Is 19:23; 40:3; 62:10. Through John the Baptizer, God prepared the "highway" for the Savior, Jesus Christ (Mk 1:2–4). Jesus himself is the only "way" to the Father and to eternal life (Jn 14:6).[9]

---

8 These proverbs have a parallel in the Wisdom of Amenemope, chapter 6 (9:7–8). See *ANET*, 422; *ANET*, 239. See also the excursus "The Words of Wise People (Prov 22:17–24:22) and Its Relationship to the Wisdom of Amenemope" in the commentary on Proverbs 22.

9 See the excursus "The Metaphor of the Path in Solomon's Wisdom" in the commentary on Proverbs 10.

Proverbs 15:20–16:7

Advice to a Wise Son, Part 1

Translation

15 [20]A wise son brings joy to [his] father,
but a foolish man despises his mother.
[21]Stupidity is a delight to a person who lacks sense,
but a person who has understanding stays straight on course.
[22]Plans are thwarted without confidential advice,
but with many advisors they succeed.
[23]A person's delight is in the answer from his own mouth,
and a word at the right time—oh, how good!
[24]The path of life leads upward for a person with insight,
so that he may turn away from Sheol below.

[25]Yahweh tears down the house of haughty people,
but he establishes a boundary for a widow.
[26]The plans of a wicked person are a disgusting thing to Yahweh,
but pleasant words are pure [to him].
[27]A person who is greedy for ill-gotten gain troubles his own household,
but a person who hates bribes will live.
[28]The heart of a righteous person contemplates [how] to answer,
but the mouth of wicked people spouts evil things.
[29]Yahweh is far away from wicked people,
but he hears the prayer of righteous people.
[30]A twinkle in the eyes delights the heart,
and good news is felt down to the bone.
[31]An ear that listens to a life-giving warning
will find a home among wise people.
[32]A person who ignores discipline despises himself,
but a person who listens to a warning acquires [good] sense.
[33]The fear of Yahweh is discipline that leads to wisdom,
and humility precedes honor.

16 [1]The plans of the heart belong to a man,
but from Yahweh comes a tongue's answer.
[2]All of a person's ways are pure in his own eyes,
but Yahweh weighs motives.
[3]Commit your efforts to Yahweh,
and your plans will be established.
[4]Yahweh has made everything for his own purpose,
even a wicked person for a day of trouble.

[5]Everyone with an arrogant attitude is a disgusting thing to Yahweh.
Be sure of this: that person will not go unpunished.
[6]Through mercy and faithfulness, iniquity is atoned for,
and through the fear of Yahweh [a person] turns away from evil.
[7]When Yahweh is pleased with a man's ways,
he makes even his enemies to be at peace with him.

Textual Notes

15:20 בֵּ֣ן חָ֭כָם יְשַׂמַּח־אָ֑ב—The imperfect (יְשַׂמַּח) can express facts that occur and are true at all times (GKC, § 107 f; Joüon, § 113 c).

וּכְסִ֥יל אָ֝דָ֗ם—This construct phrase, literally, "a fool of a man" (see Waltke-O'Connor, § 9.5.3i, example 58), recurs in 21:20. See "כְּסִיל, 'Fool,' and כְּסִילוּת, 'Foolishness' " in "Fools in Proverbs" in the introduction. The noun אָדָם, here used somewhat superfluously after the substantive, can be used similarly but preceding a substantive, as in 12:23a and 17:18a.

15:21 אִ֭וֶּלֶת שִׂמְחָ֣ה לַחֲסַר־לֵ֑ב—See "אֱוִיל, 'Stubborn Fool,' and אִוֶּלֶת, 'Stupidity' " and "חֲסַר־לֵב, 'Lacking Sense' " in "Fools in Proverbs" in the introduction.

וְאִ֥ישׁ תְּ֝בוּנָ֗ה יְיַשֶּׁר־לָֽכֶת׃—For the Piel (D) of יָשַׁר meaning "go straightforward on one's path," see the textual note on 9:15 and BDB, Piel, 1. Here the imperfect is followed idiomatically with the infinitive construct of הָלַךְ. In this construction the second verb is the main verb, and the first verb serves adverbially, "walks straightly," that is, "stays straight on course."

15:22 הָפֵ֣ר מַ֭חֲשָׁבוֹת בְּאֵ֣ין ס֑וֹד—The Hiphil (H) of פָּרַר means "break, violate" or "frustrate (plans)" (see *HALOT*, 2 b). An infinitive absolute (הָפֵר) can serve as a present tense verb (Joüon, § 123 w (4)), and its nuance needs to be determined by context. There is no expressed subject of the action ("break plans"), and it is best translated as a passive: "plans *are thwarted* when there is no counsel" (cf. "plans *fail*," Waltke-O'Connor, § 35.5.2a, example 7). The noun סוֹד (also in 3:32; 11:13; 20:19; 25:9) connotes confidentiality and here emphasizes receiving advice from those who can give sage counsel without betraying a confidence. See the second textual note on 3:32.

Another negative proverb about "plans" (מַחֲשָׁבוֹת) is in 15:26, but then 16:3 promises that by entrusting your efforts to Yahweh, "your plans will be established" (וְיִכֹּנוּ מַחְשְׁבֹתֶיךָ).

וּבְרֹ֖ב יוֹעֲצִ֣ים תָּקֽוּם׃—The feminine plural noun מַחֲשָׁבוֹת, "plans," in the preceding clause apparently is considered a collective and is the subject of the feminine singular verb תָּקוּם (Joüon, § 150 g). The feminine singular can be used in an abstract sense: "*it* will succeed." For the sake of English it is rendered as plural, matching מַחֲשָׁבוֹת ("plans") in the preceding clause.

15:23 בְּעִתּ֣וֹ—Literally, "in its time" here carries the meaning of the right time for a word, since עֵת can signify the proper time for an event (*HALOT*, 6).

15:24 אֹ֣רַח חַ֭יִּים לְמַ֣עְלָה לְמַשְׂכִּ֑יל—The noun חַיִּים, "life," has the eschatological sense of everlasting life by God's grace, as also in, for example, 3:2, 18, 22; 4:10, 13, 22–23.

The Hiphil (H) participle מַשְׂכִּיל is Wisdom vocabulary for a faithful believer, as also in, for example, 10:5 and 16:20.

לְמַעַן סוּר מִשְּׁאוֹל מָטָּה׃—"Sheol" is synonymous with everlasting death and hell. See the first textual note and the commentary on 1:12. That it lies below or downward is implied in many passages, for example, 1 Sam 2:6 and Ezek 31:15–18.

15:25 וְיַצֵּב גְּבוּל אַלְמָנָה׃—The Hiphil (H) of נָצַב is used also in Deut 32:8 and Ps 74:17 to state that Yahweh "establishes, fixes" a "boundary." Those verses use the feminine counterpart, גְּבוּלָה, of the masculine word גְּבוּל, "boundary," used here. The form of the verb here is jussive, but it apparently has the same meaning as an imperfect (cf. Joüon, § 114 l).

15:26 תּוֹעֲבַת יְהוָה—In this pericope, this recurs in 16:5. See the first textual note and the commentary on 3:32. See also the excursus " 'Disgusting Thing' (תּוֹעֵבָה) in Solomon's Proverbs" in the commentary on Proverbs 11.

וּטְהֹרִים אִמְרֵי־נֹעַם׃—In contrast to "a disgusting thing," the adjective טָהוֹר, "clean, pure," implies that the "words" (אִמְרֵי) are acceptable to Yahweh. The noun נֹעַם, "pleasantness, pleasure," is cognate to the verb נָעֵם, "to be pleasant, delightful." See the second textual note on 2:10. Here and in 16:24, נֹעַם serves as an adjectival genitive: "*pleasant* words."

15:27 עֹכֵר בֵּיתוֹ בּוֹצֵעַ בָּצַע—Literally, this is "a person who is greedy for ill-gotten gain [בּוֹצֵעַ בָּצַע] troubles his house." עָכַר, "to trouble," involves eschatological judgment for the sinner that also affects his whole family (as in Josh 7:24–25); see the textual note on 11:17. For the cognate accusative phrase בּוֹצֵעַ בָּצַע, see the first textual note on 1:19. The phrase is spelled בצע בצע in 4QProv[b], a defective spelling of the participle (to be vocalized בֹּצֵעַ) that has the same meaning as the MT's plene spelling.[1] The participle and noun of the same root highlight the illicit nature of the enterprise pictured in this saying. The root בצע often is connected with a corrupt desire for wealth (cf. 28:16).[2]

וְשׂוֹנֵא מַתָּנֹת יִחְיֶה׃—This is "but a person who hates bribes will live." The participle is spelled defectively, ושנא, in 4QProv[b], but that has the same meaning as the MT's plene spelling.[3] The verb חָיָה, "to live," connotes everlasting life; see the third textual note on 4:4 and also, for example, 7:2a and 9:6a.

15:28 יֶהְגֶּה לַעֲנוֹת—Literally, this is "contemplates [how/what] to answer." The Qal (G) imperfect יֶהְגֶּה is missing in 4QProv[b], probably an accident due to haplography.[4]

וּפִי רְשָׁעִים יַבִּיעַ רָעוֹת׃—For the Hiphil (H) of נָבַע, "to spout, gush forth," in a similar context, see the second textual note on 15:2.

---

1 Ulrich et. al., *Qumran Cave 4.XI*, 186; Clifford, "Observations on the Text and Versions of Proverbs," 49.

2 Cf. J. N. Oswalt, "בָּצַע," *TWOT* 1:122–23.

3 Ulrich et. al., *Qumran Cave 4.XI*, 186; Clifford, "Observations on the Text and Versions of Proverbs," 49.

4 Ulrich et al., *Qumran Cave 4.XI*, 183, 186; Clifford, "Observations on the Text and Versions of Proverbs," 49.

15:29 וּתְפִלַּת צַדִּיקִים יִשְׁמָע׃—"The prayer of righteous people he [Yahweh] hears" implies that he does not "hear"—in the sense of "graciously respond to"—the prayer of the wicked or unbelievers. In this verse, God hearing the prayer of those justified through faith corresponds to him answering the prayer of upright believers according to his "favor, grace" in 15:8. Because of God's omniscience, it would be wrong to say that God does not "hear" (at all) the prayers of unbelievers, for example, Muslims, Hindus, Buddhists, and atheists. However, only those prayers uttered with faith in the God who dwelt in Israel (1 Ki 8:28–43) and who has become incarnate in his Son, Jesus Christ, are acceptable to God and have the promise that he will answer graciously (Jn 14:13–14).

15:30 מְאוֹר־עֵינַיִם—Literally, this is "a light of/in the eyes." The equivalent English idiom is "a twinkle in the eyes." ("A light in the eyes" could be misunderstood by English readers as a blinding light.) It denotes a cheerful, upbeat expression on one's face. The ancients did not always envision light simply impacting the eye; sometimes the eye was considered to be a source of light.[5]

שְׁמוּעָה טוֹבָה תְּדַשֶּׁן־עָצֶם׃—Literally, "a good report fattens a bone," this signifies the deep and enduring emotional response to good news. The translation above reflects the equivalent English idiom.

15:31 תּוֹכַחַת חַיִּים—The genitive indicates a quality that is imparted by the lead noun, hence the "warning" imparts "life." For a similar construction, see the first textual note on 15:33. For תּוֹכַחַת, "warning, correction," which in this pericope recurs in 15:32, see the first textual note on 1:23. The noun חַיִּים, "life," often has the eschatological sense of everlasting life by God's grace, as in, for example, 3:2, 18, 22; 4:10, 13, 22–23.

תָּלִין׃—The subject of the feminine verb is אֹזֶן, the listening "ear" at the beginning of the verse. The Qal (G) of לוּן or לִין can mean to "abide, remain" (BDB, 2) or "endure" (forever).

15:32 פּוֹרֵעַ מוּסָר—"A person who ignores discipline" is also in 13:18. For the noun, see "מוּסָר, 'Discipline,' and יָסַר, 'to Discipline' " in "Wisdom in Proverbs" in the introduction. In this pericope מוּסָר recurs in 15:33.

קוֹנֶה לֵּב׃—For קָנָה, "to acquire, possess," see the first textual note on 8:22. The noun לֵב often means "heart," but also may denote the seat of intelligence and cognition. In this case it refers to the type of reasoning ability often called "[good] sense" in English.

15:33 יִרְאַת יְהוָה מוּסַר חָכְמָה—See the first textual note and the commentary on 1:7 and "יִרְאַת יְהוָה, 'the Fear of Yahweh,' and יְרֵא יְהוָה, 'One Who Fears Yahweh' " in "Wisdom in Proverbs" in the introduction. In this pericope יִרְאַת־יְהוָה recurs in 16:6. In the construct chain מוּסַר חָכְמָה, "discipline of [that imparts] wisdom," the genitive denotes the result, the divine gift imparted through the "discipline" of fearing (believing in) Yahweh.

[5] See Mt 6:22–23 and Gibbs, *Matthew 1:1–11:1*, 355–57.

וְלִפְנֵי כָבוֹד עֲנָוָה׃—Literally, this is "before glory, humility [is required]." This expresses classic theology of the cross. For Christ himself, see Jn 12:28; 13:31–32; 17:5; and Phil 2:6–11. For believers, see Rom 8:17.

16:1 לְאָדָם מַעַרְכֵי־לֵב—The noun מַעֲרָךְ, "arrangement," from the verb עָרַךְ, "arrange, set in order," is found only here in the OT. In the construct phrase with לֵב, it refers to the "*arrangements* (plans) *of the mind*" (BDB, s.v. מַעֲרָךְ).

16:2 כָּל־דַּרְכֵי־אִישׁ זַךְ בְּעֵינָיו—It is unusual for a construct chain with כָּל־ in construct with a plural noun (דַּרְכֵי־) to be construed as singular, but that is the case here since the singular זַךְ is the predicate (cf. Joüon, § 150 o). The adjective זַךְ recurs in 20:11 and 21:8 and means "pure, righteous" (see BDB, 2).

וְתֹכֵן רוּחוֹת יְהוָה׃—Literally, this is "the one who evaluates spirits is Yahweh." The Qal (G) participle of תָּכַן, "measure, evaluate," recurs in 21:2 and 24:12, again with Yahweh as the subject, and with human "hearts" as the object. The object here, "spirits," refers to the human spirit, and by metonymy, to a person's spiritual thoughts, desires, and "motives" (NASB, NIV), especially regarding spiritual matters (cf. 1 Cor 2:13–15; Eph 1:3; 1 Pet 2:5). In all three of the Proverbs verses, the object is translated as "motives."

16:3 גֹּל אֶל־יְהוָה מַעֲשֶׂיךָ—The Qal (G) imperative of גָּלַל, literally, "roll (upon)," in this context means "entrust, commit" to Yahweh "your efforts, works" (מַעֲשֶׂיךָ). The identical clause גֹּל אֶל־יְהוָה in Ps 22:9 (ET 22:8) means "he trusts in/relies on Yahweh," as quoted in Mt 27:43. See also the nearly identical clause in Ps 37:5: גּוֹל עַל־יְהוָה דַּרְכֶּךָ, "commit your way to Yahweh." The divine promises of redemption (Pss 22:9 [ET 22:8]; 37:5) and success (Prov 16:3) for those who entrust themselves to Yahweh did not prevent Jesus from enduring crucifixion (Mt 27:35–43), but they were fulfilled in his resurrection. Likewise, these promises are properly applied to believers only in an eschatological way and should not be misunderstood as assurances of worldly success in this life.

וְיִכֹּנוּ מַחְשְׁבֹתֶיךָ׃—The promise with the passive Niphal (N) of כּוּן, "and your plans *will be established*," implies that Yahweh (named in the preceding clause) is the agent of the action. This is explicit in 16:9, which uses the causative Hiphil (H) of כּוּן to state that, literally, "Yahweh establishes his [the believer's] step."

16:4 כֹּל פָּעַל יְהוָה לַמַּעֲנֵהוּ—It is unusual for a word that is already definite because of a pronominal suffix also to have the article, but the article is indicated by the pointing of לַמַּעֲנֵהוּ, "for his/its own purpose" (cf. GKC, § 127 i; Joüon, § 140 c). The pronominal suffix is ambiguous. It could refer to כֹּל, "everything," or to יְהוָה, "Yahweh," as translated above.

16:5 כָּל־גְּבַהּ־לֵב—The adjective גָּבֹהַּ, "high, haughty," is in construct with the noun לֵב: "one who is arrogant of heart," referring to the disposition in the heart/mind, that is, an attitude.

יָד לְיָד לֹא יִנָּקֶה׃—Literally, "hand to hand, he will not be considered innocent," this idiom is repeated from 11:21, where רָע, "evil person," was added. See the first textual note on 11:21. לֹא יִנָּקֶה is a recurring clause in Proverbs; see the second textual note on 6:29.

16:6 בְּחֶסֶד וֶאֱמֶת יְכֻפַּר עָוֺן—For the first two nouns, see the first textual note and the commentary on 3:3. "Iniquity is atoned for" (יְכֻפַּר עָוֺן) uses a verb (כָּפַר) and a noun (עָוֺן) that are each common in the sacrificial provisions in Leviticus for the forgiveness of sins. They both occur in Lev 10:17.

וּבְיִרְאַת יְהוָה סוּר מֵרָע׃—For this vocabulary, see 1:7 and 3:7. See also the first textual note on 15:33.

16:7 בִּרְצוֹת יְהוָה דַּרְכֵי־אִישׁ—For the verb רָצָה, "be favorable (toward), be pleased (with)," which is cognate to the noun רָצוֹן, "favor, grace," see the second textual note on 8:35.

גַּם־אוֹיְבָיו יַשְׁלִם אִתּוֹ׃—Who is the subject of the causative Hiphil (H) imperfect יַשְׁלִם, "he makes (someone) to be at peace"? And who is the referent of the pronominal suffixes on אוֹיְבָיו, "his enemies," and אִתּוֹ, "with him"? Is it Yahweh or the man who is righteous through faith? See the commentary.

Commentary

Advice to a Wise Son (15:20–17:24)

This third informal section (15:20–17:24) of Solomon's Proverbs in 10:1–22:16 is once again prefaced with a saying about a wise son.[6] This section concentrates on advice to a son who seeks to be wise and righteous in his faith and life. The advice to a wise son comes in two parts, the first in 15:20–16:7 and the second in 16:25–17:6. In the middle of these two parts is a collection of sayings that concentrate on a wise ruler (16:8–24), one of the roles for which Solomon was trying to prepare his son and successor. This section ends with a collection of proverbs about fools and foolishness (17:7–24). This conclusion serves as a transition to the next section of Solomon's proverbs (17:25–19:12), which begins with a saying about a foolish son (17:25).

The proverbs in 15:20–17:24 concentrate on practical advice, but one should not read them simply as instructions for everyday life, nor as moralizing guidance. Instead they are to be understood as Law and Gospel within the Gospel setting of the book as a whole.[7] They contain occasional reminders of this setting, such as the heavenward orientation of the person who possesses Gospel-revealed insight (15:24), and God's gracious promise to hear the prayer of the righteous person (15:29). In fact, 15:29 introduces a set of four proverbs (15:29–31, 33, within a group of five) that direct one to the Gospel. Prov 15:30 speaks of the renewing power of any good news, and the Gospel is the greatest good news, which renews a person by the power of Christ's resurrection (Rom 1:4–6). Prov 15:31 speaks of those who heed a life-giving warning: the second use of the Law is to warn of divine judgment as the consequence of one's own

---

[6] For the loose sections in this part of the book, see the excursus "The Organization of the Sayings in Solomon's Proverbs in Proverbs 10:1–22:16" in the commentary on Proverbs 10. For earlier addresses by Solomon as a father to his son or sons, see the excursus "Proverbs 1–9, Christ, and the Ten Commandments" in the commentary on Proverbs 1.

[7] See further "Law and Gospel in Proverbs" in the introduction.

sin, and this warning drives one to the Gospel and its gift of forgiveness, yielding everlasting life. Prov 15:33 uses the familiar phrase "the fear of Yahweh," which is not simply fear of God's wrath, but a loving relationship with Yahweh that comes from the Gospel. Other notable places where the Gospel appears in this section are 16:9, 20, and the final saying in this section, 17:24.

Five Proverbs Linked by Wordplays (15:20–24)

15:20 This proverb is nearly identical to 10:1b–c. Both verses have a string of three couplings of opposites. Each contrasts a "wise son" with a "foolish son" (10:1) or a "foolish man" (15:20), and "brings joy to" with an opposite expression, "brings grief to" (10:1) or "despises" (15:20). Both refer to a man's "father" and "his mother."

15:21 This verse is linked to the preceding one by the noun שִׂמְחָה, "delight, joy," which is from the same root as the verb יְשַׂמַּח, "brings joy to," in 15:20. This saying also forms an ironic contrast to 15:20 in that a senseless person finds delight in stupidity, whereas a wise son takes delight in giving his father a reason to rejoice.

15:22 This saying is linked to 15:20–21 by paronomasia involving the consonants שׂמח ("brings joy to," 15:20; "delight," 15:21) rearranged in the word מַחֲשָׁבוֹת, "plans." One cannot overestimate the value of sage advice for helping oneself to understand which pitfalls to avoid and to confirm what is a good course of action.

15:23 This continues the chain of proverbs by returning to the root שׂמח ("brings joy to," 15:20; "delight," 15:21). This time a person's "delight" (שִׂמְחָה) is in providing an answer to a question or giving wise advice in a timely way. This is another reason to ask the advice of other faithful believers (cf. 15:22): it gives them an opportunity for joy as they contribute to the well-being of the counselee.

15:24 This is the final link in the chain of proverbs that began in 15:20, once again using paronomasia as the connection. This saying uses the Hiphil (H) participle מַשְׂכִּיל, "a person with insight," which has two of the same consonants as שׂמח ("brings joy to," 15:20; "delight," 15:21, 23), and the third consonant has a similar sound (כ and ח). Here wisdom, in the form of God-given insight, leads a person upward and away from Sheol below.

Some critics would eliminate or minimize the word "upward" (לְמַעְלָה) in this proverb by contending that the proverb is not intended to teach about eternal life, a doctrine that, these critics contend, does not appear in Proverbs.[8] However, they can only make this claim after eliminating what other proverbs teach about the hope of eternal life, but this procedure contradicts the text (see the commentary on 3:18; 11:19, 30; 14:27, 32 and the textual note on 10:11). "Upward" here, in contrast to Sheol "below" (מָטָּה), means that "the path of life" leads to a realm of life above and beyond this present existence, just as surely as

[8] McKane, *Proverbs*, 479–80; Toy, *Proverbs*, 314.

"Sheol below" refers to a realm of horror extending downward beyond physical death. Moreover, לְמַעְלָה, "upward," must be retained also because it is an integral part of the sound pattern involving ל and מ in this proverb.[9]

A Chain of Proverbs about Yahweh and His Way among Humans (15:25–16:7)

Prov 15:25–16:7 is a long chain of proverbs linked by catchwords and paronomasia:

- יהוה, "Yahweh" (15:25–26)
- יהוה, "Yahweh" (15:26), and יִחְיֶה, "will live" (15:27; paronomasia)
- יִחְיֶה, "will live" (15:27), and יֶהְגֶּה, "contemplates" (15:28; paronomasia)
- צַדִּיק, "righteous person" (15:28), and צַדִּיקִים, "righteous people" (15:29)
- יִשְׁמָע, "hears" (15:29), and שְׁמוּעָה, "report, news" (15:30; from the same root, שׁמע)
- שְׁמוּעָה, "news" (15:30), and שֹׁמַעַת, "listens" (15:31; from the same root, שׁמע)
- שֹׁמַעַת, "listens" (15:31), and שׁוֹמֵעַ, "person who listens" (15:32; participles of the same verb, שָׁמַע)
- יהוה, "Yahweh" (15:33–16:7)

15:25 This verse repeats Yahweh's opposition to haughty people (see, e.g., 6:17; 8:13) and also promises his protection for the "widow," representing the most vulnerable in society, who were often the targets of the unscrupulous and the greedy. The "boundary" that is established is the boundary of the land that belongs to the widow. Taking a widow's land was easy to do, since boundary markers could be moved (22:28; 23:10). This is the only verse in Proverbs that mentions a widow, though other vulnerable people are mentioned elsewhere, such as orphans (23:10). The frequent biblical admonition to look out for the welfare of the helpless, who are often among the poorest segments of society, is reflected in this proverb. In the modern era, the helpless include unborn children, threatened by death through abortion; those born with disabilities, who face infanticide; and the elderly, threatened by euthanasia. The biblical mandate to protect these kinds of people is a religious obligation as well as a social one, as James reminds us:

> Religion that is pure and undefiled before (our) God and Father is this: to care for orphans and widows in their affliction, and to keep oneself unstained from the world. (James 1:27; cf. Deut 24:19–21; 26:12–13; 1 Tim 5:3)

15:26 This verse once again uses Yahweh's approbation to curb a sin that cannot be easily regulated by human justice. Yahweh alone knows all immoral plans and thoughts, and therefore he can punish them. On the other hand, pleasant words are "pure" to God. טָהוֹר, "clean, pure," usually describes something or someone who is morally or ritually pure and therefore acceptable to God. For instance, only animals that are טָהוֹר, "clean," were to be eaten or sacrificed

[9] McCreesh, *Biblical Sound and Sense*, 68–71.

(Gen 8:20; Leviticus 11; 20:25–26). The words of believers are "pure" because they speak God's truth. Everything in creation "is sanctified by the Word of God and prayer" (1 Tim 4:5; cf. Mk 7:18–19; Acts 10:10–16).

15:27 This verse begins with an observation of how sinful behavior adversely affects not only oneself, but also others, especially members of one's household. Ill-gotten gain is also mentioned as the desire of a person who is enticed to join a gang (1:19). The second line highlights the believer's inner revulsion toward sins (specifically "bribes"), and the eschatological promise that the person who shares God's hatred toward sin (see 6:16–19; 8:13; 13:5; cf. Rev 2:6) "will live" (cf. Prov 15:24).

15:28 This verse commends the righteous for giving thoughtful, considered answers, not simply off-the-cuff replies with no depth of thought. The second line is similar to the second line of 15:2. Athanasius applies this proverb to warn of those who claim to preach the Gospel, but are actually proclaiming false doctrine; see the quotation in the commentary on 12:6.

15:29 This verse is similar to 15:8. While some proverbs stress God's nearness, this compares his distance from wicked people to his nearness to righteous people, since he is close enough to hear their prayers. While the sin of wicked people is what distances them from God, righteous people do not draw themselves near to God by their acts; instead they are reconciled to God through the righteousness of Christ, imputed to them through faith alone. See the commentary on 4:18 and also Romans 4–5.

15:30 This verse highlights the theme that messages sent by other people can change one's demeanor (cf. 15:13–15). Both changes described here are for the better. The external stimulus may be as simple as the light or twinkle in someone's eye, or it can be good news that is so momentous it enlivens one's very bones. "Good news" here is probably to be understood as generic (cf. Gen 45:27), but it certainly applies to the Gospel above all other good news (Is 40:9; 52:7; 61:1; Lk 2:10; 4:18, 43).

15:31 This verse is an observation that those who listen to serious warnings will not only save their lives, but they will also commend themselves as wise and be welcomed among other wise people. This is especially applicable to those who listen to the warnings in God's Law and are driven to the Gospel to live among others who have received wisdom from God (e.g., Acts 2:37–47; 16:31).

15:32 This verse continues the theme of listening to a warning. One who does so acquires wisdom (15:32b). In contrast, one who ignores the discipline intended for his own welfare "despises himself" (15:32a). To reject discipline—whether it comes through parents, teachers, or ministers, or directly from God's Word—is to injure oneself spiritually, emotionally, intellectually, and physically. This is self-destructive and shows the fool's contempt for himself, a contempt he often does not realize that he has (see Acts 13:27; Rom 10:3; 2 Pet 2:12; 3:16).

15:33 This verse defines exactly the "discipline that leads to wisdom." "The fear of Yahweh," a positive, filial relationship with the heavenly Father through faith in his Son,[10] is a discipline formed by the Word, which is the guidance for the life of faith, the path of all who have been reconciled to God through the Gospel.

The second line explains what the fear of Yahweh is: it is the humble confession of one's sin and reception of God's gift of forgiveness, with the promise of everlasting glory. The believer knows that no one can claim any right to stand before God or demand a place in his presence. This humility precedes the honor that God graciously will bestow on his people (Rom 8:30). The second line of this saying is repeated as the second line of Prov 18:12.

16:1 This verse reminds readers that no matter what plans people may have, God determines the course of human events and even provides the words for believers to furnish wisdom to others. God can even control answers given by unbelievers so that he changes and guides historical events in the world. An example is the prophecy of Caiaphas that it was better that one man (Jesus) die for the people rather than for the entire nation to perish. Caiaphas did not understand the greater implications of his words (Jn 11:49–53).

16:2 This verse states that God assesses humans differently than they assess themselves. A sinful person may consider his acts to be "pure" (זַךְ denotes that no contamination exists). Our sin blinds us to our own faults, and we tend to minimize the selfish ulterior motives we may have. However, God weighs motives on his perfect balance of holiness—even motives that people themselves are not aware of. Thus this proverb reminds us that we all fall far short of God's standard of theological, ethical, and moral purity (Rom 3:23).

16:3 This verse builds on 16:2. Because each of us is sinful, none of our actions are pure, and it would be easy for us believers to fall into despair and think that we cannot succeed in anything (cf. Romans 7). However, this proverb points to the solution for the human inability to accomplish anything that is pure and holy: God brings success to those who entrust their plans to him instead of relying on their own plans, which, no matter how sincere, are always tainted with sin. Similar is the message of Prov 3:5–6.

16:4 This verse first affirms that God carries out his good and gracious purpose for his entire creation. See 8:22–31 and also, for example, Jn 1:3; Rom 11:32–36; 1 Tim 2:4.

The second line of this verse should not be interpreted as a statement that God has predestined some people for punishment; that would contradict the clear teaching of Scripture (Ezek 33:11; 1 Tim 2:3–4; 2 Pet 3:9; see further FC SD XI 41–42). Rather, it teaches about the final punishment on the Last Day of the person who rejects God's mercy and grace. Because of the sinful nature

---

[10] See "Wisdom in Proverbs" in the introduction. See also the commentary on 1:1–7; 3:13–20; 8:22–31; 30:1b–10; and the excursus "Proverbs 8, Wisdom, Christology, and the Arian Controversy" in the commentary on Proverbs 8.

inherited from our first parents as a result of their fall into sin (Genesis 3), people naturally are enemies of God (Rom 5:10; cf. Phil 3:18). When a person despises God's Word, that person's heart becomes even more hardened as a result of that sin, as happened to Pharaoh in the book of Exodus (see also, e.g., Jn 12:40; Rom 1:21–28; Heb 3:13). In this way God allows a wicked person to make himself even more deserving of the day of trouble (cf. Rev 22:11). The person's obduracy is not a consequence of God's eternal will, but of the person's own stubbornness (FC SD XI 84–86).

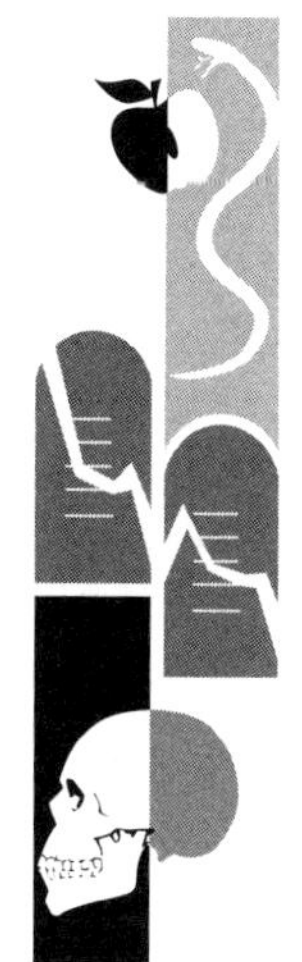

Luther cites this proverb as he explains the doctrine of original sin and how God continues his work as Creator despite the corruption of human nature because of Adam's disobedience:

> [Genesis 3 narrates] how man became evil when he was deserted by God and left to himself. From this man, thus corrupted, all are born ungodly, including Pharaoh, as Paul says: "We were by nature children of wrath like the rest" [Eph. 2:3]. God therefore did create Pharaoh ungodly, that is, out of an ungodly and corrupt seed, as it says in The Proverbs of Solomon: "The Lord has made everything for its purpose, even the ungodly for the day of trouble" [Prov. 16:4]. Hence it does not follow that because God has created the ungodly man, therefore the latter is not ungodly. How can he help being ungodly when he comes from an ungodly seed? As [LXX/Vulgate] Psalm 50 [MT 51:7; ET 51:5] says: "I was conceived in sin," and Job: "Who can bring a clean thing out of an unclean?" [Job 14:4]. For although God does not make sin, yet he does not cease to fashion and multiply the nature that has been vitiated by sin through the withdrawal of the Spirit, as a wood-carver might make statues out of rotten wood. Thus as is human nature, so are men made, God creating and fashioning them out of such a nature.[11]

16:5 This verse explains why the "wicked person" deserves the "day of trouble" in 16:4. The wicked person's arrogant attitude toward God and other people disgusts God and ultimately leads to punishment.

16:6 This verse states that iniquity is forgiven because of "mercy/grace" (חֶסֶד) and "faithfulness/truth" (אֱמֶת), but it does *not* say or imply that human efforts at mercy and faithfulness atone for sin. The passive Pual (Dp) verb יְכֻפַּר, "is atoned for," grammatically hides the agent of the action, who is the source of "mercy" and "faithfulness," namely, Yahweh (see Ex 34:6). The NT applies this language specifically to Jesus Christ, who is the source of "grace" and "truth" (Jn 1:14–17).

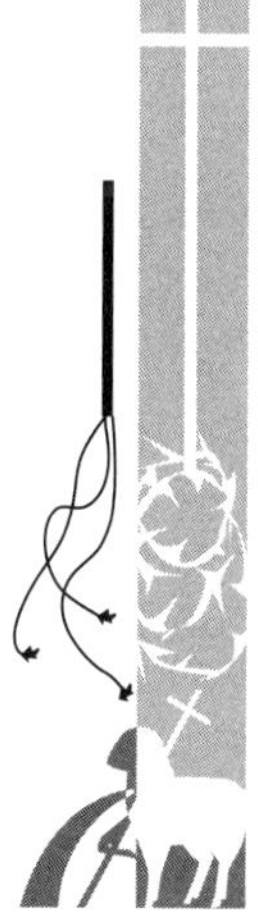

The second line of this proverb clearly identifies the divine source of forgiveness for sins. "The fear of Yahweh" involves fear of his wrath, and also love and trust in him as the merciful God who provides atonement for sin. This is what makes a person wise (1:7) and enables a forgiven sinner to turn away from sin and death to God's gift of life (3:7; 4:27; 13:14; 15:24).

16:7 This verse ends this string of proverbs that mention Yahweh (15:33–16:7) by building on the previous line about a person with the fear of

[11] AE 33:174–75.

Yahweh turning from evil. God has reconciled all people to himself through Jesus Christ, even while we were still his enemies (Rom 5:10; cf. Acts 9:4–5; Phil 3:18). Thus Christ could be the person whose ways are pleasing to God and who causes the enemies to be at peace with the Father; believers have peace with God through Christ (Rom 5:1). Unbelievers remain "enemies" of God and ultimately will be defeated and made a "footstool" for God the Son (Psalm 110, cited in Lk 20:43; Acts 2:35; Heb 1:13; 10:13). Yet the believer may also be the referent of this proverb, since the person guided by faith walks in ways that are pleasing to God. His actions not only commend him to God, but even his enemies may be disarmed by his integrity and live peacefully with him.

Proverbs 16:8–24

Wisdom for a King and His Subjects

Translation

16 [8]**Better a little with righteousness**
than a large income without justice.
[9]**A man's mind plans his way,**
but [only] Yahweh can make his step secure.
[10]**God's decisions are on the king's lips.**
His mouth should not betray justice.
[11]**An accurate balance and scales belong to Yahweh.**
He has made all the weights in the bag.
[12]**It is a disgusting thing to kings to do wickedness,**
for a throne is established by righteousness.
[13]**The favor of kings is toward righteous lips.**
He loves a person who speaks upright things.
[14]**The king's anger is a messenger of death,**
but a wise person can assuage it.
[15]**There is life in the light of a king's face,**
and his favor is like a cloud of [that brings] spring rain.
[16]**How much better it is to acquire wisdom than gold,**
and to acquire understanding is to be chosen rather than silver.
[17]**The highway of upright people is to turn away from evil.**
The person who guards his way preserves his life.

[18]**Arrogance precedes a disaster,**
and a haughty attitude precedes a fall.
[19]**Better to be humble in spirit with oppressed people**
than to share in stolen goods with haughty people.
[20]**The person who pays attention to [God's] Word finds good,**
and the person who trusts Yahweh—he is blessed.

[21]**The person who is truly wise will be called discerning,**
and sweetness of [with] the lips increases instruction.
[22]**Good sense is a fountain of life to the person who possesses it,**
but the instruction of [taught by] stubborn fools is stupidity.
[23]**The heart of a wise person makes his mouth intelligent**
and increases instruction upon his lips.
[24]**Pleasant words are honey from a honeycomb:**
sweet to the spirit and healing for the bones.

Textual Notes

16:8 בִּצְדָקָה—See "The Relationship between Wisdom and Righteousness in Proverbs" in "Wisdom in Proverbs" in the introduction, the commentary on 8:18, and the second textual note and the commentary on 10:2.

16:9 לֵב—See the first textual note on 2:10.

16:10 קֶסֶם—This word occurs eleven times in the OT, usually with a negative connotation meaning "divination, occultism." In this passage it appears to refer to the king's role as supreme judge of the nation, serving as God's spokesman to hand down justice, so it is translated as "God's decisions" (see *HALOT*, 4). Davies has suggested that the word implies that the king used lots to determine a verdict.[1]

בְּמִשְׁפָּט לֹא יִמְעַל־פִּיו׃—Literally, this is "in justice his mouth should not be unfaithful." The verb מָעַל means "be untrue, unfaithful" or "violate one's legal obligations" (*HALOT*), in other words "betray" those who have entrusted responsibility to the subject of the verb. The king has a responsibility to God to ensure that he rules justly, since governing authorities have been established by God (Rom 13:1–7).

16:11 פֶּלֶס | וּמֹאזְנֵי מִשְׁפָּט—This is a rare instance where two nouns are both in construct with a third noun, literally, "a balance of and scales of justice" (see Joüon, § 129 a, note 5; GKC, § 128 a, note 1; Waltke-O'Connor, § 9.3b, note 6). מִשְׁפָּט, in this context translated as "accurate," is used as an attributive genitive and modifies both "a balance" and "scales." The noun פֶּלֶס, "a balance," occurs only here in Proverbs. For מֹאזְנַיִם, "(pair of) scales," see the first textual note on 11:1, which has an antonymous construct phrase. God's Torah requires that scales and measures be accurate (Lev 19:36; Deut 25:13; contrast Amos 8:5).

מַעֲשֵׂהוּ כָּל־אַבְנֵי־כִיס׃—Literally, this is "his work is all stones of [in] a bag." Weights used with balances were typically made of stone and were carried in a bag.

16:12 תּוֹעֲבַת מְלָכִים—Usually in Proverbs תּוֹעֵבָה refers to something that is "a disgusting thing" to Yahweh. Here it is a disgusting thing to kings, the representatives of Yahweh. See the excursus " 'Disgusting Thing' (תּוֹעֵבָה) in Solomon's Proverbs" in the commentary on Proverbs 11.

16:13 רְצוֹן מְלָכִים שִׂפְתֵי־צֶדֶק—Usually in Proverbs the noun רָצוֹן refers to God's gift of "favor, grace" (see the second textual note on 8:35). However, in 16:13, 15 (and also in 14:35; 19:12), it refers to the king's favor or goodwill. In the construct phrase שִׂפְתֵי־צֶדֶק, literally, "lips of righteousness," צֶדֶק functions as an adjectival genitive: "righteous lips."

16:14 חֲמַת־מֶלֶךְ מַלְאֲכֵי־מָוֶת—Since "anger of a king" is singular, literally, "messengers of death" may be an intensive plural, implying quick retribution.

וְאִישׁ חָכָם יְכַפְּרֶנָּה׃—The Pual (Dp) of כָּפַר in 16:6 refers to iniquity that "is atoned for" and forgiven by God, so that his wrath is averted. Here the Piel (D) means "assuage" the king's anger. The feminine suffix on יְכַפְּרֶנָּה refers back to חֵמָה (in construct) at the head of the preceding clause.

---

1 Davies, "The Meaning of *Qesem* in Prv 16, 10."

16:15 בְּאוֹר־פְּנֵי־מֶלֶךְ חַיִּים—Compare this clause with the nouns אוֹר, "light," and פָּנִים, "face," to Num 6:25: "may Yahweh make his face [פָּנָיו] to shine [יָאֵר, the Hiphil (H) of the cognate verb אוֹר] upon you."

מַלְקוֹשׁ—This noun denotes the rain of March and April that is vital to the survival of all living things in Palestine.

16:16 קְנֹה־חָכְמָה מַה־טּוֹב מֵחָרוּץ—Literally, this is "to acquire wisdom—how much better than gold." For קָנָה, "acquire," in reference to wisdom, see the first textual note on 8:22. קְנֹה is an unusual form of the infinitive construct; the usual form, קְנוֹת, is in the next clause. The noun חָרוּץ is used with the preposition מִן ("than gold") also in 3:14; 8:10, 19.

וּקְנוֹת בִּינָה נִבְחָר מִכָּסֶף׃—The Niphal (N) participle of בָּחַר, "choose," is used similarly in 22:1 (cf. 8:10, 19).

16:18 שֶׁבֶר ... כִּשָּׁלוֹן—The downfall of the arrogant is literally portrayed as "a shattering" and "a stumbling." While the noun כִּשָּׁלוֹן occurs only here in the OT, it is cognate to מִכְשׁוֹל, "a stumbling block/stone," in, for example, Is 8:14. Jesus Christ is the rock at whom many take offense and over whom many stumble to their eternal condemnation (Rom 9:32–33; 1 Cor 1:23; 1 Pet 2:8). Contrast the Gospel promise in Jude 24–25.

16:19 טוֹב שְׁפַל־רוּחַ—In form שְׁפַל could be the Qal (G) infinitive construct, "*to be lowly of/in* spirit," and the subject of this nominal clause with טוֹב, "... is better" (BDB, s.v. שָׁפֵל, Qal, 2, and Waltke-O'Connor, § 36.2.1b, including note 12). Or it could be the adjective שָׁפָל, "lowly," in construct, as in the construct phrase שְׁפַל־רוּחַ in Is 57:15 and Prov 29:23.

16:20 וּבוֹטֵחַ בַּיהוָה אַשְׁרָיו׃—For אַשְׁרֵי, see the first textual note on 3:13. For similar blessings pronounced upon a believer who merely "trusts in" (בָּטַח בְּ) Yahweh, see Jer 17:7 and Ps 84:13 (84:12).

16:21 לַחֲכַם־לֵב יִקָּרֵא נָבוֹן—The construct phrase, literally, "one wise of heart," denotes someone who not only appears to be wise, but is in fact wise. For נָבוֹן, "discerning person," see the second textual note on 1:5.

וּמֶתֶק שְׂפָתַיִם—This is, literally "and sweetness of lips." The noun מֶתֶק is cognate to מָתוֹק in 16:24, which expands on the metaphor by referring to honey.

יֹסִיף לֶקַח׃—This clause, "he/it increases instruction," is repeated at the end of 16:23. For an almost identical clause, see the first textual note on 1:5.

16:22 מְקוֹר חַיִּים—For "fountain of life," see the textual note and the commentary on 10:11. This phrase is also in 13:14 and 14:27.

וּמוּסַר אֱוִלִים אִוֶּלֶת׃—Literally, this is "and the discipline of stupid people/stubborn fools is stupidity." See "מוּסָר, 'Discipline,' and יָסַר, 'to Discipline' " in "Wisdom in Proverbs" in the introduction and "אֱוִיל, 'Stubborn Fool,' and אִוֶּלֶת, 'Stupidity' " in "Fools in Proverbs" in the introduction. Some interpreters understand מוּסָר here to refer to "punishment," but usually מוּסָר refers to "discipline" administered with the goal of helping to correct and instruct the recipient, so it is better to render it here as "instruction" taught by "stubborn fools" (אֱוִלִים).

16:24 צוּף־דְּבַשׁ אִמְרֵי־נֹעַם—The noun צוּף means "honeycomb," and the imagery is reinforced by דְּבַשׁ, "honey." נֹעַם, "pleasantness, pleasure," serves as an adjectival genitive referring to gracious words also in 15:26. It is cognate to the verb נָעֵם, "be pleasant, delightful," for which, see the second textual note on 2:10.

Commentary

For the place of these verses in the third section (15:20–17:24) of 10:1–22:16, see "Advice to a Wise Son (15:20–17:24)" in the commentary on 15:20–16:7 as well as the excursus "The Organization of the Sayings in Solomon's Proverbs in Proverbs 10:1–22:16" in the commentary on Proverbs 10.

The five proverbs in this section that mention a king (16:10, 12–15) dominate this section. Many of the other proverbs also relate to kings and their concerns: justice (16:8), commerce (16:11), acquiring wealth (16:16), and the temptation to arrogance (16:18–19).

16:8 This verse is another proverb that teaches about the relative value of material blessings.[2] The priority of spiritual and ethical concerns over the gaining of wealth is highlighted here as it was in 15:16–17.

16:9 This verse can be interpreted as a rebuke, a statement of God's Law: no matter what we plan, he alone determines the outcome.[3] But it also has a Gospel application: God can and does accomplish even more than we ask or imagine (Eph 3:20). This he has already done by redeeming us in Jesus Christ and preparing for us an eternity beyond our comprehension (1 Cor 2:9).

16:10 This verse is a reminder that rulers are God's representatives and that they are to be respected and obeyed, since "there is no authority except from God" (Rom 13:1–7). At the same time, it is a reminder to rulers that they should not abuse the authority vested in them but govern according to God's will and Word (cf. Jn 19:11).

16:11 This verse is connected to 16:10 by the catchword מִשְׁפָּט, "justice," here translated adjectivally as "accurate." On the surface, this proverb appears to be about commerce and the Seventh Commandment,[4] speaking of God's intimate involvement in honest transactions among people.[5] In the context of royal "justice" (16:10), however, it takes on another shade of meaning: God wants righteousness and fairness in the courts with the scales of justice and the weights used on them reflecting God's standards of holiness.

16:12 This verse is the first of four proverbs about royal matters, each using מֶלֶךְ, "king." In 16:12 and 16:13 it is plural, whereas in 16:14 and 16:15 it is singular. In addition, this saying is linked to 16:13 by a catchword from the

---

[2] This saying has an inexact parallel in the Wisdom of Amenemope, chapter 13 (16:13–14). See *ANET*, 423; *ANE*, 241. See also the excursus "The Words of Wise People (Prov 22:17–24:22) and Its Relationship to the Wisdom of Amenemope" in the commentary on Proverbs 22.

[3] A similar thought is in the Wisdom of Amenemope, chapter 18 (19:16–17). See *ANET*, 423; *ANE*, 241.

[4] See the excursus "Proverbs 1–9, Christ, and the Ten Commandments" in the commentary on Proverbs 1.

[5] A similar expression, though in the negative, is found in the Wisdom of Amenemope, chapter 16 (18:4–5). See *ANET*, 423; *ANE*, 241.

root צדק: צְדָקָה, "righteousness" (16:12), and צֶדֶק, literally, "righteousness" (16:13). This proverb encourages rulers to think about the long-term stability of their position rather than the immediate wealth and power that can be gained through corruption.

16:13 This verse reminds those who serve or interact with government officials that good rulers who wish to govern well (16:12) appreciate honesty.

16:14 This verse is also a reminder for those in contact with high officials. Sudden or irrational outbursts of anger by a king can be directed at those in close proximity. A person who is wise will not exacerbate the king's anger, since capital punishment is not far behind. Instead a wise person will appease royal anger (the verb יְכַפְּרֶנָּה, "assuage," suggests propitiation and suitable atonement) and bring calm.

16:15 This verse is the opposite of 16:14. An official's favor can be beneficial. The spring rain is especially helpful in watering the crops in the weeks before the harvest so that they do not wither prematurely.

16:16 This verse is a saying about the relative value of wisdom and wealth. Both have advantages, but even worldly wisdom has more value because it can be applied in situations where wealth alone cannot help, such as when the king is angry (16:14). How much more precious is godly wisdom that leads to eternal life![6]

16:17 This verse is a reminder that righteous behavior is not only the theologically and morally correct path, but it is also is the safer path and the only path to everlasting life. Kings are not well-disposed toward those who would threaten their reign with unrighteous behavior (16:12), and they wield the death penalty (16:14).

16:18 This verse begins a string of three proverbs united by catchwords. Prov 16:18 is bound to 16:19 by the catchwords רוּחַ, "spirit," which is translated as "attitude" in 16:18 and is joined with "humble" in 16:19, and גאה, the root of גָּאוֹן, "arrogance" (16:18), and גֵּאִים, "haughty, arrogant people" (16:19). This proverb has a general application to everyone, since all sinful people have a tendency to become arrogant; to violate and disbelieve God's Word is the height of arrogance. In this context the saying especially warns those who deal with powerful people—especially God—to avoid prideful self-aggrandizement, since those who are higher have the means to cause the downfall of the arrogant.

16:19 This verse contrasts humility with arrogance, which is associated with unrighteousness (the "haughty people" have "stolen goods"). The king who seeks to rule well will tolerate neither arrogance nor criminal activity, and the person involved in both is doubly vulnerable to punishment. The better choice is to remain humble, even if that places one among the oppressed. See

---

[6] See "Wisdom in Proverbs" in the introduction. For Jesus Christ as the eternal source and the incarnation of divine Wisdom, see also the commentary on 1:1–7; 3:13–20; 8:22–31; 30:1b–10; and the excursus "Proverbs 8, Wisdom, Christology, and the Arian Controversy" in the commentary on Proverbs 8.

Mt 5:10–12; 1 Pet 2:19–24; 3:14. This proverb is tied to the next by the repeated Hebrew word טוֹב, "better" (Prov 16:19), "good" (16:20).

16:20 This verse completes this trio of proverbs by directing one's attention back to God's Word of Law and Gospel. In the keeping of the God's Law one can find good from temporal authorities, who should reward righteous behavior (16:12–13). Through trust (faith) in the Word of the Gospel, one receives everlasting blessing from God.[7]

16:21–24 These verses are about speech and are united by several catchwords:

- חָכָם, "wise" (16:21, 23)
- מֶתֶק, "sweetness" (16:21), and מָתוֹק, "sweet" (16:24)
- שְׂפָתַיִם, "lips" (16:21), and שְׂפָתָיו, "his lips" (16:23)
- יֹסִיף, "increases" (16:21, 23)
- לֶקַח, "instruction" (16:21, 23)
- שֵׂכֶל, "good sense" (16:22), and יַשְׂכִּיל, "makes intelligent" (16:23)

16:21 This verse notes the consequences of wise speech: it enhances one's reputation and influence. Uttered winsomely and without undue offense, one's words will be received more favorably. This is especially true of the proclamation of the Gospel, even though God's wisdom in Jesus Christ inevitably causes offense to those who reject it (see, e.g., Acts 17:5, 13, 32; 1 Cor 1:17–24).

16:22 This verse is the last of four proverbs that mention "a fountain of life" (see the first textual note on this verse). Good sense, a gift of God, is a source for life that God grants to the baptized believer (Jn 3:5; 4:14; 7:38–39). The negative counterpart in the stubborn fool is stupidity that, by analogy, overflows into punishment. The context suggests castigation by the king as well as everlasting divine judgment for the foolish unbeliever in the arid fire of hell (Lk 16:24).

16:23 This verse, like 16:21, notes that intelligent and insightful words come from an inner intelligence. For "heart" as the source of intelligence, see the first textual note on 2:10. Scripture depicts the "heart" as the location of the indwelling Holy Spirit, the font of wisdom and life.[a]

(a) E.g., Ezek 11:19–20; 36:25–27; Ps 51:8, 12–13 (ET 51:6, 10–11); Rom 5:5; cf. Jer 17:13; Zech 13:1

16:24 This verse notes the effect of speech that expresses divine wisdom. The comparison to honey recalls that Jonathan was strengthened by honey (1 Sam 14:27). The prophet Ezekiel and the apostle John ingested God's Word so they could preach it, and they found it to be as sweet as honey (Ezek 2:8–3:4; Rev 10:9–11; cf. Jer 15:16).

[7] See further "Law and Gospel in Proverbs" in the introduction.

Proverbs 16:25–17:6

Advice to a Wise Son, Part 2

Translation

16 [25]There is a way that appears to be correct to a person,
but its end is the way of death.
[26]A laborer's appetite labors for him,
because his mouth drives him on.

[27]A good-for-nothing person constantly plots evil,
and it is on his lips like a scorching fire.
[28]A perverse person spreads conflict,
and a gossip separates intimate friends.
[29]A violent person entices his neighbor
and leads him on a way that is not good.
[30]The person who winks his eyes is plotting something perverse.
Whoever purses his lips has completed some evil [plot].

[31]Gray hair is a beautiful crown.
It is found in the way of righteousness.
[32]Better to be a patient person than a hero,
and [better to be] a person who controls his temper than one who captures a city.
[33]The lot is thrown into a lap,
but Yahweh determines its every decision.

17 [1]Better a bit of stale food and quietness with it
than a house filled with sacrificial feasts of [with] quarreling.
[2]A slave with insight will rule over a shameful son
and will have a share in the inheritance [divided] among brothers.
[3]A crucible is for [refining] silver and a smelter for [refining] gold
as Yahweh is the one who examines hearts.
[4]An evildoer pays attention to wicked lips.
A liar feeds upon a destructive tongue.
[5]One who makes fun of a poor person insults his Maker.
A person who rejoices over [someone else's] misfortune will not escape punishment.
[6]Grandchildren are a crown to elderly people,
and the pride of children is their parents.

Textual Notes

16:25 See the textual notes on 14:12, which is identical to this verse.

16:26 נֶפֶשׁ עָמֵל עָמְלָה לּוֹ—The noun עָמֵל denotes a "laborer, workman," as in Judg 5:26. The cognate feminine verb עָמְלָה, "works, labors," has as its subject the feminine noun נֶפֶשׁ in the sense of "appetite."

כִּֽי־אָכַ֖ף עָלָ֣יו פִּֽיהוּ׃—The verb אָכַף, "press, urge, impel" (see BDB), occurs only here in the OT. In this context פִּיהוּ, "his mouth," means "his hunger" and is a synonym of "appetite."

16:27 אִ֣ישׁ בְּ֭לִיַּעַל כֹּרֶ֣ה רָעָ֑ה—For the compound בְּלִיַּעַל, see the first textual note on 6:12. The verb כָּרָה means "dig" or "excavate," and its participle in this proverb metaphorically signifies constant evil scheming. Here it might mean "**make deep** [evil] thoughts" (*DCH*).

וְעַל־שְׂפָתָ֗יו כְּאֵ֣שׁ צָרָֽבֶת׃—The Qere is the singular שְׂפָתוֹ, "his lip," while the plural Kethib, שְׂפָתָיו, "his lips," is supported by most of the ancient versions. The prepositional phrase "on his lip(s)" could imply that the reader is to supply as the subject "his words" or "his speech," as in most English translations. Or the subject could be the feminine singular noun רָעָה, "evil," in the preceding clause, which agrees with the feminine singular predicate, כְּאֵשׁ צָרָבֶת, "like a scorching fire." The translation above supplies "it," referring to "evil," as in NKJV. The adjective צָרָב, "scorching" (BDB), occurs only here in the OT and the cognate verb צרב only in Ezek 21:3 (ET 20:47).

16:28 אִ֣ישׁ תַּ֭הְפֻּכוֹת יְשַׁלַּ֣ח מָד֑וֹן—For the noun תַּהְפֻּכוֹת, "perversity," which in this pericope recurs in 16:30, see the second textual note on 2:12. Here it serves as an adjectival genitive in the construct phrase אִישׁ תַּהְפֻּכוֹת, "a perverse person." For the Piel (D) of שָׁלַח and the object noun מָדוֹן, literally, "send out strife/conflict," see the third textual note on 6:14.

וְ֝נִרְגָּ֗ן מַפְרִ֥יד אַלּֽוּף׃—Literally, this is "and a gossiper separates a close friend." The Niphal (N) participle נִרְגָּן refers to a "backbiter" (BDB), "slanderer" (*HALOT*), or "gossiper," and recurs in 18:8; 26:20, 22. אַלּוּף signifies an intimate, trusted friend or confidant. It is used to describe a woman's husband in 2:17. It is again the object of the Hiphil (H) participle of פָּרַד, "to separate," in 17:9.

16:29 אִ֣ישׁ חָ֭מָס יְפַתֶּ֣ה רֵעֵ֑הוּ—See the Piel (D) of פָּתָה, "to entice," in a similar context in 1:10.

16:30 עֹצֶ֣ה עֵ֭ינָיו לַחְשֹׁ֣ב תַּהְפֻּכ֑וֹת—Literally, this is "a person shutting his eyes [does so] to plot perversity." The verb עָצָה is hapax legomenon and means "shut" (BDB), but here it probably refers to a wink as a signal.

קֹרֵ֥ץ שְׂ֝פָתָ֗יו—The verb קָרַץ means "to close, narrow." It is used of winking in 6:13 and 10:10. With reference to lips, the corresponding English idiom is "purse one's lips."

16:32 ט֤וֹב אֶ֣רֶךְ אַ֭פַּיִם מִגִּבּ֑וֹר—For the construct phrase אֶרֶךְ אַפַּיִם, "(one who is) long of anger," meaning "(one who is) slow to anger," see the first textual note on 14:17 and the textual note on 14:29. For "better … than" (מִן … טוֹב) proverbs, see "Direct Comparisons" in the introduction.

וּמֹשֵׁ֥ל בְּ֝רוּח֗וֹ—The verb מָשַׁל, "to rule," often takes the preposition בְּ, "(rule) over," as also in 17:2. English versions are agreed that this idiom, literally, "one who rules over his spirit," signifies someone who can control his temper.

16:33 בַּ֭חֵיק יוּטַ֣ל אֶת־הַגּוֹרָ֑ל—The noun הַגּוֹרָל, "the lot," is marked by the sign of the definite direct object (אֶת־) even though it is the subject of the passive verb, the Hophal (Hp) of טוּל, "throw, cast." See GKC, § 121 b.

17:1 פַּת חֲרֵבָה—A פַּת can denote a morsel of food. This phrase is, literally, "a dried morsel," a small piece of food that has become stale.

זִבְחֵי־רִיב׃—Literally "sacrifices of strife," this refers to the worshipers' portion of their sacrifices that they could take home from the temple and feast upon. However, in this case the sacrificial feasts are eaten in the midst of quarreling. Ironically, it was the *peace* offering (Lev 7:11–21) that provided meat that the layman who furnished the sacrifice could then take home for consumption in his house.[1]

17:2 עֶבֶד־מַשְׂכִּיל יִמְשֹׁל בְּבֵן מֵבִישׁ—The Hiphil (H) participles מַשְׂכִּיל, "having good sense, insight," and מֵבִישׁ, "acting shamefully" or "causing disgrace," are contrasted also in 10:5 and 14:35.

וּבְתוֹךְ אַחִים יַחֲלֹק נַחֲלָה׃—Literally, "among brothers he will divide (the) inheritance," this means that the slave with insight (עֶבֶד־מַשְׂכִּיל) will be treated as an equal brother when it comes time to receive a share of the family inheritance. By implication, the slave replaces the "shameful son," who receives no share of the inheritance.

17:3 וּבֹחֵן לִבּוֹת יְהוָה׃—The initial *waw* may serve to join this clause to the preceding clause as a comparison (Joüon, § 174 h): "*as* Yahweh …" God is likened to the "crucible" and "smelter" in the preceding clause.[a]

(a) See Is 48:10; Ezek 22:18–22; Zech 13:9; Mal 3:3; 1 Pet 1:7; Rev 3:18

17:4 מֵרַע מַקְשִׁיב עַל־שְׂפַת־אָוֶן—This verse has three Hiphil (H) participles, מֵרַע, מַקְשִׁיב, and מֵזִין. The Hiphil (H) participle of רָעַע, "evildoer," recurs in the plural in 24:19. For מַקְשִׁיב, literally, "paying attention," see the textual note on 1:24. The evildoer pays attention עַל־שְׂפַת־אָוֶן, literally, "to a lip of wickedness," that is, to a person whose lips utter wickedness. A similar construct chain ends the next clause.

שֶׁקֶר מֵזִין עַל־לְשׁוֹן הַוֺּת׃—The abstract noun שֶׁקֶר, "falsehood, deception," here has the concrete meaning of a person who is "a liar," equivalent to the hypothetical phrase אִישׁ־שֶׁקֶר (see BDB, s.v. שֶׁקֶר, 5). מֵזִין is probably the Hiphil (H) participle of זוּן, "to feed," whose Hophal (Hp) is the Kethib in Jer 5:8 in some manuscripts. The verb זוּן, "feed," also occurs in Aramaic (in the Hithpeel [HtG]) in Dan 4:9 (ET 4:12), and the cognate noun מָזוֹן, "food," is in Hebrew in Gen 45:23 and 2 Chr 11:23, and in Aramaic in Dan 4:9, 18 (ET 4:12, 21). However, according to GKC, § 68 i, מֵזִין is a defective form of מַאֲזִין, "listening, giving ear," the Hiphil (H) participle of the verb אָזַן, which is a denominative from the noun אֹזֶן, "ear." This verb would occur only here in Proverbs, but it is common elsewhere in the OT. Two Hebrew manuscripts read מַאֲזִין, and most English translations reflect that understanding. However, מֵזִין is more vivid and need not be emended. The liar "feeds on" (repeats and expands) lies spoken by other people. He feeds עַל־לְשׁוֹן הַוֺּת, literally, "on a tongue of disasters," which describes the destructive power of a malicious tongue.

17:5 לֹעֵג לָרָשׁ חֵרֵף עֹשֵׂהוּ—This clause has three Qal (G) participles. The participle לֹעֵג, "(one who) makes fun of," occurs only here in Proverbs, but is a synonym of the common participle לֵץ, for which, see "לֵץ, 'Mocker,' and לָצוֹן, 'Mocking, Scoffing' " in "Fools in Proverbs" in the introduction. Finite forms of לָעַג are in 1:26 and 30:17. For the participle (sometimes spelled רָאשׁ) of רוּשׁ or רִישׁ, "be poor," see the first textual

[1] Cf. Kleinig, *Leviticus*, 38, 168–74.

note on 10:4. For חֵרֵף עֹשֵׂהוּ, "insults his [the poor person's] Maker," that is, God, see the first textual note on 14:31.

לֹא יִנָּקֶה׃—See the second textual note and the commentary on 6:29.

17:6 בְּנֵי בָנִים ... אֲבוֹתָם׃—Literally, these are "sons of sons" and "their fathers." In this context these terms should not be limited in gender, hence "grandchildren" and "their parents." Since the noun אָב, usually "father," can denote a more distant ancestor, אֲבוֹתָם in the second line could be translated as "their grandparents" to match "grandchildren" in the first line. Both could be rendered more generally to apply to further generations, for example, "descendants" and "their ancestors."

Commentary

For the place of these verses in the third section (15:20–17:24) of 10:1–22:16, see "Advice to a Wise Son (15:20–17:24)" in the commentary on 15:20–16:7 as well as the excursus "The Organization of the Sayings in Solomon's Proverbs in Proverbs 10:1–22:16" in the commentary on Proverbs 10.

16:25 See the commentary on 14:12, which is identical to this verse.

16:26 This verse is an observation of life. "Mouth" is used to refer to hunger or appetite through metonymy. Eccl 6:7 adds the thought that the appetite is never fulfilled.

16:27 This verse is one of three proverbs that use the word בְּלִיַּעַל, "good for nothing" (6:12; 19:28; see the first textual note on 6:12). In all three cases, the people described by this term are characterized by malicious speech.

16:28 This verse, like 16:27 and 16:29, opens with the word אִישׁ, "a person." This saying expands on the theme of 16:27 by warning of the dissension and ill will that can be caused by malicious gossip and rumormongering.

16:29 This verse speaks of the enticing path of violence that can influence people. This proverb recalls the enticement to join a gang of sinners in 1:10–19.

16:30 This verse is linked to the previous set of three sayings by the word תַּהְפֻּכוֹת, "perversity, someone/something perverse," which also occurs in 16:28. This proverb warns that evil comes not only in overt ways, such as violence (16:29), but also in underhanded and hidden plots, which can be indicated by subtle clues in people's behavior such as body language.

16:31 This verse speaks of the blessing of a long life that God gives to those who follow his path of "righteousness." This promise is connected with the Fourth Commandment (Ex 20:12; Deut 5:16; Eph 6:2–3).[2] While faithful believers may enjoy long life in this world, this is an eschatological promise that will be fulfilled in the resurrection to eternal life for all who are righteous through faith. Believers have now already received this life that shall never end (see, e.g., Jn 5:28–29; 11:25–26). Similar is the teaching of other proverbs with the eschatological promise of "life" (חַיִּים, e.g., Prov 3:2, 18, 22; 4:10, 13,

---

2 See the excursus "Proverbs 1–9, Christ, and the Ten Commandments" in the commentary on Proverbs 1.

22–23). Wisdom offers "righteousness" to all by grace alone (8:18–21). God's gift of imputed "righteousness" saves from death (10:2; 11:4). On the path of "righteousness," one receives "life," and there is "no death" (12:28).[3]

16:32 This verse commends patience over the hasty desire to accomplish some feat that will bring fame or reward. Since such feats are often foolhardy, risky, and dangerous, patience is commended. Its rewards may not appear to be as glorious, but they are enduring (Rom 2:7; Gal 5:22; Col 1:11; James 5:11).

16:33 This verse speaks of the practice of determining a course of action by casting lots.[b] As this proverb states, this was not a random way of choosing what to do, since God controlled the outcome. This is seen most clearly in the case of the apostles choosing a successor for Judas. They left the matter in God's hands through the casting of lots:

(b) See, e.g., Lev 16:8–10; Num 26:55–56; 36:2–3; Neh 10:35 (ET 10:34); 11:1; Jonah 1:7; Lk 1:8–17

> While praying they said, "You, Lord, who know the hearts of all, reveal which one of these two men you have chosen to take the place in this ministry and apostleship from which Judas deviated to go to his own place." They cast lots for them, and the lot fell to Matthias, and he was numbered with the eleven apostles. (Acts 1:24–26)

17:1 This verse observes that circumstances can change what should be a good thing (feasting on the meat of sacrifices offered to God) into a miserable experience. It counsels a wiser choice of more humble circumstances where one can have peace and quiet.

17:2 This verse notes that a wise slave is of greater worth than a son who dishonors his parents. The son is disinherited, and the wise slave is treated like a son; he gains a son's share of the inheritance. This is a warning not to rely on privilege and position, but on wisdom.

The NT expands this thought by stating that all baptized believers in Christ are adopted as God's children and are heirs of his promises (Gal 3:26–4:7; 4:21–31). All in Christ—Jewish and Gentile believers alike—comprise the "Israel of God" (Gal 6:16). In contrast, those who reject Christ, no matter how privileged their ethnicity and standing, remain slaves of sin and children of the devil (Jn 8:31–47).

17:3 This verse is not merely stating that God looks at the inner person, but it is also noting that God uses his examination to refine a person as silver or gold are refined. Examples are in Genesis 22 and Exodus 16. The first line of this proverb is identical to the first line of Prov 27:21.

17:4 This verse notes that those who abandon God's way of wisdom find it appealing to break the Eighth Commandment.[4] Such persons are to be avoided. Even more are they to be shunned if they promulgate false doctrine contrary to the Word of God (Rom 16:17–20; 2 Tim 2:16–19; 3:1–5).

---

3 See further "The Relationship between Wisdom and Righteousness in Proverbs" in "Wisdom in Proverbs" in the introduction.

4 See the excursus "Proverbs 1–9, Christ, and the Ten Commandments" in the commentary on Proverbs 1.

17:5 This verse warns against delighting in the misery of another, whether it is mocking the poor or ridiculing victims of some calamity.[5] A person who does this, though he may not realize it, insults God the Creator, who made all people (see the commentary on 14:31). In addition, he invites God's punishment to fall on himself.

17:6 This verse is an observation about family ties and love. It extols the family as a gift of God and a place where his blessings can be found. Similar are Lev 19:32 and Psalm 128. The due reverence spoken of by this proverb is to be evident especially in the household of faith, the family of God consisting of all in Christ. Paul follows the wisdom of this proverb as he instructs the young pastor Timothy about supportive relationships in the church (1 Tim 5:1–7).

---

[5] This same theme is found in the Wisdom of Amenemope, chapter 25 (24:9–10). See *ANET*, 424; *ANE*, 243. See also the excursus "The Words of Wise People (Prov 22:17–24:22) and Its Relationship to the Wisdom of Amenemope" in the commentary on Proverbs 22.

Proverbs 17:7–24

Introduction to Fools and Foolishness: The Consequences of Being a Fool

Translation

17 [7]Lips producing excess [words] are not fitting for a complete fool;
how much less [are] lying lips [not fitting] for a ruler!
[8]A bribe is a gem in the opinion of those who own it.
Wherever they turn, they prosper.
[9]A person who covers a transgression promotes love,
but whoever repeats a matter separates intimate friends.
[10]A reprimand impresses a person with understanding,
more than lashing a fool a hundred [times impresses the fool].
[11]An evil person promotes only rebellion,
and a cruel messenger will be sent against him.
[12]Let a bear robbed of her cubs meet a man,
and [let] not [a man meet] a fool in his stupidity.
[13]A person who repays evil for good—
evil will never leave his house.
[14]The beginning of a quarrel is like opening a floodgate,
so before fierce fighting breaks out, abandon the dispute.
[15]Acquitting the guilty person and convicting the innocent person—
both of them are a disgusting thing to Yahweh.
[16]Why is there money in the hand of a fool to buy wisdom,
yet he doesn't have a mind [for it]?

[17]A friend loves at all times,
and a brother is born for trouble.
[18]A person without sense strikes hands [to confirm a deal],
guaranteeing a loan for his neighbor.

[19]A person who loves sin loves a squabble.
A person who builds his gate high is seeking destruction.
[20]A crooked mind does not find good,
and a person with a perverted tongue will fall into disaster.

[21]The man who fathers a fool has grief,
and the father of a complete fool will never rejoice.
[22]A cheerful attitude is good medicine,
but a stricken spirit dries up [one's] bone.

[23]A wicked person secretly accepts a bribe
to pervert the ways of justice.

**[24]Wisdom [remains] right in front of a person with understanding,
but a fool's eyes [wander] to the end of the earth.**

Textual Notes

17:7 לֹא־נָאוָה לְנָבָל שְׂפַת־יֶתֶר—This is, literally, "not appropriate for a complete fool is a lip of excess." For the noun נָבָל, see "נָבָל, 'Complete Fool,' and נָבֵל, 'to Be a Complete Fool' " in "Fools in Proverbs" in the introduction. The feminine noun שָׂפָה (in construct), "lip," is the subject of this nominal clause, whose predicate is the feminine form of the adjective נָאוֶה, "beautiful; fitting, appropriate," which is negated again in the two other proverbs where it occurs, describing what is inappropriate for a fool (19:10; 26:1). The noun יֶתֶר means "excess; remainder." Many translations and commentaries understand "a lip of excess" to mean that the fool indulges in "excellent" or "arrogant" speech. However, it is not necessary to look for such derived meanings. Instead, the phrase refers to excessive words.

The LXX apparently read the singular שְׂפַת־ as plural (שִׂפְתֹת־) and יֶתֶר as יֹשֶׁר, "lips of uprightness," that is, "upright lips," since it translated with χείλη πιστά, "faithful lips."

אַף כִּי־לְנָדִיב שְׂפַת־שָׁקֶר׃—After a positive statement, the combination אַף כִּי can mean "how much more," but following a negative statement, as here, it can mean "how much less" (BDB, s.v. אַף כִּי, 3, under אַף II). As in the preceding clause, the singular construct of שָׂפָה, "lip," is translated as plural for the sake of English. For, literally, "lip(s) of falsehood [שֶׁקֶר]," see also 10:18 and 12:22 (cf., literally, "a tongue of falsehood," in, e.g., 12:19).

17:8 אֶבֶן־חֵן הַשֹּׁחַד בְּעֵינֵי בְעָלָיו—"The bribe" (הַשֹּׁחַד) is called, literally, "a stone of favor [אֶבֶן־חֵן] in the eyes of its masters." The construct phrase has been translated in different ways, including "magic stone" (ESV, NRSV) and "charm" (NIV, NASB). The translation here understands it as a precious stone, that is, a gem. Elsewhere in Proverbs the noun חֵן usually refers to God's "grace," which is freely available through accepting divine wisdom in faith (e.g., 1:9; 3:4, 34). Here the force of חֵן is that a bribe gains the "favor" of people who accept it, but ironically it elicits God's wrath rather than his "grace." Some interpreters understand בְּעָלָיו, "its masters," as the persons who offer the bribe, while others understand it to refer to the persons who receive it. It most likely refers to those who offer a bribe and then receive "favor" from the recipients.

אֶל־כָּל־אֲשֶׁר יִפְנֶה יַשְׂכִּיל׃—The two verbs in this clause (יִפְנֶה יַשְׂכִּיל, literally, "he turns, he prospers") are singular, but they are translated as plurals to match the implied subject, which is the suffixed plural בְּעָלָיו, "those who own it [the bribe]," in the preceding clause. Usually in Proverbs the Hiphil (H) of the verb שָׂכַל and its cognate noun refer to having insight through divine wisdom; see "שֵׂכֶל, 'Good Sense,' and הִשְׂכִּיל, 'to Act Sensibly' " in "Wisdom in Proverbs" in the introduction. Here, ironically, יַשְׂכִּיל means that the person who bribes others "prospers" in a worldly sense at the same time that he foolishly evokes God's judgment, which will result in his everlasting poverty.

17:9 מְכַסֶּה־פֶּשַׁע מְבַקֵּשׁ אַהֲבָה—This is, literally, "one who covers transgression seeks love." For the idiom "cover transgression" (the Piel [D] of כָּסָה with the object noun פֶּשַׁע), see the second textual note on 10:12, where too אַהֲבָה refers to God's gracious "love" as the motivation for his people to display "love" in their relationships with other people.

Here the Piel (D) participle מְבַקֵּשׁ has the sense "promotes" or "seeks to accomplish something" (see *HALOT*, 2). The person who covers sin is not simply seeking love in the sense of trying to get others to love him; instead he is seeking to show love to others by forgiving them, and this promotes gracious relationships, even between the other forgiven people.

In 17:11 the Piel imperfect of the same verb, יְבַקֶּשׁ, has a similar force but in a negative context: "an evil person [רָע] promotes [יְבַקֶּשׁ] only rebellion [אַךְ־מְרִי]." He does not desire others to rebel against himself, but instead he promotes rebellious behavior among others, ruining their relationships.

וְשֹׁנֶה בְדָבָר מַפְרִיד אַלּוּף׃—The verb שָׁנָה, "do a second time, repeat," is related to the numeral for "two" (שְׁנַיִם) and here refers to repeating (publicizing) what should have remained confidential. בְּדָבָר is similar to the English idiom "*by word* of mouth." For מַפְרִיד אַלּוּף, see the second textual note on 16:28. The implication is that the intimate friend (אַלּוּף) has conveyed private information to a trusted confidant, who then betrays the friend by passing on the information to others. This destroys the prior relationship of trust and intimacy.

17:10 תֵּחַת גְּעָרָה בְמֵבִין—This is, literally, "a reprimand descends into a person with understanding." For the feminine noun גְּעָרָה, "a reprimand," see the second textual note on 13:1. It is the subject of the feminine Qal (G) imperfect of נָחַת, "descend," here meaning "intrude deeply" (*HALOT*, 3) or "make [an] impression" (BDB, 2). The form of the verb is unusual because the *nun* is assimilated even though the second radical is a guttural (GKC, § 66 f). The verb takes the prepositional phrase בְמֵבִין, that is, "makes an impression *on* [בְּ] *a person with understanding*." For מֵבִין (as in, e.g., 8:9 and again in 17:24), the Hiphil (H) participle of בִּין, see "בִּינָה, 'Understanding,' and Related Words" in "Wisdom in Proverbs" in the introduction.

מֵהַכּוֹת כְּסִיל מֵאָה׃—The preposition מִן on the Hiphil (H) infinitive construct of נָכָה, "to strike, smite," has a comparative sense: the "reprimand" given a wise person in the preceding clause is "more" effective "than" beating or flogging a "fool" (כְּסִיל), even "a hundred" times (מֵאָה is an adverbial accusative). See "כְּסִיל, 'Fool,' and כְּסִילוּת, 'Foolishness' " in "Fools in Proverbs" in the introduction.

17:11 וּמַלְאָךְ אַכְזָרִי יְשֻׁלַּח־בּוֹ׃—The "cruel messenger/angel" (מַלְאָךְ אַכְזָרִי) who "will be sent" (יְשֻׁלַּח) to punish the "evil person" (רָע in the previous clause) could be the destroying angel (Ex 12:23; 2 Sam 24:16; 1 Cor 10:10) or one of the angelic men depicted in Genesis 19 or Ezek 9:1–7.

17:12 פָּגוֹשׁ דֹּב שַׁכּוּל בְּאִישׁ—The Qal (G) infinitive absolute פָּגוֹשׁ here is equivalent to a jussive: "*let* a bear robbed of its whelps *meet* a man" (Waltke-O'Connor, § 35.5.2a, example 3; so also GKC, § 113 cc). This clause needs to be understood in light of the next one. The two clauses together could be translated as a comparative: "it is *better for* a bear … to meet a man *than for* [a man to meet] a fool in his stupidity." The modified subject of the infinitive is דֹּב שַׁכּוּל, "a bear bereaved, childless," that is, "robbed of her cubs." The fierceness of such a mother bear is also evident in 2 Sam 17:8 and in Hos 13:8, where Yahweh is like a bear as he encounters (פָּגַשׁ) his apostate people. Usually

פָּגַשׁ takes an accusative; only here does the preposition בְּ introduce the person (בְּאִישׁ) whom the subject (the bear) meets.

וְאַל־כְּסִיל בְּאִוַּלְתּוֹ׃—Literally, this is "and not a fool in his stupidity." The negative אַל presupposes a jussive verb, to be supplied from the infinitive absolute in the preceding clause: "and [let] not [a man meet] a fool" (see GKC, § 152 g). See the previous textual note for an alternate translation of this line as the second part of a comparative.

17:13 מֵשִׁיב רָעָה תַּחַת טוֹבָה—A participle can introduce a *casus pendens* (Joüon, § 156 g). This entire line, beginning with the Hiphil (H) participle מֵשִׁיב, "a person who returns, pays back," is suspended (*pendens*) since the reader is left in suspense about the message until he reads the second line. The translation indicates this syntactical construction by the dash at the end of the first line. The second line is connected to the first line by means of the pronominal suffix on מִבֵּיתוֹ, "*his* house," which refers back to the participle מֵשִׁיב, the "person who repays."

17:14 פּוֹטֵר מַיִם רֵאשִׁית מָדוֹן—The construct phrase רֵאשִׁית מָדוֹן is the subject in this clause: literally, "the beginning of a quarrel [is] releasing water." The verb פָּטַר means "let out, set free." This portrays the initiation of a fight as releasing uncontrollable floodwaters. It pictures quarreling as being like opening a floodgate on a dam, so that otherwise tranquil and pent-up waters rush down in a destructive torrent.

וְלִפְנֵי הִתְגַּלַּע הָרִיב נְטוֹשׁ׃—This clause is joined to the preceding one with *waw*, "so …" It states the consequent behavior that the wise person should practice because of the truth of the preceding clause. לִפְנֵי, "before," has the temporal meaning. The verb גָּלַע occurs three times in the OT, always in Proverbs and always in the Hithpael (HtD), meaning to "burst out" (*DCH*) or "break out" (BDB) in fierce, intense fighting. In 18:1 and 20:3 the verb itself denotes fighting, even without a subject noun that means "a fight." Here הָרִיב, the noun רִיב, "a quarrel, fight, dispute," with the article, could be the subject of הִתְגַּלַּע, which could be the perfect (so BDB), as reflected in "so quit before the quarrel breaks out" (RSV, ESV; similar is NIV).

However, the disjunctive accent on the verb suggests that וְלִפְנֵי הִתְגַּלַּע forms a phrase that means "before fierce fighting breaks out." The verb probably is the infinitive construct (so *DCH*). Then הָרִיב would be the direct object of the imperative נְטוֹשׁ: "abandon the dispute." This understanding of the syntax is reflected in, for example, KJV and NKJV (cf. NASB).

17:15 מַצְדִּיק רָשָׁע וּמַרְשִׁיעַ צַדִּיק—The ironic Hebrew is, literally, "declaring righteous a wicked person and declaring wicked a righteous person." Both of the two Hiphil (H) participles (מַצְדִּיק ... וּמַרְשִׁיעַ) have the legal, forensic meaning, as when a judge pronounces a verdict. The Hiphil of צָדַק means "justify, declare righteous, acquit [as innocent]" (as in, e.g., Is 53:11), and the Hiphil of רָשַׁע means "pronounce [someone to be] wicked, condemn, convict [as guilty]." These Hiphil verbs are causative; a judge's verdict makes or causes a person to be justified or condemned. Ironically, each of the verbs takes as its object an antonymous adjective from the other root used substantivally: רָשָׁע, "wicked/guilty person," and צַדִּיק, "righteous/innocent person." Therefore both declarations are unjust.

The verb צָדַק occurs in Proverbs only here. The only other instance in the book of the verb רָשַׁע is the Hiphil (H) in 12:2, where too it is forensic. Some call these Hiphil verbs "delocutive," meaning that a judge's declaration (locution) causes a person to be justified or condemned (see Waltke-O'Connor, § 27.2e, including example 18b).

תּוֹעֲבַת יְהוָה גַּם־שְׁנֵיהֶם׃—This is, literally, "a disgusting thing to Yahweh [are] both of the two of them," referring to the two wrongly performed forensic actions in the preceding line. See the excursus " 'Disgusting Thing' (תּוֹעֵבָה) in Solomon's Proverbs" in the commentary on Proverbs 11. This entire clause is repeated in 20:10b, and גַּם־שְׁנֵיהֶם recurs in 20:12. The adverb גַּם, "also, both," is similarly used with the suffixed numeral שְׁנַיִם, "two," in, for example, Gen 27:45. The dual numeral שְׁנַיִם, "two," also recurs with the same suffix, שְׁנֵיהֶם, in Prov 24:22; 27:3; 29:13, and in each case it is translated as "both of them."

17:16 וְלֶב־אָיִן׃—This literally states about the fool, "and a mind does not exist [in him]." For לֵב, "heart," as the seat of wisdom, the "mind," see the first textual note on 2:10. This phrase occurs only here in Proverbs, but the synonymous reversed construct phrase אֵין לֵב describes foolish Israel in Jer 5:21 and Hos 7:11. A phrase with similar meaning, חֲסַר־לֵב, literally, "lacking a mind, mindless," is common in Proverbs; see the textual note on 17:18.

17:17 בְּכָל־עֵת אֹהֵב הָרֵעַ—This is, literally, "at every time the friend [הָרֵעַ] loves [אֹהֵב]." For the temporal use of בְּ, see Waltke-O'Connor, § 11.2.5c, example 7.

וְאָח לְצָרָה יִוָּלֵד׃—In light of the preceding clause, "and a brother is born for distress/trouble" must mean that God gives us brothers in order to help us during our times of trouble.

17:18 אָדָם חֲסַר־לֵב תּוֹקֵעַ כָּף עֹרֵב עֲרֻבָּה—The adjectival construct phrase חֲסַר־לֵב is often used substantivally in Proverbs, so the use of אָדָם, "a man," here is pleonastic. For a similar construction with two nouns, see the first textual note on 6:12. For the adjectival construct phrase here, see "חֲסַר־לֵב, 'Lacking Sense' " in "Fools in Proverbs" in the introduction. The phrases תּוֹקֵעַ כָּף, literally, "striking a hand," and עֹרֵב עֲרֻבָּה, literally, "guaranteeing a guarantee [a loan]," are business terminology. See the first and second textual notes on 6:1, which has perfect forms of the same verbs whose participles (תּוֹקֵעַ ... עֹרֵב) are here.

17:19 מַגְבִּיהַּ פִּתְחוֹ—Literally, "(the person who) makes high his opening," this phrase is difficult to interpret and is expressed many different ways in various translations. The Hiphil (H) participle מַגְבִּיהַּ is of גָּבַהּ, "be high," a verb that recurs in Proverbs only in 18:12, in the Qal (G), where it describes the heart of an arrogant person. Cognate terms associate "high" (16:5) and "height" (16:18) with human haughtiness and hubris. Therefore this phrase likely describes some kind of display of arrogance. The noun פֶּתַח, "opening," could refer to the person's mouth, since the cognate verb פָּתַח, "open," is used with "mouth" as its object in 24:7; 31:8–9, 26. If so, the phrase could be a metaphor for opening one's mouth wide in order to speak boastful words; this would fit with the "perverted tongue" in 17:20. However, the noun פֶּתַח does not refer to a "mouth" elsewhere in the OT. Most often it refers to the "doorway" or "entrance" of a building, or to the gate in a city wall, which was the major defense for an ancient city (see BDB).

In Judg 9:52 it refers to the entrance to a tower. The phrase here probably refers to constructing some kind of high defensive fortification.

17:20 עִקֶּשׁ־לֵב—The construct phrase "crooked of heart" is parallel to the phrase in the next clause וְנֶהְפָּךְ בִּלְשׁוֹנוֹ, literally, "and perverted in [regard to] his tongue." For the adjective עִקֵּשׁ, "crooked," see the first textual note on 2:15. The Niphal (N) of הָפַךְ, "turn," occurs only here in Proverbs, but נֶהְפָּךְ is a synonym of other terms for "perverted," the translation of עִקֵּשׁ in 11:20. See also the Piel (D) of סָלַף, "make crooked, pervert" (13:6; 19:3; 21:12; 22:12), discussed in the second textual note on 13:6.

17:21 יֹלֵד כְּסִיל לְתוּגָה לוֹ—The Qal (G) of יָלַד usually is used in the feminine to refer to a mother who "gives birth," but occasionally it can refer to a father. Since the Qal participle of יָלַד, "give birth," is masculine, as is the pronominal suffix on לוֹ, this clause must refer to a man who "fathers" (יֹלֵד) a "fool" (כְּסִיל) rather than to a mother. This is confirmed by the following parallel clause with אָב, "father." The prepositional phrases describe the result for such a father: לְתוּגָה לוֹ, "unto grief for himself." For the noun תּוּגָה, "grief," see the third textual note on 10:1.

וְלֹא־יִשְׂמַח אֲבִי נָבָל׃—The negative phrase with the Qal (G) verb, לֹא־יִשְׂמַח, literally, "the father of a complete fool *will not rejoice*," is the direct opposite of the promises in 10:1; 15:20; 29:3 (cf. 27:11) with the causative Piel (D) of שָׂמַח that a wise son will "make" his father "rejoice" (see also the Qal in 23:15, 24–25). It also contrasts with the first clause of 17:22. For נָבָל, see "נָבָל, 'Complete Fool,' and נָבֵל, 'to Be a Complete Fool' " in "Fools in Proverbs" in the introduction.

17:22 לֵב שָׂמֵחַ יֵיטִב גֵּהָה—Literally, this is "a rejoicing heart makes a cure good." The causative Hiphil (H) verb יֵיטִב, "makes good," with the object noun גֵּהָה, "cure, healing," is translated adjectivally as "good medicine." גֵּהָה is a hapax legomenon. The noun's root is the verb גָּהָה, which occurs in Hos 5:13, where it clearly refers to healing. Compare this verse to proverbs that refer to "healing" with the noun מַרְפֵּא.[a] There is no need to emend גֵּהָה to גְּוִיָּה, "body," following the Syriac and Targum.

(a) Prov 4:22; 12:18; 13:17; 14:30; 15:4; 16:24

וְרוּחַ נְכֵאָה תְּיַבֶּשׁ־גָּרֶם׃—Literally, this is "and a stricken spirit dries out a bone." For the adjectival phrase רוּחַ נְכֵאָה, "a stricken spirit," see the second textual note on 15:13. In OT thought, dry bones represent despair and death, with no hope for life except by a divine miracle of resurrection.[b] In contrast, moist or fat bones represent vitality and prosperity (Job 21:24; Prov 15:30).

(b) See Ezek 37:1–14; Ps 102:4 (ET 102:3); cf., e.g., Pss 6:3 (ET 6:2); 22:15, 18 (ET 22:14, 17); 38:4 (ET 38:3); 51:10 (ET 51:8)

17:23 שֹׁחַד מֵחֵיק רָשָׁע יִקָּח—The adjective רָשָׁע, used substantivally, "a wicked person," is the subject of the verb יִקָּח, "takes, accepts." The direct object is שֹׁחַד, "a bribe," a noun used also in 6:35; 17:8; 21:14. The prepositional phrase מֵחֵיק, "from the bosom," modifies the "bribe" but can be translated adverbially as "*secretly* accepts." The bribe is hidden in the bosom of the briber, who then pays it in secret so that others will not know what has been done.

17:24 אֶת־פְּנֵי מֵבִין חָכְמָה—Since the following clause in antithetical parallelism refers to the fool's eyes straying בִּקְצֵה־אָרֶץ, literally, "at the end of the earth," that is, looking far away as he covets what he does not have, the phrase אֶת־פְּנֵי מֵבִין, literally, "with the face of a person with understanding," must mean that the understanding person keeps "wisdom" (חָכְמָה) right in front of him. As he keeps his eyes on the divine wisdom set before him, he travels straight ahead.

Commentary

These verses conclude the third loose section (15:20–17:24) of 10:1–22:16. See "Advice to a Wise Son (15:20–17:24)" in the commentary on 15:20–16:7, as well as the excursus "The Organization of the Sayings in Solomon's Proverbs in Proverbs 10:1–22:16" in the commentary on Proverbs 10.

17:7 This verse contrasts the corrupt ruler with a fool who speaks too much. The ruler is worse than the fool because his words have the force of law.

17:8 This verse notes that a person who gives a bribe often receives special considerations. It does not recommend this behavior. The taking of a bribe is proscribed by the Law (e.g., Ex 23:8), and thus the giving of one would also be sinful. Moreover, this proverb depicts the giver of the bribe as self-deluded.[1] The payment is a gem "in the opinion of" (בְּעֵינֵי, literally, "in the eyes of") the one who gives it. Several times in Proverbs, this phrase with a suffix בְּעֵינָיו, literally, "in his own eyes," denotes someone who thinks he has something that he does not: a right way (12:15; 21:2), purity (16:2; 30:12), or wisdom (26:5, 12, 16; 28:11). Moreover, the subject of the self-delusion expressed with this phrase can be a fool (26:5; cf. 26:12), a stubborn fool (12:15), or a lazy person (26:16). Thus the person who offers a bribe considers his action to be clever and a way to prosperity, *but ironically he is only deceiving himself*, because he has incurred God's wrath as he attempts to corrupt justice for his own ends. His actual end will be to suffer divine judgment.

17:9 This verse notes two differing approaches to dealing with sin. The first and best way involves repentance, forgiveness, and confidentiality. If the transgressor is repentant and seeks divine mercy, he will be forgiven (Prov 16:6; see also Psalms 32; 51; 85). The person against whom the sin was committed, and any person to whom the sin has been confessed—especially a pastor—should forgive the contrite transgressor and say nothing more about the sin to anyone else.[2] In this way the person who absolves the repentant sinner and maintains confidentiality "covers a transgression" and "promotes love." A person does not show true love if he simply ignores sin and fails to call the sinner to repentance (Ezek 3:17–21; Gal 6:1). Jesus called for the application of both Law and Gospel[3] when he instituted the office of the keys, which is the basis for the church's practice of confession and absolution (Mt 16:19; Jn 20:22–23; Rev 1:18; 3:7; cf. Is 22:22). See also James 5:19–20, where the brother of the

[1] Montgomery, "A Bribe Is a Charm," 139.

[2] The ordination vows for a Lutheran pastor include the solemn question "will you promise never to divulge the sins confessed to you?" to which the pastor assents, "Yes, I will [promise never to divulge the sins confessed to me], with the help of God" (*LSB Agenda*, p. 166).

[3] See further "Law and Gospel in Proverbs" in the introduction.

Lord alludes to Prov 10:12, which is similar to this proverb. This verse is a condensed version of what Jesus commands his disciples to do:

> If your brother sins against you, go and reprove him, just between you and him. If he listens to you, you have gained your brother. But if he does not listen, take with you one or two others, that "out of the mouths of two or three witnesses every charge may be confirmed" [LXX Deut 19:15]. If he refuses to listen to them, tell it to the church. And if he refuses to listen even to the church, let him be to you as a Gentile and a tax collector. Truly, I say to you, whatever you bind on earth shall be bound in heaven, and whatever you loose on earth shall be loosed in heaven. (Mt 18:15–18)

This way of love has the ultimate goal of reconciling the sinner to God through repentance and faith in Christ.

In contrast, the second line of the proverb states that those who spread gossip and indulge in scandalmongering destroy relationships—both among people and with God. This is a sinister way of hatred.

17:10 A "reprimand" impresses a wise person, who learns from his mistakes and confesses his sins (see the commentary on 17:9), whereas a fool cannot be impressed (and does not repent) even when the result of his actions goes beyond rebuke to corporal punishment. This is a reminder to those who seek wisdom that they should listen to correction. It is also a way to recognize and distinguish a wise person from a fool.

17:11 This verse warns that a person should not rebel against those with proper authority, or else he can expect severe punishment. Paul makes the same point when urging obedience to those who govern:

> But if you do what is wrong, be afraid, for he [the authority] does not bear the sword in vain. For he is a servant of God, an avenger for [carrying out God's] wrath on the person who does wrong. (Rom 13:4; cf. Rom 13:1–7)

Even if an evil person escapes punishment by the civil authorities, he should expect to be sentenced by God to everlasting punishment on the Last Day.

Unstated here is the converse biblical truth: if an authority demands that a believer do something that is contrary to God's Word, then of course the believer is called to "obey God rather than men" (Acts 5:29), as the Christian martyrs have done (Rev 6:9).

17:12 This verse uses the metaphor of an angry bear sow robbed of her cubs. Those who frequent areas inhabited by bears know not to place themselves between a bear and her cubs, much less provoke her by stealing them. Yet even that is not as dangerous as encountering a fool caught up in his stupidity, spreading mayhem and destruction in the lives of those around him.

17:13 This verse notes that a person who repays a kindness with maliciousness is asking for trouble. It is foolish enough to repay evil for evil, escalating a minor infraction into a feud. To show ingratitude by attacking one's benefactor invites lasting enmity (cf. Mt 18:23–35; 21:33–44).

17:14 This verse first counsels one to avoid starting a fight. A quarrel is compared to a flood not only because both bring destruction, but also because there is no way to predict the damage that will be done or of controlling the course of events once it is unleashed. The second line adds that if a fight has already begun, one should quit before it becomes too fierce.

17:15 This verse proscribes actions whose foolishness should be obvious to all, but is not. Society is never served well when the innocent are punished and the guilty go free, but throughout human history many have used judicial systems to these ends. God, however, finds such behavior repulsive. Judges and governments are to act on God's behalf as they administer justice according to his Word (Rom 13:1–7; 1 Pet 2:13–14).

Note the forensic use of the verb צָדַק in the Hiphil (H), "pronounce righteous, acquit [as innocent]," which corresponds to δικαιόω, "justify," in the NT. God's own gracious form of justice is to be the one who "declares righteous/ justifies the ungodly" (Rom 4:5) through faith in Jesus Christ (Acts 13:38–39; Rom 3:20–30; 5:1). This justice does not simply ignore or dismiss sin; rather it is based on the atonement of Christ. Even though he was innocent, God allowed him to be convicted in order to suffer vicariously for us (Is 53:4–12; Mt 27:4, 19; Jn 18:38; 19:4, 6). The sinless one "became sin for us, that in him we might become the righteousness of God" (2 Cor 5:21). Such passages are the foundation for the biblical doctrine of forensic justification, in support of which the Lutheran Confessions cite Prov 17:15 (FC Ep III 7 and FC SD III 17).

17:16 This verse notes the futility of a fool attempting to purchase wisdom when his spiritual aptitude will prevent him from learning it. The money in his hand suggests simony (Acts 8:18–23): the fool thinks he can buy the priceless yet free gift of God by his grace (e.g., 3:13–15; 9:1–6; see also Is 55:1–3; Rev 22:17). In the same way, it is impossible to impart spiritual insight to those who continue to reject God and his Gospel. Jesus warns his disciples not to throw pearls before swine (Mt 7:6). Only as God the Holy Spirit works repentance and faith in those who hear God's Word are they enabled to receive and grow in wisdom by grace alone (e.g., Prov 1:3–7).

17:17 This verse is a definition of true friendship, which, like wisdom itself (17:16), cannot be secured by any amount of money. The brother here is not necessarily a biological relative, but a brother in the faith (Ps 133:1). A believer in the one true and triune God can provide enduring support in times of trouble. Such a faithful friend, bound by God's own gracious love, is a more certain source of love than a biological brother (Prov 18:24). See the friendship in faith between David and Jonathan (1 Sam 18:1), and between Naomi and Ruth the Moabitess.

17:18 This verse, like 6:1; 11:15; and 22:26, is a saying about ill-advised business deals. See the commentary on 6:1–5. This proverb is connected to the previous one by the catchword רֵעַ, translated "neighbor" here and "friend" in 17:17. The placement of this proverb in this position helps readers contemplate the difference between true friendship (17:17) and associations formed by economic circumstances (17:18; cf. 17:16).

17:19 This verse notes that those caught up in sin enjoy seeing and promoting strife. The meaning of the second line is disputed (see the textual note). The translation above takes it as a description of a bellicose man who builds his gate high as a defensive fortification, like a tower built on top of an ancient city wall, in anticipation of conflict. His excessive defensiveness invites attack by those who are just as contentious as he who builds the lofty means of self-protection.

17:20 This verse is somewhat ambiguous, since the negated imperfect verb in לֹ֣א יִמְצָא־ט֑וֹב could mean that the crooked mind "*will not* find good," "*cannot* find good," or "*does not* find good." The main point seems to be that those with sinful mindsets, who reject the work of the Holy Spirit, will not find the good that God offers in the Gospel because they are incapable of receiving it. "The mindset of the flesh is hostile toward God; it does not submit to the Law of God because it is not able [to do so]" (Rom 8:7; cf. 1 Cor 2:14). A crooked mind is straightened out and renewed when a person is baptized into Christ and raised to new life by the Spirit (Rom 6:1–4, 22; 7:22–8:11; 12:2). Baptized believers in Christ live "according to the Spirit," and they set their minds "on the things of the Spirit" (Rom 8:5).

The second line extends the "crooked mind" to its results in sinful speech and its everlasting consequence: eschatological "disaster."

17:21 This verse reminds those who read it of the importance of parents instructing their children in the wisdom of the Gospel so that their sons and daughters will not be fools (see also, e.g., 1:8–9; 2:1–5; 3:1–2; 4:3–4). This is good from the standpoint of parental love for children, a love that wants not only temporal good for them, but also their eternal good (see Deut 6:6–7; Prov 3:11–12; 22:6; Eph 6:4). Tragically, it also is a reminder of the consequences of failing to teach the Gospel to one's children (see 1 Sam 2:12, 34; 3:13; Mk 13:12; Rom 1:30; 2 Tim 3:2).

17:22 This proverb is connected to the previous one by a catchword, the root שׂמח: יְשַׂמַּ֣ח, "will … rejoice" (17:21), and שָׂמֵ֗חַ, "cheerful" (17:22). This verse repeats a theme from other proverbs: one's attitude can affect one's health (e.g., 14:30). Believers can have a spiritual disposition of rejoicing in the Lord always (see, e.g., 1 Sam 2:1; Pss 9:15 [ET 9:14]; 35:9; Phil 3:1; 4:4) because of his promise of "the resurrection of the body" to "life everlasting" (Apostles' Creed). This is the ultimate healing cure for sinners by the Great Physician.

17:23 This verse, like Prov 17:8 and 17:15, is about perverting justice, but it adds the emphasis of the secret payoff. Those who enter into such deals do not wish to have their actions known (see the commentary on 9:17). This is a caution against entering into secret deals that affect the public welfare. They may initially appear to be unobjectionable to those secretly involved, but they will be perceived as sinister when they come to light. Eventually, all will be made known (Mt 10:26–27).

17:24 This verse resembles Prov 4:25–27, which counsels the believer to keep his eyes (of faith) pointed straight ahead, and not to deviate to the right or left. The believer persists in the way of the Gospel by keeping divine wisdom in front of him (see Pss 16:8; 18:23 [ET 18:22]; 26:3; 56:14 [ET 56:13]).[4] He does not allow his eyes to be distracted, lest he wander far and wide in search of another "gospel," as fools do (Gal 1:6–9).[c]

(c) Cf. Amos 8:12; Pss 54:5 (ET 54:3); 119:21; Mt 24:23–26; Eph 4:14–15; 2 Tim 4:3–5

[4] For the relationship between wisdom and the Gospel, see "Wisdom in Proverbs" in the introduction. See also the commentary on 1:1–7; 3:13–20; 8:22–31; 30:1b–10; and the excursus "Proverbs 8, Wisdom, Christology, and the Arian Controversy" in the commentary on chapter 8.

Proverbs 17:25–18:24

Avoiding Fools and Foolishness, Part 1

Translation

17 [25]A foolish son is an aggravation to his father
and bitterness to her who bore him.
[26]It is neither good to fine a righteous person
nor to flog officials because of [their] uprightness.
[27]A person with knowledge is a person who restrains his words,
and a person with understanding is even-tempered.
[28]Even a stubborn fool who keeps silent will be considered wise.
He who keeps his lips shut [will be considered] a person with understanding.

18 [1]A loner seeks his own desire.
He fights against all sound judgment.
[2]A fool finds no pleasure in understanding,
but [he finds pleasure] only in revealing his own opinion.
[3]When a wicked person comes, contempt also comes,
and with dishonor [comes] disgrace.
[4]The words from a person's mouth are deep waters.
The fountain of wisdom is a flowing stream.
[5]It is not good to be partial toward a wicked person,
[thereby] depriving a righteous person of justice.

[6]A fool's lips enter a fight,
and his mouth invites beatings.
[7]A fool's mouth is his destruction,
and his lips are a trap for his soul.

[8]The words of a gossiper are like delicacies:
they go down to one's innermost being.
[9]A person who fails to do his work
is a brother to a vandal.

[10]The name of Yahweh is a strong tower:
a righteous person runs inside it and is protected.
[11]A rich person's wealth is his strong city;
in his conceit it is like a high wall.

[12]A person's heart is haughty before [his] destruction,
but humility precedes honor.
[13]The person who answers before he listens
has stupidity and dishonor.

[14]A person's spirit can endure illness,
but who can bear a stricken spirit?
[15]The heart of a discerning person acquires knowledge,
and the ear of wise people seeks knowledge.
[16]A person's gift makes room for him
and leads him into the presence of great people.

[17]The first person [to state] his case [appears to be] right,
[until] his neighbor comes and cross-examines him.
[18]The lot ends disputes
and decides between powerful people.
[19]An offended brother is more [impregnable] than a strong city,
and disputes are like a bar [across the gate] of a fortress.

[20]From the fruit of a man's mouth his stomach is satisfied;
he is satisfied with the harvest of his lips.
[21]Life and death are in the power of a tongue,
and those who love it will eat its fruit.

[22]The man who finds a wife finds a good thing,
and he obtains favor from Yahweh.
[23]A poor man speaks in pleas,
but a rich man answers confidently.
[24]A person with many friends may come to ruin,
but there is a kind of person who loves [you] and sticks [with you] even more than a brother [does].

Textual Notes

17:25 כַּעַס לְאָבִיו בֵּן כְּסִיל—The noun כַּעַס means "annoyance, aggravation," as in 12:16. For בֵּן כְּסִיל, "a foolish son," see the third textual note on 10:1.

וּמֶמֶר לְיוֹלַדְתּוֹ׃—The noun מֶמֶר, "bitterness," is a hapax legomenon, but its root verb, מָרַר, is relatively common. The suffixed Qal (G) participle of יָלַד (with לְ) is feminine, so לְיוֹלַדְתּוֹ refers to the foolish son's mother: "to *her* who bore him."

17:26 גַּם עֲנוֹשׁ לַצַּדִּיק לֹא־טוֹב—Note the play on words with 17:28, which also begins with גַּם, but in a different sense. The sequence of the particle גַּם, literally, "also," and negative לֹא, "no, not," means "neither … nor" (BDB, s.v. גַּם, 1; cf. GKC, § 153). The infinitive construct עֲנוֹשׁ, "to fine," is the subject of this nominal sentence, and the infinitive construct לְהַכּוֹת is the subject of the next clause (Joüon, § 124 b). עָנַשׁ, "to fine," is a legal penalty in Ex 21:22 and Deut 22:19. It recurs in Prov 21:11; 22:3; 27:12 (see also the cognate noun in 19:19). For the adjective צַדִּיק, here used substantivally, "righteous person," see "The Relationship between Wisdom and Righteousness in Proverbs" in "Wisdom in Proverbs" in the introduction. The phrase לֹא־טוֹב, literally, "(it is) not good," in combination with גַּם, goes with both lines of this proverb: "it is neither good … nor …"

לְהַכּוֹת נְדִיבִים עַל־יֹשֶׁר׃—Here עַל has the causal sense "because of, on account of." For the noun יֹשֶׁר, "straightness, uprightness," which is a synonym of צְדָקָה, "righteousness," see the first textual note on 2:13.

17:27 חוֹשֵׂךְ אֲמָרָיו יוֹדֵעַ דָּעַת—The participle חוֹשֵׂךְ is also used in 10:19 for "a person who restrains" or keeps in check his own speech. For the cognate accusative construction יוֹדֵעַ דָּעַת, literally, "a person knowing knowledge," see "דַּעַת, 'Knowledge,' and יָדַע, 'to Know' " in "Wisdom in Proverbs" in the introduction, as well as the commentary on 1:4, 7.

וְקַר־רוּחַ אִישׁ תְּבוּנָה׃—In this context the Kethib וְקַר, "and *cool* of spirit," makes better sense than the Qere, יְקַר־, "*precious* of spirit," which probably is a secondary reading caused by the confusion of *yod* in place of *waw*. "Cool-spirited" signifies an even temper that is not easily aroused or provoked to anger. The construct phrase קַר־רוּחַ is the opposite of קְצַר־רוּחַ, "short of spirit," that is, "short-tempered" or "impatient" (14:29).

The noun תְּבוּנָה, "understanding," which in this pericope recurs in 18:2, is cognate to בִּינָה and to the Niphal (N) participle נָבוֹן in 17:28 and 18:15. See "בִּינָה, 'Understanding,' and Related Words" in "Wisdom in Proverbs" in the introduction.

17:28 גַּם אֱוִיל מַחֲרִישׁ חָכָם יֵחָשֵׁב—See "אֱוִיל, 'Stubborn Fool,' and אִוֶּלֶת, 'Stupidity' " in "Fools in Proverbs" in the introduction. The Hiphil (H) of חָרַשׁ, "keep silent, be quiet," is used similarly to refer to a person of understanding in the second clause of 11:12. Its participle, מַחֲרִישׁ, has the durative nuance of one who "*keeps* silent," like the participle אֹטֵם in the next clause. Regarding חָכָם, "wise," see "חָכְמָה, 'Wisdom,' and Related Words" in "Wisdom in Proverbs" in the introduction.

אֹטֵם שְׂפָתָיו נָבוֹן׃—The Qal (G) participle אֹטֵם, "keeping shut," recurs in 21:13 but with "his ear" as the object instead of "his lips" (שְׂפָתָיו) here. Probably אֹטֵם שְׂפָתָיו is the subject of the implied verb יֵחָשֵׁב, "will be considered (to be)," in the previous clause, and the verb does double duty. The object נָבוֹן, "(considered) a person with understanding," is parallel to חָכָם in the preceding clause.

18:1 לְתַאֲוָה יְבַקֵּשׁ נִפְרָד—The prepositional phrase לְתַאֲוָה, literally, "for a desire," means "for the sake of his own desire." The subject of יְבַקֵּשׁ, "seeks," is the Niphal (N) participle נִפְרָד, which means a person who "separates himself" (see *HALOT*, s.v. פרד, Niphal, 2 b) from others (see Judg 4:11), that is, "a loner." This is an example of a Niphal (N) verb with a reflexive force, as a Greek verb in the middle voice can have.

בְּכָל־תּוּשִׁיָּה יִתְגַּלָּע׃—The preposition בְּ has the force of disadvantage, "against." For the noun, see "תּוּשִׁיָּה, 'Sound Judgment' " in "Wisdom in Proverbs" in the introduction. For the Hithpael (HtD) verb יִתְגַּלָּע, see the second textual note on 17:14.

18:2 כִּי אִם־בְּהִתְגַּלּוֹת לִבּוֹ׃—The combination כִּי אִם־ is restrictive: "but only." The verb in the preceding clause, the Qal (G) imperfect יַחְפֹּץ, "he delights, finds pleasure in [בְּ]," does double duty and is implied here. This explains the preposition בְּ on the Hithpael (HtD) infinitive construct of גָּלָה, which has some reflexive force, "reveal *oneself*" (*DCH*, s.v. גלה, Hithpael), since the fool displays the contents of לִבּוֹ, "his heart." Here the "heart" refers to his inner inclination and disposition (*HALOT*, 4), which becomes manifest outwardly in his thoughts and opinions.

18:3 רָשָׁע—Many scholars propose emending the concrete "wicked (person)" to the abstract noun רֶשַׁע, "wickedness," in an attempt to make it match the parallel abstract noun קָלוֹן, "dishonor."[1] However, the emendation is not needed, since Proverbs contains many inexact parallels. McCreesh notes: "The MT form [רָשָׁע] is quite acceptable since the impersonal terms are qualities adhering in a person and are the *result* of wickedness. The way to understand the proverb would be to see it as building disaster upon disaster with the arrival of the *rāšāʿ* ['wicked person']: *bûz* ['contempt'] followed by *qālôn* ['dishonor'], followed by *ḥerpâ* ['disgrace']."[2] The noun קָלוֹן, "dishonor," is followed by the noun חֶרְפָּה, "disgrace," also in 6:33.

18:4 מַיִם עֲמֻקִּים—"Deep water(s)" recurs in 20:5. The water imagery continues in the next clause.

נַחַל נֹבֵעַ מְקוֹר חָכְמָה׃—The noun נַחַל usually refers to a "wadi" that may run with torrents of water during the rainy season, but dries up in the summer (cf. 1 Ki 17:1–7).[3] However, here it is modified by the Qal (G) participle of נָבַע, which has the intransitive meaning that this wadi is always "flowing" with water. Compare the second textual note on 1:23, which has the transitive Hiphil (H) of נָבַע, "to pour out."

In place of the unique construct phrase מְקוֹר חָכְמָה, "fountain of wisdom," the LXX apparently was influenced by the more frequent מְקוֹר חַיִּים, "fountain of life" (10:11; 13:14; 14:27; 16:22), and so translated this as πηγὴ ζωῆς, "fountain of life." However, there is no reason to depart from the MT. The metaphor of a fountain providing divine wisdom is similar to Wisdom providing wine to drink in 9:5. Compare the water imagery in 5:15–18, including מָקוֹר, "fountain," in 5:18. Flowing water to drink and the outpouring of water are associated with gracious gifts from God also in, for example, Is 44:3–4; 55:1; Zech 13:1; Pss 1:3; 23:2; Jn 3:5; 4:10–14; 7:38–39; Rev 22:17. In the Sacrament of Christian Baptism, the application of water is accompanied by the outpouring of the Holy Spirit, the forgiveness of sins, and the gifts of faith and eternal life, all of which can be subsumed under the biblical meaning of divine "wisdom."[4]

18:5 שְׂאֵת פְּנֵי־רָשָׁע לֹא־טוֹב—Literally, "to lift up the face of a wicked person" is to treat him with partiality or unfair bias, to show favoritism to him (see *HALOT*, s.v. נשׂא, 5).

לְהַטּוֹת צַדִּיק בַּמִּשְׁפָּט׃—Literally, "to thrust aside a righteous person in judgment" is to ignore or suppress his legal claim and deny him justice (*HALOT*, s.v. נטה, Hiphil, 6). The Hiphil (H) infinitive construct (הַטּוֹת) with לְ forms a result clause: showing favoritism to the wicked (18:5a) has the result, intended or not, of depriving the righteous of justice (18:5b).

18:6 שִׂפְתֵי כְסִיל יָבֹאוּ בְרִיב—Literally, this is "the lips of a fool arrive at a fight." The verb יָבֹאוּ is masculine even though its subject, the dual of שָׂפָה, "lip," is feminine (GKC, § 145 u). The Qal (G) is intransitive. Many scholars advocate repointing it to

---

1 McKane, *Proverbs*, 521; Scott, *Proverbs, Ecclesiastes*, 112; Toy, *Proverbs*, 355; NIV; NJB; NRSV.

2 McCreesh, *Biblical Sound and Sense*, 125.

3 L. J. Coppes, "נַחַל," *TWOT* 2:570; L. A. Snijders, "נַחַל," *TDOT* 9:335–40.

4 See "Wisdom in Proverbs" in the introduction.

the transitive Hiphil (H) יָבִאוּ, the "lips bring strife" (NASB, NRSV), that is, cause a fight. However, that does not fit with the preposition בְּ on בְרִיב. The MT is understandable: a fool's lips come to a fight and make their presence known by contributing to the strife.

וּפִיו לְמַהֲלֻמוֹת יִקְרָא׃—The idiom קָרָא לְ, literally, "call to," can mean "summon, invite." The noun מַהֲלֻמוֹת occurs in the OT only here and in 19:29, both times plural, meaning "beatings" (*DCH*) or "blows" (BDB).

18:8 דִּבְרֵי נִרְגָּן כְּמִתְלַהֲמִים—This whole verse is repeated in 26:22. This clause means "the words of a gossiper are like delicacies." For נִרְגָּן, "gossiper," see the second textual note on 16:28. כְּמִתְלַהֲמִים is the Hithpael (HtD) participle (with כְּ) of the verb לָהַם, which occurs in the OT only here and in 26:22. The meaning is uncertain.[5] BDB understands the verb to mean "swallow greedily" (*HALOT* and *DCH* are similar). The Hithpael participle then apparently functions as a noun meaning "delicious food eagerly swallowed," that is, "delicacies" (*HALOT* and *DCH*; BDB is similar).

וְהֵם יָרְדוּ חַדְרֵי־בָטֶן׃—This clause introduced with explicative *waw* explains why the preceding clause is true: it is because, literally, "they [the words, like delicacies] descend into the innermost chambers of the belly." This refers to one's most inner being, as חַדְרֵי־בָטֶן means also in 20:27, 30; 26:22 (all with the pausal form בָטֶן).

18:9 גַּם מִתְרַפֶּה בִמְלַאכְתּוֹ—The Hithpael (HtD) participle of רָפָה refers to "a person who fails to do, perform," and בִמְלַאכְתּוֹ means "in his work." For the verb, see the textual note on 24:10.

אָח הוּא לְבַעַל מַשְׁחִית׃—Literally, this is "a brother is he to a master of destruction." בַּעַל, "master, owner," often is used in combination with another noun to designate a skill, inclination, or occupation. Here "master of destruction" refers to a "destroyer" (BDB, s.v. מַשְׁחִית) or "vandal." See the second textual note on 1:17.

18:10 מִגְדַּל־עֹז—Literally, this is "a tower of strength." עֹז is translated as an adjectival genitive: "strong tower," as also in the construct phrases קִרְיַת עֻזּוֹ, "his strong city" (literally, "the city of his strength"), in 18:11, and מִקִּרְיַת־עֹז, "than a strong city," in 18:19.

וְנִשְׂגָּב׃—The Niphal (N) of שָׂגַב can mean "be high" (see וּכְחוֹמָה נִשְׂגָּבָה, "(and) like a high wall" in 18:11) or "be exalted." Here it probably means that the righteous person is "(safely) *set on high*" (BDB, 2), that is, "protected" by Yahweh through the strength of his name. In Psalms the cognate noun מִשְׂגָּב often refers to God as the "refuge, stronghold" of his people.[a]

(a) E.g., Pss 9:10 (ET 9:9); 46:8, 12 (ET 46:7, 11); 59:10, 17–18 (ET 59:9, 16–17)

18:11 בְּמַשְׂכִּיתוֹ׃—The noun מַשְׂכִּית, from the root שׂכה, usually refers to idolatrous carved figures. Here and in Ps 73:7, it refers to a person's "imagination" or "conceit" (BDB, 2). A meaning such as "conceit" or "arrogance" is supported by the language of the next clause (18:12a).

18:12 לִפְנֵי־שֶׁבֶר יִגְבַּהּ לֵב־אִישׁ—Literally, "before a shattering, the heart of a man is high," this warning about arrogance has some of the same vocabulary as and a message similar to 16:18.

5 See the discussions in Delitzsch, *Proverbs*, 2:6–7; Toy, *Proverbs*, 359–60.

וְלִפְנֵי כָבוֹד עֲנָוָה׃—This repeats the second line of 15:33.

18:13 מֵשִׁיב דָּבָר בְּטֶרֶם יִשְׁמָע—Literally, "one who returns a word before he hears" is a person who gives an answer before listening to the person to whom he is responding (ESV, NASB, NIV, NRSV).

אִוֶּלֶת הִיא־לוֹ וּכְלִמָּה׃—Literally, "stupidity is it to him, and shame." The feminine pronoun הִיא, "it," refers to the abstract idea of the action (answering before listening) in the preceding clause. For the noun אִוֶּלֶת, see "אֱוִיל, 'Stubborn Fool,' and אִוֶּלֶת, 'Stupidity' " in "Fools in Proverbs" in the introduction.

18:14 רוּחַ־אִישׁ יְכַלְכֵּל מַחֲלֵהוּ—The verb כּוּל appears only here in Proverbs, and its Pilpel (D) can mean "sustain," "contain," or, as here, "endure." Literally, "a spirit of a man can endure his weakness/disease" must refer to the spirit of a believer, who is sustained through faith and joy despite his affliction. For comparable affirmations, see 14:30a; 15:13a; 17:22a. See also 1:23, where divine Wisdom promises the repentant, "I will pour out my Spirit for you," referring to the gift of the Holy Spirit, who sustains believers through all kinds of suffering until God brings them to the resurrection to everlasting life (Ps 51:14 [ET 51:12]; Rom 5:1–5; 8:6–11, 23; 14:17; 15:13).

וְרוּחַ נְכֵאָה מִי יִשָּׂאֶנָּה׃—Literally, this is "but a stricken spirit—who can bear it?" For רוּחַ נְכֵאָה, "a stricken spirit," see the second textual note on 15:13. The imperfect of נָשָׂא has a feminine pronominal suffix (with assimilated energic *nun*; Waltke-O'Connor, § 31.7.2a, including example 4), יִשָּׂאֶנָּה, "bear/endure *it*," which refers to the feminine noun רוּחַ, "spirit."

18:15 לֵב נָבוֹן יִקְנֶה־דָּעַת—This is identical to first line of 15:14 except for the verb יִקְנֶה, "acquires" (see the first textual note on 8:22), in place of "seeks." For לֵב נָבוֹן, "the heart of a discerning person," see the first textual note on 14:33. The noun דַּעַת (pausal: דָּעַת) is the direct object in both clauses of this verse. See "דַּעַת, 'Knowledge,' and יָדַע, 'to Know' " in "Wisdom in Proverbs" in the introduction, as well as the commentary on 1:4, 7.

18:19 אָח נִפְשָׁע מִקִּרְיַת־עֹז—The Niphal (N) participle נִפְשָׁע means that the "brother" (אָח) has been "sinned against, offended" (see *HALOT*). The comparison "than a strong city" apparently means that it is harder to win back the offended brother than it is to capture a fortified city.

The LXX has ἀδελφὸς ὑπὸ ἀδελφοῦ βοηθούμενος ὡς πόλις ὀχυρὰ καὶ ὑψηλή, "a brother who is helped by a brother is like a strong and high city." Similar are the Syriac, Targum, and Vulgate. These versions have prompted some to propose that נִפְשָׁע should be emended to מוֹשִׁיעַ or שׁוֹעַ,[6] which would make the parallelism with the second line antithetical. However, the text of this verse is clear, and it exhibits synonymous parallelism. This saying is in a collection of proverbs that rarely uses antithetical parallelism. See the excursus "The Organization of the Sayings in Solomon's Proverbs in Proverbs 10:1–22:16," including figure 11, "Predominant Kinds of Parallelism in Proverbs 10:1–22:16."

---

[6] *BHS* footnote; see also RSV.

18:20 מִפְּרִי פִי־אִישׁ תִּשְׂבַּע בִּטְנוֹ—The verb שָׂבַע, "be filled," with the preposition מִן, "from" (on מִפְּרִי), has the metaphorical meaning "be satisfied." See the second textual note on 1:31. Here the feminine noun בֶּטֶן, "belly, stomach," with suffix (בִּטְנוֹ), is the subject of the feminine verb תִּשְׂבַּע.

תְּבוּאַת שְׂפָתָיו יִשְׂבָּע׃—In this clause the man himself is the subject of the masculine verb יִשְׂבָּע, "he is satisfied," and the construct phrase תְּבוּאַת שְׂפָתָיו is an accusative of the material with which he is filled: "(with) the harvest of [provided by] his lips." For תְּבוּאָה, "harvest," see the textual note on 3:9.

18:21 מָוֶת וְחַיִּים בְּיַד־לָשׁוֹן—"Death and life are in the hand of a tongue" sounds like a mixed metaphor, but the noun יָד, "hand," here means "power" (ESV, NASB, NIV, NRSV). Both of the nouns מָוֶת, "death," and חַיִּים, "life," have a spiritual and eschatological meaning: each person faces either everlasting death in hell (מָוֶת in, e.g., 2:18; 5:5; 7:27; 8:36; 10:2) or the resurrection to everlasting life (חַיִּים in, e.g., 3:2, 18, 22; 4:10, 13, 22–23; 12:28).

וְאֹהֲבֶיהָ יֹאכַל פִּרְיָהּ׃—For the same figurative meaning of אָכַל, "eat," see the first textual note on 1:31. The feminine suffixes on אֹהֲבֶיהָ, "those who love *her/it*," and פִּרְיָהּ, "*her/its* fruit," refer to the feminine noun לָשׁוֹן, "tongue," at the end of the first line of the verse.

18:22 מָצָא אִשָּׁה מָצָא טוֹב—This is a conditional sentence (GKC, § 159 h; Joüon, § 167 a (1)): "*if* he finds a wife, he finds good." This impersonal expression conveys a truth applicable to any man, so it could be rendered as "*whoever* finds …" The same verb as used here, מָצָא (but imperfect), and the noun אִשָּׁה (but in construct) are in 31:10: אֵשֶׁת־ … מִי יִמְצָא, literally, "a wife … who can find?"

וַיָּפֶק רָצוֹן מֵיְהוָה׃—This is identical to the last line of 8:35; see the second textual note on that verse (cf. also 12:2a).

18:23 תַּחֲנוּנִים … עַזּוֹת׃—The contrasting modes of speech of the poor man and the rich man are, literally, "pleas for mercy" versus "strong things," respectively. The wealthy person "answers" with "strong things" produced by the backing of riches. This can be translated adverbially: "answers confidently."

18:24 אִישׁ רֵעִים לְהִתְרֹעֵעַ—This line has a play on the similar spelling and sounds of the plural of רֵעַ, "friend," and the Hithpael (HtD) infinitive לְהִתְרֹעֵעַ. The construct phrase אִישׁ רֵעִים, "a man of friends," means "a man who has many friends" (cf. 19:4). There is a cognate verb רָעָה, "be a friend," whose Hithpael (HtD) occurs in 22:24, but its infinitive (with לְ) would be לְהִתְרָעוֹת, "to make friends." Some advocate emending the text to that form on the basis of several ancient versions.[7] Some translations take the plural noun and the verb as cognates, including KJV and NKJV ("a man *who has* friends must himself be friendly").

However, the form לְהִתְרֹעֵעַ probably is from רָעַע II, "break, shatter." Its Hithpoel (HtD) also is found in Is 24:19, where it has a passive meaning, "be broken in pieces,"

[7] *BHS* footnote and BDB, s.v. רָעָה II, Hithpael, which also emends אִישׁ to יֵשׁ. These emendations are reflected in the RSV. Apparently *HALOT* also presupposes the emendation of אִישׁ to יֵשׁ, "there are friends who … ," since it gives a reciprocal meaning for the verb, "smash one another" (s.v. רעע II, Hithpoel, 2).

as is the case here. The infinitive probably has a hypothetical meaning, "a man who has many friends *may* come to ruin." Similar are NIV, ESV, and NASB.

וְיֵשׁ אֹהֵב דָּבֵק מֵאָח׃—For the construction יֵשׁ plus a participle, see the first textual note on 11:24. Here the construction has the participle אֹהֵב, meaning "there is a kind of person who loves ..." The adjective דָּבֵק, "clinging, sticking to," is cognate to the verb דָּבַק, "cling," which refers to relatives who remain close friends in faith (Ruth with Naomi) in Ruth 1:14 and to the union of a husband with his wife in Gen 2:24. The verb refers to faithful adherence to God and his Word in, for example, Deut 10:20; 11:22; 13:5 (ET 13:4); 30:20; Josh 22:5; 23:8.

Commentary

A Foolish Son: Avoiding Fools and Foolishness (17:25–19:12)

This fourth loose section (17:25–19:12) of Solomon's proverbs in 10:1–22:16 begins with a saying about a foolish son.[8] The proverbs in this section concentrate on teaching people how to avoid foolish behavior and fools. These proverbs discourage foolish actions and speech, discourage one from associating with others that display foolish behavior, help one identify fools and their foolishness, and encourage attitudes and acts that will lead away from foolishness toward wisdom.

Earlier Solomon established the Gospel basis for his proverbs.[9] In this section Solomon introduces few explicit references to the Gospel, but he now expects readers to understand that the Gospel supports all that is said here. Among the few proverbs that explicitly point to the Gospel in this section are the fountain and flowing stream of divine wisdom (18:4); the commending of knowledge and wisdom, which ultimately are the knowledge and wisdom of God in the Gospel (18:15; 19:8); and the power of the word (18:20–21). Prov 18:21 pertains especially to the power of the proclaimed Word of God, since his Law condemns sinners to "death," but his Gospel forgives sinners and grants them new and eternal "life" (18:21).

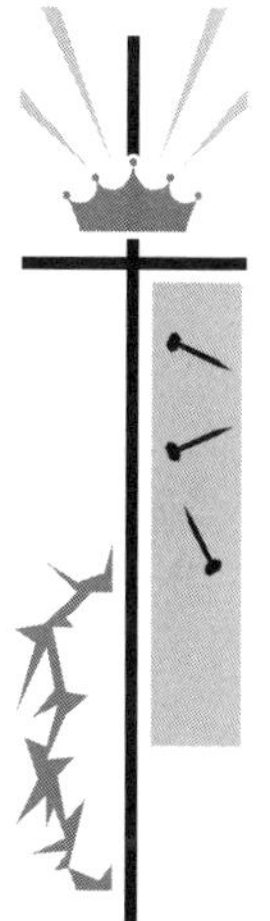

Avoiding Fools and Foolishness, Part 1 (17:25–18:24)

17:25 This verse contrasts with 10:1 and 15:20 in that the foolish son is said to be a detriment to both father and mother. In those two earlier proverbs the foolish son is connected with his mother, while the wise son is connected with his father. However, both parents are involved in, for example, 1:8 and 4:3.

17:26 This verse observes the counterproductive nature of punishing those who are righteous and upright. It does not explore the reasons why such

---

[8] The reasons for considering this to be a section are discussed in the excursus "The Organization of the Sayings in Solomon's Proverbs in Proverbs 10:1–22:16" in the commentary on Proverbs 10.

[9] See especially the commentary on 1:1–7; 3:13–20; 8:22–31; 30:1b–10; and the excursus "Proverbs 8, Wisdom, Christology, and the Arian Controversy" in the commentary on chapter 8. See also "Law and Gospel in Proverbs" in the introduction.

punishment is evil, nor does it dwell on the necessity of the theology of the cross for believers (see Acts 14:22; 1 Pet 4:12–19). Many practical reasons can also be given for why it is bad for society to persecute those who are doing good (see Prov 18:5). This proverb's silence about these further matters simply implies that persecution of the righteous is intrinsically evil, but God will rectify this injustice according to his own schedule. On the Last Day believers will be publicly vindicated and glorified.

17:27 This verse equates controlling one's words with being even-tempered. Often a lack of self-control manifests itself in a torrent of thoughtless words.

17:28 This verse is the antithetical counterpart of 17:27. Even the most empty-headed fool who does not speak could be considered wise, since his stupidity has not been exposed by his own vacuous words.

18:1 While נִפְרָד, literally, "one who separates himself," has been understood as a hermit (NRSV, NJB) or as unfriendly (NIV), it is best to understand this person as "a *loner*," a person who isolates himself socially, even if he lives among others or if he is outwardly friendly. This person is isolated because he seeks only his own desires and fights against all תּוּשִׁיָּה, "sound judgment," which is connected with the welfare of others (2:7).

18:2 This verse helps define foolishness: it is a failure to accept wisdom from God (see 1:7) or from others who have understanding. It usually is accompanied by a proclivity to promulgate one's own opinions as if they were beyond criticism.

18:3 This verse notes that sinful behaviors have consequences. The proverb does not state whether the wicked person shows contempt toward the others he meets or whether it is the wicked person himself who elicits contempt from others. Perhaps the idea is that the contempt is mutual.

18:4 This verse is difficult because of the enigmatic "deep waters" (also in 20:5). The most probable meaning of the first line is that a person's words reveal what is deep inside him. The second line compares the source of wisdom (ultimately God himself, and secondarily, people who have received his wisdom) to a stream that is never exhausted. Unlike a common wadi that is merely a dry riverbed during most of the year, in this case there is never a lack of water in the stream or a lack of wisdom from its source.

Note the parallel depiction of the life-giving water issuing from God's temple in Ezek 47:1–12 and also the words of Jesus himself in Jn 4:14 and 7:38–39, fulfilled in Baptism (see the second textual note on Prov 18:4). God's grace never runs dry, and it provides forgiveness and life for all who drink from it. In fact, wisdom here is depicted as flowing from God's favor toward humanity, even as Ezekiel depicts the ever-flowing stream in the new Jerusalem, with the tree of life growing on its banks (see also Rev 22:1–2, 14).

18:5 This verse again (see Prov 17:26) takes up the theme of justice as it relates to human jurisprudence and governance. Favoring the wicked and depriving the righteous is not good—not only because of the practical consequences for order in society, but especially because this is contrary to God's nature.[b] Those who administer justice are God's representatives for civil life. He expects them to be fair and impartial, even as he is (e.g., Deut 16:19; 2 Chr 19:7; Rom 2:11; Eph 6:9).

(b) See, e.g., Deut 20:16–18; Lk 20:21; Acts 10:34; Rom 2:11; Gal 2:6; Eph 6:9; Col 3:25; 1 Pet 1:17

18:6 This verse is a reminder that fools get themselves into trouble by their words even when their words are not intended to provoke a fight.

18:7 This verse is linked to 18:6 by theme and by wording. Note the chiasm:

A A fool's lips (שִׂפְתֵ֣י כְ֭סִיל, 18:6a)
  B And his mouth (וּ֝פִ֗יו, 18:6b)
  B' A fool's mouth (פִּֽי־כְ֭סִיל, 18:7a)
A' And his lips (וּ֝שְׂפָתָ֗יו, 18:7b)

This saying goes beyond 18:6 as it widens the application from the temporal trouble a fool invites by his foolish talk to the eternal destruction his words will bring him (see Mt 12:37; Lk 19:22).

18:8 This verse compares the temptation to break the Eighth Commandment to the appeal of delicious food. The commandment is violated both by the gossiper who spreads rumors and by those who listen and believe the tales. The statement that the gossip goes down to one's innermost being is a commentary on the profound and lasting personal corruption caused by gossip and the prejudice it creates. This proverb is repeated in 26:22.

18:9 This verse states that there is no such thing as benign neglect when it comes to work. The lazy person may not think of his failure to work as destructive, but it is insidiously damaging. It is less obvious than a vandal's harm, but it is just as hurtful as the vandal's willful act.

18:10 This verse is one of several proverbs that use military imagery (18:19 is another in this chapter). This is the only verse in Proverbs that uses the phrase "the name of Yahweh." This saying is a positive application of the Second Commandment.[10] Those who trust in God are pictured as fleeing to him for protection, which he surely provides. Since God has given us his name, he is pleased when we use it properly (see LC I 63–74). This is a Gospel invitation: "everyone who calls on the name of Yahweh/the Lord will be saved" (Joel 3:5 [ET 2:32]; Acts 2:21; Rom 10:13).

18:11 This verse is tied to 18:10 by military imagery and by the catchwords עֹז, translated as "strong," and the Niphal of שָׂגַב, translated as "is protected" (18:10) and "high" (18:11). At the same time an implicit contrast is created by these two proverbs. Here the protection is afforded by wealth, whereas in 18:10 it was Yahweh's saving name. The first line of this proverb is identical to the first line of 10:15.

---

10 See further the excursus "Proverbs 1–9, Christ, and the Ten Commandments" in the commentary on Proverbs 1.

18:12 This verse combines the thought of 16:18 in the first line with the second line of 15:33. In this way it creates a contrast between arrogance and humility.

18:13 This verse is another proverb about the foolishness of speaking in ignorance. It is impossible to reply to the concerns of others if one does not first listen to them.[11] Not listening to others is a mark of stupidity.

18:14 This verse notes that a good spiritual attitude can aid during physical illness. Ultimately, the cure God promises all believers is the resurrection of the body to be glorious and incorruptible (1 Corinthians 15). Conversely, "a stricken spirit" implies a lack of faith in the resurrection; such a person is without hope (cf. 1 Cor 15:13–19).

18:15 This verse begins with a variation of the first line of 15:14. The only difference is that in this saying the heart "acquires" (יִקְנֶה) knowledge, whereas in 15:14 it "seeks" (יְבַקֶּשׁ) it. Earlier in Proverbs, divine Wisdom calls on others to seek and acquire knowledge (e.g., 9:1–6). This proverb notes that those whose hearts have been given the gift of wisdom seek it out and find it. Thus Peter urges his readers who know the wisdom of the Gospel, "Like newborn infants, crave pure spiritual milk, that by it you may grow up in salvation" (1 Pet 2:2).

18:16 This verse observes that often in life people gain influence by what they provide for others. This proverb is not, however, endorsing bribery, which is condemned in, for example, 17:8, 23. The phrase, literally, "the gift of a man" (מַתָּן אָדָם) is not necessarily a subjective genitive (a gift given by a person). It could be an objective genitive, "a person's gift" given to him by God, which he then uses faithfully for the benefit of others, who promote and reward him. For example, Joseph used his God-given gift of interpreting dreams to benefit others, and he in turn was promoted to such a position of influence that he was able to save his relatives (Genesis 40–47). This interpretation of Prov 18:16 is supported by 18:20 and the reference in 18:14 to the gift of being able to endure disease and suffering. It is also supported by the many proverbs in which divine Wisdom promises to give beneficial gifts to those who repent and believe (e.g., 1:2–9, 23, 33; 2:1–10).

18:17 This verse is a warning about the ease in which justice can be swayed by partiality. Both sides of a dispute need to be heard, and each must be cross-examined.

18:18 This verse continues the theme of disagreements and lawsuits begun in 18:17. Here the lot is an appeal to divine guidance (see the commentary on 16:33). The casting of lots was not merely a random way of deciding a matter, but was an impartial way of determining God's will (see, e.g., Josh 18:8–10; Acts 1:24–26). In some disputes between powerful people, only God, the most powerful, can enforce a decision.

---

[11] McKane, *Proverbs*, 515.

18:19 This verse is connected to 18:18 by the catchword מִדְיָנִים, "disputes." An offended friend (the probable meaning of "brother" here) is harder to win over in a dispute because of a sense of betrayal. The wall erected by such offense is easy to put up, but hard to tear down.[12]

18:20 This verse is the first of a pair of proverbs about the power of speech. They are linked by the catchword פְּרִי, "fruit." This saying speaks of the ability of a good speaker to make a living from his words (see also 12:14; 13:2). This is especially pertinent for a faithful preacher of God's Word, the Gospel of Jesus Christ (Jn 4:35–36; 1 Cor 9:14; 1 Tim 5:17–18).

18:21 This verse goes beyond the economic power of speech to its power to change, give, and even take life. Spoken words have consequences that can result in temporal life or death, as when a judge or jury acquits or convicts. The Word of God coming from a person's tongue has the power of the Gospel to give everlasting life to all believers and the force of the Law to condemn unbelievers eternally to hell. Every Christian applies this power when he rebukes an erring brother or forgives another in the name of Christ. In the church, this power is wielded by the pastor as he exercises the office of the keys and pronounces absolution upon the penitent or retains the sins of the impenitent. This may also involve excommunication of the unrepentant sinner (1 Cor 5:3–5, 13) and gracious reinstatement of the sinner who repents (2 Cor 2:5–11). See further the commentary on Prov 17:9.

The second line states that "those who love" the tongue "will eat its fruit." This might be understood in a negative sense: the proclaimed Word of God condemns the preacher's own sins even as it condemns those of his hearers. Yet the context supports a positive understanding: evangelists and preachers benefit from the Gospel, just as those who hear them benefit if they believe the Good News. This is true about spiritual benefits and also applies to pastors who earn their living from their faithful ministries (see the commentary on 18:20).

18:22 This verse says the blessings of marriage can include Yahweh's favor (cf. 31:10–31). Note the parallel between finding a wife and obtaining wisdom (compare this verse with 8:35; see also Gen 2:18). It is worth great effort to obtain a godly wife because of the way in which marriage strengthens both believing spouses in the faith, through which each receives God's gracious favor. See Genesis 24, and contrast Gen 27:46. Christian marriage involves the "great mystery" of Christ the Savior and his redeemed church (Eph 5:21–33).

18:23 This verse is one of several proverbs that note the weak and dependent position of poor people in contrast to the independence and confidence that riches can provide (see also 10:15; 14:20; 18:11; 19:4, 7; 22:7). This is an observation about life rather than a divine endorsement of earthly wealth. Yet it can apply to the confidence evident in those who possess the infinite treasure

---

[12] Kidner, *Proverbs*, 130.

of God's riches in Christ, no matter how poor or uneducated they may be (see Acts 4:13).

18:24 This verse first notes the fickle nature of many human relationships. The first line may mean that friends can turn against one another (compare Job 2:11 with Job 12:4; 16:20; see also Ps 41:10 [ET 41:9], quoted by Jesus in Jn 13:18). Or it may mean that having many friends cannot prevent a person from self-destructing (see the first textual note on this verse). Human friendships are not able to save as Yahweh does (Prov 18:10), nor are ordinary friendships as valuable as a good wife (18:22).

The second line perhaps alludes to a godly, faithful spouse (18:22) as a believer who will, by God's grace, remain a constant and loving friend.[13] It may also refer to God as the one who steadfastly loves and remains with a believer forever.[c]

(c) Deut 31:6–8; Josh 1:5; Jn 14:3, 23; 15:14–15; Heb 13:5

[13] In Song 5:1 the chorus calls the married lovers "friends," רֵעִים, the same word as in Prov 18:24a. In context this means that the husband and wife are best "friends" to each other.

Proverbs 19:1–12

Avoiding Fools and Foolishness, Part 2

Translation

19 1 Better is a poor person walking in his integrity
than a person with crooked lips who is a fool.
2 Also without knowledge, desire is not good,
and a person who rushes with [his] feet sins.
3 A person's own stupidity distorts his way,
and his heart rages against Yahweh.
4 Wealth adds many friends,
but a poor person is separated from his friend.
5 A false witness will not go unpunished;
he breathes lies and will not escape.
6 Many seek the good will of a ruler,
and everyone is a friend to a person who gives gifts.
7 The entire family of a poor person hates him.
How much more do his friends keep their distance from him!
Though he chases them with words, they are not [near him].
8 A person who acquires a mind loves himself.
A person who guards understanding finds a good thing.
9 A false witness will not go unpunished;
he breathes lies and will perish.
10 Luxury is not fitting for a fool,
much less [is it fitting] for a slave to rule over princes.
11 A person's good sense makes him slow to anger,
and it is to his credit that he overlooks an offense.
12 The king's anger is like a lion's growl,
but his favor is like dew on grass.

Textual Notes

19:1 טֽוֹב־רָ֭שׁ הוֹלֵ֣ךְ בְּתֻמּ֑וֹ—This clause is repeated in 28:6. For "better … than" (טוֹב … מִן) proverbs, see "Direct Comparisons" in "Authorship and Date" the introduction. For the substantival participle רָשׁ, "poor person," which recurs in this pericope in 19:7, see the first textual note on 10:4. For the noun תֹּם, "integrity, blamelessness," a synonym of "righteousness" through faith alone, see the second textual note on 2:7.

מֵעִקֵּ֥שׁ שְׂ֝פָתָ֗יו וְה֣וּא כְסִֽיל׃—For the adjective עִקֵּשׁ, "crooked" (here with מִן), see the first textual note on 2:15. It is in construct with שְׂפָתָיו, "his lips," meaning that this person's crookedness is evident specifically in his speech. He is also called כְּסִיל, "a fool." See "כְּסִיל, 'Fool,' and כְּסִילוּת, 'Foolishness' " in "Fools in Proverbs" in the introduction.

Prov 28:6 is identical to 19:1 except that in the second clause it has דְּרָכַיִם, literally, “two ways,” in place of שְׂפָתָיו, “his lips,” and עָשִׁיר, “a rich man,” in place of כְסִיל, “a fool.” In many Hebrew manuscripts of 19:1, שְׂפָתָיו is replaced by דְּרָכָיו. Some interpreters wish to emend כְּסִיל in this verse to עָשִׁיר, as in 28:6,[1] which would make a stronger antithetical parallel to “poor.” עָשִׁיר is not found in 19:1 in any Hebrew manuscript, but it is supported by the Syriac. However, most likely the MT retains the original wording of 19:1, and copyists of some manuscripts inadvertently harmonized wording in 19:1 to match 28:6.

19:2 גַּם בְּלֹא־דַעַת נֶפֶשׁ לֹא־טוֹב—Literally, “also with no knowledge, a soul/desire is not good.” See “דַּעַת, ‘Knowledge,’ and יָדַע, ‘to Know’ ” in “Wisdom in Proverbs” in the introduction, as well as the commentary on 1:4, 7. Here נֶפֶשׁ could refer to the “soul” of a person (KJV, NKJV) or his “desire” (ESV).

וְאָץ בְּרַגְלַיִם חוֹטֵא׃—The verb אוּץ, “hasten, rush, hurry,” occurs in Proverbs only as the Qal (G) participle (also 21:5; 28:20; 29:20). For חוֹטֵא, see the first textual note on 8:36.

19:3 אִוֶּלֶת אָדָם תְּסַלֵּף דַּרְכּוֹ—For אִוֶּלֶת, see “אֱוִיל, ‘Stubborn Fool,’ and אִוֶּלֶת, ‘Stupidity’ ” in “Fools in Proverbs” in the introduction. The feminine noun אִוֶּלֶת is the subject of תְּסַלֵּף. For the Piel (D) of סָלַף, “pervert, twist, distort,” see the second textual note on 13:6. Regarding דַּרְכּוֹ, “his way,” see “The Metaphor of the Path in Solomon’s Wisdom” in the commentary on Proverbs 10.

19:4 וְדָל מֵרֵעֵהוּ יִפָּרֵד׃—In 18:1 the Niphal (N) participle of פָּרַד, “separate,” has a reflexive meaning (“a loner” who separates himself from others), but here its Niphal (N) imperfect has a passive meaning: “a poor person [דָּל] is separated [יִפָּרֵד] from his friend [מֵרֵעֵהוּ].” The fickle “friend” abandons his fellow when he becomes poor (cf. 18:24).

19:5 עֵד שְׁקָרִים לֹא יִנָּקֶה וְיָפִיחַ כְּזָבִים לֹא יִמָּלֵט׃—Most of this vocabulary is repeated from earlier. See the first textual note on 6:19 and the second textual note on 6:29. The *waw* on וְיָפִיחַ could have concessive force, “*although* he breathes lies,” or causal force, “*because* he …” The Niphal (N) of מָלַט means “escape, be delivered,” and occurs also in 11:21 and 28:26. That verb negated, לֹא יִמָּלֵט, “he will not escape,” is equivalent to יֹאבֵד, “he will perish,” since 19:5 is repeated in 19:9 but with יֹאבֵד in place of לֹא יִמָּלֵט.

19:6 רַבִּים יְחַלּוּ פְנֵי־נָדִיב—The verb חָלָה II always occurs in the Piel (D) with פְּנֵי (“the face of” someone) as its object, meaning “entreat the favor of” someone (see BDB, s.v. חָלָה II). This is an idiom for seeking to be in someone’s good graces (see *HALOT*, s.v. חלה I, Piel, 1). Usually the idiom refers to a person seeking God’s grace, but here and in Ps 45:13 (ET 45:12) and Job 11:19, it refers to seeking favor from another person.

וְכָל־הָרֵעַ לְאִישׁ מַתָּן׃—Literally, “everyone is the friend to a man of gift(s),” this means that everyone tries to befriend a gift-giver. The noun מַתָּן, “gift,” is also in 18:16 and 21:14 and is derived from the verb נָתַן, “to give.”

---

[1] Scott, *Proverbs, Ecclesiastes*, 115; Toy, *Proverbs*, 368.

19:7 כָּל אֲחֵי־רָ֨שׁ ׀ שְֽׂנֵאֻ֗הוּ—The noun אָח, "brother," can more generally denote blood relatives of all sorts (*HALOT*, s.v. אָח II, 3). Here its plural in, literally, "all brothers of a poor person" denotes the poor person's entire extended family.

אַ֣ף כִּ֣י מְ֭רֵעֵהוּ רָחֲק֣וּ מִמֶּ֑נּוּ—The combination אַף כִּי means "how much more" (also in 11:31; 15:11; 21:27) or "how much less" (17:7; 19:10). The singular noun מֵרֵעַ (with suffix, מְרֵעֵהוּ) occurs only here in Proverbs and has the collective meaning "friends," as also in 2 Sam 3:8, where too it is parallel to אַחִים, "brothers" (there with a suffix). Hence the singular is the subject of the plural verb רָחֲקוּ, literally, "are/stay far away."

מְרַדֵּ֖ף אֲמָרִ֣ים לֹא־הֵֽמָּה׃—This phrase is difficult. Following the Kethib לֹא (rather than the Qere, לוֹ), it, literally, says, "the one who pursues words, not they." The singular participle מְרַדֵּף, "pursues," must refer to the singular "poor person" (רָשׁ) in the first clause of the verse. אֲמָרִים may be an adverbial accusative, "pursues with/using words, verbally chases." The plural pronoun הֵמָּה, "they," must refer to his "brothers" (אֲחֵי־) or "his friends" (מְרֵעֵהוּ). The meaning of the line must be something like the translation offered above.

Nearly all commentators would omit this third line of 19:7 as a corrupt line, especially since none of the other three hundred seventy-four proverbs in 10:1–22:16 contain a third line.[2] After the first two lines of 19:7, Delitzsch attempts a reconstruction on the basis of the LXX.[3] His conjecture is not convincing. This line may be a remnant of an original proverb by Solomon that was corrupted by a copyist.

19:8 קֹֽנֶה־לֵּ֭ב אֹהֵ֣ב נַפְשׁ֑וֹ—For קָנָה, "acquire," see the first textual note on 8:22. On לֵב as "mind," see the first textual note on 2:10. In the phrase אֹהֵב נַפְשׁוֹ, the suffixed object נַפְשׁוֹ has a reflexive meaning: "loving himself" (Joüon, § 146 k).

שֹׁמֵ֥ר תְּ֝בוּנָ֗ה לִמְצֹא־טֽוֹב׃—This is, literally, "keeping understanding to find good." In such a context an infinitive construct (לִמְצֹא) can have the force of an imperfect verb expressing a promise to be fulfilled soon: "will find" (Waltke-O'Connor, § 36.2.3g, example 48). Some have proposed changing the infinitive to the imperfect יִמְצָא on the basis of the LXX's εὑρήσει. However, the Hebrew grammar is perfectly fine, and the preposition לְ fits the sound pattern of the proverb.[4]

19:9 See the textual note on 19:5.

19:10 לֹא־נָאוֶ֣ה לִכְסִ֣יל תַּעֲנ֑וּג—For לֹא־נָאוֶה, "not fitting," see the first textual note on 17:7. Here the subject of the nominal clause is the masculine noun תַּעֲנוּג, "luxury," which is not fitting for a fool, because in his self-absorbed arrogance, he will not appreciate it as God's blessing.

אַ֤ף כִּֽי־לְעֶ֬בֶד ׀ מְשֹׁ֬ל בְּשָׂרִֽים׃—"How much less" (אַף כִּי־) is it fitting for a "slave" (עֶבֶד) "to rule over" (מְשֹׁל בְּ) "princes" (שָׂרִים).

19:11 הֶאֱרִ֣יךְ אַפּ֑וֹ—Literally, "he lengthens [the time before] his anger," this idiom with the Hiphil (H) of אָרַךְ, "lengthen, prolong," is similar to the meaning of the phrase

---

2 Garrett, *Proverbs*, 171, n. 358; McKane, *Proverbs*, 527; Murphy, *Proverbs*, 141; Scott, *Proverbs, Ecclesiastes*, 112; Toy, *Proverbs*, 370.

3 Delitzsch, *Proverbs*, 2:25.

4 McCreesh, *Biblical Sound and Sense*, 100.

with the cognate noun, אֶרֶךְ אַפַּיִם, literally, "long of anger" or "slow to anger," for which, see the textual note on 14:29.

וְתִפְאַרְתּוֹ עֲבֹר עַל־פָּשַׁע׃—Literally, this is "and his glory (is) to pass over a transgression." The noun תִּפְאֶרֶת means "fame, honor" (see *HALOT*, 3) or "glory." The translation "it is to his credit" is intended in the sense that faith is credited to the believer as righteousness (Gen 15:6). God promises to reward faithfulness and a forgiving spirit, whether or not people appreciate this trait (Gen 15:1; Mt 5:7). This proverb conveys an eschatological promise to be realized on the Last Day (Ps 84:12 [ET 84:11]; Dan 12:3; Jn 17:24).

The verb עָבַר, "pass over," in this case means "overlook, forgive." This can involve confession by the transgressor and absolution by the person with good spiritual sense (see the commentary on 17:9 and 18:21), rather than simply ignoring sin or pretending that it is not evil (see 28:13). פֶּשַׁע (pausal: פָּשַׁע), "transgression," recalls earlier proverbs about forgiveness that use this term (10:12; 17:9).

19:12 נַהַם כַּכְּפִיר זַעַף מֶלֶךְ—Literally, "a growl like [that of] the lion is the indignation of a king," this is repeated as the first line of 20:2 except with the synonymous phrase אֵימַת מֶלֶךְ, "the fearful anger of a king," instead of זַעַף מֶלֶךְ, "the indignation/anger of a king."

וּכְטַל עַל־עֵשֶׂב רְצוֹנוֹ׃—The noun רָצוֹן usually refers to God's gift of "favor, grace" (see the second textual note on 8:35). Here, however, and in 14:35; 16:13, 15, it refers to the king's favor or goodwill.

Commentary

These verses (19:1–12) conclude the fourth section (17:25–19:12) in 10:1–22:16. This loose section began with the saying about a foolish son in 17:25.[5]

19:1 This verse is one of several proverbs that state that it is preferable to live in poverty as a faithful believer than it is to prosper in sin (see also 16:19; 19:22; 28:6). The second line equates dishonesty with being a fool. This is because God sees through dishonesty, and it is foolish to incur his punishment, which will be for all unbelievers to perish eternally (19:5, 9).

19:2 This verse is connected with 19:1 by טוֹב, "better/good." This saying emphasizes that without knowledge (i.e., without faith in God's Word, which affords knowledge of his wisdom and ways), a desire for gain leads to outcomes that are bad ("not good"). The second line applies this to a person who is in a hurry to receive quick rewards for his effort and is willing to cut corners ethically to reach his goals.

19:3 This verse notes that spiritual stupidity distorts one's way of life and causes rebellion in anger against God. This saying clearly connects stupidity to

---

5 The reasons for considering this to be a section are discussed in the excursus "The Organization of the Sayings in Solomon's Proverbs in Proverbs 10:1–22:16" in the commentary on Proverbs 10. See also "A Foolish Son: Avoiding Fools and Foolishness (17:25–19:12)" in the commentary on 17:25–18:24.

hatred for God (see Rom 1:30; Rev 16:9, 11). It thereby implies that wisdom leads to the opposite: love for God (see Deut 6:5; Pss 31:24 [ET 31:23]; 97:10).

19:4 This proverb needs to be interpreted in light of 19:1. It is not a commendation of wealth gained unscrupulously, but an observation about how wealth influences friendships (cf. 18:23). In this life the rich enjoy certain advantages over the poor (see also, e.g., 10:15; 13:8; 14:20; 18:23). At the same time, this proverb serves as a warning to the rich about the fickle nature of many of their friendships (cf. 18:24; 19:6).

19:5 This verse is one of five proverbs that describe false witnesses as breathing lies (the others are 6:19; 14:5, 25; 19:9). This saying and 19:9 observe that such a liar will not be able to lie his way out of being punished by God. The devil is the father of lies and of liars who reject God's truth in Jesus (Jn 8:42–45). The parallel between "will not escape" in 19:5 and "will perish" in 19:9 shows that unless they repent and believe in Christ, such liars will be punished by everlasting perdition.

19:6 This verse notes that a person who can bestow favors on others by using his power or wealth will have many friends. Like 9:4, it is a tacit warning to those who attract such friends that their friendships may not be lasting or based on love (cf. 18:24).

19:7 This verse is a direct contrast to 19:6 and is connected to it by the catchword כֹּל, "everyone/entire," and the synonymous cognates רֵעַ, "friend" (19:6), and מֵרֵעַ, "friend(s)" (19:7). Poverty is preferable compared to sin (19:1), but it is not without its disadvantages.

19:8 This verse encourages the search for wisdom, especially the understanding of God that comes through faith in his Gospel.[6] This is the knowledge that is termed a good thing here. Contrast 1 Cor 8:1, where St. Paul warns against another kind, the presumption of wisdom used as a pretext for offensive behavior: "Concerning food sacrificed to idols, we know that 'we all have knowledge.' Knowledge puffs up, but love builds up."

19:9 See the commentary on 19:5.

19:10 Luxury is not fitting for a fool because in his self-absorbed arrogance, he will not appreciate it as God's gracious, undeserved blessing. It is even less fitting for a slave to govern princes because of the arrogance he would exhibit by usurping their God-given authority. Even though all believers are equal members of God's kingdom (Gal 3:26–29), God calls each of us to submit to the proper authorities (see Eph 6:5–9; cf. Philemon 15–17).

19:11 This verse links patience with clemency. Rather than losing one's temper, it is better to forgive, even as God in Christ has forgiven us (see Mt 18:34–35; Lk 11:4).

---

6 See "Law and Gospel in Proverbs" and "Wisdom in Proverbs" in the introduction. See also the commentary on 1:1–7; 3:13–20; 8:22–31; 30:1b–10; and the excursus "Proverbs 8, Wisdom, Christology, and the Arian Controversy" in the commentary on chapter 8.

19:12 This verse continues the theme of anger, noting that a king's anger is like an aroused lion's growl. Both indicate that an attack will soon overwhelm whomever has provoked it. In contrast the king's favor is benevolent, like the "dew" that waters the grass—a term that can describe God's blessings of grace (Gen 27:28; Micah 5:6 [ET 5:7]; Ps 133:3; Prov 3:20), even the resurrection (Is 26:19; Ps 110:3).

Proverbs 19:13–29

Dealing with Fools, Part 1

Translation

19 [13]A foolish son is a disaster to his father,
and a quarrelsome wife is constantly dripping water.
[14]Home and wealth are an inheritance from ancestors,
but a wife with good sense is from Yahweh.

[15]Laziness makes one fall into a deep sleep,
and an idle person will go hungry.
[16]The person who keeps a command guards his life.
The person who despises his [Yahweh's] ways will die.
[17]The person who is gracious to the poor lends to Yahweh;
he will repay him in full.

[18]Discipline your son while there is hope,
and do not make yourself responsible for his death.
[19][A person with] great anger is responsible for [paying] a fine.
If you rescue [him] you will have to do it repeatedly.
[20]Listen to advice and accept discipline,
so that you will be wise in the future.
[21]Many plans are in a man's heart,
but it is Yahweh's counsel that will prevail.
[22]A person's desire [should be for] his [Yahweh's] mercy,
so it is better to be poor than a liar.
[23]The fear of Yahweh [leads] to life,
and [one who has it] rests content. He will not be disturbed by trouble.

[24]A lazy person buries his hand in a dish,
yet he does not bring it back to his mouth.

[25]Strike a mocker, and a gullible person will learn to be prudent.
Warn a person with understanding—he will gain knowledge.
[26]A person who assaults his father and causes his mother to flee
is a son who acts disgracefully and shamefully.
[27]Stop listening to discipline, my son,
[only if you wish] to stray from words of knowledge.
[28]A malicious witness mocks justice,
and the mouth of wicked people swallows evil.
[29]Punishments have been prepared for mockers,
and beatings for the back of fools.

Textual Notes

19:13 הַוֹּת לְאָבִיו בֵּן כְּסִיל—Literally, this is "disasters for his father (is) a foolish son." The plural of הַוָּה, "destruction, disaster," is also in 17:4.

וְדֶלֶף טֹרֵד מִדְיְנֵי אִשָּׁה׃—NIV renders this as a comparison: "and a quarrelsome wife is *like* a constant dripping" (emphasis added). But the Hebrew is a metaphorical statement: literally, "and a dripping that is constant (is) a quarrelsome wife." The noun דֶּלֶף, "a dripping," and verb טָרַד, "be continuous, constant," occur in the OT only in the participial phrase דֶּלֶף טֹרֵד here and repeated in 27:15 (where the participle is spelled plene). For the noun מִדְיָנִים, "fights, quarrellings," see the third textual note on 6:14, where it is the Qere. In the construct phrase מִדְיְנֵי אִשָּׁה, literally, "quarrellings of a wife," the genitive, אִשָּׁה, could be understood as a subjective genitive, "a wife's quarrellings" (see ESV, RSV); a genitive of source, "quarrels that a wife produces"; a genitive of specification, "quarrellings with respect to (one's) wife"; or an objective genitive, "quarrellings against (one's) wife." Four later proverbs have the reversed construct phrase אֵשֶׁת מִדְיָנִים, "a wife of quarrels," that is, "a quarrelsome wife" (see the second textual note on 21:9; the phrase is also the reading with the Qere in 21:19; 25:24; 27:15). That probably is the intended meaning here too and is adopted in the translation above. The masculine equivalent אִישׁ מִדְיָנִים, "a man of quarrels, a quarrelsome man," is the reading with the Qere in 26:21.

19:14 וּמֵיְהוָה אִשָּׁה מַשְׂכָּלֶת׃—The highest commendation is that "from Yahweh" comes "a wife with good sense." מַשְׂכָּלֶת, the feminine Hiphil participle of שָׂכַל, corresponds to the common masculine participle מַשְׂכִּיל used for wise men (e.g., 10:5, 19). For another commendation of the value of a wise wife, see 31:10–31.

19:16 שֹׁמֵר נַפְשׁוֹ—This participial phrase, "keeps his soul/life," is also in 13:3; 16:17; 22:5. נַפְשׁוֹ (like נַפְשֶׁךָ in 19:18) has a reflexive meaning, referring to oneself (Joüon, § 146 k). The message is similar to Jesus' promises of eternal life in Mt 10:39; 16:25; Jn 8:31–32; 14:23.

בּוֹזֵה דְרָכָיו יוּמָת׃—In contrast, this is a warning of everlasting death. The pronominal suffix on דְּרָכָיו, "one who despises *his* ways," could be understood as reflective ("despises his own ways"), but more probably is an oblique reference to Yahweh, just as Yahweh is the implied subject of the second line of the following proverb, 19:17. The Qere is the (intransitive) Qal imperfect יָמוּת, "he will die," whereas the Kethib is the (passive, causative) Hophal imperfect יוּמָת, "he will be put to death." Either way, God is the implied agent of the judgment on the unbeliever.

19:17 וּגְמֻלוֹ יְשַׁלֶּם־לוֹ׃—Literally, this is "and his [the gracious man's] reimbursement he [Yahweh] will repay to him." This indicates that God will repay the "debt" in full to the man who "lends [to] Yahweh" (מַלְוֵה יְהוָה).

19:18 יַסֵּר בִּנְךָ כִּי־יֵשׁ תִּקְוָה—Here כִּי could be causal (BDB, 3), "discipline your son *because* there is hope" that he will repent and live eternally, or temporal (see BDB, 2 a), "*while* there [still] is hope." The next clause implies that hope remains for the son as long as he is still alive. Compare the thief who repented and was saved just before his death (Lk 23:40–43).

וְאֶל־הֲמִיתוֹ אַל־תִּשָּׂא נַפְשֶׁךָ׃—Literally, "and to kill him do not lift up your soul," this is difficult. The idiom נָשָׂא נֶפֶשׁ אֶל, "lift up one's soul for," can mean "desire, wish/hope for" (see BDB, s.v. נָשָׂא, Qal, 1 b (9), and *DCH*, 1 g, both of which cite this verse and others). This clause would warn against wanting to kill one's son, no matter how much grief and trouble he may cause for his parents (cf. 10:1; 17:21; 19:13). However, the translation proposed here understands the verb נָשָׂא in the sense of "bear responsibility for" (cf. BDB, 2 b, and *DCH*, 3 a–b), as in the next proverb, 19:19, and also 9:12. In light of the first clause of 19:18, this would mean that a parent who fails to discipline his child bears responsibility for the child's death.

19:19 גְּרָל־חֵמָה נֹשֵׂא עֹנֶשׁ—The Kethib could be גְּרַל־, a defective spelling of גּוֹרָל, "lot," in construct, which makes little sense in the context. Or else the Kethib is an otherwise unknown word. The Qere, גְּדָל, is a defective spelling of the adjective גָּדוֹל, "great," in construct, and "great of wrath" as a descriptive phrase for a person with great anger makes good sense in the context. The Kethib may be the result of a scribe who made the common mistake of confusing ד with ר.

The noun עֹנֶשׁ, "a fine," occurs elsewhere only in 2 Ki 23:33, but the cognate verb is well attested, including in Prov 17:26; 21:11; 22:3; 27:12.

19:20 שְׁמַע עֵצָה וְקַבֵּל מוּסָר—For the two nouns, see "עֵצָה, 'Advice,' and יוֹעֵץ, 'Advisor' " as well as "מוּסָר, 'Discipline,' and יָסַר, 'to Discipline' " in "Wisdom in Proverbs" in the introduction.

19:21 וַעֲצַת יְהוָה הִיא תָקוּם׃—The feminine pronoun הִיא refers to the feminine noun עֵצָה in construct (עֲצַת). This unnecessary pronoun is emphatic, literally, "the counsel of Yahweh—*it* is what will endure," in contrast to the many, fleeting human plans in the first line of the verse. In this context the imperfect of קוּם, "stand, endure" (as in Is 40:8, quoted in 1 Pet 1:25), can be translated as "prevail" since unlike human plans, God's Wisdom alone has the power to accomplish the originator's purposes (see Prov 8:22–31).

19:22 תַּאֲוַת אָדָם חַסְדּוֹ—Literally, this is "the desire of a man (is) his mercy." Many translations recognize that תַּאֲוָה does not refer to the natural "desire" of sinful man, but instead refers to what God desires for people to show in their lives, hence "what is desired/desirable in a man" (see RSV, ESV, NKJV, NASB). Likewise, the pronoun on חַסְדּוֹ, "his mercy/faithfulness," cannot refer to any innate quality in fallen humanity, since "all its חֶסֶד" is merely like a flower that quickly withers (וְכָל־חַסְדּוֹ in Is 40:6). Instead, it must refer to Yahweh's, since "his mercy/faithfulness endures forever" (e.g., the refrain in Psalms 118 and 136).

וְטוֹב־רָשׁ מֵאִישׁ כָּזָב׃—For "better … than" (טוֹב … מִן) proverbs, see "Direct Comparisons" in "Authorship and Date" in the introduction. For רָשׁ, see the first textual note on 10:4. In the phrase אִישׁ כָּזָב, "a man who is a liar," אִישׁ need not be translated, hence simply "a liar." See the first textual note on 6:12.

19:23 יִרְאַת יְהוָה לְחַיִּים—"The fear of Yahweh (is) for life" recalls 1:7 and the eschatological promises of everlasting "life" in, for example, 3:2, 18, 22; 4:10, 13, 22–23; 12:28.

וְשָׂבֵעַ יָלִין בַּל־יִפָּקֶד רָע׃—Literally, this is "being full he remains/spends the night; he is not visited [by] evil."

19:25 לֵץ תַּכֶּה וּפֶתִי יַעְרִם—For the participle לֵץ, which in this pericope recurs in 19:29 in the plural, see "לֵץ, 'Mocker,' and לָצוֹן, 'Mocking, Scoffing' " in "Fools in Proverbs" in the introduction. The imperfect יָלִיץ, "mocks," is in 19:28. Here the participle לֵץ is the direct object of תַּכֶּה, the Hiphil imperfect of נָכָה, "you should strike," which functions as an imperative (cf. GKC, § 144 h). It is parallel to הוֹכִיחַ in the next line (see the next textual note). The clause וּפֶתִי יַעְרִם may indicate purpose and/or result: "strike ... *so that* a gullible person will become prudent." This result would be achieved if the "mocker" (לֵץ) is "gullible" (פֶּתִי) but repents at the rebuke and receives wisdom in faith. See "פֶּתִי, 'Gullible Person' " in "Fools in Proverbs" in the introduction. The Hiphil imperfect יַעְרִם is cognate to common words for wisdom. See "עָרוּם, 'Prudent,' and עָרְמָה, 'Prudence' " in "Wisdom in Proverbs" in the introduction and the first textual note on 1:4.

וְהוֹכִיחַ לְנָבוֹן יָבִין דָּעַת׃—In form הוֹכִיחַ appears to be a Hiphil infinitive construct of יָכַח, but in context it functions as an imperative: "warn." See also the first textual note on 3:12. The object is the Niphal participle נָבוֹן, "a person with understanding," which then is also the subject of the cognate Qal imperfect יָבִין, literally, "a person of understanding will understand" more "knowledge" (דַּעַת). See "בִּינָה, 'Understanding,' and Related Words" in "Wisdom in Proverbs" in the introduction. The idea is similar to that expressed by Jesus in Lk 8:18a and 19:26a.

19:26 מְשַׁדֶּד־אָב—In the Qal, the verb שָׁדַד means "violently destroy." The Piel occurs in the OT only here and in 24:15, both times meaning to "perpetrate an act of violence" (*HALOT*, 1) or to "assault" (BDB). The genitive is objective: אָב, the "father," is the victim of the assault.

בֵּן מֵבִישׁ וּמַחְפִּיר׃—Literally, "a son acting disgracefully/shamefully" is also in 10:5 and 17:2. The second Hiphil participle, מַחְפִּיר, "behaving shamefully," is a synonym that reinforces the first one, מֵבִישׁ. The verb חָפֵר occurs elsewhere in Proverbs only at the end of 13:5, where its Hiphil imperfect means "causes shame."

19:27 מוּסָר ... דָעַת׃—See "מוּסָר, 'Discipline,' and יָסַר, 'to Discipline' " as well as "דַּעַת, 'Knowledge,' and יָדַע, 'to Know' " in "Wisdom in Proverbs" in the introduction.

19:28 עֵד בְּלִיַּעַל—For בְּלִיַּעַל, here translated as "malicious," see the first textual note on 6:12. For phrases with עֵד, "witness," that have a similar meaning, see the first textual note on 6:19.

19:29 נָכוֹנוּ לַלֵּצִים שְׁפָטִים—The noun שֶׁפֶט signifies a "punishment" that is administered as the result of divine "justice," מִשְׁפָּט, in 19:28.

וּמַהֲלֻמוֹת לְגֵו כְּסִילִים׃—This is "and beatings for the back of fools." Similar are lines in 10:13, וְשֵׁבֶט לְגֵו חֲסַר־לֵב, "but a rod (is) for the back of someone who lacks sense," and 26:3, וְשֵׁבֶט לְגֵו כְּסִילִים, "and a rod (is) for the back of fools."

Commentary

A Foolish Son: Dealing with Fools and Foolishness (19:13–22:16)

Once again an informally organized section of Solomon's proverbs is introduced with a saying about "a foolish son" (19:13). This is the fifth and final section in the proverbs of Solomon in 10:1–22:16.[1]

This section (19:13–22:16) contrasts to the previous one in that instead of advising how to avoid fools, it is advice on how to deal with them, since they cannot always be avoided. Many of these proverbs also offer counsel on how to deal with one's own sinful inclination to foolishness, so that one can deal internally with one's own foolishness and then also deal with the foolish behavior of others (cf. Mt 7:4–5). This section will conclude with a collection of sayings that tend to contrast wise and foolish behavior (21:1–22:16).

Like the previous section, these proverbs seldom mention the Gospel directly and explicitly. Instead Solomon expects that those who have learned his lessons on wisdom earlier in the book will read these sayings in light of the Gospel. Thus when he speaks of "the fear of Yahweh" leading to "life" in 19:23, he expects readers to understand the Gospel underpinnings of "the fear of Yahweh" and to understand "life" to be more than temporal existence; it includes the promise of the resurrection to eternal life and redemption from everlasting death (see also 19:16). Likewise, when God through Solomon promises that "the person who pursues righteousness and mercy will find life, righteousness, and honor" (21:21), this proverb speaks of believing the Gospel (see Mt 6:33; 7:7; Col 3:1; 1 Pet 3:11) and receiving the free rewards of grace that God gives to all who trust in Christ's own righteousness (see Pss 45:5, 8 [ET 45:4, 7]; 51:16 [ET 51:14]). Many of the other proverbs in this section find their ultimate meaning only when read with the Gospel in view, as indeed is true of all the OT Scriptures (Lk 24:44–47).

Dealing with Fools, Part 1 (19:13–29)

19:13 This verse begins this section with another proverb about a foolish son. However, this proverb, like 13:1, is different from the other three verses (10:1; 15:20; 17:25) that begin sections in 10:1–22:16 because it does not contain the pair father/mother. Instead, the second line is a warning about a quarrelsome wife. The father should avoid allowing his son to become a disaster and also prevent his marriage from deteriorating so that his wife becomes an enduring annoyance (cf. 27:15–16). The father can accomplish both by exercising divine wisdom, first of all, by walking in God's ways himself, and second, by living according to God's Law and Gospel in his relationships with others. The temptation for the father is to wield only the Law and to attempt to coerce

---

[1] See the excursus "The Organization of the Sayings in Solomon's Proverbs in Proverbs 10:1–22:16" in the commentary on Proverbs 10.

his wife and children to honor him, but above all else he must show the love of God to them (see Eph 5:21–33; 6:1–4).

19:14 This verse is tied to 19:13 by the words אָב, "father/ancestor," and אִשָּׁה, "wife." The juxtaposition of this proverb with 19:13 is striking. Solomon does not want those who read these proverbs to be misogynistic, but he wants instead to lead everyone to see the blessing from Yahweh that comes in a good spouse. Those who are unmarried should seek a godly spouse and marry "in the Lord" (1 Cor 7:39). Those who are already married are not to divorce, but to cherish and nurture their spouse (see Mt 19:1–12; 1 Corinthians 7).

19:15 This verse notes that laziness feeds on itself in a downward spiral, leading to both lethargy and hunger. The sleep mentioned here, תַּרְדֵּמָה, may be "first sleep."[2] In the days before widespread artificial light, the natural sleep pattern of humans was segmented sleep—a cycle of two periods of sleep during the night with a period of wakefulness between the two lasting for several hours and beginning around midnight.[3] The first segment was characterized by deep sleep that often included dreams. If this is the case, then the sage is noting that laziness leads to premature "first sleep," perhaps even before the sun has set. This saying is linked to the following one by the catchword נֶפֶשׁ, "person/life." The sin spoken of here is against the Seventh Commandment, since laziness robs from one's employer and from God (contrast 19:17) as well as from oneself.[4]

19:16 This verse is usually understood to be a contrast between a person who is respectful of authority and one who is careless.[5] However, the contrast is between a person who is careful to keep *God's* command (especially here the Seventh Commandment [19:15, 17]) and one who despises *God's* ways, since the unexpressed antecedent of the pronoun on דְּרָכָיו, "*his* ways" (19:16),

---

[2] Holladay, "Indications of Segmented Sleep in the Bible," *CBQ* 69 (2007), 220. While some occurrences of תַּרְדֵּמָה, "deep sleep," in the Bible are divinely induced (Gen 2:21; Is 29:10) or divinely extended (1 Sam 26:12), Holladay notes that in other passages it seems to be a natural phenomenon that probably should be understood as "first sleep" (Job 4:13; 33:15; Prov 19:15). Note that in Abraham's case its onset is linked with sundown (Gen 15:12). Holladay discusses the following passages that probably involve the waking interval in natural, segmented sleep: Judges 7; 16:3; 1 Sam 28:8–25; Jer 6:5; Micah 2:1–2; Pss 36:5 (ET 36:4); 63:7 (ET 63:6); 77:7 (ET 77:6); 119:55, 62, 148; Ruth 3:8–13; Song 3:1–5; 5:2–8; Judith 11:17; 12:5–6; Mt 25:1–13 (especially Mt 25:9–10); Mk 14:40–43; Lk 11:5; Acts 16:11–40. I would also add the entire cycle of segmented sleep as mentioned in Gen 41:1–7 and Dan 2:1. Holladay also proposes that Gen 28:10–17; 1 Ki 3:5; and Wisdom 18:14–19 mention the dreams that typically come at the end of first sleep.

[3] A. Roger Ekirch, "Sleep We Have Lost: Pre-industrial Slumber in the British Isles," *American Historical Review* 106 (2001): 343–86, and *At Day's Close: Night in Times Past* (New York: Norton, 2005); Paul Bohannan, "Concepts of Time among the Tiv of Nigeria," *Southwestern Journal of Anthropology* 9 (1953): 251–62.

[4] See the discussion by Luther in LC I 225.

[5] So NASB, NIV, NJB, NRSV.

is Yahweh.[6] One's attitude toward God's Word is shaped by one's faith. Those who have received the Gospel in faith respect God's Law, whereas those who reject God's offer of forgiveness and life despise God's ways—both in the Gospel, where he offers blessing, and in the Law, where he threatens punishment (see 1:7, 31; 13:13; 14:2).

19:17 This verse promises God's reward for those who are gracious and kind to the poor. Similar is the divine counsel of the Lord Jesus in Lk 14:12–14. The promise that God himself will "repay" is eschatological, pointing to the resurrection on the Last Day, when the children of God shall receive the reward earned for them by the merits of Christ alone. This promise invites us to trust Yahweh, who provides for all our needs, so that we are moved to share our bounty with others, even if they will never be able to repay us in this life.

The use of one's wealth to aid others is a way of keeping the Seventh Commandment, which not only forbids taking the property of others, but also enjoins all of us to use our own property for the good of others.[7] Irenaeus connects this proverb to Mt 25:34–36:

> For even as God does not need our possessions, so do we need to offer something to God; as Solomon says: "He that hath pity upon the poor, lendeth unto the Lord" [Prov 19:17]. For God, who stands in need of nothing, takes our good works to Himself for this purpose, that He may grant us a recompense of His own good things, as our Lord says: "Come, ye blessed of My Father, receive the kingdom prepared for you. For I was an hungered, and ye gave Me to eat: I was thirsty, and ye gave Me drink: I was a stranger, and ye took Me in: naked, and ye clothed Me; sick, and ye visited Me; in prison, and ye came to Me" [Mt 25:34–36].[8]

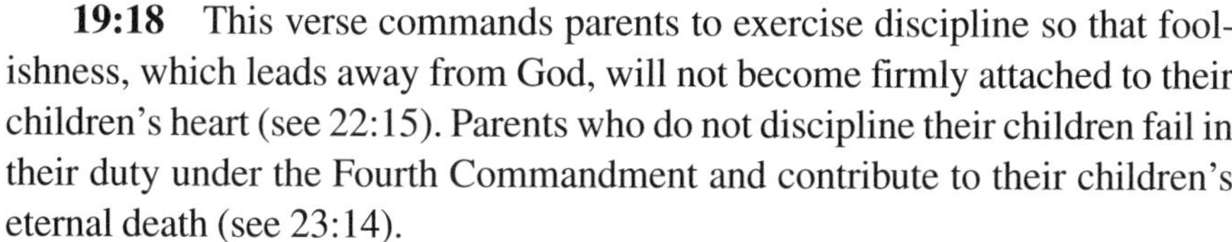

19:18 This verse commands parents to exercise discipline so that foolishness, which leads away from God, will not become firmly attached to their children's heart (see 22:15). Parents who do not discipline their children fail in their duty under the Fourth Commandment and contribute to their children's eternal death (see 23:14).

19:19 This verse is coupled with 19:18 by the verb נָשָׂא, translated in both sayings with the meaning "bear responsibility for." One reason for discipline is to rid a child of a short temper. This proverb counsels against softening the punishment for habitual sinful behavior, since sparing a person from the consequences of his actions will not solve the problem. Proper discipline administers correction that is needed.

19:20 This verse continues the theme of "discipline," expressed by the verb יִסֵּר in 19:18 and by the cognate noun מוּסָר in 19:20. This proverb advises

---

6 So also Emerton, "Notes on Some Passages in the Book of Proverbs," 206–9. However, it is not necessary to emend דְּרָכָיו ("his ways") to דַּרְכֵי־יהוה ("Yahweh's ways") as Emerton proposes.

7 See the discussion by Luther in LC I 250–53.

8 Irenaeus, *Against Heresies*, 4.18.6 (*ANF* 1:486). See also Clement of Alexandria, *The Instructor*, 3.4 (*ANF* 2:279).

the person reading these sayings to be receptive to good advice because of its long-term effect. It is easy to resent advice and discipline, even when one knows that it is good. However, accepting it, no matter how offensive it may appear at the time, leads to lasting benefits. The Hebrew verse concludes with בְּאַחֲרִיתֶךָ, literally, "in your future" or "at your latter time," which hints at the resurrection and the glorious eternity that awaits all who are wise through faith (see 19:17 and also Dan 12:2–3).

19:21 This verse is connected to 19:20 by the use of the catchword עֵצָה, "advice, counsel." It also begins a string of three proverbs that each mention Yahweh, either directly (19:21, 23) or indirectly (the pronominal suffix on חַסְדּוֹ, "*his* mercy," 19:22).[9]

This saying urges the wise person to go beyond his personal plans by seeking God's wisdom. Human plans are subject to the sinful passions that reside in all people, even those with the best of intentions. God's advice in his Word serves as a way to expose selfish motives and helps the wise person avoid foolish mistakes. Yahweh's counsel ultimately is his plan of salvation, which he has now carried out in Jesus Christ.[10] All the human schemes that sought to thwart this plan have failed, and so his counsel has prevailed (see Psalms 2 and 110; Acts 4:23–30). Those who reject God's plan shall perish, but all who repent and take refuge in him (Prov 3:5–6; see also Ps 2:11–12) have the promise of everlasting "life" (Prov 19:23).

19:22 This verse reminds us that if we desire God's mercy we should not lie.[11] Lying can be seen as not showing חֶסֶד (which means both "mercy" and "fidelity, loyalty") towards Yahweh, thereby rejecting his mercy (Mt 18:23–35). It is better, therefore, to be poor than to gain wealth through deceit (see Prov 19:1).

19:23 This verse connects "the fear of Yahweh" (see the first textual note and the commentary on 1:7) with "life." No permanent trouble will disturb the person who through the Gospel has been given this positive relationship with God. Not even death will disturb him (see 14:27) because everlasting "life" awaits.

19:24 This verse makes fun of the lazy person who is too lethargic to feed himself. His laziness may not prevent him from starting a project, but it keeps him from finishing it. This proverb is nearly identical to 26:15, differing from it slightly in the second line.

---

[9] Apart from "Yahweh," this saying is similar to one in the Wisdom of Amenemope, chapter 18 (19:16–17). See *ANET*, 423; *ANE*, 241. See also the excursus "The Words of Wise People (Prov 22:17–24:22) and Its Relationship to the Wisdom of Amenemope" in the commentary on Proverbs 22.

[10] See "Wisdom in Proverbs" in the introduction. See also the commentary on 1:1–7; 3:13–20; 8:22–31; 30:1b–10; and the excursus "Proverbs 8, Wisdom, Christology, and the Arian Controversy" in the commentary on chapter 8.

[11] As in 19:16, the unexpressed antecedent of the pronominal suffix is Yahweh.

19:25–29 These verses are a group of proverbs united by the contrast between discipline, which serves as a corrective, and punishment for those who refuse to be corrected.

19:25 This verse reminds readers that correction can be a learning experience for those who observe it being meted out to others. The mocker, who has become incorrigible in his foolishness, will not learn from his own punishment, but the gullible person who has not become enamored with his own foolishness may. This hope is similar to the divine purpose expressed in 1:4 that a "gullible person" will gain "prudence" through believing divine wisdom. This involves both Law and Gospel (see 19:21, 23), repentance and faith.[12]

The second line affirms that a person who possesses understanding does not need physical punishment to catch his attention; a verbal warning is enough for him. Compare the English proverb "a word to the wise is sufficient," based on the Latin proverb *verbum sat sapienti*.

19:26 This verse describes the ultimate way to break the Fourth Commandment. It is shameful enough to despise one's parents (see 15:20). To seek to cause them harm is even worse. According to the Torah physical abuse against either parent was punishable by death (Ex 21:15). Alluding to that passage and also to this verse, Paul notes that "the Law is not laid down for the righteous, but for the lawless and disobedient, for the ungodly and sinners, for the unholy and profane, *for patricides and matricides*, for murderers" (1 Tim 1:9).

19:27 This verse is ironic, since it is phrased with an imperative and two infinitives, which express a purpose clause, literally, "stop listening ... in order [for you] to stray" (חֲדַל ... לִשְׁמֹעַ ... לִשְׁגוֹת). It continues the theme of a disgraceful son since it uses בֵּן, "son," as in 19:26. Thus the proverb is not really encouraging the son to stop listening; rather the biting sarcasm is a way of discouraging contempt for discipline, especially God's discipline for those whom he loves as his sons and daughters.

> For the Lord disciplines one whom he loves,
> and he chastises every son whom he receives. (Heb 12:6; see also Heb 12:9–10)

19:28 This verse points to the problems caused by a person who breaks the Eighth Commandment with malevolence in his heart. It also notes that such wicked people feed on evil. Some commentators are bothered by the image of the wicked swallowing evil and have suggested that the verb יְבַלַּע, "swallows," in the second line should be changed to יַבִּיעַ, "spouts" (as in 15:28).[13] However, there is a similar image in Job 15:16.[14] In addition, the sound pattern of the proverb confirms the MT since it contains a play on words between

[12] See further "Law and Gospel in Proverbs" in the introduction.

[13] Scott, *Proverbs, Ecclesiastes*, 117; Toy, *Proverbs*, 381–82.

[14] Delitzsch, *Proverbs*, 2:38.

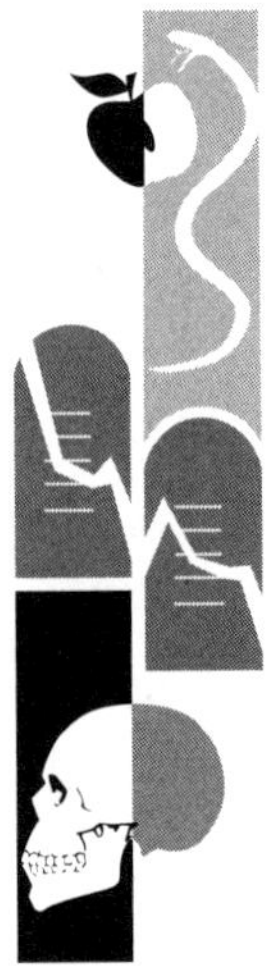

בְּלִיַּעַל, "malicious," and יְבַלַּע, "swallows." The similar sounding words draw attention to the synonymous phrases "a malicious witness" and "the mouth of wicked people."[15]

19:29 This verse observes that those who cannot accept discipline administered for the good purpose of changing their wrong attitude can have only their outward behavior curbed by punishment. It is linked to 19:28 by the roots ליץ (יָלִיץ, "mocks," 19:28; לֵצִים, "mockers," 19:29) and שׁפט (מִשְׁפָּט, "justice," 19:28; שְׁפָטִים, "punishments," 19:29). Note the similarity of the second line of this saying and the final line of 10:13 and 26:3.

That such punishments "have been prepared" (the Niphal perfect נָכוֹנוּ) gives the statement an eschatological meaning. See the declaration in Mt 25:41, which Jesus will speak on the Last Day, in contrast to what is "prepared" for believers in Mt 25:34; Mk 10:40; 1 Cor 2:9; Rev 21:2. The threat of corporal punishment is similar to Jesus' eschatological warning in Lk 12:47–48.

15 McCreesh, *Biblical Sound and Sense*, 79–81.

Proverbs 20:1–30

Dealing with Fools, Part 2

Translation

20 [1]**Wine is a mocker, and beer is noisy;**
whoever is intoxicated with it is not wise.
[2]**The king's fearful anger is like a lion's growl;**
whoever intrudes on him endangers his life.
[3]**It is to a man's glory that he stops quarreling,**
but every stubborn fool is prone to fighting.
[4]**A lazy person does not plow after autumn.**
He expects something in the harvest, but there is nothing.
[5]**The advice in a person's heart is deep water,**
but a person with understanding can draw it out.
[6]**Many people claim to be loyal,**
but who can find a faithful person?
[7]**A righteous person walks in his integrity.**
Blessed are his children after him.
[8]**When a king is sitting on his throne as judge,**
he is winnowing out all evil with his eyes.
[9]**Who can say, "I have purified my heart;**
I am cleansed from my sinfulness"?
[10]**Differing weights and differing measures—**
both of them are a disgusting thing to Yahweh.
[11]**Even a child makes himself known by his acts,**
whether his conduct is pure and upright.
[12]**An ear that hears and an eye that sees—**
Yahweh made both of them.
[13]**Do not love sleep, or you will become poor.**
Keep your eyes open, and you will have enough to eat.
[14]**"Bad! Bad!" says the buyer,**
but as he goes away, then he brags.
[15]**There are gold and many jewels,**
but lips that have knowledge are precious gems.
[16]**Take the garment of someone who guarantees a loan for a stranger,**
and hold it in pledge [when someone pledges] on behalf of foreigners.
[17]**Food gained dishonestly is sweet to a person,**
but afterward his mouth will be filled with gravel.
[18]**Plans are confirmed by [getting] advice,**
and wage war with guidance.
[19]**Someone who reveals a confidence goes about spreading gossip,**
so do not get involved with a person whose lips are always open.

20 The person who curses his father and his mother—
his lamp will be snuffed out in total darkness.
21 An inheritance quickly obtained in the beginning
will not be blessed in the end.
22 Do not say, "I'll get even [with you]!"
Wait for Yahweh, and he will rescue you.
23 Differing weights are a disgusting thing to Yahweh,
and dishonest scales are not good.
24 The steps of a man are from Yahweh;
how can a person understand his way?
25 It is a trap for someone to say impulsively, "It is holy,"
and afterwards to reconsider [his] vows.
26 A wise king winnows out the wicked;
he rolls the wheel over them.
27 A man's spirit is the lamp of Yahweh,
which searches his entire innermost being.
28 Mercy and truth protect a king,
and he maintains his throne with mercy.
29 The beauty of young men is their strength,
but the glory of old men is their gray hair.
30 Wounds and bruises scour away evil,
and blows [scour] the innermost being.

Textual Notes

20:1 לֵץ הַיַּיִן הֹמֶה שֵׁכָר—Only here in Proverbs does the participle לֵץ, "mocker," refer to an inanimate object (הַיַּיִן, "wine," with a generic article) rather than a person. See "לֵץ, 'Mocker,' and לָצוֹן, 'Mocking, Scoffing' " in "Fools in Proverbs" in the introduction. The masculine participle (הֹמֶה) of הָמָה, "be loud, boisterous," recalls the feminine participles of הָמָה that refer to Folly herself (9:13) and an adulteress (7:11). שֵׁכָר, "beer, strong drink," does not denote distilled liquor, which was unknown in ancient times. Instead it denotes alcoholic beverages made from grain, primarily barley (*HALOT*). It occurs twenty-three times in the OT, almost always with יַיִן, "wine," as here. Its only other occurrences in Proverbs are in 31:4, 6, where too it is accompanied by יַיִן.

וְכָל־שֹׁגֶה בּוֹ לֹא יֶחְכָּם׃—This involves a pun on two possible meanings of the verb שָׁגָה. Usually it means "go astray, err, sin" (as in 5:23; 19:27; 28:10), in which case וְכָל־שֹׁגֶה could refer to "everyone who strays" from the path of wisdom. Yet שָׁגָה can also mean "be intoxicated" (as in 5:19–20), "meander, reel" in drunkenness (see BDB, 2), which is the likely meaning here with בּוֹ, "by/with it," referring to "wine" (הַיַּיִן) and/or "beer" (שֵׁכָר). When שָׁגָה is followed by an object marked with the preposition בְּ, it refers to the effects of the object upon a person (5:19–20). See the textual note on 5:19–20, 23.

20:2 נַהַם כַּכְּפִיר אֵימַת מֶלֶךְ—See the first textual note on 19:12. The construct phrase here, אֵימַת מֶלֶךְ, could mean "the fear (one has) of the king" (Joüon, § 129 e) or "fear due a king" (Waltke-O'Connor, § 9.5.2e, example 15; cf. GKC, § 128 h). However, it more likely refers to the king's own "fearful anger" at his subjects.

מִתְעַבְּרוֹ חוֹטֵא נַפְשׁוֹ׃—For the Hithpael (HtD) participle מִתְעַבֵּר, here translated as "whoever intrudes," see the second textual note on 14:16. Its masculine suffix (וֹ-) probably refers to the (masculine) "king," מֶלֶךְ, rather than the feminine noun אֵימָה, his "fearful anger," hence "intrudes *on him.*" The phrase חוֹטֵא נַפְשׁוֹ, literally, "sins against his own life," is usually understood to mean "endangers" or "forfeits his own life" (see *HALOT*, s.v. חטא, 7; this understanding is reflected in ESV, NASB, NIV, NRSV).

20:3 כָּבוֹד לָאִישׁ שֶׁבֶת מֵרִיב—The construct phrase שֶׁבֶת מֵרִיב is the subject of this nominal clause, literally, "ceasing from a quarrel (is) glory to a man." This is not the noun שֶׁבֶת, "sitting, dwelling," from יָשַׁב, but a homograph from שָׁבַת, "to cease," meaning "cessation/stopping." This noun occurs elsewhere only in Ex 21:19 and perhaps Is 30:7. "From quarreling" (מֵרִיב) is the preposition מִן with the noun רִיב, which also occurs, for example, in 15:18; 17:1.

וְכָל־אֱוִיל יִתְגַּלָּע׃—See "אֱוִיל, 'Stubborn Fool,' and אִוֶּלֶת, 'Stupidity' " in "Fools in Proverbs" in the introduction. For the Hithpael (HtD) of גָּלַע, "break out in fighting," see the second textual note on 17:14.

20:4 מֵחֹרֶף עָצֵל לֹא־יַחֲרֹשׁ—The preposition מִן, on מֵחֹרֶף, has a temporal sense, "from (the time of), after." חֹרֶף denotes the autumn harvest time. The right time for plowing and planting was after the harvest, when the rainy season had begun. However, the "lazy person" (עָצֵל) is so slothful that "he does not plow" (לֹא־יַחֲרֹשׁ) in the season provided by God the Creator.

יִשְׁאַל בַּקָּצִיר וָאָיִן׃—Literally, this is "he asks during the harvest, but there is nothing." After the imperfect יַחֲרֹשׁ in the preceding clause, either the Qere, וְשָׁאַל (perfect with *waw* consecutive), or the Kethib, the imperfect יִשְׁאַל, fits. The Qal (G) of שָׁאַל can mean "ask," "seek," or "beg" (see BDB, 1 c, and *HALOT*, 5). The word is probably used here with a double entendre. The lazy person "expects" to receive produce during the harvest, although he has planted nothing. Therefore he is reduced to "begging."

20:5 מַיִם עֲמֻקִּים עֵצָה בְלֶב־אִישׁ—This clause is similar to the first clause in 18:4, which also has the expression "deep water(s)." For עֵצָה, see "עֵצָה, 'Advice,' and יוֹעֵץ, 'Advisor' " in "Wisdom in Proverbs" in the introduction.

וְאִישׁ תְּבוּנָה יִדְלֶנָּה׃—Literally, "a man of understanding" uses the noun תְּבוּנָה, which is cognate to other common terms. See "בִּינָה, 'Understanding,' and Related Words" in "Wisdom in Proverbs" in the introduction. The verb דָּלָה usually means "draw water," and so it builds on the metaphor "deep water" in the first clause. The feminine suffix on יִדְלֶנָּה (literally, "he draws *it* out") refers to the feminine noun עֵצָה, "advice," in the first clause. Compare 18:4b, which has the water metaphor "fountain of wisdom."

20:6 רָב־אָדָם יִקְרָא אִישׁ חַסְדּוֹ—This difficult clause may literally mean "a multitude of man proclaims (himself to be) a man of his fidelity." Given the parallelism with the next clause, which has אִישׁ אֱמוּנִים, literally, "a man of faithfulness," that is, "a faithful person," the phrase אִישׁ חַסְדּוֹ, "a man of his fidelity," probably means "a loyal person," yielding "many people claim to be loyal." Is 40:6 warns that all human fidelity (וְכָל־חַסְדּוֹ) is merely like a fading flower.

וְאִ֥ישׁ אֱ֝מוּנִ֗ים מִ֣י יִמְצָֽא׃—Another rhetorical question with מִי and an imperfect recurs in 20:9. Here the construction (see GKC, § 107 r, t) "who can find?" implies that it would be impossible to find "a faithful person" among sinful humanity apart from the grace of God, which alone enables a person to be faithful. Similar is the implication of מִ֣י יִמְצָ֑א when it recurs in 31:10, where instead of a man, the query asks about finding a virtuous woman/wife.

20:7 מִתְהַלֵּ֣ךְ בְּתֻמּ֣וֹ צַדִּ֑יק—The Hithpael (HtD) of הָלַךְ has the iterative meaning, "walk about," as in 6:22. One's walk reflects one's way of life. See the excursus "The Metaphor of the Path in Solomon's Wisdom" in the commentary on Proverbs 10. For the noun תֹּם, "integrity, blamelessness," see the second textual note on 2:7. For צַדִּיק, a person who is "righteous" through faith, see "The Relationship between Wisdom and Righteousness in Proverbs" in "Wisdom in Proverbs" in the introduction.

אַשְׁרֵ֖י בָנָ֣יו אַחֲרָֽיו׃—For "blessed," see the first textual note on 3:13. The theme of a father teaching wisdom to his sons runs throughout Proverbs 1–9. See the excursus "Proverbs 1–9, Christ, and the Ten Commandments" in the commentary on Proverbs 1.

20:8 מֶ֣לֶךְ ... מְזָרֶ֖ה—A "king" is described as "winnowing" also in 20:26. Compared to the (literal) Qal (G) of זָרָה, the Piel (D) participle מְזָרֶה used in these two proverbs may indicate that the meaning is metaphorical (cf. Waltke-O'Connor, §24.3.2b, example 1b).

20:9 מִֽי־יֹ֭אמַר זִכִּ֣יתִי לִבִּ֑י טָ֝הַ֗רְתִּי מֵֽחַטָּאתִֽי׃—The verb זָכָה, "be pure," occurs in Proverbs only here, and the Piel (D) has a factitive sense: זִכִּיתִי, "I have made pure, purified." The cognate adjective זַךְ in 20:11 (also 16:2; 21:8) means "pure, righteous" (BDB, 2). As in 20:6b, the rhetorical question (מִֽי־יֹ֭אמַר, "who can say … ?") points to the impossibility of righteousness through works or human effort. No sinful person can make his own heart pure; only God in his grace can accomplish this. The same is true for the second part of the question: only through God's gracious action and gift of forgiveness through faith alone can a believer say, טָ֝הַ֗רְתִּי מֵֽחַטָּאתִֽי, "I am clean/cleansed from my sin." See טָהֵר also in Ezek 36:25, 33; Ps 51:4, 9 (ET 51:2, 7); Job 4:17. It is a common verb in Leviticus 13–15 for purification, made possible only by God's gracious provisions for sacrificial and sacramental rites of atonement and cleansing. In the NT, see, for example, Mt 8:3; 10:8; Eph 5:26; Titus 2:14; 1 Jn 1:7–9.

20:10 אֶ֣בֶן וָ֭אֶבֶן אֵיפָ֣ה וְאֵיפָ֑ה—The repetition, literally, "stone and stone, ephah and ephah" indicates diversity of weights and measures (Joüon, § 135 d; GKC, § 123 f; Waltke-O'Connor, § 7.2.3c). Other instances of repetition are in Ps 12:3 (ET 12:2); 1 Chr 9:27; 26:13; 28:14–15; 2 Chr 8:14; 11:12; 19:5.

תּוֹעֲבַ֥ת יְ֝הוָ֗ה גַּם־שְׁנֵיהֶֽם׃—This is identical to the second line of 17:15. See the second textual note on 17:15. גַּם־שְׁנֵיהֶם recurs at the end of 20:12.

20:13 פְּקַ֖ח עֵינֶ֣יךָ שְֽׂבַֽע־לָֽחֶם׃—The verb פָּקַח, "to open," is a synonym of פָּתַח, but פָּקַח is only used with "eyes" (here עֵינֶיךָ) or, once (Is 42:20), with ears. Its imperative, פְּקַח, here has a durative force: "*keep* your eyes *open.*" The second imperative here, שְׂבַע, has the force of a promise: literally, "… and you *will be* satisfied [with] food" (see GKC, § 110 h; Joüon, § 116 i), which means "you will have enough food, have enough to eat."

20:15 יֵ֣שׁ זָ֭הָב וְרָב־פְּנִינִ֑ים—For זָהָב, "gold," see also, for example, 11:22 and 22:1. For פְּנִינִים, "jewels," see the first textual note on 3:15.

וּכְלִ֥י יְ֝קָ֗ר שִׂפְתֵי־דָֽעַת׃—The singular noun כְּלִי can have a wide range of meanings, including "jewels" (BDB, 1) or "gems," as implied here by יְקָר, literally, "preciousness," and the parallel nouns in the preceding clause. יְקָר is an adjectival genitive: "*precious* gems."

20:16 לְקַח־בִּ֭גְדוֹ כִּי־עָ֣רַב זָ֑ר—This verse is repeated almost identically in 27:13. Here, however, the rare imperative form לְקַח, "take" (elsewhere only in Ex 29:1; Ezek 37:16), retains the לְ whereas the common form, קַח, is in Prov 27:13. For עָרַב, "guarantee a loan," see the first textual note on 6:1.

וּבְעַ֖ד נָכְרִ֣ים חַבְלֵֽהוּ׃—Literally, this is "and on behalf of foreigners hold him/it." The Kethib is נָכְרִים, "foreigners." The masculine singular נָכְרִי is in 5:10 and 27:2, but the masculine plural נָכְרִים occurs in Proverbs only as the Kethib here, and it also occurs in Is 2:6; Obad 11; and Lam 5:2. Many follow the Qere, נָכְרִיָּה, "a foreign woman," which is used in the nearly identical proverb in Prov 27:13 and also in, for example, 2:16 and 5:20. חָבַל can mean "bind, obligate someone by holding something from him as a pledge, guarantee," in which case the suffix on חַבְלֵהוּ ("hold *him* in pledge") would refer to the person in the first line of the verse who gives the garment, and to the person in the second line who gives some kind of pledge (similar are BDB, 2, citing Prov 20:16 and 27:13, as well as KJV, RSV, NASB). Or the verb can mean "hold [something] in pledge" (BDB, 2, citing other verses), in which case the suffix ("hold *it* in pledge") would refer to "his garment" (בִּגְדוֹ) in the first line, the article of clothing that secures the pledge. This second option is reflected in the translation above and in ESV, NIV, NKJV. For the pointing of the suffixed Qal (G) imperative חַבְלֵהוּ with *patach* (חַ-) caused by the guttural ח, see GKC, § 63 l.

20:18 מַ֭חֲשָׁבוֹת בְּעֵצָ֣ה תִכּ֑וֹן—The feminine plural noun מַחֲשָׁבוֹת, "plans," apparently is construed as a collective since it is the subject of the feminine singular Niphal (N) verb תִּכּוֹן, "be confirmed" (see Joüon, § 150 g). The preposition בְּ indicates means: בְּעֵצָה, "by [means of soliciting] advice" from wise people and pondering their godly counsel.

וּ֝בְתַחְבֻּל֗וֹת עֲשֵׂ֣ה מִלְחָמָֽה׃—Literally, this is "and with guidance make war." The vocabulary is repeated in 24:6a but with the verb עָשָׂה in the imperfect. As in the preceding clause, the preposition בְּ indicates that a person should only wage war בְתַחְבֻּלוֹת, "by [after receiving sage] guidance." For the abstract plural noun, see "תַּחְבוּלוֹת, 'Guidance' " in "Wisdom in Proverbs" in the introduction.

20:19 גּֽוֹלֶה־סּ֭וֹד הוֹלֵ֣ךְ רָכִ֑יל—This repeats 11:13a except that the phrases are reversed and the participle here, גּוֹלֶה־, is Qal (G) instead of the Piel (D) מְגַלֶּה־ there.

וּלְפֹתֶ֥ה שְׂ֝פָתָ֗יו לֹ֣א תִתְעָרָֽב׃—Literally, this is "and in relation to a person (constantly) opening his lips—you shall not have fellowship." The Hithpael (HtD) of עָרַב, "have fellowship" with a person (BDB, s.v. עָרַב II, 2 a), recurs with the same meaning in 24:21, where again it is negated. It also is negated, but with a slightly different meaning, in 14:10b. It may be another form of the same verb whose Qal (G) (עָרַב) was in 20:16a (so BDB, s.v. עָרַב II, but not *HALOT*, s.v. ערב II).

20:20 מְקַלֵּל אָבִיו וְאִמּוֹ—A nearly identical clause with the Piel (D) participle of קָלַל, "to curse," is in Ex 21:17, which prescribes the death penalty for cursing one's parents, as also does Lev 20:9, which uses imperfect and perfect forms of the verb.

יִדְעַךְ נֵרוֹ בֶּאֱשׁוּן חֹשֶׁךְ׃—The Kethib, followed by the LXX, Syriac, and Vulgate, has בְּאִישׁוֹן, "*in the pupil (of the eye)* of darkness," meaning utter darkness. See the textual note on 7:9, which uses אִישׁוֹן similarly. The Qere is בֶּאֱשׁוּן, the preposition בְּ with the noun אֱשׁוּן, which occurs nowhere else. Perhaps אֱשׁוּן means the "beginning" (*DCH*) of darkness, which would point to swift judgment as soon as night falls. A cognate in Rabbinic Hebrew means "dense vapor, steam" (Jastrow, s.v. אֲשׁוּנָה).

20:21 נַחֲלָה מְבֹחֶלֶת בָּרִאשֹׁנָה—This refers to an "inheritance" (נַחֲלָה) that is "hastily gained" (BDB, s.v. בָּהַל, Pual) according to the Qere, the feminine Pual (Dp) participle מְבֹהֶלֶת. The Kethib is another feminine Pual (Dp) participle, מְבֻחֶלֶת, a hapax legomenon that could mean "gained by greed" (*DCH*, s.v. בחל II).

וְאַחֲרִיתָהּ לֹא תְבֹרָךְ׃—The referent of the feminine suffix on וְאַחֲרִיתָהּ and the subject of the feminine verb תְבֹרָךְ is the feminine noun נַחֲלָה, "inheritance," in the preceding line. "Will not be blessed" is a circumlocution or litotes for "be cursed (by God)." Compare 20:20 and "cursed" in Gen 3:14, 17 and Mt 25:41.

20:22 אֲשַׁלְּמָה־רָע—The cohortative verb with its object "let me repay evil" is a threat to retaliate and is idiomatically equivalent to "I'll get even."

קַוֵּה לַיהוָה וְיֹשַׁע לָךְ׃—These two clauses express salvation through faith alone (see also, e.g., Rom 3:21–28). The Piel (D) imperative קַוֵּה, literally, "hope, wait" (for Yahweh), is a synonym of "believe, trust in." It is followed by the jussive וְיֹשַׁע, "and he will save/rescue" you. For the verb sequence, see Joüon, § 116 d. Both verbs here take an object introduced by the preposition לְ (לַיהוָה and לָךְ, which is pausal for לְךָ).

20:23 See the textual notes on 20:10.

20:24 מֵיְהוָה מִצְעֲדֵי־גָבֶר—This is, literally, "from Yahweh (are) the steps of a man." Similar wording is in 16:1, 9. This implies that his steps are "ordered by" (RSV) or "directed by" (NIV) Yahweh. "Ordained by" (NASB) overstates the Hebrew and could be misconstrued to support a doctrine of double predestination (see the commentary).

וְאָדָם מַה־יָּבִין דַּרְכּוֹ׃—This clause begins with a *casus pendens*: literally, "and a man—who can discern his (own) way?"

20:25 מוֹקֵשׁ אָדָם יָלַע קֹדֶשׁ—Probably this means "it is a snare of a person [when] he rashly declares [something to be] 'holiness.' " This is a warning against hasty vows of dedication to God. However, the verb יָלַע is uncertain. Probably it is the Qal (G), or perhaps Hiphil (H), imperfect of לָעַע, and a Qal perfect form of the same verb probably occurs in Job 6:3. Most likely it means to speak without thoroughly considering one's words: "talk wildly" (BDB, s.v. לוּעַ II) or "speak rashly" (see *HALOT*, s.v. לעע I).

לְבַקֵּר׃—This Piel (D) infinitive construct (with לְ) of בָּקַר means "to reflect upon" (see *HALOT*, 2), hence "to reconsider." The infinitive construct expresses a result clause (cf. GKC, § 114 i): after his hasty, ill-considered vows, the person is forced to reconsider them.

20:26 מְזָרֶה ... וַיָּשֶׁב עֲלֵיהֶם אוֹפָן׃—The Piel (D) participle מְזָרֶה, "winnows," has a present-tense meaning, as does the Hiphil (H) imperfect with *waw* consecutive, וַיָּשֶׁב,

"and he returns" a wheel, that is, "he rolls" it. For the verb sequence, see Joüon, § 118 r. Most English versions and many commentators agree that, literally, "he returns the wheel upon them" refers to the rolling of a threshing wheel over the harvested shocks of grain to force the seed off of the stalks, which metaphorically represents the way a wise king (and eschatologically, God) "winnows" his subjects to separate the righteous from the wicked.

20:27 נֵר יְהוָה נִשְׁמַת אָדָם—Literally, "the breath of a man is the lamp of Yahweh" is a unique statement. Other OT passages refer to the "lamp of God" in the tabernacle (1 Sam 3:3; cf. Ex 40:25; Lev 24:4) or call Yahweh himself the believer's "lamp" (2 Sam 22:29) or the one who "gives light to my lamp" (Ps 18:29 [ET 18:28]; cf. Pss 119:105; 132:17; Job 29:3). Here the "lamp" that God has placed into a man is his "breath." See Gen 2:7, where God breathed the "breath of [נִשְׁמַת] life" into the first man. See also נְשָׁמָה, "breath," in Is 42:5; Job 27:3; 32:8; 33:4, where God or his Spirit is the source of human life and understanding.

חֹפֵשׂ כָּל־חַדְרֵי־בָטֶן׃—The subject of the masculine participle חֹפֵשׂ, "searches," must be one of the masculine nouns in the construct phrase נֵר יְהוָה, "the lamp of Yahweh" (in the first line of the verse), most likely the lamp, which Yahweh uses to search the (dark) inner recesses of the person. The object phrase, literally, "all the innermost chambers of the belly," refers to one's innermost being. In this pericope, חַדְרֵי־בָטֶן recurs in 20:30 (see also 18:8; 26:22).

20:28 חֶסֶד וֶאֱמֶת—These two nouns are paired also in 3:3; 14:22; 16:6. See the first textual note on 3:3.

20:30 חַבֻּרוֹת פֶּצַע תַּמְרִיק בְּרָע—The noun חַבּוּרָה, "wound," is applied to the Suffering Servant in Is 53:5. Its feminine plural is in the construct phrase, literally, "wounds of injury/bruise," which is translated as "wounds and bruises." Apparently the feminine plural noun is construed as a collective feminine singular subject of the feminine Kethib verb תַּמְרִיק. The Qal (G) of מָרַק means "rub, scrape, polish," so this Hiphil (H) has the force of "to clean" (*HALOT*) or "scour." The Kethib is preferable to the Qere, the noun תַּמְרוּק from the same root, meaning "a rubbing" (see BDB), as in Esth 2:3, 9, 12.

Commentary

These verses continue the section about dealing with fools and foolishness that extends from 19:13 through 22:16. This section was introduced by the proverb about a foolish son in 19:13. The reasons for considering that proverb (19:13) to mark the beginning of a section are discussed in the excursus "The Organization of the Sayings in Solomon's Proverbs in Proverbs 10:1–22:16" in the commentary on Proverbs 10. See also "A Foolish Son: Dealing with Fools and Foolishness (19:13–22:16)" in the commentary on 19:13–29.

20:1 This verse is connected to 19:28–29 by catchwords from the root ליץ (יָלִיץ, "mocks," 19:28; לֵצִים, "mockers," 19:29; לֵץ, "mocker," 20:1). This is the first proverb to warn about the abuse of alcohol. Subsequent proverbs that do so include 23:20–21, 29–35; 31:4–7. The NT extols being filled with the Holy Spirit instead of alcoholic drink (Eph 5:18; cf. Rom 14:17). Christians are incorporated into the body of Christ and are given the Spirit to drink in Baptism

(1 Cor 12:13; cf. Jn 7:38–39). For God-pleasing water imagery, see Prov 20:5 and possibly 20:9.[1]

20:2 This verse begins with a line nearly identical to the first line of 19:12. This saying warns against meddling with a powerful person, especially when he is angry, since his anger may turn and be directed at the intruder. If this is true about a human king, how much more should a person fear God and take refuge in Christ, who has propitiated God's wrath (Rom 3:25; 5:9).

20:3 This verse is a warning against needless strife. The fool looks for a fight. The honorable person seeks to avoid conflict when it is not necessary (see Rom 12:18). "Glory, honor" (כָּבוֹד) has an eschatological dimension, as in, for example, 3:16, 35; 8:18; 15:33; 22:4 (see also Ps 73:24). God promises eternal glory for those who promote spiritual peace (Mt 5:9; cf. Eph 2:17) and trust in Christ (Jn 17:22, 24; Rom 5:2; 8:18).

20:4 This verse is a saying not merely about farming, but also about work in general. The lazy person does not do his work when the opportunity presents itself, but he is foolish enough to think that he should profit later. At God's harvest on the Last Day, he shall receive nothing.

20:5 This verse speaks of the "advice, counsel" that God pours into those who are wise through faith (see the commentary on 18:4). Divine wisdom flowing and welling up within the believer (see Jn 4:14; 7:38–39) motivates him and acts as his advisor and guide. A wise person can draw out this profound wisdom like one draws water from a deep well.

20:6 This verse is joined to 20:5 by אִישׁ, "a person," which is used twice in each of these proverbs, once in each line. This saying builds on the theme of Spirit-given motives deep within a person (20:5) by noting that claims of loyalty are not the same as true fidelity. The noun in the difficult clause translated as "loyal" is חֶסֶד, for which, see the first textual note and the commentary on 3:3. There it is rendered as God's "mercy," and that proverb promises that God's "mercy and truth" attend those who are wise by faith (see also, e.g., 11:17; 14:22; as well as Jn 1:17). God's grace alone enables a person to be faith-filled and thereby to be faithful to God and other people. A wise person can discern and encourage such loyalty in others.

20:7 This verse begins a string of three proverbs that each begin with the letter *mem* (מ). The person whom God has forgiven and declared righteous strives to live according to God's righteous ways. The blessing he receives also benefits his children, who learn of God's righteousness from him (see Ex 20:4–6). See also grandchildren as beneficiaries in Prov 13:22 (cf. 17:6).

20:8 This verse depicts the king as supreme judge. His task is to separate wrongdoing from innocence and to punish those who have done wrong. This proverb and 20:26 compare the adjudicating king to a harvester who is "winnowing" (מְזָרֶה), separating the grain from the chaff (cf. Psalm 1). For details,

---

1 The textual note on 20:9 (with "cleansed") point out other passages where cleansing is associated with washing.

see the commentary on Prov 20:26. This proverb serves as an ideal for all who serve as magistrates and also is a warning to those who would attempt to defraud the court.

20:9 This verse uses a rhetorical question to remind all humans that they are sinful; only God's grace justifies and sanctifies. This serves as a subtle reminder not to judge others more harshly than we judge ourselves.[2] See the words of Jesus in Mt 7:1–5, especially Mt 7:2: "with the judgment by which you judge, you will be judged; and with the measure by which you measure, it will be measured to you."

20:10 This verse brings God's approbation upon fraud in using inaccurate weights and measures, a type of corrupt business practice condemned also in 20:23 as well as Amos 8:5. This injustice may be hard for human authorities to detect, but God sees and will judge it. The application of this proverb may be wider than simply the world of commerce. Since it is placed after 20:9, it may also speak of God's disgust with those who would hypocritically use a different measure of sin for themselves than they do for others (again, see Mt 7:1–5). God's standard is perfection (Mt 5:48), which he gives to his people by grace alone (Rom 12:2; Eph 4:13; Col 1:28; James 1:4).

This proverb also begins a series of three sayings that use the particle גַּם, "even, also, both."

20:11 This verse offers advice to parents. It reminds them to observe their child's behavior and cultivate conduct that is pleasing to God.

20:12 This verse states that God created human senses and the members of the body. It also implies that they are to be used in his service and to his glory. Only the gracious action of God the Holy Spirit can enable sinful humans to hear and believe God's Word, and to see the redemptive work God has accomplished for the salvation of all (see Is 6:9–10; Mt 13:9–17).

20:13 This verse is linked to 20:12 by the word עַיִן, "eye." Like 20:4, this proverb warns about the consequences of laziness. In contrast to 20:4, it also speaks of the rewards of diligence. Especially in spiritual matters, one must remain awake and alert (see Mt 25:13; Mk 13:33–37; 1 Thess 5:6).

20:14 This verse is a humorous description of haggling and bargaining. It teaches those with little experience in business deals to be on guard for misrepresentations and deceit by those with whom they are dealing. So too must believers have discernment to guard themselves against spiritual misrepresentations (Mt 24:5, 11; 1 Jn 4:1).

20:15 This verse favorably compares the value of knowledgeable words to gold and jewels, a theme found in the introductory chapters of Proverbs. It reminds Christians of the riches we have in Christ. See the commentary on 2:4; 3:14–15; 8:10–11, 19.

---

2 Similar wording is in the Wisdom of Amenemope, chapter 18 (19:18). See *ANET*, 423; *ANE*, 241. See also the excursus "The Words of Wise People (Prov 22:17–24:22) and Its Relationship to the Wisdom of Amenemope" in the commentary on Proverbs 22.

20:16 This verse is advice about holding people to the pledges they have made, especially when there is a great risk of default. See the commentary on 6:1. This proverb is repeated in 27:13 (see the textual notes on 20:16).

20:17 This verse is connected to 20:16 and 20:19 by a play on words: עָרַב, "guarantee a loan" (20:16), עָרֵב, "sweet" (20:17), and תִתְעָרָב, "get involved with" (20:19). Anything obtained dishonestly seems good at first (see 1:10–14; 9:17), but in the end it brings only judgment and death (see 1:15–19; 9:18).

20:18 This verse emphasizes wise planning though consulting the wisdom of other believers, as do several other proverbs (11:14; 15:22; 24:6). Jesus gives similar wisdom about the need to take counsel before engaging in a war (Lk 14:31–32), and in context this seems to refer to accepting peace with God through faith in Christ (Rom 5:1). An unbeliever who rejects the Gospel foolishly wages war against God the King and will be overwhelmingly defeated.

20:19 This verse begins with a line that is similar to 11:13a. Whereas that proverb distinguishes between a gossip and a person who can keep a secret, this one counsels avoiding people who do not show a potential for keeping secrets.[3]

The warning not to "have fellowship" or "get involved" with a person who cannot keep his mouth shut can be compared to the same negated verb in 24:21, a warning not to have fellowship with those who do not fear Yahweh. Both proverbs anticipate St. Paul's warning to avoid those who cause schisms by their smooth talk and false doctrine (Rom 16:17–18; cf. Prov 7:21) and his command for the faithful pastor to rebuke such persons (1 Tim 1:3–7; 6:3–5).

20:20 This verse notes the seriousness of violating the Fourth Commandment.[4] Those who call God's curses down upon their parents are defying God's authority. The penalty prescribed for this in the Torah was death (Ex 21:17; Lev 20:9; cf. Deut 27:16), the snuffing out of the offender's lamp of life. "Total darkness" is similar to the depictions of everlasting perdition in, for example, Jude 6, 13. See also Prov 21:4, and contrast Yahweh's "lamp" in 20:27.

20:21 This verse contrasts with the enduring wealth proffered in 20:15 and the everlasting inheritance promised the believer in, for example, 3:35 as well as Mt 25:34; Eph 1:11, 14; 1 Pet 1:4. It once again notes that haste in obtaining riches is often a sign of foolishness, since such wealth does not last (see also 13:11; 28:20). The end of those who pursue it is judgment (cf. 1 Cor 6:9–10; Jude 10–19).

A person could gain an "inheritance" quickly (or "by greed"; see the first textual note) by facilitating the death of his father. Therefore this proverb relates to the cursing of parents in Prov 20:20. Taken together, these proverbs suggest that attempting to obtain (or even desiring) an inheritance prematurely is a form of cursing one's parents. The father in Lk 15:12 was astonishingly generous

---

[3] This proverb is often compared to the Wisdom of Amenemope, chapter 21 (22:13–14), but the connection is weak. See *ANET*, 424; *ANE*, 242.

[4] See further the excursus "Proverbs 1–9, Christ, and the Ten Commandments" in the commentary on Proverbs 1.

because he bequeathed to his prodigal son a share of the inheritance while he, the father, was far from dead; the son's request was tantamount to a death wish for his father.

20:22 This verse counsels reliance on Yahweh to execute vengeance and to rescue his believers (see also 25:21–22 as well as Deut 32:35; Rom 12:19–20).[5] This does not forbid using public and orderly ways to obtain redress when one is injured by the actions of someone else, because government is one of God's ways of exacting punishment on those who do wrong (Rom 13:1–7; Ap XVI 6–8). However, this saying does forbid private revenge. See Rom 12:17–21, especially Rom 12:19: "beloved, never avenge yourselves, but leave it to the wrath [of God]" (cf. Mt 5:25; 1 Cor 5:12–6:8).

20:23 This verse repeats the thought of 11:1 and 20:10.[6] For תּוֹעֲבַת יְהוָה, "a disgusting thing to Yahweh," see the excursus " 'Disgusting Thing' (תּוֹעֵבָה) in Solomon's Proverbs" in the commentary on Proverbs 11. For the construct phrase מֹאזְנֵי מִרְמָה, "dishonest scales," see the first textual note on 11:1.

20:24 This proverb begins another set of three that start with the letter *mem* (מ), as did 20:7–9. This verse observes that no person has autonomy. Yet this proverb should not be construed to mean that God is the agent of evil or that he guides unbelievers to perdition in hell. The rest of Proverbs (e.g., 9:1–6) makes clear that God extends his guiding wisdom to all people through his Word and in the person of his Son.[7] He desires everyone to believe his wisdom and be guided by it along his way into the fullness of salvation. But those who reject his wisdom thereby travel down the other way, which seems appealing and right to them because they do not discern its end (see 7:27; 9:18; 14:12; 16:25).

The second line affirms that sin still clouds the minds of believers even as they walk their pilgrimage along God's path in this life (cf. Jer 17:9–10; Rom 3:9–20). God alone knows the ways of their hearts and their every deed, even secret and inadvertent sins of which they are not aware (Deut 29:28 [ET 29:29]; Jer 16:17; Ps 19:13 [ET 19:12]). Therefore it is imperative to rely on God and his Word to guide one to salvation instead of leaning on human understanding, even one's own intellect (see Prov 3:5–6; 14:12; 16:25; Jer 17:5–8; Jn 14:6).

20:25 This verse warns against making rash vows or oaths that dedicate something to God as holy. This risks violating the Second Commandment (Ex 20:7; Deut 5:11) and profaning the holy name of Yahweh (Lev 19:12). God expects those who make a pledge, especially one taken in his name, to fulfill it. The Torah provided a way to buy oneself out of a hastily made vow, but it was expensive (Lev 27:1–24). Jesus counsels his disciples not to swear at all, but

---

[5] A similar theme is found in the Wisdom of Amenemope, chapter 21 (22:1–6). See *ANET*, 424; *ANE*, 242.

[6] This proverb is said to be similar in thought to the Wisdom of Amenemope, chapter 16 (17:18–19). See *ANET*, 423; *ANE*, 241.

[7] See "Wisdom in Proverbs" in the introduction. See also the commentary on 1:1–7; 3:13–20; 8:22–31; 30:1b–10; and the excursus "Proverbs 8, Wisdom, Christology, and the Arian Controversy" in the commentary on chapter 8.

simply to use "yes" and "no" (Mt 5:33–37; cf. James 5:12). Only rarely in the apostolic era did some disciples of Jesus voluntarily take a vow (Acts 18:18; 21:23; contrast Acts 23:12, 14, 21). The *Didache* teaches the Christian not to swear (οὐκ ἐπιορκήσεις, 2:3) and to exercise restraint in speech (2:3–5).

20:26 This verse, like 20:8, uses imagery of the harvest to speak of a king's role in judging. The king "winnows out the wicked." The first step in winnowing was to thresh, to drag or roll something heavy over the stalks to force the grain to separate from its pod. This is probably the image used in the second line of this proverb. The king forces the good to be separated from the wicked when he judges wisely. This saying speaks of the usefulness of judges and courts that seek justice by sparing the innocent but convicting the guilty. Solomon is the prime OT example of the adjudicator with divine wisdom (1 Ki 3:9, 16–28), but Jesus is the "one greater than Solomon" (Mt 12:42). On the Last Day he shall separate the righteous from the wicked as one separates the wheat from the tares (Mt 13:38–43; cf. Mt 25:31–48).

20:27 Yahweh alone kindles the lamp of spiritual life that will never be snuffed out (contrast 20:20). Jesus is the light of the world (Jn 8:12; 9:5). God scrutinizes a person down to his most secret thoughts (cf. Mt 10:30; Acts 1:24; 15:8). Thus God judges the heart and knows those who are his (1 Sam 16:7; 2 Tim 2:19). In Rev 2:23 the exalted Christ claims the ability ascribed to Yahweh in this proverb. St. Paul seems to draw on this proverb as he speaks of God as the one who "searches" human hearts and knows the mind of the Spirit (Rom 8:27), and when he affirms that the Spirit "searches" everything, even the deep things of God (1 Cor 2:10).

20:28 This verse is an observation that rulers cannot make their position secure using tyranny, corruption, or bloodshed. The only way a ruler can remain secure is to do God's will and show mercy while upholding truth. This is how Christ the King reigns; he is God the Son (Psalm 2; Ps 45:7 [ET 45:6]; Heb 1:8).

20:29 This verse notes that in youth men are valued for their strength, an asset that is not always used wisely. Old men are valued for their wisdom (and righteousness [see 16:31]) that has allowed them to attain an old age and gray hair. This points beyond advanced earthly years (cf. Is 65:20) to God's promises of everlasting "life" through wisdom (e.g., 3:2, 18, 22; 4:10, 13, 22–23).

20:30 This verse speaks of the theology of the cross. God can use suffering to refine his people as his Holy Spirit works their inner renewal (2 Cor 4:16) through his Word and Sacraments:

> And not only this, but we also boast in our tribulations, knowing that tribulation brings about perseverance; and perseverance, character; and character, hope; and hope is not put to shame, because God's love has been poured out in our hearts through the Holy Spirit, who was given to us. (Rom 5:3–5; see also 2 Cor 12:5–10; James 1:2–4)

Proverbs 21:1–31

Wise and Foolish Behaviors, Part 1

Translation

21 **[1]A king's heart in the hand of Yahweh is streams of water:**
he directs it wherever he desires.
[2]A person considers his every way to be upright,
but Yahweh weighs motives.
[3]Doing righteousness and justice
is more acceptable to Yahweh than a sacrifice.
[4]Haughty eyes and an arrogant heart:
[this] lamp of wicked people is sin.
[5]The plans of a hardworking person [lead] only to abundance,
but every person in a hurry [progresses] only toward poverty.
[6]Making a fortune by a lying tongue
is a fleeting vapor and snares of death.
[7]The violence of wicked people will drag them away,
because they refuse to do what is just.
[8]A guilty person's way is very crooked,
but the conduct of a pure person is straight.
[9]Better to live on the corner of a roof
than in a home shared with a quarrelsome wife.
[10]The soul of a wicked person craves evil.
His neighbor is not viewed mercifully in his eyes.
[11]When a mocker is punished, a gullible person becomes wise,
and when a wise person is instructed, he gains knowledge.
[12]The Righteous One pays attention to the house of a wicked person.
He is turning wicked people toward ruin.
[13]The person who shuts his ear to the cries of a poor person—
he too will cry out and not be answered.
[14]A gift [given] in secret soothes anger,
and a secret bribe [soothes] great fury.
[15]It is a joy for a righteous person to do justice,
but destruction is for those who do evil.
[16]A person who wanders from the way of understanding
will rest in the company of the souls of the dead.
[17]Whoever loves pleasure will be a poor person.
Whoever loves wine and olive oil will never be rich.
[18]The wicked person is a ransom for a righteous person,
and the treacherous person [is a ransom] in place of upright people.
[19]Better to live in desert country
than with a quarrelsome and ill-tempered wife.

[20]A pantry of choice food and olive oil are in the dwelling of a wise person,
but a foolish person will devour it [his own goods].
[21]The person who pursues righteousness and mercy
will find life, righteousness, and honor.
[22]A wise person can attack a city of warriors
and pull down the strong defenses in which it [that city] trusts.
[23]The person who guards his mouth and his tongue
guards himself from troubles.
[24]The haughty arrogant person: his name is Mocker.
He behaves with overwhelming arrogance.
[25]A lazy person's craving will kill him,
because his hands refuse to work.
[26]All day long [a wicked person] craves something,
but a righteous person gives and does not hold back.
[27]A sacrifice offered by wicked people is a disgusting thing—
how much more when they bring it with evil intent!
[28]A lying witness will perish,
but a person who listens will subdue [him] forever.
[29]A wicked person puts on a bold front,
but an upright person thinks about his way.
[30]There is no wisdom, no cleverness,
and no advice [that can stand up] against Yahweh.
[31]A horse is made ready for a day of battle,
but the victory belongs to Yahweh.

Textual Notes

21:2 וְתֹכֵ֖ן לִבּ֣וֹת יְהוָֽה׃—The verb תָּכַן, "measure, evaluate," occurs as a Qal (G) participle with Yahweh as the subject in 16:2; 21:2; 24:12. In all three verses the object is translated as "motives." In the latter two verses, the object is, literally, human "hearts," but the noun לֵב is used with the meaning "will, intention" (*HALOT*, 6), hence, "motives." See the second textual note on 16:2, where the object is, literally, human "spirits."

21:3 עֲ֭שֹׂה צְדָקָ֣ה וּמִשְׁפָּ֑ט נִבְחָ֖ר לַיהוָ֣ה מִזָּֽבַח׃—"Righteousness" and "justice" are paired also in 8:20 and 16:8 and frequently in the Prophets. The infinitive construct עֲשֹׂה, literally, "to do," is the subject of the Niphal (N) participle נִבְחָר, "is preferable" to Yahweh (see *HALOT*, 2), "is more acceptable" to Yahweh (see Waltke-O'Connor, § 23.3d, example 18, and ESV, NIV, NRSV), or "is desired by" Yahweh (NASB). The preposition מִן on the noun זֶבַח (pausal: זָבַח) is comparative: "than sacrifice." Samuel uses מִזֶּבַח to express the same theological point in 1 Sam 15:22.

Similar to מִשְׁפָּט ... עֲשֹׂה, "to do ... justice," is לַעֲשׂ֣וֹת מִשְׁפָּ֑ט in 21:7.

21:4 רוּם־עֵ֭ינַיִם וּרְחַב־לֵ֑ב—"High eyes" and "a wide heart" are idioms describing arrogance and egotism (*HALOT*, s.vv. רוּם, 2 b; רָחָב I, 3).

נִ֖ר רְשָׁעִ֣ים חַטָּֽאת׃—"The lamp of wicked people is sin" recalls 20:20 and contrasts with 20:27. The noun נֵר is a defectively spelled instance of נִיר, a "lamp" (BDB, s.v. נִיר I, under the root נור), not the homograph נִיר that means "fallow land, land ready to be farmed.” Many Hebrew manuscripts point it as נֵר, “lamp,” a synonym from the same root as נִיר I. Either pointing is supported by λαμπτήρ in the LXX.

21:6 הֶבֶל נִדָּף מְבַקְשֵׁי־מָוֶת׃—Wealth gained by lying is called “a fleeting vapor,” apparently “[*for*] those who are seeking death.” This would designate liars as foolishly “seeking death.” This could allude to earlier proverbs where fools are seduced into “death” (e.g., 7:27) and are said to love “death” (8:36), which has an eschatological sense pointing to eternal perdition in hell. However, many emend the participle מְבַקְשֵׁי־, “those who are seeking,” to וּמוֹקְשֵׁי־, “and snares of” death, on the basis of several Hebrew manuscripts, the LXX (παγίδας), and the Vulgate (*laqueos*).

21:7 שֹׁד־רְשָׁעִים יְגוֹרֵם—The noun שֹׁד, “violence,” recurs in 24:2. The genitive is subjective: “violence done by wicked people.” שֹׁד is the subject of the singular verb יְגוֹרֵם. The rare verb גָּרַר, “drag away,” occurs in the Qal (G) also in Hab 1:15, where Babylon drags away apostate Israelites like fish caught in a net.

21:8 הֲפַכְפַּךְ דֶּרֶךְ אִישׁ וָזָר—The adjective הֲפַכְפַּךְ, “crooked,” occurs only here in the OT. Its reduplicated form suggests an intensive meaning: “*very* crooked.” It is derived from the verb הָפַךְ, as also is the noun תַּהְפֻּכוֹת in, for example, Prov 2:12, 14.

The first part of the clause, literally, “crooked is the way of a man,” is clear enough, but the meaning of וָזָר is unknown. As pointed, it seems to be an adjective modifying אִישׁ, “a man/person.” Most understand it as “guilty” (*DCH*) based on Arabic cognates (see *HALOT*). Others repoint it to וְזָר, “and strange,” and assume that it modifies דֶּרֶךְ, “way.” Sometimes דֶּרֶךְ is feminine, but here it is construed as masculine since it is already modified by the masculine adjective הֲפַכְפַּךְ. Some would change אִישׁ וָזָר to אִישׁ כָּזָב, “a man who is a liar.”[1] Others would rewrite the entire first line.[2]

However, these emendations ignore the striking sound pattern between וָזָר and וְזַךְ that links the two halves of the saying as well as other sound patterns in the saying that depends on these two words.[3]

וְזַךְ יָשָׁר פָּעֳלוֹ׃—The adjective זַךְ (also in 16:2; 20:11) means “pure, righteous” (see BDB, 2), and here is used as a substantive: literally, “but *a pure person*—straight [is] his action/conduct.” The adjective יָשָׁר, “straight, right,” is an antonym of הֲפַכְפַּךְ in the preceding clause.

21:9 טוֹב לָשֶׁבֶת עַל־פִּנַּת־גָּג—The infinitive construct שֶׁבֶת, from יָשַׁב, “live, sit,” is the subject of this nominal sentence: literally, “to live on a corner of a roof is better …” (see Joüon, § 124 b A 1).

מֵאֵשֶׁת מִדְיָנִים—The construct phrase אֵשֶׁת מִדְיָנִים, “a wife of quarrels,” is repeated as the reading with the Qere in 21:19; 25:24; 27:15. The contexts show that this refers to a wife who is prone to causing unjustified quarrels with her husband, so it is probably either a subjective genitive, “a wife of (who provokes) quarrels,” or an adjectival genitive, “a quarrelsome wife,” as adopted in the translation above. See the second textual note on 19:13.

---

1 *BHS* footnote; Scott, *Proverbs, Ecclesiastes*, 123.

2 Driver, “Problems in the Hebrew Text of Proverbs,” 185.

3 McCreesh, *Biblical Sound and Sense*, 58–59.

Lest Proverbs be misinterpreted as misogynistic, the masculine equivalent אִישׁ מִדְיָנִים, "a man of quarrels, a quarrelsome man," is the reading with the Qere in 26:21. Positive phrases about a wife in laudatory contexts include אִשָּׁה מַשְׂכָּלֶת, "a wife with good sense" (19:14), and אֵשֶׁת־חַיִל, "a wife with strong character" (31:10).

וּבֵית חָבֶר׃—Literally, "and a house of association" means "and a shared home" (see BDB, s.v. חָבֶר I, 2, and *HALOT*, s.v. חָבֶר I, 1 b). The two phrases loosely joined, "a quarrelsome wife *and* a shared home," mean "*in* a home shared *with* a quarrelsome wife."

21:10 לֹא־יֻחַן בְּעֵינָיו רֵעֵהוּ׃—The verb יֻחַן is a Qal passive (Gp) imperfect of חָנַן, "be gracious, merciful" (see Waltke-O'Connor, § 22.6, including n. 32). Its subject is רֵעֵהוּ, so the clause means "his neighbor is not viewed mercifully in his eyes."

21:11 בַּעְנָשׁ־ ... וּבְהַשְׂכִּיל—Both lines of the verse begin with an infinitive construct with בְּ forming a temporal clause: "when ..." Both infinitives have no expressed subject, but each has an object. The translation renders each verb as a passive with its object as its subject: "a mocker [לֵץ] is punished" and "a wise person [חָכָם] is instructed," respectively.

21:12 מַשְׂכִּיל צַדִּיק ... מְסַלֵּף—The "Righteous One" (צַדִּיק) is the subject of the participle מַשְׂכִּיל, which has the intransitive meaning "pays attention." He is also the subject of the participle that begins the next line of this verse. The lack of an article on צַדִּיק may be "indeterminateness for the sake of amplification" in reference to God (GKC, § 125 c). For his identity as the subject of this proverb, see the commentary.

מְסַלֵּף רְשָׁעִים לָרָע׃—For the Piel (D) of סָלַף, see the second textual note on 13:6. Since the implied subject of the participle is "Righteous One" in the preceding line, the preposition and noun לָרָע should not be taken to refer to an evil purpose, as the expression did in 1:16 (see the textual note on 1:16). Instead, it denotes result: God "turns toward ruin" the "wicked" (רְשָׁעִים) as a result of their refusal to be corrected (see 21:7) and their persistence in their wickedness.

21:13 אֹטֵם אָזְנוֹ—The participle אֹטֵם, literally, "one who keeps shutting," is also in 17:28, but with "his lips" as its object and in a good sense, instead of "his ear" here and in a bad sense.

21:14 בַּסֵּתֶר ... בַּחֵק—To match "in secret," the parallel בַּחֵק, literally, "in the bosom," is translated as "secret." See the textual note on 17:23, which has מֵחֵיק.

21:15 שִׂמְחָה לַצַּדִּיק עֲשׂוֹת מִשְׁפָּט—Literally, this is "joy for the righteous person (is) to do justice." The infinitive construct עֲשׂוֹת takes the noun מִשְׁפָּט as its accusative object (Joüon, § 124 i).

21:16 מִדֶּרֶךְ הַשְׂכֵּל—The Hiphil (H) infinitive absolute הַשְׂכֵּל has the meaning of a noun in construct here: "from the way *of understanding*" (see Waltke-O'Connor, § 35.3.3, including example 10).

רְפָאִים—This noun, repeated from 2:18 and 9:18, denotes those who are both physically and spiritually dead. Their souls have departed their bodies for שְׁאוֹל, "Sheol" (9:18; see the first textual note and the commentary on 1:12). After the resurrection of all people, they will be consigned to everlasting perdition in hell (Is 66:24; Dan 12:2; Rev 20:15).

21:19 מֵאֵשֶׁת מִדְיָנִים וָכָעַס׃—Literally, this is "than a wife of quarrels and of vexation." For the two words in the first construct chain, see the second textual note on 21:9. The third word here, the noun כַּעַס, is an unusual second genitive, a second word also in construct with אֵשֶׁת.

21:20 אוֹצָר ׀ נֶחְמָד וָשֶׁמֶן—An אוֹצָר can refer to a "treasure" or "wealth," as in 21:6. Or it can refer to a "treasury," as when God promises to fill the "treasuries" of believers by his Wisdom (8:21), or a "storeroom" (see *HALOT*, 1 a). It is modified by the Niphal participle נֶחְמָד, "desired, desirable." "A desirable storehouse" probably means "a pantry with choice food," since the phrase is followed by a food item, "and (olive) oil" (וָשֶׁמֶן). This culinary interpretation fits the verb "swallow, devour" in the next clause.

וּכְסִיל אָדָם יְבַלְּעֶנּוּ׃—For כְּסִיל אָדָם, literally, "a fool of a man," see the second textual note on 15:20. The parallelism to the first clause implies that the masculine singular suffix on the verb יְבַלְּעֶנּוּ, "he will swallow *it*," must refer to the fool's stored food, which he does not save for the future, but immediately devours. בָּלַע, "swallow, devour," is also used in 1:12 and 19:28 for greedy and wicked people whose insatiable appetite causes them to rob and slander—to their own destruction (1:18–19).

21:22 עִיר גִּבֹּרִים עָלָה חָכָם—The idiom "go up" (עָלָה) against "a city" (עִיר) means to attack it. In this context the verb in this line and the next both have a potential meaning: "*can* attack … *(can)* pull down." The verbs do not state what a wise person must do or is expected (by God) to do (cf. Mt 17:20; 21:21).

וַיֹּרֶד עֹז מִבְטֶחָה׃—The feminine suffix on the noun מִבְטֶחָה, literally, "*its* (object of) trust," refers back to the feminine noun עִיר, "city," and by metonymy, this refers to the city's inhabitants as the ones who trust in its defenses. The suffix (normally הּ-) on מִבְטֶחָה may lack *mappiq* because the word is in pause (Joüon, § 94 h).

21:24 זֵד יָהִיר לֵץ שְׁמוֹ—The adjective זֵד, "insolent, presumptuous, arrogant," here used as a substantive, is cognate to the noun זָדוֹן, "insolence, arrogance" in the second line of the verse. The adjective יָהִיר, "haughty, proud," occurs elsewhere only in Hab 2:5. The participle לֵץ or other forms of the verb לִיץ occur eighteen times in Proverbs, always in the sections by Solomon. See "לֵץ, 'Mocker,' and לָצוֹן, 'Mocking, Scoffing' " in "Fools in Proverbs" in the introduction.

21:26 כָּל־הַיּוֹם הִתְאַוָּה תַאֲוָה—Literally, this is "all the day he craves a craving." The Hithpael (HtD) of אָוָה takes the cognate accusative noun תַּאֲוָה. See Joüon, § 125 q, and Waltke-O'Connor, §10.2.1g, including example 37 and note 12. This kind of construction is favored in Hebrew, but avoided in English.

21:27 זֶבַח רְשָׁעִים תּוֹעֵבָה—The first line of this proverb is identical to the first line of 15:8 except that it has the absolute form of תּוֹעֵבָה, "a disgusting thing," instead of the construct phrase תּוֹעֲבַת יְהוָה, "a disgusting thing to Yahweh." See the textual note and the commentary on 15:8.

21:28 עֵד־כְּזָבִים יֹאבֵד—Literally, "a witness of lies" is "a lying/false witness," like those in Mk 14:56–59.

וְאִישׁ שׁוֹמֵעַ לָנֶצַח יְדַבֵּר׃—This might literally mean "a man listening, forever he will speak." But most probably יְדַבֵּר is not the common verb for "speak" but a homograph. The Piel (D) form here may mean "he will destroy, subdue" (see *DCH*, s.v. דבר II). For other occurrences of this verb, see Pss 18:48 (ET 18:47); 47:4 (ET 47:3).[4] The implied object would be the "false witness." A less likely proposal is that the verb means "he will leave behind descendants [forever]" (Waltke-O'Connor, § 24.4e, example 2).

21:29 הֵעֵ֤ז אִ֣ישׁ רָשָׁ֣ע בְּפָנָ֑יו—Literally, this is "a wicked man [אִ֣ישׁ רָשָׁ֣ע] makes strong [הֵעֵ֤ז] with his face [בְּפָנָ֑יו]." This is an idiom for attempting to look bold or fearless. For the use of the preposition בְּ after the Hiphil (H) verb (הֵעֵ֤ז), see Joüon, § 125 b.

וְ֝יָשָׁ֗ר ה֤וּא ׀ יָכִ֬ין דַּרְכָּֽיו׃—For both of the last two words, the Qere, יָבִ֬ין דַּרְכּֽוֹ, is to be preferred: literally, "an upright person—he thinks about his way." This reading is also found in one Hebrew manuscript. The Kethib is יָכִ֬ין דַּרְכָּֽיו, "he establishes his ways," but only God can do that. Yahweh is the stated subject of active forms of כּוּן, "establish," in 3:19; 8:27; 16:9, and he is the implied agent of passive forms of the verb ("be established") in, for example, 4:26 and 16:3.

21:31 וְ֝לַיהוָ֗ה הַתְּשׁוּעָֽה׃—The noun תְּשׁוּעָה refers to "victory" in a military context also in 24:6, and probably in 11:14 as well. It is cognate to the similar noun יְשׁוּעָה, "salvation," which is common in the OT, especially in the Prophets. See לַיהוָ֥ה הַיְשׁוּעָ֑ה, "to Yahweh belongs (the) salvation," in Ps 3:9 (ET 3:8).

Commentary

These verses continue the section about dealing with fools and foolishness (19:13–22:16), a section introduced by the proverb about a foolish son in 19:13. The reasons for considering that proverb (19:13) to mark the beginning of a section are discussed in the excursus "The Organization of the Sayings in Solomon's Proverbs in Proverbs 10:1–22:16" in the commentary on Proverbs 10. See also "A Foolish Son: Dealing with Fools and Foolishness (19:13–22:16)" in the commentary on 19:13–29.

21:1 This verse is the first of three sayings mentioning Yahweh. A king wields great power, but when his heart is in the hand of Yahweh, God directs his heart wherever he (God) wants it to go. God's gracious will causes the king's heart to be like streams of water, providing life for the people. Wisdom itself is a "fountain of life" (10:11; 13:14; 14:27; 16:22; cf. 18:4).

This proverb is a reminder that every leader is to govern as God wills. No matter how powerful a ruler may be, God is in control (Jn 11:51; 19:11; Rom 13:1). This is not only a warning for rulers who may think they are supreme over everything, but it is also comfort to God's people even when government is corrupt and evil because they know that God is in charge, ruling the world for the sake of the advent of his kingdom in Christ (Rev 11:15).

21:2 This verse is linked to 21:1 by the mention of "Yahweh" and the catchwords כָּל, "wherever/every," and לֵב, "heart/motives." This proverb, like 16:2, whose second line is similar, reminds us that while humans look primarily at their actions, God weighs motives. He will be the Judge on the Last Day.

21:3 This verse emphasizes that saving faith results in righteous deeds throughout daily life as well as in worship. God-given "righteousness" saves a

---

[4] Emerton, "The Interpretation of Proverbs 21,28."

person from death (10:2; 11:4) and confers eternal life (11:19) even as it guides one's way of life (8:20; 11:5; 13:6). "Religion that is pure and undefiled before (our) God and Father is this: to care for orphans and widows in their affliction, and to keep oneself unstained from the world" (James 1:27).

21:4 This verse appears to say that the "lamp" or light that guides wicked people in their arrogance is their own sin.

21:5 The first line about the "hardworking person" (חָרוּץ) recalls similar proverbs with that term (10:4; 12:24, 27; 13:4). The second line cautions that those who are in a hurry to amass riches often get the opposite result because of the foolish and sinful short cuts they take (see also 13:11; 20:21; 28:20). Compare the English proverb "haste makes waste."

21:6 This verse shares with 21:5 the theme of acquiring possessions wrongly. The problem with gaining riches through deceit is that the riches do not last and the sins committed carry the threat of eternal death.

21:7 This verse notes that wicked people will become victims of their own violence, as in 1:18–19. The violence they commit only begets more violence directed at them, either by rivals engaged in the same activities or by authorities, who are seeking to stop crime. In the end, God will punish them. Though they may protest when violence is directed at them, they have no valid grounds to complain because they had refused to do what is right. See "refuse" (the Piel [D] of מָאֵן) also in 1:24 and 21:25.

21:8 This verse has a difficult first line (see the textual note), but it is clear that it contrasts the crooked way of an unbeliever with the straight conduct of a righteous person, who can be recognized by what he does.

21:9 This verse is the first of two proverbs in this chapter that speak of a quarrelsome spouse; the other is 21:19. In this case the seeming disadvantage of braving the elements on a roof is better than the apparent blessing of cozy shelter when constant bickering is present. This proverb is repeated almost verbatim in 25:24 (see the commentary there).

21:10 This verse points out the incompatibility of evil desire versus grace. The sinful nature craves evil, but God's grace in Christ moves us to be gracious toward one another. Showing mercy often requires putting aside one's personal preferences and selfish interest for the sake of another person's good. Jesus' parable of the master and his debtors illustrates this (Mt 18:23–35).

21:11 This verse first notes how the application of punishment according to God's Law can be instructive to "a gullible person," that is, someone who has not yet learned wisdom but who is also not an incorrigible fool. Wisdom in, for example, 1:4 and 9:4 invites the "gullible" to learn. Such people see punishment, and the fear of it leads them away from foolishness. The threat of punishment drives them toward the wisdom of God in the Gospel.[5]

---

5 See "Wisdom in Proverbs" in the introduction. See also the commentary on 1:1–7; 3:13–20; 8:22–31; 30:1b–10; and the excursus "Proverbs 8, Wisdom, Christology, and the Arian Controversy" in the commentary on chapter 8.

The second line refers to a wise person. The wise are people who believe the Gospel and are motivated to love God and their neighbor. They are instructed by the Word and gain knowledge. The Law keeps them aware of the sinful nature that still clings to them in this life. In this way they do not fall back and begin relying on their own holiness and piety (see FC SD VI 18–25).

This proverb is tied to the following one by Hiphil (H) forms of the verb שָׂכַל, "instructed/pays attention."

21:12 This verse first notes that God is aware of what the wicked do, even when it may not appear that way. Then it states that even when they appear prosperous, God will turn wicked people to destruction. His will is to save all people (1 Tim 2:4), but if they remain impenitent they will fall under his judgment.

Many understand צַדִּיק in this verse to be a "righteous" human instead of God, since this term is only used of God in one other passage, Is 24:16. However, many passages use cognate terms to describe God as righteous and to refer to his righteousness. Moreover, Proverbs never depicts righteous people as acting to cause the ruin of the wicked. The doom of the wicked is only in God's hands.

21:13 This verse is a warning to those who have no mercy that they cannot expect to receive mercy when they will need it. This theme is also found in the NT: Mt 18:23–35 (the master and his ungrateful forgiven debtor) and Lk 16:19–31 (the rich man and Lazarus). Contrast Mt 5:7: "blessed are the merciful, for they shall receive mercy."

21:14 This verse is not an endorsement of bribery, but an observation of the effect of such gifts (see also 17:8; 18:16). It cautions that bribery works among sinful people, even if it is not right (see also 15:27; 17:23). The use of "gift" and "bribe" in parallel lines may be an indication that it is not always easy to distinguish one from the other.[6]

21:15 This verse characterizes the righteous as rejoicing in justice. As just people—justified by God's grace alone—they have nothing to fear from the performance of God's justice. They also truly love God and his justice. They joyfully use opportunities to act justly and exult when they see other people or God carrying out justice.

The second line of this saying is identical to the second line of 10:29, whose first line clarifies that the "destruction" comes from Yahweh's judgment upon those who practice evil. They cannot rejoice, but have the fear of punishment because of their penchant for ignoring, belittling, and breaking God's Law.

21:16 This verse repeats a familiar theme in Proverbs: those who do not stay on the way of wisdom will perish eternally (see, e.g., 2:18; see also Mt 7:13–14).

21:17 Instant gratification and constant indulgence in luxuries lead to "poverty" (מַחְסוֹר), either lack of wherewithal because it has been foolishly

[6] Kidner, *Proverbs*, 143.

spent or spiritual poverty that is rich in things but poor toward God. The point is not that a person should not enjoy God-given pleasures, but that a person who is focused on them, rather than on the diligence and virtue that bring such pleasures, will not attain them—a point already made in 13:4.

This is the first of three proverbs in this chapter whose second line repeats an important term from the first line, here אֹהֵב, "who loves." The other two are 21:21, 23 (cf. the textual note on 21:24).

21:18 This verse is difficult because of the word כֹּפֶר, "ransom." What does it mean that a wicked person somehow is a ransom price paid to free the righteous? Commentators have offered many solutions to this dilemma, most of them unsatisfactory. The most that can be safely said about this proverb is that it offers an assurance that ultimately on Judgment Day, the righteous—who are not sinless, but are righteous by faith alone in Christ (Gen 15:6; Is 53:11)—will be delivered from all punishment for sin. However, the wicked will not be delivered from judgment.

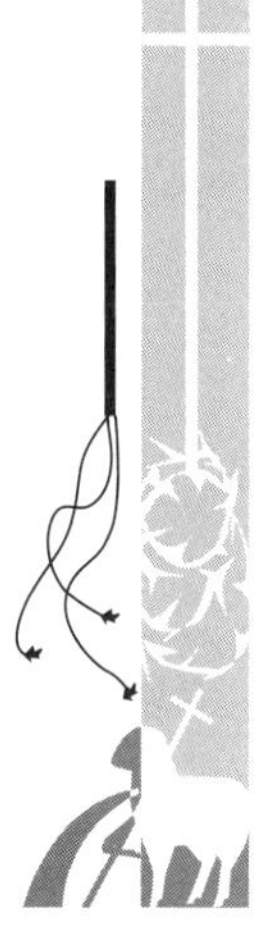

Considered within the whole of Holy Scripture, this proverb states the Gospel: "a wicked person" is a vicarious, substitutionary sacrifice for the salvation of the "righteous." This is fulfilled by Jesus Christ, the sinless Son: "him who knew no sin [Christ] he [God] made to be sin for our sake, so that we might become the righteousness of God in him" (2 Cor 5:21).

21:19 This verse is similar in thought to 21:9. The comparison in this saying is between living alone or with refractory companionship. While companionship is generally a good thing, a solitary existence is better than choosing companionship with a contentious spouse. However, for those already married, God calls the believing spouse to continue to forgive and live with the unbeliever as long as a marriage relationship is possible (1 Cor 7:10–16).

21:20 This verse notes the difference between the wise and foolish when it comes to foresight. The wise have the foresight to look to the future, recognize what truly is treasure, and store up good things, while the foolish person lives only for the present and consumes whatever is available now. This saying is not limited in its application to wealth or food, or even just to worldly foresight. The "pantry of choice food" (literally, "desirable storehouse") and "olive oil" point to the spiritual wealth described in 21:21: "righteousness," which brings everlasting "life" (see, e.g., Eph 1:7, 18; 2:7). The importance of spiritual foresight is a constant theme of Proverbs 1–9 (1:4; 2:11; 3:21; 5:2; 8:12). Tragically, the foolish lack foresight and so will be found wanting on Judgment Day (see also 21:16–17).

21:21 This verse encourages the foresight praised in 21:20. The person who pursues God's "righteousness" (see also, e.g., 1:3; 2:9; 8:18, 20) and "mercy," which are to be found and are available to all only in Christ, finds them and more ("my cup overflows," Ps 23:5; "running over," Lk 6:38). In the proverb the believer seeks two things, "righteousness" and "mercy," but receives more—three things. The first is eternal "life" (see also, e.g., Prov 3:2, 18, 22; 4:10, 13, 22–23). The second is the "righteousness" he seeks (see Mt 6:33).

The third is "glory/honor" from God (see also, e.g., Prov 3:16, 35; 8:18; 15:33; Mt 5:6; Rom 8:18; 1 Pet 5:1). Imputed "righteousness saves from death" (Prov 10:2; 11:4) and results in "life" also in 11:19 and 12:28.

On the basis of the LXX, some commentators would delete the second occurrence of צְדָקָה, "righteousness."[7] However, this misses the point of the proverb (that through faith a person receives the "righteousness" he seeks [see Mt 6:33]). It also fails to account for other proverbs in this immediate context that also repeat an important word from the first line in the second line (21:17, 23; cf. the textual note on 21:24).

21:22 This verse describes the superiority of wisdom in military terms (see also 24:5–6; 31:10; and Eccl 9:13–16). Wisdom from God enables one to fight and win spiritual warfare (Eph 6:10–18). The point being made is that just as strategy can overcome strength, the insight and blessings given by God's wisdom can overcome the apparent strength of the world (see also 1 Sam 17:1–51). The greatest victory promised to all believers is over death through the power of Christ's resurrection (1 Cor 15:26, 54–57).

21:23 This verse is an application of the Eighth Commandment.[8] Those who consider their words and do not speak what is false or harmful to others avoid the problems their own words can cause for themselves as well as for others.

21:24 This verse is one of many proverbs about mockers. Yet this proverb is unique in that it speaks of the attitude that makes a person such: arrogance without limit. A mocker submits to no authority, even that of God, but considers his own judgment and opinion to be supreme.

21:25 This verse characterizes the lazy person's craving as the reason why he takes the easy way out of hard work. He values his comfort over the things that can be gained from labor. However, his craving "will kill him." The causative (Hiphil [H]) verb תְּמִיתֶ֑נּוּ can refer to physical, temporal death, and it also connotes spiritual and everlasting death in hell. The same is true of intransitive Qal (G) forms of מוּת, "to die," in, for example, 5:23; 10:21; 15:10; 23:13. Many proverbs are multivalent in their application, and to restrict them (e.g., to only a physical or only a spiritual meaning) is to rob them of their ingenuity and power.

21:26 This verse is connected to 21:25 by the root אוה, "a craving/to crave." This proverb contrasts the unbeliever who is so greedy that he can think only of his own sinful desires with a righteous person, who gives generously as God has given to him (see also 22:9, as well as Pss 110:3; 112:9; 2 Cor 9:9; James 1:5). The ultimate example of this is Christ himself:

7 McKane, *Proverbs*, 556–57; Scott, *Proverbs, Ecclesiastes*, 124–25; Toy, *Proverbs*, 407.

8 See the excursus "Proverbs 1–9, Christ, and the Ten Commandments" in the commentary on Proverbs 1.

> For you know the grace of our Lord Jesus Christ, that although he was rich, yet for your sake he became poor, so that you through his poverty might become rich. (2 Cor 8:9)

21:27 This verse once again repeats a theme common in Proverbs and the OT in general: the rejection by God of the worship of wicked people.[a] Added here is that wicked people can make their sacrifice even more disgusting to God by bringing it with an evil intent, probably the intent to deceive others in some way. Instead of humbly seeking God's mercy, they might wish to display their piety so that other people admire them (see Mt 6:1–2; Lk 18:9–14).

(a) See, e.g., 1 Sam 15:22; Is 1:10–17; Ps 40:7–9 (ET 40:6–8); Prov 15:29; 21:3, 27; 28:9

21:28 This verse urges wise people to listen carefully to testimony in order to expose false witnesses. Witnesses are not to be taken at their word, but they are to be evaluated for their trustworthiness. When the character of a witness's testimony is not taken into consideration, injustice can result (see, e.g., the men who testified against Naboth in 1 Ki 21:11–13). Above all, a person should listen to and believe the true testimony of Jesus (e.g., Jn 5:31–36; 8:13–18).

This saying is linked to Prov 21:29 by the catchword אִישׁ, "person."

21:29 This verse first describes a wicked person, who refuses to examine his life and confess his sin, preferring to present the world and his Maker with a false front. He is contrasted with an upright person, who examines himself, discerns, and admits his sin (see Psalm 51). Such a person throws himself on God's mercy and also receives the power of God's Gospel of forgiveness and life. The Gospel transforms how he lives and thinks and cleanses him of his sinful behavior (1 Jn 1:8–2:6).

21:30 This verse reminds readers that human wisdom can succeed only if it is aligned with, and derived from, God's own wisdom. This is a warning for believers not to trust their own understanding (see 3:5–6) because of the sin that still clings to all people in this life, even the spiritually wise, that is, the regenerate (see FC SD VI 7–9). It is important to compare our thoughts and desires to God's will as revealed in his Word to ensure that they are not skewed by our sinful inclinations.

21:31 This verse continues the thought of 21:30 and is united with it by the catchword יהוה, "Yahweh." This proverb is not intended to discourage preparations and planning, but is intended to keep readers from claiming that their own efforts made success possible apart from God's blessing. Thus Christians are not to take credit for what they have done, but to give all the credit to God (see Ps 20:8 [ET 20:7]; Lk 17:7–10), who has fully accomplished our salvation by his grace alone, and who gives us "the victory" (הַתְּשׁוּעָה, Prov 21:31) in our crucified and risen Lord Jesus Christ (1 Cor 15:54–57).

Proverbs 22:1–16

Wise and Foolish Behaviors, Part 2

Translation

22 [1]A good reputation is to be chosen rather than great wealth.
Favor is better than silver and gold.
[2]Rich and poor have this in common:
Yahweh is the Maker of all of them.

[3]A prudent person sees trouble and hides,
but gullible people keep going and pay the penalty.
[4]The consequence of humility [and] the fear of Yahweh
is wealth, honor, and life.
[5]Thorns [and] traps are in the way [taken by] a crooked person.
The person who guards himself will stay far away from them.
[6]Consecrate a child according to the way he should go,
and even when he becomes old, he will not turn from it.

[7]A rich person rules over poor people,
and a borrower is a slave to a lender.
[8]Whoever sows injustice reaps trouble,
and the rod of his fury will be destroyed.
[9]A generous person will be blessed,
because he gives some of his food to the poor.

[10]Drive away a mocker, and conflict leaves.
Quarrels and insults cease.
[11]A person who loves a pure heart—
his lips are gracious; a king will be his friend.
[12]The eyes of Yahweh watch over knowledge;
he overturns the words of a treacherous person.
[13]A lazy person says, "There's a lion outside!
I'll be murdered in the streets!"
[14]The mouth of women who are strangers is a deep pit.
The man who is under Yahweh's wrath will fall into it.

[15]Stupidity is bound tightly to a child's heart.
A rod of discipline will drive it far from him.
[16]The person who oppresses the poor to enrich himself
or the person who gives to the rich—
surely [both end up in] poverty.

Textual Notes

22:1 נִבְחָר שֵׁם מֵעֹשֶׁר רָב—The Niphal (N) participle נִבְחָר means "chosen," and describes high quality gold in 8:10 and high quality silver in 8:19 and 10:20. Here, as in 16:16 and 21:3, נִבְחָר is used with the preposition מִן on another noun to state that something "is preferable to" or "to be chosen rather than" something else (here מֵעֹשֶׁר, "than wealth"). The subject of the participle is שֵׁם, "a name," an idiom for a good reputation. This can include a person's standing before God as well as the regard of other people. For שֵׁם as "reputation," see Deut 22:14, 19; Ezek 22:5; Ruth 4:11; Eccl 7:1 Neh 6:13.

מִכֶּסֶף וּמִזָּהָב חֵן טוֹב׃—For חֵן, "grace, favor," which here refers to God's as well as that received from other people, see the first textual note on 1:9. In this pericope, it recurs in 22:11, there in reference to gracious speech. The combination of טוֹב, "good, better," and the preposition מִן (on both מִכֶּסֶף וּמִזָּהָב) forms a "better than" proverb. See "Direct Comparisons" in "Authorship and Date" in the introduction.

22:2 עָשִׁיר וָרָשׁ נִפְגָּשׁוּ—The verb פָּגַשׁ in the Niphal (N) means "meet one another" (*HALOT*). In this proverb it is used metaphorically to mean "a rich person and a poor person have something in common." For רָשׁ, "poor (person)," which in this pericope recurs in the plural in 22:7, see the first textual note on 10:4.

עֹשֵׂה כֻלָּם יְהוָה׃—The participle of עָשָׂה refers to Yahweh as "Maker, Creator," also in 14:31 and 17:5. He is the subject of the perfect in 20:12.

22:3 עָרוּם ׀ רָאָה רָעָה וְיִסְתֵּר—For עָרוּם, "prudent (person)," see "עָרוּם, 'Prudent,' and עָרְמָה, 'Prudence' " in "Wisdom in Proverbs" in the introduction and the first textual note on 1:4. עָרוּם is the subject of both of the following verbal clauses, which are sequential. Note the alliteration of the first verbal clause: רָאָה רָעָה, *ra'ah ra'ah*, literally, "sees evil." For the second verb, the Niphal (N) of סָתַר, "hide oneself," either the Qere or the Kethib fits in this context. The Qere is the Niphal (N) perfect וְנִסְתָּר, which is the form in the parallel verse 27:12. The Kethib is the Niphal (N) imperfect וְיִסָּתֵר.

וּפְתָיִים עָבְרוּ וְנֶעֱנָשׁוּ׃—For the subject, פְּתָיִים, see "פֶּתִי, 'Gullible Person' " in "Fools in Proverbs" in the introduction. The verb עָבַר here probably plays on two of its possible meanings: "cross over," that is, "keep going," and "transgress, sin." The Niphal (N) of עָנַשׁ means "be fined," and refers to a fine levied by a court as punishment. Here is it used metaphorically to denote the price of foolish behavior. The identical Niphal verb recurs in 27:12 (see also the Qal infinitive in 17:26; 21:11). It is cognate to the noun עֹנֶשׁ, "a fine," in 19:19.

22:4 עֵקֶב עֲנָוָה יִרְאַת יְהוָה—The noun עֵקֶב, "a consequence, result," occurs only here in Proverbs. Although יִרְאַת lacks a *waw*, it probably should be understood as joined to the preceding noun עֲנָוָה, so that this clause means "the consequence of [having] humility [*and*] the fear of Yahweh (is) …" The predicate of the nominal sentence consists of the three nouns in the second half of the verse: עֹשֶׁר וְכָבוֹד וְחַיִּים.

22:5 צִנִּים פַּחִים בְּדֶרֶךְ עִקֵּשׁ—"Thorns" is the meaning usually assigned to צִנִּים on the basis of the LXX's τρίβολοι. However, its meaning is uncertain. For the adjective עִקֵּשׁ, here used as a substantive, "crooked *person*," see the first textual note on 2:15.

22:6 חֲנֹךְ לַנַּעַר עַל־פִּי דַרְכּוֹ—This is, literally, "consecrate a child according to the mouth of his way." The imperative חֲנֹךְ is of the verb חָנַךְ, "consecrate," which occurs only five times in four verses in the OT. In the other three verses it refers to the consecration of a building, either the dedication of a new house (Deut 20:5 [twice]) or the hallowing of the Jerusalem temple (1 Ki 8:63 || 2 Chr 7:5). See also the cognate noun חֲנֻכָּה, "consecration, dedication," used for the altar of the tabernacle (e.g., Num 7:10), for the altar of the temple (2 Chr 7:9; cf. Ps 30:1 [ET: superscription]), and for the city wall of Jerusalem (Neh 12:27). In the other passages, the verb takes an accusative direct object. Here it is used with the preposition לְ on נַעַר, "a child, young person," with the article.

The common view is that this is the only OT passage where the verb חָנַךְ means "train up" (BDB, 1; *HALOT*, 1, also, e.g., KJV, ESV, NASB). However, this is based on Mishnaic Hebrew, where the verb can mean "*to train, initiate* (a child)" as well as "*to inaugurate, prepare for office* [e.g., the high priest]; *to dedicate*" (Jastrow). For example, in Talmud, *Nazir*, 29a, it refers to training a son into the performance of his religious duties for when he reaches maturity: לחנכו, "to train him."

The phrase עַל־פִּי, literally, "according to the mouth of," simply means "according to" (see *HALOT*, s.v. פֶּה, 10 c). For the force of the suffix on דַרְכּוֹ, literally, "*his* way," see the commentary.

גַּם כִּי־יַזְקִין לֹא־יָסוּר מִמֶּנָּה׃—Literally, this is "also when he is old, he will not depart from it." The Qal (G) of the stative verb זָקֵן means "be or become old." Its Hiphil (H) occurs only here and in Job 14:8, and both times it is synonymous with the Qal. The Qal of סוּר, "turn aside, depart," is commonly used in Proverbs in exhortations to avoid evil (e.g., 3:7; 13:19; 14:16). Here it means that the now-old youth will not deviate from the way of divine wisdom, similar to סוּר in 5:7 (cf. the Hiphil [H] in 28:9). The feminine suffix on the preposition מִמֶּנָּה, "from *it*," refers back to the feminine noun דֶּרֶךְ in the first line (דַרְכּוֹ, literally, "his way").

22:7 וְעֶבֶד לֹוֶה לְאִישׁ מַלְוֶה׃—The verb לָוָה in the Qal (G) means "borrow" (*HALOT*), and לֹוֶה is a participle used substantivally: "a borrower." In the Hiphil (H) the verb means "lend," and מַלְוֶה is a Hiphil participle used substantivally: "a lender." In the phrase אִישׁ מַלְוֶה, the two nouns are in apposition, and the second indicates a species of the first (see the first textual note on 6:26).

22:8 Following the translation of this saying, the LXX adds ἄνδρα ἱλαρὸν καὶ δότην εὐλογεῖ ὁ θεός ματαιότητα δὲ ἔργων αὐτοῦ συντελέσει, "God blesses a cheerful and generous man, but he will bring to an end the foolishness of his works." The first clause of that addition may be the background for Paul's assurance ἱλαρὸν γὰρ δότην ἀγαπᾷ ὁ θεός, "for God loves a cheerful giver" (2 Cor 9:7).

22:9 טוֹב־עַיִן הוּא יְבֹרָךְ—Literally, this is "good of eye, he will be blessed." As the second clause makes clear, this is an idiom for a generous person (see ESV, NASB, NIV, NRSV). It is the opposite of רַע־עָיִן, literally, "evil of eye," a miserly and tight-fisted person (23:6; 28:22). The Pual (Dp) יְבֹרָךְ has the passive meaning "be blessed" by God (also in 20:21) corresponding to the active Piel (D), "bless," with God as subject, for which, see the textual note on 3:33.

מִלַּחְמוֹ—The preposition מִן is partitive: "*some of* his food."

22:11 אֹהֵב טְהָור־לֵב—Literally, this is "a person who loves (one who is) pure of heart." Both the Qere (טְהָר) and Kethib (טְהוֹר) are forms of the adjective טָהוֹר, "clean, pure," in construct. This could refer to another person who is "pure in heart," or it could refer to the person himself who loves to be "pure of heart." Most English translations render the phrase abstractly: "loves *a pure heart*."

חֵן שְׂפָתָיו—This could literally mean "grace [is on] his lips" or "his lips [are] grace." Either way, it is a more forceful expression than the corresponding English, "his lips are gracious." The person may speak the Gospel itself, or he may simply reflect the Gospel in his gracious manner of speech toward others.

22:13 בַחוּץ בְּתוֹךְ רְחֹבוֹת—See the textual notes on 1:20.

22:14 זְעוּם יְהוָה—The Qal passive (Gp) participle of זָעַם, "be wrathful, indignant; curse," is in construct with יְהוָה as the agent of the action: "a person shown wrath by Yahweh" or "cursed by Yahweh." In some other verses Yahweh is the subject of active forms of זָעַם (e.g., Is 66:14; Mal 1:4; Ps 7:12 [ET 7:11]).

22:15 אִוֶּלֶת קְשׁוּרָה בְלֶב־נָעַר—For אִוֶּלֶת, see "אֱוִיל, 'Stubborn Fool,' and אִוֶּלֶת, 'Stupidity' " in "Fools in Proverbs" in the introduction. That stupidity is literally "fastened" (קְשׁוּרָה, translated as "bound tightly") to the heart of a youth contrasts with the commands in 3:3; 6:21; 7:3 to "fasten" divine wisdom to one's body. See the second textual note on 3:3 and the excursus "The Use of Deuteronomy 6:4–9 in Proverbs 3:1–12 and 6:20–22" in the commentary on chapter 3.

שֵׁבֶט מוּסָר יַרְחִיקֶנָּה מִמֶּנּוּ׃—See "מוּסָר, 'Discipline,' and יָסַר, 'to Discipline' " in "Wisdom in Proverbs" in the introduction. The feminine suffix on the Hiphil (H) verb יַרְחִיקֶנָּה, "cause *it* to be far away, remove *it*," refers back to the feminine noun אִוֶּלֶת, "stupidity," in the first clause of the verse. The masculine suffix on מִמֶּנּוּ, "from *him*," refers back to נַעַר (pausal: נָעַר), the "child."

22:16 עֹשֵׁק דָּל לְהַרְבּוֹת לוֹ—Literally, this is "one oppressing a poor person in order to make [wealth] abundant for himself." For עֹשֵׁק דָּל, see the first textual note on 14:31. The verb רָבָה when used in the Hiphil (H), "multiply, make numerous," and followed by a לְ marking a person means "acquire a great deal" for that person (*HALOT*, Hiphil, 3 b). Here לוֹ has the reflexive meaning: literally, "for himself."

Commentary

These verses conclude the section about dealing with fools and foolishness (19:13–22:16). This last section of 10:1–22:16 was introduced by the proverb about a foolish son in 19:13. The reasons for considering that proverb (19:13) to mark the beginning of a section are discussed in the excursus "The Organization of the Sayings in Solomon's Proverbs in Proverbs 10:1–22:16" in the commentary on Proverbs 10. See also "A Foolish Son: Dealing with Fools and Foolishness (19:13–22:16)" in the commentary on 19:13–29.

22:1 This verse extols the value of a good reputation by comparing it favorably to great wealth, and it praises being viewed with favor by God and others by favorably comparing that to silver and gold. The Eighth Commandment protects one's reputation as a valuable possession.[1] This proverb reminds those

1 See also the commentary on 21:23 and the excursus "Proverbs 1–9, Christ, and the Ten Commandments" in the commentary on Proverbs 1.

who ponder it to guard their reputation by seeking to live by the divine wisdom, fully revealed in the person of Jesus Christ.[2] In Proverbs only wisdom and its benefits (3:14; 8:10, 19; 16:16) or wise speech (25:11) are compared to gold and silver.

22:2 This verse is linked to 22:1 by the root עשׁר, "wealth/rich," and it is the first of three consecutive proverbs that begin with the consonant ע. This saying encourages respect for all people as creatures originally made by God in his image. It is a reminder that it is easy to consider the poor as less valuable because of their economic status or to take advantage of their poverty to oppress them (see 14:31; 17:5; 29:13). Instead we are to avoid favoritism for the rich or condescension toward the poor. "Have no partiality/favoritism as you hold to the faith in our Lord of glory, Jesus Christ" (James 2:1; see James 2:1–13).

22:3 This verse is a saying that highlights the difference between a prudent person and a gullible one. The prudent person has the foresight to see trouble coming and avoid it. The gullible person does not have the wisdom to guide himself away from such situations. This proverb is nearly identical to 27:12. The only differences are three conjunctions here that are not present in 27:12 and a different form of the verb סָתַר, "hide" as the Kethib in this verse.

22:4 This verse links two spiritual gifts with three rewards. The rewards are not a result of one's actions, but God's blessings on the person to whom he has given humility and fear of God, which is not just fear of his wrath according to his Law, but also includes faith and love for him because of his Gospel.[3] Through repentance and faith come wisdom and righteousness. Note that wisdom, which is intimately connected with the fear of Yahweh (1:7; 9:10; 15:33), is specifically connected with "wealth/riches," "glory/honor," and "life/length of days" also in 3:16. "The fear of Yahweh" is connected with "life" several times (also in 14:27; 19:23; see also 10:27), and חַיִּים, "life," has the eschatological sense of everlasting life by God's grace also in, for example, 3:2, 18, 22; 4:10, 13, 22–23; 12:28. In addition, "humility" (repentant faith) twice previously is said to be a prerequisite for everlasting "glory/honor" (כָּבוֹד, 15:33; 18:12).

22:5 This verse makes the point that those who are sinful choose a life that harms themselves (see also 1:18–19; 8:36), even though they may not be aware of the consequences of their choice. Indeed, sinful choices are so tempting because they *appear* to be beneficial. The point of this proverb is that a circumspect person will look ahead and have the foresight to see the harm he is inviting by choosing sin over righteousness. Note how this proverb relates to the following one by the metaphor of the path, even using the catchword דֶּרֶךְ,

---

[2] See "Wisdom in Proverbs" in the introduction. See also the commentary on 1:1–7; 3:13–20; 8:22–31; 30:1b–10; and the excursus "Proverbs 8, Wisdom, Christology, and the Arian Controversy" in the commentary on chapter 8.

[3] See the first textual note and the commentary on 1:7 and "יִרְאַת יְהוָה, 'the Fear of Yahweh,' and יְרֵא יְהוָה, 'One Who Fears Yahweh' " in "Wisdom in Proverbs" in the introduction.

"way," to bind the two together. See the excursus "The Metaphor of the Path in Solomon's Wisdom" in the commentary on chapter 10.

22:6 This verse is one of the most discussed proverbs in the book. Part of the challenge in understanding this saying has to do with the translation of the first word, since "train up" is a meaning not attested elsewhere in Biblical Hebrew (see the first textual note). While the word may here imply training, it primarily denotes consecrating and starting a child along a certain course in life. After the coming of Christ, this is fulfilled by parents who lead their children to become disciples of Jesus by Christian Baptism and by teaching them to observe all that Jesus has commanded in his Word (Mt 28:19–20). In this way children are incorporated into Christ (Col 2:11–14), who is himself "the way" (Jn 14:6), are given the Holy Spirit, and become heirs of all God's promises (Acts 2:38–39; Gal 3:26–29). From infancy children should be taught the Scriptures, which will continue to make them wise unto salvation (see 2 Tim 3:15; cf. Eph 6:4).

Another challenge is in understanding עַל־פִּי דַרְכּוֹ, literally, "according to the mouth of his way," which means "according to his way." Every person (save Jesus) is conceived and born in sin (Ps 51:7 [ET 51:5]), so the natural, innate way of a child is not the morally correct one, but a foolish and evil one (Prov 19:18; 22:15; see also 3:5; 14:12; 16:25). Proverbs consistently portrays human nature as inclined toward sin and death.

"According to his way" may mean that parents are to instruct the child according to his age, capabilities, and/or aptitude for learning.[4] If the one training a child takes advantage of his interests and talents, the youngster is more likely to grasp what he is being taught. Approaches that best suit the child will help him hold on to the truth and not depart from it. Teaching must be adapted to the child's abilities in order to be effective. Of course, it is the Holy Spirit who works through the Word and Sacraments to instill saving faith and to preserve the person in that faith throughout life. If a person (perhaps a young adult) asserts his sinful nature by rejecting the Gospel and departing from the faith, the Spirit has the power to remind him of God's Law and his Gospel promises in his Word, so that, eventually, the person may repent and return to the faith he once had (cf. Lk 15:11–32).

It is also true that parents ought to help steer a child to take advantage of his God-given abilities and talents. This will give him a good start in life and also serve him well throughout his entire life, both as he works in society and as he serves in the church.

---

[4] See, for example, Delitzsch, *Proverbs*, 2:86–87; Garrett, *Proverbs, Ecclesiastes Song of Songs*, 188; Kidner, *Proverbs*, 147; Toy, *Proverbs*, 415. Note also Archer, "Proverbs 22:6 and the Training of Children," 274, who tries to combine this meaning with "the way he should go."

Many interpreters[5] and most English translations take the phrase as meaning that the parents should train the child in "the way he should go." This understands the suffix on דַּרְכּוֹ, "his way," not as indicating source (the child decides the way) nor as possessive, but as datival: "the (best) way *for* him." This fits with dominant themes in Proverbs, including the need for the wise father and mother to instruct their son in the way of divine wisdom[6] and the theme that divine wisdom is the only good "way, path."[7]

Another issue is how to understand the noun נַעַר, normally translated as "child" here. In the OT it can refer to a child from infancy through young adulthood (e.g., Gen 22:12; 1 Sam 1:22–27) or to an adult who is a servant or assistant (e.g., 1 Sam 2:13; 9:3). The term does not always focus on age, whether "a child," "youth," or "(young) adult." In many passages, including some other proverbs, it pertains more to the status of being a dependent or apprentice, that is, a person in training under the tutelage of his actual father, a father-figure, or a leader.[8] Thus the נַעַר could be learning how to become a leader himself—in the military, in the king's court, in government, or in the priesthood.[9]

Therefore, this proverb teaches that parents are to consecrate, discipline, and educate their children according to the Word of God in the way of wisdom, which is the way of faith and everlasting life. This spiritual training is a lifelong process that continues well into adulthood (as parents of adult children can attest). This religious instruction enables youth and adults to grow into positions of leadership both in society and in the church. As these consecrated learners mature and themselves become teachers and elders, they will in turn train up the next generation.

The promise "and even when he becomes old, he will not turn from it" is an observation of life, based on what usually happens by God's grace. It is also an eschatological promise. Many young adults explore the different possible paths in life, and only later may they settle down and return to the firm faith and righteous way of life they were taught as children. Practically speaking, many young adults do not resume faithful church attendance until they marry, and especially after they have children of their own. Then they realize that they want their children to have the same secure Christian foundation for life that they were given.

Does this proverb promise that every child who wanders away from faith in Christ will eventually return at some later point in life before he dies, and so

5 E.g., McKane, *Proverbs*, 564; Ross, "Proverbs," 1061.

6 This theme is especially prominent in chapters 1–9. See the excursus "Proverbs 1–9, Christ, and the Ten Commandments" in the commentary on Proverbs 1.

7 See the excursus "The Metaphor of the Path in Solomon's Wisdom" in the commentary on chapter 10.

8 The noun נַעַר, "child, youth," is also in 1:4; 7:7; 20:11; 22:15; 23:13; 29:15. In Proverbs the main emphasis is not on chronological age, but that such a person should (continue to) learn divine wisdom and grow in knowledge.

9 Cf. Hildebrandt, "Proverbs 22:6a: Train Up a Child?" 10–14.

be saved eternally? Many parents pray that it would be so, and God hears such prayers (cf. Mt 9:18; 15:22).

22:7 This verse is an observation of life without moral evaluation of either rich or poor. The rich have advantages over the poor simply by virtue of being rich. While Proverbs has much to say about the way one gains riches, it does not condemn all rich people.

22:8 The metaphor of reaping what one sows is common in the Bible.[a] The difficulty in this proverb comes in understanding the "rod of his fury" in the second line. It has been understood in various ways and has also been subject to emendation to make sense of it,[10] but none of the emendations are convincing. The second line probably means that the person who uses injustice as a weapon to satisfy his anger will perish, and his malevolent methods and instruments will be destroyed too. It could also mean that the man who sows injustice will perish when he experiences the punishing "rod" of God's "fury": "and [by] the rod of his [God's] fury, he [the one who sows injustice] will be destroyed" (cf. Prov 22:14b).

(a) E.g., Hos 8:7; 10:12–13; Job 4:8; Prov 11:18; Rom 6:21–22; 2 Cor 9:6; Gal 6:7–9

22:9 This verse uses the idiom טֽוֹב־עַ֭יִן, literally, "good of eye," to denote a gracious generosity. The opposite expression, רַע עָ֑יִן, literally, "evil of eye" (23:6; 28:22), denotes a malicious stinginess. The source of the blessing for generous people is not stated here, but it is God, as stated in 19:17 (cf. 14:31; 21:13). While the poor may bless those who are generous, the great blessing comes from God, who has compassion for the poor and watches over them. "Has not God chosen the poor of the world to be rich in faith and heirs of the kingdom that he has promised to those who love him?" (James 2:5; see also Prov 3:16; 8:18; Rom 10:12; 1 Tim 6:17).

22:10 This verse ascribes conflict to a mocker. Since such a person has no respect for anyone, he is constantly showing his contempt for others and their opinions. Because no peace can be had as long as such a person is present to make trouble, the only solution is to get rid of such a person. In modern society, such a person could be kicked out of his house, fired from his job, or isolated in prison. The church is to excommunicate flagrant sinners who refuse to repent and cease their transgressions, which damage the whole body of Christ (see 1 Corinthians 5; 1 Tim 1:20).

The LXX assumes the setting for this proverb is a meeting that is disrupted and unable to pursue its work. It translated the second half of the saying with this: ὅταν γὰρ καθίσῃ ἐν συνεδρίῳ πάντας ἀτιμάζει, "for when he sits in a council, he dishonors everyone."

22:11 This verse forms a contrast with 22:10. A "pure heart" is created in the penitent believer by God, who justifies and sanctifies the sinner by grace alone: "create in me a pure heart, O God" (לֵ֣ב טָ֭הוֹר בְּרָא־לִ֣י אֱלֹהִ֑ים, Ps 51:12 [ET 51:10]). In this proverb a pure heart leads to gracious speech, unlike the

[10] See, for example, McKane, *Proverbs*, 570; Scott, *Proverbs, Ecclesiastes*, 127; Toy, *Proverbs*, 416–17.

mocker, whose contempt leads to constant strife. Not only does the pure person bring peace and progress through his gracious words, but he also commends himself to those in authority, especially God. This proverb, therefore, is not commending insincere flattery and sycophancy, but it also encourages honest words motivated by pure intentions. See the divine promises for the "pure in heart" in Ps 73:1 and Mt 5:8.

22:12 This verse is the third of five sayings concerned with speech. This proverb notes that while humans may not always be able to distinguish speech that derives from a pure heart from that which comes from sinister motives, God can. He will make sure that truth prevails and that deception is uncovered and banished.

22:13 This verse parodies the silly excuses of a lazy person who will say anything to avoid work. His claim in an urban context that a lion is near and will attack him is ridiculous since lions did not live in the regions of Palestine with concentrated human populations. Rather, they were found in areas where humans did not live: the dense vegetation surrounding the Jordan River (Jer 49:19), the forests in Lebanon (Song 4:8), and the Negev (Is 30:6).[11] His second statement is even more absurd. He does not describe the result of the lion's attack with a verb for "kill" (e.g., הָרַג or טָרַף or the Hiphil [H] of מוּת), but with "murder" (רָצַח), as in Ex 20:13 and Deut 5:17. He thereby ascribes moral culpability to a beast. This proverb is similar in thought and imagery to 26:13.

22:14 This verse expresses God's judgment on a man who commits adultery. It is the only proverb outside of chapters 1–9 to mention a woman who is a "stranger," that is, any woman who is not the wife of the man (see 2:16; 5:3, 20; 7:5). A "prostitute" is labeled by the same designation, a "deep pit," in 23:27. The "mouth" of the women here that constitutes a "deep pit" may refer to all of their seductive charms, including words and kisses (see the commentary on 5:3; 7:13–21).

22:15 This verse notes the inbred sin of all humans that tends to lead them away from God from their first days (see Gen 8:21). It advises parents that discipline with the threat of punishment is often necessary to curb the innate human affinity for stupidity. Yet this verse should not be misused as a license for excessive corporal punishment or child abuse; see the commentary on 13:24.

22:16 This verse inveighs against two seemingly different ways of gaining wealth and influence: first, the easy and tempting practice of economic manipulation of the poor, and second, squandering money (bribes?) on those who are already rich and do not need more. Both lead to poverty. God will punish those who oppress the poor (see the commentary on 14:31). It is difficult to buy the favor of the rich with more of what they already have in abundance. How much less can a person purchase the favor of God, who already owns everything (see Ps 50:7–15).

---

[11] *FF*, 50.

Proverbs 22:17–24:22

The Words of Wise People

Excursus	*The Words of Wise People (Prov 22:17–24:22) and Its Relationship to the Wisdom of Amenemope*
22:17–21	Introduction to the Words of Wise People
22:22–23:14	Advice for Living with Your Neighbor
23:15–24:22	Advice from Your Father

Excursus

The Words of Wise People (Prov 22:17–24:22) and Its Relationship to the Wisdom of Amenemope

Since the discovery of the Egyptian wisdom document the Wisdom of Amenemope and Budge's publication of the text in the early 1920s,[1] scholars have debated the relationship between certain sayings in Amenemope and Proverbs, especially Prov 22:17–24:22. There is a general consensus that some relationship between Proverbs and Amenemope exists. Amenemope is organized into thirty chapters,[2] and some have been quick to emend Prov 22:20 to read, "have I not written to you thirty [sayings]?" But this is a procedure that is not without its own difficulties since the Words of Wise People does not contain thirty distinct sections as Amenemope does (see the first textual note on 22:20). A generally accepted list of sixteen parallels is shown in figure 14.

Some of these parallels are close. Prov 23:4–5 and Amenemope, chapter 7 (9:14–10:5), both use the metaphor of riches flying away like birds.[3] The prohibition of moving boundary stones is found in Prov 22:28 and 23:10–11 and Amenemope, chapter 6 (7:12–15; 8:9–10).[4] However, other parallels are so vague and deal with such different subjects that it is difficult, if not impossible, to see them as true parallels (Prov 22:21 and Amenemope, prologue [1:5–6]; Prov 23:6–8 and Amenemope, chapter 11 [14:5–10, 17–18]).[5] Clearly the Words of Wise People and the Wisdom of Amenemope sometimes contain true parallels and other times contain verbal similarities without thematic parallels or thematic parallels without verbal correspondence.[6] One example is the supposed

---

1 In 1922 Budge published a partial translation and synopsis in "The Precepts of Life by Amen-em-apt, the Son of Ka-nekht." In 1924 he published a translation of the entire text in *The Teaching of Åmen-em-åpt, Son of Kanekht*, 140–79. Excerpts from the Wisdom of Amenemope can be found in *ANET*, 421–24, and *ANE*, 237–43.

2 Citations from Amenemope commonly include both the chapter number in Amenemope as well as the column of the papyrus (British Museum Papyrus 10474) and the line number(s) in that column. For example, "chapter 2 (4:4–5)" refers to lines 4–5 of the fourth column of the papyrus, which are part of the second chapter of Amenemope.

3 See Ruffle, "The Teaching of Amenemope," 323–24.

4 See Ruffle, "The Teaching of Amenemope," 326.

5 Ruffle, "The Teaching of Amenemope," 321, 325.

6 See the discussion in Ruffle, "The Teaching of Amenemope," 299–317, where he identifies a number of thematic parallels shared not only by Proverbs and Amenemope but also by other Near Eastern wisdom writings. For examples of other Near Eastern wisdom, see *ANET*, 412–21, 425–40, or *ANE* 234–37, 244–52.

parallel between Prov 24:11 and Amenemope, chapter 8 (11:6–7), where the correspondence is so slight that most commentators doubt that it is an actual parallel and do not bother to comment on it.[7]

Another problem with the relationship between the two documents is the differing order in which they appear. Figure 14 follows the order of the biblical verses, but note that the corresponding chapter numbers from Amenemope are not in any particular order. When this randomness is combined with the observation that forty-eight of the seventy verses in the Words of Wise People have no parallel in Amenemope, it is difficult, if not impossible, to posit a direct connection with Amenemope.

This is not to say that there is no connection whatsoever. Instead we should note that throughout the book of Proverbs, Solomon frequently urges others to learn from wise people. In addition, 1 Ki 3:1 records that Solomon did marry a daughter of the Egyptian Pharaoh, providing a possible avenue for a link between his writings and Egyptian wisdom. 1 Ki 5:9–10 (ET 4:29–30) specifically compares Solomon's wisdom to that of the Egyptians, the only nation singled out for such a comparison. In addition, it appears that the Wisdom of Amenemope predates Solomon by at least a hundred years.[8] A version of it could easily have been brought to Israel with the entourage that accompanied the Egyptian wife of Solomon, if it had not been known in Israel earlier. Thus it is entirely possible that Solomon took his own advice and learned from other wise people and their writings, including the Wisdom of Amenemope.

However, Prov 22:17 specifically says that 22:17–24:22 is the compilation of the words of more than one wise person; note the plural חֲכָמִ֑ים, "wise men/ people." One of those wise people was most likely Amenemope, whose words may have influenced this section of proverbs and the thought found in several other proverbs in the Solomonic collections[9] (see figure 15). While Murphy avoids attributing these proverbs to Solomon, his conclusion is probably correct:

> The Israelite writer is remarkably independent. Only a third of this collection [the Words of Wise People] corresponds to the sayings of Amenemope, and then in an order differing from the Egyptian work. He has freely imitated and reworked the material, rather than simply taking it over. As W. Richter … remarks of 24:23 ["these also are by wise people"], the title [of 22:17–24:22:

[7] For instance, Overland, "Structure in *The Wisdom of Amenemope* and Proverbs," does not consider 24:11 to have a parallel to Amenemope.

[8] Washington, *Wealth and Poverty*, 11–24. The earliest surviving copy of Amenemope is from Egypt's twenty-first dynasty (1069–945 BC). Since this copy was produced as a student's learning exercise, Amenemope must be older than that copy of it. Based on paleographical data, personal names, loanwords, and chapter headings, the Wisdom of Amenemope is most probably from the twentieth dynasty, 1186–1069 BC, at least a hundred years before Solomon's reign (970–930 BC).

[9] This refers to the sections of Proverbs either authored by Solomon (chapters 1–9; 10:1–22:16; 25:1–29:27) or collected by him (22:17–24:22; 24:23–34).

> "the words of wise people"] hardly designates authorship, but rather the group (wise men) that was associated with the "words."[10]

In addition, Overland has noted that the sayings drawn from Amenemope were, for the most part, significantly positioned in that source document, either at the end or the beginning of a chapter in Amenemope. He concludes:

> This pattern of borrowing (and sometimes adapting) significantly positioned phrases implies that the Israelite sage was aware of the way chapters in *Amenemope* tended to be structured, with key sentences appearing toward the beginning and end. In view of the structure evident in other parts of Proverbs, it is not surprising to find that, when he encountered a foreign document that was already structured, the Israelite sage was sensitive to that structure and made use of it as he sought to distill foreign material for the benefit of an Israelite audience.[11]

Thus we may conclude that Solomon probably used the Wisdom of Amenemope, or perhaps some document related to or derived from it, as one source for his compilation of words of wise people. However, Solomon felt free to adapt, change, and improve the sayings as he saw fit under God's inspiration. He placed them into a new context, since, unlike Amenemope, the book of Proverbs is about the wisdom of the God of Israel—the one true and triune God, whose preexistent Wisdom became incarnate in the fullness of time in the person of Jesus Christ.[12]

Figure 15 lists possible parallels between the Wisdom of Amenemope and proverbs in the Solomonic collections outside of the Words of Wise People, although many of these parallels may simply be independent proverbs that happen to share similar wording or themes.

---

[10] Murphy, *Wisdom Literature*, 74, citing Wolfgang Richter, *Recht und Ethos* (Munich: Kösel, 1966), 27.

[11] Overland, "Structure in *The Wisdom of Amenemope* and Proverbs," 291.

[12] See "Wisdom in Proverbs" in the introduction. See also the commentary on 1:1–7; 3:13–20; 8:22–31; 30:1b–10; and the excursus "Proverbs 8, Wisdom, Christology, and the Arian Controversy" in the commentary on chapter 8.

Figure 14

Parallels between the Words of Wise People (Prov 22:17–24:22) and the Wisdom of Amenemope*

Proverbs	*Amenemope*
22:17–18	chapter 1 (3:9–11, 13, 16)
22:19	prologue (1:7)
22:20	chapter 30 (27:7–8)
22:21	prologue (1:5–6)
22:22	chapter 2 (4:4–5)
22:23	*no parallel*
22:24	chapter 9 (11:13–14)
22:25	chapter 9 (13:8–9)
22:26–27	*no parallels*
22:28	chapter 6 (7:12–13)
22:29	chapter 30 (27:16–17)
23:1–3	chapter 23 (23:13–18)
23:4–5	chapter 7 (9:14–10:5)
23:6–7	chapter 11 (14:5–10)
23:8	chapter 11 (14:17–18)
23:9	chapter 21 (22:11–12)
23:10–11	chapter 6 (7:12–15; 8:9–10)
23:12–24:10	*no parallels*
24:11	chapter 8 (11:6–7)
24:12–22	*no parallels*

* This list is from *ANET*, 424, n. 46, citing D. C. Simpson, "The Hebrew Book of Proverbs and the Teaching of Amenophis," *Journal of Egyptian Archaeology* 12 (1926): 232–39.

Figure 15

Further Parallels between Proverbs and the Wisdom of Amenemope

Proverbs	*Amenemope*
12:22a	chapter 10 (13:15–16)
12:23	chapter 21 (22:15–16)
14:15	chapter 13 (16:1–2)
15:16–17	chapter 6 (9:7–8)
16:8	chapter 13 (16:13–14)
16:9	chapter 18 (19:16–17)
16:11	chapter 16 (18:4–5)
17:5	chapter 25 (24:9–10)
19:21	chapter 18 (19:16–17)
20:9	chapter 18 (19:18)
20:19	chapter 21 (22:13–14)
20:22	chapter 21 (22:1–6)
20:23	chapter 16 (17:18–19)
25:21–22	chapter 2 (5:5–6)
27:1	chapter 18 (19:12–13)

Proverbs 22:17–21

Introduction to the Words of Wise People

Translation

22 [17]Open your ears and listen to the words of wise people,
and set your heart on my knowledge,
[18]for it is pleasant when you keep them within you;
they will be established together on your lips
[19]so that your trust will be in Yahweh.
Today I make [them] known to you—especially to you.
[20]Have I not written to you already
with advice and knowledge
[21]in order to make known to you truth, reliable words,
so that you may reply truthfully to those who send you?

Textual Notes

22:17 הַט אָזְנְךָ—Literally, "extend your ear," this is rendered as "open your ears." See the textual note on 4:20. The imperative and the suffix ("your") are singular, just as in earlier passages where Solomon exhorts his (singular) son to listen to his wisdom. See the excursus "Proverbs 1–9, Christ, and the Ten Commandments."

וְלִבְּךָ תָּשִׁית לְדַעְתִּי׃—This idiom with the verb שִׁית, "set," the direct object noun לֵב, "heart," and the preposition לְ, "to, on," recurs in 27:23 and, without לְ, in 24:32. The Qal (G) imperfect תָּשִׁית has a modal nuance, "you *should* set," and is equivalent to an imperative, like the imperatives in the preceding line (see Joüon, § 113 m; Waltke-O'Connor, § 31.5b, including example 3). For the indirect object noun, see "דַּעַת, 'Knowledge,' and יָדַע, 'to Know' " in "Wisdom in Proverbs" in the introduction, as well as the commentary on 1:4, 7. The suffix on לְדַעְתִּי, "on *my* knowledge," again recalls Solomon's earlier exhortations as a father to his son. However, it also resembles the earlier first-person speeches by God's Wisdom in, for example, 1:20–33 and 8:22–31. Not just Solomon, but God himself is speaking through these proverbs. Compare the "one greater than Solomon" who speaks in Mt 12:42.

22:18 כִּי־נָעִים כִּי־תִשְׁמְרֵם בְּבִטְנֶךָ—The first כִּי is causal, "*for* it is pleasant," and the second כִּי is temporal, "*when* you keep them." For the adjective נָעִים, "pleasurable, pleasant," which recurs in 23:8 and 24:4, see the second textual note on 2:10, which has the cognate verb נָעֵם. There is no obvious masculine referent for the singular adjective נָעִים, since דַּעַת ("knowledge," 22:17) is feminine, and דִּבְרֵי ("the *words of* wise people," 22:17) is plural. Probably "*it* is pleasant" refers to the overall spiritual state of the person who keeps the wise words internally. בְּבִטְנֶךָ is, literally, "in your belly." Compare the Wisdom of Amenemope, chapter 1 (3:13): "Let them rest in the casket of thy belly."[1]

---

1 *ANET*, 421; *ANE*, 237. See the excursus "The Words of Wise People (Prov 22:17–24:22) and Its Relationship to the Wisdom of Amenemope" before this pericope.

יִכֹּנוּ יַחְדָּו עַל־שְׂפָתֶיךָ׃—The subject of the Niphal (N) plural verb יִכֹּנוּ, "they will be established," is the "words" (דִּבְרֵי) in 22:17a. Other proverbs similarly use Niphal (N) forms of כון to promise that paths, plans, or lips (speech) that rely on divine wisdom will "be established" (e.g., 4:26; 12:19; 16:3). Some interpreters would emend יַחְדָּו to כְּיָתֵד, "like a tent peg," based on the Wisdom of Amenemope, chapter 1 (3:16).[2] However, considering the many ways in which this section is different from similar passages in Amenemope, this is a dubious procedure.

22:19 לִהְיוֹת בַּיהוָה מִבְטַחֶךָ—The Hebrew word order emphasizes Yahweh by placing the prepositional phrase before the main noun: literally, "to be *in Yahweh* your trust," that is, "so that your trust will be in Yahweh." Saving faith is simple trust in the triune God alone. The noun מִבְטָח, "trust," is similarly used in 14:26.

הוֹדַעְתִּיךָ הַיּוֹם אַף־אָתָּה׃—The Hiphil (H) of יָדַע often takes two accusative objects: "to make someone know something" (see the first textual note on 22:21). Here the pronominal suffix on הוֹדַעְתִּיךָ is the first object ("make *you* know"), and the second object ("them") is unstated but implied to be the "words" in 22:17a.[3] Since the verb has a suffix (ךָ-), the personal pronoun (אַף־אָתָּה, "also *you*") is redundant and emphatic. Both forms translated as "you" are singular in Hebrew, continuing the singular form of address from 22:17, as from a father to his son.

22:20 הֲלֹא כָתַבְתִּי לְךָ שָׁלְשׁוֹם—The Kethib is the adverb שִׁלְשׁוֹם, "formerly; the day before yesterday." Etymologically, it is related to שָׁלֹשׁ, "three," and using the OT method of counting inclusively, "the day before yesterday" is the third previous day. Of the twenty-five occurrences of this word, this is the only one where it is not preceded by a variant of the adverb תְּמוֹל, "yesterday," to form the idiom "yesterday and the day before," meaning "formerly; at any previous time." Because of the absence of תְּמוֹל here, שִׁלְשׁוֹם has been seen as awkward.

The Qere, שָׁלִישִׁים, "officers," is even more difficult, and perhaps implies "excellent things" as the object of the verb "written" (so KJV, NKJV, NASB). This plural noun does not agree with the singular suffix on לְךָ, so the text cannot mean "I have written to you officers," even though English uses "you" as a plural. The LXX uses the adverb τρισσῶς but alters the meaning of the line to καὶ σὺ δὲ ἀπόγραψαι αὐτὰ σεαυτῷ τρισσῶς, "but also you, write them out for yourself *three times*," which is probably the translator's guess as to the meaning.

Based on the Wisdom of Amenemope, which has thirty chapters, some scholars have suggested that the Hebrew word is a scribal corruption of an original שְׁלֹשִׁים, "thirty" (RSV, ESV, and NIV have "thirty sayings"). However, this conjecture creates

---

[2] Footnote in *BHS*; Scott, *Proverbs, Ecclesiastes*, 135. For the saying in the Wisdom of Amenemope, see *ANET*, 422; *ANE*, 237.

[3] Waltke-O'Connor, § 27.3c, cites this proverb as example 12 and calls a Hiphil that can take a subject and two direct objects "a three-place *Hiphil*." It notes that when such a Hiphil has only one direct object, as is the case here, the stated object usually is a person (here "you"), and the implied second direct object usually is an abstract noun or a speech act (here "words," 22:17).

more problems than it solves. First, it differs from both the Qere and the Kethib, so it is not supported by any Hebrew text. Second, it requires supplying another noun such as דְּבָרִים, "sayings," since Hebrew requires the object that is counted or enumerated to be explicitly stated unless it is a commodity (see Waltke-O'Connor, § 15.2.2b). Third, and most problematic, there is no clear indication that there are thirty sayings or units in the Words of Wise People (22:17–24:22), though some scholars have proposed various conflicting schemes that divide this section into thirty parts.[4] These schemes are creative, but far from convincing. In fact, there are twenty-nine sayings in this section; see the commentary on 22:22–23:14 and 23:15–24:22.[5] Fourth, the statement "have I not written to you thirty [sayings] of counsels and knowledge?" would fit best at the *end* of this collection, not at its beginning. Note that the proposed parallel statement in Amenemope occurs in its final (thirtieth) chapter (27:7–8).[6]

All things considered, it is best to read the text as it stands with an anomalous, but understandable, use of שִׁלְשׁוֹם, "formerly." Solomon is asking, "Have I not written to you *already* with counsels and knowledge?" This question implies that God has already inspired Solomon to write *his own, original* sayings of divine wisdom in Prov 1:1–22:16, and now he is relating advice and knowledge that he has, under inspiration, adapted from other wise people.

If this clause alludes to Amenemope in any way, it is probably a play on the word שְׁלֹשִׁים, "thirty" (a word not actually in the text), as a veiled reference to that older work from which the ideas and imagery (but not exact wording) of some of the sayings in this section may have originated. See further the excursus "The Words of Wise People (Prov 22:17–24:22) and Its Relationship to the Wisdom of Amenemope" before this pericope. This may explain the omission of תְּמוֹל, "yesterday," a variant of which is elsewhere always used with שִׁלְשׁוֹם. By omitting תְּמוֹל, Solomon calls attention to שִׁלְשׁוֹם and its similarity to שְׁלֹשִׁים. Yet he thereby creates an ironic statement, since there are only twenty-nine sayings in Solomon's collected Words of Wise People. This different number in 22:17–24:22 shows that the biblical proverbs are not simply copied from the extrabiblical Wisdom of Amenemope.

בְּמֹעֵצֹת וָדָעַת׃—Literally, this is "with counsels and knowledge." The plural noun מוֹעֵצֹת may denote wise counsel offered on several occasions or several pieces of advice given at the same time. This is treated collectively in the English translation above as

---

[4] See the discussion in Ruffle, "The Teaching of Amenemope," 320, and Emerton, "The Teaching of Amenemope and Proverbs XXII 17–XXIV 22." The differences between the various proposals as to how the Words of Wise People ought to be divided into thirty sections are an indication that the text does not support these proposals. Some of them, such as the proposal by Scott (*Proverbs, Ecclesiastes*, 135–47; see especially p. 141), require rearranging the text to make the scheme work.

[5] Waltke (*Proverbs*, 1:22–23) has proposed that the introduction (Prov 22:17–21) be counted as the thirtieth saying. He argues that there are more affinities between 22:17–21 and the first chapter of Amenemope than there are between 22:17–21 and the prologue of Amenemope. However, 22:17–21 clearly is an introduction to the proverbs that follow. It should be interpreted according to its function in Proverbs and not forced to correspond to a section of that Egyptian work.

[6] *ANET*, 424; *ANE*, 243.

"advice," which denotes the sum of several wise suggestions one might receive. The only other occurrence in Proverbs of מוֹעֵצָה, "advice, counsel," is in 1:31, where too it is plural, but there it refers to the schemes of malefactors. It is cognate to other vocabulary that is common in Proverbs; see "עֵצָה, 'Advice,' and יוֹעֵץ, 'Advisor' " in "Wisdom in Proverbs" in the introduction.

The noun דַּעַת occurs thirty-three times in 1:1–22:16 (out of a total of thirty-nine times in Proverbs and eighty-eight occurrences in the entire OT). See "דַּעַת, 'Knowledge,' and יָדַע, 'to Know' " in "Wisdom in Proverbs" in the introduction, as well as the commentary on 1:4, 7. "With counsels and knowledge" may not refer to two different kinds of writings, but just one: "counsels (that teach divine) knowledge," that is, wisdom sayings that impart saving faith and "knowledge" of God (1:4, 7).

22:21 לְהוֹדִיעֲךָ קֹשְׁטְ אִמְרֵי אֱמֶת—The Hiphil (H) infinitive construct of יָדַע takes a double accusative: its suffix and the following noun, literally, "to make *you* know *truth*." The unusual vocalization of the noun קֹשְׁטְ suggests that it is probably a loanword from Aramaic. The Aramaic word is used in Dan 2:47; 4:34 (ET 4:37). In apposition to קֹשְׁטְ is a construct phrase with the common Hebrew synonym אֱמֶת: אִמְרֵי אֱמֶת, "words of truth," with אֱמֶת translated as an adjectival genitive: "*reliable/true* words." אֱמֶת, "truth," recurs in the second line of the verse and also in, for example, 3:3; 12:19; 16:6.

לְהָשִׁיב אֲמָרִים אֱמֶת לְשֹׁלְחֶיךָ׃—The idiom with the Hiphil (H) of שׁוּב, "cause to return," with an object noun for "word(s)" (here אֲמָרִים) means "reply, give an answer/response," as also in 18:13; 24:26; 27:11 (all with the noun דָּבָר). Whereas the preceding line had the construct phrase אִמְרֵי אֱמֶת, here אֱמֶת, "truth," could be in apposition to the absolute state plural אֲמָרִים, "*words* (which are) *truth*" (GKC, § 131 c; cf. Waltke-O'Connor, § 12.3c, including example 11; Joüon, §§ 131 c and 154 e (5); similar are KJV, NKJV). Or אֱמֶת may be an adverbial accusative modifying the infinitive construct לְהָשִׁיב, which forms a purpose clause, "so that you may reply *truthfully*," "give a true answer" (RSV, ESV), or "correctly answer" (NASB).

The participle לְשֹׁלְחֶיךָ may be a true plural: "to your sender*s*." Or it could be a plural of majesty (Joüon, § 136 e; cf. GKC, § 124 k; see also the second textual note on 10:26). If so, God may be the one who has sent each person in mission to the world, and all people will eventually be required to give an answer to God. The biblical Gospel enables each person who believes it to give a truthful and acceptable response on the day of reckoning.

Commentary

This introduction to the Words of Wise People (22:17–24:22) is similar to the introductory words of Solomon's addresses to his son in Proverbs 1–9.[7] The call to pay attention (22:17) recalls the beginning of the sixth and seventh addresses to a son (4:20; 5:1; cf. 4:1; 7:24). The phrase דִּבְרֵי חֲכָמִים, "words of wise people," is used in the book's preface (1:1–7), where readers are told that Solomon's proverbs are given to allow one to understand the words of wise peo-

---

7 See the excursus "Proverbs 1–9, Christ, and the Ten Commandments" in the commentary on Proverbs 1.

ple (1:6). Now that Solomon has presented his own original proverbs, inspired by God, he presents a selection of sayings from other sages. He does not simply duplicate their words, but refines and adapts them under divine inspiration as he arranges them within their larger context in Proverbs, which teaches the wisdom of saving faith in the one true and triune God.[8]

Solomon follows his call to pay attention with two promises in 22:18. The first is that it is pleasant, even pleasurable, to believe and incorporate the wise words internally (literally, "in your belly"). In the prayer traditionally called the Collect for the Word, God's people pray: "Blessed Lord, You have caused all Holy Scriptures to be written for our learning. Grant that we may so hear them, read, mark, learn, and inwardly digest them."[9]

The second promise in 22:18 is that these words "will be established together" on the lips of the believer. This second promise seems to point to the ability to understand how the sayings of these sages relate to one another as they are established "together," not separately, on the lips. The adverb יַחְדָּו, "together," implies that the words are harmonious with each other and form a unity. What is true about these proverbs is true of all the Scriptures: they were written through diverse authors from different times and places, and each has its distinctive voice, yet all teach and support the same divine truth of Law and Gospel, without contradicting each other.[10]

Note that the goal of these sayings is to inculcate trust in Yahweh (22:19). "*Today* I make [them] known to you" suggests that every time these Scriptures are read, God is calling each hearer or reader to open his ears and listen (22:17) in faith—to repent, believe, gain wisdom, and be saved eternally (see Ps 95:7–8; Heb 3:7–8, 15; 4:7). Instilling this trust is the same goal as in the previous portions of the book, as Solomon notes when he asks, "Have I not written to you *already* with counsels and knowledge?" (22:20). God has caused his holy Word to be recorded in writing in the Scriptures for the benefit of subsequent generations. Solomon is implying that readers should supplement the divine wisdom in the earlier part of the book with these words adapted from other wise people. Moreover, Solomon says that the words he has already given have engendered wisdom so that his readers can answer with reliable words to the One who entrusts them with tasks (22:21). These divine words are trustworthy and true (cf. Rev 21:5; 22:6) and enable believers to be reliable themselves—that is, truthful and true (Prov 22:21; cf. Ps 119:42; 1 Pet 3:15; 1 Jn 5:20; 3 Jn 12).

---

[8] See "Wisdom in Proverbs" in the introduction. See also the commentary on 1:1–7; 3:13–20; 8:22–31; 30:1b–10; and the excursus "Proverbs 8, Wisdom, Christology, and the Arian Controversy" in the commentary on chapter 8.

[9] *LSB*, p. 308 (cf. *TLH*, p. 14).

[10] See further "Law and Gospel in Proverbs" in the introduction.

Proverbs 22:22–23:14

Advice for Living with Your Neighbor

Translation

22 [22]Do not rob a poor person because he is poor,
and do not crush an oppressed person in the [city] gate,
[23]because Yahweh will defend their cause
and deprive those who deprive them of life.
[24]Do not befriend a hot-tempered person,
and do not associate with a hothead,
[25]otherwise you will learn his path
and set a trap for yourself.
[26]Do not be among those who strike hands,
among those who guarantee debts.
[27]If you do not have enough to repay,
why should he take your bed out from under you?
[28]Do not move an ancient boundary marker
that your ancestors made.
[29]Do you see a person who is efficient in his work?
He will serve kings;
he will not serve unknown people.

23 [1]When you sit down to eat with a ruler,
consider carefully what is in front of you,
[2]and put a knife to your throat if you have a big appetite.
[3]Do not crave his delicacies;
it is deceptive food.
[4]Do not wear yourself out getting rich.
Have the insight [to know when] to stop.
[5]Will your eyes glimpse it before it is gone?
For it will quickly make a pair of wings for itself;
like an eagle it will fly into the sky.
[6]Do not eat the food of a tightfisted person.
Do not crave his delicacies,
[7]because as he calculates [the cost] to himself, this is what he does:
"Eat and drink," he says to you,
but he doesn't mean it.
[8]You will vomit the little bit you ate
and spoil your pleasant conversation.
[9]Do not speak directly to a fool,
because he will despise your sensible words.
[10]Do not move an ancient boundary marker,
and do not enter the fields of orphans,

11because their redeemer is strong.
He will defend their cause against you.
12Apply your heart to discipline
and your ear to words of knowledge.
13Do not withhold discipline from a child,
for if you beat him with a rod, he will not die.
14Beat him yourself with a rod,
and you will rescue his soul from Sheol.

Textual Notes

22:22 אַל־תִּגְזָל־דָּל כִּי דַל־הוּא—The Qal (G) of גָּזַל, "steal, rob," recurs in 28:24. Its passive Niphal (N) is in 4:16. For דַּל, "poor (person)," see the first textual note on 14:31. The force of כִּי is causal, and the line can be rendered as "do not rob a poor person [even though it is easy and tempting to rob him] *because* he is poor."

וְאַל־תְּדַכֵּא עָנִי בַשָּׁעַר׃—The Piel (D) of דָּכָא, "crush," is used with בַשַּׁעַר, "in the [city] gate," and refers to oppression in the location where elders assembled to serve as the court of law in the ancient Near East (e.g., Gen 23:10, 18; Ruth 4:1, 10–11). Therefore this refers to legal injustice, depriving someone of his civil rights. Job 5:4 has a similar clause with the Hithpael (HtD) of דָּכָא and בַשַּׁעַר. For עָנִי, "oppressed (person)," see the textual note on 3:34.

22:23 כִּי־יְהוָה יָרִיב רִיבָם—The cognate accusative construction with the verb רִיב and the noun רִיב could be rendered as "for Yahweh will litigate their litigation," that is, legally defend them. The same cognate accusative construction is in 23:11, and one using an imperative is in 25:9. A different cognate accusative construction is in the next clause of this verse.

וְקָבַע אֶת־קֹבְעֵיהֶם נָפֶשׁ׃—This is another cognate accusative construction: the Qal (G) perfect of קָבַע with *waw* consecutive takes as its direct object the suffixed plural participle of the same verb: "and he will deprive those who deprive them of life." This line is challenging on two counts: the verb קָבַע occurs only here and in Mal 3:8–9, and its exact meaning is unknown.[1] It is often translated as "rob" on the basis of the meaning it is assumed to have in Mal 3:8–9. The other challenge is the syntax, particularly in understanding how נֶפֶשׁ is coordinated with the rest of the sentence. Most likely it is an accusative of respect: קֹבְעֵיהֶם נָפֶשׁ means "those who deprive them [in regard to their] life," that is, "those who deprive them [poor and oppressed people] of life."

22:24 אַל־תִּתְרַע אֶת־בַּעַל אָף—The Hithpael (HtD) תִּתְרַע is of the verb רָעָה, "befriend, associate with" someone, for which, see the second textual note on 13:20. בַּעַל אָף, literally, "a master of anger," is "a hot-tempered person." See the second textual note on 1:17.

---

1 For a suggestion similar to the translation above, though based on a doubtful Arabic cognate, see Cody, "Notes on Proverbs 22,21 and 22,23b," 425–26.

אִישׁ חֵמוֹת—For, literally, "a man of rages" meaning "a hothead," see the textual note on 15:18, which has אִישׁ חֵמָה. The plural here, חֵמוֹת, is an abstract (Joüon, § 136 g).

22:25 וְלָקַחְתָּ מוֹקֵשׁ לְנַפְשֶׁךָ׃—Literally, this is "you shall receive a snare for your soul." Similar is 18:7b, and see also 12:13a and 29:6a, as well as Heb 12:1; 1 Tim 3:7; 6:9. Escape from such a snare is a metaphor for God's salvation in Ps 124:7 (cf. 2 Tim 2:26).

22:26 בְתֹקְעֵי־כָף בַּעֹרְבִים—"Strike the hand" (תָּקַע כָּף) and "guarantee" (עָרַב) a debt are technical terms for entering into legal agreements. See the textual notes on 6:1.

22:28 אַל־תַּסֵּג גְּבוּל עוֹלָם—This identical clause also begins 23:10. The Hiphil (H), here the imperfect, of סוּג and the object noun גְּבוּל means "move/displace a boundary marker." The same idiom is in Deut 19:14; 27:17; Hos 5:10.

22:29 חָזִיתָ אִישׁ ׀ מָהִיר בִּמְלַאכְתּוֹ—The verb חָזָה, "see, observe," recurs in 24:32 and 29:20. The object is, literally, "a man quick in his work." מָהִיר occurs only four times in the OT. The cognate verb מָהַר means "hurry, rush, do quickly" and occurs in negative contexts in Proverbs (1:16; 6:18; 7:23; 25:8) but can also be used in a good sense, out of urgency to accomplish something beneficial (e.g., Gen 18:6–7). In this case מָהִיר probably means "efficient" and perhaps "skilled," as in Ps 45:2 (ET 45:1) and Ezra 7:6 (see *HALOT*).

לִפְנֵי־מְלָכִים יִתְיַצָּב—Literally, "before kings he will be stationed," in this context it refers to the high honor of serving royalty. The Hithpael (HtD) of יָצַב has a similar meaning when used with the preposition עַל to mean "stand before" Yahweh, ready to serve him (Zech 6:5; Job 1:6; 2:1), and "present oneself before" King Rehoboam, at his service (2 Chr 11:13).

חֲשֻׁכִּים׃—This adjective of the root חשך, "be dark," occurs only here in the OT and is used substantivally to mean "people of darkness," hence "unknown, obscure people."

23:1 בִּין תָּבִין—This form of the infinitive absolute (בִּין instead of בּוֹן) is used for the sake of assonance with the following imperfect (Joüon, §§ 81 e and 123 q).

23:2 וְשַׂמְתָּ שַׂכִּין בְּלֹעֶךָ—Literally, "you shall place a knife at your throat" probably refers to "restraining oneself from indulgence in food" (BDB, s.v. לֹעַ, under the root לוע I). The noun שַׂכִּין, "knife," and the noun לֹעַ, "throat," both occur only here in the OT. No words cognate to שַׂכִּין are attested in the OT, but it has cognates in other Semitic languages (see BDB). לֹעַ is from the verb לוּעַ or לָעַע, "swallow," which occurs only in Obad 16.

אִם־בַּעַל נֶפֶשׁ אָתָּה׃—Literally, "if you are a master of an appetite" refers to having a big appetite. See the second textual note on 1:17.

23:3 אַל־תִּתְאָו לְמַטְעַמּוֹתָיו—This clause is repeated in 23:6. The Hithpael (HtD) of אָוָה, "desire, crave," also occurs in 13:4; 21:26; 24:1. The object noun, the suffixed plural of מַטְעָם, "a delicacy, savory food," occurs elsewhere only referring to the tasty meal Isaac desired to eat before he would bless his son and die (the plural מַטְעַמִּים in Gen 27:4–31).

וְהוּא לֶחֶם כְּזָבִים׃—The singular pronoun הוּא, "*it* is," refers to the delicacies in the preceding clause even though לְמַטְעַמּוֹתָיו is plural. The construct chain לֶחֶם כְּזָבִים, literally, "food of lies," contains an adjectival genitive: "lying/deceptive food." This does not refer to the food itself but to the deceptive motives of the ruler who offers it to his subordinate.

23:4 מִבִּינָתְךָ חֲדָל׃—The preposition מִן here has a causal meaning: literally, "because of your insight, stop!" For the suffixed noun to which it is attached, see "בִּינָה, 'Understanding,' and Related Words" in "Wisdom in Proverbs" in the introduction. The Qal (G) imperative חֲדַל (pausal: חֲדָל), "stop!" is also used in 19:27.

23:5 הֲתָעוּף ... וְעָיֵף—Note the play on the first and second-to-last words of the verse. The wordplay suggests that even in this close parallel to a saying in the Wisdom of Amenemope,[2] a Hebrew sage, perhaps Solomon himself, has reworked this proverb before its inclusion in this collection. Both verbs probably should be read as Qal (G) forms of עוּף, "to fly," hence literally, "Will your eyes *fly/alight* on it? … It will *fly away*." Each verb has a variant Hebrew reading due to confusion of י and ו. The first verb, according to the Kethib, is the interrogative -הֲ on the feminine singular imperfect תָּעוּף with the feminine dual subject עֵינֶיךָ, literally, "will your eyes fly/alight on it?" More difficult is the Qere (also with the interrogative -הֲ), הֲתָעִיף, which could be the Qal (G) imperfect of a by-form עִיף or the Hiphil (H) imperfect of עוּף, whose Hiphil would occur only here. In either case the meaning must be the same.

The masculine suffix on בּוֹ, "fly/alight on *it*," must refer back to the wealth for which the person wears himself out in 23:4a, even though 23:4–5 lacks any Hebrew word for this wealth. It must also be the referent of the suffix on וְאֵינֶנּוּ, literally, "and *it* is not/no more," as well as the subject and referent of the masculine singular forms יַעֲשֶׂה־לּוֹ, "*it* will make for *itself*." The dual כְנָפַיִם means "a *pair* of wings."

The Qere of the second-to-last word is יָעוּף, the masculine imperfect of עוּף, "fly (away)." The difficult Kethib is the adjective וְעָיֵף, "and *weary*."

23:6 רַע עָיִן—See the first textual note on 22:9.

23:7 כִּי ׀ כְּמוֹ־שָׁעַר בְּנַפְשׁוֹ כֶּן־הוּא—Literally, this is "for as he calculates in himself, thus [is] he," and the following quote explains "thus" (כֵּן). This is the only proverb with כְּמוֹ, the preposition כְּ with enclitic *mem*, and here it has a temporal sense, "as, while." The verb שָׁעַר occurs only here in the OT, though the related noun שַׁעַר, "a calculation, reckoning" (i.e., a unit of measure; see BDB), is used in Gen 26:12. The LXX translated שָׁעַר here as τρίχα, apparently reading it as the more common noun שֵׂעָר, "hair," and paraphrased the MT in an attempt to make sense of it. However, to read שֵׂעָר and to suppose that the tightfisted person is like a swallowed hair that causes one to vomit (an idea introduced in the next verse) requires a number of other emendations to this verse that are dubious at best.[3]

---

2 Wisdom of Amenemope, chapter 7 (10:4–5). See *ANET*, 422; *ANE*, 239. See also the excursus "The Words of Wise People (Prov 22:17–24:22) and Its Relationship to the Wisdom of Amenemope" in the commentary on Proverbs 22.

3 See, for example, the attempt of McKane, *Proverbs*, 384–85.

וְלִבּוֹ בַּל־עִמָּךְ׃—Literally, "but his heart is not with you" means he is insincere, that his kind words don't match his malevolent thoughts (cf. *HALOT*, s.v. לֵב, 6). This use of the negative בַּל with a preposition in a nominal clause is unusual (see GKC, § 152 t (f)).

23:9 בְּאָזְנֵי כְסִיל אַל־תְּדַבֵּר— Literally, "in the ears of a fool do not speak" is not referring to placing one's mouth directly opposite the fool's ear. Rather it means "do not speak directly to a fool" since the result will be what the next clause describes.

כִּי־יָבוּז לְשֵׂכֶל מִלֶּיךָ׃—The verb בּוּז, "despise," characterizes a fool's attitude toward wisdom (1:7; 13:13). "Because he will despise the good sense of your words" can be translated as "… your sensible words." See "שֵׂכֶל, 'Good Sense,' and הִשְׂכִּיל, 'to Act Sensibly' " in "Wisdom in Proverbs" in the introduction. This is the only proverb with the noun מִלָּה, "a word," a synonym of the more common nouns דָּבָר and אֵמֶר.

23:10 אַל־תַּסֵּג גְּבוּל עוֹלָם—See the textual note on 22:28.

23:11 כִּי־גֹאֲלָם חָזָק—The verb גָּאַל, "redeem," most often has God as its subject and refers to him saving his people from bondage in Egypt (e.g., Ex 6:6), from exile (e.g., Jer 31:11), or from other evils including death (e.g., Ps 103:4; Lam 3:58). The participle גֹּאֵל is similarly used as a divine title for God, the national and personal "Redeemer" of his people (e.g., Is 44:6; 54:5; Ps 19:15 [ET 19:14]; Job 19:25). Yet גֹּאֵל can also refer to a kinsman who acts as protector of a family and its heritage (see the commentary). The Hebrew could refer to God and/or to such a kinsman. Hebrew lacks the English distinction between capital and lowercase letters by which we make this distinction ("Redeemer" versus "redeemer").

הוּא־יָרִיב אֶת־רִיבָם אִתָּךְ׃—See the first textual note on 22:23, where Yahweh is the explicit subject. He is the implied subject here.

23:12 לַמּוּסָר … דָּעַת׃—For these two nouns, see "מוּסָר, 'Discipline,' and יָסַר, 'to Discipline' " and "דַּעַת, 'Knowledge,' and יָדַע, 'to Know' " in "Wisdom in Proverbs" in the introduction. מוּסָר recurs in the next verse.

23:13 כִּי־תַכֶּנּוּ בַשֵּׁבֶט לֹא יָמוּת׃—The Hiphil (H) imperfect of נָכָה, "strike," is used with the prepositional phrase בַּשֵּׁבֶט, literally, "with the rod," again in 23:14a.

The promise that the disciplined son "will not die" (לֹא יָמוּת) is parallel to the last clause of 23:14: literally, "and his soul from Sheol you will save" (וְנַפְשׁוֹ מִשְּׁאוֹל תַּצִּיל). Taken together these clauses speak of the everlasting spiritual welfare of the son. Compare the repeated promise "righteousness saves from death" (וּצְדָקָה תַּצִּיל מִמָּוֶת, 10:2; 11:4; see also 11:6a). These are promises of everlasting life.

Commentary

The words of wise people that follow the introduction (22:17–21) divide into two sections with a total of twenty-nine sayings: 22:22–23:14 and 23:15–24:22. Of the proverbs in this first section, scholars usually claim that nine of the twelve sayings have parallels in the Wisdom of Amenemope,[4] whereas the other section of the Words of Wise People (23:15–24:22) has no parallels in Amenemope. It

---

4 See the excursus "The Words of Wise People (Prov 22:17–24:22) and Its Relationship to the Wisdom of Amenemope" before the commentary on 22:17–21, including figure 14.

seems clear that Solomon's arrangement of these proverbs was based at least partially on their possible source. This section appears to have drawn from the Wisdom of Amenemope or perhaps from some condensation or other writing related to Amenemope. However, the invocation of Yahweh—the God of Israel and the only true God—in the very first saying (Prov 22:22–23) demonstrates that these proverbs are not simply repetitions of sayings drawn verbatim from the Egyptian Wisdom of Amenemope. Instead they may be the result of the reworking and adapting of Amenemope by Solomon or by some other Israelite sage or sages ("wise men/people," 22:17; 24:23) under the influence of the Holy Spirit. These proverbs are part of the Scriptures inspired by the one triune God, the second person of whom has become incarnate in Jesus Christ, the Wisdom of God revealed already in the book of Proverbs.[5]

This section is divided into twelve sayings:

Saying	*Verses*	*Topic*
1	22:22–23	Warning against oppressing the poor
2	22:24–25	Warning about intemperate people
3	22:26–27	Warning about economic speculation
4	22:28	Prohibition of land fraud
5	22:29	Observation about competence
6	23:1–3	Warning about rulers and their ulterior motives
7	23:4–5	Warning about excessive ambition for wealth
8	23:6–8	Warning about false generosity
9	23:9	Warning about wasting wisdom
10	23:10–11	Warning about defrauding orphans
11	23:12	Invitation to learning
12	23:13–14	Command to discipline children

Ten of these sayings (all but 22:29; 23:12) contain a negative imperative construction (אַל plus an imperfect verb), and nine of them begin with this construction.[6] (Prov 23:1–3 is the lone exception, where the negative imperative

[5] See "Wisdom in Proverbs" in the introduction. See also the commentary on 1:1–7; 3:13–20; 8:22–31; 30:1b–10; and the excursus "Proverbs 8, Wisdom, Christology, and the Arian Controversy" in the commentary on chapter 8.

[6] The negative imperative construction is a characteristic of the Words of Wise People (22:17–24:22). It is used twenty-seven times in this part of Proverbs. By contrast, it occurs thirty-seven times in chapters 1–9, which is a much longer section; only three times in the further proverbs of Solomon (10:1–22:16); only ten times in the proverbs copied by Hezekiah's men (chapters 25–29); four times in Agur's proverbs (chapter 30); and once in Lemuel's words (31:1–9); and it is absent from the final poem (31:10–31). It is almost evenly distributed between the two sections of the Words of Wise People, occurring thirteen times in 22:22–23:14 and fourteen times in 23:15–24:22.

ends a saying.) These prohibitions emphasize the Law that is stressed in this section. Since this wisdom may draw on non-Israelite sources, it is not surprising that it emphasizes natural law, including observations from life and insights supported by the general revelation of God in his creation. Natural law is known to all people, because God has written it in all human hearts, although knowledge of it is clouded by human sin, which also makes it impossible for unbelievers to do God's will (see Rom 1:18–21; 2:14–15; LC II 67–69; FC SD VI 5). The special revelation of God in the Scriptures sets forth God's will clearly, but the scriptural Law condemns human sin (Rom 7:7–14).

The Gospel can only be known by God's special revelation, which shows that God the Creator is also God the Redeemer. "For the God who said, 'Let light shine out of darkness,' he is the One who has shone in our hearts to give the light of the knowledge of the glory of God in the face of Christ" (2 Cor 4:6; see also LC II 67). The Gospel comes through God's Word and centers in Jesus Christ, the Word incarnate. We should not expect to encounter the Gospel in sayings from Egypt or elsewhere outside of Israel. The overt message of these twelve sayings is much more about the Law than the Gospel, although the Gospel is present implicitly in, for example, the affirmation that God is the Redeemer and defender of the defenseless (22:23; 23:11).[7] Solomon was inspired by God to include these proverbs for our instruction, so that we can be guided in wise and holy living.

22:22–23 Saying 1 warns against taking advantage of a poor or an oppressed person. Such people have the least amount of protection, making them easy prey. The robbery here may signify legal but unethical means to take their property, as well as simple theft. The reason for not taking advantage of the poor is that Yahweh is their Maker too (14:31; 17:5; 22:2), and he is the Redeemer (23:11) of the lowly and vulnerable. Though the poor or oppressed may appear to have no means to ward off those who would plunder what little they have, they have a surer defense (Psalm 46) than the rich who rely on their riches, since God can take away life itself from those who victimize the poor. Proverbs frequently warns about the dangers of "Sheol" and everlasting death.[8]

22:24–25 Saying 2 advises against associating with those who are rash and quick-tempered. Such people often make decisions based on the emotions of the moment and not on sober judgment. Their anger, even if directed elsewhere, can harm their innocent companions.

22:26–27 Saying 3 repeats a warning found elsewhere in Proverbs (6:1; 11:15; 17:18). The thought added here is that a person may lose his own property

---

[7] See further "Law and Gospel in Proverbs" in the introduction.

[8] "Sheol," is synonymous with everlasting death and the grave (1:12; 5:5; 7:27; 9:18; 15:11, 24; 23:14; 27:20; 30:16). See the first textual note and the commentary on 1:12. "Death" has an eschatological sense pointing to eternal perdition in hell in, for example, 2:18; 5:5; 7:27; 8:36; 10:2. So too does the verb "to die," in, for example, 5:23; 10:21; 15:10; 23:13.

("your bed") because he attempts to gain riches. The risk of personal loss may not appear great at the time the deal is struck, but this danger is to be taken into account by the prudent person, who avoids such pitfalls. This proverb is the first of six consecutive sayings (22:26–23:8) dealing with economic matters.

22:28 Saying 4 is a warning against a specific type of theft: land fraud. Since modern surveying techniques were not available in ancient Israel, property lines were established by markers, usually stones placed on the ground. Moving the marker to gain land at the expense of one's neighbor was easy, but hard for the neighbor to prove in a court of law. Therefore the fear of God himself was the best deterrent. This crime is prohibited in the Torah (Deut 19:14), and a perpetrator was condemned in the strongest terms according to the covenant curses (Deut 27:17; cf. Hos 5:10).

The first half of this proverb is identical to the first line of 23:10.

22:29 Saying 5 notes that competence earns recognition and reward. This proverb encourages learning one's craft well instead of focusing on one's advancement. Those who seek success without expending the effort to increase their competence risk losing any advantages and offices they may have gained when it becomes obvious to those who promoted them that they are not worthy of their position.

This proverb is a general observation about life. It is not a divine promise that a talented person always will be recognized and promoted by his human supervisors; a capable worker may be passed over for any number of reasons. Eschatologically, however, the believer can trust that his faithful labor will receive God's commendation on the Last Day, with a more glorious promotion (Mt 25:21, 23).

While three-line sayings are relatively rare in Proverbs, the final line of this saying should not be viewed as superfluous, but a vital part of the proverb that is integrated into it by use of a number of phonetic devices including assonance and consonance.[9]

23:1–3 Saying 6 warns about taking advantage of a superior's largesse and is a counterbalance to the previous saying's counsel about advancement. Those in power often have motives that are not apparent. Accepting what they offer may hurt one's chance for true promotion and one's spiritual well-being. A person can be discharged from service (or suffer a worse fate) if he appears too anxious to receive a superior's wherewithal for his own advantage. The food of the ruler is deceptive because the ruler has brought the underling into his service for his own (often unstated) purposes, under false pretenses, not for the good of the underling. This is illustrated by the narrative of Saul bringing David into his service (1 Samuel 17–24).

23:4–5 Saying 7 warns that an unbridled ambition for wealth endangers one's health, damages family and social relationships, and creates enemies. It is

---

[9] McCreesh, *Biblical Sound and Sense*, 136–38.

futile to wear oneself out pursuing affluence because as soon as one sets eyes on it, it will fly away. This suggests the transitoriness of earthly life (Psalm 90). At death a person leaves all his wealth and possessions behind for others to enjoy (cf. Prov 10:2; 21:6; Eccl 2:11, 18–23).

The wisdom in using this proverb comes in recognizing the point where one ought to stop before exhaustion. One must also realize when or that he has enough already. The desperately poor may never reach this point. Even the fabulously wealthy may never realize that this point has long since passed. Most people are somewhere in between poverty and the excessive wealth of a person such as Solomon himself. Every person needs to assess his situation and know when to stop chasing wealth.

23:6–8 Saying 8 is the last of six economic proverbs. It focuses on the person who is tightfisted (in Hebrew רַע עָיִן, literally, "evil of eye"; the expression is also used in 28:22). This warning is about the lack of sincerity of such a person. He invites his guests to enjoy themselves but is all the while calculating the cost and what he can gain from them. This ulterior motive will eventually show in his demeanor and spoil the dinner conversation—and the friendship.

The proper motive for a host's hospitality is taught by Jesus in Lk 14:7–14. Diverse motives by those gathered for table fellowship with Jesus are revealed in Lk 7:36–50.

23:9 Saying 9 warns against trying to correct a fool by speaking directly to him, since he will only respond by despising your good sense. This will do no good, and you will increase his animosity toward you. This proverb implies that one should seek ways of communication that will be most effective. In some cases it is best to correct a person obliquely by directing comments toward someone else who will have more influence.

23:10–11 Saying 10 shares its first line with 22:28. However, this proverb is not simply about property theft. Instead, it is about taking advantage of the weak and powerless, a theme already encountered in 22:22–23. In this saying, "move an ancient boundary marker" may be a concrete example that represents more broadly any manipulation of the legal system. This would include changing laws and customs to the disadvantage of the weak and defenseless. It would also apply to frivolous lawsuits, harassment, and perpetration of injustices that may now be considered legal. For society to legalize and approve of things long recognized as immoral is to "move an ancient boundary." For example, such evils as abortion, euthanasia, and pornography have proliferated in many societies that formerly enforced biblical morality but now have changed their standards of right and wrong.

To "enter the fields of orphans" may be a metaphor for using one's might to intimidate them. Though these orphans themselves are powerless to stop such aggression, they have on their side the omnipotent God, who is גֹּאֲלָם, "their redeemer." In ancient Israelite society, גֹּאֵל ("redeemer") could signify a prominent male family member responsible for defending and rescuing the weaker and more vulnerable members of his clan (e.g., Lev 25:25; Num 35:19; Ruth

3:12–13; 4:1, 14). Since orphans are without such relatives to defend them, God himself will act as their relative and Redeemer. As a designation for God, גֹּאֵל, "Redeemer," is a synonym of "Savior" (מוֹשִׁיעַ), and both titles occur together in Is 49:26 and 60:16. The NT, of course, identifies Jesus Christ as the Redeemer of the world and the Savior of all who believe. Offenses against even the least of God's children will incur his wrath (Mt 18:6, 10).

23:12 Saying 11 is an invitation to learn. It calls on the reader to be self-disciplined in gaining wisdom.

23:13–14 Saying 12 follows 23:12 to instruct those placed over young people to rear them by giving them the discipline they need. These verses do not necessarily mandate corporal punishment; the discipline should be appropriate and only as harsh as needed to help instill "knowledge" (23:12). See the commentary on 13:24, where the key word is "loves," and compare 22:15. This proverb encourages parents not to neglect punishment out of a false sense of compassion that cannot bear any suffering by the child. Instead appropriate discipline administered wisely and in love will train the child not to wander away from the faith and into sin. As in Eph 6:4, the parents' ultimate goal is to rescue their child from everlasting death in hell and preserve him in the true faith to everlasting life. This is precisely what the heavenly Father does for his children (Heb 12:5–11).

Proverbs 23:15–24:22

Advice from Your Father

Translation

23 [15]My son, if your heart is wise,
my heart will rejoice as well.
[16]My innermost being will celebrate
when your lips speak upright things.
[17]Do not allow your heart to envy sinners.
Instead have the fear of Yahweh all the time.
[18]Indeed, there is a future,
and your hope will never be cut off.
[19]Listen, my son, and be wise,
and make your heart go straight on the way.
[20]Do not be among those who drink too much wine,
with those who eat too much meat,
[21]because a drunk and a glutton will become poor,
and drowsiness dresses a person in rags.
[22]Listen to your father, who begot you,
and do not despise your mother when she is old.
[23]Buy truth and do not sell [it];
[buy] wisdom, discipline, and knowledge.
[24]The father of a righteous person will cheerfully rejoice.
The man who begets a wise person will find joy in him.
[25]Your father and your mother will find joy,
and she who gave birth to you will rejoice.
[26]My son, give me your heart,
and let your eyes be pleased with my ways,
[27]because a prostitute is a deep pit,
and a foreign woman is a narrow well.
[28]She is also like a robber waiting to ambush [someone],
and she increases treacherous men among humanity.
[29]Who has trouble?
Who has misery?
Who has quarrels?
Who has complaints?
Who has wounds for no reason?
Who has glazed eyes?
[30]Those who linger over wine,
those who go to search for mixed wine.
[31]Do not look at wine when it is red,
when it sparkles in the cup,
when it goes down smoothly.

[32]Later it bites like a snake,
and it strikes like a venomous viper.
[33]Your eyes will see strange things,
and your heart will speak perverse things.
[34]You will be like someone lying down [in a boat] on the high seas
and like someone lying down on top of the rigging.
[35]"They struck me, but I felt no pain.
They beat me, but I didn't know it.
When will I wake up so I can look for a drink again?"

24 [1]Do not envy evil people,
and do not wish to be with them,
[2]because their heart plans violence,
and their lips speak trouble.
[3]With wisdom a house is built;
with understanding it is established;
[4]and with knowledge its rooms are filled:
[with] every kind of riches, [both] valuable and pleasant.
[5]A wise man [grows] strong,
and a person of knowledge becomes more powerful,
[6]because with advice a battle is yours,
and many advisors [bring] victory.
[7]Matters needing wisdom are too difficult for a stubborn fool;
in the city gate he cannot open his mouth.
[8]Whoever plans to do evil
will be called a master schemer.
[9]A stupid scheme is a sin,
and a mocker is a disgusting thing to people.
[10]If you fail to act in times of trouble,
your strength is deficient.
[11]Rescue captives condemned to death,
and spare those staggering toward a slaughter.
[12]If you say, "We didn't know about this,"
won't the one who weighs motives notice,
and won't the one who guards your life know [about it],
and won't he repay a person according to what he has done?
[13]My son, eat honey, because it is good,
and flowing honey is sweet upon your palate.
[14]In the same way, know that wisdom is [like this] for your soul.
If you find [it], then there is a future,
and your hope will never be cut off.
[15]You wicked person, do not ambush a home of a righteous person;
do not destroy his house,
[16]because a righteous person may fall seven times, but he will get up,
while wicked people will stumble in misfortune.

[17]Do not be joyful when your enemy falls,
and do not inwardly rejoice when he stumbles.
[18]Otherwise Yahweh will see it and consider it evil,
and he will turn his anger away from him.
[19]Do not get angry about evildoers;
do not be jealous of wicked people,
[20]because there is no future for an evil person:
the lamp of wicked people will be extinguished.
[21]Fear Yahweh, my son, and [fear] a king.
Do not associate with those who are rebellious,
[22]because their disaster will happen suddenly,
and who knows what ruin both of them [Yahweh and a king] will cause?

Textual Notes

23:15 יִשְׂמַח לִבִּי גַם־אָנִי׃—Literally, this is "my heart will rejoice—also I."

23:16 וְתַעְלֹזְנָה כִלְיוֹתָי—Literally, "and my kidneys will rejoice" indicates deep-seated joy. The verb עָלַז denotes extreme joy that manifests itself in singing and shouting.[1] Whereas in Hebrew the לֵב, "heart," is the usual seat of intellect and emotion, the kidneys (the plural of כִּלְיָה) are the seat of extreme emotion (cf. BDB, s.v. כִּלְיָה, 2; *HALOT*, 2). Thus this clause is translated as "my innermost being will celebrate."

מֵישָׁרִים׃—This abstract plural, literally, "uprightness, fairness," is derived from the root ישׁר, "be straight," in contrast to words for "twisted" or "crooked," for example, עִקְּשׁוּת in 4:24; 6:12; נִפְתָּל in 8:8; נָלוֹז in 2:15; 3:32; 14:2; and הֲפַכְפַּךְ in 21:8.

23:17 כִּי אִם־בְּיִרְאַת־יְהוָה כָּל־הַיּוֹם׃—Literally, this is "but rather in the fear of Yahweh all the day." See the first textual note and the commentary on 1:7 and "יִרְאַת יְהוָה, 'the Fear of Yahweh,' and יְרֵא יְהוָה, 'One Who Fears Yahweh' " in "Wisdom in Proverbs" in the introduction.

23:18 יֵשׁ אַחֲרִית—This clause is repeated in 24:14. The noun for "end" or "future (time)" has an eschatological meaning, pointing to eternal life, as also in 19:20. In other verses it is used negatively to refer to everlasting perdition (e.g., 5:4; 14:12).

וְתִקְוָתְךָ לֹא תִכָּרֵת׃—This clause too is repeated in 24:14. And it too has an eschatological meaning. "And your hope will not/never be cut off" means that it will be fulfilled. See Rom 5:1–5; 8:24–25; Titus 1:2; 2:13. In contrast, the "hope" of the wicked "will perish" along with them (Prov 10:28; 11:7).

23:20 אַל־תְּהִי בְסֹבְאֵי־יָיִן—In contrast to the common verb שָׁתָה, which simply means "drink," the verb in 23:20–21 is סָבָא, "drink excessively/too much." Usually סָבָא occurs as a participle, and in construct here with יַיִן, "wine," the participle could be rendered as "those who *get drunk* on wine."

בְּזֹלְלֵי בָשָׂר לָמוֹ׃—The verb זָלַל means "be thoughtless or rash." Those who are, literally, "thoughtless ones of meat" are gluttonous consumers of meat (*HALOT*, 1). The

[1] C. Schultz, "עָלַז," *TWOT* 2:670; G. Vanoni, "עָלַז," *TDOT* 11:118–20.

participle recurs in this sense but in the singular in the next verse, and the plural participle recurs in 28:7. לָמוֹ in pause, לָֽמוֹ, is the sole instance in Proverbs of the preposition לְ with enclitic *mem*. This form can function as if it has a pronominal suffix of any person, gender, and number. Here it serves as the equivalent of לָהֶם with a reflexive sense, "for themselves," although it need not be reflected in translation.

23:22 שְׁמַע לְאָבִיךָ זֶה יְלָדֶךָ—Here זֶה is used as a relative pronoun rather than a demonstrative: "listen to your father, *who* begot you" (see Waltke-O'Connor, 19.5b, including example 1; Joüon, § 145 c).

23:23 אֱמֶת קְנֵה וְאַל־תִּמְכֹּר—For אֱמֶת, "truth," see the first textual note on 8:7. For the verb קָנָה, "acquire," see the first textual note on 8:22. Here it can be translated as "purchase, buy," in contrast to the following verb, מָכַר, "sell."

חָכְמָה וּמוּסָר וּבִינָה׃—These are synonyms of אֱמֶת, "truth," used in the first line of the verse. See "חָכְמָה, 'Wisdom,' and Related Words"; "מוּסָר, 'Discipline,' and יָסַר, 'to Discipline' "; and "בִּינָה, 'Understanding,' and Related Words" in "Wisdom in Proverbs" in the introduction.

23:25 וְתָגֵל יֽוֹלַדְתֶּךָ׃—The first verb is the feminine Qal (G) jussive of גִּיל, "rejoice." The second is the suffixed feminine Qal (G) participle of יָלַד, "*she* who gave birth to you." יוֹלַדְתּוֹ is in 17:25.

23:26 וְעֵינֶיךָ דְּרָכַי תִּרְצֶנָה׃—The Kethib, תִּרְצֶנָה, is the feminine plural imperfect of רָצָה, literally, "your eyes, my ways, *let them look with favor*," that is, "let your eyes look favorably on my ways." The Qere is תִּצֹּרְנָה, from נָצַר, "let them guard/observe." The difference between the two involves a metathesis of ר and צ. The LXX (τηρείτωσαν), Syriac, Vulgate, Targum, and some modern translations and commentators follow the Qere.[2] However, the Qere is a more common verb, perhaps a substitution for a less common one, making it suspect. In addition, the Kethib fits the context better. The father is exhorting his son to be pleased with his wise ways instead of being pleased by a prostitute.

23:27 כִּי־שׁוּחָה עֲמֻקָּה זוֹנָה—Most of this vocabulary is in the first clause of 22:14, but that verse does not explicitly refer to a זוֹנָה, "prostitute."

23:28 אַף־הִיא כְּחֶתֶף תֶּאֱרֹב—For the verb אָרַב, "lie in wait, ambush," see the first textual note on 1:11, the textual note on 1:18, and the commentary on those two verses. In this pericope it recurs in 24:15. The noun חֶתֶף is hapax legomenon from the verb חָתַף, "seize, snatch away," which occurs in the OT only in Job 9:12. Probably חֶתֶף is an abstract noun ("seizure, robbery") that here has a concrete meaning. כְּחֶתֶף could refer to the man she seeks to ambush and mean "*as* for *prey*" (BDB, s.v. חֶתֶף). Or it could refer to the woman herself and mean "like a robber" (see *HALOT*).

23:29 חַכְלִלוּת עֵינָיִם׃—This is the last effect of intoxication listed in this verse. Most consider the feminine noun with the abstract ending, חַכְלִלוּת, to derive from the root חכל, "be dull." English versions exhibit a variety of translations, including "redness of eyes" (e.g., ESV, NASB) and "bloodshot eyes" (NIV). The LXX translates the phrase

2 E.g., NIV; ESV; NRSV; Garrett, *Proverbs, Ecclesiastes, Song of Songs*, 197; Toy, *Proverbs*, 437.

as πέλειοι οἱ ὀφθαλμοί, "pale eyes." Whatever the exact meaning, in English "glazed eyes,"[3] signaling inattention and stupor, fits well.

23:31 כִּֽי־יִתֵּ֣ן בַּכּ֣וֹס עֵינ֑וֹ—Literally, this is "when it gives in the cup its eye/appearance." English translations are generally agreed that this means "when it sparkles in the cup" (cf. *HALOT*, s.v. עַיִן, 3 b).

23:32 אַחֲרִית֗וֹ כְּנָחָ֥שׁ יִשָּׁ֑ךְ—The noun נָחָשׁ, "a serpent," is used with the verb נָשַׁךְ, "bite," also in, for example, Num 21:6, 9; Amos 5:19; 9:3. For the form of the Qal (G) imperfect יִשָּׁךְ, see Joüon, § 32 c.

וּֽכְצִפְעֹנִ֥י יַפְרִֽשׁ׃—The noun צִפְעֹנִי refers to a venomous viper, as in Is 11:8. The verb here is a hapax legomenon, but Semitic cognates confirm that it means "pierce" (BDB, s.v. פרשׁ II, Hiphil) or "strike."

23:34 בְּלֶב־יָ֑ם—Literally, "in the heart of the sea" does not signify that this person has sunk to the bottom; instead it depicts the drunken person's sensation of motion even when lying still. He feels as if he is lying on a ship's pitched deck on the high seas.

חִבֵּֽל׃—This noun for a ship's "rigging" is a hapax legomenon. It derives from the verb חָבַל, "bind," and is related to two nautical terms: חֶבֶל, "ropes" used to secure a sail (Is 33:23), and חֹבֵל, "sailor" (Ezek 27:8, 27–29; Jonah 1:6). Here the drunken person is depicted as lying in the constantly moving rigging of the ship.

23:35 בַּל־חָלִ֗יתִי—Here the verb חָלָה, "be sick, weak," means "feel pain" (*HALOT*, 3).

מָתַ֥י אָקִ֑יץ א֝וֹסִ֗יף אֲבַקְשֶׁ֥נּוּ עֽוֹד׃—Three imperfect verbs occur in rapid succession here. Semantically, the second two (א֝וֹסִ֗יף אֲבַקְשֶׁ֥נּוּ) are subordinated to the first (אָקִ֑יץ): literally, "when shall I arise? I will continue, I will search for it again," means "when will I wake up *so* I can search/look for it again?" (see GKC, § 120 c). The masculine singular suffix on אֲבַקְשֶׁ֥נּוּ, literally, "I will search for *it*," refers back to יַיִן, "wine," in 23:31, which is the subject of the masculine singular verbs and the referent of the masculine singular pronouns in 23:31–32. The translation of 23:35 simply renders "it" as "a drink."

24:3 בְּ֭חָכְמָה יִבָּ֣נֶה בָּ֑יִת—This clause with the בְּ of means and the passive Niphal (N) of בָּנָה, "by/with wisdom a house is built," recalls the statement in 9:1 with the active Qal (G) of בָּנָה: "wisdom has built her house" (see also 14:1; cf. 24:27).

24:5 גֶּֽבֶר־חָכָ֥ם בַּע֑וֹז—Literally, this is "a wise man (is) with strength." Usually בַּע֑וֹז is translated as "is strong" or "grows strong," as the second clause of the verse clearly means. This use of the preposition בְּ is commonly called the *bet essentiae*.

24:6 This verse repeats vocabulary from 11:14; 20:18b; and 21:31b.

24:7 רָאמ֣וֹת לֶאֱוִ֣יל חָכְמ֑וֹת—Probably this means "(too) high for a fool are matters of wisdom." The feminine plural רָאמ֣וֹת could mean "corals," since the identical form refers to this costly merchandise in Ezek 27:16; Job 28:18. However, probably it is a variant spelling of רָמוֹת, the Qal (G) participle of רום, "be high, lofty," hence "too difficult."[4] (For a similar form, see the first textual note on 10:4, which has רָאשׁ, the Qal participle of רושׁ or רִישׁ.) The subject of the feminine plural participle is חָכְמ֑וֹת, which here is a true plural of חָכְמָה, meaning "matters of wisdom, matters that require wisdom

3 Murphy, *Proverbs*, 173.

4 So Luther: *Weisheit ist dem Narren zu hoch* (WA DB 10/2.79).

to understand." (For the abstract plural חָכְמוֹת as a personified or hypostatized singular, "Wisdom," see the first textual note on 1:20.) For the indirect object לֶאֱוִיל, see "אֱוִיל, 'Stubborn Fool,' and אִוֶּלֶת, 'Stupidity' " in "Fools in Proverbs" in the introduction.

בַּשַּׁעַר לֹא יִפְתַּח־פִּיהוּ׃—"The city gate" (שַׁעַר) served as the place for the court of law and for transacting business matters (see 22:22; 31:23). The imperfect verb יִפְתַּח probably has the nuance "he *cannot* open his mouth" because the matters of wisdom under discussion are beyond the fool's comprehension. Or it could mean "he *should* not …" because if he talks, he would not contribute, but only reveal his own stupidity.

24:8 מְחַשֵּׁב לְהָרֵעַ—The Piel (D) of חָשַׁב, "to plan," has a similar meaning in 16:9. The infinitive construct הָרֵעַ is of the Hiphil (H) of רָעַע, "to do/cause evil." Other forms of its Hiphil (H) are in 4:16 and 17:4, as well as 24:19, which has the participle with preposition בַּמְּרֵעִים, "at/about evildoers."

לוֹ בַּעַל־מְזִמּוֹת יִקְרָאוּ׃—Literally, this is "to him [the planner] 'a master of schemes' they will call." The impersonal plural verb יִקְרָאוּ can be translated as a passive: "he will *be* called." For the construct phrase בַּעַל־מְזִמּוֹת, literally, "a master of schemes," see the second textual note on 1:17. For מְזִמּוֹת meaning "schemes, wicked plans," see the second textual note on 12:2.

24:9 זִמַּת אִוֶּלֶת חַטָּאת—The singular noun זִמָּה, "a scheme," is cognate to the plural מְזִמּוֹת in the second line of 24:8. It is in construct with the feminine abstract noun אִוֶּלֶת, "stupidity," which is cognate to אֱוִיל, "stupid fool," in the first clause of 24:7. אִוֶּלֶת functions as an adjectival genitive: "a *stupid* scheme."

וְתוֹעֲבַת לְאָדָם לֵץ׃—This is one of the few proverbs that refer to something that is "disgusting" in human estimation, rather than in God's estimation. See the excursus " 'Disgusting Thing' (תּוֹעֵבָה) in Solomon's Proverbs" in the commentary on Proverbs 11. This is the last occurrence of the participle לֵץ in Proverbs. See "לֵץ, 'Mocker,' and לָצוֹן, 'Mocking, Scoffing' " in "Fools in Proverbs" in the introduction.

24:10 הִתְרַפִּיתָ בְּיוֹם צָרָה צַר כֹּחֶכָה׃—Although there is no hypothetical particle, this begins a conditional sentence: "*if* you fail to act …" Another conditional sentence begins in 24:12 with כִּי־.

In the Qal (G) רָפָה often refers to hands that "drop, hang limp," meaning that a person loses heart and is discouraged (e.g., 2 Sam 4:1). It occurs three times in the Hithpael (HtD). In Josh 18:3 it is used to characterize the Israelites' failure to act on the success of Joshua's campaigns and take the land that God had placed before them. In Prov 18:9 it describes a lazy person's failure to do his work. Here it addresses a person who "fail[s] to act" and does not do what God requires. Translations such as "if you faint" (ESV), "if you falter" (NIV), or "if you are slack" (NASB) miss its force in this context.

Note the play on words with צָרָה צַר. The noun צָרָה is a feminine substantive formed from the adjective צַר. The phrase בְּיוֹם צָרָה means "on a day of trouble, adversity, distress" (see *HALOT*, s.v. צָרָה; ESV; NASB; NIV). The last phrase, צַר כֹּחֶכָה, uses the adjective צַר itself to mean "your strength is meager" (see *HALOT*, s.v. צַר I, 1 b) or "deficient." The noun כֹּחַ has a second masculine singular pronominal suffix with the unusual spelling כָה- (Joüon, § 94 h).

24:11 וּמָטִים לַהֶרֶג אִם־תַּחְשׂוֹךְ׃—Ordinarily this line would mean "and those staggering to a slaughter—*if* you would spare [them]." The hypothetical particle אִם normally means "if" and begins a conditional clause. However, the first clause of the verse begins with the imperative הַצֵּל, "save/rescue," and this second clause too must be a command or exhortation. אִם could be understood as a hortatory particle as in Ps 139:19[5] or as an oath formula.[6]

24:12 הֲלֹא־תֹכֵן לִבּוֹת ׀ הוּא־יָבִין—The verb תָּכַן, "measure, evaluate," occurs as the Qal (G) participle תֹּכֵן with Yahweh as the subject in 16:2 and 21:2. Here Yahweh is the implied subject; he is the "one" who performs the action in this clause and the following two lines in the verse. Both in 21:2 and here in 24:12, the object that God "weighs, evaluates" is לִבּוֹת, human "hearts." See the second textual note on 16:2, where the object is, literally, human "spirits." In all three verses, the object is translated as "motives."

The resumptive pronoun הוּא refers back to תֹּכֵן and is emphatic: literally, "will not the one who weighs motives—*he* will notice?" The final verb in the line, יָבִין, here means "notice, become aware of" (*HALOT*, 1, gives "see").

וְהֵשִׁיב לְאָדָם כְּפָעֳלוֹ׃—The Hiphil (H) perfect of שׁוּב, "cause to return, pay back, repay, recompense," is used with לְאָדָם in a distributive sense, literally, "to each man, person" (cf. Joüon, § 147 d). The prepositional phrase כְּפָעֳלוֹ with the noun פֹּעַל, "deed, action," means "according to his work, what he has done." A similar phrase occurs in 24:29 but with the verb in the imperfect, אָשִׁיב, and with לָאִישׁ instead of לְאָדָם.

24:14 כֵּן ׀ דְּעֶה חָכְמָה לְנַפְשֶׁךָ—This is, literally, "thus know wisdom for your soul." דְּעֶה is an unusual form of the Qal (G) imperative of יָדַע, "know" (see GKC, § 48 l; Joüon, § 29 f (A)).

וְיֵשׁ אַחֲרִית וְתִקְוָתְךָ לֹא תִכָּרֵת׃—See the textual notes on 23:18, which has virtually identical wording.

24:15 אַל־תֶּאֱרֹב רָשָׁע לִנְוֵה צַדִּיק—For אָרַב, "ambush," see the first textual note on 1:11, the textual note on 1:18, and the commentary on those two verses. Since the negated verb תֶּאֱרֹב ("do not ambush") is second person, the noun רָשָׁע must be a vocative, "*you* wicked person." Some commentators are bothered by a vocative here since all of the other vocatives in these sayings address a son.[7] They either omit it or interpret it as if the prefixed preposition כְּ, "like/as," is implied (see also NIV, NRSV, ESV). However, there is no need for these changes. Since this section is a compilation of proverbs from several wise people (see 22:17; 24:23), it is altogether possible that it came from a context where this vocative was not out of place.

רִבְצוֹ׃—"His resting place, bed" (see *HALOT*, s.v. רֵבֶץ) is used by metonymy to denote the entire house or home (so ESV, NIV, NRSV) of the צַדִּיק, "righteous (person)."

24:17 וּבִכָּשְׁלוֹ אַל־יָגֵל לִבֶּךָ׃—The expected form of the Niphal (N) infinitive construct (with preposition and conjunction) would be וּבְהִכָּשְׁלוֹ, "and when he stumbles," but the ה has been elided after the preposition בְּ (GKC, § 51 l; cf. Waltke-O'Connor, § 23.2.1a, example 4). The following command, literally, "do not let your heart rejoice," has the jussive יָגֵל with לִבֶּךָ as its subject. This idiom is used in Zech 10:7 in a positive context of rejoicing in Yahweh (cf. Pss 13:6b [ET 13:5b] 16:9). The command here is to

---

5 Toy, *Proverbs*, 446.

6 Murphy, *Proverbs*, 179; Waltke-O'Connor, § 40.2.2b.

7 Murphy, *Proverbs*, 179–80; Toy, *Proverbs*, 447–48.

not find joy in someone's misfortune, even joy that you do not show outwardly, hence the translation "do not inwardly rejoice."

24:18 וְרַע בְּעֵינָיו—Literally, this is "it will be evil in his eyes." וְרַע is not the adjective רַע, "evil," but the *waw* consecutive with the Qal (G) perfect of the verb רָעַע, "be evil." This describes God's attitude. The equivalent English idiom is "consider it evil." For בְּעֵינֵי־, see the second textual note on 3:4.

וְהֵשִׁיב מֵעָלָיו אַפּוֹ׃—Literally, "and he [God] will turn his anger from him" means that God will turn his anger "away from" the fallen wicked person in 24:17. It suggests that the anger that God diverts away from the wicked person will now be directed against the gloating person.

24:19 אַל־תִּתְחַר בַּמְּרֵעִים—The shortened Hithpael (HtD) imperfect תִּתְחַר is the sole occurrence in Proverbs of the verb חָרָה, "be angry." The object of the anger with בְּ is the Hiphil (H) participle of רָעַע, meaning "evildoers, those who cause evil." See 17:4, which has a singular Hiphil participle.

24:20 נֵר רְשָׁעִים יִדְעָךְ׃—This sober warning about the lamp of wicked people being extinguished occurs also in 13:9b. Similar is the second line of 20:20. For positive affirmations about a lamp, see 6:23a; 20:27a; and 31:18b.

24:21 יְרָא־אֶת־יְהוָה בְּנִי וָמֶלֶךְ—The imperative יְרָא, "fear," takes two direct objects. First in word order and in importance is אֶת־יְהוָה, "Yahweh." The verbal expression here is cognate to the nominal "fear of Yahweh" theme. See the first textual note and the commentary on 1:7 and "יִרְאַת יְהוָה, 'the Fear of Yahweh,' and יְרֵא יְהוָה, 'One Who Fears Yahweh' " in "Wisdom in Proverbs" in the introduction.

The second direct object, וָמֶלֶךְ, "and a king," is indefinite (not "*the* king") and is relegated to the final position in the word order, after the vocative בְּנִי, "my son." This suggests a subordination of any human ruler to God. The believer is to fear a human authority only because—and insofar as—he is enforcing God's will. If the government contradicts God's will and Word, then the believer must "obey God rather than men" (Acts 5:29).

עִם־שׁוֹנִים אַל־תִּתְעָרָב׃—The Qal (G) participle שׁוֹנִים is, literally, "those who change." The most probable interpretation of this difficult word is that these are "rebellious" people who wish to change the Law of God or the laws set by the king and society in order to suit their own evil purposes. An expression with a causative form of the same verb (לְהַשְׁנָיָה זִמְנִין וְדָת) is used in the Aramaic of Dan 7:25 to refer to the Antichrist's efforts "to change" God's "Law" and divine worship "times."[8]

For the verb תִּתְעָרָב, "have fellowship with, associate with," see the second textual note on 20:19, where it is negated with לֹא.

24:22 וּפִיד שְׁנֵיהֶם מִי יוֹדֵעַ׃—Literally, this is "the ruin of [caused by] the two of them—who knows?" The rare noun פִּיד, "ruin, disaster," occurs elsewhere only in Job 12:5; 30:24; 31:29. It is a synonym of אֵיד, "disaster," in the preceding line (אֵידָם, "their disaster"). Both nouns, "disaster" and "ruin," refer to the devastating punishment of people who incur the wrath of either of, literally, "the two of them" in 24:21: either Yahweh

8 See Steinmann, *Daniel*, 363, 373–74.

or a king, who is God's agent of punishment (Rom 13:1–7). For שְׁנֵיהֶם, literally, "the two of them," translated as "both of them," see the second textual note on Prov 17:15.

Commentary

This section (23:15–24:22) of the Words of Wise People (22:17–24:22) differs from the first section (22:22–23:14) in two important ways. First, this section has no parallels to the Wisdom of Amenemope.[9] Second, this section contains six vocatives ("my son," 23:15, 19, 26; 24:13, 21, and "you wicked person," 24:15), whereas the previous section contains none. This section is framed by the vocative "my son" in 23:15 and 24:21, which casts the entire section as fatherly advice.

This section is divided into seventeen sayings, which can be numbered consecutively after the twelve sayings in the previous section:

Saying	*Verses*	*Topic*
13	23:15–18	Do not envy sinners, but have the fear of Yahweh
14	23:19–21	Avoid drunkenness and gluttony
15	23:22–25	Learn wisdom from your father
16	23:26–28	Avoid sexual immorality
17	23:29–35	The dangers of drunkenness
18	24:1–2	Do not envy evil people
19	24:3–4	Building a life with wisdom
20	24:5–6	Growing strong with wisdom
21	24:7	Wisdom is too difficult for a fool
22	24:8	Those who get reputations as schemers
23	24:9	The results of sinful thoughts and attitudes
24	24:10–12	Courage in troubling times
25	24:13–14	The sweetness of wisdom
26	24:15–16	Warning against attacking a righteous person
27	24:17–18	Warning against gloating over someone's misfortune
28	24:19–20	Warning against envying the apparent success of wicked people
29	24:21–22	Warning against associating with rebellious people

These sayings contain more explicit Gospel than those in the first section of the Words of Wise People (22:22–23:14). Especially prominent in this regard are the thirteenth and the twenty-fifth sayings, which speak of the everlasting hope that divine wisdom brings (see the commentary on 23:15–18 and 24:13–14). Therefore, it is very likely that this section derives at least in part

[9] See the excursus "The Words of Wise People (Prov 22:17–24:22) and Its Relationship to the Wisdom of Amenemope" before the commentary on 22:17–21, including figure 14.

from native Israelite sages, whose sayings Solomon incorporated (perhaps with some adaptations) into this collection. Some of these Israelite sages could be those mentioned in 1 Ki 5:11 (ET 4:31): Ethan the Ezrahite, as well as Mahol's sons Heman, Calcol, and Darda.

(a) See Is 42:1; Mt 3:17; 12:18; 17:5; Jn 6:38; 10:17–18; Gal 1:3–5

23:15–18 Saying 13 begins with an address that urges the son to be wise. It harnesses the son's natural desire to please his father by noting that the son's wisdom will delight his father. Jesus, the Son of God, through his perfect and sinless life in our stead (2 Cor 5:21), best exemplifies this filial relationship, to the delight of God the Father.[a]

This saying contrasts envying sinners with fearing Yahweh. The wisdom of this saying lies in its insight that the worldly success of those who ignore God's Word can tempt the faithful person to imitate the sins of the evil person. However, the wise person will look beyond the temporary advantages that sin may offer to the eternal promises of God and his wisdom in Jesus Christ.[10] Such a person has an unlimited future in the eternal life that God grants freely to his people. What they hope for according to God's promise will never fail.

23:19–21 Saying 14, like the previous one, also begins with a call to a son, this time to listen and learn. This saying assumes that the son's heart has been trained in the way of Yahweh and urges the son to remain in that way. Like the previous saying, this one promotes long-term planning over immediate gratification. This is the mind of Christ (Phil 2:5–11), who looked at the ultimate goal rather than the immediate consequences. He was able to be faithful unto death, even death on the cross, so that we have the promise of resurrection to glory with him.

The temptation of substance abuse, be it alcohol and food or the illicit drugs of modern invention, is so powerful that it continues to destroy lives. The "drowsiness" to which the saying refers is probably the physical aftereffect of the drinking and gluttony.

23:22–25 Saying 15 is the third of four consecutive sayings that begin with an appeal from parent to child. This saying does not refer to the hearer as "son" but does call him to listen to his "father" and to not despise his "mother." This saying is framed by the same nouns and verbs in its beginning and ending verses:

> Listen to *your father* [אָבִיךָ], who *begot you* [יְלָדֶךָ],
> and do not despise *your mother* [אִמֶּךָ] when she is old. (23:22)
>
> *Your father and your mother* [אָבִיךָ וְאִמֶּךָ] will find joy,
> and *she who gave birth to you* [יוֹלַדְתֶּךָ] will rejoice. (23:25)

The advice is to acquire truth and never to let it go. Truth is defined in this saying as wisdom, discipline, and knowledge. All of these are understood

---

[10] See "Wisdom in Proverbs" in the introduction. See also the commentary on 1:1–7; 3:13–20; 8:22–31; 30:1b–10; and the excursus "Proverbs 8, Wisdom, Christology, and the Arian Controversy" in the commentary on chapter 8.

throughout Proverbs as deriving from God. Therefore, the father is guiding his son to divine revelation as truth (see Jn 17:17). This, of course, guides the son to Christ (Jn 14:6). In turn, Christ makes a person righteous and wise (Prov 23:24). Like the thirteenth saying (23:15–18), this one uses the son's natural urge to please his parents as motivation.

23:26–28 Saying 16 not only calls for the son to give his heart to his father, but also to find the father's ways pleasing. This proverb implies that the father's way of life has been shaped by God's Word and that the father is now calling on the son to follow the same Word of God, including the Decalogue in the Torah of Moses.[11] In particular, the father is teaching his son about the Sixth Commandment. This saying parallels several sections of Proverbs 1–9. See the excursus "Wisdom and the Adulteress in Proverbs 1–9" in the commentary on Proverbs 2.

However, the characterizations of "deep pit" and "narrow well" (23:27) are not used in chapters 1–9. The mouth of "women who are strangers," that is, all women other than the man's wife, is characterized as a "deep pit" in one of Solomon's proverbs (22:14), where the metaphor is carried through when the foolish man is depicted as falling into it. Here the "prostitute" (זוֹנָה, as in 6:26; 7:10; 29:3) is called a "deep pit" (23:27), and the metaphor is left unexplained, though the obvious implication is that a man will not be able to extricate himself from it and faces death in it, as Joseph (Gen 37:22–28) and Jeremiah (Jer 38:1–13) almost perished in literal pits before they were taken out of them.

The "foreign woman" (נָכְרִיָּה) in the second clause of 23:27 is not necessarily a woman from outside of Israel, but one who is "foreign" to a man because she is not his wife and most probably is someone else's wife (see the textual notes on 2:16). Therefore she can be called an "adulteress," as נָכְרִיָּה can be translated also in, for example, 2:16; 5:20; 6:24; 7:5. Metaphorically she is "a narrow well" (בְּאֵר צָרָה, 23:27). Like the "deep pit" in the preceding clause, this means that a man who falls into her may not be able to escape and may perish in her. It may also suggest that the "well" is too constricted or deep to allow a person to draw water from it (cf. Jn 4:11). This would contrast to the metaphors in Prov 5:15–18, where a man's own wife is a "cistern," "well," and "fountain" who provides abundant flowing water for her husband (see also Song 4:12, 15).

Another image is added when this adulteress is described as being like a robber waiting to ambush a man (23:28). The stealth depicted here is not obvious to a man, since the adulterous woman may be in plain view, rather than hiding. See 7:10–12 and note that the identical verb תֶּאֱרֹב, "she ambushes, lies in wait," is in 7:12 and 23:28. The hidden ambush consists of the consequences that await a man who falls into an adulterous affair. He will suffer shame, disgrace, and loss of his position in the community of faith (the church)

---

[11] See the excursus "Proverbs 1–9, Christ, and the Ten Commandments" in the commentary on Proverbs 1.

and in society. Even more serious is that he risks losing his faith and salvation. While good works do not contribute to salvation, sins and evil deeds erode saving faith and can cause a person to fall from grace, thereby coming under everlasting condemnation.[12]

This woman is also depicted as increasing the number of treacherous men in humanity. A person who commits adultery acts treacherously by sinning against God and his family. He will also go to great lengths to try to conceal his indiscretion. A person who commits this unfaithful act cannot be trusted to be faithful in other ways.

23:29–35 Saying 17 is the longest of the sayings in the Words of Wise People.[13] It begins with a series of rhetorical questions that form a riddle (23:29). The questions begin with the most general and become more specific, leading to a possible solution to the riddle. The answer is the habitual drinker (23:30). The person characterized here is one who craves drink. While this may apply to a person addicted to drink, it need not have reached that point. The sage is warning about the person who misuses alcohol and makes it an important part of his life. The sage then warns about desire for alcohol.

Looking at the wine "when it is red" (23:31) is probably a reference to drinking undiluted alcohol. It was common in the ancient world to dilute alcohol when it was used as a beverage. The sage is warning about serious drinking that is intended to intoxicate, telling his son to not even look at undiluted wine in the cup.

There is also a play on words between 23:29 and 23:31. Wine gives the drunk "glazed eyes" (23:29), and it has an eye of its own: literally, "its eye" is its sparkle in the cup (עֵינ֑וֹ, 23:31). The wine may go down smoothly, but its easy way bites back in the end (23:32). The sage's description of the effects of intoxication are comical: hallucinatory effects and a loosening of inhibitions so that one says things that one should not and normally would not say (23:33), as well as the heaving sensations of apparent motion (23:34).

The saying ends with a comical, yet pathetic, quotation from the drunkard: He was physically abused, but did not know it. Yet he cannot wait to go back to the same substance that made him vulnerable to abuse. The sage's skillful rhetoric in this extended proverb is a powerful and memorable warning against substance abuse.

24:1–2 Saying 18 returns to the theme of the thirteenth saying (23:15–18). This proverb recalls the warning for the son not to join the violent gang of sinners, who will come to a violent end (1:10–19). It does not attempt to persuade one to put aside envy for sinners by calling upon the parental relationship, as

12 See Luther's discussion in SA III III 41–45. Luther refers to King David's adultery.

13 Andrew, "Variety of Expression in Proverbs XXIII 29–35," outlines this proverb as having the following parts: riddle (23:29); answer (23:30); instruction (23:31); consequence of disobeying the instruction (23:32); consequence in direct address (23:33–34); and a quotation from the drunkard's own words (23:35).

23:15 does, nor by pointing to God's promise of eternal life, as 23:18 does. Instead it simply depicts the treachery of such people as undesirable character traits.

24:3–4 Saying 19 is advice on wisely building one's house, that is, one's household and family. This saying was perhaps included as a contrast to 9:1, where wisdom has built her own house. The possessions that are kept in this house first of all consist of "knowledge" (דַּעַת), which in Proverbs is always divinely imparted knowledge that includes saving faith.[14] The second line of 24:4 characterizes knowledge as consisting of all kinds of riches. This knowledge from God is described as "valuable" and "pleasant." This is a promise connected with wisdom intended to make it attractive. Since this proverb was placed immediately after 24:1–2, it is probably to be understood as purposely drawing a contrast between the unpleasantness of evil people and the pleasant nature of wisdom and its gifts.

Moreover, the image of creation through the agency of wisdom here clearly enjoys a close connection with divine Wisdom in 3:19–20. In both passages the terms "wisdom," "understanding," and "knowledge" occur (in that order). Moreover, both use the verb "establish" (כּוּן) in connection with "understanding." The act of building is a common motif connected with wisdom in Proverbs (9:1; 14:1; 24:3). Wisdom is portrayed as a divine hypostasis in 3:19–20, that is, as God the Son (see the commentary on 3:19–20). Here in 24:3–4 wisdom is a gift from God to his people. It leads the believer to build in the family and in the church, and it fills/provides for all in the household: "with knowledge its rooms are filled: [with] every kind of riches, [both] valuable and pleasant."

24:5–6 Saying 20 depicts a wise person as growing in the power that comes from divine knowledge and wisdom. This growth comes from the willingness to take advice, a theme that is frequently connected to gaining wisdom (see also 8:14–15; 9:9; 13:10; 15:22; 19:20). The connection of advice with victory has already been treated in Solomon's proverb in 20:18. The second line of 24:6 is identical to the second line of 11:14.

24:7 Saying 21 forms a contrast with the previous proverb. While the wise person grows in wisdom, the stubborn fool, who has rejected wisdom, cannot even make sense of lofty matters and so does not dare say anything when they are being discussed.

24:8 Saying 22 is advice aimed at helping one avoid a bad reputation as a cold, calculating schemer who is only interested in his own selfish interests and advancement. The schemer may be crafty and astute, capable of calculating ingenious schemes, but spiritually he is a stupid fool who is not able to grasp true wisdom (see 24:7).

24:9 Saying 23 is linked to the previous saying by the root זמם, "schemer/scheme," and to 24:7 by the root אול, "stubborn fool/stupid." Like the previous

[14] See "דַּעַת, 'Knowledge,' and יָדַע, 'to Know' " in "Wisdom in Proverbs" in the introduction, as well as the commentary on 1:4, 7.

saying (24:8) this one warns of the bad reputation that schemers and mockers acquire. This is what makes their schemes stupid even from a human perspective. The theological term "a sin" (חַטָּאת) indicates that they also will face God's wrath on Judgment Day.

24:10–12 Saying 24 concerns spiritual and moral courage in the face of grave danger. Each person should act according to God's Word and his conscience and seek to rescue others even when he faces personal risk. The fear of death should not deter a person from trying to save others who are condemned to die (24:11). All unbelievers are captives to sin and will be condemned to eternal death, but they can be saved through the Gospel proclaimed by a courageous believer. The Bible contains many accounts of heroic faith by which a person refuses to let fear of death dissuade him from testifying to God's truth (e.g., Daniel 3; Acts 7) or prevent him from boldly snatching others from destruction despite personal peril (e.g., Joshua 2; 1 Samuel 17).

Pleading ignorance or powerlessness about the fate of others who are perishing may convince human authorities that inaction was acceptable or even prudent, but it will not convince God. He is the "one who weighs motives" and "guards your life," and "he" will "repay" (24:12). He can save your life in times of danger—and will save all believers for eternity. Jesus calls his disciples to proclaim his Gospel for the salvation of all who believe, and to ignore the potentially fatal dangers of poverty, rejection, and persecution. At the same time he warns that those who spurn his missionaries will face judgment on the Last Day (Mk 6:7–13).

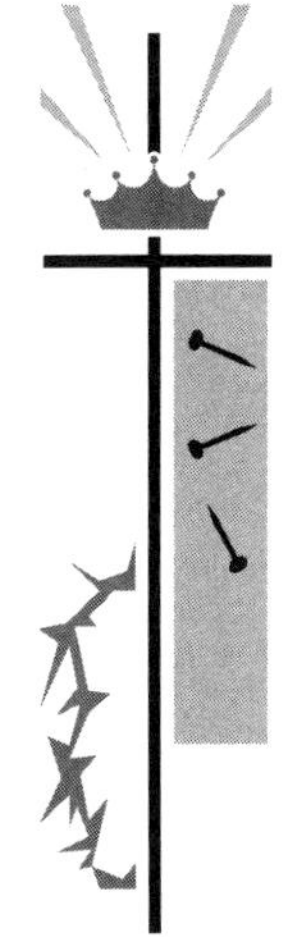

Therefore, the fear of losing one's life should not override one's fear and trust in God, who raises the dead. Christ himself became "obedient to the point of death" (Phil 2:8). Therefore "God has highly exalted him" (Phil 2:9). He promises, "Whoever loses his life for the sake of me and the Gospel will save it" (Mk 8:35). That God will "repay a person according to what he has done" (Prov 24:12) is a warning of condemnation according to the Law for unbelievers (cf. Ps 28:4) but is a Gospel promise for believers (Mt 25:34–40; Rev 14:13).

24:13–14 Saying 25 compares the sweetness of honey to wisdom. Honey is both healthful and good tasting. In the same way wisdom is beneficial and pleasant. The benefit of wisdom highlighted in this proverb is that of eternal life. Wisdom that comes from God leads to righteousness before him through Jesus Christ.[15] Finding this wisdom ensures that a believer always has the hope for an unlimited future in the eternal life that God grants freely to his people. This saying essentially repeats the promise of the thirteenth saying (23:15–18).

24:15–16 Saying 26 builds on the previous proverb. The wicked person who seeks to further his future by destroying someone else's prosperity

---

[15] See "Wisdom in Proverbs" in the introduction. See also the commentary on 1:1–7; 3:13–20; 8:22–31; 30:1b–10; and the excursus "Proverbs 8, Wisdom, Christology, and the Arian Controversy" in the commentary on chapter 8.

is warned that a righteous person can never be brought to permanent ruin.[16] As elsewhere in Proverbs, the number seven signifies comprehensiveness (6:16, 31; 9:1; 26:16, 25; see the commentary on 30:11–33 and 31:10–31). In this case, the meaning is that no matter how many times a righteous person falls, he gets up again. This implies that God has given the believer an eternal future, as promised in the previous proverb. Jesus promises to raise each believer to everlasting life on the Last Day (Jn 6:40, 44, 54; cf. James 5:15).

On the other hand, wicked people do not get up from even one fall (Prov 24:16), because they do not rely on God to uplift and sustain them. They will lie down to everlasting pain (Is 50:11).

24:17–18 Saying 27 is a warning about gloating over an enemy's downfall. It is connected to the previous saying by the verb נָפַל, "to fall." This is a warning to both the righteous person and the wicked person. While the previous proverb warns the wicked person that he should not cause the downfall of a righteous person, this saying is especially aimed at a righteous person who may be tempted to gloat over the downfall of a wicked person and celebrate because that person got what he deserved. This saying reminds the righteous person that he would thereby commit his own evil sin and incur God's wrath.

The righteous person must ever trust in God's grace and not become arrogant by thinking that he could not fall if God were to abandon him and leave him to his own devices. If God so chooses, he can aid the wicked person and help him recover from adversity. This in fact is what the godly person does: help even his enemy in times of trouble, as advised in Prov 25:21–22 and quoted by Paul in Rom 12:20–21, so that they can "overcome evil with good."

24:19–20 Saying 28 repeats a theme already found in the eighteenth saying (24:1–2), that of jealousy over the apparent advantages of those who prosper in worldly life even though they disbelieve and violate God's Word. This proverb counsels both against abiding anger over their actions and against jealousy over what they have gained by their actions. Instead by stating that evil people who have rejected God have no eternal "future" (אַחֲרִית, 24:20), this proverb draws a contrast with the thirteenth (23:15–18) and twenty-fifth (24:13–14) sayings, where the righteous person is promised a "future" (אַחֲרִית) of eternal life.

The second line of 24:20 is virtually identical to the second line of 13:9. The picture of a wicked person's lamp being snuffed out is also found in 20:20. This is in direct contrast to the righteous person's lamp, which is God's Word (6:23; see also Ps 119:105; 2 Pet 1:19) and Yahweh himself (2 Sam 22:29; cf. Ps 18:29 [ET 18:28]; Prov 20:27). Jesus is "the light of the world" (Jn 8:12; 9:5), the light that the darkness cannot overcome (Jn 1:5; cf. Mt 17:2; Acts 26:13; 2 Cor 4:6; Rev 1:16).

---

[16] See "The Relationship between Wisdom and Righteousness in Proverbs" in "Wisdom in Proverbs" in the introduction.

24:21–22 Saying 29 combines the fear of Yahweh and the fear of the king's power. In this case it counsels against association with those who seek to change God's immutable Law or the king's law. They wish to rebel and become their own masters (cf. Ps 2:2–3, where the human kings set themselves against Yahweh and his Christ). The coupling of Yahweh and the king implies that governments are given their power to rule by God himself (see Prov 8:15–16; Rom 13:1–7). The reason that one is not to associate with rebellious people is that one will be in danger of harm if the king should mete out punishment, as God and his King surely will (Psalms 2:4–12; 110). But those who "kiss the Son" (cf. Lk 7:37–38) in homage and "take refuge in him" shall be saved and blessed (Ps 2:12).

Proverbs 24:23–34

More Words of Wise People

Proverbs 24:23–34

More Words of Wise People

Translation

24 [23]These also are by wise people:
To show partiality when administering justice is not good.
[24]Whoever says to a wicked person, "You are righteous,"
people will curse him;
nations will denounce him.
[25]However, it will be pleasant for those who convict [the wicked],
and a wonderful blessing will come upon them.
[26]One who gives a straight answer kisses the lips.
[27]Prepare your work outside,
and get it ready for yourself in the field.
Afterward build your house.
[28]Do not be a witness against your neighbor without cause
or deceive with your lips.
[29]Do not think, "I'll do to him what he did to me.
I'll pay the man back for what he did."
[30]I passed by a lazy person's field
and by a vineyard of a person without sense.
[31]It was overgrown with thistles
and covered with nettles.
Its stone wall was broken down.
[32]When I saw this, I took it to heart.
I observed [and] learned a lesson:
[33]A little sleep, a little slumber,
a little folding of the hands to lie down,
[34]and your poverty will come [like] a drifter,
and your need like a bandit.

Textual Notes

24:23 גַּם־אֵלֶּה לַחֲכָמִים—The collection in 22:17–24:22 is characterized by the construct phrase דִּבְרֵי חֲכָמִים, "words of wise people" (22:17). This short collection (24:23–34) is described as לַחֲכָמִים, "belonging to" or "by wise people." Probably the preposition לְ is a *lamed auctoris* (GKC, § 129 c). Even though other sages originally authored these sayings, Solomon would have reworded and adapted them as needed for them to fit in the context of Holy Writ about the one true and triune God.

הַכֵּר־פָּנִים בְּמִשְׁפָּט בַּל־טוֹב׃—"To recognize faces in adjudication" is an idiom for "to show partiality when administering justice." The Hiphil (H) infinitive absolute הַכֵּר, linked by *maqqeph* to its object פָּנִים (see Joüon, § 13 d), is the subject of this nominal sentence (Joüon, § 123 b). See the Hiphil of נָכַר with the object פָּנִים also in Deut 1:17; 16:19; Job 34:19; Prov 28:21. This results in injustice, as elaborated in 24:24.

This clause is repeated in 28:21 but without בְּמִשְׁפָּט and with לֹא instead of בַּל (for "*not* good"). For the less common negative בַּל, see Joüon, § 160 m V.

24:24 יִקְּבֻהוּ עַמִּים—The verb קָבַב is one of the strongest possible terms in the OT for "to curse." While God, when he curses someone or something, can be the subject of אָרַר (e.g., Gen 5:29) or the one who says, "Cursed" (אָרוּר, e.g., Gen 3:14), only once is God is the subject of קָבַב.[1] Elsewhere people are the subjects of קָבַב, as here and also in 11:26. It occurs most often in the narrative of Numbers 22–24, where Balak hired Balaam to curse Israel, but he was unable to do so because God had not done so. Instead he was constrained to bless Israel because God had done so. The human cursing here reflects God's own curse. See also the second textual note on 24:25.

24:25 וְלַמּוֹכִיחִים יִנְעָם—Literally, this is "but for those who convict it will be pleasant." The Hiphil (H) of יָכַח in its forensic sense refers to the proceedings of a court.[2] Here the Hiphil (H) participle refers to those who render the verdict of condemnation for the guilty. It is stronger than the common use of the Hiphil (H) of יָכַח to mean "warn" (see the first textual note on 3:12).

For the verb נָעֵם, "be pleasant, delightful," see the second textual note on 2:10. The verb here is impersonal, with no explicit subject (cf. Waltke-O'Connor, § 22.7b, including example 7), and it expresses a promise about the everlasting fate of those who believe and live according to God's Word. Compare the cognate adjective in the resurrection promise נְעִמוֹת בִּימִינְךָ נֶצַח, "pleasant things at your [God's] right hand forever," in Ps 16:11.

וַעֲלֵיהֶם תָּבוֹא בִרְכַּת־טוֹב׃—This clause is antonymous to the cursing in 24:24b. Literally, "a blessing of good," this includes human benediction. However, the proverb ultimately promises God's own eschatological blessing, as do other proverbs with the noun בְּרָכָה, for example, 10:6, 22; 11:11, 26, and proverbs with the cognate verb בֵּרַךְ, "bless," for example, 3:33; 22:9.

24:26 שְׂפָתַיִם יִשָּׁק מֵשִׁיב דְּבָרִים נְכֹחִים׃—The Hiphil (H) of שׁוּב with the object דָּבָר, literally, "return a word," means "answer." In this verse the participial phrase beginning with מֵשִׁיב, literally, "a person returning/answering straight words," is the subject of the verb יִשָּׁק (imperfect of נָשַׁק), "he kisses." The direct object is the first word of the verse, the dual שְׂפָתַיִם, "(two) lips." Kissing the lips was (and still is) the most intimate expression of love (Song 1:2; 8:1).

24:27 הָכֵן ... וְעַתְּדָהּ ... אַחַר וּבָנִיתָ בֵיתֶךָ׃—This verse has two clauses with imperatives: the Hiphil (H) הָכֵן, "prepare," and the Piel (D) עַתְּדָהּ, "get it ready." The feminine suffix on עַתְּדָהּ ("it") refers back to the suffixed feminine noun מְלַאכְתֶּךָ, "your work."

The third clause has the adverb אַחַר, "afterward," and the perfect with *waw* consecutive וּבָנִיתָ, which expresses consequential action (Waltke-O'Connor, § 32.2.2a). It

---

[1] In Num 23:8, Balaam is speaking, and he declares that "God has *not* cursed" Israel.

[2] Cf. G. Mayer, "יכח," *TDOT* 6:65–68; G. Liedke, "יכח," *TLOT* 2:542–43; P. R. Gilchrist, "יָכַח," *TWOT* 1:376–77.

could be rendered as "afterward, *then* you can build your house." The force of the verb is that he who has worked hard will be able to build, since he will have enough savings in reserve.

24:28 וְהִפִּיתָ בִּשְׂפָתֶיךָ׃—The verb has the interrogative הֲ, which can express a rhetorical question expecting a negative answer (BDB, s.v. הֲ, 1 b), "should you … ?" meaning "you should not …" The Piel (D) of פָּתָה can mean "entice" (as in 1:10) or, as here, "deceive" (BDB, 2). בְּ has the instrumental meaning: "*with* your lips."

24:29 אַל־תֹּאמַר—In addition to "say, speak," the verb אָמַר often refers to thoughts that precede speech and actions—one's inner conversation with oneself.[a] Here it could be rendered as "do not even think …"

(a) See Gen 20:11; 26:9; 1 Sam 20:26; 2 Sam 5:6; 12:22; 2 Ki 5:11; Mal 1:7; Ruth 4:4

כַּאֲשֶׁר עָשָׂה־לִי כֵּן אֶעֱשֶׂה־לּוֹ—Literally, this is "just as he did to me, so I will do to him." The speaker has in mind a particular person who, he thinks, has done him an injustice.

אָשִׁיב לָאִישׁ כְּפָעֳלוֹ׃—For similar wording, see the second textual note on 24:12, where God is the subject. The vengeful person here intends to take the place of God by carrying out retribution in the way that only God himself properly does. The definite article on לָאִישׁ, "to *the* man," refers to the particular person ("he … him") in the preceding line who, in the speaker's estimation, has mistreated him.

24:30 אָדָם חֲסַר־לֵב׃—For this phrase, "a man lacking sense," see the textual note on 17:18. See also "חֲסַר־לֵב, 'Lacking Sense' " in "Fools in Proverbs" in the introduction.

24:31 עָלָה כֻלּוֹ ׀ קִמְּשֹׂנִים—Literally, "all of it [כֻלּוֹ] came up [עָלָה] thistles [קִמְּשֹׂנִים]," this means that the vineyard was overgrown with thistles (see GKC, § 117 z; Joüon, § 125 o). The noun קִמּוֹשׁ is a general word for any kind of weed, the exact species of which cannot be determined.[3] It is mentioned also in Is 34:13 and Hos 9:6. Its plural occurs only here, and its form, קִמְּשֹׂנִים, has an inserted *on*, -נ- (GKC, § 85 u, note 1).

כָּסּוּ פָנָיו חֲרֻלִּים—This is, literally, "its face [פָנָיו] was covered [the Pual [Dp] perfect כָּסּוּ] [with] nettles [חֲרֻלִּים]." The noun חָרוּל probably refers to one of the four species of the nettle genus *Urtica* that is native to Palestine. These plants are weeds that grow in untended gardens and once-cultivated areas that have been neglected. They are annuals with broad, notched leaves, having stems and leaves covered with stinging hairs. They produce small green flowers.[4] The singular חָרוּל refers to this kind of nettle in Zeph 2:9 and Job 30:7.

וְגֶדֶר אֲבָנָיו נֶהֱרָסָה׃—Literally, this is "and the wall of its stones was broken down." Usually גָּדֵר, "wall," is masculine, but here it may be construed as feminine and as the subject of the feminine singular Niphal (N) perfect נֶהֱרָסָה, "broken down, ruined." Or the feminine verb may be the result of the proximity of the suffixed plural of the (normally) feminine noun אֶבֶן, "stone," whose plural may be construed as a collective singular subject of the verb: "the wall of its stones—they [the stones] were thrown down."

---

[3] See *FF*, 184–86.

[4] *FF*, 152.

24:32 וָֽאֶחֱזֶ֣ה אָ֭נֹכִי אָשִׁ֣ית לִבִּ֑י—Every word in this line is or has a first-person form, emphasizing the subject: literally, "and I saw—I myself—I set [it in] my heart.

לָ֝קַ֗חְתִּי מוּסָֽר׃—Literally, "I received discipline" is rendered as "I learned a lesson."

24:33–34 These verses are nearly identical to 6:10–11; see the textual notes there. The only three differences are in 24:34: (1) the Hithpael (HtD) participle of הָלַךְ here, מִתְהַלֵּ֣ךְ instead of the Piel (D) participle with preposition כִּמְהַלֵּ֣ךְ in 6:11, although both participles likely have the same meaning; (2) the spelling change of רֵישֶׁ֑ךָ ("your poverty") compared to רֵאשֶׁ֑ךָ in 6:11; and (3) the plural וּ֝מַחְסֹרֶ֗יךָ, literally, "and your needs/lacks," versus the singular וּ֝מַחְסֹרְךָ֗ in 6:11.

Commentary

These additional words of wise people (24:23–34) form a short appendix to the preceding collection of words derived from other wise people in 22:17–24:22. Like the preceding collection, this collection too consists of proverbs that apparently originated from wise people other than Solomon (24:23a). Like the first set of sayings in 22:22–23:14, this additional set of proverbs has more emphasis on the Law than on the Gospel, and perhaps some of them were originally derived from non-Israelite sources. However, these sayings were then compiled and adapted by Solomon under divine inspiration to comprise this section of Holy Scripture. They are God's Word and teach God's will.

These proverbs consist of six sayings arranged in two sets of three:[5]

Conduct in court	1. Impartiality and just judgments (24:23b–25)	4. A true witness (24:28)
Responding	2. A right answer (24:26)	5. A wrong, vindictive response (24:29)
Work	3. Constructive labor (24:27)	6. Lazy neglect of labor (24:30–34)

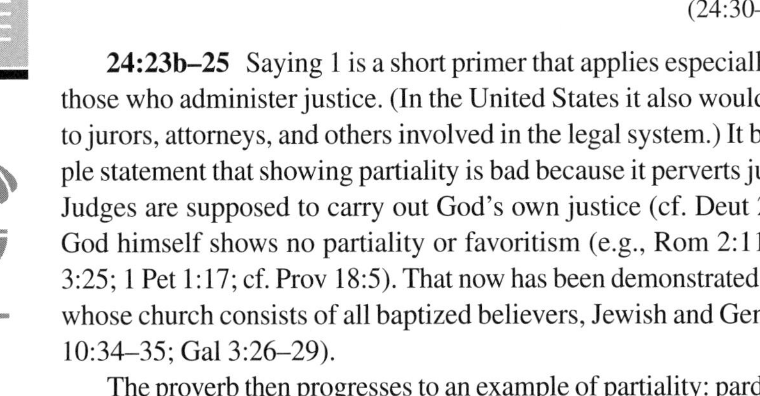

24:23b–25 Saying 1 is a short primer that applies especially to judges and those who administer justice. (In the United States it also would directly apply to jurors, attorneys, and others involved in the legal system.) It begins by a simple statement that showing partiality is bad because it perverts justice (24:23b). Judges are supposed to carry out God's own justice (cf. Deut 20:16–18), and God himself shows no partiality or favoritism (e.g., Rom 2:11; Eph 6:9; Col 3:25; 1 Pet 1:17; cf. Prov 18:5). That now has been demonstrated in Jesus Christ, whose church consists of all baptized believers, Jewish and Gentile alike (Acts 10:34–35; Gal 3:26–29).

The proverb then progresses to an example of partiality: pardoning a wicked person (24:24). Such a miscarriage of justice will rightfully bring curses and

---

[5] Cf. Meinhold, *Die Sprüche*, 410.

denunciation upon the corrupt judge. The opposite will happen to the judge who refuses to be partial, but convicts a person who is guilty of a crime: he will please the citizenry and be blessed by them (24:25). He is a faithful servant acting on behalf of God himself (Rom 13:1–7).

This advice can also be applied to the relationships between Christians in the church (see James 2:1–13). It pertains to ministers, who are to proclaim God's condemning Law and his justifying Gospel faithfully, without showing favoritism. Pastors can face the temptation not to rebuke the sins of influential church members, or to minimize the time and effort they spend ministering the Gospel to the lowlier members of the congregation, who can do little for them in return.

24:26 Saying 2 is a terse, direct metaphor. A person who gives honest, open answers is a true friend, as if he kisses the lips of his grateful hearers. For familial and fraternal kisses, see, for example, Gen 27:26; 31:28; 2 Sam 19:40 (ET 19:39); 20:9; Ruth 1:9, 14. See also the "holy kiss" shared by early Christians, men and women alike (Rom 16:16; 1 Cor 16:20; cf. Lk 7:45). On the other hand, not even a kiss can disguise dishonesty, as Judas discovered (Lk 22:47–48).

24:27 Saying 3 encourages productive labor. Its literal setting is to advise a young man to labor in the field to amass the requisite amount of wealth before building a house—not just a structure, but also a large family. Its wider application is to counsel the believer to plan ahead, prepare, and expect hard work to come before enjoying the benefits of one's labor.

24:28 Saying 4 prohibits serving as a witness without due cause, giving false testimony, or committing perjury. The second line is a broader injunction against any kind of deceptive speaking. Therefore this saying relates to both the Second and the Eighth Commandments.[6]

24:29 Saying 5 forbids plotting revenge. The implication is that the believer should trust that God himself will see that justice is done (20:22; 24:12).

24:30–34 Saying 6 is a proverb that demonstrates how wisdom is intended to work: A wise person observes the world (24:30–31). He then thinks about his observation (24:32). Lastly, he draws a general conclusion (24:33–34). In this case the sage notes that he observed the condition of a lazy person's field as he was passing by: it was full of noxious weeds instead of productive crops. The lesson he learned is that bit-by-bit procrastination leads to poverty that can seem to come upon one randomly, like a drifter that happens along or a bandit whose choice of victims seems arbitrary and opportunistic. The combination of "a little" with the plural forms of "sleep" and "slumber" serves to show the son how ridiculous the excuses of a lazy person can be (24:33).

---

[6] See the excursus "Proverbs 1–9, Christ, and the Ten Commandments" in the commentary on Proverbs 1.

This skillful portrayal of the consequences of choices one may make shows the sage's skillful application of the Law to discourage unwise and self-destructive behavior. Such warnings prepare the reader to receive with joyful faith God's saving wisdom.[7]

---

[7] See further "Law and Gospel in Proverbs" in the introduction.

Proverbs 25:1–29:27

Solomon's Proverbs Copied by Hezekiah's Men

Excursus	*The Organization of Solomon's Proverbs Copied by Hezekiah's Men (Prov 25:1–29:27)*
25:1	**Superscription to Solomon's Proverbs Copied by Hezekiah's Men**
Excursus	*Luther on Proverbs*
25:2–27	**Advice for Kings and Leaders**
25:28–27:4	**All about Fools**
27:5–22	**Dealing with Family, Friends, and Other People**
27:23–29:27	**More Advice for Kings and Leaders**
27:23–27	Pay Attention to Your Flock
28:1–11	Better to Be Poor and Maintain Your Integrity
28:12–28	Beware of Wicked People
29:1–15	Wicked People Endanger a Kingdom
29:16–27	Final Advice for Kings and Leaders

Excursus

The Organization of Solomon's Proverbs Copied by Hezekiah's Men (Prov 25:1–29:27)

Like the appearance of the collection of the proverbs of Solomon in 10:1–22:16,[1] the collection of Solomon's proverbs in chapters 25–29 might appear to be a collection of sayings with little or no organization. However, closer inspection reveals that these sayings were not merely collected by Hezekiah's men, but also underwent some sort of editorial process to arrange them. While it is not always clear exactly what the editor or editors had in mind, several studies have highlighted the connections that tie together groups of sayings in this collection into a number of sections.[2] There is general agreement that chapters 25–27 and chapters 28–29 form two units within this collection.

Proverbs 25–27

In terms of literary style, the first three chapters (Proverbs 25–27) rely heavily on metaphors and similes in sayings that are in the form of comparisons, whereas only one proverb in Proverbs 28–29 is that type of comparison saying (28:15; cf. 28:6, which is the only "better ... than" comparison in this section). These three chapters have very little antithetical parallelism.

Many thematic connections between the sayings are evident in 25:2–27. Regarding the primary audience, some scholars persuasively argue that 25:2–27 is a collection of sayings intended for the instruction of kings and for those who would serve at the royal court.[3]

Beginning with 25:28 the proverbs begin to speak almost exclusively about fools and foolish behavior. In 27:5 the proverbs switch to speaking about social relationships, especially centering on family and friends.

Proverbs 28–29

The break between the two major sections in chapters 25–29 is signaled by one of the few sayings in these chapters that extends over more than one verse: 27:23–27.[4] This saying about tending one's flock serves as an introduction to

---

1 See the excursus "The Organization of the Sayings in Solomon's Proverbs in Proverbs 10:1–22:16" in the commentary on chapter 10.

2 Bryce, "Another Wisdom-'Book' in Proverbs"; Finkbeiner, "An Analysis of the Structure of Proverbs 28 and 29"; Malchow, "A Manual for Future Monarchs"; Van Leeuwen, *Context and Meaning in Proverbs 25–27.*

3 See further the commentary on 25:2–27.

4 Other extended sayings include 25:6–7, 9–10, 21–22; 26:18–19, 24–26; 27:15–16.

the second major section, a collection of sayings that appears to be guidance for kings and governing faithfully. This section is organized into groups of proverbs by the use of sayings that contrast a righteous person and a wicked person (28:1, 12, 28; 29:2, 16, 27).[5] Within each section the proverbs are connected by catchwords and paronomasia.

The organization of Proverbs 28–29 can be outlined as follows:[6]

28:1	Introductory saying: the righteous and the wicked
28:2–11	First collection: ten proverbs
28:12	Transitional saying: the righteous and the wicked
28:13–27	Second collection: fifteen proverbs
28:28	Transitional saying: the righteous and the wicked
29:1	Theme proverb: Listening to warnings
29:2	Transitional saying: the righteous and the wicked
29:3–15	Third collection: thirteen proverbs
29:16	Transitional saying: the righteous and the wicked
29:17–26	Fourth collection: ten proverbs
29:27	Concluding saying: the righteous and the wicked

As this outline demonstrates, chapters 28–29 consist of four collections of proverbs held together by six sayings contrasting righteous and wicked people. Moreover, 29:1 stands at the center of these chapters. Its advice to heed warnings serves to call the king and his courtiers to pay attention to the advice given in these proverbs. It stands almost directly in the center of these proverbs, with twenty-eight sayings before it and twenty-six after it.

Who organized these sayings? Was this the editorial work of Solomon himself, with the men of Hezekiah merely serving as copyists of Solomon's manuscript? Or was the editorial arrangement the work of Hezekiah's men, who copied a number of scattered sayings from Solomon and assembled them into their present organization?[7]

It may be impossible to decide with absolute certainty, but a number of factors indicate that the arrangement of chapters 25–29 was the work of Hezekiah's men. First, the arrangement of these proverbs seems to indicate that they were selected for use in the royal court. Solomon's work in 1:1–22:16 was consistently addressed to his sons.[8] Second, while the words צַדִּיק, "righteous

---

[5] Malchow, "A Manual for Future Monarchs," 239.

[6] Cf. Malchow, "A Manual for Future Monarchs," 240.

[7] See also the discussion in "Conclusion about Authorship" in "Authorship and Date" in the introduction.

[8] See the excursus "Proverbs 1–9, Christ, and the Ten Commandments" in the commentary on Proverbs 1, and the excursus "The Organization of the Sayings in Solomon's Proverbs in Proverbs 10:1–22:16" in the commentary on Proverbs 10. The only saying to directly address a "son" in chapters 25–29 is 27:11.

(person),"[9] and רָשָׁע, "wicked (person)," occur many times in 1:1–22:16, they never are used as an organizing principle for sections within those proverbs by Solomon. Finally, the entire collection of proverbs in chapters 25–29 seems to be organized around the king's reign, opening and closing with advice for kings. This same organizational principle is confined to only one section in the previous collections of proverbs arranged by Solomon himself, namely, 16:8–24.

Therefore, it would appear that Hezekiah's men were not just the copiers of Solomon's proverbs in chapters 25–29. They also engaged in editorial activity by choosing particular proverbs by Israel's wisest king that would speak to any king and his court, and by carefully arranging these sayings to emphasize their usefulness and relevance for all who govern and are governed.

Reading These Proverbs

Originally the proverbs in these chapters applied to rulers in ancient Israel, who not only wielded political authority over God's chosen, covenant people, but also were to govern in conformity with God's Word and uphold it. The proverbs also applied to Israelites called to serve in some capacity in the royal administration and more generally to all Israelites, who lived and served within the nation called to be the people of God. For modern believers in Christ, these proverbs are especially relevant for pastors, who minister, preach, and teach God's authoritative Word of Law and Gospel for the benefit of the church, the new Israel of God (Romans 9–11; Gal 6:16). More broadly, these proverbs also pertain to all believers in Jesus Christ as citizens who serve both in the kingdom of God—the church—and in their vocations within the particular nation, social network, and family in which they reside.

These proverbs contain the special revelation of God's Word, and they also affirm the general revelation of God that is evident throughout his creation. Divine wisdom contains practical elements that apply to the lives of all people as they live within any human society. Every people has a system of government and leadership that ultimately rests upon God, his authority, and his will for his creatures.[a] Therefore these proverbs can apply to Christian leaders in government and business, who wield power for the benefit of all citizenry.

(a) Cf. Mt 28:18; Acts 1:7; Rom 13:1–10; Eph 1:20–21; 3:14–15; Col 2:10

While righteousness and wickedness[10] are theological categories describing the status of a person before God (either justified through faith or an unbeliever), they also can describe civil righteousness or lack thereof. All human nations are built on universal moral categories of good and right behavior, although these absolutes may be evident in a particular nation's laws only to a greater or to a lesser extent. Those behaviors, institutions, and relationships that are

---

[9] See "The Relationship between Wisdom and Righteousness" in "Wisdom in Proverbs" in the introduction.

[10] "Righteous (person)" and "wicked (person)" are prominent words in Proverbs 28–29. See above.

fundamentally good are constructive for society, whereas immoral, dishonest, and unlawful behavior destroys nations, social relationships, and individuals.

God's eschatological plan is to allow human leaders and governments to stand as long as they serve his purposes. His will is for them to foster conditions under which his church can grow through the proclamation of the Gospel and be purified by suffering. In the end, all human authorities will be abolished in God's final judgment, when he will finally answer all the prayers of his people, deliver them from all the effects of sin and wickedness, and establish his eternal kingdom in which all believers will reside forever under Christ their King (see, e.g., Psalms 2 and 110; 1 Cor 15:24–25; Rev 2:26–27; 6:9–11; 11:15).

This collection of proverbs teaches about these things.

Proverbs 25:1

Superscription to Solomon's Proverbs Copied by Hezekiah's Men

Translation

25 [1]These also are the proverbs of Solomon, which the men of King Hezekiah of Judah transcribed.

Textual Notes

25:1 גַּם־אֵ֭לֶּה מִשְׁלֵ֣י שְׁלֹמֹ֑ה—The identical construct phrase מִשְׁלֵי שְׁלֹמֹה, "the proverbs of Solomon," is in 1:1 as the title of the whole book and as the introduction to Solomon's proverbs in chapters 1–9. It is also in 10:1 as the introduction to the collection of Solomon's proverbs in 10:1–22:16. The prefatory גַּם־אֵלֶּה, literally, "also these (are) ..." is repeated from 24:23.

This phrase shows that the editor or editors of Proverbs 25–29 ("these ... proverbs") were aware of the previous collections of Solomon's proverbs at the time when chapters 25–29 were placed here. The editor(s) intended these chapters to come after the preceding chapters of proverbs from Solomon.

אֲשֶׁ֥ר הֶ֝עְתִּ֗יקוּ אַנְשֵׁ֤י ׀ חִזְקִיָּ֬ה מֶֽלֶךְ־יְהוּדָֽה׃—Literally, the proverbs "which the men of Hezekiah, king of Judah, transcribed." The verb הֶעְתִּיקוּ is a Hiphil (H) perfect of עָתֵק, "move (forward)," and thus means "caused to be moved, transfer," or in this context, "transcribed" (see BDB, 3).[1] Whether this means that "the men of Hezekiah" (אַנְשֵׁי ׀ חִזְקִיָּה) merely copied this collection of proverbs by Solomon or whether it refers to them as the editorial shapers of chapters 25–29 cannot be ascertained from the verb or this entire clause. See the excursus "The Organization of Solomon's Proverbs Copied by Hezekiah's Men (Prov 25:1–29:27)" before this pericope.

This is a shorter, less common form of a name meaning "Yah is (my) strength": חִזְקִיָּה, *hizqiyyah*, "Hezekiah."[2] This form is used thirteen times in the OT, referring to three or four different men: 2 Kings (eight times); Zeph 1:1; Prov 25:1; Neh 7:21; 10:18 (ET 10:17); 1 Chr 3:23. In Nehemiah; in 1 Chr 3:23 (where it is often spelled Hizkiah in English); and possibly in Zephaniah, it refers to a Hezekiah other than King Hezekiah, but here in Prov 25:1 the phrase in apposition, "king of Judah," leaves no doubt about which Hezekiah is intended.

The most common form of the king's name is חִזְקִיָּהוּ, *hizqiyyahu*, which has the fuller form of the theophoric element (*-yahu*) that refers to Yahweh. This longer form is used in 2 Kings, Isaiah, Jeremiah, and Chronicles a total of seventy-four times.

---

[1] Cf. H. Schmoldt, "עתק," *TDOT* 11:456.

[2] In addition to the form given below, the name is also spelled as יְחִזְקִיָּה and יְחִזְקִיָּהוּ.

Commentary

This short notice is about Proverbs 25–29. It names the original author, Solomon, and the transcribers, "the men of Hezekiah." The notice appears have been written in imitation of 1:1; 10:1; and 24:23. It begins with the same words as 24:23, גַּם־אֵלֶּה, "these also (are)," and then adds מִשְׁלֵי שְׁלֹמֹה, "the proverbs of Solomon," as in 1:1 and 10:1. The description of this Hezekiah as חִזְקִיָּה מֶלֶךְ־יְהוּדָה, literally, "Hezekiah, king of Judah," is reminiscent of the description of Solomon himself in 1:1 as שְׁלֹמֹה ... מֶלֶךְ יִשְׂרָאֵל, "Solomon ... king of Israel [still united]." The designation of Hezekiah as "king" also ties the superscription (25:1) to the following section of proverbs, which are about kings (25:2–5) and how to deal with kings (25:6–15).

This imitation of the previous notices of authorship in Proverbs (especially the use of גַּם, "also") and the use of the perfect aspect of the verb הֶעְתִּיקוּ, "transcribed," leave the impression that the final editor of the book penned this notice. This editor probably was the one who also added 30:1–33 and 31:1–9 after this last collection of Solomonic proverbs, and he may have composed 31:10–31.[3]

This notice is an important attestation of literary activity in ancient Israel during the reign of Hezekiah, the king of Judah from 715 to 686 BC, a time period when Isaiah and other prophets preached and wrote. It helps show that the biblical writings were not simply preserved orally, but were also written down by the original authors and were faithfully transcribed. This copying could be done by royal scribes, as in this case, and/or by priests, as was the case for the Torah of Moses (see, e.g., Deut 17:18; 31:9, 26; cf. 2 Ki 22:8; 2 Chr 17:9).[4]

For the sections in the collection consisting of Proverbs 25–29, see the excursus "The Organization of Solomon's Proverbs Copied by Hezekiah's Men (Prov 25:1–29:27)" before this pericope.

---

3 See the commentary on 31:10–31 and also "Authorship and Date" in the introduction.

4 See further Steinmann, *The Oracles of God*, 59–61, 111–13.

Excursus

Luther on Proverbs

"Proverbs is an excellent book. Rulers ought to read it," said Luther.[1] In this exhortation Luther recognized the major purpose behind the proverbs transmitted by King Hezekiah's men (chapters 25–29) and a theme that can also be found elsewhere in Proverbs (see especially 16:8–24; 31:1–9). Reading this excellent book, along with the rest of the Scriptures, of course leads to good government, which is itself a gift of God:

> When God wishes a region well, He gives the people good princes and governs them according to the statement in Proverbs: "By Me princes rule, and rulers decree what is just" (8:16, 15). This cannot take place except through divine wisdom, which rules princes for the welfare of their subjects, that is, when it speaks with kings and princes and not only speaks but also interprets what it says. Such empires are surely the best and the most flourishing, for the prince will have thoughts worthy of a prince (cf. Is. 32:8) and will persevere in nobility of spirit.[2]

Moreover, Luther clearly articulated the significance of the key concepts of Proverbs—wisdom and foolishness:

> In Proverbs and Ecclesiastes folly is to savor earthly and transitory and carnal things, when spiritual and eternal things have been lost. To savor the latter constitutes wisdom.[3]

Luther loved proverbs of all types, and he frequently quoted German and Latin proverbs in his writings. In fact, Luther even quoted some German proverbs in his prefaces to Proverbs in his German translation of the Bible.[4] Yet as fond as Luther was of proverbs, even of sayings from the biblical book of Proverbs, he seldom attempted to explain their meaning. Instead he often simply quoted a proverb in order to reinforce some point he was making.

Indeed, that is how the book of Proverbs was most frequently used by those before Luther. The practice of quoting a saying from Proverbs to prove a

---

1 Table talk, § 5541 (AE 54:450).

2 AE 7:150.

3 AE 11:162–63.

4 Luther wrote two prefaces to Proverbs. The first appeared in a 1524 installment of his German Bible (AE 35:261–63), while the second, a part of a longer preface to the books of Solomon, was used for the first time in the 1534 edition, with subsequent revisions through 1545 (AE 35:258–61). The following German proverbs are quoted by Luther in these prefaces:

> It is intended for you, but not imparted. (1524 preface; AE 35:262, including n. 70)
>
> Fortune gains the bride. (1524 preface; AE 35:262, including n. 71)
>
> You may escape me, but you will not escape the hangman. (1545 preface; AE 35:259)
>
> The older they are, the worse they get. (1545 preface; AE 35:259)
>
> Age is no cure for folly. (1545 preface; AE 35:259)

point, without subsequent discussion of its meaning, is well attested from the church fathers onward. Perhaps it has also been the most frequent kind of use of Proverbs since the time of Luther. After all, proverbs share a trait with truisms, maxims, axioms, and even jokes: their meaning and application must be at least partly self-evident to the intended audience in order to be effective. A proverb, adage, or dictum encapsulates wisdom in a concise way that is memorable and comprehensible even without extended explanation. Such a pithy saying invites the hearer to ponder and contemplate all that it means. But a saying that defies comprehension apart from a lengthy clarification will not be recognized nor remembered as a proverb. Neither will a saying that is lame or insipid.

Thus it is difficult to find extended discussions of the book of Proverbs or of individual sections of Proverbs in Luther or in early Lutheran theologians.[5] Nevertheless, Luther did have a few intriguing comments on Proverbs. In his 1545 preface to the books of Solomon he said: "It may properly be called a book of good works, for in it he [Solomon] teaches how to lead a good life before God and the world."[6] Clearly, Luther saw much of Proverbs as guidance for the believer's life, which doctrinally can be called the third use of the Law, as this commentary has also asserted.[7]

It is impossible for unbelievers to lead lives and do good works that are pleasing to God (e.g., Jn 3:18–21; Heb 11:6). Only believers, justified by the Gospel of Jesus Christ through faith alone, are able to do so (e.g., Phil 4:18; Col 1:10; 1 Tim 2:3; Heb 13:16, 21). God's Word can function as the third use of the Law only for believers, and this use presupposes the justifying Gospel. Therefore, it is not surprising that Luther often also found Christ and the Gospel in Proverbs. Thus he, like the church fathers, identified Christ as the divine Wisdom portrayed in Proverbs 3 and 8:

> Arius was unable to deny that Christ existed before the creation of the world, because Christ also says (John 8:58): "Before Abraham was, I am." And it is written in Proverbs (8:27): "Before the heavens were, I am." Therefore he shifted to the position that Christ, or the Word, was created before all things and later on created all things and was the most perfect creature, but that He had not always been in existence. This insane and wicked opinion must be countered with the fact that Moses briefly says "in the beginning" [Gen 1:1]

---

5 Philip Melanchthon lectured on Proverbs, but his lectures, published in Latin (*Paroimiai, sive Proverbia Solomonis, filii Davidis: Explicatio proverbiorum cum adnotationibus Philippi Melanchthonis* [Haganoae: Secerius, 1525]) and in German with Luther's translation of Proverbs (*Die Spruch Salomo* [Erfurt, 1526]), are rare. I have located only six Latin copies and two German copies in the United States.

6 AE 35:258.

7 See further "Law and Gospel in Proverbs" in the introduction. Also relevant is the excursus "Proverbs 1–9, Christ, and the Ten Commandments" in the commentary on Proverbs 1. The Lutheran Confessions speak of the new obedience of the believer as he is instructed by Scripture to do good works (AC VI; FC Ep and SD III; FC Ep and SD IV). The role of Scripture as the normative teaching and guide for a believer's life is also called the third use of the Law (FC Ep and SD VI).

and does not assert that anything else was in existence before the beginning except God, to whom he gives a name in the plural number.[8]

Luther affirmed the biblical doctrine of the Trinity when he also said:

The Lord, who is Wisdom, that is, the Son of God, who was to become incarnate, was with him; for in Proverbs Solomon also undoubtedly calls wisdom the Son among the divine Persons, and on the basis of what Paul says we also teach that Christ led the people of Israel out of Egypt (1 Cor. 10:4).[9]

Luther understood Proverbs from a Gospel perspective. He comments on Prov 16:9, which expresses a truth found in many other proverbs:

This bears out the proverb, "Man proposes, but God disposes" [Prov. 16:9]. That is, God turns things around and brings to pass something different from that which man had planned. Thus in this one respect alone it is not possible for us to deny that our lives and actions are under the guidance, not of our prudence, but of the wonderful power, wisdom, and goodness of God. Here we see how often God was with us when we neither saw nor sensed it, and how truthfully Peter has said, "He himself cares for us all" [I Pet. 5:7].[10]

The biblical dynamic of Law and Gospel is evident in many proverbs. Luther observed this as he affirmed the interpretation of Prov 31:26 by the church father Augustine (AD 354–430):

Thus St. Augustine, too, in the ninth chapter of his book *On the Spirit and the Letter*, where he treats of the statement in the last chapter of Proverbs (31:26), "Law and kindness are on her tongue," makes the most excellent remark: "Therefore it is written of wisdom that she bears law and kindness on her tongue for this reason—law, in order that she may render the proud guilty; kindness, in order that she may justify the humbled."[11]

Luther saw Law and Gospel at work when the believer confesses his own sinfulness, yet is also justified and saved by Christ:

And this is the true definition of the righteous man in Proverbs 18[:17]: "The righteous man is his own first accuser"; therefore, he is righteous because he accuses himself. From this it follows, "His friend (Christ) comes and examines him," that is, he will search for him and will not let him perish; he will deliver him even from the depth of hell.[12]

---

[8] AE 1:13. See further the excursus "Proverbs 8, Wisdom, Christology, and the Arian Controversy" in the commentary on Proverbs 8. When Luther speaks about "a name in the plural number" he is referring to אֱלֹהִים, "God" (e.g., Gen 1:1–12). This Hebrew form is often called a plural of majesty, yet it can be seen as pointing to the mystery of the Trinity. The three persons of the triune God—God the Father and Creator; God the Son, the Word; and God the Holy Spirit—are revealed already in Genesis 1, where God creates the earth (Gen 1:1), the Spirit of God hovers over the deep (Gen 1:2), and God creates by the power of his spoken Word (e.g., Gen 1:3, 6).

[9] AE 7:109.

[10] AE 42:131.

[11] AE 27:274 (cf. *NPNF*[1] 5:89).

[12] AE 39:29.

Finally, we should note that Luther understood Proverbs, like the rest of Scripture, to be the powerful Word of God in Law and Gospel, which is the only sure source and norm for the Christian faith and life:[13]

> Moses has not forgotten anything; he has stopped all gaps which might enable us to consult and seek knowledge outside of God's word [Deut 18:9–12; cf. Deut 18:13–22; 30:11–20]. Therefore he has condemned our self-conceit and natural reason many times, especially in Deuteronomy 12[:8], "You shall not do whatever is right in your own eyes," and in Proverbs 3[:5], "Be not wise in your own eyes and do not rely on your own insight." He does this so that we may see that it is not the will of God that we should follow either what is in our reason or beyond it; rather we should follow his word alone, as Isaiah said so well above [Is 8:19–20]: We should consult neither the living nor the dead, but God alone in his law.[14]

Thus, although Luther never produced an extended work on Proverbs, he most certainly understood its important themes, and he was able to articulate a theology of Proverbs that is in harmony with Scripture's teaching of God's Law and the Gospel of Jesus Christ, who is the Wisdom of God incarnate.[15]

---

[13] The Lutheran Confessions affirm that "the prophetic and apostolic writings of the Old and New Testaments are the only rule and norm according to which all doctrines and teachers alike must be appraised and judged. … Holy Scripture remains the only judge, rule, and norm according to which as the only touchstone all doctrines should and must be understood and judged as good or evil, right or wrong" (FC Ep, Rule and Norm, 1, 7).

[14] AE 52:182.

[15] This commentary affirms the traditional Christian and Lutheran view of Christ as the Wisdom of God. See "Wisdom in Proverbs" in the introduction; the commentary on 1:1–7; 3:13–20; 8:22–31; 30:1b–10; and the excursus "Proverbs 8, Wisdom, Christology, and the Arian Controversy" in the commentary on chapter 8.

Proverbs 25:2–27

Advice for Kings and Leaders

Translation

25 [2]It is the glory of God to hide a matter
and the glory of kings to investigate a matter.
[3][Like] heaven for height and earth for depth,
so there is no searching the heart of kings.
[4]Remove impurities from silver;
then a vessel is cast by a silversmith.
[5]Remove a wicked person from a king's presence;
then his throne will be established with righteousness.
[6]Do not honor yourself in a king's presence,
and do not stand in a place [reserved for] great people,
[7]because it is better to be told, "Come up here,"
than for you to be humiliated before a ruler whom your eyes have seen.
[8]Do not be in a hurry to go to court.
Otherwise, what will you do afterwards, when your neighbor humiliates you?
[9]Argue your case with your neighbor,
but do not reveal someone else's secret.
[10]Otherwise, the person who hears [it] will shame you,
and your bad reputation will never leave you.
[11]Golden apples in silver settings [are]
a word spoken at the right time.
[12]A gold ring and a gold ornament [are]
correction from a wise person to ears that listen.
[13]Like the coldness of snow on a harvest day
is a trustworthy messenger to those who send him.
He revives his masters' soul.
[14]Clouds and wind but no rain [are]
a person who brags about a gift that is never given.
[15]By patience a ruler can be persuaded,
and a soft tongue can break a bone.
[16]When you find honey, eat only what you need.
Otherwise you will be filled with it and vomit it.
[17]Let your foot seldom be in your neighbor's house.
Otherwise he will have too much of you and hate you.
[18]A club, a sword, and a sharp arrow [are]
a person who bears false witness against his neighbor.
[19]A broken tooth or a lame foot [is]
confidence in an unfaithful person in time of crisis.

[20]Taking off a coat on a cold day [or] vinegar on baking soda [is]
singing songs to a despondent heart.
[21]If your enemy is hungry, give him something to eat;
if [he is] thirsty, give him something to drink,
[22]because you will heap burning coals on his head,
and Yahweh will repay you.
[23]A north wind gives birth to rain,
and a whispering tongue [gives birth] to angry faces.
[24]Better to live on the corner of a roof
than in a home shared with a quarrelsome wife.
[25]Cold water for a weary person [is]
good news from a distant country.
[26]A muddied spring or a polluted fountain [is]
a righteous person swayed before a wicked person.
[27]To eat much honey is not good,
but an investigation of difficult things is glorious.

Textual Notes

25:2a כְּבֹד אֱלֹהִים הַסְתֵּר דָּבָר—Literally, this is "the glory of God (is) to hide a matter." הַסְתֵּר is an unusual Hiphil (H) infinitive construct, whose expected form would be הַסְתִּיר (see GKC, § 53 k).

25:2b–3 וּכְבֹד מְלָכִים ... וְלֵב מְלָכִים—The second line of 25:2 and the second line of 25:3 begin with *waw*, here signaling a comparison to the preceding line (GKC, § 161 a; Joüon, § 174 h). This could be reflected by translating the verses like this: "it is the glory of God to hide a matter *just as* it is the glory of kings to investigate a matter" and "heaven is for height and earth is for depth; *so likewise* there is no searching the heart of kings." This can also be reflected by inserting "like" at the start of the first line, as does the translation above for 25:3. A translation as a simile would also be possible for 25:11, 12, 14, 18–20, 25–26, but instead those verses are translated as containing metaphors. See the first textual note on 25:11.

חֲקֹר ... חֵקֶר:—Note the play on the root חקר. The second line of 25:2 has the Qal (G) infinitive of the verb חָקַר, which means that kings "explore, search out" (*HALOT*) or "investigate." Compare 18:17, where the verb means "cross-examine." The cognate noun חֵקֶר in the second line of 25:3 has the nuance of "a search" conducted in the hope of discovery, but the noun is negated by the particle אֵין, literally, "there is no (successful) search" that can be conducted in the heart of kings. They search (25:2b) but cannot be searched (25:3b).

25:3 וָאָרֶץ—As in Is 65:17, this word is pointed as if it were in pause even though it is not the final word of the line (cf. GKC, § 29 i, note 1).

25:4 הָגוֹ סִיגִים מִכָּסֶף—The infinitive absolute הָגוֹ recurs at the beginning of 25:5, and both times it is translated as an imperative. It is of the verb הָגָה II, "remove" (BDB), which occurs elsewhere in the OT only in Is 27:8. (The homograph הָגָה I, "utter, contemplate," is in Prov 8:7; 15:28; 24:2.) The plural of the noun סִיג, traditionally "dross" (*HALOT*), denotes the impurities that are removed when refining silver.

וַיֵּצֵא לַצֹּרֵף כֶּלִי׃—Literally, this is "and a vessel [כֶּלִי] comes out for the smelter/smith." The verb יָצָא can be used as a technical term in metallurgy for casting,[1] as in Ex 32:24 (the golden calf "came out," i.e., "was cast"); Is 54:16; and Job 23:10.

Some propose repointing the *waw* consecutive וַיֵּצֵא to a *waw* conjunctive, וְיֵצֵא, "and will (be) cast,"[2] to match the (Niphal [N]) imperfect with *waw* conjunctive, וְיִכּוֹן, in the second clause of 25:5. However, this emendation is not needed. The *waw* consecutive וַיֵּצֵא denotes simple chronological sequence (Waltke-O'Connor, § 33.2.1a). The smith first removes impurities from the silver, and then he casts it into a useful and valuable vessel. Moreover, this natural sequence forms a nice contrast with the next verse. This verse describes the casting in the normal sequence as it always has been done, whereas the next verse prescribes taking away the wicked person, with the promise that by doing so the royal throne "will be established" (וְיִכּוֹן, with *waw* conjunctive).

25:5 הָגוֹ רָשָׁע לִפְנֵי־מֶלֶךְ—The "wicked person" (רָשָׁע) to be removed here is parallel to the "impurities" (סִיגִים) in the corresponding clause beginning 25:4. Then the removal of this wickedness corresponds to the "righteousness" (צֶדֶק) in the second clause of 25:5. See "The Relationship between Wisdom and Righteousness in Proverbs" in "Wisdom in Proverbs" in the introduction.

וְיִכּוֹן בַּצֶּדֶק כִּסְאוֹ׃—"His throne is established with righteousness" is almost identical to the second clause of 16:12: "for a throne is established by righteousness [בִּצְדָקָה]." In addition to the same preposition בְּ as in 16:12, here the article is used with the abstract noun בַּצֶּדֶק (GKC, § 126 n (c); Waltke-O'Connor, § 13.5.1g, including example 46).

25:6 אַל־תִּתְהַדַּר לִפְנֵי־מֶלֶךְ—The verb הָדַר in the Hithpael (HtD) has a reflexive or middle sense: "honor/glorify *yourself*." The verb occurs only here in Proverbs (and this is its only Hithpael form in the OT), but the cognate noun הָדָר, "glory, honor," is in 20:29 and 31:25.

25:7 כִּי טוֹב אֲמָר־לְךָ עֲלֵה הֵנָּה—The phrase beginning with the infinitive construct אֲמָר־, literally, "to say to you, 'Come up here,' " is the subject of the nominal sentence (Joüon, § 124 b A 1). The predicate is טוֹב, "good," translated as "better" because of the following preposition מִן (on מֵהַשְׁפִּילְךָ), "than." For the construction טוֹב ... מִן, see "Direct Comparisons" in "Authorship and Date" in the introduction.

מֵהַשְׁפִּילְךָ לִפְנֵי נָדִיב אֲשֶׁר רָאוּ עֵינֶיךָ׃—The causative Hiphil (H) infinitive construct (with מִן) מֵהַשְׁפִּילְךָ, "than to make you low, humiliate you," has no explicit subject or agent of the action, so it is rendered as a passive, "than for you to be humiliated." The most likely antecedent of the relative pronoun אֲשֶׁר is the preceding noun נָדִיב, "a noble person, ruler." Nevertheless, most translations, beginning with the LXX (ἃ εἶδον οἱ ὀφθαλμοί σου λέγε, "the things your eyes have seen, declare ..."), and commentators understand the אֲשֶׁר clause as the beginning of the next saying (25:8).[3] Their assump-

---

1 Van Leeuwen, "A Technical Metallurgical Usage of יצא."

2 Driver, "Problems in the Hebrew Text of Proverbs," 190; footnote in *BHS*; see the LXX: καθαρισθήσεται, "will be purified."

3 NIV; NJB; ESV; NRSV; Clifford, *Proverbs*, 220; Murphy, *Proverbs*, 187; Scott, *Proverbs, Ecclesiastes*, 153; Toy, *Proverbs*, 460.

tion seems to be that the relative pronoun אֲשֶׁר cannot be accusative ("whom" instead of "who") since there is no resumptive pronoun later in the clause. However, a resumptive pronoun is not absolutely required for the relative pronoun to be accusative (Waltke-O'Connor, § 19.3a). Thus several translations and commentators rightly understand this clause as belonging with the rest of 25:7, as in the translation above.[4]

25:8 אַל־תֵּצֵא לָרִב מַהֵר—This is, literally, "do not go to litigate quickly." The imperfect of יָצָא is combined with the infinitive construct of the verb רִיב, which often refers to participating in a judicial court case, arguing as a plaintiff or a party in a legal dispute (as God does in 22:23; 23:11; see also the first textual note on 25:9). Together the two verbs mean "go to court (as a party to a dispute)." In form מַהֵר is a Piel (D) infinitive absolute, but it is often used as an adverb, "quickly, hastily." When used as an adverb, it always immediately follows a verb.

בְּאַחֲרִיתָהּ—Literally, "in its end," this is translated as "afterwards." The context has no feminine noun to serve as the referent for the feminine suffix (־תָהּ). However, the feminine gender can be used for an abstract idea, as here, where it refers to the action of going to court hastily.

25:9 רִיבְךָ רִיב אֶת־רֵעֶךָ—The imperative רִיב, "litigate, argue," takes the suffixed cognate accusative noun רִיבְךָ, "your (legal) case," which is in emphatic first position in the clause, preceding the verb. A similar cognate accusative construction with רִיב is in 22:23 and 23:11. Here אֶת־ is the preposition, "*with* your neighbor," not the sign of another definite direct object.

וְסוֹד אַחֵר אַל־תְּגָל—Literally, this is "and the secret of another person you shall not divulge." The noun סוֹד denotes something that should be kept private and confidential, such as a personal matter or confession (cf. *HALOT*, 2 b). This noun is the object of the Qal (G) of גָּלָה, "reveal," in 20:19, and the object of the Piel (D) of גָּלָה in 11:13, as also here. תְּגָל is shortened (apocopated) from תְּגַלֶּה (GKC, § 75 bb). Both of those other proverbs (11:13; 20:19) likewise condemn those who publicize an intimate secret.

25:10 פֶּן־יְחַסֶּדְךָ שֹׁמֵעַ—The indefinite participle שֹׁמֵעַ could be translated as "*anyone* who hears" the matter that should have been kept confidential (סוֹד in 25:9). The participle is the subject of the Piel (D) verb יְחַסֶּדְךָ, a verb that occurs only here in the OT. It means "put to shame, reproach" (see BDB, s.v. חָסַד II), and it is cognate to the noun חֶסֶד II, "shame, reproach" (BDB), for which, see the second textual note on 14:34.

וְדִבָּתְךָ לֹא תָשׁוּב׃—The feminine noun דִּבָּה denotes a "report" or "rumor" (see *HALOT*) that is damaging to a person's reputation, as in 10:18 as well as, for example, Gen 37:2 and Ezek 36:3. It is the subject of the negated feminine verb תָשׁוּב, meaning that one's sullied reputation as an untrustworthy person "will not turn away, leave, depart."

25:11 תַּפּוּחֵי זָהָב בְּמַשְׂכִּיּוֹת כָּסֶף—"Apples of gold in settings of silver" probably refers to valuable jewelry. See the metaphor of jewelry also in 25:12 and, for example, 1:9; 3:15; 4:9; 8:11; 31:10. Elsewhere the noun מַשְׂכִּית, from the root שׂכה, usually refers

---

4 So also KJV; NKJV; NASB; Delitzsch, *Proverbs*, 2:152–53; Garrett, *Proverbs, Ecclesiastes, Song of Songs*, 205.

to idolatrous carved figures condemned by God (Lev 26:1; Num 33:52; Ezek 8:12), although it has a different nuance in Prov 18:11 (see the textual note there). Here, however, it has a positive connotation and is part of a construct phrase with an adjectival genitive: "silver carvings/settings."

The comparisons in this proverb and in 25:12, 14, 18–20, 25–26 are direct metaphors. Most English translations render them as similes, but the Hebrew does not have any terms for "like" or "as" (which would make them similes). Many English translations also reverse the order of the lines in order to conform to normal English usage, which is to place the reality first, and the metaphor second: "a word … *is like* apples of gold" (NKJV). The order of the Hebrew lines appears to an English reader to be backward, because the first line is the metaphor and the second line refers to the reality depicted by the metaphor. Thus the Hebrew lines of 25:11 are literally as follows:

Golden apples in silver settings
  a word spoken at the right time.

The direct metaphors in 25:11, 12, 14, 18–20, 25–26 prompt the reader to stop and think about the features shared by the metaphor and the reality. This rhetorical strategy is designed to slow down the reader so that he does not miss the point. To reflect this strategy, the translation of these proverbs uses "is" or "are" placed in brackets at the end of the first line, instead of at the beginning of the second line, which would correspond more closely to customary English.

דָּבָ֗ר דָּבֻ֥ר עַל־אָפְנָֽיו׃—Literally, "a word spoken according to its circumstances" means an appropriate, fitting, timely word that properly addresses the situation. Note the alliteration (*dabar dabur*) of the noun דָּבָ֗ר as the subject of the Qal passive (Gp) participle דָּבֻ֥ר. The noun אֹפֶן probably means "circumstance, condition" (BDB), but it is a hapax legomenon whose precise nuance is uncertain.

25:12 נֶ֣זֶם זָ֭הָב וַחֲלִי־כָ֑תֶם—The noun נֶזֶם often refers to a "ring" worn in the nose by women (e.g., Is 3:21). Such a nose ring was given as a betrothal gift for a bride (Gen 24:22, 30, 47; probably also Ezek 16:12; Hos 2:15 [ET 2:13]; contrast Prov 11:22). Whenever its material is stated, a נֶזֶם is always made of gold, as here (זָ֭הָב). The noun כֶּתֶם is a less common synonym for "gold."

מוֹכִ֥יחַ חָ֝כָ֗ם עַל־אֹ֥זֶן שֹׁמָֽעַת׃—Literally, this is "a wise man warning/correcting upon an ear listening." חָ֝כָ֗ם is the subject of the Hiphil (H) participle מוֹכִ֥יחַ. For the Hiphil of יָכַח, "warn," see the first textual note on 3:12. Since אֹזֶן, "ear," is feminine, it is modified by the feminine Qal (G) participle (in pause), שֹׁמָֽעַת, "listening."

25:13 צִ֥יר נֶ֭אֱמָן לְשֹׁלְחָ֑יו—The noun צִיר, "a messenger," modified by the Niphal (N) participle נֶאֱמָן, "faithful," is similar in meaning to the construct phrase צִ֣יר אֱמוּנִ֣ים, for which, see the second textual note on 13:17.

For לְשֹׁלְחָ֑יו, see the second textual note on 10:26. As there, the plural here could be one of majesty and so suggest that God is the one who sends the messenger (Joüon § 136 e; cf. GKC, § 124 k). Similarly, the plural in the next clause, אֲדֹנָ֣יו, could refer to "his" (the messenger's) important human "master," such as a king, or allude to God as "his Master."

25:14 בְּמַתַּת־שָׁקֶר׃—It is generally agreed that, literally, "a false gift" is a gift never given (ESV, NIV, NRSV). Ironically then, the noun מַתַּת, "gift," is from נָתַן, "give."

25:15 בְּאֹרֶךְ אַפַּיִם יְפֻתֶּה קָצִין—For the idiom meaning "by patience" (shown here by a subject dealing with a ruler), see the textual note on the similar expression in 14:29. The Piel (D) of פָּתָה has negative connotations ("entice, deceive") when it occurs in Proverbs (1:10; 16:29; 24:28), but its Pual (Dp), which appears in Proverbs only here (יְפֻתֶּה), has a neutral connotation: "be persuaded" (BDB, 1). קָצִין, "ruler," is also in 6:7.

וְלָשׁוֹן רַכָּה תִּשְׁבָּר־גָּרֶם׃—Compare "a gentle/soft tongue" to מַעֲנֶה־רַךְ, "a gentle answer," in 15:1. גֶּרֶם, "a bone," is also in 17:22, where too it metaphorically represents the inner disposition, spirit, or will of a person.

25:16 וַהֲקֵאתוֹ׃—The Hiphil (H) of קִיא, "to vomit," is also in 23:8. The cognate noun קֵא, "vomit," is in 26:11.

25:17 הֹקַר רַגְלְךָ מִבֵּית רֵעֶךָ—"Make your foot rare from the house of your neighbor" means "do not frequently set your foot in your neighbor's house." The verb יָקַר, "be precious, costly," is used here in the Hiphil (H), the imperative הֹקַר, which has a causative meaning, "to make [something] rare, uncommon."

25:18 אִישׁ עֹנֶה בְרֵעֵהוּ עֵד שָׁקֶר׃—The vocabulary of, literally, "answering against your neighbor false testimony" is the same as in the Eighth Commandment (Ex 20:16) and also Deut 19:18 (but with "brother" in place of "neighbor"). This is another example of how Solomon affirms the Torah of Moses. See the excursus "Proverbs 1–9, Christ, and the Ten Commandments" in the commentary on Proverbs 1.

25:19 שֵׁן רֹעָה וְרֶגֶל מוּעָדֶת—The feminine noun שֵׁן, "a tooth," is modified by רֹעָה, which apparently is the feminine Qal (G) participle (GKC, § 67 s) of רָעַע II, "to break," here with the intransitive meaning, "be broken." Modifying another feminine noun, רֶגֶל, "a foot," is מוּעָדֶת, probably a feminine Qal passive (Gp) participle of מָעַד, "slip, slide, totter." The translation "lame foot" fits the parallel "broken tooth."

25:20 מַעֲדֶה בֶּגֶד—The rare verb עָדָה I occurs only in the Qal (G) in Job 28:8, meaning "advance, proceed," and here in the Hiphil (H), where the participle with בֶּגֶד as its object apparently refers to someone "taking off a garment/coat."

נָתֶר—"Natron" is a natural form of sodium bicarbonate, better known as baking soda.

וְשָׁר בַּשִּׁרִים עַל לֶב־רָע׃—Literally, this is "and (a person) singing with songs to a bad heart." The participle of שִׁיר, "sing," is used with the cognate noun שִׁיר, "a song." The expression לֶב־רָע, can denote "a bad heart," one that is filled by anxiety or worry (see *HALOT*, s.v. רַע, A 9), hence "a despondent heart." The same expression is used in 26:23 to designate "an evil heart." Compare the similar expressions יֵרַע לְבָבֵךְ (1 Sam 1:8) and רֹעַ לֵב (Neh 2:2).

25:22 גֶּחָלִים אַתָּה חֹתֶה—The pronoun and the participle with direct object literally mean "coals you *are* (thereby) heaping."

25:23 רוּחַ צָפוֹן תְּחוֹלֵל גָּשֶׁם—Literally, this is "a wind of (the) north writhes in birth pangs (with/for) rain." The feminine noun רוּחַ is the subject of the feminine Polel (D) imperfect of חוּל or חִיל, whose Polal (Dp), "I was given birth," was in 8:24–25.

וּפָנִים נִזְעָמִים—The plural Niphal (N) participle of זָעַם, "be angry, indignant," modifies פָּנִים, which here is a true plural, "faces" of multiple people.

לְשׁוֹן סָתֶר׃—In the construct phrase with the nouns לָשׁוֹן and סֵתֶר (in pause), סֵתֶר is an adjectival genitive: literally, "a *hidden* tongue." This difficult phrase probably refers to speaking within earshot of others, but concealing one's words from them as when holding a conversation in whispers.

25:24 See the textual notes and commentary on 21:9, which is identical, except that here the infinitive construct שֶׁבֶת lacks the preposition לְ. The reading מִדְיָנִים, as in 21:9, is the Qere here.

25:26 מַעְיָן נִרְפָּשׂ—The plural of מַעְיָן, "spring," is in the metaphorical water imagery of 5:16 representing a man's wife within the context of a faithful marriage relationship. In 8:24 Wisdom refers to the time before springs were created. However, here, literally, "a trampled spring," with the Niphal (N) participle of רָפַשׂ, is one that has been "muddied" (*HALOT*) and fouled by the feet of careless people and beasts seeking its water. The same verb (רָפַשׂ) and a cognate noun are used in Ezek 34:18–19 for rams and goats (Ezek 34:17)—metaphors for Israel's arrogant and unfaithful leaders—that muddy the water so that it is no longer potable for the rest of the sheep (God's people).

וּמָקוֹר מָשְׁחָת—The noun מָקוֹר, "fountain," is used in 5:18 in the context of the water imagery relating to marriage in 5:15–18. See also מְקוֹר חַיִּים, "fountain of life," in 10:11; 13:14; 14:27; 16:22, and מְקוֹר חָכְמָה, "fountain of wisdom," in 18:4. Here, however, מָקוֹר is modified by the Hophal (Hp) participle of שָׁחַת, "ruined, corrupted, polluted."

צַדִּיק מָט לִפְנֵי־רָשָׁע׃—The verb מוט is used in 24:11 for people "staggering" toward slaughter. Here its participle, מָט, refers to a "righteous person" (צַדִּיק) who "slips, totters, is moved," or is "swayed" because of the pressure and influence of a "wicked person" (רָשָׁע).

25:27 אָכֹל דְּבַשׁ הַרְבּוֹת לֹא־טוֹב—Literally, this is "to eat honey excessively (is) not good." The infinitive absolute אָכֹל is the subject of this nominal sentence.[5] A similar construction with an infinitive absolute and לֹא־טוֹב is in 28:21. Here the Hiphil (H) infinitive construct הַרְבּוֹת serves as an adverb, "excessively, too much." Normally this meaning is expressed by the Hiphil infinitive absolute הַרְבֵּה (BDB, s.v. רָבָה, Hiphil 1 e (3)).

וְחֵקֶר כְּבֹדָם כָּבוֹד׃—This is, literally, "an investigation of their glory is glory." The vocabulary is simple, but this clause is difficult, if not impossible to understand, especially since the context has no masculine plural noun to serve as a referent of the suffix on כְּבֹדָם, "*their* glory." Many divergent interpretations have been proposed. Contrary to most of them, the translation above assumes that the verse is written in antithetical parallelism. In addition, it reads כְּבֹדָם as a defective spelling of the plural כְּבֵדִים, "weighty, difficult things," though this meaning is not attested elsewhere.

---

5 See GKC, § 113 b; Joüon, §§ 123 b B, 123 t, and 154 b (3); Waltke-O'Connor, §§ 4.4.1a, including example 5, and 35.3.3a, including example 3.

Commentary

Prov 25:2–27 is a collection of sayings intended for the instruction of kings or those who would serve them.[6] Scholars have persuasively argued that 25:2–27 forms a unit.[7] The organization of 25:2–27 is as follows:[8]

25:2–5		Introduction: kings (25:2–3) and wicked people (25:4–5)
	25:6–15	Section 1: dealing with kings
	25:16–26	Section 2: dealing with wicked people
25:27		Concluding saying

This section is held together by repetition of words from the introduction (25:2), a verse on the seam between the two sections (25:16), and the conclusion (25:27). These form a chiastic structure:[9]

Glory (25:2)
    Honey (25:16)
    Honey (25:27)
Glory/glorious (25:27)

This chiasm is highlighted in Hebrew by the reversal of elements from these verses:

כְּבֹד ... וּכְבֹד ... חֲקֹר ... חֵקֶר, the glory... and the glory ... to investigate ... investigation/searching (25:2–3)
    דְּבַשׁ ... אֱכֹל, honey ... eat (25:16)
    אֱכֹל דְּבַשׁ, to eat honey (25:27)
וְחֵקֶר כְּבֹדָם כָּבוֹד, an investigation of their glory is glory (25:27)

The skillfully composed section of 25:2–27 also serves as the introductory section of chapters 25–29. It deals with matters of the king and his court, which have modern applications to those in government and the church.[10]

Prov 25:2–27 relies heavily on comparison proverbs, either in the form of similes using כְּ, "like," or metaphors that make direct comparisons. Among the twenty-three proverbs in this section, there are thirteen comparison proverbs (25:2, 3, 11, 12, 13, 14, 18, 19, 20, 23, 24, 25, 26) and one set of proverbs that together form a comparison (25:4–5).

---

[6] See further the excursus "The Organization of Solomon's Proverbs Copied by Hezekiah's Men (Prov 25:1–29:27)" before the commentary on 25:1.

[7] Bryce ("Another Wisdom-'Book' in Proverbs") goes so far as to understand this passage as a separate wisdom book that was later incorporated into Proverbs, whereas Van Leeuwen (*Context and Meaning in Proverbs 25–27*, especially pp. 36, 39, 72–73, 101, 146) simply views it as a separate "proverb poem." While not endorsing either of those views, this commentary acknowledges that their cases for recognizing 25:2–27 as a distinct section in Proverbs are strong ones. However, instead of seeing it as a separate composition, it is more accurate to describe it as a collection of Solomon's proverbs skillfully arranged by Hezekiah's men into a coherent section, in harmony with the superscription in 25:1.

[8] Cf. Bryce, "Another Wisdom-'Book' in Proverbs," 151.

[9] Bryce, "Another Wisdom-'Book' in Proverbs," 153.

[10] See "Reading These Proverbs" in the excursus "The Organization of Solomon's Proverbs Copied by Hezekiah's Men (Prov 25:1–29:27)" before the commentary on 25:1.

Since this section concentrates on the king and his concern for maintaining order and promoting civil righteousness, it focuses on God's Law, especially applications of the Fourth Commandment from the viewpoints of both ruler and subjects.[11] It has little extended or explicit teaching about the Gospel. Nevertheless, the believer naturally will connect language from these proverbs to Gospel themes such as God's glory (Prov 25:2; cf., e.g., Jn 1:14; 2:11); the refining process (Prov 25:4; cf. Zech 13:9; Mal 3:3; 1 Pet 1:7; Rev 3:18); "righteousness" (Prov 25:5; cf., e.g., Phil 3:9); the humble person who is exalted (Prov 25:6–7; cf. Lk 14:8–11); being reconciled (Prov 25:8–9; cf. Mt 5:25–26); loving even enemies (Prov 25:21; cf. Mt 5:44; Rom 12:20); and "good news" (Prov 25:25; cf. Is 40:9; 52:7; 61:1; Mt 11:5; Lk 2:10).

25:2 This verse explores a paradox: God's glory comes in what is hidden about him from human understanding, while a king's glory comes in investigating and making things known. We know only what God chooses to reveal about himself (Deut 29:28 [ET 29:29]). The treasures of God's wisdom and knowledge are hidden in Christ (Col 2:3; cf. Col 1:26; 3:3), who spoke in parables both to reveal and to conceal (Mt 11:25; 13:35; Lk 8:10). However, a good king investigates matters in his kingdom to expose wrongdoing and bring it into judgment publicly so that all may take warning.

25:3 This verse is a contrast to the last line of 25:2. Whereas kings are to investigate, their intentions frequently are unknowable to their subjects. Rulers must keep matters of state confidential, and their motives may be concealed because of their superior wisdom, or perhaps because of their personal quirks or hidden agendas.

25:4–5 These verses are two related sayings. The first one has many applications since its message is to get rid of wickedness so that a task can be accomplished. The second proverb makes a specific application to governance: those who govern can only be secure if they rid themselves of those whose sinful behavior will besmirch their character and ruin their plans. The best intentions of a ruler cannot overcome the corruption of his aides.

25:6–7 These verses form one saying that advises against seeking honor for oneself, which is unseemly, or thinking more highly of oneself than one ought. Humility can lead to elevation by others, but hubris can only lead to humiliation in front of the king himself. To have an audience with a king was a rare privilege for many people. To be in the king's presence only to be under his scorn and disapproval would be the worst outcome for the privilege one was granted.

This proverb likely is part of the background for Jesus' advice in Lk 14:8–11. Self-abasement through repentance and trust in Christ alone (not self) will, in the end, result in exaltation before God, while the arrogance of unbe-

---

[11] See further "Law and Gospel in Proverbs" in the introduction and also the excursus "Proverbs 1–9, Christ, and the Ten Commandments" in the commentary on Proverbs 1.

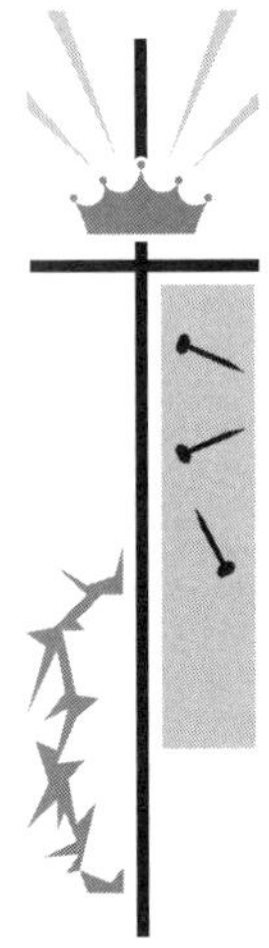

lief will be punished. This theology of the cross is embodied in Jesus himself (Phil 2:6–11).

25:8 This verse advises against a litigious mindset. Those who are always ready to go to the authorities for adjudication of every perceived slight may find themselves humbled when the magistrate rules in favor of their neighbor. In the same way, we should not be quick to call our neighbor to judgment before God when we may be vulnerable to that same judgment (Mt 7:1–5; 18:21–35).

25:9–10 These verses are connected to 25:8 by the words רִיב, "go to court, argue," and רֵעֲךָ, "your neighbor," as well as the adversative פֶּן, "otherwise." This saying continues the thought of settling a dispute out of court, but warns against revealing a secret in the course of doing so. This will bring the shame of being known as someone who is untrustworthy in keeping the confidences of others and leave a lasting mark on one's reputation.

This proverb may lie behind Jesus' advice to come to terms quickly with one's accuser (Mt 5:25–26). Of greatest importance is to be reconciled to God through Christ, the crucified and risen Savior; otherwise a person will have to face God as accusing Judge (Rom 5:9).

25:11 This verse notes that a well-spoken and well-timed comment is as beautiful as gold and silver jewelry. The saying, however, does not say what the particular comment and the proper time are. Only the person who acquires wisdom from God's Word and observes life's workings in the world can learn this.

25:12 This verse is linked to 25:11 by זָהָב, "gold." In this case gold jewelry is compared to the value an astute learner places on the correction offered by a wise person.

25:13 This verse has been the subject of much speculation because of the reference to snow at harvest time. It probably does not refer to actual snowfall during the harvest, which took place during the hot summer. Such a meteorological event would be highly unlikely, as stated in 26:1, and it would be disastrous for the crop (see the commentary on 26:1). The most likely explanation is that a wealthy and gracious landowner dispatches a few of his servants to bring some snow down from the mountains (e.g., Mount Hermon) to cool and refresh the hot, hardworking harvesters. In the same way a messenger who can be trusted to complete his mission and adequately represent his master's wishes is refreshing to the authority who is relying on him.

Every faithful ambassador of Christ, and those who receive his emissaries, will be commended on the Last Day (Mt 10:40–42; 1 Cor 4:1; 2 Cor 5:20).

25:14 This verse is linked to 24:13 by the reference to precipitation. Rain is critical to the survival of agricultural people, including the Israelites in ancient Palestine, where many parts of the land would receive less than eight inches of precipitation each year. A cloud that looked like it was bringing rain but did not was a great disappointment and annoyance. So also is a person who promises gifts, but never gives them. This is advice against promising what one cannot deliver.

25:15 Patience is so great of a virtue that eventually it may persuade a ruler that the longsuffering believer holds the correct position (cf. 1 Pet 2:17–25; 4:14–19). Similarly, "a soft tongue can break a bone" refers to a gentle, respectful answer that deflects the hostility of others. A lion can inflict a bone-crushing bite to defeat its prey (cf. Num 24:8; Zeph 3:3; Dan 6:25 [ET 6:24]). However, a loving tongue that articulates the Gospel is even more powerful (cf. Mt 8:8, 16; Jn 4:50; Acts 3:6).

25:16 This verse advises moderation. It reminds us that overindulgence in any good material blessing can transform it into a cause of discomfort or even into a detriment.

25:17 This verse with פֶּן־יִשְׂבָּעֲךָ, literally, "otherwise, he [your neighbor] will be full [that is, sick] of you," is linked to 25:16, which has another imperfect form of the same verb, פֶּן־תִּשְׂבָּעֶנּוּ, "otherwise you will be filled/gorged with it [honey]." In both verses the verb שָׂבַע, which normally means "be filled with" in a good sense, has the negative connotation "have too much of." The themes are also similar: moderation is the key to both. In this case, your neighbor may have too much of you if you visit too often, just as a person can have too much honey. Both will become repulsive and be expelled. Compare this proverb to the English adage "don't wear out your welcome."

25:18 This verse says that a false witness is destructive. His words can be as indiscriminate in their harm as a crude club, as cutting as a sword, and as targeted and piercing as a sharp arrow. In every case the injury inflicted can be fatal.

25:19 This verse notes that faithfulness is needed especially in a crisis, not just in good times. A person who cannot be counted on in an emergency is just as painful as a broken tooth and as useless as a lame foot, because it is for such a time that someone has put confidence in him. Compare the English proverb "a friend [when you are truly] in need is a friend indeed."

25:20 This verse is linked to 25:19 by similar phrases with nearly identical sounds:

> בְּיוֹם צָרָה, *beyom tsarah*, in a time of crisis (25:19)
> בְּיוֹם קָרָה, *beyom qarah*, on a cold day (25:20)

Also similar are the participle בּוֹגֵד, "an unfaithful person" (25:19), and the noun בֶּגֶד, "a coat" (25:20). This proverb notes two counterproductive behaviors: taking off a coat on a cold day and neutralizing both vinegar and baking soda by mixing them with each other. These futile actions are compared to attempting to cheer up a person who is in the midst of deep despair simply by singing songs to him. To alleviate his depression he needs far more substantial counsel and encouragement from God's Word.

25:21–22 These verses form a contrast with 25:20, since they counsel what appears to be counterproductive behavior: helping one's enemy. However, doing so will accomplish two things. First, the enemy will be given a guilty conscience and perhaps will cease from his hostility. Second, God himself will reward the believer's extraordinary, Christ-like compassion.

Jesus calls his followers to love their enemies in Mt 5:44. Paul quotes this proverb in Rom 12:20, after which he applies it by advising Christians to conquer evil with good (Rom 12:21). In order to reconcile us to God, Jesus himself demonstrated extraordinary love by dying for us even while we were sinners and God's enemies (Rom 5:6–10).

25:23 Some commentators have disagreed with this verse because it appears to say that a north wind brings rain, which normally comes instead from the west. However, the proverb does not actually say that. Instead, it states that a north wind, literally, "writhes" and eventually "gives birth" to rain (see the first textual note on this verse). That is, the north wind signals the coming of a low-pressure system and the ensuing west wind with its rain. In the same way a whispering tongue gives birth to angry looks from those who have been excluded from the open, yet secret conversation.

25:24 Prov 21:9 was almost identical. The point of this proverb is first of all to warn that it is wise to avoid marrying a contentious person, so that the unpleasant situation depicted will not develop. However, a believer who reads this verse may already be married to a difficult spouse. This proverb contains a secondary message for such a situation. While the husband prefers isolation on the roof over bickering inside the house, the proverb envisions that he will continue to reside there. The verse does not counsel the believer to abandon the house altogether and desert the argumentative spouse. Instead the proverb is in harmony with the apostle's directives in 1 Cor 7:10–16 about believers persevering within their marriages.

25:25 Good news from a distant place probably is unexpected, yet delightful and invigorating, especially if it is about a friend or loved one. All the more is this true about *the* Good News about the events in Jerusalem, to be proclaimed to the ends of the earth (Is 52:7; Mt 28:18–20; Acts 1:8).

25:26 A righteous person can, by God's grace, be a "spring" or "fountain" providing wisdom and life for others, as some proverbs indicate (see the first and second textual notes on this verse). Jesus himself offers living waters with the power of the Spirit (Jn 4:14; 7:34–38). But if the righteous person is "swayed" by a wicked one, he can offer only foul, polluted water. A righteous person who cannot stand up for his principles in the face of opposition from evil people has spoiled his principles and his reputation.

God's righteousness never fails. Those whom he has declared righteous in his Gospel are also given his power for sanctification so that they live righteous lives. He promises that a righteous person "will never be moved" (בַּל־יִמּוֹט, Prov 10:30; 12:3), and that remains true as long as the person retains faith, and especially after he is received into eternal glory. Tragically here, another form of the same verb is used to state that the righteous person allows himself to be "swayed" or moved by evil influences. Those who fail to rely on God's gracious power in his Gospel will falter in the face of wickedness.

25:27 This verse repeats the thought of 25:16. The second line is notoriously difficult (see the second textual note on this verse). It probably is a contrast to the first line. One can eat too much honey, but one can never overindulge in gaining wisdom by investigating difficult but glorious things. Kings can never learn too much about the state of their kingdom or about how to govern wisely. For Christians, this proverb especially applies to studying God's Word and pondering spiritual matters, such as learning to distinguish and apply Law and Gospel—one of the most difficult of theological skills, but also the most glorious (see FC SD V 1).

Proverbs 25:28–27:4

All about Fools

Translation

25 [28]A city broken into [and] without a wall [is]
a person who lacks self-control.

26 [1]Like snow during the summer and rain during the harvest,
so honor is not fitting for a fool.
[2]Like a migratory bird or a flying swallow,
so a gratuitous curse does not come [to rest].
[3]A whip is for the horse, a bridle is for the donkey,
and a rod is for the back of fools.
[4]Do not answer a fool according to his stupidity.
Otherwise you too will be like him.
[5]Answer a fool according to his stupidity.
Otherwise he will consider himself wise.
[6]Cutting off feet, drinking violence, [is]
a person who sends messages in the hand of a fool.
[7]The legs of a lame person dangle,
and a proverb [dangles] in the mouth of fools.
[8]Binding a stone in a sling
is like giving a fool honor.
[9]A thorn comes up into a drunkard's hand,
and a proverb [comes up] into a mouth of fools.
[10]Many [people] destroy everything,
like hiring a fool [destroys everything]
and hiring drifters [destroys everything].
[11]Like a dog returns to his vomit,
a fool repeats his stupidity.
[12]Have you seen a person who considers himself wise?
There is more hope for a fool than for him.

[13]A lazy person says, "There's a ferocious lion in the street.
There's a lion in the public squares!"
[14]A door turns on its hinges,
and a lazy person [turns] on his bed.
[15] A lazy person buries his hand in a dish.
He is too tired to return it to his mouth.
[16]A lazy person considers himself wiser
than seven people who answer sensibly.

[17]A person who grabs a dog by the ears [is]
a passerby who meddles in a quarrel that is not his.

[18]A madman who shoots flaming arrows, arrows, and death,
[19]is like a person who deceives his neighbor and then says,
"[Didn't you know] I was [only] joking?"
[20]When there is no more wood, a fire goes out,
and without a gossiper, a quarrel dies down.
[21]As charcoal is to coals and as wood is to fire,
so is a quarrelsome person to kindling a fight.
[22]Words of a gossiper are like easily swallowed food;
they go down to one's innermost being.

[23]A cheap silver glaze covering a clay pot [is]
smooth lips and an evil heart.
[24]A person who hates disguises himself [his hatred] with his lips,
but inwardly he harbors deceit.
[25]When he makes his voice sound gracious, do not believe him,
because seven disgusting things are in his heart.
[26] [His] hatred covers itself with craftiness,
but his evil will be revealed in the congregation.
[27]The person who digs a pit will fall into it.
The person who rolls a stone—it will roll back over him.
[28]A lying tongue hates those it crushes,
and a smooth mouth causes ruin.

27 [1]Do not boast about tomorrow,
because you do not know what a day may beget.
[2]Let a stranger praise you, not your own mouth—
a foreigner, not your own lips.

[3]A stone is heavy and a load of sand is weighty,
but aggravation from a stubborn fool is heavier than both of them.
[4]Cruelty of wrath and a flood of anger [are devastating],
but who can stand before jealousy?

Textual Notes

25:28 Like several proverbs in 25:2–27 and like 26:6, 17, 23 in this pericope, the first line of this proverb is metaphorical and the second line describes the reality depicted by the metaphor(s). See the first textual note on 25:11.

אִ֗ישׁ אֲשֶׁר אֵין מַעְצָר לְרוּחוֹ׃—Literally, "a man who—there is no restraint for his spirit" refers to someone with no "self-control" (*HALOT*, s.v. מַעְצוֹר and מַעְצָר, which occurs in the OT only here).

26:1 כַּשֶּׁלֶג ... וְכַמָּטָר ... כֵּן—The preposition כְּ (here repeated) begins the protasis (literally, "*like* the snow … and *like* the rain …"), and the adverb כֵּן begins the apodosis ("so …"). This construction forms a comparative clause (Joüon, § 174 c). The same comparative construction is used in 10:26; 26:2, 8; 27:8, 19.

26:2 כְּצִפּ֣וֹר לָ֭נוּד כַּדְּר֣וֹר לָע֑וּף—Literally, this is "like the bird to wander, like the swallow to fly." Each of the two Qal (G) infinitive constructs (לָנוּד … לָעוּף) with לְ is best translated adjectivally: "like a *homeless/migratory* bird" (see *HALOT*, s.v. נוּד, 2) and "a *flying* swallow." Though צִפּוֹר is rendered as "sparrow" by many translations, it is a general noun for "bird." The point of this proverb is that the curse does not come to rest on its object, just as migratory birds have no permanent home. A "swallow" (דְּרוֹר) is an insectivore. Therefore, its flight as it darts about in search of food appears erratic and restless.

קִֽלְלַ֥ת חִ֝נָּ֗ם—Rarely does a construct phrase consist of a noun in construct with an adverb (Joüon, § 129 l). Here the noun קְלָלָה, "a curse," is in construct with the adverb חִנָּם, "in vain, without good reason, unjustifiably," meaning a curse without due cause (see *HALOT*, s.v. חִנָּם, 3), "a gratuitous curse."

לֹ֣א תָבֹֽא׃—The subject of the feminine verb תָבֹא is the noun קְלָלָה, "a curse," in the preceding phrase. Almost all translations follow the Kethib, לֹא, "will *not* come," which is supported by the LXX and the Targum. The Qere, לוֹ, "will come *to him*," apparently means that the curse will be inflicted on the person who gratuitously pronounced it.

26:3 וְ֝שֵׁ֗בֶט לְגֵ֣ו כְּסִילִֽים׃—Some proverbs express a comparison simply by begining the second or (as here) the third clause with *waw*. A *waw* at the beginning of the second clause forms a comparison in 26:9, 14 (Joüon, § 174 h). The vocabulary here is also in 10:13, which has וְשֵׁבֶט לְגֵו, "and/but a rod (is) for the back of … ," and 19:29, which has לְגֵו כְּסִילִים, "for the back of fools."

26:4 אַל־תַּ֣עַן כְּ֭סִיל כְּאִוַּלְתּ֑וֹ—This proverb uses the second person singular imperfect of עָנָה, "to answer," whose imperative (עֲנֵה) begins 26:5. For the noun אִוֶּלֶת, which recurs with כְּ and the same suffix (אִוַּלְתּוֹ) in 26:5, see "אֱוִיל, 'Stubborn Fool,' and אִוֶּלֶת, 'Stupidity' " in "Fools in Proverbs" in the introduction.

פֶּן־תִּשְׁוֶה־לּ֥וֹ גַם־אָֽתָּה׃—This clause has a superfluous, emphatic subject pronoun: literally, "lest you be like him—also you!"

26:5 פֶּן־יִהְיֶ֖ה חָכָ֣ם בְּעֵינָֽיו׃—Literally, "lest he will be wise in his (own) eyes," this is translated as "otherwise he will consider himself wise." See the first textual note on 3:7. חָכָם בְּעֵינָיו recurs in 26:12, 16; 28:11.

26:6 Like 25:28 and 26:17, 23, this proverb is a direct metaphor. See the first textual note on 25:28. Here participles are used for the two metaphors and for the reality: literally, "a person cutting off [מְקַצֶּה] feet, a person drinking [שֹׁתֶה] violence, [is] a person who sends [שֹׁלֵחַ] …"

26:7 דַּלְי֣וּ שֹׁ֭קַיִם מִפִּסֵּ֑חַ—This is, literally, "a pair of thighs/legs [שֹׁקַיִם] dangle [דַּלְיוּ] from a lame person [מִפִּסֵּחַ]." The verb form דַּלְיוּ is difficult. It appears to be a Qal (G) perfect of דָּלָה, which usually has the transitive meaning "draw (water)," but here would have the intransitive meaning "*hang down* (helpless)" (BDB, s.v. דָּלָה, Qal). However, the דָּלָה here may be a by-form of דָּלַל, "hang down, dangle, languish." See GKC, § 75 u. Some suggest emending דַּלְיוּ to a Qal (G) form that clearly is from דָּלַל, such as דַּלּוּ or דָּלֲלוּ, "dangle."

וּמָשָׁל—The word מָשָׁל, "proverb," recurs in this pericope in 26:9. It is also the first word of the book, in the title. See the textual note on 1:1.

26:8 כִּצְרוֹר אֶבֶן בְּמַרְגֵּמָה—Here צְרוֹר is the Qal (G) infinitive construct of צָרַר, "bind, tie up." (The OT attests two homographic nouns spelled צְרוֹר, meaning "a bundle, pouch," and "a pebble.") Its object is אֶבֶן, "a stone." The noun מַרְגֵּמָה (with בְּ) is a hapax legomenon whose meaning is uncertain. The phrase is usually translated as "in a sling" on the basis of LXX's translation, ἐν σφενδόνῃ, though some prefer to translate מַרְגֵּמָה as "heap of stones."[1]

26:10 רַב מְחוֹלֵל־כֹּל—This could mean "a master produces/begets everything" (see BDB, s.v. חוּל I, Polel, 2) if the participle מְחוֹלֵל is of the same verb חוּל or חִיל that was in 25:23. Similar is "the great *God* who formed everything" (NKJV). Often רַב can mean "captain, chief," but that seems unlikely here. רַב could also mean "archer," as in Jer 50:29 and Job 16:13, and as it is often translated in this verse (NASB, NIV, NRSV, ESV). If so, then מְחוֹלֵל probably would be the Poel (D) participle of the verb חָלַל I, "bore, pierce, wound," whose feminine Poel participle occurs in Is 51:9, and whose Poal (Dp) participle is in Is 53:5. This clause would then mean "an archer pierces everything" or "an archer wounds everyone." While an archer's arrows may pierce many things, it is unlikely that they literally could pierce everything or wound everyone, even in battle. Perhaps the word should be repointed to רֹב, "multitude," that is, "a crowd destroys everything." Whatever the precise meaning, this clause most likely speaks about destruction, since the following two participial clauses speak of actions that likely would cause damage.

וְשֹׂכֵר כְּסִיל וְשֹׂכֵר עֹבְרִים׃—The repeated Qal (G) participle שֹׂכֵר is of שָׂכַר, "to hire." The participle עֹבְרִים, literally, "those passing through," probably denotes "drifters" or "vagabonds."

26:11 כְּכֶלֶב שָׁב עַל־קֵאוֹ—"Like a dog returns to his vomit" uses the noun קֵא, a hapax legomenon that is cognate to the verb קִיא, "to vomit," in 23:8 and 25:16.

כְּסִיל שׁוֹנֶה בְאִוַּלְתּוֹ׃—The Qal (G) participle שׁוֹנֶה here means "do again, repeat," as in 17:9. For אִוַּלְתּוֹ, see the first textual note on 26:4.

26:12 רָאִיתָ אִישׁ חָכָם בְּעֵינָיו—The verb רָאִיתָ is translated as a question: "have you seen … ?" Hebrew questions need not have an interrogative marker. A similar unmarked question begins 29:20. For חָכָם בְּעֵינָיו, see the textual note on 26:5.

תִּקְוָה לִכְסִיל מִמֶּנּוּ׃—This clause is repeated in 29:20. The preposition מִן (with suffix, מִמֶּנּוּ) has a comparative sense: literally, "(there is) hope for a fool (rather) *than* for him" means "there is *more* hope for a fool than for him." תִּקְוָה can refer to the enduring "hope" of wise believers (e.g., 19:18; 23:18; 24:14).

26:13 אָמַר עָצֵל שַׁחַל בַּדָּרֶךְ אֲרִי בֵּין הָרְחֹבוֹת׃—A similar exaggeration by a "lazy person" (עָצֵל) about a "lion" (אֲרִי, and here also שַׁחַל) in the "streets/public squares" (רְחֹבוֹת) is also in 22:13.

---

[1] See the discussion in Toy, *Proverbs*, 475.

26:15 נִלְאָה לַהֲשִׁיבָהּ—The Niphal (N) perfect of לָאָה, "be weary, tired," is used with the Hiphil (H) infinitive construct לַהֲשִׁיבָהּ, whose feminine suffix refers back to the suffixed feminine noun יָדוֹ, "his hand," in the first line of the verse. This clause could mean "he (the sluggard) *gets weary* by returning it (his hand) to his mouth" (Waltke-O'Connor, § 23.3c, example 9; similar is the explanation for this verse in BDB, s.v. לָאָה, Niphal). This would imply that he keeps eating until he is exhausted by the effort. Or it may form an elliptical comparison: "he is *too* tired to return it" (cf. Joüon, § 141 i). This second possibility is supported by the parallel phrase in 19:24, a proverb that is almost identical to 26:15, but has לֹא יְשִׁיבֶנָּה, literally, "he *does not* return it."

26:16 מְשִׁיבֵי טָעַם׃—The Hiphil (H) participle in construct with the noun טַעַם is, literally, "those who return (words) of taste, good judgment, discretion." The noun טַעַם is also in 11:22, and the cognate verb is in 31:18. The translations that have "answer discreetly" (NIV, NRSV) miss the point, since that implies that the seven men answer secretly or in private. Instead the point is that the lazy person considers himself wiser than seven people who can give a public answer that displays discretion and good judgment.

26:17 עֹבֵר מִתְעַבֵּר עַל־רִיב לֹּא־לוֹ׃—Note the play on words with the two participles of the verb עָבַר (*ʿober mitʿabber*). The Qal (G) participle עֹבֵר denotes "a person passing by," and the Hithpael (HtD) participle מִתְעַבֵּר describes him as one "who meddles" or "intrudes" (see the second textual notes on 14:16 and 20:2). Another wordplay describes the "dispute, quarrel" (רִיב) as לֹּא־לוֹ, *llo' lo*, "not his," a very terse relative clause (GKC, § 155 e).

26:18 כְּמִתְלַהְלֵהַּ—"Like a madman," this is a participle with כְּ. The only other occurrence of the verb לָהָה is in Gen 47:13, where its Qal (G) means "languish, waste away." The form here is a Hithpalpel (HtD), a rare conjugation. With the exception of the hollow verb חִיל, only geminate verbs display the pattern of this conjugation (also מָהָה, גָּלַל, מָרַר, עָרַר, קָלַל, שָׁעַע, שָׁקַק, תָּעַע).

26:19 כֵּן־אִישׁ רִמָּה אֶת־רֵעֵהוּ—This contains a relative clause, "so is a man *who* deceives his neighbor." The verb רָמָה occurs only in the Piel (D), meaning "deceive, beguile," and only here in Proverbs. The cognate noun מִרְמָה, "deceit," is found in eight proverbs, including 26:24.

26:20 וּבְאֵין נִרְגָּן יִשְׁתֹּק מָדוֹן׃—The Niphal (N) participle נִרְגָּן, "a gossiper," recurs in this pericope in 26:22. This person is associated with מָדוֹן, "strife," also in 16:28. The verb שָׁתַק, "quiet down," occurs elsewhere in the OT only in reference to the stormy sea (Jonah 1:11–12) or people at sea (Ps 107:30).

26:21 אִישׁ מִדְיָנִים—Literally, "a man of quarrels, a quarrelsome man," is the masculine equivalent to the feminine construct phrase אֵשֶׁת מִדְיָנִים, "a quarrelsome wife," repeated in four proverbs. See the second textual note on 21:9.

לְחַרְחַר־רִיב׃—The verb חַרְחַר is the reduplicated Pilpel (D) infinitive construct of חָרַר, "scorch, burn, kindle."

26:22 דִּבְרֵי נִרְגָּן כְּמִתְלַהֲמִים—See the first textual note on 18:8, which has the identical clause.

:וְהֵם יָרְדוּ חַדְרֵי־בָטֶן—See the second textual note on 18:8, which has the identical clause. חַדְרֵי־בָטֶן refers to one's innermost being (also in 18:8; 20:27, 30).

26:23 כֶּסֶף סִיגִים—Literally, "silver dross," this is the leftover byproduct from refining silver; see the first textual note on 25:4. It is mostly lead oxide with only a small amount of residual silver. It is translated as "a cheap silver glaze," and it is the subject of the Pual (Dp) participle in מְצֻפֶּה עַל־חָרֶשׂ, "covered over pottery." The conjecture that כֶּסֶף סִיגִים should be emended to כְּסַפְסַג, "like glaze," based on the Ugaritic *spsg* and the Hittite *zapzagay(i)a* or *zapzaqaya*, "glaze,"[2] is widely adopted by translations (NIV, NRSV, ESV) and commentaries,[3] but it has been questioned.[4]

דֹּלְקִים—This masculine plural form is used even though it refers to the feminine dual noun שְׂפָתַיִם, "(two) lips," because of the general Hebrew preference for masculine forms (GKC, § 145 u). This participle, "burning," could be the result of a scribal mistake caused by the confusion of ד for an original ח.[5] Therefore, the translation above reads "smooth lips," following the LXX's χείλη λεῖα, which reflects a Hebrew text reading שְׂפָתַיִם חֲלָקִים.[6]

26:24 בִּשְׂפָתָו יִנָּכֵר שׂוֹנֵא—The subject of this clause and the implied subject of the second clause is the participle שׂוֹנֵא, "a person who hates." The verb שָׂנֵא, "to hate," recurs in this pericope in 26:28, and the cognate noun שִׂנְאָה, "hatred," is in 26:26. The Niphal (N) verb יִנָּכֵר has a middle meaning, literally, "makes himself a stranger," that is, "disguises himself." Similar is the meaning of the first clause in 26:26. This verb is cognate to the adjective (sometimes used substantively) נָכְרִי, "a stranger," in 27:2; the word occurs also in, for example, 2:16; 5:10, 20; 6:24, where it has a negative connotation. It makes little difference whether one follows the singular Kethib, בִּשְׂפָתוֹ, "with his lip," or the plural Qere, בִּשְׂפָתָיו, "with his lips."

:וּבְקִרְבּוֹ יָשִׁית מִרְמָה—Literally, "but in his innards he sets deceit" means that the hateful person harbors ill will against his neighbor. The noun מִרְמָה, "deceit," is cognate to the verb רִמָּה, "deceives," in 26:19.

---

[2] See Albright, "A New Hebrew Word for 'Glaze' in Proverbs 26:23"; Driver, "Problems in the Hebrew Text of Proverbs," 191; footnote in *BHS*.

[3] E.g., Clifford, *Proverbs*, 230; Garrett, *Proverbs, Ecclesiastes, Song of Songs*, 215, including n. 31; Scott, *Proverbs, Ecclesiastes*, 158.

[4] Waltke-O'Connor, § 1.6.3e, note 73, notes that based on the external evidence, this emendation has been questioned by Dietrich, Loretz, and Sanmartín, "Die angebliche ug.-he. Parallele *spsg* || *sps(j)g(jm)*."

[5] Murphy, *Proverbs*, 197, argues that the MT should be retained, since the emendation to "smooth lips" is "so obvious it is suspicious." Some translations attempt to make sense of this unique phrase by translating it as "fervent lips" (e.g., NIV). However, the verb דָּלַק, "burn," is rare (nine occurrences in the MT) and is not used elsewhere in Proverbs. When it does not refer to actual fire, it is used metaphorically to mean "hot pursuit" of someone except in Is 5:11, where it means to be intoxicated ("inflamed by wine"). דָּלַק is never used in connection with speech. In addition, the concept of "burning speech" is foreign to Proverbs. Moreover, while חָלַק, "be smooth," is the obvious choice since it often associated with speech in Proverbs (2:16; 7:5; 28:23; 29:5; see also the cognates in 7:21; 26:28), it is especially appropriate here for deceptive speech.

[6] Cf. Clifford, *Proverbs*, 229, 234; Scott, *Proverbs, Ecclesiastes*, 159; Toy, *Proverbs*, 479.

26:25 כִּי־יְחַנֵּן קוֹלוֹ—Here כִּי has a temporal meaning: "when." In Proverbs the verb חָנַן, "be gracious," occurs only here in the Piel (D), which has a factitive or causative meaning: "make something [קוֹלוֹ, 'his voice'] be/sound gracious" (cf. Waltke-O'Connor, § 24.4g, including example 16). Other forms of חָנַן have positive meanings in, for example, 14:21; 19:17. For the cognate noun חֵן, "grace, favor," see the first textual note on 1:9.

תּוֹעֵבוֹת—See the excursus " 'Disgusting Thing' (תּוֹעֵבָה) in Solomon's Proverbs" in the commentary on Proverbs 11. For תּוֹעֲבַת יהוה, "an abomination/a disgusting thing to Yahweh," see the first textual note and the commentary on 3:32.

26:26 תִּכַּסֶּה שִׂנְאָה בְּמַשָּׁאוֹן—The feminine noun שִׂנְאָה, "hatred," is the subject of the feminine Hithpael (HtD) imperfect תִּכַּסֶּה. This noun lacks a suffix, but the parallel noun in the second clause, רָעָתוֹ, "*his* evil," suggests that שִׂנְאָה should be understood as "(his) hatred." The Hithpael of כָּסָה, "to cover," has a middle meaning, "to cover/conceal oneself." The Hithpael preformative ת has been assimilated and is marked by the *daghesh forte* in -כּ- (Joüon, § 53 e). The full spelling of the verb would be תִּתְכַּסֶּה (with *daghesh lene* in the *kaph*: -כּ-). The conjugation is called a Hippael by Waltke-O'Connor (§§ 21.2.3c, including note 30, and 26.1.1c, including example 28). The noun מַשָּׁאוֹן, "craftiness, deception, guile," is a hapax legomenon, but it clearly is derived from the verb נָשָׁא, "deceive, beguile."

26:27 כֹּרֶה־שַּׁחַת בָּהּ יִפֹּל וְגֹלֵל אֶבֶן אֵלָיו תָּשׁוּב׃—These two lines have parallel syntactical structures: a Qal participle (כֹּרֶה, "the person who digs," and גֹּלֵל, "the person who rolls"), a feminine object noun (שַׁחַת, "a pit," and אֶבֶן, a stone"), a prepositional phrase (בָּהּ, "into it [the pit]," and אֵלָיו, "over him [the roller]"), and finally a Qal imperfect (יִפֹּל, "he will fall," and תָּשׁוּב, literally, "it [the stone] will return"). In both clauses the hostile strategy backfires. The first line is similar to Pss 7:16 (ET 7:15); 9:16 (ET 9:15); 57:7 (ET 57:6); Eccl 10:8. Other OT passages speak of rolling (גָּלַל) a stone (אֶבֶן), but always in a literal sense (e.g., Gen 29:3, 8), without the retribution theme that is here. Compare Mt 27:66; 28:2; Mk 16:3–4.

26:28 לְשׁוֹן־שֶׁקֶר יִשְׂנָא דַכָּיו—For the construct phrase, literally, "a tongue of falsehood" with שֶׁקֶר as an adjectival genitive, "a lying tongue," see the second textual note on 6:17. Often in the OT לָשׁוֹן is construed as feminine, but here it is masculine—the subject of the masculine verb יִשְׂנָא and the referent of the masculine suffix on דַכָּיו. Thus the lying tongue "hates those it crushes." The adjective דַּךְ elsewhere has the metaphorical meaning "oppressed" (Pss 9:10 [ET 9:9]; 10:18; 74:21), but here it can be rendered literally as "crushed." Its suffix denotes the agent of the verbal action: דַכָּיו, literally, "its crushed ones," means "those people who are crushed by it [the lying tongue]."

וּפֶה חָלָק—Only here in the OT does the adjective חָלָק, "smooth, deceptive, seductive, flattering," modify the noun פֶּה, "mouth." However, see the second textual note on 5:3, where חָלָק describes the "palate" as an organ of speech. See also the second textual note on 2:16, where the cognate verb חָלַק refers to seductive speech.

27:3 כֹּבֶד־אֶבֶן וְנֵטֶל הַחוֹל—These are nominal clauses, literally, "heaviness of a stone and weight of the sand." For the sake of English they are translated verbally: "a stone *is* heavy and a load of sand *is* weighty." The noun כֹּבֶד, "heaviness," is cognate to כָּבֵד in the next clause.

וְכַעַס אֱוִיל כָּבֵד מִשְּׁנֵיהֶם׃—Literally, this is "but the aggravation of a stubborn fool is heavier than the two of them." The noun כַּעַס means "vexation" (*HALOT*) or in more current English, "aggravation," as also in 17:25. See "אֱוִיל, 'Stubborn Fool,' and אִוֶּלֶת, 'Stupidity' " in "Fools in Proverbs" in the introduction. Probably כָּבֵד is the adjective "heavy" (so BDB, 1 a) or "weighty, burdensome," and so this is a nominal clause, although the form could also be the Qal perfect of the stative verb כָּבֵד, "be heavy." For שְׁנֵיהֶם, literally, "the two of them," translated as "both of them," see the second textual note on 17:15.

Commentary

This section (25:28–27:4), like the previous one (25:2–27), relies heavily on comparison proverbs.[7] Of the thirty sayings in this section, seventeen are metaphors or similes.[a] Since this section is concerned with fools—avoiding them, not imitating their destructive behavior, and dealing with them—it is heavily oriented toward God's Law. The Gospel of the forgiveness of sins does not receive extended exposition in any of the sayings in this group.[8] However, the reader needs to remember that the wise person is wise because true wisdom comes from the Gospel of Jesus Christ.[9] These proverbs presuppose the Gospel, which enables one to recognize foolish behavior and grants the sanctifying power to avoid it.

(a) Prov 25:28; 26:1, 2, 3, 6, 7, 8, 9, 11, 14, 17, 18–19, 20, 21, 22, 23; 27:3

25:28 This verse serves as the introductory saying to this section. A lack of self-control is a defining characteristic of the "fool" described in the later proverbs in this section. Someone who has rejected God and his Gospel therefore does not have the power of the Spirit, who works through the Gospel, to subdue sin and its cravings. Such lack of self-control is a result of the original sin inherited from Adam (cf. Rom 5:12–21; 1 Cor 15:21–22, 49). The sinful human nature holds the unbelieving fool in bondage (cf. 2 Tim 3:2–5).

This saying links lack of self-control with vulnerability. A person who cannot control his sinful passions leaves himself open to attack, eventuating in death. In contrast, God grants to all believers self-control through the Holy Spirit (Rom 8:13–14; 1 Cor 6:11; Gal 5:16–25; 2 Tim 1:7).

26:1–12 Of the first twelve sayings in chapter 26, eleven (all but 26:2) mention the "fool" (כְּסִיל). These twelve proverbs are arranged in two interlocking chiasms as shown in figure 16.

---

[7] See further the excursus "The Organization of Solomon's Proverbs Copied by Hezekiah's Men (Prov 25:1–29:27)" in the commentary on Proverbs 25. See also the start of the commentary on 25:2–27.

[8] For the distinction between Law and Gospel, see "Law and Gospel in Proverbs" in the introduction.

[9] See "Wisdom in Proverbs" in the introduction. See also the commentary on 1:1–7; 3:13–20; 8:22–31; 30:1b–10; and the excursus "Proverbs 8, Wisdom, Christology, and the Arian Controversy" in the commentary on chapter 8.

Figure 16

The Chiastic Structure of Proverbs 26:1–12

A Honor is not fitting for a fool (26:1)

  B Inconsequential curse (26:2)

    C Double comparison: disciplining a fool (26:3)

      D Not answering a fool (26:4)

      D' Answering a fool (26:5)

    C' Double comparison: the folly of using a fool for important business (26:6)

  B' Inconsequential proverb (26:7)

A' Honor is not fitting for a fool (26:8)

E1 A fool's stupidity (26:4)

  E2 A fool's stupidity is his wisdom (26:5)

    F The folly of using a a fool for important business (26:6)

      G A proverb in the mouth of fools (26:7)

        H Honor is not fitting for a fool (26:8)

      G' A proverb in the mouth of fools (26:9)

    F' The folly of using a fool for important business (26:10)

E1' A fool's stupidity (26:11)

  E2' A fool's wisdom (26:12)

While the parallels in these chiasms are mainly thematic, one parallel is by form: the double comparison (26:3, 6). Several of the parallels also contain repeated words: לִכְסִ֣יל כָּבֽוֹד, literally, "to a fool, honor" (26:1, 8); כְּסִיל כְּאִוַּלְתּוֹ פֶּן־, "a fool according to his stupidity, otherwise … " (26:4–5); וּמָשָׁל בְּפִי כְסִילִים, "and a proverb in(to) the mouth of fools" (26:7, 9); אִוַּלְתּוֹ, "his stupidity" (26:4, 5, 11); חָכָם בְּעֵינָיו, literally, "wise in his own eyes," that is, "will consider/considers himself wise" (26:5, 12). Note that in the second chiasm, the outer element—E and E', a fool's stupidity and wisdom—is split between two proverbs at both the beginning and the end. These interlocking chiasms also highlight the importance of 26:4 and 26:5. These two proverbs have drawn much attention and comment, since they appear to contradict each other. However, in the view of Hezekiah's men (25:1), these two proverbs embody the contradictions that are characteristic of all fools. Thus those editors made these sayings the central element of the first chiasm (D) and the beginning outer element of the second chiasm (E).

26:1 This verse makes two related meteorological observations about Palestine. First, snow would be highly unlikely in the hot summer. Second, rain would be unexpected and inappropriate during harvest, which took place in the summer dry season. Either of these events would force the harvesters to stop their work, since the usual processes of harvesting with a sickle, threshing, and winnowing required the crop to be dry and brittle. These events could also ruin the crop since the moisture could result in mildew or rot. Like this verse, 25:13 refers to "snow" (שֶׁלֶג) and the "harvest" (קָצִיר). Apparently that verse refers to snow being transported from the mountains to provide cooling relief to sweltering harvesters. However, snow would not fall during the harvest season, since such untimely precipitation would be contrary to all forecasts.

In the same way, honor is singularly inappropriate for a fool. Instead, God's Word forecasts everlasting ignominy for those who reject divine wisdom (e.g., 3:35; 13:5; 18:3). This saying functions as a warning to those in positions of power about the dangers of handing out honors without appropriate cause.

26:2 This verse compares the behavior of birds to pronouncing a curse for no good reason. Neither come to rest permanently. Only God can allow a curse to be effective (contrast Numbers 22–24 with Deut 27:9–26; 28:15–68). One foolishly pronounced without condemning sin on the basis of God's Law will have no chance of being fulfilled. Neither will a malediction spoken against a person justified by faith (see Gen 12:3).

26:3 This verse is the first of ten consecutive proverbs that mention a "fool" (כְּסִיל) or "fools" (כְּסִילִים). This saying notes that fools, like stubborn animals, often respond only to corporal punishment. The final line of this proverb combines wording in the final lines of 10:13 and 19:29.

26:4–5 These verses are probably the best-known pair of proverbs in the book and have received much attention from commentators. General agreement exists that these two proverbs speak of differing circumstances. The first states that, in general, it is foolish to engage in dialogue with fools (26:4). However, the second affirms that on some occasions a fool's words are so dangerous that they must be answered and refuted (26:5) or else he (and any others listening to him) will think that he has presented the truth. The same apparent contradiction exists in proverbs in the English language. Compare, for example, "look before you leap" and "he who hesitates is lost." Each truism must be applied to the right situation.

26:6 This verse notes that sending a fool as a spokesman is dangerous on two levels. First is the danger that the message will not be delivered, as if the sender is "cutting off [the] feet" of his own messenger. Second, even if the fool accurately reproduces the words, he may present or deliver them in a way that stirs up trouble, so that the sender is "drinking violence" to be perpetrated against himself (cf. "wine obtained by violence they drink" in 4:17). See also the lazy messenger in 10:26, and contrast the faithful messenger in 25:13.

26:7 This verse observes that a fool may be able to quote a proverb, but it does not ring true and dangles limply in his mouth because he does not possess the wisdom to make use of it.

26:8 Tying a stone into a sling would prevent the proper use of the sling, which is to release and hurl a stone at a target. Only a person who does not understand a sling's purpose would abuse it in that way. So also, only a person who does not understand honor and its purpose would bestow it upon a fool. For the misuse of honor, see also 26:1. For the rightful bestowal of honor, see, for example, 3:16; 11:16; 21:21; 22:4.

26:9 This verse refers to a thorn that pierces the hand of a clumsy drunken person. Due to the anesthetizing effect of alcohol, he will not feel the sharpness of the pain until later, when he emerges from his stupor. So is a wise proverb in the mouth of fools: their spiritual foolishness anesthetizes them from feeling the painful judgment of God's Law, even when it is found in their own words! Later, unless they repent and believe the Gospel, they will feel the sharpness of everlasting condemnation.

26:10 This verse notes the folly of hiring incompetents or relying on unbelievers for spiritual matters. Fools are destructive when entrusted with important work, just as a mob can be destructive. So too, drifters, who have no ties to a community, often destroy by their shoddy or neglectful work.

26:11 Not only do fools repeat their mistakes, they do so thoughtlessly, just like a dog's instinctive behavior. This proverb is quoted in 2 Pet 2:22, where it is applied to baptized believers who had escaped the world's defilements through faith and knowledge of the Lord and Savior Jesus Christ, but who then turn from the way of righteousness and become apostate. The apostle Peter then quotes a similar proverb, perhaps from Heraclitus: "a sow, after washing herself, wallows in the mire."

26:12 A person who is enamored with his own wisdom is beyond help, since he will reject all other advice as inferior. Such a person is even more incorrigible than a fool, who is nearly impossible to help.

Note the parallel proverb in 29:20. The first lines of both proverbs have the same grammatical structure, and the second lines are identical.

26:13 This is the first of a set of four proverbs about the "lazy person" (עָצֵל). It is similar to 22:13; see the commentary there. It ridicules the lazy person who will try any excuse to avoid labor. His ruse is to claim that a lion is near and would attack him if he were to go outside to work. However, this is ridiculous since lions did not live in the urban regions of Palestine ("in the street … in the public squares"), but were found in wild areas (Is 30:6; Jer 49:19; Song 4:8).[10] He pretends that work would literally kill him.

[10] *FF*, 50.

26:14 This verse observes the ease in which a lazy person turns in bed, his natural place. This proverb is a good example of the use of humor to emphasize a truth.

26:15 This verse makes fun of the lazy person who is too lethargic even to feed himself. The laziness may not prevent him from starting a project, but it keeps him from finishing it. This proverb is nearly identical to 19:24, differing from it by only slightly in the second line.

26:16 This verse rounds out this section on the lazy person with the same concept that closes the chiasms on fools (26:12): considering oneself wise. In this case the lazy person thinks he is wise by avoiding work. He believes he has outsmarted others by shirking his responsibility and causing others to pick up the slack and make up for his lack of effort. More sensible people cannot persuade the lazy person of the advantages of carrying out his vocation in life. Seven is used here, as elsewhere in Proverbs, to signify comprehensiveness (6:16, 31; 9:1; 24:16; 26:25; see the commentary on 30:11–33 and 31:10–31). In this case the "seven people who answer sensibly" represent a comprehensive explanation of the usefulness of constructive labor. Those who serve faithfully not only benefit society, but they also please God and can look forward to an eternal reward of rest (see Is 14:3; Dan 12:13; Mt 11:28–29; Rev 6:11; 14:13). The lazy person shows that he does not care about the welfare of others and that he also merits everlasting condemnation (see 2 Thess 3:6–12).

26:17 This verse begins a series of five comparison proverbs that concern strife. All but this one note the role of sinful speech in creating or sustaining fights. The dog mentioned here is not a domesticated pet, but a wild dog, like the ones that often roamed the streets in ancient Israel in packs.[b] The person who meddles in a quarrel to which he is not a party is like someone who grabs such a wild dog by the ears: he cannot hold on and he cannot let go. If he holds on, the other members of the dog's pack will maul him. If he lets go, the dog itself will attack him. Compare the English saying that a person "has a tiger by the tail."

(b) See, e.g., Ex 22:30 (ET 22:31); 1 Sam 17:43; 1 Ki 14:11; 16:4; 21:19–24; 22:38; 2 Ki 9:10, 36; Jer 15:3; Pss 22:17–21 (ET 22:16–20); 59:7, 15 (ET 59:6, 14)

In the same way a person who meddles by getting involved in someone else's quarrel cannot stay in the fight without being harmed, and he cannot get out of the quarrel without being harmed. Even if he abandons the dispute, the person he tried to help will think of him as a traitor, and the other party will consider him a coward.

This humorous picture reminds us that some quarrels are not ours to solve, no matter how helpful we might desire to be.

26:18–19 These verses form one saying. It refers to a person who causes trouble for his neighbor through his words and then claims he was only jesting (26:19). He is compared to a madman who attacks an army, first by shooting "flaming arrows" (זִקִּים) to cause general havoc among the enemy, then shooting "arrows" (חִצִּים) to kill warriors at a distance, and then bringing "death" (מָוֶת) in hand-to-hand combat.

26:20 Quarrels are often sustained by gossip and innuendo. Gossipers are not interested in trying to help solve problems. Instead they seek to attract attention to themselves and satisfy their own appetite for juicy information about others.

26:21 This verse uses the same metaphor as in 26:20 of wood as fuel for fire, this time focusing on the role of a habitually contentious person in igniting fights.

26:22 This proverb is identical to 18:8. The Eighth Commandment is violated both by the gossiper, who spreads rumors and innuendo, and also by those who listen to the gossip and spread the stories.[11] These half-truths "go down to one's innermost being," that is, they corrupt the soul and ruin relationships. See James 1:26; 3:1–18.

26:23 This verse begins a set of four proverbs about schemers. This one notes that a schemer attempts to display a veneer of goodwill through his words. This façade covers an evil heart. However, to the wise person the veneer is detectable, just as a cheap silver glaze cannot hide a pot that is no more than common earthenware.

26:24–26 This is an extended saying that explores the theme already touched upon by 26:23: the person who seeks to conceal evil schemes with his appealing words. This proverb is advice on how to identify a schemer, noting that a schemer full of hatred has seven disgusting things in his heart, a reference to 6:16–19 (see the commentary there). Though this person has gone to great lengths to conceal his hatred, it will eventually be revealed for all to see. This ultimately refers to Judgment Day (Lk 8:17; Rev 20:11–15; cf. Zech 4:10; Heb 4:13).

26:27 This verse notes that those who lay traps for others may well end up being caught in them (see the commentary on 1:17–19). This proverb is similar in meaning to the familiar English saying "what goes around comes around." Hippolytus notes that this is the central plot element in Susannah, and Augustine made a similar observation concerning Daniel 6.[12]

26:28 This verse observes that lying and deceiving words are acts of hatred and the equivalent of violence.

27:1 This verse is the first of a pair of proverbs that warn about bragging. They are bound together by the verb הָלַל, which occurs in the Hithpael (HtD) תִּתְהַלֵּל in 27:1, "to boast, brag," and in the Piel (D) יְהַלֶּלְךָ in 27:2, "to praise." This saying cautions that no one can boast about the future—even just the next day—since the future is unknown, except to God. The return of Christ will bring all earthly activities to an end, and God alone knows that day (Mt 24:36; 1 Thess 5:2). Therefore, presumption about the future is foolhardy. The

---

[11] See also the excursus "Proverbs 1–9, Christ, and the Ten Commandments" in the commentary on Proverbs 1.

[12] Hippolytus, *On Susannah*, verse 61 (*ANF* 5:193–94); Augustine, Letter 93.19 (*NPNF*[1] 1:389).

only boasting allowed is by way of faith in the Lord (1 Cor 1:31; 2 Cor 10:17). James warns of the same thing, telling his readers:

> Come now, you who say, "Today or tomorrow we will go into such a town and work there a year and do business and make a profit"—yet you do not know anything about tomorrow. Of what sort is your life? For you are a mist that appears for a little time and then vanishes. Instead you ought to say, "If the Lord wills, we will live and do this or that." Now you boast in your arrogance. All such boasting is evil. (James 4:13–16)

27:2 This verse is a reminder that praising oneself is conceited. The only praise that rings true is that which comes from others. Above all, the true praise one should seek is that from God, which he will bestow upon all believers—all who are faithful through faith in Jesus Christ.[c]

27:3 This verse is an argument from two lesser evils to a greater evil. In this case the two lesser evils are the heaviness of a stone and the weight of sand. The greater burden is the aggravation caused by a fool, which weighs one down much more than physical burdens. A believer should avoid such a person (Prov 20:19; Rom 16:17; 1 Cor 5:9–11; Eph 5:7).

27:4 This verse is coupled with 27:3 because it is also an argument from two lesser evils to a greater one. The cruelty of wrath and an abundance ("flood") of anger can be devastating enough, but even more destructive are attacks that derive from "jealousy" (קִנְאָה), which runs far deeper and is much more persistent than the brief flare of anger. Song 8:6 notes that "jealousy" (קִנְאָה) is "as fierce as Sheol" (parallel to "strong as death"). Infidelity or betrayal can provoke a spouse or friend to jealousy so intense that it can lead to murder. How much more must a person avoid provoking the anger of the "jealous God" (אֵל קַנָּא) by unbelief or idolatry (e.g., Ex 20:5; 34:14; Deut 6:15; see also 1 Jn 5:20–21; Rev 9:20–21)!

(c) Eph 1:1; Col 1:2; see also Pss 31:24 (ET 31:23); 101:6; Prov 28:20; Lk 19:17; Rom 2:29; Rev 2:10

Proverbs 27:5–22

Dealing with Family, Friends, and Other People

Translation

27 [5]Open correction is better than concealed love.
[6]The wounds caused by someone who loves [you] are reliable,
but the kisses from someone who hates [you] are many.
[7]A satisfied appetite spurns honey,
but to a hungry appetite, everything bitter is sweet.
[8]Like a bird that wanders from its nest,
so is a person who wanders from his place.
[9]Olive oil and incense bring joy to a heart,
and the sweetness of a friend is better than one's own advice.
[10]Do not abandon your friend or your father's friend,
and do not go to your relative's house when disaster strikes you.
A neighbor who is near is better than a relative who is far away.

[11]Be wise, my son, and bring joy to my heart,
so that I may answer anyone who taunts me.
[12]A prudent person sees trouble and hides,
but gullible people keep going and pay the penalty.
[13]Take the garment of someone who guarantees a loan for a stranger,
and [hold it] when someone pledges on behalf of a foreign woman.
[14]Whoever blesses his neighbor in a loud voice early in the morning
will be considered to have cursed him.
[15]Constantly dripping water on a rainy day
and a quarrelsome wife are alike.
[16]Those who hide her hide the wind,
and his right hand calls [her] olive oil.
[17]Iron sharpens iron,
and a man sharpens his neighbor's face.
[18]A person who tends a fig tree eats its fruit,
and a person who attends to his master will be honored.

[19]As water reflects one's face,
so the person's heart reflects the person.
[20]Sheol and Abaddon are never satisfied,
and a person's eyes are never satisfied.

[21] A crucible is for [refining] silver and a smelter for [refining] gold,
and a person [is tested] according to his praise.
[22]Even if you pulverize a stubborn fool in a mortar with grit using a pestle,
his stupidity will not leave him.

Textual Notes

27:5 טוֹבָה תּוֹכַחַת מְגֻלָּה מֵאַהֲבָה מְסֻתָּרֶת׃—For the combination טוֹבָה and the preposition מִן (on מֵאַהֲבָה), "better … than," see "Direct Comparisons" in "Authorship and Date" in the introduction. The feminine טוֹבָה is used here (instead of טוֹב) as the predicate adjective because of the feminine nouns תּוֹכַחַת, "correction, warning," and אַהֲבָה, "love." For תּוֹכַחַת, see the first textual note on 1:23. אַהֲבָה is also in 5:19; 10:12; 15:17; 17:9.

The adjectival feminine Pual (Dp) participle מְגֻלָּה is of גָּלָה, "reveal." English translations are agreed that תּוֹכַחַת מְגֻלָּה, literally, "correction revealed," means "open correction" given its antithetical parallelism to אַהֲבָה מְסֻתָּרֶת, literally, "love hidden."

27:6 נֶאֱמָנִים פִּצְעֵי אוֹהֵב—The noun פֶּצַע, "a wound/bruise," is also in 20:30 and 23:29. Here its plural is in construct with a genitive of source: "wounds from/caused by one who loves [the participle אוֹהֵב]." The Niphal (N) participle נֶאֱמָנִים, "faithful, trustworthy," here is used as a predicate adjective meaning "reliable" or "effective": the wounds accomplish the purpose intended by the loving relative or friend.

וְנַעְתָּרוֹת נְשִׁיקוֹת שׂוֹנֵא׃—The Niphal (N) participle נַעְתָּרוֹת has unusual pointing (GKC, § 63 c). It is most likely from the verb עָתַר II, "be abundant" (BDB). This verb occurs elsewhere only in Ezek 35:13, where it is Hiphil (H). A cognate noun, עֲתֶרֶת, "abundance," is in Jer 33:6. A number of commentators propose alternative meanings or an emendation for this participle.[1] However, the generally accepted meaning is "be many, profuse," which makes good sense here.[2]

The noun נְשִׁיקָה, "a kiss," is found elsewhere in the OT only in Song 1:2. The participle שׂוֹנֵא is used substantively, "a person who hates," as also in these other verses in this section (25:1–29:27): 25:21; 26:24; 28:16 (where the Kethib is plural); 29:24. Like פִּצְעֵי אוֹהֵב in the preceding clause, the construct phrase נְשִׁיקוֹת שׂוֹנֵא has a genitive of source: "kisses *from* someone who hates."

27:7 נֶפֶשׁ שְׂבֵעָה תָּבוּס נֹפֶת—Literally, this is "a full appetite tramples honey." The feminine noun נֶפֶשׁ here and in the next line means "appetite," related to its use for the "throat" (*HALOT*, 1). It is the subject of the feminine imperfect (תָּבוּס) of בּוּס, which usually means "tread down, trample," but here has the figurative meaning "reject, loathe." נֹפֶת, "honey," is used positively in 24:13 but for seduction by an adulteress in 5:3.

וְנֶפֶשׁ רְעֵבָה כָּל־מַר מָתוֹק׃—English requires adding "to" before "a hungry appetite—everything bitter is sweet." The adjective מָתוֹק, "sweet," is cognate to the noun מֶתֶק, "sweetness," in 27:9.

27:9 שֶׁמֶן וּקְטֹרֶת יְשַׂמַּח־לֵב—Usually when a compound subject, here שֶׁמֶן וּקְטֹרֶת, "(olive) oil and incense," precedes the verb, the verb is plural, but here it is singular: יְשַׂמַּח, literally, "makes rejoice" (see Joüon, § 150 p, and GKC, § 146 e). The verb יְשַׂמַּח

---

1 Murphy, *Proverbs*, 205; Scott, *Proverbs, Ecclesiastes*, 161.

2 This or a similar meaning is advocated by NIV; ESV; NRSV; Delitzsch, *Proverbs*, 2:201–2; McKane, *Proverbs*, 610–11; Waltke, *Proverbs*, 2:367, including n. 6.

is a causative Piel (D): “make [something; here לֵב, ‘a heart’] rejoice, bring joy to.” It is masculine, which agrees with שֶׁמֶן, but not with the feminine noun קְטֹרֶת.

:וּמֶתֶק רֵעֵהוּ מֵעֲצַת־נָפֶשׁ—Literally, this is “and sweetness of his friend from advice of soul.” This line is difficult, which makes the meaning of the whole proverb uncertain. The translation above is one possible interpretation.

27:10 רֵעֲךָ וְרֵעה אָבִיךָ—The Qere of the second word is וְרֵעַ, “friend of … ,” a repetition of the first word but in construct and without a suffix. The Kethib is the synonym וְרֵעֶה.

וּבֵית אָחִיךָ—Literally, this is “and the house of your brother.” Here and in the next line, אָח is translated more broadly as “relative.”

בְּיוֹם אֵידֶךָ—Literally, “on the day of your calamity” is expressed more idiomatically in English as “when disaster strikes you.”

27:11 חֲכַם בְּנִי וְשַׂמַּח לִבִּי—The imperative of חָכַם, “be wise,” is addressed to בְּנִי, “my son,” also in 23:19, but in the reverse word order. The verb חָכַם is cognate to the common noun for divine wisdom. See “חָכְמָה, ‘Wisdom,’ and Related Words” in “Wisdom in Proverbs” in the introduction.

The clause with the Piel (D) imperative שַׂמַּח, “make rejoice, bring joy to,” and suffixed object noun לִבִּי, “my heart,” recalls the clause with the imperfect verb יְשַׂמַּח־לֵב, literally, “makes a heart rejoice,” for which, see the first textual note on 27:9. Here the two imperatives together form a consecutive or consequential idea: “*if/when* you are wise, my son, *then the result will be that* you will bring joy to my heart.”

:וְאָשִׁיבָה חֹרְפִי דָבָר—The idiom with the Hiphil (H) of שׁוּב and the object noun דָּבָר, literally, “return a word,” means “answer, reply.” The suffixed participle חֹרְפִי, literally, “my reviler,” is rendered as “anyone who taunts me.”

27:12 This verse is a variant of 22:3. See the textual notes on 22:3. The only differences are that the Niphal (N) perfect here, נִסְתָּר, “he hides (himself),” is the Qere in 22:3, and there are three conjunctions in 22:3 (וְנִסְתָּר/וְיִסָּתֵר וּפְתָיִים ... וְנֶעֱנָשׁוּ) that are not present here.

27:13 קַח־בִּגְדוֹ כִּי־עָרַב זָר—This verse is almost identical to 20:16. Its first line has the rare imperative form לְקַח, “take,” compared to the common form of that imperative here, קַח. For עָרַב, “guarantee a debt/loan,” see the first textual note on 6:1. For the adjective זָר used substantively, “a stranger,” see the first textual note on 2:16, which has its feminine form זָרָה, “a woman who is a stranger.”

:וּבְעַד נָכְרִיָּה חַבְלֵהוּ—See the second textual note on 20:16. נָכְרִיָּה, “foreign woman,” is the Qere in 20:16. Here the LXX has ἀλλότρια, “foreigners.” Apparently the LXX followed the Kethib in 20:16, which is the masculine plural נָכְרִים, “foreigners.”

27:14 מְבָרֵךְ רֵעֵהוּ ׀ בְּקוֹל גָּדוֹל בַּבֹּקֶר הַשְׁכֵּים—Blessings could be uttered on many different occasions. The Piel (D) participle מְבָרֵךְ, “whoever blesses,” in this context apparently refers to a benediction spoken “in the morning” (בַּבֹּקֶר) as a greeting, perhaps like the greeting benedictions in Ruth 2:4. The Hiphil (H) infinitive absolute הַשְׁכֵּים is used as a temporal adverb: “early” in the morning (Joüon, § 123 r; Waltke-O’Connor, § 35.4a, including example 5).

:קְלָלָה תֵּחָשֶׁב לוֹ—Literally, “a curse will be reckoned to him” means that the man who blessed too loudly and early will be considered to have uttered a curse instead of a benediction. The feminine noun קְלָלָה, "a curse," is an antonym of בְּרָכָה, "a blessing,"[a] which is cognate to the Piel of בָּרַךְ, used in the first line. Here קְלָלָה is the subject of the feminine Niphal (N) imperfect תֵּחָשֶׁב, "be reckoned, considered, regarded." The suffix on the preposition לוֹ, "to him," refers back to the participle מְבָרֵךְ, "whoever blesses."

(a) See, e.g., Gen 27:12; Deut 11:26, 29; 23:6 (ET 23:5); 30:1, 19

27:15 דֶּלֶף טוֹרֵד בְּיוֹם סַגְרִיר—The phrase דֶּלֶף טוֹרֵד, literally, "a dripping that continues," is also in 19:13. The noun סַגְרִיר, "steady, persistent rain" (BDB), is a hapax legomenon. It is from the root סגר II with a reduplicated final consonant. It can be called a Qatlīl form (Joüon, § 88J a).

וְאֵשֶׁת מִדְוָנִים—For the construct phrase אֵשֶׁת מִדְיָנִים, "a quarrelsome wife," see the second textual note on 21:9. The Qere here is מִדְיָנִים, while the Kethib, מְדוֹנִים, would have the same meaning.

נִשְׁתָּוָה׃—This is translated as "are alike." The unusual form here, pausal for נִשְׁתְּוָה, is a Nithpael perfect of שָׁוָה. The feminine singular form of this verb is used, apparently because the closest member of its compound subject ("constantly dripping water … and a quarrelsome wife") is feminine singular. The Nithpael conjugation combines features of the Niphal (N) and of infixed "t" patterns, as in the Hithpael (HtD), yielding a reciprocal meaning: to be "like each other."[3] This conjugation is used with two other verbs, כָּפַר (in Deut 21:8) and יָסַר (in Ezek 23:48). Because of its rarity some interpreters have suggested that this form should be emended and the ת should be dropped to make a simple Niphal (N) form.[4]

27:16 וְשֶׁמֶן יְמִינוֹ יִקְרָא׃—The Masoretic accents indicate that this obscure line literally says, "and his right hand [יְמִינוֹ] calls/names [יִקְרָא] olive oil [שֶׁמֶן]." Most likely the quarrelsome wife in 27:15 is being compared to olive oil, which her husband vainly tries to hold in his right hand, but it slips and drips through his hand despite his efforts.

Some interpreters emend יִקְרָא to יִקְרֶה, "his right hand *will meet* olive oil,"[5] and translate that the husband attempts to "grasp olive oil in his right hand."[6] However, there is no evidence that קָרָה, "meet," can have the sense of "hold, grasp." Even if emended, the implication would remain the same: if a person tries to grasp and hold olive oil in his cupped hand, eventually it will leak through.

27:17 בַּרְזֶל בְּבַרְזֶל יָחַד—The verb יָחַד is the Qal (G) jussive of חָדָה I, "be sharp," which occurs in the OT only in this verse, twice. Therefore this clause literally means "let iron by means of iron grow sharp" (BDB, s.v. חָדָה I, Qal). However, it is commonly translated as "iron sharpens iron."

וְאִישׁ יַחַד פְּנֵי־רֵעֵהוּ׃—The verb יַחַד is the Hiphil (H) imperfect of חָדָה I, meaning "make sharp, sharpen." Literally, "and a man sharpens the face of his neighbor" has

---

3 See GKC, § 55 k (9); Waltke-O'Connor, § 23.6.4. Although Waltke, *Proverbs*, 2:369, n. 20, calls this form "reflexive," that would require the meaning "to be like oneself." In this proverb two things are like each other, which indicates a reciprocal, not reflexive, meaning. At times the Hebrew Hithpael (HtD) can have a reciprocal meaning.

4 GKC, § 75 x; cf. Toy, *Proverbs*, 489.

5 See Waltke, *Proverbs*, 2:369, who has "and oil meets his right hand" (see also 2:383).

6 Similar are NASB, NIV, ESV, NRSV.

been interpreted in several ways. The most common is that is signifies improving the neighbor's wits.[7]

27:18 תְּאֵנָה—The "fig tree" was, like the olive tree and the grape vine, one of the most important fruit-producing plants in ancient Palestine. The metaphor of a well-tended fig tree is especially appropriate in this proverb. When the owner of a fig tree kept its ground cultivated and regularly tended the tree, it would produce two bountiful harvests each year, one in June and another in August and September.[8]

יְכֻבָּד׃—The Pual (Dp) imperfect, "will be honored, glorified," recalls earlier proverbs with eschatological promises of glory for the faithful. Prov 13:18 uses the same verb. The cognate noun כָּבוֹד, "honor, glory," is in, for example, 3:16, 35; 8:18; 15:33; 21:21.

27:19 כַּמַּיִם הַפָּנִים לַפָּנִים—Literally, "as water the face to the face" is understood by most English translations to mean "as water reflects the face." See also the next textual note.

כֵּן לֵב־הָאָדָם לָאָדָם׃—This similar repetitive idiom, literally, "so the heart of the man to the man," is usually understood to mean that a person's heart reflects himself.

27:20 שְׁאוֹל וַאֲבַדֹּה לֹא תִשְׂבַּעְנָה—The use of a feminine plural verb, תִשְׂבַּעְנָה, the Qal (G) imperfect of שָׂבַע, implies that both proper nouns in the compound subject (שְׁאוֹל וַאֲבַדֹּה) are here construed as feminine. For שְׁאוֹל, "Sheol," see the first textual note and the commentary on 1:12. It is paired with אֲבַדּוֹן, "Abaddon," in 15:11, and that is probably the next term here. The unusual spelling here, which can be transliterated as *ʾAbaddo*, could be a variation on the usual name or possibly a result of multiple scribal errors. The Qere in Codex Leningradensis is וַאֲבַדּוֹ, while in some manuscripts the Qere is the usual name וַאֲבַדּוֹן. The Qere in Leningradensis reflects a type of haplography: the loss of the final letter ן- due to the similarity of its form to the preceding letter, ו-. The Kethib, וַאֲבַדֹּה, may be due to aural confusion of the final long vowel, וֹ-, and ה-.

27:21 וְאִישׁ לְפִי מַהֲלָלוֹ׃—A comparison between the first and second lines of this proverb is indicated simply by the *waw* beginning this second line (Joüon, § 174 h). Literally, this line is "a man/person by the mouth of his praise." The combination of לְ and פֶּה (in construct) could mean "according to" or "in proportion to" (see BDB, s.v. פֶּה, 6 c; cf. 6 b (*b*)). The noun מַהֲלָל, "praise," is a hapax legomenon, but it is derived from the common verb הָלַל, "to praise." Most likely the suffix on מַהֲלָלוֹ is objective and the clause means that a person is tested according to the praise he does (or does not) receive from others (so BDB, s.v. מַהֲלָל), especially from God. If the suffix were subjective, then the clause could mean that a man is tested according to the praise he gives to others.

27:22 אִם תִּכְתּוֹשׁ ... בַּמַּכְתֵּשׁ ... בַּעֱלִי—The verb כָּתַשׁ, "to pound, pulverize," is a hapax legomenon. It is cognate to the rare noun here, מַכְתֵּשׁ, which has the preposition בְּ in a

---

[7] NIV; McKane, *Proverbs*, 615.

[8] *FF*, 118.

local sense: "in a mortar." The noun עֱלִי, "a pestle" (BDB, under עָלָה), is another hapax legomenon, and it has the preposition בְּ in an instrumental sense: "using a pestle."

הָאֱוִיל ... אִוַּלְתּוֹ:—See "אֱוִיל, 'Stubborn Fool,' and אִוֶּלֶת, 'Stupidity' " in "Fools in Proverbs" in the introduction.

הָרִיפוֹת—This plural noun with the article is rendered "grit." Its exact meaning is unknown. Its only other occurrence is in 2 Sam 17:19, where its meaning is probably not "grain," as in many translations, but rather "dirt, sand." Here it probably signifies some gritty, abrasive substance that aids the grinding action.

Commentary

The proverbs in this section (27:5–22) form a contrast to the ones in the previous section (25:28–27:4) in several ways.[9] The most obvious is that fools (the singular or plural of כְּסִיל) are frequently mentioned in the previous section, but they are never mentioned in this section. Only the closing proverb mentions any type of fool, and it uses a different Hebrew term than כְּסִיל, namely, the "stubborn fool" (אֱוִיל, 27:22), who is also mentioned near the end of the previous section (27:3). A second difference between the two sections is that this one depends less on comparison proverbs.[10] Finally, a third difference is that in the previous section the literary device of pairing proverbs is used only once, in 27:1–2. In contrast, 27:5–22 contains many proverbs that are paired, usually by catchwords. The paired proverbs in this section include these:

- 27:5–6: Each verse has a word derived from the root אהב, "to love."
- 27:7–8: Each of these verses has an internal catchword. There is an inner repetition of the noun נֶפֶשׁ, "appetite," in 27:7. Both a feminine participle (נוֹדֶדֶת) and a masculine participle (נוֹדֵד) of נדד, "wanders," are in 27:8.
- 27:9–10: The noun רֵעַ, "friend," is used once in 27:9 and twice in 27:10.
- 27:19–20: The first clause of 27:19 has an inner repetition of פָּנִים, "face," and the second clause has an inner repetition of אָדָם, "person." Then 27:20 uses אָדָם, "person," once in its second clause, and both clauses end with לֹא תִשְׂבַּעְנָה, "are never satisfied/full."

Despite the artistic structure and organization that Solomon and the editors (25:1) gave to these proverbs, many of them are difficult to understand due to cryptic wording. This section contains the greatest concentration of enigmatic sayings in the entire book.

As in the previous section, there are no sayings in this collection that explicitly proclaim the Gospel of Jesus Christ.[11] Instead the reader is expected to read these proverbs primarily as God's Law, especially according to its third use:

---

[9] See further the excursus "The Organization of Solomon's Proverbs Copied by Hezekiah's Men (Prov 25:1–29:27)" in the commentary on Proverbs 25.

[10] Prov 25:28–27:4 contains seventeen comparison proverbs among its thirty sayings (almost sixty percent), whereas 27:5–22 contains seven or eight comparison proverbs among its seventeen sayings (less than fifty percent).

[11] For sections of Proverbs that do clearly proclaim the Gospel, see the commentary on 1:1–7; 3:13–20; 8:22–31; 30:1b–10; and the excursus "Proverbs 8, Wisdom, Christology, and the

as a guide for the justified believer.[12] The third use of the Law presupposes the believer's faith and knowledge of the Gospel. Certain wording in this section points the reader to the Gospel, which is expressed in other portions of Scripture more clearly and fully with the same or similar language and themes. These include "love" (27:5–6); joy in the heart and "the sweetness of a friend" (27:9); "be wise, my son, and bring joy to my heart" (27:11); and the promise that a faithful servant "will be honored, glorified" (27:18).

27:5 This verse makes a counterintuitive observation: correction can be better than love. Love that is concealed, that is, inactive and unexpressed, is not helpful and is not genuine love. True love takes action to correct a character flaw in a child or underling, or to rebuke a brother or sister who strays from the faith and needs to be called to repentance. Open correction is more loving and helpful even if the person being corrected does not immediately perceive it as flowing from love. This is not only advice for children and underlings to accept correction, but also it is advice for parents and masters: they need to express their love, even if it pains them do it by handing out discipline and administering correction (see Mt 18:15–22; Lk 17:3; Gal 5:6; 6:1).

27:6 This verse is linked to 27:5 by the catchword אָהַב, "to love," which is cognate to the noun אַהֲבָה, "love," in 27:5. This saying builds on the thought of the previous one. Correction that comes from love is "reliable" because it is much more effective than trying to change other people simply out of anger or resentment. The person being corrected will eventually realize that the true motive is love, which seeks the best for others. God's Law tells us his demands for how we are to live and be, but the Law alone is only able to condemn us, not reform us. God's love and grace come through the Gospel by the power of the Holy Spirit, who is active in the Word and Sacraments to transform our hearts and minds. As we daily die to sin and rise to new life with Christ, God wounds and heals us (Deut 32:39; Hos 6:1–3; Job 5:18). By the wounds of Christ, all believers are healed through the forgiveness of sins with the promise of bodily resurrection (Is 53:5; 1 Pet 2:24).

In contrast, feigned affection from an enemy is useless. The phrase "kisses from someone who hates" is similar to the way in which Judas betrayed the Son of Man (Lk 22:47–48).

27:7 A person who thinks he has everything he needs has no incentive and is difficult to motivate, even by the sweetest of rewards, whereas a person who feels a need or deficiency in life is motivated by that need and looks forward to even the smallest fulfillment.

Arian Controversy" in the commentary on chapter 8. See also "Wisdom in Proverbs" in the introduction.

[12] See further "Law and Gospel in Proverbs" and "Reading and Understanding Proverbs" in the introduction. See also the excursus "Proverbs 1–9, Christ, and the Ten Commandments" in the commentary on Proverbs 1. In the Lutheran Confessions, see FC Ep and SD VI, "The Third Use of the Law."

27:8 This verse uses the figure of a bird who is lost and without a safe haven because it has wandered far away from its nest. A person who wanders away from the safe haven of home and family that God provides may also find himself lost and vulnerable in the world. This proverb has many applications: as a warning about lack of appreciation for family, as a warning against adultery (see also 5:8; 7:10–12; 9:13–18), or as a warning against an arrogant spirit of independence. Believers who wander from God's house are away from the place they belong. All need to be strengthened by God's Word and Sacraments in regular worship with fellow Christians (Ps 122:1; Acts 2:41–47; Heb 10:25).

27:9 The exact import of this proverb is uncertain because the meaning of the second line is puzzling (see the second textual note on this verse). The first line describes the joy given by olive oil and incense. And the second line could mean that friendship is better than the advice one gives oneself (see, e.g., ESV and NASB for other possible understandings). "Oil" could mean perfume, for which the oil served as a base, to which spices were added. See Ex 25:6 and 37:29 for the holy, spiced anointing oil. Incense too was mixed with spices and was burned on the incense altar to provide an aroma pleasing to God (Ex 30:1–8, 34–38; cf. Ps 141:2).

27:10 This verse is a rare three-line saying. The first line counsels loyalty to friends, especially family friends. The second line advises against automatically imposing upon family members every time you have an emergency. The third line ties the two thoughts together as it notes that a close friend is better than a distant relative. This may not just refer to physical distance, but also or instead to nearness or remoteness in terms of the strength and depth of the relationship.

27:11 This verse serves as an introduction to a short section that contains a number of repetitions from Solomon's proverbs in 10:1–22:16. This section, 27:11–18, interrupts the paired proverbs in 27:5–10 and is followed by another set of paired proverbs, 27:19–20. Like the introductions to sections in the earlier collection of Solomon's proverbs in 10:1–22:16, this saying addresses a son.[13] It urges the son to "be wise," which will allow his father to rejoice because he will have a ready answer for those who criticize his execution of his parental duties or those who would fault him for his son's foolishness. The language of 27:11 is reminiscent of 23:15.

27:12 This saying repeats 22:3. It highlights the difference between a prudent person and a gullible one. The prudent person has the foresight to see trouble coming and avoid it. Gullible people do not have the divine wisdom that would guide them away from such situations. They fall into sin and pay the price (cf. Rom 6:23).

---

[13] See the excursus "Proverbs 1–9, Christ, and the Ten Commandments" in the commentary on Proverbs 1.

27:13 This verse, a variant of 20:16, is advice about holding people to the pledges they have made, especially when there is a great risk of default. See the commentary on 6:1.

27:14 A blessing, prayer, or compliment, even if spoken with the best of intentions, can elicit an adverse reaction if the beneficiary is not prepared for it or is in a foul mood. A greeting or salutation that is exaggerated, insincere, or ill-timed will not be received favorably, but as its opposite: a curse.

Because of the length of the first line of this proverb, some commentators have suggested that it contains a gloss that was added later and that has made the two lines imbalanced.[14] However, there are at least two reasons why the first line should not be emended. First, the sound pattern of the line would be disrupted,[15] and second, the length of the first line may be intended to mock by imitation the pretentious greeting that it describes.[16]

27:15–16 These verses are a warning against marrying a wife whose temperament leads her to be constantly contentious. Prov 27:15 is a variation of the second line of 19:13, using all of the words of that line and adding three more: בְּי֣וֹם סַגְרִ֑יר, "on a rainy day," and נִשְׁתָּוָֽה, "are alike." The first line of 27:16 is clear: no one can hide a quarrelsome wife from public view, and she will always have the potential to embarrass her husband. However, the meaning of the second line is uncertain (see the textual note). Most translations and commentators understand it in light of the previous line: restraining such a contentious wife is no more possible than holding olive oil in one's hand without it slipping through one's fingers.

27:17 This verse notes that human relationships often have a reciprocal effect, benefitting both people. Debaters can interact like dueling swordsmen. One person sharpens his skills on the other, who is sharpened. He in turn can challenge and sharpen the first person.

27:18 This verse is a comparison between farming and life in a king's court. Cultivation of a fig tree requires diligence and hard work, but it also offers a good return for one's efforts. In the same way, working for the king or another high official can be long, hard work, but it also offers great reward. Note that the proverb does not say that a human master himself would reward his servant, allowing for the possibility that the honor could come from others such as the general populace or the king if one worked for one of the king's officials. The greatest honor is to serve God and to be glorified by the Master at the resurrection on the Last Day—a promise he makes to all believers (Rom 8:16–17, 30; cf. also Mt 25:21, 23).

27:19 This verse notes the reflective properties of water's surface, so that it can act as a mirror. The second line is enigmatic however. It is unclear how

---

[14] Scott, *Proverbs, Ecclesiastes*, 162–63; Toy, *Proverbs*, 488.

[15] McCreesh, *Biblical Sound and Sense*, 43–45.

[16] Delitzsch, *Proverbs*, 2:209.

the heart reflects a person. Perhaps the meaning is that one can learn one's true personality by introspection: when one looks at one's heart and compares it to God's Law, the heart reveals one's sins and faults, and from out of the sinful heart come evil actions that can be seen by others (Mt 15:19; Mk 7:21). Yet the heart of a believer will also show evidence of God's redeeming and sanctifying work by the power of the indwelling Spirit (Ezek 11:19; 36:26–27; Ps 51:12 [ET 51:10]; 2 Cor 1:22; 4:6).

This saying is connected to the next by the catchword אָדָם, "person."

27:20 This verse has a variant spelling of אֲבַדּוֹן, "Abaddon, place of perdition," paired with שְׁאוֹל, "Sheol." See the commentary on 15:11, where they are also paired.

In this saying the emphasis is on death, which is a constant in this world. Death is never satisfied with those who have already died, but continues to take others. The devil is never content with the people he has brought to hell but always seeks to lead more souls to their eternal ruin.

In the same way, sinful human desires and cravings are never satisfied, so that the "eyes" are always looking for more, especially what appears to be novel. This saying is a subtle warning intended to curb the desire to seek and admire what is new merely because it is different. It warns against insatiable greed, lust, and materialism (see Mk 7:21–22; Lk 12:15; Rom 1:29; Eph 5:3; Col 3:5). People often think that if they could have just a little more, then they would be happy. However, if a person lacks appreciation for the gracious gifts God has already given, he will never be content (cf. 2 Cor 12:9–10; Phil 4:11–12; 1 Tim 6:6–11; Heb 13:5).

27:21 This verse shares its first line with the first line of 17:3. Just as gold and silver ore are refined in fire to reveal the pure metals, praise can reveal the true character of a person. A wicked person may receive no praise from others, or if he does, he may congratulate himself in a self-righteous way that inflates his ego. A humble believer can respond to praise in a self-effacing way and ascribe to God alone all the glory, since "God is the one who works in you both to will and to work for his good pleasure" (Phil 2:13). Our goal should be to seek praise from God instead of from other people (see Rom 2:29). God allows suffering to refine and purify his redeemed people, and they yearn to hear his praise—his commendation by grace—by which he promises to welcome them into paradise on the Last Day.[b]

(b) See, e.g., Zech 13:9; Mal 3:3; Mt 25:34; Titus 2:14; 1 Pet 1:7; Rev 3:18

27:22 This verse speaks of the intractable foolishness of the אֱוִיל, "stubborn fool." It is a warning that a person who remains obstinately impenitent in his foolishness cannot be changed by any human effort. Those who try to change him and fail will be frustrated. Only God's Word has the power to bring a fool to repentance and saving faith, but this becomes more difficult the more the fool hardens his heart. As throughout Proverbs, "fool" (as opposed to "wise") especially applies to a person's spiritual state:

> Those who have once been enlightened, who have tasted the heavenly gift, and who have shared in the Holy Spirit, and who have tasted the goodness of

the Word of God and the powers of the age to come, if they then fall away, it is impossible to restore them again to repentance as they are crucifying once again to themselves the Son of God and are holding him up to contempt. For land that has drunk the rain that often falls on it, and bears a crop useful to those for whose sake it is cultivated, receives a blessing from God. But if it bears thorns and thistles, it is worthless and near to being cursed, whose end is burning. (Heb 6:4–8; cf. 1 Jn 5:16)

Proverbs 27:23–27

Pay Attention to Your Flock

Translation

27 **[23]Be certain you know well the condition of your flock.**
Pay attention to [your] herds,
[24]because wealth is not forever,
nor a crown from generation to generation.
[25]The hay is removed and new growth appears,
and grass from the mountains is gathered in.
[26]Lambs [provide wool] for your clothes,
and the price of a field [can be earned from] goats.
[27]Moreover, there will be enough goats' milk for your food,
for your household's food,
and life for your girls.

Textual Notes

27:23 יָדֹ֣עַ תֵּ֭דַע פְּנֵ֣י צֹאנֶ֑ךָ—An infinitive absolute (here יָדֹ֣עַ) used together with a finite form of the same verb (תֵּ֭דַע) can express a number of different emphases. Here it could be rendered as "make sure you get to know very well …" (cf. Joüon, § 123 j). The construct phrase that is the direct object, פְּנֵ֣י צֹאנֶ֑ךָ, literally, "the face of your flock," is an idiom for "the condition of your flock" (see *HALOT*, s.v. פָּנֶה, A 3 f).

שִׁ֥ית לִ֝בְּךָ֗ לַעֲדָרִֽים׃—Literally, "set your heart to" (שִׁ֥ית לִ֝בְּךָ֗ לְ-) is an idiom for "pay attention to" (see *HALOT*, s.v. שִׁית, 3 b β).

27:24 חֹ֑סֶן—This noun for "wealth" appears elsewhere in Proverbs only in 15:6, where it refers to that of a righteous person. Solomon was not only the wisest, but also the wealthiest king on earth (1 Kings 10). Yet later, speaking through Jeremiah, Yahweh warns that he will give Jerusalem's "wealth," along with "the treasures of the kings of Judah," as plunder to their Babylonian enemies (Jer 20:5), proving the transitory nature of royal "wealth" as this proverb states.

וְאִם־נֵ֝֗זֶר לְדֹ֣ור ׀ דֹּֽור׃—The hypothetical particle אִם can serve as a negative, especially when it follows a negative, like לֹ֣א in the preceding clause. Here אִם is best translated as "nor is a crown …" (see Waltke-O'Connor, § 38.6b). The noun נֵזֶר, "a crown," occurs only here in Proverbs. It denotes a royal crown in 2 Sam 1:10 and 2 Ki 11:12, but refers to a crown on the turban of the high priest in Ex 29:6; 39:30; Lev 8:9. Many interpreters object to the royal imagery here and emend the text in various ways.[1] However, royal imagery is appropriate here in light of the advice for royalty that opens and closes these proverbs compiled by Hezekiah's men (25:2–27; 28:1–29:27). See the excursus "The Organization of Solomon's Proverbs Copied by Hezekiah's Men (Prov 25:1–29:27)" in the commentary on chapter 25.

---

[1] Clifford, *Proverbs*, 236–37; Scott, *Proverbs, Ecclesiastes*, 162; Toy, *Proverbs*, 492–93.

Whether one follows the Qere לְדוֹר וָדוֹר or the Kethib לְדוֹר דּוֹר, the repetition means "from generation to generation."

27:25 גָּלָה חָצִיר—The noun חָצִיר, "hay," is a general word for grass-like vegetation. It is the subject of גָּלָה, which usually has a transitive meaning, "reveal, uncover [something]," but here it has the intransitive meaning "depart" (BDB, Qal, 2) or "be removed." This suggests that the hay has been cut and harvested.

וְנִרְאָה־דֶשֶׁא—The noun דֶּשֶׁא, "new growth," is the subject of the Niphal verb נִרְאָה, "be seen, appear." This refers to the sprouting of a new crop after the old one has been harvested.

וְנֶאֶסְפוּ עִשְּׂבוֹת הָרִים׃—In the plural of עֵשֶׂב, a general noun for "grass," the sibilant (-שּׂ-) has a euphonic *daghesh* (see GKC, § 20 h). It is the subject of the Niphal of אָסַף, "be gathered (into a barn)," which again suggests that a harvest has taken place.

27:27 וְדֵי ׀ חֲלֵב עִזִּים—The substantive דַּי, "what is enough, sufficient," is also in 25:16. This is the only OT passage where דַּי is in construct with the commodity that is sufficient, literally, "enough of (the) milk of goats."

וְחַיִּים לְנַעֲרוֹתֶיךָ׃—This means "and life for your girls." In this context חַיִּים is not just "life" in the abstract, but includes the concrete meaning of nourishment, which is necessary to sustain life. See BDB, s.v. חַיִּים, 3, which cites only this verse for such a meaning.

Commentary

More Advice for Kings and Leaders (27:23–29:27)

The extended saying about tending one's flock (27:23–27) serves as an introduction to the second major section (Proverbs 28–29) of the proverbs copied by Hezekiah's men (25:1–29:27). Proverbs 28–29 is a collection of sayings that contains guidance for kings and leaders in governing God's people on his behalf for their higher good.[2]

Introduction: Leaders as Shepherds (27:23–27)

On the surface this introductory proverb (27:23–27) is about attending to one's own responsibilities, including the stewardship of God-given possessions, as God intended already in the pristine creation (Gen 1:26–30; 2:8, 15).[3] This attention is needed because earthly wealth does not last (Prov 27:24), especially if one neglects domesticated animals and agricultural crops. It also

---

2 See further the excursus "The Organization of Solomon's Proverbs Copied by Hezekiah's Men (Prov 25:1–29:27)" in the commentary on Proverbs 25.

3 At the time of the Reformation, some Roman Catholics cited "know well the condition of your flocks" from Prov 27:23 as a biblical mandate for the practice of requiring confession and penance (see Ap XII 106). However, the Lutheran reformers called attention to the literal meaning of this passage as a mandate for the head of a household "to pay diligent attention to his own property and leave other people's alone, but warning him not to be so preoccupied with the increase of his holdings that he neglects the fear of God or faith or his concern for God's Word." Yet the Lutheran confessors do concede that the passage could by analogy be applied as a commandment for a pastor to pay diligent attention to the conduct of the members of his church.

reminds the reader that just as God renews his creation (27:25), so his people need constant renewal and growth. This saying also advises special diligence in tending to those things that provide for an adequate income for oneself and one's family (27:26–27).

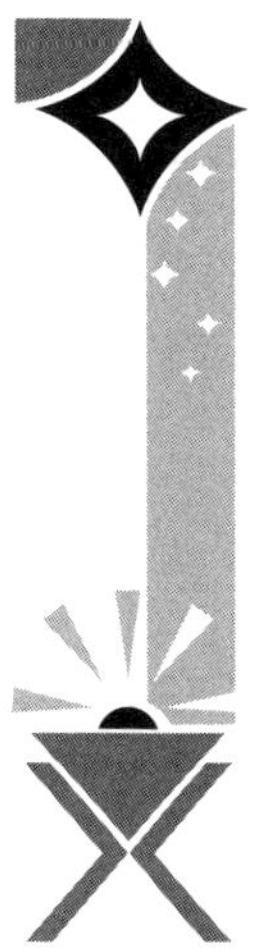

Furthermore, by including this extended saying immediately before the advice for monarchs that begins in 28:1, this proverb takes on the character of a parable. Kings in the ancient Near East were often depicted as shepherds who governed on behalf of their gods and whose duty was to attend to their flock, the people.[4] Moreover, in the Scriptures "shepherd" is a title often used for Israel's kings (e.g., 1 Ki 22:17; Jer 6:3; Ezekiel 34; Ps 78:70–71). Yahweh himself is the Shepherd of the patriarchs (Gen 48:15; 49:24) and of King David (Ps 23:1). God promises that the Messiah, the preexistent and eternal Ruler, will be born in Bethlehem. He will shepherd his people and even raise up seven (the number of divine completeness) undershepherds to fend off and defeat the adversaries of his people (Micah 5:1–5 [ET 5:2–6]).

Prov 27:24 is especially appropriate for kings, since it mentions not only "wealth" but also a "crown" (see the textual notes on 27:24). Therefore, a king who is concerned about establishing and continuing a dynasty is warned that self-absorption that leads to neglect of his people endangers his own dynasty. Instead, just as God renews the land and its bounty (27:25), so a king needs to be constantly renewing and reforming his rule according to God's Word. Then the people of the faithful leader will provide for him and his family (Prov 27:26). In keeping with the metaphor of the king as shepherd, the king's subjects are pictured as wool-providing "lambs" (כְּבָשִׂים, 27:26). The male "goats" (עַתּוּדִים, 27:26) that provide income may represent the people as a whole (as in Jer 51:40; Ezek 34:17) or the princes and leaders (as in Is 14:9; Ezek 39:18; Zech 10:3). Further support comes from female "goats" that produce "milk" (חֲלֵב עִזִּים, Prov 27:27). This prosperity will benefit the king and all his relatives, which would include his sons and successor—and not just the men in his family, but also his daughters and other women in his household (Prov 27:27).

How did Solomon intend this extended proverb to be read: as general advice on animal husbandry and agriculture, or as a parable about the king's responsibilities to attend to his people? We may never know with certainty. However, the editors in Hezekiah's day (25:1) clearly intended it to be read on both levels by placing it at the end of a section of proverbs about more general concerns of life (27:5–22) and before advice for kings (28:1–29:27). In this way it provides a natural and subtle transition from the earlier theme to the next.

Of course, this passage is fulfilled ultimately in Jesus Christ, the everlasting messianic King (2 Sam 7:8–16, which recalls David's vocation as a shepherd; Is 9:5–6 [ET 9:6–7]; Psalms 24 and 110). Paradoxically, the Lamb of God who takes away the sin of the world (Jn 1:29, 36; see also Lk 22:15; 1 Cor 5:7) is

4 Malchow, "A Manual for Future Monarchs," 244–45.

also the Good Shepherd, who lays down his life for his sheep (Jn 10:11, 15). In this way Christ serves as *the* faithful Shepherd who provides for the eternal welfare of his flock (Lk 12:32; Jn 10:16) and who also reigns as King over all kings (1 Tim 6:13–16). This proverb also applies to Christian pastors and church workers, who are called to shepherd God's flock on behalf of Christ himself, anticipating his return (Acts 20:28–29; 1 Cor 9:7; 1 Pet 5:1–4).

The miscellaneous advice that follows in the next two chapters of Proverbs (28:1–29:27) is intended to help Judah's monarchs learn to imitate the promised messianic King as they contemplate God's wisdom in light of the Gospel. Thus starting with 28:4, תּוֹרָה, "instruction, teaching" takes on a decidedly religious meaning. In this collection of Proverbs, תּוֹרָה (28:4, 7, 9; 29:18) denotes both the "instruction" of the Law and—more importantly—the revelation of God's mercy and grace in the Gospel (cf. Jn 1:17). The attention in these proverbs that is devoted to having mercy on the poor (e.g., Prov 28:8, 27) serves as a way for the righteous, wise person to reflect God's love for his people, since he has loved poor humanity by sending his precious Son to die for all, that through faith in Christ all believers may inherit the riches of eternal salvation.[a]

(a) E.g., Mt 5:3; Lk 4:18; 2 Cor 6:10; 8:9; 9:9; Eph 1:7, 18; 2:7; James 2:5

Proverbs 28:1–11

Better to Be Poor and Maintain Your Integrity

Translation

28 [1]**A wicked person flees even though no one is pursuing [him],**
but righteous people are like a lion that is confident.
[2]**In a rebellion, a land has many rulers,**
but with a person who has understanding and knowledge, stability endures for a long time.
[3]**A man who is poverty stricken and who oppresses poor people**
is a driving rain [that leaves] no food.
[4]**Those who abandon instruction praise the wicked,**
but those who keep instruction oppose them.
[5]**Evil men do not understand justice,**
but those who seek Yahweh understand everything.
[6]**Better is a poor person walking in his integrity**
than a person who is twisted [in his] ways and is rich.
[7]**The person who guards instruction is a son with understanding,**
but a companion of gluttons brings shame upon his father.
[8]**The person who increases his wealth through usury and price gouging**
gathers it for someone who is gracious [to] needy people.
[9]**A person who turns his ear away from hearing instruction—**
even his prayer is a disgusting thing.
[10]**A person who misleads upright people along an evil way will himself fall into his own pit,**
but people of integrity will inherit good.
[11]**A rich person considers himself wise,**
but a needy person with understanding will expose him.

Textual Notes

28:1 נָסוּ וְאֵין־רֹדֵף רָשָׁע—The singular adjective used as a substantive רָשָׁע, "wicked person," is the subject of the Qal (G) perfect of נוּס, which is plural in Codex Leningradensis: נָסוּ, "they flee." The verb is singular, נָס, in another Masoretic manuscript, and the LXX translates it as singular: φεύγει. The plural could be explained if רָשָׁע has a collective meaning, "wicked (people)," or it might be the result of dittography of the *waw* that begins the following word (if נס ואין became נסו ואין).

וְצַדִּיקִים כִּכְפִיר יִבְטָח׃—Literally, this is "the righteous (are) like a lion [that] trusts/ is confident." The plural צַדִּיקִים, "righteous people," stands in a comparison introduced with כְּ on the singular noun כְּפִיר, "a lion," which must be the subject of the singular Qal (G) imperfect יִבְטָח. Nevertheless, almost all English translations translate as if the subject of the verb were צַדִּיקִים, for example, "the righteous are bold as a lion" (ESV).

28:2 בְּפֶשַׁע אֶרֶץ רַבִּים שָׂרֶיהָ—This is, literally, "in a rebellion of a land, many are her princes." The feminine suffix on שָׂרֶיהָ, "her princes," refers back to the feminine noun אֶרֶץ, "a land." The basic meaning of פֶּשַׁע is "rebellion." "The fundamental idea of the root is a breach of relationships, civil or religious, between two parties."[1]

וּבְאָדָם מֵבִין יֹדֵעַ—In the larger context of the advice to kings in chapters 28–29, this phrase probably refers to a ruler: a land is ruled, literally, "by a man who discerns and knows." Most translations render the two participles, מֵבִין יֹדֵעַ, "who discerns and knows," as nouns, "of/who has *understanding* and *knowledge*." These two verbs occur often in Proverbs but even more common are their cognate nouns. This vocabulary refers to faculties given by God in his grace and received through saving faith. The Hiphil (H) participle מֵבִין is cognate to בִּינָה, for which, see "בִּינָה, 'Understanding,' and Related Words" in "Wisdom in Proverbs" in the introduction. Regarding יֹדֵעַ, see "דַּעַת, 'Knowledge,' and יָדַע, 'to Know' " in "Wisdom in Proverbs" in the introduction, as well as the commentary on 1:4, 7.

כֵּן יַאֲרִיךְ׃—Biblical Hebrew has several homographs spelled כֵּן, perhaps as many as six (so *DCH*). Some translations take כֵּן as the adverb, "so, thus," and consider "the land" in the first clause of the verse to be the implied subject of the internally transitive Hiphil (H) imperfect יַאֲרִיךְ, for example, "so it endures" (NASB). However, the verb is masculine. Therefore it is more likely that כֵּן is the subject of the verb and that כֵּן is an adjective or noun. One כֵּן is an adjective or substantive meaning "right, what is right/true" (see BDB, s.v. כֵּן I, under the root כון I), so this clause could mean "right will be prolonged" (NKJV). Another כֵּן is a masculine noun that usually refers to a "base" or "pedestal" (*HALOT*, s.v. כֵּן III, 2; BDB, s.v. כֵּן III, under the root כנן I). That word could be used metaphorically here to mean "stability," as in RSV, ESV, and the translation above. Or the word here may be another homographic noun that means "stability" and that occurs in a few other OT passages (so *DCH*, s.v. כֵּן III).

28:3 גֶּבֶר רָשׁ וְעֹשֵׁק דַּלִּים—This construction with גֶּבֶר, "a man," is similar to that in 24:5; 29:5; and other proverbs that use אָדָם or אִישׁ, "a man," with a more specific substantive; see the first textual note on 6:12. For רָשׁ, the participle of רוּשׁ or רִישׁ, "be/become poor, in need," see the first textual note on 10:4. Here רָשׁ is rendered as "poverty stricken" and in 28:6 as "a poor person." For the participle עֹשֵׁק, "who oppresses," see the first textual note on 14:31. Here and in 14:31 and 22:16, those who are oppressed and who are the object of עֹשֵׁק are denoted by a form of דַּל, "poor." Ironically here, a synonym of דַּל, namely, רָשׁ, a "poverty stricken" man, is the one who is oppressing "poor people."

מָטָר סֹחֵף וְאֵין לָחֶם׃—The verb סָחַף means "wash away" (*HALOT*). A "rain" (מָטָר) that "washes away" is called a "driving rain" in English. Literally, "and there is no food" (לָחֶם is pausal for לֶחֶם) shows that the torrential rain is destructive, causing erosion, flooding, and crop failure.

28:4 עֹזְבֵי תוֹרָה—The plural participle of עָזַב, "leave, abandon, forsake," is in construct with its direct object, the noun תּוֹרָה, "teaching," for which, see the second textual

[1] G. H. Livingston, "פָּשַׁע," *TWOT* 2:741.

note on 1:8. This noun recurs in 28:7, 9. For the cognate verb, the Hiphil (H) of יָרָה, "teach," see the first textual note on 4:4.

28:5 אַנְשֵׁי־רָע—In this construct phrase, literally, "men of evil," רָע is an adjectival genitive: "*evil* men."

לֹא־יָבִינוּ מִשְׁפָּט—The noun מִשְׁפָּט, "justice, justification," is a synonym of "righteousness," as in 2:9, where both nouns are objects of the same verb as used here, בִּין, "understand." For מִשְׁפָּט, see also the second textual note and the commentary on 1:3.

וּמְבַקְשֵׁי יְהוָה—The Piel (D) of the verb בָּקַשׁ, "seek," with Yahweh as its object implies repentance, saving faith, and a yearning to learn more from God. See this identical participial construct phrase in Is 51:1; Ps 105:3; 1 Chr 16:10, and see other phraseology for "seek Yahweh" in, for example, Deut 4:29; Hos 3:5; Zech 8:21–22; Ps 27:8.

28:6 See the textual notes on 19:1. The first line is repeated from the first line of 19:1. The second line is similar to the second line of 19:1, but there the person was crooked in terms of שְׂפָתָיו, literally, "his lips," and here he is crooked in regard to דְּרָכַיִם, a dual form, "two ways." Most translate the second line with a plural, "ways." For the virtue of תֹּם, "integrity, blamelessness," given a believer who is righteous through faith, see the second textual note on 2:7. The feminine synonym תֻּמָּה is in 11:3. The cognate adjective תָּם occurs in 29:10. Also cognate is the plural of תָּמִים in 28:10.

28:7 בֵּן מֵבִין—Note the alliteration: *ben mebin*. This participial phrase, literally, "a son who understands," recalls the earlier addresses by divine Wisdom and by Solomon calling a "son" to listen and gain understanding. See the excursus "Proverbs 1–9, Christ, and the Ten Commandments" in the commentary on Proverbs 1. See also, for example, 23:15 and 27:11.

וְרֹעֶה זוֹלְלִים—This verb רָעָה means "associate with, be a friend to," and the participle רֹעֶה serves as a noun, "a companion," as also in 13:20 and 29:3. For the plural participle of זָלַל, "gluttons," see the second textual note on 23:20.

יַכְלִים אָבִיו׃—The Hiphil (H) of כָּלַם, "put to shame, make [someone] ashamed," is also in 25:8. The theme of bringing shame on one's father by foolish living is also in, for example, 17:21, 25; 19:13, 26.

28:8 מַרְבֶּה הוֹנוֹ בְּנֶשֶׁךְ וּבְתַרְבִּית—The Hiphil (H) participle of רָבָה, "be large, great," has the causative meaning: "a person who increases, multiplies." The object is הוֹנוֹ, the suffixed noun הוֹן, "wealth," which is common in Proverbs (e.g., 1:13; 3:9; 28:22; 29:3). The noun נֶשֶׁךְ refers to "usury" or "interest" charged on a loan. The Torah prohibited the practice of charging this from fellow Israelites (Ex 22:24 [ET 22:25]; Lev 25:36–37; Deut 23:20 [ET 23:19]). In Lev 25:36 נֶשֶׁךְ is paired with תַּרְבִּית, as also here. "Price gouging" is an interpretive translation of תַּרְבִּית. The Kethib, וּבְתַרְבִּית, includes the preposition בְּ in an instrumental sense, "through, by." The Qere is וְתַרְבִּית, *waw* with just the noun תַּרְבִּית, which means "increase" and can mean "profiteering" (*HALOT*). Several different translations have been proposed for this word, but all of them understand the practice to be some form of economic oppression.[2]

---

2 E.g., NASB: "usury"; Clifford, *Proverbs*, 241: "surcharge"; Murphy, *Proverbs*, 211: "overcharging"; Toy, *Proverbs*, 498: "increase." NIV and NRSV have "by exorbitant interest" for the phrase בְּנֶשֶׁךְ וּבְתַרְבִּית.

לְחוֹנֵן דַּלִּים יִקְבְּצֶנּוּ׃—The participle מַרְבֶּה in the preceding line, "the person who increases" his wealth unjustly, is the subject of the imperfect verb here, יִקְבְּצֶנּוּ, "(he) gathers it." The masculine suffix on the verb ("it") refers back to הוֹנוֹ, "his wealth." The person for whom he unwittingly is gathering his wealth is denoted by the participial phrase לְחוֹנֵן דַּלִּים, literally, "one who is gracious [toward] needy people." The verb חָנַן does not simply mean "be kind, compassionate" in a humanitarian sense, but implies that the person who acquires the evil man's wealth "shows God's grace" by sacrificial giving, even as Jesus Christ fully revealed God's grace by sacrificially giving himself on the cross (cf. εὐαγγελίσασθαι πτωχοῖς, "to preach the Gospel to the poor," Lk 4:18). The Qal (G) participle חוֹנֵן, "be gracious, show grace," is in similar contexts in Prov 14:31 and 19:17, as is מְחוֹנֵן, the Poel (D) participle of the same verb, in 14:21.

28:9 תּוֹעֵבָה׃—See the excursus " 'Disgusting Thing' (תּוֹעֵבָה) in Solomon's Proverbs" in the commentary on Proverbs 11.

28:10 מַשְׁגֶּה יְשָׁרִים ׀ בְּדֶרֶךְ רָע—The Qal (G) of שָׁגָה, "wander, go astray," is in earlier proverbs (5:19–20, 23; 19:27; 20:1), but this is the only saying with the causative Hiphil (H), the participle מַשְׁגֶּה, "lead [others] astray, mislead." For the object, the plural of יָשָׁר, "straight, right," used as a substantive, "upright person, just/righteous person," see the first textual note and the commentary on 2:7. בְּדֶרֶךְ רָע, literally, "in a way of evil," recalls a frequent metaphor; see the excursus "The Metaphor of the Path in Solomon's Wisdom" in the commentary on Proverbs 10.

בִּשְׁחוּתוֹ הוּא־יִפּוֹל—Literally, "into his own pit he himself will fall," the word order and the pronoun הוּא (which refers back to מַשְׁגֶּה) both make this warning emphatic. The noun שְׁחוּת, "pit," is a hapax legomenon, probably from the root שׁחח. It may be a variant spelling of the noun שְׁחִית, "pit" (Ps 107:20; Lam 4:20), perhaps due to graphic confusion of י and ו. It is probably related to other words for "pit" from the root שׁוח, including שׁוּחָה, שִׁיחָה, and שַׁחַת in Prov 26:27, which has a similar message.

וּתְמִימִים יִנְחֲלוּ־טוֹב׃—The plural תְּמִימִים is of תָּמִים, "person of integrity, blameless person," for which, see the second textual note on 2:21. טוֹב, what is "good," is God's gift by grace through divine wisdom (8:19; 13:21; 16:16).

28:11 חָכָם בְּעֵינָיו אִישׁ עָשִׁיר—Literally, "wise in his (own) eyes is a rich man," this is translated as "a rich person considers himself wise." See the first textual note on 3:7. חָכָם בְּעֵינָיו is also in 26:5, 12, 16.

וְדַל מֵבִין יַחְקְרֶנּוּ׃—The Qal (G) of חָקַר can mean "to search" or "examine thoroughly, so as to expose weakness in a case," as in 18:17 and also Job 29:16 (see BDB, 2 d).[3] Its suffix refers back to עָשִׁיר. Here the verb refers to the result of the examination: after the needy person with understanding conducts an investigation, he "will expose him," that is, be able to show publicly that the rich man is not wise, but a fraud; his wisdom is a sham.

[3] Cf. H. Wolf, "חָקַר," *TWOT* 1:318.

Commentary

Proverbs 28–29 is a section that contains advice for kings and faithful leadership.[4] This section begins with an introductory saying about righteous and wicked people (28:1) and then contains ten sayings, many about treatment of the poor. These sayings share a cluster of common words: the verb בִּין, "understand, have understanding" (28:2, 5 [twice], 7, 11); the noun תּוֹרָה, "instruction" (28:4 [twice], 7, 9); the adjective and substantive דַּל, "poor/needy, a poor/needy person" (28:3, 8, 11); the adjective and substantive רָשׁ, "poor, a poor person" (28:3, 6); the adjective and substantive עָשִׁיר, "rich, rich person" (28:6, 11).[5] In the proverbs copied by Hezekiah's men (Prov 25:1–29:27), these words occurs only in chapters 28–29, and in the case of each of these words, it occurs as many times or more times in these ten sayings as it does in the rest of chapters 28–29.[6]

In addition, the ten sayings of 28:2–11 are arranged in two parallel stanzas of five sayings based on these catchwords as shown in figure 17.

28:1 This verse, as the introduction, sets the tone for the following collection of ten proverbs. It is intended to encourage righteous people by directing them to the source of their confidence: God, who has forgiven them and declared them righteous through the promises of his Gospel.[7] Wicked people have no such confidence, so they are afraid even when there is no reason for anxiety. Their fear is the result of their (conscious or sub-conscious) awareness of their own sin and God's condemnation. They are wicked because they reject God's Law and refuse to trust in the promises in his covenant, as demonstrated by the other occurrences of "flee even though no one is pursuing," which are in covenant curses upon Israelites who apostatize (Lev 26:17, 36). In this context this proverb encourages a ruler to do what is right despite the desire to enrich himself and the pressure to please the powerful. This same divine counsel is applicable to all people.

28:2 This verse reminds those in authority that understanding combined with knowledge is essential to bring stability to a nation. They should not think that they or their nation would survive without these two important attributes. Those who are enlightened by the knowledge of God through his Law and Gospel have saving faith and are guided by the Holy Spirit according to God's Word.[8] This enables them to govern with God's own wisdom and understanding.

---

4 See further the excursus "The Organization of Solomon's Proverbs Copied by Hezekiah's Men (Prov 25:1–29:27)" in the commentary on Proverbs 25. See also the commentary on 27:23–27, which serves as the introduction for chapters 28–29.

5 Cf. Finkbeiner, "An Analysis of the Structure of Proverbs 28 and 29," 7.

6 The other instances of these words in 28:1–29:27 are בִּין, "understand," in 29:7, 19; תּוֹרָה, "instruction," in 29:18; דַּל, "poor/needy," in 28:15; 29:7, 14; and רָשׁ, "poor," in 28:27; 29:13. עָשִׁיר, "rich," does not occur elsewhere in chapters 25–29.

7 See further "Law and Gospel in Proverbs" in the introduction.

8 See the second textual note on 28:2.

Figure 17

The Catchword Arrangement of Proverbs 28:2–11*

First Stanza	*Second Stanza*	*Catchword*
1. Stability through understanding (28:2)	1. Honor through understanding (28:7)	מֵבִין, "(one who has) understanding"
2. Oppression of poor/needy people (28:3)	2. The one who engages in economic oppression gathers wealth for someone who is gracious to poor/needy people (28:8)	דַּלִּים, "poor/needy (people)"
3. Those who abandon instruction are contrasted to those who keep it (28:4)	3. Those who do not listen to instruction (28:9)	תּוֹרָה, "instruction"
4. Evil men are contrasted to those who seek Yahweh (28:5)	4. Those who mislead along an evil way are contrasted to those with integrity (28:10)	רַע, "evil"
5. A poor person is contrasted to a rich one (28:6)	5. A rich person who purports to be wise is exposed by a poor person with understanding (28:11)	עָשִׁיר, "rich (person)"

*This analysis is partly based on Finkbeiner, "An Analysis of the Structure of Proverbs 28 and 29," 7–8.

Unbelievers who reject God's Word can only govern well in so far as they nevertheless still obey God's Law as written on their hearts and as evident in the natural order of creation.

On the other hand, a people's wickedness overturns good order in society. This leads to instability and many competing authorities. This is perhaps intended as admonishment to those in authority to restrain wicked behavior because it endangers their own position as well as their people's welfare.

28:3 This verse observes the heartless behavior of one poor person oppressing another (see the commentary on 14:31). A poor person should have a sympathetic connection with others who share his lot in life. This proverb makes the point that at times a poor person will lack such compassion and will instead oppress other destitute people in an attempt to climb out of his own poverty. Such a person is compared to a driving rain that beats down the crops and destroys the harvest, leaving nothing to eat. Rulers need to be diligent in stopping wicked behavior, even when it does not involve the rich and influential. The same is true for a pastor and his flock (see the commentary on 27:23–27).

28:4 This verse states that one's attitude toward God's Word determines one's attitude toward those who are opposed to God. תּוֹרָה, "instruction," takes on a decidedly religious meaning in this chapter (see 28:7, 9). It is the same Hebrew term that in other contexts refers to the Torah or Pentateuch, especially the covenant given through Moses.[a] It is not exclusively "Law" in the narrow sense of signifying only statutes and regulations. Instead, it signifies God's whole revelation of divine teachings, including both Law and Gospel. As Law, it requires obedience (28:7). As Gospel it enlightens and saves those who hear, believe, and learn it (28:5).

(a) E.g., Deut 31:24; 33:4; Josh 1:7; 8:31–32; Mal 3:22 (ET 4:4); Ezra 3:2; Neh 8:1

28:5 This verse is a statement that points to the enlightenment given by the Holy Spirit to those who seek God in faith according to his promises in his Word. Evil people, who do not have this enlightenment, cannot have a true understanding of justice. In the fullest sense, God's justice not only includes the condemnation of sin, but also the vicarious atonement of Jesus Christ and justification, the imputation of righteousness to all in Christ (2 Cor 5:21). Those who have been justified through faith and enlightened by the Spirit continue to seek Yahweh throughout their life as believers. He gives them growth in understanding and knowledge through his Word.

This proverb may be part of the OT background of 1 Cor 2:9–16, where the apostle Paul states that by nature a person without the Spirit—an unbeliever—cannot understand spiritual things, but through the work of the Spirit, God enables believers in Christ to have the mind of Christ and to discern or judge all things.

This proverb is a reminder for rulers that in appointing magistrates they need to carefully consider the character of those whom they elevate to high position. Those who cannot fully comprehend God's justice will not provide for the eternal welfare of the citizenry nor contribute to the stability of the king's reign under God.

28:6 This verse makes the point that riches in themselves are not an unmitigated blessing. This saying notes instead that integrity is a higher blessing than wealth and is to be chosen over wealth, if that choice must be made. While the saying does not deny that one could have integrity and be rich or have twisted ways and be poor, it is primarily designed to promote integrity as a high moral value.

28:7 This verse contrasts a person who values instruction—given by God through parents as his representatives—with a person who prefers the company of gluttons. Parents who instruct their children in godly virtues teach them to avoid decadent lifestyles. Someone who becomes a companion of those with degenerate habits thereby brings shame to his parents. The parents may assume that they failed in their duty to teach their children or that they did not properly discipline their children (cf. the commentary on 22:6b).

The filial language in this proverb about a faithful believer as a "son" relies on a positive relationship between a believing father and his child that motivates the child to please his father as well as God. This type of relationship involves both Law and Gospel. It is akin to the relationship that one is to have with Yahweh and that is summarized as "the fear of Yahweh." See the first textual note and the commentary on 1:7.

28:8 This verse speaks about divine justice at work in human events. It is a warning that wealth obtained in ways that impoverish others is a target for God's intervention in the course of daily life. The person who gains riches by dishonest, corrupt, or abusive methods will lose them—perhaps through a personal financial crisis or a natural disaster, and certainly at the time of his death (see 28:10 and the "fool" in Lk 12:15–21).[9] Then God will mete out justice through the agency of another person who is gracious and kind to the needy. In this way God redistributes the ill-gotten riches to those from whom it was taken.

28:9 This verse warns about God's judgment on those who despise his Word. God rejects those who reject his Word when they bring their words to him. This proverb does not say who finds the prayer disgusting. Perhaps this is purposeful. While one might naturally first consider God as the one who finds such prayers abhorrent, God's people might also find them equally repulsive since they would demonstrate the hypocrisy of the one offering a prayer after rejecting God's Word (see 1:28).[b]

(b) See also Is 1:15; 59:2; Jer 11:3, 11, 14; Ezek 8:18; Zech 7:11–13; Lk 18:9–14

28:10 This verse finds its strength as a saying in the irony of a person being caught in his own trap. This is a theme found at the very beginning of Proverbs (1:15–19). This saying also is a subtle warning to upright people that those with less than righteous motives can mislead them. They need to be on their guard against schemers.

---

[9] At death, the righteous too will leave behind all their possessions (cf. Psalm 90; Job 1:21; Eccl 2:16–19, 21, 26; 1 Tim 6:7).

The second line commends the righteous. A hardworking and honest person generally will "inherit good" through his integrity. This promise applies most fully to believers, to whom God gives integrity by grace alone, which enables a life of fidelity according to God's Word. Those who follow God's guidance not only avoid being deceived by those with evil motives, but God also promises them an everlasting inheritance. This is an eschatological promise. See "inherit" also in 3:35; 13:22, and, for example, in Mt 5:5; 19:29; 25:34, and "inheritance" in Eph 1:11, 14, 18; 1 Pet 1:4.

28:11 This verse is a reminder of the corrupting power of riches. A rich person may be tempted to think of his riches as something he has earned by his own wisdom, ability, and cleverness, giving him a pretentious, self-important attitude. Instead he ought to regard wealth as a blessing bestowed out of God's kindness and favor. This saying observes that a poor believer has an understanding of God's ways that is far more valuable and powerful than anything possessed by a rich person who does not discern God's ways. The poor person can expose the folly of the rich person who attributes his wealth to his own wisdom rather than to God's grace.

Throughout this section (28:1–11), the reader learns of God's love and compassion toward those who are poor, and the value of faith over worldly possessions. James reminds his readers that God opposes rich people who oppress others, but favors poor believers with heavenly riches:

> Listen, my beloved brothers, did not God choose those who are poor in the world to be rich in faith and heirs of the kingdom, which he has promised to those who love him? But you have dishonored the poor. Are not the rich the ones who oppress you and drag you into court? Are they not the ones who blaspheme the honorable name invoked over you? If you really fulfill the royal Law according to the Scripture, "You shall love your neighbor as yourself," you are doing well. But if you show partiality, you are committing sin and are convicted by the Law as transgressors. (James 2:5–9)

Moreover, Jesus demonstrated the proper attitude toward the poor. Far from oppressing the poor, he became poor for our sakes so that he would be able to share his heavenly riches with us (2 Cor 8:9). Therefore, the wise person not only receives the grace of God in Christ as a free gift to him in his spiritual poverty, but he also learns to reflect Christ's attitude by learning and applying these proverbs in his relationships.

Proverbs 28:12–28

Beware of Wicked People

Translation

28 [12]When righteous people rejoice, there is much glory,
but when wicked people rise, a person is hidden.
[13]A person who conceals his sins will not prosper,
but a person who confesses and abandons [them] will be shown mercy.
[14]Blessed is the person who is always reverent,
but the person who hardens his heart will fall in a calamity.
[15]A growling lion or a charging bear [is]
a wicked ruler over a poor people.
[16]A prince lacking in understanding [is] also [a man of] much corruption,
but the person who hates ill-gotten gain prolongs [his] days.
[17]A person burdened with guilt from bloodshed
will be a fugitive until [he goes down to the] pit.
No one should offer him assistance.
[18]A person who walks with integrity will be saved,
but a person whose ways are crooked will fall all at once.
[19]The person who works his land will have plenty of food,
but whoever pursues fantasies will have plenty of poverty.
[20]A trustworthy person has many blessings,
but a person in a hurry to get rich will not go unpunished.
[21]Showing partiality is not good.
However, for a piece of bread, a man may sin.
[22]A tightfisted person is in a hurry to get rich,
and he does not know that poverty is coming to him.
[23]A person who disciplines someone will afterward find more favor
than a person with a smooth tongue.
[24]A person who robs his father and his mother and [then] says, "It's not a sin,"
is a companion of a vandal.
[25]A greedy person stirs up strife,
but a person who trusts in Yahweh will prosper.
[26]A person who trusts in his own thoughts is a fool,
but a person who walks in wisdom will be kept safe.
[27]A person who gives to a poor person will lack nothing,
but the person who closes his eyes [to a poor person will have] many curses.
[28]When wicked people rise, a person hides,
but when they perish, righteous people increase.

Textual Notes

28:12 בַּעֲלֹץ צַדִּיקִים—The Qal (G) infinitive construct of עָלַץ with בְּ forms a temporal clause: "when righteous people rejoice." This is often translated as "when the righteous *triumph*" (NASB, NIV, ESV, NRSV; emphasis added) based on the assumption that the rejoicing is occasioned by the rise of righteous people to prominent positions. This assumption is partly supported by the parallel infinitive construct of קוּם with בְּ in the next line, וּבְקוּם, "but when wicked people *rise*." However, there is no good evidence that עָלַץ itself can mean "triumph."[1] It is better to translate the verb literally as "rejoice" and allow the reader to infer from the context the possible reasons why the righteous rejoice.

וּבְקוּם רְשָׁעִים יְחֻפַּשׂ אָדָם׃—The Pual (Dp) of חָפַשׂ, "search for," has a passive meaning, "a man is searched for," that is, "is hidden" (see BDB), not a middle or reflexive meaning, "hides himself," despite this kind of rendering in many translations (NASB, NIV, NJB, NRSV). Many commentators propose emending this verb to a Hithpael (HtD), יִתְחַפֵּשׂ, which would mean "disguises/hides himself," or to a form of another verb such as חָפַז, "hurry, be alarmed," or חָפַשׁ, "be free."[2] Apparently the many translations that render the verb here as if it were a Hithpael (HtD) have been influenced by the first line of 28:28, which is identical to this clause except that יְחֻפַּשׂ is replaced by יִסָּתֵר, and the Niphal (N) of סָתַר usually has the middle or reflexive meaning "to hide (oneself)."

28:13 מְכַסֶּה פְשָׁעָיו לֹא יַצְלִיחַ—The Piel (D) of כָּסָה, "to cover," is used with פֶּשַׁע, "transgression, sin," also in 10:12, but in that context the phraseology connotes forgiving sin, whereas the phrase here means "conceals his sins." (The expression has that meaning also in 17:19.) The negated verb יַצְלִיחַ is the Hiphil (H) of צָלַח, which occurs in Proverbs only here. It could have the transitive, causative meaning that the concealing person "will not make [his endeavors] succeed," but more likely it has the intransitive meaning that "he (himself) will not prosper."

וּמוֹדֶה וְעֹזֵב יְרֻחָם׃—The first two verbs are participles: the Hiphil (H) of יָדָה, "confess, acknowledge," and the Qal (G) of עָזַב, "leave, forsake, abandon," participles of which are also in 2:13, 17; 10:17; 15:10; 28:4, all in a negative sense. Here, however, the implied object of both participles is פְּשָׁעָיו ("his sins") in the preceding clause: "a person who confesses and abandons/ceases" his sins. The verb רָחַם, "be merciful, show mercy," occurs only here in Proverbs, and the Pual (Dp) has the passive meaning, "receive/be shown mercy." Active forms of the verb describe God as showing mercy in, for example, Ex 33:19; Deut 30:3; 2 Ki 13:23; Is 30:18; 55:7; Ps 116:5. It can also refer to a human authority showing mercy, as in Ps 103:13, where Yahweh is likened to a father who shows mercy to his children.

---

1 Emerton, "Notes on Some Passages in the Book of Proverbs," 214–20, proposes that Hebrew has two roots עלץ, one of which means "prevail, come to power." His argument, however, is unconvincing. See G. Vanoni, "עָלַז," *TDOT* 11:115–20, who treats עָלַץ as a by-form of עָלַז.

2 F. Maass, "חָפַשׂ," *TDOT* 5:112–13. The meaning of the Pual (Dp) of חָפַשׂ in Ps 64:7 (ET 64:6) is also disputed.

28:14 אַשְׁרֵי אָדָם מְפַחֵד תָּמִיד—For אַשְׁרֵי אָדָם, "blessed is the man/person," see the first textual note on 3:13. The force of the Piel (D) participle מְפַחֵד is "who is reverent." While this verb usually means "shake, be terrified," in a number of passages words from the root פחד denote fear and faith with respect for God and his Word (the noun פַּחַד in 2 Chr 19:7 and negated in Ps 36:2 [ET 36:1]; the verb פָּחַד in Sirach 7:29; 37:12).[3] Thus it can be compared to the theme of the "fear of Yahweh." See the first textual note and the commentary on 1:7 and "יִרְאַת יְהוָה, 'the Fear of Yahweh,' and יְרֵא יְהוָה, 'One Who Fears Yahweh' " in "Wisdom in Proverbs" in the introduction.

28:15 אֲרִי־נֹהֵם— In this proverb the first line is metaphorical and the second line states the reality ("a wicked ruler") that is described by the metaphors in the first line. See the first textual note on 25:11. This phrase with the participle of נָהַם, "to growl," can be compared to the nominal phrases with the cognate noun נַהַם, the "growl" of a lion, in similes describing an angry king (19:12; 20:2). A lion growls as it attacks in order to paralyze its prey with fear. This serves as a metaphor for Yahweh as he proclaims his wrath through his prophet in Amos 1:2; 3:4, 8 (using the synonymous verb שָׁאַג).

וְדֹב שׁוֹקֵק—This participial phrase denotes a bear on the attack (*HALOT*, s.v. שׁקק I, b). Bears begin their attack on humans by charging at them. Compare the bears in 1 Sam 17:34–37; 2 Ki 2:24; Hos 13:8; Prov 17:12; contrast Is 11:7.

28:16 נָגִיד חֲסַר תְּבוּנוֹת—The plural of תְּבוּנָה, "understanding," is replaced in the LXX with προσόδων, "income," which may imply that the translator had a Hebrew text that read תְּנוּבוֹת, "income, produce" (as in Deut 32:13), with metathesis of the ב and the נ. This change may have been facilitated by בֶּצַע, "ill-gotten gain," in the second line.[4]

וְרַב מַעֲשַׁקּוֹת—The noun מַעֲשַׁקָּה occurs only here and in Is 33:15. It is derived from the common verb עָשַׁק, "oppress, extort," as in 14:31; 22:16; 28:3, 17. It denotes some type of ill-gotten gain. In this case, it is profit made by a ruler's misuse of power. Therefore, instead of the more specific "extortion," it is best translated more generally as "corruption."

שֹׂנְאֵי בֶּצַע יַאֲרִיךְ יָמִים׃—The Kethib is the Qal (G) plural participle שֹׂנְאֵי in construct: "haters of …" However, it does not fit as the subject of the singular verb יַאֲרִיךְ. The Qere is preferable: the singular participle שֹׂנֵא, "one who hates," agrees in number with the singular verb יַאֲרִיךְ, of which it is the subject. The Hiphil (H) of אָרַךְ and the object יָמִים, literally, "to prolong (one's) days," means to enjoy long and everlasting life. This idiom occurs in divine promises here and in, for example, Ex 20:12 || Deut 5:16; Deut 4:40; 5:33; 32:47. See the textual note on Prov 3:2, which has the phrase with the cognate noun, אֹרֶךְ יָמִים, "length of days" (also in 3:16).

28:17 אָדָם עָשֻׁק בְּדַם־נָפֶשׁ—This phrase with the Qal passive (Gp) participle of עָשַׁק, "oppress" (see the second textual note on 28:16), literally, "a man oppressed with blood of life," means he is "burdened with guilt from bloodshed" (cf. ESV, NASB, NIV, NRSV).

---

3 H.-P. Müller, "פָּחַד," *TDOT* 11:523–24; H.-P. Stähli, "פחד," *TLOT* 2:981.

4 Murphy, *Proverbs*, 212–13, prefers the reading of the LXX.

בּוֹר—For "pit," which connotes eternal perdition in hell, see the second textual note on 1:12.

אַל־יִתְמְכוּ־בוֹ׃—Literally, this is "may they not take hold of him." תָּמַךְ can mean "uphold, support" and is used here of offering assistance (*HALOT*, s.v. תָּמַךְ, 4 c α). With this meaning it often takes the preposition בְּ attached to the person who is supported (BDB, s.v. תָּמַךְ, 2). The suffix on בוֹ refers back to אָדָם at the start of the preceding line.

28:18 הוֹלֵךְ תָּמִים יִוָּשֵׁעַ—Here תָּמִים serves as an adverbial accusative modifying the participle הוֹלֵךְ: literally, "a person walking [הוֹלֵךְ] as one with integrity [תָּמִים]." For the adjective תָּמִים, often used as a substantive, "a person of integrity, blameless person," see the second textual note on 2:21. The promise here is that יִוָּשֵׁעַ, "(he) will be saved," the Niphal (N) imperfect of יָשַׁע, which occurs elsewhere in Proverbs only in the Hiphil (H) in 20:22, where Yahweh "will save/rescue" those who wait for him in faith.

וְנֶעְקַשׁ דְּרָכַיִם יִפּוֹל בְּאֶחָת׃—The verb עָקַשׁ, "be crooked, twisted," occurs in the Niphal (N) only here, while the Piel (D) is in 10:9. It is cognate to the adjective עִקֵּשׁ, "crooked," for which, see the first textual note on 2:15. The construct phrase נֶעְקַשׁ דְּרָכַיִם has a genitive of respect: literally, "crooked (regarding his) two ways." As in 28:6, most translations simply treat the dual form דְּרָכַיִם ("*two* ways") as a plural. The prepositional phrase בְּאֶחָת, "in one (incident, time)" serves as an adverb modifying יִפּוֹל, "will fall," and could be rendered as "suddenly, unexpectedly, precipitously."

28:19 יִשְׂבַּע—This repeated verb, literally, "be full, satiated with," is translated as "have plenty of."

רֵקִים—For "fantasies," see the textual note on 12:11.

28:20 אִישׁ אֱמוּנוֹת—This is the only OT occurrence of the plural of the noun אֱמוּנָה, and it probably is an abstract plural for the quality of trustworthiness (see Waltke-O'Connor, § 7.4.2a, including example 2, and Joüon, § 136 g). Its use in this construct phrase is as an adjectival genitive: literally, "a man of trustworthiness" is "a trustworthy person." אֱמוּנָה, "trustworthiness, faithfulness," is primarily an attribute of God (e.g., Deut 32:4; Pss 36:6 [ET 36:5]; 40:11 [ET 40:10]; Lam 3:23). God establishes this quality in believers, and those who have this quality through faith are both faithful to him (e.g., 2 Chr 19:9) and trustworthy in their dealings with others (e.g., 2 Ki 22:7).[5]

לֹא יִנָּקֶה׃—Literally, "he will not be declared innocent" means "he will be condemned, punished" on the Last Day, if not before. For this expression, repeated seven times in Proverbs, see the second textual note on 6:29.

28:21 הַכֵּר־פָּנִים לֹא־טוֹב—See the second textual note on 24:23, which has these same words except that its negative is בַּל instead of לֹא.

וְעַל־פַּת־לֶחֶם יִפְשַׁע־גָּבֶר׃—Here the preposition עַל has the nuance "for the sake of," that is, in order to acquire פַּת־לֶחֶם, "a piece of bread." The verb פָּשַׁע, "to sin, transgress," here in the Qal (G), occurs elsewhere in Proverbs only in 18:19, where it is in the Niphal (N), but the cognate noun פֶּשַׁע, "a sin," is common, as in, for example, 28:13, 24.

---

5 Cf. J. B. Scott, "אֱמוּנָה," *TWOT* 1:52; H. Wildberger, "אֱמוּנָה," *TLOT* 1:147–51; A. Jepsen, "אֱמוּנָה," *TDOT* 1:316–20.

28:22 נִבֳהָל לַהוֹן אִישׁ רַע עָיִן—This is, literally, "in a hurry for wealth is a man (with) an evil eye." The Niphal (N) of בָּהַל usually means "to be terrified," but it means "to be hasty, to hurry" here and in Eccl 8:3 (cf. BDB, 2). The Niphal (N) participle נִבֳהָל has unusual pointing (GKC, § 10 h). For the idiom רַע עָיִן meaning "tightfisted" and the opposite of "generous," see the first textual note on 22:9.

חֶסֶר יְבֹאֶנּוּ׃—Literally, this is "poverty will come to him." The noun חֶסֶר, "lack, need, absence," is found elsewhere only in Job 30:3 and Prov 10:21, unless the construct form there (בַּחֲסַר) is of the common adjective חָסֵר, "lacking." A suffix on a verb need not always be the verb's *direct* object; it can serve as an *indirect* object with a datival force, hence יְבֹאֶנּוּ can be translated as "is coming *to* him" (see Joüon, § 125 ba).

28:23 מוֹכִיחַ אָדָם אַחֲרַי חֵן יִמְצָא—The Hiphil (H) participle מוֹכִיחַ is of יָכַח, "warn, discipline," for which, see the first textual note on 3:12. The preposition אַחֲרֵי often means "after," but the form here is pointed אַחֲרַי, as if with a pronominal suffix, "after me." This form might be an adverb meaning "afterward" and may recur as the Kethib in Neh 3:30 (so *DCH*, s.v. אַחֲרַי). One solution is to follow a medieval manuscript that has אַחֲרָיו,[6] "after it," that is, after the disciplinary action. The subject of יִמְצָא is מוֹכִיחַ, and its object is חֵן, "grace, favor," for which, see the first textual note on 1:9.

מִמַּחֲלִיק לָשׁוֹן׃—The preposition מִן on the Hiphil (H) participle, מַחֲלִיק, forms a comparative clause: literally, "*more* grace *than* a person who makes his tongue smooth," that is, who flatters. For the Hiphil (H) of חָלַק, "make smooth, slippery," in reference to speech that is deceptive and seductive (2:16; 7:5; 28:23; 29:5), see the second textual note on 2:16.

28:24 פָּשַׁע—This is not the verb פָּשַׁע, for which, see the second textual note on 28:21. Rather, it is the pausal form of the noun פֶּשַׁע, "a sin, transgression," as also in 28:13.

חָבֵר הוּא לְאִישׁ מַשְׁחִית׃—Literally, this is "an associate is he to a man who destroys." For the similar phrase אָח הוּא לְבַעַל מַשְׁחִית, see the second textual note on 18:9.

28:25 רְחַב־נֶפֶשׁ—The idiom, literally, "wide of appetite" refers to "a greedy person" (see *HALOT*, s.v. רָחָב I, 3). This phrase signifies someone whose desire for material possession is rapacious.

יְגָרֶה מָדוֹן—The identical clause, "(he) stirs up strife," is in the first line of 15:18. It recurs in 29:22.

וּבוֹטֵחַ עַל־יְהוָה יְדֻשָּׁן׃—This is, literally, "and one who trusts upon Yahweh will be fattened." The Pual (Dp) of דָּשֵׁן, "be fat," is in promises of prosperity also in 11:25; 13:4. For the verb בָּטַח, "to trust," referring to faith in the one true God, see also 3:5; 16:20; 29:25. However, the participle בּוֹטֵחַ recurs in the next verse in the opposite sense.

28:26 בּוֹטֵחַ בְּלִבּוֹ הוּא כְסִיל—The pronoun הוּא is emphatic, and so the line could be translated as "one who trusts in his (own) heart—*he is the one who is* a fool" (see Joüon, § 154 j). Such a person contradicts the counsel in 3:5 to "trust in Yahweh with all your heart." He is an unbeliever. Here לֵב, "heart," can be translated as "thoughts" (see the first textual note on 2:10).

---

[6] Footnote in *BHS*.

28:27 נוֹתֵן לָרָשׁ אֵין מַחְסוֹר—Literally, "he who gives to a poor person, there is no lack" means that the benefactor will lack nothing. Compare the cognate verb in לֹא אֶחְסָר in Ps 23:1. For the participle רָשׁ, "poor (person)," see the first textual note on Prov 10:4.

וּמַעְלִים עֵינָיו רַב־מְאֵרוֹת׃—רַב־מְאֵרוֹת, literally, "many of curses," modifies מַעְלִים, the person who closes his eyes: that person "[will have] many curses." "Curses" translates the plural of מְאֵרָה (from the root ארר), which refers to Yahweh's curse upon the wicked in 3:33. This is the strongest antonym to the words for "blessed" in 28:14 and "blessings" in 28:20.

Commentary

This portion of the proverbs of Solomon copied by Hezekiah's men (Prov 25:1–29:27)[7] opens and closes with two similar transition proverbs about the righteous and the wicked (28:12, 28). The second line of 28:12 is nearly identical to the first line of 28:28, and their other two lines share common vocabulary. The proverbs between these two transition sayings share the common topic of wicked people and behavior. At least one proverb (28:16) refers to a ruler, and at least one more (28:21) has advice about the administration of justice. These proverbs help connect this set of proverbs with the larger context of chapters 28–29, which pertains especially to wise leadership and just government.

28:12 This verse notes the difference it makes among God's people and in society in general when the righteous are able to rejoice. The righteous are believers, justified through faith and endowed with divine wisdom.[8] They give glory to God, and God promises them everlasting glory. When the people have righteous leaders, they are able to exult more than when they are dominated by wicked ones. With wicked rulers come corruption and justice that is administered arbitrarily or with favoritism (see 28:21). Under such circumstances society's stability is compromised and righteous people are not able to contribute as much to the common good.

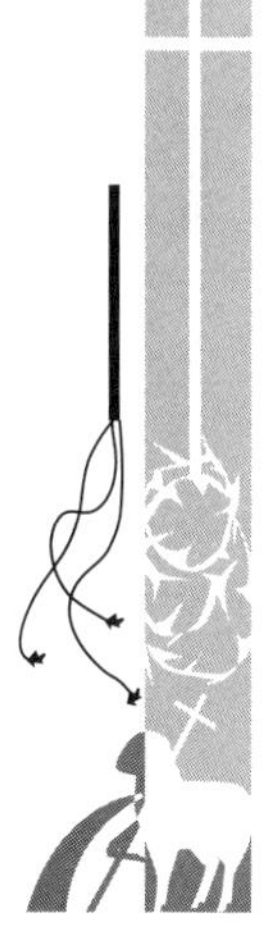

28:13 This unique verse may be the proverb that most clearly and directly discusses the mercy found by those who confess their sins (cf. Ps 32:1–5; Prov 10:12; 1 Jn 1:6–9). Note that the passive construction in the proverb (יְרֻחָם, "will be shown mercy") does not specifically mention God as the one who shows mercy. While God's mercy is certainly in view here, the proverb may also apply to human mercy toward those who are forthright in their confession of their wrongdoings instead of engaging in vain attempts to hide their wrongs from public view. Note that this proverb also speaks about the change that follows repentance in that the person is said to abandon his former sins.

---

7 See further the excursus "The Organization of Solomon's Proverbs Copied by Hezekiah's Men (Prov 25:1–29:27)" in the commentary on Proverbs 25, as well as the commentary on 27:23–27, which serves as the introduction for chapters 28–29.

8 See "The Relationship between Wisdom and Righteousness in Proverbs" in "Wisdom in Proverbs" in the introduction.

The Lutheran Confessions expound this same theology of repentance and faith, confession and absolution, and the new obedience of the baptized believer living under grace.[a]

(a) See, e.g., AC VI and XX; Ap XII 131–32, 170, 174; SC V 16–29; LC IV 74–76

28:14 This verse notes that a person who respects God and his Word (see the textual note) receives blessing, not because this attitude earns him a blessing, but because through faith he receives the gracious promises of God and by faith obeys God's Law, which guards him from falling into sin and harming himself and his neighbor. This proverb is a beatitude that, like 3:13, for example, and those in the NT (e.g., Mt 5:3–11; Rev 14:13), is fulfilled in Christ but will be fully realized only on the Last Day. For the Christological character of such wisdom beatitudes, see the commentary on Prov 3:13–20.

The opposite person, who will fall under God's curse, is one who hardens his heart and refuses to listen to God's commands and warnings or to trust his promises.[b]

(b) Cf., e.g., Ex 4:21; 7:3, 13–14, 22; 8:11, 15, 28 (ET 8:15, 19, 32); 9:7, 12, 34–35; 10:1, 20, 27; 11:10; 14:4, 8,17; Deut 2:30; 15:7; Josh 11:20; 1 Sam 6:6; Ezek 2:4; 3:7; Ps 95:8; Dan 5:20; 2 Chr 36:13; Mt 19:8; Mk 10:5; Rom 9:14–24; Heb 3:8, 15; 4:7

28:15 This verse explains that a wicked ruler is especially vicious when he governs a poor people. His wickedness exacerbates their poverty. To improve their standard of living, he would have to establish justice and law, things that are against his sinful nature. That the people are "poor" implies that they are powerless to mitigate or oppose his ruthless reign. Thus such governance is compared to the vicious attacks of a lion or a bear.

28:16 This verse connects a prince's tyranny (28:15) with a lack of understanding. It does not deny the prince's intelligence, but his ability to apply that intelligence in a godly, productive way. Without an understanding of justice and truth, which would cause him to regulate his own corrupt acts, he is bound to be a tyrant who preys upon his people.

However, a just ruler, who respects others' lives and property, avoids ill-gotten gain. He is promised prolonged days, which may imply a longer reign than he would otherwise have, as well as everlasting life. Typically his people will love and support him, and he will not face the threat of rebellion among them.

Luther notes this in his comments on this verse:

> That is a large subject, and there are too many lawbooks already, although if a prince is himself no wiser than his jurists and knows no more than what is in the lawbooks, he will surely rule according to the saying in Proverbs 28: "A prince who lacks understanding will oppress many with injustice" [28:16]. For no matter how good and equitable the laws are, they all make an exception in the case of necessity, in the face of which they cannot insist upon being strictly enforced. Therefore, a prince must have the law as firmly in hand as the sword, and determine in his own mind when and where the law is to be applied strictly or with moderation, so that law may prevail at all times and in all cases, and reason may be the highest law and the master of all administration of law.[9]

28:17 This verse is a warning not to interfere with justice, which can be meted out directly by God or indirectly by him through human authorities. The

[9] AE 45:118–19.

burden carried by a murderer includes a guilty conscience and probably also the fear of knowing that he is being pursued by judicial authorities. In any event, no one is to aid and abet him, lest the helper become an accomplice to murder. If the murderer is fleeing from human authorities, one must not help him avoid justice. If he is attempting to flee from his guilty conscience, one must not help him justify or deny his sin and avoid repentance. Instead the proper course is to allow God's Law to convict him of sin so that he becomes aware that he deserves death (see Rom 3:23; 6:23), and then he can be led to the Gospel, where he alone can find relief from the burden of sin.

However, the forgiveness of sins, which God freely gives to all who repent and believe in Christ, does not necessarily mean that a criminal can escape the civil penalties prescribed by the nation's laws. There have been murderers on death row who have become Christians and have been absolved by a chaplain, but who still received capital punishment by the state before being received into eternal life.

28:18 This verse was placed after 28:17 in order to draw a contrast between the sinner who flees and the righteous person who walks with integrity. People whose life is shaped by God's Word are safe, not because they earn or deserve that safety, but because of God's promise to keep them safe.[c] No matter what vicissitudes may affect believers during this life, they can rely on their eternal safety under God's protection. The Gospel motivates their integrity, and in gratitude for God's grace, they follow his Law. However, a person whose life is contrary to God's Word can expect a sudden downfall. This proverb looks beyond judgments that may or may not come upon the wicked in this life to the sudden fall into perdition for all those who die in their sins.

(c) Prov 2:8, 11; 3:26; 4:6; 6:22, 24; 13:6; 20:22

28:19 This verse is nearly identical to 12:11. Only the last two Hebrew words are different: 12:11 ends with חֲסַר־לֵב, "lacks sense," while this proverb ends with יִשְׂבַּע־רִישׁ, "will have plenty of poverty" (cf. 28:22b). This saying commends faithfully carrying out one's vocation using God-given resources. A believer should do whatever work or service he is called to perform, using the tools and means available within proper relationships on the job or in the family, rather than pursuing unrealistic goals or sinful schemes. Although grand schemes may appear to promise riches, they lead instead to poverty. Get-rich-quick strategies such as gambling or pyramid (Ponzi) schemes[d] appeal to a person's greed but normally cause monetary loss, and spiritual poverty leads to eternal ruin (Mt 25:24–30).

(d) Cf., e.g., Prov 11:4, 15, 28; 13:11, 22; 22:16; 27:24; 28:8, 20, 22

28:20 This verse points to the many divine blessings that will come to a trustworthy and faithful believer. He will inherit inestimable blessings from God on the Last Day, and perhaps some tangible rewards already in this life—from God and from humans, such as a civil authority or an employer who recognizes his faithful diligence and promotes him.

However, the person who is in a hurry to get rich cannot be trusted. He will betray relationships in his pursuit of wealth, and he will find that he will be held accountable for his actions by God even if he evades human justice (cf. 28:17, 19b).

28:21 The first line of this proverb is similar to the second line of 24:23. This verse teaches that partiality is wrong and also that it is an easy sin to commit, since the perpetrator might think that he is simply doing what he needs to do "for a piece of bread." An underling can readily play favorites in order to gain a promotion and may justify it by rationalizing that if he gets ahead, he can better provide for his family. A leader easily shows partiality toward those who can strengthen his own position of authority. This proverb is a warning to those who exercise power not to be easily corrupted.

28:22 Being stingy is often caused by the love of money (cf. 1 Tim 6:10; Heb 13:5). This person, like the one mentioned in 28:20, is in a hurry to get rich. He does not share his bounty with those who are in need for fear that he may not be as wealthy. Instead he overlooks the fact that poverty can come upon him (as it does for the person in 28:19b) despite his miserly practices, since wealth is a gift from God and he can also withhold or remove it (see Job 1:21; cf. Lk 12:20; Acts 5:1–10).

28:23 This verse is a caution to those who would avoid administering discipline in an effort to gain favor with their children or with those over whom they exercise authority to train or supervise. In some cases a supervisor can be tempted to withhold discipline from a person who is in some way related to a higher authority, and a pastor can be tempted to avoid condemning the sins of a major donor or a friend or relative of an influential person, for example, the son of a church elder. A smooth tongue that says only good things and temporarily makes others feel good does not gain enduring respect nor God's commendation. Discipline that teaches and saves someone from trouble will eventually garner favor, probably from that person and certainly from God.

28:24 This verse focuses on the combination of two sins: failure to respect parents and theft. This combination is a grave insult to one's parents and a highly antisocial act comparable to senseless vandalism. It not only is a misuse of the property of others, but it also brings grief and shame to one's parents. Throughout Proverbs parents are held in high esteem. The person depicted in this proverb contradicts that value by claiming that his action is not sinful. Jesus condemned the Pharisees and scribes for committing a similar kind of sin (Mk 7:10–13).

28:25 This verse notes that the self-centered attitude of greed starts fights because it pits one self-interested person against another. Greed ultimately is trust in and worship of wealth—a form of idolatry (Col 3:5). Instead trust in Yahweh, that is, saving faith, is what leads to prosperity that cannot fail (see Mt 6:19–21; Lk 12:33–34).

28:26 This verse is linked to 28:25 by the catchword בּוֹטֵחַ, "a person who trusts." In this case the trust is not in God but in one's own intellect. This proverb clearly defines what a fool is: someone who trusts in his way rather than in the divine wisdom from God.

28:27 In this verse God first promises that those who have compassion for the poor will be rewarded (cf. Mt 5:7; 19:21; 26:11; Lk 14:13–14). It is also a threat that those who disregard the needy around them can expect many curses. The source of the curses is not stated. They may be curses from the poor themselves, but the word especially points to curses from the compassionate God who commands compassion.[e]

(e) See, e.g., Ex 23:11; Lev 19:10; 23:22; 25:25, 35, 39; Deut 15:7, 11

28:28 This verse is a transition saying that once again compares the wicked to the righteous. Like the first transition saying, 28:12, it warns that with wicked rulers come corruption and capriciously administered justice. Under such circumstances society's stability is compromised and righteous people are not able to contribute as much to the common good. However, when a wicked ruler perishes, the righteous can once again flourish, since the threat of injustice and persecution has passed.

The advice in this section is aptly summarized by Paul in a quotation from Menander: "bad company ruins good morals."[10] Throughout both the Old and New Testaments, Christians are encouraged to seek the company of believers and avoid those whose influence could lead them into sin, idolatry, apostasy, and eternal death. Instead they are to walk with the triune God, who graciously comes into their presence through his Word and Sacraments, Baptism and Holy Communion, to make his people his temple, with the promise of everlasting life. The apostle Paul attests this exhortation and promise with a catena of OT citations:

> Do not be unequally yoked with unbelievers. For what partnership has righteousness with lawlessness? Or what communion has light with darkness? What agreement is there between Christ and Belial? Or what portion does a believer share with an unbeliever? What agreement has the temple of God with idols? For we are the temple of the living God, as God said, "I will tabernacle in them and walk among them, and I will be their God, and they shall be my people. Therefore go out from their midst, and be separate from them, says the Lord, and touch no unclean thing; then I will welcome you, and I will be your Father, and you will be my sons and daughters, says the Lord Almighty." (2 Cor 6:14–18)

[10] 1 Cor 15:33, quoting Menander, *Thais*, 218.

Proverbs 29:1–15

Wicked People Endanger a Kingdom

Translation

29 [1]**A person who has often been disciplined yet remains stubborn**
all at once will be broken, and there will be no remedy.
[2]**When the righteous increase, a people rejoices,**
but when a wicked person rules, a people groans.
[3]**A person who loves wisdom brings joy to his father,**
but a companion of prostitutes destroys wealth.
[4]**A king brings stability to a land by justice,**
but a person who accepts bribes tears it down.
[5]**A man who flatters his neighbor**
is spreading a net for his steps.
[6]**An evil person sets a trap with sin,**
but a righteous person sings and rejoices.
[7]**A righteous person knows the legal rights of the poor,**
but a wicked person does not understand [such] knowledge.
[8]**Scoffers stir up a city,**
but wise people turn away anger.
[9]**When a wise person seeks justice from a stubborn fool,**
he rants and laughs, but there is no peace.
[10]**Bloodthirsty people hate a person of integrity,**
but upright people seek [to save] his life.
[11]**A fool vents all his emotions,**
but a wise person calmly restrains them.
[12]**[If] a ruler listens to lies,**
all his officials [will become] wicked.
[13]**A poor person and an oppressor have this in common:**
Yahweh is the one who gives light to the eyes of both of them.
[14]**[If] a king judges poor people with truth,**
his throne will be established permanently.
[15]**A rod used for discipline gives wisdom,**
but a neglected child disgraces his mother.

Textual Notes

29:1 אִ֣ישׁ תּ֭וֹכָחוֹת—For the noun תּוֹכַחַת, "warning, chastisement," see the first textual note on 1:23. In this context the construct phrase, literally, "a man of chastisements" denotes a person who has needed to *receive* discipline many times, rather than one who has meted out discipline often. Ps 39:12 (ET 39:11) clearly refers to Yahweh disciplining a sinful "man" (אִ֗ישׁ) "with chastisements" (בְּֽתוֹכָח֨וֹת). Similar is the construct phrase אִישׁ תְּרוּמוֹת, literally, "a man of contributions," that is, a man who has accepted many bribes, in 29:4. Compare אִישׁ מַכְאֹבוֹת, "a man of (many) pains," describing the Suffering Servant in Is 53:3.

מַקְשֶׁה־עֹרֶף—Literally, "one who stiffens (his) neck," this means he "remains stubborn." מַקְשֶׁה is the Hiphil (H) participle of קָשָׁה, whose Hiphil, meaning "make stiff, stiffen," is used with the object noun עֹרֶף, "neck," eleven times in the OT.[a] In every case it refers to a person who displays a stubborn attitude toward God by rejecting his Word and will.

(a) Deut 10:16; 2 Ki 17:14; Jer 7:26; 17:23; 19:15; Prov 29:1; Neh 9:16–17, 29; 2 Chr 30:8; 36:13

פֶּתַע יִשָּׁבֵר וְאֵין מַרְפֵּא׃—These two clauses are repeated verbatim from the end of 6:15. See the textual note on 6:15. Compare פֶּתַע יִשָּׁבֵר, "all at once (he) will be broken," to יִפּוֹל בְּאֶחָת, "(he) will fall all at once," in 28:18.

29:3 יְשַׂמַּח אָבִיו ... יְאַבֶּד־הוֹן׃—The parallel Piel (D) imperfects of שָׂמַח and אָבַד both have a causative meaning: literally, "(he) makes his father joyful" and "(he) causes wealth to perish." The Piel (D) of שָׂמַח is used with the object אָב also in 10:1 and 15:20, where "a wise son brings joy to [his] father." See also 17:21 and 23:24–25, where a father does (or does not) rejoice (the Qal [G] of שָׂמַח) because of his wise (or foolish) son.

וְרֹעֶה זוֹנוֹת—This is the verb רָעָה that means "associate with, be a friend to," and its participle, רֹעֶה, serves as a noun, "a companion," as also in 13:20 and 28:7. זוֹנוֹת is the plural of the feminine participle זוֹנָה, "a prostitute," whose singular is in 6:26; 7:10; 23:27.

29:4 מֶלֶךְ בְּמִשְׁפָּט יַעֲמִיד אָרֶץ—Literally, this is "a king by justice causes a land to stand/endure." For the noun מִשְׁפָּט, "justice, justification" (a synonym of "righteousness," as in 2:9), see the second textual note and the commentary on 1:3. The Hiphil (H) imperfect of עָמַד here takes on the causative sense of extending the existence of something (*HALOT*, 3 b). Thus the king "brings stability" to his realm.

וְאִישׁ תְּרוּמוֹת יֶהֶרְסֶנָּה׃—Literally, "a man of contributions" in this context probably is a leader who frequently accepts bribes or similarly engages in graft. He is the subject of the verb יֶהֶרְסֶנָּה, "(he) tears it down," whose feminine suffix ("it") refers back to אֶרֶץ ("a land") in the preceding line.

29:5 מַחֲלִיק—This participle is the Hiphil (H) of חָלַק, "make smooth, slippery," which is used to describe speech that is deceptive and seductive also in 2:16; 7:5; 28:23. See the second textual note on 2:16. In Ps 5:10 (ET 5:9) the Hiphil is used with לָשׁוֹן, "tongue," as its object, meaning "flatter." Although this proverb does not use לָשׁוֹן or any other word that directly refers to speech, most agree that it describes flattery (so *HALOT*, s.v. חלק I, Hiphil, 2).

רֶשֶׁת פּוֹרֵשׂ עַל־פְּעָמָיו׃—This is, literally, "a net he is spreading out for his steps." The suffix on פְּעָמָיו, "*his* steps," probably refers back to רֵעֵהוּ, "his neighbor," as the intended victim, although the flatterer unwittingly could be laying a trap into which he himself will fall: "his *own* steps." A similar idea is in 26:27 and 28:10. The noun רֶשֶׁת, "a net," is also in 1:17, where it refers to a trap set for birds.

29:6 בְּפֶשַׁע אִישׁ רָע מוֹקֵשׁ—Literally, this is "in/by a transgression of an evil man, a snare [is set]." The Masoretic accents indicate that אִישׁ רָע is an adjectival phrase: "an evil man." When an accent (here the conjunctive *munach*) is repeated on adjacent words, its force is stronger on the first word than on the second word, hence אִ֣ישׁ is joined more strongly (by its *munach*) to רָ֣ע than רָ֣ע is joined (by its *munach*) to מוֹקֵ֑שׁ. For the noun מוֹקֵשׁ, "a snare," see the first textual note on 12:13, where too the context has בְּפֶשַׁע, literally, "in/by a transgression."

וְ֝צַדִּ֗יק יָר֥וּן וְשָׂמֵֽחַ׃—For צַדִּיק, "righteous (person)," see "The Relationship between Wisdom and Righteousness in Proverbs" in "Wisdom in Proverbs" in the introduction. Most likely יָרוּן is an unusual Qal (G) imperfect of רָנַן, "shout" in joy/triumph (so GKC, § 67 q, and Joüon, § 82 l), but its expected form would be יָרֹן. In this context וְשָׂמֵחַ likely is the *waw* consecutive with the Qal (G) perfect of the stative verb שָׂמַח or שָׂמֵחַ, "rejoice," rather than the adjective שָׂמֵחַ, "rejoicing."

29:7 דִּ֣ין—This noun denotes a legal claim, a case in law, or a judgment (*HALOT*, 1–3). Here it is used generally of the "legal rights" of the poor (דַּלִּ֑ים), who are often deprived of their rights because their poverty renders them powerless in a society where money buys influence.

29:8 אַנְשֵׁ֣י לָ֭צוֹן יָפִ֣יחוּ קִרְיָ֑ה—For the noun לָצוֹן, see "לֵץ, 'Mocker,' and לָצוֹן, 'Mocking, Scoffing' " in "Fools in Proverbs" in the introduction. Literally, "men of scoffing" are "scoffers." Elsewhere in Proverbs the Hiphil (H) of פּוּחַ, "breathe, blow," means "utter" and usually has "lies" as the object spoken; see the first textual note on 6:19. Here the object is קִרְיָה, "a city." Here the verb could mean to "excite, inflame" the city (BDB, Hiphil, 2 c), a meaning that would be found only here. Many English translations have "set a city aflame" (RSV, ESV, NKJV, NASB), perhaps assuming that it denotes blowing on a fire to enhance combustion. However, it is preferable to render it more generally as "stir up" (NIV).

Note the alliteration between the two parallel Hiphil (H) verbs, יָפִ֣יחוּ ... יָשִׁ֣יבוּ, *yaphiḥu* ... *yashibu*, "stir up ... turn away."

29:9 אִֽישׁ־חָכָ֗ם נִ֭שְׁפָּט אֶת־אִ֣ישׁ אֱוִ֑יל—This forms the protasis of a conditional sentence: literally, "*if/when* a man who is wise litigates with a man who is a stubborn fool." The Niphal (N) of שָׁפַט usually has a reciprocal meaning (BDB, 1), which could be rendered as "go to court [as a plaintiff] with someone [a defendant] to seek justice from him." For אֱוִיל, see "אֱוִיל, 'Stubborn Fool,' and אִוֶּלֶת, 'Stupidity' " in "Fools in Proverbs" in the introduction. For the constructions here with אִישׁ, "a man," in construct with a more specific noun or substantive, see the first textual note on 6:12.

וְרָגַ֥ז וְ֝שָׂחַ֗ק—The verb רָגַז means "be agitated, excited, anxious." Since the following verb שָׂחַק, "he laughs," indicates a context of oral expression, וְרָגַז probably means "(and) he rants." The subject of both of these verbs must be אִ֣ישׁ אֱוִ֑יל, the "stubborn fool," who refuses to go through the legal process rationally or take it seriously.

וְאֵ֣ין נָֽחַת׃—The noun נַחַת (pausal: נָחַת), "rest, quiet, tranquility," describes the state of those who will be saved by God in Is 30:15. Here "there is no [אֵין] quiet/peace" while the impenitent fool rants and raves.

29:10 אַנְשֵׁ֣י דָ֭מִים יִשְׂנְאוּ־תָ֑ם—Some Hebrew nouns when plural signify a natural item in an unnatural state. The singular דָּם can denote "blood" still in a body (e.g., Gen 9:4;

Lev 17:10–14), but its plural, דָּמִים, often signifies blood that is shed. Literally, "men of shed blood" are murderous "bloodthirsty people."

The adjective תָּם, "blameless, having integrity," is used as a substantive, and it occurs in Proverbs only here. It is a synonym of the more common adjective תָּמִים, also used as a substantive, "person of integrity, blameless person," for which, see the second textual note on 2:21. Both terms are appropriate for a believer, who is justified by grace alone and enabled by God to lead a sanctified life that God deems blameless (see Eph 1:4; 5:26–27; Phil 2:15; Col 1:22).

It is also true that unbelievers who lead a life of civil righteousness, outwardly conforming to God's Law in significant ways (as, e.g., Mormons or Muslims may do), may be hated by the more grossly sinful and lawless members of society, and Christians may come to the rescue of those who are persecuted for their Law-abiding behavior or views.

וִ֝ישָׁרִ֗ים יְבַקְשׁ֥וּ נַפְשֽׁוֹ׃—Literally, this is "upright people seek [to rescue] his life." For יָשָׁר, "straight, right," used as a substantive, "upright/righteous person," a believer, see the first textual note and the commentary on 2:7. The idiom with the Piel (D) of בָּקַשׁ and the object נֶפֶשׁ, "seek a life," normally signifies a hostile action, "seek to kill someone."[1] However, since the subject of the verb is "upright people" (וִ֝ישָׁרִ֗ים), that is clearly not the meaning here. A nearly identical idiom is used in the sense of "seek to save life" in Esth 7:7. That is most probably the meaning intended in this saying.

29:11 כָּל־ר֭וּחוֹ יוֹצִ֣יא כְסִ֑יל—Literally, "all his spirit a fool causes to go out" probably means that a fool is always displaying his inner state, all thoughts that come to his mind. The translation "a fool vents all his emotions" is an attempt to say this in idiomatic English while preserving some concept of ר֫וּחַ, "spirit/wind/breath," by using the verb "vent."

וְ֝חָכָ֗ם בְּאָח֥וֹר יְשַׁבְּחֶֽנָּה׃—Literally, "but a wise man in the end calms it" is difficult. The verb שָׁבַח occurs only twice elsewhere in the OT, and both times it refers to calming the sea: the Piel (D) in Ps 89:10 (ET 89:9) and the Hiphil (H) in Ps 65:8 (ET 65:7). The Piel imperfect here, יְשַׁבְּחֶנָּה, has a feminine suffix that refers back to רוּחוֹ in the preceding clause. This could mean that the wise man calms "his [the fool's] spirit/emotions/temper," but more likely the suffix that refers to רוּחוֹ should be understood in a reflexive sense: "the wise man calms *his own* spirit/emotions." The translation above seeks to bring out the apparent meaning.

29:12 מֹ֭שֵׁל מַקְשִׁ֣יב עַל־דְּבַר־שָׁ֑קֶר—Although they lack any conditional particles, both this clause and the first clause of 29:14 form the protasis of a conditional sentence, "if … ," and the second clause of each verse is the apodosis, "(then) … will …" (see GKC, § 159 i). The first clauses of both verses have the same construction: a substantive (here the participle מֹשֵׁל, "a ruler") followed by a participle that functions verbally

---

[1] See BDB, s.v. בָּקַשׁ, Piel, 2 a, which wrongly includes Prov 29:10 as having this meaning. The idiom is used thirty times in this sense: Ex 4:19; 1 Sam 20:1; 22:23 (twice); 23:15; 25:29; 2 Sam 4:8; 16:11; 1 Ki 19:10, 14; Jer 4:30; 11:21; 19:7, 9; 21:7; 22:25; 34:20–21; 38:16; 44:30 (twice); 46:26; 49:37; Pss 35:4; 38:13 (ET 38:12); 40:15 (ET 40:14); 54:5 (ET 54:3); 63:10 (ET 63:9); 70:3 (ET 70:2); 86:14.

(Joüon, § 121 k, including note 1, referring to 29:14). Here the Hiphil (H) participle מַקְשִׁיב, "listens to, pays attention to," implies that the ruler not only hears, but also gives credence to false reports and takes action based on believing them. The construct phrase דְּבַר־שָׁקֶר, "a word of falsehood," means "a lie" (Waltke-O'Connor, § 9.7a, example 2). Since the participle מַקְשִׁיב indicates habitual or repeated action, the construct phrase is translated as plural, "lies" (not just one lie heard at one time).

כָּל־מְשָׁרְתָיו רְשָׁעִים׃—This is a nominal sentence: "all his assistants (are) wicked." However, as the apodosis of the conditional sentence begun with the preceding clause, it is best translated with the verb in the future tense: "all his officials *will become* wicked." This is supported by the parallel construction in 29:14, whose second clause has an imperfect verb, יִכּוֹן, "*will be* established."

29:13 רָשׁ וְאִישׁ תְּכָכִים נִפְגָּשׁוּ—For רָשׁ, "poor (person)," see the first textual note on 10:4. The noun תֹּךְ, "injury, oppression," occurs in the singular thrice elsewhere in the OT, but this is the only instance of the plural. The construct phrase אִישׁ תְּכָכִים, literally, "a man of oppressions," denotes an "oppressor" (BDB, s.v. תֹּךְ, under the root תכך). For the Niphal (N) verb נִפְגָּשׁוּ meaning "have something in common," see the first textual note on 22:2.

מֵאִיר־עֵינֵי שְׁנֵיהֶם יְהוָה׃—Literally, this is "the one who enlightens the eyes of the two of them (is) Yahweh." מֵאִיר is the Hiphil (H) participle of אוֹר, "to be light," whose Qal is used in 4:18b. The Hiphil has a causative sense, "enlighten, provide light, make [something] shine." For שְׁנֵיהֶם, "the two of them," translated as "both of them," see the second textual note on 17:15.

29:14 מֶלֶךְ שׁוֹפֵט בֶּאֱמֶת דַּלִּים—As in 29:12, here too a participle functions verbally in the protasis of a conditional sentence: "[if] a king judges [שׁוֹפֵט] poor people in/with truth." For אֱמֶת, "truth, faithfulness," see the first textual note on 8:7.

כִּסְאוֹ לָעַד יִכּוֹן׃—"His throne for ever is established," the noun כִּסֵּא, "throne," is the subject of יִכּוֹן, the Niphal (N) imperfect of כּוּן, "be established," also in 16:12 and 25:5, both of which promised that a throne would be established "by/with righteousness." לָעַד, the preposition לְ and עַד, "for ever, eternity," is also in the promise in 12:19 that "a truthful lip is established forever." This proverb suggests that any leader who governs faithfully under God could be blessed with a long reign. Its literal meaning ("forever") is fulfilled by the everlasting reign of Christ the King over God's people, redeemed by his grace. See 2 Sam 7:13, 16; Is 9:5–6 (ET 9:6–7); Lk 1:32–33.

29:15 שֵׁבֶט וְתוֹכַחַת יִתֵּן חָכְמָה—The compound subject, literally, "a rod and correction," consists of a masculine noun (שֵׁבֶט) and a feminine noun (תּוֹכַחַת), but the verb יִתֵּן ("*gives* wisdom") is masculine singular, not plural. Therefore the two nouns may be intended as a hendiadys: "a rod of [used for] discipline" or "a correcting rod." שֵׁבֶט denotes a "rod" for punishment also in 10:13; 13:24; 22:15; 23:13–14; 26:3.

מְשֻׁלָּח מֵבִישׁ אִמּוֹ׃—The masculine Pual (Dp) participle מְשֻׁלָּח, "be sent away, set free," here means "unrestrained" or "left to himself" (see *HALOT*, s.v. שׁלח I, Pual, 1 b; similar are KJV, RSV, NIV, ESV). A son who "gets his own way" (NASB) is "neglected" when he does not receive proper discipline and guidance. According to the first clause of the verse, a person who is never disciplined will never gain wisdom. Earlier proverbs speak of a son who "brings/causes shame" using the Hiphil (H) participle מֵבִישׁ

(10:5; 17:2; 19:26). A wayward son brings grief to "his mother" (אִמּוֹ) in 10:1 (cf., e.g., 1:8; 15:20; 23:25).

Commentary

These sayings begin with the central proverb in Proverbs 28–29, two chapters that form a section within the larger collection of proverbs by Solomon that were copied by King Hezekiah's men (Prov 25:1–29:27).[2]

29:1 This verse is a warning about stubbornness and rejecting discipline. It is placed in the center of chapters 28–29 as advice about not rejecting the divine guidance offered in these proverbs. The stubbornness to which this proverb refers is specifically a rejection of God's Word and guidance (see the second textual note on 29:1). The implication of the second line is that God will mete out judgment on such a person and that God's everlasting punishment cannot be undone. There will be no "healing" (מַרְפֵּא) or remedy for those who die in unbelief, since they will not participate in the bodily resurrection to eternal life, which is the full meaning of מַרְפֵּא, "healing" (see the second textual note and the commentary on 4:22 and the commentary on 12:18). Instead the stubbornly impenitent will be raised and cast—body and soul—into everlasting torment (7:27; 9:18; Mt 5:29–30; 10:28). This threat of extreme punishment uses fear to dampen a stubborn person's willful rejection of God's will.

Note that the second line of this saying is identical to the second line of 6:15.

29:2 This verse is another transition proverb that contrasts righteous and wicked people (as are 28:12, 28; 29:16).[3] The blessing of righteous people lifts up entire nations. Not only do their godly lives lead to honesty and civic virtues, but also, more importantly, their righteousness before God through his grace leads to rejoicing before God in thanks for his mercy toward his people. However, one wicked ruler can bring misery to a people as he sponsors apostasy (as did many of Israel's kings), causes injustice, and allows corruption to spread through society.

29:3–15 These verses form a subsection of proverbs that speak of the necessity of possessing wisdom in order to avoid foolish and evil behaviors and people. This advice is appropriate for all believers, but is especially important for godly kings and leaders who seek to govern well on God's behalf. The words חָכָם, "wise (person)" (29:8–9, 11), or חָכְמָה, "wisdom" (29:3, 15), are concentrated here and occur five times in these thirteen sayings. In contrast, words from the root חכם ("wise, wisdom") are found only seven times in the rest of chapters 25–29 (25:12; 26:5, 12, 16; 27:11; 28:11, 26).

---

[2] See further the excursus "The Organization of Solomon's Proverbs Copied by Hezekiah's Men (Prov 25:1–29:27)" in the commentary on Proverbs 25. See also the commentary on 27:23–27, which serves as the introduction for chapters 28–29.

[3] See the excursus "The Organization of Solomon's Proverbs Copied by Hezekiah's Men (Prov 25:1–29:27)" in the commentary on Proverbs 25.

This subsection is enclosed by two sayings that describe how wisdom or its absence affects the relationship between a child and a parent: a wise child brings joy to his father in 29:3, while an undisciplined, wisdom-less child disgraces his mother in 29:15. Moreover, two of the three central proverbs in this section mention "wise person(s)" (חֲכָמִים in 29:8 and חָכָם in 29:9). And all three central proverbs begin with a plural or singular form of the word אִישׁ, "man, person," in construct. They are arranged chiastically, since the plural begins 29:8, the singular begins 29:9, and the plural begins 29:10:

אַנְשֵׁי לָצוֹן, literally, "men/people of scoffing" (29:8)
אִישׁ־חָכָם, literally, "a man/person who is wise" (29:9)
אַנְשֵׁי דָמִים, literally, "men/people of shed blood" (29:10)

29:3 This verse includes a contrast. Joy comes to a godly father whose offspring love wisdom, which especially means that the children believe the Gospel of the Savior.[4] Bitter disappointment comes from seeing one's son frequent prostitutes, a sin that squanders the family wealth and inheritance, as also in Lk 15:30 (cf. Lk 15:13). This unfaithful behavior destroys God's physical blessings (cf. Prov 6:26) and shows a spiritual rejection of his eternal blessings.

This saying is joined to the transitional saying in 29:2 by the repetition of the verb שָׂמַח, whose Qal (G) is in 29:2, "rejoices," and whose Piel (D) is in 29:3, "brings joy."

29:4 This verse notes the blessings of justice. When the government administers justice according to God's Word, a country is stable and the church is not hindered from carrying out its mission to proclaim the Gospel faithfully. The people can invest their time and money in the church and in other worthy projects and charities without fear of being defrauded or having the fruit of their labors capriciously confiscated. Moreover, they can count on social stability that affirms civil righteousness and punishes immoral acts. However, corruption in government officials makes a sham of all economic investment and all morality. Unfaithful leadership diverts a church from carrying out the Great Commission (Mt 28:19–20).

29:5 This verse is a warning about flattery. False praise in an attempt to influence someone is just as destructive as bribery (29:4b). The second line is ambiguous as to the prey for whom the flatterer is spreading a net: for the person he flatters or for himself. Perhaps the ambiguity is intended to evoke both possibilities. One can flatter someone and trap him when he becomes overconfident and prideful. However, one's flattery can backfire and entrap the flatterer when it reveals his insincerity and evil motives.

29:6 This verse shares a common concept with 29:5, which has רֶשֶׁת, "a net," by its use of the synonym מוֹקֵשׁ, "a trap." It also has same ambiguity as

---

4 See "Wisdom in Proverbs" in the introduction. See also the commentary on 1:1–7; 3:13–20; 8:22–31; 30:1b–10; and the excursus "Proverbs 8, Wisdom, Christology, and the Arian Controversy" in the commentary on chapter 8.

the previous proverb: does the evil person's sin entrap others or himself? As in 29:5, the divine intent probably is both. This proverb has two possible applications. It may say that an evil person commits the iniquity of trying to trap others in sin and bring them misfortune, whereas a righteous person rejoices in the salvation and success of others. Or it may observe that a wicked person traps himself with his own sin (see 1:17; 26:27; 28:10; Jn 8:34), whereas a righteous person can sing and rejoice without fear of sin's power, because God has rescued him from bondage to sin and death (Rom 6:16–22).

29:7 This verse identifies the righteous person with a godly attitude: concern and sympathetic knowledge of the plight of poor people (see Pss 41:2 [ET 41:1]; 72:4, 12; Rom 15:26; Gal 2:10). Wicked people are alienated from God and cannot possess this knowledge.

29:8 This verse contains advice that a ruler can apply as he chooses what type of people to place in positions of power to enable God's people to be peaceful and productive. Those who mock the concept of morality and obligations and have no respect for godly behavior only stir up problems. These people are to be avoided (cf. Rom 16:17–20). However, wise people "turn away anger." They bring calm to heated disputes and seek peace, harmony, and mutual forgiveness. They do this because they know the grace and mercy of God shown to them, and they seek to bring it to others. An example of a prior historical fulfillment of this saying by Solomon is when ungodly scoffers brought fiery divine judgment on the city of Sodom, but God promised to avert his wrath from the city if righteous people could be found in it (Genesis 18–19).

29:9 This verse is paired with 29:8 by חָכָם, "wise person," and also serves as a corrective for a misplaced application of 29:8 that would understand the wise person as seeking peace at the expense of justice and truth. This proverb observes that a fool whose folly is firmly rooted in his heart will allow no one peace when he is forced to account for his unjust actions. Some have read this as a proverb that discourages taking a fool to court.[5] Instead it is a warning as to what to expect when a fool is called to account for his actions. It will be an unpleasant but necessary task.

29:10 This verse helps define "a person of integrity" (תָּם) by speaking of those who seek to destroy him and those who try to preserve his life. Integrity involves not only doing what is right but also opposing what is wrong, even in the face of an imminent threat to one's own life (see Mk 8:35; 10:29–30). Upright people appreciate such a person of integrity and show their own integrity by providing help and aid when it would be easy to look the other way. See, for example, how upright people saved the lives of Jeremiah (Jer 38:8–13) and Paul (Acts 9:20–25), and how the Israelite spies were saved by justified Rahab (Joshua 2; Heb 11:31; James 2:25).

---

5 Ross, "Proverbs," 1113; Toy, *Proverbs*, 509.

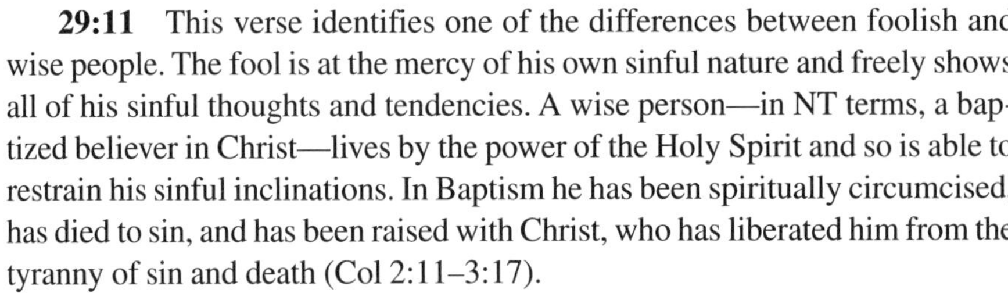

29:11 This verse identifies one of the differences between foolish and wise people. The fool is at the mercy of his own sinful nature and freely shows all of his sinful thoughts and tendencies. A wise person—in NT terms, a baptized believer in Christ—lives by the power of the Holy Spirit and so is able to restrain his sinful inclinations. In Baptism he has been spiritually circumcised, has died to sin, and has been raised with Christ, who has liberated him from the tyranny of sin and death (Col 2:11–3:17).

(b) E.g., Num 6:25; Pss 31:17 (ET 31:16); 67:2 (ET 67:1); 80:4, 8, 20 (ET 80:3, 7, 19); 118:27; 119:135; cf. Dan 12:3; Mt 13:43; 2 Cor 4:6; Eph 5:14

29:12 This verse reminds those in power that they set the tone for all activities that happen under them. If a ruler listens to deception and flattery, his officials will adjust their behavior accordingly. His bad character and decisions have evil repercussions for his staff and his people. His administrators, who take their cue from their leader, eventually will become just as corrupt as he is.

29:13 Earlier proverbs speak of the "light" (the noun אוֹר) that God gives through his Word, enabling believers to see and walk on the righteous path (4:18; 6:23; 13:9a; cf. 16:15). For Yahweh to cause light to shine on someone (the Hiphil [H] of the verb אוֹר) usually refers to him showing grace, saving, and bestowing eternal life.[b] In contrast, the "lamp" of the wicked will be snuffed out (13:9b; cf. Rev 18:23). Therefore this proverb's statement that Yahweh gives light for the oppressor as well as the poor probably describes the work of the triune God as Creator (cf. Gen 1:14–18; Prov 3:19; 8:27–28), life-giver, and preserver of the world. He causes his sun to shine on the both the wicked and the righteous (Jer 31:35; Ps 136:7–8; Eccl 11:7; Mt 5:45). His goal in so showing his goodness and clemency is to lead all to repentance and faith (Rom 2:4; 2 Pet 3:9).

This verse notes that regardless of status or power in this life, all people are subject to God. This saying serves as a reminder to the king that he must be impartial when dealing with his subjects, because all of them are creatures of God.

29:14 This verse builds on the theme of 29:13 by encouraging justice and truth when dealing with poor people. A judge is neither to favor the poor because he feels sorry for them nor to favor the powerful simply because they can use their influence to help him (Ex 23:3, 6; Lev 19:15).

29:15 This verse matches 29:3 with its emphasis on wisdom and parents. Whereas 29:3 speaks of a child who loves wisdom, this proverb notes that discipline and punishment are necessary to teach wisdom. Because of the totally depraved sinful nature that every person has from the moment of conception (Gen 6:5; Psalm 51; Rom 3:9–20) and that stubbornly persists even in believers until natural death (Romans 7), all people, including children, need correction and the threat of punishment according to God's Law in order to restrain and destroy their sinful inclinations and self-righteous attitude. Even children who are not baptized and have not been led to faith in Christ can at times be kept from disgracing their parents outwardly because of the Law's civic use in threatening punishment. This threat discourages and curbs shameful behavior.

A child—whether young or now an adult—who does not receive this necessary application of the Law will disgrace his believing mother because the Law was not used to show him his sin and drive him to the only solution for sin: God's forgiveness and justifying grace in Jesus Christ. It is the Gospel that gives the true wisdom of God in Christ.[6] The concern of Prov 29:15 is also the concern of Paul's admonition: "Fathers, do not provoke undue anger in your children, but bring them up in the discipline and instruction of the Lord" (Eph 6:4). Examples of Christian mothers who rightly could have been proud of the children they raised in the faith are Lois and Eunice, the grandmother and mother of Timothy, who was taught the Scriptures from infancy (2 Tim 1:5; 3:15–17).[7]

---

[6] See "Wisdom in Proverbs" and "Law and Gospel in Proverbs" in the introduction. For Christ as the Wisdom of God, see also the commentary on 1:1–7; 3:13–20; 8:22–31; 30:1–10; and the excursus "Proverbs 8, Wisdom, Christology, and the Arian Controversy" in the commentary on chapter 8.

[7] Christian artwork traditionally shows young Timothy being taught the Scriptures by both his grandmother Lois and by his mother, Eunice. A stained glass window that shows these two Christian mothers instructing the child Timothy with the Scriptures is featured in the Chapel of Saint Timothy and Saint Titus on the campus of Concordia Seminary, St. Louis, Missouri.

Proverbs 29:16–27

Final Advice for Kings and Leaders

Translation

29 **[16]When wicked people increase, sin increases,**
but righteous people will see their downfall.
[17]Discipline your son, and he will give you rest,
and he will give delight to your soul.
[18]Without a prophetic vision, a people is unrestrained,
but the person who follows [God's] instruction is blessed.
[19]A servant cannot be disciplined with words,
although he understands, [he will show] no response.
[20]Have you seen a person who is hasty with his words?
There is more hope for a fool than for him.
[21][If] a person pampers his servant from the time he is young,
later on he will have grief.
[22]A hothead stirs up a fight,
and a quick-tempered person [commits] many sins.
[23]A person's haughtiness will humble him,
but a humble spirit will attain honor.
[24]A person who shares with a thief hates his own life.
He hears a curse but does not reveal [anything].
[25]Fear of a person sets a trap,
but a person who trusts in Yahweh will be secure.
[26]Many people seek a ruler's favor,
but a person gets justice from Yahweh.
[27]An unjust person is a disgusting thing to righteous people,
but a person whose way is upright is a disgusting thing to a wicked person.

Textual Notes

29:16 בִּרְב֣וֹת רְ֭שָׁעִים יִרְבֶּה־פָּ֑שַׁע—The plural substantive רְשָׁעִים, "wicked people," is the subject of the Qal (G) infinitive construct רְבוֹת, from רָבָה, "to increase," with the preposition בְּ in a temporal sense, "when." Then the noun פֶּשַׁע (in pause: פָּ֑שַׁע) is the subject of the Qal imperfect of the same verb, יִרְבֶּה. Similar to "sin increases" is the phrase רַב־פָּֽשַׁע (literally, "abundant of sin") in 29:22, with the adjective רַב, which is cognate to the verb רָבָה here, and the same pausal form of the noun פָּשַׁע.

וְ֝צַדִּיקִ֗ים בְּמַפַּלְתָּ֥ם יִרְאֽוּ׃—The noun מַפֶּלֶת, "downfall" (from the verb נָפַל), can refer to the "ruin" or "overthrow" of a group of people. Its plural suffix refers back to רְשָׁעִים, the "wicked people" in the first clause. It has the preposition בְּ to form the idiom רָאָה בְּ, which can mean "triumphantly to look at" a defeated foe, for believers "to see" divine justice carried out through the punishment of those who persecuted God's people (see BDB, s.v. רָאָה, Qal, 8 a (6)).

29:17 מַעֲדַנִּים—"Delight" is a plural noun. It can mean "delicacies" (Gen 49:20; Lam 4:5). Here the plural is employed to indicate the multiple times that a disciplined son will delight his parents.

29:18 חָזוֹן—"Prophetic vision" is a noun that frequently refers to God's explicit verbal revelation of his Word (whether or not accompanied by a visual revelation) to a prophet (e.g., Is 1:1; Obad 1; Nah 1:1; Dan 8:1; 1 Chr 17:15). The Hebrew term is *never* used to mean "vision" in the human sense of a person's envisioned goals, aspirations, persuasive powers, or imaginative leadership, even though this proverb has often been misinterpreted along those lines.

יִפָּרַע עָם—The Qal (G) of פָּרַע has the negative meaning "to ignore, neglect" divine Wisdom and discipline in 1:25; 8:33; 13:18; 15:32. Here the Niphal (N) has a similar passive meaning: the "people" (עָם) are "let loose" in the negative sense of "be unrestrained" by God's Word, that is, they feel free to violate God's Word, since there is no prophetic revelation of it, and to indulge in all kinds of sinful behaviors. Similar is the meaning of the Qal in Ex 32:25 (twice), where Aaron led Israel into idolatrous worship of the golden calf, apparently accompanied by gluttony and sexual sins (Ex 32:6).

וְשֹׁמֵר תּוֹרָה אַשְׁרֵהוּ׃—This is the opposite of the situation depicted in the first clause. Here a person or a people "keeps Torah" by following the teaching or instruction of God, especially Scripture. For תּוֹרָה, see the second textual note on 1:8 and also, for example, 3:1. אַשְׁרֵהוּ is defectively spelled for אַשְׁרֵיהוּ, "blessed is he." For beatitudes with אַשְׁרֵי, see the first textual note and the commentary on 3:13. Prov 8:32 too uses אַשְׁרֵי with שָׁמַר to pronounce a blessing on those who "keep, follow" the ways of divine Wisdom.

29:19 וְאֵין מַעֲנֶה׃—This is, literally, "there is no answer." Although the noun מַעֲנֶה (as in 15:1, 23; 16:1) has no suffix, the context implies that it is the "servant" (עָבֶד, pausal of עֶבֶד) who shows no response.

29:20 חָזִיתָ אִישׁ אָץ בִּדְבָרָיו—A similar unmarked question begins 26:12. See the first textual note there.

תִּקְוָה לִכְסִיל מִמֶּנּוּ׃—See the second textual note on 26:12, which has the identical clause.

29:21 The immediately preceding and following proverbs (29:19–20, 22) are entirely negative, including the description of the incorrigible servant in 29:19. Therefore it is most likely that this saying about a servant is negative too, although some English versions render it positively or even as a promise.

מְפַנֵּק מִנֹּעַר עַבְדּוֹ—The Piel (D) participle מְפַנֵּק is of the verb פָּנַק, a hapax legomenon in the OT. However, its Piel is attested in Rabbinic Hebrew, and Pael (D) cognates are in Aramaic (פְּנַק) and Syriac (ܦܢܩ). Most likely it has a negative connotation and means "pamper, indulge." However, in Rabbinic Hebrew it can mean "treat as a freeman" or "treat tenderly" (see Jastrow, s.v. פָּנַק, Piel), as reflected in KJV: "he that delicately bringeth up his servant." In any case the object of the participle is עַבְדּוֹ, "his servant." "From youth" (נֹעַר plus מִן) must refer to the childhood of the servant, not of the pamperer.

וְאַחֲרִיתוֹ יִהְיֶה מָנוֹן׃—The noun מָנוֹן is a hapax legomenon whose meaning is uncertain. Rabbinic interpretation of this verse understood מָנוֹן to mean "manager, executor" (Jastrow, s.v. מָנוֹן). *HALOT* and *DCH* cite the same word in Sirach 47:23 and give "insolent" among other possible meanings.[1] Most English translations take this clause as a promise: "in the end" the servant will be "his heir" (RSV, ESV) or even his "son" (KJV, NKJV, NASB). However, this clause may instead mean, literally, "(in) his end, he will be (a source of) grief" (similar is NIV). This is supported by the LXX, which diverges somewhat from the MT: "whoever lives in luxury from his youth will become a slave, and in the end he will have grief over himself [ὀδυνηθήσεται ἐφ' ἑαυτῷ]." Some propose emending מָנוֹן to מָדוֹן, "strife," which is common in Proverbs (e.g., 15:18).

The suffix on אַחֲרִית, "end, later time," may refer to עַבְדּוֹ, "his servant," so וְאַחֲרִיתוֹ would refer to the servant's adulthood, in contrast to his "youth" (נֹעַר in the preceding clause). Or the suffix could refer to מְפַנֵּק, in which case וְאַחֲרִיתוֹ refers to the old age of the pamperer. In any event, the feminine noun אַחֲרִית cannot be the subject of the masculine verb יִהְיֶה. Its subject could be עַבְדּוֹ, "his servant," or the noun מָנוֹן, "there will be grief (?)."

29:22 אִישׁ־אַף יְגָרֶה מָדוֹן—This is the same as the first line of 15:18 except that this substitutes אַף, "anger," for the synonym חֵמָה, "rage." "A man of anger" (אִישׁ־אַף) is one who is prone to fits of anger, a "hothead," the same translation used in 15:18.

וּבַעַל חֵמָה רַב־פָּשַׁע׃— Literally, "a possessor/master of rage" is "a quick-tempered person." See the second textual note on 1:17. Literally, "abundant of transgression/sin" (רַב־פָּשַׁע) means he commits many sins.

29:23 גַּאֲוַת אָדָם תַּשְׁפִּילֶנּוּ—The feminine noun גַּאֲוָה, "arrogance," is also in 14:3. Here it is the subject of the feminine Hiphil (H) imperfect תַּשְׁפִּילֶנּוּ, whose masculine suffix refers to אָדָם, literally, "the arrogance of a man will make him low, bring him down" or "humble him." The verb is cognate to the adjective in the next clause.

וּשְׁפַל־רוּחַ יִתְמֹךְ כָּבוֹד׃—The construct phrase שְׁפַל־רוּחַ, literally, "low of spirit," occurs also in Is 57:15 and probably also Prov 16:19 (see the textual note there). The adjective שָׁפָל, "low, humble," is cognate to the verb in the preceding clause. The construct phrase serves as the subject of the verb: "(a person with) a humble spirit will take hold of/attain glory." The imperfect of תָּמַךְ, "take hold of, attain," is used with the object כָּבוֹד, "glory, honor," also in 11:16, with "a gracious woman" as the subject.

29:24 שׂוֹנֵא נַפְשׁוֹ—Literally, "(one who) hates his own life," this idiom with the reflexive use of נֶפֶשׁ could also be rendered as "hates himself" (see Joüon, § 146 k).

29:25 חֶרְדַּת אָדָם יִתֵּן מוֹקֵשׁ—The construct phrase חֶרְדַּת אָדָם has an objective genitive: literally, "trembling of (at) a man" means "undue fear of offending or angering another person." This clause is a rare example where the verb does not agree with the noun in construct (the feminine noun חֲרָדָה) but instead with the genitive noun (the masculine אָדָם), since the verb is masculine, יִתֵּן, "gives/causes/sets" a snare (see Joüon, § 150 n). For the noun מוֹקֵשׁ, "a snare, trap," see the first textual note on 12:13.

---

[1] *HALOT* also gives "arrogant" and "rebellious," while *DCH* gives "weak" and "pained" as two other possible homographs spelled מָנוֹן.

Proverbs repeatedly enjoins the "fear of Yahweh" (e.g., 1:7), and fear of people should not be allowed to compromise or erode one's trust in God (see the next clause) or obedience to his Word. Jesus exhorts his disciples to fear God but not to fear man or human persecution, since such fear could lead a person to deny Christ and so be denied before God (Lk 12:4–12). The second clause stands in antonymous parallelism to the first clause: the opposite of, and antidote for, fearing people is faith in God.

וּבוֹטֵחַ בַּיהוָה יְשֻׂגָּב׃—The participial phrase וּבוֹטֵחַ בַּיהוָה, "and one who trusts in Yahweh," is also in 16:20. The participle is the subject of the Pual (Dp) imperfect יְשֻׂגָּב, "*be set* (securely) *on high*" (BDB). Elsewhere in Proverbs שָׂגַב occurs only in the Niphal (N): in 18:10 the meaning is similar to the Pual here, and in 18:11 the participle functions as an adjective meaning "high."

29:26 רַבִּים מְבַקְשִׁים פְּנֵי־מוֹשֵׁל—Literally, this is "many are seeking the face of a ruler." The Hebrew idiom "seek" (the Piel [D] of בָּקַשׁ) someone's "face" (פָּנִים) means to seek his favor. It is often used to describe seeking God's favor.[a]

(a) E.g., Hos 5:15; Pss 24:6; 27:8; 105:4; 1 Chr 16:11; 2 Chr 7:14

וּמֵיְהוָה מִשְׁפַּט־אִישׁ׃—As in 29:25, the second, antonymous clause of the verse gives the God-pleasing counterpart to the anthropocentric first clause. Literally, "from Yahweh (comes) the justice/justification of a man" shows that he is the true Ruler whose favor people should seek as their highest priority (see Mt 6:33). For the noun מִשְׁפָּט, "justice, justification," which is a synonym of "righteousness" (as in Prov 2:9), see the second textual note and the commentary on 1:3.

29:27 תּוֹעֲבַת צַדִּיקִים אִישׁ עָוֶל—In Proverbs תּוֹעֵבָה usually is in construct with "Yahweh" as the one who considers something to be "a disgusting thing." See the excursus " 'Disgusting Thing' (תּוֹעֵבָה) in Solomon's Proverbs" in the commentary on Proverbs 11. Here it is in construct with צַדִּיקִים, "righteous people," who show the same disgust toward unrighteousness as Yahweh. The construct phrase אִישׁ עָוֶל, literally, "man of unrighteousness," has an adjectival genitive: "unjust person."

יְשַׁר־דָּרֶךְ׃—For the adjective יָשָׁר, "straight, right," used as a substantive, "upright, righteous person," see the first textual note and the commentary on 2:7. This construct phrase, literally, "upright of (in respect to his) way," relates to the theme of the "way, path." See the excursus "The Metaphor of the Path in Solomon's Wisdom" in the commentary on Proverbs 10.

Commentary

This section concludes the proverbs by Solomon that were collected and arranged by men who served under righteous King Hezekiah. Like the rest of chapters 28–29, these proverbs are especially relevant for rulers and administrators as they seek to lead and govern in accord with God's will and Word. See the excursus "The Organization of Solomon's Proverbs Copied by Hezekiah's Men (Prov 25:1–29:27)" in the commentary on Proverbs 25, and the commentary on 27:23–27, which serves as the introduction for chapters 28–29.

29:16 This verse is the last transition proverb in the set of proverbs that begins in 28:1 and ends in 29:27. It is a reminder to those in authority that when wicked attitudes and behaviors are allowed to increase and are not reprimanded by punishment and discipline, they multiply. Often it seems to believers that society, and perhaps even the church, will continue the spiral of increasing sin with no end in sight.

However, the second line in this proverb promises that righteous people eventually will see the downfall of wicked people. Yet it does not say how or when. This promise of God is ultimately fulfilled in God's final judgment upon the return of Jesus Christ. Only then will he fully answer the prayers of his oppressed people, deliver them from all the effects of sin, death, and wickedness (1 Cor 15:35–58; 2 Thess 1:5–10; Rev 6:9–11), and raise them to everlasting life in the new paradise with the "tree of life."[2]

29:17–26 These verses are sayings arranged mainly by catchwords. Elsewhere in Proverbs catchwords usually occur in adjacent proverbs,[3] but only three of these catchword links are in consecutive sayings. Instead these sayings mainly are connected by catchwords in alternate proverbs:

- יַסֵּר, "discipline" (29:17), and יִוָּסֶר, "be disciplined" (29:19), both forms of the verb יָסַר
- לְנַפְשֶׁךָ, "to your soul" (29:17), and נַפְשׁוֹ, "his own life" (29:24)
- בְּאֵין, literally, "when there is no" (29:18), and וְאֵין, literally, "and there is no" (29:19)
- חָזוֹן, "prophetic vision" (29:18), and חָזִיתָ, "have you seen?" (29:20), both words from the root חזה
- בִּדְבָרִים, "with words" (29:19), and בִּדְבָרָיו, "with his words" (29:20)
- עֶבֶד, "a servant" (29:19), and עַבְדּוֹ, "his servant" (29:21)
- אִישׁ, "a man/person" (29:20), and אִישׁ, "a man/person" (29:22)
- אָדָם, "a man/person" (29:23), and אָדָם, "a man/person" (29:25)
- בַּיהוָה, "in Yahweh" (29:25), and וּמֵיְהוָה, "but … from Yahweh" (29:26)

Note that every saying in this section except 29:24 is connected to another saying that is either adjacent to it or has one intervening proverb. While these connections by means of catchwords do not yield a tight, regular pattern, they do give a semblance of unity to this small collection of sayings. At the same time they also prompt the reader to draw other connections within this collection and to proverbs outside of it with the same or similar words. Thus in keeping with the tradition of wisdom throughout Proverbs, the reader is expected to make a three-dimensional web of connections among the wisdom sayings while also noticing the cohesion among a small groups of sayings.

---

[2] For the tree of life, see 3:18 (also 11:30; 13:12; 15:4); Ezek 47:1–12; Rev 2:7; chapters 21–22. In Proverbs "life" and "live" often have the eschatological sense of everlasting life by God's grace. See, for example, the noun חַיִּים, "life," in 3:2, 18, 22; 4:10, 13, 22–23; 12:28. For the verb חָיָה, "to live," see 4:4; 7:2; 9:6; 15:27. The promise of the bodily resurrection is also latent in the proverbs that speak of God bestowing "healing" (מַרְפֵּא). See the second textual note and the commentary on 4:22 and the commentary on 12:18, as well as Ezek 47:12; Rev 22:1–2.

[3] See, for example, the commentary on 10:13; 11:3–11; 18:11, 19, 20; 19:7, 15, 21; 20:1; 21:2, 28, 31; 28:26.

29:17 This verse speaks of the blessings that disciplined children will bring to their parents. While other proverbs hint at this (10:1; 15:20), this is the only proverb that directly connects parental discipline to its benefits for the parents who must administer it, especially a "son" who will bring delight to his father (the three Hebrew pronouns ךָ-, translated as "your" and "you," are masculine singular, pointing to the father). This encouragement to discipline motivates parents through the promise given here, rather than through the threat of harm to the child (19:18) or grief to the parents if they fail to discipline (17:25; 19:13). The promise is cast in the future tense (the Hebrew imperfects translated as "he *will* give you rest … he *will* give delight"), which implies that parents may have to wait (years or perhaps decades) until they see the full benefits of the godly way in which they raised their children. See 22:6 and the commentary on 29:15 (cf. Deut 6:6–7).

29:18 This verse observes the necessity of God's revelation for keeping order in society as well as preserving God's people in faith. The "prophetic vision" (חָזוֹן) received and preached by prophets usually had a strong initial emphasis on condemnation according to God's Law.[4] Without the order imposed on people through the threat of punishment for those who transgress God's Law, a nation is unrestrained and the people spiral downward into ever-increasing sin (29:16).

The second line of this proverb, however, clearly extends beyond the Law to include all of God's revelation, both Law and Gospel.[5] The "instruction" of God (תּוֹרָה, *torah*, as in 1:8) confers divine wisdom (1:2–7), "grace" (1:9), and the Holy Spirit (1:23). God's gifts of "blessing" and "life" are found in the Torah, which promises them to all who believe and keep it (Deut 30:15–20). Theologically, these promises are Gospel, the Good News of God's forgiveness with the eschatological promise of his richest blessings by grace alone. The person who follows God's instruction—who trusts in him (Prov 29:25) according to his Word—receives these promises through faith alone (Pss 86:5; 103:2–5). The believer lays claim to the promised blessings already now, even though the Gospel promises will not be fully realized until the Last Day.

29:19 This verse speaks of a servant who must be disciplined more firmly than with words because he fails to respond to warnings. Eli's sons failed to listen to their father's warnings (1 Sam 2:22–25), and later God judged the father for not taking stronger measures to restrain his sons (1 Sam 3:13). Like children, servants need discipline that is sufficient to compel them to do what is right, or else they will never learn to be self-disciplined.

---

4 For example, much of Isaiah 1–39; most of Ezekiel 1–32; and almost all of the book of Amos consist of prophecies of condemnation against Israel and the surrounding nations, but the latter parts of these books have powerful Gospel promises (Isaiah 40–66; Ezekiel 33–48; Amos 9:11–15). The OT prophets have the same dynamic of condemning Law and comforting Gospel that characterizes Christian (and notably Lutheran) theology and biblical preaching.

5 See "Law and Gospel in Proverbs" in the introduction.

29:20 This verse is similar to 26:12. The second lines of these proverbs are identical to each other. The first lines are syntactically and morphologically identical, but three of the four vocabulary words are different.

This proverb calls the reader to contemplate his observations in life and remember seeing people who speak hastily without thinking of the meaning or consequence of their words. Such people are even more incorrigible than a fool,[6] who would be hopeless without the possibility that he may be brought to repentance and faith through the power of God's Word.

29:21 This verse relates to the counsel in 29:19. It warns that allowing a servant to grow up with no discipline will only lead to grief later in life because he will not possess the wisdom to serve his master well. This is similar to warnings about the result of raising children without sufficient discipline (e.g., 13:24; 22:15; 23:13–14).

29:22 This verse contains two warnings about the consequences of failing to control one's temper: it will lead to quarrels and to sin. Other proverbs make similar points about the consequences of anger, including 14:17, 29; 15:18; 19:19; 22:24; 27:4.

29:23 This verse is ironic in tone. An arrogant person who considers his thoughts and ways better than those of others eventually will be humiliated, and his arrogance will be shown to have been misplaced trust in himself (see 3:5; 28:26). Outwardly he appears to be on the verge of seizing honor, and he may attain great power in this life, but he will receive no eternal glory. On the other hand, a man with a humble spirit knows his sinfulness and lack of ability to reach out and seize divine glory, but God will reward his faith with everlasting honor. See Phil 2:1–11, and note οὐχ ἁρπαγμόν, "not something to be seized" (Phil 2:6).

29:24 This verse notes that a person who partners with a thief as his companion or accomplice is endangering his own well-being. The "curse" or "oath" (אָלָה) mentioned in the second line probably is in a legal setting or court. This term (אָלָה) refers to a legal oath in Lev 5:1 and Num 5:21, and it can refer to a curse from God (e.g., Num 5:23; Deut 29:18–20 [ET 29:19–21]). The friend of the thief is called to testify and is put under oath, which invokes God to punish any witness who lies or does not come forward with evidence of a crime. Compare the legal oaths invoking God that are imposed on a witness in Josh 7:19 and Mt 26:63. However, the thief's friend remains silent and refuses to testify, thus falling under the curse. He may know of the thief's crimes, but he will keep silent due to his friendship. Such a person is liable to punishment from God, even if he evades the human legal authorities. He falls under the covenant curses (e.g., Deut 27:19, 26) and violates the Eighth Commandment (Ex 20:16; Deut 5:20) because his silence is a form of false testimony.

---

6 See "Fools in Proverbs" in the introduction.

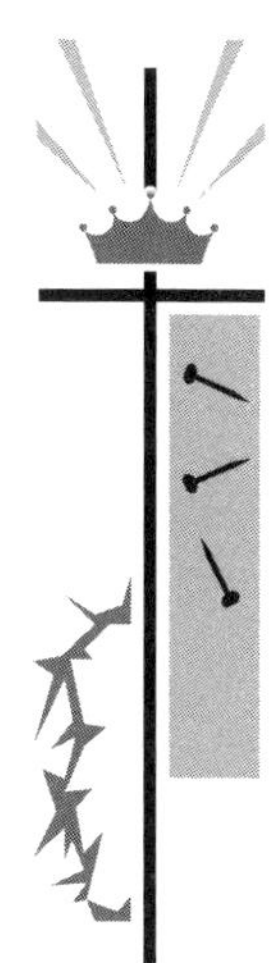

29:25 This verse draws a contrast between fear of humans and trust in Yahweh. Fear of what other humans can do sets a trap by allowing their actions and threats to control one's life. Far better off is the person who trusts Yahweh and does not allow the influence of others to control his life. He is secure because God promises to reward faithfulness with eternal blessings, whereas humans can only affect events in this world, and even then only as God allows. Jesus commanded, "Do not fear those who kill the body but are not able to kill the soul. Instead fear him who is able to destroy both soul and body in Gehenna/hell" (Mt 10:28). Jesus himself did not let fear of rulers deter him from fulfilling his mission through his crucifixion and resurrection (Lk 13:31–33). Neither did the apostles cease preaching the Good News of Jesus after being imprisoned and facing possible death, for they chose to obey God rather than men (Acts 5:25–33; see also Stephen the protomartyr in Acts 7).

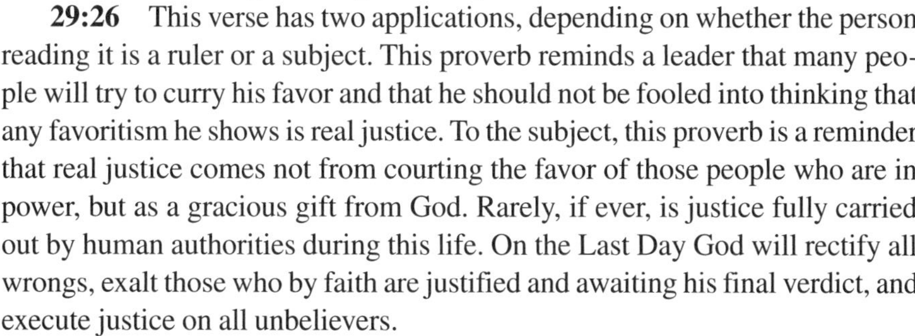

29:26 This verse has two applications, depending on whether the person reading it is a ruler or a subject. This proverb reminds a leader that many people will try to curry his favor and that he should not be fooled into thinking that any favoritism he shows is real justice. To the subject, this proverb is a reminder that real justice comes not from courting the favor of those people who are in power, but as a gracious gift from God. Rarely, if ever, is justice fully carried out by human authorities during this life. On the Last Day God will rectify all wrongs, exalt those who by faith are justified and awaiting his final verdict, and execute justice on all unbelievers.

29:27 This verse is the closing proverb of the Solomonic collection that began in 25:1. The mutual disgust of the righteous and the wicked is caused by the incompatibility of each other's spiritual disposition and lifestyle. This revulsion is a reminder of the wide gulf between the wise person, who trusts God and judges life according to God's standards in his Word, and the fool, who trusts his own sinful inclinations and therefore detests anything godly or anyone who tries to live a godly life—much less a righteous person who rebukes the fool's views and sinful behavior.

This proverb is a warning that the two contrasting attitudes—faith versus unbelief—cannot be reconciled (cf. 1 Ki 18:21). Those in power should not try to force a compromise between the two, which would only draw the righteous into sin and endanger the ruler's own position (cf. 29:4, 12, 14, 16). Nor should any of Christ's disciples try to alleviate the inevitable conflict the church has with the world by accommodating it. To compromise the truth is to lose it (cf. Jn 14:6; Acts 4:12). "In the world you will have tribulation. But be courageous, for I have achieved the victory over the world" (Jn 16:33; cf. 1 Jn 5:4).

Proverbs 30:1–33

Agur's Proverbs

30:1a	Superscription to Agur's Proverbs
30:1b–10	Agur's Prayers and Advice
30:11–33	Agur's List Proverbs

Proverbs 30:1a

Superscription to Agur's Proverbs

Translation

30 [1a]The words of Agur son of Jakeh. His prophetic revelation.

Textual Notes

30:1a דִּבְרֵ֤י ׀ אָג֘וּר—The name "Agur" (אָגוּר) is explained by many commentators as deriving from the verb גּוּר, "to sojourn," in which case it may mean "I am a sojourner."[1] However, it is also possible to understand the name as deriving from the verb אָגַר, "to gather," which occurs in 6:8 and 10:5, in which case the name may mean "gatherer, assembler."[2] The LXX apparently pointed the first word as דְּבָרַי and took the name as an imperative of the homographic verb גּוּר, "to fear," since it translated 30:1a as "son, fear my words, and having received them, repent!" The Syriac Peshitta transliterated the first word as a name and closely followed the MT: ܡܠܘܗܝ ܕܐܓܘܪ ܒܪ ܝܩܐ, "the words of Agur son of Jaki."

No other person in the OT bears this name. Jewish tradition took it to be a pseudonym for Solomon himself.[3] This was probably done as part of an effort to assign the entire book to Solomon, but there is little evidence for identifying Agur with Solomon. It is probably best to consider Agur, the author of Proverbs 30, to be an otherwise unknown Israelite.

בִּן־יָקֶ֗ה—Usually the construct form of בֵּן, "son," is בֶּן־, but sometimes it is בִּן־ (see GKC, § 96, s.v. בֵּן). No other person in the OT bears the name "Jakeh" (יָקֶה). Some have proposed that this name derives from יקה, which is the root of the noun יְקָהָה, "obedience," in Gen 49:10 and Prov 30:17. Others have proposed that בִּן־יָקֶה ("son of Jakeh") does not refer to the name of Agur's father but instead means "an obedient man" in the same way that בֶּן־חַיִל (literally, "son of valor") means "mighty man" (e.g., 1 Sam 14:52; 18:7; 2 Sam 2:7; 13:28; 17:10).[4] According to this view, Prov 30:1 would then mean "the words of Agur, a man of faith/understanding." However, בֵּן, "son," is never used in this way to introduce a personal characteristic when it immediately follows a proper noun (here "Agur"). Instead it always designates the preceding person as a "son" of the following person.

Jerome in the Vulgate apparently understood this name as deriving from the verb קִיא, "vomit" (23:8; 25:16), and translated as the superscription as *verba congregantis filii vomentis*, which probably he intended to mean "the words of the assembler, son of one who spews forth [preaches words]."

---

1 See Murphy, *Wisdom Literature*, 80.

2 See Toy, *Proverbs*, 518.

3 Delitzsch, *Proverbs*, 2:260.

4 Franklyn, "The Sayings of Agur in Proverbs 30," 239.

As creative as these proposals are, it is best to understand בֶּן־יָקֶה as "son of Jakeh," with יָקֶה being a proper name of an otherwise unknown Israelite.

הַמַּשָּׂא—Literally, "the prophetic revelation" is the meaning of this word as it stands in the MT. מַשָּׂא recurs in Proverbs in 31:1, where it characterizes the following proverbs from King Lemuel. Elsewhere in the OT it often refers to the God-given content of the preaching of a prophet.[a] The proverbs of Agur are a prophecy fulfilled in Jesus Christ; see especially the commentary on Prov 30:4. The NT affirms that all OT prophecy is fulfilled in Jesus Christ (e.g., Lk 4:16–21; 18:31; 24:44; 2 Pet 1:16–21). The only NT book that is designated as a "prophecy" or "prophetic revelation" is Revelation (προφητεία, Rev 1:3; 22:7, 10, 18–19).

Many commentators have proposed emending הַמַּשָּׂא here to הַמַּשָּׂאִי, "the Massaite," or maintain that even if not emended, it must mean something like "a person from Massa."[5] Massa was a tribe from north Arabia (Gen 25:14; 1 Chr 1:30). The argument for emendation usually begins with at least one of two objections. First, it claims that if הַמַּשָּׂא meant "the prophetic revelation," then the word נְאֻם, "utterance, oracle, declaration," which immediately follows in Prov 30:1b, would be redundant. Second, it claims that since מַשָּׂא appears without the article in Prov 31:1, the same word would not have the article if it appeared here, so a different word must be here.

(a) E.g., 2 Ki 9:25; Is 13:1; 15:1; 17:1; Nah 1:1; Hab 1:1; Mal 1:1

However, neither objection is substantial enough to warrant the emendation, which is completely conjectural.[6] Note that both Num 24:3 and Num 24:15 begin with the verb נָשָׂא, "lift up; utter," which is the root of the noun מַשָּׂא, "prophetic revelation," and then each of these verses has two occurrences of נְאֻם, "utterance, oracle." No commentators object to the redundancy in those verses, so the repetitiveness of מַשָּׂא and נְאֻם in Prov 30:1 should not pose a problem. Moreover, מַשָּׂא is perfectly natural without the article in 31:1, where it refers to *a* prophetic revelation (indefinite: one of many revelations) received by King Lemuel. Its presence here is also natural, and the article is used to designate the proverbs in chapter 30 as "the" (only) divine revelation that Agur received. This use of the Hebrew definite article is best rendered in English by a personal pronoun: "*his* prophetic revelation."[7]

Commentary

This superscription introduces Proverbs 30 as the words of Agur and tells us that they are not simply his wisdom, but a revelation from God with prophetic authority. Since we do not know who Agur was, it is impossible to know precisely when these words were spoken or how they came to be included in the book of Proverbs. However, we can make some inferences from their position in

---

5 Clifford, *Proverbs*, 259–60; Longman, *Proverbs*, 518; Murphy, *Proverbs*, 225–26; Scott, *Proverbs, Ecclesiastes*, 176.

6 Franklyn, "The Sayings of Agur in Proverbs 30," 239–40, takes that position. Murphy, *Proverbs*, 225–26, favors reading "the Massaite," but admits that this is a purely conjectural reading.

7 The article marks a noun as definite in the mind of the writer and designates it as belonging to a particular person. See Waltke-O'Connor, § 13.5.1e, citing, for example, 1 Sam 16:23: וְלָקַח דָּוִד אֶת־הַכִּנּוֹר, "David would take *his* harp" (see also examples 12–13).

the book. They follow the proverbs of Solomon that were copied by Hezekiah's men (chapters 25–29), so we can be reasonably certain that they were added to the book no earlier than the time of King Hezekiah and that they could have been written during his reign.[8]

This superscription is held by some to indicate the authorship of only 30:1–14, since 30:15–33 contains numerical sayings.[9] Furthermore, the LXX places 30:1–14 after 24:22, whereas it places 30:15–31:9 after 24:34. However, these are unconvincing reasons to limit the superscription to designating the authorship only of 30:1–14 and not also of 30:15–33.

Clearly, 30:11–14 is a list saying about four different kinds of persons, although it does not mention the number four. In the same way, 30:32–33 is a list saying about three different effects of, literally, "pressing" (מִיץ). The word is repeated three times in 30:33, but the saying does not mention the number three. Thus Agur's numerical sayings in 30:11–33 are framed by two numerical sayings in which the number is implicit but not explicit.[10] Therefore, it is artificial to split Proverbs 30 into two units by dividing the chapter between 30:14 and 30:15. And since the LXX included the sayings of Lemuel (31:1–9) with 30:15–33, it is obvious that it was not making divisions based on authorship. In addition, it should be noted that the LXX or its Vorlage probably rearranged the material at the end of Proverbs to make it appear as if the entire book should be attributed to Solomon.[11] There is no good objection to viewing all of Proverbs 30 as composed by Agur. The MT (reflected in English translations) likely preserves the original arrangement of the text of Proverbs, and the order in the LXX is a secondary development.

The sayings of Agur that follow this superscription treat three estates that God has established for human welfare. These estates can be outlined as follows:

1. God's kingdom of grace: the church (30:1b–10)
2. God's kingdom of good order (30:11–33)
    a. The family
    b. Civil government

First, 30:1b–10, with its emphasis on God's Word and the person of Christ, relates to God's people as his children—called, adopted, and preserved in faith by his grace alone. This is the estate God has established especially for our eternal welfare, with the promise of the resurrection to everlasting life in the

---

[8] See further "Authorship and Date" in the introduction, including figure 1, "The Authors of the Sections of Proverbs," and figure 3, "The Growth of Proverbs."

[9] Murphy, *Wisdom Literature*, 80–81.

[10] See further the commentary on 30:11–33.

[11] Washington, *Wealth and Poverty*, 126–27. Note that the LXX omits all references to authors other than Solomon. In 22:17 it adds "and hear my [Solomon's] word" in order to attribute "the words of wise people" to Solomon, and it omits references to wise people in 24:23, the authorship of Agur in 30:1, and the authorship of Lemuel (or his mother) in 31:1.

new creation. This is the sphere of the church, established by God to guide us to eternal salvation through his Word, which centers on the person and work of Jesus Christ.[12]

In the second part of his sayings, 30:11–33, Agur treats two estates established by God for our welfare during this earthly life: family and government. This is a highly organized section that emphasizes how each of these two estates is vitally important for our well-being. The family is the universal means God created to bring people into this world and to nourish and educate children into adulthood. Civil government is a universal means by which God restrains sin and harmful behavior and promotes what is good for all people.

These three estates are not disconnected, but are overlapping spheres of life in which God works for our good. All believers are members of all three estates at the same time. The specific ways in which each believer participates in each of the estates depends on his or her vocations or callings in relation to God and other people. For example, a man may be a clergyman or a member of a congregation. Every person is a child, and many are also siblings and parents, and each of those vocations brings responsibilities to serve God within family relationships. A person may wield authority as part of the civil government, and every person is called to live and serve within the boundaries established by God-pleasing laws and rulers. A large number of proverbs elsewhere in the book likewise counsel how to live faithfully as a believer and how to carry out God's calling as a member of the family and as a citizen of the state.[13]

---

[12] See "Wisdom in Proverbs" in the introduction. See also the commentary on 1:1–7; 3:13–20; 8:22–31; and the excursus "Proverbs 8, Wisdom, Christology, and the Arian Controversy" in the commentary on chapter 8.

[13] The entire book of Proverbs reveals the divine wisdom that gives, preserves, and strengthens saving faith so that the believer will enter the fullness of everlasting life. Parts of the book have more specific emphases. For example, 27:23–27 is overtly relevant for pastors as shepherds of God's people. The emphasis on the family can be seen in the way much of Proverbs 1–9 is worded as divine wisdom addressed by a loving father to his son. See, for example, the excursus "Proverbs 1–9, Christ, and the Ten Commandments" in the commentary on Proverbs 1. In contrast, much of 28:1–29:27 is about kings and leadership, offering wisdom for those who govern and also for all who are governed.

Proverbs 30:1b–10

Agur's Prayers and Advice

Translation

30 [1b]This man's declaration:
I'm weary, God.
I'm weary, God, and worn out,
[2]because I am [more] stupid than a [normal] person,
I don't [even] possess human understanding,
[3]I haven't learned wisdom,
and I don't have knowledge of the Holy One.

[4]Who has gone up to heaven and come down?
Who has gathered wind in the palms of his hands?
Who has wrapped water in a garment?
Who has set up all the ends of the earth?
What is his name and the name of his Son?
Certainly you know!

[5]Every word of God has been refined.
He is a shield to those who take refuge in him.
[6]Do not add to his words.
Otherwise he will correct you, and you will be shown to be a liar.

[7]Two things I've asked of you.
Don't keep them from me before I die:
[8]Keep worthless speech and lies far away from me.
Don't give me poverty or riches.
Feed me [only] my allotted food.
[9]Otherwise I may feel satisfied and deny you
and say, "Who is Yahweh?"
Or on the other hand, I may become poor and steal
and profane the name of my God.
[10]Do not slander a servant to his master.
Otherwise he will curse you, and you will be found guilty.

Textual Notes

30:1b Most English translations follow the Masoretic accentuation. The *athnach* on the first לְאִֽיתִיאֵ֑ל indicates two phrases, apparently with two proper names, the first of which is repeated:

Declaration of the man to Ithiel,	נְאֻ֤ם הַגֶּ֗בֶר לְאִֽיתִיאֵ֑ל
to Ithiel and (to) Ucal.	לְאִֽיתִיאֵ֣ל וְאֻכָֽל׃

The only other occurrence of the name אִיתִיאֵל in the OT is in Neh 11:7, where it refers to a Benjaminite. Some older interpreters assumed that Ithiel was a pupil of Agur, hence it is repeated with the preposition לְ, indicating instruction "to" him. Probably Ithiel means "with me is God" (so BDB, s.v. אִיתִיאֵל, under אֵת II, "with"). אֻכָל is not attested elsewhere, as a proper name or as any other part of speech.

However, it is unclear how these names would relate to the rest of the chapter. Also, the repetition of the Hebrew name "to Ithiel, to Ithiel" would be unusual and hard to understand in this context. In some other passages a Hebrew name is repeated (with no intervening Hebrew words) in a time of extreme stress related to someone's death. See "Absalom" in 2 Sam 19:5 (ET 19:4), and "Absalom" with "my son" in 2 Sam 19:1 (ET 18:33). Apparently in Mt 27:46–49 some thought that Jesus, while dying on the cross, was repeating the name of Elijah. However, there does not seem to be any dire circumstance here in Proverbs.

Because of the uncertainties and difficulties in interpreting these words, almost all modern commentators assume that this text was corrupted in some way. Most maintain that by accident the consonantal text was not properly divided into words and that the Masoretes pointed it in such a way as to attempt to make sense of the consonants that were not sufficiently separated into words.[1] Other, more radical, emendations have been proposed to make sense of the MT,[2] but the one followed in this commentary is both the least intrusive and the most widely accepted.

נְאֻם הַגֶּבֶר—Literally, this is "the declaration of the man." The article on הַגֶּבֶר in this phrase is anaphoric, referring to the previously mentioned "Agur" in 30:1a (see Waltke-O'Connor, § 13.5.1d). It ought to be translated as "*this* man's declaration." The most common use of the noun נְאֻם (perhaps the passive participle of נָאַם, "to utter") is in the phrase נְאֻם (אֲדֹנָי) יהוה, "the declaration of (the Lord) Yahweh" (three hundred sixty-five times in the MT). The same phrase that occurs here, נְאֻם הַגֶּבֶר, is used to introduce oracles by prophets in Num 24:3, 15 and 2 Sam 23:1.

לְאִיתִיאֵל לְאִיתִיאֵל—This commentary follows an emendation that involves only a minimal adjustment in the text by dividing the name Ithiel into two separate words and by leaving the vowels unchanged: לָאִיתִי אֵל לָאִיתִי אֵל, "I am weary, God. I am weary, God." The repeated verb form would be the first common singular Qal (G) perfect of לָאָה, "be weary," which is used in the Qal (G) in Gen 19:11 and Job 4:2, 5. The usual vocative form for addressing אֵל, "God," is with the article, הָאֵל, but the OT does attest

[1] Almost all but the shortest ancient inscriptions in Hebrew and Aramaic and other related languages had word dividers or spaces between words, and it is most often assumed that the OT was originally written with spaces or word dividers. Some very short ancient Hebrew inscriptions, such as those on seals, were written without spaces or dividers between words since there would be little chance of confusion to the reader. This is in contrast to Greek, which most often was written without any indication of boundaries between words. However, unlike English or Hebrew, almost all Greek words end with one of only eight letters, making it possible to write intelligible text without words being visually divided from one another.

[2] See, for example, the Aramaizing proposal in Torrey, "Proverbs, Chapter 30," 96:

לָאִיתַי אֵל לָאִיתַי אֵל וְאֻכַל

I am not a god, I am not a god, that I should have power.

the vocative use of אֵל without the article (Num 12:13; Ps 83:2 [ET 83:1]). Such repetition of clauses for emphasis in poetry is possible. See, for instance, Ps 29:1 (cf. 1 Chr 16:28 || Ps 96:7):

הָבוּ לַיהוָה בְּנֵי אֵלִים
הָבוּ לַיהוָה כָּבוֹד וָעֹז׃

Give to Yahweh, you sons of God,
give to Yahweh glory and strength.

See also Prov 31:4:

אַל לַמְלָכִים ׀ לְמוֹאֵל
אַל לַמְלָכִים שְׁתוֹ־יָיִן

It is not for kings, Lemoel,
it is not for kings to drink wine.

וְאֻכָל׃—The translation "and I am worn out" is based on the repointing to וָאֵכֶל, the Qal (G) imperfect first person singular of כָּלָה. This repointing is supported by the LXX's καὶ παύομαι and Aquila's καὶ τέλεσον. The MT reading וְאֻכָל, a form that occurs only here, could be a Qal (G) imperfect first person singular of יָכֹל, "I am able, have power." Or the MT might be a Qal passive (Gp) form of אָכַל, meaning "consumed," as אֻכָּל means in Ex 3:2, but that might require the addition of a *daghesh* in the *kaph* in the form here, וְאֻכָל (cf. GKC, § 52 s). However, אָכַל ("eat, consume") is never used metaphorically to mean mental exhaustion and despair.[3]

The interpretation that Agur confesses that he is "weary" and "worn out" fits much better with the following self-deprecating verses (30:2–3) than the interpretation that the opening half-verse (30:1b) is an address to two people by their proper names (Ithiel and Ucal).

30:2 כִּי בַעַר אָנֹכִי מֵאִישׁ—The preposition מִן on מֵאִישׁ forms a comparative clause: literally, "because *more* stupid am I than a [typical] man." See "בַּעַר, 'Stupid' " in "Fools in Proverbs" in the introduction.

וְלֹא־בִינַת אָדָם לִי׃—The negative לֹא usually is used with verbs, but here it negates a nominal sentence. The preposition לְ (with suffix: לִי) is used in the sense of possession: literally, "there is no understanding [typical] of a man *belonging to me*." For the noun in construct (בִּינַת), see "בִּינָה, 'Understanding,' and Related Words" in "Wisdom in Proverbs" in the introduction.

30:3 וְדַעַת קְדֹשִׁים אֵדָע׃—This appears to be a positive affirmation, "knowledge of the Holy One I know," but the negative לֹא that begins the verse probably does double duty and negates this second clause too. Almost all translations take the two clauses of the verse as parallel, for example, "I have not learned … nor have I knowledge …" (ESV). However, this second clause may be a consecutive clause: "I have not learned wisdom *so that I could know* knowledge of the Holy One" (see GKC, § 166 a). The result would still be that the author says he lacks such knowledge. The identical construct phrase

---

3 Krantz, "A Man Not Supported by God," 550–51.

וְדַעַת קְדֹשִׁים is also in 9:10 (see the second textual note and commentary there). For the noun דַּעַת and the verb אֵדָע here, see "דַּעַת, 'Knowledge,' and יָדַע, 'to Know' " in "Wisdom in Proverbs" in the introduction, as well as the commentary on 1:4, 7.

30:4 כִּי תֵדָע׃—This clause employs the emphatic or asseverative use of כִּי, "certainly you know!" (see *HALOT*, s.v. כִּי II, A 1). This sarcastic tone is intended to instill humility and repentance.

30:5 כָּל־אִמְרַת אֱלוֹהַּ צְרוּפָה—The subject in this sentence is the three-word construct chain "every word of God." This is the only proverb that uses אֱלוֹהַּ for "God" instead of אֵל or אֱלֹהִים. This divine term is common in Job and mostly found in poetic OT texts. The predicate is the feminine Qal passive (Gp) participle (צְרוּפָה) of צָרַף, "refine, smelt (a metal)," which agrees in gender with אִמְרָה, "word." The verb צָרַף is used metaphorically to speak of Yahweh or his Word testing a person (Pss 17:3; 26:2; 66:10; 105:19), of divine judgment and purification (Is 1:25; Jer 6:29), and of the authenticity and trustworthiness of God's Word (2 Sam 22:31 || Ps 18:31 [ET 18:30]; Pss 12:7 [ET 12:6]; 119:140).

מָגֵן הוּא לַחֹסִים בּוֹ׃—"A shield is he to those who trust in him," this expresses salvation through faith alone, since saving faith consists of simple trust. The wording here is slightly expanded in 2 Sam 22:31 || Ps 18:31 (ET 18:30) to לְכֹל הַחֹסִים, "a shield is he to *all* who trust in him." The metaphor that God is a מָגֵן, "shield," is used with the verb חָסָה, "to trust, take refuge in," also in 2 Sam 22:3 || Pss 18:3 (ET 18:2) and Ps 144:2.

30:6 אַל־תּוֹסְףְּ עַל־דְּבָרָיו—This prohibition or negative command has an unusual form of the second masculine singular Hiphil (H) imperfect of יָסַף, "to add." The regular form is תּוֹסִיף, and here one would expected the usual shortened form תּוֹסֵף (GKC, § 10 k).

פֶּן־יוֹכִיחַ בְּךָ וְנִכְזָבְתָּ׃—For the Hiphil (H) of יָכַח, "to correct, warn," see the first textual note on 3:12. The verb כָּזַב, "to lie, be a liar," occurs in the Niphal (N) only here and in Job 41:1 (ET 41:9), and both times it means "to be shown/proven to be a liar" (see BDB). This verb is cognate to the noun כָּזָב, "a lie," as in 30:8, where דְּבַר־כָּזָב (literally, "a word of a lie") is translated collectively as the plural "lies."

30:8 רֵאשׁ וָעֹשֶׁר אַל־תִּתֶּן־לִי—For the noun רֵאשׁ, "poverty," see the first textual note on 6:11. Its antonym here, עֹשֶׁר, "wealth," is common in Proverbs, often as a positive term for the divine gift of wisdom (e.g., 3:6; 8:18; 22:4), but sometimes as a reference to worldly wealth that can be an object of false trust (11:28), here leading to apostasy (30:9).

הַטְרִיפֵנִי לֶחֶם חֻקִּי׃—The Qal (G) of טָרַף can refer to the action of wild beasts that violently "tear, rend" their prey (e.g., Gen 37:33). The Hiphil (H) occurs only here, and its imperative apparently has the neutral sense "feed, give food." The noun חֹק can refer to a "*prescribed portion*, or allowance of food" (BDB, 2, under the root חקק). The construct phrase לֶחֶם חֻקִּי, literally, "the food of my portion," has an epexegetical genitive: just "my allotted portion of food" needed for daily life.

30:9 וְכִחַשְׁתִּי—The Piel (D) of כָּחַשׁ can mean to "deceive" (BDB, 1) or, as here, to "*act deceptively* against," to "seem to acknowledge, but not really do so" (BDB, 2). Thus it means to "deny" God even if still showing an outward pretense of godliness. This is similar to Jesus' exhortations, as in Mt 23:23–27, about the need for inner repentance and faith, not just an outward veneer of obedience to God. See also Rom 2:26–29.

וְתָפַשְׂתִּי שֵׁם אֱלֹהָי׃—The verb תָּפַשׂ usually means "grasp, seize, use skillfully." Only here does it apparently mean "*seize* (do violence to)" God's name (BDB, Qal, 1), "desecrate, profane" (*HALOT*, 3) "the name of my God" by misusing and abusing it.

30:10 אַל־תַּלְשֵׁן עֶבֶד אֶל־אֲדֹנָו—The noun לָשׁוֹן, "tongue," is common in Proverbs (e.g., 18:21; 31:26). The denominative verb לָשַׁן appears only twice in the OT, and both its Poel (D), used in Ps 101:5, and its Hiphil (H) here mean to "use the tongue" to "slander" (BDB; see also Waltke-O'Connor, § 27.4a, including example 8). The Kethib אֲדֹנוֹ, "his master," is the suffixed singular form of the noun, whose suffixed singular almost always refers to a human lord. The Qere, אֲדֹנָיו, also means "his master," but this plural form of the noun can refer to God as Lord or to a human master. Rom 14:4 commands one Christian not to judge another Christian (on the basis of diet) because the other is a servant who is answerable to his own Lord, that is, the Lord Jesus.

פֶּן־יְקַלֶּלְךָ וְאָשָׁמְתָּ׃—The Piel (D) imperfect of קָלַל, "to curse," recurs in 30:11 and its participle is in 20:20, all referring to one person cursing another. The subject here is unstated, but it must be one of the people in the preceding clause. The "master" could curse the person who slandered his servant, or the "servant" could be the one who curses the person who slandered him. More likely this proverb speaks of the way a servant could obtain justice: by invoking God's curse on the person who wronged him. The master would have the power to take other measures to punish the slanderer besides simply pronouncing a curse. The helpless servant must rely on God to fulfill the curse in order for the servant to obtain a measure of justice. Regardless of the human subject of "will curse," the verb וְאָשָׁמְתָּ, "and you will be found/held guilty," suggests not only human condemnation, but also (eventual) divine judgment on the slanderer.

Commentary

This first section of Agur's words concerns God's work to bring us Christ through his holy Word. This is the activity of the church, where the Word is preached to bring God's promises to us and to bring us to trust in them. Agur skillfully uses both Law and Gospel in his prophetic preaching to guide his hearers to God's grace in Christ and to guide them in their life as children of God.[4]

Agur's prophecy begins with a meditation on Scripture in the form of prayers alternating with addresses to his audience, as shown in figure 18.

[4] See also the commentary on 30:1a, the superscription, which discusses the origin and arrangement of Proverbs 30.

Figure 18

The Basis of Agur's Meditation

Agur's Words	*The Basis of His Meditation*
Prayer: Agur confesses his lack of true wisdom (30:1–3)	Prov 12:1; 9:10
Address: Challenge concerning the name of God and his Son (30:4)	Deut 30:11–14; Job 38–39
Address: Advice about honoring the sanctity of God's Word (30:5–6)	2 Sam 22:31 ‖ Ps 18:31 (ET 18:30); Deut 4:2
Prayer: Request to be kept from misusing God's name (30:7–9)	Deut 5:11, 20
Address: Advice about avoiding slander (30:10)	Deut 5:20; Num 5:6

Agur begins his first prayer to God with the admission that he has worn himself out (Prov 30:1). This weariness did not come to him from physical labor, but from the work associated with trying to get wisdom (cf. Eccl 1:13, 17–18). Yet Agur considers himself "stupid" (בַּעַר, Prov 30:2a). This is a reference to 12:1, where the person who hates discipline is said to be "stupid" (בַּעַר). Agur extends this thought by way of reference to 9:10:

> The fear of Yahweh is the beginning of *wisdom.*
> The knowledge of the Holy One is understanding. (9:10)

> I don't [even] possess human *understanding*,
> I haven't learned *wisdom*,
> and I don't have *knowledge of the Holy One*. (30:2b–3)

Agur claims not to have any wisdom, not even the first part of wisdom, which is the fear of Yahweh. In his prayer he has confessed to not dining at wisdom's banquet (9:1–6). Note the vocabulary he has adopted from 9:10: "wisdom" (חָכְמָה), "knowledge of the Holy One" (דַּעַת קְדֹשִׁים), and "understanding" (בִּינָה).

Agur's claim is not false humility. Instead this is a sincere, repentant heart that knows how it has failed to attain God's ideal. Though Wisdom constantly invites, even the most pious among God's people fail to learn all they should from God's Word. The Old Adam infects all people, and Agur, like the rest of God's people, confesses that he has not learned wisdom.[5] Instead he must rely on God's mercy to supply the wisdom he is lacking (see 1 Cor 1:18–29).

---

[5] Thus Agur's words are not, as Scott (*Proverbs, Ecclesiastes*, 175–76) maintains, the words of a skeptic. Scott's contention is refuted by Franklyn, "The Sayings of Agur in Proverbs 30," and Moore, "A Home for the Alien."

Agur next turns his attention to his hearers or readers. They may think that they have succeeded where he failed. He begins with a rhetorical question based on the words of Yahweh through Moses in Deut 30:11–14:

> Surely, this commandment that I am commanding you today is not too difficult for you, nor is it far away. It is not in heaven [that you should say], "*Who will go up to heaven* for us and get it for us so that we can hear it and do it?" Nor is it across the ocean [that you should say], "Who will cross to the other side of the ocean and get it for us so that we can hear it and do it?" Surely, the Word is very near to you. It is in your mouth and in your heart so that you may do it.

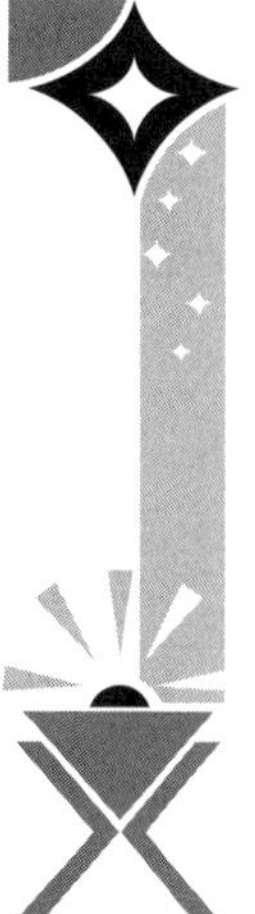

Agur's question (Prov 30:4) challenges his audience to understand that none of them have acquired—nor can acquire—wisdom through their own effort. Instead he wants them to see that God's Word of wisdom is near to them and has been given to them in Solomon's proverbs, which Agur had studied. It is also earlier in Moses' writings. This connection between wisdom and Moses' teachings recalls the connection that Solomon made with Deuteronomy at the very beginning of Proverbs.[6] Centuries later Paul would make the same theological points as Agur as he too draws on Deut 30:11–14. The apostle states that Jesus Christ is the divine Word who has descended from heaven in order to reveal God's salvation to us. The preached and confessed Gospel of Christ brings to us the saving knowledge of God that we could never attain by our own efforts (Rom 10:6–17).

Agur continues with five more questions that challenge his audience's pretensions. These are based on God's challenging questions to Job (Job 38–39).[7] He makes this connection clear by ending his challenge with the same clause God used to challenge Job: "certainly you know!" (Prov 30:4; Job 38:5). The first four questions, like the questions in Job, ask about creation and the One who has the power to control it. The fifth question challenges his audience's wisdom by asking the name of the One who has created the world and sustains it.

Moreover, Agur asks them to supply the name of his Son. This question connects God's Son with wisdom. Throughout Proverbs 1–9 wisdom was conveyed to a son,[8] and this emphasis on a son learning wisdom was continued in 10:1–22:16.[9] Agur is asserting that Solomon's proverbs are not mere human wisdom from a very intelligent mind, but the inspired Word of God brought near to humans. *The person who can master all of them can claim the designation as God's Son.* However, his audience (including present day readers) falls

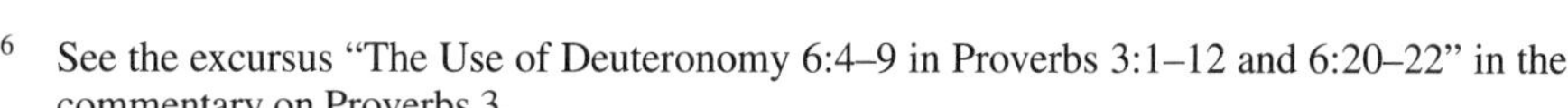

6 See the excursus "The Use of Deuteronomy 6:4–9 in Proverbs 3:1–12 and 6:20–22" in the commentary on Proverbs 3.

7 The questions that begin with "who?" are in Job 38:2, 5–6, 8, 25, 28–29, 36–37, 41; 39:5.

8 See the excursus "Proverbs 1–9, Christ, and the Ten Commandments" in the commentary on Proverbs 1.

9 See the excursus "The Organization of the Sayings in Solomon's Proverbs in Proverbs 10:1–22:16" in the commentary on Proverbs 10.

short. This question can only be answered affirmatively by Jesus Christ, who is God's Wisdom (see the commentary on 8:22–31).[10]

The same Christological understanding of this passage was set forth by Augustine:

> And what is Christ but the Wisdom of God? Again, in another place in the book of Proverbs, he says: "God hath taught me wisdom, and I have learned the knowledge of the holy. Who hath ascended up into heaven and descended? who hath gathered the winds in His fists? who hath bound the waters in a garment? who hath established all the ends of the earth? What is His name, and what is His Son's name?" [Prov 30:3–4] Of the two questions concluding this quotation, the one referred to the Father, namely, "What is His name?"—with allusion to the foregoing words, "God hath taught me wisdom,"—the other evidently to the Son, since he says, "or what is His Son's name?"—with allusion to the other statements, which are more properly understood as pertaining to the Son, viz. "Who hath ascended up into heaven and descended?"[11]

Having preached the Law to his audience to show them the inadequacy of human efforts to know wisdom, Agur moves on to point them to the Gospel in God's Word with a paraphrase of 2 Sam 22:31 (|| Ps 18:31 [ET 18:30]):

אִמְרַ֥ת יְהוָ֖ה צְרוּפָ֑ה
מָגֵ֣ן ה֔וּא לְכֹ֖ל הַחֹסִ֥ים בּֽוֹ׃

> The Word of Yahweh has been refined.
> He is a shield to all those who take refuge in him. (2 Sam 22:31)

כָּל־אִמְרַ֣ת אֱל֣וֹהַּ צְרוּפָ֑ה
מָגֵ֥ן ה֝֗וּא לַחֹסִ֥ים בּֽוֹ׃

> Every Word of God has been refined.
> He is a shield to those who take refuge in him. (Prov 30:5)[12]

Agur is pointing his audience to the wisdom of God in the Gospel. God here acts as a shield for those who trust him and his Word. This is far different from attempting to gain wisdom through human effort—a task that is just as impossible for the readers of Proverbs as it was for Agur (30:1–3). Here God graciously protects his people, surrounding them with salvation. Even though they failed to acquire wisdom on their own, by faith they take refuge in him, and he gives them the unfailing wisdom of his Word.

Next, Agur adds a warning against adding to God's Word (30:6). His thought is based on the same command in Deut 4:2. Agur's command is especially aimed at guarding the Gospel, though it certainly also applies to those who would add

---

[10] See especially the commentary on 8:22–31. See also "Wisdom in Proverbs" in the introduction; the commentary on 1:1–7 and 3:13–20; and the excursus "Proverbs 8, Wisdom, Christology, and the Arian Controversy" in the commentary on chapter 8.

[11] Augustine, Letter 102.29 (*NPNF*[1] 1:422).

[12] In his paraphrase Agur avoids using God's name, Yahweh, the name he just demanded from his audience with "what is his name?" in 30:4. Also, he moves כֹּל, "all, every," from before הַחֹסִים, "those who take refuge in him," and places it before אִמְרָה, "word."

laws that God has not commanded. See the words of Jesus in Mt 15:9 and the comments of the Lutheran confessors in AC XXVI 8–11 and Ap XII 143–45. Human additions to the Gospel rob believers of its comfort by foisting upon them the necessity to meet requirements not given by God. This is why Agur adds the warning that God himself will correct any person who is guilty of corrupting his Gospel. God, who is shield and protector, will protect his people by defending his pure and saving Word.

Even though the OT canon was only partially complete at the time Agur wrote Prov 30:6, it applies to more than just "his prophetic revelation" (30:1a) and to the book of Proverbs. This divinely inspired warning applies to the entire OT and NT canon of Scripture. At the end of the Bible a similar admonition warns that God will deal with any person who either adds to or subtracts from the final "prophecy" in the Scriptures (Rev 22:18–19). No one should tamper with any of the books in the canon nor with their message of Law and Gospel given by the holy God himself.

Agur's second prayer begins with a request for two things (Prov 30:7–8). First, he asks to be kept from sinning in his speech. Just as God's Word is pure (30:5), so Agur asks that God, by his sanctifying power, keep this believer's word pure. The noun Agur uses to describe sinful utterances as "worthless speech" (שָׁוְא, 30:8) is used in both the Second Commandment (Ex 20:7; Deut 5:11, where it is usually translated adverbially: "you shall not take the name of the Yahweh your God *in vain*") and also in the second record of the Eighth Commandment (Deut 5:20, where it is usually translated adjectivally: "*false* witness").[13] Agur's second request is that he be neither impoverished (cf., e.g., Prov 6:10–11) nor made rich. Instead he requests that God feed him only his allotted food, that is, daily provide him with only what he needs for this body and life each day. Indeed God had given Israel only the sufficient daily allotment of manna (Exodus 16), and he graciously promised that he would bless his people in, for example, Deut 6:11; 28:3–5, 11–12. Even so, Jesus teaches his disciples to pray, "Give us today our daily bread" (Mt 6:11; Lk 11:3).[14]

Agur's two requests are related to one another (Prov 30:9). On one hand, if a believer receives more than he needs and becomes rich, he faces the temptation to rely on his own success and riches and "deny" God, saying, "Who is Yahweh?" that is, "Who needs Yahweh?" Those who deny the Son will be denied by him before his Father on the Last Day (Mt 10:33; cf. Acts 3:13–14). On the other hand, if a believer has too little to provide for the needs of himself and his family, he faces the temptation to abandon his trust in God and take matters into his own hands by becoming a thief or a swindler. Since God's people bear his name, their sinful actions can also profane his name (Ezek 36:17–23;

[13] שָׁוְא is not used in the Eighth Commandment in Ex 20:16, making it likely that Agur's prayer is based on Deuteronomy.

[14] For Luther's exposition of this petition of the Lord's Prayer, see LC III 71–84. For an exegetical discussion of the possible meanings of ἐπιούσιος, usually translated as "*daily* bread," see Gibbs, *Matthew 1:1–11:1*, 316–17 and 331–35, who prefers the translation "our bread *that is coming*" (emphasis added).

Rom 2:17–24), thereby breaking the Second Commandment (Ex 20:7; Deut 5:11). Therefore, Agur, who confesses Yahweh as "my God" (Prov 30:9), asks that he be kept from poverty.

Agur extends the theme of being kept from "worthless speech" (30:8) in his address to his audience concerning slander (30:10). Here he explores the implications of the Eighth Commandment (Ex 20:16; Deut 5:20). Agur warns about slandering an underling to someone who has authority over him.[15] This may seem like a sin that has no consequent punishment for the slanderer if the person in authority believes the slander. There is little the underling can do in such situations. However, Agur notes that the subservient person may call down a divine curse upon the slanderer, and God will find the person guilty, even if human authorities do not. Agur probably has in mind Num 5:6, which uses the same verb אָשַׁם, "to be (found) guilty," in a similar way, referring to the objective guilt God assigns to those who sin, whether or not they feel guilty or are judged by other people as guilty. The worst kind of slander would be to revile faithful believers and call upon God to punish them, but Jesus assures us that such faithful believers in him are the opposite of cursed, namely, blessed (Mt 5:10–12; cf. Jn 16:2; 2 Pet 2:10; Jude 8, 10).

Thus Agur's words in Prov 30:1–10 are a meditation on God's Word of Law and Gospel. He recognizes Numbers, Deuteronomy, 2 Samuel (and/or Psalm 18), Job, and Proverbs as God's inspired Word that brings salvific wisdom. "His prophetic revelation" (Prov 30:1a) was placed after the proverbs of Solomon to emphasize the divine nature of the wisdom spoken by Solomon.[16] They are as authoritative and inspired as the words of Moses and David and the NT apostles and evangelists.

Moreover, Agur's words point forward to Christ, the Son of God, who alone has the answers to the rhetorical questions Agur raises (30:4). In fact, as a "prophetic revelation" (30:1a), these OT words carry the same weight as the words of Christ himself, for they testify to him (cf. Lk 24:27, 44; Jn 5:39). He has descended to earth to redeem his people and ascended to heaven to reign over them in grace at the right hand of the Father. Though no one in Agur's day could give the proper name of God's Son, the chosen people were told that he would be "Immanuel" (Is 7:14; cf. Is 9:5 [ET 9:6]), Yahweh's "Servant" (Is 42:1; 52:13; 53:11), the righteous "Branch" (Jer 23:5; 33:15), his "Anointed One" (Ps 2:2), and his "Son" (2 Sam 7:14; Ps 2:7, 12). The Christian can now answer Agur's question: his name is "Jesus," meaning "Yahweh/the Lord saves," because he is the one who has saved his people from their sins (Mt 1:21; cf. Phil 2:10).

---

[15] The meaning is not as narrow as "slave" and "his master," as some translations indicate (NASB, NJB). Considering that much of the advice in Proverbs concerns kings and those in authority, in this context the term עֶבֶד probably refers to any kind of subservient person or underling, which in modern terms could apply to an employee under an employer and similar hierarchical relationships.

[16] For the collections of Solomonic proverbs that make up Proverbs 1–29, see "Authorship and Date" in the introduction, including figure 3, "The Growth of Proverbs."

Proverbs 30:11–33

Agur's List Proverbs

Translation

30 [11]A certain kind of person curses his father
and does not bless his mother.
[12]A certain kind of person considers himself to be pure
but is not washed of his own feces.
[13]A certain kind of person—how haughty and arrogant he is!
[14]A certain kind of person—his teeth are swords,
and his fangs are knives
in order to devour oppressed people from the earth,
and poor people from among humanity.

[15]The leech has two daughters: Give! [and] give!
Three things are never satisfied;
four never say, "Enough!":
[16]Sheol and a barren womb;
land, which is never satisfied with water;
and fire, which never says, "Enough!"

[17]An eye that makes fun of [its] father
and despises obedience due [its] mother—
ravens of the valley will peck it out,
and young vultures will eat it.
[18]Three things are too wonderful for me,
and four I cannot understand:
[19]the way of an eagle in the sky,
the way of a snake on a rock,
the way of a ship on the high seas,
and the way of a man with a virgin.
[20]This is the way of a woman who commits adultery:
she eats and wipes her mouth and says, "I haven't done anything wrong."

[21]Under three things the earth trembles,
and under four it cannot bear up:
[22]under a slave when he becomes king
and [under] a complete fool when he is filled with food;
[23]under a woman who is hated when she is wed
and [under] a slave when she replaces her mistress.

[24]Four things are small on the earth,
yet they are wiser than the wisest people:

[25]Ants are a species without strength,
but they store their food in summer.
[26]Rock badgers are a species without power,
but they make their home in a cliff.
[27]Locusts have no king,
but they all go forth in ranks.
[28]A lizard you can hold in [your] hands,
but it is in palaces of a king.

[29]Three things stride with majesty,
four walk with majesty:
[30]a lion, the mightiest among the animals—
it does not turn away from anything;
[31]a rooster or a male goat;
and a king presiding over his army.

[32]If you are such a complete fool as to inflate your own ego,
or if you have been scheming,
[put your] hand over [your] mouth,
[33]because churning milk produces butter,
and punching a nose brings forth blood,
and pressing [one's] anger produces a fight.

Textual Notes

30:11–14 דּ֣וֹר—This noun usually refers to a "generation" of people, but in these proverbs it is used to denote a class or kind of person ("there are those," NIV, ESV, NRSV; "there is a kind," NASB).

30:11 דּ֭וֹר אָבִ֣יו יְקַלֵּ֑ל—The Piel (D) of קִלֵּל, "to curse," is used in 20:20 with both "his father" (אָבִ֫יו, as here) and "his mother" (אִמּ֫וֹ) as the direct objects. This crime merits the death penalty according to Ex 21:17 and Lev 20:9.

וְאֶת־אִ֝מּ֗וֹ לֹ֣א יְבָרֵֽךְ׃—"And his mother he does not bless" is equivalent to "and he curses his mother." The Piel (D) of בֵּרַךְ, "to bless," is a direct antonym of "to curse." See בֵּרַךְ in, for example, 3:33; 20:21; and 22:9.

30:12 טָה֣וֹר בְּעֵינָ֑יו—Literally, "clean in his own eyes" means "considers himself to be pure." See the first textual note on 3:7.

וּ֝מִצֹּאָת֗וֹ לֹ֣א רֻחָֽץ׃—The noun צֹאָה is probably derived from the root צוא (so BDB), although it may be derived from the verb יָצָא, referring literally to "what comes out" from a person (cf. Mt 15:17–20). רֻחָץ could be a Pual (Dp) perfect, but since רָחַץ, "to wash," is common in the Qal (G) and does not occur in the Piel (D), this form is most likely a Qal passive (Gp) perfect, is not "washed." A similar perfect form is in Ezek 16:4.

30:13 דּ֭וֹר מָה־רָ֣מוּ עֵינָ֑יו וְ֝עַפְעַפָּ֗יו יִנָּשֵֽׂאוּ׃—Literally, this is "a kind of person—how high are his eyes, and [how] his eyelids are lifted up." These expressions denote arrogance. See the first textual notes on 6:17 and 21:4. For עַפְעַף, "eyelid," see the textual note on 4:25.

30:14 וּמַאֲכָלוֹת מְתַלְּעֹתָיו—The noun מַאֲכֶלֶת denotes a "knife" as a utensil for eating, and it is derived from the verb אָכַל, "eat." The noun מְתַלְּעוֹת occurs elsewhere only in Joel 1:6 and Job 29:17, always as a feminine plural. It probably means "incisors" (BDB, s.v. מְתַלְּעוֹת, under the root תלע) and is translated as "fangs." Its suffixed plural, מְתַלְּעֹתָיו, "his fangs," stands in synonymous parallelism to שִׁנָּיו, "his teeth," in the preceding clause.

עֲנִיִּים מֵאֶרֶץ וְאֶבְיוֹנִים מֵאָדָם׃—In these two phrases the repeated preposition מִן could be partitive: "(some of the) oppressed people *from* the earth … *from* humanity." However, it more likely has a privative sense: "to devour (all of the) oppressed people *from* the earth," so that none are left; all are consumed.

30:16 שְׁאוֹל וְעֹצֶר רָחַם—The first of the four things that are never satisfied (30:15) is שְׁאוֹל, "Sheol," synonymous with everlasting death and the grave; see the first textual note and the commentary on 1:12. The accents *ʿole veyored* (-ָ֥ -ֶ֫-) on עֹצֶר רָחַם indicate that these two nouns go together, literally, "restraint/closure of a womb," and they conclude the first line of the verse. For a "womb" (רָחַם, pausal of רֶחֶם or רַחַם) to be restrained or closed means that it is barren; no child is conceived in it nor emerges from it. See Gen 20:18, where the verb עָצַר with the object רֶחֶם means that Yahweh "closed … the wombs" of all the women in the household.

30:17 וְתָבוּז לִיקֲּהַת־אֵם—The noun יִקְּהָה, "obedience," occurs in the OT only here and in Gen 49:10. Some believe that the name of Agur's father, יָקֶה, Jakeh, derives from the same root (יקה) as this noun. See the second textual note on 30:1a.

נָשֶׁר׃—נֶשֶׁר denotes a large bird of prey in general,[1] such as a "vulture" or an "eagle." It recurs in 30:19. The English translations above were selected to fit the context.

30:18 וְאַרְבָּע לֹא יְדַעְתִּים׃—The Kethib is the masculine form of the numeral (with *waw*), וְאַרְבַּע, while the Qere is the feminine form, וְאַרְבָּעָה. An implied relative particle follows the numeral, and the verb יְדַעְתִּים has a resumptive or retrospective suffix that refers back to the "four" things: literally, "four [things that] I do not know *them.*"

30:19 בְּלֶב־יָם—For "on the high seas," see the textual note on the same expression in 23:34.

בְּעַלְמָה׃—This means "with a virgin." The noun עַלְמָה denotes "a virgin" (Is 7:14; cf. Mt 1:18–25; Lk 1:26–34), whether still "a girl" or "a young woman of marriageable age." The women referenced by this noun are often virgins by implication: Rebekah in Gen 24:43; Moses' sister in Ex 2:8; the women who would like to marry Solomon in Song 1:3; 6:8. In the case of this proverb, virginity is clearly in view.[2]

---

1 *FF*, 82–85.

2 The word עַלְמָה in the verses cited above can be compared and contrasted with בְּתוּלָה, "a woman [of any age] who has never been married." This other word, בְּתוּלָה, is often taken to mean "a virgin," but note Gen 24:16 and Judg 21:12. Those contexts emphasize that a particular בְּתוּלָה was a virgin by adding a phrase like "who had not known a man" (Judg 21:12). Thus בְּתוּלָה means a woman who had never been married or had not publicly been known to be promiscuous or otherwise had intercourse, but was not necessarily a virgin, though probably was presumed to be by the community. Note that this is precisely the kind of woman a high priest was to marry (Lev 21:14).

30:20 אִשָּׁה מְנָאָפֶת—"A woman who commits adultery" obviously forms a contrast to the "virgin" in 30:19. מְנָאָפֶת (as in Ezek 16:32; Hos 3:1) is the feminine Piel (D) participle of נָאַף, "commit adultery," whose Qal (G) is in the Sixth Commandment (Ex 20:14; Deut 5:18; cf. Lev 20:10). The masculine Qal participle refers to a man "who commits adultery" in Prov 6:32.

30:21 תַּחַת שָׁלוֹשׁ רָגְזָה אֶרֶץ—The preposition תַּחַת, "under," occurs four times in 30:21–23. Here the "earth" (the feminine noun אֶרֶץ) is said to "quake, tremble" (the feminine verb רָגְזָה) under the weight or injustice of "three" (שָׁלוֹשׁ) things. The verb רָגַז often has eschatological and cosmological implications, pointing to the universal judgment on the Last Day. Thus pagan nations "tremble" when God vanquishes Egypt and redeems Israel through the exodus (Ex 15:14; Deut 2:25). All peoples and the whole earth will "shake, quake" (רָגַז) on the day God executes his wrath against sinful humanity.[a]

(a) E.g., 2 Sam 22:8 || Ps 18:8 (ET 18:7); Is 13:13; 23:11; Joel 2:10; Amos 8:8; Ps 99:1

וְתַחַת אַרְבַּע לֹא־תוּכַל שְׂאֵת׃—The feminine noun אֶרֶץ, "earth," in the preceding clause is the implied subject of the negated feminine imperfect of יָכֹל, namely, לֹא־תוּכַל, "it is not able," followed by the Qal (G) infinitive construct of נָשָׂא as a verbal complement, שְׂאֵת, "to bear (up), carry, endure."

30:22 וְנָבָל—For this adjective used as a substantive, "a complete fool," see "נָבָל, 'Complete Fool,' and נָבַל, 'to Be a Complete Fool' " in "Fools in Proverbs" in the introduction. The cognate verb נָבַל is used in 30:32.

30:23 תַּחַת שְׂנוּאָה כִּי תִבָּעֵל—The feminine Qal passive (Gp) participle of שָׂנֵא, "to hate," literally means "a hated woman." This is used to describe a wife whom the husband does not favor or love as much as he loves other wives (e.g., Leah in Gen 29:31, 33; see also Deut 21:15–17). Therefore it may be translated as "an unloved woman" (so NIV, ESV, NASB here). This woman is the implied subject of the Niphal (N) imperfect תִבָּעֵל, literally, "be possessed, taken," meaning "be wed, married." The cognate noun בַּעַל, "owner, master, lord," can refer to a woman's "husband" (see the noun and verb in Gen 20:3 and the noun in, for example, Ex 21:3, 22; Prov 12:4; 31:11, 23, 28).

וְשִׁפְחָה כִּי־תִירַשׁ גְּבִרְתָּהּ׃—The noun שִׁפְחָה denotes a female slave or handmaiden who serves "her mistress" (גְּבִרְתָּהּ). For example, Hagar was such a female slave (שִׁפְחָה) to her mistress Sarai/Sarah (Gen 16:1–8). Zilpah was Leah's handmaid, and Bilhah was Rachel's female slave (שִׁפְחָה, Gen 29:24, 29). In all three cases, the wife (the mistress of the female slave) eventually allowed her handmaid to have conjugal relations with her husband (Abraham; Jacob), resulting in children. In theory, the female slave (now a concubine) could replace the wife, and the slave's son could become the husband's heir. That would be the situation indicated here by the verb תִירַשׁ, "she replaces/inherits," the imperfect of יָרַשׁ. However, God told Abraham to comply with Sarah's demand that he expel Hagar and Ishmael, leaving only Sarah as Abraham's wife and Isaac as his rightful heir (Gen 21:8–21; cf. Gal 4:21–31). In the case of Jacob, the two handmaidens and their children did not *replace* the two wives and their children, but in effect became equals in terms of legal standing and inheritance rights. All twelve of Jacob's sons became heirs and fathers of the tribes of Israel.

30:24 קְטַנֵּי־אָרֶץ—The plural of the adjective קָטָן, "small," in construct with "earth" may simply mean "small things of/on earth," or it could be a superlative: "the *smallest* things on earth" (see GKC, § 133 g).

וְהֵמָּה חֲכָמִים מְחֻכָּמִים׃—Literally, this is "and they are wise, having been made wise." The Pual (Dp) participle מְחֻכָּמִים is translated by many as an adverb: "but they are *exceedingly* wise" (ESV, NKJV, NASB; emphasis added). The translation above uses a comparative and superlative: "they are *wiser* than the *wisest* people." The repointing of the participle מְחֻכָּמִים to מֵחֲכָמִים, the plural adjective with the preposition מִן, is based on τῶν σοφῶν in the LXX.[3]

30:25 הַנְּמָלִים עַם לֹא־עָז—Literally, "ants are a people [that is] not strong," is a litotes meaning "that seems weak." The harvester ant (נְמָלָה, as in 6:6) is found throughout Palestine. It stores grain in its nests.[4] The ant is used as an illustration of industriousness (30:25). The damage it causes to farmers is not mentioned here, and this is not a concern of the author, who is using the ant as an illustration of foresight.

וַיָּכִינוּ בַקַּיִץ לַחְמָם׃—Like the preceding clause, this verbal clause (with an imperfect with *waw* consecutive) has a gnomic, timeless, or present-tense meaning: "they store up …" (see Waltke-O'Connor, § 33.3.4c, including example 7; cf. Joüon, § 118 r). The Hiphil (H) verb וַיָּכִינוּ, "they prepare, store," and the suffix on לַחְמָם, "their food," are masculine plural to match הַנְּמָלִים, "the ants" in the previous clause. The same message and vocabulary is in 6:8a, but feminine singular forms are used there to match the feminine singular נְמָלָה, "ant," in 6:6.

30:26 שְׁפַנִּים—"Rock badgers," or Syrian coneys, are herbivorous animals about the size of a hare. Their feet contain toes with broad nails (four toes on the front paws, three on the back). On the underside of their feet they have pads that enable them to keep their footing on rocks. Their fur is yellow and brown. They have short ears and a very small tail. Rock badgers live among the rocks from the valley of the Dead Sea to Mount Hermon.[5]

וַיָּשִׂימוּ בַסֶּלַע בֵּיתָם׃—The preceding nominal clause has a general, present-tense meaning ("rock badgers are …"). After it, the verb וַיָּשִׂימוּ here, the Qal (G) imperfect of שִׂים with *waw* consecutive, also has a general, present-tense meaning: "they set/make in a cliff their home." See Joüon, § 118 r, and the second textual note on 30:25.

30:27 וַיֵּצֵא חֹצֵץ כֻּלּוֹ׃—The verb חָצַץ means "divide into groups." Here locusts are depicted as a well-organized army that "goes forth in ranks—all of it," prepared for battle.

30:28 שְׂמָמִית בְּיָדַיִם תְּתַפֵּשׂ—The feminine noun שְׂמָמִית is a hapax legomenon whose exact meaning is unknown. It is translated above as "lizard" and as the direct object of the verb תְּתַפֵּשׂ, which then would be second masculine singular: literally, "a lizard in two hands [בְּ with the dual יָדַיִם] you can hold." Similar are RSV, NIV, ESV, NASB. In

---

[3] See Murphy, *Proverbs*, 233.

[4] *FF*, 1.

[5] *FF*, 69–70.

such a context a second masculine verb could be translated as third person: "a person can hold …" (see GKC, § 144 h).

Based on the context in this verse, another possible meaning for שְׂמָמִית is "spider."[6] This feminine noun could be the subject of the verb תְּתַפֵּשׂ, which then would be third feminine singular: "a spider grasps with [her] two hands" (similar are KJV, NKJV). Luther understands this creature to be a spider: *die Spinne wirckt mit iren henden*,[7] "the spider works with its hands."

30:29 שְׁלֹשָׁה הֵמָּה מֵיטִיבֵי צָעַד וְאַרְבָּעָה—The feminine form of the numerals שְׁלֹשָׁה, "three," and אַרְבָּעָה, "four," are used even though all four things in 30:30–31 are male: לַיִשׁ, "a lion," זַרְזִיר מָתְנַיִם, "a rooster (?)", תַיִשׁ, "a male goat," מֶלֶךְ, "a king" (see Joüon, § 152 g).

The plural Hiphil (H) participle of יָטַב, "do good," is in construct with the pausal form of the noun צַעַד, "a step": literally, "three things are they (that are) doing good [in their] stride." This refers to a majestic stride (cf. *HALOT*, s.v. יָטַב, Hiphil, 3). The first line of the verse is translated as "three things stride with majesty."

מֵיטִבֵי לָכֶת׃—Here the plural Hiphil (H) participle of יָטַב, "do good," is in construct with the Qal (G) infinitive construct לֶכֶת, of הָלַךְ, literally, "(that are) doing good at walking," translated as "walk with majesty."

30:30 לַיִשׁ גִּבּוֹר בַּבְּהֵמָה—Literally, "a lion, a warrior among the beasts," this can be a superlative phrase: "a lion, the *mightiest* among the animals."

וְלֹא־יָשׁוּב מִפְּנֵי־כֹל׃—Literally, this is "he shall not turn from the face of all." The combination of לֹא and כֹּל forms an absolute negative: "he shall not turn away from anyone/anything whatsoever" (see GKC, § 152 b (*a*)).

30:31 זַרְזִיר מָתְנַיִם—This is, literally, "one girded about the loins." It is translated above as "rooster." Several other animals have been suggested that fit this context, including the greyhound and the warhorse.[8]

וּמֶלֶךְ אַלְקוּם עִמּוֹ׃—This could mean "and a king (when) a band of soldiers (is) with him," if אַלְקוּם denotes a "band of soldiers" (BDB, s.v. אַלְקוּם, under אַל I). Another possibility is that אַלְקוּם is a compound name for God as the one against whom no one can arise or stand (the negative אַל plus the Qal [G] infinitive קוּם), so that this line means "and a king—God is with him" (*DCH*, s.v. אַלְקוּם). The translation above, "and a king presiding over his army," is based on the emendation of אַלְקוּם עִמּוֹ to קָם אֶל־עַמּוֹ, "(who is) standing to his people/troops." עַם means "troops, army" in several passages; see its twenty-six occurrences in 1 Samuel 14. Another acceptable emendation is עִמּוֹ לֹא־קָם, "with him no (one) arises," meaning "against whom there is no rebellion."[9]

30:32 אִם־נָבַלְתָּ בְהִתְנַשֵּׂא—Literally, "if you act foolishly by lifting yourself up," this is translated as "if you are such a complete fool as to inflate your own ego." As the

---

6 *FF*, 78.

7 WA DB 10/2.101.

8 See BDB, s.v. זַרְזִיר, under the root זור III; *FF*, 17. "Greyhound" is Luther's understanding: *ein Wind von guten lenden* (WA DB 10/2.101), literally, "a greyhound [*Wind* is an archaic equivalent of *Windhund*] of good loins," that is, "a well-bred greyhound."

9 See Driver, "Problems in the Hebrew Text of Proverbs," 194.

context suggests, this is not necessarily an outward act that can be observed by others, but an inner arrogance. For the verb נָבַלְתָּ, see "נָבָל, 'Complete Fool,' and נָבַל, 'to Be a Complete Fool' " in "Fools in Proverbs" in the introduction.

30:33 מִיץ ... וּמִיץ ... וּמִיץ —"Churning," "punching," and pressing" are three contextual translations for this same word. It could be a verbal noun, which would mean "squeezing, pressing" (BDB, s.v. מִיץ), "pressure" (*DCH*, s.v. מִיץ I), or "churning" (*DCH*, s.v. מִיץ II). Or it could be the Qal (G) infinitive construct of מִיץ, "churn (milk), press, stir up" (*DCH*, s.v. מיץ II). In any case, the word occurs only here in the OT, although הַמֵּץ ("the oppressor") in Is 16:4 may be related.

Commentary

It should be noted that the break between this section of Agur's prophecy and his previous section (30:1–10) is not a sharp one.[10] While 30:10 is linked thematically with the saying that precedes it, 30:10 is also linked by the catchword קָלַל, "to slander, curse," to 30:11. In addition, these are not the only proverbs by Agur built around numbers or lists. Prov 30:7–9 also employs a number, "two," in its construction. Instead the difference between these two sections is mainly in the mode of address. In 30:1–10 Agur directly addresses God or his audience. This kind of direct address is lacking in 30:11–33 until the very end. Agur's direct address to his audience in 30:32–33 serves to bind 30:11–33 to 30:1–10 and give the chapter an overall unity.

In this section of Agur's prophecy, he treats life in this world under God's established order in family and in government. Both are gifts of God for our benefit in this life, and therefore they are to be respected and honored. Agur has organized both of these temporal estates by a skillful pattern based on proverbs that are, for the most part, in the form of lists.

In these list proverbs Agur teaches first about family and then about government, so that his hearers will perceive that the family is the basic unit for every society, the building block created by God upon which all human civilization depends, including every government. The family and the government are not mere human inventions, but estates established by God.[11]

Every government has the obligation to protect and promote the family structure created and hallowed by God. This includes the sanctity of marriage as the lifelong union of one husband and one wife (cf. 30:20, 23) and the sanctity of each person from the moment of conception to the natural end of life. God has designed the family to provide, among other things, for the procreation and raising of children, so that they may be taught to walk in his ways even as

---

[10] See also the commentary on the superscription to Agur's proverbs, 30:1a, which discusses the origin and arrangement of Proverbs 30.

Much of the following commentary is based on Andrew E. Steinmann, "Three Things … Four Things … Seven Things: The Coherence of Proverbs 30:11–33 and the Unity of Proverbs 30," *Hebrew Studies* 42 (2001): 59–66.

[11] See also the commentary on the superscription to Agur's proverbs, 30:1a.

the parents are called to do.[12] Attempts to redefine marriage in ways that allows for frivolous divorce or same-sex unions are sinful and dangerous because they undermine the very foundation of society. God's creatures cannot endure very long if their civilization is in open rebellion against their Creator (see Gen 11:9; chapters 18–19). Likewise, a society that allows abortion and other abuses of children is destroying its own future.

The sayings of Agur in Prov 30:11–33, which follow his opening prayers and advice (30:1b–10), are mainly a collection of list sayings. This cleverly constructed collection's most noticeable feature is the graded numerical sayings in the pattern "three (things) … four (things)." In a subtle way Agur has used these two numbers to unite this entire section: the number "three" (שָׁלוֹשׁ or שְׁלֹשָׁה) is used four times (30:15, 18, 21, 29), while the number "four" (אַרְבַּע or אַרְבָּעָה) is used five times (30:15, 18, 21, 24, 29). Four list sayings use this pattern "three (things) … four (things)" (30:15b–16; 30:18–19; 30:21–23; 30:29–31), while four list sayings do not use this pattern (30:11–14; 30:15a; 30:24–28; 30:32–33).

Prov 30:11–33 opens with a list of four kinds of people in 30:11–14, although this passage does not use the number "four." It closes with a list of three actions in 30:32–33, though this final list does not use the number "three." Moreover, this section consisting of list sayings (30:11–33) is arranged chiastically into seven (the sum of three plus four) units. See figure 19, which gives chiastic parallels in italics.

Note that 30:17 and 30:20 are not list sayings. Instead they are connected to the list saying in 30:18–19 by catchwords. Prov 30:17 is connected to 30:19 by the catchword נֶשֶׁר, "vulture, eagle," and 30:20 is connected to 30:19 by the catchword דֶּרֶךְ, "way."

As with other sections of Proverbs, the arrangement (in this case a chiasm) is not as tightly organized as in non-Wisdom literature. None of the units are completely parallel with their counterparts. This looseness allows the reader not only to see a connection to the chiastic parallel, but also to draw connections in other directions, including other chapters of the book of Proverbs. This is, of course, similar to the loose constructions found in many sections of Solomon's proverbs (chapters 1–29).

Nevertheless, Agur has carefully and intricately arranged his sayings in 30:11–33 into a cohesive section that explores three main topics: (1) family; (2) government; and (3) foolishness (in contrast to wisdom). The first four units (30:11–14; 30:15–16; 30:17–20; 30:21–23) concern family in some way: fathers, mothers, daughters, birth (womb), and marriage. The fourth unit speaks both of government ("king" in 30:22) and of family ("wed" in

[12] A dominant theme in Proverbs 1–9 is a father's instruction to his son to enable him to live by divine wisdom. See, for example, the excursus "Proverbs 1–9, Christ, and the Ten Commandments" in the commentary on Proverbs 1.

Figure 19

The Organization of Agur's List Sayings

Unit	*Features*
A 30:11–14	*A list saying without a number;* a list of four.
B 30:15–16	*A list saying beginning with a number: "three (things) ... four (things)"; a list of four in two pairs* (13:15b–16). This list saying is preceded by a short list saying (30:15a). Both sayings are united around the theme of insatiability.
C 30:17–20	*A list saying beginning with a number:* "three (things) ... *four (things)"; a list of four* (30:18–19). This list saying is preceded by a non-list saying (30:17) that is linked to it with the catchword נֶשֶׁר, "vulture, eagle," and it is followed by a non-list saying linked to it with the catchword דֶּרֶךְ, "way."
D 30:21–23	A list saying beginning with תַּחַת, "under"; "three (things) ... four (things)"; תַּחַת, "under," is used four times; a list of four in two pairs.
C' 30:24–28	*A list saying beginning with a number: "four (things)"; a list of four.*
B' 30:29–31	*A list saying beginning with a number: "three (things) ... four (things)"; a list of four in two pairs.* These four are chiastically arranged: A A lion with characterization B A rooster B' A male goat A' A king with characterization
A' 30:32–33	*A list saying without a number;* a list of three.*

*Note that 30:11–14 and 30:32–33 are parallel even though 30:11–14 is a list of four kinds of people and 30:32–33 is a list of three actions. The parallel consists of the fact that they are the only lists in this section without an explicit number.

30:23). Therefore the theme of the family in the first four units overlaps with the theme of government, which is evident in the fourth through sixth units (30:21–23; 30:24–28; 30:29–31), each of which refers to a "king." (Note again the organization involving three and four.) The seventh and final unit (30:32–33) serves as a warning to those who are foolish enough to have an inflated ego about their own wisdom. This final unit cautions against the notion that if one can comprehend these sayings, one has mastered wisdom (contrast the self-aggrandizement warned against in this unit with Agur's confession in 30:1b–3).

That Agur has chosen to arrange his list sayings into seven units is no accident. Like other passages in Proverbs that involve seven (6:16–19; 6:31; 9:1; 24:16; 26:16; 26:25), he is signaling comprehensiveness: in the case of 30:11–33, the comprehensiveness of God's wisdom as it encompasses all of temporal life in both the estates of family and of government. Moreover, Agur has implicitly used the number seven to link the list sayings in 30:11–33 with the sayings about the estate of the church in 30:1–10, since there are a total of seven numerical sayings in Proverbs 30 (30:7–9; 30:15a; 30:15b–16; 30:18–19; 30:21–23; 30:24–28; 30:29–31).

30:11–14 Unit A (see figure 19) lists four kinds of people with attitudes that are opposed to wisdom. All these people are lacking in wisdom because of their opposition to God. Prov 30:11, which describes the first person, is reminiscent of 20:20, where we are told that a person who curses father and mother will be subject to judgment when his lamp is snuffed out. Opposition to parents is a rejection of God's wisdom throughout Proverbs, as is stated already in 1:8.

The second person (30:12) is a person who considers himself "pure, clean" (טָהוֹר, 30:12), without fault and presentable to God, though he is unwashed and anything but pure. This is a person who does not repent of his sins. Jesus speaks of the necessity of being washed by him (Jn 13:8–10), and the "clean water" (מַיִם טְהוֹרִים, Ezek 36:25) that God promises to pour out on his people in order to give them a new heart and the Holy Spirit (Ezek 36:25–27) is fulfilled in Christian Baptism. Through this Sacrament, God bestows the Holy Spirit and salvation as he works repentance and saving faith (Acts 2:38–39; 13:24; 19:4; Rom 6:1–4; Titus 3:4–7; 1 Pet 3:18–22).

The third person (Prov 30:13) is related to the second, because he has a haughty attitude. The expression רָמוּ עֵינָיו, literally, "his eyes are high," denotes an arrogant attitude toward God (see the similar expressions in 2 Ki 19:22 || Is 37:23; Pss 18:28 [ET 18:27]; 131:1) and is a disgusting thing to Yahweh (see Prov 6:17). The person with this attitude, like the one who curses father and mother, will have his lamp darkened (21:4).

The final person (30:14) is the most brutal of all, because he not only refuses to help the poor and needy, he actively harms them. In this way he insults God, his Maker and the Maker of the poor and oppressed (14:31).

30:15–16 Unit B begins with a short list of the twin daughters of a leech (30:15a). This is a reference to a person who is a parasite, living off of the work of others. Such a person is never satisfied and seems even to have two mouths (the "daughters: Give! [and] give!"), like a leech with two suckers.

The second list saying in this unit enumerates four more insatiable things. These four are grouped in two pairs. The first pair is positioned at the two ends of life: death and birth. Sheol never has enough because it is always ready to receive one more life. A barren womb never has enough because it can never reach the goal for which God created it: the birth of a child. Scripture portrays the anguish of mothers who were barren until God interceded on their behalf (Sarah, Rachel, Hannah, Elizabeth). However, many believing women never conceive a child, yet they should not conclude that God is displeased with them, for all who hear and believe the Word of God are blessed (Lk 11:27–28).

The second pair notes the insatiability of land and fire. A dry land such as Palestine seems as if it can never be watered enough. Similarly, feeding a fire will not satisfy it, but only make it burn more strongly. A blaze will continue to burn and spread as long as it can find fuel. It is this fourth element in the list that is the climax of the saying. Fire is a metaphor for quarreling in Prov 26:20–21. As long as one adds fuel to a quarrel it will continue to rage. A long-running feud can even extend from one generation to the next. The only way to quench it is to deprive it of all fuel.

30:17–20 Unit C contains three proverbs. The first (30:17) returns to the theme of disrespect for parents (cf. 30:11). The despising eye is probably meant to tie the haughty person of 30:13 with the disrespectful person of 30:11. To despise godly parents is to despise God himself because they are in the place of God in this life (see Ex 20:12; Deut 5:16; LC I 126; cf. Lev 19:32). Such a person may consider himself טָהוֹר, "clean, pure" (Prov 30:12), but his judgment will be to have his carcass picked clean by unclean birds.

The central proverb in this unit (30:18–19) lists four things that Agur claims he cannot understand. The mystery common to the first three is locomotion without legs, which neither follows a visible path nor leaves footprints behind. The fourth element, however, is the climactic one. The focus of Agur's amazement is the mystery of human love. A man woos his virgin bride, and their love leads to betrothal and marriage, with the physical expression of their love at the consummation of the marriage. This great gift of God to humans is a source of pleasure and joy, comfort and companionship (Gen 2:18–25; 24:67; Song 4:9–5:1; 7:2–14 [ET 7:1–13]). While extolling the expression of Christian love within marriage, St. Paul exclaims that this union is bound up in the greater mystical union—the "great mystery" of Christ and his church, his washed and cleansed bride (Eph 5:22–33).

The third saying in this unit (Prov 30:20) stands in contrast but is linked to the preceding list saying by the catchword דֶּרֶךְ, "way." It comments on the adulteress who does not honor marriage as a gift from God, but instead shows contempt for God's gift by denying that adultery is a sin. This woman eats, that is, she engages in illicit sex (see the commentary on 9:17), but she refuses to see her assault on God's institution of marriage as wrong. This condemnation of the adulteress balances the earlier warnings by Wisdom that a son (a man) must avoid adultery to escape condemnation in hell (Prov 6:24–29; 7:5–27; 9:13–18). The unregenerate typically are not able to discern the severity of their own sins (see Rom 1:21–32). This is partly because they lack the Holy Spirit, who convicts believers of their sins (Jn 16:7–13), and partly because their standards generally are based on merely comparing themselves to the behaviors of other sinners (see Lk 18:11), rather than to the holy and perfect standards of God (Pss 19:8–12 [ET 19:7–11]; 119:66, 86, 137–38).

30:21–23 Unit D is the only graded numerical saying in this section not to begin with a number. Instead it begins with the preposition תַּחַת, "under," and uses this word as the organizing principle for the four things that are unbearable. These four things are intolerable because they invert the proper order of the world.

The first two unbearable situations are grouped together by תַּחַת at the start of 30:22, where it does double duty for both clauses of the verse ("under a slave … and [under] a complete fool …"). This pairing recalls the similar pairing of a slave become king and a fool made comfortable in 19:10. The two situations here are unbearable because of the arrogance they engender in both the slave and the fool. The slave is likely to be full of overweening pride because of his ascension to ultimate power, and the fool is arrogant once he feels no hunger, which would normally curb his arrogance. Instead he can freely pour forth foolish words and alienate whomever he wishes because he has been freed from need and social responsibility. The truth of this verse often becomes evident when a person quickly becomes rich or experiences a sudden rise to power. Such a person may be exceptionally conceited because he has not learned humility and wisdom through the lengthy time of hard labor that normally is a prerequisite for power and wealth.

The second two situations are likewise paired in 30:23 by תַּחַת, which again does double duty ("under a woman … and [under] a slave …"). The pairing of the hated woman and the slave woman notes the two unfortunate marriages into which these women are taken. In 30:22 the promoted slave and the satiated fool cause others to suffer, but in the pair in 30:23, it is the hated woman and the slave girl who suffer. The hated woman has a life of bitterness because she is not loved by her husband (see the first textual note on 30:23). The slave woman might be able to replace her mistress, such as when Hagar provided Ishmael as a potential heir for Abraham while Sarah was still barren (see the second textual note on 30:23). She might also replace her mistress if her mistress dies. However, even if she replaces the rightful wife, she has an impossible task, because she will in some sense always be a slave in the eyes of her husband. She will not be as fully loved and valued as the former wife was.

The fourth element is the climax in 30:21–23. The first three are all possible—a slave can become a king, a fool can be filled with food, and a woman can be unloved when married. However, a slave girl cannot really replace her mistress, making this the climax in its irony.

While most modern societies do not allow slavery or polygamy, the truths in 30:23 are still relevant and may become evident in abusive marriages, in divorce, and in the tensions that are sometimes seen in "blended families" when divorced spouses remarry.

30:24–28 Unit C' abandons the "three (things) … four (things)" formula in favor of simply listing four animals that exhibit wisdom despite their small size and seeming powerlessness. The ant's wisdom (30:25) comes in its apparent foresight in working while the time still presents the opportunity. This example employs language drawn from Solomon's description of the ant in 6:6, 8.

Rock badgers (30:26) are wise because, without being powerful themselves, they can live in a cliff as their powerful fortress. They make the best uses of their resources.

Locusts (30:27), individually tiny and vulnerable, are wise because they find strength in their corporate self-discipline and organization even without the benefit of a leader.

Like the other lists of four, the fourth element of this list (30:28) is the climax: a lizard is wise. Although it appears to be subject to the whims of ordinary humans, who can pick it up in their hands, it can gain access to the king—something most of the king's subjects cannot do!

30:29–31 Unit B' reverts to the familiar graded numerical saying of "three (things) … four (things)." This saying is about the majesty of the gait of four creatures. These creatures are paired chiastically:

A A lion, the mightiest among the animals …
    B A rooster
    B' A male goat
A' A king presiding over his army

The outer pair is characterized by an additional phrase or phrases, whereas the inner pair is simply listed. This pairing points out the climax in the list. The king is paired with the lion. The lion is majestic because as the mightiest animal it does not have to yield to any creature. The king likewise is displaying his might as he parades at the head of his army. As one is cautious and avoids approaching the lion, so also one should be cautious in risking the king's wrath by interrupting his display of regal authority and power (see also 20:2, 26; 24:21; 25:5). Authorities delight in displaying the prerogatives of their office (Lk 22:25). A wise person does nothing to deny them their honor (Rom 13:7), yet fears God above all else (e.g., Prov 1:7; 3:7; 24:21; 29:25).

30:32–33 Unit A' closes out Agur's proverbs with a warning involving a list of three consequences of applying pressure (מֵּיץ). The person who thinks of himself more highly than he ought or who has been scheming (presumably to hatch some plot at the expense of others) should keep his mouth shut. A person who expresses the opinion that he is superior to others or who reveals his schemes to get ahead and take advantage of others will be seen as aggressive, adding tension and pressure to society. Such self-aggrandizement is like punching someone in the nose or allowing one's anger to flare so that a fight ensues. The wise person instead keeps his sinful thoughts to himself until he recognizes them as sinful, and then he repents of them and receives God's pardon (see 10:12; 14:9; 28:13). The fool ignores this advice and precipitates a fight like a butter churn coagulates butter from milk.

While the previous section of proverbs by Agur focuses on the estate of the church and has obvious expressions of the Gospel of Jesus Christ (see the commentary on 30:1–10), this section seems to have few such overt connections. However, it should be noted that this section (30:11–33) focuses on the estates of family and government, both of which are created by God.[13] The believer renders God-pleasing service as he or she lives faithfully within these estates (see, e.g., Rom 13:1–7; Eph 5:22–6:4).

Moreover, both estates were important in the life of Christ himself. The preexistent Son of God (Prov 8:22–31) assumed his human nature at his incarnation. The moment he was conceived of the Virgin Mary by the power of the Holy Spirit, he became a member of a human family (his relatives are noted in Mt 13:55; Lk 8:19–20; Jn 2:12). Jesus was subject to his parents (Lk 2:51). He was also subject to governing authorities (Mt 17:24–27; 22:15–21; Jn 19:10–11). In all of these cases, God used these two estates to fulfill his purpose to redeem all people through the sinless life, sacrificial death, and victorious resurrection of his Son. The Gospel of Christ, who is Wisdom incarnate,[14] enables believers to live wisely in the realms of family and governed society in order to bring glory to God (see 1 Cor 10:31–33; 1 Tim 4:3–5; Heb 13:4; 1 Pet 2:12–17).

---

[13] See further the commentary on the superscription to Agur's proverbs, 30:1a.

[14] See "Wisdom in Proverbs" in the introduction. See also the commentary on 1:1–7; 3:13–20; 8:22–31; 30:1b–10; and the excursus "Proverbs 8, Wisdom, Christology, and the Arian Controversy" in the commentary on chapter 8.

Proverbs 31:1–9

King Lemuel's Proverbs

Proverbs 31:1

Superscription to King Lemuel's Proverbs

Translation

31 [1]The words of Lemuel, a king. A prophetic revelation that his mother used to discipline him.

Textual Notes

31:1 דִּבְרֵי לְמוּאֵל מֶלֶךְ—The Masoretic accents, with *athnach* on מֶלֶךְ, indicate that these words form the first part of the superscription. The second part (see the next textual note) will show that the construct phrase דִּבְרֵי לְמוּאֵל, "the words *of* Lemuel," may have objective genitive: "words taught/addressed *to* Lemuel" by his mother (so GKC, § 128 h). However, he in turn became the source and author of these words as now recorded in Scripture, so the construct phrase can also be said to have a genitive of authorship (so Waltke-O'Connor, § 9.5.1c, including example 7).

The king's name, here לְמוּאֵל, "Lemuel," is vocalized לְמוֹאֵל, "Lemoel," in 31:4. The *shureq* in לְמוּאֵל might reflect an archaic nominative plural ending, as it apparently does in other similarly formed proper names (Waltke-O'Connor, § 8.2b). This name is unique, and this person cannot be positively identified with any other person named in the OT. The LXX translated it as ὑπὸ θεοῦ, "from God" in 31:1, apparently because it read this name as the words לְמוֹ אֵל. The combination לְמוֹ is the preposition לְ with enclitic *mem* (an archaism), as in, for example, Job 27:14; 29:21. Perhaps the name should be understood as לְמוֹ אֵל, meaning "dedicated to God." See the name לָאֵל, "(belonging) to God," in Num 3:24.

At the same time, "Lemuel" may also be a pseudonym for a faithful king. These proverbs (31:1–9) are positioned in the book after the Solomonic proverbs that were compiled by the men of Hezekiah (25:1–29:27). (They also follow chapter 30, the proverbs of Agur, whose identity and dates are unknown.) Therefore, if "Lemuel" is a pseudonym for one of Israel's faithful kings, and he lived during the time of Hezekiah (715–686 BC) or later, he would have to be a king of Judah, since the Northern Kingdom of Israel had been conquered by Assyria in 723 BC.[1] Only two kings of Judah from that era are commended in Scripture as having been faithful to God, namely, Hezekiah (2 Ki 18:1–5) and Josiah (2 Ki 23:24–25). Since a large portion of the book of Proverbs (chapters 25–29) is clearly associated with Hezekiah (25:1), he is a likely candidate. The several Aramaisms in 31:1–9 indicate a time when Aramaic was well-known in the Judean court, which would indicate a time from at least Hezekiah onwards (2 Ki 18:26). However, we cannot be certain that לְמוּאֵל is a pseudonym.

---

[1] For 723 BC as the date for the fall of Samaria, see Thiele, *The Mysterious Numbers of the Hebrew Kings*, 137, 163–68.

The noun מֶ֫לֶךְ lacks the definite article, hence "*a* king." It is clearly not to be taken as a title of Lemuel; "King Lemuel" would be expressed by לְמוּאֵל הַמֶּלֶךְ. Instead מֶ֫לֶךְ is an appositive that defines for us who Lemuel was, perhaps indicating that "Lemuel" is an alternate name of one of the faithful Judean kings.

מַ֝שָּׂ֗א אֲשֶׁר־יִסְּרַ֥תּוּ אִמּֽוֹ׃—The Masoretic accents indicate that these words go together and form the second part of the superscription. For the noun מַשָּׂא, "a prophetic revelation," see the third textual note and the commentary on 30:1a. מַ֝שָּׂ֗א is the antecedent of the following relative clause, which begins with אֲשֶׁר־, meaning "(the prophetic revelation) *with* which his mother disciplined him." אִמּֽוֹ, "his mother," is the subject of יִסְּרַ֥תּוּ, the feminine Piel (D) perfect of יָסַר, "to discipline," with a third masculine singular suffix that refers back to לְמוּאֵל, "Lemuel," in the first part of the verse. יָסַר is a common verb in Proverbs for imparting divine wisdom through the proper application of Law and Gospel. See "מוּסָר, 'Discipline,' and יָסַר, 'to Discipline' " in "Wisdom in Proverbs" in the introduction, as well as "Law and Gospel in Proverbs" in the introduction.

Some commentators have disregarded the Masoretic accents and have instead connected מַשָּׂא to the preceding words ("Lemuel, a king") instead of to the following relative clause. They argue that מַשָּׂא does not have its normal meaning, "a prophetic revelation," but rather means "a person from Massa."[2] They maintain that the phrase לְמוּאֵל מֶ֫לֶךְ מַ֝שָּׂא should be translated as something similar to "King Lemuel of Massa." Massa was a tribe from north Arabia (Gen 25:14; 1 Chr 1:30). To support this argument some contend that the Aramaic word בַּר, "son," in 31:2 and the Aramaizing plural מְלָכִין, "kings," in 31:3 point to a non-Israelite origin for 31:1–9. However, the use of the Aramaic בַּר instead of the Hebrew בֵּן is not conclusive evidence for connecting מַ֝שָּׂא to Massa because Massa was not an Aramean tribe, but rather is identified as an Arabic tribe. Moreover, Israelite poetry can on occasion incorporate familiar Aramaic words, as demonstrated by the use in Psalm 2 of both בֵּן (Ps 2:7) and בַּר (Ps 2:12) for "son."

In addition, if מַ֝שָּׂא is taken to be a place name ("Massa") instead of "a prophetic revelation," then the antecedent of אֲשֶׁר would be דִּבְרֵי: "the *words* of … , *which* his mother used …" This would leave open the question of why the words of Lemuel's mother, no matter how sagacious they are, were added to the book of Proverbs after the divinely inspired wisdom of Solomon (chapters 1–29) and Agur (chapter 30). But if we understand the text according to the clear meaning of מַ֝שָּׂא, "a prophetic revelation," and follow the syntax indicated by the Masoretic accents, it is obvious why the words recorded in 31:1–9 were recognized to be on par with the inspired, revelatory words of Solomon and Agur, and worthy of inclusion in the book of Proverbs.

Commentary

This superscription identifies 31:1–9 as the words of Lemuel's mother, which she used to discipline and instruct him, probably from the time of his childhood onward. Lemuel recognized that her words were an authoritative

---

2 Clifford, *Proverbs*, 268–69; Murphy, *Proverbs*, 239.

"prophetic revelation." He remembered and recorded them since they are the very words of God himself.

Many other proverbs speak of the "mother" as involved in the spiritual education and formation of children. See, for example, 1:8; 6:20; 23:25. Similarly, the NT indicates that a Christian mother and also a grandmother can have a vital role in teaching the Scriptures to children from infancy, as was done for Timothy (2 Tim 1:5; 3:15–17), who became an influential pastor in the apostolic church (see the commentary on Prov 29:15). God can inspire women (as well as men) to speak a divine revelation that he intends to be recorded and preserved as part of his authoritative Word, as perhaps best illustrated by Elizabeth's blessing of the Virgin Mary (Lk 1:42–45) and the Magnificat (Lk 1:46–55) by the θεοτόκος, "she who begot God" or "the mother of God" (FC Ep VIII 12; FC SD VIII 24).

"A king" (מֶלֶךְ) in Prov 31:1 helps the reader understand that 31:2–9 is a revelation of wisdom that Lemuel found to be especially relevant for himself as a king and how he is to govern. Lemuel now passes on this wisdom for the benefit of other leaders among God's people. Thus 31:2–9 contains not simply observations about kings, but also counsel for them, as confirmed by the exhortations to "kings" in 31:3–4.

The superscription calling these proverbs "the words of Lemuel, a king," may indicate that they were preserved in his official chronicles, the royal archives of Israel. This probably applies only to 31:1–9 and does not designate the authorship of 31:10–31, which is shown to be a separate composition by its acrostic structure.[3] Moreover, 31:1–9 has little in common with 31:10–31. While 31:10–31 is about an ideal wife, the only mention of women in 31:1–9 is a warning about the misuse of sexuality (31:3), which resonates with the many Solomonic proverbs that warn against adultery in order to safeguard the believer's spiritual relationship to God as part of his church, the virgin bride of Christ.[4]

---

[3] Even Garrett, *Proverbs, Ecclesiastes, Song of Songs*, 247, who favors the view that 31:10–31 contains the words of Lemuel or his mother, admits that there is no strong evidence for this position.

[4] See the excursus "Wisdom and the Adulteress in Proverbs 1–9" in the commentary on Proverbs 2; see also the discussion of the Sixth Commandment in the excursus "Proverbs 1–9, Christ, and the Ten Commandments" in the commentary on Proverbs 1.

Proverbs 31:2–9

Three Pieces of Advice for Kings

Translation

31 [2]What, my son?
What, my very own son?
What, son of my vows?

[3]Do not give your strength to women
nor your ways to those women who destroy kings.

[4]It is not for kings, Lemoel,
it is not for kings to drink wine
nor for rulers to crave liquor.
[5]Otherwise he will drink and forget what is decreed
and change legal standards for all those who are oppressed.
[6]Give liquor to someone who is perishing
and wine to those whose soul is bitter.
[7]He will drink and forget his poverty,
and he will no longer remember his trouble.

[8]Speak out for those who cannot speak,
for the rights of all those who are defenseless.
[9]Speak out, judge fairly,
and defend the oppressed and needy.

Textual Notes

31:2 מַה־בְּרִי—"What, my son?" is designed to command attention from the mother's son. In this verse בַּר, the usual Aramaic noun for "son," occurs three times. The Hebrew OT prefers בֵּן, but בַּר does occur in some Hebrew passages. Psalm 2 uses both בֵּן (Ps 2:7) and בַּר (Ps 2:12) for "son" (cf. the second textual note on 31:1).

בַּר־בִּטְנִי—The force of "son of my womb" is "my very own son."[1]

בַּר־נְדָרָי׃—"Son of my vows" could have a genitive of source if the mother made "vows" to God and he responded by enabling her to conceive and bear a son. See 1 Samuel 1.

31:3 וּדְרָכֶיךָ לַמְחוֹת מְלָכִין׃—The word לַמְחוֹת is translated as the feminine plural Qal (G) participle of מָחָה, "blot out, exterminate," with the preposition לְ and the definite article (-לַ), "to those women who exterminate kings" (see BDB, s.v. מָחָה, Qal, 3). The construct phrase has an objective genitive. מְלָכִין has the usual Aramaic masculine

[1] Deist, "Prov. 31:1."

plural ending ין־ (see GKC, § 87 e; Joüon, § 90 c; Waltke-O'Connor § 7.4b, and the second textual note on 31:1) rather than the Hebrew ending: מְלָכִים (twice in 31:4).

A second possibility is that לַמְחוֹת is the Hiphil (H) infinitive construct of the same verb, מָחָה, with the preposition לְ. Both the Qal (G) and the Hiphil (H) of מָחָה are used elsewhere in the OT with the same meaning, "blot out, exterminate" (see BDB, s.v. מָחָה, Hiphil). The infinitive would begin a result clause, but the syntax would be rougher: "do not give your strength … or your ways … (so as) to exterminate kings."

31:4 אַל לַמְלָכִים שְׁתוֹ־יָיִן—The Qal (G) infinitive שְׁתוֹ־ is of שָׁתָה, "to drink." However, it is uncertain whether this is the infinitive construct (usually spelled שְׁתוֹת) or the infinitive absolute.[2] The infinitive absolute can be spelled שָׁתוֹ (Is 22:13), but here may be pointed שְׁתוֹ־ because of the syntax, since it is joined with יָיִן. In any event, the meaning is clear: "it is not for kings to drink wine."

וּלְרוֹזְנִים אֵו שֵׁכָר׃— The noun שֵׁכָר, "liquor," is also in 20:1, as is יַיִן, "wine," and both nouns recur in 31:6. The first and third words of this line, לְרוֹזְנִים … שֵׁכָר, "for rulers … liquor," are parallel to the corresponding words in the previous line, "for kings … wine." Because of the parallelism one might expect the word represented by the Kethib או or the Qere אֵי to be an infinitive with a meaning similar to that of שְׁתוֹ־, "to drink," in the preceding line. Driver has observed that the consonants could be vocalized אַוֹ, which could be a defectively written form of the Piel (D) infinitive absolute (אַוֹּו or אַוֹּה) of the verb אָוָה, "to desire." Driver has also noted that אַו may be an Aramaizing form of that same infinitive absolute.[3] This commentary ("to crave") and many translations (RSV, NIV, NASB) follow his proposal. Piel (D) and Hithpael (HtD) forms of אָוָה, "to desire," occur elsewhere in Proverbs (13:4; 21:10, 26; 23:3, 6; 24:1). Another possibility is that אַו is a noun meaning "desire," a hapax legomenon whose construct form could be אוֹ (so BDB, s.v. אַו, under אָוָה).

The Qere, the interrogative אֵי, "where?" would require an implied verb for speaking or asking, for example, "nor for rulers *to say*, 'Where is liquor?' " While that is less likely, the resulting message of the line would be similar. Other attempts at emendation are unconvincing.[4] KJV simply omits any translation of אַו, which lets "to drink" in the preceding line do double duty for this line too.

31:5 פֶּן־יִשְׁתֶּה וְיִשְׁכַּח מְחֻקָּק—The Qal (G) imperfect of שָׁתָה, "to drink" (whose infinitive, שְׁתוֹ, is in 31:4), is repeated in the identical form in 31:5 and 31:7, יִשְׁתֶּה, "he will drink." Each time it is immediately followed by the Qal imperfect וְיִשְׁכַּח, "and he will forget," implying a causal relationship between drinking alcohol and a faulty memory.

The Pual (Dp) participle מְחֻקָּק, "what is decreed" (see BDB), is from the verb חָקַק, "enact (a law), decree (legislation)." It could refer to the legal system previously established by God in the Torah and/or by earlier monarchs or to what the drunk and forgetful king himself promulgated: "forget what he himself decreed." The same possibilities pertain to the next clause.

---

2 See GCK, § 75 n, and Driver, "Problems in the Hebrew Text of Proverbs," 194–95.

3 Driver, "Problems in the Hebrew Text of Proverbs," 195.

4 E.g., Thomas, "אַו in Proverbs XXXI 4."

וְישַׁנֶּה דִּין—The Qal (G) of שָׁנָה I, with the intransitive meaning "change," is in 24:21 (see the second textual note on that verse). Here the Piel (D), וִישַׁנֶּה (the imperfect with conjunctive *waw*), has a transitive meaning: "and *he will change* legal standards." This may be a technical legal idiom denoting a violation of legal precedent or changing a decision that has already been handed down by a judge.[5]

Note the play in this section on דִּין. Here in 31:5 it is a noun with the connotation "legal standards." In 31:8 it is a noun with the connotation of "legal rights" (see *HALOT*, 1), whereas in 31:9 it is a Qal imperative of the verb דִּין, meaning "judge."

כָּל־בְּנֵי־עֹנִי׃—Literally, "all sons of oppression," this means "all those who are oppressed." The plural construct בְּנֵי־, "sons of," is used similarly in the construct phrase כָּל־בְּנֵי חֲלוֹף in 31:8 to refer to all people who share a certain characteristic. Here the shared status in life is denoted by the noun עֳנִי (pausal: עֹנִי), "affliction, oppression."

31:7 וְיִשְׁכַּח רִישׁוֹ וַעֲמָלוֹ לֹא יִזְכָּר־עוֹד׃—The noun רִישׁ, "poverty," is part of a frequent theme in Proverbs. It occurs in 6:11 (רֵאשׁ); 10:15; 13:18; 24:34; 28:19; 30:8 (רֵאשׁ). Note the chiastic word order in the synonymous parallelism here, literally:

A And he will forget (וְיִשְׁכַּח)
  B His poverty (רִישׁוֹ)
  B' And his trouble (וַעֲמָלוֹ)
A' He will not remember again (לֹא יִזְכָּר־עוֹד)

31:8 פְּתַח־פִּיךָ לְאִלֵּם—Literally, this is "open your mouth for a mute person." In this context it refers to rising to the defense of someone who cannot serve as his own advocate, hence, "speak out" (NRSV; similar is NIV). The imperative and direct object, פְּתַח־פִּיךָ, are repeated at the start of 31:9.

אֶל־דִּין כָּל־בְּנֵי חֲלוֹף׃—The literal meaning may be this: "for the legal right of all sons of defenselessness." For this use of בְּנֵי, see the third textual note on 31:5. The word חֲלוֹף is a hapax legomenon. In form it is the infinitive construct of חָלַף, which can mean "pass by, pass away, vanish," although this may be a noun derived from that verb (so BDB, s.v. חֲלוֹף). Note the various translations: "destitute" (NIV, NRSV), "unfortunate" (NASB),[6] "dispossessed,"[7] and "weak."[8] The meaning may best be expressed by "defenseless," that is, people who are easily deprived of their legal rights and who would pass away and vanish (be marginalized or die) unless others with influence speak out on their behalf.

31:9 שְׁפָט־צֶדֶק—The imperative of שָׁפַט, "to judge," does not simply mean "to condemn," but "to carry out justice," including the rescue of the innocent, the acquittal and vindication of those who are unfairly oppressed. The noun צֶדֶק, "righteousness," serves as an adverbial accusative: "judge *righteously, justly, fairly.*" See "The Relationship between Wisdom and Righteousness in Proverbs" in "Wisdom in Proverbs" in the intro-

---

5 Paul, "Unrecognized Biblical Legal Idioms," 231–35.

6 Also Scott, *Proverbs, Ecclesiastes*, 183.

7 Murphy, *Proverbs*, 239.

8 Clifford, *Proverbs*, 269.

duction. God is the ultimate judge who justifies (declares righteous) all sinners who trust in him and rely on his gracious forgiveness.

וְדִ֝֗ין עָנִ֥י וְאֶבְיֽוֹן׃—The verb דִּין can imply condemnation and mean "act as judge, administer judgment" (BDB, Qal, 1). Yet it can imply redemptive action and mean "plead the cause" of an orphan or other defenseless person (BDB, Qal, 2 a). Its imperative here with the adjectives "oppressed" and "needy" as its objects has the contextual meaning "defend," as a synonym of שְׁפָט־ in the preceding clause. The verb דִּין can have God himself as the subject in the sense that he "will vindicate" his persecuted believers (Ps 54:3 [ET 54:1]). The exalted Messiah is the King who will "judge" or "rule" over all nations and execute those who have opposed him (Ps 110:6; cf. Ps 2:6–12; Mt 21:41).

Commentary

Lemuel's mother gave him three pieces of advice preceded by three questions in 31:2 that draw attention to her authority and responsibility to teach him. These three pieces of advice are linked to one another by means of repeated words and phrases. Three times the negative אַל is used with the plural of מֶלֶךְ, "… not … kings" (31:3–4). Another three verses use דִּין, a noun ("legal standards, rights," 31:5, 8) and verb ("defend," 31:9), and twice the noun דִּין is followed by כָּל־בְּנֵי־, literally, "all sons of …" (31:5, 8). See figure 20.

Figure 20

The Organization of King Lemuel's Proverbs

1. Warning about sexual promiscuity (31:3)	אַל … מְלָכִין, "not … kings" (31:3)
2. Advice about alcohol (31:4–7)	אַל לַמְלָכִים, "it is not for kings" (31:4)
	אַל לַמְלָכִים, "it is not for kings" (31:4)
	דִּין כָּל־בְּנֵי־עֹנִי, "legal standards for all those who are oppressed" (31:5)
3. Call to ensure that the defenseless receive justice (31:8–9)	דִּין כָּל־בְּנֵי חֲלוֹף, "the rights of all those who are defenseless" (31:8)
	וְדִ֝֗ין עָנִ֥י וְאֶבְיֽוֹן׃,"defend the oppressed and needy" (31:9)

The pattern that links these three sayings is unique to these verses in Proverbs. The first saying introduces a line that is repeated (with variation) twice in the second proverb. The second proverb, likewise, introduces a phrase that is repeated in the third. These proverbs also move from prohibition to encouragement. The first saying (31:3) is strictly prohibition of a harmful behavior,

namely, sexual sin. The second saying moves from prohibition of harmful behavior (31:4–5) to encouraging a helpful behavior (31:6–7). The final saying encourages a helpful behavior (31:8–9).

31:2 This verse contains the introductory questions that point to the authority of Lemuel's mother to teach her child. By referring to Lemuel as her "son" three times, she asserts her God-given vocation to instruct him in faith and for life. First she calls him "my son." Then by calling him her "very own son," she strengthens her claim to have the responsibility as well as the authority to direct him. Then by calling him "son of my vows," she asserts that she has a sacred duty to instruct him because it is a fulfilling of a vow she has made to God. Perhaps God even enabled her to conceive and bear her son Lemuel after she had made a holy vow about him, as Hannah did for Samuel (1 Samuel 1).

31:3 This verse is a warning that a harem could be more than a distraction for a king. Sexual promiscuity may cause his downfall and destroy his kingdom. The problem lies not with the women, but with the king's indulgence in a sin readily available to him. This saying may have in mind Solomon's fall into idolatry under the influence of his heathen wives (1 Ki 11:1–8), contrary to the prohibition in Deut 17:17. Solomon was the last king over united Israel; after his death the kingdom was split and both northern Israel and southern Judah eventually fell to other nations. Despite his wisdom recorded in Proverbs 1–29, Solomon was led astray by his own passions.

While civilized society no longer permits powerful rulers to keep harems nor tolerates polygamy (cf. 1 Tim 3:2, 12), any believer, especially a leader or one with money and power, can fall prey to the same kind of ruinous temptation. Many modern societies tolerate sexual promiscuity and even the abominations of homosexuality and lesbianism. They wrongly view sex outside of marriage as normal and natural. Instead sex is a gift from God that he commands to be used only within marriage (Gen 2:24), that is, the lifelong union of one man and one woman (Mt 19:4–6). God ordains this sacred context (Heb 13:4) for the good of both spouses and for the well-being of the entire community. To contravene God's design for sexuality is to provoke his destructive judgment on the entire society (Genesis 18–19; Rom 1:18–32; Revelation 18).

31:4–7 This is a saying about another passion that can ruin kings: alcohol. It is a reminder that even the finest fruits of God's creation can be abused and that substance abuse by those in power can lead to grave injustices throughout society. Alcoholism may cloud the ruler's mind with one or both of these two results: First, he may not enforce good laws that he himself or others before him have instituted. Second, he may change long-established laws upon which his kingdom is built. The greatest destruction is caused by a failure to govern according to God's Word, as noted often in Proverbs 25–29. The degeneration of the monarchy and innovations in the legal system are especially harmful for those who are least able to defend their rights: "those who are oppressed" (31:5; see further 31:8–9).

However, this misuse of alcohol should be balanced against its proper use according to Scripture. This is signaled by the two ways in which the prohibition of 31:4–5 is linked to the encouragement of 31:6–7. First, both the prohibition and the encouragement imply that the result of drinking is to forget: יִשְׁתֶּה וְיִשְׁכַּח, "he will drink and forget" (31:5, 7). Second, both use the same terms for alcoholic beverages, but the order is reversed when the prohibition, "wine … liquor" (31:4), is compared to the encouragement, "liquor … wine" (31:6).

In 31:6–7 Lemuel is encouraged to supply wine to the poor and suffering so that they may find some pleasure in life and, perhaps at least temporarily, forget about their misery (see Ps 104:15). The Qal (G) participle אוֹבֵד in 31:6 suggests that the recipient is "(already) perishing" and could benefit from liquor to anesthetize his pain, not that liquor is given for the purpose of hastening his demise. This might be compared to modern ethical health care practice in which a terminal patient, perhaps at a hospice, is given increasing doses of medication as needed to alleviate the suffering, even though some of the drugs administered (e.g., morphine) may be addictive. Of course it would be unethical and contrary to Scripture to euthanize a person by a fatal dose, but Christian compassion calls for allowing enough to relieve the pain.

This passage does not, however, endorse drunkenness, which is universally condemned in the Scriptures, including Proverbs (20:1; 21:17; 23:29–35). Neither is it a license for substance abuse or alcoholism. Resignation to such a lifestyle can be an expression of unbelief in God and a denial of the resurrection and life of the world to come. The apostle Paul quotes Is 22:13: "If the dead are not raised, then 'let us eat and let us drink, for tomorrow we are going to die' " (1 Cor 15:32). The biblical teachings of the indwelling of Christ and the Holy Spirit (Prov 1:23) and the promise of the resurrection of the body ("healing" in Prov 4:22; 16:24) call believers to glorify God by the way they use their bodies (Rom 8:9–11; 1 Cor 3:16; 6:9–20; Col 1:27).

The same dual view of alcohol can be found in the NT. Paul condemns drunkenness (Rom 13:13; Gal 5:19–21; 1 Pet 4:3), but encourages the moderate use of alcohol when it can be beneficial (1 Tim 5:23). Of course the most salutary use of wine is in the Lord's Supper, which Christ instituted to grant his disciples communion in his blood (1 Cor 10:16), which was shed for the forgiveness of sins and which established the new covenant (Mt 26:28; 1 Cor 11:25).

The proper use of alcohol has generally been accepted by Christians throughout church history. For instance, the early church father John Chrysostom (ca. 345–407) cites this proverb as he distinguishes the acceptable use of wine from its abuse through drunkenness:

> Wouldest thou know where wine is good? Hear what the Scripture saith, "Give strong drink unto him that is ready to perish, and wine unto the bitter in soul" [Prov 31:6]. And justly, because it can mitigate asperity and gloominess, and drive away clouds from the brow. "Wine maketh glad the heart of man" [Ps 104:15], says the Psalmist. How then does wine produce drunkenness? For it cannot be that one and the same thing should work opposite effects. Drunkenness then surely does not arise from wine, but from intemperance. Wine is bestowed upon us for no other purpose than for bodily health; but this purpose also is thwarted by immoderate use. But hear moreover what

> our blessed Apostle writes and says to Timothy, "Use a little wine for thy stomach's sake, and thine often infirmities" [1 Tim 5:23].[9]

Another early church father, Gregory of Nyssa (ca. 331–ca. 396), says this:

> Moreover console each other with the following words; it is a good medicine that Solomon has for sorrow; for he bids wine be given to the sorrowful; saying this to us, the labourers in the vineyard: "Give," therefore, "your wine to those that are in sorrow" [Prov 31:6], not that wine which produces drunkenness, plots against the senses, and destroys the body, but such as gladdens the heart, the wine which the Prophet recommends when he says: "Wine maketh glad the heart of man" [Ps 104:15].[10]

31:8–9 These verses go beyond encouraging Lemuel to soothe the pain of the needy and oppressed to encouraging him to be an advocate for the defenseless, who will have no other defender unless the believer speaks up with conviction. Lemuel's mother echoes Scripture's expectations for all good kings when she states that she expects him to place a high value on justice and righteousness so that the rich and powerful may not take advantage of the poor and weak. The rich and powerful need no defenders because they have the resources to defend themselves. Yet those in high positions in government are often swayed by their friendships with the rich and influential people of society. The result is government favoritism and policies that, intentionally or not, deny justice for the powerless. This saying reminds those in high office of the potentially corrupting effect of friendship with the mighty.

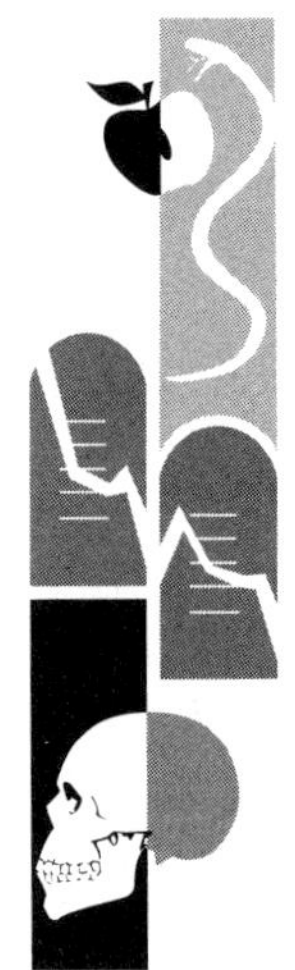

In modern times, abortion of unwanted children has become commonplace, and even infanticide is increasingly tolerated, as also is euthanasia and the selective denial of life-preserving care (even the basic necessities of food and water) when a person is judged to be a burden or no longer useful to society. Infants still in the womb cannot physically speak for themselves; they are wholly dependent on God and their mothers to protect their lives. Many who are incapacitated or elderly likewise cannot protest inhumane treatment. Even those who have the physical ability to speak may be deprived of due rights to defend themselves in the judicial and legal systems.

These proverbs remind those in power, and indeed all believers, that God calls them to defend the defenseless. Wise leaders are friends of God, who watches over the poor and lowly (Prov 3:34; 14:31). Believers who serve as advocates reflect Christ, the righteous one who is the sole and universal advocate for sinners before God the Father (Job 16:19; 1 Jn 2:1–2).

---

9 John Chrysostom, *Homilies on the Epistle of Saint Paul to the Ephesians*, 19 (*NPNF*[1] 13:138).

10 Gregory of Nyssa, *Funeral Oration on Meletius* (*NPNF*[2] 5:517).

Proverbs 31:10–31

An Acrostic Poem about a Godly Wife

Proverbs 31:10–31

An Acrostic Poem about a Godly Wife

Translation

31 א[10]Who can find a wife with strong character?
Her value is beyond that of jewels.
ב[11]Her husband's heart trusts her,
and he never lacks spoils.
ג[12]She does him good and not evil
all the days of her life.
ד[13]She seeks wool and flax,
and she eagerly works with her hands.
ה[14]She is like merchant ships:
from afar she brings her food.
ו[15]She rises while it is still night,
and she gives food to her household
and allotted portions to her female servants.
ז[16]She considers a field and acquires it.
From the fruit of her hands, she plants a vineyard.
ח[17]She straps strength around her waist,
and she rolls up her sleeves.
ט[18]She perceives that her profit is good.
Her lamp does not go out at night.
י[19]She stretches out her hands for the distaff,
and the palms of her hands grasp the spindle.
כ[20]She spreads out the palm of her hand to the oppressed,
and she stretches out her hands to the needy.
ל[21]She does not fear for her household on account of snow,
because her entire household is clothed in scarlet clothes.
מ[22]She makes bedspreads for herself.
Fine linen and purple [cloth] are her clothing.
נ[23]Her husband is known at the city gates
when he sits with the elders of the land.
ס[24]She makes linen garments and sells them,
and she delivers belts to the merchants.
ע[25]Strength and honor are her clothing,
and she laughs at the days to come.
פ[26]She opens her mouth with wisdom,
and kind instruction is on her tongue.
צ[27]She keeps a close eye on the conduct of her household,
and she does not eat the bread of laziness.
ק[28]Her sons rise up and bless her;
her husband [rises up] and praises her:

ר29"Many women show strong character,
but you have surpassed all of them."
ש30Charm is deceptive, and beauty is a fleeting vapor.
A woman with the fear of Yahweh—she should be praised.
ת31Give her [rewards] from the fruit of her hands,
and let her accomplishments praise her in the city gates.

Textual Notes

31:10 אֵֽשֶׁת־חַיִל מִי יִמְצָא—Literally, "a wife of valor, who can find?" uses חַיִל, which often denotes strength, bravery, and/or military prowess. For its translation as "strong character" both here and in 31:29, see "A Wife with Strong Character" in the commentary below.

וְרָחֹק מִפְּנִינִים מִכְרָהּ׃—The adjective רָחֹק means "distant, far." Here with the preposition מִן (on מִפְּנִינִים) in a comparative sense it means "far beyond" (BDB, s.v. רָחֹק, 1 a). For פְּנִינִים, translated as "jewels," see the first textual note on 3:15. The noun מֶכֶר means "value, price, worth," and the feminine suffix on מִכְרָהּ, "her value," refers back to אֵשֶׁת־, "wife of/with …"

31:11 בָּטַח בָּהּ לֵב בַּעְלָהּ—As expected, this second verse of the acrostic begins with the second Hebrew letter, ב. Moreover, three of the four words in this clause begin with ב, and every word contains it: *b*atach *b*ah le*b* *b*aʿlah. The noun לֵב in the construct phrase לֵב בַּעְלָהּ, "the heart of her husband," is the subject of the verb in the predicate, בָּטַח בָּהּ, "trusts in her."

וְשָׁלָל לֹא יֶחְסָר׃—The implied subject of "spoils he does not lack" is בַּעְלָהּ, "her husband," in the preceding clause. The noun שָׁלָל, "spoils," refers to stolen goods in 1:13 and to the plunder taken from defeated foes and shared by the conquerors in 16:19. The verb חָסַר, "to lack," has a negative connotation in its other occurrence in Proverbs, in 13:25, as also does the common cognate adjective חָסֵר, "lacking" (e.g., 6:32). However, the negated verb here has the positive force of "never lacks," equivalent to "always has."

31:12 גְּמָלַתְהוּ טוֹב וְלֹא־רָע—This is "she does him good and not evil." The verb גְּמָלַתְהוּ is the Qal (G) third feminine singular perfect of גָּמַל, "to do to," with a third masculine singular suffix that serves as an indirect object, "to him," referring back to בַּעְלָהּ, "her husband," in the first clause of 31:11. גָּמַל refers to beneficial action also in 11:17 and to not doing evil also in 3:30 (לֹא גְמָלְךָ רָעָה).

כֹּל יְמֵי חַיֶּיהָ׃—The final word in this construct chain, "all the days of her life," is pointed anomalously in Leningradensis: חַיֵּיה. Many manuscripts have the expected pointing for the feminine suffix: חַיֶּיהָ.

31:13 דָּרְשָׁה צֶמֶר וּפִשְׁתִּים—This means "she seeks wool and flax." צֶמֶר usually occurs with פִּשְׁתִּים as raw materials for textiles. "Flax" here denotes a processed form of the plant, probably the fibers prepared to be spun into linen thread for weaving into cloth.[1]

---

1 Nouns denoting vegetable matter in the plural indicate a processed state, whereas the singular indicates the material in its natural state (Waltke-O'Connor, § 7.4.1b).

וַתַּעַשׂ בְּחֵפֶץ כַּפֶּיהָ׃—Literally, "and she works with the delight of her hands" means that she is eager and happy to work with her hands (*HALOT*, s.v. חֵפֶץ, 1).

31:14 הָיְתָה כָּאֳנִיּוֹת סוֹחֵר—This is, literally, "she is like ships of a merchant." The participle סוֹחֵר is of the verb סָחַר, "travel about (to conduct business, commerce)." The construct phrase אֳנִיּוֹת סוֹחֵר can be rendered as having an adjectival genitive: "merchant ships" or "commercial/freighter ships." Note the cognate noun סַחַר, "profit (gained from commerce)," in 31:18. That noun is used twice in 3:14 to extol the surpassing "profit, gain" given by divine Wisdom.

מִמֶּרְחָק תָּבִיא לַחְמָהּ׃—This could be rendered causally since it explains the reason for the simile in the preceding clause: "she is like merchant ships *because* from afar she brings her food." The noun מֶרְחָק, "a far-away place" (with the preposition מִן, "from afar," מִמֶּרְחָק), is cognate to the adjective רָחֹק in the second clause of 31:10.

31:15 וַתָּקָם ׀ בְּעוֹד לַיְלָה—The preposition בְּ on עוֹד, "still, yet," begins a temporal clause: "she arises *while* (it is) *still* night." This action to provide food might be compared to Ruth 3:14–17 and, for a different purpose, to the women who arose on Easter morning when "there still was darkness" (σκοτίας ἔτι οὔσης, Jn 20:1).

וַתִּתֵּן טֶרֶף לְבֵיתָהּ—Two different meanings are possible for the noun טֶרֶף: "she gives *prey/food* to her household" (see *HALOT*, s.v. טֶרֶף, 1–2). Most often the noun refers to "prey" (BDB, 1) captured and killed by a lion or sometimes by another predatory animal such as a wolf (e.g., Gen 49:9; Ezek 22:25, 27; Amos 3:4; Ps 104:21). Only in a few passages does it refer to "food" for people (BDB, 2, citing Mal 3:10; Ps 111:5; Job 24:5; Prov 31:15). For the significance of this wordplay, see "A Wife with Strong Character" in the commentary below.

וְחֹק לְנַעֲרֹתֶיהָ׃—The noun חֹק refers to an allotted, appropriate "portion" of food also in 30:8. The singular here must have a collective sense because of the following plural: daily she gives "portions" לְנַעֲרֹתֶיהָ, "to (all of) her female servants."

31:16 זָמְמָה שָׂדֶה וַתִּקָּחֵהוּ—In 30:32 the verb זָמַם means "plan/devise evil." Only here in the OT does it have the positive meaning "consider" (BDB, 1) in the sense of contemplating and evaluating a possible business transaction, which the wife with strong character decides to complete: "she considers a field and she takes it." The masculine suffix on וַתִּקָּחֵהוּ (from לָקַח) refers to שָׂדֶה, "a field."

מִפְּרִי כַפֶּיהָ נָטְעַ כָּרֶם׃—After acquiring the field, she can afford to purchase seed or seedlings in order to cultivate it. מִפְּרִי כַפֶּיהָ, "from the fruit of her hands," is a poetic way of referring to the profit from her labor (*HALOT*, s.v. פְּרִי, 4). The Qere of the verb is נָטְעָה, "she plants," the preferred reading. The Kethib probably would be vocalized as נְטֹעַ and would be the infinitive construct of the same verb. נָטַע, "to plant," often has the direct object כֶּרֶם (pausal: כָּרֶם), "a vineyard" (e.g., Gen 9:20), and this clause is in prophetic promises of everlasting life in the new creation, the new heavens and new earth, in Is 65:21 and Amos 9:14.

31:17 חָגְרָה בְעוֹז מָתְנֶיהָ—The noun עֹז (here plene: עוֹז), "strength," is in earlier proverbs as one of the gifts God gives through faith, divine wisdom, and the fear of Yahweh (14:26; 18:10; 24:5). It recurs in 31:25, where it metaphorically refers to an article of clothing. This clause may mean "she girds [חָגְרָה] with strength [בְעוֹז] her loins [מָתְנֶיהָ],"

with the metaphorical meaning "she wraps strength around her waist." Or it could have the more concrete meaning "she uses a strong belt to secure her garment around her waist." A further possibility is that the noun עֹוז with the preposition בְּ could function adverbially: "she strongly girds her loins," "she tightly wraps her garment about her waist." In any case, gathering the loose garment around the waist enables easier and quicker movement with the legs. See חָגַר מָתְנַיִם in, for example, Ex 12:11 and 2 Ki 4:29.

וַתְּאַמֵּץ זְרֹועֹתֶיהָ׃—Literally, this is "and she strengthens her arms." This probably means that she "binds her sleeves or upper garment to free her arms for work."[2] The equivalent English idiom is "she rolls up her sleeves." This clause is parallel to the previous clause about her action with her waist. This is the only place in the OT where the Piel (D) of אָמֵץ takes זְרוֹעַ as a direct object. A similar idiom in Tannaitic and Amoraic Hebrew is the Piel of קָשַׁר with the plural of כָּתֵף as a direct object, and it too means to fasten one's upper garment to free one's arms for work. That Rabbinic Hebrew idiom is often accompanied by the same idiom as in the preceding clause here: "to gird [the Qal (G) of חָגַר] the loins/waist [direct object מָתְנַיִם]."[3]

31:18 טָֽעֲמָה כִּי־טֹוב סַחְרָהּ—While the common meaning of the verb טָעַם is "to taste," it can be used more generically to mean "to perceive" (*HALOT*, 3). The verb occurs only here in Proverbs, but the cognate noun טַעַם, "taste, good judgment, discretion," is in 11:22; 26:16. The identical suffixed form (סַחְרָהּ) of the noun סַחַר, "profit," refers to that gained by receiving divine Wisdom in 3:14.

לֹא־יִכְבֶּה בַלַּיְל נֵרָהּ׃—Several earlier proverbs warn that the "lamp" (נֵר) of the wicked or unbelievers will be extinguished (13:9; 20:20; 24:20), meaning that they will perish in eternal darkness. However, Yahweh and his Word serve as the "lamp" for believers (6:23). That the godly woman's "lamp" does not go out even "in the night" (the Qere is בַלַּיְלָה) suggests not only that she works into the night, but also that her enduring faith is continually sustained by God and his Word.

31:19 יָדֶיהָ שִׁלְּחָה בַכִּישֹׁור—The idiom with שָׁלַח (here in the Piel), the object יָד, and the preposition בְּ, "stretch out one's hand on/to, reach out and grasp," is used at least twenty times in the OT.[4] The idiom often has an aggressive or hostile connotation of action "against" someone or something (BDB, s.v. שָׁלַח, Qal, 3 a). This is also true of שָׁלַח with the object יָד when no preposition or a different preposition is used, as when Jael, the wife of Heber, grabbed a tent peg to kill Sisera (Judg 5:26, using the Qal and the preposition לְ).[5] Here, however, the item the wife takes hold of is a כִּישׁוֹר, "distaff," a noun that occurs only here in the OT. The idiom (with לְ) recurs in 31:20b with a gracious and generous connotation: וְיָדֶיהָ שִׁלְּחָה לָאֶבְיֹון, "and she stretches out her hands to the needy."

---

2 Novick, "She Binds Her Arms," 111.

3 Novick, "She Binds Her Arms," 109–11.

4 Cf. Humbert, "Etendre la main."

5 Wolters, "Proverbs XXXI 10–31 as Heroic Hymn," 453–54.

וְכַפֶּיהָ תָּמְכוּ פָלֶךְ׃—Literally, this is "her palms grasp the spindle." The noun פֶּלֶךְ means "spindle" also in 2 Sam 3:29.

31:21 לֹא־תִירָא לְבֵיתָהּ מִשָּׁלֶג—This is, literally, "she does not fear for her house from snow." The verb יָרֵא, "to fear," is negated here, but this lack of fear about worldly threats is based on the positive statement about the woman "with the fear of Yahweh" in 31:30. She knows that her gracious God is in control of all things, and her faith in him casts out her fear of temporal dangers (cf. 1 Jn 4:18).

כִּי כָל־בֵּיתָהּ לָבֻשׁ שָׁנִים׃—The singular suffixed masculine noun בֵּיתָהּ, "her house," refers to all the people in her household. It is the subject of the masculine singular Qal passive (Gp) participle לָבֻשׁ, from לָבַשׁ, "wear, be clothed." (The cognate noun לְבוּשׁ, "clothing," is in 31:22, 25.) Passive forms of verbs for donning clothing often take an accusative noun that describes the material of the clothing (Joüon, § 121 o). Here the accusative is the plural שָׁנִים, "scarlet." The LXX apparently read it as שְׁנַיִם and translated it as δισσάς, "doubly" (the first word in LXX 31:22), a translation favored by Luther[6] and some modern commentators,[7] since the plural of שָׁנִי, "scarlet," is rare and a double layer of clothing seems appropriate for the snow. However, the plural שָׁנִים, "scarlet," does occur in Is 1:18, where the context refers to שֶׁלֶג, "snow," as in the preceding clause of 31:21, and "scarlet" is appropriate. Scarlet-dyed clothing was expensive, and a heavy wool garment that was dyed scarlet would speak well of the woman's ability to provide for her household.

31:24 סָדִין—This singular noun must be a collective, hence "linen garments." This material is listed among the attire of the rich women in Is 3:23, and it also occurs in Judg 14:12–13.

וַחֲגוֹר נָתְנָה לַכְּנַעֲנִי׃—The singular noun חֲגוֹר too must be a collective here: "belts." The gentilic כְּנַעֲנִי usually means "Canaanite," but it can also be used as a common noun meaning "merchant" (see *HALOT*, 2).

31:26 וְתוֹרַת־חֶסֶד עַל־לְשׁוֹנָהּ׃—Literally, this is "teaching of mercy/faithfulness is on her tongue." For חֶסֶד, see the first textual note and the commentary on 3:3, where it is a gift from God's wisdom. See also 16:6, where sin is atoned for by "mercy." The precise meaning of חֶסֶד depends on its context. In reference to God, it denotes his gracious disposition and faithfulness to his covenant promises. The Scriptures repeatedly assure us that Yahweh's חֶסֶד endures forever.[a] Thus חֶסֶד often points to God's grace, his attitude toward humans who cannot by their own merits expect his mercy or kindness. When חֶסֶד is displayed by a believer, as by the godly wife here, it refers to the fruit of faith: a gracious disposition, Gospel-laden speech, or a pattern of merciful action toward others—all of which exceed what is normal and expected among sinful humans.

(a) Jer 33:11; Pss 100:5; 106:1; 107:1; 118:1–4, 29; 136:1–26; Ezra 3:11; 1 Chr 16:34, 41; 2 Chr 5:13; 7:3, 6; 20:21

31:27 צוֹפִיָּה הֲלִיכוֹת בֵּיתָהּ—"She keeps a close eye" is a Qal (G) participle feminine singular of צָפָה, "keep watch" (*HALOT*, s.v. צָפָה I, 1). Its direct object is the construct phrase הֲלִיכוֹת בֵּיתָהּ, literally, "the walkings of/in her house." The noun הֲלִיכָה, "walking," here is used generically in the plural to mean "doings" (*HALOT*, 3) or "conduct."

---

6 WA DB 10/2.102–3.

7 Clifford, *Proverbs*, 272, 276; Murphy, *Proverbs*, 244; Scott, *Proverbs, Ecclesiastes*, 185.

Some commentators have proposed that the participle צוֹפִיָּה, *tsophiyah*, "watching," is intended to be a play on the Greek word σοφία, *sophia*, "wisdom," giving this line a double meaning: "wisdom is the conduct of her household."[8] They contend that the word here is a rarer form of feminine participle: the more common form of feminine participle expected for a verb ending in ה- (originally י-) would be צוֹפָה, but instead the poet intentionally used the older form that retained the original consonant ending the verb, י-. These commentators argue that since this is allegedly a play on a Greek word, this poem dates to sometime after the conquest of Palestine by the Greek conqueror Alexander the Great (332 BC).

However, there are at least two problems with this argument. First, although Greek influence in Palestine became pervasive after Alexander, Greeks had been in contact with that part of the world for centuries before Alexander. The presence of one word that may be a play on a Greek word is flimsy evidence for a Hellenistic date when there are no other signs of Greek words or Hellenistic thought (or reaction against it) in the entire poem.

Second, the contention that the form of the feminine singular ending on the participle צוֹפִיָּה is rare and optional (for the roots that use it) is erroneous.[9] For III-ה verbs, this ending is quite common. The Qal (G) feminine singular participle in the absolute state is used for nineteen III-ה roots in Biblical Hebrew.[10] Fifteen of these roots use the form without י.[11] Yet five roots use the form with י.[12] Moreover, only one root (המה) is found with both forms, and הוֹמִיָּה is favored over הוֹמָה by a ratio of three to one.[13] Far from being rare, the form with the י is found in over a quarter of the III-ה roots that have a feminine singular participle. Moreover, for most roots the two forms are not interchangeable or available, since only one form of their feminine participle exists.

Thus there is no evidence that the author of this poem chose the form צוֹפִיָּה to imitate the Greek word σοφία. Instead by coincidence this word may simply be similar in sound to that Greek word for wisdom.

וְלֶחֶם עַצְלוּת לֹא תֹאכֵל׃—The abstract feminine noun עַצְלוּת, "laziness," occurs only here in the OT, but it is cognate to the adjective עָצֵל, "lazy, lazybones," for which see the textual note on 6:6.

---

8 Wolters, "*Ṣôpiyyâ* (Prov 31:27) as Hymnic Participle and Play on *Sophia*." This idea is endorsed by Murphy, *Proverbs*, 244, and Rendsburg, "Bilingual Wordplay in the Bible."

9 This contention is based on a misreading of GKC, § 75 v, which notes that this ending is present on some III-ה verbs. However, nowhere does GKC state that this form is rare for III-ה verbs or that it is an optional form for most of the roots that use it.

10 There are six uses of Qal (G) feminine singular participles of III-ה roots in the construct state: פֹּרָת (root פרה), Gen 49:22 (twice); הוֹרָתָם (root הרה), Hos 2:7 (ET 2:5); הוֹרָתִי (root הרה), Song 3:4; חוֹלַת (root חלה), Song 2:5; שֶׁחוֹלַת (root חלה), Song 5:8.

11 These roots are גלה, היה, המה, זנה, חלה, חנה, ינה, סעה, עלה, עשׂה, פתה, צעה, ראה, רעה, and שׁתה.

12 These roots are בכה, המה, עטה, פרה, and צפה.

13 Is 22:2 and Prov 7:11; 9:13 versus 1 Ki 1:41. It should be noted that this is also the only root that shows both of the two possible forms of its feminine plural: הֹמִיּוֹת (Prov 1:21) and הֹמוֹת (Ezek 7:16).

31:28 קָמוּ בָנֶיהָ וַֽיְאַשְּׁר֑וּהָ בַּ֝עְלָ֗הּ וַֽיְהַֽלְלָֽהּ׃—The verb קוּם, "arise," shows a posture of her sons' deference to her. The Piel (D) of אָשַׁר, "bless, pronounce [someone to be] blessed," occurs in Proverbs only here. Its Pual (Dp) in 3:18 has the corresponding passive meaning. It is cognate to the declaration אַשְׁרֵי that forms the beatitude in 3:13. See the first textual note on 3:13. The Piel (D) of הָלַל, "to praise," recurs in 31:31.

Song 6:9 has the same suffixed verbs in the same sequence, although the second verb is plural. Moreover, the syntax and theological meaning of both verses in their larger context are comparable:

רָא֤וּהָ בָנוֹת֙ וַֽיְאַשְּׁר֔וּהָ
מְלָכ֥וֹת וּפִֽילַגְשִׁ֖ים וַֽיְהַלְלֽוּהָ׃

Sons see her and bless her,
queens and concubines, and they praise her.

Joüon, § 119 za, suggests that Song 6:9 is modeled after Prov 31:28, but since the Song is by Solomon and this verse is by a later author, this verse is probably patterned after Solomon's praise for his Shulammite wife.[14]

31:29 רַבּוֹת בָּנוֹת עָשׂוּ חָיִל—A Hebrew adjective usually follows the noun it modifies, but when the adjective רַב has the sense of "many," it often precedes the noun it modifies (Waltke-O'Connor, § 14.3.1b, including example 9; Joüon, § 141 b). Literally רַבּוֹת בָּנוֹת is "many daughters," but the plural of בַּת, "daughter," in this context has the more general meaning "women." The predicate, עָשׂוּ חָיִל, is, literally, "(they) do valor," with the same noun חַיִל that is in the construct phrase that characterizes the godly wife in 31:10, "a wife with strong character." However, the women here are not designated by a corresponding plural construct phrase, but rather by this verbal phrase, translated as "show strong character."

וְאַתְּ עָלִית עַל־כֻּלָּֽנָה׃—The pronoun אַתְּ, "you" (feminine singular), is redundant before the inflected verb (עָלִית, second feminine singular), and so it is emphatic: literally, "you *yourself* have ascended above all of them." The verb עָלָה, "ascend, be high," is used here to mean "surpass" (*HALOT*, 3 c). כֻּלָּנָה is כֹּל, "all," with the form of third feminine plural suffix usually found "in great pause" (Joüon, § 94 h), hence "all of them," referring to the בָּנוֹת, "women," in the preceding clause.

31:30 שֶׁקֶר הַחֵן—Usually חֵן means "grace, (divine) favor." See the first textual note on 1:9. Here, however, it refers only to outward appearance, and its predicate noun in the nominal clause is שֶׁקֶר "falsehood." Therefore חֵן is best translated as "charm," which can be feigned or affected, not sincere.

וְהֶבֶל הַיֹּפִי—The predicate noun הֶבֶל refers to a "fleeting vapor," as in 21:6b, where too it is associated with שֶׁקֶר, "falsehood," and also with death. This noun is used most memorably by Solomon in Ecclesiastes, traditionally translated as "vanity" (e.g., Eccl 1:2).

---

[14] See the textual notes and exposition of Song 6:9 in Mitchell, *The Song of Songs*, 1003–5 and 1016–18.

The subject noun יֹפִי (pausal: יֹּפִי), "beauty," occurs elsewhere in Proverbs only in 6:25, where it refers to a seductive adulterous woman whom the wise, believing man is to avoid. This noun is cognate to the adjective יָפֶה, "beautiful," found in Proverbs only in 11:22, where it describes a "beautiful woman" (אִשָּׁה יָפָה) who does not have God's gift of wisdom, and so she is likened to a gold ring in the snout of a pig. Therefore 31:30 is consistent with those earlier proverbs in its rejection of outward beauty as a characteristic that—by itself, without faith and wisdom—could qualify a woman to be a godly wife. The next clause of 31:30 is yet another clause in this poem that stresses the one essential characteristic: the fear of Yahweh, that is, faith in God and love for him and for others.

אִשָּׁה יִרְאַת־יְהוָה הִיא תִתְהַלָּל׃—Literally, this is "a woman fearing Yahweh—*she* should/will be praised." Here יִרְאַת־ is the construct form of the feminine participle (יְרֵאָה) of יָרֵא, "to fear," which is also in 31:21. Its form is identical to the noun יִרְאָה in construct, as in the phrase יִרְאַת יְהוָה in, for example, 1:7, 29. The participle here is adjectival, modifying אִשָּׁה, "a woman fearing/who fears Yahweh." The pronoun הִיא, "she," is emphatic. The Hithpael (HtD) of הָלַל, "to praise" (as in 31:28, 31) has the passive meaning "shall be praised" (GKC, § 54 g; see also Waltke-O'Connor, § 26.3a, including example 1).

31:31 תְּנוּ־לָהּ מִפְּרִי יָדֶיהָ—Since the masculine imperative תְּנוּ, "*give* to her," is plural, it is directed to more than just her husband. It would include her sons (31:28) and also all the people of the church and community, as implied by "city gates" in the next clause. "From the fruit of her hands" (מִפְּרִי יָדֶיהָ) could indicate the source of the rewards, that is, she is to benefit from her own productiveness by enjoying the products she has made and the profits she has earned. The preposition מִן could also have a causal sense: she is to be rewarded "because of" what she has accomplished.

וִיהַלְלוּהָ בַשְּׁעָרִים מַעֲשֶׂיהָ׃—Literally, this is "and her deeds will praise her in the city gates." Similar are the eschatological promises about the good works of believers in Christ in Rev 14:13; 22:12. On the Last Day Christ will publicly commend believers for their good works (and ignore their forgiven sins), even though all that they have accomplished has been solely by his grace (Mt 25:31–40). Thus the basis for the acquittal of believers at the judgment ultimately is not the good works themselves, which are the fruit of saving faith, but that the believers' names are written in God's book of life by grace alone (see Rev 20:12–15 and also Ex 32:32; Ps 139:16; Phil 4:3; Rev 3:5; 13:8; 21:27).

Commentary[15]

"A Wife with Strong Character"

This section is praise for a wife who is described as אֵשֶׁת־חַיִל, "a wife with strong character" (31:10). This phrase is used in only two other places in the OT: Prov 12:4 and Ruth 3:11. From the parallel in Prov 12:4, framed by references

[15] לרבקה אשתי: ממנה לא הבינותי המשל הזה, "To my wife, Rebecca: without her I would not have understood this proverb."

to the "righteous" (12:3, 5), who are justified by grace alone, this phrase carries the primary denotation of strong spiritual and moral character. This woman has not achieved this status simply by human effort, since it is impossible for an unbeliever to please God by attempting to fulfill his holy Law. Rather, this woman is characterized by saving faith in the triune God. By the power of his Gospel he calls sinners to faith so that they are justified and sanctified, and he enables them to grow in faith and good works as they anticipate the life of the world to come.[16] Justification through faith alone is also essential for the corresponding description of Ruth the Moabitess (Ruth 3:11), a former pagan who was converted to saving faith in the one true God and who expressed confidence in the promise of resurrection to eternal life on the Last Day (Ruth 1:16–17).[17]

When we look at the masculine counterpart to this phrase, אִישׁ־חַיִל, "a man of valor," we find that it may carry three different denotations, depending on context.[18] First, its emphasis can be on spiritual and moral strength of character (Ex 18:21, 25), which specifically includes "fearing God" (אַנְשֵׁי־חַיִל יִרְאֵי אֱלֹהִים, "men of valor, fearing God," Ex 18:21). Second, it can denote skill and expertise (Gen 47:6). Third, it most often denotes ability to serve as a soldier (e.g., Judg 20:46; 2 Sam 11:16; Jer 48:14; Nah 2:4 [ET 2:3]; Ps 76:6 [ET 76:5]).

All three of these possible denotations for a man are present in this poem's description of the good wife. First and most prominently, she has strong faith in the one true God and firm moral values: she fears Yahweh (31:30), does good and not evil (31:12), and is able to teach divine wisdom (31:26). All of these characteristics are found elsewhere in Proverbs in descriptions of believers endowed with God's gift of Wisdom. The major theme in Proverbs of "the fear of Yahweh" centers on saving faith, which leads to wise actions: doing good, avoiding evil, and imparting wisdom to others through one's words.[19] Since the divine Wisdom portrayed in Proverbs is a hypostasis of the second person of the Trinity, namely, the preexistent Son of God, the agent of creation, the

---

16 See further "Law and Gospel in Proverbs" in the introduction.

17 For a discussion of Ruth's conversion and her implicit confession of belief in the resurrection of the body, so that not even death would separate her from believing Naomi, see Wilch, *Ruth*, 25–28, and 168–75, commenting on Ruth 1:16–17.

18 Wolters, "Proverbs XXXI 10–31 as Heroic Hymn," 453–55, says that אֵשֶׁת־חַיִל, "a wife with strong character" (31:10), is a feminine counterpart to גִּבּוֹר חַיִל, literally, "a warrior of valor," that is, a heroic soldier. However, this is not the comparison implied in 31:10–31. If it were, the poet could have called the woman something like אֵשֶׁת־גְּבוּרָה, "a wife of/with military might," or גִּבּוֹרַת־חַיִל, "a female warrior of valor" (although the OT does not attest any feminine forms of גִּבּוֹר). Instead he chose a feminine phrase that has a masculine counterpart that has a wider semantic range. Nevertheless, Wolters has useful observations about the military connotations of several words and phrases used in this poem, and these insights are incorporated in this commentary.

19 See "Wisdom in Proverbs" in the introduction. See also the first textual note and the commentary on 1:7 and "יִרְאַת יְהוָה, 'the Fear of Yahweh,' and יְרֵא יְהוָה, 'One Who Fears Yahweh' " in "Wisdom in Proverbs" in the introduction.

faith of the godly wife is an OT expression of faith in Jesus Christ.[20] This faith and many of the other features of a "man/person [אִישׁ] who fears Yahweh" as described in another acrostic poem, Psalm 112, are also present in this poem.[21]

Second, the poet gives us a picture of an accomplished wife. This is shown in the progressive nature of her handcrafts. She first seeks out the materials to use: wool and linen yarn (31:13). She next spins these materials into useful form with the distaff and spindle (31:19). Finally, she produces clothing for her children (31:21), bedspreads and clothing for herself (31:22), and even extra garments to sell in market (31:24). In addition, she is to be rewarded for her achievements, called "the fruit of her hands" (פְּרִי יָדֶיהָ, 31:31).

Finally, her character and actions are described with terms that often are associated with military prowess. She brings her husband "spoils" (שָׁלָל, 31:11), the fruit of military victory. The food she serves her household is called טֶרֶף, which often refers to defeated "prey" (see the second textual note on 31:15). She girds herself with strength like a warrior preparing for battle (31:17), and she possesses strength (31:25).[22] Even when "she stretches out her hands for the distaff," this poem employs an idiom for reaching and grabbing that elsewhere often has an aggressive connotation[23] (see the first textual note on 31:19). In this way the poet has depicted the well-rounded, complete wife as boldly skillful and courageous in faith. This helps correct any misunderstanding that "the fear of Yahweh" (31:30) would imply timidity or lack of courage in the skillful execution of her responsibilities.

This poem, then, serves as a survey of the attributes of this woman by noting her faith, skills, and accomplishments. Interestingly, it can be contrasted to the poems that praise the physical attributes of Solomon and his Shulammite bride, who are the married lovers in the Song of Songs.[24] Those metaphorical

---

[20] See the commentary on 1:1–7; 3:13–20; 30:1b–10; and especially 8:22–31 and the excursus "Proverbs 8, Wisdom, Christology, and the Arian Controversy" in the commentary on chapter 8.

[21] Wolters, "Proverbs XXXI 10–31 as Heroic Hymn," 448. The parallels between the believers depicted in Prov 31:10–31 and Psalm 112 include wisdom, wealth, children, compassion and generosity to the poor, and a fearless attitude toward the future.

[22] Wolters, "Proverbs XXXI 10–31 as Heroic Hymn," 453.

[23] Cf. Wolters, "Proverbs XXXI 10–31 as Heroic Hymn," 453, including n. 32, citing Humbert, "Etendre la main," 387.

[24] Song 4:1–7; 5:10–16; 6:4–10; 7:2–10 (ET 7:1–9). Only Song 5:10–16 is about Solomon; the other three depict his Shulammite bride or wife. For an analysis of how these poems fit into the structure of the Song and contribute to its theological message, see Mitchell, *The Song of Songs*, 148–54, 284–96, 809–20. Implicit in these bodily descriptions is forensic justification: the believing spouse sees the other as perfect and without blemish, just as God in Christ forgives the believer's sin and regards him or her as clothed with the perfect righteousness of Christ himself. Solomon praises his bride by calling her "my perfect one" (Song 5:2) and declares, "you have no fault" (Song 4:7), just as God regards his church and the individual baptized believer in Christ as perfect and blameless. See Gal 3:26–29; Eph 1:4; 5:25–27; Col 1:22; 1 Thess 5:23; Jude 24; and, after the second coming and the bodily resurrection, the bride of Christ in Rev 21:2, 9–11, 27. One can also compare the glorious portrait of Solomon

portraits of idealized physical features, seen through the eyes of the spouse's forgiving faith and love ("the flame of Yah[weh]," Song 8:6), are part of a marriage celebration. However, this poem is in some ways the opposite of them and serves as a canonical counterbalance.[25]

> The physical appearance of the woman in question [Prov 31:10–31] is altogether ignored. Rather, throughout the extended encomium, it is the deeds and character traits of the אשת חיל ["wife with strong character," Prov 31:10] that are serially lauded. A number of the woman's body parts do garner the poet's attention. For example, her arms are mentioned seven times in the poem (31.13, 16, 17, 19 [twice] and 20 [twice]), but their shape, skin tone and beauty are never referenced. Instead, the limbs and hands are invoked as symbols of the woman's initiative and capability. …
>
> This notion is conveyed consistently in Proverbs. Wisdom, as a quality, or a personified woman, is compared to jewels and precious metal (e.g. Prov. 1.9; 2.4; 3.14–15; 8.10–11, 18–19) and praised as life sustaining (1.33; 2.21–22; 3.2, 16–18; 4.10, 22; 8.34–35). Beauty, however, even as a metaphor, is never ascribed to Wisdom. Conversely, physical attractiveness is a trait possessed by the אשה זרה, the "Strange or Foreign Woman" [2:16; 7:5]. The reader is enjoined, אל תחמד יפיה בלבבך ("Do not covet her beauty in your heart," Prov. 6.25).[26]

The first clause of the second-to-last verse of this poem is especially striking in this regard because it repudiates a culture (ancient or modern) that would worship physical beauty apart from godliness (see the textual notes on 31:30, and see also Prov 6:25; 11:22). Then the second clause of 31:30 reinforces the priority of faith for marriage (see also 1 Cor 7:39; 9:5; 2 Cor 6:14) and solidifies the connection of this poem to "the fear of Yahweh" theme that extends throughout Proverbs:

> Charm is deceptive, and beauty is a fleeting vapor.
> A woman with the fear of Yahweh—she should be praised. (31:30)

Thus, like the discourses on Wisdom in Proverbs 1–9, this final poem in Proverbs shuns outward beauty as the reason for attraction to a woman and marriage to her as a wife.[27] Instead a wise man who is searching for a good wife should be attracted to—above all else—godly wisdom. Moreover, this wise

---

in Song 5:10–16 with portraits of the risen and exalted Christ in, for example, Dan 7:13–14; 10:5–6, 16; Rev 1:13–16 (see also his transfiguration in Mt 17:2).

[25] However, the contrasts should not be overemphasized so that one loses sight of the similarities. For example, both the woman of Prov 31:10–31 and the bride in the Song work in a vineyard (Prov 31:16; Song 1:6; 8:12). Both women exhibit strong faith and a courageous determination to serve their husbands in love, even at the risk of personal danger (compare Song 5:2–8 to Prov 31:14, 21, 25).

[26] Bernat, "Biblical *Wasfs* beyond Song of Songs," 342–43. The poems in Song 4:1–7; 5:10–16; 6:4–10; and 7:2–10 (ET 7:1–9) are sometimes called by the Arabic term *wasf.*

[27] For the theme in Proverbs of the attractive, seductive woman who is a stranger and/or a prostitute, see the excursus "Wisdom and the Adulteress in Proverbs 1–9" in the commentary on Proverbs 2.

woman demonstrates her God-given faith and skillful industriousness by furnishing her house and nourishing everyone in her household (31:14–15, 19, 21–22, 27), just as God has furnished the entire creation by divine Wisdom and provides the food of eternal life in his Son.[28]

The Structure of the Acrostic Poem in Proverbs 31:10–31

This poem is a highly structured composition. It is a complete acrostic: each verse begins with a successive letter of the Hebrew alphabet, covering the total of the twenty-two Hebrew letters. It also is organized into four parts: a nine-verse characterization (31:10–18), a two-verse chiastic unit (31:19–20), a nine-verse characterization (31:21–29), and a two-verse closing (31:30–31).[29] The author signals the parallel nature of the two nine-verse units by a chiastic arrangement of the first verses of the first unit and the last verses of the second unit:

חָיִל, "strong character" (31:10)
    בַּעְלָהּ, "her husband" (31:11)
    בַּעְלָהּ, "her husband" (31:28)
חָיִל, "strong character" (31:29)

The two-verse unit in the center of the poem is also chiastic, literally:

יָדֶיהָ שִׁלְּחָה בַ-, "she stretches out/puts her hands on" (31:19a)
    וְכַפֶּיהָ, "and her palms (of her hands)" (31:19b)
    כַּפָּהּ, "her palm (of her hand)" (31:20a)
וְיָדֶיהָ שִׁלְּחָה לָ-, "and she stretches out her hands to" (31:20b)

Moreover, the two-nine verse characterizations balance one another by their sevenfold description of this woman:

Characterization	*First Unit*	*Second Unit*
Strong character	31:10	31:29
Benefits her husband	31:11	31:23
Good works and wise speech	31:12	31:26
Expertise at handcrafts	31:13	31:21–22, 24
Industriousness	31:14–15, 18	31:27
Commercial benefit to her family	31:16	31:24
Strength	31:17	31:25

This sevenfold characterization is no accident, but is used to signal her comprehensive grasp of all of the godly virtues of an ideal wife. This is consistent with the use of the symbolism of the number seven throughout Proverbs to indicate divine completeness (6:16–19; 6:31; 9:1; 24:16; 26:16; 26:25; see the commentary on 30:11–33).

---

[28] See the commentary on Prov 3:19–20; 8:22–31; and 24:3–4, and compare those passages to Jn 1:1–5; Col 1:15–20; 2:2–3, 9.

[29] Lichtenstein, "Chiasm and Symmetry in Proverbs 31." The treatment of this poem's structure follows Lichtenstein's model and observations, with a few additional observations.

Each nine-verse unit is divided into eight subunits. The first nine-verse unit contains the subunits 31:10, 11, 12, 13, 14–15, 16, 17, 18. The industriousness of the wife is the theme of two of the eight subunits (31:14–15, 18), one of which is a two-verse subunit (31:14–15). The second nine-verse unit contains the subunits 31:21–22, 23, 24, 25, 26, 27, 28, 29. Expertise at handcrafts is a two-verse subunit (31:21–22) and this expertise is combined with commercial benefit to her family in one of the seven other subunits (31:24). Another one-verse subunit is used to introduce her husband's and children's praise of her strong character (31:28).

The two-verse closing (31:30–31) unites its two verses by the use of the verb הָלַל, "to praise," that occurs in both verses. Just as the two nine-verse units balance one another, the two-verse closing is balanced with the two-verse chiastic unit (31:19–20). The chiastic unit couples the practical good works with the spiritual and moral virtues of the woman (handcrafts and generosity to the poor), and the closing unit couples her spiritual and moral virtues with her more practical achievements. These are also balanced chiastically:

A Practical virtue: use of her hands at the distaff and spindle (31:19)
    B Spiritual virtue by faith: generosity to the poor (31:20)
    B' Spiritual virtue by faith: fear of Yahweh (31:30)
A' Practical virtue: her achievements (פְּרִי יָדֶיהָ, "the fruit of her hands") and accomplishments (31:31)

Scholars have debated whether the woman in this poem is an ideal wife or whether she is intended to be another picture of Lady Wisdom, who is portrayed in several passages in Proverbs 1–9 (see 1:20–33; 9:1–6). While this woman is surely wise and embodies wisdom, she is not Wisdom. Lady Wisdom is never depicted as a mother or a wife.[30] This woman is both. She has apprehended wisdom, and so she exhibits some of the qualities of Lady Wisdom. Since throughout the book men are urged to acquire wisdom, this poem urges them to acquire another lady with wisdom: a wife with strong character.

Because of the strong links of this poem with other parts of Proverbs, it is likely that it is the composition of the final editor or compiler of the book.[31] He uses it to connect this woman with Lady Wisdom in the first major section of the book, Proverbs 1–9. He opens with the rare phrase אֵשֶׁת־חַיִל, "a wife with strong character" (31:10), which also is used in 12:4. This connects his poem to the sayings of Solomon in 10:1–22:16 and chapters 25–29. He uses the technique of subtly employing the number seven in imitation of Agur's similar technique ("three … four") in 30:11–33 (see the commentary on 30:11–33). He even surpasses Agur's technique by never mentioning any number. Finally, he places his poem immediately after the words of Lemuel's mother (31:1–9) to counteract any negative connotations concerning women that a misreading of 31:3

[30] Hawkins, "The Wife of Noble Character in Proverbs 31:10–31," 17.

[31] See "Authorship and Date" in the introduction.

could give (see the commentary on 31:3). And he positions the poem at the end of the book to balance Lady Wisdom at the beginning of the book (1:20–33).

Thus the reader of Proverbs is told to search for this kind of wise woman as a wife. She embodies all that is good for a wife to be. In the same way, the good wife becomes a paradigm of what God's people, as his bride, are now through faith and ought to be. The Gospel of Jesus Christ, active through God's Word and Sacraments, endows his betrothed bride, the church, with all the qualities she needs (Eph 5:25–27), just as God endows husbands and wives with the qualities they need to serve each other and their families—all based on the sacrificial self-giving of Jesus Christ on the cross, and the church's response in love (Eph 5:21–33). As readers contemplate the qualities that make a good wife, they also are led to contemplate the qualities that God gives to the bride of Christ, his church, through the "great mystery" of his union with her (Eph 5:32). Though the virtues of the church may go largely unseen or unacknowledged by the rest of the world, she has Christ's promise that after his return, her eternal glory, which she possesses now by faith, will be fully revealed and permanently established. Then the "bride" will become "the *wife* of the Lamb" (Rev 21:9).[32]

The Description of a Godly Wife (31:10–31)

31:10 This verse opens this poem with a rhetorical question about an ideal wife followed by a statement of her worth. By comparing her to "jewels" (פְּנִינִים), the poet is immediately signaling that this woman is wise, because the priceless treasure of Wisdom is worth more than "jewels" (3:15; 8:11).

31:11 This verse notes the trust her husband can place in her. She delivers on that trust by bringing him "spoils," like the spoils of war. "Spoils" (שָׁלָל) may be a reference to 1:13, where a gang of sinners (1:10–19) seeks to entice a young man to join them and divide the "spoils/plunder" (שָׁלָל, 1:13) they gain from their crimes. The poet may be indicating that a young man should instead be joined to a virtuous wife, since she will give him better benefits than those of the outlaw gang.

31:12 This verse immediately follows 31:11 and drives home the virtue of the wife's spoils over the gang's spoils. She brings no evil, but only good for a lifetime (the phrase "all the days of her life" points to eternal life through faith). In contrast, the sinful gang of 1:13 plots murders (1:11–12, 16), only does "evil" (1:16), and leads to a premature (and everlasting) death for the gang members themselves (1:18–19).

31:13 This verse begins the theme of handcrafts that runs throughout this poem. The godly wife begins by searching for wool and flax, the raw materials of the textile process. Even at this early stage, her hands are eager to work.

---

[32] For an overview of the OT and NT theme of God's people as his bride and wife, and the theological implications in terms of Law, Gospel, the means of grace, and eschatology, see Mitchell, *The Song of Songs*, 40–66.

31:14–15 These verses move on to the wife's industriousness in providing for her family. She does not give them only what is convenient for her to obtain, but she finds them food from distant places. She does not feed them only when it is convenient for her, but she rises early to feed her entire household, including the servants. By serving the servants she emulates the one who came not to be served, but to serve and give his life as a ransom for many (Mt 20:28; Jn 13:1–16).

31:16 This verse notes the wife's business acumen. She is skilled at obtaining real estate and in making enough profit to plant a vineyard, abilities often associated with men in the OT and NT, although the bride in the Song of Songs too labors in a vineyard (Song 1:6; 8:12). The godly wife is a capable counterpart to her husband, and her skills transcend gender distinctions. Metaphorically, all disciples of Christ are laborers in God's vineyard (Mt 20:1–16; 21:28–43; cf. Jn 15:1–8; 1 Cor 9:7).

31:17 This verse continues the normally male-linked attributes of this woman. It depicts her in terms similar to that of a warrior as she arms for battle with her waist girded and her arms freed of constraints that would hinder movement. She might be compared to Solomon's bride in the Song of Songs, who is sometimes described with military imagery (e.g., "terrifying like bannered [troops]," Song 6:4, 10) and with terminology that also can apply to her husband.[33] Likewise, in the NT the church militant (Eph 6:10–18) can be described as the virgin bride of Christ (2 Cor 11:2) or as an army of male virgins (Rev 14:1–5).

31:18 This verse once again describes this woman's industriousness, as she perceives (טָעַם, literally, "to taste") whether her profits are sufficient. She also fulfills her domestic duty by keeping the household lamps burning throughout the night. In the dark nights of ancient Palestine, where there was no public lighting on the night streets, houses would be especially dark in the middle of the night. The wife often had the duty to make sure the household's oil lamps were filled with enough oil to last the night so that those who rose during the night could find their way around the house without stumbling and injuring themselves.

Jesus employs this language as a metaphor: the church is to keep her lamps brightly burning through faith, so that all may see by her light, which is Christ, the light of the world (compare Prov 6:23; 13:9 to Mt 25:1–13; Lk 8:16; 11:33–36; 12:35; 15:8; 2 Pet 1:19; Rev 21:23).

---

[33] For example, Song 5:10 describes Solomon himself as "bannered," just as the Shulammite is in 6:4, 10. See further "Interchangeable Terminology" in Mitchell, *The Song of Songs*, 408–12, which notes descriptive terms used for both the bride and the husband. Some of the military language depicts the bride as the church militant. See, for example, Song 3:6–8; 4:4; 6:4, 5, 10; 7:5 (ET 7:4); 8:10, and Mitchell, *The Song of Songs*, 414–16, as well as the commentary on those verses.

31:19 This verse returns to the theme of handcrafts. This woman is skilled in the use of the distaff and spindle, devices used to spin fibers into thread and yarn.

31:20 This verse shows that her hands are not merely for domestic crafts, but also benefit others as she shows her compassion to the poor and needy, just as a wise man is called to do.[b] A wise wife knows that God has compassion on the poor, and she imitates his provision for the poor. This act becomes part of her service to God, as indicated by the combination of the verb פָּרַשׂ, "stretch out," and the object noun כַּף, "hand." The most common use of the combination of this verb and noun is to signify prayer to God.[c]

(b) E.g., Prov 14:21, 31; 17:5; 19:17; 22:9, 22; 31:9

(c) E.g., 1 Ki 8:22, 38, 54; Is 1:15; Ps 44:21 (ET 44:20); Ezra 9:5; 2 Chr 6:12–13, 29

31:21–22 These verses return to the wife's handcrafts, this time noting the products she has made for her family: warm clothes for them in the cold weather. Her industriousness has also benefited her, since she will not worry about their health. In addition, it has benefited her because she also has fine clothing and even bedspreads for her bed to share with her husband. Her clothes are of the highest quality (fine linen) and value (purple, a very expensive dye, often used for royal clothing). These cloths furnished the garments worn by the rich man in Lk 16:19, and they are named as luxury items in Rev 18:12, 16. Compare the conversion of Lydia, a godly woman who sold purple cloth (Acts 16:14). "Fine linen," but white in color and bright, is the cloth of the garments given to the faithful followers of Jesus Christ (Rev 3:4–5, 18; 19:8, 14), since the baptized are clothed with Christ himself (Gal 3:26–29). See also the nuptial "garments of salvation" and "robe of righteousness" in Is 61:10.

"Bedspreads" (מַרְבַדִּים, Prov 31:22) are mentioned in only one other passage in the entire OT, Prov 7:16, where the adulterous woman mentions her bedspreads to entice an unwitting young man into her bed. In contrast to that passage, this woman manufactures bedspreads for herself and her husband so that they can enjoy the sexual union that God has given them. Within the sacred context of marriage, God's blessing rests upon the entire relationship of the believing couple, including their intimacy.[d]

(d) See, e.g., Song 1:4; 4:12–5:1; 7:2–14 (ET 7:1–13); Mt 19:4–6; Jn 2:1–11; Heb 13:4

31:23 This verse picks up the hint of the presence of her husband in 31:22 by implying that her husband has an honored position among the leaders of the community,[34] in part because of her accomplishments. The city gate was the place where elders would gather in order to conduct business transactions and decide legal cases, which were to be adjudicated according to God's Word. In Ruth 4 the elders of Bethlehem gathered at the city gate to settle a matter that involved marriage, inheritance, and redemption.

This picture of loving service in marriage as benefiting oneself and one's spouse (31:22–23) points to God's design of this institution for human good, and as a testimony to the "great mystery" of Christ's union with his church (Eph 5:21–33).

---

[34] Wolters, "Proverbs XXXI 10–31 as Heroic Hymn," 455.

31:24 This verse expands further on the benefit this wife brings to the household as her industriousness and commercial enterprises provide funds for the entire family. Her work is so highly prized that the merchants accept her merchandise for resale.

31:25 This verse observes that she is clothed not only with the best of clothes (see the commentary on 31:21–22), but also with fine virtues. Because her honor and strength come from God (31:30), she can laugh at the days to come. She knows that her future is in his hands and that no one can snatch her out of his hands.[e]

(e) Jn 10:28–29; cf. Deut 33:27; Ps 119:73; Lk 23:46; Jn 13:3

31:26 This verse builds upon 31:25. Since her relationship with God has brought her true wisdom, she can speak wisely and instruct her children, just as the addresses from the father to his son(s) do in Proverbs 1–9.[35] Once again, she proves to be a capable counterpart to her husband. Other proverbs speak of *torah*, divine "teaching, instruction," taught by a mother to her son (1:8; 6:20) and of the joy wise children bring to their mother and father (23:25). Prov 31:1–9 is a divine, prophetic revelation taught to Lemuel by his mother (see 31:1), and in Song 8:2 Solomon's wife recalls how she had been taught by her mother.[36]

Scripture's depiction of God-pleasing roles of women often transcend overly narrow gender distinctions. Yet this proverb should not be misused to contradict what this and other Scripture passages declare about the proper roles and relationships for men and women.[37]

31:27 This verse emphasizes the wife's industriousness as she both keeps a watchful eye on the conduct of her household and also watches herself so that she does not become lazy and unproductive.

31:28 This verse reflects the value of this woman's contribution to the family. She receives from her sons and her husband the highest praise. As she has given to them, they now in turn give her praise and acknowledge her value, just as the poet acknowledged her inestimable value at the beginning of his poem (31:10). Indeed her greatest praise is not that spoken by her family, but the commendation by grace that she will hear spoken by her Lord on the Last Day, welcoming her into the city gates of the new Jerusalem (Rev 22:14; cf. Heb 10:19). She is a reflection of the value of the church, the bride of Christ, whom he purchased at the inestimable cost of his precious blood (1 Pet 1:18–19), that

---

[35] See the excursus "Proverbs 1–9, Christ, and the Ten Commandments" in the commentary on Proverbs 1.

[36] For an exposition of Song 8:2, see Mitchell, *The Song of Songs*, 1165–67.

[37] All of the passages cited above are in harmony with the biblical model for the family and with the divine mandate that only qualified men are to be ordained into the office of pastor (e.g., 1 Cor 14:33–38; 1 Tim 3:1–7; Titus 1:5–9). See "Women Teaching Women: The Shulammite Teaches the Daughters of Jerusalem Just As Her Mother Had Taught Her" in Mitchell, *The Song of Songs*, 181–93. See also the dictum of the early church father Cyprian: "Now one cannot have God as Father who does not have the church as mother" (*The Unity of the Catholic Church*, 6 [PL 4:519]).

she may be washed in that blood (Rev 7:14; cf. Is 4:4; Zech 13:1; Ps 51:4, 9 [ET 51:2, 7]; 1 Cor 6:11) and be cleansed, "without spot or stain or any of such things, but that she may be holy and without blemish" (Eph 5:27).

31:29 This verse contains the actual words of praise from the woman's (sons and) husband (31:28). He values her above all women. In his eyes she is the most valuable, and he acknowledges this. In a similar way, Solomon and the women of his court utter the highest praise of his Shulammite wife and acclaim that she is blessed by God (Song 6:9).

31:30 This verse begins the poet's final observations about the ideal wife. His observation of the fleeting nature of physical appearance heightens his praise of a woman who fears Yahweh, that is, who perseveres in faith until she is called to the fullness of everlasting life. This observation is intended to serve as a guide for young men evaluating the marital potential in those they are pursuing as mates. Beauty is the first and most important criterion that some men consider when picking a wife. However, the poet urges believing men to look for a woman who embodies the wisdom of Proverbs through her inner beauty by faith, which is far more precious. This will outlast physical beauty, and both the woman and her husband will be rewarded with God's blessing. A similar point is made by the apostle Peter about the imperishable spiritual beauty of a Christian woman (1 Pet 3:1–6), in contrast to the vain worldly glory that quickly perishes (1 Pet 1:23–25).

31:31 This verse ends the poem with the poet urging husbands not only to praise their wives (31:28–30), but also to reward their wives. Their accomplishments are to be acknowledged not only among the family, but also in public. Praise at the city gates was the highest, most prominent praise because it would be in the presence of the town's elders, leaders, and wisest men. Moreover, it places the wife in the same position of honor as her husband: "the city gates" (31:23).

This reciprocity and mutuality of grace and praise demonstrates the ideal to which God calls all married couples (Eph 5:21–33; 1 Pet 3:1–7). Every spouse—and every Christian—is first called to give of himself or herself before expecting any rewards, and indeed to give all of oneself in sacrificial love even when no human reward will be returned (Lk 14:11–14; cf. the women in Mt 28:1–9). That is what the Bridegroom has done for his bride, the church (Eph 5:25; cf. Mt 22:1–10), so that her faith may be firmly founded on the promise of her gracious reward "at the resurrection of the righteous" (Lk 14:14).

As the poet began his poem with a reference that was applied to Ruth,[38] so he now ends it with what may be another allusion to her, for Ruth too received the blessing of the elders at the city gates of Bethlehem (Ruth 4:11–12; cf. the blessing by the women of Bethlehem in Ruth 4:14–15). That blessing was fulfilled as this foreign woman, converted to faith, became an ancestress of King

---

[38] The Hebrew phrase translated as "a wife with strong character" in Prov 31:10 is used to describe Ruth in Ruth 3:11.

David and of King Solomon—the author of most of Proverbs—as well as of the Son of David, the Savior of all believers, Jewish and Gentile alike (Ruth 4:22; Mt 1:5; Rev 5:5; 22:16).[39]

[39] That the women Rahab and Ruth are included in the genealogy of Christ may portend that he is the Redeemer who calls believing Gentiles as well as believing Jews into the kingdom of God. For the significance of the genealogy from Ruth to David to Jesus Christ, and of the inclusion of the women (also Tamar) in Mt 1:3, 5, see Wilch, *Ruth*, 382–85, and Gibbs, *Matthew 1:1–11:1*, 86–89.

Index of Subjects

Index of Passages

Apocrypha, Old Testament Pseudepigrapha, and Other Jewish Literature

Early Christian Literature

Ecumenical Creeds

Lutheran Confessions

Works of Martin Luther

Lutheran Hymnals

Ancient Near Eastern Literature

Classical Literature